COMPLETE GUIDE TO

FOCUS ON THE FAMILY

BABY

& CHILD CARE

PRIMARY AUTHOR PAUL C. REISSER, MD

TYNDALE HOUSE PUBLISHERS, INC., CAROL STREAM, ILLINOIS

THE OFFICIAL BOOK OF

THE FOCUS ON THE FAMILY PHYSICIANS RESOURCE COUNCIL, U.S.A.

Visit Tyndale's exciting Web site at www.tyndale.com

TYNDALE and Tyndale's quill logo are registered trademarks of Tyndale House Publishers, Inc.

Focus on the Family is a registered trademark of Focus on the Family, Colorado Springs, Colorado.

Complete Guide to Baby & Child Care

Designed by Jennifer Ghionzoli

Published in 1997 as The Focus on the Family Complete Book of Baby and Child Care by Focus on the Family under ISBN 0-8423-0889-X (hc) and ISBN 0-8423-3512-9 (sc).

Scripture taken from the HOLY BIBLE, NEW INTERNATIONAL VERSION,® NIV.® Copyright © 1973, 1978, 1984 by Biblica, Inc.® Used by permission of Zondervan. All rights reserved.

For information about special discounts for bulk purchases, please contact Tyndale House Publishers at csresponse@tyndale.com, or call 1-800-323-9400.

The Library of Congress has cataloged the first edition as follows:

Reisser, Paul C.
   The Focus on the Family complete book of baby and child care / The Focus on the Family Physicians Resource Council ; primary author, Paul C. Reisser.
      p.   cm.
   Includes bibliographical references and index.
   ISBN 0-8423-0889-X (alk. paper)
      1. Pediatrics—Popular works.   2. Child care.   3. Child development.
I. Focus on the Family Physicians Resource Council.   II. Title.
RJ.R4165   1997
618.92—dc21   97-23617

ISBN 978-1-4964-3647-4

Printed in the United States of America

24   23   22   21   20   19   18
 7   6   5   4   3   2   1

To the children of this and future generations

Table of Contents

Foreword by
Dr. James Dobson

If you've picked up this book, it is likely that you are a parent, soon to be one, or know someone who is. Maybe you and your spouse are expecting your first child. Pregnancy has been an experience more precious and indescribable than you could ever have imagined. Ultrasound photos provide incontrovertible evidence of your baby's developing hands and feet, the shape of his or her head, the not-yet-seeing eyes. As this fragile life takes shape, you can't help being filled with wonder at the intricate, unfolding miracle of God's handiwork.

Perhaps your scenario is not so idyllic. Maybe you are not yet out of high school. The father of your baby conveniently excused himself when he learned of your condition. You've lived at home with your mom and dad throughout your pregnancy, or perhaps in a halfway house with other girls in crisis pregnancies.

Or your grown daughter has rejected her own baby, and now you're being asked to bring up your grandchild. Or you're a single dad trying to find your way in a world that fails to recognize that sometimes daddies have to be mommies too. Perhaps your baby is no longer a baby at all, but a troubled teen flirting with drugs and premarital sex—what do you do? This book was written with you in mind too.

Under the best of circumstances, rearing kids is a challenging assignment. As a parent, you will be called on to don a variety of hats, among them teacher, doctor, psychologist, friend, and pharmacist. As you contemplate the challenges ahead, you may feel overwhelmed by the responsibility. How can you nurture healthy self-esteem in your children? How can you teach them to protect themselves from unhealthy ideas, attitudes, habits, and associations? How can you build within them discernment and self-discipline? How can you develop in them, day by day, the values that are so basic to their well-being? And—one of the toughest questions of all—how can you guide them into independence until they themselves are walking with God in wisdom and truth, rather than simply following you?

The most discerning, vigilant, and competent parents ultimately find themselves feeling inadequate to accomplish these important tasks. A parent must have support, guidance, and encouragement—from other parents, from friends and family, from physicians and pastors. And we believe that, ultimately, each child must be entrusted to the care, love, and protection of Jesus Christ. I urge you not to shortchange your children by underestimating the importance of biblical precepts—either in the values you teach or in the way you conduct your own life. The stakes are simply too high.

Here at Focus on the Family, we recognize that parenting a child involves the care and nurture of the whole person—body, mind, *and* soul. That's why I'm particularly excited to be able to introduce to you this wonderful offering from Tyndale House Publishers, the Focus on the Family *Complete Guide to Baby & Child Care*. This comprehensive, well-researched volume offers detailed advice from more than fifty of the country's most highly respected physicians and medical authorities. Some have appeared as guests on the *Focus on the Family* broadcast, and many are members of Focus's prestigious Physicians Resource Council. This book is full of practical, specific guidance on every aspect of the child-rearing process—from infancy through the teen years and beyond. Additionally, the book contains hundreds of topical definitions, as well as charts, graphs, illustrations, and resource listings.

And what truly sets this book apart is the spiritual guidance and encouragement woven throughout its pages. You will find countless helpful hints for instilling in your little ones the timeless truths of Scripture—and the foundation of faith upon which rest our ultimate hope and salvation.

You yourself may have gotten a rough start in life. You may not have received the nurturing and encouragement you deserved as a child. Maybe you've struggled with issues of low self-esteem and feelings of rejection from your own parents. If that's your story, I have good news for you: Starting here, you *can* do better by your own child. It begins with dedicating yourself and your baby to the care of the only truly perfect parent—the Lord Jesus Christ.

Whatever your parenting situation—be it by choice or by chance, whether the circumstances are ideal or heartbreaking, whether yours is a background of poverty or privilege—it matters not. What does matter is that you have been charged by God with a profound and sacred trust: that of shaping and nurturing a human life. Handle it with care. God bless you!

James C. Dobson, PhD

Acknowledgments

The first edition of this book was the result of the diligent and cooperative effort of many talented individuals over a period of nearly three years. The preparation of the revised edition extended over more than eighteen months and involved a number of the original team members as well as many new recruits. To all of them we are deeply indebted. While we cannot fully acknowledge the full length and breadth of their contributions, the following is our attempt to give credit where it is most certainly due.

First of all, a standing ovation is due to the members of the original Physicians Resource Council (PRC) review team, who spent endless hours in conference calls and many days (sometimes in cramped quarters) reviewing literally every letter of the manuscript. We thank you for your dedication, perseverance, patience, professionalism, and commitment. Another ovation is owed to the PRC members who diligently reviewed every page of the first edition, offered their insights and recommendations, and then reviewed all of the revisions, updates, and new material for the second edition. All of the PRC members who have served as reviewers for one or both editions are listed below:

THE FOCUS ON THE FAMILY PHYSICIANS RESOURCE COUNCIL REVIEW TEAM AND CONTRIBUTING EDITORS

Peter F. Armstrong, MD
ORTHOPAEDICS—TAMPA, FLORIDA

Byron Calhoun, MD
MATERNAL-FETAL MEDICINE—
CHARLESTON, WEST VIRGINIA

Douglas O. W. Eaton, MD
INTERNAL MEDICINE—LOMA LINDA, CALIFORNIA

Larry Farmer, DO
EMERGENCY MEDICINE—
HENDERSONVILLE, NORTH CAROLINA

J. Thomas Fitch, MD
PEDIATRICS—SAN ANTONIO, TEXAS

Patricia O. Francis, MD
PEDIATRICS—MORAGA, CALIFORNIA

Cynthia Go, MD
OTOLARYNGOLOGY—HINSDALE, ILLINOIS

W. David Hager, MD
GYNECOLOGY—LEXINGTON, KENTUCKY

Leanna Hollis, MD
INTERNAL MEDICINE—BLUE SPRINGS, MISSISSIPPI

Gaylen M. Kelton, MD
FAMILY MEDICINE—INDIANAPOLIS, INDIANA

Richard D. Kiovsky, MD
FAMILY MEDICINE—INDIANAPOLIS, INDIANA

In addition to the members of the Physicians Resource Council, we would like to thank the many contributors who provided research, written material, and reviews of topics in their fields of expertise:

Jane Anderson, MD
PEDIATRICS—SAN FRANCISCO, CALIFORNIA

Karl Anderson, MD
UROLOGY—SAN FRANCISCO, CALIFORNIA

Brian L. Burke Jr., MD
PEDIATRICS—GRAND RAPIDS, MICHIGAN

Sarah Chandler, MD
FAMILY MEDICINE—LUBBOCK, TEXAS

Robin Cottle, MD
OPHTHALMOLOGY—VANCOUVER, BRITISH COLUMBIA

M. C. Culbertson Jr., MD
PEDIATRIC OTOLARYNGOLOGY—DALLAS, TEXAS

William G. Culver, MD
ALLERGY-IMMUNOLOGY—LOVELAND, COLORADO

Russell Engevik, MD
EMERGENCY MEDICINE—JULIAN, CALIFORNIA

Joyce Fischer, MD
PEDIATRICS—BLUFFTON, INDIANA

Linda Flower, MD
FAMILY MEDICINE—TOMBALL, TEXAS

Lawrence P. Frick, MD
FAMILY MEDICINE—CHILLICOTHE, OHIO

Stanley Hand, MD
OPHTHALMOLOGY—ORLANDO, FLORIDA

John Hartman, MD
FAMILY MEDICINE—KISSIMMEE, FLORIDA

Duke Johnson, MD
FAMILY MEDICINE—TUSTIN, CALIFORNIA

W. Kip Johnson, MD
FAMILY MEDICINE—IRVINE, CALIFORNIA

Ronald Jones, MD
PEDIATRICS—SPRINGFIELD, MISSOURI

Paul Liu, MD
PEDIATRICS—PHOENIX, ARIZONA

Margaret Meeker, MD
PEDIATRICS—TRAVERSE CITY, MICHIGAN

Carl Meyer, DO
PEDIATRICS—GREENVILLE, PENNSYLVANIA

Michael C. Misko, MD
FAMILY MEDICINE—HOLDEN, MISSOURI

D. Brett Mitchell, MD
FAMILY MEDICINE—DENISON, TEXAS

John Moyer, MD
PEDIATRICS—DENVER, COLORADO

Steve Parnell, MD
FAMILY MEDICINE—FAIRMONT, MINNESOTA

Jan Payne, MD
PATHOLOGY—ST. PAUL, ALASKA

John C. Rhodes, MD
FAMILY MEDICINE—LAS VEGAS, NEVADA

David Sadowitz, MD
PEDIATRIC HEMATOLOGY/ONCOLOGY—
CAMINUS, NEW YORK

Bodo Treu, MD
FAMILY MEDICINE—OMAHA, NEBRASKA

G. Scott Voorman, MD
OTOLARYNGOLOGY—THOUSAND OAKS, CALIFORNIA

James C. Wilkes, MD
PEDIATRICS/PEDIATRIC NEPHROLOGY—LEXINGTON,
KENTUCKY

Franklin D. Wilson, MD
ORTHOPAEDICS—INDIANAPOLIS, INDIANA

Gentry Yeatman, MD
ADOLESCENT MEDICINE—TACOMA, WASHINGTON

We would like to thank the following individuals for reviewing segments of the completed manuscript for accuracy:

Mary Beth Adam, MD
ADOLESCENT MEDICINE—TUCSON, ARIZONA

Stephen Apaliski, MD
PEDIATRIC ALLERGY—FORT WORTH, TEXAS

Sarah Blumenschein, MD
PEDIATRIC CARDIOLOGY—FORT WORTH, TEXAS

Paul Bowman, MD
PEDIATRIC HEMATOLOGY/ONCOLOGY—
FORT WORTH, TEXAS

Preston W. Campbell, MD
PEDIATRIC PULMONOLOGY—
NASHVILLE, TENNESSEE

James Cunningham, MD
PEDIATRIC PULMONOLOGY—FORT WORTH, TEXAS

Mary Davenport, MD
OBSTETRICS/GYNECOLOGY—BERKELEY, CALIFORNIA

Mary A. Eyanson, MD
PEDIATRICS—CEDAR RAPIDS, IOWA

EDITORIAL STAFF

Paul C. Reisser, MD, PRIMARY AUTHOR

Melissa R. Cox, MANAGING EDITOR

David Davis, FOCUS ON THE FAMILY EDITOR

Vinita Hampton Wright, TYNDALE EDITOR

Lisa Jackson, TYNDALE EDITOR

Jan Pigott, TYNDALE COPY EDITOR

Kimberly Miller, TYNDALE COPY EDITOR

FOCUS ON THE FAMILY

Bradley G. Beck, MD,
MEDICAL ISSUES ADVISOR

Linda Beck, ADMINISTRATIVE SUPPORT

Lianne Belote, ADMINISTRATIVE ASSISTANT

Lisa D. Brock, RESEARCH EDITOR

Bob Chuvala, RESEARCH EDITOR

Vicki L. Dihle, PA-C,
MEDICAL REVIEW ANALYST

Kathleen M. Gowler,
ADMINISTRATIVE SUPPORT

Karen Sagahon,
ADMINISTRATIVE SUPPORT

Keith Wall, RESEARCH EDITOR

Larry Weeden, BOOK PUBLISHING EDITOR

Special thanks to:

Glenn Bethany

Kurt Bruner

Charmè Fletcher

Anita Fuglaar

Al Janssen

Mark Maddox

Dean Merrill

Craig Osten

Barbara Siebert

Mike Yorkey

Rolf Zettersten

TYNDALE HOUSE PUBLISHERS

Douglas R. Knox, PUBLISHER

Richard L. Regenfuss, SENIOR DIRECTOR,
FOCUS ON THE FAMILY ALLIANCE

PRODUCTION

Amanda Haring, PROJECT MANAGER

Joe Sapulich, ART DIRECTOR

Jennifer Ghionzoli, DESIGNER

Sandy Jurca, TYPESETTER

Keith Johnson & Mary Choate, PRINT BUYERS

ART REVIEWERS

Bradley G. Beck, MD

John Livoni, MD

Curtis Stine, MD

Last but certainly not least, a heartfelt thank you to Teri Reisser, Alan Cox, and the many loving (and patient) spouses of all who worked for so many months on this project. Neither edition of this book would have been possible without your support, wisdom, and inspiration.

Introduction to the
First Edition

The *Focus on the Family Complete Book of Baby and Child Care* has been designed to assist you throughout the course of the most rewarding and challenging job of your life: parenting. Whether you are expecting your first baby in the near future or have years of parenting experience, we hope that you will find this book helpful—not only as a useful resource but also as a source of inspiration, especially when the going gets a little tough (or extremely difficult).

This book is divided into two major sections:

The first section is a detailed chronological tour of a child's life from conception through infancy, toddlerhood, preschool and school years, adolescence, and finally the release of a young adult to independent living. Chapters in this section are intended to be read in their entirety, but you may also benefit from reviewing specific topics contained within them. The chapters include:

- Details about physical, mental, and emotional development at each age
- Practical information about basic topics such as feeding, sleep, safety, and common illnesses
- Suggestions for building strong bonds with your child, providing appropriate discipline through a balance of love and limits, and instilling moral and spiritual values
- Encouragement for strengthening marriage, meeting the special challenges of single parenting, avoiding burnout, managing conflicts, and generally surviving and thriving throughout the entire journey of parenthood

The second major section is a health-care reference containing hundreds of entries, arranged alphabetically, including:

- Definitions or brief descriptions of a wide variety of medical conditions
- Explanations of many health-related terms
- More extensive reviews of common health problems in childhood (for example, sore throats, headaches, and allergies) and conditions affecting specific parts of the body (for example, the eyes and teeth)

This book contains a number of additional features:

- Special Concerns sections dealing with topics that are important to parents of children in all age-groups: adoption, discipline, conflicts within the family, educational issues, the impact of divorce on children, and many others
- An overview of a number of **orthopaedic conditions** (those related to muscles, bones, and joints), from congenital deformities to everyday bumps and bruises
- A section devoted to **emergency care** and **first aid**
- A listing of **resources**, including addresses, phone numbers, and Web sites of organizations that can assist you in gathering additional information about specific problems

As you begin to use the *Focus on the Family Complete Book of Baby and Child Care*, it is important that you keep these cautionary points in mind:

- This book is intended to serve as a road map to help orient and guide you through your parenting journey. It does not provide detailed directions for every conceivable situation you might encounter along the way, nor is the advice it contains cast in concrete. The basic principles set forth in this book must be molded and adjusted to fit you and your own child.
- This book is not intended to serve as a substitute for specific input that you will receive from your child's physician. You will be encouraged many times throughout these pages to contact a doctor or, if the situation is urgent, take your child directly to a medical facility, for a variety of specific problems. *No book can substitute for a direct assessment of your child by a qualified health-care professional.*
- Despite our best efforts to include the most up-to-date information, in the field of health care, the "current wisdom" changes continuously, especially in areas such as immunization guidelines. What was hot news when this book went to press may be outdated in a matter of months. This is another reason to check with your child's doctor if you have any questions about a particular situation you might encounter.

For the physicians who serve on the Focus on the Family Physicians Resource Council, this book has indeed been a labor of love. Having spent countless hours over the past three years preparing the information and advice contained within this book, our heartfelt desire is that it will be a valuable resource for you while enhancing the life of your child(ren) for many years to come.

May you find joy in your parenting journey,

John P. Livoni, MD, MPH, Chair
Focus on the Family Physicians Resource Council
May 1997

Introduction to the Revised Edition

In many ways, the preparation of the *Focus on the Family Complete Book of Baby and Child Care* (the first edition of this book) resembled the process of parenting a child from infancy to adulthood. Our "baby" was born in 1994 over the course of several enthusiastic brainstorming sessions, during which exciting and formidable proposals were set in motion. During the book's infancy, as the first chapters and reference topics were written, we slowly began to appreciate the amount of time, effort, and patience that would be required before our "young adult" would be ready to meet the world.

But there was no turning back. We eventually hit our stride over a period of months as more chapters and topics were written, reviewed, debated, revised, and reviewed again—often as many as nine or ten times over the course of several months. Our "child" grew and matured and received ongoing prayer, loving attention, and correction until another rite of passage arrived: an "adolescence" of sorts, when hundreds of pages of manuscript were presented to Tyndale House Publishers. More questions, suggestions, and insights from Tyndale's team led to further refinements, sometimes after spirited (but inevitably fruitful) discussions.

Finally graduation day arrived in the fall of 1997. Our offspring vacated the nest and began what would prove to be a successful independent career. More than 350,000 hard- and softcover copies of the book, including special editions for parents of newborns, toddlers, and teenagers, have been sold over the past decade. But ten years have brought many changes in medicine and society, and we are pleased to introduce a new edition, now entitled *Complete Guide to Baby & Child Care*, that has been carefully updated, revised, and expanded. Some of the many changes include:

- Several new Special Concerns sections addressing a variety of topics, including the premature infant, the overweight child and adolescent, safety in cyberspace, bullying, and the teenage driver.
- Numerous updates on facts and figures, safety advice, and approaches to medical problems that have changed over the past decade. For example, the use of syrup of ipecac, once a staple of the medicine cabinet that would induce vomiting in a child who had accidentally swallowed a toxic substance, is no longer recommended.

- New reference sections covering the length and breadth of immunizations and some ABCs of nutrition.
- Updates on the impact of changing media and technologies on children and teenagers, especially immersive video games and the explosive growth of electronic interactions such as text messaging, the sharing of digital photos and video via cell phone and computers, and social networking Web sites (for example, MySpace.com). All of these have created new and significant challenges for parents, especially those who aren't particularly technosavvy, and we made an effort to provide some timely advisories on these topics.

What *hasn't* changed since 1997 are the predictable developments in body and mind from infancy through adolescence and the critical role of the parenting assignment during those crucial years. Rearing children hasn't gotten any easier, nor is it any less fulfilling. Furthermore, the moral and spiritual principles that have served as the foundation for all of Focus on the Family's work and publications, including this one, are unchanging, and they may be found in this new edition from one end to the other.

Paul C. Reisser, MD, Primary Author
February 2007

Preparing for Parenthood

Whether you are just beginning to think about starting a family
    . . . or have just learned that you are going to be a mother or a father in a few
        months
    . . . or are a day or two away from an expected delivery date
    . . . or are planning an adoption
    . . . or have a baby (or two) in your arms
    . . . or have a house full of toddlers, school-age children, adolescents,
        or a combination of all ages
    . . . or are proud grandparents,
this book is dedicated to enhancing the journey you have started.

Parenting is an adventure, a source of incredible fulfillment, a humbling responsibility, and a unique privilege. It's a voyage of discovery with a long learning curve. On many occasions, it brings both laughter and tears. It is, above all, a priceless gift from God—one that deserves to be received with joy and treated with the utmost respect.

Many people enter parenthood unexpectedly, at times even suddenly, often in a state of panic. Nearly everyone who accepts the assignment develops qualms at some point. You may have already progressed from "Am I really ready for all the responsibility of bringing up a child?" to "What am I going to do if _____ happens?" to "How in the world did I get into this?"

If any of those questions have passed through your mind, take heart, and remember some fundamental truths of parenting:

- You're not alone. Many millions have traveled the path before you.
- You probably know a lot more than you think.
- It's never too late to learn, to mold your attitudes and refine your skills.

Whether you're aware of it or not, the process of becoming a mother or a father actually begins well before the doctor announces, "It's a boy!" or "It's a girl!" It begins before conception. In fact, it begins before the physical intimacy that sets the biological marvel of reproduction in motion.

And for an event of this importance, it's nice, as much as is humanly possible, to be prepared. This chapter is all about getting ready, but it's worth reading even if a lot of water has already passed under your parental bridge.

Fearfully and Wonderfully Made: How a Baby Develops

Many authors and poets, after hearing the cry and seeing the first flailing movements of tiny arms and legs at the moment of birth, have declared that the process of coming into the world is a miracle.

But while childbirth is truly awe inspiring, the real miracles began long before this transition of the baby from one environment to another. If you are expecting an arrival in the near future, be assured that a host of wondrous and marvelous events have already taken place. Just six days after **conception**, the union of egg and sperm that created a new person, a tiny cluster of 64 to 128 cells embedded in the thickened lining of the uterus. Within seventy-two hours of establishing a temporary residence in the warm sanctuary of the womb, this new human being sent a powerful hormonal signal to override the mother's monthly cycle, preventing the shedding of her uterine lining.

Then began the astonishing process of differentiation, as new cells took on particular shapes, sizes, and functions, aligning themselves into tissues and organs, eyes and ears, arms and legs. Each of these cells contained all of the information needed to make any of the multitudes of cell types in the body. Yet during the process of constructing and organizing, integrating and communicating with one another, individual cells began to express unique qualities in very short order, but in a seamless and orderly pattern. The intricacy and timing of these events are nothing less than masterpieces of planning and engineering.

See color insert for photos of fetal development, page A1–A3.

Before the end of the first six weeks of life, your child's heart has started to beat, eyes are developing, the central nervous system is under construction, most internal organs are forming, and small buds representing future arms and legs have sprouted. One cell created by the union of egg and sperm has now become millions, and your new daughter or son has reached the length of one-quarter of an inch (0.6 cm).

By the end of eight weeks, the fingers and toes have been formed. Heart, lungs, and major blood vessels have become well developed. Taste buds and the apparatus needed for the sense of smell have appeared. Tiny muscles have generated body movements, which at this point a mother cannot feel.

When twelve weeks of growth have ended, your baby has reached a length of three inches (7.6 cm). The heartbeat can be heard using an electronic listening device. All of the organs and tissues—including heart, lungs, brain, digestive system, kidneys, and reproductive organs—have been formed and are in place. The only necessary remaining ingredient is time: six more months for growth and maturation.

Sixteen weeks after conception, eyebrows and hair are growing. Your baby, now measuring six to seven inches (about 15 to 18 cm) and weighing nearly as many ounces (about 170 to 200 gm), kicks, swallows, hiccups, wakes, and sleeps. Soon the mother can begin feeling movement inside, an important milestone still referred to as quickening.

You created my inmost being; you knit me together in my mother's womb.

Psalm 139:13

At twenty weeks, with weight now approaching one pound (about 450 gm), your baby can hear and react to sounds, including Mom's heartbeat and stomach rumblings, as well as noise, music, and conversations outside the uterus. (Whether any of these sounds are recognized or become part of early memories is uncertain.)

At twenty-six weeks of life, breathing movements are present, although there is no air to be inhaled. Depending on their weight, babies born prematurely at this time have a 60 to 80 percent chance of survival with expert care, although complications are common.

With each additional week that passes within the mother's womb, the baby's likelihood of surviving a premature delivery improves, the risk of long-term complications declines, and the medical care needed after birth usually becomes less complex.

8 MONTHS' GESTATION

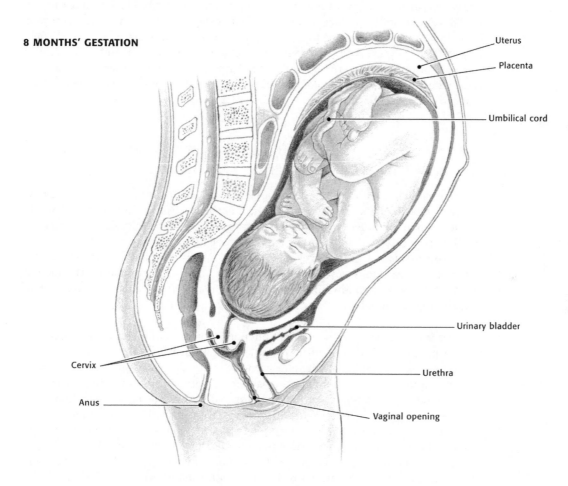

The final fourteen weeks are the homestretch, during which your baby grows and gains weight very rapidly. *By the end of thirty-two weeks,* the bones are hardening, the eyes are opening and closing, the thumb has found its way into the mouth, and the arms and legs are stretching and kicking regularly. Your baby is sixteen to seventeen inches (about 40 to 43 cm) long and weighs almost four pounds (about 1.8 kg). Over the next four weeks, the weight nearly doubles, and you feel all sorts of kicks, prods, and pokes much more strongly. A baby born at this age needs some assistance with feeding and keeping warm and could still develop more complicated medical problems as well. However, the vast majority of those born a month or so ahead of schedule do very well.

Finally, after a few more weeks of rapid weight gain (about half a pound per week during the last six weeks of gestation), your baby is fully developed and ready to meet you.

Every mother and father awaits the birth of a child with a mixture of anticipation, excitement, and anxiety. Who is this new person? Will this be a son or a daughter (or more than one)? What will he or she be like? Will she have her mother's eyes? Will he have his father's chin? Will everything be in the right place? Could there have been any problems that occurred silently during the time between conception and birth?

Some of these questions—but certainly not all of them—may be answered by ultrasound or other types of tests before the moment of birth. Furthermore, a baby may have some initial problems that clear up quickly and easily, while a more serious disturbance may not be apparent until a number of days, weeks, or even months have passed. Obviously, everyone involved in the debut of a new life is hoping, praying, and working toward the safe arrival of a healthy baby to a healthy mother. While no one can guarantee this happy outcome, there are many positive steps and basic precautions that can dramatically increase the likelihood of a joyful "special delivery."

Planning Ahead: Lifestyle and Health Questions for the Mother- (and Father-) to-Be

In a very real and practical sense, parenting begins well before the news arrives that a new family member is on the way. The state of the union of the parents-to-be and particularly the health of the mother *before* pregnancy strongly affect her health *during* pregnancy, which in turn plays a vital role in the baby's well-being both before and after delivery.

If you are planning to begin a family, or even if your pregnancy is well under way, you would be wise to review the following list of self-assessment questions. Much of what follows is directed toward the mother, but the ongoing health and habits of *both* parents are very important. (Expectant fathers, please read on.)

One important note: This book is not intended to be a comprehensive resource on pregnancy and childbirth. The information given in this and the next chapter is intentionally limited to parenting before the delivery—matters that specifically affect the health of the baby to be born. This is not to imply that a mother's health is any less important or that her well-being and her child's are not intimately connected. Nevertheless, the length, breadth, and depth of pregnancy care are beyond the scope of this book. If you are pregnant (or may be soon), it is very important that you find a physician who will not only guide you through pregnancy but also recommend books and other materials from which you can learn more about this miraculous process.

How well are you taking care of your (one and only) body?

Imagine what would happen if a strict law were passed declaring that you could buy only one automobile in your lifetime. Suppose the law also included a stiff penalty for riding in anyone else's vehicle. If your car ever became seriously damaged or fell apart, you would have to walk—everywhere. How well would you take care of your one and only car if the only alternative would be a pair of very sore feet? Would you fill its tank with the cheapest grade of no-name gas or find the highest-octane premium fuel on the market? Would you get the oil changed, engine tuned, and wheels aligned on a regular basis or wait for rumbles, rattles, and warning lights to appear before heading for the service station? When you weren't using it, would you keep the car snug in the garage or let the elements beat on it mercilessly day and night?

The analogy to your one and only body should be obvious: If it deteriorates and malfunctions, you can't borrow anyone else's. *And neither can your baby*. Poor nutrition, smoking, and the use of alcohol and drugs can have a serious impact on your baby's development, especially during the first eight weeks, when the vital organs are under construction. But your pregnancy may not even be confirmed until this period has already passed. Therefore, *the habits you develop well before you even think about having a child are very important*.

So how are you treating yourself? Specifically:

How's your nutrition?

Contrary to what you may hear on talk shows and infomercials or what you may read on Web sites that promote eccentric diets and expensive supplements, good nutrition does not involve magic formulas, rigid restrictions, or tackle boxes full of vitamins. At the same time, "eating right" isn't just something you should do during pregnancy and then return to a collection of unhealthy food habits. (If your four favorite foods are burgers, soft drinks, doughnuts, and chips, for example, you need to start making some serious changes.)

Instead, you can and should make a decision to choose high-quality foods for a lifetime—not only for yourself, but for your child(ren) as well. In fact, you are probably already familiar with some basic principles of healthy eating that continue to be reinforced by research and consensus among health professionals. You can review these in "Some ABCs of Good Nutrition," beginning on page 771, but for now we want to emphasize a few key points:

- When we say that a pregnant woman is "eating for two," it doesn't mean that she should double her food intake. In fact, her overall energy requirements increase by only about 15 percent—roughly 300 calories per day, or the amount contained in a modest snack such as a combination of an apple, an ounce (30 g) of cheese, and an eight-ounce (240 ml) glass of skim milk.
- The amount of protein recommended during pregnancy is about 60 grams per day—10 grams more than for a nonpregnant woman. This should not be difficult to obtain from dietary sources such as lean meat, poultry (minus skin), fish, eggs, nuts, dried beans, and peas. Unless specifically advised otherwise by your obstetrician or a registered dietitian, additional high-protein supplements or beverages should not be necessary. A cup (240 ml) of cottage cheese, for example, contains nearly 30 grams of protein, as does half a chicken breast or a quarter pound (120 g) of ground beef. Two eggs contain 12 to 13 grams.
- Eat lots of fresh fruits and vegetables—seven or more servings per day. These provide wholesome nutrients, fiber, vitamins, minerals, and a diverse group of compounds called **phytochemicals** that help protect us from heart disease, cancer, and other disorders. Sample widely from a variety of colors—green, red, yellow, orange, blue, and tan/white—because phytochemicals

Metric conversions are given for some—but not all—measurements and temperatures in this book. If you'd like to find a metric equivalent for one that isn't provided in the text, see "Metric Conversion Charts" on the inside back cover.

associated with different colors of fruits and vegetables appear to provide a variety of health benefits.

- Gravitate toward whole-grain foods rather than those made from refined or processed grains. Fiber, vitamins, and minerals are lost during refining and processing (though some are replaced), while whole-grain products contain a variety of useful compounds, including antioxidants, phytochemicals, folic acid, B vitamins, iron, and vitamin E.

If you are a vegetarian, you should be able to continue through an entire pregnancy without difficulty, provided that you include a wide variety of foods. If you eat absolutely no animal products, such as milk, eggs, or cheese, you may become short-changed on protein and calories, as well as on iron, calcium, vitamin B_{12}, and zinc. Careful attention to the protein content of foods such as legumes (beans and peas), nuts, soy products, and grains, as well as vitamin and mineral supplementation under the guidance of your obstetrician or a registered dietitian would be advisable.

FISH, METHYLMERCURY, AND PREGNANCY

You have probably heard of **omega-3 fatty acids**, and perhaps you're aware that they are considered to be beneficial nutrients. Indeed, they play vital roles in several important functions in the body, including immunity, clot formation, and many others. Two omega-3 fatty acids with tongue-twisting names—**eicosapentaenoic** and **docosahexaenoic acids**, better known by their initials **EPA** and **DHA**—have been identified as particularly important to the well-being of the heart, blood vessels, and nervous system. DHA is an important component of cell membranes in the brain, and both EPA and DHA are considered crucial to brain (as well as eye) development before birth and during infancy. DHA is transferred to the baby before birth via the placenta and is present in breast milk. (In fact, it is now being added to infant formula.)

Our bodies manufacture EPA and DHA from **linolenic acid**, a compound that is called an **essential fatty acid** because we cannot make it ourselves and thus must obtain it from food. Unfortunately, linolenic acid is not as plentiful as other types of fatty acids in a typical Western diet. (It is found in flaxseed, walnuts, soybeans, canola, and their oils—not exactly staples at the drive-through—and it is also present in dark green leafy vegetables, though in lesser amounts.)

A widely recommended response to the research supporting the benefits of omega-3 fatty acids is to add some to our diet in the form of fatty, cold-water fish—salmon, mackerel, lake trout, albacore tuna, herring, and sardines. These contain the beneficial fatty acids EPA and DHA already formed and in more generous amounts than in their leaner counterparts, such as cod, orange roughy, sole, and flounder. In addition to containing variable amounts of beneficial omega-3 fatty acids, fish is an excellent source of protein, with smaller amounts of saturated fats than many other types of meat.

A pregnant or nursing mother would appear to be a particularly good candidate to eat fish regularly in order to obtain adequate supplies of DHA and EPA for the developing brain and eyes of her growing baby. But some fish contain

What about vitamins and other supplements? Theoretically, a woman who eats a variety of fresh, high-quality foods should not need to take supplemental vitamins and minerals. But certain substances are so critical to a healthy pregnancy that most physicians will prescribe **prenatal vitamins** to make up for any deficiencies in the mother's diet. Remember, however, that *supplements are not a replacement for healthy eating habits.*

There is evidence that taking supplemental **folic acid** will reduce the likelihood that the newborn will have one of several types of major problems known as **neural tube defects**. Within the first month after conception, a tubelike structure forms from which the brain and spinal cord develop. If the tube does not close properly, serious abnormalities of these vital structures can result. Unfortunately, neural tube defects may occur before you know you are pregnant. Therefore, the Institute of Medicine (see margin note on page 10) recommends that *all women of childbearing age take 0.4 mg of folic acid* daily to reduce the risk of a neural tube defect occurring in an unexpected pregnancy. Once a woman becomes pregnant, she should take 0.6 mg of folic acid daily. Most prenatal vitamins contain at least this amount. (You may see these amounts of

a worrisome amount of **methylmercury**, a form of mercury that can harm a baby's central nervous system if he or she is exposed to it regularly. Mercury circulates in the atmosphere as a result of natural events and the release of industrial pollutants. Some of this accumulates in rivers, streams, and larger bodies of water, where bacteria convert it to methylmercury. Fish in turn absorb this compound during their feeding, and as a result most contain tiny amounts of it that are not harmful to humans. However, fish that are closer to the top of the food chain—especially the oldest and largest types that eat fish that have eaten other fish—are likely to have accumulated a fair amount of methylmercury before being pulled aboard the fishing boat.

The most likely candidates to carry unwholesome quantities of mercury are shark, swordfish, king mackerel, and tilefish (sometimes called golden bass or golden snapper), and the FDA therefore recommends that pregnant women and nursing mothers, as well as young children, avoid eating them. They should also consider limiting their tuna consumption to less than six ounces (180 g) per week, based on recent concerns that have been raised about the presence of mercury in this popular fish. (The amount may vary depending on the type of tuna—tuna steaks and canned albacore tuna typically contain more mercury than canned light tuna, for example.)

What about other fish? Women who are pregnant (or may become so) and young children can enjoy up to twelve ounces (360 g) of other types of fish per week without risk. Shrimp, salmon, catfish, and pollock are lower in mercury content. A typical serving is about three to six ounces (90 to 180 g), and while eating more than this amount in a given week isn't a big danger, cutting back during the following week(s) to keep the overall average at twelve ounces (360 g) is advisable.

For updated advisories regarding mercury in fish, check the FDA Web site (http://www.fda.gov). Once there, in the "A–Z Index," go to "M" and click on "Mercury in Fish." ∎

folic acid expressed in **micrograms**—a tiny amount equal to a thousandth of a milligram, often abbreviated mcg or µg. For example, a vitamin label may say that a tablet contains 400 mcg of folic acid, which is the same amount as 0.4 mg.)

If you have already had a child with a neural tube defect, a higher dose of folic acid—4 mg per day—is recommended for a month prior to the time you plan to become pregnant and should be continued through the first three months. (This amount of folic acid requires a doctor's prescription.) You can, of course, obtain folic acid through foods such as dark green leafy vegetables, cereals, whole-grain breads, citrus fruits, bananas, and tomatoes. However, in light of the research favoring supplementation, you should check with your physician about the amount of folic acid recommended for your pregnancy.

A pregnant woman needs additional **iron**, both for her increased blood volume as well as for the growing tissues and iron stores within her baby. Iron is necessary for the formation of **hemoglobin**, the protein within red blood cells that binds to oxygen, thus allowing red cells to deliver oxygen to every cell in the body. If the supply of iron in a mother's food is inadequate to meet this increased need, iron deficiency anemia will eventually result. This can cause her to feel extremely tired—more so than she would normally expect from the pregnancy itself.

An intake of about 30 mg of elemental iron per day will meet the need of most pregnant women. (Those who are already iron deficient may require 60 mg or more to correct this problem.) Since a typical diet provides only 5 or 6 mg of elemental iron per one thousand calories of food, and because consuming five thousand calories per day would be both unwise and impractical, iron should be included in your prenatal vitamin regimen. Absorption of iron is improved when foods containing vitamin C are eaten at the same time.

A woman's daily **calcium** intake normally should be 1,000 mg per day during the childbearing years but should increase to 1,200 to 1,500 mg per day during pregnancy because of the new skeleton under construction inside her uterus. You should eat at least four servings per day of foods that contain calcium, which is necessary to build and maintain both your and your baby's bones and teeth. Dairy products (such as low-fat or nonfat milk, cheese, and yogurt), green leafy vegetables, tofu, canned salmon (with bones), and calcium-fortified products (such as some brands of orange juice and breakfast cereal) are good sources of calcium. For example, you can get nearly 300 mg from a cup (eight ounces, or 240 ml) of nonfat milk, 300 to 400 mg from a cup of yogurt, and 200 to 250 mg from a cup of cooked spinach.

If you can't tolerate dairy products (or are a vegetarian who does not eat any type of animal products), you should consider taking a supplement containing 600 mg of calcium during pregnancy.[1] Your doctor may recommend a specific calcium supplement, since prenatal vitamins alone typically do not include the full amount. Calcium carbonate or calcium citrate are the forms that are most easily absorbed.

Do you weigh enough or too much?

Obesity is a health hazard for many reasons, all of which are heightened during pregnancy. Excessive weight during pregnancy is a risk factor for **high blood pressure** and **diabetes**, both of which can lead to significant problems for mother and baby. The aches and pains (especially in the lower back) that are so common during the later stages of pregnancy can become intolerable when there is already an extra burden on muscles and joints. Obesity is associated with a higher risk of miscarriage, an increased

The Institute of Medicine (IOM) is a private, nonprofit organization originally chartered in 1970 as a component of the National Academy of Sciences (now called the National Academies). The IOM provides information and advice regarding health to policymakers and professionals within both the government and the private sector, as well as to the general public.

likelihood of needing a cesarean delivery, and a greater risk for complications after a cesarean. Infants carried by obese pregnant women are more likely to be stillborn or premature, to have neural tube defects (regardless of the mother's folic acid intake), and to be obese themselves during childhood.[2]

But being underweight before or during pregnancy is no great advantage either because the nutritional needs of the baby may be compromised. This can result in a baby of low birth weight who is at risk for a variety of problems, including difficulty maintaining normal temperature or blood sugar level after birth.

If you have had a history of erratic nutritional habits or even a full-blown eating disorder (such as **anorexia** or **bulimia**), you and your baby will benefit greatly from ongoing counseling and coaching from a dietitian before, during, and after pregnancy. Similarly, if you are struggling with excessive weight, a gradual process of reduction (ideally under the guidance of a dietitian) *prior* to becoming pregnant would be wise. Attaining a stable weight prior to pregnancy will help prevent rapid regaining of weight after pregnancy begins. If you are already pregnant, however, a weight-loss program is not a good idea because the nutritional needs of both you and your baby could be jeopardized. Pregnancy would be a good time, however, to modify eating habits toward healthy patterns that will serve you well for the rest of your life.

Are you exercising your muscles, heart, and lungs?

A sedentary lifestyle—that is, one without deliberate exercise—has been specifically identified as a health risk for both women and men. Unfortunately, despite the numerous and well-publicized benefits of regular exercise, a majority of Americans still do not take part in any form of planned physical activity. But a regular habit of exercise established now will serve as an investment in long-term health and also improve the way you feel throughout pregnancy.

Several normal changes during pregnancy put new physical demands on your body. Aside from a normal weight gain of twenty-five to thirty-five pounds (about eleven to sixteen kilograms), your heart will be dealing with a 50 percent increase in blood volume. Muscles and ligaments in the back and pelvis will be stretched and subjected to new tensions and strains. Unless you have a scheduled cesarean section, you will also go through the rigors of labor—which is aptly named—and the birth itself. These are physically challenging events, and those who are well conditioned will usually fare better. In fact, their labor may even be shortened.

The increased stamina and muscle tone resulting from regular exercise will also increase your energy level, improve sleep, reduce swelling of the legs, and probably reduce aches and pains in the lower back. If you are on your feet all day, it may seem ridiculous to spend precious time for additional muscle motion. But unless you are a professional athlete, it is unlikely that your daily activities, no matter how exhausting, will specifically condition your heart and lungs. The good news is that you don't need to become a marathon runner to see some benefit in your health.

If you are not used to exercising, a goal of thirty minutes three or four times per week is reasonable. It is always better to do light or moderate exercise on a regular basis than heavy exercise intermittently. While stretching and muscle strengthening are worthwhile, aerobic conditioning—in which increased oxygen is consumed continuously for a prolonged period of time—has the greatest overall benefit.

The most straightforward and least costly aerobic activity is walking. No fancy equipment, health-club membership, or special gear (other than a pair of comfortable, supportive shoes) is needed. Pleasant and safe surroundings, a flat surface, and agreeable weather are advisable, however, as well as a companion. Another person (whether your husband, an older child, a relative, a friend, or another pregnant woman) will add accountability to the process, and the conversation can be enjoyable and help the time pass quickly. Gentle stretching for a few minutes before and after is a good idea in order to warm up and then cool down leg and back muscles.

Alternatives to walking include:

- *A home treadmill.* Advantages: No concerns about weather, aggressive dogs, or finding someone to watch your children. You can be flexible about the time of day you use it. Disadvantages: Cost, size, and noise.
- *An exercise video or book geared to pregnant women.* Advantages: Same as above, with less cost. Disadvantage: Repetition could become boring.
- *A prenatal fitness class at a local hospital or health club.* Advantage: Interaction with instructor and other women can be helpful and motivating. Disadvantages: Cost. Also, scheduling and child-care needs may be complicated.
- *Swimming.* Advantage: Good aerobic conditioning involving many muscle groups, with no added strain on sore muscles and joints of the lower back and pelvis. Disadvantage: You need access to a pool.

HOW MUCH WEIGHT SHOULD YOU GAIN DURING YOUR PREGNANCY?

The short answer is, "Check with your obstetrician," because your specific weight gain will depend on a number of factors. Why does weight matter? If you gain too little, you risk having a baby with a low birth weight (less than 5½ pounds, or 2.5 kg). If you gain too much, you risk having not only a large baby but also a number of health problems of your own. The basic guidelines for weight gain during pregnancy are related to your **body mass index (BMI)**, a calculation based on height and weight defined as follows (depending on whether you use metric or standard English measurements):

$$BMI = \frac{weight\ in\ kilograms}{(height\ in\ meters)^2} \qquad BMI = \frac{weight\ in\ pounds}{(height\ in\ inches)^2} \times 703$$

If you don't have a calculator handy, you can find BMI calculators on several Web sites, such as http://nhlbisupport.com/bmi/bmicalc.htm or http://www.cdc.gov/nccdphp/dnpa/bmi/index.htm.

BMI correlates with body fat—not perfectly, but well enough to serve as a general indicator of the health risk associated with your current height and weight. In 1998 the National Institutes of Health established the following categories for weight based on BMI among adults twenty years and older. These are now widely utilized among health professionals and researchers:

BMI	Weight Status
Below 18.5	Underweight
18.5 to 24.9	Normal
25.0 to 29.9	Overweight
30.0 to 39.9	Obese
Over 40.0	Extremely obese

- *Stationary cycling.* Advantages: Good aerobic conditioning and (depending on your anatomy) probably less strain on your lower back than from walking. Disadvantage: Many women become increasingly uncomfortable on this equipment as pregnancy progresses.

If you are already well conditioned, you should be able to continue your specific exercise routine. If you are already a confirmed jogger or an accomplished tennis player, you can probably continue these activities through the early months of pregnancy. Snow skiing, surfing, water skiing, and horseback riding all pose specific risks during pregnancy because of the possibility of falls—especially as your center of gravity shifts and your balance becomes less reliable as the uterus enlarges. All of these activities should be reviewed with your physician throughout the course of your pregnancy. Note: Scuba diving is not recommended at any time during pregnancy.

A few special precautions about exercise during pregnancy:

- Pregnancy is *not* a good time to take on a new, intense form of exercise, especially if it involves jumping, jerking, high-impact motion, or sudden changes in direction.

The Institute of Medicine has made the following recommendations for weight gain during pregnancy:

- A woman who begins her pregnancy at a *normal* weight should gain twenty-five to thirty-five pounds over nine months.
- A woman who is *underweight* prior to becoming pregnant should gain about twenty-eight to forty pounds.
- A woman who is *overweight* when she becomes pregnant should not attempt to lose weight during her pregnancy but should target a gain of fifteen to twenty-five pounds. For an *obese* woman, the target should be fifteen pounds.
- A woman carrying twins should gain thirty-five to forty-five pounds over nine months, and for triplets, fifty pounds.[3]

During the first trimester (three months) of pregnancy, a gain of two to eight pounds is typical, although some women lose a little weight during this time. During the second and third trimesters, however, a woman normally gains about a pound per week. Those who are underweight should gain a little more than a pound per week, and a woman who is overweight at conception should try to gain about two-thirds of a pound per week during this period.

Remember that these are only general guidelines, and the progress of your weight during pregnancy must ultimately be assessed and guided by your obstetrician (who may, when appropriate, recommend some input from a dietitian as well). ▪

- Exercise should not be so vigorous or prolonged as to cause exhaustion, over-heating, or dehydration. During pregnancy your heart rate should stay below 140, regardless of the type of exercise you are doing.
- After the first trimester (three months) of pregnancy, you should avoid exercises that require you to lie on your back, since this could restrict blood flow to the uterus.
- Exercise should not continue if any of the following pregnancy-related problems develop: preterm rupture of membranes; poor growth of the baby (**intrauterine growth restriction**); vaginal bleeding; high blood pressure; preterm labor; or cervical incompetence, a condition in which the cervix or "neck" of the uterus isn't strong enough to prevent a premature delivery. Exercise may also be limited if you are pregnant with more than one baby.
- If you have specific health problems such as heart disease, high blood pressure, irregular heart rate, epilepsy, fainting episodes, asthma, arthritis, or anemia, review any exercise plans with your physician, whether or not you are pregnant.

In addition to aerobic activity, a variety of gentle stretching and muscle-conditioning activities can help prepare your body for the changes of late pregnancy and labor. Your doctor and/or childbirth class instructor will have a number of suggestions for such exercises.

Are you taking or inhaling any substances that might harm you or your baby?
As a result of widespread public-health announcements, most people are aware that smoking cigarettes, drinking excessive amounts of alcohol, and using illicit drugs are risky and destructive, especially during pregnancy. Yet it's often difficult to believe that "this could happen to me"—that we might actually suffer any of the consequences we hear so much about. Furthermore, even if one is convinced of the dangers of these substances, gaining freedom from their grip can be a real uphill battle. If you need any additional reasons to separate yourself from cigarettes, alcohol, or illegal drugs, or if you need some extra resolve to remain free of these unhealthy habits, consider carefully the following facts:

Cigarette smoking. This is a form of legalized drug addiction that is harmful to the smoker, those around the smoker, and especially the baby growing inside the smoker. Thousands of chemicals in cigarette smoke flow directly from the mother's lungs into her bloodstream and then directly into the baby. According to the Centers for Disease Control and Prevention (CDC), smoking during pregnancy is the single most preventable cause of illness and death among mothers and their infants.[4] Nicotine specifically causes constriction of blood vessels in both the placenta and the baby, thus reducing the baby's supply of vital blood and oxygen. Carbon monoxide in smoke binds tightly to red blood cells and displaces oxygen. The overall effect is a recurrent choking of the baby's oxygen supply, resulting in smaller (by an average of half a pound, or 225 g) and shorter babies. Unfortunately, these infants (whom doctors refer to as small-for-dates) are more likely than their normal counterparts to have a variety of medical problems after birth.

The smoker's baby is more likely to be born prematurely or to be stillborn. The tragedy of **sudden infant death syndrome (SIDS)** occurs two to three times as frequently when the child's mother has smoked throughout pregnancy, and this increased risk continues if there is continuing exposure to secondhand smoke after birth.[5] Smoking *anywhere* in the home increases a young infant's risk of SIDS, so going to another room to smoke is not a reasonable alternative to a completely smoke-free home.[6]

Exposure to cigarette smoke after birth is linked to colds, ear infections, and asthma. And the child who sees Mom and Dad smoke is also much more likely to pick up the habit than are his peers who live in homes where there are no smokers.

Let's not forget smoking's effect on the mother. Aside from the long-term risks of chronic lung disease, heart disease, ulcers, and diseased blood vessels, she is more likely to have unexpected vaginal bleeding during her pregnancy.

The only good news about smoking is that *quitting early in pregnancy reduces the baby's risk of problems to the level of a child born to a nonsmoker.* For many women, the emotional impact of a threat to the baby is powerful enough to override the compulsion to light up, and a pregnancy usually lasts long enough to help temporary abstinence lead to a smoke-free life.

But cigarettes are so powerfully addictive that additional support may be necessary to kick the habit. If you are a smoker, it's never too late—or too early—to stop. A successful decision to quit usually requires:

- A well-defined list of reasons that have some emotional power. ("I don't want to starve my baby of oxygen" or "I want to live long enough to see my kids grow up.") Since resistance to quitting often hinges on an emotional attachment to cigarettes, your reasons for giving up smoking should likewise motivate you on an emotional level.
- A specified quitting date that is announced to family, friends, and coworkers. Some gentle peer pressure can be a powerful motivator.
- Participation in a stop-smoking class. These are available in most communities through hospitals or local chapters of national organizations (American Lung Association, American Heart Association, American Cancer Society).
- A firm declaration that your home, car, and workplace are smoke-free zones. Nobody, but nobody—spouse, in-laws, guests, visiting heads of state—lights up in your airspace.
- If you are not yet pregnant, you may wish to consider using nicotine patches or chewing gum to assist you through the withdrawal process. These are now available on both a prescription and nonprescription (or over-the-counter) basis. You should not smoke while using nicotine patches or gum. These nicotine-replacement products are generally not recommended for use during pregnancy, although some research has suggested that short-term use to help end a tobacco habit may be preferable to ongoing smoking by a pregnant woman. You should review any concerns about their proper use (especially during or after pregnancy) with your physician.

According to the Centers for Disease Control and Prevention (CDC), if just one percent of the number of pregnant women who smoke would quit, about 1,300 cases of low birth weight infants would be prevented each year.

Alcoholic beverages. We'll start and end this section with some critical bottom-line statements:

- When a pregnant woman drinks alcohol, her baby does as well.
- *Any* amount of alcohol consumed by a mother at *any* time during pregnancy can be potentially harmful to her baby.

A baby exposed to alcohol before birth is at risk for suffering a number of irreversible problems that are collectively known as **fetal alcohol spectrum disorders (FASDs)**.

The most extreme manifestation of these is **fetal alcohol syndrome (FAS)**, which is considered one of the leading causes of preventable birth defects and mental retardation. Babies with this disorder may have a variety of abnormalities of the head, face, heart, joints, and limbs, including growth deficiency. In addition, the central nervous system can be affected, causing mental retardation, hyperactivity, and behavioral problems. Memory, communication, attention span, vision, and hearing may be affected throughout life.

When a pregnant woman drinks alcohol, her baby does as well. Any amount of alcohol consumed by a mother at any time during pregnancy can be potentially harmful to her baby.

For every child with FAS it is estimated that there are three or more who have some but not all of its manifestations. These tend to fall into two specific subgroups: Those with **alcohol-related neurodevelopmental disorder** (or **ARND**) primarily manifest mental and behavioral disturbances, while those with **alcohol-related birth defects** (or **ARBD**) have problems with one or more body structures such as the heart, kidney, or bones.

Fetal alcohol syndrome occurs most often among infants born to women who chronically abuse alcohol (typically consuming four or more drinks daily), but ARND and ARBD can occur when mothers drink much less. Some research has suggested that babies born to women who have had as little as one drink per week during pregnancy may be at higher risk for behavior problems later in life.[7] Furthermore, fetal alcohol spectrum disorders can occur in a child whose mother drank at *any* stage of her pregnancy. Birth defects (such as heart abnormalities) are more likely to arise from alcohol consumption during the first three months of pregnancy; growth disturbances can occur when a mother drinks during the last few months; and adverse effects on the brain can result from a mother's alcohol use at any time while pregnant.[8]

Here's the bottom line again, stated another way:

- There is no amount of alcohol that can be considered safe for a woman to drink during pregnancy.
- There is no time during pregnancy when consuming alcohol can be considered safe for the developing baby.

Because a woman may become pregnant without realizing it, and because many pregnancies are unplanned, a woman who is *thinking* about becoming pregnant (or who even remotely suspects that she might be pregnant) should not consume any alcohol. If abstaining from alcohol is hard for you or if you tend to lose control of the amount you drink at any given time, you would be wise to seek help *before* you become pregnant, whether in a group setting (such as a church support group or Alcoholics Anonymous) or individually with a professional counselor.

Illegal drugs. The use of illegal drugs continues to be a fearsome epidemic in our culture. The popular term *recreational drug use* is a contradiction because the word *recreation* implies an activity that has a positive, restoring, re-creating effect on mind and body. These substances, however, have just the opposite effect, draining away the resources, health, and ultimately the life from their users. When the user is a pregnant woman, two lives (at least) are being damaged.

Regular **marijuana** users may deliver prematurely and even at term are more likely to have smaller babies. **Cocaine** use during pregnancy can cause not only a miscarriage or premature labor but also the eventual delivery of a small, irritable baby who may have serious, lifelong problems. Aside from any difficulties that might arise from premature delivery, cocaine itself can damage the infant's central nervous system, urinary tract, and limbs by constricting their blood supply. Increased irritability during the newborn period, developmental delays, and difficulty with learning and interacting with others may also be attributable to cocaine use by the mother. (Frequently cocaine users consume substances such as alcohol and tobacco as well, complicating the question of identifying specific consequences of cocaine.) Long-term memory and learning problems may also occur in the child whose mother has taken the popular mood-altering drug **ecstasy** during pregnancy. **Amphetamine** use during pregnancy can compromise the supply of nutrients to the growing baby. It can even cause a dangerous event known as **placental abruption**, in which the placenta prematurely separates from the uterus, threatening the lives of both baby and mother.

A mother's use of narcotics such as **heroin** or **methadone** throughout her pregnancy may subject the baby to a difficult withdrawal after birth. Symptoms, which usually begin during the first day or two after birth, can include increased irritability, tremors, a high-pitched cry, constant hunger, sweating, and sneezing. In severe cases, seizures, vomiting, diarrhea, and difficulty with breathing can occur. Furthermore, if these drugs are taken intravenously (that is, injected into the veins), the mother risks becoming infected with one or more dangerous pathogens, including the viruses that cause hepatitis B and C as well as AIDS. Any of these could not only shorten the mother's life drastically but could infect her baby as well. Furthermore, a woman addicted to one or more drugs may resort to exchanges of sex for cash or drugs, thus greatly increasing her risk for acquiring a sexually transmitted infection.

As serious as all these health concerns are, they do not encompass the vast waste of resources and the chaotic lifestyle that so often accompany the use of illegal drugs. Chronic drug abusers are usually unable to deal consistently with the daily demands of child care. Food preparation, safety in the home, and basic health practices are likely to be compromised. Run-ins with the law and difficulty maintaining steady employment are not uncommon. Healthy relationships with friends and family members may be in short supply. The disturbances and distractions of chronic drug use seriously compromise a parent's ability to bring up healthy children. Whether or not you are pregnant, the time to stop using any of these toxic substances is *now*, and seeking help to do so should be an immediate priority.

Caffeine. This stimulant abounds in everyday beverages such as coffee, tea, and soft drinks, as well as some headache remedies and pain relievers. A daily intake of up to 300 mg (the amount in two or three five-ounce cups of coffee) is widely considered safe during pregnancy. Larger amounts (over 500 mg per day) will keep both you and your baby awake, and his or her increased activity levels before birth may lead to a lower birth weight. If you consume coffee by the pot or sodas by the six-pack, you should begin cutting back on your intake of these drinks to reduce your daily caffeine to well below 300 mg (see table on page 18) before you become pregnant or reduce immediately if you are already expecting. Decreasing the brewing time for coffee or tea will also cut caffeine content. (If you're trying to become pregnant, you should be aware that some evidence suggests that consuming more than 300 to 500 mg of caffeine per day may delay conception.) One additional thought: While coffee and tea (with or without caffeine) contain antioxidants that may actually provide some long-term health benefits, soft drinks contain a lot of sugar (or artificial sweetener) and zero nutritional value. If they are part of your daily nutritional routine, demoting them to an occasional indulgence or phasing them out entirely would be a wise decision.

CAFFEINE CONTENT OF FOOD AND BEVERAGES

Food Source	Amount	Caffeine Content
Regular coffee	8 oz (240 ml)	100–300 mg
Instant coffee	8 oz	80–100 mg
Decaf coffee	8 oz	3–5 mg
Tea	8 oz	60–65 mg
*Regular cola	12 oz (360 ml)	36 mg
Diet cola	12 oz	36–47 mg
Chocolate bar	1 oz (30 g)	20 mg

* Read labels to determine the presence of caffeine in specific soft drinks, such as Mountain Dew and Dr. Pepper.

Prescription and over-the-counter (OTC) drugs. In general, you should try to avoid using any type of medication that isn't specifically prescribed or approved by your physician. *Always be sure to inform any physician who treats you that you are or might be pregnant, since this could have a significant impact on the medication(s) he or she might recommend.*

The fact that you can buy a drug off the shelf at the supermarket doesn't necessarily mean that it is wise to use it during pregnancy. Pain relievers, cold tablets, laxatives, and other medications, as well as vitamin, herb, and food supplements, may seem harmless merely because they are easily accessible or advertised as "natural." A number of these are, in fact, quite safe during pregnancy, but you should consult your physician, who is familiar with your medical history and the details of your pregnancy, before using any of them. Common examples of OTC medications include the following:

Pain relievers. Acetaminophen (Tylenol and other brands) is generally recognized as safe for both mother and baby during pregnancy when used in the recommended dosage, but it can be toxic to the liver in an overdose. This drug reduces aches, pains, headaches, and fever. Aspirin and the anti-inflammatory drugs **ibuprofen** (Advil, Motrin, and others) and **naproxen** (Aleve) may increase the risk of bleeding in both mother and baby, especially around the time of birth. Anti-inflammatory medications taken late in pregnancy also may inhibit the onset of labor. Furthermore, they can cause a structure in the infant's heart known as the **ductus arteriosus** to close, resulting in potential circulatory problems after birth. While such complications are very unusual, you should avoid these medications during pregnancy (especially during the final three months) unless they are recommended for a specific purpose by your physician.

Cold tablets. Decongestants, antihistamines, cough syrups, and nasal sprays are sold in a bewildering array of combinations and preparations. All are intended to relieve symptoms, but these drugs rarely have a direct effect on the course of an upper-respiratory illness. Some of the ingredients in cold remedies are considered safe during a normal pregnancy, but you should check with your physician and pharmacist before using any of them. Rest, fluids, and time will take care of the vast majority of these infections. However, you should also contact your doctor if your runny nose, sore throat, or cough continues for more than a week; if you are producing thick, discolored drainage from nose or chest; or if you are running a fever over 100°F (37.8°C). If the doctor you speak with is not the one who is caring for your pregnancy, be sure that he or she knows you are pregnant.

Antacids. Many pregnant women develop heartburn and indigestion because of changes in the intestinal tract produced by the growing uterus. Antacids are generally considered safe during pregnancy when used in recommended doses, but they may provoke diarrhea and can interfere with the absorption of prescription drugs. If neither antacids nor simple measures (such as eating smaller amounts of food more frequently and avoiding lying down within an hour after eating) are controlling these symptoms, the nonprescription medications **cimetidine** (Tagamet) and **ranitidine** (Zantac) are generally considered both effective and safe during pregnancy. As with nearly all medications, you should consult with your obstetrician before using any of these during the first three months of pregnancy. (A similar drug, **nizatidine** [Axid], is *not* recommended during pregnancy because of adverse effects in animal studies.)[10]

Laxatives. Constipation is common during pregnancy, but chemical laxatives are not the preferred method of treatment. Lots of fluids and juices, additional fiber in the diet (whether directly from food sources or from psyllium-seed supplements such as Metamucil or Citrucel), and regular exercise are the best first-line remedies. If you are not able to have a bowel movement for a few days at a time, you should review additional options with your physician.

Are you exposed to any environmental hazards?

During the course of your pregnancy, and especially during the first three months, you should minimize your exposure to **X-rays** (also called **ionizing radiation**). Exposure to very large doses during the early weeks, when the baby's tissues and organs are under construction, could lead to birth defects. Fortunately, the X-ray exposure involved in common medical examinations is a tiny fraction of the amount generally considered risky. If you have had one or more diagnostic X-rays and then discover you were pregnant at the time, it is extremely unlikely that your baby will be affected. Nevertheless, if this occurs you should review with your physician what procedures were done.

Some reasonable precautions to minimize your (and your baby's) exposure to X-rays include these steps:

- If X-rays (including those in the dentist's office) have been recommended, be sure to tell both your physician or dentist and the X-ray technician if you are or might be pregnant.
- If at all possible, postpone X-rays until after the baby is born, or at least wait until the first three months of pregnancy have passed. Procedures that do not utilize ionizing radiation, such as **ultrasound** or **magnetic resonance imaging (MRI)**, may be alternative options that can supply the necessary diagnostic information. (It is currently assumed but not proven that an MRI study is safe in early pregnancy.) If X-rays are needed in an emergency situation, techniques that limit exposure (such as shielding the abdomen with a lead apron or limiting the number of films taken) may be utilized. (It is generally recommended that a woman of reproductive age have her abdomen shielded when she has *any* type of X-ray.)

- If you work around sources of ionizing radiation (for example, in an office or hospital area where X-rays are taken), be sure to follow carefully the occupational guidelines in your facility for minimizing and measuring any ongoing exposure.
- Depending upon location, dose, and timing during pregnancy, radiation therapy for cancer may—or may not—pose a significant hazard to a developing baby. The difficult problem of managing a cancer arises only in about one in one thousand pregnancies. Should this occur, however, the benefits and risks of any proposed treatment—as well as the consequences of postponing treatment—must be reviewed in detail and decisions made after careful deliberation and prayer.

Over the past several years concerns have been raised about the effects of exposure of pregnant women to **nonionizing radiation**—microwaves, radio waves, electromagnetic fields (such as those associated with power lines), and infrared light. Thus far, problems arising from these forms of radiation have not been clearly demonstrated. Specifically, research has not shown an increased risk of birth defects among pregnant women who work at video display terminals (VDTs) such as computer monitors for several hours per week. Similarly, adverse effects of living near power lines have not been established.

Some concerns have been raised about prolonged exposure to high temperatures in **hot tubs**, **whirlpools**, and **saunas**. The American College of Obstetricians and Gynecologists recommends that a woman avoid core body temperatures above 102.2°F (39°C) during the first three months of pregnancy because of an increased risk of her baby having a birth defect. Because a maximum safe amount of exposure to high temperatures cannot be established with complete certainty, and because ten to twenty minutes in a hot tub can raise a person's body temperature to 102° (38.9°C) or more, it is best to avoid hot tubs or extremely hot baths altogether during the course of your pregnancy (and especially during the first three months).

Do you have any medical problems that need to be addressed?

Before 1900, a pregnant woman typically had only one prenatal visit with a physician prior to her delivery, during which her due date was determined—and little else. When

LAB TESTS COMMONLY DONE DURING PREGNANCY

- A complete blood count (CBC) to check for anemia and other abnormalities of blood components.
- A urinalysis to check for infection, protein (which normally is minimally present in urine), blood, or other signs of disease.
- Blood type and Rh factor. This is important because differences between your blood type or Rh and the baby's could lead to complications in the newborn. For women who do not have the Rh factor (that is, they are Rh-negative), additional screening is done later in the pregnancy.
- A blood test for immunity to rubella (German measles).
- Tests for syphilis, hepatitis B, chlamydia, and HIV, and possibly for gonorrhea (see Special Concerns "Sexually Transmitted Infections: Their Impact on You and Your Unborn Child," page 73).
- Blood glucose to check for diabetes.

next seen, she might be near term and in perfect health—or severely ill with an infection or a complication of her pregnancy. One of the major advances in public health in the early twentieth century was the recognition that a number of health problems that affect both mother and child could be detected, and in many cases corrected, through screening during pregnancy.

Many experts now not only advocate starting prenatal care as soon as possible after a pregnancy is diagnosed but even recommend a **preconception visit** for those who are thinking about starting a family. Whether before or during pregnancy, a thorough history and physical examination, including a review of important areas such as family background, habits, lifestyle, and general health, are wise. Some basic laboratory tests may also be done. Since all these areas can affect the health of both mother and child during pregnancy and thus the quality of a baby's start in life, an ounce or two of prevention and protection can save several pounds of costly cure. Areas to consider include:

Family background. If there is a history of any diseases that are passed by inheritance (such as cystic fibrosis, sickle cell disease, or Tay-Sachs disease) within the family of either parent-to-be, genetic counseling can help to determine the potential risk of having a baby with a similar problem. This information can in turn guide decisions about having certain tests done during pregnancy to detect possible problems in the child (see Special Concerns, "Birth Defects and Prenatal Testing," page 85).

Previous pregnancies. If you have had a prior pregnancy loss, a complication during labor or delivery, or a child born with a congenital problem of any type, specific tests and preparations may be in order before or during another pregnancy.

General health. Pregnancy is not a disease, of course, but it does have a significant impact on the way a woman's body functions. Furthermore, a number of medical problems can have a profound effect on her pregnancy and the health of her baby. The most important of these are diabetes, high blood pressure (hypertension), epilepsy, heart disease, asthma, kidney disease, and the so-called autoimmune disorders such as rheumatoid arthritis or systemic lupus erythematosus. Any of these problems should

- A Pap test (smear) to check the cells of the cervix (the opening of the uterus) for abnormalities, including cancerous or precancerous cells. This is normally carried out during the first prenatal visit if it has not been done during the previous year.
- Screening for bacterial and viral infections in the vagina and cervix. This is often performed during pregnancy. Specifically, a woman who has had a premature delivery in the past may be screened during her first prenatal visit for bacterial vaginosis, the presence of certain bacteria in the vagina that could increase the risk for premature rupture of membranes and subsequent labor. A culture for group B streptococci, which can infect and harm the newborn after delivery, is generally done during the last few weeks of pregnancy.
- Other tests may be appropriate, based on your history or exam findings. For example, if you have high blood pressure, an assessment of kidney function and other tests may be necessary. ■

be addressed and controlled, if at all possible, *before* becoming pregnant or as soon as possible after pregnancy is confirmed.

Infections and immunity. Most acute illnesses (such as colds) that might occur during a pregnancy are weathered without difficulty by both mother and baby. However, some types of infections in a pregnant woman can have adverse effects on her unborn child. When one of these occurs, the ultimate outcome will depend on (among other things) the type of organism, the severity of the infection, and the stage of pregnancy during which it occurs. While the more troublesome infections are uncommon, it is well worth taking some basic precautions in order to avoid them.

Rubella (German or **three-day measles)** is a viral infection that causes fever, aches, and a rash for a few days. If a woman becomes infected with rubella during the first three months of pregnancy, her baby will have a significant risk of developing one or more serious defects, which together are known as **congenital rubella syndrome**. These can include delayed growth, mental retardation, eye disorders, deafness, and heart disease. Congenital rubella syndrome rarely occurs if the mother is infected with rubella after the halfway point of the pregnancy (twenty weeks).

We will look at rubella in more detail, and the importance of immunizing a child against it, in "Immunizations— Which Ones, Why, and When?" beginning on page 739.

Any woman who might become pregnant should have a blood test to see if she is immune to this disease. A vaccine that protects children and adults from developing rubella has been available since 1969, and its widespread use has drastically reduced the number of cases of both the infection and congenital rubella syndrome in the United States over the past few decades. Most young women have had at least one MMR (measles/mumps/rubella) injection—two doses during childhood have been recommended since 1990—*but this does not guarantee that they are protected.*

If a blood test does not detect antibodies to rubella, a woman should have an immunization *before* she becomes pregnant. Most experts recommend waiting for one month after the injection before becoming pregnant,[11] although congenital rubella syndrome has not been reported even when the injection has been accidentally given during pregnancy. (If a woman is breastfeeding, the rubella vaccine can be administered without any apparent risk to the nursing child.)

Chickenpox (varicella) is another viral infection that usually occurs during childhood, although susceptible adults (including pregnant women) can also develop this illness—often causing a more difficult course than the one their younger counterparts experience.

A developing baby can be infected with the mother's chickenpox, and the consequences will depend on the timing of the illness. If she becomes ill during the first twelve weeks of pregnancy, there is a 0.4 percent risk (stated another way, a one in 250 chance) of her baby developing a **congenital varicella syndrome**, which may include any of several defects of the eyes, heart, and limbs. If the infection occurs between thirteen and twenty weeks of the pregnancy, the risk of congenital varicella syndrome is about 2 percent. There is no way to determine whether the baby has been affected at the time of the mother's infection. Unfortunately, women who are infected with chickenpox during the first half of pregnancy may be advised that they should have an abortion without being told that the risk of a congenital problem is quite low.

After twenty weeks of pregnancy, chickenpox in the mother does not result in harm to her baby unless the infection occurs from five days before to two days after delivery. (Before birth, the baby can be infected through the mother's blood via the umbilical cord. If the mother is infected shortly after giving birth, the baby can contract the illness by direct exposure.) When this occurs, a severe infection can result because the baby may acquire the virus without also receiving any of the mother's protective antibodies. If this occurs, the baby should receive an injection called varicella-zoster immune globulin (or VZIG), which provides a temporary protective dose of "borrowed" antibody.

If you are pregnant and do not believe you have had this disease, you should be careful to avoid any child who has or might have chickenpox, as well as any adult with an outbreak of shingles, which can spread the same virus. If you are uncertain whether or not you have had chickenpox in the past and wish to find out prior to or during pregnancy, your doctor can order a blood test that detects antibodies to the virus. If the test indicates that you are not immune and you are not yet pregnant, discuss with your physician the possibility of receiving the varicella vaccine, which is given in two doses four to eight weeks apart. You should avoid becoming pregnant for at least one month after receiving either dose of the vaccine.[12]

Group B streptococci are bacteria that are present in the vagina of approximately 20 to 25 percent of pregnant women and can infect the baby during birth, especially if labor is premature or if the woman's membranes are ruptured for more than eighteen hours prior to delivery. Overall, about one of every one thousand infants is infected during birth, often with severe consequences including pneumonia and meningitis. Your doctor may recommend a culture to detect this bacteria at some point during your pregnancy. A baby born to a woman who is a carrier of group B streptococci has a one in two hundred chance of being infected if the mother is not treated with antibiotics at the time of delivery. If she is treated, however, the risk of group B strep infection drops twentyfold to one in four thousand.

The term *ruptured membranes* refers to the breaking open of the amniotic sac (known more familiarly as the "bag of waters") that contains amniotic fluid in which the baby floats prior to birth.

Toxoplasmosis is an infection caused by a one-celled parasite (*Toxoplasma gondii* is its official name) that usually causes few or no symptoms in children or adults who have normal immunity. However, if a woman becomes infected with *Toxoplasma* just before or during her pregnancy, her baby may become infected as well. The infant may not have any symptoms, or he may develop a disease that can affect the skin, central nervous system, vision, and/or hearing. Premature delivery, a head that is small (microcephaly) or large (macrocephaly), enlargement of liver and spleen, and anemia (a low red cell count) may also occur. Seizures and mental retardation may be late manifestations. If recognized in mother and/or infant, toxoplasmosis can be treated with antibiotics. Unfortunately, this infection can be difficult to diagnose, and treatment may or may not change the outcome. Because toxoplasmosis is potentially very hazardous to a preborn infant but difficult to diagnose and treat, *preventing* the disease is critical.

Cats play a pivotal role in the transmission of toxoplasmosis, passing millions of parasites in their feces for about three weeks after eating birds, rodents, or other animals that have been infected. The cat feces in turn can spread *Toxoplasma* wherever they are deposited—in a litter box, a garden, or a feed lot. Animals such as pigs or sheep that eat contaminated feed can develop cysts containing the parasite in their muscles, which can then infect the unwary individual who eats undercooked meat. To minimize your risk of getting toxoplasmosis, you need to mind how you handle your cat (if you have one) and your food (even if you don't have a cat).

According to the Centers for Disease Control and Prevention (CDC), more than 60 million Americans have been infected by *Toxoplasma gondii*. Each year between four hundred and four thousand infants are infected before birth, and as many as eighty die of toxoplasmosis.[13]

- If you have an indoor cat, keep her that way.
- Don't feed your cat raw meat. Stick with canned or dry cat food.

- If you're pregnant, don't get a new cat—especially a stray. Note that kittens and younger cats are more likely to spread *Toxoplasma* than older cats.
- If you're pregnant, have someone else clean the litter box. Daily removal of feces reduces the likelihood of transmission because the parasite is not infectious until at least a day after it has been passed by the cat.
- If no one else can clean the litter box, wear disposable gloves, clean it daily, and wash your hands thoroughly after doing so.
- Because cats pass *Toxoplasma* in their feces for only a few weeks after becoming infected, testing their stools for the parasite is not recommended.
- Wash your hands thoroughly after handling soil, sand, raw meat, or unwashed fruits and vegetables.
- Cook your meat thoroughly, making sure there is no visible pink color, until it reaches an internal temperature of 160°F (71.1°C). Don't sample meat that is still cooking.
- Wash your cutting boards and other food preparation surfaces with hot water and soap after you have used them.
- Wash and/or peel fresh fruits and vegetables before you eat them.

Listeriosis is an infection caused by a type of bacteria (known as *Listeria monocytogenes*) that can be transmitted through a variety of ready-to-eat foods derived from animals.[14] It is particularly hazardous for the elderly, those with impaired immunity, pregnant women, and unborn children. (One in three cases of this disease occurs during pregnancy.) Even if the mother does not become ill, *Listeria* can be transmitted to her baby during pregnancy and may cause miscarriage, stillbirth, or premature delivery. A baby infected near the end of pregnancy is at risk for serious illness after birth and a number of potentially serious long-term problems involving the central nervous system, heart, or kidneys.

As with toxoplasmosis, listeriosis can be prevented by taking some basic precautions involving the handling, preparation, or outright avoidance of certain types of food:

- Do not eat unpasteurized milk or any foods that contain it.
- Do not eat unpasteurized soft cheeses such as feta, brie, Camembert, or cheeses such as *queso blanco fresco* (fresh white cheese) that are popular in Hispanic cuisine. Pasteurized cheeses, cottage cheese, cream cheese, and hard cheeses are safe.
- Hot dogs, lunch meats, and deli meats should not be eaten *unless* heated until steaming hot.
- Do not eat smoked seafood that you find in the refrigerated section of the store or the deli counter. These include fish such as salmon, trout, tuna, whitefish, cod, and mackerel, variously described as smoked, lox, kippered, jerky, or nova-style. (This type of fish may be eaten if it is an ingredient in a fully cooked dish.)
- Perishable foods that are ready to eat or precooked should be eaten as soon as possible, even if kept in the refrigerator. (Unlike many bacteria, *Listeria* can grow at 40°F [4.4°C] or below.)
- Clean your refrigerator regularly.
- Wash raw vegetables thoroughly before peeling or eating them.

Parvovirus causes an infection, seen commonly in schoolchildren but also in other age-groups, called **erythema infectiosum**, or **fifth disease**. Typically seen in winter and spring months, fifth disease is most well known for producing a so-called slapped-cheek rash on the face, although a lacy eruption may be seen on the arms, legs, and upper body as well. Adults who are infected may develop the rash but also typically develop aching joints. However, both children and adults can become infected without any symptoms at all. Unfortunately, this disease is contagious for up to three weeks *before* the rash breaks out, so it is virtually impossible to prevent exposure of other family members.

If a woman becomes infected with parvovirus during pregnancy, it's very likely that there will be no adverse effects on her baby. However, sometimes the mother's infection results in a severe anemia in the baby, which in turn can cause congestive heart failure. This may result in the death of the preborn baby, leading to miscarriage or stillbirth, especially if the infection occurs during the first half of the pregnancy. Therefore, a pregnant woman who is exposed to this infection should have a blood test to determine whether she is immune to it. If she is, there should be no cause for concern. If not, testing may be recommended later in the pregnancy to determine whether she has become infected.

If infection with parvovirus appears to have taken place during pregnancy—with or without symptoms—the baby should be monitored with ultrasound exams prior to birth for signs of heart failure resulting from anemia. Should heart failure or anemia develop, the baby may require medication, early delivery, or even a transfusion prior to birth (one of the many forms of medical intervention now available for the preborn).

Cytomegalovirus (CMV) has the dubious distinction of causing the most common congenital infection in the United States while being both untreatable and rarely (if ever) preventable. Fortunately, significant CMV disease in newborns is very uncommon. Approximately one to 3 percent of pregnant women experience a primary (first-time) infection with CMV, but the vast majority have no symptoms. About 30 to 40 percent of infected mothers transmit the virus to their babies, but only about 10 to 15 percent of infected infants will have some form of noticeable disease at birth. Sadly, about 20 percent of those with symptoms of CMV infection at birth will die, and 90 percent of the survivors will have long-term neurological problems. In addition, about 15 percent of infected infants who do not have symptoms at birth will develop problems (such as mental retardation, vision and hearing loss) during the first two years of life. At the present time, pregnant women are not screened for their susceptibility to CMV because there is no effective treatment for this infection. However, if a woman develops an illness during pregnancy that resembles mononucleosis—with fever, sore throat, enlarged lymph nodes in the neck, and marked fatigue—her physician may at some point request blood tests or even cultures to help determine if CMV might be involved. If this diagnosis is made, she will need careful and accurate counseling regarding the risk of the baby having congenital disease.

Approximately twenty different **sexually transmitted infections (STIs)** pose significant risks to both mother and baby. Many STIs are passed during intimate contact with people who look perfectly well and have no signs of illness. *Unfortunately, the first indication that an infection has taken place may be the birth of a very sick baby, a miscarriage or stillbirth, or even a woman's inability to become pregnant.* The Special Concerns section on page 73 has details about STIs and pregnancy, including descriptions of their symptoms, risks to an unborn child, treatment, and prevention. Even if you consider yourself at low risk for having a sexually transmitted infection, you would be wise to review this

Erythema infectiosum (which literally means "infectious redness") was given the name fifth disease because it was originally fifth on a list of common childhood infectious diseases that were accompanied by rash. The first four were measles, rubella (German measles), scarlet fever, and a viral infection called scarlatinella.

information. (An in-depth look at the impact of STIs on adolescents and young adults is contained in a Special Concerns section beginning on page 539.)

Personal and Spiritual Preparations: What Sort of World Will Your Child Live In?

As important as it is to have a safe and satisfactory childbirth, in the long run the most critical assignments of parenthood involve much more than preparing for the delivery date. Once the cord is cut and the first breaths of air are taken, your child's world has permanently and dramatically changed. If she is going to thrive, and not merely survive, that world needs to be safe, stable, and loving, especially during the first three years of life.

The task of parenting is too scary on our own, and there is not enough knowledge in the books to guarantee the outcome of our duties. We desperately need divine help to do the job properly!

The New Dare to Discipline
By Dr. James Dobson

It is a sad reality that the world at large is anything *but* safe, stable, and loving. It is full of "many dangers, toils, and snares," to quote the writer of the hymn "Amazing Grace," so much so that some young adults are not sure they are willing to bring a child into a world so torn by upheaval and uncertainty.

But for children (especially the very young), the world they experience is primarily the creation of the people around them. The sights, sounds, and touches of parents and family and a general sense of order, comfort, and predictability can be an island of love and sanity, even when the culture outside the front door is volatile or even violent. The reverse is also true: The prettiest home in the nicest neighborhood may be hell on earth for a young child, who will carry the aftermath of damaging experiences into adulthood.

Whatever else you do as you bring up your child, you must convey a crucial message that she can hear, see, and *experience* in hundreds of different ways, especially when she is young:

> You are loved, you are important, and you always will be, no matter what happens. I care enough about you to provide for you, stand with you, coach you, correct you, and even die for you if necessary. My commitment to you is not based on what you do or don't do, how you look, whether your body is perfect or handicapped, or how you perform in school or sports. It is based on the fact that I am your parent and you are my child, a priceless gift whom God has loaned to me for a season. Eventually I will release you to live your own life, but while you are growing up, I consider caring for you an assignment of utmost importance.

Obviously, a newborn baby will not understand these words, and even an older child will not fully grasp their meaning. But embracing these words as a mind-set and a fundamental attitude toward your child will shape thousands of interactions that ultimately convey its message. Indeed, most of the other details and techniques of child rearing—feeding, toilet training, education, and the rest—pale in comparison to the importance of communicating this attitude to your child, week in and week out for years.

The question to ponder, therefore, is this: Are you ready to deliver this message to your child and to strive to make your child's world safe, stable, and loving?

This is certainly a more complicated question to answer than "Are you smoking cigarettes?" or "Is your blood pressure too high?" The answer has a lot to do with how *you* were brought up and with the decisions you have made up until now. The answer is also affected by the way you see yourself in relation to the baby, to any other children you may have, to your mate, to your own parents, to the world in general, and ultimately to God. To get a better grasp on this issue, consider carefully the following questions, perhaps writing down your thoughts in a journal for future reference:

- What did your mother and father teach you about love, safety, and security? Did you see them express affection for one another? Did they build one another up or barrage one another, and everyone else, with criticism? (If you were reared by one parent, the same questions apply in connection with that parent or other caregivers.)
- Did you hear and feel that you were loved unconditionally? Were consistent limits set and enforced? Was discipline administered in a context of teaching and love, or did unpredictable punishments occur in outbursts of anger? Was your home a safe or a dangerous place? Were you abused as a child—or as an adult?
- Are you expecting your baby to give you love? Are you hoping to derive significance from the role of being a mother or a father? Or do you already feel loved and believe that your life is significant and useful?
- How do you feel when
      you are interrupted frequently?
      someone needs you constantly?
      you have ongoing responsibilities?
      sudden changes rearrange your plans?
      you don't get enough sleep?

The messages you received from one or both parents can have a profound impact on the messages you in turn give to your own child. If your world was safe and secure, and if you felt loved and accepted by the most important people in your life—even when you were being corrected or disciplined—you are more likely to transmit that same sense of belonging and security to your own child. If the opposite was true, you may have a difficult time communicating warmth and acceptance to a child because you are probably still seeking them yourself.

You may be looking for love, acceptance, and significance from the role of being a mother or a father (and the recognition from others that ideally should come with the role) or even directly from your child. *But for babies or small children, nearly all of the loving and caring flows in a one-way direction: from you to them.* The newborn baby in particular is totally incapable of offering any affection before the first genuine smile appears at about the age of one month. His or her crying—especially if there is a lot of it—may sound downright hostile to the mother or father who is looking for a little appreciation for all the effort, pain, and sleepless nights.

If you are not sure—or are not happy—about your answers to these questions, you are not alone. No one has had perfect parents, and no one has lived a life free of mistakes and bad decisions. We are all on a learning curve, especially when it comes to parenting, and it's never too late to make course corrections. Here are some ways to get started:

Tap into a support team. By seeking guidance and input from your pastor, a professional counselor, a relative, or someone with parenting experience whom you respect, you can gain valuable encouragement and support. Many churches have ongoing small-group studies available for young parents, and these can be water in the desert during some of the challenging periods of child rearing. A counselor may be efficient at sorting through your particular personal issues, but a great deal can also be accomplished with a person (or a couple) who is willing to serve as a mentor. If you have been verbally, physically, or sexually abused as a child (or adult), it is particularly important that you work with someone who is qualified to help you in the process of healing the wounds that are an inevitable consequence of such experiences.

Take advantage of books, CDs, audiocassettes, and DVDs/videotapes that can be utilized at your own pace. There is an abundance of materials that can educate and inspire you or supplement counseling about a particular problem.

Maintain a regular quiet time. Setting aside time to read Scripture, reflect, and pray elevates the entire project of child rearing to a different plane. However, if you already have one or more small children at home, sitting down for a peaceful quiet time may seem about as easy as flying to Mars. Some planning, creativity, and perseverance will definitely be necessary. (For example, this activity may have to take place during nap time or after the children are in bed, assuming you can stay awake and ignore whatever mess needs to be picked up. Or you may try to think and pray while taking a walk around the block, with or without a stroller.) Whatever effort is spent carving out some time for personal renewal will definitely pay off—perhaps in ways you may not appreciate until months or years have passed.

God is clearly presented in both Old and New Testaments as the perfect parent: not only our Creator but a loving, patient, wise Father who cares enough to guide and correct His children on a daily basis. When we truly begin to grasp the lengths to which God has gone in expressing His love for each of us and His desire to be involved in the details of our lives, our ultimate sense of identity, security, and significance takes on a whole new meaning. If we were brought up in an atmosphere of inconsistency, neglect, or hostility and violence, God is willing and able to parent us, even as adults. And that in turn leads us into a new capacity for loving and cherishing our own children.

Prayer forges powerful links not only to God but also to those we care about most. It's never too late (or too early) to give thanks for our children, to release the health and well-being of each child to God's provision since they ultimately belong to Him anyway, and to pray for those who will influence that child in the future—friends, teachers, pastors, and eventually a mate.

For the parent who is married: Cultivate your relationship with your spouse. Kids whose parents are openly affectionate, do kind things for one another, and treat one another with respect will feel secure indeed. *Your relationship with your husband or wife cannot be put on hold when children begin to arrive.* Eventually they will leave the nest, and you definitely want to have a healthy and thriving marriage, with a long-lasting supply of conversation and worthwhile projects, after they are gone.

Some thoughts for the expectant and new father

As your wife progresses through her pregnancy, your original commitment to "love, honor, and cherish" will take on some important new dimensions. She is going through some significant physical changes, including radical variations in hormone levels, which can affect energy, appetite, and mood. At any given time, she may feel tired (especially if there are other small children at home), nauseated, ungainly, and unattractive. After your baby is born, she may feel terrific, but she could also feel exhausted or depressed. Unfortunately, for all of these reasons, pregnancy and the months that follow are times when someone else who isn't tired or nauseated or irritable might begin to look attractive to you—in other words, when there may be an increased risk of infidelity. Your job, therefore, is to honor the commitments you made at the altar on your wedding day and to say and do things that communicate a consistent message:

> You are loved, you are important, and you always will be, no matter what happens. I care enough about you to provide for you, stand with you, protect you, and even die for you if necessary. My commitment to you is not based on how you look, whether your body is perfect, how much you accomplish, or whether we can have sex. It is based on the fact that I am your husband and you are my wife and that our union is a priceless gift that God has so graciously provided. I consider looking out for your well-being to be an assignment of utmost importance as long as we live.

Sound familiar? Cultivating this attitude toward your wife is the foundation for communicating the same message to your child. Some practical suggestions include:

Take the time to communicate. If you have been separated from your wife all day, debriefing with her is far more important than browsing through the evening paper or watching the six o'clock news. This is particularly important if she is caring for small children at home, since most women crave adult conversation after a day full of toddler talk. You can begin with the simple "How was your day?" type of questions—and pay attention to the answers—but on a regular basis (weekly, if not more often) both of you should also ask and answer some important "checking in" questions as well:

1. What was the high point of your week (or day)?
2. What was the low point?
3. What are you most worried about right now?
4. Is there anything I can do right now to help you with what you are worried about (or anything else)?

Here's another important tip: Throughout your married life (and not just during pregnancy and the child-rearing years), make it a habit to ask these or similar questions, and listen carefully to the responses. Otherwise, after a few years you may find yourselves not knowing who your spouse has become.

Learn how to listen. If she's had a bad day, hear her out. Very often a husband will go into troubleshooting mode when his wife is unhappy, but it's usually much more important to let her vent than for you to try to "fix" everything. If you're not sure, by the way, whether she is looking for a fix-it or a sympathetic ear (or perhaps some of each), it's okay to ask. (Important tip for wives: Don't require your husband to read your mind. Let him know what you need most at the moment.)

Offer to take on some tasks that might not normally be your turf at home. Better yet, just do them without saying anything about it. Shoo her out of the kitchen, clean up the kids' mess, or offer to do the grocery run if you're not doing so already. Give her the opportunity to go out for a few hours to do something she enjoys or simply let her put her feet up or take a warm, uninterrupted bath.

Maintain (or start) a date night every week or at least twice a month. Spending a lot of money is not the object—but spending time together is. She needs to know that she is still desirable and that you appreciate her.

Unexpected flowers and cards always make an amazingly positive impact, as they have for generations.

A number of constructive approaches to dealing with marital and family issues can be found in Special Concerns, "Conflict within the Family," beginning on page 425.

Pray regularly for and with your wife.

On the warnings and cautions side, remember the following:

Learn to deal with conflict constructively. Most people do not automatically know how to discuss differences of opinion, especially strong ones, in a manner that is mutually respectful. If you find that discussions are generating more heat than light, take the time and effort to work with a pastor or counselor on your specific issues. Better yet, find a husband-wife team you both respect and who would be willing to serve as mentors, particularly in improving the basic way you approach disagreements.

Choose your timing carefully when you discuss conflicts and problems. If you are both tired, distracted, or irritated, the conversation will likely be unproductive.

Eliminate from your vocabulary words and phrases that insult or degrade your wife. If common courtesy would prevent you from saying them to a coworker or a complete stranger, you have no business saying them at home.

Never, under any circumstances, strike, shove, or in any way make physical contact with your wife as an expression of anger or with intent to injure her. There is never justification for taking this type of harmful action, but it is particularly destructive when she is pregnant. If you are angry and have run out of words, walk away from the situation and calm down. If you have hit your wife (or any woman in your life) in the past or feel the urge to do so, seek help from a pastor or counselor. This is a serious issue that must not be ignored or denied.

For the mother-to-be who is single

All of the recommendations mentioned earlier—finding a support team, taking advantage of helpful books and tapes, and establishing a quiet time—are especially important for you and perhaps worth reading again. It is a courageous but often very difficult task to raise a child on your own, and you should not hesitate to seek whatever help is available within your family, church, or community at large. Most significantly, on many occasions you will also need to remember that God is keenly aware of all your needs and that He will be your "silent partner," standing beside you during those times when you feel you've reached the end of your resources.

At the same time, you will need to be careful with the attitudes you cultivate about your child. Watch out for the dangerous but all too common feeling that he is a burden, a hassle, or an obstacle to what you *really* would like to do with your life. (This viewpoint isn't unique to single mothers, by the way.) Because you might not have someone to share the workload, the time your child is dependent upon you may seem like an eternity. In fact, it is but a season, and one that will never return. It may take effort to do so, but remember—especially when what you want most is a good night's sleep, one that isn't interrupted by crying—to cherish this new person in your life.

So . . . Are You Ready to Bring Up a Child?

This is a trick question.

As important as it is to plan ahead and prepare for parenthood, it is impossible to be *completely* ready. Even those who feel ready, willing, and able; have had all their checkups; have gone to the childbirth classes; and have decked out the nursery to look like a designer showcase may be thrown a major curveball with the arrival of their new baby. An unexpected physical abnormality, a sudden medical problem during or after delivery, or perhaps a difficult temperament in an otherwise normal child can turn the lives of the most well-equipped parents inside out.

For most parents, there is never a perfect time to have a baby. There will always be problems and circumstances to deal with: education, career paths, money, living space, health problems, and most of all, the basic maturity to nurture a child—especially the first one. Unfortunately, our culture has become so fixated on idealized notions of what constitutes a "wanted" pregnancy that in the United States there is one abortion for every three babies born.

Many women have not actually been trying to become pregnant when they find out they are carrying a child, and a number are in difficult circumstances. This is a particularly acute issue when the mother is young, single, and limited in resources. Those who need help dealing with the circumstances surrounding their pregnancy should not have to fend for themselves. The good news is that help is available. Hundreds of nonprofit centers have been established across North America, all dedicated to helping pregnant women (both single and married) and those close to them tackle the challenges of pregnancy and parenthood. Their services, all given without charge, range from locating a shelter and medical care to providing baby supplies and single-parent support groups.

An organization that provides these types of services may be called a pregnancy resource center, crisis pregnancy center, pregnancy care center, or women's resource center. To locate one in your community, call 800-395-HELP or check www.optionline.org on the Internet.

The bottom line is that circumstances will *never* be perfect. No pregnancy, childbirth, or newborn baby will be flawless. But one major advantage of having nine months between conception and delivery is that it allows both Mom and Dad time to adjust and prepare for this major change in their lives. With time to reflect and draw on inner resources and assistance from family and community, the most turbulent beginnings of parenthood can ultimately have a successful outcome.

Developing a Birth Plan and Preparing the Nest

Just as every child is a unique and irreplaceable creation, each baby's entry into the world is a one-of-a-kind event. No two births are alike, even for parents who have had a number of children and feel like old pros. One critical aspect of childbirth never changes: Everyone involved in this momentous process wants the same outcome—a healthy baby and a healthy mother. Whether everything has moved like clockwork or nothing has gone as planned, this outcome is what matters most. This goal must be kept in mind during all phases of planning and experiencing birth and must override every other consideration.

There are many possible routes to the destination called healthy baby–healthy mother. A number of choices must be made along the way, although some parents may have more options than others. Who will provide the prenatal and delivery care? What type of childbirth-preparation classes are available? Who will be present at the delivery, and who will serve as coach? Will medications or anesthesia be used to relieve pain? Who will examine the baby after delivery? Will the baby stay with Mom the entire time or spend time in the nursery? What about breastfeeding versus bottle-feeding?

You may have strong convictions about all of these topics, or they may seem like a bewildering array of details to sort through when all you care about is getting everyone through the big event safe and sound. No doubt you will receive an earful of opinions from friends and relatives, if you haven't already. There is no shortage of books, magazine articles, Web sites, DVD and videocassette programs, and other materials containing information and opinions about childbirth and all that follows it.

Like everything else in parenthood, wisdom about childbirth begins by avoiding extremes. Ignoring the inevitable due date and "letting it happen" without any preparation could result in a truly unpleasant experience, if not a full-blown disaster. But holding rigid expectations about every detail of the "perfect" birthing experience could lead to disappointment and frustration—or even an all-out battle with those who are providing care during labor and delivery. Either of these approaches will get the parent-child relationship off to a shaky start.

Instead, thoughtful consideration of the following questions will help you formulate a sense of direction as you approach the due date. Write down some of the things you would like—and not like—to be part of your birthing experience, as well as the areas about which you are uncertain. Seek advice from a few mature people who have been down the road before you, and don't be dismayed if you hear differences of opinion. Be sure to review these topics with your health-care provider, preferably before the first contractions of labor begin!

Who Is Going to Provide Your Care during Pregnancy and Childbirth?

Depending upon the community in which you live and the type of health-care coverage you have, you will be dealing with one or more of the following types of providers:

An **obstetrician/gynecologist (ob/gyn)** has completed four years of medical school, followed by at least four years of residency training specializing in the female reproductive system. An ob/gyn is prepared to handle both routine and problem deliveries and can perform cesarean sections. Some have additional training in treating infertility. A **maternal-fetal medicine specialist** (sometimes known as a **perinatologist**) is an ob/gyn who has expertise in dealing with unusually difficult or high-risk pregnancies.

Many **family physicians** (**FPs**, also called **family practitioners**) provide care for pregnant women. (In Canada, FPs take care of most uncomplicated deliveries.) Following medical school, an FP completes a three-year residency that encompasses the gamut of health care, including adult internal medicine, pediatrics, ob/gyn, and surgery. A family physician can provide routine obstetric care, and baby and child care as well. Most do not take care of women with high-risk pregnancies or complicated deliveries, so FPs will routinely have an ob/gyn available for backup if trouble arises.

While most obstetricians and family physicians hold the familiar **MD** degree, a number of doctors who hold a **DO** (Doctor of Osteopathy) degree are equally qualified to serve as primary-care physicians during pregnancy and childbirth. However, this is not the case with chiropractors, naturopaths, and other alternative practitioners, whose training does not qualify them to provide prenatal care or deliver babies.

Nonphysician providers of prenatal care include the following:

A **certified nurse–midwife (CNM)** is a registered nurse who has additional hospital experience in labor and delivery and has completed training in midwifery at a program accredited by the American College of Nurse–Midwives. (There are nearly fifty such programs in the United States.) After passing a certification exam and obtaining a state license, a CNM can follow a normal pregnancy through delivery. The practice patterns of midwives in a given community will vary, depending upon the facilities and medical backup available to them. In a best-case scenario, they collaborate actively with ob/gyns and FPs, providing care for patients in hospitals or adjacent birth centers that handle uncomplicated deliveries.[1]

In some physicians' offices, a **nurse practitioner (NP)** or **physician assistant (PA)** may provide basic prenatal care under a doctor's supervision but will not actually deliver the baby. A nurse practitioner is a registered nurse (RN) who has completed advanced training in diagnosing and managing common medical conditions and illnesses through graduate nursing school. Nurse practitioners are often trained in a specific area of interest, such as gynecology or pediatrics, and when training is completed, the NP's scope of practice is limited to the chosen specialty. In many states, nurse practitioners do not have to practice under the supervision of a physician, although most do. A physician assistant has completed a two- to three-year training program (usually an extension of an accredited medical school) that includes both classroom and clinical training, comparable to the first and third years of medical school. After graduation, a physician assistant must pass a national board certifying exam to earn the title PA-C (physician assistant–certified). A PA can carry out routine exams, treat common medical problems, and prescribe medication under the supervision of a physician. NPs and PAs generally play similar roles in health-care settings.

Who Is Going to Provide Care for the Baby?

Your options for the baby's health-care provider may include the following:

Pediatricians have a medical degree and have taken at least three years of residency training in the care of infants, children, and adolescents. Like family physicians and ob/gyns, pediatricians are considered **primary-care physicians**—that is, they serve as the point of entry into the health-care system. They provide routine checkups and manage the vast majority of illnesses and other health problems of children. Some spend additional years developing expertise in subspecialty fields such as pediatric cardiology, neurology, and gastroenterology. (These physicians normally serve as consultants for specific problems rather than providing primary care. In Canada pediatricians generally function as consultants.) Some pediatricians focus more specifically on older children and teenagers, practicing what is called **adolescent medicine**. A **neonatologist**, at the other end of the age spectrum, specializes in the care of premature infants and sick newborns, usually in an intensive-care unit.

Family practitioners (whether holding MD or DO degrees) care for all age-groups, including infants and children. Depending upon their practice setting, FPs may request consultation from pediatricians or subspecialists when dealing with more difficult cases.

Pediatricians and family physicians may also employ nurse practitioners and physician assistants, who are trained to provide basic services in an office setting. Some parents wonder whether they get their money's worth if they do not actually see a doctor during their visit. But these nonphysician health-care providers are not only likely to be more readily accessible, especially for same-day appointments, but they also may be able to spend more time answering questions and working through common problems.

> *If any of you lacks wisdom, he should ask God, who gives generously to all without finding fault, and it will be given to him.*
>
> **James 1:5**

Choosing Health-Care Providers for Mother and Baby

This is an important issue because the qualifications of your health-care providers and the quality of your relationship with them can have a major impact on your childbirth—and child-rearing—experiences. Ideally you will be working with someone (or a team) who

- is competent. The greatest bedside manner in town can't compensate for lack of knowledge or poor judgment.
- treats you with respect. Courtesy, willingness to answer questions and explain clearly what is going on, and a feeling of collaboration rather than condescension are essential to good health care.

- is available. Whether you are dealing with a solo practitioner or a multispecialty group, you should be able to make contact with someone who can answer questions or respond to a problem within a reasonable period of time. That person may be the doctor, a colleague on call, an office nurse, a nurse practitioner, or a physician assistant.
- shares, or at least respects, your basic value system.

Finding all of these qualities in a practitioner may be easier said than done. Depending on their community and health-insurance coverage, some families will have more choices than others. If you have options—for example, a list of preferred providers available through your insurance—don't hesitate to make inquiries. Most hospitals have referral lists of physicians who are permitted to admit patients to their facility. This will tell you that they have passed some level of scrutiny regarding their basic competence but not much else about their practice patterns or office routines.

If you already know someone in the medical community—a longtime family physician or a neighbor who is a nurse, for example—ask for recommendations. Take an informal poll of families with children in your church or neighborhood to see which names are mentioned most often. Families with pro-life convictions often prefer to see physicians who do not perform abortions. Local pregnancy resource centers that assist women with alternatives to abortion (see page 31), or other pro-life organizations, usually maintain a list of these physicians.

If you have narrowed your list but aren't sure of your choice, you may want to set up a meet-the-doctor session. Such a visit should allow you to:

See how you are treated on the phone. Does the person at the other end of the line sound friendly, pleasant, and willing to talk, or harried and hostile?

HOW TO HAVE A GREAT RELATIONSHIP WITH YOUR DOCTOR

The best relationships between physicians and their patients, both young and old, are built on two basic qualities: mutual respect and flexibility. From the health-care provider's side, these are manifested by listening to you (and your child), providing understandable explanations, answering questions, and being willing to discuss options and alternatives to normal routines. From the patient's side, respect and flexibility involve acknowledging the value of the provider's training and experience, being willing to change course (especially during labor and delivery) if things are not going the way you had expected, and understanding that no one can guarantee a perfect outcome.

If you find yourself seeing a doctor who insists on "my way or the highway," who talks down to you like a schoolteacher addressing a misbehaving child, who races in and out of the exam room like the White Rabbit in *Alice in Wonderland*, or who won't take time to answer your questions, you should consider choosing another practitioner.

Assuming that you have a decent working relationship with your health-care provider, you can get even more out of your visits by following a few basic suggestions:

- *Do* let the doctor know at the outset of your visit what you want to talk about. If you have a number of concerns and want to make the most of

Check out the office itself. Do you (or your children, if they are going to be seen there) feel comfortable and welcome? Is the waiting area tidy or a wreck? Does it feel like a bus station, a funeral parlor, or a nice place to relax? If children are going to be seen, are there things for them to do or look at?

Meet the doctor. If you make it clear up front that you want to talk briefly and not become a patient yet, you can also ask whether there will be a consultation fee. You may not be charged, in which case you shouldn't expect a half-hour conference. If you have a lot of questions about the practice, someone on the office staff may be able to answer them for you. A large, multidoctor practice may even have a designated patient-relations representative who will be more than happy to answer questions and show you around. Whatever you do, don't set up a get-acquainted visit and then suddenly ask, "By the way, can you look in Meagan's ear?" If you want medical attention, ask for it ahead of time and sign in as a patient.

Questions you may want to ask the physician who is going to take care of you during pregnancy and childbirth:

- What is the routine for prenatal visits?
- With whom does she share after-hours coverage? Ideally you should have a chance to get to know any and all of the people who might deliver your baby.
- What will happen when labor begins? Are there routines, such as electronic fetal monitoring, that are expected as a part of every childbirth? Any problems with moving around during labor? If you want to have an unmedicated childbirth, will the physician support that decision? If you desire pain relief, what options will be available? What is the physician's approach to an **episiotomy** (an incision to widen the opening of the birth canal just before delivery)?

your time, give him a list of your questions, letting him know what's most important to you.
- *Do* make friends with the nurses and other office staff. They'll often be able to help you solve problems more quickly than the doctor will.
- *Do* respect your doctor's off-call boundaries. If you run into her at church or in a supermarket, don't ask for medical advice.
- *Don't* utter the dreaded phrase "by the way . . ." at the end of the visit. That new problem may need more time than the other things you've already discussed.
- *Don't* bring surprise patients. ("While I'm here, could you look at Tyler's throat?")
- *Don't* insist you will "talk with the doctor and no one else," except in very unusual or highly confidential situations. Many physicians rely heavily on a nurse to screen calls and questions, and refusing to talk with her may delay getting your problem solved.
- *Don't* challenge every recommendation he makes. Good dialogue is healthy, but if you find yourself arguing more than agreeing, you should probably seek care from someone else. ■

- Don't be afraid to bring up the *M* word—*money*. How much will the prenatal and delivery care cost? How much more will it cost if a cesarean section is necessary? Is a checkup afterward included? How much will be covered by the insurance plan? (Before this discussion takes place, you would be wise to become familiar with the extent of your health-insurance coverage.)
- How long should you expect to stay in the hospital after the delivery?

WHAT ABOUT BIRTH CENTERS AND DELIVERIES AT HOME?

Some hospitals have established **birth centers** on or adjacent to their campus, staffed by midwives, family physicians, and/or obstetricians who are affiliated with the hospital. These facilities are geared toward women with low-risk, straightforward pregnancies, offering pregnancy-and-delivery care in one location. Usually prenatal visits are carried out in the same location and by the same health-care providers as the childbirth. The cost of birth-center care may be significantly less than the formal hospital setting. There is a relaxed familiarity to the surroundings and typically few surprises for the parents-to-be. Should a significant problem develop, however, mother and baby can be moved quickly into the main hospital for definitive care.

Freestanding birth centers operate independently and geographically separate from hospitals. According to the National Association of Childbearing Centers (NACC), as of 2004 there were 170 independent birth centers operating in the United States (compared with 125 in 1984). These are often staffed by midwives, with one or more obstetricians available for consultation and assistance should a problem arise. They offer services similar to birth centers located on or adjacent to a hospital campus, though with one distinct disadvantage: If a major problem should develop, mother and baby must be transferred to the nearest hospital. This process can be upsetting, time-consuming, costly (if an ambulance is needed), and potentially risky.

The largest study to date dealing with outcomes of birth-center deliveries, the National Birth Center Study, was published in 1989 in the *New England Journal of Medicine*.[2] The researchers analyzed 11,814 births at eighty-four freestanding birth centers in the United States. Overall, nearly 16 percent (or one woman in six) were transferred to a hospital, and 2.4 percent (or about one woman in 40) required an emergency transfer. It should be noted that 29 percent (more than one in four) of women delivering their first baby required hospital transfer, while only 7 percent of those who already had one or more deliveries required a transfer. (The rates of emergency transfers were the same for both groups.)

If you are considering using a freestanding birth center, you should consider the following:

- Do you have a high-risk pregnancy? If you have diabetes, high blood pressure, a baby who is premature or overdue, a multiple birth (twins, triplets, or more), a baby who is not in the head-down position, a history

Questions you may want to ask of the physician who is going to care for the baby:

- How soon after birth will the baby be examined? If there is a need for cesarean delivery, will another doctor be called to care for the baby? (Some hospitals allow only pediatricians to tend to the newborn at the time of a cesarean birth. In these facilities, if a family practitioner had originally been designated as the

of complications during or after a previous delivery, or any number of other problems that a qualified and experienced provider has identified during your pregnancy, *you do not belong in a birth center.*
- Is this your first delivery? If so, you have a greater likelihood of being transferred to a hospital than if you have had one or more babies already.
- Is the birth center accredited by the Commission for the Accreditation of Birth Centers? Is it licensed in your state?
- What are the professional qualifications of the center's staff?
- How far is the center from your home?
- What will happen if there is a problem? If the facility is staffed by midwives, who serves as the backup obstetrician(s)? How far away is the nearest hospital, and how long would it take to get there?
- What percentage of the center's patients are transferred to a hospital?
- Are the center's fees covered by your health insurance?

Home birth remains a controversial practice in the United States and other countries with well-developed obstetrical resources. Proponents of home birth argue that it is the most natural and least intrusive way to bring a child into the world. But the American College of Obstetricians and Gynecologists, as well as the obstetricians who serve on Focus on the Family's Physicians Resource Council, do not endorse home deliveries for one very important reason: An apparently uneventful labor or delivery can suddenly go sour in a matter of minutes. If a serious problem develops suddenly—an unfortunate but very real possibility, even with a low-risk pregnancy—the woman and her caregivers are at a serious disadvantage, and a catastrophe could occur in the time it takes to pack up and move to the nearest hospital. Even if a problem is less severe or develops more slowly, resources at home are extremely limited. Furthermore, home birth is not considered mainstream health care in our society and may attract fringe practitioners whose credentials and skills are questionable.

If you are thinking about having your baby at home, you should carefully review your reasons and ask whether the apparent convenience and comfort at home are really worth risking a lifetime of damage—or a loss of life. In the final analysis, if you really have your heart set on a nonhospital type of delivery, a birth center directly affiliated with an adjacent hospital would be the preferable option—assuming, of course, that your pregnancy is uncomplicated. ■

baby's physician, he would usually assume care after the baby's condition has been judged stable.)

- What are the physician's views regarding breast- or bottle-feeding? Will you receive support for either decision? What is his opinion regarding feeding on demand as opposed to attempting to establish a schedule?
- What is the routine for checkups and immunizations after the baby is born?
- Does he have strong opinions about discipline? (This topic may be too far-reaching to cover during a visit of this type, although it should be brought up as the baby approaches the toddler months.) Are there any books or other materials regarding child rearing that he recommends? (This may provide you a glimpse of the practitioner's worldview and approach to basic values.)

Birth in the Hospital Setting

While interest in birth centers and home deliveries has waxed and waned over the past few decades (see page 40), in North America, hospitals remain the most widely utilized birth setting for a number of reasons. The first and most obvious is that most pregnant women seek care from obstetricians and family practitioners—all of whom are trained, and for the most part continue to practice, in hospitals.

But a more compelling reason, and the overwhelming advantage of a hospital delivery, is the availability of definitive care for both mother and baby if something goes wrong. This is particularly important when a pregnancy is known to be complicated by medical problems such as diabetes, high blood pressure, prematurity, twins or multiples, or an unusual position of the baby in the uterus. Even a straightforward pregnancy can have a stormy conclusion, especially if it is your first, and the rapid availability of a full range of medical, surgical, and pediatric services is a reassuring safety net. In addition, more options for pain relief, if needed, are available within the hospital than in other settings.

Some expectant parents have concerns about interventions and procedures they might experience during a hospital delivery, perhaps wondering if they leave their autonomy and options at the door when they check in. But over the years most hospitals have revised their maternity-care policies to become much more parent-friendly.

In response to patients' desires (and common sense), most hospitals have drastically altered their maternity-care areas to create **labor/delivery/recovery (LDR) rooms**. Traditionally, women in hospital maternity-care areas have labored in one room, delivered the baby in another, recovered and stabilized in a third, and finally spent one or more days in a regular hospital room. In contrast, LDR rooms are usually large and nicely decorated (often with a couch, TV, and ample space for family members). The entire labor-and-birth process can proceed without the disruption of moving in and out of four different rooms.

In some facilities, mother and baby remain in the LDR for the duration of their stay, in which case the room is called an **LDRP**, the *P* standing for *postpartum*, meaning "after delivery." A variation on this theme, the **birthing suite**, may offer even more amenities, such as a whirlpool tub, a fully equipped kitchen, and a living room with a sofa bed, TV, and stereo for family members. Because they combine the best of both worlds—a family-friendly environment with high-tech capabilities—LDRs, LDRPs, and birthing suites in hospitals have enjoyed wide acceptance by both parents and health-care providers. In addition to the more pleasant surroundings, labor-and-delivery policies in most hospitals have also shifted to a more family-friendly, flexible, collaborative approach.

You can take a number of steps to become better prepared for a birth experience at a hospital:

Visit the facility and become acquainted with the labor-and-delivery area. Familiarity with the environment and the staff can greatly increase confidence and comfort during labor. Most hospitals host prenatal classes, tours, maternity teas, and other outreach activities. Hospital staff enjoy caring for women in labor, so get to know them, look things over, and feel free to ask lots of questions.

See if the hospital has specific policies regarding the number of people allowed in the delivery area. A husband's participation is almost always desired by the hospital, but you may wish to have other family members or close friends present as well. Are there any restrictions?

Find out what will happen to your baby after the birth. Will your baby stay with you? Is "rooming in" the rule or the exception? What routines are part of the baby's care? Is the hospital equipped to handle medical problems of the newborn? If your baby is premature, has an infection, or needs intensive care, will he be transferred to another facility?

Ask about the kind of teaching and assistance available after delivery. Does the staff provide "basic training"? If you have trouble breastfeeding, is a lactation consultant available to help?

Take care of the paperwork ahead of time. Most hospitals allow you to preregister, check insurance coverage, and deal with other business details so this won't be a distraction during labor. Also, find out from your insurance carrier how many days in the hospital they will cover, assuming there are no unexpected problems. Some policies are more restrictive than others, and your doctor should be aware of any financial constraints you may have.

ATTENTION FATHERS: BE AVAILABLE WHEN THE TIME ARRIVES

Once upon a time, fathers were routinely shuttled off to a smoke-filled waiting area while their children were being born. Those days are long gone, and fathers are encouraged to play an active role in the delivery process through attending childbirth classes and acting as coaches (or at least loving supporters) during labor. But one additional, very practical detail involves being careful with the calendar.

The last month of your wife's pregnancy is probably not the best time to schedule several double work shifts or back-to-back business trips to the other side of the country. Obviously, no one can know for sure the exact due date, but it would be a shame to work diligently through the preparation process and then miss the actual event. This may require giving your employer a fair amount of advance notice about the upcoming delivery and your desire to be present for it. The same type of advance planning is also important for the person who serves as coach for a single mother during her labor. ■

What Type of Childbirth Classes Will You Take?

Notice that the question was not *whether* you will take childbirth classes. The normal process of moving a baby from the womb to the outside world is called labor for a reason—it's work. One reason so many women were heavily sedated during childbirth several decades ago is that few were adequately prepared for what would happen once labor started. As the contractions of the uterus became more uncomfortable, fear and anxiety would multiply the pain until virtually all control would be lost. In 1944 the groundbreaking book *Childbirth without Fear* by British physician Grantly Dick-Read introduced the concept that a woman who understood what was happening during labor and learned how to work with it could have a calm, controlled, and far more comfortable birth experience.

Over the next several years, a variety of prepared childbirth approaches and techniques were developed as the goal of having a "natural" childbirth gained popularity and acceptance. Some advocates of natural childbirth campaigned for labor and delivery completely devoid of any medical intervention, at times putting expectant parents who subscribed to these ideas at odds with their physicians. In response, many doctors complained about "natural childbirth fanatics" who challenged every detail of the hospital routine. But over time, physicians observed that well-informed couples working as a team had a much better experience—and usually had an easier time from a medical

SHOULD YOUR CHILDREN WATCH THE BABY BEING BORN?

A few decades ago, only doctors and nurses welcomed the vast majority of American newborns into the world. Once the "husband barrier" was broken and fathers became active in the delivery process, some couples wanted childbirth to become a family affair. Why not let the other children watch the birth of their new brother or sister?

Some enthusiasts describe positive experiences with children as young as four years of age watching siblings being born. But the likelihood of an emotional jolt for the children, potential distraction for the adults, and the issue of violating the boundaries of modesty within a family are all good reasons to keep your kids out of the delivery room. A better option would be to have the children prepared to see their new sibling soon after delivery—when both mother and baby appear to be okay and have had a few minutes to allow things to settle down.

If you choose to video the delivery for future viewing by your children or other family members, consider carefully who ought to see what. A living-color, full-frame shot of Mom's pelvic region isn't exactly appropriate viewing for the general public. There are lots of other interesting things to capture (especially facial expressions) during childbirth, and it would be prudent to talk over your wishes with whoever is shooting your video for you. If your video does indeed directly view the moment of birth, consider creating an edited, G-rated version for the kids to see later on. This might include, for example, shots of the birth from a vantage point looking over the mother's shoulder.

You should be aware, by the way, that many hospitals no longer allow births to be recorded. Check your hospital's video policy before you pack up your equipment to take to the labor-and-delivery room. ■

perspective—than terrified, unprepared patients who spent the entire labor and delivery in a state of panic and uncontrolled pain.

Childbirth classes are now considered a routine component of prenatal care. They come in all shapes and sizes and may be presented in hospitals, homes, or community centers. Instructors may emphasize one or another school of thought or blend ideas from several sources. Needless to say, some classes will be more organized and detailed than others. The leader should be a certified childbirth educator. Your doctor will probably have a referral or two, but you would be wise to ask some parents who have recently experienced childbirth for their recommendations as well.

Some hospitals or large medical groups also offer early-pregnancy classes dealing with nutrition, exercise, and general self-care. If available, these are well worth attending.

Normally you will begin childbirth-preparation classes during the sixth or seventh month of pregnancy, with a goal of being finished two weeks before the baby's due date. Most meet one evening per week for eight to twelve weeks, though in some communities late starters can take a crash course in one or two weekends. Childbirth preparation is intended to be a team effort of the mother and another person who will be available for the entire course as well as the birth itself. Usually this team will be a husband-wife pair, but in some situations (especially with a single mother), a relative or close friend may be serving as the teammate. Some mothers/couples also hire a **doula**, a nonmedical assistant who attends to the physical and emotional comfort of a woman during labor and delivery.

The following areas should be covered as part of the curriculum:

- What happens during pregnancy and childbirth: basic anatomy and physiology, including the development of the baby; changes in the mother; and the stages of labor and birth.
- Basic self-care: nutrition, exercise, sexuality, and maintaining a healthy lifestyle.
- Managing the contractions: relaxation, breathing, and pain-control techniques; positions during labor; and the final pushing stage.
- Details of the birth setting: when and where to go; what will happen in the LDR/LDRP/birthing suite (or birth center); how the labor will be monitored; possible interventions; and pain-medication options, if and when needed.
- Possible problem areas and their treatment: failure to progress, fetal distress, premature labor, prolonged rupture of membranes, or cesarean section and its aftereffects.
- Preparing for the first days of baby care, including feeding techniques.

The approach most commonly taught in childbirth classes is the **Lamaze method** or some variation of it. This method was introduced by French obstetrician Fernand Lamaze in his 1958 book *Painless Childbirth*. In America, Lamaze's techniques have been called **psychoprophylaxis** (literally, "mind protection"), and the organization that accredits its teachers was originally called the American Society for Psychoprophylaxis in Obstetrics, or ASPO. It is now called Lamaze International. Along with other information, Lamaze teaches a variety of techniques—breathing, relaxation, movement and positioning, massage, and a number of others—that can help a woman manage and cope with the labor process.

Another widely utilized method was launched in 1965 when Denver obstetrician Robert Bradley published *Husband-Coached Childbirth*. Along with stressing the involvement of the mother's husband as a coach (a term men could relate to), the **Bradley**

method teaches deep relaxation techniques and tends to discourage pain medications and other interventions more vigorously than Lamaze.

Some childbirth educators teach their own homegrown blend of both approaches. Regardless of the method you choose, the object of your preparation should not be to become a walking encyclopedia, reform the entire health-care system, or nurture unrealistic expectations of a problem-free childbirth experience. Training should combine a broad base of general knowledge, adequate time to practice pain-reducing techniques, reassurance that you can handle both normal and unexpected developments, and a healthy dose of reality.

If you truly desire an unmedicated childbirth but find that you can't manage the pain, accepting medication is not a moral failure. One approach that relieves pain while allowing you to remain awake and alert is the **epidural anesthetic**, which may be given either by the obstetrician (if he or she is trained to do so) or an anesthesiologist. This involves the injection of pain-relieving medication through a small plastic catheter into the space just adjacent to the fibrous sack that surrounds the spinal cord. Pain is dramatically reduced without paralysis of the lower half of the body, and the ability to push during the final stage of labor is usually not affected. The catheter can be left in place if more medication is needed, and if a cesarean birth takes place, this medication can provide a great deal of nondrowsy pain relief.

If you forget some of the finer points of your breathing or relaxation techniques during the heat of the moment, you won't be the first to do so. If an uneventful labor suddenly takes a surprise detour at the last minute, you need to be ready to ask intelligent questions, weigh the options, make an informed decision, and remain calm if things don't turn out the way you expected. *Remember: A healthy baby and a healthy mother are ultimately more important than a perfect childbirth experience.* You want to be as prepared as possible, and you should work diligently toward a controlled labor and joyous delivery, but you're not going to be graded on your performance.

As was already mentioned in chapter 1, this book does not contain step-by-step information about the childbirth process. You should be learning those details through your physician and childbirth classes.

What Does the New Arrival Need at Home?

As important as it is to prepare for the birth itself, there are some important and practical details to consider about life *after* your baby's arrival. New parents-to-be are often concerned about the amount of clothing and equipment they will need when their son or daughter finally arrives—and how much it will cost. If you have the financial resources to outfit a designer nursery and a four-season infant wardrobe, you will find no shortage of catalogs and showrooms to accommodate you. But most young couples with growing families are stretching their pocketbooks in several directions. You should be relieved to know that it is possible to meet a new baby's needs exceptionally well without creating a newborn penthouse. After all, infancy is the one stage in children's lives when they are not interested in material things. Newborns don't care where their clothes and equipment came from. Modest surroundings that are rich in parental love and tenderness will yield far better results than showcase environments that are emotionally impoverished. Remember—the greatest person who ever lived was born in a stable.

Actually, it is extremely unlikely that you will have to buy everything you need and want for the new baby. If you have older children or friends and relatives with children, a number of items can usually be handed down or borrowed for the new arrival. Friends may throw a baby shower or two for you before the delivery, and after the big event, indulgent grandparents and other well-wishers will perhaps descend on you with all manner of gifts. If you are a single parent or you have had to deal with opposition and obstacles to your pregnancy, your local pregnancy resource center can assist you with a variety of baby supplies. Many new parents are able to obtain needed supplies at a fraction of the original cost by visiting local garage sales and thrift shops. Babies and children outgrow their clothes so quickly that many secondhand items that have been worn very little (and look brand-new) can be purchased for a few dollars. Used nursery furniture and equipment can also be picked up at bargain prices, but make sure that whatever you buy meets current safety standards, especially if it is more than a few years old (see page 49).

It's a good idea to create your need/wish list *before* you start purchasing items for the nursery. You can use your list to keep track of what you've already acquired so that shopping trips for baby gear will be shorter and more focused. The goods you will need, commonly referred to as a **layette**, will fall into the following basic categories:

Clothing

While there is no magic formula for deciding how many of each type of garment to acquire, the following list covers the basics:

- Small, lightweight (receiving) blankets—3 or 4
- Sleeper sets with feet—3 or 4
- Light tops (gowns or sacques)—2 or 3
- T-shirts or undershirts—3 or 4
- Socks or booties—3 or 4
- Sweaters—2 (heaviness depends on climate and season)
- Hats or bonnets—2 (level of protection depends on climate and season)
- Baby washcloth and towel—1 or 2 sets

As you acquire clothing for your baby, remember three important principles:

Think ahead. Most newborns outgrow newborn-size clothes in a very few weeks, if not days, so favoring somewhat larger sizes for much of the wardrobe is a wise idea. This is especially true for those cute but costly dress-up outfits that may hang idly in the closet after a few outings. If you receive a number of these as gifts, don't remove the tags or original packaging, and consider doing some discreet trades for bigger sizes at the store where they were bought. If you are buying outfits for the next few months, consider what the future may hold weather-wise.

Think safety. Be sure that no garment is too snug around your baby's neck, hands, and feet, and completely avoid any accessory such as a necklace or a long ribbon that could become tangled around the neck. Buttons, beads, and other small objects attached to shirts or pants may be a hazard if they can become detached and find their way into little hands, mouths, and airways; it's a good idea to reinforce buttons and bows, which requires only some time, a needle, and thread. Snaps are

> *A relationship that is characterized by genuine love and affection is likely to be a healthy one, even though some parental mistakes and errors are inevitable.*
>
> The New Strong-Willed Child
> *By Dr. James Dobson*

safer and handier. Infant and toddler clothing should be flame-retardant—a safety feature that will be stated on the label. Prewash the baby clothes you buy, whether secondhand or fresh from the department store. Use detergents without perfumes or other ingredients that might irritate the baby's skin. (Many brand names offer such products—check the label.) This will assure not only that used garments are sanitary but also that new clothing is free from any detergents or other chemicals used during the finishing processes.

Don't worry about shoes at this point. Not only are they unnecessary before a baby can walk, but they may interfere with normal growth of the feet.

Think convenience and comfort. Since diaper changing is a frequent activity with babies, easy access is preferable to a complicated, multilayered outfit when cleanup is necessary.

Diapers

You will need to decide whether you want to use cloth or disposable diapers, or at least which you would like to start with.

Disposable diapers are abundant in every supermarket, and they are most notable for their convenience. When it's time for a change, take them off, dump any solid waste into the toilet, fold them up, and throw them away. Manufacturers also compete with one another to see who can create the most leak-proof diaper by combining superabsorbency (which also tends to keep a baby's skin drier, thus reducing the likelihood of diaper rash) with cleverly engineered configurations that prevent urine or stool from escaping onto bedding or furniture. (Nurseries or day-care centers may prefer—or require—disposable diapers for babies left in their care since they are less likely to leak.) For all of these advantages, however, disposable diapers have their drawbacks. Not only are they potentially more costly than cloth diapers, but they do not disintegrate, raising environmental concerns. (Over two thousand diapers enter dumps and landfills every year for each baby using disposables.)

Cloth diapers can be less expensive to use if you launder them yourself. If you choose this route, wash them separately from other clothing after rinsing them out in the toilet. Use hot water and a double rinse and avoid fabric softeners and scented additives, which can provoke rashes on some infants' skin. Since newborns will soil as many as ten or more diapers a day, you will need a stockpile of three or four dozen. You will also need pins or clips (unless you use the newer models with Velcro fasteners) and some type of waterproof protective covering, unless you buy the all-in-one versions. If you have any difficulty finding cloth diapers with some of these features at your local retail outlet, look online. Typing the words "cloth diapers" into your favorite search engine will put you in touch with dozens of businesses that offer a wide variety of products and prices.

Diaper services bring the convenience level of cloth diapering nearly up to that of disposables, at roughly the same cost. Shop around for prices, delivery schedules (twice weekly is typical), and policy regarding whether you rinse first or simply toss the diaper, waste and all, into the pail the service provides. Diaper services are readily available in some parts of the country and more scarce in others. If you have trouble locating a service where you live, check the Internet by typing "diaper services" into a search engine. The price of the service should be weighed against the cost of laundry supplies and utility bills when you do the job yourself, as well as your time and energy, which may be in very short supply. While cloth diapers may appear kinder to the environment, it should be noted that diaper services (or parents at home) must consume considerable amounts of water and energy to clean them. Ultimately your choice between disposable and cloth diapers should be compatible with your family's time and budget constraints.

Furniture and other hardware

This is where your biggest onetime expenses may lie and where some judicious borrowing of equipment from friends and family will be helpful.

A **cradle** or **bassinet** is a portable sleep space, allowing you the convenience of changing your newborn's sleeping quarters relatively easily. In some families, a cradle whose gentle rocking has calmed restless infants for many decades is handed down from generation to generation. Bassinets don't sway, but they do have the advantage of being portable. Be certain that the legs of the bassinet are stable and sturdy so it cannot accidentally collapse.

If you want the new baby right next to your own bed or elsewhere in the house, a cradle or bassinet will allow you more flexibility. However, within three or four months your baby will outgrow it, and he will need to graduate to a crib.

A **crib** can be the newborn's sleeping place from day one and will be in use for two to three years. Since your baby will spend time in a crib without direct supervision, this must be a completely safe environment. In order to prevent falls and other types of accidents, cribs manufactured since 1985 have had to comply with a number of safety requirements. If your baby is going to be using an older model, you will need to check the following:

- The **slats** in the crib should be no wider than two and three-eighths inches (six centimeters) apart.
- Unless they are supporting a high canopy, **corner posts** that extend above the rails are a potential hazard because they may entangle loose clothing. They should be unscrewed or cut off.
- **Paint** on an old crib may contain lead, and any flakes of paint accidentally swallowed by a curious baby could cause lead poisoning.

When in doubt, you should have the old coat removed and replaced with some new enamel. Removing lead-based paint (whether from a crib or from surfaces

CRADLE

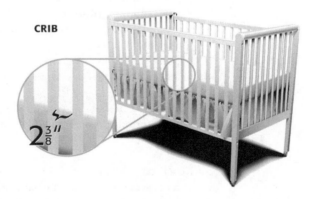

CRIB

$2\frac{3}{8}''$

in an old home) can be a hazardous process because sanding, scraping, or using chemical removers can generate dust or fumes that contain lead. You would be wise to have this done by a professional who is trained to remove lead-based paint (or obtain a crib that you know was manufactured after 1985).

- The **headboards** and **footboards** should be solid and without decorative cut-outs that could trap a head, hand, or foot.

In addition, you should check the following before you place your baby in any crib, new or old:

- The **mattress** should fit snugly into the frame. If you can wedge more than two fingers between the mattress and the crib side, the mattress is too small. Remove any extraneous tags and thin plastic wrappings. If you use a mattress cover, be sure it is made of thick plastic that, ideally, can be zipped around the pad. Don't place pillows or any soft bedding material other than a fitted sheet under the baby. His head or face might become accidentally buried in the soft folds, especially if he happens to be facedown, which could lead to suffocation. (This may be one of the conditions leading to the tragedy of sudden infant death syndrome, or SIDS. See sidebar, page 154.) Sheepskin, down mattresses, feather beds, and wavy water beds pose similar risks.
- **Bumper pads**, securely tied into place, may line the inside of the crib. When your baby can pull up to a standing position, the pads should be removed, since they can assist a baby's attempts to climb over the rail. The same is true of large stuffed animals that a toddler might use as a soft step or launching pad for a trip over the side.
- The **side rails** should latch securely in place, with the release mechanism out of reach of exploring fingers. When fully raised, the rails should extend at least twenty inches (fifty-one centimeters) above the top of the mattress. As your baby grows and eventually stands up, the mattress will need to be lowered. If the distance from the mattress to the top of the crib rail is less than three quarters of a child's height (or if the rail is below the level of his nipples when he stands up), he is too big for the crib and at risk for falling out.
- If you hang any **mobiles** above the crib, be sure they remain out of reach a few months from now when your baby begins to move toward (and grab for) interesting objects.
- For many reasons—sun exposure, shades, cords, and worst of all, the possibility of a disastrous fall—never put a crib next to a window, whether open or shut.

A **changing table** can be a convenient one-stop location for diaper duties at home. But it is also notorious for being the place from which a baby takes his first fall. If you use a changing table:

- Never step away, turn around, or otherwise divert your attention from the job at hand unless you pick up the baby to do so. Babies seem to choose this moment to show off their new ability to roll over—and then take a fast trip to the floor. Never answer the phone or the door if it means walking away from your baby.
- To reduce the likelihood of such a fall, make sure you have all the changing gear—new diaper, wipes, etc.—within reach before you start.

- The table should have a two-inch guardrail around its edge and a safety strap to help you secure the baby. However, these should not be considered a substitute for your undivided attention when your infant is on the changing table.
- Don't distract an older baby by letting him handle a can of baby powder (which he might accidentally unload into his or your airspace), play with a disposable diaper, or suck on some other miscellaneous object on the changing table.

Car seats

Unlike a changing table, a **car seat** is an absolute necessity. Automobile accidents are a leading cause of death in children, and proper use of car seats could prevent hundreds of tragic losses every year. As a result, every state has passed laws requiring their use. Hospitals will not allow you to take your new baby home without one, and many will loan or rent you a seat if you cannot buy one.

Each infant, toddler, and young child must be properly secured into an appropriate car seat *every* time she rides in a car—no exceptions. Holding a baby in your lap, even if you are wearing a seat belt, can cause her to be crushed between you and the dashboard in an accident—assuming that she hasn't been thrown through the windshield first. Even if the time needed to buckle everyone in place will be far longer than the drive itself, *do it anyway*, because most accidents occur within a few miles of home at speeds below thirty miles an hour. The death of a child for any reason is always a horrendous loss for a family, but the pain is greatly magnified when that loss could have been prevented.

The car seat for a newborn should be either an **infant-only** or **convertible** model manufactured within the last ten years. (Some manufacturers recommend that car seats only be used for five to six years. Check with the manufacturer to find out how long the company recommends using their seat.) Because the newborn has no head control, she must face backward in the car to prevent dangerous, rapid forward movement of the head during a sudden stop. The seat should position her so

INFANT CAR SEAT
Infant in car seat carrier facing rear of car

TODDLER CAR SEAT
Toddler in car seat facing forward

NOTE: Children under the age of 12 should always ride in the backseat.

that her upper body is angled upward but not sitting upright, since she can't keep her head from flopping forward. You may need to use small rolled-up towels or diapers to pad the seat and keep her from slouching. (Many models come with padding designed for the seat that serves this purpose.) The center of the backseat is the safest location for her, and thus you should avoid putting her in the front passenger seat. This means that, should she start to fuss, you will have to resist the temptation to turn around and tend to her while your vehicle is in motion. *Do not put an infant in a front passenger seat that has an air bag* (see page 53).

An infant-only car seat can have the distinct advantage of doubling as a carrier or even a comfortable napping spot for a small baby even when not in the car. Many are designed to snap in and out of a detachable base that can be secured in the backseat; if your baby is a frequent rider in more than one car, you can buy additional bases to facilitate taking her in and out of these vehicles. (Some also snap into compatible strollers.) However, the reverse is not true: You should never use an infant carrier as a car seat. Once your baby outgrows the infant-only car seat, it will have little use until another baby enters your life.

A convertible seat can be reconfigured to face forward when your baby reaches her first birthday *and* weighs twenty pounds (just over nine kilograms). It should accommodate her until she weighs forty pounds. However, it will be too cumbersome to serve any other purpose. Some infant-only seats are designed for infants weighing up to twenty-two pounds, and some convertible seats allow children to remain in the rear-facing position at higher weights. If you are using one of these seats, continue using the rear-facing position until your child has reached the weight (and height) limits set by the manufacturer.

Some important reminders about car-seat safety

We've come a long way since the days when parents drove with a baby propped next to them on the front seat of the family sedan, or when older children would lie in the space between the backseat and the back window, or when Mom multitasked by nursing her newborn while speeding down the freeway. Unfortunately, although buckling infants or children into car seats is now both the norm and the law, they aren't always used correctly. Common errors include:

- Using a seat that's the wrong size for the infant or child
- Using an outdated car seat
- Not securing the child correctly in the seat
- Not securing the seat properly in the vehicle
- Having the seat turned the wrong direction
- Not adjusting the shoulder harnesses correctly
- Putting a rear-facing car seat in front of an air bag
- Not securing the child completely because "We're just going up the street."

Far too many avoidable injuries or deaths occur every year because adults haven't taken the time to understand how to install and use a car seat correctly, or they don't use it *every* time a child is a passenger. Needless to say, there's more to securing an infant or child safely in a car than "click and go." Because people of all ages are the most precious cargo you will ever carry in your vehicle, consider the following very carefully:

- Before you buy a car seat, make sure that it's the right size for your child and that it will fit properly in your vehicle.
- If you're using or buying a used seat, make sure that it isn't more than ten (or better yet, five or six) years old, and that you have the manufacturer's instruc-

tions for its proper use. Don't count on a prior owner's oral tutorial. Write to the manufacturer for the instructions or download them from the manufacturer's Web site, and then read them carefully.

- Do not use a car seat that has been in a crash (even if it looks intact) or has cracks in its frame.

New car seats are clearly marked with expiration dates.

- If you're not sure whether your baby or child seat is properly installed, *get some help*. Local law-enforcement agencies, fire stations, health departments, or organizations such as AAA may offer this service or can direct you to resources in your area where certified child passenger safety (CPS) technicians can check your car-seat installation. You can also find help at the Web site of the National Highway Traffic Safety Administration (http://www.nhtsa.gov), where there is extensive information about child passenger safety. One NHTSA service will guide you to local car-seat inspection stations by state or zip code.
- Who else is going to chauffeur your child(ren)? You need to be sure that Grandma and Grandpa, other relatives, or friends who might serve in this role understand clearly how to use the car seat(s) properly.
- *If your car has a passenger-side air bag, never place your baby in the front passenger seat.* As was just noted, even without the air bag, the backseat is a safer location for an infant seat. But if an air bag is present, it can cause serious or even fatal injuries to a baby if it inflates during an accident. The exception to this rule would be in a vehicle that does not have a backseat and has an air-bag on/off switch, such that the air bag can be turned off if the baby's car seat is in the front passenger seat.
- When your car is sitting in the sun, cover the infant seat with a towel, since plastic and metal parts can become hot. Even if a towel has been used, check the temperature of the seat, belts, and buckles with your hand to be sure you're not depositing your baby into a veritable frying pan.
- At some time (or perhaps most of the time), your baby will wail indignantly when put into the car seat. Make sure there is nothing physically annoying

If you buy a new car seat, fill out the registration form and send it to the manufacturer. This information will be important if there is a need to notify you of a product defect or recall that might occur in the future.

him (such as a hot buckle or a stray toy poking his leg), talk or sing sweetly to him, and press on. But do not give in and take him out of the seat to restore calm to the car. If for some reason your baby's crying has reached an unusually distracting pitch, pull off the road and tend to his needs. But then buckle him in before you continue.

- *Do not, under any circumstances, ever leave your baby—or any children—unattended in your car.* Amazing and terrible things can happen while you "just dash into the cleaners for thirty seconds." Aside from physical risks to your baby, such as becoming overheated on a warm day or chilled when it's cold, there's always the exciting possibility that an older child will discover how to release the brake—or at least find the horn. And, while we would rather not think about such horrific possibilities, children left unattended in a car present a prime opportunity for a predator who is seeking his next victim to abduct and abuse.

(For more information about automobile safety for older children, see page 850.)

Baby carriers—front and back

See color insert for photos of baby products, page A8.

Many parents find front and back carriers extremely helpful during the first several months of a child's life. They allow a parent to tend to a variety of activities with hands free and baby close and secure. Front carriers are most useful for the first three to six months, after which a baby's increasing size, weight, and activity may begin to strain a parent's back and shoulders. Carriers may be configured so the baby is in an upright position with legs dangling through leg holes (like a backpack worn backwards) or in a "sling" arrangement in which the baby can lie horizontally as in a hammock. Of the two, the sling is somewhat more versatile; the baby can be placed in a variety of orientations (not merely staring at Mom's or Dad's chest), the weight can be adjusted or shifted to either shoulder, and some parents are able to continue carrying babies this way comfortably well past the first birthday. One variation on the sling is configured to allow an infant four months or older to be carried on one hip, an arrangement some parents find more comfortable.

When buying a front carrier, you may want to wait until you can take your baby with you and then "try him on for size." Pay attention to these details:

- How would you rate the padding, distribution of weight, and general comfort? Would you be able to walk around for extended periods of time with your baby in this particular carrier?
- How easy (or difficult) is it to put on and adjust, or remove, the carrier?
- How well supported are the baby's head and body?
- Does your baby seem contented in this arrangement? Some babies will be more calm and comfortable in a sling, while others may seem to prefer a vertical carrier.

If you choose a front carrier, you may find that carrying your baby for extended periods of time in a front pack is convenient for you, soothing for your new baby, and a bonding experience between the two of you. Some parents whose babies seem to cry a great deal if not held may find that a comfortable front carrier calms the infant—and maintains the parents' sanity. However, *you must not use a carrier when you are driving or riding in a car.*

A backpack is most useful after a baby has gained steady head control, at which point you won't need to worry about the position and support of the head (which you cannot see). If both parent and passenger find the backpack agreeable, it may remain in service through the toddler years. As with front carriers, it is a wise idea to try on various models with the baby in place. One potential disadvantage of this arrangement is that you can't see or talk directly to the baby. This may become a bigger problem if she is irritable or begins to shift herself around by pushing against the frame. When using a backpack you must also remember to bend your knees if you are tending to something close to the ground. If you bend at the waist, the baby may topple out.

Carriages and strollers

These familiar items are useful when you have some distance to cover with your baby and you don't want to carry him. They come in a variety of shapes, sizes, and prices—some plain and simple and others loaded with bells and whistles. There are convertible models that can be changed from one configuration in which a newborn can lie flat to another that permits an older, mobile baby to sit up. There are also jogging (or even racing) strollers for those who want to do some serious exercise while the baby comes along for the ride.

Unfortunately, according to the U.S. Consumer Product Safety Commission, there are more than ten thousand emergency-room visits every year involving children who have been injured in carriages or strollers. If you acquire one of these now or during the coming months, look beyond price and durability to these safety features as well:

- Look for a wide base that will not tip over easily.
- Check the seat belt. Is it securely attached to the frame? Is it strong? Is it easy for you to fasten and unfasten?
- Check the brakes. Do they securely lock the wheels? Are there brakes on two wheels rather than on just one? Are they easy to use? Will they be out of reach of inquisitive fingers when your baby becomes a curious toddler?
- If there is a basket that holds your supplies or parcels, for stability it should be placed low and in front of or directly over the rear wheels.

Your safety awareness will need to continue, as you will utilize a carriage or stroller for months into the future:

- Make sure the equipment is appropriate for the baby's size. Once a baby can sit up on his own, it won't be long before he can fall out of a carriage, so he must graduate to a stroller into which he can be more securely fastened.
- Always use the seat belt, even if your baby (or older child) protests.
- Don't hang a purse or shopping bag over the handle—the leverage may tip the carriage or stroller backward.
- Keep older children away from the stroller as you fold or unfold it.

"Ready or Not, Here I Come!"

In a few short years you will probably hear your child call out this familiar phrase during some energetic neighborhood game. But now as you await your baby's arrival, you will also hear (and feel) the same message as your baby begins the inevitable passage from the womb to the outside world. Ready or not, your daughter or son will soon be arriving.

We hope that well before the delivery date you will have the time (and energy) to make some of the important physical, financial, emotional, and spiritual preparations that have been outlined in this and the previous chapter. If you haven't yet, and the due date is fast approaching, don't panic. You can jump on the learning curve at any time—even well after your baby has been born.

Speaking of births, the time has come to shift our focus to that exciting first meeting with your baby and the first eventful days of your child's life.

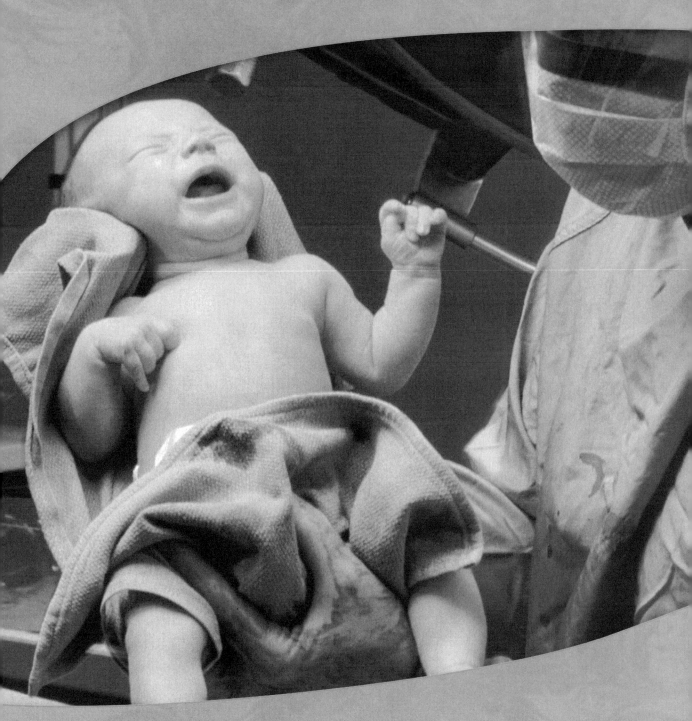

The Moment Arrives

After months of anticipation, some emotional highs and lows, and (usually) a number of hours of labor, the waiting will finally be over. All your hopes and preparations are about to culminate in the arrival of the tiny new person (or perhaps more than one!) whom you will soon be holding in your arms. Without question, your first look, touch, and embrace of this newest member of your family will be an intense experience, one that we hope will be joyous and fulfilling as well. What can you expect to see?

What Happens during the First Few Minutes after Birth?

The moment your baby exits the birth canal (or the uterus in a cesarean delivery), she will begin a rapid and radical transition from the warm liquid "inner space" of amniotic fluid—in which the placenta efficiently provided for all her needs by way of the umbilical cord—to the outside world. Within seconds she must begin breathing for herself, within minutes begin regulating her own temperature, and within hours begin actively taking nutrients.

As soon as her body is out (or sometimes when the head alone has just been delivered), her nose and mouth will be gently cleared of fluid. The umbilical cord will be clamped and then cut. (By prior arrangement, Dad may be offered this privilege.) In order to prevent heat loss and a drop in body temperature, the baby will be dried quickly, often while being checked to be sure she is breathing adequately. The mild rubbing that occurs during drying will actually stimulate breathing. (No one swats a newborn on the fanny after birth, by the way.) You may hear a little whimper, a continuous noisy howl of protest, or something in between during these exciting first few moments.

How quickly you are able to hold your newborn will depend on your condition and the baby's. In many uncomplicated births, the baby practically makes a nonstop flight from birth canal to mother's chest. In others, the need for some immediate attention to deal with a problem will delay this initial moment of contact. If the delivery was particularly difficult or was a cesarean birth, the mother may not have as much freedom or may be too preoccupied to attend to her baby. If the baby's breathing is slow to start or sluggish and inadequate, she will be quickly placed on a warmer. Further gentle stimulation will continue, and if needed, oxygen or assistance with a bag and mask will be given until the problem stabilizes.

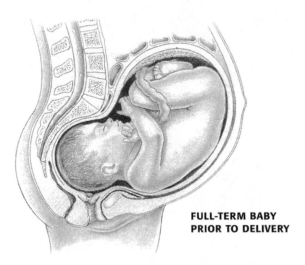

FULL-TERM BABY PRIOR TO DELIVERY

Some babies need more attention to the vocal cords and airway because of the presence of **meconium** in the amniotic fluid. Meconium is a thick, tarlike material that accumulates in the baby's intestines starting at about the fourth month after conception. Normally it is not seen until after birth, but up to 20 percent of babies will pass some beforehand. Meconium is usually harmless to a baby, even if swallowed. But if a large amount is present before delivery, and if she makes any breathing or gasping attempts before birth or during delivery, meconium may have been inhaled into her airway. This can cause a number of respiratory problems that are called **meconium aspiration syndrome (MAS)**, and thus if your baby exits the birth canal amidst some meconium-stained fluid, her mouth, nose, and possibly her airway should be cleared of this material as soon as possible. (Roughly one in ten infants

FULL-TERM BABY BEING DELIVERED

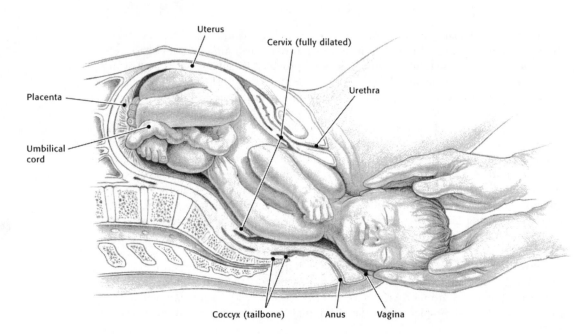

Uterus

Cervix (fully dilated)

Placenta

Urethra

Umbilical cord

Coccyx (tailbone)   Anus   Vagina

born with meconium staining will experience some degree of MAS.) While the need for these sorts of interventions is the exception rather than the rule, the possibility of an unexpected respiratory problem in the newborn is one of the reasons most health-care providers prefer not to deliver babies away from the hospital.

Assuming things go smoothly, you should have an opportunity to spend time with your new baby immediately after birth. While keeping her warm and covered, both mother and father can gently touch and caress her, check out the tiny details of her hands and feet, allow her to grasp their fingers, and look into her eyes if they are open. This is a close, emotional time, and you should feel free to laugh, cry, say a prayer of thanksgiving, or just be silent and savor the moment.

The baby may or may not be interested in trying to nurse right away, but you need not be in any hurry. She has plenty of extra fluid in her newborn system, and you may want to try the first feeding later when you are a little more comfortable. The doctor will usually be attending to some after-birth details—collecting a sample of blood from the umbilical cord, delivering the placenta, checking for and repairing any damage, and generally cleaning up, so this may not be the ideal setting in which to get positioned for the first nursing.

The baby's first report card and other details

At one minute and five minutes after birth, a nurse or doctor will do a quick survey of your baby and then assign an **Apgar score**. This simple point system was devised by anesthesiologist Dr. Virginia Apgar during the early 1950s as a tool to predict which infants might need closer observation or more intense care after birth. A baby is given 0, 1, or 2 points on each of five variables: appearance (specifically color), respirations, pulse rate, response to stimulation, and activity (including muscle tone).

APGAR SCORECARD			
	Score		
Sign	**0**	**1**	**2**
Appearance	pale or blue	body pink, extremities blue	completely pink
Respirations	absent	slow and irregular	good, crying
Pulse	not detectable	below 100	above 100
Reflex irritability	no response to stimulation	grimace	cough, sneeze, or cry
Muscle tone	limp or weak movement	some movement	active motion

Scores determined for each sign are totaled. The highest possible score is 10. By five minutes of age, most healthy babies have scores of at least 7. A score less than that indicates that the baby warrants careful watching.

Few babies receive a perfect 10 at five minutes because most have some dusky or bluish coloration of the hands and feet. (Note that references to pink or blue coloration in the table have nothing to do with the racial or ethnic origin of the baby.) If the score is 6 or less at five minutes, the baby will be given closer attention. It serves as a cue or a red flag for the level of care a baby may need immediately after birth.

Eventually the health-care staff will weigh and measure your baby, take footprints, apply an armband, and carry out a few other standard procedures. There is no reason your baby should be unceremoniously carted off to the nursery for these details two minutes after birth. On the other hand, you don't need to be upset if you are separated from the baby for a few minutes once you've had a comfortable time to get acquainted.

Soon after the baby is born, the nurse will bathe her to remove the thick, whitish material called **vernix**, which served as a protective covering for her skin while she was in the womb. The baby will also receive three routine medical treatments:

- One dose of **antibiotic eye ointment or drops**. Eye infections caused by gonorrhea or chlamydia acquired during birth can be serious enough to cause blindness. These are effectively prevented by this treatment. Even if you feel certain that you could not possibly carry these organisms, all states by law require this treatment.
  - A shot of **vitamin K**. Newborn infants have a relatively low level of this vitamin, which is necessary for normal blood clotting. Rarely, the level is so low that the baby may be at risk for internal bleeding that can cause significant damage (a syndrome known as **hemorrhagic disease of the newborn**). A single injection of vitamin K prevents this problem.
  - A **plastic clip** on the remnant of the umbilical cord. The clip will be removed before discharge or will be left in place and removed at the doctor's office during a follow-up visit.

Not all babies have vernix, and its absence is not an indication of any problem.

A closer look: physical appearance and behavior of your newborn baby

Your newborn will not look like the smiling image you have seen beaming from a jar of baby food. (The "newborns" you see in movies and TV-show delivery rooms are nearly always a few weeks old.) She, in fact, will have a unique appearance immediately after birth. Be sure to take plenty of pictures—this phase will be very short.

Depending on the course of labor, her head may develop an oval shape known

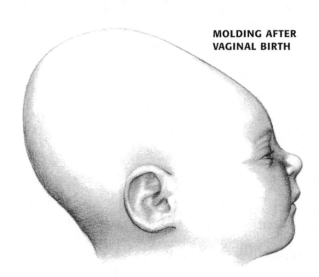

MOLDING AFTER VAGINAL BIRTH

as **molding**, resulting from compression of the soft bones of the skull during the trip through the birth canal. This may be accentuated if her head is large and if labor was long. Pressure against her mother's pelvis may also produce some puffiness of the scalp. If blood vessels break under the skin, a collection of blood called a **cephalhematoma** will form, although it may not be obvious for a day or two after birth. Normally all these conditions resolve without difficulty or any specific treatment. However, a cephalhematoma may take months to disappear and may harden in the process.

When you gently run a finger over the top of a newborn's head, you will feel the **fontanelles**—the two indentations where the bones of the skull have not yet joined. These so-called soft spots, the largest of which will be felt toward the front of the skull, are actually covered with a thick protective membrane. They are usually flat, but they may bulge slightly when the baby cries or pushes out a bowel movement. If you watch the hair on the scalp covering her anterior (or forward) fontanelle, you may even see some gentle pulsations.

A newborn may be nearly bald, endowed with thick hair, or have an amount in between. Don't be too impressed (or upset) with the hair you see; color, texture, and amount will usually change to some degree during the first year. You may also notice some soft, thin, fuzzy hair called **lanugo** along the back and shoulders. Lanugo is more obvious in some babies than others, but if at first it looks conspicuous, you need not worry about your newborn growing a fur coat. This will disappear within several weeks.

Her face, and especially her eyelids, will be puffy. A closer look at the eyes usually reveals some shade of blue gray or blue brown in Caucasian babies, or brown in dark-skinned infants. Unless she is born with dark brown eyes, the final color of her eyes may not be known for at least six months. The newborn can focus on and follow a slowly moving object at close range and may be particularly attentive to a nearby face. Some of the most emotional moments in parenting occur when a new baby and a loving parent gaze into one another's eyes. Because her brain will need some time to assemble these visual images into meaningful patterns, your smile will not be returned for a while. (She will begin this direct socializing at four to six weeks of age.) You may notice some bright red spots on the white portion (the **sclera**) of one or both eyes. These are areas where tiny blood vessels ruptured during labor. They are not a sign of damage and will disappear on their own in several days.

A newborn has well-developed hearing and will appear startled (with sudden jerking movements) in response to a sudden loud noise. While her environment doesn't need to be hushed like a library, it is a good idea to keep the sounds around a new baby at a comfortable level. If a noise is loud enough to annoy you, it will

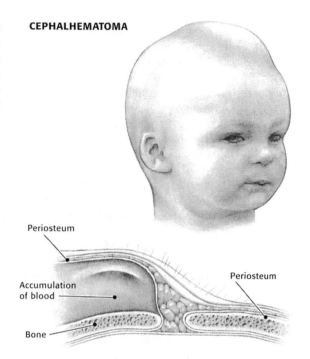

CEPHALHEMATOMA

Periosteum

Periosteum

Accumulation of blood

Bone

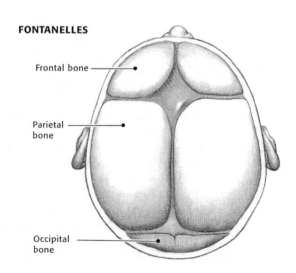

FONTANELLES

Frontal bone

Parietal bone

Occipital bone

certainly not be pleasant for her. Soothing voices, humming, singing, and soft music are definitely welcome in her world of new sounds.

The newborn's nose is relatively flat, and her nasal passages are quite narrow. Since she breathes primarily through her nose rather than her mouth, you may often hear a noisy, snorting type of breathing, especially if she is excited. Furthermore, she may sneeze from time to time in order to clear mucus out of her nose. This by itself does not mean that she has a cold. However, if you notice mucus draining from the nose or if you are not sure whether the breathing sounds are normal, ask the doctor to check it. You may also hear your baby hiccuping, as she may have done inside the womb. This does not require any specific treatment.

The skin of the newborn is usually smooth, but in postmature (late-arriving) babies it tends to appear more wrinkled. Some (or much) of her skin may be covered by vernix, especially in the creases of the arms and legs. This material, which helped protect the skin while she floated in amniotic fluid, will be much more noticeable if she is premature. Many babies have areas of dry, flaky skin, especially on the hands and feet. These do not need to be treated with lotion, but dryness will persist if a baby is bathed too frequently. She may have a dusky color for the first few minutes until her newly functioning lungs send blood with higher levels of oxygen through her circulatory system. As this process continues, she will "pink up," although hands and feet may maintain a bluish tinge for a longer period of time. Some babies develop a ruddy coloration or may appear flushed when they cry. In nonwhite infants, the dusky color will be more pronounced, but lips, tongue, and fingernails will appear pink once the blood is carrying more oxygen.

When you have had time to inspect her from "stem to stern" in more detail, you may notice some unique markings on her skin. A small red **salmon patch** occurs on the nape of the neck (some might call it a "stork bite") in 30 to 40 percent of all infants. One or more of these may also appear on the eyelids or on the forehead between the eyebrows (where it may be called an "angel's kiss"). Eyelid patches will disappear by three to six months of age, while those on the neck will fade but may last for years. Areas of increased pigmentation known as **Mongolian spots** are common on the back and buttocks of dark-skinned newborns, although they may be found in all racial and ethnic groups. These spots may even have a greenish or bluish tinge like a bruise and will disappear gradually over a few years' time. Tiny cysts known as **milia** appear on the nose, cheeks, and forehead of many newborns. (The same type of cysts are nearly always seen on the roof of the mouth and have been dubbed **Epstein's pearls**.) Between one and two days of life, many newborns develop a number of red spots with a slightly raised pale center. This eruption, unique to newborns, is known as **erythema toxicum**, but it is not a sign of any illness or toxicity. Both milia and erythema toxicum disappear without treatment.

In baby boys the testicles will normally be present in the scrotum, having made a short but important journey from within the abdomen to the scrotal sac during the final weeks of pregnancy. When one (or both) has not moved into position at birth, the baby is said to have an undescended testicle, a condition that will be evident at the time of the first exam. This occurs in approximately 3 percent of full-term male infants and up to 21 percent of premature newborns. Fortunately about three-quarters of undescended testes will enter the scrotum during the first three months of life.[1]

The scrotum of a baby boy may appear puffy or even swollen, a change that normally resolves within a few days. In about 10 percent of male infants, a collection of fluid called a **hydrocele** may persist for six to twelve months. A hydrocele normally resolves on its own, but sometimes it is accompanied by a swelling in either groin that often appears during crying or straining. This is a **hernia**, a sac that may contain a small portion of bowel. If you feel that your infant may have a hernia, have his doctor check this area during an office visit. If one is indeed present, it will need to be corrected surgically. Rarely, the contents of a hernia sac become stuck (or **incarcerated**)

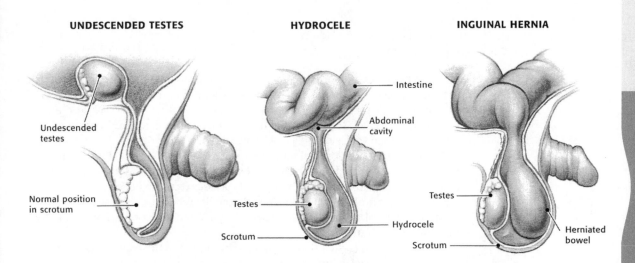

UNDESCENDED TESTES

Undescended testes

Normal position in scrotum

HYDROCELE

Intestine

Abdominal cavity

Testes

Hydrocele

Scrotum

INGUINAL HERNIA

Testes

Herniated bowel

Scrotum

in the abdominal wall, restricting blood flow and causing increased swelling and pain. Emergency surgery may be needed to prevent damage to the bowel. If your infant's groin becomes markedly swollen or tender (provoking crying when touched), you should call the doctor immediately.

The baby girl's genital area—specifically the **labia** or "lips" at the opening of the vagina—may also appear swollen. In addition, a little mucus or even a small amount of blood may drain from the vagina during the first few days of life. Both are caused by sudden changes in hormone levels after birth and will disappear on their own. (For more information, see "genital care and concerns" in Reference Section, page 672.)

While a newborn is awake, his legs will tend to be flexed frog-style, with fists closed and drawn toward the face. In fact, he may accidentally scratch himself. Some newborn shirts enclose the hands to prevent scratching, but if necessary long nails can be carefully trimmed. A newborn's feet will tend to be turned inward and the legs bowed. During sleep, arms and legs will relax and unfold.

As you watch his arms and legs move around, don't expect any purposeful movements. A newborn cannot deliberately reach for anything, kick in a specific direction, or turn his head toward a sound. However, he does have a number of reflex behaviors that are already programmed into the nervous system at the time of birth. When you gently stroke one of his cheeks, he will turn his head in that direction. This is called the **rooting reflex**, and it helps the baby locate his food source. Place a nipple (or fingertip) in his mouth, and he will begin to suck on it. This **sucking reflex** will in turn set off the **swallowing reflex**. These nourishment-seeking behaviors are necessary for survival.

The **Moro** or **startle reflex**, on the other hand, is not. If a newborn is startled or if his head or body moves suddenly downward, his arms will quickly arch over his chest, as if trying to embrace the nearest solid object. The Moro reflex will disappear after the first few months of life. The **grasp reflex** is easy to demonstrate: Place your finger in a newborn's hand, and he will grasp it tightly for a short period of time. This reflex will disappear around the age of two months, but shortly thereafter he will be deliberately grabbing everything within reach.

Getting Further Acquainted with Your Baby: The Bonding Process

Over the past several years, much has been written about the importance of bonding with a newborn, especially in an era when family structures and commitments have seemed so shaky. What exactly establishes the deep emotional ties with a child that will cause a parent to spend untold hours feeding, bathing, rocking, changing, and attending to the seemingly unending needs of a new baby? Is the bond locked into the genetic code of mothers and set loose by the flow of hormones during pregnancy? Is it biologically preexistent in fathers, or does it develop as a man watches role models in his family, as an extension of his love for his wife, or by an act of the will? Does it spring to life when the baby is first seen at the moment of birth? And what secures the attachment of a newborn to his mother and father?

Parents are given the privilege of taking the raw materials that comprise a brand-new human being and then molding him or her day-by-day into a mature, disciplined, productive, and God-fearing adult who will someday live in eternity.

The New
Strong-Willed Child
By Dr. James Dobson

Some have suggested that there is a critical time in the baby's first hours of life when a special connection will be made, especially between mother and child, that will affect the quality of their relationship for years to come. But this assumption raises a troubling question: What happens when mother or baby (or both) have special medical problems and cannot be together during those early hours or days? What if the new mother has a cesarean delivery and thus only momentary contact with her baby after birth, not to mention the potential distraction of pain during her recovery? What if the baby is born prematurely and must spend weeks in a high-tech hospital setting?

The answers hinge on the fact that human behavior is highly complex and not rigidly stereotyped or predictable like a computer program. As a result, bonding is a process that begins well before the baby is born and continues for years thereafter. It is certainly influenced by biology, hormones, and genetics. But it is also shaped by the upbringing of the new mother and father, their personal and spiritual values, their commitment to one another, and some everyday decisions they must make. Furthermore, human babies are not like newly hatched ducklings, which attach themselves to the first object they see.

Throughout this book we will be looking at the process of building and nurturing the bonds between parents and children and suggesting practical ways to carry out this important assignment. Here are several specific ideas to put into practice during childbirth and the time immediately following it:

If at all possible, keep sedating medications to a minimum during the hour or two before delivery. It is indeed nice if both mother and baby are awake and alert when they meet for the first time. However, it is not a sign of moral failure to request pain relief during labor (especially in the later stages when discomfort can become much more intense). If you do receive medication that produces drowsiness immediately after birth, you will have plenty of opportunity to begin enjoying and interacting with your baby in very short order.

Stop, look, listen, and touch. Whether immediately after birth, a few hours later, or better yet, many times over the next several months, take the time to sit quietly and enjoy your new family member. Study his features. Let him grip your finger. Smile and talk and sing to him. Count his toes. Marvel at the handiwork of God's creation, and thank Him for loaning this child to you for a season.

Look into rooming in. Continuous contact with the baby while in the hospital can give a new mother more practical and realistic preparation for the first few days at home. A pattern for nursing can be established, problems can be talked over with the nurses and other staff members, and (more important) there is more time for everyone to get acquainted with the new baby. Most hospitals today are flexible about these post-delivery arrangements, and some will assign a single nurse to attend both mother and child in a more coordinated fashion.

Some mothers prefer a variation on this theme, known as modified rooming in: The baby spends most of the day in the room with Mom and then goes to the nursery during the late-night and early-morning hours. This can be particularly helpful for a mother who has had a long, exhausting labor. Occasionally, when one or more small children are waiting at home and Mom already knows the basics of feeding and newborn care, she will actually prefer *not* to have full-time responsibility for the new baby in order to get a time-out and rest for a day or two. However, this relatively quiet interlude should include a generous amount of one-on-one time with the newborn, since the other children will want some attention once everyone arrives home.

In one sense, it might seem easier to spend time forming attachments with the new baby by getting out of the hospital and returning home as soon as possible. But home is also where your responsibilities are. Someone needs to prepare meals, do laundry, feed the dog, maintain order, and tend to any other children in the family, all of which could compete with your attention to your newborn. Ideally, prior arrangements can be made with the father, relatives, friends, or live-in help to take on some of these daily assignments. Preparing for this phase of childbirth can be every bit as important as all the classes and exercises during the last months of pregnancy.

Feeding and bonding. There are numerous advantages to breastfeeding, which we will review in detail in the next chapter. One that many mothers have described is a feeling of special closeness and nurturing that comes from a combination of skin-to-skin contact with the baby, the satisfaction of providing him nutrients and watching him grow as a result, and possibly the release of hormones triggered by nursing. For these and many other reasons, medical authorities consider breastfeeding to be the optimal form of infant nourishment. (The American Academy of Pediatrics recommends that it be the exclusive form of nourishment for the first four to six months of a baby's life.)

Because of the unique relationship between mother and baby during breastfeeding, fathers may feel that they have less to offer, at least for the first several weeks. On the contrary, there are plenty of hours left in the day when the baby can be held, rocked, talked to, and generally enjoyed by his father. In addition, while Dad may be tired from hours of coaching during labor and delivery, he will not have suffered the same physical exhaustion from the childbirth process that Mom did, and he should be given the opportunity to tend to their newborn child as often as possible.

If you cannot or choose not to breastfeed, you need not lose sleep wondering whether your bonding with your child is going to be impaired. For one thing, both parents can interact with the baby during bottle-feeding. And remember that feeding is only one of many components of the attachment process.

What about bonding after a cesarean delivery?

The need to deliver the baby by cesarean section may arise suddenly, or it may be known for some time in advance. The reasons this surgery may be recommended and the techniques used to carry it out will not be detailed here. (They should be covered in detail in your childbirth classes.) However, in most cases there should be time to carry out an epidural anesthetic, which allows the mother to be awake and alert during the delivery. Furthermore, the father or coach is typically allowed to sit at the head of the operating table, near the anesthesiologist. Only a small minority are so-called "crash" surgeries, in which an emergency requires that a general anesthetic be given.

When your baby is delivered by cesarean section, as soon as her cord is clamped and cut, she will be taken to a warmer for a brief examination. (While this is going on, the obstetrician and an assistant will check your uterus and abdomen, then begin the process of closing the multiple layers of tissue between the uterus and skin.) If all appears satisfactory, the baby will be brought to the head of the table where you can look at and touch her briefly. Unfortunately, the logistics of a cesarean delivery make a prolonged time with her difficult, and any attempt to nurse immediately after birth is impossible. After the surgery, you will go to a recovery area, where you may have further contact with your baby.

The first minutes (or even hours) after a cesarean delivery are usually not what most couples hoped for as a postchildbirth bonding experience. But catching up can be done over the next few days. Here are a few suggestions to help the process go more smoothly:

Explore your pain-relief options. A cesarean is major surgery, and pain control will be necessary for the first few days. Injections of narcotics every few hours can cause wide swings between drowsy relief and wide-awake discomfort, either of which can interfere with your interaction with your baby. An alternative that is widely used involves the delivery of analgesic (pain-relieving) medication through a **patient-controlled analgesia (PCA)** pump. This is an intravenous system that injects the pain medication at a rate you control, within specified limits. The effect is smoother, without extremes of pain or sleepiness. Some anesthesiologists will leave the small tube for the epidural block in place for a few hours, through which they can give a long-acting pain medication that allows for very effective pain relief without any drowsiness at all.

Don't give up on nursing. Breastfeeding after a cesarean delivery is challenging because the usual positions for holding the baby can be quite uncomfortable. But it can be done and is worth the effort (see chapter 4, page 114).

Try to recruit some extra help at home. The discomfort and fatigue that are so common in the wake of major surgery can turn the most basic tasks at home into major projects, leaving little energy (or enthusiasm) for the pleasantries of bonding. If your husband can't take extra time away from work to be home, consider having someone lend a hand for a few hours a day or even serve as a live-in to take care of some of the daily necessities. This person could be a relative (perhaps one of the baby's grandmothers), a volunteer from church, or someone specifically hired for this job.

Additional Events before Going Home

The newborn examination. Sometime during the first twenty-four hours after birth, your baby's pediatrician or family physician will carry out a formal examination. (Of course, if problems are apparent at birth, an evaluation will be carried out immediately.) Unless you go home within a few hours, a second checkout exam may be done before discharge. You should receive feedback from these checkups, especially if there are any problems. In addition, you may have questions about basic care and follow-up visits. You will get more out of these conversations if you write your questions down ahead of time.

Newborn screening blood tests. Newborns in every state and U.S. territory are routinely tested for a number of uncommon conditions that may not be apparent at birth but may have profound (or even fatal) effects later in life if not recognized and managed appropriately. These screening tests are performed on a few drops of blood collected from the baby's heel within the first two or three days of life. (If the blood is collected within the first twenty-four hours, retesting should be done a week or two later.) If any of the test results are abnormal, follow-up tests will be recommended to confirm the specific diagnosis.

What tests might be carried out? The answer depends on which state you live in, and it may change over time. All states and territories in the United States screen for the following three conditions:

Phenylketonuria (**PKU**), which affects one in 10,000 to 25,000 infants, was the first condition for which a newborn screening test was implemented, beginning in the early 1960s. PKU involves the inability to process **phenylalanine**, an amino acid (one of the building blocks of protein) that is found in many foods. When phenylalanine accumulates in the body, brain damage and mental retardation may result. However, an infant with PKU who is fed formula that is low in phenylalanine and who subsequently adheres to a special diet can live a normal life.

Congenital hypothyroidism is the most common of the newborn conditions currently screened, affecting about one in five thousand infants. It involves a low level of **thyroid hormone** (which regulates the overall rate of metabolism) and can lead to serious problems in growth and brain development. An infant who is diagnosed at birth and treated with a daily oral dose of thyroid hormone can live a normal life.

Galactosemia is an uncommon condition (affecting one in fifty thousand infants) in which the sugar **galactose**, found in milk, cannot be converted to glucose. Avoidance of milk and all dairy products throughout life can prevent severe problems, including blindness, mental retardation, and even death.

In addition, most states screen for the following:

Sickle cell disease involves an alteration of hemoglobin (the molecule that carries oxygen within red blood cells) that can cause those cells to become crescent or "sickle" shaped. Affected individuals may suffer anemia, sudden bouts of severe pain, damage to important organs, and serious infections. Unlike PKU or congenital hypothyroidism, sickle cell disease is not prevented by following a certain diet or taking a specific supplement, but appropriate medical care significantly affects its course and complications.

Congenital adrenal hyperplasia is a group of conditions that results in reduced levels of a critical hormone called **cortisol** (and sometimes another called **aldosterone**). Appropriate medical treatment can prevent a variety of problems, ranging from reproductive problems among those who are mildly affected to death in more severe cases.

Some states test not only for these but also for many other conditions. A technology called **tandem mass spectrometry** (which is abbreviated **MS/MS**) allows for screening more than twenty congenital metabolic problems from one blood specimen. These syndromes are extremely uncommon, but when twenty or more are screened at the same time, the odds of discovering any abnormality rise to about one in four thousand—higher than the likelihood of finding any of the disorders that are universally screened (PKU, congenital hypothyroidism, and galactosemia, as described above).

You can obtain an up-to-date list of the tests routinely carried out in your state at the Web site of the National Newborn Screening and Genetics Resource Center (http://genes-r-us.uthscsa.edu), a cooperative project of the federal Maternal and Child Health Bureau and the Department of Pediatrics at the University of Texas Health Sciences Center. The NNSGRC also provides information about laboratories (both commercial and nonprofit) that offer MS/MS screening if you wish to have your newborn tested for a wider array of metabolic disorders than those routinely carried out in your state. You may want to discuss this with your baby's physician, who in turn can check the NNSGRC Web site for updated information. (This is an area of medicine and public policy that is in transition, and a number of professional organizations are calling for uniform national policies for newborn screening.)

Newborn screening for hearing loss. More than thirty states have universal newborn hearing screening programs, and many health centers in other states promote this type of screening as well. Every year an estimated two to four in one thousand infants are born with significant hearing loss and are at risk for delays in speech and language development. Before newborn screening became a widespread practice, the average age for diagnosing moderate to severe hearing loss was thirteen months, and seventeen months for infants with milder loss.[2] In many cases the problem was not identified until the child was two, three, or even older.

The screening test for hearing is typically done before a baby leaves the hospital. It is quick and painless and can in fact be carried out while the infant is asleep. If he does not pass the screening test shortly after birth, it should be repeated at about one month of age. If he fails the second screen, a more detailed evaluation should be carried out. For more information about hearing screening in newborns and young children, check the Web site of the National Center for Hearing Assessment and Management (established at Utah State University in 1995) at http://www.infanthearing.org.

Circumcision. Circumcision is the removal of the foreskin, the half inch of skin that covers the head of the infant's penis. It has been a religious and cultural tradition in many parts of the world for thousands of years and was the norm for newborn boys a generation ago. More recently, some consumer groups and professional organizations have questioned the wisdom of routine circumcision.

The advantages of circumcision are primarily hygienic. The circumcised penis is easier to keep clean, whereas uncircumcised boys and men must learn to retract (gently pull back) the foreskin to clean the head of the penis. Otherwise, the accumulation of debris and bacteria may lead to an inflammation known as **balanitis**. Some evidence suggests that uncircumcised infants are at higher risk for infections of the urinary tract. Also, it has long been assumed that being uncircumcised is a risk factor for developing cancer of the penis (a rare form of cancer) among older men. Newer research suggests that the risk may be more specifically related to poor hygiene (which can result in a buildup of **smegma**, a mix of dead cells, secretions, and bacteria under the foreskin) and multiple sexual partners—uncircumcised men appear to be at increased risk for infection with human papillomavirus (HPV). As we will discuss later, certain strains of HPV are linked with the development of genital and anal cancers in both men and women (see pages 74 and 541). In addition, circumcision appears to reduce the risk of heterosexually acquired HIV infection in men.

On the other hand, circumcision is a minor surgery and thus carries with it a very slight risk of complications, specifically moderate bleeding, infection, or even injury to the penis. If there is a family history of bleeding problems, the procedure should not be done until the baby's clotting status has been checked. Babies who have not had a vitamin K injection (sometimes the case when the baby was born at home) tend to bleed more freely after the procedure. (Interestingly, the biblical mandate for circumcision of male babies in the nation of Israel called for the procedure to be done on the eighth day—which, prior to the use of vitamin K, was precisely the time clotting-factor levels would peak, thus reducing the risk of bleeding.)

Typically circumcision is done by the baby's pediatrician or family doctor or by Mom's obstetrician before the baby leaves the hospital, although it can be arranged anytime during the first few weeks. It should not be done if there is any question about the newborn's stability, especially during the first twenty-four hours. The physician will use a local anesthetic to relieve pain, and a pacifier dipped in a sucrose (sugar) solution may be used to soothe the baby during the procedure. Circumcision is generally carried out when the infant's stomach is empty, but he can be nursed immediately afterward. A small dressing will be applied to prevent bleeding, and

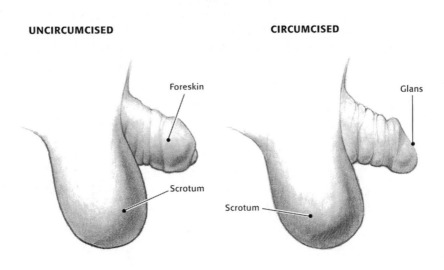

UNCIRCUMCISED

Foreskin

Scrotum

CIRCUMCISED

Glans

Scrotum

it will fall off on its own within a day or two. The head of the penis will appear somewhat raw, and a small amount of petroleum jelly will keep it from sticking to the inner surface of his diaper. If the circumcision has been done with a device called a Plastibell, the small plastic bell will fall off on its own in about one to two weeks, leaving a healed surface.

If a baby boy is not circumcised, the foreskin should be left alone until it can be retracted easily, which may occur anytime before puberty. Occasionally problems with the foreskin develop later in life, and in some cases a circumcision becomes a medical necessity for an older child or adult.

Whether or not to have a baby boy circumcised is a straightforward decision for some families and a quandary for others. Despite some potential health advantages, there is no medical consensus specifically supporting or condemning routine infant circumcision. For many families, religious or other traditions are the main considerations. In others, the father or an older brother has been circumcised, and the parents want everyone to look alike. Foreskin uniformity in the family, however, is not really necessary for a child's emotional well-being.

If you are uncertain about your decision, take some time to discuss the pros and cons with the baby's physician and with your spouse (assuming you are married). The bottom line is that you can and should be comfortable with your decision.

When Do Mother and Baby Go Home?

After a hospital birth, mother and baby typically return home in one or two days following a vaginal delivery and three or four days after a cesarean. Obviously this will change if mother or baby needs further care. The length of stay should be determined by the physician's assessment of what is medically appropriate. If the newborn is premature or develops an unexpected problem that requires a longer stay, most hospitals are prepared to offer parents as much ongoing contact with the baby as possible.

Whether after a few hours, a day or two, or an extended stay, the gathering together of mother, father, baby, other family members, and your assorted new baby gear (including flowers, balloons, gifts, and other items that may have suddenly appeared after the delivery) for the trip home is a true graduation, a family commencement. Savor the moment and make sure someone captures it in pictures or on video. You are about to begin the next great adventure in parenting.

Sexually Transmitted Infections (STIs): Their Impact on You and Your Unborn Child

Syphilis is caused by a spiral-shaped organism known as a **spirochete**, which easily passes from mother to baby during pregnancy and can cause serious problems in many of the baby's organs. It may even result in stillbirth. Fortunately, the infection can be detected by a blood test, which is normally obtained as part of the first prenatal visit. If the test is positive, additional tests are necessary to confirm the diagnosis. If a woman becomes infected later in her pregnancy, however, the diagnosis might be missed, with disastrous consequences for the baby. Many of the problems caused by syphilis can be avoided if this infection is promptly diagnosed and treated (usually with penicillin).

Gonorrhea is a bacterial infection that continues to infect more than one million Americans every year. A pregnant woman with an active infection can transmit it to her baby during childbirth. The eyes of the newborn are extremely sensitive to this bacterium, and severe damage or even blindness can result if they become infected. For this reason antibiotic eye ointment or drops (required by state law) are given to every newborn, regardless of the mother's history. Gonorrhea prior to or during pregnancy can be treated with antibiotics; the type of antibiotic, dose, and length of treatment will depend on the extent and severity of the infection.

Chlamydia is an organism that has risen from relative obscurity in the 1970s to become the most common bacterial STI in the United States. As with gonorrhea, a chlamydia-infected woman may pass the organism to her baby during delivery. Not only may the baby's eyes become infected, but a stubborn pneumonia can also develop. When an infection with chlamydia is diagnosed, treatment with antibiotics can and should be carried out.

Herpes simplex virus (HSV) is notorious for a property it shares with a number of other organisms: Once a person is infected, HSV remains for life. HSV type 1 typically causes eruptions known as cold sores or fever blisters around the mouth or nose, although it can also cause genital infections through oral-genital contact.

A baby born to a mother with HSV could be infected during vaginal delivery if there is a herpes outbreak on the mother's genital area. The risk of transfer is much higher (33 to 50 percent) if this is the mother's first outbreak rather than a recurrence (4 percent or less).[1] (One to 2 percent of pregnant women with recurrent HSV infection could transmit the virus at the time of delivery without any visible outbreak.) For the newborn, an HSV infection can be disastrous. About 45 percent of infected infants will have surface (skin and mucous membrane) involvement only. Another 35 percent will have disease primarily involving the central nervous system. Of these, 15 percent will die, and two out of three will have major consequences, including blindness, seizures, and mental retardation. About one in five infants infected with HSV at birth will have the most devastating type of HSV infection in which the virus spreads to multiple organs throughout the body. Sixty to 80 percent of these will die.[2]

If you have a history of genital herpes, it is important to inform your physician, and both of you should be watchful for any recurrences. If there is an outbreak within a week before birth, your physician will probably recommend a cesarean delivery to minimize the risk of contact between virus and newborn. While cold sores around the mouth are less likely to cause trouble, you should be cautious if one is present when you give birth. You should avoid touching your mouth, wash your hands frequently, and wear a surgical mask over your mouth when handling your baby until the sore heals. (Be sure to check with your doctor to confirm that you are dealing with an HSV outbreak.)

Genital warts are caused by the **human papillomavirus (HPV)**. As many as 65 to 75 percent of sexually active individuals will be infected with HPV, though most will clear their infection without medical treatment. Some strains of HPV cause soft, wartlike growths in the genital area. During pregnancy these may grow dramatically, and surgery, cautery, or laser treatment may be needed to remove them. Fortunately HPV transmission from mother to newborn during delivery appears to be extremely uncommon; however, if it does occur, the virus may cause recurrent growths on the vocal cords. Of greater concern is the association of certain strains of HPV—typically *not* those that cause genital warts—with cancer of the mother's cervix (the opening of the uterus). Any woman who has ever had sexual intercourse (whether or not she has had genital warts) should have regular Pap smears to detect and treat changes that might be caused by HPV infection in the cervix. Doing so can significantly reduce her risk of developing this type of cancer.

Bacterial vaginosis is an overgrowth of certain types of bacteria in the vagina that can be (but is not always) sexually transmitted. Because this condition can increase the risk of premature rupture of membranes and preterm (early) labor, screening for it may be performed during the second half of pregnancy.

Acquired immune deficiency syndrome (AIDS) is caused by the **human immunodeficiency virus (HIV)**. The vast majority of HIV infections are transmitted during sexual contact, through contaminated needles and syringes used during the injection of illegal drugs, or by transfer from infected mother to baby during pregnancy. (Transmission of HIV during blood transfusions is now extremely rare.) Infants can also become infected by nursing from an infected mother.

After gaining access to the body, HIV multiplies quietly within the immune system over a period of many months or years, gradually destroying its ability to deal with invading microorganisms. The eventual result is full-blown AIDS, in which a person becomes vulnerable to a variety of devastating infections and some forms of cancer. Although this condition has been almost universally fatal, the development of new drug regimens may extend the life span and improve the quality of life for those with this disease, while researchers continue to seek a cure. Pregnancy does not increase the progression of HIV infection to AIDS but can worsen the disease in a woman who is already severely ill.

Pregnancy itself does not worsen the health of an HIV-infected woman, but she has a 20 to 30 percent risk of transmitting the virus to her baby if no preventive treatment is given.[3] About one in five infected newborns will develop AIDS-related illness by one year of age, and most of these will die from overwhelming infection by the age of four. The rest have a slower rate of disease progression and may not develop AIDS until later in childhood or even adolescence. Needless to say, HIV infection among pregnant women and their children is a serious health issue anywhere it occurs, but it is particularly devastating in developing nations. According to UNICEF, about one percent of the world's pregnant women are infected with HIV, and the vast majority of these live in Africa. In the United States, fewer than four hundred infants acquire HIV from their mothers every year, but worldwide the number is greater than seven hundred thousand, with 90 percent living in developing nations. (For a more detailed look at the child with HIV/AIDS, see "HIV infection/AIDS" in Reference Section, page 684.)

Screening tests for HIV detect a person's antibody response to the virus and not the virus itself. If such screening indicates that one has HIV (is HIV positive), further investigation will be necessary to determine the status of the infection and guide treatment decisions. It is strongly recommended that testing for HIV be carried out as part of routine prenatal screening for the following reasons:

- A woman can become infected with HIV even if she has not been involved in a high-risk lifestyle. A single sexual encounter with an infected individual or a onetime experiment with intravenous drugs can transmit the virus.
- The signs and symptoms of HIV/AIDS may not appear for years after the initial transmission, so a woman may have no idea that she is infected.
- Medical treatment of an HIV-infected pregnant woman may decrease her odds of transmitting the virus to her baby to less than 2 percent.
- An HIV-infected mother should not breastfeed her infant, because doing so carries a 10 to 14 percent risk of transmitting the virus to the baby.

Hepatitis B is a viral infection of the liver that is transmitted through the same mechanisms as HIV. About 70 percent of adults and children five and older who are infected experience a flulike illness with fever, nausea, and jaundice (a yellow discoloration of the skin and eyes), typically occurring about three months after exposure. The majority of these recover completely, but between 2 and 6 percent develop a chronic infection that can lead to **cirrhosis** (scarring) or even cancer of the liver. Furthermore, chronic carriers—of which there are about 1.25 million in the United States—can transmit the virus to sexual partners or to a baby during pregnancy or delivery.

While adults infected with hepatitis B are likely to experience an acute illness and then recover, infants and children tend to have a different course. Acute symptoms are less common among the young, but they are much more likely to develop a chronic infection. Among infants and children infected with hepatitis B, 30 percent of those one to five years of age and 90 percent of infants (including those who are infected at birth) develop the chronic form of the infection and are at risk for long-term complications.

A blood test for hepatitis B surface antigen should be a part of routine prenatal screening. If it is positive, further testing can determine if a woman has a new infection, an old infection that has resolved, or a chronic infection. Depending on the results, appropriate plans can be made to help provide the newborn with an antibody injection that offers more immediate protection, if needed, along with the routine hepatitis B vaccine normally given shortly after birth.

A final word on STIs

Sexually transmitted infections can have lifelong and life-threatening consequences for both parents and their children. Yet they are definitely preventable for those who are willing to commit to a "no risk" sexual lifestyle. In a best-case scenario, this means that a man and a woman abstain from sexual relations until marriage and then remain strictly monogamous in a mutually exclusive relationship. Medically, this eliminates a significant number of risks, and it greatly enhances the stability of the environment for raising children.

The threat of HIV/AIDS sparked a national campaign for what has been dubbed "safe sex" (or, somewhat more realistically, "safer sex"), which has placed a heavy emphasis on condom use to prevent the spread of STIs. But while condoms offer some degree of risk reduction, they are far from foolproof, and their effectiveness depends on correct and consistent use. When used correctly 100 percent of the time during sexual encounters, condoms offer about an 80 to 90 percent risk reduction for transmission of HIV. For a number of common STIs, such as chlamydia, gonorrhea, syphilis, and herpes simplex, risk reduction provided by consistent condom use is 50 percent or less. (One reason for decreased effectiveness is that many of these can occur on areas of the genitals that are not covered by condoms.) Until recently most authorities, even those who strongly advocated condom use, considered condoms to offer little if any protection against infection with human papillomavirus (HPV). While newer research suggests that condoms, when used consistently and correctly, might reduce the risk of spreading or acquiring HPV, condoms still do not offer complete protection against the virus.

If you are unmarried, it would be wise to remain abstinent until you enter a permanent, monogamous relationship.

If you have had one or more sexual partners prior to marriage, you should discuss STI screening with your physician. This is especially important if you are pregnant, because so many STIs have more serious consequences for the baby if they are acquired during pregnancy. In addition, it is important for a pregnant woman to be both candid and thorough in reviewing her sexual history—including any prior symptoms of vaginal discharge, pelvic discomfort, or surface changes in the genital area—with her physician, because important screening tests may be recommended based on this information.

The Adopted Child

Approximately 125,000 children are adopted every year in the United States, and of these about 15 percent involve children born in other countries (now called **intercountry adoptions**). Each of these adoptions represents a unique set of circumstances in which the paths of adults and children who (with rare exception) do not share biological ties converge. Adopting a child can fulfill a couple's most cherished dreams and desires while meeting a child's deepest needs for love and stability. But as honorable, compassionate, and joyous as this process might be, it is also rarely accomplished without considerable effort, significant (but surmountable) challenges, and occasional heartaches.

Because this book is primarily concerned with rearing children, most of the issues and details of events prior to bringing an adopted child home will not be discussed here. Concerns related to adoption agencies, attorneys, regulations, foreign governments, finances, paperwork, the home study, and, above all, the endless patience often required of adoptive parents-to-be are all very important but ably covered in a variety of other books and materials. One topic that will be addressed here is the nature of the relationship between the adoptive parents and the birth parents (especially the mother), assuming that one or both of the birth parents are involved in the adoption process, since their interactions can have a significant impact on the child's upbringing.

Closed and Open Adoptions

When a pregnant woman decides that she is going to release her baby for adoption, two basic scenarios may occur, each having many variations. In what is called a **closed adoption**, the birth mother has very little (if any) contact with her infant immediately after delivery, and no contact with the adoptive parents. Confidentiality regarding the parties involved in the adoption prevents future interactions between them. Closed adoptions were the norm in previous generations (and remain so in Canada) and are still carried out in significant numbers in the United States. Those who favor this approach feel that it brings about more timely and effective closure for all concerned, allowing the birth mother to move on with her life and the adoptive parents to focus their attention exclusively on the baby. Others raise concerns that closed adoption may leave the birth mother with a significant emotional crater to fill, as she can only imagine what her child's life will be like during the ensuing months and years. Also, unless specific arrangements have been made (as is done in Canada and in some adoption agencies in the United States through a registry system), the child of a closed adoption would be unable to fill an important gap in his own personal history if he should desire to meet his birth mother when he is an older adolescent or adult.

In recent decades the partially or completely **open adoption** has become more common. This means that there is some degree of interaction between the birth mother or both birth parents and the adoptive family. In many cases, the birth mother actually selects who will rear her child from a number of potential candidates presented by an adoption agency. The couple may then become involved with the birth mother through an extended period of her pregnancy, and one or both adoptive parents might even attend the birth of the baby. The birth mother or both birth parents may relinquish the baby directly to the adoptive parents at the hospital or shortly after the birth in a physical gesture of release. Such a relationship can be fulfilling for all concerned, and it also offers the adoptive parents more knowledge of the baby's prenatal care and family health history. But it is not without potential pitfalls. Childbirth and adoption are emotionally charged events, and open adoption raises the possibility for complications in both the immediate and distant future. If you are going to be involved in an open adoption, consider the following:

The relationship between the adoptive parents and the birth mother, and everyone's expectations for the future, should be carefully considered and discussed before the baby is born. For example, if the prospective parents offer a generous amount of attention and affection (and even material goods within the legal limits set by the state) to the birth mother prior to the delivery, they might satisfy some deep needs in the birth mother's life. But once the baby arrives, the parents' attention quite understandably shifts dramatically to the infant. The birth mother may then feel like a nonentity, someone who was valued only because she was carrying the prized baby inside her. Depression, bitterness, even second thoughts about the adoption decision could result from this turn of events. If the adoptive parents do not want or intend to have an ongoing relationship with the birth mother after the birth, they should be careful about the signals they send beforehand.

It is very important that expectations be clarified regarding the amount of contact between mother and adoptive family once the baby is born. The birth mother may want to visit her baby, which can help her develop a clear mental picture of the setting in which her child will be brought up. But ongoing visits might also become uncomfortable for the adoptive parents if they begin to feel that they are "on trial" when the birth mother is present. These visits can also be emotionally difficult for the birth mother, who sees her baby relating to another woman as "Mommy."

What about long-term contact between the birth mother and the adoptive family? In some cases regular visitation continues for years, but it is more common for interaction to be limited to pictures and an update from the adoptive parents once or twice a year. For many birth mothers, the need for closure leads them to a decision to walk away both physically and emotionally, bringing ongoing contact with the child to an end. Many experts in this field argue that long-term contact can be unhealthy for the birth mother because it could prevent her from moving forward with her life. Furthermore, the birth mother's continued involvement in her child's life might become disruptive if she interferes with decisions the adoptive parents must make on a day-to-day basis. Everyone must have a clear understanding that the adoptive parents *are* the parents and that they have the final say in the way the child is brought up. Honest conversation and counseling will help clarify expectations and minimize the risk of conflict.

Everyone involved in an adoption must understand that the birth mother will undergo a significant grieving process that normally lasts many months, even under the best of circumstances. It is very important for the birth mother to receive competent and compassionate counseling before—but especially after—the birth, to work through the grieving and releasing process. It is not enough for an agency or an attorney to say that counseling is available "if she needs it" and then leave it up to the birth mother to initiate the process. Adoptive parents would be wise to see to it that counseling takes place and to cover its cost if necessary. Not only does this ensure that the birth mother's emotional needs are taken seriously, but it also reduces the likelihood of a reversal—a heart-wrenching event in which the birth mother decides after a few weeks or months that she wants to keep her baby after all. All too often the seeds of a reversal are sown when the normal grieving process leads the birth mother to think that the adoption choice was a mistake.

Throughout this section, the term *birth mother* will be used to designate the woman who is giving birth to the child. *Birth parents* refers to both the birth mother and the biological father.

All of these concerns, especially the need for counseling before and after the baby's birth, most certainly apply to the biological father also, assuming that he remains involved and is engaged in the ongoing decision making.

Sometimes the adoption process takes place much more rapidly, and adoptive parents may find themselves meeting a birth mother or both birth parents for the first time at the time of the birth. While there might not be much opportunity for building a relationship on such short notice, the exploration of everyone's expectations should still take place, even if in a somewhat condensed time frame.

What If an Adoption Falls Through or Is Reversed?

Two of the most emotionally charged events related to the adoption process are the "failed placement" (the placement that has been arranged with considerable effort but then falls through for whatever reason) and the reversal (the baby has actually arrived in the adoptive parents' home for several days, or even a few months, only to be taken away when one or both biological parents have a change of heart before their legal rights to the baby have been terminated). Both of these situations (especially the reversal) can be extraordinarily difficult and will generate virtually the same full force of grief that would occur with the loss of any child. *The severity of the loss must be acknowledged, and the need for grieving must not be ignored.* (Although some may try to lessen the parents' pain by saying or implying, "This wasn't really your child, after all," the loss is real, and lack of biological ties has nothing to do with it.) Counseling, whether individually or through a support group, can be very helpful, especially when the question of trying to arrange another adoption is to be broached.

Common Concerns of Adoptive Parents

Parents who are considering adopting a baby or a child often have a number of qualms and concerns, most of which are quite normal (and similar to those of parents anticipating caring for their own new baby).

Will I be able to love this child as if he were my own flesh and blood (especially if I already have one or more biological children)? The process of adding children to any family raises similar questions ("Is there enough love in me for this new baby on the way?"). But God is able to open a parent's heart to "make room" for the newcomer. After a very short while it becomes virtually impossible to imagine life in the family without him.

Will I be able to treat each child in my family the same way, especially if I have both biological and adopted children? Actually, no two children in any family can be treated in exactly the same way because each child is a unique creation. Remember that no child is perfect, that all children will give you grief at some point, and that one child will probably cause more overall difficulty than another. The issue isn't treating everyone exactly the same way, but rather being firmly committed to each child's well-being and surrounding each one with both unconditional love and appropriate limits.

Can I discipline a child who has been abused or abandoned? Absolutely—in fact, not doing so is a worse form of abandonment. Discipline does not merely consist of negative consequences or punishment imposed for misbehavior; it encompasses the entire process of building a child's character and imposing appropriate limits. (See Special Concerns, "Principles of Discipline and Training: Balancing Love and Limits," page 259.)

Am I up for this? Doubts and feelings of inadequacy about parenting are normal. (Even if you believe that you have child rearing completely figured out, the next bundle of joy God sends will most likely change that opinion.) However, if you feel major persistent qualms about your ability to parent, by all means spend time with a qualified counselor to sort through your specific concerns.

Special Issues in Caring for Adopted Children

The most basic needs of an adopted child are the same as those of any other child: physical, emotional, and spiritual nurturing in an environment where love, stability, and appropriate limits are clearly evident. Nearly all of what you will read in this book or other resources about parenting will apply to your adopted child. However, several specific concerns that may arise during or after the adoption process are worth a brief review.

Unity of purpose on the home front

While in nearly every case the prospective parents share equally the desire to adopt a child, occasionally one may be less enthusiastic about this undertaking than the other. It is unwise for a person to merely "go along" with an adoption primarily to please his or her spouse. The commitment of both parents to the adopted child should be as strong as if he were biologically their own.

What if there are one or more other siblings at home at the time of the adoption? Ideally, they should be prepared in the same manner they would be if Mom were expecting a new baby. Tell them the facts in basic language they can understand, and describe the adoption in a positive light. There will be a new brother or sister who will be sharing in the love of the family and who will be treated with the same love and respect that everyone at home receives. If the adopted child has any special problems or will be of different racial or ethnic origin, discuss this in a matter-of-fact way. It should go without saying that parents in such situations will need to be both fair and abundantly affectionate to all the children, striving to see that no one feels left out or is treated with favoritism—just as in any family where more than one child is present.

Nursing an adopted baby

Believe it or not, it is not necessary for a woman to bear an infant in order to nurse one. A woman who would like to breastfeed an adopted baby may be able to produce her own milk through a combination of medication that stimulates lactation and repeated stimulation of her breasts, either by using a pump prior to the adoption or allowing the baby to nurse after he arrives.

This process is usually more successful with infants younger than eight weeks of age, although it can also be attempted with an older baby. While nursing an adopted child can yield many of the benefits that breastfeeding affords to infants and mothers (see chapter 4, page 114), it will also require considerable commitment and effort. Furthermore, it is very likely that the adoptive mother's production of milk will be less than adequate to meet all of the growing baby's nutritional needs. Supplementation with formula will thus be necessary in such cases. Plans to nurse an adopted baby should be discussed in advance with a knowledgeable physician or lactation consultant.

Adopting an older baby or child

Parents of newborns are normally concerned about the process of bonding with their new baby, often wondering if even brief periods of separation will interfere with it. But what if you are going to begin parenting a baby who has lived with someone else for several weeks or months—or perhaps a toddler or older child who cannot even understand your language?

In such circumstances you cannot necessarily expect an instantaneous bonding experience or a picture-perfect first meeting, where a child throws her arms around your neck in a display of unrestrained gratitude. In fact, in some cases the initial contact will be strained. A baby might be frightened, fussy, fidgety—or oddly quiet, especially if she has been raised in an environment where crying yielded little response from her adult caretakers. An older child who has not had a stable environment or who has been ignored or mistreated in the past might be reserved or even sullen. Any parent adopting such a child should be aware that neglect, trauma, or abuse early in that child's life may have resulted in long-term or even permanent developmental and relational problems. Children who are not nurtured and stimulated as infants sometimes have great difficulty ever attaching to other people, no matter how much those people express love and affection for them. In addition, a baby or child arriving from a foreign country may be tired, poorly nourished, and overloaded by the entire experience. Whether coming from across town or halfway around the world, she may actually show signs of grieving for whatever familiar faces and environment she has left behind.

Getting acquainted with and then getting close to an older adopted child will take time and a fair amount of patience. Obviously it is helpful if information about the child's background and previous experiences is available. If you have not yet had a child, you would be wise to read about the normal developmental milestones for the age of the child you will be adopting. In general, voices that are calm and reassuring, touch that is soft and soothing, and sensitivity to the cues given by the child will go a long way toward a harmonious adjustment. If all your best efforts to form a mutually satisfying attachment seem to be a resounding failure, don't hesitate to seek help from your child's physician, the adoption agency (assuming that one was involved), or a counselor, preferably one who has experience with adoptive parents and children.

Adopting a child with a physical, mental, or emotional handicap

A special-needs child can be a great blessing to a family, but it is important to have a clear understanding of problems that are likely to arise during his life. (In some cases a handicap may require special education and care well into the child's adulthood.) Support services, including other parents who have raised a child with similar problems, should be consulted both before and after the adoption.

Medical concerns

You should obtain as much information as possible about the medical history of the baby or child you are planning to adopt. Details of the family history, the mother's pregnancy and delivery, congenital problems, illnesses, and immunizations are helpful, if available. However, in some cases you may not even be certain of your child's birth date, and some evaluation based on physical and behavioral characteristics will be necessary. (This may not be easy if the child has been malnourished or raised in a deprived setting that has delayed his growth and developmental milestones.)

If your adopted child appears to be well, you might want to wait for several days (or even a few weeks) before taking him for a medical evaluation so that he can become comfortable with you before entering the unfamiliar realm of the doctor's office. A child from a foreign country may require a more extensive examination soon after arrival—even if he has been examined before leaving his country of origin—because of the possibility that he might have acquired one or more infections (such as tuberculosis, hepatitis B, or intestinal parasites) that are more common in other areas of the world or conditions (such as particular forms of anemia) seen in certain racial and ethnic groups. If the child appears ill upon arrival, he should be evaluated as soon as possible.

Cross-cultural and cross-racial adoptions

From an infant's standpoint, his ethnic background is not initially a major source of concern, although the adoptive parents might need to deal with occasional inappropriate reactions, such as "Why would you adopt a child of a different race?" As the child becomes older, however, you will need to deal with questions raised by differences in appearance within the family. Most can be handled during the ongoing process of talking to him about his adoption (see next section). Exploring your child's racial or ethnic heritage as a means of enhancing his overall understanding of his "story" would be beneficial to both you and your child. Your child should be encouraged to develop and maintain friendships within his minority community. This will make him more comfortable moving in and out of his own subculture. Keep in mind, though, that your child's basic sense of identity should focus primarily on qualities of character and bonds of love that have been established in your family over a period of years.

Talking to a Child about His Adoption

In bygone generations it was common not to reveal to a child his status as an adopted child, apparently out of fear that this would cause him undue pain or alienation. Unfortunately, this approach usually had the opposite effect. Very often it was during adolescence—a time already full of great upheaval, self-doubt, and issues of an emerging identity—that he would learn of his adoption, often by accident (such as a relative's careless slip of the tongue). And so, with all the other concerns of this age-group already in full swing, he would now have to contend with harrowing questions such as "Why did my mother abandon me?" and "What else don't I know about my family?"

Just as children should be given age-appropriate information about sexuality on a need-to-know basis, so should the adopted child's unique question, "Where did I come from?" be met with answers that are straightforward, tactful, and truthful. Ideally, a child should not grow up remembering a time when he did not know that Mom and Dad were not his biological parents. *The events leading to his adoption should be described as a unique and positive story.* The decision of his birth mother very often can be understood as one born out of love and concern rather than an act of abandonment. But even if the child was abandoned by his birth mother, he can be told, quite truthfully, that *God did not abandon him and never will.* Whatever the circumstances might have been, a child can be led to understand that God not only "knit him together in his mother's womb" but also entrusted him to his adoptive parents, who are continually joyful that he has become an important member of their family.

Some adoptive families put together a scrapbook that tells the child's story. This might include pictures of the birth mother, if available, and if possible a note from her to the child explaining what she did, her feelings about him, how happy she was about the family that was adopting him, and so forth. Baby pictures, documents, a map of his country of origin if he came from a foreign land, and any other such memorabilia are of great interest to children, who will look through them over and over as they grow up.

What if an older child or teenager expresses a desire to meet one or both of his birth parents? These feelings are not unusual or inappropriate, and in most cases they should not be squelched. (An exception would be a situation in which an adopted teenager who is struggling against parental ground rules believes that "things would be better if I could be with my real mom." A grass-is-greener fantasy should not be the primary motivation for contacting a birth parent, and this process should not move forward until the issues at home have been resolved.) In many cases, meeting one or both biological parents could take some of the mystery out of an adopted child's origins and identity and also help him appreciate his adoptive parents. If there have been on-going contact and friendly relationships over the years, a meeting may not be terribly difficult, either logistically or emotionally. However, if contact has been lost, this will be difficult to arrange without a fair amount of detective work. If you know that a birth parent is unstable or involved in a lifestyle you disapprove of, it might be prudent to forestall such a meeting until the child is mature enough to deal with it. This may not occur until he is a young adult.

Birth Defects and Prenatal Testing

Every parent-to-be anticipates the arrival of a new son or daughter with a strong sense of excitement but also with a certain level of concern in the back of his or her mind: *What if there is something wrong with my baby?* For some, a known family risk of a particular disease or a child already born with a birth defect usually brings this concern to the forefront of prenatal considerations: *How can we find out ahead of time whether or not this baby will be normal?*

What Are Birth Defects, and How Common Are They?

Birth defects, also called **congenital disorders**, are abnormalities that are present at birth, whether or not they are diagnosed at that time. These disorders sometimes involve visible changes in one or several parts of the body, or they can affect the baby on a less visible metabolic or microscopic level. More than three thousand specific birth defects have been identified, ranging from conditions that are barely noticeable to some that are catastrophic.

According to the March of Dimes Birth Defects Foundation, some type of birth defect is present in one out of every twenty-eight babies born in the United States, resulting in more than eight thousand deaths every year—the most common cause of death during the first year of life in this country. There is untold personal grief underlying these statistics, and yet we bear only a fraction of the world's burden of birth defects. The March of Dimes estimates that worldwide, 7.9 million infants are born every year with a serious birth defect that is entirely or partially of genetic origin. Hundreds of thousands more have defects that develop between conception and birth, arising from exposure to toxins such as alcohol, infections (rubella, syphilis, and others), and various forms of nutritional deficiencies. Worldwide every year 3.3 million children under five die because of birth defects. More than 90 percent of these defects and deaths occur in middle- and low-income countries.[1]

What Causes Birth Defects?

While the underlying causes of many types of birth defects are understood, *in roughly two out of three cases the specific reason is unknown* and thus assumed to be the result of a complex interaction of genetic and nongenetic factors during the intricate process of the baby's development within the womb. Birth defects in which a specific cause can be identified fall into the following categories:

Genetic abnormalities

Genetic abnormalities arise directly from the transmission of genetic information from one generation to the next. In what is truly a marvel of engineering, all of the information necessary to form and maintain a human being is coded on long strands of the spiral molecule known as **deoxyribonucleic acid**, or **DNA**. An extended segment of DNA that serves a specific function (such as providing the blueprint for a certain protein) is called a **gene**, and it is estimated that somewhere between twenty thousand and one hundred thousand of these genes govern the physical attributes of each individual. Rather than being randomly dispersed throughout the cells whose functions it governs, DNA is packed into forty-six dense bodies known as **chromosomes**, all of which easily fit within the nucleus of a cell. Our forty-six chromosomes consist of twenty-three pairs, of which twenty-two are known as nonsex, or **autosomal**, while one pair consists of the sex chromosomes designated X and Y.

Most of our 60 trillion cells contain all of our genetic code; notable exceptions are the egg and sperm cells, which contain only a single set of twenty-three chromosomes. At the time of conception, twenty-three chromosomes from the mother's egg and twenty-three from the father's sperm combine to begin a new human being. These include an X chromosome contributed by the egg and either an X or a Y chromosome from the sperm. If the final product contains two X chromosomes, the baby will be a girl, while an XY combination of chromosomes will result in a boy.

While this extraordinarily complex activity normally proceeds without mishap, at times it does not function as originally designed. This might result in profound abnormalities in the number or structure of the chromosomes, such that the fertilized egg may fail to divide properly, may not implant within the mother's uterus, or may not develop beyond a very early stage. In such cases a woman will have an early miscarriage or the new life will end without her ever being aware that it had started. However, a number of genetic abnormalities do not end this way, and the pregnancy may continue to term. There are two main types of genetic abnormalities:

Single-gene abnormalities involve a defect in a particular strand of DNA, which in turn causes a specific malfunction within the body. These abnormalities are further subdivided into three categories: dominant, recessive, and X-linked. These variations arise from the fact that genes are paired—that is, the genes on a chromosome inherited from the mother have a corresponding gene on the chromosome provided by the father. The effect of one gene may override the other, or they might make an equal contribution to a particular trait.

A **dominant genetic disorder** (for example, Huntington's chorea) needs only one gene (which can come from either parent) to be manifested. If one parent is affected, there is a 50 percent chance that his or her child (of either gender) will have the same abnormality. Some dominant disorders run in families, while others result from a mutation that occurred in an individual egg or sperm.

A **recessive genetic disorder** (for example, cystic fibrosis) is one that will occur only when an abnormal gene that causes it is contributed by both parents. A child who receives an abnormal recessive gene from only one parent usually will not manifest that defect, although he or she will be a carrier of the disorder. If both parents of a child are carriers of a recessive disorder, the child has a 50 percent chance of being a carrier, a 25 percent chance of having two normal genes, and a 25 percent chance of being affected. Recessive genetic defects often cluster in particular racial, ethnic, or geographic groups.

X-linked genetic disorders (for example, hemophilia) are carried only on the X chromosome and may be dominant or recessive, although the latter are more common. Females with an abnormal X-linked gene usually are not affected by the problem because they typically have a normal gene on their other X chromosome, which will override the abnormal gene.

Chromosomal abnormalities involve significantly larger amounts of genetic material than do single-gene defects. Either part or all of a chromosome may be missing or duplicated. Often the results are not compatible with development of the fetus within the womb, and a miscarriage results. (It is estimated that half of all miscarriages that occur during the first three months of pregnancy are caused by chromosomal abnormalities.) The abnormality may be passed on from one or the other parent or may occur during the development of egg or sperm.

The risk of a child having a chromosomal abnormality increases steadily with the age of his mother. The risk of a twenty-five-year-old woman having a baby with **Down syndrome**—the most common disorder of this type—is about one in 1,250. At age thirty it is one in 1,000; at thirty-five, one in 400; at forty, one in 100; and at forty-five, one in 30.[2]

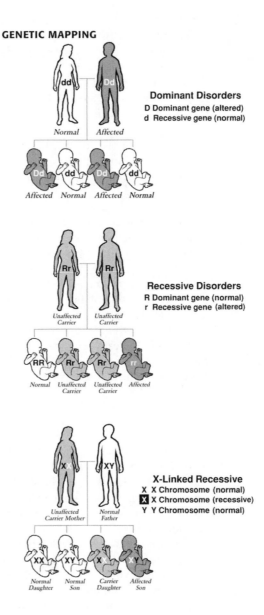

GENETIC MAPPING

Dominant Disorders
D Dominant gene (altered)
d Recessive gene (normal)

Normal *Affected*

Affected *Normal* *Affected* *Normal*

Recessive Disorders
R Dominant gene (normal)
r Recessive gene (altered)

Unaffected Carrier *Unaffected Carrier*

Normal *Unaffected Carrier* *Unaffected Carrier* *Affected*

X-Linked Recessive
X X Chromosome (normal)
X X Chromosome (recessive)
Y Y Chromosome (normal)

Unaffected Carrier Mother *Normal Father*

Normal Daughter *Normal Son* *Carrier Daughter* *Affected Son*

Infections and other medical problems

Infections passed from mother to baby that can cause birth defects and illness are discussed in detail in chapter 1. In addition, medical problems in the mother, such as diabetes, high blood pressure, and heart disease, can affect the development of the baby growing within her. Detecting and managing any maternal conditions are key factors of prenatal care and a major reason regular visits with a qualified physician are so important during pregnancy.

Substances that pass from mother to baby

While the uterus, placenta, and amniotic fluid are usually very effective in providing a safe environment for the growing baby before birth, certain chemical compounds that enter the mother's bloodstream are capable of causing harm to her preborn child. The degree of damage can vary enormously depending upon the amount of the substance involved and the stage(s) of development at which the exposure to the unborn child takes place. These substances include:

- Drugs—prescription and nonprescription, legal and illegal
- Alcohol and tobacco
- Chemical and occupational pollutants

The use of drugs, alcohol, and tobacco is discussed in detail in chapter 1 (see page 14). The gamut of potential environmental exposures, especially in the workplace, is well beyond the scope of this book. However, if you are pregnant (or might become so in the near future), you should become knowledgeable about any chemical compounds to which you are exposed on a regular basis. The Occupational Safety and Health Administration in Washington, D.C., which has established standards designed to reduce the likelihood of work-related injury or harm, requires that information be made available to any employee regarding potentially harmful compounds present in the workplace. In order to arrive at a bottom line that reduces risks to your (and your unborn child's) health, you may need some help from your physician in interpreting the Medical Safety Data Sheets (MSDS) or any other input you receive regarding harmful materials to which you may be exposed.

How Are Congenital Defects Identified Prior to Birth?

A few decades ago, an expectant mother had little to inform her about her baby's condition other than the size of her abdomen, the movements that she felt inside it, her own sense of well-being or illness, and some very rudimentary input from her doctor. Advances in medical technology have changed that situation dramatically so that even the most uneventful pregnancy is now likely to be assessed with one or more prenatal screening tests.

This section will briefly describe a number of screening and diagnostic procedures utilized during pregnancy, along with their potential benefits and risks. Their role and significance in your pregnancy will depend upon your personal and family history as well as how far your pregnancy has progressed. You should be aware that tests will vary in their accuracy and predictive value. *Depending upon the procedure, abnormal results may not predict defects with absolute certainty, nor do normal results guarantee a problem-free baby.*

Ultrasound

Ultrasound (also called **diagnostic ultrasonography** or **sonogram**) is an extremely useful tool that utilizes high-frequency sound waves to create images of a woman's uterus and the baby growing within it. Sound waves are sent through a handheld transmitter called a transducer that is gently applied to a woman's abdomen or early in pregnancy may be placed inside the vagina using a narrow probe. (Placing the ultrasound transducer inside the vagina does not pose any risk for either mother or baby.) The sound waves reflect back to the transducer from internal structures in patterns that vary depending upon their shape and density. The images are displayed on a monitor and may even be recorded on videotape or DVD. (Some of the images may be printed for the expectant parents to take home as their first "baby picture.")

When is it performed? Ultrasound may be carried out during any stage of pregnancy. The timing for this procedure will depend to some degree upon its purpose, the state of your pregnancy, any problems that are developing, and your physician's approach to following a normal pregnancy. Many doctors recommend routine ultrasonography between the sixteenth and twentieth weeks of pregnancy, at which point many details (including the chambers of the baby's heart) can be visualized.

How is it performed? A woman having an ultrasound may be instructed to drink a few glasses of water and hold off on voiding until the procedure is completed because a full bladder serves as a useful landmark. (A full bladder is not necessary for a vaginal ultrasound.) A conducting gel will be applied to the abdomen, and the transducer is then gently pressed against it in a number of locations. A basic evaluation, which can be carried out in the doctor's office, will usually not take more than twenty minutes, while a more detailed study (sometimes called a level two, targeted, or comprehensive exam) could take an hour or more. The latter might be done if there is concern about an abnormality for which more detailed information and sophisticated equipment are needed.

Normally you will be able to see the monitor during an ultrasound, and the technician or physician will usually point out a variety of highlights of your "tour" of the uterus and its occupant. Parents are often delighted and deeply moved by the first sight of their new child and may be surprised by the amount of movement if the baby is active at the time of the procedure. In many settings you may be able to take home some images of your son or daughter on CD, DVD, or videotape.

Is it safe? Ultrasound has never been reported to cause harm to mother or baby, even during the earliest stages of pregnancy. No X-rays are involved, and the mother's skin is not punctured. Sometimes there is mild discomfort when the transducer is pressed against a full bladder.

What information does it provide? This test can provide a great deal of information:

- Verification that pregnancy is in fact under way within the uterus. A tiny sac can be visualized three weeks after conception, and a week later the baby's body can be seen within it. Ultrasound is also useful in diagnosing an **ectopic pregnancy** (one that is growing outside of the uterus).
- An accurate determination of the age of the baby and whether or not more than one baby is present.
- An assessment of the growth rate and movements of the baby.
- Detection of major structural abnormalities of the head, spinal cord, chest, abdomen, or limbs.

- The location and appearance of the placenta and the amount of amniotic fluid.
- Identifying structures (such as the placenta) that are important to diagnostic tests such as amniocentesis and chorionic villus sampling (see page 92).

A number of medical centers and physicians' offices have 3-D ultrasound equipment that provides three-dimensional images of the growing baby, often with startling and nearly photographic clarity. These can be particularly useful when certain types of structural defects are suspected. A 4-D ultrasound displays movement of the 3-D images. Some commercial enterprises offer 3-D and 4-D ultrasound "baby pictures" for eager parents and family members, but these are not formal medical studies, and the individual(s) performing them may not be trained to interpret them accurately. Mainstream medical authorities generally discourage these types of "shopping mall" ultrasounds.

Maternal blood tests: alpha-fetoprotein, beta-HCG, and estriol

These are considered to be *screening* (rather than *diagnostic*) tests because:

- They are relatively easy and inexpensive to perform.
- While they detect pregnancies in which the baby may be at higher risk for certain problems, they do not make a specific diagnosis.
- They can be carried out on large numbers of pregnant women to determine who might benefit from more complex diagnostic testing.

The most widely used maternal blood test is a screen for the level of **alpha-fetoprotein (AFP)**, one of two major proteins that circulate in the blood of the developing fetus. The other protein, **albumin**, is found also in the bloodstream of adults, while AFP is unique to the fetus. Normally during pregnancy a small amount of AFP finds its way into the **amniotic fluid** (fluid surrounding the fetus in its closed sac) and from there into the mother's bloodstream. A certain amount of AFP can thus be measured in the mother's bloodstream, and the level gradually rises during the first twenty weeks of pregnancy. A number of conditions can increase the amount of AFP that passes from fetus to mother at any given point in the pregnancy:

- A leak of fetal blood into the amniotic fluid or a defect in the placenta that allows more AFP to pass into the mother's bloodstream.
- Twins, because the two fetuses produce more AFP than one.
- An abnormality in which some of the fetus's internal tissue is exposed, allowing an increased amount of AFP to escape into the amniotic fluid. Examples of such conditions are open neural tube defects (anencephaly or spina bifida), which expose nerve tissue at the top or bottom of the spinal column (see page 9), or abdominal wall defects (omphalocele or gastroschisis) in which part of the intestinal tract may be present outside of the abdomen.

The screening test for a mother's blood level of AFP is quite sensitive: 80 to 85 percent of fetuses with neural tube defects can be detected through elevated levels of this protein in the mother's blood. However, the test is not very specific, since so many other conditions also cause the AFP to be elevated. As a result, out of one hundred cases in which maternal AFP is abnormally high, more than ninety will prove to be false alarms in which no neural tube defect or other significant problem is identified.

How is the screening done? AFP is measured in a sample of blood drawn from the mother. The screening is most accurate if done between sixteen and eighteen weeks after the last menstrual period, although the tests can be done between fifteen and twenty-two weeks. Results are usually available for review within about a week. Because of the steady rise of AFP during pregnancy, *accurate dating of the pregnancy is very important for a meaningful interpretation of this test.* In addition, the mother's age, weight, and race are taken into account when determining what level of AFP should be considered normal.

What if the AFP level is abnormally high? Your physician may want to repeat the test to confirm that the results are definitely abnormal. Even when the lab results are consistently high, however, a high AFP does not necessarily mean that the baby has a significant problem. Usually the next step will be an ultrasound examination, which can help specifically to

- confirm the accuracy of the date of the pregnancy. One of the most common reasons for an unexpectedly high level of AFP in a mother's bloodstream is that her pregnancy is actually further along than was originally estimated.
- determine whether there is a multiple pregnancy (twins or more).
- detect abnormalities such as neural tube defects.

Very often the ultrasound study will make the diagnosis, but if it does not provide an explanation for the high AFP level, an amniocentesis (see page 92) may be carried out to determine the level of AFP in the amniotic fluid. This test is much more accurate than maternal AFP levels at predicting the presence or absence of neural tube and abdominal wall defects. A combination of a normal amniotic fluid level of AFP and a normal ultrasound would indicate that one of these problems is extremely unlikely. (However, an elevated AFP not caused by an open neural tube defect or twins has been associated with a greater chance of late-pregnancy complications.)

What if the AFP is abnormally low? Elevated levels of AFP are quite sensitive for detecting neural tube defects, but what about low levels? A low AFP may indicate an increased likelihood that the baby has Down syndrome or a much less common chromosomal abnormality known as **trisomy 18** (or **Edward syndrome**).

By itself, however, AFP is not a highly accurate test, identifying less than half of babies with Down syndrome in pregnant women under age thirty-five. However, some confirmation of this risk may be obtained from two other maternal blood tests, which are commonly carried out at the same time. **Unconjugated estriol** is an estrogen hormone whose level in the mother will be affected by the status of both the fetus and the placenta. **Beta-HCG (human chorionic gonadotrophin)** is a hormone produced by the placenta soon after conception, rising to levels that are detectable by the time the first menstrual period is missed.

If a low maternal AFP is present in combination with a low level of estriol and a high level of beta-HCG, the likelihood that the baby will have Down syndrome is definitely greater than if the AFP alone is abnormal. The results of these tests are combined with the mother's age to determine the probability that her baby will have Down syndrome. A combination of low levels of all three compounds is associated with a higher risk of trisomy 18.

Occurring in one in six thousand births, trisomy 18 is much less common than Down syndrome but also much more serious, causing severe mental retardation, heart abnormalities, and numerous other defects that usually lead to death within the first year of life.

The combination of AFP, estriol, and beta-HCG is often referred to as the triple screen. Some laboratories measure another substance in the mother's blood called **inhibin-A**, which increases the accuracy of predicting the presence of Down syndrome. When this fourth test is done, the combination is often called a quad screen. A triple screen will lead to the diagnosis of about 65 percent of infants with Down syndrome before birth, while a quad screen increases the prenatal diagnosis rate to 75 percent. Remember, however, that these tests cannot actually make this diagnosis. This requires other studies, which will be discussed shortly.

First trimester testing: Nuchal thickness (NT) ultrasound, pregnancy associated plasma protein-A (PAPP-A), and beta-HCG

A more recent addition to the list of potential screening tests during pregnancy is a combination of a specific ultrasound study of the baby and a blood test for the mother carried out during the first trimester (three months)—specifically, at eleven to fourteen weeks, about a month earlier than the triple or quad screen. The ultrasound study measures the thickness of a clear area of tissue at the back of the baby's neck, referred to as nuchal lucency or simply nuchal thickness. (The word *nuchal* comes from the Latin word for the nape of the neck.) The combination of this ultrasound (performed and interpreted by properly trained technologists and physicians) and two blood tests—pregnancy associated plasma protein-A (PAPP-A) with beta human chorionic gonadotropin (beta-HCG)—can predict a number of problems early in the pregnancy. They are particularly sensitive for Down syndrome (about 90 percent) and trisomy 18 (more than 95 percent), and may detect a number of other abnormalities (such as heart or skeletal defects) as well. They also tend to have fewer false positives—that is, abnormal results that prove to be false alarms in normal infants. Of equal (if not greater) importance, when normal, they may reduce the need for more invasive tests such as amniocentesis (see below). These studies are likely to become more widely used among pregnant women at higher risk for having a baby with Down syndrome.

For more information about Down syndrome, see page 656.

Amniocentesis

Amniocentesis is the withdrawal of a small amount of amniotic fluid from the sac that surrounds the fetus. Both the contents of the fluid and the fetal cells that are present within it can be studied to diagnose a variety of problems before birth.

How is it done? When used to diagnose birth defects, amniocentesis is usually carried out between the fifteenth and twentieth weeks of pregnancy. Whether done in a physician's office or in a hospital, an ultrasound is routinely done first to assess (among other things) the size and position of the fetus, the location of the placenta, and the amount of amniotic fluid present. Then an appropriate site is selected on the mother's abdomen, antiseptic solution is applied, and often a local anesthetic is injected. (However, the anesthetic cannot numb the wall of the uterus, so a brief stinging or cramping pain might be felt when it is punctured.) Under ultrasound guidance, a long needle is inserted through the abdominal wall and into the amniotic fluid. Between 15 and 30 ml (or one-half to one ounce) of fluid is removed before the needle is withdrawn.

What kind of information is obtained from studying amniotic fluid?
- *Chromosome analysis.* Fetal cells within the fluid are cultured for one to two weeks and then specially treated so the chromosomes within them can be identified and

studied. Extra or missing chromosomes are seen in disorders such as Down syndrome, in which the nucleus of each cell contains three chromosome 21s rather than the usual two. The analysis can also provide advance notice of the baby's gender, although amniocentesis will not be done strictly for this purpose. Results of chromosome analysis are usually ready within two weeks after the procedure.

- *Measurement of alpha-fetoprotein (AFP) in the amniotic fluid*, when screening tests done on the mother's blood reveal abnormal levels of this protein, as just described.
- *Identification of genetic markers* for certain diseases (for example, cystic fibrosis) where there is a family history or increased risk.
- *Assessment of the maturity of the baby's lungs.* This is evaluated toward the end of pregnancy in situations where a need to induce labor must be weighed against the possibility that the baby's lungs will not be mature enough to function normally once out of the womb. The compounds lecithin and sphingomyelin are measured within the amniotic fluid, and when the **lecithin/sphingomyelin (L/S) ratio** is more than 2, the baby can be expected to breathe adequately on his own after birth.

What kinds of birth defects will amniocentesis not detect?
- Specific, isolated structural abnormalities that do not have genetic or chromosomal causes. Examples would be cleft lip or palate, club foot, absent fingers or limbs, or heart defects.
- Disorders in the fetus arising from alcohol, tobacco, or drugs used by the mother.

What are the risks of amniocentesis? The mother might experience mild cramping for a few hours after the procedure. Occasionally local infection or leaking of amniotic fluid occurs at the puncture site. Unfortunately, the risks for the baby are more significant. It is generally understood that between one in 200 and one in 400 amniocentesis procedures in early pregnancy will result in a miscarriage, although some researchers have suggested that the risk may be as low as one in 1,600. The risk of this complication occurring in a pregnancy will depend upon a variety of factors, including the size of the baby and the experience of the physician who performs the test. Miscarriage most commonly results from damage to the placenta, which may bleed and separate from the uterus, or from infection, which can begin if bacteria are accidentally carried by the needle into the amniotic fluid. Rarely, amniocentesis provokes early labor.

In what situations might amniocentesis be recommended for detecting a birth defect?
- When a woman has had another child with a chromosomal abnormality.
- When either parent has a chromosomal abnormality.
- When the mother's alpha-fetoprotein screen or triple/quad screen is abnormal and the reason cannot be determined by ultrasound alone.
- When there is an increased risk of a genetically transmitted disorder for which additional information may be provided through analysis of amniotic fluid or the cells it contains.
- When a pregnant woman is over thirty-five. At this age, the chances of finding a chromosomal abnormality (about one in 400 for Down syndrome, one in 200 for all chromosomal defects) are roughly equal to the risk of a miscarriage from the amniocentesis (see above). This is the most common reason that amniocentesis might be recommended during the first half of pregnancy. Unfortunately,

in some instances a woman may be given the impression that she *must* have amniocentesis if she is over age thirty-five and that the pregnancy *must* be terminated if an abnormality is found. However, there is no requirement, legal or otherwise, that this test be carried out, regardless of a pregnant woman's age, and certainly no situation in which an abortion is mandated.

Chorionic villus sampling

Chorionic villus sampling (CVS) is a procedure in which cells are taken from tiny, fingerlike projections of the placenta (called villi, which literally means "shaggy hairs"). These cells contain the same genetic material as the baby and can be cultured for chromosomal analysis and other genetic tests.

When and how is it done? CVS can be carried out between the tenth and twelfth weeks of pregnancy. Using ultrasound for guidance, a needle is introduced through the abdominal wall into the uterus, or more commonly a catheter is inserted into the vagina and through the cervix (the opening of the uterus). The needle or catheter is then used to aspirate a small amount of tissue from the edge of the placenta.

What information can be obtained from CVS? The cells obtained from chorionic villus sampling can be cultured and then analyzed for chromosomal and genetic abnormalities, yielding information similar to that gained from amniocentesis. However, this procedure can be carried out more than a month earlier than amniocentesis, and more cells are available at the outset, so results can be ready within a week to ten days. But CVS cannot diagnose neural tube defects because it does not obtain amniotic fluid. Also, while normal results can be considered highly reassuring, CVS is slightly more likely than amniocentesis to yield results that are inconclusive. When abnormal results are obtained, there is a small possibility that the baby will in fact be normal. (This can occur because of chromosomal changes in the placenta that are not present in the fetus.) Thus when tests run on a CVS specimen are abnormal, a follow-up amniocentesis later in the pregnancy may be considered to verify these results.

What are the risks of CVS? As with amniocentesis, the mother may experience some cramping as well as pain at the puncture site if the specimen is obtained through the abdomen. (The vaginal approach is generally painless.) Vaginal bleeding and local infection are possible complications of the abdominal approach. Of greater concern is the risk of miscarriage, which occurs after one in 100 to 200 procedures—at least twice the rate for amniocentesis. In addition, CVS has been linked to limb abnormalities (missing or undeveloped fingers and toes) in the baby and cases of severe infections in the mother's uterus. (It appears that the risk of limb defects is increased minimally, if at all, when CVS is carried out after the tenth week of pregnancy.)

These risks, along with the slight but not insignificant possibility of a false positive result (that is, one that suggests an abnormality when the baby is in fact normal), raise particular concerns about CVS. The presumed advantage of this test over amniocentesis is that it allows for an earlier identification of the baby's genetic status—and thus an earlier abortion if the mother has decided that she will end her pregnancy if the baby is abnormal. If abortion is not an option that she intends to exercise, however, there would appear to be little purpose to expose her and her baby to this procedure's risks.

How Do You Decide Whether or Not to Have Amniocentesis or Chorionic Villus Sampling?

Make this decision carefully, prayerfully, and with all the facts you can possibly gather. You should be properly counseled and fully informed regarding the following:

- What potential birth defect(s) will the procedure help to identify?
- How high is the risk that the baby might be affected with a particular defect?
- How does the risk of the baby's having the abnormality compare with the risk of the procedure? It would be of questionable value to perform any procedure if the chance of provoking a miscarriage was significantly greater than the likelihood of identifying a problem, and it would be undeniably sad to lose a baby under such circumstances—especially in situations where infertility has been a problem.
- What have the complication rates been for the specific physician or medical center that would be performing the procedure? CVS, in particular, requires special expertise and experience.
- What would be the specific benefits of having information about the defect prior to birth? Are there interventions available that might help the baby while still within the uterus? Would preparations be needed for expert care at the time of delivery or shortly thereafter? Would it help the parents to learn about the condition ahead of time and make their own adjustments to cope with it?
- Is the primary purpose of the procedure to determine whether or not to continue the pregnancy? CVS is done to identify genetic abnormalities early in the pregnancy so that an abortion, if chosen, might be carried out with less difficulty. Amniocentesis, on the other hand, in a number of situations provides information that can improve the care of the baby either before or after delivery. There could thus be instances in which a woman who knows she would not have an abortion might nevertheless benefit from having an amniocentesis.
- What costs would be involved with this procedure? These would include not only physician fees but also laboratory costs and other expenses incurred at the facility where the procedure is to be performed.

With this information clearly in mind, you need to consider not only the medical aspects of the decision but also the personal and ethical dimensions. Your own values will significantly affect your response to the information you receive from prenatal testing—or whether you decide to have one or more procedures done in the first place.

In particular, you should consider ahead of time how you might respond to the unsettling news that your baby might have a birth defect. This is an extremely difficult question, even for those who value human life at all stages and in all conditions. How do you currently view people who have a significant physical, intellectual, or emotional handicap? How would you feel if such a person were your own child, living with you and depending on you for his daily needs, possibly for many years?

On a much broader scale, how do you view adverse events that occur in your life? Are they the meaningless cruelties of a mechanical universe? Are they divine punishment for something you have or haven't done? Or are they the fallout from a broken world, trials that God nevertheless can redeem and even use for a greater purpose in your life—and perhaps in the lives of many others?

These might seem rather weighty considerations to bring into a discussion of the pros and cons of a few medical tests, but these questions apply profoundly to the realm of prenatal evaluation of the baby. If you feel that a baby who will be born with one or more significant defects represents a biological mistake—a life that shouldn't be lived—and that caring for him would be an exercise in futility, this viewpoint will seriously influence your response to any bad news you hear from your physician. Your reaction to such news could be quite different if you believe that life's trials are not pointless or punitive and that, to quote the apostle Paul, "we also rejoice in our sufferings, because we know that suffering produces perseverance; perseverance, character; and character, hope. And hope does not disappoint us, because God has poured out his love into our hearts by the Holy Spirit, whom he has given us" (Romans 5:3-5).

Undoubtedly, some people undergo prenatal testing in order to identify a significant disorder in time to abort the fetus. However, depending on the specific condition, there may be other measures that can help the child with a defect (and the parents) before the birth. In certain situations knowledge that a baby will be born with a particular defect will allow physicians to prepare for his arrival and begin corrective measures in a timely manner. Advances in medical and physical therapy may also change the long-term outlook for a child with a particular defect.

THE PERINATAL HOSPICE

The technology to identify a number of prenatal defects has raised wrenching issues for many parents who receive the devastating news that their son or daughter yet to be born has a disorder that will prove fatal soon after birth. Not only must they deal with intense grief and soul-searching, they must also make some difficult decisions: *Do we terminate the pregnancy? Do we have the baby and then do everything medically possible to prolong his life? We can't just let him die, can we?* The options that are presented to the parents of a terminal infant all too often point toward an inevitable conclusion that ending his life before birth—even if that involves a late-term abortion—is somehow more humane than allowing him to be born even if he will live only a few hours, days, or weeks. Those who choose not to end the pregnancy are at risk for feeling abandoned and hopeless. *Do we really want to go through with this exercise in futility?*

In recent years, the concept of the **perinatal hospice** has been gaining support among health-care professionals as a viable alternative to aborting an infant with a lethal defect. The perinatal hospice idea has been implemented in a number of medical centers in the United States. In a best-case scenario, a multidisciplinary program provides comprehensive support from the time of diagnosis through the delivery and death of the infant, as well as its aftermath. Ideally the breadth of services includes

- support before and during labor by nurses and other caregivers trained in grief management;

What If the Results of Prenatal Screening or Diagnostic Tests Are Abnormal?

Your response will, of course, depend on the test that was done and the specific defect that may be involved. It is important, first of all, to have a clear understanding of the reliability of the test(s) and the implications of the results. Was the test a screen, such as the alpha-fetoprotein blood test, that could prove to be a false alarm after further testing? Is there more than one possible explanation for the results? Does a repeat test or follow-up study need to be done to confirm the diagnosis? All of these questions should be reviewed carefully after receiving the news of abnormal results on any test.

Assuming that a birth defect has been identified with some certainty, what else might you do upon receiving this information? Again, this will depend significantly on the type of problem and its long-term implications. Down syndrome, for example, in which the child has a relatively normal life expectancy, is vastly different from anencephaly, in which most or all of the brain is missing and death follows very soon after birth. You will in fact need to deal with news of a birth defect on a number of levels.

Your *emotional response* will probably be intense and will need to be acknowledged and expressed among those whom you love and trust. Don't be surprised if you experience a wide range of feelings, including:

- Shock
- Denial—*This can't be happening.* Accepting the diagnosis might be extremely difficult, even when the same diagnosis is given by further testing or another consultant.

- basic comfort measures for the infant once the diagnosis is confirmed by a maternal-fetal medicine specialist after birth;
- support for whatever degree of contact with the infant that family members find comfortable and comforting; and
- support from social service and pastoral caregivers for the family's emotional and spiritual needs.

The American Association of Pro Life Obstetricians and Gynecologists, in their position statement on the concept of perinatal hospice, has described the benefits for families who participate in such a program:

> The care of these patients has been accomplished without any notable maternal complications, and the response of parents to this philosophy of care has been overwhelmingly positive. . . . These parents are . . . allowed to fully experience the birth of their child and the bonding that occurs during the antepartum and immediate postpartum period. This bonding helps provide a firm foundation for obtaining closure with the death of their child. They may rest secure in the knowledge that they shared in their baby's life, however brief, and treated their child with the same dignity afforded other terminally ill individuals under the best of circumstances.[3]

For information about perinatal hospice programs, see http://perinatalhospice.org. ■

- Sorrow and grief—over many losses: the loss of hopes and dreams for a normal child or for the baby's life itself if the defect is one that will seriously shorten her life.
- Anger—at oneself (*What did I do wrong?*), at someone else, or even at God (*Why have You allowed this to happen?*).
- Impatience—wanting more information, answers to difficult questions, and perhaps more testing immediately.

This is the time for solidarity and teamwork between husband and wife. Blaming or finger-pointing is a luxury no one can afford.

Your *practical and problem-solving response* should be to find out more about the defect. What does it involve? Can anything be done to correct or improve it before or after birth? Reading about it, doing research in the library or on the Internet, or talking with other parents who have dealt with the same problem can help you understand more clearly what you may be dealing with later on.

Your *support-gathering response* is extremely important. An impending birth defect is not the type of problem that is discussed easily. Those with whom you are closest among family, friends, and church members need to be brought up to speed on your problem. You will need shoulders on which to lean and cry, open ears and hearts, and knees ready to bend in prayer for you and your child.

Finally, your *spiritual response* is crucial. During this time you may wonder if God is making any sense or if He hears your cries and prayers. Don't be surprised (and try not to get upset) if you hear simplistic or unkind "answers" from well-meaning individuals; don't let such responses prevent you from drawing near to God, who really does care about this situation more than you can imagine. Indeed, its ultimate significance—what it will mean, how it will affect you and your family, what you will learn from it, and how this difficulty and sorrow will be redeemed—may not be clear for many years or even during this lifetime.

In Conclusion: A Note of Encouragement

You might feel a great deal of pressure to end a pregnancy by means of abortion, especially if the defect is severe. You might wonder if it wouldn't be more merciful to all concerned if this imperfect life and all the trials that will accompany it would not be brought into the world in the first place.

We certainly don't want to trivialize the sorrow, difficulty, and expense involved when a child has a serious defect. But it is important to remember that no child you bear will be free of defects and imperfections. Even if all the body parts and systems are completely normal when a baby is born, other profound problems could develop later in life. A "normal" child might suffer injuries and illness after birth or break your heart eventually by making poor lifestyle choices. On the other hand, a baby who is malformed or destined for subnormal intelligence or a very short life could become the greatest blessing of your life.

> *As you do not know the path of the wind,*
> *or how the body is formed in a mother's womb,*
> *so you cannot understand the work of God,*
> *the Maker of all things.*
> Ecclesiastes 11:5

Baby Blues, Postpartum Depression, and Postpartum Psychosis

Many mothers who have just had a mountaintop experience in the delivery room are often dismayed to find themselves in a dark, turbulent emotional valley during the first weeks after the baby is born. Between 50 and 80 percent of women are affected by a temporary emotional slump commonly known as baby blues, while 10 percent suffer from a more severe disturbance known as postpartum (literally, "after the delivery") depression. A much less common—but far more severe—disturbance known as postpartum psychosis occurs after about one in 1,000 deliveries.

When one considers all of the intense physical and psychological changes that accompany the birth of a new baby, it's actually surprising that storm clouds aren't a part of *every* mother's emotional weather after childbirth.

There are a number of physical factors that can affect the emotions of a new mother:

- Dramatic shifts in the levels of a number of hormones (estrogen, progesterone, prolactin, cortisone, and others) after delivery. No one has identified which one (or perhaps a combination) might play a dominant role. There are probably differences in the sensitivity of women to changing hormone levels, as occurs in premenstrual syndrome.
- Physical exhaustion following the demands of labor.
- Blood loss during and after delivery.
- Pain after childbirth, especially following a cesarean section. Drugs that may be needed to kill pain can also affect mood and energy level.
- Loss of sleep, perhaps starting with an all-night labor and continuing with the round-the-clock needs of a newborn.
- Genetic factors. Depression, anxiety syndromes, panic attacks, and even more severe disturbances have a definite biochemical component. Because vulnerability to these syndromes can be inherited, they may run in families, much like diabetes, heart disease, or other medical problems. A woman with a prior history of depression, whether or not related to pregnancy, has a one in four risk of experiencing postpartum depression with any future pregnancies.[1]

Personal and family issues that could also affect the emotions include:

- A difficult labor and delivery during which very little went according to plan.
- Problems with the baby. These might include a complex medical concern such as prematurity or a normal baby with feeding problems or unusual irritability.
- A mismatch of expectations. The amount of time and effort involved in caring for a newborn may come as a shock to some, especially first-time mothers, who may have never experienced being on call twenty-four hours a day.
- Lack of family support. If Dad is gone most of the day (or there is no dad in the picture) and relatives are not available to lend a hand, taking care of a newborn can be overwhelming. This will be worsened if a marriage is shaky or if a new mother is getting negative input: "Why are you so tired? I've been working hard all day—all you've had to do is sit around with the baby!"
- Perfectionism. With a new baby (or even with one or more older children), it is not possible to be the Mother of the Year, keeper of the showcase home, rising young executive, and amorous wife. Childbirth and baby care bring one's limitations into striking and sometimes distressing focus.
- Financial pressure. Budgets are often tight in new families, and the expenses surrounding childbirth will add new stress to the family finances.
- Feelings of being stuck or trapped in the new role. A woman who has been pursuing a rewarding career or who is accustomed to a relatively carefree lifestyle might begin to feel that nonstop responsibility for a helpless newborn is a ball and chain—especially if family support or financial resources are limited.

Postpartum Blues

Baby blues, the most common mood problem related to childbirth, usually develops during the first week after delivery. Symptoms can include irritability, tearfulness, anxiety, insomnia, lack of energy, loss of appetite, and difficulty concentrating. This emotional and physical slump typically resolves by itself within two weeks. However, it should not be met with an attitude of "ignore it and it will go away." Support and reassurance from husband, family, and friends are very important. In addition, help with the baby, housekeeping, and other practical details can make a major difference.

Postpartum Depression

While many of its symptoms are very similar to those of baby blues, **postpartum depression (PPD)** is a more serious condition. Not only does it last longer, but its impact on both mother and baby is more profound. A mother with PPD may be so intensely depressed that she has difficulty caring for her baby, or she may develop extreme and unrealistic anxiety over the infant's health. Furthermore, ongoing disruption of mother-child interactions can have adverse effects on the infant's long-term development.

PPD can begin at any time during the first six months after childbirth and may resolve on its own after several months, but this problem should not be left to run its course. Like a major depression at any other time in life—including one that might occur *during* pregnancy as well as after the baby is born—PPD is not a situation in which a little attitude adjustment is all that is needed. If symptoms such as those listed above for baby blues continue for more than two weeks, professional help should be sought. Treatment might involve extended counseling, the use of antidepressant medication, or both. Medication is sometimes very helpful in normalizing biochemical mechanisms in the central nervous system that affect mood, sleep patterns, and fatigue. However, if a mother is breastfeeding, input from the baby's doctor will be needed if medications are being considered.

Postpartum Psychosis

In the relatively rare but very serious disorder called **postpartum psychosis**, a woman experiences not only a disturbance in mood but also a break with reality. At some time during the first month after delivery, she may become confused and experience hallucinations and delusions. She may even consider harming herself or her baby. Current research indicates that 5 percent of women with postpartum psychosis kill themselves, and an equal percentage kill their baby. Because of this dire risk for suicide or infanticide, *postpartum psychosis should be considered a medical emergency* and must be evaluated immediately by a qualified psychiatrist—even though it will probably be difficult to convince the woman that this is necessary. This condition can and should be treated with appropriate medication. There is, furthermore, a 30 to 50 percent chance that postpartum psychosis will recur with a subsequent pregnancy.

It is important to note that postpartum depression and psychosis can occur without warning. A woman's mood during her pregnancy does not necessarily predict how she will feel after the baby comes home. However, if a woman has a history of depression or other significant emotional problems or if they have occurred in her immediate family, those close to her should be alert for signs of turbulence during the days and weeks following childbirth. *A mother who has suffered postpartum psychosis in the past must be observed carefully for any signs of recurrence after future deliveries.*

Preventing Emotional Problems after Childbirth

The first chapter of this book includes a section that contains recommendations for parents anticipating the birth of their child (see page 28). These include tapping into a support team, maintaining a personal quiet time, and (for married couples) building the relationship with one another. All of these are important *after* the baby is born as well. Fathers should pay particular attention to the items under "Some thoughts for the expectant and new father." Expressions of love and respect, help with the daily tasks of living, and ongoing prayer for and with a new mother can certainly help prevent an emotional upheaval during the weeks after a baby arrives.

The Premature Infant

When the psalmist described how God "knit me together in my mother's womb"(Psalm 139:13), he not only declared a spiritual truth but a biological one: A mother's uterus (womb) is truly the best place for an infant to live before he is fully "knit together" and ready to be born. If he should leave that sanctuary ahead of schedule, a host of problems can develop. Thankfully, medical advances now allow premature infants—"preemies" in medical jargon—who would not have survived a few decades ago to live and thrive, though even the most sophisticated and expert care cannot prevent or overcome some complications. Depending on a host of factors, a premature infant's first few days, weeks, or months outside the womb may be relatively straightforward or incredibly challenging, both for him and for his parents.

Some Basic Facts and Figures

An infant is considered premature if he is born less than thirty-seven weeks after his mother's last menstrual period. The percentage of preterm births has risen gradually since 1980 to the current rate of about 11 percent of live births in the United States. Not surprisingly, the earlier an infant is born before his due date, the more complex and potentially serious his medical problems are likely to be.

The time between the mother's last menstrual period and birth, also called the **gestational age**, is normally forty weeks, and a baby born at thirty-seven weeks or later is considered **full term**. Infants born before the thirty-seventh week of gestational age may weigh less than 2,500 grams (5 pounds, 8 ounces), which is considered **low birth weight**. Most of the significant problems associated with prematurity occur when a baby is born before the thirty-second week of gestation, when his weight is likely to be 1,500 grams (3 pounds, 5 ounces) or less—what is called **very low birth weight**. Infants born between twenty-two and twenty-six weeks are considered **extremely premature**, and will weigh less than 1,000 grams (2 pounds, 3 ounces), referred to as **extremely low birth weight**. Few infants born at twenty-two weeks survive, and among extremely premature babies every additional week spent within the womb has a significant impact on the likelihood of survival.

What causes premature birth?

Preterm or **premature** labor and delivery may arise from a problem with mother or baby. More often than not, the cause of spontaneous onset of premature labor is unknown. About 15 to 20 percent of premature deliveries are initiated by a physician in order to deal with a serious problem that threatens mother, infant, or (most commonly) both. (These are referred to as **indicated** premature births, meaning that they were initiated for a specific and necessary reason.)[1]

Factors that can contribute to spontaneous premature labor and delivery include:

- **More than one baby** within the uterus (twins, triplets, or more). These **multiple pregnancies** account for about 15 percent of premature deliveries.[2]
- **Bacterial infection** that spreads to the uterus (usually from the vagina or urinary tract) can provoke both premature contractions and rupture of the amniotic sac that contains the fluid in which a baby lives prior to birth.
- **Structural or functional problems with the uterus** such as weakness of the opening (referred to as an **incompetent cervix**), one or more **fibroid tumors** (benign growths of uterine muscle that can distort the uterus), or other abnormalities of uterine anatomy such as a **septum** (a wall of tissue that divides part or all of the inner cavity of the uterus).
- **Premature separation of the placenta from the inside of the uterus** (the medical term is **placental abruption**), a situation that can pose a serious threat to both mother and infant.
- **Situational and behavioral issues involving the mother**, including substance abuse (tobacco, alcohol, or illegal drugs—especially cocaine), poor nutrition, age (under nineteen or over thirty-five), and poor prenatal care.
- **One or more prior induced abortions.** The likelihood of premature birth appears to increase with the number of prior abortions.

What can go wrong when a baby is born prematurely?

A number of problems arise when a baby's body isn't ready to function on its own outside of the mother's womb. These can include:

- **Difficulty maintaining body temperature.** Infants with a gestational age younger than thirty-four weeks must be kept in a warm environment—typically an **Isolette** or **incubator**—in order to maintain an adequate body temperature.
- **Inability to feed by mouth.** Infants younger than thirty-two to thirty-four weeks' gestation cannot feed by mouth because of an inability to suck and swallow, as well as their small stomachs. Until they can take milk or formula on their own, they will receive **gavage** feedings via a small tube inserted through the mouth or nose into the stomach or small intestine. The tube may be left in place or removed after each feeding. Infants who are very premature or ill may need to receive fluid and nutrients directly into the bloodstream through an intravenous (IV) line.

Physicians and nurses who care for premature infants routinely track their tiny patients' weight in grams (a unit in the metric system) rather than the more familiar pounds and ounces.

Labor and delivery that occurs before the twentieth week of gestation is referred to as a miscarriage.

- **Difficulty with breathing.** Premature infants may have underdeveloped lungs and also may lack the energy and muscular strength needed to move adequate amounts of air in and out of them. These infants may also lack a substance called **surfactant** that coats the inner surfaces of lung tissue and allows them to expand properly. (Products are now available to help stimulate surfactant function.) A variety of breathing problems (the most common of which is called **respiratory distress syndrome** or **RDS**) may necessitate oxygen or even a ventilator while the lungs mature and other treatments are given.
- **Pauses in breathing (apnea).** Because of immaturity of the neurological system which (among many other functions) controls respiration, premature infants (especially those born at or before thirty weeks) may have **apneic** episodes during which they stop breathing for twenty seconds or more. When air isn't moving, both heart rate and blood oxygen can fall to dangerous levels. Premature infants are routinely monitored for apneic episodes, which can be treated with measures ranging from gentle stimulation to the use of medication or even mechanical devices to maintain a stable flow of air into the lungs.
- **Anemia (too few red blood cells).** For a variety of reasons, premature infants may have an inadequate number of red blood cells, which are needed to carry oxygen throughout the body. They typically don't make as many new red cells during the first few weeks of life as they will later on, and the cells they do produce have a shorter life span. Even medical care can unintentionally contribute to anemia because of the number of blood tests that may be necessary during the first weeks of the premature newborn's life. In some cases, one or more transfusions may be needed to supply an adequate number of red blood cells.

In addition to these functional problems, premature infants may be vulnerable both to infections and to a wide range of complications that can involve virtually any organ system. Because of the complexity of these problems, babies born at or before thirty-two weeks' gestation require care from specialists (called neonatologists) in intensive care environments (known as **neonatal intensive care units**, or **NICUs**) staffed by physicians, nurses, respiratory therapists, and other highly trained personnel. If the hospital in which a baby is born does not have a NICU, he may be transferred to a regional center where proper care can be provided.

How Do You Cope with All of These Problems?

If you have a premature infant, dealing with his appearance, medical difficulties, and care may feel (at least at first) like an overwhelming challenge. The tiny body, the monitors and other equipment that seem to engulf it, the Isolette, the swirl of medical personnel and the technical vocabulary they use, the anxiety that each new problem stirs, the fact that the NICU may be many miles from home—all of these are likely to be a far cry from what you envisioned for your baby's first few days or weeks of life. You might have to make some harrowing decisions about medical procedures or the extent of ongoing care for your baby. Don't be surprised if you experience a gamut of emotions—disappointment, anger, guilt, discouragement, apprehension, feelings of abandonment, even depression. In order to cope, you will need to draw on a number of resources:

God, first and foremost. Even with the best medical care, your baby's life (and yours too) is ultimately in His hands. You may have to walk through many "Why me? Why my baby? What does this mean?" questions without getting clear answers. (Indeed, try not to be impatient with well-meaning people who attempt to comfort you with pat answers to tough problems.) This is the time to climb into God's lap and be comforted, not to withdraw or slide into bitterness. Pray for your baby's recovery and health, for yourself, for the caregivers, and for your family, and ask others to do likewise.

The medical staff. These hardworking professionals may become like an extended family before your baby's time in the NICU is completed. They have worked through difficult scenarios hundreds of times, and they want to help you and your baby get through yours. They will explain the medical problems, the treatments, and the equipment. They will guide you through what you can and can't do when touching and handling your baby. You should feel free to ask as many questions as you need (and if necessary, ask them again at a later date) to understand what is going on. You should also ask if the facility provides brochures or other printed materials that explain in more detail any of the problems your baby might be facing.

Other professional caregivers. You may want to seek help and guidance from a counselor, a social worker in the hospital, a chaplain, and your own pastor as you deal with personal concerns and emotional fallout, especially if your baby has a stormy medical course.

Other parents of premature infants. The hospital may have a support group, or at least be able to refer you to parents who have been through similar experiences.

Your family, friends, and church. When you are dealing with a premature newborn son or daughter, especially if the medical problems are complicated, you may feel as though any semblance of a normal life has evaporated. This is not the time to try to be the Lone Ranger. You will need all kinds of practical help—caring for one or more older children, for example, especially if the NICU isn't near your home—and you shouldn't be shy about asking for it.

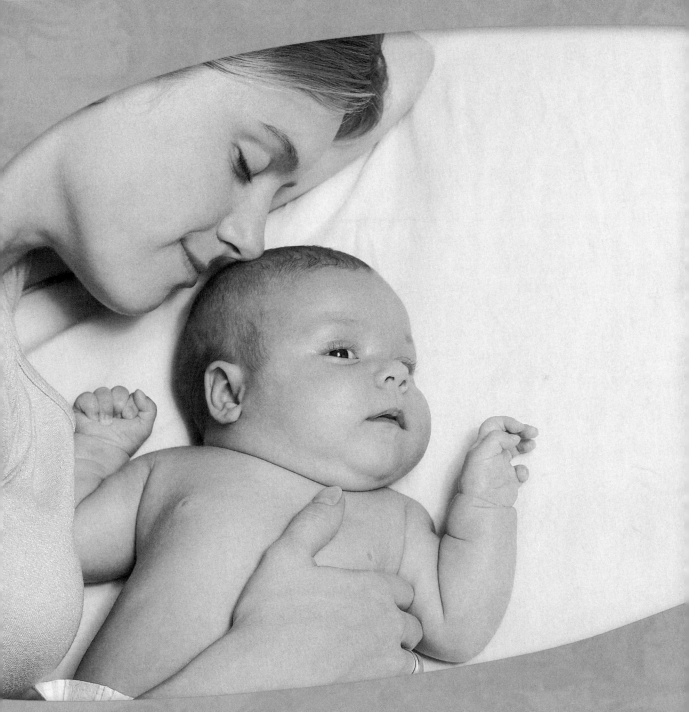

The First Three Months, Part One: Family Adjustments, Feeding the New Arrival, and Dealing with Basic Health Concerns

Now that the efforts of labor and delivery are over, within a few hours or a few days after your baby's birth (with rare exception), you will be bringing your son or daughter home. If this is your first child, you will most likely have some apprehensions about the coming weeks—or, for that matter, about the first night. Will he get enough nourishment? How often should he be fed? Where should he sleep? Will *you* get any sleep? What if he starts crying—and won't stop? If there are other children at home, how will they respond to the new arrival?

Many of these questions have probably already been addressed in a childbirth or parenting preparation class. And if you have older children at home, you have already dealt with most of these concerns before and may not feel the need for any further "basic training." But just in case you didn't get all the bases covered, this chapter and the next one will cover the ABCs of new baby care.

Before we begin, remember:

- The information in this book assumes that your baby is full-term, has been examined, and is basically healthy. If he was born prematurely or has medical problems that require special care, you should follow the specific directions of your physician.
- In the coming months, you will be getting all sorts of advice from friends, relatives, and other resources. Much of it will be helpful and appropriate, at least for most babies. But if something you read or hear doesn't make sense or doesn't work, don't be afraid to get a second opinion. And if you get conflicting advice, don't panic. Newborns are much more sturdy and resilient than you might think, and there are very few mistakes that loving, attentive parents might make that cannot be straightened out later on.
- While it is normal to feel some anxiety over the responsibility of full-time care for a new baby, the process of parenting a newborn should not be dominated by fear and uncertainty. Be confident that you and your baby can and will survive and thrive, even while all of you are learning. Since every parent-child

combination is unique, some adjusting and improvising will be a necessary part of the process. But it is neither necessary nor wise to wade through the first months or years purely on blind instinct.

First Things First for Couples: Mom and Dad's Partnership

With all the excitement and changes that come with the role of parenting, whether for the first time or with a new addition, *it is extremely important that mother and father continuously reaffirm the importance of their own relationship.* For many reasons, it is common for a new baby to take center stage and for parents, especially new ones, to put the maintenance of their marriage at the bottom of the daily priority list. Remember that the two of you became a family with the exchange of vows, before children were in the picture. You will remain a family after the children have grown and left your home. While they are under your roof, a rock-solid partnership, continually renewed and refreshed, will be the foundation for the security of any and all children you add to your original family of two. Your new baby is to be loved and cherished, but he must not, for his own sake, become the permanent center of gravity around which everything else in your home revolves.

Preventing turmoil in the nest

You might assume that the awe and wonder of having a newborn at home would automatically forge a powerful bond between the proud parents. But it is also quite possible for the new demands of baby care to generate some unexpected friction, resentment, or jealousy in the marriage.

If the new baby is breastfed rather than bottle-fed, much of a young mother's time and energy will be occupied with feeding, not to mention the many other details of infant care. (This can also occur, of course, when a baby is bottle-fed, although in this case others can take turns with feeding sessions.) As a result, a father might begin to feel left out and could even resent a nursing child who seems to have displaced him from his wife's affections.

This may be aggravated by unspoken assumptions about mothers' and fathers' roles, especially with newborns. If one parent believes that tending to a baby is "women's work" and that Dad need not report for duty until his son or daughter can throw a ball or is ready to ride a bike, a wedge can develop between mother and father. He may become weary of seeing her attention directed toward meeting the newborn's seemingly endless needs. She may become irritated if he isn't pulling his weight at home, especially if he seems to expect her to meet a lot of his needs when she is thoroughly exhausted.

How can you prevent a newborn nest from becoming a "house divided"?

Hot tips for Mom: Make sure your husband knows that he hasn't been relegated to the back burner of your affection and interest. Beware of total and absolute preoccupation with your new baby, as normal as that desire might seem to you. If you nurse, carry, rock, caress, and sleep with your baby twenty-four hours a day without offering some attention to your mate, before long your marriage may be a shadow of its former self.

Whenever possible, try to give some attention to your own needs and appearance, even if you're feeling exhausted. It's important that you establish a pattern of taking care of yourself even in these early days of motherhood, because from now on it will be tempting to neglect yourself when there are so many needs and tasks surrounding you. Taking care of yourself, even in small ways, can help you avoid baby-care burnout—not only now but also in the days and seasons to come.

Your husband and others will appreciate seeing you take steps to maintain your health and appearance as well.

Hot tips for Dad: Pay lots of attention to your newborn, for whom you can do all sorts of things (such as cuddling, rocking, and changing). Wives tend to become very enamored with husbands who clearly cherish their babies. Don't expect to be treated like another child at home, waiting for a weary housekeeper to fix your meals, do your laundry, and clean up your messes. Roll up your sleeves and pitch in. Finally, take another look at the material in chapter 1 entitled "Some thoughts for the expectant and new father" (page 28). Your commitment to "love, honor, and cherish" has no expiration date.

Patterns you establish now in your marriage may well continue as your new baby and other children at home grow to maturity. Ultimately their sense of security will rise or fall with the visible evidence of stability, mutual respect, and ongoing love of their mother and father for one another. Overt demonstrations of affection not only fulfill deep and abiding needs between husband and wife, but they also provide a strong, daily reassurance for children that their world will remain intact. The same can be said of time set aside by parents for quiet conversation with one another before (and after) the children have gone to bed. Make it a point to start or maintain the habit of asking each other a few key "checking in" questions, such as those on page 29, on a regular basis (at least weekly), and then listening carefully to the answers. These attentive conversations are an important safeguard against losing track of your spouse's thoughts and emotions, and they can help prevent an alarming realization months or years later: *I don't know my spouse anymore.*

Equally significant is a regular date night for Mom and Dad, which should be instituted as soon as possible and maintained even after the kids are grown and gone. These time-outs need not be expensive, but they may require some ongoing creativity, planning, and dedication. Dedication is necessary because child-care needs, pangs of guilt, and complicated calendars will conspire to prevent those dates from happening. But the romance, renewal, and vitality they generate are well worth the effort.

A special note to single parents

Taking care of a new baby is a major project for a couple in a stable marriage. For a single parent—who usually, but not always, is the mother—the twenty-four-hour care of a newborn may seem overwhelming from the first day. But even without a committed partner, you *can* take care of your baby and do it well. The job will be less difficult if you have some help.

Hopefully, before the baby was born, you found a few people who would be willing members of your support team. These might be your parents, other relatives, friends, members of your church, or volunteers from a pregnancy resource center. By all means, don't hesitate to seek their help, especially during the early weeks when you are getting acquainted with your new baby. If your parents offer room, board, and child-care assistance, and you are on good terms with them, you would be wise to accept. Or if a helpful and mature family member or friend offers to stay with you for a while after the birth, give the idea careful consideration. (Obviously, you should avoid situations in which there is likely to be more conflict than help.)

Even after you have a few weeks or months of parenting under your belt, at some point you may need a brief time-out to walk around the block, or advice on how to calm a colicky baby. But no one will know unless you ask. Many churches and pregnancy resource centers offer ongoing single-parent groups in which you can relax for a few hours on a regular basis, swap ideas, and talk with others who know firsthand the challenges you face. You might also make a short list of the names and numbers of trusted friends or relatives who have offered to be "SOS" resources—people you can call at any hour if you feel you've reached the end of your rope. Keep this list in a handy spot where you can find it at a moment's notice.

Preparing other children for the new arrival

Parents often worry about how the arrival of a new baby will affect other children in the family. Children's responses are as different as the children themselves. Some siblings will struggle with jealousy for a while; others will welcome the new baby excitedly, eager to be "big sister" or "big brother." But most children, especially if they are younger than age six or seven, will experience a range of emotions: happiness, jealousy, possessiveness toward the baby, protectiveness, fear of being forgotten by the parents, fear that there won't be enough love in the family to go around. While parents can't prevent the onset of these emotions, they can do much to prepare children for an additional person in the family.

Talk about the baby's coming well in advance. When Mom's abdomen begins to grow, the other children may ask about it; this is a good time to begin talking about the new sister or brother to come. Allow your other children to enjoy the anticipation along with you.

Include your other children in discussions about the baby. Let them join in the conversations about names for the baby and preparations for the nursery.

Be careful about how much the arrangements for the baby will impinge on other children's space in the house and schedule. Be sure to prepare children if they are going to get moved out of a bedroom or if their possessions are going to be displaced. Don't disturb their routine any more than necessary, both in preparation for the new baby and after the baby has come home.

Make plans for other relatives to pay attention to the other children. Since Mom and Dad are going to have their hands extra full the first several weeks after the baby comes home, arrange for Grandma and Grandpa or some other relative(s) to do some special things with the other children. And make sure Mom and Dad are relieved of baby duty part of the time so they can spend time with the other children.

Pay attention to signs of jealousy or other forms of upset. Don't take lightly difficult emotions your children may be experiencing. Respond to them, talk to them, let them know they are still important, and continually assure them of your love for them.

Small children are quite capable of harming infants, often without realizing the seriousness of their actions. If a child is acting angry or jealous toward the new baby, don't leave them alone together.

Direct visitors' attention to the other children. Visitors will ooh and aah over the new baby and often neglect siblings. Bring big brother and sister into the circle. Praise their accomplishments. Talk about how much they help you with the baby.

Remember that much of the negative emotion young children feel toward a new baby is rooted in their own fear of being forgotten or not loved by you. As long as you continually express your love for them and their importance to your family, most of their jealousy will subside with time.

Life with a Newborn: What Can You Expect?

If you are bringing home a new baby for the very first time, you have probably been wondering what your life will be like on a day-to-day basis. Perhaps you have envisioned your new parenthood as a tranquil scene from a greeting card or a TV commercial: a contented mother and father sitting by the fireside, smiling softly at the tiny cherub who sweetly coos her love in return. Or you may have heard tales of misery from family or friends who have complained about sleepless nights, relentless fatigue, and no life at all away from the seven-pound tyrant who demands attention every moment. Some young mothers arrive at parenthood believing that caring for their new baby will be like bringing a puppy home from the pet store. If you already have children, you know that none of these visions accurately encompass the breadth and depth of caring for a newborn.

Babies are always more trouble than you thought—and more wonderful.

Charles Osgood

In one sense, a newborn has a relatively simple agenda: eating, sleeping, crying, being quietly alert, and eliminating urine and stool, repeated over and over each day. Therefore, it wouldn't seem all that difficult or complicated to care for her. After all, she won't be feverishly exploring every cupboard in the house, struggling with overdue homework assignments, or arguing with you over access to the car.

But there are countless variations on these basic activities, and there's some unpredictability in the way each baby behaves from day to day. If you have had two or more children, you are already aware that as unique human beings, each of your offspring has displayed various differences from the others since day one, or even *before* day one.

Furthermore, the first few days of life at home may seem unsettled for both you and your baby. You may be coping for the first time with the profound reality of being responsible for a tiny, helpless human twenty-four hours a day and wondering if you will ever "have a life" again. It may take several character-building days for both baby and parents to establish a predictable pattern of eating and sleeping—or to become used to the absence of a predictable pattern. In response to her new surroundings, your baby may also be more fussy or sleepy after she first arrives home.

For all these reasons, cookbook approaches to baby care, with step-by-step directions for every situation, are unrealistic. Instead, as we look at the elements of your new baby's daily routine, we will outline some basic facts and principles that you can then adapt and fine-tune to your family's unique circumstances. Above all, try your best to relax and trust that you and your baby will in fact eventually settle in (and settle down) together.

Feeding Your Newborn

For a new baby and her parents, feeding time represents far more than "open mouth, insert milk." In the course of receiving life-sustaining calories, nutrients, and fluids from multiple feedings every day, your baby is also having a series of important multisensory experiences. The receptors of sight, hearing, touch, taste, and smell are all actively gathering information during feedings. More important, emotional bonds are forming as the discomfort of hunger is repeatedly ended by a loving parent. Hopefully you will come to look forward to each feeding as a special, satisfying, and relaxing event rather than a time-consuming chore or a source of anxiety. Like so many other aspects of parenting, how you approach and prepare for this activity will have a major impact on its success.

There is no finer investment for any community than putting milk into babies.

Winston Churchill

The vast majority of newborn babies are ready, willing, and able to take in the milk offered to them. As mentioned in the last chapter, they come equipped with rooting, sucking, and swallowing reflexes that are quite efficient at transporting milk from nipple to stomach. Although babies may show differences in feeding styles, and some may seem more adept than others at the outset, you should assume from the beginning that you and your baby are very capable of learning to work together to accomplish this important goal.

Breast or formula?

Over the past few decades a mountain of scientific evidence has validated what is, in fact, a very straightforward observation: Human mothers are beautifully designed to feed their own babies. Breast milk, with extremely rare exception, is the best—and should normally be the complete—source of nutrition during the first months of a child's life, without additional water, juice, cereal, or other foods.

While there is clear medical consensus that breastfeeding is the preferred source of fuel for the newborn, it should not be viewed as a sacred rite. If you need or choose to bottle-feed, you can do so with the assurance that your baby will do well physically and emotionally. There are a variety of formulas available that will meet a baby's nutritional needs quite adequately, and either Mom or Dad can provide a warm, nurturing experience while feeding an infant from a bottle.

Whether you feed your baby breast milk or formula (or a combination of the two), it is important to understand that *she does not need other types of food or fluids during the first four to six months.* Juice, cow's milk from the dairy case, cereal, fruit, and other solids are all unnecessary and inappropriate for your baby at this stage of her life.

Details about formula feeding begin on page 130. However, if you are planning to use formula but have the option to breastfeed, or if you are not sure which approach to use, take time to consider carefully the following information before you make your final decision.

What are the advantages of breastfeeding?

Human milk is uniquely suited to human babies. It is not only nutritionally complete and properly balanced, but it is also constantly changing to meet the needs of a growing infant. The fat content of breast milk increases as a feeding progresses, creating a sense of satisfied fullness that tends to prevent overeating. Indeed, a number of studies indicate that being breastfed as an infant may offer modest protection against becoming overweight and developing diabetes later in life. Furthermore, the fat and cholesterol content of breast milk is higher in the early months, when these compounds are most needed in a baby's rapidly growing brain and nervous system. The primary proteins in all forms of milk are whey and casein, but in human milk, whey, which is easier to absorb, predominates. Compared to cow's milk, the carbohydrate component of breast milk contains a higher percentage of lactose, which appears to play an important role in both brain development and calcium absorption.

Vitamins and minerals are adequately supplied in mother's milk. Vitamins and minerals (including trace elements such as copper and zinc) are present in the right amounts, and iron is present in breast milk in a form that is easier for the baby to absorb than that found in any other type of milk. As a result, no supplements are needed for the normal breastfed infant—with one exception. Breast milk alone does not contain enough vitamin D to ensure proper bone development. This vitamin is manufactured in the skin in response to exposure to sunlight. But since direct exposure to sunlight can pose potential hazards to the sensitive skin of a young infant (see page 181), professional organizations such as the American Academy of Pediatrics (AAP) recommend routine use of sunscreen. In order to provide adequate vitamin D without risking sun damage to an infant's skin, the AAP recommends that an infant who is fed only breast milk also receive 200 international units (IU) of vitamin D every day by dropper, starting at about two months of age. Infant formula contains vitamin D, and a baby who drinks seventeen ounces (about 500 cc) or more per day will receive an adequate amount of this vitamin.

> *As a mother comforts her child, so will I comfort you; and you will be comforted over Jerusalem.*
>
> Isaiah 66:13

Breast milk is absorbed extremely efficiently, with little undigested material passing into stool. Experienced diaper changers are well aware that formula-fed infants tend to have smellier stools, a by-product of the nutritional odds and ends (especially certain fats and proteins) that are not thoroughly absorbed on their trip through the bowel.

From day one, breast milk contains antibodies that help protect babies from infections. The first product of the breast after birth, known as **colostrum**, is particularly rich in antibodies known as **immunoglobulin A**, which help protect the lining of the intestine from microscopic invaders. As the mother comes in contact with new viruses and bacteria, her immune system generates the appropriate microbe-fighting antibodies and passes them on to her baby, thus reducing—but by no means eliminating—the newborn's risk of becoming infected. This is particularly important in the first several months of life, when the newborn's immune system is less effective at mounting a defense against microscopic invaders. While formula manufacturers have labored mightily to duplicate the nutritional mixture of breast milk, they cannot hope to supply any of these complex immune factors. Current research has provided strong evidence that feeding infants with human milk decreases the incidence (number of cases) and severity of a wide range of infectious diseases, including otitis media (middle ear infections), diarrhea, respiratory infections, bacterial meningitis, and urinary tract (bladder and kidney) infections.[1]

Breastfeeding may reduce the risk of a variety of serious health problems. Some research indicates a reduced risk of sudden infant death syndrome (SIDS) among breastfed infants. Older children and adults who were breastfed as infants may be less likely to develop diabetes, obesity, elevated cholesterol levels, asthma, and certain types of cancer (specifically leukemia, lymphoma, and Hodgkin's disease).[2]

Breast milk is free. It is clean, fresh, warm, and ready to feed, anytime and virtually anyplace. It does not need to be purchased, stored (although it can be expressed into bottles and frozen for later use), mixed, or heated.

Breastfeeding offers several health benefits for Mom. Stimulation of a mother's nipples by a nursing infant releases a hormone called **oxytocin**, which helps her uterus to contract toward what will become its nonpregnant size. The hormonal response to nursing also postpones the onset of ovulation and the menstrual cycle, providing a natural—although not foolproof—spacing of children. Nursing mothers also tend to reach their prepregnancy weight more quickly. In addition, some research indicates that breastfeeding may reduce a woman's chance of developing breast and ovarian cancer, osteoporosis, and hip fractures later in life.

Breastfeeding lends itself to a sense of closeness, intimacy, and mutual satisfaction. The skin-to-skin contact, the increased sensory input for the baby, and the mother's satisfaction in being able to provide her child's most basic needs can help establish strong bonds between them.

Are there any reasons *not* to breastfeed?

There are a few medical situations in which breastfeeding poses a risk for the baby. HIV, the virus responsible for AIDS, can be transmitted from an infected mother to a noninfected infant through nursing, and thus a woman infected with HIV should not breastfeed her infant. A mother with active, untreated tuberculosis should not nurse her baby. Hepatitis C is not transmitted through breast milk, but it is spread through infected blood. A nursing mother with hepatitis C should temporarily stop nursing if her nipples or the area surrounding them become cracked or bleed.

Obviously, breastfeeding may be extremely difficult or even unsafe for both mother and child if the mother has a serious illness. Furthermore, virtually all medications show up to some degree in breast milk, and some are potentially harmful for infants. If a new mother needs to take one or more drugs that are necessary to preserve her life and health but are unsafe for a baby (for example, cancer chemotherapy), formula feeding should be used. Careful consultation with both mother's and baby's physicians is in order when making this decision.

Previous breast surgery may affect a mother's ability to nurse. A biopsy or local lump removal in the past normally will not cause difficulty. Even after a mastectomy, it is possible to feed a baby adequately using the remaining breast. Breast-reduction surgery, however, may result in an inadequate milk supply if the majority of milk-producing tissue has been removed. Previous breast-enhancement/implant surgery should not cause a problem for nursing unless the ducts that carry milk to the nipple were cut during the procedure.

Infants born with phenylketonuria (PKU) or galactosemia, rare metabolic disorders that are detected by routine screening tests after birth, must be fed special formulas to prevent a variety of serious consequences.

Congenital problems such as a cleft lip or palate, heart disease, and Down syndrome can create special challenges for nursing. However, the benefits of mother's milk for these infants are usually well worth the extra effort needed to provide it for them, even if they cannot obtain milk directly from the breast. A team effort involving parents, physicians, and a lactation consultant will be necessary.

A number of nonmedical concerns might cause a woman to be reluctant to breastfeed or to consider abandoning it too quickly. These are worth some review and reflection.

A previous bad experience. "I had a baby who wouldn't nurse/couldn't nurse/didn't want to nurse. She wouldn't stop crying until we gave her a bottle. After days of frustration, tears, and sore nipples, I felt like a total failure."

If you had difficulty nursing a baby in the past, remember that each newborn is different. There is no rule that says history must repeat itself, and there are, in fact, very few women who simply are unable to supply enough milk to sustain their offspring.

Physical problems. "My breasts are too small/too big. My nipples are flat/dimpled/inverted."

Your milk is supplied by **mammary** (milk-producing) **glands** whose function is not related to breast size. In response to large amounts of hormones circulating during pregnancy—especially prolactin (literally, "for milk"), estrogen, progesterone, and human placental lactogen (which, as its name indicates, is secreted by the placenta)—the mammary glands enlarge, mature, and become capable of producing milk. However, the actual process of creating milk is held in check during pregnancy by these same elevated hormone levels. When your baby is born and the placenta delivered, the abrupt loss of placental hormones allows milk production to begin in earnest—whether you plan to nurse or not. This interplay between multiple hormones and structures within the body is intricately designed, and you can assume that it will function as intended.

Nipples may vary in shape, and some may be easier for infants to grasp and suck than others. Those that clearly protrude may look like better nursing candidates than those that are flat, dimpled, or inverted. What matters most, however, is what happens when the infant attempts to latch on and suck. To get a preview, gently squeeze *behind* the nipple using thumb and index finger.

If your nipple clearly extends outward in response to this squeeze, your baby should have little difficulty. If your nipple flattens or inverts further, however, you may have tiny adhesions under the skin that are preventing it from extending outward. Normally, changes in the breast related to pregnancy will help correct this problem. However, if the squeeze test is still yielding a flat or inverted nipple by the last trimester of pregnancy, a **breast shield** may help. This is a simple plastic device, worn inside the bra, that exerts constant gentle pressure on the areola and gradually helps the nipple protrude. If help is needed after birth, a shield can be worn between feedings.

Don't try to toughen up your nipples by pulling or rubbing them before or during pregnancy. Not only will this fail to prevent any soreness during nursing, but it might stimulate the release of hormones that can cause the uterus to contract or even begin labor prematurely. (Nursing an older child may also cause premature contractions. If this happens, the child must be weaned immediately.)

Lifestyle issues. "I don't want to be the only one who can feed the baby. I've seen women whose babies are like appendages stuck permanently on their chests. They have no life—they can't go anywhere or do anything without their baby."

Breastfeeding does take more of Mom's time, but it need not be a ball-and-chain experience. After nursing has become a well-established routine, milk can be expressed into a bottle and stored for Dad, grandparents, or babysitters to use at a later date. And if you need to get away for a long evening or even overnight, it won't harm your baby to have a formula feeding or two if you don't have enough of your own milk in the freezer. Don't forget that nursing means being free from the expense and hassle of buying formula; preparing it; and dealing with nipples, bottles, bottle liners, and other items.

Keep in mind that it is hardly a major setback if nursing slows your life down for a while. Your body needs time for rest and restoration after accomplishing the formidable tasks of completing pregnancy and childbirth. Do you really need to accelerate immediately back into the fast lane of your prepregnant lifestyle? This very dependent season of your child's life—whether she is breastfed or bottle-fed—is relatively short, and it would be beneficial for both of you if you could settle back and enjoy it as much as you can. (This applies whether or not you need to return to a full- or part-time job outside the home or have other children making demands on your time.)

Returning to work. "I need to return to my job in two months, and I don't see how I can spend eight or ten hours in the office at the same time I'm trying to nurse."

Even one or two months of nursing are worth doing, and believe it or not, with some planning, creativity, and assistance on the home front, it is possible for a breast-feeding mother to return to work. The adjustments will vary considerably with the age of the baby, the location of the job, and the hours involved.

Breastfeeding Basics

As mentioned in chapter 3, your new baby may be nursed for the first time immediately after delivery or some time later if you or the baby has medical needs that require immediate attention. A newborn is alert and most ready to nurse during the first hour after birth; therefore many physicians recommend that a mother offer the breast during that time if at all possible. However, even if your first feeding must be delayed several hours or even days, you can still get off to a good start.

Whenever you begin, you and your baby should be able to find a position that not only is comfortable but also allows him to latch on to the breast properly. This occurs when his mouth closes over the **areola** (the dark area surrounding the nipple) and forms a seal with his gums. When properly attached, a baby should grasp the entire areola and not just the nipple itself. His tongue should be positioned against the underside of the nipple, and then with wavelike motions compress it, emptying the milk-containing ducts just below the areola.

If he repeatedly clamps down on the nipple only and not the areola, you will probably develop some major pain and cracking in the nipple before long—and have a frustrated baby as well because he won't get much milk this way. Some babies at first seem more interested in licking or nibbling than in grasping the breast properly. While it is a good idea in general to avoid bottle feedings during the first several days unless absolutely necessary, it is particularly important that these "lick and chew" newborns stay away from formula and pacifiers until they catch on to latching on.

If you nurse immediately after delivery, it will usually be easiest to lie on your side with the baby's entire body facing you, stomach to stomach. This position will also be very useful in the days following a cesarean delivery, in order to prevent the weight of the baby from pressing on your sore abdomen. In this position you will need to lift your breast with the opposite hand to move the areola next to his mouth. More common is the *sitting cuddle position*, in which the infant's head is cradled in the bend of your elbow with your forearm supporting his back and your hand holding his bottom or upper leg. An alternative sitting position, called the *football hold*, places your baby's body at your side, supported by your arm with your hand holding his head. This position can be helpful if you have had a cesarean birth, since it minimizes pressure on your incision site, and it is also useful for mothers of twins who wish to nurse both babies simultaneously. The football hold can also help babies who are having a harder time getting attached properly, since they face the breast straight on without having to turn their heads.

Once you are positioned comfortably, gently lift your breast and stroke your baby's cheek or lower lip with your nipple. This will provoke his rooting reflex. When his mouth opens wide, gently pull him to you so that your areola enters his mouth. You will need to make this move relatively quickly before his mouth closes. Be sure not to meet him halfway by leaning forward, or else you will have a very sore back before long. It helps to compress your breast slightly between thumb and palm or between two fingers in a scissorlike position, using your free hand, but stay a couple of inches behind the areola when you do so.

When your baby begins sucking, nerve endings in the nipple send a message to the pituitary gland at the base of your brain. The pituitary in turn secretes the hormone **prolactin**, which stimulates more milk production, and oxytocin, which causes tiny muscles that surround the milk ducts to squeeze milk toward the areola. This event is called the **let-down reflex**, which you will probably feel as a change of pressure or, less commonly, as a tingling within the breasts. Some women, however, can't feel the let-down reflex at all. Once your milk has come in, you may notice anything from a slow drip of milk to a full-blown spray during let-down. Many women will experience let-down not only in response to their baby's sucking but also when their baby—or someone else's—begins to cry. During the first days after delivery, you will also feel contractions of the uterus in response to the oxytocin released by the pituitary gland. While these might be uncomfortable, they are carrying out the important function of reducing the size of your uterus.

BREAST ANATOMY

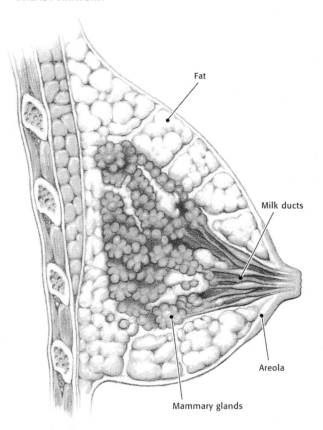

Fat

Milk ducts

Areola

Mammary glands

The let-down reflex may be inhibited by certain drugs, as well as by smoking. Let-down also may not function as well if you are upset or tense. It is therefore important that your nursing times be as relaxed and calm as possible. You might consider setting up a comfortable "nursing corner" at home, where your favorite chair (very often a rocker) and a table with soft light, a few key supplies, soft music, and even something to read are within easy reach. A small stash of healthy snack food and some water or juice would be an appropriate addition as well. Not only is it important that mothers remain well hydrated while nursing, but they often experience considerable thirst during let-down.

If you live in a multistory setting, you may want to set up one of these nursing stations on each floor. Take the phone off the hook and savor these moments, not worrying about whatever else you think you should be doing. Watch your baby, caress him, talk or sing softly to him, or take some time to pray quietly. These can be sweet times of reflection and meditation during otherwise busy days.

Remember that for the first three or four days you will be producing colostrum, the yellowish, high-protein liquid full of antibodies and white blood cells. With rare exception, this is all your baby will need, since he was born with extra fluid in his system that compensates for the relatively low fluid volume of colostrum. When your milk supply begins to arrive, you will notice some increased fullness, warmth, and probably tenderness. During this process, your breasts are said to be **engorged**, and they may actually swell so much that your baby will have trouble latching on to them. Should this occur, you can gently express some milk from each breast, softening it so your baby can grasp more easily. To express milk, grasp the edge of the areola between thumb and fingers and then repeatedly squeeze while pushing gently toward your chest. (A warm compress or hot shower may be needed to get the milk flowing.) Engorgement typically lasts only a day or two (see page 123).

NURSING POSITION—
SIDE

Nursing patterns

Each baby has a unique style of nursing, and yours may mesh easily with your milk supply and lifestyle or may require that you make some adjustments. Some infants get right down to business, sucking vigorously and efficiently without much hesitation. These "barracudas" contrast sharply with the "gourmet" nursers, who take their sweet time, playing with the nipple at first, sampling their meal, and then eventually getting started. Some babies vary the gourmet approach by resting every few minutes, as if savoring their feeding, or even falling asleep one or more times during the nursing session. The "suck and snooze" types may exasperate a mother who feels that she doesn't have all day to nurse. While it's all right to provide a little mild stimulation (such as undressing him) to get Sleepy back on task and complete his feeding, some downsizing of your expectations for the day's activities may be necessary to prevent ongoing frustration.

Newborns also vary in the frequency with which they need to nurse. A typical span between feedings will be two to three hours, or eight to twelve times per day, but during the first days after birth, the interval may be longer, with only six to eight feedings in a twenty-four-hour period. The baby will feed more often than usual during growth spurts. The time involved in a feeding will also vary, but a typical feeding will take ten to fifteen minutes per breast.

As with nearly every aspect of life, what is said to be "typical" may not match with what happens in reality—especially with newborns. For example, your first nursing experiences in a hospital setting may be somewhat confusing, especially if you are not rooming in and the nursery adheres to the tradition of bringing out all the babies to their mothers for feeding on a fixed schedule. Since newborns don't necessarily synchronize to Nursery Standard Time and may be sound asleep for these nursing "appointments," this arrangement could lead to frustration for mothers whose zonked-out newborns seem to have little interest in latching on, let alone sucking, during the first few days after birth. In a worst-case scenario, a baby who hasn't been ready to nurse with Mom might wake up and sound off when he's parked in the nursery, only to have his crying ignored or answered with a bottle. A better approach is to have the nursery staff bring newborns to their mothers when they're hungry rather than in fixed shifts. Better yet, rooming in gives everyone a chance to get acquainted and, more important, nurse when the baby is awake and hungry.

Don't worry if your baby doesn't seem terribly interested in frequent nursing during the first few days. That will change, often just after you bring him home. The early phase of sleepiness that occurs as he adjusts to the outside world will usually give way to more active crying and nursing—sometimes every few hours—after the first week. Some parents are aghast when this happens. The mellow baby they enjoyed in the hospital suddenly seems wired and insatiable just a few days later. Don't panic. Instead, look at this as a time to hone your nursing skills with a very willing partner.

The newborn baby will announce his desire for milk every two to four hours in a number of ways. Some of these are subtle—looking alert, fidgeting a little, moving his mouth or tongue—and some more overt, such as sucking on his hand or rooting toward your breast (or the chest of whomever is holding him). Insistent crying is a *late* sign of hunger, and there's no point in waiting for him to reach that level of discomfort before offering the breast. (Indeed, nursing is likely to proceed more smoothly if he is calm rather than agitated.) If he is showing signs of hunger, it is appropriate to tend to him promptly, change him if necessary, and then settle in for a feeding.

For five to ten minutes you will notice him swallowing after every few sucks, and then he will shift to a more relaxed mode or even seem to lose interest. He can then be burped, either by lifting him and placing his head over your shoulder, or by sitting him up with your hand under his jaw and gently patting him on the back. You can also place him facedown across your lap, with head supported and chest a little higher than abdomen, and gently pat his back. (See diagram on page 123.)

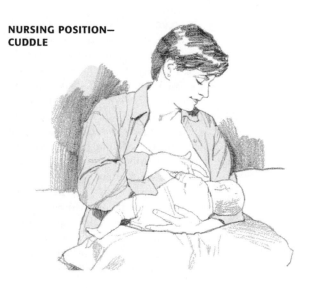

NURSING POSITION—CUDDLE

Once he burps, he may show interest in the other breast. (If he doesn't burp and yet appears comfortable, you can still proceed with the feeding.) Since the first side may be more completely emptied during the feeding, it is wise to alternate the breast from which he starts. (A small pin or clip that you move from one side of your nursing bra to the other can help remind you where to begin next time.)

Relatively frequent nursing is typical after the first days of life, and it will help stimulate your milk production and let-down reflex. A newborn who seems to be very content with infrequent feedings (more than four hours apart) should probably be checked by your physician to confirm that his activity level is satisfactory. He may in fact need to be awakened to feed every three hours to ensure adequate weight gain during the first two or three weeks.

Problems and concerns with nursing

"How do I know if she's getting enough?" During the first few days after birth, this concern often prods new mothers toward bottle-feeding, where they have the security of seeing exactly how much the baby is consuming. Remember that the quantity of milk you produce during a feeding will start with as little as half an ounce (15 ml) of colostrum during the first day or two and increase to an ounce (30 ml) as the milk supply arrives by the fourth or fifth day. After the first week, your milk output will range from two to six ounces (about 60 to 180 ml) per feeding. Obviously, there is no direct way for you to measure how much your baby is sucking from your breast, but other signs will indicate how the two of you are doing:

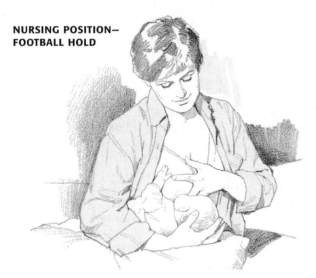

NURSING POSITION— FOOTBALL HOLD

- When the room is quiet, you will hear your baby swallowing.
- Once your milk has arrived, you may notice that your breasts soften during a feeding as they are emptied of milk.
- After the first four or five days, you should be changing six to eight wet diapers each day. In addition, you will notice one or several small, dark green stools—sometimes one after every feeding—that become lighter after the first (meconium) stools are passed. As your milk supply becomes well established, your baby's stools will take on a yellowish color and a soft or runny consistency. Later on, stools typically become less frequent.
- Tracking your baby's weight will give you specific and important information. *It is normal for a baby to drop nearly 10 percent of her birth weight (about eleven or twelve ounces, for example, for a seven-pound baby, or 0.31 to 0.34 kg for a baby weighing 3.2 kg) during the first week.* Usually she will have returned to her birth weight by two weeks of age, and thereafter she should gain about two-thirds to one ounce (or about 20 to 30 grams) per day. Obviously, you can't track these small changes at home on the bathroom scale. Instead, it is common to have a checkup during the first week or two after birth, during which your baby will be weighed on a scale that can detect smaller changes. If there is any question about appropriate weight gain, your doctor will ask you to return every week (or more often, if needed) to follow her progress. Some physicians' offices allow mothers to bring in their newborns for a quick "weigh-in" without charging for the visit.

One of the most important—and hardest—things to remember if you are concerned about the adequacy of your nursing is to *relax*. If you approach every feeding with fear and trembling, you may have difficulty with your let-down reflex. Furthermore, newborns seem to have an uncanny sense of Mom's anxiety, and their jittery response may interfere with smooth latching on and sucking. Remember that for many women, breastfeeding requires time, effort, and learning. Even if your first few feedings seem awkward or your baby doesn't seem to be getting the hang of it immediately, you should be able to make this process work. Take a deep breath, take your time, and don't be afraid to ask for help if you are truly having trouble getting started.

"It hurts when I nurse!" No one wants to spend a good portion of the day in misery, and a strong dose of pain with every feeding can demoralize even the most dedicated breastfeeding mother. Discomfort can have one or more causes. Many mothers, for example, feel aching during the let-down reflex, and some may even notice a brief shooting pain deeper in the breast after nursing as the milk supply is refilling. For some women, the engorgement of the breasts prior to each nursing session can be very painful. It is possible, in fact, to have intense pain with engorgement even when your nursing technique is correct and nothing specific is wrong with your breasts. Some mothers who are unprepared for such severe discomfort may give up on nursing too soon. But becoming comfortable with nursing may, in fact, take a few days or even a few weeks as your baby learns and your body adjusts to this new function. The following may help reduce pain from engorgement:

- Nurse frequently, especially during the first few days—every two hours during the day and at least every four hours at night.
- Express or pump your milk if your baby isn't emptying the breast or if you miss a feeding.
- Take acetaminophen (Tylenol) or ibuprofen as directed on the bottle.
- Apply cool packs (such as crushed ice in a plastic bag or even frozen vegetables such as corn or peas, wrapped in a thin towel) between feedings.

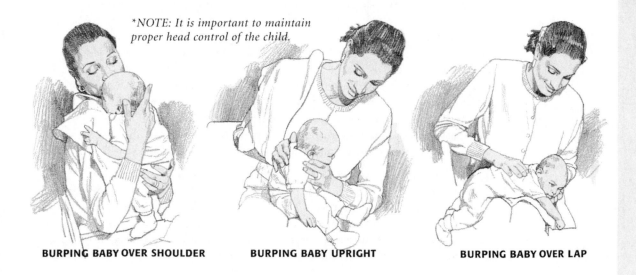

*NOTE: It is important to maintain proper head control of the child.

BURPING BABY OVER SHOULDER   **BURPING BABY UPRIGHT**   **BURPING BABY OVER LAP**

In most cases, pain serves as a warning that should not be ignored. If you have significant, ongoing pain with nursing, you should review this with your doctor and attempt to identify one of the causes that can and should be treated.

There will likely be at least a few, if not many, times during your breastfeeding career when you will not be able to nurse your baby for several hours (or days) at a time. These occasions might involve anything from an evening out for dinner, an unexpected trip, a time-out to allow irritated nipples to heal, or even the desire to supply breast milk to a premature infant who must be fed by tube. Nursing mothers who begin or resume work outside the home may have to contend with daily absences of several hours from their babies. While formula can be a satisfactory substitute in these situations, it is also possible to maintain your baby's nourishment with your own milk.

Guidelines for Expressing Milk—for Immediate or Future Use
- First, hands should be thoroughly washed with soap and water each time you collect milk. (The breasts do not need to be washed, however, but should be free of any lotions or creams.)
- Next, before any milk is expressed, each breast should be gently massaged. Using the palm of the hand, stroke several times from below, above, and the sides of the breast toward the nipple, applying gentle pressure.
- After massaging, milk can be expressed from each breast, either by hand or with the assistance of a breast pump. Either method is acceptable, and the choice of one or the other approach can be based on effectiveness, comfort, convenience, and cost.
- As with the first days of nursing, you may find it easier to begin expressing milk for three to five minutes at a time and then gradually progress to ten- or fifteen-minute sessions if you are collecting milk on a regular basis.

To express by hand. Sit in a comfortable position and lean over the container into which you will be collecting the milk. Place the thumb and index finger of one hand about an inch to either side of the nipple and then press toward your chest while gently squeezing the fingers toward one another. At first, you may see a few drops, a literal spurt, or nothing at all.

When the milk stops flowing, release your fingers, rotate to another position around the nipple, and squeeze again. If you don't see much milk, keep trying and don't give up—becoming adept at expressing milk may take practice. You may find that massaging again improves your flow. It may also be helpful to alternate between breasts rather than expressing all the milk from one before moving to the other.

To express using a breast pump. Breast pumps utilize a funnel or bicycle-horn-shaped apparatus that is placed against the breast. A vacuum is created, either by manually moving a piston or by an electrically powered device, and milk is sucked into an appropriate container. Electrical pumps are more expensive but are more efficient, especially for a mother who needs to express milk on a regular basis. (Some models can pump from both breasts simultaneously.) It is usually possible to rent one from

Intense discomfort can arise from traumatized, cracked, or inflamed nipples, which of course are sensitive areas to begin with. If the nipple is irritated at the tip, it is probably entering your baby's mouth at an upward angle and rubbing on her palate. During

a medical-supply company, hospital, or other local resource in order to confirm its usefulness before actually buying one.

To make an airtight seal between the pump and your breast, a little water or milk can be applied to the skin where contact is made. The apparatus should be applied snugly enough to make a good seal but not pressed so tightly as to restrict the flow of milk. Pumping can continue until after the milk has stopped flowing for a minute or so. After you are finished, use soap and water to wash whatever components of the pump came in contact with the milk and then allow them to air dry. (Check the manufacturer's directions for specific details about cleaning and proper handling of the equipment you are using.)

Collecting and Storing Milk

Your milk can be collected in a clean baby bottle or a breast-milk storage bag that attaches directly to the pump. Your baby can immediately drink what you have just expressed (which would be the case, for example, if you are expressing milk while sore nipples are healing), but you can also store milk for future use.

Remember that breast milk is a perishable food. Here are some guidelines for handling it so it will maintain its nutritional value and not become contaminated:

- If you plan to refrigerate or freeze milk, do so as soon as you have finished collecting it. You can use plastic or glass bottles with sealable tops, or sealable plastic bags designed specifically for storing breast milk. Label and date the containers.
- You may feed a baby fresh breast milk that has been left at room temperature for up to ten hours, after which the milk should be discarded.
- Breast milk that has just been expressed may be kept in the refrigerator for seven days, but any that is thawed from the freezer must be used within twenty-four hours and should not be refrozen.
- Various time limits for safe storage of breast milk in the freezer have been recommended; they range from two weeks (in a refrigerator freezer compartment that is opened frequently and whose temperature thus varies) to six months (in a deep freeze). A reasonable guideline would be to store frozen milk no longer than one month. Mark each bottle or plastic bottle liner with the date you collected it, and use the oldest milk first.
- You can combine the milk from both breasts into a single bottle or plastic bottle liner. If a particular pumping session has not yielded enough milk, you can freeze it and then add more cooled milk to the same container later—but don't change the date on your label.
- When you want to feed your baby expressed milk, thaw it by placing the bottle or bottle liner in warm (but not hot) water. Heating milk in a microwave is not recommended because it may cause "hot spots" in the milk that could burn the baby's mouth. Overheating may also destroy some nutrients in breast milk. ■

the latching-on process, try holding your breast so the nipple points downward. This is often easier if you are sitting, using the cuddle or football hold.

If the nipple is more tender at the base, it is more likely being chewed during feedings. Remember that your baby needs to take the entire areola into her mouth when she latches on, so your nipple lies against her tongue. If she won't open her mouth fully or slides off the areola after latching on, your nipple will be gummed continually while you nurse. To add insult to injury, your baby may not get enough milk when this occurs. The combination of miserable Mom and crying newborn is often enough to send Dad out into the night in search of formula.

To help your baby latch on to the whole areola (and not just your nipple), wait for her to open her mouth wide enough, and then gently pull her to the breast. If you are engorged and she is having difficulty forming a seal around the areola, you can express or pump some milk so that area will be softer. You may have to utilize the football hold (see page 118) to give your hand better control of her head and thus keep her from sliding off the areola. If she seems to lose her position during the feeding, don't be afraid to pull her gently from the breast and then reattach. If she has a strong hold, you should first loosen it by gently pulling downward on her chin or inserting a finger into the corner of her mouth to release the vacuum seal formed by her gums.

Other causes of painful irritation of one or both nipples, or even full-blown inflammation known as **dermatitis**, include:

- Overzealous use of soap and water that can remove the skin's own moisturizers. Rinse your breasts during your normal shower or bath, but keep soap away from your nipples.

PACIFIER POINTERS

Some parents say they could not have survived their baby's infancy without these gadgets, while others (and some breastfeeding advisers) see them as an abomination. While pacifiers are not exactly a threat to world peace, you would be wise to limit their use in a very young infant who has not established stable and efficient nursing patterns. The feel, texture, taste, and smell of a pacifier are clearly different from that of Mom's nipples, and sucking a pacifier too soon may interfere with a baby's learning the real thing. But after two weeks or more, assuming nursing is going well, a pacifier can help calm a baby who

- is already fed and full but still wants to suck;
- doesn't have anything else, such as a wet diaper, bothering him; and
- will suck on it with apparent satisfaction.

In addition, a number of research studies suggest that pacifier use during sleep is associated with a significant reduction in the risk of sudden infant death syndrome (SIDS). There are a number of possible explanations for this finding, and the effect appears to be greater among infants who sleep in more hazardous environments, such as soft bedding. (We discuss SIDS and guidelines for safe infant sleep in the next chapter, beginning on page 154.)

- Continuous moisture on the skin's surface. This can occur when the breast is not allowed to dry off after a feeding or when the pads of a nursing bra are moist. Air-drying for a few minutes after nursing is the simplest solution. (Make certain that your nursing bra is dry as well.)
- An allergic reaction to breast creams or oils. Paradoxically, traditional remedies for breast soreness such as vitamin E preparations or impure lanolin may make the problem worse if they provoke an allergic dermatitis. If your nipple develops redness, swelling, and a burning sensation, stop using any nipple cream. If the problem persists or worsens, see your doctor. You may have to use a mild anti-inflammatory prescription cream for a few days to calm this problem down more quickly.
- An infection with the yeast organism known as **Candida albicans**, which will also be present in the baby's mouth. In this case, the irritation may not only burn but also itch. *Candida* may appear after you have been nursing without any problems. A tip-off is the presence of small, white patches inside your baby's cheeks. *Candida* infection in the baby's mouth (also known as **thrush**) is not a dangerous condition, but it can be a persistent annoyance.

  Candida infections usually respond to treatment with an antifungal cream (check with your doctor). At the same time, your baby should be given antifungal drops by mouth. If both of you are not treated concurrently for several days, the infection may bounce back and forth between you. Furthermore, in order to prevent reinfection, you will need to change nursing pads after every feeding. If your baby is receiving any feedings from a bottle or is using a pacifier, you will need to boil the rubber nipples and pacifiers every day until the infection clears.

Remember that inserting a pacifier in an infant's mouth must not be a substitute for normal feeding, parental nurturing, or checking to see if something is wrong. If you decide to use a pacifier, make sure you get a one-piece model with a soft nipple—either the straight bottle shape or the angled "orthodontic" type. (Don't waste your money on those "gag" pacifiers that make a baby appear to have buck teeth or fangs—they're a silly joke at a young infant's expense.) Never use the nipple assembly from a feeding bottle as a pacifier because the nipple can come loose and choke your baby. Make sure you have the right size for babies younger than six months and that it is designed to survive boiling or trips through the dishwasher. For the first six months, you will need to clean pacifiers frequently in this way to reduce the risk of infection.

Babies are unable to replace pacifiers that fall out of their mouths, so you will have to do this for them. *Do not, under any circumstances, tie a pacifier to a string or ribbon around a baby's neck to keep it in place. This solution to a wandering pacifier could strangle your baby.*

If you find a pacifier that your baby likes, buy several. They have a knack for disappearing into the sofa, under the car seat, or into the bottom of the diaper bag, so lots of backups are a good idea. ■

- Rarely, an ongoing **eczema** problem that has appeared on other parts of your body will erupt on the breast during nursing. You will want to consult with your doctor about appropriate treatment, which may involve the short-term use of a mild anti-inflammatory cream.
- A potentially more serious cause of pain is **mastitis**, inflammation of breast tissue that arises from a plugged milk duct or represents a potentially serious infection involving bacteria that gain entry into breast tissue, usually through a cracked nipple. Symptoms include pain, swelling, heat, redness, and tenderness in a localized area of one breast, accompanied by generalized aching and fever.

  A breastfeeding mother who feels as though she has the flu should consider the possibility that she has mastitis, even if localized redness and tenderness haven't yet developed. If there is no fever, she probably has a plugged duct and does not require antibiotics.

  With or without fever, however, it is important to contact your physician if these symptoms develop. Antibiotics that are safe for both mother and baby will normally be prescribed, and acetaminophen may be used to reduce both pain and temperature. Alternating application of warm and cold compresses can assist in the treatment. Warmth (as in a bath or applied in a warm, moist towel) may enhance local circulation. Crushed ice in a plastic bag (or even frozen vegetables) wrapped in a thin towel to protect the skin may help reduce pain and swelling. Gently massaging the inflamed area may also help empty the plugged duct. *In addition, it is important to continue nursing,* although you may be more comfortable with more frequent, shorter sessions. Your baby will not become ill by nursing from an infected breast, and emptying the breast of milk helps clear the infection.

Aside from some of these specific treatments for breast and nipple pain, how else do you spell *relief* until the cracking or irritation heals?

- Don't attempt to toughen your nipples, either before or after the birth, by rubbing, stretching, or pinching them.
- Acetaminophen (or ibuprofen) may be taken thirty to sixty minutes before you nurse. Of course, it is wise to take medications only when necessary while nursing, but a short-term pain reliever that helps you continue nursing will be a worthwhile exception.
- Take some measures to "move things along" during your feedings. Express a little milk before your baby latches on, and then gently massage your breasts while nursing to help them empty more quickly. Think in terms of shorter but more frequent feeding times.
- Rotate the type of "hold" you are using so that the orientation of the breast to the baby's mouth varies with each feeding.
- Air-dry your nipples for several minutes after you nurse. Some mothers find that ice applied to the nipple just before nursing may reduce pain when the baby latches on. Many traditional remedies such as breast creams, oils, vitamin E capsules, or even tea bags have fallen out of favor, especially since some may actually increase the irritation. However, a *pure* lanolin preparation applied after nursing, or simply expressing breast milk onto the nipple and allowing it to air-dry, may help restore normal skin moisture and decrease pain.

- When it is not possible to expose your nipples to air, you can wear dome-shaped plastic **breast shells** that prevent sore nipples from being rubbed by your clothing. (Don't confuse breast shells with **nipple shields**, which can help women with inverted nipples prior to and after birth. Nipple shields are not helpful for sore breasts.)
- If your baby forms a strong suction with her gums, be sure to release her grip before you pull her from your breast.
- If all else fails, consider pumping your breasts and allowing your baby to accept your milk from a bottle while your nipples are healing, especially if they have been bleeding. This is less desirable during the first several days while she is still learning the ropes, but it's better than giving up on nursing altogether.

Remember that a temporary time-out from breastfeeding to allow for healing or for any other reason (for example, an illness affecting either mother or baby) does not mean that you cannot resume nursing when things calm down. Pumping your breasts at feeding time will help you maintain your milk supply. Furthermore, even if your baby has spent a fair amount of time with a bottle, she can learn (or relearn) to obtain nourishment successfully from your breast.

"My baby wants to nurse all the time. I'm getting sick of being a human pacifier."
All babies derive comfort and satisfaction from sucking, but some are true enthusiasts who would be more than happy to turn every nursing session into a ninety-minute marathon. You may be happy with this arrangement, but more likely it can lead to sore nipples and a gnawing concern that your entire existence has been reduced to being a mobile restaurant. Fortunately, you are not without options.

A healthy newborn, properly attached to the breast and sucking continuously, will empty about 90 percent of the milk available on each side within ten minutes. You can usually hear and feel the transition from intense sucking and swallowing to a more relaxed, pacifying sucking after five to ten minutes on each side, at which point you can decide how long you want to continue. If you're both feeling cozy and comfortable, relax and enjoy it. But if it's the middle of the night and you need sleep, or other children need your attention, or you're getting sore, you won't destroy your baby's personality by gently detaching her.

A problem can arise, however, if your baby sounds terribly unhappy and indignant when you decide enough's enough. How do you respond? The answer depends on how far along and how well established you are in your nursing relationship. In the earliest days when milk is just arriving or you're not sure whether she is truly swallowing an adequate volume, it is probably better to give her the benefit of the doubt and continue for a while longer. This is especially true if you are blessed with a casual "gourmet" or "suck and snooze" baby who may not empty your breast very quickly.

But watch the indicators of your progress: good swallowing sounds, frequent wet diapers, weight gain, and softening of your breast after feeding. If you notice these and feel you have developed a smooth nursing routine after two or three weeks, you can consider other calming maneuvers, including the use of a pacifier (see sidebar on page 126). *If your soothing maneuvers aren't working, however, or your baby doesn't seem to be gaining weight, contact your baby's doctor for further evaluation and recommendations.*

Some mothers make the mistake of assuming that every sound from a baby should be answered with nursing, when something else (or nothing in particular) may be bothering her. If, for example, she just finished a good feeding thirty minutes ago and begins to fuss after being put down for a nap, it is reasonable to wait and listen for a while, since she may settle down on her own, rather than trying to nurse her again. Otherwise you may find yourself spending nearly every minute of the day and night with your baby attached to your breast. As the days pass, you will become more discerning about the meaning of your baby's various crying messages.

A final note: If you are having a significant problem with breastfeeding—whether it be latching on, anatomy problems, sore nipples, a sluggish nurser, slow weight gain, or anything else—seek out a **lactation consultant** for some additional help. This is a health-care professional whose wealth of knowledge and practical suggestions can help both mother and baby succeed at breastfeeding, even when the going gets very tough. Your baby's doctor or a local hospital should be able to give you a referral. You don't need (or want) to wait until a crisis has developed before seeking help. Some early troubleshooting by a lactation consultant may help prolong breastfeeding (and all of its benefits) and prevent you from switching to formula when problems first arise.

Bottle-Feeding Basics

Choosing a formula

First things first: *For the first year, do not feed your baby cow's milk from the dairy section at the store.* Cow's milk that has not been specifically modified for use in infant formulas is not digested well by human infants; it contains significant loads of protein that your baby's kidneys will have difficulty processing, and it contains inadequate amounts of vitamin C, vitamin E, and iron. It also contains inadequate amounts of fat, which provides 50 percent of the calories in human milk and formula, and the fat that is present may be more difficult for the baby to digest and absorb. Furthermore, the new baby's intestine may be irritated by cow's milk, resulting in a gradual but potentially significant loss of red blood cells. This may lead to anemia, which in turn may be aggravated by an insufficient supply of iron. Finally, some of the protein in cow's milk may be absorbed through the baby's intestine in a way that can lead to allergy problems later in life.

The vast majority of bottle-fed infants are given iron-fortified commercial formulas, whose manufacturers have gone to great lengths to match mother's milk as closely as possible. The most commonly used formulas are based on cow's milk that has been *significantly* altered for human consumption. Among other things,

BOTTLE-FEEDING BABY

the protein is made more digestible and less allergenic, lactose is added to match that of human milk, and butterfat is removed and replaced with a combination of other fats more readily absorbed by infants.

Soy formulas are based on soy protein and do not contain lactose, which is the main carbohydrate in cow's milk. These are used for the small percentage of infants who are allergic to the protein in cow's milk or (much less commonly) cannot digest lactose and thus develop excessive gas, cramps, and diarrhea when they consume regular formula. In addition, bottle-fed infants who have diarrhea resulting from a viral or bacterial infection may develop a temporary difficulty processing lactose. During their recovery, these babies may tolerate soy formulas better than cow's milk formulas. Infants from families with a strong history of cow's milk allergy have traditionally been started on soy formulas as a precautionary measure. However, this has not been shown to prevent the development of cow's milk allergy, and up to 50 percent of infants who are allergic to cow's milk will prove to be allergic to soy formula as well. Furthermore, because of some subtle differences between the protein in soy and cow's milk, as well as a tendency for calcium and certain other minerals to be absorbed less efficiently from soy milk, soy-based formulas should be reserved for full-term infants who are clearly intolerant of cow's milk. Soy formulas should *not* be fed to premature infants.

There are a variety of formulas that have been designed for special needs. Infants who are allergic to both cow's milk and soy formulas may use what are called **protein hydrolysate** formulas, in which the proteins are essentially predigested. Special formulas are also available for babies with phenylketonuria (PKU) and for premature infants.

Check with your baby's physician regarding the type(s) of formula he or she recommends. Once you have made your choice, you can stock up with one or more of the three forms in which they are normally sold:

- **Ready-to-feed** is just that. Put it into a bottle if it isn't already packaged in one, make sure the temperature is right, and you're all set. While extremely convenient, this format is also the most expensive.
- **Concentrate** must be mixed with water in the exact amount recommended by the manufacturer. If it is too diluted (mixed with too much water), your baby will be shortchanged on nutrients. But if it is too concentrated (mixed with too little water), diarrhea and dehydration may result. The unused portion of an opened can of concentrate may be sealed and stored in the refrigerator for twenty-four hours, after which it should be discarded.
- **Powdered formula** is the least expensive form and must be mixed exactly as recommended, using the measuring scoop provided. A bottle of formula prepared from powder can be kept in the refrigerator for up to twenty-four hours and then should be discarded.

Whatever type of formula you use, be sure to check the expiration date on the bottle or can before feeding it to your baby.

In order to prevent your baby's formula from being contaminated by potentially harmful bacteria, it's important to take some basic precautions during preparation:

- Wash your hands before you begin handling formula, water, bottles, and nipples.

- If the formula you are using comes from a can, wipe the top before you open it. Use a separate can opener specifically designated for this purpose, and clean it on a regular basis.

- What about sterilizing bottles and nipples, and boiling water to be used in mixing formula? Over the past few decades the health-advisory pendulum has swung from boiling everything that might come near the baby's mouth to a more relaxed approach—using tap water for formula and hot soapy water or the dishwasher for bottles and nipples—and now more recently back again to more rigorous measures. While the vast majority of public water supplies in the United States are safe, an infant—especially during the first few weeks of life—is more vulnerable to infectious organisms, and protecting him is worth a little extra effort to boil the water you plan to mix with concentrated or powdered formula. A couple of minutes should be adequate; then let it cool. Bottled water should also be boiled unless it is specifically labeled as sterile.

- Well water should be checked for bacterial contamination and should always be boiled before you use it. In addition, well water may contain **nitrates**, components of plants and fertilizers that can be toxic to infants, especially those younger than three months of age. If a well is your water source, have it tested on a regular basis for nitrate content before using it to mix formula for your baby. When in doubt, it would be best to use ready-to-feed formula or to mix bottled water with concentrated or powdered formula.

- Similarly, bottles, nipples, and utensils should be boiled for five minutes before preparing formula, although automatic dishwashers in which water temperature reaches at least 180°F (82°C) appear to do an adequate job of sterilizing.[4] After each use, bottles and nipple assemblies should be washed with hot, soapy water, using a bottle brush to clean the inside thoroughly, and then rinsed out. They can then be boiled or run through the dishwasher prior to the next time they are used for a feeding.

You can prepare a day's worth of bottles at one time, storing the ones you don't immediately need in the refrigerator for up to twenty-four hours. It's not necessary to warm a bottle, although younger babies prefer tepid or room-temperature formula. To warm a bottle you've stored in the refrigerator, let it sit for a few minutes in hot water. Warming the bottle in a microwave is *not* recommended because uneven heating may cause pockets of milk hot enough to scald a baby's mouth. Before feeding, shake the bottle well and let a drop or two fall on your hand. It should be barely warm and definitely not hot. Also check the flow rate from the nipple. An ideal flow is about one drop per second when the bottle is held upside down. If the nipple allows milk to flow too quickly, your baby may choke on it. If it flows too slowly, he may swallow air while he tries to suck out his meal.

You can use four- or eight-ounce (120 or 240 ml) bottles made from plastic or glass. (Later on, however, when he can hold his own bottle, glass bottles should be replaced with plastic.) Many parents prefer the nurser style in which formula is poured into a plastic bag that attaches to a plastic shell and nipple assembly. Babies tend to swallow less air from the bags, but they cost more in the long run. It is important not to use the bags to mix concentrate or powder because you cannot measure accurately with them.

Why the renewed interest in boiling and sterilizing? Perhaps the most compelling reason was a series of at least ten outbreaks of diarrhea caused by the parasite *Cryptosporidium parvum* in various public water supplies between 1990 and 2000. The most notable of these occurred in Milwaukee, Wisconsin, in 1993, affecting more than four hundred thousand people.[3]

What about making your own formula? If for some reason you can't find or buy commercial formula, a *temporary* solution would be to mix 13 ounces of *evaporated* (not condensed) milk and 2 tablespoons of corn syrup in 19 ounces of boiled water.[5] This can be poured into sterilized bottles and kept in the refrigerator up to forty-eight hours until used. This do-it-yourself formula is not recommended for long-term use because it lacks the nutritional fine-tuning that is now the norm in commercial formulas.

As with breastfeeding, bottle-feeding should be relaxed and unhurried, preferably in a comfortable and quiet area of your home. Hold your baby across your lap with his upper body slightly raised and his head supported. A flat position during feedings not only increases the risk of choking but also allows milk to flow into the passageways, called **eustachian tubes**, that lead into the middle ears. Frequent ear infections may result. Stroke the nipple across his cheek or lower lip to start the rooting reflex, and be sure to keep the bottle elevated enough so the milk completely covers the inside of the nipple. Otherwise he may start sucking air.

The fact that milk is flowing from a bottle does not mean that the feeding should switch to autopilot. Take time to lock eyes with your infant, talk or sing softly to him, gently caress him, and pray about this new life with which you've been entrusted. Your baby should not be left unattended with a bottle propped in his mouth. This practice puts your baby at an unnecessary risk for ear infections or choking.

According to the American Academy of Pediatrics, an estimated 15 million families use unregulated wells as their water source, and 2 million of these do not meet federal standards for nitrate content.

Formula-fed newborns typically will consume two or three ounces (60 to 90 ml) every two to four hours, gradually increasing to a routine of taking about three to four ounces (90 to 120 ml) every four hours by the end of the first month. The amount per feeding will then increase by about an ounce every month, up to a maximum of eight ounces (240 ml) at a time. A general rule of thumb is that a normal baby will need between two and two and one-half ounces of formula per pound of body weight each day (up to fifteen pounds), with a maximum of thirty-two ounces of formula per day. (In metric equivalents, that would be about 130 to 165 ml of formula per kilogram, up to 6.8 kg, with a maximum of 960 ml of formula per day.) As we noted earlier, normally he will give a number of cues (such as looking more alert, fidgeting, or sucking on his hand) when he is hungry—remember that crying is a *late* sign of hunger—and will turn his head away or push the nipple out of his mouth with his tongue when he is full. If the bottle isn't empty, don't force the issue. However, during the first few weeks, it is wise to awaken him to feed if he is sleeping for stretches of more than four or five hours during the day.

As with breastfeeding, every baby's pattern of bottle-feeding (both in timing and amounts of formula taken) will be a little different. It's more important to become familiar with your own baby's cues for being hungry or full rather than trying to follow a particular formula (no pun intended) to the letter. If you're wondering whether he is getting enough, or if you're concerned that he seems to want too much, by all means have him checked by your physician. It will help if you keep a simple log—how much formula he is taking and when, and how many wet diapers you are changing every day—for a couple of days before the visit.

EUSTACHIAN TUBE

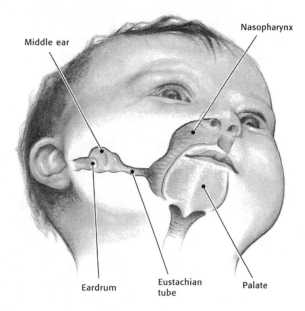

Middle ear

Nasopharynx

Eardrum

Eustachian tube

Palate

When (if ever) should the baby's formula be changed?

Most doctors will recommend that bottle-fed infants begin with an iron-fortified cow's milk formula, and if doing well with it, use it through the first year of life. (Iron is not absorbed as efficiently from formula as from breast milk, and the amount added to iron-fortified formula ensures that your baby will get what he needs.) Additional vitamin supplementation isn't needed.

One of the headaches that most bottle-feeding parents eventually face is figuring out whether irritability, especially if accompanied by gas or loose stools, means that baby and formula are not getting along. There are no clear-cut answers to this dilemma.

If you think your baby might be having a problem with the current formula, discuss it with his physician. It may be appropriate to try another brand, or even a different form of the same brand, and observe the results. Sometimes persistent crying, irritability, and poor sleep at night—definitely one of the most disturbing situations for new parents—will provoke a switch to soy-based formula. If it seems to help, stay with it. Beware of making changes too quickly or attributing every one of your baby's problems to his current formula, because you won't be able to sort out cause and effect, and you may overlook some other cause of his discomfort. You would also be wise to read carefully the section entitled "What if the baby becomes ill?" beginning on page 136. Unfortunately, some of the problems we have just mentioned—persistent crying or irritability, for example—could also be signs of illness in a newborn. If you have any doubt, give your baby's physician a call, especially during the first three months of life.

Occasionally there may be such frustration and expense associated with finding a tolerated formula that **relactation**—resuming breastfeeding after it has been interrupted for a period of time—may be considered, even if several weeks (or even longer periods) have passed without nursing. Input from a lactation consultant would definitely be helpful if you are considering this option.

Health Concerns during the First Three Months

When should the baby be seen for checkups?

Your pediatrician or family physician will ask that you follow a specific routine of well-baby visits; there is a definite purpose to this plan that involves monitoring the baby's progress and administering immunizations that are very important to her health. If you have been sent home from the hospital within twenty-four hours of your baby's birth, your baby should be checked within the next twenty-four to forty-eight hours. If all is going smoothly, you can expect to take your baby back for a checkup between two and four weeks of age and then again at two months.

During these visits, the baby will be weighed and measured and the results plotted on a standardized growth chart, which allows the health-care provider to track her progress over time. You will be asked how she is feeding, sleeping, and eliminating urine and stool. At the one- and two-month visits, specific behavioral milestones such as smiling and head control will probably be discussed. The baby will be examined from head to toe, so be sure to put her in an outfit that can be removed easily.

It is important that you bring up any problems or concerns you have, no matter how minor they seem. If you have a number of questions, write them down and present them at the beginning of the visit so the practitioner can see what's on your mind. Don't suddenly pull them out as a list of "by the way" items after everything else is done. If the examiner seems rushed and uneasy about taking time to deal with your concerns, find out how and when you can go over them. Some large practices have well-trained nurses or other health educators who can answer most of the questions you might have.

Your physician will recommend that your baby receive a number of routine immunizations during the first three months of life. These will be given to protect her against a number of dangerous diseases—whooping cough (pertussis), diphtheria, tetanus, polio, rotavirus infection, and hepatitis B—as well as against pneumococcus and *Haemophilus influenzae* type B, bacteria that can cause meningitis, pneumonia, and other serious infections. Many parents are anxious about the prospect of their tiny infant receiving these vaccines, and some have read literature suggesting that they are dangerous or ineffective. But overwhelming evidence indicates that immunizations do in fact drastically reduce the

TAKING AN ACCURATE TEMPERATURE

Y ou cannot accurately judge your baby's temperature by placing your hand on his forehead or anywhere else. *Skin temperature strips are no better.* Furthermore, you cannot get an accurate reading using an oral thermometer in babies and small children because they can't cooperate in keeping the little bulb under the tongue. Electronic ear thermometers will give you a ballpark number, but results may vary somewhat depending on your technique. Therefore, for your young infant you'll need to rely on a rectal digital thermometer when you want an accurate temperature reading. (For decades, glass thermometers containing mercury were the gold standard for taking temperatures in infants and adults alike. However, their tendency to break and spill this hazardous substance has led the American Academy of Pediatrics to recommend that they be discarded in favor of digital thermometers, which are now inexpensive, simple to use, and usually quite accurate.)

Your baby should be lying tummy-down on a bed or crib, or across your knees if he is very small. Keep one hand firmly in control of his lower back and don't try to take the temperature while he is actively squirming or resisting you. Lubricate the tip of the thermometer with petroleum jelly, and put a little around the baby's anus as well. Then gently insert the thermometer into the child's rectum about one-half to one inch. Do not force the thermometer into the rectum. Hold it until you hear the beep (usually about a minute), then remove it and read the temperature. Afterward cleanse the tip with rubbing alcohol or soap and water, then rinse. If you're having trouble getting a reading, be sure to review the instructions that came with the thermometer.

What about taking the temperature in the baby's armpit? This is referred to as an **axillary** reading, and it is taken by placing the tip of a digital thermometer in the armpit and holding the arm snugly against the chest until you hear the beep. An axillary temperature can provide a convenient, ballpark reading if you're wondering whether a fever is present. But because a fever in a very young infant could indicate a potentially serious problem, it is well worth the extra effort to get a more accurate rectal reading if you have any question about his temperature. ■

If you need to dispose of a mercury thermometer, *don't throw it into the trash.* If it breaks it could expose others to this hazardous substance. Mercury thermometers must be disposed of properly through a local hazardous waste collection program. You can find out about state and local collection programs for mercury-containing devices at the Environmental Protection Agency's Web site: http://www.epa.gov/epaoswer/hazwaste/mercury/collect.htm.

risk of your baby becoming ill with a number of serious or even fatal infections. And the odds of having a problem from any of the vaccines are far less than the odds of contracting the disease if no vaccine is given. For a detailed look at immunizations and the diseases that they prevent, see "Immunizations—Which Ones, Why, and When?" beginning on page 739. We recommend that you review this information carefully.

What if the baby becomes ill?

Because newborns normally receive a healthy donation of Mom's antibodies through the umbilical cord blood supply prior to birth, they usually escape common illnesses such as colds and flu during the first several weeks, as long as they are well nourished and their environment is kept reasonably clean. Nursing infants have the added advantage of ingesting their mother's antibodies at every feeding.

This is indeed providential because an illness in a baby younger than three months of age is a completely different situation from one in an older baby. For one thing, your new baby has very few ways to notify you that something is wrong. You will not have the luxury of language and specific complaints ("My ear hurts" or "I have a headache") to guide you. You won't have months or years of experience with this particular child—or, if this is your first baby, perhaps with any child—to sense what is "normal" for her.

In addition, your baby's defense system is still under construction, and her ability to fight off microscopic invaders will not be fully operational for a number of months. As a result, a seemingly minor infection acquired during the first several weeks can turn into a major biological war.

Also—and this is the most unsettling reality of all—an illness can go sour much more rapidly in a newborn than in older children. If bacteria are on the move, they can spread like wildfire. If fluids are being lost through vomiting or diarrhea, dehydration can develop over several hours rather than days.

These warnings are not meant to generate undue anxiety but rather to encourage you to notify your baby's health-care provider if you think something is wrong, especially during the first three months of life. You can also reduce your newborn's risk of infection by keeping her out of crowded public places, preventing if possible direct contact with individuals who are ill with contagious infections, and minimizing group child-care situations, especially during the first few weeks after birth.

What are the signs that a baby might have a problem?

Some of the danger signals in infants are similar to those that will alert you to problems later in life. But in newborns, several of these signals are more critical and require a more immediate and detailed evaluation than in older babies and children. Here are some important newborn distress signals:

Fever. There will be many occasions in the coming months and years when your child will feel hot, and the thermometer will agree. In babies over three months of age, this may or may not be cause for alarm, depending on what else is going on. *In a baby under three months of age, however, a rectal temperature over 100.4°F (38°C) should be considered cause for an immediate call to the doctor's office.*

If your baby seems perfectly well, his temperature is slightly above 100.4°F, and there is a possibility that he was overdressed or in a hot environment, you can remove some clothing and try taking his temperature again in thirty to forty-five minutes. A temperature that is closer to normal will be reassuring—but you should run the story by your baby's physician anyway. Do not give the baby acetaminophen (Tylenol) or a tepid bath in this situation because you need to know whether the fever will come down on its own. Besides, the fever itself is not dangerous. It is the possible causes of the fever that you need to worry about.

If there is no doubt about the presence of fever, your baby needs to be evaluated right away, either by his own physician or at the emergency room. You may be surprised or even alarmed by the number of tests that may be requested after your baby is examined. The problem is that a newborn fever can indicate a serious bacterial infection that could involve the lungs, urinary tract, or the tissues that surround the brain and spinal cord (these tissues are called **meninges**). Bacteria could also be present in the bloodstream, in which case the baby is said to have **sepsis**.

It is not unusual for a doctor to recommend that a newborn with a fever undergo blood tests, an evaluation of the urine, and a lumbar puncture (or spinal tap), all of which obtain specimens to be cultured for bacteria. A chest X-ray may be ordered if there is any question about pneumonia. In addition, the baby may be admitted to the hospital for two or three days so antibiotics can be given intravenously (that is, through a vein) while the cultures are growing in the laboratory. If he is doing well and no bacteria are growing in the cultures, he will be sent home. How this scenario ultimately unfolds will depend upon a number of factors, including the age of the baby, the history of his illness, his appearance and behavior, and the physician's examination. Many of these measures may seem rather drastic in response to a simple fever, but babies in this age-group are more vulnerable to the spread of bacteria—especially into the bloodstream and meninges. If left untreated, the results could be disastrous.

Feeding poorly. Lack of interest in nursing, poor sucking, or failing to awaken for feeding well beyond the expected time could be an important indicator of a medical problem. If you contact a physician with a concern that your newborn is ill, the physician will want to know, among other things, how the baby appears to be feeding.

Vomiting. As we will discuss later in this chapter, you will need to distinguish between spitting up and vomiting, since the latter is much more significant in a newborn (see page 140).

Decreased activity or alertness. A baby who is listless—with eyes open but little spontaneous movement, an indifferent response to stimulation, or very floppy muscle tone—may be quite sick. Believe it or not, a vigorous protest by a baby during an examination is a reassuring finding. At this age, remaining quiet and disinterested while being poked and prodded by the doctor is not a sign of being a "good" patient but rather an indication of probable illness.

Nonstop crying. As will be described in the next chapter, many babies enter a "crying season" between two weeks and three months of age, without any specific medical cause. But you can't assume that prolonged, inconsolable crying is normal until the baby has been evaluated by his physician.

Abnormal movements. Unusual jerking of arms, legs, or head, especially if sustained for several seconds, may represent a seizure or other significant problem affecting the nervous system. Contact your baby's doctor immediately for further advice if you observe this type of activity.

Unusual color. A pale or mottled color of the skin or bluish discoloration of the lips could indicate a change in normal circulation patterns.

What Are Some Common Medical Problems during the First Three Months of Life?

Jaundice is a yellow orange discoloration of skin caused by the buildup of a substance called **bilirubin** in the bloodstream. Bilirubin is a by-product of the breakdown of red blood cells, which normally circulate for about four months until they wear out. (New red cells are constantly produced within the bones in tissue called **marrow**.) Removing and recycling the contents of red cells require the liver to process bilirubin, which before birth is largely managed through the mother's circulation. After birth, the newborn's liver takes a few days to gear up for this job, and the level of bilirubin in the bloodstream will increase by a modest amount. If a significant backlog of bilirubin develops, the baby's skin will take on a yellow orange hue, beginning with the head and gradually spreading toward the legs. (Why jaundice progresses from the head downward rather than evenly over the entire body is unknown, but this peculiarity may give an examiner a rough idea of its severity.)

Whether or not jaundice is significant will depend upon several factors, including the level of bilirubin, how soon and how fast it has risen, the suspected cause, and whether the baby was full-term or premature. In some instances, extremely high bilirubin levels can damage the central nervous system, especially in the premature infant. *Therefore, if you notice that your new baby's skin color is changing to pumpkin orange, the white area of the eyes is turning yellow, and/or your baby is feeding poorly, see your doctor immediately.*

If there is any concern, the doctor will order blood tests to check the bilirubin level, and other studies may be done to look for underlying causes. Normally the jaundice will resolve on its own, although some healthy babies will carry a slight yellow orange tint for weeks. Occasionally a little extra help is needed. This may involve five approaches, as directed by the baby's physician:

- Treat any underlying cause (such as an infection), if possible.
- Increase the baby's fluid intake by feeding him more often.

- Expose the baby to *indirect* sunlight—that is, undress him down to his diaper in a room bright with sunlight *that does not shine directly on his sensitive skin*. Since indirect sunlight has only a modest effect on clearing bilirubin, don't use this approach unless you are sure that your baby won't become too hot or cold in the room you use.
- In some cases of jaundice, an enzyme found in mother's milk may interfere to a modest degree with the clearing of bilirubin. Occasionally your health-care provider may ask you to stop breastfeeding briefly and use formula until the problem improves, after which nursing can resume. In such a case, it is important that you continue to express milk so your breasts will continue to produce it and will be ready when your baby is able to resume breastfeeding. This should *not* be an occasion to stop nursing altogether.
- A treatment called **phototherapy** may be utilized if the bilirubin level needs to be treated more actively. Under a physician's direction, the baby, wearing protective eyewear, lies under a special intense blue light like a sunbather at the beach. In addition, or as an alternative, a baby can lie on a thin plastic light source called a **BiliBlanket**. Whether carried out at a hospital or at home (using equipment provided by a home-health agency), phototherapy usually reduces bilirubin gradually within two or three days, if not sooner.

Colds and other **respiratory infections** are relatively uncommon in this age-group. The breathing patterns in a newborn baby, however, may cause you some concern. He will at times move air in and out noisily, with snorting and sniffing sounds emanating from his small nasal passages, even when they are completely dry. Some sneezing now and then isn't uncommon, but watery or thick drainage from one or both nostrils is definitely abnormal. A call to the doctor's office and usually an exam are in order when this "goop" appears in a baby under three months.

If your newborn has picked up a cold, you can gently suction the excess nasal drainage with a rubber-bulb syringe, since a clogged nose will cause some difficulty breathing while he is feeding. *Do not give any decongestant or cold preparations to a baby this young unless given very specific directions—not only what kind, but exactly how much—from your baby's physician.* (In general, research evidence has suggested that such medications are not terribly effective in babies and young children.)

Even when his nose is clear, your baby's breathing rate may be somewhat erratic, varying with his activity and excitement level. A typical rate is thirty to forty times per minute, often with brief pauses, sighs, and then a quick succession of breaths. If he is quiet and consistently breathing fifty or more times per minute, however, he may have an infection or another problem with his lungs or heart. Flaring of the nostrils, an inward sucking motion of the spaces between the ribs, and exaggerated movement of the abdomen with each breath suggest that he may be working harder than usual to breathe. An occasional cough probably doesn't signal a major problem, but frequent or prolonged bouts of coughing should be investigated, especially if there are any other signs of illness.

Infections of the middle ear (known as **otitis media**) may complicate a cold in any baby, including a newborn. There are, however, no specific signs of this important problem in a young baby. (At this age, movement of the hands around the side of the head are random, and your baby cannot deliberately point to or try to touch any area that is bothering him.) Furthermore, an ear infection can be much more serious in this age-group. If he is acting ill, irritable, running a fever, or all of these, he will need to have his ears checked by his doctor.

Some babies always seem to be overflowing with tears in one eye. This is caused by a **narrowing of the tear duct** near the inner corner of each eye, which acts like a drain for the tears that are produced constantly to keep the eye moist. Aside from causing a nonstop trail of tears down one side of the face, this narrowing can lead to a local infection manifested by goopy, discolored drainage; crusting; and if more widespread, a generalized redness of the eye known as **conjunctivitis**. The crusting and drainage will need to be removed gently using moist cotton balls, which should be promptly thrown away after being used since they may be contaminated with bacteria. In addition, the baby's health-care provider will probably prescribe antibiotic eye drops or ointment for a few days. He or she may also suggest that you gently massage the area between the inner corner of the eye and the nose to help displace and move any mucous plug that might have formed.

Usually the clogged tear duct will eventually open on its own, but if it continues to be a problem after six months, talk to your baby's doctor, who may refer you to an ophthalmologist.

Spitting up breast milk or formula is not uncommon during the first weeks of life, and some babies return a little of their feedings for months, sometimes if they are not promptly burped. As long as he is otherwise doing well—gaining weight and making developmental progress—this can be considered a temporary annoyance that will correct itself. However, if a baby in this age-group begins **vomiting**, with stomach contents returning more forcefully, some prompt medical attention is in order.

If there is also a marked increase in the amount of stool (usually indicating that an infection has developed in the intestinal tract), the baby will need careful observation for signs of dehydration. These signs include poor feeding, a decrease in urine output (manifested by fewer wet diapers), sunken eyes, decreased tears or saliva, persistent fussiness or listlessness, and cool or mottled skin. A baby under three months of age with any of these problems should be evaluated immediately.

Projectile vomiting is an alarming event in which the stomach's contents fly an impressive distance. A young baby with this problem should be checked promptly. In a few cases, forceful vomiting is caused by a thickening muscle in the portion of small intestine known as the **pylorus**, just past the stomach, which can begin to cause trouble after the second week of life. This condition, known as **pyloric stenosis**, has traditionally been considered a problem of firstborn males, but a baby of either gender or any birth-order position can be affected. In a young baby with forceful vomiting, a combination of an examination with an ultrasound or an X-ray study of the stomach will usually clarify the diagnosis. If pyloric stenosis is present, surgical correction is a must and should be carried out as soon as possible. The surgery is relatively simple, however, and is very well tolerated by the vast majority of infants.

Settling in at home and getting a good start with your baby's feeding are important accomplishments during the first few weeks of life. But there are other concerns to deal with and new parenting skills to master as you and your baby become better acquainted. In the next chapter we will look at your baby's other important behaviors, especially sleeping and crying; a number of guidelines and ground rules for common-sense baby care; and some survival skills for new parents.

The First Three Months, Part Two: Sleeping, Crying, and Other Newborn Pursuits (. . . and Survival Skills for New Parents)

From the moment you see, touch, and begin to live with your new baby, one basic reality will become abundantly clear: She can do nothing to meet her own needs. She can't feed herself, lift her head, change position, or scratch where she itches. She can—and will—let everyone know when she is unhappy, but she can't communicate exactly what is bothering her.

The fact that she is totally dependent on those who care for her may not sink in until your first day and night at home. Assuming that your baby was born in a hospital, it is likely that nurses and other health-care personnel provided at least some, and perhaps most, of her care. Now you're on your own with this little person who needs you for everything. Don't feel strange if this thought creates a sense of mild anxiety or near panic. Almost every parent has experienced these emotions, along with an unsettling sense of inadequacy. *Am I really up to this task? Have I got what it takes to do this job?*

For many young parents, a combination of grandparents, other relatives, and friends who are baby veterans is available to lend a hand, a few helpful hints, and a shoulder to lean on during these first weeks. Remember, however, that some of the advice you receive from others may not be medically accurate. Grandparents and other relatives may suggest—perhaps with considerable enthusiasm—approaches to baby care that differ from your own or even from your doctor's advice. Many of these are more a matter of style than substance, but if any differences of opinion seem significant, seek input from your baby's physician.

If you are isolated from your family or are a single parent, you may feel as if you're drowning in this new, nonstop responsibility. Most likely your discouragement won't last long, especially as you get used to the basic routines of baby care. *But don't be afraid to seek help if you feel that you are going down for the count.* Your church, a local pregnancy resource center, or even the social-services department of the nearest hospital should be able to provide both emotional and practical support. As we mentioned in the previous chapter, you might also create a short list of the names and numbers of trusted friends or relatives who have offered to be "SOS" resources—people you can call at any hour if you feel you've reached the end of your rope. Keep this list in a handy spot where you can find it at a moment's notice.

Remember that your baby's need for total care has a time limit. Indeed, one of the most important tasks of your child's first two decades will be the gradual process of becoming completely independent of you. As she develops new skills, she will need and want you to do less and less for her—and she'll probably be quite vocal about telling you so. All too soon you will face the ultimate challenge of releasing her to live on her own. During those times of emerging independence, you will find yourself thinking back, perhaps misty-eyed, to the time when she needed you so much.

Special Considerations of a Newborn's Total Dependence

Your baby's total dependence on you has a number of practical as well as emotional ramifications that should be kept in mind as you begin your first weeks of parenthood.

HOLDING A NEWBORN PROPERLY
Hold infant with your hand protecting the child's neck from sudden movement.

Controlling the head

Because a newborn's head is so large relative to his body size—more so than it will ever be in the future—and because his neck muscles are not strong enough to control it, his head must be constantly supported. Allowing it to flop freely in any direction could injure both his head and neck. Always pick him up with two hands, one of which should support and control the baby's head. Once you have picked him up, you can cradle him in one arm with his head resting in your hand. Never pick him up quickly, especially if you don't have control of his head, and *never shake him for any reason, because this can cause brain damage and/or blindness.*

Temperature and clothing

A newborn is less capable of regulating his body temperature than he will be in just a few months. This doesn't mean that he should be bundled in arctic gear twenty-four hours a day or that your thermostat at home should be set at greenhouse levels. Keep his environment at a temperature that's comfortable for you, and dress him in about the same number of clothing layers that you would want for yourself, with a light receiving blanket added during the first few weeks. Typically this will involve a diaper and an infant T-shirt covered by a gown or sleeper set. If the weather is hot and you don't have air-conditioning, you can dispense with everything but the diaper and T-shirt. In cold weather, extra layers will be needed if you take him outside. Because he can lose a considerable amount of heat from the surface of his head, keep it covered when he is outside in chilly weather.

When dressing or undressing your young baby, be careful with his head and hands. Don't pull a shirt or sweater over his head in a way that drags the material forcefully past his skin, ears, and nose. Instead, use your hand to spread the shirt's neck wide open, then maneuver it over his head so there's little if any pressure of the garment against his skin. Once his head is through, don't try to push his hands through the narrow opening of the sleeves. Instead—one sleeve at a time—reach through the opening, gently grasp his hand, and carefully pull the sleeve over it. When removing a top, reverse the procedure, pulling the garment over his hands first and then his head.

Diaper Duty

Before your child passes her final exam in Toilet Training 101, you can look forward to changing about five thousand diapers. (Actually the number may seem more like 43 trillion, especially if you have more than one baby in diapers at the same time.) Since

DIAPERING STEPS
Place baby on diaper with tabs facing up.

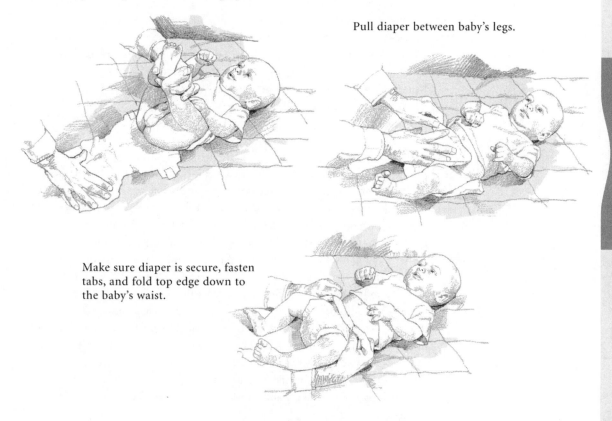

Pull diaper between baby's legs.

Make sure diaper is secure, fasten tabs, and fold top edge down to the baby's waist.

your newborn will need to be changed eight to ten times a day, you'll have plenty of opportunities to practice this skill.

As discussed in chapter 2 ("Developing a Birth Plan and Preparing the Nest"), you'll need to decide whether your baby will spend most of her time in disposable or cloth diapers. You'll also need supplies to clean up dirty bottoms, either small washcloths that can be moistened with warm water or commercial baby wipes, which are convenient when you are away from home. Some babies' skin may be sensitive to fragrances or irritated by the alcohol contained in some wipes, but fragrance free and alcohol free varieties are also available. Baby powder isn't necessary and can be left out of the changing procedure altogether unless your baby's health-care provider recommends it for a moist rash. If you do need to use powder, shake a little into your hand and then apply it directly to the infant's skin. Don't shake out clouds of powder, which can be irritating if inhaled. And keep the powder container out of the reach of older babies and children.

You'll want to check your baby's diaper for moisture or stool every two or three hours when she's awake. You don't need to rouse a sleeping baby if you notice a wet diaper unless you are trying to calm down a rash. Urine alone is normally not irritating, although stool left in contact with skin can provoke a rash because of its acidity.

DEALING WITH DIAPER RASH

Nearly every baby will develop diaper rash at some point. Causes can include:

- Prolonged exposure to urine or stool, especially after solid foods are started.
- Chemical or fragrance irritants in baby wipes, detergents used to wash diapers, or soaps used during bathing. Some babies will even react to the material used in a specific brand of disposable diaper.
- Infections with bacteria or, more commonly, yeast (*Candida*). Yeast infections tend to cause a more intense irritation, often with small extensions or "satellites" around the edges of the rash.

Steps you can take to calm a diaper rash include:

- Change the diaper as soon as possible after it becomes wet or soiled. Once a rash develops, ongoing contact with urine and stool can irritate it further. Superabsorbent diapers, while more convenient, tend to be changed less frequently, which may unintentionally increase contact of urine with skin.
- Try to eliminate other types of irritants. Change to fragrance- and alcohol-free wipes. If you are washing your own cloth diapers, use soap and hot water rather than detergent (this will be marked on the label), and double rinse. If using disposable diapers, try another brand.
- Let your baby's bottom air-dry after it is cleaned. If you feel particularly adventurous, leave it open to the air for a while before putting on a new diaper.
- Ointments such as Desitin or A and D may have a soothing effect. If the rash is severe, your baby's physician may prescribe a mild cortisone cream for a few days. If yeast appears to be involved, an antifungal cream, either alone or in a blend with cortisone, will usually calm the rash within a few days. ■

When it's time to change a diaper, gather all your supplies before you begin. This is particularly important if you are using a changing table. *Remember—you must not walk away from a baby lying on a table or, for that matter, on any open surface above the floor.* Unfasten the diaper while you gently grasp her feet by the ankles and pull them upward to expose the genital area. Use the diaper to remove the bulk of any stool that remains on the baby's skin, and then use your washcloth or wipe to clean the skin. Be careful to cleanse the creases between her legs and upper body. Then lift up her ankles again to slide the new diaper under her bottom, and fasten it into place. A baby girl's bottom should be cleaned from front to back to avoid spreading bacteria from her rectal area to the vagina or urinary tract, and you don't need to wipe between the labia (the folds of skin that border the opening of the vagina) unless stool is present. If you are using diaper pins, keep your finger between the cloth and her skin. If the pin strays, you'll tolerate the point far better than your baby's sensitive abdomen will.

Changing diapers certainly isn't anyone's favorite activity, and the job shouldn't be left solely to Mom. Dad can and should learn to become adept at this task, along with any preadolescent or teenage children at home. Even if you're squeamish about cleaning up stool, avoid making a "yuck" face and groaning at every mess you find. As often as they occur during the day, diaper changes should be times when you communicate love and reassurance, not repulsion (even in fun). Some babies routinely put up a howl during these cleanup sessions, but with rare exception they eventually get used to the process. After two or three months, your baby may even coo at you during diaper changes.

Bathing Your Baby

Aside from daily cleansing of the diaper area, newborns and young babies don't need to be bathed more than two or three times a week. Before the umbilical remnant falls off, don't immerse your baby in water. Instead, give him a simple sponge bath, using a soft washcloth and a basin of warm water (comfortable to your touch) containing a small amount of a mild baby soap.

The remnant of your baby's umbilical cord may generate some goopy material, and for the first several days the area around the umbilical stump should be kept clean and dry. Fold the top of the diaper below the stump so that the stump is exposed to air rather than urine. Check with your baby's doctor about swabbing the base of the stump once or twice daily with rubbing alcohol. Some continue to recommend this time-honored measure, while others suggest forgoing it. (Research has suggested that avoiding the rubbing alcohol may shorten the healing of the stump site by a couple of days.[1]) When you change your baby's diaper, check for

BATHING NEWBORN

and gently remove any debris that might accumulate on or around the stump. Use soap and water on a soft washcloth, then dry it off with a soft dry cloth. The remnant of the cord will shrivel and fall off within two or three weeks—you don't need to pull it off yourself. You may notice small spots of blood at the umbilical site for a few days.

Occasionally, local bacteria will get a foothold at the stump site, generating pus, tenderness, and redness. Contact your baby's physician if this occurs or if there is any persistent swelling and moisture several days after the stump is gone. This area will normally be examined during the first few routine checkups, but be sure to bring it to the practitioner's attention if you don't like the way it looks.

If your baby was circumcised, he may have a small dressing wrapped around the area from which the foreskin was removed. The dressing will normally fall off within a day or two, and it does not need to be replaced. If a Plastibell was used for the circumcision, it will begin to separate after a couple of days. Don't try to pull it off; let it come loose by itself. A small dab of lubricating jelly applied to any moist or raw surfaces will prevent them from sticking to the diaper. Later on, you can use a soft, warm, moist washcloth to remove (gently) any debris that remains on the penis.

You can sponge-bathe your baby while he lies on any surface that is adequately padded. To keep him from losing body heat, cover him with towels, except for the area you are washing. Start with the head, using water only (no soap) around the eyes and mouth. Then, using the washcloth dipped in soapy water, work your way down, saving the diaper area for last. Be sure to cleanse the skin creases of the neck, behind the ears, under the arms, in the groin, and beneath the scrotum in boys.

After the umbilical stump is dry, you can bathe your baby in an infant tub specifically designed for this purpose or even in the sink. As with the sponge bath, water should be comfortably warm but not hot (test with your elbow or wrist) and no more than a couple of inches (a few centimeters) deep. Make sure you have all your supplies (washcloth, soap, shampoo, towel) ready before you undress your baby. If you have forgotten something you need or the phone rings, pick your baby up out of the water and take him with you. *Never leave a baby unattended in a bath, even if it contains only a very small amount of water.*

If he has a dirty diaper at the time you undress him, clean the area as you normally would *before* he goes into the water. You may choose to give him a sponge bath just as you did before the umbilical cord remnant fell off and then rinse him off in the bathwater. If you plan to use shampoo (not necessary with every bath, especially if he isn't endowed with a lot of hair), be sure to control his head so the shampoo and water used to rinse it don't get in his eyes, nose, or mouth.

Your baby will have no interest in rubber ducks or other bath toys at this age. Some babies fuss when put into water, but usually the sensation of warmth and rubbing by a pair of loving hands will have a calming effect. At this age, long baths are neither necessary nor wise since the effect of prolonged contact with water may dry out his skin and cause rashes. (This is also the reason he should not be bathed every day.) In a few months, as he comes to enjoy splashing and playing in water, baths can extend beyond the time it takes to be cleaned.

Because he can lose body heat so quickly when he's wet, be ready to wrap him in a towel as soon as you bring him out of the water. This will also improve the stability of your hold on him. The last thing you want is to have a wet, wiggly baby slip out of your hands.

A Newborn's Skin

A new baby's skin is so sensitive that at times looking at her cross-eyed may seem to provoke a new rash. You will see spots and splotches come and go, especially in the first several weeks, but most don't need special treatment.

The characteristics of newborn skin and some common conditions, including erythema toxicum, milia, and salmon patches, were mentioned in chapter 3. In addition, during the first few weeks, many babies develop pimples on the face, neck, and upper back, which in some cases look like acne. (A full-blown eruption is sometimes referred to as **neonatal acne**.) These pimples most likely are a response to some of Mother's hormones acquired just before birth, and with rare exception they will resolve without treatment. If they become progressively worse, however, have them checked by your baby's health-care provider.

Another common skin problem in early infancy is **seborrheic dermatitis**, an inflammation of those areas of skin where the oil-producing sebaceous glands are most abundant: the scalp, behind the ears, and in the creases of the neck and armpits. The most striking form is **cradle cap**, a crusty, scaly, oily eruption of the scalp, which may persist for months. Fortunately, cradle cap is neither contagious nor uncomfortable, but you can help shorten its appearance with a few simple measures. Washing the hair with a gentle baby shampoo every two or three days, followed by gentle brushing, will remove much of the scaly material. Baby oil applied for a few minutes before shampooing may help soften more stubborn debris, but use it sparingly and be sure to wash all of it off. In more severe cases, your baby's doctor may recommend an antidandruff shampoo. A mild cortisone cream or lotion may also be prescribed, especially if there are patches of seborrhea on other parts of the body.

Another common rash appears on the chin and upper arms and is caused by excessive heat. **Heat rash** produces tiny red bumps rather than overt pimples and can usually be remedied by removing excess clothing.

A newborn's skin is easily dried out by excessive exposure to water, so if her skin seems dry or flaky, you may use a little baby lotion on the affected areas. Stay away from baby oil, which plugs pores and can actually provoke rashes. Keep your new baby completely out of direct sunlight because even very brief exposure can cause sunburn.

A Newborn's Behavior Patterns

As you settle into your routines with a new baby, you'll begin to notice patterns developing in a number of his behaviors. Although a newborn has only a few basic activities that occupy his first days and nights, he will carry them out in ways that are uniquely his. Mothers are often aware of differences between their children well before birth, as they feel the kicks and prods inside. The initial cry, the first waving of arms and legs, the attachment at the breast, and the willingness to cuddle will be some of the first strokes of a unique signature for this person you have brought into the world.

While every child is one of a kind, there are certain common threads and trends in behavior that have been observed in many newborns. Harvard pediatrician T. Berry Brazelton, MD, who has studied and written extensively about newborn behavior, has described three basic types of babies, which he has dubbed "quiet," "active," and "average."

Quiet newborns sleep a lot—up to eighteen hours a day, even while nursing. They may sleep through the night very early and snooze through daytime feedings.

They fuss or cry for about an hour each day and may communicate their needs quietly by sucking on their hands or wriggling in their cribs.

Active newborns behave quite differently. They sleep about twelve hours a day and spend half of what's left crying and fussing. They seem extremely sensitive to the environment, arouse easily, and may be slow to calm. When they're hungry, everyone will know about it. When it's time to nurse, they may clamp onto the breast or bottle frantically, gulping and swallowing air and then burping back a partial refund on whatever went down.

Average babies fall into the middle ground, sleeping fifteen hours or so each day, crying and fussing for about three hours a day. While more reactive to light and sound around them than quiet newborns are, they may calm themselves back to sleep if aroused. They'll let you know whenever they're hungry, but they usually settle fairly quickly when fed.

These are thumbnail sketches rather than detailed portraits, and no baby's behavior will fit precisely into one category or another. Furthermore, these characteristics are not necessarily previews of permanent coming attractions. During their first few days at home, many newborns go through a transition period that is marked either by seemingly endless sleeping or nonstop fussing. They may then shift gears after the first week, behaving quite differently as they adjust to their new surroundings. The newborn who is more active for the first weeks or longer may become much calmer later on, and vice versa.

What is most important for parents to know is that *these patterns are all inborn variations of normal behavior, not the result of child-rearing techniques, the phase of the moon, or the virtues or sins of the parents*. Some newborn behaviors, however, may be altered if drugs or alcohol was used by the mother during pregnancy.

These characterizations of babies should not be taken as value judgments. Because the quiet baby may not seem very demanding, it could be tempting to think of him as "sweet," "good-natured," or "mellow." On the other hand, the active baby might bring to mind a different vocabulary: "a handful," "high-strung," "a real pistol," or "exhausting." In fact, the weary parents who were not prepared for an active baby may find themselves bleary-eyed at 3 a.m., wondering if their child is still under warranty and whether it's too late to trade for another model.

Parents should not waste too many hours gloating over their angelette who sleeps peacefully all the time or reminiscing about the good old days before their baby kept them up for hours every night. The quiet baby may become lost in the shuffle, especially in a house already busy with the activities of older children, unless parents deliberately take the time and effort to interact with him. Worse, his low-key nursing style could lead to an inadequate intake of calories and poor weight gain. If you have a quiet baby, you and the doctor will need to keep a close watch on his weight and possibly deliberately awaken him (at least during the day) to nurse at more frequent intervals. The active baby, on the other hand, for all of his intensity, will tend to be more social and interactive when he's not fussy. He may seem like a "taker" much of the time, especially during the first three months of life, but he will also give back quite a bit to those who hang in there with him.

"Sleeping like a Baby"

This timeworn phrase is reinforced whenever we behold a baby in deep, relaxed sleep. Wouldn't it be nice if we could sleep like that?

Well, not exactly.

During the first three months of life, a baby's sleeping patterns are quite different from those she will experience the rest of her life. A newborn sleeps anywhere from twelve to eighteen hours every day, but this is not unbroken slumber. Her small stomach capacity and her round-the-clock need for nutrients to fuel her rapid growth essentially guarantee that her life will consist of ongoing three- or four-hour cycles of feeding, wakefulness, and sleep. Like it or not, two or three feedings will be on the nighttime agenda for the first several weeks.

Furthermore, the patterns of brain activity during sleep are unique in a newborn. All of us experience cycles of two different types of sleep—rapid eye movement, or REM, and non-REM—throughout the night. During REM sleep, the brain is active with dreams, manifested by movements of the eyes and frequently other body parts as well. We may twitch, roll, or thrash, and we may be more easily awakened if the bed is cold, the bladder full, or the environment noisy. Non-REM sleep, during which little, if any, dreaming takes place, passes through phases of light, deep, and very deep sleep. There is less movement, deeper and slower breathing, and increasing relaxation of muscles when we pass through these stages in repeated cycles throughout the night. Adults spend about one-fourth of their sleep time in REM sleep and the rest in non-REM.

People who say they sleep like a baby usually don't have one.

Rev. Leo J. Burke
(1911–1980)

Babies also manifest these types of sleep but spend equal time in each, alternating about every thirty minutes. During non-REM or quiet sleep, they will appear very relaxed, breathing regularly and moving very little. During REM or active sleep, they seem to come to life, moving arms and legs, changing facial expressions, breathing less regularly, and perhaps making a variety of sounds. They may be experiencing their first dreams during these periods.

Adults and children older than about three months pass through the increasing depths of non-REM sleep before they enter an REM phase. But *newborns reverse this pattern,* starting with a period of REM sleep before moving into non-REM stages. As a result, the new baby who has just fallen asleep may be easily awakened for twenty minutes or more until she moves into her non-REM phases.

This accounts for those character-building situations for some parents in which they feel they are dealing with a little time bomb with a short fuse. A fed, dry, and apparently tired baby fusses and resists but finally succumbs to sleep after prolonged cuddling and rocking. But when placed ever so gently into the cradle or crib, she suddenly startles and sounds off like a fire alarm. The cycle repeats over and over until everyone, baby included, is thoroughly exhausted and frustrated. The problem is that this baby isn't getting past her initial REM phase and happens to be one who is easily aroused out of it. If all else fails, the problem usually will resolve itself by the age of three months, when she shifts gears and enters non-REM sleep first.

Helping a new baby enter the slumber zone

For those parents who don't want to wait twelve weeks, there are two basic but quite different approaches to helping this baby—or, for that matter, any baby—fall asleep. Each approach has advocates who tend to view their ideas as vital to a happy, stable life for both parent and child, while seeing the other as producing troubled, insecure babies. In reality, both have something to offer, and neither will work for every baby-parent combination.

One method calls for parents to be intimately and directly involved in all phases of their baby's sleep. Proponents of this approach recommend that she be nursed, cuddled, rocked, and held continuously until she has fallen asleep for at least twenty minutes.

She can then be put down in her customary sleeping place, which may be Mom and Dad's bed. The primary advantage of this approach is that it can help a baby navigate through drowsiness and REM sleep in the comfort and security of closeness to one or both parents. Those who favor this approach claim that a baby does best when she has more or less continuous contact with a warm body, having just exited from inside of one. Those who challenge this approach argue that she may become so accustomed to being "manipulated" into sleep that she will not be able to fall asleep on her own for months or even years. Every bedtime or nap time will thus turn into a major project, and parents (or whoever is taking care of the baby) will be hostage to a prolonged routine of feeding and rocking well into the toddler years.

The other approach suggests that a baby can and should learn to "self-calm" and fall asleep on her own. Rather than nursing her to sleep, she can be fed thirty to sixty minutes before nap or bedtime and then put down before she is asleep. She may seem restless for fifteen or twenty minutes or even begin crying but will likely settle and fall asleep if left alone. Proponents of self-calming feel this approach frees Mom and Dad from hours of effort to settle their baby and allows the baby to become more flexible and independent without her security being dependent on their immediate presence at all times. Critics argue that leaving her alone in a bassinet or crib represents cruel and unusual treatment at such a young age. Some even suggest that this repeated separation from parental closeness leads to sleep disorders (or worse) later in life.

You may be relieved to know that neither of these methods was carved in stone on Mount Sinai along with the Ten Commandments. You should tailor your approach to your baby's unique temperament and style and to your (and your family's) needs. Whatever you do will probably change over time as well. What works for your first baby may fail miserably for the second, and what helps this month may not the next. When dealing with newborns and very young infants, a fair amount of adjusting and pragmatism are not only wise but necessary. "Let's see if this works" is a much more useful approach than "We have to do it this way," except for a few ground rules dealing with safety.

Most babies give clues when they are ready to sleep—yawning, droopy eyelids, fussiness—and you will want to become familiar with your child's particular signals. If she is giving you these cues, lay her down in a quiet, dimly lit setting and see if she will fall asleep. If she is clearly unhappy after fifteen or twenty minutes, check on her. Assuming that she is fed and dry, comfort her for a while and try again. If your baby is having problems settling herself, especially during the first few weeks of life, do not attempt to "train" her to do so by letting her cry for long periods of time. *During the first few months of life, it is unwise, for many reasons, to let a baby cry indefinitely without tending to her. Babies at this stage of life are not capable of being manipulative and cannot be "spoiled" by adults who are very attentive to their needs.*

If you need to help your new baby transition into quiet sleep, any of these time-honored methods may help:

- Nursing (or a bottle, if using formula) may help induce sleep, especially at the end of the day. However,
  - (a) Don't overfeed with formula or, worse, introduce solids such as cereal at this age in hopes of inducing a long snooze. A stomach that is too full will interfere with sleep as much as an empty one. Solids are inappropriate at this age and will not lengthen sleep.

(b) Never put a baby to bed with a bottle propped in her mouth. Not only can this lead to a choking accident, but it also allows milk to flow into her eustachian tubes (which lead into the middle ears), increasing her risk of ear infections. (Also, an older baby who has become accustomed to going to bed with a bottle of milk or juice will be at risk for developing tooth decay.)

- Rocking gently while you cuddle your baby can calm both of you. If this works for your baby, relax and enjoy it. A comfortable rocking chair is a good investment, by the way, if one hasn't been handed down from earlier generations of your family.
- One alternative to the rocking chair is a cradle—again, rocked smoothly and gently. Another alternative is a baby swing, but it must be one that is appropriately designed for this age-group.
- Many new babies settle more easily if they are swaddled—wrapped snugly in a light blanket.
- Quiet sounds such as the whirring of a small fan (not aimed toward the baby), a tape or CD recording of the ocean, or even small devices that generate monotonous "white noise" may help settle your baby and screen out other sounds in the home. For the musically inclined, there are several lovely anthologies of lullabies, quiet classical music, or gospel songs and hymns that might soothe a fussy baby.
- A gentle touch, pat, or massage may help settle a baby who is drowsy in your arms but squirmy in her bed.
- The gentle vibrations of a car ride are often effective at inducing a baby to fall asleep. Occasionally a frustrated parent who is dealing with a wakeful baby during the night may take her out for a 3 a.m. automobile trip—although this does not guarantee that she will stay asleep once the ride is over. Since staggering out into the night isn't much fun, especially in the dead of winter, some high-tech baby catalogs offer a device that attaches to a crib and simulates the motion of a car. Needless to say, both of these measures should be considered only as last-resort maneuvers for a very difficult sleeper.

All of the above, except for the white noise and the swaddling, involve ongoing parental activity to help settle a baby. In some situations, however, prolonged rocking, jostling, patting, and singing may be counterproductive, keeping a baby awake when she needs *less* stimulation in order to settle down. If a few weeks of heroic efforts to induce sleep don't seem to be working, it may be time to take another look at self-calming. Steps that may help the self-calming process when a baby has been put down but is not yet asleep include the following:

- Guide a baby's flailing hand toward her mouth. Many infants settle effectively by sucking on their hand or fingers.
- Identify a simple visual target for the baby's gaze, such as a single-colored surface; a small, nonbreakable mirror in her crib; or a nearby window or night-light, and place her in a position where she can see it. (Complex visual targets such as moving mobiles or busy patterns may not be as useful for settling during the earliest weeks, especially when a baby is very tired.)
- But make sure she is on her back before falling asleep. This is an important measure to help prevent the tragedy of sudden infant death syndrome (SIDS), as we will discuss in the sidebar on the next page.

What about sleeping through the night?

Newborns do not typically sleep in long stretches during the first several weeks of life, nor do they know the difference between day and night. By two months, however, they are capable of lasting for longer periods without a feeding. Most parents will go through the pulse-quickening experience of awakening at dawn and realizing that the baby didn't sound off in the middle of the night. "Is he okay?" is the first breathless concern, followed by both relief and quiet exultation: "He slept through the night!"

SAFE SLEEP: REDUCING THE RISK OF SUDDEN INFANT DEATH SYNDROME (SIDS)

Sudden infant death syndrome (SIDS), also called **crib death**, has been the subject of intense research for a number of years. SIDS remains the most common cause of death for babies between the ages of one and twelve months in the United States, claiming 2,500 very young lives every year. While the exact cause is uncertain, SIDS appears to represent a disturbance of breathing regulation during sleep that occurs when three types of risk factors converge in a particular infant. (This is sometimes referred to as the "triple risk" model for SIDS.) The three components of infant vulnerability are:

- Subtle abnormalities in areas of the brain stem that regulate respiration, heart rate, body heat, and arousal from sleep
- A critical developmental period—specifically, the first six months of life—during which rapid growth and change may affect the stability of an infant's inner controls of critical functions
- External stressors, such as exposure to tobacco smoke, overheating, sleeping facedown, and/or a recent respiratory infection

SIDS occurs most often between the first and fourth months of life, with a peak incidence between the second and third months.

Ninety percent of cases occur by the age of six months. It is more common in the fall and winter months, perhaps because (at least in some cases) parents overcompensate for cold weather by overheating an infant's room and increasing the layers of clothing and blankets in his sleeping environment. Also, colds and flu, which occur prior to SIDS in a significant number of cases, are more common at this time of year.

SIDS is more common in males with low birth weight and in premature infants of both sexes. African-American and Native American infants are two to three times more likely to die from SIDS than white infants. Breastfed babies, on the other hand, may have a reduced risk. In addition, some potential contributing factors to SIDS can be minimized by taking a few basic preventive measures:

- *Stay completely away from cigarettes during pregnancy, and don't allow anyone to smoke in your home after your baby is born.*
- *Lay your baby down on his back.* For decades, child-care guidebooks recommended that new babies sleep on their stomachs, based on the assumption that this would prevent them from choking on any material they might unexpectedly spit up. However, recent evidence suggests that this position might be a risk factor for SIDS. *Therefore, it is now recommended that a newborn be positioned on his back to sleep.* Since the 1994 initiation of the Back to Sleep campaign—

By three months of age, much to their parents' relief, a majority of babies have established a regular pattern of uninterrupted sleep for seven or eight hours each night. However, some will take longer to reach this milestone. A few actually drift in the wrong direction, sleeping peacefully through most of the day and then snapping wide-awake—often fidgeting and fussing—just when bleary-eyed parents are longing for some rest. If you have a baby who favors the wee hours, you will want to give him some gentle but definite nudges to use the night for sleeping:

a program designed to spread the word that young infants should sleep on their backs—the number of SIDS deaths in the United States has dropped by 40 percent. Similar results have been observed in other countries.

Exceptions to this guideline are made for premature infants, as well as for some infants with deformities of the face that might cause difficulty breathing when lying faceup. In addition, your doctor may advise against the faceup position if your baby spits up excessively. If you have any question about sleeping position, check with your baby's doctor. Sometime after four months of age, your baby will begin rolling over on his own, at which point he will determine his own sleeping positions. By this age, fortunately, SIDS is extremely rare.

- *Put your baby to sleep on a safe surface.* Don't place pillows or any soft bedding material other than a fitted sheet under the baby. His head or face might become accidentally buried in the soft folds (especially if he happens to be facedown), which could lead to suffocation. Sheepskin, down mattresses, and feather beds pose a similar risk. For similar reasons, don't put your baby to sleep on a wavy water bed or beanbag chair. On one of these plastic surfaces, a baby whose face shifts to the wrong position could suffocate.
- *Don't overbundle your baby.* Overcompensating for the cold of winter by turning up the thermostat and wrapping a baby in several layers of clothing should be avoided. If he looks or feels hot and sweaty, start peeling off layers until he appears more comfortable.
- *Offer your baby a clean, dry pacifier when he is going to sleep.* A convincing body of recent research has associated pacifier use with a dramatic reduction in the risk of SIDS.

A few parents experience the terror of seeing their baby stop breathing, either momentarily or long enough to begin turning blue. It is obviously important in such cases to begin infant CPR and call 911 if he does not start breathing on his own (see Emergency Care, page 836). A careful evaluation by your doctor or at the emergency room is mandatory. It is also likely that this baby will be sent home with an **apnea monitor**, which will sound off if a breath is not taken after a specified number of seconds.

Parents who have suffered the loss of an infant for any reason must work through a profound grieving process. When SIDS is the cause, they may also feel a great sense of guilt as well as great anxiety over the safety of their other children. It is important that they obtain support from family, church, and if available, a local support group for families who have dealt with such a loss. ■

- Make a specific effort to increase his awake time during the day. Don't let him fall asleep during or right after eating, but instead provide some gentle stimulation. Talk or sing to him, lock eyes, change his clothes, play with his hands and feet, rub his back, or let Grandma coo over him. Don't make loud noises to startle him, and do not under any circumstances shake him. (Sudden movements of a baby's head can cause physical damage to the brain.) Let him nap only after he has been awake for a while after nursing. This can also help prevent a baby from becoming dependent on a feeding to fall asleep.

- If your baby is sleeping for long periods during the day and fitfully at night, consider gently awakening him while he is in one of his active sleep phases when a nap has lasted more than three or four hours.

- By contrast, make nighttime interactions—especially those middle-of-the-night feedings—incredibly boring. Keep the lights low, the conversation minimal, and the diaper change (if needed) businesslike. This is not the time to party.

- Remember that babies frequently squirm, grunt, and even seem to awaken briefly during their REM sleep phases. Try to avoid intervening and interacting with him during these times because you may unknowingly awaken your baby when he was just shifting gears into the next phase of sleep. This may require some adjusting of your sleeping arrangements.

- If your baby tends to awaken by the dawn's early light and you don't care to do likewise, try installing shades or blinds to block out the first rays of sunlight. Don't assume that his rustling around in bed necessarily means he is waking up for good. Wait for a while before tending to him because he may go back to sleep. Sometimes, however, he will wake up with the local roosters no matter what you do, at which point you may want to consider adjusting your schedule to follow the famous "early to bed, early to rise" proverb until a few more months pass.

- During these early weeks of nighttime feedings and daytime naps, it may be necessary to "sleep when the baby sleeps" in order to get an adequate amount of rest. This may be challenging when there are other tasks that need to be done. But if you're exhausted, your baby's daytime naps may be a much-needed opportunity to recharge your own batteries. You may even try to synchronize your newborn's and older sibling's naptime(s). If you succeed, give yourself permission to take the phone off the hook and lie down.

Where should your baby sleep?

By the time your baby arrives home for the first night, you will have had to address a basic question: Will she sleep in her own room, in a cradle or bassinet next to your bed, or in your bed right next to you? There are advocates for each of these arrangements.

Those who espouse sleeping with your baby (often called **co-sleeping** or **shared sleep**) point out that this is widely practiced throughout the world and claim that it enhances parent-infant bonding, facilitates breastfeeding, and gives the newborn a sense of security and comfort she won't feel in a crib. Shared-sleep advocates also argue that this practice reduces the risk of sudden infant death syndrome (SIDS), although the National Institute of Child Health and Human Development states that there is no scientific proof to support this claim.[2]

Furthermore, in 2002, the U.S. Consumer Product Safety Commission (CPSC) issued a warning about the potential hazards of infants sleeping in adult beds, citing reports of more than one hundred deaths of children under the age of two during a three-year period.[3] Proponents of shared sleep contended that the CPSC's information was misleading and that this arrangement is safe if certain safety guidelines are followed. Needless to say, it is critical that parents who desire to share their bed with an infant take careful note of these precautions (see sidebar below).

Critics of shared sleep have also raised other concerns about the potential disruption of parental sleep, intimacy, and privacy. New babies don't quietly nod off to sleep at 10 p.m. and wake up calmly eight hours later. They also don't typically sleep silently during the few hours between feedings. As they pass through their REM sleep phases, they tend to move around and make all sorts of noises, often sounding as if they're waking up. All of this activity isn't easy to ignore, especially for new parents who tend to be tuned in and concerned, if not downright worried, about how their new arrival is doing. Unless you learn to screen out these distractions and respond to your infant only when she is truly awake and in need of your attention, you may find yourself woefully short on sleep and patience within a few days.

IF YOU ARE GOING TO SHARE YOUR BED WITH AN INFANT . . .

Elsewhere in this chapter we outline several measures to reduce the risk of sudden infant death syndrome (SIDS). One of the key points is that an infant needs a **safe sleep environment** in which suffocation or disrupted breathing is unlikely to occur. Critics of shared sleep argue that the parents' bed is more likely to be unsafe than a properly equipped crib. Proponents claim otherwise, provided that a number of important safeguards are followed.

In one sense, the critics are right: Many common sleeping environments for older children or adults are not appropriate for infants. *If you are thinking about co-sleeping with your baby, you must be willing and able to abide strictly with all of the following:*

- You must use a wide bed with a firm mattress. Do not sleep with your baby on a water bed, sofa, or beanbag chair.
- Do not use fluffy bedding or cover your baby with your comforter.
- Your baby must sleep on her back.
- There must not be any gaps between the mattress and a wall or bed frame in which your baby might become trapped.
- The baby should sleep next to her mother but not between her mother and father.
- Don't let your baby fall out of bed. If the baby is going to be positioned on the side of the mattress from which she could potentially fall, use a mesh guardrail that fits flush against the mattress.
- Do not sleep with your baby if you are using alcohol, sedatives, sleeping pills, or any medication that might affect your ability to awaken.
- Don't sleep with your baby if you are a smoker. The risk of sudden infant death syndrome associated with co-sleeping is significantly higher among smokers. Important: Exposure to cigarette smoke increases *any* baby's risk of dying of SIDS.
- Older siblings or babysitters should not sleep with the baby.
- Don't leave a baby sleeping unattended in an adult bed. ▪

The other issue to consider is the effect on the mother and father's relationship. If Mom and Dad are equally enthused about having a new bedmate, great. But many young couples aren't prepared for the demands a new baby may place on them and especially on a mother who may have little energy left at the end of the day for maintaining her relationship with her husband. A father who feels that his wife's attention is already consumed by the baby's needs may begin to feel completely displaced if the baby is in their bed too.

Many parents prefer to place their newborn in a cradle next to their bed. This arrangement allows for both a safe sleep environment and a close proximity to Mom that facilitates breastfeeding. The baby can be fed when she first becomes aroused by hunger, though parents may find themselves awakened repeatedly through the night by their baby's assorted movements and noises during sleep. They will also have to fine-tune their responses in order to avoid intervening too quickly during a restless period, which can accidentally interrupt a baby's transition from active to quiet sleep.

Parents who are contemplating having their baby sleep in another room (whether during the newborn period or after the first few months of life) may wonder whether they will hear her if she needs them. They can be assured that an infant who is truly awake, hungry, and crying during the night is difficult to ignore. And new parents, especially moms, are uniquely tuned in to their baby's nighttime vocalizing: They will normally awaken at the first sounds of crying, even after sleeping through louder sounds such as the rumble of a passing truck. On the other hand, as we noted in the previous chapter, crying is a late sign of hunger in the newborn, and it is often easier (for all concerned) if you nurse or feed an infant before she reaches a point of frantic crying.

If you are truly concerned about hearing your baby when she first begins to cry, you can purchase an inexpensive wireless electronic baby monitor, which will allow you to hear what's happening in the nursery long before crying reaches even a modest intensity. In fact, the monitors can be so sensitive that you may find yourself hearing (and possibly being kept awake by) "false alarms" as your baby stirs and makes a variety of sounds without actually awakening, just as if she were in the room with you. And, like the rooming-in arrangement, you will have to train yourself not to respond immediately to every rustle or chirp you hear over the speaker because you may unintentionally awaken a baby who is simply transitioning from one phase of sleep to another. On the other hand, it would be unwise to leave your baby in a place where you would be totally unable to hear her and then rely on a monitor to be your electronic ears. If the monitor failed for some reason, your baby might lie uncomfortable, crying, and unattended for an extended period of time.

As with the techniques you choose to help your baby settle down to sleep, you will need to determine which sleeping arrangements work best for your family and be flexible about the various possibilities. Moreover, it is important that parents keep their communications about this subject open with each other. If Mom is the one getting up to nurse a fussy baby and as a result spends more hours in the baby's room than in her own bed, Dad may need to assume a larger share of the nighttime duties. He could, for example, bring the baby to Mom for nursing and then return her to her crib when the feeding is done. Similarly, if Dad is feeling an increasing distance from Mom because of a baby in their bed, Mom may need to be willing to empty the nighttime nest of offspring.

One of the tricky issues for parents who share their bed with one or more children is deciding when and how to reclaim their bed for themselves. Most children are more than happy to sleep with Mom and Dad well into or beyond their toddler years, and making the transition to their own bed may be easier said than done. Parents who routinely allow one or more babies and children in bed with them for months or years should regularly take stock of the effect this custom is having on their marriage. Regaining sexual intimacy after the birth of a child normally requires some time and effort for both parents. It may be far more challenging if there are more than two bodies in the marriage bed.

Crybabies: What Happens When the Tears Won't Stop?

One of the greatest mental and emotional adjustments new parents must make is sorting out the meanings of, and their responses to, the new baby's crying. In most cases, crying is a clear signal that a stomach is empty or a diaper full, and the appropriate response will quiet it. Even in these routine circumstances, however, the newborn cry has distinct qualities—insistent, edgy, and downright irritating. Indeed, it can sound almost like an accusation—"I don't like the care you're giving me!"

Lord, you are our Father. We are the clay, you are the potter; we are all the work of your hand.

Isaiah 64:8

If your new baby's cry gives you a twinge of discomfort or even annoyance, don't panic; your response is quite normal. If you're a mother acutely short on sleep and sore in body (especially if you've had a cesarean delivery), with hormones shifting in all directions, you may find yourself harboring some troubling thoughts about your crying newborn. These feelings can enter the minds of even the most dedicated parents.

How should you feel about and deal with your baby's crying? First of all, it's important to understand the function of crying. Remember that a newborn baby is totally helpless and cannot do *anything* for himself other than suck on a breast or bottle given to him (or one or two of his own fingers that have accidentally found their way into his mouth). Unless someone meets his most basic needs on an ongoing basis, he will not survive. Crying is his only means—but a very effective one—of provoking a parent into action. It's *designed* to be annoying and irritating, to create all sorts of unpleasant feelings, especially among those closest to him. The responses that usually stop the crying—food, clean diapers and clothing, cuddling and cooing—are what keep him alive.

During these first three months of your baby's life, assume that when he cries, it's for a good reason. His crying is definitely not a deliberate effort to irritate you, manipulate you, or test parental limits. Therefore, it is appropriate to take action in response to your baby's crying as opposed to ignoring it and hoping it will go away. *You cannot spoil a baby at this young age,* and for now it is far better to err on the side of giving too much attention than too little. He needs comfort, open arms, and ongoing love from those around him, even though he cannot express any signs of gratitude or even pleasure in response to all you give him. This is not the time for any misguided attempts to "train, mold, and discipline" your child. (In several months you will begin to have plenty of opportunities to carry out that important assignment.)

What is your baby trying to tell you when he cries? Most likely, one of these things:

- He's hungry and wants to be fed.
- He has a wet or dirty diaper.
- He's wet, hot, cold, or uncomfortable in some other way.
- He wants to be held.

- He's had too much stimulation and needs a quieter environment for a while.
- He's ready to go to sleep.

At some point, usually between two weeks and three months, there will be at least one occasion when you suspect that something has gone terribly wrong. Just a day or so ago you could comfort your baby regularly and predictably. A feeding every few hours, dry diapers, and a little rocking and cooing would end crying fairly quickly. Now, however, he starts fussing late in the afternoon or early in the evening, and nothing works for an hour . . . or two . . . or three. Or he suddenly lets out an ear-piercing wail or screams for no apparent reason in the middle of the night. What's going on? You may never know for sure. But it may help if you understand that many babies cry like this now and then, some do it every day, and a few seem determined to set a world record for the longest crying episode in history.

Dealing with colic

According to a long-standing definition, if your baby cries three hours a day three days a week for three weeks, and he's between two weeks and three months of age, he has **colic**. A simpler definition, without counting hours and days (and more to the point), is "a whole lot of crying that doesn't calm down with the normal measures, and the doctor says there's nothing really wrong with him." True colicky episodes tend to occur around the same time each day, usually in the late afternoon or evening, and are marked by intense activity on the baby's part, such as flailing about or pulling his knees to his chest. From all appearances, he acts like he's feeling a lot of discomfort—and undoubtedly he is.

The classic theories about the cause of colic have assumed that the baby's intestinal tract is at fault—that it goes into uncontrollable spasms, perhaps because of immaturity or a reaction to something in Mom's milk or the current formula. Other proposed explanations include a problem interacting with parents, often assuming that Mother is tense or high-strung, and as a result the baby is also. But changing feeding patterns or formulas may or may not help, and colicky babies may land in families that are intact or disjointed, relaxed or uptight. Basically, a universal cause for colic has yet to be determined.

If your baby begins having long stretches of crying, you will need to address two basic concerns:

1. Does he have a medical problem?
2. How is everyone—baby included—going to get through this?

The first question needs to be answered relatively quickly because a medical illness can be a much more serious problem during the first three months of life than when the baby is older. Some indicators of a disturbance that might need a physician's care include:

- Any fever over 100.4°F (38°C) taken with a rectal thermometer (see sidebar, page 135)
- Poor sucking at the breast or bottle
- Change in color from normal pink to pale or bluish (called **cyanosis**) during feeding or crying

- Overt vomiting, as opposed to spitting up (When a baby spits up, the partially digested food burps into his mouth and dribbles down his chin and clothes. When he vomits, this material becomes airborne or is voluminous.)
- A marked increase in the amount and looseness of bowel movements
- Unusual jerking movements of the head, eyes, or other muscles that you don't recall seeing before

If any of these occur, you should contact your physician, and your baby should be checked—especially if he has a fever. If he is crying up a storm but seems okay otherwise, he should still have a medical evaluation, either as part of a routine checkup or at an appointment specifically for this purpose. The more specific information you can give the doctor, the better. When did the crying start? How long does it last? Does anything seem to set it off? Is it improved or worsened after a feeding? Are there any other symptoms?

Assuming your baby is doing well otherwise (gaining weight, arriving at his developmental milestones more or less on time, showing no apparent signs of medical illness), your primary tasks during his crying episodes are to *be there* for him and to make ongoing efforts to comfort him. *You are not a failure, and you should not give up if your measures do not succeed in stopping the crying.* Eventually each crying episode will end, and the crying season overall will come to a close, in nearly all cases by the third to fourth month of age.

So what do you do for a colicky baby, assuming that he is fed, dry, and not sick? You can try any or all of the following, once or many times. If a particular measure helps one time but doesn't the next, don't panic. You may get impressive results today with something that failed miserably last week.

Soothing movements. Gentle rocking or swaying in someone's arms is a time-honored baby comforter. Unfortunately, when a baby is wailing at full volume, you may unconsciously begin moving faster or more forcefully—but you should *avoid rapid, jerky movements,* which not only make the problem worse but may even injure the baby. Cradles and baby swings that support the body and head can also provide this type of movement.

Soothing sounds. Provide humming, gentle singing, white noise, or pleasant recorded music.

Soothing positions. Some colicky babies respond to being held tummy-down against your forearm like a football or across your thigh. Others seem to calm down while being carried close to Mom's or Dad's body in a baby sling. Swaddling in a light blanket and resting on one side or the other might help.

Soothing environments. Spending time in a quiet, dimly lit room can help calm a baby who may be in sensory overload at the end of the day. Turn down the TV and unplug the phone if you have to.

Soothing trips. A ride in the car or a stroller may provide the right mix of gentle movement and sound to soothe the crying.

Soothing touch. Gentle touching or stroking of the back, stomach, or head may help.

Soothing sucking. Nursing may seem to calm the crying, even if he just had a feeding. A pacifier may also work. If your baby doesn't seem satisfied by any of your feedings, you should check with his physician and possibly a lactation consultant as well. This is particularly important if he's not gaining adequate weight because the problem may be that his hunger is never satisfied. If your colicky baby is formula-fed, you may at some point want to try a different brand or a different type of formula—for example, switching from cow's milk to soy-based formula. (Check with your baby's health-care provider on this.) Sometimes a change will bring about some noticeable improvement.

Self-soothing. Sometimes all the rocking, singing, touching, and pacifying maneuvers unwittingly overload the baby's capacity to handle stimulation. The self-soothing measures mentioned in the previous section on sleep (page 153) may work wonders when everything else has failed.

What can you do for yourself while all of this is going on?

Keep reminding yourself that "this too will surely pass." You will deal with crying problems for only a short period of your child's life. Believe it or not, before you know it there will come a time when you'll wonder where all those baby years went.

If you find yourself reaching the end of your rope, don't take it out on the baby. Mounting frustration and anger are indications that you need a brief time-out. If that time arrives, don't allow yourself to become a martyr or a child abuser. Sounding off verbally at the baby will accomplish nothing, and *you must not carry out any physical act of anger*—picking him up or putting him down roughly, shaking him, hitting him, or anything else that inflicts pain or injury—no matter how upset you may feel. Instead, put him in his cradle or crib and *walk away* for fifteen or twenty minutes until you have a chance to collect your thoughts and calm down. It won't hurt him to cry by himself for that period of time, and you can then try comforting him again. He may have expended enough energy to become more responsive to calming efforts at this point. If necessary, call a friend or relative and get your frustration off your chest, or let someone else come look after your baby for a while (see sidebar on next page).

A famous Erma Bombeck quote: "Never go to a doctor whose office plants have died." A Dave Barry quip about parenting: "I've noticed that one thing about parents is that no matter what stage your child is in, the parents who have older children always tell you the next stage is worse."

If at all possible, husband and wife should pass the baton during a prolonged crying episode. Let Dad hold the baby while Mom takes a walk around the block and vice versa. Single moms—and for that matter, married ones—shouldn't be embarrassed to seek help from an experienced relative or friend. If Grandma wants to help you for a while during a rough evening, by all means let her do it. She may have a few tricks up her sleeve that aren't in any book.

Try to find some humor in all this to maintain your perspective. Pretend you are the next Erma Bombeck or Dave Barry (both of whom have brought smiles to millions with their wry observations about everyday life) and jot down some of your observations. If you have one or more books that have made you laugh out loud, by all means keep them close at hand.

Try to maintain "self-preservation" activities as much as possible. A quiet time for reflection and prayer may have to occur during a feeding, but it will provide important perspective and strength. Having a world-class wailer is a humbling experience, and it is during these rough times that special intimacy with God often develops. The question to ask Him isn't "Why did You give me such a fussy baby?!" but "What do You want me to learn about myself and life in general through this experience?" You may be surprised at the answer.

If you have "gone the distance," repeatedly trying every measure listed here (and perhaps a few others as well) without success, check back with your baby's doctor. Be prepared to give specific information—for example, how many hours the baby has been crying, not just "He won't stop!" Depending upon your situation and the baby's crying pattern, another medical evaluation may be in order.

Milestones and Memories

Even though nursing, sleeping, and crying may dominate the landscape during the first several weeks, you'll be happy to know that your baby will also be taking in all kinds of information and learning new ways to respond to it. Young babies manifest six

TO GRANDPARENTS AND OTHER PARENT SUPPORTERS: THE GIFT OF TIME

If you have experience as a parent, whether recently or in the more distant past, one of the greatest gifts you can offer a relative or friend with a fussy baby is a brief respite. This is particularly important for single moms, but even a married mother may have a husband who isn't much help when the baby is having full-throttle colic. And a baby who cries nonstop can wear out both Mom and Dad before much time has passed.

The sound of someone else's baby crying is not nearly as nerve-racking as it is for the mother or father of the child. You may also be able to model some perspective, a reminder of the preciousness of this new life, by cooing and fussing over a baby who may not seem very lovable to her parents at this particular moment.

Take the initiative in asking a new parent how life with the new arrival is going, and in particular if there are any problems with fussing and crying. If you have time, energy, and child-rearing skills, offer to look after the baby for a while. You might suggest a specific time ("How about if I come over tomorrow or Wednesday night around six so you can get out for a couple of hours?") rather than something vague ("Let me know if I can help you"), which may be more difficult to accept without sounding utterly desperate. Your offer to provide a time-out for a frazzled parent may be far more valuable than any baby-shower gift.

If you know a new parent with a particularly fussy baby and you're willing to make a priceless offer, give the mom or dad a piece of paper with your phone number and instructions to call at any time—24-7—if one or both feel they have reached the end of their rope. This is particularly meaningful if you've been there yourself in the past and they know that you understand how awful it feels when nothing seems to calm a crying baby. It is likely that merely having this note at their bedside may get them through some very tough times, even if they rarely or never call. ■

different levels of consciousness: quiet sleep, active sleep, drowsiness, quiet alertness, active alertness, and crying.

Quiet alertness occupies about 10 percent of your baby's time at first, but you will want to watch for these moments of calm attentiveness, during which you can begin to have some genuine interaction. Enjoy them, file them in your memory bank, and if you have time, you may want to jot your impressions in a personal journal. As the weeks pass, you will begin to notice that your baby is spending more time in calm and active alertness, during which you will see several wonderful developments in a variety of areas:

Vision. During the first few weeks, a baby focuses best on objects eight to fifteen inches (about 20 to 40 cm) from her face. You may find her staring intently at the fist at the end of her outstretched arm, which happens to be in her focusing range. She will prefer to study plain, high-contrast, black-and-white images such as stripes, checks, or spirals, or a simple drawing of a face. She may gaze intently into a small, unbreakable mirror attached to the inside of her crib. But her favorite subject to scrutinize will be the face of another person, about a foot away from hers. She will not respond directly to a smile for a few weeks, but a lot of smiles are what she should see.

Your baby will be able to follow an object with her eyes only momentarily at first. You can give her some practice at this ability by moving your face or a brightly colored object slowly from side to side across her field of vision. Around two months of age, she will be able to coordinate her eye movements to stay locked on an interesting visual target that passes through a semicircle in front of her. She will also be interested in more complex shapes and patterns and will be able to hold her head steady enough to fixate on simple, high-contrast objects hung from a mobile over her crib. By three months of age, her distant vision will be increased to the point that she will recognize you halfway across a room.

Responses to color also develop over the first several weeks. At first she will pay attention to objects with bright, strongly contrasting colors. Ironically, the soft colors that are so often used in decorating a baby's room won't be particularly interesting to her at first. It will take a few months before her color vision has matured enough to distinguish a full palette and varieties of shades.

From time to time, all babies will briefly cross their eyes as they develop their tracking skills. But if she frequently appears to have crossed eyes at the age of three months or later, she should be checked as soon as possible by her physician and an ophthalmologist. Why is this important? If the position of her eyes is constantly presenting two images instead of one to her brain, she will shut down the information arriving from one eye or the other, resulting in **amblyopia**, or lazy eye. (See "eye care and concerns" in Reference Section, pages 661–662, for information about cross-eye and amblyopia.)

Hearing. Newborns vary in their sensitivity to sounds. Some infants seem capable of sleeping through a violent thunderstorm, while others appear to startle when a cat crosses the street a block away. If a young infant is placed in a very noisy environment, he may appear to "shut down," markedly reducing his activity level. This is a protective mechanism, an internal withdrawal from a situation that is overloading him. While you don't need to maintain a hushed silence around your newborn, you should try to keep the noise level around him at a comfortable level—no more than, for example, the intensity of pleasant conversation between two or three people. If you want to go to a ball game or a concert (or even a church service) where the sound is likely to be pumped up, leave the baby at home.

Within a few weeks, he will appear to pay attention to certain sounds, especially the voices of those who regularly care for him. By two months of age, he may begin to shift his eyes and head toward your voice. He may also show some movements and expressions indicating that he recognizes this familiar and comforting sound. As he continues toward three months of age, you will notice him starting to turn toward other interesting sounds, such as a tinkling bell. If the sound is repeated over and over, however, he will tune it out and stop responding to it.

Smell. A very young baby is capable of responding to a variety of smells and can distinguish the smell of his mother's breast from those of other nursing mothers by the end of the first week of life.

Touch. All of us are strongly affected by touch, but a baby is particularly sensitive. She will startle in response to scratchy surfaces, rough handling, or sudden temperature changes—especially when her skin makes contact with something cold. Cuddling, caressing, and stroking may help calm a crying episode, but these shouldn't be used merely to stop tears. Touch is an important expression of love and will nourish her emotions before she can understand any words. It should be as routine a part of her day as her feedings.

These developments set the stage for your baby's first true **socializing**, which will probably begin just as you are starting to wonder whether all the nursing and diapers and nonstop caregiving are worth it. You may first notice a brief flicker of a grin after a feeding. Was that a smile or a gas pain? Maybe it was both or maybe neither, but it felt like a puff of fresh air on a hot day. Suddenly—at about the age of four to six weeks—it will be unmistakable: You will lock eyes with your baby, and a big grin will flash across her face. It will be an unforgettable moment, and the next time she smiles will be equally rewarding because you'll know that this milestone was for real.

Over the next month, you will catch smiles in response to your own grinning, cooing, talking, or singing to your baby. You may notice special enthusiastic body movements in response to familiar voices and the turning of eyes and head to seek them out. Even more pleasant are your first "conversations." At about two months, your baby will begin to coo, often in response to your speaking to her in soft, soothing tones. At this age, she will not understand the words you speak, but the tone of your voice will communicate volumes.

Even at this young age, your baby may show some selectivity in her responses. Not everyone will necessarily receive the big grin and happy sounds. More often than not, it will go to the most familiar faces and voices. Your baby is already starting to sort out who is important in her life, so whoever wants to be included in that category will need to log some time with her. This is particularly important for fathers, who may find it harder to interact with a squirmy two-month-old than an older child who likes to "wrestle" on the carpet or play catch. Mothers who are weighing decisions about work outside the home also need to ponder how much time the baby should spend with other caregivers.

Growth and movement. Babies lose and then regain several ounces (about a tenth of their birth weight) during the first ten days of life. From then on, you can anticipate a weight gain of about two-thirds to one ounce per day, or one to two pounds per month (20 to 30 gm per day, or 450 to 900 gm per month). Your baby will add between one and one and a half inches (or about 2.5 to 4 cm) in height each month as well. These amounts will vary, of course, depending on your baby's feeding patterns and on genetics, which will affect whether this growing body will ultimately resemble a ballerina or a fullback. During each medical checkup, your baby's height, weight, and head circumference will be measured and then plotted on a growth chart. Tracking your baby's growth will be an important tool for her health-care provider to confirm how well she is doing.

During the first three months, you will see dramatic changes in your baby's movement patterns. At birth her arms and legs flail and jerk, her chin may twitch, and her hands may tremble. Many of her movements are reflexes, such as rooting, sucking, and grasping. In addition, you may see her do a "fencing" maneuver known as the **tonic neck reflex**: If her head is turned in one direction, you may see the arm on that side straighten and the other arm flex, as if she were about to enter a sword fight. In addition, if you gently hold her body upright, supporting her head, and then lower her gently until her feet touch a firm surface, she will begin stepping motions. This has nothing to do with how soon she will begin walking, and this so-called **stepping reflex** will be gone by the age of two months. However, she will kick her legs quite vigorously when awake and active while lying on her back or stomach.

Hand and arm movements will gradually become less jerky and almost appear purposeful. Between two and three months, she will begin to spend more time with her hands open rather than clenched and will bring them toward her mouth or in front of her face, where she may appear to study them. She still won't have the coordination to reach directly for something that interests her, although she will tightly grasp a small object placed in her hand. In fact, you may have to help her let it go.

At two months she will have developed enough control of her neck muscles to hold her head in one position while lying on her back. When lying on her stomach, she will be able to raise her head briefly, just long enough to turn it from one side to another. But her head control overall will not be secure until three to four months of age, so you must support her head whenever you hold or carry her.

Other people in your baby's life

Just as it is important for you to handle your newborn carefully and appropriately, any older brothers or sisters in the family will need to be supervised during their interactions with the baby. They should have been given plenty of advance warning, in language they could understand, about the sibling on the way, and perhaps they will have had a chance to say hello to her while Mom was still in the hospital. For very young children, fascination with the wiggly little person will be mixed with an overriding concern about whether there is enough love to go around.

With everyone oohing and aahing over the new baby, your toddler or preschooler may conclude that the best way to get attention is to act like the baby. You may notice him trying to climb into the baby's crib or suddenly forgetting all his potty-training skills. Rather than spending a lot of energy rebuking this behavior, take time to affirm his capabilities and point out some of the advantages of being older. ("You're such a big boy now—you can go to the park and ride on the swings! The baby is too little to do that.") He needs reassurance that he is special and unique, and he needs one-on-one time with Mom and Dad. If Mom is worn out or recovering from surgery, Dad or a grandparent should be prepared to take on this assignment.

Equally (if not more) important is the need to ensure the new baby's safety around children who are not likely to be well versed in the details of newborn care. Toddlers and preschoolers who want to touch and caress the new baby must be shown how to do so gently, avoiding the baby's eyes, nose, and mouth, and they should be clearly told that they can only touch the baby while Mom or Dad is there watching them. They should not be allowed to carry a new baby, play any of their physical games with the baby, or touch the baby with anything but their hands that have just been washed. If they have runny noses or a cough, they'll need to wait until the illness is gone before getting near the baby.

If you see an older sibling talking or acting aggressively toward a new baby, immediately separate the two, find out what's going on, and make certain the issue (usually jealousy) is settled before allowing any further contact. Small children, especially if they are upset (for whatever reason), are quite capable of injuring babies, whether or not they fully realize what they are doing. One- and two-year-olds are particularly incapable of processing the moral and physical reasons they should not act aggressively toward a baby, although it is appropriate to define limits for them in this as in other arenas (see chapters 7 and 8, pages 203 and 234). Parents and other caregivers will thus need to remain constantly on guard to protect a young infant from the older sibling—who was himself a baby not long ago.

The same rules about colds and acute illnesses apply to relatives and friends who may want to handle your baby. Because her immune system is not as competent as it will be in a few months, you should be careful to expose her to as little risk of infection as possible. This means that, at the risk of upsetting a well-meaning friend or relative, you may need to be firm about keeping your new baby away from anyone with an acute infection, especially one involving sneezing and coughing (which can easily spread contaminated droplets). Adults and older children will have a much easier time getting over their temporary disappointment than your newborn will have recovering from an acute infection. Your protective stance for the first two to three months of your baby's life should also include keeping her out of crowds in general and group nurseries in particular, unless it is absolutely necessary to do otherwise. (Don't hesitate to say that the doctor advised you to take these precautions to protect your baby from infections; it's sometimes easier for others to accept these restrictions if they come from a medical authority.)

Don't hesitate to ask well-wishers to come back at a later date if you are feeling overwhelmed by all your new responsibilities. If the baby is fussy and you're running on empty with too little sleep, keep visitors to a minimum, place a polite sign on the door asking not to be disturbed, and let the answering machine take care of incoming calls so you can get some extra rest. You'll have plenty of time to socialize and show off your pride and joy in the coming months.

CHAPTER 6

Three to Six Months: Expanding Horizons

As your baby grows and slowly graduates from the newborn stage, you will find your-self entering a phase of increased enjoyment and satisfaction in parenting. During these months, your baby will progress from being a pure "taker" of your love and energy to a "giver" as well, someone who can flash a smile and carry on irresistible interactions with nearly anyone who will give him the time of day. For a baby, these months are full of intense exploration. No longer restricted to crying as his only method of gaining atten-tion, your baby is now finding all sorts of new ways to investigate and affect what goes on around him. While he isn't exactly capable of propelling himself out the front door while your back is turned, his wondrous new skills will create some safety challenges.

Physical Developments: Arms, Legs, and Bodies in Motion

During his first three months, one of your baby's major accomplishments was simply learning to keep his head still enough to focus on an object or track a moving object with his eyes. Now he is starting to use larger muscle groups that will eventually allow him to sit up on his own. This begins with more decisive head control, which you will notice when he is lying on his stomach while awake. He will make a more deliberate effort to keep his head elevated so he can see what's going on in front of him. You can encour-age the exercise of these upper back and neck muscles by placing a small toy or brightly colored object—or your smiling face—in front of him while he is in this position.

He will then progress to lifting his entire upper chest, with or without help from his arms. When he combines this with vigorous kicking, you will see surprisingly active rocking, and by five or six months, the right combination of movements will send him rolling over front to back. Rolling back to front will not be far behind. (A few babies roll back to front first.) Invariably, he will accomplish this skill for the first time when you least expect it, so never leave him alone on any elevated surface, such as a bed or changing table, or he may add free-falling to his new movement experiences.

At this stage he will enjoy being propped on pillows in a sitting position, although he must be watched because he can easily topple forward. He will soon figure out how to sit in a hunched position with one or both hands on the floor, precariously maintaining his balance. He can still topple easily, so make sure his landing will be on a soft surface. At six months of age at the earliest, he will be able to maintain a sitting position without using his hands, although he is still a few months away from maneuvering himself into a sitting position.

Another adventure for him at this age is being held by the upper body and "standing" in someone's lap. Most babies love to flex their legs and bounce up and down, as if ready to bear their weight in a standing position. They are, of course, nowhere near achieving this milestone, and the playful bouncing won't bring it along any sooner. But it also won't cause any harm to growing muscles and bones. However, you should not suspend or lift a baby's full weight by holding his hands or arms.

Your baby's ability to use his hands will develop dramatically during these three months. As a newborn, he spent most of his time with his little fists clenched and could only respond with a tight reflex grip to objects placed in his hands. Now he will spend more time with open palms, and more important, he will begin to reach deliberately toward interesting things that catch his eye. He will grasp as if his hand were in a mitten, thumb against the other fingers, or rake an item into his hand. (Independent use of the fingers and the ability to pick up an object between the thumb and index finger will not develop until about nine months of age.) You will not be able to tell whether he is right- or left-handed at this point, since this characteristic is not clearly manifested until about the age of three years.

But even without fine-tuning, your baby will become a first-class grabber by the age of six months. Not only will he reach for toys in his immediate vicinity (or his own feet), but when someone holds him, he will expertly seize hair, earrings, glasses, or the pen in Dad's shirt pocket. Furthermore, all of these items will be inspected carefully and fearlessly, not only with eyes and fingers but invariably with his mouth. You will now need to enter a state of perpetual vigilance for small objects that you would rather not see entering his mouth, either because they are disgusting or because they might be accidentally swallowed and block his airway.

As his reaching and grasping skills become more developed, he will also discover the joy of letting go. During these three months, you will see him transfer an object from one hand to the other, which requires that one hand release what the other hand takes. At some point he will also discover gravity, as he begins to drop things and observe what happens as a result. In later months, this may become a serious pastime as toys, food, and other unidentified nonflying objects are released from various heights (such as a crib or high chair) in order to watch them career or bounce or even shatter. All of this activity is exploratory and not a sign of a destructive streak or a future career in sports. But he will eventually need to be taught what items can be tossed and where.

Vision and hearing

During these three months, your baby will continue to gain in the ability to see and hear what's going on around her. By six months she will be able to focus on people or objects several feet away and follow movement in all directions. She will show interest in more complex patterns and subtle shades of color, so this is a great time to hang a mobile over her crib. (Make sure that she can't reach it, however—if she grasps it and pulls it loose, a mobile could fall on her or she could become entangled in its strings.) She will also find stroller rides stimulating times to take in a passing parade of new colors and shapes.

She will become more skillful at localizing the source of sounds and turning her head in the direction of your voice or an interesting noise in her vicinity. In addition, you will begin hearing a wider range of sounds—babbles, belly laughs, bubbling noises, and even a screech or two for good measure. Sometimes she will even alter her "speech" patterns, raising and lowering her voice as if giving an oration in a language only she understands. Rather than parroting back her assorted sounds, which is often irresistible, you can begin to transform some of her favorite syllables into simple words such as *baby*, *doggie*, and *Mommy* and feed them back to her. By seven months of age, she should begin imitating sounds you make.

Social Developments: The Joys of Interacting

For many parents, this stage of a baby's life is one of the most pleasant they will experience, a time when a true personality emerges from the seemingly endless cycles of feeding, sleeping, and crying during the first three months. All of her new skills in movement, vision, hearing, and noisemaking seem to converge and complement each other as she shows off for family, friends, and complete strangers. When her face lights up for Aunt Mary, she'll likely get a big grin and a lot of sweet talk in return. When she babbles and gurgles for Grandpa, she'll probably hear a few new funny noises in response. Even older brothers and sisters will enjoy making the new baby smile.

In all of these encounters, your baby is finding out what kind of world she lives in. What sights and sounds envelop her, and what happens when she tries to make an impact, in her own way, on her surroundings? Does she see smiles and bright colors, hear laughter and pleasant voices, and feel hugs, kisses, and cuddling? Is she in a place that is safe physically and emotionally? Even during her first stirrings of independence, she is still completely helpless, depending on the adults around her for her physical needs and her most basic sense of security. She may not be able to understand your words, but she'll get a strong message about her importance to you and your family.

Everyone who cares for your baby plays a role in this process. It is particularly important for Dad to interact with her at this point. Playing with a baby this age isn't all that difficult. With rare exception, your baby can now be entertained simply by laying her across your lap and playing with her hands and feet, making faces, and giving her interesting objects to handle. She will love to wave rattles and toys that make sounds or musical tones. She will enjoy looking at books or magazines with bright pictures. She will like touching and squeezing soft toys, especially if they have an interesting texture.

There will probably be grandparents and favorite uncles and doting aunts around who will also enjoy these simple pleasures. Sometimes a relative who hasn't had all the day-to-day responsibilities and interrupted sleep for the past few months can give you a fresh perspective on your baby, a reminder that tending her is not only worthwhile but a source of enjoyment. This is especially important if you are a single parent, because you will need the break from being on call twenty-four hours a day and the reassurance that raising your child is worth the effort.

Feeding: New Adventures

If your baby is nursing, he will typically need to fill his tank about five times a day and soon should be skipping the late-night feeding(s) if he isn't already. By six months, if he is waking up two or three times during the night, it is far more likely to be for reasons other than hunger (see page 178).

Some mothers who are breastfeeding quite successfully will, for a variety of reasons, begin to think about shifting from breast to bottle before their baby reaches six months of age. If at all possible, however, continue nursing during these months, for all of the reasons outlined in chapter 4 (page 114). If you need to start or resume employment outside the home and cannot nurse your baby during work hours, you do not necessarily need to switch your baby entirely to formula. Depending upon your schedule and your baby's feeding patterns, you may be able to nurse before and after work and even express milk (which can be used at a later feeding) during the time you are away from home. (If you intend to shift from breastfeeding to bottle-feeding, see sidebar, page 208.)

A formula-fed baby will similarly be consuming five bottles every day, each containing five to eight ounces (about 150 to 240 ml) of formula, depending on his weight. You can discuss the amount with your physician at the four- and six-month checkups, but a ballpark amount for a given feeding is an ounce of formula for every two pounds of weight (30 ml for every 900 g). By the way, it's too early to begin drinking from a cup at this age. That adventure can begin after your baby reaches the six-month mark.

Parents of babies in this age-group often wonder if this is a good time to introduce solid foods. Thirty years ago, physicians routinely advised parents to begin feeding their babies rice cereal at two months and then speedily progress to other types of foods. Your baby's grandmother may have started you on cereal practically from day one, and perhaps one of your friends has announced with some satisfaction that her baby is already taking all sorts of fruits and vegetables at two months of age. But consuming solids is not a sign of advanced intelligence or motor skills. In fact, there are reasons you don't need to be in any hurry to introduce solids before your baby is six months old:

Breast milk or formula can supply all of the fluid, calories, and nutrients your baby needs for his first six months of life, and it is more easily digested than other foods. The efficiency of the intestinal tract in absorbing other foods increases significantly between the fourth and sixth months.

Babies who are fed solids early may develop food allergies. If there is a strong history of allergies in either parent or other family members, you would be wise to wait. After six months, infants are better equipped to process a variety of foods without this risk.

Solid foods are best managed by a baby who has some basic developmental skills in place. (See sidebar, page 175.)

First experiences with solid foods

While you don't need to be in a rush to start solids, most babies are given their first taste of foods other than breast milk or formula between four and six months of age. Like many other everyday concerns in child rearing, directions for introducing solids to babies were not included in the Ten Commandments. Even the American Academy of Pediatrics (AAP) acknowledges a difference of opinion among its own experts on this topic. The AAP's Section on Breastfeeding (a subcommittee that makes policy recommendations on this subject) recommends breastfeeding exclusively for the first six months of life, while its committee on nutrition proposes that other foods (if safe, nutritious, and age appropriate) can be introduced between four and six months of age. Needless to say, families have made this transition for thousands of years in thousands of ways, with or without the input and approval of panels of experts. What follows are basic guidelines to help you navigate this passage smoothly, along with a few cautions about certain foods and feeding practices that would best be avoided.

Before you decide to let your baby try something other than breast milk or formula, consider your timing. First, she should be ready developmentally (see sidebar below).

The other timing question to consider is the specific setting of your baby's first experience with solids. Pick a time when you aren't going to be rushed or hassled, and take the phone off the hook for good measure. Your baby shouldn't be tired, cranky, ravenously hungry, or completely full. Give her part of a feeding of breast milk or formula before you try the new stuff. *Remember that when you begin solids, they will only supplement milk feedings, not substitute for them,* so the normal feeding should be finished after whatever solid food she has eaten.

What should you start with? The general consensus is that rice cereal specifically formulated for babies is best. It is well absorbed, contains iron, and rarely causes allergic reactions. Whether premixed in a jar or prepared by you with water or formula, it can be adjusted to whatever thickness your baby prefers. You should feed her from a small spoon and not a bottle with an enlarged hole in the nipple. If she sucks solids out of a bottle, she may get too much volume and become obese if this is done repeatedly. And she will delay learning how to swallow solids without sucking.

DEVELOPMENTAL SIGNS THAT YOUR BABY IS (OR ISN'T) READY FOR SOLID FOOD

- While sucking at the breast or bottle, a newborn first protrudes her tongue, pushing it against the nipple as she sucks and swallows. This tongue-thrusting reflex, which gradually subsides over the first six months, interferes with the process of taking food from a spoon and moving it to the throat, where it can be swallowed. A baby who repeatedly pushes her tongue against the spoon probably isn't ready for solids.
- Accepting food from a spoon is much easier for a baby who can control her head position, a skill which will be far better developed after six months than at three or four. A young baby whose head flops everywhere if not supported should be given more time with just breast or bottle.
- By six months of age, your baby will be happily grabbing everything in sight and putting whatever she finds into her mouth, an indication that she will find a spoon worth exploring as well.
- If a couple of teeth erupt before six months of age (the usual time of the first appearance of teeth), this in itself is not a sign that your baby is ready for pizza. Your baby won't use her teeth to chew food yet for some months. In fact, even if she still doesn't have teeth at the six-month mark, she will be quite able to swallow the mushy solids you'll be feeding her. ■

Offer her about half of a small baby spoonful (or use a small coffee spoon if you wish), which should total about a quarter teaspoon (one ml). She may not know what to do with your offering and may even appear to reject it with a grimace. Talk to her in soothing tones through the entire process. When she gets the hang of swallowing this amount, she will begin opening her mouth in anticipation of more. Aim for a total of about one tablespoon (15 ml) once a day, gradually increasing to two or three tablespoons (30 to 45 ml) per feeding once or twice per day. If she simply refuses or repeatedly thrusts her tongue, don't force her. This is not a moral issue or a contest of wills. Simply wait and try again in another week or two.

When two or three tablespoons of rice cereal are going down smoothly at one feeding, you can try other cereals. Oats and barley are good for the next round, but check with your baby's doctor before trying corn or wheat cereals, which may provoke digestive problems in some infants. After cereals have been successfully consumed for a few weeks, you can think about adding other foods to the mix. Either vegetables or fruits may be the next category you try, but vegetables may hold an advantage because they will not condition your baby to sweet tastes. Fruits can be added later, and meats should be introduced last. By the time your baby is eating from three or four food groups, she will probably be eating three times per day. You may choose to raise a vegetarian and not introduce meats to your baby at all, but if you do this, be sure that you are adequately informed so your baby won't be deprived of any necessary nutrients.

Let your baby try each new food (one to three tablespoons' [15 to 45 ml] worth) for a few days before introducing another. Observe her for any signs of a reaction: diar-

THE DEBUT OF TEETH

During these months, you may notice that your baby is doing a fair amount of drooling. This does not necessarily mean that the appearance of her first teeth is imminent. The ongoing flow of saliva serves partly to protect the mouth from being traumatized by the various objects, including her feet, that your baby will stick in her mouth. Antibodies in saliva may also help prevent bacteria and viruses on those objects from gaining a foothold in her throat or intestinal tract.

Somewhere in the neighborhood of six months, the first two lower front teeth, called the central incisors, will poke through the gums. (However, don't worry if you don't see any teeth for the first year. After that, if none have appeared, check with your baby's doctor.) The central incisors will be followed sometime later by the four upper incisors and then by two more lower incisors. Your baby may ease through this or display a lot of fussiness. She may drool somewhat more than usual and may also try to gum the nearest firm object. Contrary to popular belief, teething does not generate a temperature over 100.4°F (38°C) taken rectally. If your baby has a fever, something else is wrong.

Rubbing your finger against the gum through which the tooth is erupting may help the pain, or she may prefer a teething ring—which should not come from the freezer because it will be too hard. Acetaminophen (Tylenol and others) can help, but topical preparations that are supposed to numb the gums don't usually provide impressive relief because they can't remain in place for long. ■

Adam and Eve had many advantages, but the principal one was that they escaped teething.

Pudd'nhead Wilson
(published in 1894)
By Mark Twain

rhea, irritability, runny nose, coughing or wheezing, or a rash, especially around the face. If there is any possibility that a reaction has occurred, withdraw the food, wait for the problem to calm down, and try again. If you see the same response, put that food aside for several weeks and then run the story by your baby's doctor before serving it to her again. Of course, if any feeding is followed by a more severe reaction, such as an immediate rash or difficulty breathing, contact the doctor right away. Fortunately, sudden and intense reactions to foods are very uncommon at this age.

You can obtain many foods for your baby in prepackaged forms at the store, or you can prepare them yourself. Commercial baby foods have the advantage of convenience, especially if you are traveling or are short on time for food preparation. Unlike their predecessors of a few decades ago, most are free of sugar, salt, and artificial flavorings—they contain just the straight food in a mushy consistency, ready to feed. When opening a baby-food jar, make sure the safety button in the middle of the lid pops up. If it doesn't, return the jar or throw it away. Don't feed your baby directly out of the jar because the enzymes and bacteria from her saliva may degrade or contaminate the food she doesn't finish. Instead, spoon a small amount on a plate and refrigerate what remains in the jar; it will be good for a day (or a month if left in the freezer). Whatever she doesn't finish from her plate should be thrown away.

Foods do not need to be hot; room temperature or slightly warm is just fine for most babies. If you need to warm something from the refrigerator, use the microwave with extreme caution—if at all—because of the possibility of uneven temperatures and hot spots within the food that could burn the baby's mouth. Food that is microwaved should be thoroughly stirred so the heat is distributed evenly throughout. If heating food in a baby-food jar, you can place the jar in a pan of warm water for a few minutes.

Don't become a clean-plate fanatic with your baby. When first sampling solids, she will take only small amounts—one or two tablespoons (15 to 30 ml) at a time—and then gradually increase her intake over time. Watch for signs that she is no longer hungry—turning her head, getting fussy, or general disinterest in what you are offering from the spoon. Trying to force her to eat a prescribed amount is not only an exercise in futility but may also set up a bad habit of eating when she has no appetite.

A few additional cautions about foods and feeding

Do not feed honey to your baby. Infants younger than twelve months of age who eat honey may develop infant botulism, a form of food poisoning that can cause serious damage to the nervous system or very rarely can be fatal. Infant botulism was once thought to be linked to corn syrup but more recent evidence hasn't supported this association.

Keep your baby on breast milk or infant formula (fortified with iron) rather than milk from the dairy case. Infants who drink cow's milk before their first birthday are more likely to develop an allergy to the protein it contains. Cow's milk may also interfere with the absorption of iron contained in other foods.

Steer clear of fruit juices, punch, or other sweetened drinks. Some babies can become so enamored with sweet liquids that they will favor them over more nutritious sources of calories. They may also become hard to separate from their beloved juice bottle, which unfortunately will keep their new teeth continuously bathed in cavity-provoking sweet liquids. A good time for your baby to begin enjoying juices is when she can drink them from a cup.

Don't feed your baby foods with added salt or sugar or with spicy flavors. She needs to become accustomed to the basic, unadulterated taste of high-quality foods.

Avoid feeding your baby certain vegetables that you have prepared yourself. Home-prepared spinach, beets, collard greens, turnips, and carrots may contain quantities of nitrates—components of plants and fertilizers—that can be toxic to a young infant. (You may recall from chapter 4 that well water can contain nitrates in amounts that could be harmful to a baby during the first three months of life.) Commercial baby-food preparations of these vegetables are made from produce that has been screened for nitrates, and they are safe to use.

Don't let your baby become a grazer. Some parents respond with food (breast, bottle, or snacks) whenever their baby utters any sound remotely suggesting displeasure. The result is nonstop eating by a baby who is never actually hungry or completely satisfied and who may gain excessive weight.

Remember not to put your baby to bed with a bottle of milk. If she falls asleep with anything other than water in her mouth, bacteria can damage her incoming teeth. A baby who drinks from a bottle while lying flat will also be at greater risk for developing middle-ear infections. If your baby truly seems to sleep better after a bedtime snack, be sure all of it is swallowed.

Sleep: Is It Time to Establish a Routine?

Between the fourth and sixth months, your baby will probably have settled into a sleeping routine that is more predictable and easier on everyone during the wee hours. Two naps during the day, one in the morning and one in the afternoon, are a good habit to encourage and maintain. These may last from one to three hours, and at this age you need not awaken your baby from a long nap unless it seems to be interfering with his sleep at night. (Some infants continue to catnap during this period.) Between two and four months or shortly thereafter, your baby should be skipping a night feeding. By six months, he should well be able to handle an eight-hour stretch without being fed unless he was premature or is exceptionally small. But whether this translates into uninterrupted sleep will depend on both your baby and your sleeping arrangements.

If he's down for the night by 8 p.m., he may be genuinely hungry at 4 a.m. But at that hour, unless he's crying with no sign of letting up, you may want to wait a few minutes to see if he might go back to sleep. Delaying his bedtime may help extend his and your uninterrupted sleep in the morning, but a decision to allow him to stay up later must be weighed against other family needs. Ideally, before he is put to bed, there should be some time to wind down with quiet activities—a feeding, some cuddling, some singing, and perhaps a bath. With repetition of a routine, he will begin to associate these particular activities with bedtime and a surrender to sleep. If at all possible, have different people walk through this process with him so he won't come to expect that Mom and Dad are the only people in the world who can bring the day to a close.

Now is a good time to let him learn to fall asleep on his own if he hasn't been doing so already. When he is drowsy but not yet asleep, lay him down, pat him gently, and leave the room. Make sure there's a night-light on so he can see familiar surroundings. If he fusses for more than a few minutes, you can come back for a brief reassurance (perhaps offering some gentle patting on the back) but not a full-blown recap of the nighttime routine. If he persists, let a little more time go by before you return. If there's no end in sight to the crying and you can't stand to let it continue, do whatever works to bring on sleep, and then try again at a later date, perhaps on a weekend night when you have some flexibility in your evening and morning schedules.

If he isn't able to fall asleep by himself by six months of age, the window of opportunity for learning this skill may not be open again for a while. Within the next few months, he is likely to begin demonstrating a normal behavior known as **separation anxiety**, in which a mighty howl may erupt when you or his closest caregivers are out of his sight, especially at bedtime. (We'll look at separation anxiety in more detail in the next chapter.) As a result, if after six months he's still used to being nursed, held, and rocked through several rounds of "Hey Diddle Diddle" until he's sound asleep, you can plan on repeating this ritual for months on end unless you are prepared to endure a vigorous and prolonged protest.

Remember that your baby's nighttime activity may include one or more awakenings that do not necessarily need your attention. If you rush into your baby's room to feed, cuddle, and rock him with every sound he produces, he will become quite accustomed to this first-class room service, and you may find that he is rather reluctant to give it up. Obviously, if he sounds truly miserable and is keeping everyone awake, do whatever is necessary to comfort him and calm things down. At this age it is still better to err on the side of too much attention than too little. After a few more months pass, however, you can become more hard-nosed if he seems intent on having a social hour several times a night.

Crying: More Than Just Hunger or a Wet Diaper

Your baby's growing list of skills for interacting with her surroundings also includes new expressions of displeasure, and you will notice that a "language" of sorts is developing in her cries. The sounds she makes when she is hungry will be different from those she makes when she is undressed on the doctor's examining table and very different from her reaction to an immunization. Unlike the newborn's intense, almost primitive crying in response to any and all forms of discomfort, after four months a baby may also cry in order to get attention or other action from the adults in her life. Watch and listen carefully, and you will learn to distinguish a cry that says, "I need to be fed" from one that says, "I'm bored" or "I want that toy I just threw on the floor."

Learning to discern the various intensities and inflections of her cries will also help you decide whether you need to tend to her immediately or whether she can wait a little while for you to finish what you are doing. Indeed, as she progresses in her social skills through the first year, she will also need to discover that she is not the center of the known universe. If you know that she is fed, dry, and comfortable, you may want to delay a bit your response to the cry that seems to say, "I want some attention *right this minute*."

Health and Safety Issues: Some Reminders

As your baby begins to show his first signs of mobility and starts inserting everything he can grab into his mouth, you are but a few short months away from the exciting project of keeping him and your possessions safe when he wants to check out *everything in sight*. There will be much more on this topic in the next chapter, but a few basic ground rules are worth stating and repeating.

Don't leave your baby alone on any surface such as a changing table, kitchen counter, or sofa. He will invariably pick that moment to demonstrate his ability to roll over.

Don't leave your baby unattended even for a few seconds while he is in water, whether bathing in the sink, infant tub, or adult bathtub. He can drown in an inch or two (a few centimeters) of water.

Everyone in your house, including young children, should know how to dial 911 in case of an emergency. All adults and children over twelve should be trained in infant CPR. Local hospitals normally conduct CPR classes on a regular basis.

Be extremely cautious about leaving one of your older children in charge of your baby, even for a few minutes. This assignment should be considered only for a responsible sibling more than twelve years of age who has been observed handling the baby appropriately for a number of weeks. He or she must have explicit information about your whereabouts, instructions about what to do if the baby cries or has any other type of problem, and names and phone numbers of people to call for help if needed.

Always buckle your baby securely into his car seat, no matter how short the ride. Through the sixth month, he will still be sitting facing backward. (He should not be placed in a forward-facing car seat until he is a year old *and* weighs at least twenty pounds [about 9 kg].) The center of the backseat is the safest location for him; thus you should avoid putting him in the front passenger seat. This means that, should he start to fuss, you will have to resist the temptation to turn around and tend to him while your vehicle is in motion. *If your car has a passenger-side air bag, you should never place your baby in the front passenger seat.* If the air bag inflates during an accident, it could cause serious or even fatal injuries to a baby.

Never carry your baby while you are also holding a cup of hot liquid. One strong wiggle could result in a scalding injury to one or both of you.

Keep a watchful eye for small objects scattered around your living space. These would include older children's LEGOs, marbles, action figures, and other toys that might come within your baby's reach and therefore go into his mouth. If your baby is going to spend time on the floor, put your face on his level and scan the horizon. Look for stray coins, paper clips, pins, pieces of dry pet food, plastic wrappers, electrical cords, or unstable objects that might fall on your baby if given a gentle shove.

Beware of parking your baby in an infant swing or doorway jumper and then turning your attention elsewhere. After four months, a baby with enough wiggle power may be able to squirm out of a swing or even bring the whole thing down.

Keep your baby out of walkers, which are responsible for thousands of accidents every year. These devices will not teach him how to walk or speed up his motor development. Instead, they give your active baby the opportunity to propel himself to the edge of the stairs, investigate whatever is sitting on your coffee table, or flip the walker over when he bumps into an obstruction.

Extremely vigorous play (such as tossing a baby a few inches into the air and catching him) is not a good idea at this age. Rapid accelerations and changes in direction, however playful, can have the same effect as shaking a baby, risking injury to his neck, brain, and eyes.

A baby's skin may become sunburned after as little as fifteen minutes of direct exposure to the sun. Don't allow your baby to have prolonged exposure to direct sunlight (even on a hazy or overcast day), especially between the hours of 10 a.m. and 3 p.m. This is particularly important at higher altitudes or around lakes and seashores, where the sun's ultraviolet light (which provokes the burn) can reflect off sand and water. The use of sunscreen before the age of six months has been controversial because of concerns over the absorption and metabolism of chemicals in these products by young infants.

If you take your baby outdoors for any length of time, keep him in the shade or use an umbrella, and make sure his skin is covered with appropriate clothing (including a hat or bonnet) even if he is in the shade. A small amount of sunscreen may be applied to exposed areas of skin (such as the face, back of the hands, and neck) if for some reason you are in a situation where you cannot provide physical protection from the sun using a hat, clothing, or shade.

Medical checkups and immunizations

If all goes well, your baby will have just two encounters with her doctor (or a nurse practitioner or physician assistant, depending on the practice setting) during this time period: a well-baby check at four months and another at six months. During these visits, you should be asked questions about your baby's feeding and sleeping patterns, developmental milestones, and indications that she is seeing and hearing well. Some of the practitioner's assessment of your baby's progress will hinge more on observations you have made rather than the actual examination in the office. It will help a great deal if you can offer information about your baby's head control, her use of her hands, rolling over, tracking objects with her eyes, responses to sounds, and her other activities.

Concerns you might have about whether she is "ahead" or "behind" in these areas must be put in perspective because there can be a wide variation in the time when babies accomplish various tasks. In most cases, what matters more is whether your baby is making steady progress overall. If you have questions and concerns about development—or any problems you have encountered—be sure to ask about them during these checkups. It will help if you write them down. If your list contains more than two or three items, let the doctor or nurse know at the beginning of the visit.

Your baby's height, weight, and head circumference will be measured and plotted on a growth chart. At the six-month check, it is likely that she will have doubled her birth weight. During each visit, the examiner will look "stem to stern," noting how your baby moves and responds during the entire process. Unless there are specific reasons to do otherwise, at these visits your baby will normally continue to receive routine immunizations to protect her against a number of dangerous diseases. (We will take a detailed look at immunizations and the diseases that they prevent in "Immunizations—Which Ones, Why, and When?" beginning on page 739.) Be sure to let the health-care provider know if your baby has had an unusual response to any prior immunizations.

When your baby is ill: common medical problems

You now have a more sturdy, immunologically competent baby than you had three months ago. Infections are not as likely to get out of control and turn into a major medical event or a catastrophe. Unlike the first three months of life, a fever over 100.4°F (38°C) rectally is no longer a cause for an immediate trip or call to the doctor's office or emergency room. But all of your baby's exploring with hands and mouth is certain to introduce some new viruses and bacteria into her body, and some of these will gain enough of a foothold to cause trouble.

Invaders in the air passages. By far the most common illness you will see will be an **upper respiratory infection** (**URI** in medical shorthand, or a **cold** to everyone else), involving the nose, ears, throat, and upper airway. The most obvious symptoms will be a runny nose and cough, with irritability and disturbed sleep likely as well. Remember, your baby can respond to a sore throat or headache only by fussing and crying. It will be many months before you have the luxury of your child being capable of telling you what hurts. Fever may or may not be present, and you should get in the habit of checking your baby's temperature if she appears ill. Don't rely on your sense of touch to decide whether the temperature is normal, but take the extra time to use a thermometer. If you need to discuss the illness with your baby's doctor (or whoever fields phone calls at the office or clinic where she receives her care), he or she will want to know whether a fever is part of the problem (see sidebar, page 135).

Be careful, and watch yourselves closely so that you do not forget the things your eyes have seen or let them slip from your heart as long as you live. Teach them to your children and to their children after them.

Deuteronomy 4:9

If the cause of this infection is a virus—and there are at least a hundred different varieties of the **rhinovirus**, which is the usual culprit—your baby's immune system will normally deal with it within a week and return things to normal. During these few days, your baby will want and need more cuddling and comforting. Her appetite may be less enthusiastic than usual, or she may want to nurse more often. You do not need to withhold feedings unless there is a significant airway problem, which is rare. Remember to wash your hands regularly, since you can't avoid contact with drool and drainage, and these infections are spread more commonly by contaminated hands than through airborne droplets. Your fingers, which could be hosting some unfriendly organism, make more trips every day to your eyes, nose, and mouth than you think.

Acetaminophen may be helpful for relieving aches and pains for a few hours at a time. It can also help reduce but not eliminate a fever, a capability that is useful only because it can make your baby more comfortable. Although it is an important symptom during an illness, fever rarely causes problems in and of itself, and you do not need to embark on a crusade to drive it away. If you use acetaminophen at this age, your baby will take a dose of 40 mg (0.4 ml of the infant drops that contain 80 mg per 0.8 ml) if she weighs less than twelve pounds (about 5½ kg) and 80 mg (0.8 ml of the infant drops) if she weighs more than twelve pounds.

Talk with her doctor before using a cold remedy or cough syrup to relieve symptoms. There are scores of different brands, combinations of ingredients, and dosage schedules on the market, but not many are geared for babies, and some may cause more problems than they solve. Depending on your baby's sensitivity, the ingredients in these medications (decongestants, antihistamines, cough suppressants, and even alcohol) may cause sedation, which could be confusing and worrisome. Is she getting worse, or is it the medication? Or these medications may cause her to be more irritable and wakeful.

The antihistamines in many cold preparations may also thicken the secretions in the nose or airway, making them harder to clear. (In addition, controlled studies of these medications have suggested that they are not likely to be effective in children.) But if coughing and drainage are making your baby miserable and *if your baby's doctor recommends it*, one of these products, whether a single-ingredient decongestant or a combination cold-and-cough reliever, may be tried. If it seems to help for a few hours and doesn't cause any problems, you can continue to use it as needed. Since most colds are caused by viruses, and viruses are not affected by antibiotics, don't be surprised if your baby's doctor doesn't prescribe one of these medications. (Do not pressure the doctor to use them if they're not really needed.)

Remember that you can use a rubber-bulb syringe to suck excessive secretions from your baby's congested nose. Saline nose drops may be helpful in cleansing nasal passages. Three or four drops of nasal saline solution may be instilled in each nostril (one at a time) and then suctioned out. This simple procedure may relieve congestion that is interfering with feeding. A cool-mist vaporizer may also help soothe the nose. However, a vaporizer must be cleaned and rinsed daily to prevent mold and bacteria from growing in it and then being sprayed all over the room the next time it is used. In addition, if everything in the room, including the baby, is perpetually damp from the vaporizer, you're probably using it too much. Don't use a hot-water vaporizer, which not only offers no advantage over a cool-mist device, but also adds a risk for accidental burns or scalding injuries.

Unfortunately, not all colds go away peacefully in a few days. Some allow bacteria to gain a foothold, producing a variety of illnesses for which your baby will need medical attention. One sign that bacteria have invaded is that the nasal drainage not only refuses to disappear after a week or two, but it turns and stays thick and discolored (gray, yellow, or green). If a cold persists more than two weeks or thick, discolored discharge continues more than a few days, give your doctor a call—especially if there is a fever. (This isn't a sinus infection, by the way, because at this age the sinuses are not fully formed.) Antibiotics may be necessary to help your baby deal with these invaders.

The anatomy of a baby's nose and ears may allow bacteria to travel into the middle ear by way of the eustachian tubes. The resulting infection of the middle ear—that is, the air-filled space behind the eardrum—is known as **acute otitis media**. Usually an ear infection will cause pressure to build up behind the eardrum or irritate the drum directly, producing a great deal of discomfort and often fever. Therefore, a baby with a cold who becomes increasingly irritable should definitely be checked, especially if fever is present. If otitis media is diagnosed, antibiotics will nearly always be prescribed in this age-group. (In otitis media involving children over two years of age, the doctor may choose to treat with pain measures only.) *Once started, this medication should be continued for its full course.* If your baby reacts to the antibiotic in some way—for example, with a rash or diarrhea—contact the doctor's office for further instructions.

Any virus or bacteria that infects the nose or throat can find its way into the linings of one or both eyes (known as the **conjunctivae**). These eye infections, known as **conjunctivitis** (or pinkeye), produce a reddish discoloration along with a discolored drainage. When this material dries overnight, the eyelids may be stuck together with a crusty debris you will need to remove gently with a warm, wet washcloth. Your doctor will normally prescribe antibiotic drops or ointment, which can be a little challenging to instill in the eyes of your wiggly, unhappy patient for a few days. Careful hand washing is a must for anyone handling a baby with conjunctivitis because it is very contagious—the organisms involved have a knack for spreading to others by hitching a ride on unsuspecting fingers.

Coughing will not be hard to miss, but the ultimate source may not be quite as obvious. Mucus draining into the throat from the nose (postnasal drip) can provoke coughing, as will any infection involving the larynx (vocal cords), trachea (airway), bronchial tubes, or lungs. If the very upper portions of the airway are involved, you will notice a barking sound with the cough, in addition to hoarseness and noisy respirations. This syndrome, known as **croup**, is uncommon before the age of six months.

Bronchiolitis is an inflammation of the very small tubes that lead to tiny air sacs in the lungs called **alveoli,** where oxygen is transported into the bloodstream. It may be caused by any of several types of viruses but is most commonly attributed to the **respiratory syncytial virus (RSV)**. Bronchiolitis is usually restricted to infants and young children under the age of three and may become serious enough to require hospitalization. Coughing may actually be less obvious than wheezing and difficulty breathing. **Pneumonia** is an infection of the air sacs themselves and may be caused by bacteria or viruses or, rarely, by aspiration of some foreign material such as water or food. The baby with widespread pneumonia will usually appear quite ill, with fever, rapid respirations, and signs that breathing has become hard work: grunting, flaring of the nostrils, and retracting (sucking inward) of the muscles between the ribs. Sometimes, however, the pneumonia will be so localized to a certain section of lung that coughing and shortness of breath will not be evident. Fever and irritability may be the only symptoms.

If you have any concerns about your baby's well-being during a cold or other respiratory illness, don't hesitate to call your physician for advice or an assessment. A number of situations definitely deserve a call, although the timing and urgency of your contact will depend on the condition of your baby.

If your three-to-six-month-old baby is active and feeding well, you can wait to call during office or daytime hours for

- coughing that persists more than a week or is persistent enough to interrupt sleep;
- fever under 103°F (39.4°C) accompanying a cold or cough;
- thick, discolored drainage, redness, and/or crusting from the eyes;
- watery discharge from the nose that lasts more than seven to ten days, or thick, discolored drainage for more than a few days;
- discolored drainage from one or both ears; this may indicate that your baby not only has had an ear infection but has had a spontaneous rupture of the eardrum. This event is not a disaster. In fact, it relieves pressure and pain in the ear, but antibiotics are usually prescribed.

You should call, regardless of the hour, for

- any signs of difficulty breathing other than nasal congestion; rapid respirations (more than forty per minute) or evidence of labored breathing (grunting, flaring of the nostrils, or retracting of the muscles between the ribs) should be evaluated by a physician. If your baby seems to literally gasp for breath, take her immediately to the nearest emergency room, or if you are unable to do so, call 911;
- relentless crying or listlessness, especially with a fever;
- poor color—pale, bluish, dusky, or mottled skin;
- rectal fever of 103°F (39.4°C) or more, especially if your baby is very irritable or lethargic.

You should be aware that many viruses can generate a high fever that a baby over four months of age can tolerate surprisingly well. If your baby is active, feeding well, and in reasonably good spirits despite the fever, your doctor may advise a check during office hours rather than the middle of the night.

Digestive-tract disturbances. As in previous months, you will want to keep a close watch on your baby if he begins to throw up or if his stools increase in frequency and volume. Some babies at this age may still routinely spit up some breast milk or formula after any given feeding, and it may even seem worse than a few weeks ago. That's because the muscles at the lower end of the esophagus may be looser than they were before. If height, weight, and developmental milestones are still on track, however, the primary focus can remain on minimizing the amount of spitting up. Eventually the problem should correct itself. Helpful measures in the meantime include

- more frequent, smaller feedings;
- more frequent burping during the feeding;
- enlisting gravity's assistance by keeping your baby in an upright position for a half hour after a feeding.

But if your baby's vomiting is forceful, you'll need to watch him carefully. If he is lethargic, running a fever, and/or pouring out loose stools, call the doctor's office for advice and probably a weigh-in and exam, since babies in this age-group can become dehydrated very quickly, especially if they are losing fluids from both ends.

If he throws up once but seems otherwise normal and in good spirits, you can see what happens over the next hour or two. If all is well, you can nurse him for a couple of minutes, watch him again for ten or fifteen minutes, and repeat this process for an hour. If there are no further signs of trouble, resume your normal feeding routine. The same can be done with a bottle-fed baby, except that rehydrating solutions such as Pedialyte or Enfalyte should be tried instead of formula.

A similar approach holds for diarrhea. One or two loose stools in an otherwise happy and active baby need not generate a lot of concern. It happens from time to time, and you won't necessarily know why. If your baby is formula-fed, check to see if his most recent batches of formula have been correctly measured and mixed. If stools are frequent and watery but not accompanied by vomiting or signs of dehydration (see page 186), breastfed babies can continue nursing as usual because Mom's milk is easy on the intestinal tract. Formula-fed babies, however, should be given a rehydrating solution until the stools begin to slow down and firm up. Plain water will *not* be absorbed nearly as well, and carbonated soft drinks (with or without the fizz) or juices will not contain the ideal blend of electrolytes, such as sodium and potassium, to replace what has been lost in the stool. Babies who are already taking solids can try some foods that are mildly constipating, such as rice cereal, applesauce, or banana.

After your baby has experienced an intense bout of diarrhea, your physician may suggest using a lactose-free formula, since the illness may temporarily cause lactose intolerance. *Medications used to control diarrhea in adults, such as diphenoxylate (Lomotil) or loperamide (Imodium), should generally not be given to young infants.* They don't actually treat the cause of the loose stools, and they may cause the extra stool to accumulate in the bowel rather than pass into the diaper. This could lead to a false sense of security because it looks as if the diarrhea has stopped.

If diarrhea lasts more than one or two days, especially if a fever is present, call your baby's doctor—even if the baby seems to be doing well. He should be evaluated if he is listless, passing blood with the stool, or having vomiting episodes along with the diarrhea.

Whether brought on by mild or moderate vomiting, diarrhea, or both, you should be aware of signs that **dehydration** (loss of body water) is becoming significant. A decrease in activity level, fewer wet diapers than usual, and fewer tears with crying suggest mild to moderate dehydration. If these occur, call your health-care provider for advice, which may include a doctor's evaluation.

Signs of more severe dehydration—indicating a much more urgent need for a trip to the doctor's office or emergency room—include the following:

- Dry mouth and no tears
- No urine for five to six hours, indicating that your baby is working hard to conserve his fluids
- Sunken eyes
- A sunken fontanelle (the soft spot in the skull)
- Skin texture that is no longer elastic, but more like bread dough
- Persistent fussing, especially if it is more of a moan or whine than a vigorous cry
- Cool and/or mottled skin
- Marked listlessness, with lack of interest in play or feeding. A baby this age who lies still while awake, shows little interest in people or things around him, and

WHAT CAUSES VOMITING AND DIARRHEA IN INFANTS?

Vomiting can be provoked either by an intestinal infection or by illness somewhere else in the body. When vomiting and diarrhea begin suddenly at the same time, the problem is usually **gastroenteritis** (the so-called stomach flu), most often caused by a virus. Occasionally bacteria or even parasites are at fault.

Vomiting may also signal a problem elsewhere: an ear infection, pneumonia, urinary tract infection, or even meningitis. Because of the number and variety of possible causes of persistent vomiting, a medical examination will nearly always be needed, especially in a baby less than a year old.

Diarrhea, with few exceptions, indicates a problem focused in the bowel. Usually this is an infection—most commonly viral, especially in the winter when an unsavory character known as **rotavirus** makes its rounds—but bacteria and parasites may have to be ruled out by taking samples of stool to a local laboratory for culturing and other tests. Contaminated food can be a cause of infectious diarrhea in older babies and children.

Antibiotics are a notorious cause of diarrhea in infants and children because they directly irritate the bowel or wipe out the normal bacteria in the intestine and allow less friendly organisms to multiply.

Food allergy, lactose intolerance, or a problem with formula may also provoke loose stools, though without other signs of illness such as fever or lethargy. Some detective work with your health-care provider may be needed if your baby has persistent loose or watery stools but is otherwise doing well. ■

has markedly reduced movements of arms and legs may be in serious trouble and should be evaluated immediately.

Please note: Detailed information about each of these illnesses, including treatment principles and options, can be found in the Reference Section.

FOR MORE INFORMATION

Turn to the Reference Section for more detailed information on:

- colds   page 643
- vomiting   page 734
- diarrhea   page 653
- ear infections   page 657

Are We Having Fun Yet?

As you progress toward the halfway mark of your baby's first year, you will probably find yourself increasingly settled in with this new person in your life. Feeding and sleeping should become generally more ordered and predictable so you can spend less time in maintenance mode and more in playful and pleasant interactions with him. You don't yet have the challenge of keeping track of a crawler/cruiser/toddler who is fervently seeking to explore every nook and cranny of your home. This child has yet to look you in the eye and communicate in his own unique way, "I know what you want, and I'm not giving it to you—what are you gonna do about it?"

Obviously not every infant approaching six months of age is a complete joy, and some will still be spending a lot more time fussing than cooing. But, if at all possible, this would be a good time for you to take a deep, slow breath and marvel at the wondrous gift God has entrusted to you. This project called parenting should include times when you momentarily lay aside your quest to catch up with the bills, laundry, projects brought home from work, dishes in the sink, and general clutter. Set a time at least once every week to take the phone off the hook, sit back in a comfortable chair, place your baby on your lap, and take a good long look at him. Watch his eyes; see how he is beginning to use his hands; catch the details of his toes. If you can elicit a few sounds from him, carry on a little "conversation." Jot down in a notebook some thoughts about what you now behold. In a few short years, long after you have forgotten whatever cares and annoyances were floating through this particular day, these memories will linger in your mind like a sweet song.

A babe in the house is a well-spring of pleasure, a messenger of peace and love, a resting place for innocence on earth, a link between angels and men.

Martin Farquhar Tupper
(British poet,
1810–1889)

Six to Twelve Months: Explorers

During the six months prior to her first birthday, your baby will begin a momentous transition. As Sir Isaac Newton might have put it, she will change from a "body at rest" to a "body in motion." Her blossoming ability to control arms and legs will enable her to propel herself from point A to point B, usually by way of points C, D, and E. This exciting development will also set in motion a series of conflicts that you and your child will reenact in thousands of ways over the next two decades.

She will want to investigate everything she can get her hands on but will be completely clueless about risks and consequences. And though fervently desiring to explore whatever she can see, she will also be afraid of separation from familiar faces, voices, and hugs. Your challenge will be to protect her—and her environment—while allowing her to stretch her wobbly legs and find out how the world works.

Before the end of her first year, she will also need to discover that, contrary to her own belief, she is not the center of the universe. She will need to learn about limits, that she cannot have or do whatever she wants, whenever she wants. She will need to discover that someone is in charge, and it isn't her. Your job will be to introduce her to these realities in a way that is loving, firm, consistent, and respectful.

Welcome to a whole new chapter of parenting!

Developmental Milestones: From Sitting to "Cruising" and Climbing . . .

Between six and nine months, your baby will be figuring out how to sit up and remain steady. First she will need support from pillows or the nearest adult. Then she will begin to prop herself up using her outstretched hands in a "tripod" posture. Eventually she will sit up for minutes at a time without toppling. By nine months, half of all babies are able to maneuver themselves into a sitting position from any other posture. This will give her considerable satisfaction, because her hands will be free to examine interesting objects while she remains upright.

Once your baby discovers the wonders of her world that are visible from a few inches off the floor, she will develop a keen interest in moving herself closer to whatever she spies across the room. Whether she eventually tries to roll, slither, scoot, or crawl toward them, and when she first makes the attempt, will be impossible to predict. If she takes to crawling, her skill will peak between seven and ten months, at which point you will be amazed at the speed with which she can cross the floor. She may use the traditional hands-and-knees approach, scuttle sideways like a crab, or inch forward military-style.

Some babies rarely or never crawl, and crawling doesn't actually appear on standard charts as a developmental milestone. Babies don't need to learn to crawl before they walk, and there is no correlation between this skill and future athletic or intellectual ability. Learning to crawl is not necessary for visual development, hand-eye coordination, or learning to read later in life. If other skills are moving ahead and your baby's doctor confirms that all else is going well, don't panic if she decides to skip crawling and move on to bigger and better things.

At around nine months of age, your baby will make another discovery: Standing upright is really, really fun. Usually someone in the family will pull her to a standing position next to the sofa or a soft chair, and she will gleefully remain there, using her hands to hold her position. Eventually she will figure out how to pull herself to her feet, using any available object that appears tall enough. Next comes the ultimate pre-walking thrill of "cruising" from one place to another while holding on to whatever will keep her upright.

There will be three potential problem areas during this phase of exploration. First, expect a minor commotion if she pulls herself to a stand but can't figure out how to let herself down. You can teach her to bend her knees and lower herself to the ground without a fall, a skill that will save her a few bruises and spare you several trips to wherever she has become hung up, including her crib.

Second, your baby will have no ability to judge the stability of whatever she sees around her. If she decides to pull herself up using a wastebasket, a petite end table, a houseplant, or a floor lamp, both she and her unsteady support may end up on the floor. The results can be unpleasant if she pulls down a loose tablecloth on which sits your favorite china, or dangerous and disastrous if she applies her weight to an object that is both unstable and heavy, such as a wobbly bookcase.

The third problem arises from a variation on cruising—climbing. Some babies find the lure of heights irresistible and will startle you with their ability to scale low-level furniture, stairs, or even combinations of pillows and stuffed animals to explore the upper atmosphere of the room. A few climbers will carry out remarkable acts of problem solving in their efforts to gain increased elevation. Unfortunately, their interest in heights will not be matched by an appreciation of the discomforts caused by a fall.

If your budding cruiser is going to be turned loose in a room, take a quick visual survey or a brief tour at her level to make certain that she won't find out about the force of gravity the hard way. Particularly important is keeping her off the stairs, which she will find irresistible once she discovers them. After her first birthday, she can begin to learn, with your direct supervision, how to get herself downstairs backward. But until she is clearly "stair safe" many months from now, you will need to consider getting one or more barricades if her activity areas provide potential access to a flight of stairs. These barricades should be the sturdy, horizontal gates with narrow slats (two and three-eighths inches or less apart) or plastic mesh, not the old-fashioned accordion-style, wood-slat barriers, which are less stable and are potential traps for inquisitive heads. (By the way, you won't find this style of gate on sale in any store, but they might show up at a garage sale. They might also be passed along by a well-meaning friend or relative who fished them out of an attic. Either way, this type of gate should be retired from duty.)

You will also need to choose between pressure-mounted gates (which are easier to install) and hardware-installed gates that take more effort to attach to a doorway or wall but are more stable. If you're unsure which to buy, keep in mind that you should not use pressure-mounted gates at the top of a staircase, because they're easier for a determined child to dislodge.

Letting her suffer some bruising consequences to "teach her a lesson" is a bad idea at this age. Not only will this risk unnecessary injury, but she is in fact not yet capable of understanding and judging the risks involved in her explorations. (She won't start on this learning curve until she is about fifteen months of age.)

Standing and walking

As your baby continues his relentless efforts to stay upright, he will at some point let go of his favorite support and stand on his own for a few seconds. At the same time or shortly thereafter, he will take a few shaky steps, perhaps with one or both parents cheering him on. Within a week he likely will be purposefully walking from one end of the room to the other, with or without a few unscheduled drops to the floor along the way. His legs will be bent and toes pointed outward, giving a thoroughly precarious appearance to his efforts. But all the lurching and plopping, which you may find nerve-racking to watch, won't slow him down at all. (Don't forget to grab the camera so you—and he—can enjoy seeing his first attempts at walking later.)

When will all this ambulating begin? Depending upon his size, center of gravity, genetic code, and temperament, it can begin anywhere between eight and fourteen months of age. If he is on the hefty side, he may have more difficulty hoisting his weight and maintaining his balance. The timing of his first steps has nothing to do with his future batting average or his chances of getting into college, but if he arrives at his first birthday and cannot stand even while being supported, your health-care provider—who will be doing a routine checkup at this age anyway—should be consulted.

What about shoes? Shoes serve little purpose prior to the onset of walking other than to decorate the feet for a family portrait. Once your baby starts to walk routinely, however, you may want to get shoes to protect his feet if he will be walking somewhere—such as in the backyard or a park—where terrain is more likely to contain objects that are unfriendly to little soles.

Shoes should be big enough to allow a half inch of space between his toes and the tip of the shoe, and since his feet will be growing rather rapidly, there is no sense in blowing the family budget on designer footwear. A simple pair of tennis shoes with a sole that grips will suffice. Unless prescribed by a qualified health-care professional to remedy a specific problem, he shouldn't need wedges, heel lifts, or other hardware in his shoes. He won't need arch supports because his arch is covered by a fat pad that will gradually recede over two to three years.

Furthermore, you may notice that while his toes point outward when he walks (because of looseness of the hip ligaments), his feet will tend to point inward (pigeon toes) when he lies down. Both of these situations should straighten out by the time he is about eighteen months old. If any positioning of feet or legs seems extreme or not symmetrical, have your baby's doctor (or, if necessary, an orthopedist who deals with young children) take a look. If you see your baby limp, whether now or in the future, a medical evaluation should be carried out as soon as possible. *Limping is never normal,* and it may in fact be the sign of a significant medical problem.

Eyes and hands

By seven or eight months of age, your baby's visual capabilities will have matured to the point that she can focus on people and objects across the room, though not quite with the clarity with which she sees things directly in front of her. She may find a mirror entertaining, as she watches the interesting little person who responds exactly to her own movements. She will be more attentive to a variety of colors and shapes and will be rapidly absorbing visual information about the world around her. You will at times notice her staring intently at something across the room. More often she will become fixated on, and apparently fascinated by, some tiny object directly in front of her—a wad of lint, a stray Cheerio, or a little bug.

Her increased visual skills will be matched by new abilities with hands and fingers. By nine months she will have progressed from the mitten or rakelike grasp (using four fingers as a unit against the thumb) to the more precise "pincer" grasp between thumb and one finger. She will also begin cooperative efforts between her two hands to pick up toys, pass an object from hand to hand, or smack two items together to enjoy the sound they produce.

SHOULD YOUR BABY WATCH "EDUCATIONAL" DVDS?

The promises seem a little far-fetched, but still you wonder. Can a thirty-minute video production really enhance your infant's IQ? Then one day you slip a disc into the player and, much to your surprise, you find that your seven-month-old is transfixed by the colorful images and pleasant music. In fact, you quickly find that whenever you need a twenty-minute break to start dinner or return an important phone call, you can count on one of these DVDs to hold your baby's rapt attention.

Do educational programs build your baby's brain power, or do they turn her into a budding couch potato? DVDs geared toward children two and under have become a billion-dollar business over the past decade, and their brisk sales have spawned a host of related paraphernalia such as CDs, flash cards, books, and computer software. Parents and relatives often buy these products because of the assumption, direct or implied (especially when they bear titles such as *Baby Einstein* and *Brainy Baby*), that they somehow educate babies or at least stimulate their developing intellect. But recently such claims have come under fire from some consumer groups who charge that there is no proof these products enhance a baby's brain development. In fact, these same critics have raised concerns that watching videos or DVDs might actually hinder development, and the American Academy of Pediatrics (AAP) has flatly stated that the amount of time a child under two should spend watching a video screen is *zero* minutes per day. So what's a parent to do?

The critics of "educational" baby DVDs are on target with two important points. First, any claims that these products accelerate a baby's intellectual development are more about marketing than systematic research. Rather than promoting passive viewing, child development experts emphasize the importance of parents encouraging a baby's interactions with the world around her and, more importantly, with the

Over the next three months, these investigations with hands will become more sophisticated. She will discover the joy of releasing something from her hands, or actually throwing it, and watching what happens. She will turn an item around and look at it from a variety of angles, rub it, and shake it. If it has a hole, she'll poke a finger into it. If it has parts she can move, she'll push, pull, twist, or spin them. Toward the end of the first year she will enjoy dumping small objects out of a container and then putting them back in, one at a time. She will knock something over and then set it upright, over and over. And, of course, she will bring *everything* directly to her mouth for examination by lips, gums, and tongue.

Sounds, syllables, and speech

One of the most pleasant developments between six and twelve months is watching your baby begin to make all sorts of new sounds. After six months he will begin imitating various syllables, primarily with vowels at first. By nine months, gurgling and babbling will be replaced by sounds with consonants such as *baba* or *dada*, either in short bursts or repeated at length. He will probably not assign these sounds to a particular person (for example, *Mama* for his mother) until twelve months or after.

As he progresses toward his first birthday, his "speech" will sound more sophisticated, though without much obvious meaning. Your one-year-old is likely to utilize a

people around her. Right now your baby's education is going on during every waking hour as she handles, gums, bangs, and drops everything in sight, and as she listens to older people talk to her. No DVD can duplicate these experiences.

The second concern is a direct outgrowth of the first: Weary or time-pressured parents might choose to put their infants in front of a TV screen for hours on end, based on a misguided assumption that these products are doing as good (or better) a job at stimulating budding intellects as a parent could. (Some DVDs even have a repeat play option, which allows the program to cycle in an endless loop.) Later in this book we'll talk more about the risk of allowing electronic babysitters to occupy a child's attention for extended periods of time, even if you select their content.

One additional issue: Some parents hope to accelerate their baby or toddler's intellectual development using "educational" DVDs or other materials because they want to give them an academic head start. But as we've just noted, in addition to the lack of evidence that these DVDs make a difference in a child's long-term brainpower, even more important is the fact that *little ones need to be valued for who they are*. If a perceived shortfall in terms of IQ, appearance, athletic ability, musical talent, or any other characteristic affects your love and acceptance of your child, it's time to take a hard look at your own values.

All that being said, will watching a video program once in a while harm your baby? The AAP's recommendation that a child under two never look at a TV screen may meet with a little skepticism from a busy parent. If you find that twenty or thirty minutes of a *Baby Einstein* keeps your infant or toddler occupied once in a while, by all means enjoy the break. (Many of these have sound tracks consisting of engaging arrangements of classical music, which you may enjoy as much as your child.) Better yet, watch the show together and talk to her about what you both see and hear. Remember, when it comes to learning, that type of interaction is *really* where the money is. ■

vocabulary of a few words, along with some wonderfully modulated babbling that rises and falls with the inflections of real speech. You can almost imagine that he is a visitor speaking a foreign language. He will also begin to communicate with gestures, such as pointing to something he finds interesting, waving bye-bye, or shaking his head to signify no. You may also hear exclamations such as "Uh-oh!"

While his speaking vocabulary may not be extensive at his first birthday, he can understand quite a bit more (in fact, far more than you probably realize) well before that date. After nine months he will begin responding to his own name and may show recognition of familiar people, pets, or objects. He will likely (we hope) respond to the word *no* before he starts using it himself. He may turn his head toward a person or toy you name, and before long he will surprise you by following a simple command.

You can make a major contribution to your child's language development during these months, even if you're not yet having much conversation. All day long you can name objects that you both see, talk in simple terms about what you are doing, and even look through simple picture books together. Try to keep your vocabulary straightforward and consistent, and don't expose him to hours of convoluted baby talk. Instead, coo and fuss and caress with your voice to your heart's content—using real words. His little computer will be processing all of this input, associating objects and pictures with words that you provide, and he might as well get it right the first time.

As cute as you will find his babbling, resist the temptation to repeat back his garbled versions of new words. If he points to a truck and says, "Guck!" be sure to say, "That's right, truck!" rather than leading him to believe that he has truly seen a guck. (One exception: Grandparents almost always proudly assume the names given to them by the first grandchild, such as "Nana and Papa," "Gomba and Bumpa," etc.)

Now is a good time to think about the kinds of sounds your baby will be imitating. Does everyone in the family speak in calm, pleasant tones, or do conversations sound loud and confrontational? Are compliments or complaints exchanged across the kitchen table? Is your baby likely to learn "Shut up!" before he says "I love you"? Is he hearing more words from the adults in his life or from the TV set droning in the corner? If you don't like what your baby is hearing, hold a family meeting and prayer time to help launch some new conversation patterns (and perhaps lower noise levels) at home.

Gestures and games

In addition to imitating your words and speech patterns, your six- to twelve-month-old will also begin to mimic gestures and movements. You will be pleasantly surprised one day to see him holding his toy telephone to his ear rather than banging it on the floor, or stroking his toy brush across his hair rather than gumming it. By one year of age, he will also enjoy a number of gesture games, such as peekaboo, pat-a-cake, and "so big." ("How big is Tyler?" Tyler's hands will imitate yours reaching for the sky, as you say, "So-o-o-o big!")

You can have fun with your baby and watch some developmental milestones being reached as he develops his sense of **object permanence**. At four or five months of age, if something is out of sight, it's also out of mind. If he pushes his rattle off the edge of the sofa, he won't pursue it with his eyes. But at about nine months of age, he can keep an image of something fixed in memory long enough to look for it after it disappears.

Take one of his toys, show it to him, and then hide it under a small cloth. Voilà! He will pull the cloth away to reveal the toy, much to everyone's delight. As he practices this skill, you can try putting two or more obstacles between him and the toy. With the increasing maturity of his sense of object permanence, he will be more persistent in finding it. To make the game even more exciting, you can "hide" yourself behind a chair or around a corner and then let him "find" you. (You may need to leave a foot in view or peek around the corner the first time until he gets the idea.)

Other games you can play (which for your baby are actually explorations of the world around him) include rolling a ball back and forth, building a small tower out of plastic blocks and letting him knock it over, and plopping all sorts of smaller objects into a large container and then dumping them out. There are, indeed, very few fancy gadgets that babies this age will appreciate any more than simple, inexpensive toys (or, for that matter, household items): all sizes and types of plastic containers, lightweight unbreakable bowls and cups, balls of all sizes (as long as they are too big to fit into his mouth), building blocks, toy telephones, and plastic cars, trucks, and planes (whose edges aren't sharp and whose parts won't come loose).

Safety Measures: Curiosity, Chaos, and Cautions

All of these activities with eyes and hands are not random or meaningless. On the contrary, they are vital to your baby's development. Her brain and nervous system are assimilating information at a rapid pace, and all of the staring, touching, and gumming are providing important input about how things are and the way they work. By nine months of age, your baby's curiosity will be insatiable. She will not be content merely to inspect every item within her reach. She will also be itching to get her hands on all those interesting shapes that she's been seeing for weeks on end from across the room. Her intense curiosity will thus become a driving force in advancing her motor skills.

This normal—and necessary—development will generate extra work and worry for everyone in your baby's life. Her explorations should be encouraged, but they will inevitably require some adjustment of your living arrangements. You'll need to balance your baby's healthy curiosity against her need for a safe environment and your need for some semblance of order.

Avoiding extremes is important. Confinement for hours on end in a playpen, which might be convenient for the grown-ups, will impair the flow of information to baby's developing brain. But giving her unlimited access to all parts of the home without some thoughtful preparation is an invitation to harm or disaster. *Furthermore, attempting to train a baby at this age by subjecting her to a nonstop torrent of No's! and hand slapping while she is merely trying to find out what's what in her world will make everyone miserable and exhausted.*

Some reasonable baby-proofing and commonsense precautions will spare everyone a lot of toil and grief.

Take a child's-eye tour of whatever living space will be available to your crawler/ cruiser/walker. Are there any top-heavy items—chairs, tables, floor lamps, bookshelves—that might fall if pulled by your baby? Are any electrical cords or outlets within reach? (Install plastic plugs to block unused outlets from inquisitive fingers.) Do you see any wires with frayed insulation? These are a hazard to everyone, not just the baby. What about cords dangling down from a curling or steam iron resting on a counter or ironing board? A yank on one of these could cause not only a hazardous bonk on her head or body but also a very painful burn.

Are there any small objects lying around that, upon entering her mouth, might end up in her airway? Your vigilance regarding small objects will be a daily concern if you have older children at home because their toys and games tend to have lots of tiny parts and pieces that have a way of dispersing throughout your home. How about cords attached to draperies and blinds? These should be looped or tied on a hook well out of reach to prevent the baby from getting tangled in them.

Don't leave your prized china or other valuable breakables within reach of a newly mobile baby and then demand that she not touch them. She will have no concept of the difference between a cup made by Wedgwood and one brought home from Wendy's, except, perhaps, by the distinctive sounds they make when they hit the floor. Your expensive collectibles should be displayed (or stored) out of reach during this season of your child's life.

While some recommend that your kitchen be kept off-limits to little explorers, this will probably not be a realistic option. Most parents and older children traverse the kitchen many times each day, and dealing with a barricade every time is a major nuisance. Lots of family interactions take place in kitchens, and your baby will not want to be left out.

This will mean, however, relocating cleaning compounds and other chemicals to higher ground. Bleach, furniture polish, and drain cleaners are particularly hazardous, and automatic-dishwasher powder can be extremely irritating if it gets into the mouth. Sharp objects, which of course are abundant in kitchens, must also be kept out of reach at all times. If you have an automatic dishwasher, be sure to keep the door latched when you are not loading or unloading it. A wide-open dishwasher door is not only an ir-resistible climbing spot but also a gateway to all sorts of glassware and sharp utensils.

Many families set aside a low cupboard for "baby's kitchen stuff"—a collection of old plastic bowls, cups, spoons, lids, and other safe unbreakables that she can examine and manipulate to her heart's content. (By the way, she will probably spend a fair amount of time moving the cupboard door back and forth on its hinge.) You may want to steer her toward this particular cupboard and away from the others (this will take lots of

SPECIAL TOYS, AND TOYS TO AVOID

Short attention spans and nonstop investigation of one item after another mean that you don't have to spend a lot of money on a special toy, since your young explorer probably won't spend any more time with it than with the box containing it. However, if Uncle John really wants to unload some cash on a toy for his nephew, you could steer him toward the following:

- Push toys, especially if they have a low center of gravity that allows your baby to cruise or "walk" behind them.
- Busy boxes with all sorts of switches and levers to push and noises to make.
- Bath toys that can be emptied and filled (a few plastic cups may suffice for this) or toys that float, squeak, and squirt.
- Sturdy picture books with thick cardboard pages; your baby will probably get less of a charge out of the pictures than he will from moving the pages back and forth, since they function as a colorful hinge, and many babies at this age are hinge fanatics.

repetition) or make the arrangement more formal by installing plastic safety latches in the cupboards and drawers that are off-limits.

While kitchens are difficult to barricade, bathrooms are another story. Like kitchens, they are full of potential hazards: medications, cleaners, and, most important, bodies of water. Any medications (prescription or over-the-counter, including vitamins and iron) and cleaning substances must be stored well out of reach and returned to their secure spot *immediately* after each use.

Never leave a baby unattended in the bath, even at this age, and be certain to empty the tub as soon as you're done with it. Open toilets are an irresistible destination for a cruiser. The possible consequences of a baby's investigation of an unflushed toilet are both unsafe and stomach turning. More important is the possibility that a top-heavy toddler might lean over far enough to fall in.

Never leave hair dryers, curlers, or other electrical devices plugged in after you use them. For that matter, no one should be using any of these items when the baby (or anyone else) is in the bathtub, unless you have a very large bathroom with a lengthy distance between appliance and water. If your baby or an older child tries to take the hair dryer for a swim, *even if it's turned off but plugged in,* the resulting shock could be lethal.

Unlike most kitchens, bathrooms have doors that can be shut to prevent unsupervised entry. If an enterprising explorer learns to turn door handles, an additional high latch may need to be installed.

Survey your home for "what's hot and what's not." Radiators, heaters, floor furnace grills, and fireplace screens can all become surprisingly hot, and a protective barrier between these surfaces and little fingers will be needed, at least during some times of the year.

Be sure the handles of pots on hot burners don't extend over the edge of the stove, since one healthy pull could result in a severely scalded child. Some stoves also have exposed knobs that babies and toddlers might love to twist and turn. If these are easily detachable, you may want to remove them between meals. You can also buy safety covers at a hardware store.

Toys to think twice about or avoid altogether at this age include:

- Stuffed animals. That's right, stuffed animals, especially for the baby younger than nine months who has no idea who Elmo or Mickey Mouse is and has no interest in finding out. These toys can collect dust, aggravate allergic noses, shed hair and stuffing, and lose plastic eyes and noses that might end up in someone's airway or even in an older toddler's nose. If the stuffed toys accidentally get in the line of fire when your baby spits up, they'll reek for weeks. As your baby passes the nine-month mark and separation anxiety becomes more evident, a soft something may be enlisted for duty as a transitional object to help keep him calm when you are out of the room or out for the evening. Whatever is used must be sturdy enough to survive lots of handling and washing, and must not be adorned with little decorative items that might come loose.
- Anything with sharp edges, little parts, or big parts that might easily become little parts.
- Balloons. Aside from scaring the daylights out of your baby when they pop, those little rubber fragments are very easy to choke on. ■

A similar reminder applies to hot liquids such as soups and gravies near the edge of your dining table, especially if they sit on a tablecloth that could be pulled from below. Avoid carrying your wiggly explorer and a cup of hot coffee or tea at the same time. One sudden twist on her part could fling hot liquid over both of you.

Set your hot-water heater temperature below 120°F (49°C) to minimize the risk of an accidental scald from the tap.

How about those houseplants? Infants and toddlers can be quite adept at doing some impressive pruning on your prized houseplants if they are within reach. A more worrisome possibility is that these young children might choose to sample the leaves and stems, which may be irritating to the lining of the mouth or even overtly toxic. Now is the time to move the plants out of reach, unless you know for certain that they are nontoxic and you don't care if they get mangled sometime during the next few months. In order to prevent your explorer from having a close encounter with the dirt around any plants that remain at floor level, you can cover the soil with screen mesh.

PREVENTING HOT-WATER BURNS

Pop quiz:

    1. How hot is the water that flows from your tap?
    2. How hot is too hot?

We'll answer the second question first. The chart below shows the length of time it takes for water at various temperatures to cause a burn that will need medical attention:[1]

Temperature of Water	Time to Cause a Significant Burn
150°F (66°C)	2 seconds
140°F (60°C)	6 seconds
125°F (52°C)	2 minutes
120°F (49°C)	10 minutes

The numbers speak for themselves. If the water running into your sink or bathtub is too hot, your infant or small child could suffer a painful or even life-threatening burn after only a few seconds of accidental contact.

In order to check water temperature, you'll need to measure it yourself. Run hot water into the sink for two or three minutes in the morning before anyone has taken a shower or bath, and hold an outdoor or candy thermometer under the stream until the temperature reaches its maximum level. If the thermometer reads between 120° and 125°, you don't need to make any changes. If the water is hotter than 125°, you'll need to find the temperature adjustment on your water heater and turn it down. Check the temperature again twenty-four hours after the first reading. If it's too high or low, make another adjustment and check again the next day. You may have to make several adjustments before you find the right temperature, but preventing a burn is well worth this modest amount of trouble. ■

Finally, think about your baby's introduction to the great outdoors. When the weather's nice and the family gathers in the backyard, what interesting but hazardous items might cross her path? Once again, make a baby's-eye survey of any area that she might reach (if she's a skilled crawler, keep in mind how fast she can move while your attention is diverted).

If you have a swimming pool, make sure that a childproof fence— at least four feet high, not climbable, and equipped with a self-closing and self-latching gate—surrounds it. (Some states require this safety barrier by law.) If your yard contains a spa, it should be securely covered when not in use. Pool and hot-tub drain covers should be checked periodically to make sure they are properly in place. If not, a child's hand or even hair could be pulled into the outlet by the suction created by the pump, and she might be unable to break free. Children have drowned in such circumstances. As a backup precaution, make sure that the pump's on-off switch is readily accessible.

Check the lawn for mushrooms, and if you are not absolutely certain they are nontoxic, get rid of them, because anything your baby finds at this age is likely to go straight into her mouth. Are there any garden tools, insecticides, fertilizers, or other unfriendly items lying around? The more potential dangers you can eliminate from her immediate access, the more you can enjoy your time outdoors with her.

One other outdoor hazard you must not ignore is the sun. A baby's skin is very sensitive to the ultraviolet (UV) light generated by the sun, and at peak times of the day (between 10 a.m. and 3 p.m.) as little as fifteen minutes of direct exposure can provoke an unpleasant burn. This is a particular problem at higher altitudes, where UV light is more intense, and around lakes and oceans, where UV light can reflect from water and sand. Sunburns can also occur on hazy or overcast days because UV light penetrates both haze and cloud cover.

If your baby is going to be experiencing the great outdoors for any length of time, try to avoid the 10 a.m. to 3 p.m. time of peak intensity, keep her in the shade as much as possible, and utilize appropriate clothing (as well as a hat or bonnet) for protection. An explorer who is going to be in and out of sunlight will benefit from a sunscreen with a sun protection factor (SPF) rating of at least 15, applied an hour before she ventures forth. If you are going to take her with you into the pool, use a waterproof version and reapply it after you are done. Occasionally a baby will react to the UV-protecting ingredient known as PABA, so you may want to avoid sunscreens containing this compound. If your baby has very sensitive skin, you might take your sunscreen for a "test drive" by applying some to a small area of her skin (an inch or a couple of centimeters wide) for several hours to see if any reaction develops.

What about insect repellent for your outdoor explorer? Increasing awareness of illness caused by the West Nile virus that is spread by bites from infected mosquitoes has put repellents in the spotlight, even though West Nile virus infections have been very uncommon in the United States. Nevertheless, you may want to consider using repellent for your child (and yourself) if you're going to be outside for any length of time—especially between dusk and dawn, when mosquitoes (including those that carry West Nile virus) are more likely to be biting. This is particularly important if there are reports of mosquito-transmitted disease in your area.

DEET (N,N-diethyl-m-toluamide) is widely used as an active ingredient in insect repellents and is considered safe for use in children over two months of age.[2] According to the Food and Drug Administration (FDA), products containing another active ingredient, oil of eucalyptus, are not recommended for children younger than three years old.[3]

Equally (if not more) important for safety is proper use of repellents:

- When applying repellent, put it on your hands first and then rub it on the child's skin, avoiding the eyes, mouth, and any cuts or irritated skin.
- Don't apply repellent to a child's hands (which often go into their mouths).
- Sunscreen and insect repellent can be applied at the same time (put on the sunscreen first), but products containing both should be avoided. To be effective, sunscreen usually has to be applied more often than repellent.
- When the outdoor activities are over for the day, wash the skin on which the repellent was applied.

Weather permitting, remember that clothing with long pants and long sleeves can serve as a physical barrier to bites by insects and other critters (such as ticks).

Parental vigilance . . .

Many of these guidelines represent passive restraints—fixed barriers between child and hazard. But you cannot anticipate every possible risk or create enough safeguards for a 100 percent–safe environment, unless you want to turn your home into a padded cell. You will need to take more active measures as well, involving both your own surveillance and some basic training for your baby.

From your standpoint, perpetual vigilance is the price of child rearing, at least for now. You must develop an ongoing sense of your child's whereabouts, a third eye and ear that are tuned in to him, even when he is in a confined and seemingly safe space such as his crib. You will need to monitor his activities constantly to see what new perils might cross his path in the immediate future.

The riskiest times will be those when you are distracted, frazzled, or just plain weary. You may be in the middle of a project involving hazardous tools or materials—a long overdue deep cleaning, for example. Suddenly the phone rings, or someone is at the door, or another child cries out in another room. Before you drop everything to attend to the new situation, look at what might be open, exposed, or available to your baby. Could he get to any of it? You may have to delay your response for a few moments while you ensure there is no way your baby in motion can get his hands on something dangerous.

Beware of those times in the day—especially the late afternoon—when your energy may be low, your mind preoccupied, and your patience short. One or more other children may be irritable at this time, competing for your attention. But don't lose track of your youngest crawler/cruiser/toddler, who may have just discovered something interesting that was dropped under the kitchen table.

Sometime in your parenting career, you may reach a point of such sheer exhaustion that you just have to lie down for a little while. Do you let an older child watch the baby or let him roam around your bedroom while you close your eyes for a few precious minutes? Think hard before you stretch your safety boundaries. Some cautions about using older children as babysitters were brought up in the previous chapter, but you must be even more wary when you have a new explorer. An older child is more likely to become distracted by a friend or toy, and a major problem could develop during a few moments of inattention. If you are really that tired, see if a trusted adult such as a friend, neighbor, or relative might relieve you for one or more hours' respite.

. . . and baby's boundaries

The other side of the safety coin involves your child. As her first birthday nears, she must learn that there are some boundaries in her world, even if she has been given access to a substantial amount of your living space. Of course, she will have no way of knowing what is okay to touch and what is off-limits until she is given that information. And give it you must, remembering that—for now—her driving force is nearly always her intense curiosity rather than a specific desire to put you and your limits to the test. At this stage of development, in fact, you can take advantage of her curiosity, along with her short attention span, to help shift her interest away from the things you want her to avoid.

Keep in mind that your limit setting will require a lot of legwork because you can't use much verbal "remote control" until she's a few months older. If she is examining something that is unsafe or inappropriate, it is extremely unlikely that she will understand the command ("Emily, don't eat that bug!") you issue from across the room. The tone of your voice may get her attention and perhaps stop the deed momentarily. But you will also have to separate the offending item from her fingers (or mouth) while making a simple and concrete statement about it. ("No, no—not for Emily" or "Don't touch the stove—ouch!")

Will she understand what you are saying? Probably not at first, although she will pick up your reaction about what she has been doing. More important, her amazing little computer is continually processing information about "What happens when I _____?" and you definitely want to provide a lot of the input. In particular, when setting boundaries, your tone of voice should communicate that you mean business. (You can't project much of a warning or a sense of authority if you sound like the Lullaby Lady.) On the other hand, yelling, haranguing, or (worse) sounding off without taking any action will definitely work against you. Sometimes a verbal and physical response at the same time can turn your statement into an object lesson: "Don't touch the curtains" will make more of an impact while you are physically removing her from them.

Her short attention span will usually allow you to distract her focus elsewhere after you have made your point. Most likely she will forget about whatever she found interesting if you offer her something else that is equally intriguing. But she may also forget whatever you were originally trying to tell her. If she is really intent on pursuing her investigation, she may promptly head back to the shiny knobs on the stereo or the ill-tempered cat's flopping tail, even when you have just taken her away from it—for the seventh time.

When your mobile baby seems determined to override your intentions and repeatedly bears down on the forbidden target, *don't back away from the limits you have set.* Take action every time, making your statement by using an increasingly firm tone of voice (which won't be difficult). One approach to consider when she crosses your line over and over again is to remove her completely from the temptation zone. A time-out in a crib or playpen, where her roaming privileges are temporarily curtailed for a few minutes, may be appropriate at this point.

At some point, however, you may need to take more direct and immediate action, especially if she is repeatedly reaching for something that is dangerous. A quick thump on the hand (not hard, but enough to get her attention) may need to accompany your verbal warning, but this should be done only if

- you are certain that she understands what you want (which is not likely before nine months of age);
- her safety is on the line; and
- you have no other way to separate her from the hazard.

The point of your response is not to lash out in anger and frustration but to change behavior for her benefit and protection. If she is bent on playing with the handle on the oven, for example, the brief sting of your rebuke will be far less painful than a burn on her fingers. When she cries as a result, take a moment to comfort her and talk things over. While she won't understand a lecture on burn prevention, some simple input such as "Mommy said not to touch this" will usually be understood by a baby approaching her first birthday.

Indeed, at this age your objective is not to teach great moral principles or the whys and why nots of home safety. Later, when her language and reasoning skills are more sophisticated, you will carry out that assignment on an ongoing basis. In the meantime, she must assimilate some reasonable house rules into her ever-increasing fund of knowledge about how her world works. Your consistent enforcement of boundaries, even at this preverbal stage, will establish that you are in charge and position you to handle the more overt challenges to come.

If it hasn't become apparent by now, you will soon become acutely aware that you cannot guarantee the absolute safety of your child. In addition to loving, comforting, teaching your child, and taking appropriate safety precautions where you live, now is the time to renew your commitment to pray for her as well. Remember that she is on loan, entrusted to your care for a season, and her Creator ultimately knows and loves her far better than anyone can imagine. Acknowledging that fact and seeking His wisdom on a daily basis—even for the everyday routines of parenting—will help keep your concerns in perspective and tap into strength and insight that extend far deeper than your own.

Feeding: Solid Foods—Beyond the Basics

During these six months your baby will make another important transition as he becomes nourished primarily by solid foods. Chapter 6 described the process of introducing your baby to solids in some detail (page 174), and if you are just now beginning to offer your baby any food other than milk, you should review that information.

Chapter 6 also mentioned some reasons not to begin solids too early (before four months of age), but you don't want to wait too long either. As your baby passes the sixth month, breastfeeding or formula alone will fall short of providing the calories and nutrients he needs. Between six and nine months he may be more willing to try a variety of foods than after the one-year mark. Thus, your goal at six months will be to begin solids if you haven't by now and then to expand his food horizons gradually and steadily.

By the end of the first year, the general outline of his eating patterns should resemble your own, except for amounts and textures. This raises the question of where you will take your baby nutritionally. If your family's eating habits are chaotic and your diet loaded with fat, salt, and sugar, do you want your baby to reach the same endpoint? This may be a good time to reevaluate and reconfigure your own food choices. (If you'd like to review this topic in more detail, see "Some ABCs of Good Nutrition," beginning on page 771.)

By nine months you will see some side-to-side chewing movements that signal readiness for foods with a thicker texture. This is a good time to begin trying some mashed or chopped food from the family meal and some finger foods that your baby can feed himself. The latter include items such as small pieces of soft, peeled fruit (peaches or pears, for example), little squares of bread or toast, unsalted crackers, pieces of pancake or soft waffle, and cooked soft pasta.

Don't become a clean-plate fanatic with your baby. When first sampling solids he will take only small amounts—one or two tablespoons at a time—and then gradually increase his intake over time. Watch for signs that he is no longer hungry—turning his head, getting fussy, or general disinterest in what you are offering from the spoon. Trying to force him to eat a prescribed amount is not only an exercise in futility, but it may also set up a bad habit of eating when he has no appetite.

Chapter 6 listed a number of cautions about foods and feeding. Because of their potential impact on your baby's health, these caveats will be repeated here along with some additional notes for the more experienced solid-food consumer.

- *Do not feed honey to babies under the age of twelve months* because of the risk of infant **botulism**, a form of food poisoning that can cause serious damage to the nervous system, or very rarely can be fatal. For a number of years, corn syrup was said to be a potential dietary source of the toxin that causes infant botulism, but more recent evidence has not supported this idea.
- Keep your baby on breast milk or infant formula (fortified with iron) until he reaches the age of twelve months. Infants who drink cow's milk before their first birthday are more likely to develop an allergy to the protein it contains. This may lead to the loss of small amounts of blood from the intestine. Cow's milk may also interfere with the absorption of iron contained in other foods. Both of these could lead to a shortage of red blood cells (anemia). After twelve months, when you do begin to offer cow's milk, use whole milk, not low fat or nonfat, because your baby will need the extra fat to construct his growing central nervous system.
- Keep your baby away from chocolate, peanut butter, shellfish, egg whites, citrus fruits, strawberries, and tomatoes before his first birthday; these can induce future allergies. Some physicians also add wheat and corn to this off-limits list for the same reason.
- Even more risky to your baby are foods that might cause a choking accident. Avoid any foods that are small and hard such as seeds, nuts, small candies, uncooked peas, and popcorn. Also keep your baby away from foods that are sticky, chewy, stringy, or small and round. Peanut butter and hot dogs are thus off-limits, along with grapes, uncooked vegetables, raw apples, and dried fruit. In a nutshell, foods that can't be squashed by gums or easily dissolved in saliva or that might fit snugly into a small airway don't belong in your baby's mouth.
- Don't feed your baby foods with added salt or sugar, or with spicy flavors. He needs to become accustomed to the basic, unadulterated taste of high-quality foods. Offer fruit for dessert rather than calorie-drenched sweets such as custards and puddings. By all means, don't offer your baby soft drinks, punch, or other sweetened drinks. The last thing he needs is to develop a taste for this "liquid candy."
- Keep up the variety. If your baby seems to ignore everything but one or two foods—crackers and bananas, for example—don't be frightened or blackmailed into allowing him to establish a major food rut. Hold these items and offer him a variety of alternatives from the other food groups instead. If he refuses, don't panic. When he's hungry, he'll eat what you've offered, especially if he hasn't filled his tank with milk before mealtime.
- Don't let your baby become a grazer. Some parents respond with food (breast, bottle, or snacks) whenever their baby utters any sound remotely suggesting displeasure. The result is nonstop eating by a baby who is never actually hungry

or completely satisfied and who might acquire a long-term habit of turning to food for comfort. You would be wise to avoid feeding patterns such as this that might result in overeating, especially if obesity is a problem on either side of your family. Between six and nine months, you can establish mealtime routines: breakfast, lunch, and dinner, with midmorning and midafternoon snacks if you and your baby desire. But when meals are over, let them be over.

- Don't put your baby to bed with a bottle of milk or juice. If he falls asleep with anything other than water in his mouth, bacteria can damage his incoming teeth. A baby who drinks from a bottle while lying flat will also be at greater risk for developing middle-ear infections. If your baby truly seems to sleep better after a bedtime snack, be sure all of it is swallowed and then carry out a gentle toothbrushing with water (if he has any teeth) before going to bed.

- Don't let your baby become a "juiceaholic." Some become so enamored with the sweet taste of juices that they will favor them over more nutritious sources of calories, including milk. Furthermore, juices sucked from bottles may stay in contact longer with the teeth and lead to early decay. Juice bottles have a

INTRODUCING YOUR BABY TO SOLID FOODS

1. After three tablespoons of rice cereal go down smoothly at one feeding, you may want to try other cereals such as oats and barley. Check with your baby's doctor before trying corn or wheat cereals, which provoke digestive problems in some infants.

2. After cereals have been established on the menu for a few weeks, you can introduce either fruits or vegetables. Vegetables may hold an advantage because they will not condition your baby to sweet tastes. Fruits can be added later, and meats should be introduced last. You may choose to raise a vegetarian and not introduce meats to your baby at all, but if you do so, be sure that you are adequately informed so your baby won't be deprived of any necessary nutrients.

3. Remember to let your baby try each new food (one to three tablespoons' worth) for a few days before introducing another. Observe for any signs of a reaction: diarrhea, irritability, runny nose, coughing or wheezing, or a rash, especially around the face. If there is any possibility that a reaction has occurred, withdraw the food, wait for the problem to calm down, and try again—unless the reaction is severe; then consult your baby's doctor. If you see the same response again, put that food aside for several weeks, and tell your baby's doctor before serving it to him again. If there's a more severe reaction, such as an immediate rash or breathing difficulties, contact his doctor immediately. Fortunately, sudden intense reactions to foods are very uncommon at this age.

4. Once your baby is taking food from different groups (for example, cereal and vegetables), you can feed him solids twice daily and expand to three times daily when three or more types of food are part of his daily routine. In addition, his daily intake should include about twenty-four to thirty-two ounces of breast milk or formula. (A rule of thumb is that one nursing session at this age delivers six to eight ounces of milk.)

way of becoming an entrenched habit. Hold off on juices until he can drink them from a cup. Once he has started drinking them on a regular basis, set a four-ounce daily limit, or dilute four ounces with an equal amount of water if you want to offer them more often. Since citrus fruits may provoke allergic responses during the first year, you may want to hold the orange juice until after the first birthday. (Check with your baby's doctor.)

Avoiding high-chair hazards

As your baby begins to spend more time with solids each day, you may find it easier to feed her in a high chair. As with all baby equipment, a few simple precautions will help prevent unpleasant or even serious accidents.

- As with bathtubs and car seats, rule number one with high chairs is *never leave your baby unattended while she is sitting in it.*
- Make certain that the chair has a broad base so it cannot be easily tipped over. Grandma's high chair might be a venerated family heirloom, but if it doesn't

Once he has become well acquainted with solids, you'll generally want to offer breast milk or formula *after* your baby has had other foods. (Milk can also be given between meals and at bedtime.) Solids won't hold much interest if his tank is already full of six or eight ounces of milk.

A Few Reminders about Food Preparation

If you are using commercially prepared baby food from a jar, make sure that the safety button in the middle of the lid pops up when you open it. If it doesn't, return the jar or throw it away. Don't feed your baby directly from the jar because the enzymes and bacteria from his saliva may degrade or contaminate the food he doesn't finish. Instead, spoon a small amount on a plate, and put what remains in the jar into the refrigerator, where it will be good for a day (or a month frozen). Whatever is left on his plate should be thrown away.

You may prefer to prepare your own foods rather than (or in addition to) using commercial baby-food products. At first, keep them simple: adequately cooked and then pureed in a blender or baby-food grinder, or mashed with a fork. Fruits other than bananas should be cooked rather than served raw.

Avoid salty, sugary, and spicy concoctions as well as foods that might provoke allergic reactions. When your baby has had his fill of a particular item, you can store any extra in the refrigerator. However, before serving rewarmed food to your baby at a later meal, inspect and smell for any signs of spoilage. If in doubt, toss it out.

Solid foods do not need to be hot; room temperature or slightly warm is just fine for most babies. If you need to warm something from the refrigerator, use the microwave with extreme caution—if at all—because of the possibility of uneven temperatures and hot spots within the food that could burn the mouth. Microwaved food should be thoroughly stirred so the heat is distributed evenly throughout. If heating baby food in a jar, you can place the jar in a pan of warm water for a few minutes. ■

sit rock solid on the floor, use a newer one. If you use a chair that folds, make sure it is locked into place before your baby gets in.

- Take the few extra seconds to secure your baby with the chair's safety straps. This will prevent her from wiggling and sliding out of position or standing up to survey the horizon, both of which could result in a serious injury.
- Before your baby is seated, make sure the chair is at a safe distance from the nearest wall or counter. Otherwise, a healthy shove from your young diner might topple her and the chair to the floor.
- Don't let other children play under or climb on the high chair.
- Clean food debris off the chair and tray after each meal. Your baby may have no reservations about sampling any leftovers—in various states of decay—that are within finger range.

If you use a portable baby seat that clamps onto a table when you travel or eat out, observe a few additional precautions:

MAKING THE TRANSITION FROM BREAST TO BOTTLE?

If breast milk has been your baby's primary nutrition source through the first six months of life, you will need to introduce her to solids during the coming months (if you haven't started already) as has been described on pages 206–207.

But should you switch to formula feeding as well? The answer depends entirely on you and your baby. On one hand, if the two of you are a smoothly functioning nursing team and everyone is quite happy with this arrangement, there's absolutely no need to change. Indeed, the American Academy of Pediatrics strongly supports breastfeeding as the best nutrition source for at least the first year of life. If a well-meaning relative thinks you're "getting a little carried away with this breastfeeding thing" because you're still nursing a baby who is nearly a year old and perhaps starting to walk, you can let her know, without any embarrassment, that this arrangement not only is working very nicely for you but also has the solid backing of health professionals. In other words, at this point in your baby's life, "if it ain't broke, don't fix it."

On the other hand, baby or mother (or both) may be ready to make a change during the months approaching the first birthday. As babies become more mobile and fascinated with the world around them, they may also become squirmy and distracted during nursing sessions—especially during the day when they are wide-awake and their hunger is being satisfied by other foods. They may suck a few times and then display body language that says, "Sorry to eat and run, Mom, but I've got things to do!" To add injury to insult, some babies may absentmindedly chomp on a nipple with their newly erupted teeth.

Many moms have their own reason to wean a baby from nursing to formula between six and twelve months of age. Perhaps they feel the need to devote more of their time and attention to other people and activities within the home, to educational pursuits, to outside employment, or to a combination of these interests. Some begin to long to "have my body back," especially if nursing is starting to feel more like alligator wrestling. There may be a budding (or even full-grown) desire to pursue weight reduction and physical conditioning without worrying about affecting a baby's nutritional well-being.

- Make sure the table is steady enough to support both chair and baby and that the chair is securely clamped to the table before your baby gets in. Card tables, glass tops, tables supported only by a center post, and extension leaves are not strong or stable enough for this job.
- Position the chair so your baby can't push against one of the table legs and literally "shove off" for a voyage to the floor.
- The chair should attach to the bare surface of the table, not a tablecloth or place mat that can slide off.
- Don't let older children play under the table or seat, since they might accidentally bump and dislodge it.

Dining area or "mess" hall?

Some babies are quite content to let you feed them one spoonful of food after another, while others can't wait to take matters into their own hands (literally) as soon as possible. When your ten-month-old reaches for the feeding spoon, she is primarily

Even more fundamental and important for many mothers is the realization that an inevitable passage is arriving: The totally helpless and dependent newborn, who derived all of her sustenance from her mother who carried and nursed her, is now taking the very first steps toward independence. She now needs more nourishment than she can obtain from milk. She is starting to move in all directions under her own power. She most certainly needs to be loved and cherished and must have plenty of Mom's attention if she is going to thrive, but her direct physical attachment to her is coming to a close. Whether it occurs now or sometime after the first birthday, allowing this brief season of intimate dependence to end is but one of hundreds of ways in which she will need to be released, step by tiny step, over the next eighteen to twenty years.

Whatever your reasons might be, if you are ready to move from breastfeeding to a bottle or cup:

- Substitute the bottle or cup for a feeding in which your baby tends to be distracted or not interested in a long nursing session. (Usually this is one in the middle of the day.) Each week add a bottle substitution to a different feeding. Usually bedtime nursing is the last to go.
- Eliminate nursing for reasons other than nourishment. If you need to comfort your baby, caress and rock her rather than using the breast as a pacifier.
- Cut down the duration of nursing sessions. If your baby wants a hit-and-run session, don't try to keep her at the breast longer than she seems interested.
- If your breasts are becoming engorged and uncomfortable as your baby nurses less often, express just enough milk to stay comfortable. If you empty them fully, they will produce larger quantities of milk.

A final note: If you have second thoughts during this transition and decide to maintain your nursing relationship for a few more months, you can reverse the process by having your baby nurse longer and more often. Your milk supply will increase accordingly. ■

interested in it as an object to investigate and manipulate—just like everything else she touches. It is quite unlikely that she will use it to transfer food into her mouth with any consistency until she has passed the fifteen-month mark. Instead, she will probably bang her spoon against the nearest hard object, fling it to the floor, or perhaps dip it into her food—before she bangs and flings it.

Many babies couldn't care less about the spoon, no matter who is holding it, and simply want to turn every solid into a finger food—or an unidentified flying object. Either scenario will serve as an impressive illustration of the word *mess*. After a prolonged mealtime with a self-feeder in this age-group, food may be everywhere—from head to toe on the baby, scattered over a radius of several feet around her high chair, and perhaps decorating a few walls, people, and pets as well.

One theoretical advantage of giving your baby free rein in feeding herself before her first birthday is that her prowess with the spoon might develop more quickly. However, it is questionable whether early spoon practice really matters in the long run. A more realistic benefit of self-feeding is that she'll tend to regulate her own food intake. She'll get down to business (eating and making a mess in the process) when she's truly hungry, then shift into other activities (making a mess full-time) when her appetite is satisfied. The end result is a baby who stops eating when she's no longer hungry, an eating habit that will serve her well the rest of her life, making it less likely that she will turn to food for needs other than hunger or unwittingly overeat on a regular basis. In contrast, a baby who happily accepts any and all food offered to her, even after she is no longer hungry, is at risk of becoming overweight.

The major disadvantage of a do-it-yourself feeding at this age, of course, is the extra cleaning effort needed to round up the wayward food. To protect floors and carpets, some parents buy special splash mats at stores that sell baby paraphernalia or even set up an empty plastic wading pool around the high chair. Unfortunately you can't haul all this gear to a restaurant or a friend's house, and you may grow tired of hosing off the high chair after every meal. Furthermore, just as imposing some limits on your baby's explorations is necessary for safety and sanity, imposing some semblance of order at mealtimes is a reasonable and worthwhile goal.

Some parents go to the opposite extreme, trying to control and orchestrate every bite taken by the baby. If this is your intention, keep an eye on your blood pressure, because you'll be repeatedly going to the mat with your child over the fine points of what she will or won't eat. *Whatever else you do, don't attempt to force a baby to eat when she's not hungry and don't let your concern over her lack of interest in a particular food escalate into trench warfare.* If she doesn't like bananas, for example, find some other fruit she does enjoy.

A balanced approach is for you to manage the spoon with the gooey stuff—the cereal and strained foods—for the first several months, until she is able to handle this assignment herself with a minimum of mess making. You can let her handle a spoon all she wants, of course, without getting food involved. As she passes her first birthday, see if she will imitate you as you show how it's used. At the same time, let her have some of the self-contained finger foods described on the bottom of page 204, either before or after spoon feeding. Pay attention, however, to the signs that she isn't hungry: turning her head, not accepting the spoon, getting restless, or tossing foods overboard. If she doesn't want to eat, don't try to feed her, but don't let her play with the food.

Cup control

Another skill you may want your baby to tackle while perched in the high chair is drinking from a cup. This may be a bit easier now than it was a generation or two ago because of the widespread use of spill-proof or sippy cups. These are small plastic cups with tight-fitting lids and a narrow spout through which an infant or toddler can suck or sip his favorite beverage. Bridging the gap between breast or bottle and regular cups used by older children and adults, the sippy cup effectively prevents the child from dumping liquid all over himself and everything around him—unless, of course, the lid isn't attached snugly. Many children use these until the preschool years, by which time improved coordination enables them to drink from the genuine article with less chance of a spill. On the other hand, some have raised concerns that using sippy cups long after a child can master an open cup may lead to some temporary difficulties with clarity of speech. Also, taking a sippy cup to bed with milk or juice could promote tooth decay, as does a bedtime bottle.[4]

If you are adventurous, you can always go straight to the open cup. Since this involves hand control, new swallowing skills, and liquid that might go anywhere and everywhere, take your time. The cup you choose for your baby may be easier to use if it has two handles or, depending on his preference, no handles. A weighted bottom will help keep it oriented topside up, and sturdy construction is a must. The pretty china cup illustrated with Beatrix Potter characters might be nice to look at, but for everyday use, unbreakable plastic is the only way to go. After your baby's gotten the hang of taking food from a spoon, you can try putting a little water in his cup. When you first put it to his lips, he will probably not know what to do. After you let a few drops enter his mouth, he may swallow, or let it run down his chin, or some of each. Be patient. Only one in four babies will master the skill of drinking from a cup by the age of nine months, and it may be an additional six months before most of the liquid goes where it belongs.

Health Issues: Medical Checkups

During this six-month period your baby will not need as many routine checkups as he did during the first six months of life. Normally, visits are carried out at six months, nine months, and one year of age. Your baby's doctor will, as before, measure progress in height, weight, and head circumference. A review of developmental milestones and a check from head to toe will also be on the agenda. You should feel free to ask questions about feeding or behavior problems that might concern you, and check for any specific guidelines about the introduction of solid foods. You can expect some input about safety at home as well, including directions about appropriate action to take in case your baby accidentally swallows a toxic substance or an overdose of medication (see "Poisoning," pages 831–833).

Immunizations that protect your baby against dangerous illnesses—diphtheria, tetanus, whooping cough (pertussis), polio, rotavirus infection, hepatitis B—and aggressive bacteria—*Haemophilus influenzae* type B and pneumococci—will be continued during these visits. After your baby arrives at the six-month mark, his doctor may also offer a yearly vaccine against influenza. If for any reason your baby has fallen behind on his basic immunization schedule, talk to the doctor about a timetable for catching up. Now that he has reached the six-month mark, you may be tempted to slack off on vaccinations, especially if your budget is tight. But you should press on and complete this process because the illnesses that you may prevent can be devastating (see the detailed segment dealing with immunizations, beginning on page 739). If you are short on funds, check with your local health department about the availability of low-cost immunizations. Many communities have vaccination programs that are carried out on a regular basis throughout the year.

Between the ninth and twelfth months, your baby may be given a skin test to detect contact with the bacteria that causes tuberculosis (*Mycobacterium tuberculosis*). This test is usually *not* done unless there is reasonable concern that your child may have been exposed to this organism. By the one-year checkup your baby may have blood drawn to check for **anemia** (a shortage of red blood cells) or exposure to lead. If anemia is present at this age, it usually indicates a need for more iron in the baby's diet. Your doctor will give you specific recommendations if this is the case.

For more information about TB skin testing, see the sidebar "Does Your Child Need a TB Test?" on page 346.

While it may seem a little early to be taking your baby to the dentist, the American Academy of Pediatric Dentists recommends a dental check once the first teeth come in, and no later than the first birthday. (See "teeth care and concerns" in the Reference Section, page 723.)

Common illnesses in infancy, including upper respiratory infections (colds), ear infections, intestinal upsets, and other disturbances were discussed in chapter 6 in the section entitled "When your baby is ill: common medical problems." These will not be repeated here, but if you need a quick review, turn to page 181.

Social Developments

While no two babies interact with the rest of humanity in exactly the same way, there are distinct trends you will likely notice during this very eventful six-month period.

At six months of age and for the next two or three months thereafter, babies tend to socialize easily with the world at large. As you walk by a seven- or eight-month-old who is peering over someone's shoulder in the church foyer, flash a grin and you'll probably get one in return. This sunny responsiveness—to just about anyone—is pleasant and certainly endearing, but it won't last forever. It also does not mean that a baby is equally attached to every grown-up on the planet. All the attention and care that have been given at home have been making a profound impact, and the bonds of attachments for the immediate family will continue to strengthen during these important months.

Strangers and separation

As early as six months of age, but usually between eight to twelve months, a new phase will develop. Your baby, who may have seemed so comfortable around everyone, will begin showing anxiety among unfamiliar people. The approach of someone new or someone she hasn't seen for a while will provoke a wide-eyed stare, usually followed by wailing and clinging to you for protection. This is called **stranger anxiety**.

This behavior may bother Aunt Mary, who hasn't seen your baby yet and was expecting a warm embrace from her newest grandniece. Since fear of strangers is virtually universal as the first birthday approaches and continues well into the second year, both you and Aunt Mary should relax about it. In fact, a simple strategy can help her and your baby get acquainted.

First, Aunt Mary shouldn't try to touch, kiss, or hold the baby right away. In fact, even a direct return of your baby's stare may set off a healthy cry. Instead, you should chat with Aunt Mary as if nothing else is going on. Let your baby see that this is someone you are comfortable with, and let her get used to the sight of this new person in your home. After a while, some simple exchanges of looks, touches, and eventually play will likely begin as Aunt Mary becomes one of the gang.

The flip side of stranger anxiety is **separation anxiety**, an increased unwillingness to be separated from the main caregiver—usually (but not always) Mom. Your baby may begin to cry when you simply step into another room for a moment or put her into her crib for a nap. If and when she's about to be left with a relative or a sitter, the crying may escalate into a wailing and clinging session of spectacular proportions.

Separation issues can turn into an emotional upheaval for parents and baby alike. On one hand, it's nice to know that your child thinks so highly of you, so to speak. But having your baby cling to you like superglue, hearing a prolonged chorus of protest every night at bedtime, or wondering whether you'll ever have a night (or weekend) away without massive guilt can begin to feel like a ball and chain.

Your approach to this development should be, first of all, to avoid extremes. Some parents, especially with the first baby, feel that their supreme calling in life is to prevent their child from experiencing one minute of unhappiness. Whatever it takes to prevent crying they will do, and whatever the baby seems to want they will provide, immediately and without question. But this is an exercise in futility, and a setup for creating an overindulged, selfish, and miserable child. Conversely, parents who take a very controlling approach to child rearing may not be very concerned about separation anxiety. But they also run the risk of being inattentive and neglectful of a young child's emotions in general. Both approaches stake out a path of least resistance that may seem to work for now but may also exact a terrible price in the future.

Since you are no doubt sensitive to your child's emotions but probably don't want to feel entirely controlled by her cries and moods, you'll be relieved to know that separation anxiety is a normal phase of development. It's virtually inevitable, but you can buffer its impact. For example, if a sitter is coming to your home, take an approach similar to the one just described for Aunt Mary. Have your sitter arrive a half hour early so she can get acquainted with your baby in an unhurried manner. If you are dropping the baby off at a place that is new to her, try to stick around for a while to allow your baby time to explore and get accustomed to the new environment. When it's time for you to depart, don't stoke the emotional fires with a hand-wringing send-off. Let your baby get involved in an activity with the caregiver, say a short and sweet good-bye, and then leave. (If your baby or toddler is going to spend time with a favorite set of grandparents or an aunt and uncle whom she knows well, you may find that your departure barely provokes any response at all.)

The separation process will be much more unpleasant if your baby is tired or hungry. If you can schedule your departure after a nap or a meal, it may go more smoothly. There is no harm in finding a so-called transitional object to serve as a comforting reminder of things that are familiar to her. (It can also help at bedtime—see next page.) This can be a soft toy or small blanket, much like the world-famous security blanket belonging to Linus in the "Peanuts" comic strip. Once this object has been picked out by your child, you may want to buy a duplicate (or in the case of a blanket, cut it in half) to have on hand if the original is lost or in the washer. Tattered, stained, and probably a little smelly, this item may become a treasured souvenir of your child's early years.

Separation and sleeping

For some babies separation becomes a major issue at bedtime. As was mentioned in the previous chapter, if your baby isn't used to falling asleep on her own by eight or nine months of age, you may be in for some stormy nights ahead if you try to revise her routine. If she wakes up during the night, not only will she sound off, but she may also pull herself to a stand in her crib and rattle it vigorously until you tend to her. (Make sure you have adjusted the mattress and side rails of the crib so she can't tumble out.) Even a baby who originally was doing very well at bedtime may start resisting the process, crying and clinging to you when it's time to go to sleep.

You can still work toward bringing her into a state of drowsiness (but not quite asleep) using a little nursing or formula, rocking and singing, augmented perhaps by her favorite soft object. Then lay her down, pat her gently, reassure her, say good night, and leave. The same approach should be used if she begins awakening during the night. If this is a new behavior for her, check to be sure she isn't ill, grossly wet or soiled, or tangled in her blanket. Tend to these concerns if needed, but keep your visit quick, quiet, and businesslike and then say good night. She shouldn't need any middle-of-the-night feedings at this point; if you continue offering them well after the six-month mark, you'll only be providing room service and bleary-eyed companionship, not meeting any nutritional needs.

Obviously, if interrupted sleep doesn't bother anyone, you may choose to leave things alone. Eventually your child will sleep through the night on her own—but with some children it may take many more months before this occurs spontaneously. But if you have an infant older than nine months who is still routinely rousing everyone from sleep two or three times a night, even after you have been providing a boring response for weeks, you may want to take more deliberate measures to bring this behavior to a close. One alternative approach would involve picking a time—usually on a weekend—when you say good night and then resolve not to return until the next morning—if you can handle it—no matter how often (or how long) the crying goes on. Obviously, you would not want to try this "commando" approach with a child who is sick, or on a hot summer night when the windows are open, or when you need to be wide-awake the next day, or (most important) if *both* parents are not wholeheartedly ready for it. If you try this tactic, you should greet your baby in the morning with smiles, hugs, and reassurance. Yes, indeed, you love her as much as the day is long, but nighttime is for sleeping. Normally after three, or at most, four nights (if not fewer), she will get the picture and sleep through the night thereafter (unless, of course, something else is wrong).

Relationships and security

This six-month period of your baby's life begins an extremely important phase in development, not only for his motor skills but for his intellectual and social abilities as well. The intense curiosity and exploration described earlier isn't limited to the world of objects. It also includes a huge amount of information gathering about the people around him. He will make the transition from having limited forms of communication—crying when he's uncomfortable or hungry and babbling randomly when he feels good—to owning a wide array of sounds, gestures, and body movements.

As he exercises these abilities, he will be learning how his parents, siblings, and others around him respond. If he is uncomfortable and cries as a result, does anyone come to make him feel better? Does this happen when he makes different kinds of sounds? Does crying evoke a response more often than other behaviors? If he can't get to something he wants and cries (or makes other sounds), will someone get it for him? What happens when he touches or plays with various objects he finds? If he seems unhappy when he is taken away from a particular object, is your response consistent? Who makes him feel warm and comfortable? Who smiles and makes pleasant sounds—and who doesn't?

Your baby won't be formulating these questions (he hasn't the words for them yet), but he will be paying close attention to your reactions and responses, and he will be taught by them.

He will need to know that he is deeply and consistently loved. He will flourish when someone responds to his sounds of frustration or pleasure and comes to assist him or to share in the joy of a particular discovery. Paradoxically, he will also develop some security when he learns that those who love him don't necessarily come "right this instant" every time he calls out. A little delay in getting what he needs—and not always getting what he wants—will not harm him when it occurs in a setting where there is an abundance of smiles, caresses, and sweet conversation. On the contrary, it will teach him that he is secure in your love, even when you are not immediately present or when your love for him causes you to overrule his immediate desires.

Twelve to Twenty-Four Months: Declarations of Independence

During the first twelve months of life, your baby will have undergone an incredible transformation—from a totally helpless newborn to a mobile explorer who is interacting vigorously with everything and everyone around him. During the next year of life, the physical changes you see in your child from month to month will not appear nearly as dramatic. You will, however, start the year with a "baby on wheels" and end it with a small child whose mind and body have, in fact, undergone some very significant developments.

Because of his mobility, your one-year-old will keep you hopping during nearly all of his waking hours. Track shoes, a sense of humor, and a little tolerance for disorder are a must from here on. Striving to ensure that he (and everything in his path) stays in one piece will be a full-time project, and you would be wise to review carefully the cautions regarding safety and sanity in the first half of chapter 7 (beginning on page 197).

But as much attention as this assignment rightfully requires, a common mistake made by parents of toddlers is to enter a maintenance (or, in some cases, raw survival) mode and never move beyond it. As much as they need food, safety, endless cleanups, and diaper changes, toddlers also need the important grown-ups in their life to be *fascinated* with them. "Lord, give me the strength to get through this day" may be the repeated cry of the parent's heart (usually about 5 p.m.). But with it should come a postscript: "Lord, help me understand, appreciate, and marvel at this incredible creation You have loaned to me." Your toddler is no less "fearfully and wonderfully made" now that he is tearing all over the house than he was while he was being knit together in his mother's womb.

Your need for both of these prayers may become more intense, at least at times, as your child begins to demonstrate a reality that is painfully obvious to parents and often ignored by the most learned philosophers: Little children aren't inherently virtuous. They are not born brimming with selfless instincts and kind gestures. They have no concept of other people's viewpoints or needs. In fact, they are not even morally neutral "blank slates" who will readily follow whatever direction you give to them. They come hardwired with a will, boundless energy to express their interests, and powerful emotions to display if they aren't satisfied at any given moment. They don't need to be taught to grab, fight, howl in anger, or bluntly defy you (or anyone else caring for them). If you have any doubt that humankind is a fallen race (as painfully set forth in Genesis 3 and demonstrated in every generation thereafter), you have yet to spend any length of time in close quarters with a toddler.

Your response to this reality should be, as much as possible, measured, loving, calm (at least most of the time), and like everything else, governed by an avoidance of extremes. If you don't believe that your sweet, innocent baby could ever challenge you ("Not *my* boy, whom I love so dearly . . ."), you're in for a rude shock this year. And if you aren't prepared and willing to meet him confidently when he does, you may find yourself living with a miserable, demanding two- or three-year-old, or even a full-fledged miniature tyrant.

However, if you are bound and determined to meet every departure from perfect decorum with harsh words and an iron fist, your opportunities to shape his will, impart moral standards, and serve as a role model will be squandered. Whatever good behavior you see will be based on raw fear and, once soured with a few years of resentment, will be spectacularly discarded at the first available opportunity.

During these next several months—which will pass more quickly than you might imagine—you will enter into some crucial interactions with your child. By the end of this year he needs to know and understand that you love him fervently and uncondition-ally and, at the same time, that you are in charge and he isn't. *If either or both of these messages are not clearly established by the second birthday (or within the few months that follow), your child-rearing tasks during the following years are likely to be far more difficult.* His patterns of relating to you and any other people close to him, whether generally pleas-ant or continually combative, are likely to become more firmly entrenched by the third birthday and may continue for years thereafter.

You don't need to do everything perfectly this year to bring up a healthy, delightful child, however. An isolated mistake or even getting on the wrong track for a number of weeks isn't going to ruin his life. God has granted parents a good deal of time on the learning curve and given children a great deal of resiliency. So take a deep breath, fasten your seat belt, stay on your knees (not just when you're picking up toys), and amid all the challenges, don't forget to step back once in a while to marvel at this little person you are nurturing.

Physical Developments

Height, weight, and other physical progress

If you haven't already done so during one of your child's well-baby checkups, take a look at the growth curve that should be in her medical chart. Better yet, ask the doctor or office staff for a copy you can continue updating on your own. You'll notice that the average rate of growth during the second year is slower than it was during the first twelve months. A normal one-year-old will have tripled his birth weight but then will gain only three to five more pounds (about 1.4 to 2.3 kg) by age two. Similarly, regardless of gender, your child will add roughly four inches (a little over 10 cm) of height between the first and second birthdays, less than half the height gained during the first year. Interestingly, while your child's head will increase in circumference only about an inch (2.5 cm) over the next twelve months, by age two it will have reached 90 percent of its adult size.

The percentile curves shown on the growth charts begin to diverge more noticeably after the first twelve months. In other words, the differences in height and weight between a child who is at the 90th percentile (that is, larger than 90 percent of the children his age) and one of the same age who is at the 10th percentile will become more dramatic after the first birthday. For most children, position on the growth chart depends largely on genetics, with a height and weight trajectory that will be fairly predictable after the first eighteen to twenty-four months of life have been tracked, barring an unusual problem or chronic illness. If your child is "falling off" a curve—that is, she has been at a certain percentile of weight and height for a number of months and then appears to shift to a significantly lower level during subsequent checkups—a medical or nutritional problem may be present, and your health-care provider may recommend further evaluation.

See growth charts, beginning on page 788.

Even though she will not be experiencing drastic changes in height and weight, the baby look will begin to fade away between her first and second birthdays. With more muscle motion, her arms and legs will look longer and leaner and her abdomen less prominent. Her face will gradually shift from the round, nonspecific but universally appealing look of a baby to more well-defined features that will give you a preview of her future appearance. As you watch her enthusiastically attempting to blow out two birthday candles, don't be surprised if you find yourself wondering, *Where did my baby go?*

As described in the previous chapter, the debut of walking may already have occurred two or three months before the first birthday, or it may be a few months away. By eighteen months, your child should have this skill down pat. While early starters won't have any long-term advantage over the late bloomers who are otherwise normal, they will be somewhat ahead of the game in maturity of their gait. It takes a few months to progress from the broad-based, lurching, hands-up, toes-out, frequent-faller toddling walk to a smoother, more narrow-based gait with fewer falls, improved maneuvering, and—a big thrill for many kids—the ability to use hands to carry things while on the move.

Parents watching a toddler careen around the room may wonder about the alignment of the legs: Are they turned outward too far? Does one foot point in a different direction from the other? During the first several weeks of walking, this may be impossible to answer. If you see an obvious, consistent difference in the orientation of the legs, however, you should have your toddler's health-care provider watch her move up and down the office corridor. He or she may want an opinion from an orthopedist to determine whether specific intervention is in order.

The treatment for the vast majority of toddler gait concerns is "tincture of time"— they resolve as weeks pass and coordination improves. However, an obvious limp or a toddler's sudden unwillingness to walk after she clearly knows how is always abnormal and should be evaluated medically as soon as possible.

Vision, hearing, and language

The average one-year-old can see well enough to spy small objects across the room or planes flying overhead. By the age of two he will probably approach normal vision, although it is difficult to measure accurately at this age. If he seems to be squinting a lot or bringing objects right up to his face before he interacts with them or doesn't seem to be tracking objects with his eyes, an exam by an ophthalmologist (a physician who specializes in eye problems) would be a good idea. An exam is also needed if you see obvious crossing of his eyes (even temporarily) or if they don't seem to be moving in the same direction. Ideally, you'll consult a pediatric ophthalmologist, a physician specializing in children's eye problems, although many ophthalmologists deal with all age-groups. Unless specially trained and equipped, your primary-care physician will not be able to determine the visual acuity of a one-year-old.

While major visual problems are uncommon in one-year-olds, hearing can become impaired if ear infections and colds—which are not at all unusual in this age-group—leave persistent thick fluid behind one or both eardrums (see "ear infections" in Reference Section, page 657). If the problem persists untreated for weeks or months, your child's ability to understand and generate language can be delayed.

If you have any concerns about hearing loss (see sidebar below), by all means have his ears and hearing checked—the sooner the better. While your health-care provider can usually determine whether there is fluid behind the eardrum or identify other physical problems, a detailed assessment of hearing in this age-group requires special training and equipment. A safe and painless test with the intimidating name "brainstem auditory evoked response" (also called "auditory evoked potentials") can test hearing without your child's cooperation, but you may have to travel some distance to have it done. If your toddler's physician recommends this test or a consultation with an ear, nose, and throat (ENT) specialist, don't hesitate to do so.

Assuming that hearing is normal, your child will probably have a speaking vocabulary of a few words at his first birthday and about ten times that many at his second, some of which he may combine into two- or three-word sentences. What he can *understand*, however, will become much more impressive as the year progresses. As he moves past the eighteen-month mark, he will point to all sorts of things—people, objects, body parts—when asked about them ("Where is your nose?" "Where's Auntie Linda?"). By the second birthday, the unintelligible strings of sounds that sounded like a foreign language at the beginning of the year will be honed down to simple statements

WHEN MIGHT YOU SUSPECT YOUR ONE-YEAR-OLD HAS A HEARING PROBLEM?

- He doesn't turn in response to sounds or ignores you when you call him. Many parents have had the humbling experience of repeatedly disciplining a toddler for failing to respond to them, only to find out later that he really couldn't hear them.
- He isn't using any single words (such as *Mama*) by the age of twelve to fifteen months, or his speech is unintelligible by the age of two. Babies and toddlers normally love to experiment with all sorts of sounds, and one who seems to be specializing in making noises he can feel (such as gargling or growling) may not be able to hear his own vocalizations.
- His responses to sounds seem to be selective. While you might suspect that he is choosing to pay attention to some and not others, he may be hearing low-pitched sounds better than high-pitched ones, or one ear may be affected but not the other. ■

or even questions. Even more amazing is seeing your walking baby, who not long ago lay helpless in a crib, following a simple command such as "Go get the ball."

Over the next several months, you will have the unique and important opportunity to help expand your child's language skills. You won't need a teaching credential, a master's degree, or special training in child development to do this. Instead, you will simply need to "be there" when you are with him. Keep your antennae up and be ready to give him dozens of little doses of your attention and conversation throughout the day.

Take advantage of his curiosity. When your child approaches you with an object or points to something and makes a sound (which may rise at the end like a question—"Car?"), you've got his attention. Name the object and say something simple about it ("Yes, that's Daddy's car"). He doesn't need a lecture about auto mechanics, of course, but don't be afraid to aim your comment a little beyond what you think he might understand.

Talk to him while you're doing everyday chores. Folding clothes may be boring to you, but if he's watching, it doesn't take any extra time to name the items or say what you're doing with them. Remember, his little computer is on all the time.

Read to him. Reading simple stories to your child, especially at bedtime, is an extremely worthwhile activity to begin this year, if you haven't already. (Be sure to let him see what you are reading and to identify for him anything he finds interesting in the pictures.) His interest and understanding will increase dramatically over the course of the year. By age two, in fact, he may be able to fill in the blanks in a story he knows well, anticipating and saying one or more words at favorite spots along the way.

A few cautions about language:

Remember to speak to your child using clear, meaningful words. Use a pleasant tone of voice, but avoid baby talk, and don't repeat his unique mispronunciations of words, even if they *are* cute (see page 196).

Don't make reading to him an issue if he's not interested at the particular story time you have in mind. Usually you won't meet much resistance to looking at books at bedtime, when children are attentive to just about anything that delays lights-out, but they may not be as interested during daylight hours.

Don't rely on "educational" videos to build your toddler's language skills. As we discussed in the previous chapter ("Should Your Baby Watch 'Educational' DVDs?" beginning on page 194), *Baby Einstein* and *Sesame Street* may be pleasant diversions, but you shouldn't hand the responsibility of your child's language development to Bert and Ernie. Even if he appears to pay rapt attention, live humans who are paying attention to *him* do a much better job.

Hands, minds, and safety

This year your toddler will continue to explore whatever she finds around her. Her ability to pick up and manipulate objects both large and small will become much more refined and coordinated during the coming months. By her second birthday, she will enjoy scribbling with crayons (preferably not on the walls), stacking four or five items and then knocking them over, playing with clay, and sticking pegs of various shapes into similarly shaped holes. Many toddlers also become fascinated with things that go around. Wheels that spin on toy cars, pedals on bicycles, a lazy Susan you don't need anymore, or a saucepan lid turned upside down on the kitchen floor may become objects of your child's greatest affection.

Between eighteen and twenty-four months of age, most toddlers also become enamored with balls; holding, rolling, tossing, watching them bounce around, and then chasing them hold endless interest and delight. Beware, however, of small round objects (such as marbles) that might be put in the mouth and then accidentally inhaled. Best bet: Buy your toddler her own inexpensive inflatable twelve- to eighteen-inch beach ball. It's quiet, it can't do much damage, she can carry it around when she doesn't want to throw it, and it's easy to replace.

By her second birthday, you may get a preview of your child's preference for using the right or left hand. But she may also use the spoon with her right, scribble with her left, and throw a ball with either. Don't try to push the use of one hand over the other and don't worry about speeding up the process. She'll sort out her handedness in due time.

This year your child will significantly increase her grasp of the way things work. Her sense of object permanence—the idea that something is still present even if she can't see it—will become more sophisticated. Not only will she learn to search for a toy she saw you place under two or three blankets or pillows, but she will also become a whiz at little hide-and-seek activities. If she sees you stick a toy in your pocket, she won't forget where it went. (Don't try to fake her out with some sleight of hand,

WHAT IF YOUR TODDLER SWALLOWS A POISONOUS SUBSTANCE?

Common sense dictates that if a child swallows something poisonous, the best thing to do is to have him immediately throw it up. For decades parents were advised to buy **ipecac**, a medicine that induces vomiting, for just that purpose. However, over the past several years, medical professionals have expressed some serious reservations about this routine advice. One major concern is that a host of materials and objects may cause considerable harm as they pass from stomach to mouth during vomiting. These include:

- Alkaline materials: detergents, drain cleaners, oven cleaners, bleach, and flat circular batteries. (Chemical names include lye, sodium hydroxide, potassium hydroxide, ammonia, calcium oxide, trisodium phosphate, and wood ash.)
- Acids: automobile battery fluid, toilet-bowl cleaners, soldering fluxes, antirust compounds, and slate cleaners. (Chemical names include sulfuric, hydrochloric, phosphoric, hydrofluoric, and oxalic acids.)
- Petroleum products: cleaning fluid, gasoline, kerosene, coal oil, fuel oil, or paint thinner.
- Sharp or solid objects: glass, nails, razors, and thermometers.

In addition, the idea of using ipecac was largely based on intuition rather than actual scientific studies, and more recent research doesn't support the notion that however. "Magic tricks" where items appear or disappear unexpectedly will confuse the toddler's budding sense of object permanence. Save the disappearing ball and card tricks for the older kids.)

Brief episodes of playacting and imitation will become more sophisticated over the course of the year. Watch her hold the toy phone to her ear (or yours), try to brush her hair, rock her baby, or turn the steering wheel on a toy car. As the months pass, she will try to engage you in some of these scenarios. If you can stop for a few moments to pretend to drink out of the toy cup she offers you or talk on her phone, you'll make her day. Finding the right balance between responding to these overtures often enough to satisfy your child but without endless interruption to whatever you're trying to get done is an art in parenting (see "Social and Emotional Development: The 'First Adolescence'" on page 231).

Because of your child's maturing motor and problem-solving skills, your vigilance for her ongoing safety must not only continue but become more sophisticated. Her developing fine-motor coordination will include new abilities that can lead to new hazards: turning doorknobs, manipulating latches, flipping switches, and pushing buttons. If you turn your back for a moment, she may be locked in the bathroom or out the door and down the street, peering over the edge of Grandma's swimming pool. Her interest in climbing to precarious new heights may increase, along with her ability to find new and clever ways to get to them.

Her tendency to gum everything as a means of gathering information will wane, but she may not hesitate to place small objects in her mouth. Remember to stay vigilant for any such items that might cause choking if accidentally inhaled. She may very

children who receive ipecac at home have better outcomes than those who don't. Furthermore, there has been a dramatic decline in the percentage of cases in which poison control centers in the United States have advised parents to give ipecac to their children. (The number decreased from 15 percent in 1985 to less than half a percent in 2003.) As a result, the American Academy of Pediatrics now recommends that ipecac *not* be used routinely as an intervention at home following accidental ingestion of a toxic substance. If you have any old syrup of ipecac at home, you should flush it down the toilet.

So what *should* you do if you suspect that your toddler has swallowed a toxic substance?

- If he doesn't appear ill, call the toll-free number for the U.S. Poison Control Center at **1-800-222-1222** for advice.
- If he is unconscious, breathing erratically, or having convulsions, call **911** immediately. If he has stopped breathing, you must begin CPR while someone else calls 911.

A final thought: Before you have to respond to an emergency, you would be wise to review the sections on poisoning and cardiopulmonary resuscitation (CPR) beginning on pages 831 and 836. ■

well take a swig or a bite of *anything* that looks interesting. Medicines, plants, cleaning products, dog food—you name it—nothing is off-limits for an oral sampling. You cannot assume that a bad taste will keep her from guzzling the furniture polish or anything else. This year and the next are the most risky for your child accidentally ingesting a dangerous substance. Some basic precautions can help you and your toddler avoid the trauma of a poisoning incident:

- Household products (cleaners, antifreeze, drain openers, pesticides, kerosene, and many others) and medicines must be kept where they can't find their way into a toddler's hands and mouth. Keep them in latched or locked cabinets or drawers, preferably at levels beyond a child's reach.
- Always label hazardous products clearly.
- Avoid referring to a child's medicine as "candy" or "a treat" when you're trying to get him to take it. If it tastes good, he might decide to try some on his own.
- Be sure to replace childproof caps on medications immediately after use.
- Be especially careful when you are using one or more hazardous products during a lengthy household project. When tired or distracted, you might lose track of what you have left lying within reach of curious hands.

Feeding: Establishing Patterns for Eating

By her first birthday, your toddler should have a working knowledge of a variety of foods from the well-known groups in addition to her milk. Remember that while cow's milk may be introduced after the first birthday if your child doesn't demonstrate any allergy to it, *whole* milk—not low-fat or nonfat—should be on the menu. Cholesterol is not an issue at this age, and the fat in whole milk is useful in building a number of tissues, including the central nervous system. Beware, however, of allowing a budding milkaholic to push her milk consumption past sixteen to twenty-four ounces (one to one and one-half pints) per day. Not only will this curb her interest in other types of food, but large amounts of milk may also interfere with the absorption of iron from other foods, which in turn can lead to anemia (a deficiency in red blood cells).

During this year you will want to establish a routine with meals and snacks if you haven't already. Three meals and two small snacks at generally consistent times are far preferable to nonstop grazing, which trains a child to eat for all kinds of reasons other than hunger, scatters food everywhere, and may lead to a choking accident if a toddler stumbles with food in her mouth. This is a good time to establish a routine of sitting down at the table before eating, which actually is beneficial for adults and older children as well.

A fair amount of the food she eats at a meal can consist of small portions of whatever the rest of the family is having, as long as it

- isn't too hot in temperature;
- isn't too hot in seasoning, or overly salty, sweet, or swimming in butter or grease—which isn't so great for the rest of the family either;
- is either mushy or cut into small, easily chewed pieces. Continue to avoid foods that could easily lodge in the airway: hot dogs (that aren't cut into bite-size pieces), nuts, seeds, hard candy, grapes, popcorn, peanut butter, raw vegetables, dried fruit, etc., as described in chapter 7 (see page 205).

One development on the food front that catches many parents off guard is the erratic appetite of the toddler. She may eat voraciously one day and show little interest in food the next, or consume a sizable breakfast and then quit after only a few bites of the day's other meals. With her nonstop activity during waking hours, this apparent inconsistency in fueling patterns may not make sense, but it is not uncommon. In fact, at this age her intense curiosity and compelling desire to explore the world around her will tend to limit her interest in food to two primary activities: eating it if she's hungry and examining it if she isn't. If either of these isn't happening at the kitchen table, she'll probably want to move on to more interesting pursuits. Also remember that growth is not as rapid now as it was during the first year, and that the average toddler needs only about one thousand calories a day—not a huge amount of food—to meet her nutritional needs.

Your goal should be to offer her a variety of foods in modest amounts each day. If she turns you down, don't turn your mealtime into a battle zone. Attempting to force a toddler to eat anything is an exercise in futility, and insisting that she can't leave the table or have another meal until she has finished every last speck of her vegetables (which might get a few days old while you wait) will lead to miserable, exhausting times around the dinner table. You'll also need to decide how much mess you can tolerate. Some postmeal cleanup will be necessary while your child learns the fine points of hand-spoon-mouth coordination, but you shouldn't confuse the pitching of food and fluids in all directions with her self-feeding learning curve (see chapter 7, page 209). One way to minimize the mess is to keep the serving sizes small.

Don't panic and then offer your toddler something she really likes out of fear that she won't get enough to eat. This may turn into a subtle form of dietary extortion and is a surefire way to create long-term food habits that may be nutritionally inadequate. If

MENU FOR TODDLERS

The listing below will give you a rough idea of the types of foods and quantities that are appropriate for this age-group. Remember, however, that your toddler may eat less or more than these amounts on any given day.

Breads, cereals, and other grains: four to six servings per day
One serving = 1/4 to 1/3 cup cereal; 1/4 cup pasta or rice; 1/4 to 1/2 slice bread or bagel

Milk/dairy products: two to three servings per day
One serving = 1/2 cup milk; 1/2 to 1 ounce cheese; 1/3 to 1/2 cup yogurt or cottage cheese

Vegetables: two to three servings per day
One serving = 1 or 2 tablespoons

Fruit: two to three servings per day
One serving = 1/4 cup cooked or canned; 1/2 piece fresh; 1/8 cup dried; 1/4 to 1/2 cup juice

Meat/poultry/fish, eggs, and beans: two servings per day
One serving = 2 tablespoons ground or 2 one-inch cubes meat, poultry, or fish; one egg;
   1/4 cup tofu or cooked beans ■

she doesn't want much now, put the plate back in the fridge and warm it up for the next meal. When she's hungry, she'll eat. If you are worried about her food intake, write down what she has eaten over a week's time and run it by her doctor. If she is active, showing developmental progress, and gaining on the growth chart, she's getting enough. Remember: No normal child will voluntarily starve herself. Depending upon everyone's schedule, make an effort to include your toddler at the family table for at least one meal per day. Traditions and timetables will vary, of course, but for many families, a shared meal (usually dinner) may be the one occasion when everyone at home can share conversation as well as food. (Shutting off the TV and taking the phone off the hook will enhance this experience.) While not exactly participating at the same level as everyone around the table, your one-year-old will be watching and listening and will become accustomed to being included in these gatherings. Let her see the family pause for a blessing—if you hold hands around the table, hold hers too, and soon she'll reach out spontaneously when everyone is seated. Indeed, it would be good for her to hear brief words of thanks before her other meals as well, a practice that will prepare her for that time in the near future when she begins to understand the meaning of prayer.

You should discuss with your health-care provider whether or not your toddler should be on vitamin supplements. Some use these routinely, while others feel that well-balanced food intake essentially eliminates the need for vitamins. Fluoride supple-

WHEN SHOULD YOU WEAN YOUR TODDLER FROM BREASTFEEDING?

Some authorities discourage nursing as a frequent daily activity after a toddler reaches twelve to fifteen months of age. Others (especially members of breastfeeding advocacy groups) encourage a completely open-ended approach, noting that in some cultures mothers may nurse a newborn on one breast and a child as old as five on the other. If you are pondering this question, remember that there are both nutritional and behavioral aspects to consider.

Unlike the first months of your baby's life, nursing does not serve a life-sustaining function after solids have been introduced. In fact, at this age if frequent trips to the breast are substituting for solid foods, your toddler may become anemic or even gradually undernourished. The role of nursing thus becomes increasingly social and emotional as the months (or years) pass, especially after eighteen months of age. This can be a source of ongoing nurturing, closeness, and even relaxation between mother and child. If all else is going well, there may be no compelling reason to bring it to a close in the immediate future.

On the other hand, nursing for an extended period of time could cause or prolong problems such as:

- A toddler who is overly dependent on or demanding of Mom. If she is clinging to you and your breast day and night and not spending much time exploring the world around her, she needs to expand her horizons. If she wants to nurse whenever she's unhappy or bored, she needs to learn how to find comfort in other ways (such as cuddling without the oral intake). If she refuses to take liquids from any other source but Mom, parental activities are going to be stifled. If you are still nursing because your toddler throws

ments may be recommended, however, based on the content of your local water supply. Your child's doctor or local pediatric dentist should have this information, or you can obtain it from the agency that supplies your water.

Weaning

As the year progresses, you will see improving skill in your toddler's use of the cup and spoon, which will enable you to turn more of the feeding assignment over to her. With increasing cup proficiency (see chapter 7, page 210), you can begin phasing out bottles. This process may meet with some resistance but should be started by the first birthday and accomplished by the fifteen-month mark. Plan on substituting a cup for her bottle one meal at a time (or all three at once, if you're adventurous), and then do likewise for her snacks. Usually a bottle before bedtime is the last to go, since it has a way of becoming part of the nighttime routine. Remember: No milk or juice should ever be given to your baby while she is lying down and falling asleep because this practice (which is all too easy to start as a last resort during a restless night) can lead to dental cavities and ear infections. A little snack just before bed and before brushing teeth is fine, but food should not be part of any middle-of-the-night activity at this point (see pages 213–214).

Once you've decided to bid the last bottle feeding farewell, your best bet is to pack all of them away when your toddler is asleep. If she begins to ask (or cry) for her

a tantrum whenever she can't have access to your breast, you are under siege. In this case, you may need to curtail nursing simply to gain control of your (and her) life.

- A mom who is overly dependent on the toddler. As was mentioned in the last chapter, the intimacy of nurturing a dependent young infant occurs for a special but brief season. Acknowledging that it is over is a necessary step for both mother and child. If you feel that your meaning and purpose in life are going to evaporate if you are not nursing, you may need to explore some more basic issues relating to your identity and importance as an individual. This may be worked out informally in conversations with other mothers, but more formal counseling may be appropriate as well.

- Friction in the marriage. If your husband is beginning to feel that personal and physical intimacy with you is hampered by the ongoing presence of one or more children at your breast, the duration of nursing should be open for discussion.

- Modesty problems. A small child burrowing under Mom's blouse can be an awkward event at the mall or in the neighbors' living room, and appropriate limits must be set for the location of nursing an older toddler. A preschooler who is still accessing Mom's breast may well be crossing modesty boundaries, even in the privacy of the home.

If one or more of these problems have developed, it may be time to get the weaning process under way. There is rarely, if ever, a need to do a "cold turkey" approach, however, and a gradual phaseout is likely to provoke less turmoil. The principles for shifting from nursing to bottle or cup described in the previous chapter (see sidebar on page 208) apply at this age also. ■

"baba," be matter-of-fact and upbeat: "Your bottles are gone! And you're so big, you don't need them anymore!"

If your baby is still nursing at this point and has never used a bottle, she can graduate directly from breast to cup and avoid bottles altogether. As mentioned in the previous chapter, you should still introduce your baby to drinking from a cup even if most of her fluids are coming directly from Mom. If you wait too long, you may face resistance when it's time to stop nursing.

Sleeping: Establishing a Routine

By his first birthday, your child should have been sleeping through the night for some time. If not, remember that by now his nocturnal awakenings aren't the result of any nutritional needs. Instead, he has learned that having company or a snack feels good during the night. Why go back to sleep after awakening momentarily in the wee hours when there are other pleasantries to enjoy?

If you really don't mind working the nursery night shift, you may choose to put off dealing with the inevitable protest that will break forth when you cancel room service. But if he is otherwise well, you can usually establish uninterrupted sleep for everyone within one or two days, typically over a weekend, once you decide to take the plunge (see chapter 7, pages 213–214, for details).

Even a seasoned all-night sleeper, however, may depart from his pattern during an illness, while on a trip, after a move, or perhaps because of a bad dream. Under these circumstances, you'll need to provide care and comfort (though not snacks, unless you have been specifically directed by the doctor to push fluids when he is sick) until things settle down, then nudge him back toward his old habits.

For many toddlers the *Good Ship Slumber* may be rocked in other ways. At some point, you're likely to run into bedtime resistance, manifested either by winsome appeals (requests for another kiss, one last drink, and in subsequent months, answers to riddles of the universe) or by outright rebellion against getting or staying in bed. Some of this may arise from separation anxiety, from negativism, or simply from the fact that other people are up doing interesting things, and lying in a crib or bed seems awfully boring by comparison. You may be tempted to take the path of least resistance and let him decide when he's ready to sleep—in other words, when he eventually collapses from sheer exhaustion. This is a bad idea for a number of reasons:

- You need to spend time with older children (if you have any) without an increasingly tired and irritable toddler wandering around.
- You need to spend time with your mate or by yourself without any children wandering around.
- Your toddler needs the sleep—a good ten or eleven hours at night, which probably won't happen if he's staying up until your bedtime.

If not already in place, establishing both a fixed bedtime and a fixed bedtime routine will be an important task this year. Even if his vocabulary is limited, you can talk him through the steps you choose: bath, jammies, story, song, prayer, for example, carried out in a manner that winds him down. A raucous wrestling match or chasing the dog right before bedtime probably won't help set the stage for turning in. Keep in mind that whatever bedtime routine you establish (including one that takes one or two hours to complete) may become entrenched and expected every night for years to come.

As with a blessing before meals, your child will learn the routine of a short bedtime prayer before he understands the words or the theology. Over the coming months and years, however, this brief but important moment should take on new meaning and should not become a singsong patter repeated every night for no apparent reason other than long-standing habit.

As happened (hopefully) when he was an infant, your toddler should be placed in his crib or bed sleepy but not asleep. If he becomes accustomed to falling asleep on the sofa, floor, or your bed, he is more likely to resist signing off on his own pillow—both at bedtime *and* during the night.

Parents who have maintained a "family bed" through the first year should take the baby's first birthday as an occasion to review the current sleeping arrangements. Does your child need a parental body next to him to fall or stay asleep? (If one or both parents were to go away on a retreat for a night or two, would there be a problem?) More important, how is the presence of a much larger and more mobile baby affecting your sleep and your intimacy? Mother and Father should be in complete agreement about this situation or seek to resolve any difference of opinion if they are not—even if counseling is needed. Serious and damaging rifts in a marital relationship can develop if one spouse feels displaced physically and emotionally by a child who is taking over an ever-increasing area of bed space. In general, if either Mom or Dad feels that it's time for the baby to sleep elsewhere, the other parent should oblige—not only out of respect for the other's feelings but in recognition that the marital relationship needs to be nurtured and preserved.

At the first birthday, most children are still logging three to four hours of daytime sleep, usually in two naps. The amount of daytime sleep will decline to two or three hours over the next year, and as a result, the morning nap will eventually phase out. When your toddler shifts to a one-nap-per-day routine, don't start too late in the afternoon or you may increase his bedtime resistance. (Who wants to go to bed after just getting up?) And though he may seem intent on playing through the entire afternoon, don't be conned into eliminating nap time altogether, even if he resists it. Without daytime sleep, afternoons will probably be more notable for combat than for companionship.

Social and Emotional Development: The "First Adolescence"

During the second twelve months of life, your child will display a gamut of behaviors and emotions that, depending on your frame of mind, you may find confusing, amusing, or downright exasperating. A little preparation and some insight into the emerging worldview of the one-year-old can help you sort out and manage this important developmental passage.

First and foremost, keep in mind that above all else your toddler needs to know that she is loved, accepted, and "at home" with you and that you are on her side without reservation—even when you won't give her everything she wants. She needs kind and loving words and actions all day long, and she will come to you frequently for them.

Expect overtures of all sorts, often with arms outstretched, many times during the day as your toddler seeks

- cuddles and hugs;
- comfort after a bump or bruise;
- reassurance after being frightened;
- help with a problem, such as getting something out of reach or fixing a misbehaving toy;
- your enthusiastic reaction to something she has brought you;
- your response to a simple question (or sounds that resemble a question);
- relief from being hungry, thirsty, or having a wet or dirty diaper;

AVOIDING TODDLER-CARE BURNOUT

There is no getting around it: Bringing up a toddler requires a seemingly limitless supply of time and energy. If you have other children at home, especially if one or more of them are under five, the demands on your attention may seem even more overwhelming. Simply maintaining some semblance of order can be a daunting task, and worrying about such niceties as a child's language development may sound like a fantasy if you feel immersed in total chaos.

There may be other pressures too. The parent who elects to stay at home (usually the mother, but not always) may feel that her brain is rapidly turning to mush and that the stimulating worlds of education and career are passing her by. ("I've got a degree in history, and all I'm doing is changing diapers and listening to babbling.") If both parents work or if a single parent is rearing a toddler, many of the daily responsibilities at home must be carried out after a full day working elsewhere.

Because so much is going on in your toddler's life, he needs meaningful attention and input from the most important people in his life. If you feel that you're just marking time, becoming demented, or enduring a state of slave labor, consider the following burnout-prevention ideas:

- There should be some time during your day when things become quiet. This usually can occur only after little people are in bed. You cannot collect your thoughts or anything else if kids are up until all hours of the night. Early bedtime for small children is not only good for them but necessary for you.
- Some of this quiet time should be real quiet time, designated for reflecting, reading, praying, and journaling. A daily devotional will provide not only refreshment but perspective on how your parenting tasks fit into the big picture of who God is and what He's doing.
- Don't feel as if you are wasting your time and education to focus your primary attention on your children at this age. Believe it or not, the world isn't passing you by, and there will be plenty of time to make your mark in it later on. This doesn't mean that you have to put your brain in neutral, however, or that all outside activities must come to a screeching halt.
- Try to remember that this particular period of your child's life is not only extremely important but, in fact, highly interesting. Many people take

- invitations to role-play (at her direction)—pretending to talk on her toy phone, for example; and
- confirmation that you are still "there" when she has not seen you for a few minutes.

These approaches for comfort, input, and help will not last forever, and to the best of your ability they shouldn't be ignored. For a toddler they provide some critical fact-finding about how things work, how to get help, and who cares about her. They probably will also have a major impact on the way she interacts with the world at large in subsequent years. In a very real sense, you are her launching pad, and after determining

sophisticated classes and earn advanced degrees to understand what is unfolding in front of you every day. You can, in a very real sense, become a student of child development and the human condition in your own living room by being an observer as well as a caregiver. You may even want to consider doing some additional reading about this phase of your child's life. Take time to write down some of the details of daily events in your child's life—not only the milestones, but also stories that are amusing, touching, or exasperating. You (and your child) will treasure the opportunity to read these vignettes later in life.

- Take time for yourself. If you are a full-time parent at home, you will need regular time-outs—not merely for errands but for personal refreshment. These might include exercise workouts, walking in the park or strolling through the mall by yourself, or meeting a friend for lunch. Yes, you will need someone to watch your offspring while you do this, but it's worth the trouble and expense.

- Don't become starved for adult communication. When you reunite with your mate at the end of the workday, the first order of business should be some unhurried and attentive conversation between the two of you. Your child(ren) should see you do this and should be informed (as often as necessary) that this is "your time" together and "their time" will arrive shortly. Not only will this help maintain your marriage, but children who see their parents regularly connecting and showing affection will feel much more secure about the stability of their world.

- Married couples should also maintain their date night, once a week if possible. Important news for fathers: Never stop courting your wife, especially now. Notes, flowers, and unexpected gifts speak volumes and breathe new life into your relationship.

- Build relationships with other parents who have young (or even older) children. Many parents meet regularly in small groups, whether assembled spontaneously or organized by their church.

- Local pregnancy resource centers often put together single-moms' groups and activities. In the setting of such a get-together, you can share wisdom and woes, find support and encouragement, release laughter and tears, and even receive exhortation, if necessary. ■

that her base of operations is safe and secure, she will be able to explore an expanding world around her.

You may find it difficult or impossible to stop whatever you're doing and respond immediately every time your toddler comes or calls to you. In fact, a little wait at times won't hurt: She needs to learn that she is important, but not Queen of the Domain. If you're on the phone or up to your elbows in dishwater, it's quite all right to acknowledge one of her overtures with "I hear you, and I'll help you in a few minutes."

As with everything else in parenting, extremes are best avoided. If your toddler is clinging to you every minute of the day or whining and crying if you pay attention to anything or anyone else, she may be too attached to you and not spending enough of her day exploring and learning about other parts of the known universe. In this case, you may need to be more assertive about delaying your response to her when you need to tend to other business. On the other hand, if you find yourself issuing a steady stream of brush-offs, uh-huhs, or irritated sighs ("What is it now?!"), take a few minutes to review your own state of mind or think about some ways to recharge your batteries (see sidebar, "Avoiding Toddler-Care Burnout" on page 232).

Exploring: pushing the boundaries and the advent of negativism

At some point during the second year of life, usually between fourteen and sixteen months, your child will begin a phase that may seem exasperating but is quite normal. Up until this point, his explorations of the world have been fact-finding missions. He has been finding out "what happens when I eat the mashed banana, turn the knobs on the stereo, push my toy car across the floor, flip the light switch, pull the cat's tail, bounce the ball, laugh, cry, yell, babble . . ."

Some of these acts have results that are interesting or feel good, some tweak little fingers, some get attention, some make the big people laugh or get upset, some are still under investigation. If the important people in his life have responded consistently, he will have figured out many of the ground rules of his world or at least have a good sense of the odds that a particular consequence will follow a certain deed.

Now, however, he will take his explorations a step further and up the ante. Instead of merely observing cause-and-effect relationships, he will want to find out how much power he wields. *What will happen if I push the limits? Who's really in charge here? Mom may have said not to do this or touch that, but did she really mean it? Sister's dolls are supposed to be off-limits, but will anyone do something about it if I carry one away?*

During the months that follow, most, if not all, of the limits you have set will be challenged. At times they will receive a spectacular full-frontal assault. To call him "oppositional," a developmental term applied to this period, may be an understatement. By eighteen months, his favorite word may well be *no* followed by three exclamation points. What parents usually find astonishing, and at times humorous, is the extent and irrationality of this negativity:

"Would you like some water?" you ask innocently, holding his cup.
"No!"
You put the cup on the counter.
"Waaber!" he cries, reaching for it.
You fill it and give it to him.
"No!" He pushes it away.
You put the cup on the counter.
"*Waaber*!!" he howls.

You offer him the cup.

"*No*!!" He swipes at the cup, nearly knocking it out of your hand.

What fuels this temporary insanity is, in fact, a very simple premise: If it wasn't his idea, he won't have anything to do with it.

Another startling variation on this theme is his disobeying a rule you have made abundantly clear—and making sure you're there to see it broken. This is not what was going on at eleven or twelve months, when his insatiable curiosity would override his very short memory, so he might explore an object after you have told him to leave it alone—seven times.

By eighteen months he can understand simple rules very well. Furthermore, the toddler in this phase won't always operate in stealth mode, a routine practice for older rule breakers. Instead, he may trot right over to the curtains you just told him not to touch, wait until you're watching, look you in the eyes (perhaps with a grin to boot), and give them a healthy tug. He is extremely interested in your response, and it is crucial that you give him one with more substance than "Isn't he cute. . . ."

The duration and severity of this oppositional stage will vary, but you can count on manifestations of it for at least six months. Some children who are particularly agreeable and compliant won't give you much to write home about. (There aren't too many of these.) Others who are especially strong-willed seem to put on the war paint and push the boundaries on a daily basis.

To some degree, this behavior represents an important developmental milestone for your toddler. He is developing a budding sense of identity, an awareness that it is possible to make things happen, and a compelling need to find out how far his new-found capabilities can take him. At the same time, of course, he is emotionally volatile, lacking in wisdom, and extremely primitive in his handling of relationships. And when there is a conflict, any attempt at reasoning is usually an exercise in futility.

These characteristics are, indeed, strikingly similar to some seen in another age-group—teenagers. You might think of this phase of your child's life as a preview of adolescence, a turbulent but universal passage for which there is, thank goodness, light and sanity at the end of the tunnel. As with adolescence, some parental wisdom can keep the family boat from rocking too hard. Aside from the fact that a teenager is a lot bigger than a toddler, there is one crucial difference in the way you manage these two periods of your child's life. During the teen years, your goal will be to let go, to escort your son or daughter to independent, responsible adulthood. But with a toddler, it is critical that he understand without any doubt that you are in charge.

If this fact is not established with absolute certainty (though always with an abiding sense of love and respect) by twenty-four to thirty months of age, your child may be very unpleasant to live with for months—or even years—thereafter. Indeed, for many children the "terrible twos" are but an extension of the "ornery ones," only with more horsepower. But a child who comes through this developmental stage knowing he is surrounded by unshakable love and consistent limits will generally be happier and more civilized throughout the rest of childhood.

How do you make it clear to your toddler that you are in charge? Some basic approaches and specific techniques of discipline—the word literally refers to teaching and molding, not merely corrective action or punishment—are discussed in detail in the Special Concerns section "Principles of Discipline and Training" on page 259. How to deal with tantrums, breath holding, head banging, and other spectacles is included in that section.

Relationships with other children

Very often two or more sets of parents who have toddlers of similar ages will have the bright idea of getting their offspring together for a little fun and group playtime. After all, isn't this a good time to learn how to get along and make new friends?

Believe it or not, the answer is "probably not," *especially* if the children are closer to one than to two years old.

With rare exception, a one-year-old is incapable of playing cooperatively with children her own age. Her universe is centered around herself, and she cannot comprehend such niceties as understanding the viewpoint or feelings of someone else. Parents and other adult caregivers are important to her, of course, but another small child will generate little more interest than another toy—except when each is interested in the same item.

If there's one concept that is foreign to the toddler's outlook, it is sharing. She cannot grasp the idea that one of her toys can be "borrowed" or used by someone else and still remain hers, or vice versa. She lives in the here and now, and "waiting a turn" is a meaningless phrase. Her outlook has been summarized quite amusingly by child-development expert Dr. Burton L. White:

THE TODDLER'S CREED

If I want it, it's mine.
If I give it to you and change my mind later, it's mine.
If I can take it away from you, it's mine.
If I had it a little while ago, it's mine.
If it's mine, it will never belong to anyone else, no matter what.
If we are building something together, all the pieces are mine.
If it looks like mine, it's mine.[1]

Therefore, if you turn more than one toddler loose in the same room, keep a close watch and plan to serve as referee. Having plenty of toys available will help, of course, but you will need to be ready to intervene at the first sign of combat. This is important not only as a means of keeping the flow of tears to a minimum but also to prevent physical consequences. All too often if a desired item can't be pulled easily out of the grip of another child, pushing and hitting will follow.

Should this occur, separate the opponents with a clear rebuke ("No hitting!"), tend to any wounds, and then administer consequences. In this case, immediate withdrawal of a privilege (such as access to the toy she wanted) or a time of isolation from the others and the toys is an appropriate response.

If the skirmish includes biting, you will need to take decisive action to reduce the risk of a repeat performance, because human bite wounds carry a significant risk of infection. The biter should be removed from the scene and given a firm, eyeball-to-eyeball order: "Do not bite Amanda or anyone else! Biting hurts very much." A long lecture about manners or infections isn't necessary, but you may want to maintain a steady (but not painful) grip on the upper body to prevent any wiggling or movement for a minute or so. A toddler normally becomes quite unhappy after a very short period of this restraint, and continuing it for fifteen to thirty seconds after she begins to complain will reinforce your point. (Say it again before you let go.) Do not shake or slap her, and never bite the biter in an effort to show "how bad it feels."

Along with maintaining zero tolerance for your child's biting anyone, consider some preventive measures as well. If you hear a conflict brewing between two toddlers, don't wait for them to negotiate through their disagreement because they can't (and won't) at this age. Distract, separate, take whatever is in dispute out of the picture, or simply call it a day if it looks as if everyone is tired and cranky.

Depending upon the spacing of your children, conflict between a toddler and other siblings is virtually inevitable. If your children are spaced less than two years apart, the older at first will be wary of the attention being showered on the younger and may even regress to babylike behavior in an effort to regain center stage. Once she is assured of her place in your affection, however, she probably will pay little attention to the baby—until he becomes mobile. Once this happens, the insatiable curiosity of the new explorer will inevitably lead to an invasion of big sister's possessions. If your older child isn't yet two and a half, don't expect her to embrace any high-minded ideals about sharing. Try to keep your older child's prized possessions out of harm's way, and in return, make it clear that any hitting or other physical action taken against the younger sibling will have unpleasant consequences.

Even with very basic ground rules, however, some combat is inevitable. Furthermore, when it erupts, you may not always be able to figure out who did what to whom or who was at fault. This problem often gives parents considerable grief, and you will need plenty of wisdom, prayer, and patience to deal with it. In general, your response will have to depend on the age of the children involved. With very young children, separation from one another and whatever they were fighting over should be your most common tactic. Remember that this age-group is not terribly responsive to logic and reason. Later on, more sophisticated ground rules, "rules of evidence" when stories contradict, and consequences that fit the crime will need to be carried out.

If there is a difference of a few years or more between children, the likelihood of conflict with a toddler will be reduced. Not only will the older child have her own circle of friends and interests, but depending on her age, she may serve, at least at times, as a caregiver. She should not, however, be given disciplinary authority or responsibilities that belong to you alone.

Health Issues: Checkups and Immunizations

Your toddler should have a routine exam at age one, at fifteen and eighteen months, and at age two. As before, along with the normal gentle poking and prodding, his measurements will be taken and charted, and his developmental milestones (walking, etc.) should be reviewed. Remember to bring something to entertain your toddler in case you have to wait before the visit.

Don't expect a great deal of cooperation from your toddler during these exams. Typically the same physician who was greeted with coos a few months ago will now elicit howls of terror. Most of the exam will need to be done with your child sitting on your lap, and at times (such as when his ears are being checked) you will need to hold him still, pinning arms and head to your chest in an affectionate hammerlock. Occasionally, a more prolonged look into the ears will be needed, especially when wax needs to be cleared, and you may be asked to help keep your screaming and thrashing patient quite still on the exam table while this is going on. You will be impressed at how strong your child is, how upset he sounds, and how guilty you feel. Remember, however, that he is experiencing far more fright than pain.

Everyone will have an easier time at the doctor's office if you can maintain a cheerful and confident demeanor throughout the visit. If your toddler senses that you are apprehensive or ambivalent about what is going on, his fright level may increase tenfold. When he cries or resists, don't plead with him to stop. Keep your voice mellow and reassuring, and your grip tight.

Between twelve and fifteen months of age, your child should receive a number of immunizations, including some that are new to him as well as booster doses and any catch-up shots that he needs. These are likely to include vaccines against measles, mumps, rubella, varicella (chickenpox), hepatitis A, and influenza; boosters to protect against tetanus, diphtheria, pertussis (whooping cough), pneumococci, and *Haemophilus influenzae* type B; and any remaining doses of the hepatitis B or polio series if either wasn't completed during the first year. (For more details about these immunizations, see "Immunizations—Which Ones, Why, and When?" beginning on page 739.)

If you haven't done so already, be sure to make an appointment for your toddler to see a dentist who cares for children. (See "teeth care and concerns," in the Reference Section, page 723.)

Is It Time to Start Potty Training?

Probably not.

Some children may show signs that they are ready to learn this skill before the second birthday, and you may begin the process of training them if you desire (see chapter 9, page 301). But most toddlers are still in the throes of discovering their place in the world and dealing with their emotions during this eventful year, and adding any pressure to get rid of diapers and use the toilet may create even more turmoil. Take your time.

A Note to Grandma and Grandpa

Although much of this book is addressed specifically to parents, we assume that a lot of its content would be helpful to anyone who cares for babies, children, and teenagers. While we can't provide specific advice about every possible relationship, for many young people, grandparents are among the most important and influential people in their lives. If you have the privilege of experiencing this special relationship, please spend some time thinking about the content of the next few pages. (The rest of you are welcome to look over their shoulders.)

As a grandparent, you can have a profound impact on the lives and outlook of your children and grandchildren. Your ability to appreciate and enjoy grandchildren is likely to be much greater than what you experienced with your own children, for several reasons. Without the relentless "24-7–the buck stops here" duty required during early parenthood, you have the luxury of greeting grandchildren with fresh delight each time they walk through the door. The errands and chores of life can be suspended while you are with your grandchildren because (unlike their own mom and dad) you know you will have time later, when the house is quiet once again, to tend to those details. Also, by this time you most likely realize that cultivating relationships is what really counts in life, and (most important) you will have allotted more time to do so.

The value of the perspective gained *after* raising children cannot be overstated. Even those who are happy about how their grown children turned out will often reflect on their parenting careers and wish they had put a little more emphasis on *enjoying* the relationship instead of worrying so much about messy rooms or crayon marks on the walls. Having gained that understanding (and without the responsibility for daily guidance and correction—although they can certainly make a contribution), grandparents are wonderfully positioned for a unique and highly enjoyable relationship with their grandchildren.

It is an incredible gift to help grown children see their offspring through the eyes of a hopelessly lovestruck grandparent. When Grandma's face lights up the instant Ella toddles through the front door, it helps Mom remember why she became a mommy in the first place. When Grandpa values playing with Joshua more than watching a football game, it helps Dad renew his commitment to being a good father. When grandparents regard these little ones with perpetual awe and wonder rather than seeing them as a source of nonstop responsibility, they are unintentionally (but quite happily) blessing two generations at once.

Speaking of blessing, older adults also have an opportunity to make (or continue making) a spiritual investment in their children and grandchildren. Perhaps when your children were younger, your faith was nonexistent or not sufficiently mature for you to provide much spiritual guidance as your kids were growing up. It is not too late for you to have some heart-to-heart conversations with grown children about your faith and its importance to you. You might even surprise them by having a candid conversation in which you make amends for your own shortcomings as a parent.

By the way, here's an important piece of advice about *giving* advice: If you are not in complete agreement with the way your grown children are raising your grandchildren, spiritually or otherwise, be *very* careful about the way you broach that subject, especially with a daughter-in-law or son-in-law. Remember: As parents they have the final say and responsibility for the way their children are reared, and your duty in nearly every situation is to abide by their decisions. (As one seasoned grandparent put it, "Your job is to keep your wallet open and your mouth shut.")

The exception to this guideline, of course, is when an irresponsible parent's behavior or neglect is exposing your grandchildren to harm. Otherwise, offer advice only if asked and work at building a relationship in which you can compare notes and share the benefits of your parenting experience. Needless to say, suggestions that are presented simply as "take it or leave it" opinions or observations are more likely to be welcomed than grand pronouncements.

You also have the opportunity to communicate a legacy of faith to a new generation, both by word and (more important) example. Whether your and your family's spiritual roots are old and deep or newly planted, you can pray for your children and their children daily. The impact of that time logged in conversation with God on their behalf may ultimately be more profound than any advice or gift you'll ever bestow.

When Your Child Has a Fever

In order to function properly, the human body is intricately designed to maintain its internal (also called core) temperature within very narrow limits. The normal human core body temperature is 98.6°F (or 37°C), but temperatures as low as 96.8°F (36°C) or as high as 100.4°F (38°C) are not necessarily abnormal. Normal variations in body functions brought about by a child's biological clock can cause temperatures to be lower in the early morning and higher in the later afternoon and evening. A child who has been in vigorous perpetual motion will have a higher body temperature than one who has been resting quietly.

The control center for regulating temperature is in the **hypothalamus**, a structure at the base of the brain that governs a number of critical bodily functions. The hypothalamus monitors body temperature and balances heat production and heat loss to maintain the temperature within very narrow limits. This **set point** is much like the desired temperature that you set on your thermostat at home. Heat is increased by shivering and by constriction of blood vessels at the body surface, and it is lost through sweating, breathing more rapidly, and dilation of surface blood vessels.

What Is Fever, and What Causes It?

A fever is an abnormal elevation of core temperature. Most medical practitioners define a fever as a temperature higher than 100.4°F (38°C) taken rectally in an infant and in a toddler up to three years of age.

There are several important points to remember about fever:

- *A fever is not a disease in itself* but a sign that the body's regulation of temperature has temporarily changed. Fever in children is most commonly a response to infection, and it is now known to serve a useful purpose by stimulating activity of white blood cells and other functions in the immune system.
- While it is a significant sign of an illness in progress, *fever itself is rarely dangerous for an infant or child.* A persistent temperature of 106°F (41.1°C) or higher can

be harmful, but this level occurs only in unusual circumstances such as in an extremely hot environment or during a heatstroke. Fever generated by the hypothalamus in response to an infection only occasionally exceeds 105°F (40.5°C), but essentially never rises above 106°F (41.1°C). Even at this level a fever will not cause damage except in very unusual circumstances, although it will usually be accompanied by some general discomfort (especially headache or body aches).

- *The height of the temperature does not always indicate how serious the problem is.* An infant with roseola, for example, will typically be quite active and cheerful even with a temperature climbing past 104°F (40°C). Conversely, a baby or child can be gravely ill with a temperature that is much lower.
- *Whether or not it is specifically treated, a fever may go up and down several times during the course of an illness.* Some parents mistakenly fear that a fever will climb relentlessly if they don't take active measures to lower it.

Body temperature is elevated in three ways:

- *Elevation of the body's internal thermostat.* This is by far the most common mechanism. Chemical factors released by the body in response to invasion by viruses or bacteria can raise the set point of the hypothalamus, provoking shivering and other mechanisms that raise body temperature. Rare causes of a rise in set point are certain cancers (for example, leukemia) and illnesses such as arthritis syndromes, which generate inflammation within the body but are not infections.
- *Heat production exceeds heat loss.* This can occur if heat loss mechanisms are thwarted by high environmental temperature or even when a child is wearing too many layers of clothing. Uncommon disorders such as hyperthyroidism or an overdose of certain types of drugs (for example, aspirin) may cause the body to generate excessive heat.
- *Malfunction of the body's normal heat-loss mechanisms.* This may result from an overdose of certain drugs or from the syndrome known as **heatstroke** (see "Heatstroke" in "Emergency Care" on page 831). This is also an uncommon reason for a child's fever.

Ways to Measure a Child's Temperature

There will be many occasions during your child's life when you will need to determine her body temperature as accurately as possible. Even though the touch of your hand might suggest that your child is burning up or cold and clammy, this impression based on surface temperature can be very misleading. Most fevers below 102°F (38.9°C) cannot be detected this way, and children who feel warm to the touch are as likely to have a normal temperature as an elevated one. Plastic liquid-crystal strips placed on the forehead aren't much better and may miss a fever entirely. To obtain a reliable core temperature measurement, your best bet is to use a thermometer in one of these locations:

- *Rectal* temperature most accurately and reliably reflects core temperature, especially in infants and young children. It is typically 0.9°F (or 0.5°C) higher than oral temperature. *Measuring temperature rectally is specifically recommended for infants under three months of age,* for whom significant medical decisions may hinge on the numbers that are obtained.

- Taking an *oral* temperature is usually more convenient than a rectal temperature in older children (preschool age and older), assuming they can cooperate. It will be less reliable if the child is breathing through her mouth or has taken hot or cold liquids within ten minutes prior to the reading.
- Temperatures taken using a thermometer whose tip is held in a child's *armpit* (also called **axillary readings**) are not as reliable as those properly taken rectally or orally. However, they may be more accurate than a temperature taken improperly in an uncooperative child.
- *Ear* temperatures taken with special electronic thermometers are both quick and convenient, but they may be less accurate than rectal temperatures in infants and toddlers (see below).

When talking to your physician, tell him the exact temperature and method used. Do not add or subtract a degree because this could make a significant difference in the care of your child, depending on his age.

Types of Thermometers

Glass (mercury) thermometers used to be the gold standard for taking temperatures in children and adults alike. However, their tendency to break and spill this hazardous substance has led the American Academy of Pediatrics to recommend that they be discarded in favor of other types of thermometers.

Digital thermometers use battery-driven heat sensors and take about thirty seconds to arrive at a reading (usually signaled by a beep), which is displayed on a small screen. They can be used to take temperatures orally, rectally, or under the arm. Typically costing about ten dollars or less, they are simple to use and usually quite accurate.

Ear (tympanic membrane) thermometers can give an estimate of core temperature instantly by measuring the energy emitted from tiny blood vessels within the eardrum. Many doctors' offices and clinics use them because of their speed (less than two seconds to get a reading) and convenience, since very little cooperation is required from the child. In fact, these thermometers can be used when a child is asleep. However, the readings may be less accurate, especially in infants and toddlers, because of the children's smaller external ear canals; the reliability of the reading can also be affected by the position of the thermometer's tip within the ear.

If you need to dispose of a mercury thermometer, *don't throw it into the trash*. If it breaks it could expose others to this hazardous substance. Mercury thermometers must be disposed of properly through a local hazardous waste collection program. You can find out about state and local collection programs for mercury-containing devices at the Environmental Protection Agency's Web site: http://www.epa.gov/epaoswer/hazwaste/mercury/collect.htm.

Taking a Child's Temperature

When taking a rectal temperature, your baby or child should be lying stomach-down on a bed or crib, or across your knees if he is very small. Keep one hand firmly in control of his lower back, and don't try to take the temperature while he is actively squirming or resisting you. Lubricate the tip of the thermometer with petroleum jelly and put a little around the anus as well. Then gently insert the thermometer into the child's rectum about one-half to one inch. *Do not force the thermometer into the rectum.* Hold it until you hear the "beep" (usually about a minute), then remove it and read the temperature. Afterward cleanse the tip with rubbing alcohol or soap and water, then rinse. If you're having trouble getting a reading, be sure to review the instructions that came with the thermometer.

When using an oral thermometer, the tip should be placed under the middle or back portion of either side of the tongue. The child should hold the thermometer steady with her lips and fingers, not with her teeth. Be sure your child is not biting down on the thermometer. The mouth should be closed, so she will need to breathe through her nose until the thermometer beeps, indicating that you can read the temperature. (If her nose is extremely congested, she may need to take intermittent mouth breaths, or you might want to consider using a different method of checking her temperature.)

If you use an ear thermometer, be sure to follow the manufacturer's directions for proper use, being especially attentive to the position of the tip in your child's ear. During its first few uses you may want to compare your reading with a simultaneous temperature taken by a digital thermometer, in order to confirm that you are obtaining consistent readings.

If you are taking an axillary (armpit) temperature, first make sure that this area is dry. (If damp, the reading could be inaccurately low.) Place the thermometer tip in the center of the armpit and hold the child's elbow against her chest until you hear the beep. An axillary temperature can provide a convenient, ballpark reading if you're wondering whether a fever is present. But remember that a fever in a very young infant could indicate a potentially serious problem, and thus it is well worth the extra effort to get a more accurate rectal reading if you have any question about the temperature in a baby under three months of age.

What to Do if Your Child Has a Fever

First, stay calm—which may be easier said than done if your child is very young—and then assess the situation. The actual height of the temperature is important, but equally significant are *the age of your child and what else is going on.* Before calling the doctor, determine if there are other symptoms such as coughing, runny nose, sore throat, rash, or (in children who can communicate) pain in some location.

Even more important is *the way your child is acting,* which will help you determine how urgent the problem is. A normal child will usually become somewhat irritable, less active, more clingy, and less hungry when a fever is present. (This shouldn't be surprising if you remember how you felt the last time you had a significant fever.) In a typical acute illness such as a cold, your child may act like her old self again when the fever subsides. With more serious infections, however, changes in behavior tend to be more profound, and if you are uncomfortable with—or even uncertain about—what you are seeing (for example, marked lack of responsiveness), call the doctor immediately. As we have mentioned earlier in this book, you should also call right away if a baby under three months of age has a rectal temperature over 100.4°F (38°C). (See page 136 for more information about fever in young infants.)

Most acute illnesses that generate a fever in infants and children are caused by viruses and will disappear on their own, while some illnesses may involve bacteria that will respond to specific antibiotic treatment. (Certain viral illnesses, such as influenza, may also improve more rapidly with treatment.) If the fever persists for more than twenty-four hours, a call to your child's physician and possibly an evaluation may help determine the problem. In addition, there are some other general measures that may be helpful.

Dress your infant or child in light clothing and keep her room at a comfortable temperature. Turning up the heat at home or bundling her up in hot clothes will not speed recovery, and doing so may actually keep her temperature elevated. If she is shivering, give her a light blanket for comfort. (Remember, though, that shivering is a process that will raise the body temperature.)

Give your sick child fluids of all kinds, since some body fluids will be lost during sweating. Appetite is typically reduced during an illness in which fever is present. Large or fatty meals should be avoided, since fever tends to slow movement of food through the digestive tract.

Your child does not need to be strictly confined to bed, but activities should be kept on the quiet side since vigorous exertion might increase her temperature. If the illness is potentially contagious (and most viruses are), she should be kept away from other children or anyone (such as an elderly person) whose health might be jeopardized by an acute infection.

Sponge bathing an infant or child to bring down a fever is not necessary, except in unusual situations (such as heatstroke) where temperatures exceed 106°F (41.1°C). However, sponging might help her feel more comfortable, especially if her temperature is higher than 104°F (40°C). It is helpful to give a dose of acetaminophen or ibuprofen (see pages 609 and 688) at least thirty minutes before doing so to lower the set point of your child's thermostat. (Otherwise, she will simply shiver back to her original temperature.)

Set the child in an inch or two of lukewarm water (85°F to 90°F or about 30°C to 32°C, which should feel just slightly warm to the touch). *Do not use cold water,* which will make her shiver (and thus raise her temperature), and *do not use rubbing alcohol,* which can be dangerous when absorbed through the skin or inhaled. Use a sponge or washcloth to keep body surfaces wet for thirty to forty-five minutes, during which time she will lose heat as water evaporates from her skin. You do not have to bring her temperature down to normal—lowering it a couple of degrees will help her feel better.

Using Medications to Lower Temperature

Three medications that are available without prescription can help reduce an infant's or child's fever. Before using them, keep these things in mind:

- *The primary reason to give these drugs normally will be to make your child more comfortable.* They will not make an infection disappear more quickly. If your child has a fever but is otherwise contented, you don't need to give her anything to make the fever go away.
- *The fever's response to any of these medications is not an indication of the severity of the illness.* One dose may only reduce the fever 2° or 3°F (about 1 to 1.5°C) over a couple of hours, or it may merely limit the height of an upward temperature

spike. Don't panic if the thermometer reading doesn't drop right away or if it rises again after a few hours.

- *Do not give medication to lower fever to a baby under three months of age without contacting your physician.* In this age-group, determining the *cause* of the fever is far more important than lowering the temperature itself.

There are several medications on the market that can help lower fever:

- Acetaminophen (Tylenol and other brands, as well as generic formulations) is available in a variety of oral and rectal suppository preparations and may be given every four hours as needed. While this medication has been widely and safely used for a number of years, an accidental overdose can be potentially dangerous (see "acetaminophen" in Reference Section, page 608).

  Most acetaminophen products list recommended doses based on age, but if possible, it is better to determine the dosage based on weight, especially if your infant or child is above or below average (see dosage chart on page 609).
- Ibuprofen (Children's Motrin, Children's Advil, and other brands, as well as generic formulations) has the potential advantage of a longer-lasting effect—six to eight hours per dose, as opposed to acetaminophen's four to six (see dosage chart on page 688).
- Aspirin is effective in lowering temperature and relieving aches and pains, *but it is not recommended for this purpose in anyone younger than twenty-one years of age* because of its link to an uncommon but serious disorder called **Reye's syndrome** (see Reference Section, page 709).

Febrile Convulsions

Febrile convulsions—seizures precipitated by fever—occur in 2 to 5 percent of children sometime between four months and five years of age. These seizures often begin early in an acute illness, usually during the rapid upswing of a fever (which doctors refer to as a **spike**). In fact, an infant or child whom you find hot and cranky with a 104°F (40°C) temperature is not likely to have a seizure in the immediate future because with rare exception she has already arrived at the high temperature without incident. Temperature spikes tend to occur so quickly that it is unlikely that you will be able to take a temperature while one is actually taking place (see "febrile seizures" in Reference Section, page 714).

Caregivers: Who Will Care for Your Child While You Are Away?

Even if you are the most dedicated and attentive parent(s) on earth, you cannot (and indeed should not) provide hands-on care for your child twenty-four hours a day, seven days a week, from the delivery room to the college dormitory. Many times during your child-rearing career you will need to release her to the temporary care of another person. Whether this involves an occasional time-out to run errands or a routine of several hours every workday, transferring responsibility for your child to someone else raises many questions:

- How do you choose a caregiver?
- Is it better for your child if the caregiver comes to your home, or is it okay to take him elsewhere (such as to another home or day-care center)?
- How long is it appropriate for you to be away from your child?

Without question these are extremely important topics. Like many other concerns of parenting (such as discipline), there is no surefire formula that will apply to every family or even to one family through the development of all its children. Following are a few basic—but very important—overriding principles.

Child-care issues overall cluster around two major situations:

- Extended periods of child care on a regular basis, usually occurring when both parents (or a single parent) are employed outside the home.
- Short-term or episodic care, commonly referred to as babysitting, which is discussed at the end of this section (pages 256–257).

The first of these concerns—and the question of whether the mother of one or more young children should be employed outside of the home—is by far the more complicated, emotional, and controversial of the two.

Working in and out of the Home

Whether you are a young couple enthusiastically welcoming the first baby to your nest, seasoned parents with a home full of children of all ages, a blended family, or a single mom or dad, you must deal with some of the following issues:

- How much income does the family need, and where will it come from?
- How will we divide labor in the home? Will one parent be the main income producer while the other's primary role is caring for children? Or will both parents share more equally in these tasks?
- How will bringing up one or more children mesh with one or both parents' work schedules, not to mention education and career plans?
- Is it wise for both mother and father to work outside the home? If this is done, who is going to take care of the children?
- How can a single mother or father best cope with the simultaneous demands of earning a living and rearing children?

Every family will have different circumstances that affect the answer to these questions:

- Age, abilities, and temperament of each child
- The state of the marital union or the absence of a marriage partner
- Educational background
- Job/professional skills
- Financial resources
- Relationships with immediate and extended family members
- Involvement with a church community
- Goals, plans, and dreams for the future

For some parents there will be many ways to approach these questions. For others, options are very limited and the answers will be defined by current circumstances. Most single parents, for example, have the daunting dual role of primary income provider and full-time parent. There is no standard solution that will work for every family or even for one family throughout its entire lifetime. But when thinking through these very important and often emotionally charged questions, it is important to keep some broad perspectives and reality checks in mind.

Faulty expectations, identity, and the "end of life" test

Much discontent over the question of balancing child rearing and career(s)—for both mothers and fathers—can arise from several powerful but faulty expectations:

The expectation that rearing one or more children won't require considerable effort or many changes in lifestyle. An infant cannot be fed and changed and then left to his own devices, nor can an older child be expected to grow up on his own. Not only must a child's basic health and safety be assured, but his intellectual and emotional development require continuous monitoring and frequent interaction with adults who are deeply committed to him.

The expectation that a certain lifestyle is necessary for happiness. With rare exception, whatever standard of living young parents envision for themselves in the immediate or distant future will probably require more income than expected. Remember Murphy's Law of Money: Everything costs more than you expect—both to purchase and to maintain. The belief that a particular home or car, travel, and certain experiences are necessary for contentment in life can push the budgetary limits to the point that a second income becomes a necessity. But this could have the ultimate effect of trading irreplaceable interactions with one's own children for material goods that will eventually be worn out and discarded.

The expectation that Mom can be Supermom, effortlessly managing a career, nurturing children, and experiencing extraordinary marital satisfaction—all with great style and finesse. TV commercials and magazine ads have helped create this fantasy, which more often than not leads to frustration, guilt, and most of all, fatigue. There may be a few true Supermoms around, but the other 99 percent who are more earthbound usually realize that they must accept a number of compromises at home and work in order to survive.

An issue more often (but not always) for women: The expectation that being at home will result in the evaporation of one's intellect and ambition. Women have received this message from numerous voices, including popular media, friends and acquaintances who work outside the home, even insensitive husbands and family members who either don't understand or have forgotten what is involved in running a household and nurturing children. The decision to remain at home is often made at considerable sacrifice, and many women find themselves disadvantaged later when they try to reenter the outside marketplace after a few years' absence from it. However, to assume that staying home with the children will erode a woman's mental or professional powers is to subscribe to an extremely narrow view of life.

The rewards of participating significantly in a child's development cannot be measured. A parent who chooses to stay home is aware that her children will only be home for a season and that her impact on their intellect, development, and values will probably continue for decades. Rearing children is a career that requires a host of skills as well as insight, patience, and wisdom.

The world of work is changing to accommodate parents who have decided to spend more time with their children. An increasing number of options for working part-time or from a home office are making it possible for both moms and dads to be with their children more often and more consistently. Many women for whom an outside career or interest is important have created satisfying professional options for themselves from within the home setting. These are encouraging developments, both for women who want to pursue a career outside the home (whether now or in the future) and for women who are content to make home their career but who want to pursue artistic or community interests.

An issue more often (but not always) for men: The expectation that the career track defines identity and that all other concerns pale in comparison. Men are notorious for defining themselves in terms of their occupation and position. (How often do you hear a father answer the question "What do you do?" with "I'm Trevor and Amanda's dad"?) But the danger of this orientation is that the demands of a career and the pursuit of excellence at work can result in rampant absenteeism from home and mediocrity in parenting. Many fathers and mothers buy into the myth that a few minutes of time spent with one's children every day is just fine, as long as it's "quality time."

But will a one-ounce steak be satisfying because it is "quality steak"? Or (perhaps more relevant for men) will sex every six months be adequate because it is "quality sex"?

Both mothers and fathers need to think very carefully about these issues. The truth is, a true and lasting sense of worth, identity, and satisfaction comes ultimately from being present and accounted for in God's family and going about His business every day. In the final analysis, these qualities are not derived from the initials after one's name, the title on one's door, the plaques on the walls, or the money in the bank. They do not come from being CEO of Universal Widget or having a home that is the envy of the neighborhood—or having kids who are perfect. Parents must beware of the "If only . . ." syndrome: "If only ____, then I'd be satisfied/content/happy." These are the longings of those who are perpetually restless and discontented, who never fill the gaping hole remaining in their lives, no matter how often they successfully accomplish last month's "If only . . ."

The "end of life" test. Parents who are making decisions about who will rear their children should ask themselves an important question: When you are staring down death's corridor, what in your life will really matter? Will you look back fondly at the hours spent at the office and pine over the fact that you weren't there longer? You may be the world's greatest Monopoly player—on the game table or in the real world—but eventually you will have to fold up the board, put the money back in the box, and put it in the closet. No one will remember for very long who won the game, but those who were at the table with you will long recall whether their time with you was pleasant or miserable.

More specifically, will your children arrive at your bedside and thank you for all the career goals you accomplished? They will probably remember most fondly and thank you for the times you spent with them—rocking them, listening to them, wrestling on the carpet, having lunch at their favorite restaurant, going fishing, walking on the beach, or helping them out of a jam. At that moment, what will matter most will be the people you care about, the lives you have touched, and the prospect of hearing God say, "Well done, my good and faithful servant."

Best and second best

These considerations are not intended to incite great pangs of guilt nor to say that careers launched from within or outside the home are somehow evil. They are, however, meant to raise serious questions about priorities, about what really matters, and to lay the foundation for the following observations.

While children are growing up, they should be cared for primarily by people who are *passionately and sacrificially committed to them*. In the vast majority of cases, the people who best fit this description are their own parents. However, grandparents, other relatives, or close friends may feel this way too.

People who are hired to take care of other people's children can and should be responsible, mature, kind, and attentive—but they will rarely be passionately and sacrificially committed to those children. Most paid caregivers are probably not going to develop a deep emotional bond or a relationship with a child that will last for years.

If at all possible, then, it is most desirable for children to spend the majority of their waking hours with one of their own parents or with someone else who has an equally intense commitment—especially during the first few years of life when children are dealing with basic issues of security and trust.

This will not always be possible for a variety of reasons. If it isn't and your child is going to spend a significant amount of time in the care of others, your energy should be expended not on guilt but on finding the best possible caregiver arrangements, a process that will be reviewed in the next section. As much as possible, continually seek ways to arrange schedules and time commitments that will maximize parental time with each child at home.

Seeking a Caregiver

Assuming that your child is going to be spending time on a regular basis with a caregiver other than one of his parents, what options are available?

In-home care: the caregiver comes to your child

This person might be a relative such as a grandparent, a nanny whom you hire for an extended period, or perhaps a college student or au pair from another country who provides care in exchange for room and board. There are several advantages of in-home care:

- Your child remains in a completely familiar environment—with access to his own crib or bed, toys, and yard.
- Assuming that the same person comes to your home regularly, there will be greater stability and consistency in your child's life.
- The caregiver's attention is focused specifically on your children, rather than on a larger group.
- There is no exposure to contagious diseases from other children. If your child becomes ill, care does not have to be interrupted or rearranged.
- Convenience is maximized—there is no need to transport your child and the items he needs to another home or facility.
- Depending upon the caregiver's availability, there may be more flexibility in this arrangement; your home doesn't have "closing hours."

Disadvantages of in-home care are as follows:

- If you are hiring the caregiver, in-home care is likely to be more costly. In this case, the individual will in effect be your employee, so you will need to be aware of possible tax implications and even liability concerns. (For example, who pays the bills if the caregiver is injured in your home? Your homeowner's insurance may or may not cover such expenses.)
- What do you do if the caregiver is ill or can't come for some other reason? You will always need to have Plan B ready in case such a problem arises.

Family child care: your child stays in the caregiver's home

In this arrangement, an individual (or perhaps a couple) provides care in his or her home for a number of children who may be of similar or widely variable ages. (If the caregiver is a devoted relative who is responsible only for your child, this situation may be essentially the equivalent of in-home care.) The advantages of family child care include:

- Your child remains in a home rather than a "facility" environment. If the family is someone you and your child already know, there will be some familiarity (and perhaps less separation anxiety).

- As with the in-home arrangement, having the same caregiver every day will provide consistency in your child's experiences.
- There are likely to be fewer children than in a day-care center, and thus less exposure to contagious diseases.
- Costs are sometimes less than for in-home care or a day-care facility.
- As with care in your own home, there is often more flexibility with hours.

Disadvantages of family child care include the following:

- There may be no licensing requirements for family caregivers in your state. In this case, you will need to rely more heavily on your own assessment of the caregiver and the home environment to determine if all is safe and sound. (Obviously, it is helpful if you know the family beforehand.)
- Plans may have to be rearranged (sometimes without warning) if the caregiver becomes ill, has an unexpected family problem, or simply goes on vacation.
- If the caregiver is responsible for several children, you will need to determine if she or he can give adequate attention to your child and not become overwhelmed.

Facility child care: your child stays at a day-care center operated by a church, university, or commercial entity

There are several advantages to this type of child care:

- These are normally licensed and thus accountable to regulations regarding the facility and the staff. These places may have extremely well-trained employees, age-appropriate learning programs, and physical resources (such as playground equipment) not available in homes.
- Facilities normally have predictable staffing and hours of operation. You will not need to make sudden adjustments because a caregiver is ill or unavailable.
- If care is provided by a church whose beliefs you share, your child might be exposed to songs, stories, and other input that build spiritual and moral values.

There are some disadvantages of facility child care:

- Day-care centers sometimes have relatively large child-to-staff ratios so that individual attention for your child is in short supply.
- If the facility does not offer competitive wages, it might not attract well-trained or attentive staff. Staff turnover in some centers can be rapid, leading to unpredictable relationships between the children and their adult caregivers.
- Infections are spread much more easily among groups of children who are interacting at close range and handling the same toys. Both upper-respiratory infections (including middle-ear infection) and diarrhea are more frequent among children in day-care centers.
- While hours of operation are more predictable, they might not be very flexible. What happens if you are stuck in traffic or experience some other delay at the end of the day?

All things being equal, if care is provided on a regular, ongoing basis by someone other than a parent, the order of preference for choosing a caregiver follows:

1. One or more relatives, either in your home or in theirs
2. A nonrelative in your home, such as a nanny or a live-in

3. Nonrelatives in a home setting
4. Large-group day care in a facility

This ranking is based on several key assumptions:

- A relative is more likely to be attached and attentive to your child than a non-relative would be.
- A stable, predictable situation is more desirable than one in which there is constant change.
- If there are fewer children for each caregiver, your child is likely to receive more individual attention.
- Infections are less common among small numbers of children than in large-group settings and even less frequent in your own home.

As with so many other parenting concerns, there are always exceptions to these guidelines:

- A conscientious nonrelative is preferable to an irresponsible family member.
- A large day-care center that is well maintained and staffed by adults who love children is preferable to a home setting that is unsanitary and poorly supervised.
- A caregiver whom you hire to stay in your home may not necessarily devote herself to your child's well-being while you are gone.

If you need, but do not yet have, child care, ask some trusted friends or coworkers for suggestions or referrals. Your church might have references or a bulletin board listing caregivers in your community. Newspaper and yellow-page listings are also possibilities, although with these you do not have the advantage of a specific recommendation. Ultimately you must survey the options available to you and then consider carefully which might best meet your family's needs. In doing so you will need to keep three factors in balance:

1. Is your child likely to thrive in this situation? How closely will the care duplicate (or at least resemble) the way you care for your child at home?
2. How well will the availability and location of the caregiver mesh with your own schedule and daily logistics?
3. Are the child-care arrangements affordable?

There are also specific considerations for infants and toddlers. A baby's physical and intellectual development, as well as emotional security, require ongoing adult attention. Infants need mental, emotional, and physical stimulation; they should not be left lying or sitting for hours in a crib or playpen. They need to be changed when wet, comforted when crying, and played with when awake and comfortable. They should be hand-fed; propping a bottle in an infant's mouth creates a risk of choking and of ear infections. (If you are looking into a center that provides care for infants, check to see if there are a number of comfortable chairs in which adults can hold and feed babies.)

Mobile babies and toddlers need room to explore—safely. They can neither be confined to a small enclosure nor allowed to roam far and wide without supervision. Their attention can shift as rapidly as their mood, and they are not capable of playing cooperatively with other children.

In order to give adequate attention to the needs and development of infants and toddlers, there should be

- at least one caregiver for every three children younger than two years of age. If at all possible each infant or toddler should have a main caregiver—that is, someone with whom he has an ongoing and consistent relationship.
- at least one caregiver for every four children between two and three years of age.
- at least one caregiver for every eight children between three and six years of age.

With these basic principles clearly in mind, you must also evaluate several aspects of any potential child-care arrangement, including short-term (babysitting) care:

The person or people involved. (This is the most important factor.) *You should get to know those who are going to be responsible for your child's welfare.* Don't hesitate to request one or more interviews, and take the time to observe the caregiver's interactions with your own child as well as with other children.

- Does the caregiver appear comfortable, relaxed, and pleasant with children?
- How well does the caregiver interact with *you*?
- What prior experience does the caregiver have?
- Are references available?

If you are dealing with group care in a home or day-care center, ask the following questions about the staff before you make your decision:

- Who is in charge, and what are her or his credentials?
- What is the ratio of children to caregivers?
- If assistants are used, are they at least fourteen years old and properly supervised?
- Is everyone trained in child CPR?

The child-care setting (assuming it is not your own home). Before choosing the best facility for your situation, look at the following:

- Is it clean, cheerful, and attractive to you and your child?
- Do tables, chairs, and other equipment appear to be in good repair?
- Are there any potential safety problems?
- Are electrical outlets covered?
- Are smoke detectors and fire extinguishers present?
- Are heating, air-conditioning, and overall ventilation adequate?
- Are cleaning supplies, medications, and other hazardous products inaccessible to children?
- Are appropriate toys available?
- Is the outdoor play area properly fenced and secured?
- Are enough mats, cots, cribs, or beds available for naps?
- Is there an area specifically designated for diaper changing? Is it cleaned after each use? Is it anywhere near where food is prepared?
- Are pets present? Are they child-friendly? Is your child allergic to animals?

Philosophy, policies, and programs (in day-care centers or group home care).
Consider the following when choosing your facility:

- Are there written policies and procedures you can review?
- Is the basic worldview of the caregiver or facility compatible with yours?
- Will the values you teach at home be honored?
- Is there any spiritual input for older children?
- What is the caregiver's outlook on training and discipline?
- Are the disciplinary policies delineated and followed by all caregivers?
- Does there appear to be an appropriate balance between love and limits in dealing with behavior problems?
- What types of measures are used to maintain order?
- Is disciplinary spanking ever carried out, and if so, under what circumstances?
- Is disruptive or destructive behavior handled appropriately?
- If you observe a child's behavior being corrected, is it done with respect?
- Are children adequately supervised at all times?
- What kind of food is offered to children?
- Are activities planned and available for older children?
- Do these activities enhance learning and overall development?
- Are arts and crafts available?
- Is there excessive reliance on TV or other passive activities?
- Are there opportunities for physical exertion and outdoor play?
- What happens when a child is ill?
- Do children who are sick remain in contact with those who are not?
- Are the caregivers willing and able to give prescribed medications to infants and children?
- Are parents encouraged to drop in at any time to see how things are going? (*This is very important.* Be wary of any place where your access to your child or the facility is discouraged or restricted.)
- Is the caregiving situation appropriately secure?
- Are there clear policies regarding releasing children to adults who are not their parents?
- Can the facility prevent unauthorized individuals from entering?

Red Flags

While stable and nurturing child care is desirable, *safe* child care is an absolute necessity. Injuries resulting from adult carelessness, physical or sexual abuse, or assaults on a child's emotions are a parent's nightmare—and all are unacceptable in any setting. Unfortunately, signs of neglect or wrongdoing may not be especially obvious, and even if they are, it can be impossible to prove that the caregiver was at fault. Nevertheless, you will need to keep your eyes and ears wide-open for any of these potential indicators of trouble:

- Does your child become unusually upset or fearful about being left with a particular caregiver?
- Does the caregiver appear impatient, irritable, or stressed?
- Has your child become more withdrawn or shown other signs of not being himself after spending time with a caregiver?

- Have you discovered unexplained bruises, welts, or other marks on your child's body?
- Has your child exhibited inappropriate language or sexual behavior?
- Do you feel uneasy whenever you leave your child with a particular caregiver?
- Are you discouraged from dropping in on the caregiver unannounced?
- If you have made an unexpected visit, have you found things in disarray, or have you noticed children improperly supervised or extremely upset?

If you observe one or more of these red flags, you should strongly consider removing your child from that situation until you can determine with greater certainty what is best in the long run. You may need to speak candidly to the caregiver about what you have observed and see if the response you receive is appropriate, evasive, or overtly hostile. If you believe that your or someone else's child has been abused in a child-care setting, you should contact your nearest child-protection agency and explain your concerns. Even if you are not certain whether abuse has actually taken place, it is their job to investigate more fully and take appropriate action if needed.

Babysitters

While it is vitally important to be diligent regarding the choice of a long-term caregiver for your child, it is also important to be careful about your choice of babysitters, even though the time your child spends in their care may be considerably shorter. During the first six months of your child's life, it is best to leave her in the hands of experienced relatives or other adults. As your child grows older, however, younger babysitters can be utilized. Indeed, some of the best babysitters you may find will be students in high school or middle school. In many communities, hospitals or other organizations offer short courses (including CPR training) for babysitters, and those who have completed such a program could be excellent candidates for you to consider.

It is best to build a roster of trustworthy babysitters before you actually need one. Ask other mothers of young children whom they recommend and why. Responsibility, experience, and good rapport with young children are important qualities to seek. You might find some excellent sitters and have a chance to see them in action in the church nursery or Sunday school.

Once you have potential candidates, it is helpful to spend time with each one in your home. If possible, have him or her watch your child while you do some other work at home. This will give you a chance to observe how the sitter interacts with your child; it will also allow your child time to become familiar with the babysitter, thus reducing separation anxiety (if the child is old enough to manifest it) when you leave.

When you leave your child with a sitter, always write down where you are going and how you can be reached. This will usually include your cell phone number, the location and phone number(s) of your destination(s), and (if you carry one) your pager number. You should also provide the phone number of your doctor, the local hospital, and another relative or friend who will be home in case you can't be reached. Let the babysitter know when you expect to be home and what you expect to happen while you're gone—including feeding, bathing, and bedtime routines. If a child needs medication, make sure the babysitter knows exactly how much and when to give it. The sitter should also know any other family rules, such as those applying to TV or video watching, as well as any reliable ways to comfort your child when you leave. The babysitter should allow no visitors into your home unless you have made prior arrangements. If it helps you feel comfortable, check in with the sitter by phone after you've been gone awhile to find out how things are going.

Make sure that your pay rate is clear from the start. Ask a friend what the going rate is for each age-group and don't hesitate to offer more for the best sitter on your list. If you would like the sitter to clean up dishes or straighten up elsewhere in the home, offer to pay a little extra.

If your child is old enough to understand, tell her that you are leaving and you will be back. Don't sneak out when she isn't looking, and don't be pulled into a long, emotional parting scene. Your child will survive and, with rare exception, will calm down shortly after you leave. Enjoy the night out!

A Final Note: Who Will Provide Care If You Are Gone . . . for Good?

Planning for a disaster is never enjoyable. But an accident during even the most routine errand might unexpectedly leave your children without one or both parents. If such a tragedy were to take place, who would care for your children, and how would their material needs be met?

All parents must consider this possibility, carefully decide whom they would want to care for their children—along with a number of other financial, practical, and spiritual considerations—and then express their desires in a legally binding document. The specific steps involved in the preparation of a will or a living trust should be reviewed with an attorney who is well versed in estate planning.

What matters most is that parents not succumb to the notion that "it can't happen to me" but instead take the proper measures to provide for their children should the unthinkable happen.

Principles of Discipline and Training: Balancing Love and Limits

Discipline: Training and instruction that is intended to produce a specific pattern of behavior, character development, and moral or mental improvement. (From the Latin *discipulus*: "pupil," derived from *discere*: "to learn.")

Mention the word *discipline* in connection with rearing children, and images of various forms of punishment may come to mind. But discipline encompasses the entire process of shaping and molding children's attitudes and behaviors over the years that they are entrusted to your care. This project is deserving of your diligence, fervor, humility, and prayer.

Training your children cannot be approached in a careless or haphazard manner because, left to their own devices, children rarely gravitate toward virtuous behavior, selfless attitudes, and responsible decisions. If these are not learned at home during thousands of interactions with parents and other family members, they may never be learned at all—to the detriment of the child and everyone around him.

But you don't need to live in a state of constant anxiety, wondering whether one false move on your part will unleash a career criminal years later. The discipline of children involves an overall mind-set rather than a cookbook full of behavioral recipes. ("If he does this, you should do that.") Discipline can include a variety of techniques and approaches that vary depending upon the child's age and temperament. And what brings about a desired result with one child may prove to be a dismal flop with a sibling. While you will want to have an overall plan in mind, you will have to improvise along the way.

The subject of training and discipline often raises a lot of questions, concerns, and even controversy. For example:

How do you sort out all the input and advice you get, including the impact of your own upbringing? Your approach to discipline will be influenced significantly by your own experiences as a child or adolescent. You may even overcompensate for extremes that have affected you. If you were treated harshly as a child, you may tend toward being permissive, and vice versa. You will also receive plenty of advice (some more worthwhile than others) from relatives and friends, books and magazines, sermons, radio and TV programs, child-rearing classes, and your child's physician. You will have to choose wisely from these resources, separate the wheat from the chaff, and try to avoid becoming a "Method of the Month Club" parent.

Are you too rigid or too lenient? If you don't worry about this question once in a while, you may be at risk for extreme or unhealthy discipline patterns.

How early can or should discipline begin? Based on developmental milestones, you can't expect a baby under eight months of age to follow directions, although certain behaviors (such as day and night sleeping patterns) may be shaped by parents. As your baby becomes mobile, you will need to begin establishing and enforcing limits through a variety of approaches. If you haven't started some basic molding and training of your child by eighteen months, you're off to a late start.

Why is it so difficult? And why does your child keep challenging you? Sometimes (or perhaps most of the time) bringing up children seems at best loaded with uncertainty, at worst a perpetual uphill struggle. Why? Because each child is a unique creation, a person with a mind, spirit, and will of his own. Children are not built like cars or computers; they do not arrive with instruction manuals that guarantee that B will happen if you do A. Nor do they enter your life as "blank slates" whose thoughts and actions are completely determined by whatever input you provide at home. While many of their behaviors are predictable in general terms, they are not little robots who will automatically yield to your direction.

Some children who are endowed with a particularly strong will seem bent on bucking everyone who crosses their path—beginning in the delivery room. If you have been blessed with one of these children, don't panic or give up. You won't be the first parent in your neighborhood to bring up a strong-willed child, and as you continue to shape that powerful will, you may well see not only an adolescent who resists peer pressure but later a young adult who has become an effective leader.

What about disciplinary spanking or other physical punishment? This question, which will be reviewed in some detail later on, has become increasingly controversial in recent years. Some parents use spanking (a form of corporal punishment) too frequently, too severely, and too long into childhood. A few parents abuse their children in the name of discipline. In response to these harmful extremes, many authors and organizations have concluded that *all* physical discipline, including disciplinary spanking, is inappropriate. But this position is also extreme. At the right time, for the right reasons, and with the right safeguards, spanking can be a useful tool in rearing young children.

Extremes in Discipline: What Not to Do

No mother or father disciplines children with absolute perfection, and like every other parent in the world, you will make mistakes. You may say or do something that you later regret, or you may neglect one or more worthwhile aspects of the training process.

But parenting involves a long learning curve, and children brought up in an environment where it is clear that they are deeply loved will be resilient in the face of numerous parental errors. Nevertheless, it is very important to stay away from patterns of missteps and omissions that could have a lasting negative impact on your child. If any of the following have taken root in your home, remember that it's never too late to make midcourse corrections.

Physical abuse. Punching, slapping, whipping, burning, and other horrors inflicted upon children are *not* discipline. They are abuse, pure and simple, and have no place in the rearing of a son or daughter. They do not benefit the child in any way, but merely represent unhealthy ways for a parent to vent anger or exert control over a smaller, weaker person. These behaviors indicate a basic defect in the parent's communication skills, the parent's lack of respect for the child's body and emotions, and a gross misunderstanding of a parent's responsibilities. Those who believe that cruelty inflicted on their children somehow fulfills a biblical mandate not to "spare the rod" should rethink this position—immediately. If this type of violence has occurred in your home, seek counseling now to prevent further damage. Such help is especially important if you received this sort of treatment as a child, because abusive patterns may continue through generations unless someone has the courage to break the cycle.

Verbal thrashing. Even if you don't throw sticks and stones or break any bones, your words can hurt your children. Harsh, degrading, insulting language—"You are so stupid," "I'm disgusted with you," "You little jerk"—burns its way into the memory and emotions of a child. While physical abuse scars the body, verbal abuse scars the mind and heart, and neither is a proper exercise of parental authority. If your mouth is the source of repeated harsh and hurtful assaults on your children, it is important to seek counseling to rein in these verbal beatings.

Authoritarianism. This rigid micromanagement of childhood behavior stresses pure obedience without any understanding or internalization of principles. There may be times when you need to declare, "Because I'm the mom, that's why!" But demanding knee-jerk submission in every detail of life will wear thin as the years pass. You can probably impose this regime on your children when they are younger, but as they reach adolescence, their rebellion will be a certainty—and probably will be spectacular.

Management by yelling and screaming. Some parents arrive at the mistaken conclusion that their children will respond to them only when they raise their voices in anger. This idea usually develops over time through many repetitions of a scenario in which a parent's direction is ignored by a child—and nothing is done about it. When this pattern is fully developed, a child will have learned to gauge accurately when Mom or Dad is likely to take action.

Always be nice to your children because they are the ones who will choose your rest home.

Phyllis Diller

Typically, after five or six requests or orders have been ignored, the parent's voice becomes more forceful, words are clipped, and the child's middle name is used: "John Patrick Smith, you get into that tub *now*!" The child has calculated that something unpleasant is likely to occur at this point and heads for the bathroom. The parent comes to believe that anger got the desired results, and he or she may resort to it more frequently. In fact, it wasn't the anger, but action (or the likelihood of it) that got the child moving.

Eventually, if action doesn't always follow the angry words, a child may learn to ignore even the most intense outbursts. This not only dilutes the effectiveness of all other communication within the family but may lead to a disaster in an emergency. (Imagine a child chasing a ball into the street unaware of the truck bearing down on him and ignoring, as always, his parent yelling at him to stop.)

Idle threats. Many parents attach threats of dire consequences to the orders they give a child: "You'd better not _____, *or else*!" But if the child repeatedly disobeys and "*or else*" never happens, she will learn that a lot of what Mom or Dad says is just hot air. This may escalate to some form of home terrorism; a frustrated parent whose warnings aren't taken seriously may increase the verbal artillery to abusive levels or become enraged to the point of finally making good on some extravagant threat. As with "management by yelling," it is action and consequences early in the game, not threats alone, that motivate children to follow directions.

Laissez-faire parenting: little or no adult input or involvement. This occurs when one or both parents are too busy, overwhelmed, tired, or indifferent to set and enforce consistent limits. A child who is left more or less to his own devices will probably not be very relaxed and happy but rather quite unsettled, because the boundaries that provide security are missing. Even though most kids push and shove against limits, they will become surprisingly anxious if few or none are present.

Nonstop bribery. Rewards have a definite place in training children, but parents should not haggle or make deals over every direction they give a child—especially those that are not negotiable. It would be quite inappropriate to say, "I'll give you a cookie if you get in your car seat." A child should not become used to the idea that virtue is only worthwhile if there's a prize attached. Moral values eventually need to be internalized, not merely bought and sold.

"Democratic" parenting. One of the great cultural follies of our times is the belief (often expressed with humanitarian fervor) that parents and children should have equal say in all matters and that a mother or father has no right to exert any parental authority over a child. A variation of this occurs when a parent is unwilling or unable to override a child's drives and desires, usually out of fear of rejection, an unwillingness to deal with conflict, or the mistaken notion that anything that causes an infant or child to become upset is terribly harmful.

But conflict is inevitable in any long-term human relationship, including the one between parent and child. Misguided attempts to keep a child from experiencing any unhappiness by routinely giving in to her every desire will ensure that she is miserable and unpleasant. Respect for a child's identity and feelings is important. But someone needs to be in charge while she is growing up, and for everyone's sake, it should not be the child.

Overt permissiveness. This is a more extreme and naive version of democratic parenting; it is assumed that children are born bundled with "virtue software." They are thus seen as innocent little "clean slates" who may even possess moral qualities their elders have lost. According to this misguided viewpoint, while they might be corrupted by a negative environment, children in a nurturing setting do not need correction. Some parents tolerate a great deal of dis-

The thing that impresses me most about America is the way parents obey their children.

Edward,
Duke of Windsor
(King Edward VIII)

respectful and destructive behavior in their young children based on the assumption that they are "getting it out of their system." Unpleasant surprises during late childhood and early adolescence await those who adopt this approach.

Six Basic Principles of Discipline

1. Balance love and limits.

Balance expressions of love—physical affection, kind words, comfort, help—with appropriate boundaries and consequences. Children cannot survive without experiencing consistent and unconditional love. From the first day of life through her journey into adulthood, your child must know that your love is rock solid, the foundation from which she can safely and confidently explore her world. Chapter 1 contained an important statement about a crucial message that your child needs to hear, see, and experience in hundreds of different ways from the moment she is born through the day you release her to live on her own. This message summarizes the essence of unconditional love and bears repeating here:

> You are loved, you are important, and you always will be, no matter what happens. I care enough about you to provide for you, stand with you, coach you, correct you, and even die for you if necessary. My commitment to you is not based on what you do or don't do, how you look, whether your body is perfect or handicapped, or how you perform in school or sports. It is based on the fact that I am your parent and you are my child, a priceless gift whom God has loaned to me for a season. Eventually I will release you to live your own life, but while you are growing up, I consider caring for you an assignment of utmost importance.

Children also need, and actually fervently seek, boundaries and ground rules. Expressing love and enforcing limits are not contradictory but intimately related. Allowing a child to have her way without any restraint is not an expression of love. At the other extreme, harsh, rigid, or authoritarian treatment of children, even if it produces apparent model citizens, isn't an appropriate exercise of limit setting.

2. Parents must assume leadership in the home.

For a variety of reasons—whether the nonstop attention required to rear infants and small children, fatigue, distractions, or one or more strong-willed children at home—it is possible for parents to find themselves struggling simply to maintain order and manage the demands of daily life. After a few or several years, the children may set the family's agenda and even drift into a general disrespect or disregard for the parents' authority. This is an unhealthy state of affairs for three reasons:

- Children lack the wisdom, knowledge, experience, and capabilities to train and nurture themselves.
- Children will not gain the skills and responsibility to live independently as adults without ongoing direction from parents who require that the children learn and do things that don't come naturally.
- Children want to know and will ask in a variety of ways, "Who's in charge here?" If the answer is "I guess I am," the result will be uncontrollable, disruptive, and generally unhappy children.

The critical importance of establishing your right to lead is central to the next two principles.

3. Distinguish among normal behavior, childish irresponsibility, and willful defiance—all of which need your guidance and correction but in different ways.

- The normal explorations of infants and toddlers should be encouraged—but in a manner that is safe for themselves and their surroundings.
- Throughout your child's years at home, you will have to deal with numerous episodes of childish irresponsibility—knocking over the milk, leaving your rake out in the rain, losing her new gloves, forgetting his lunch, not feeding the cat, leaving toys strewn all over the living room.

  These actions need correction, but they usually do not represent a direct challenge to your authority. A steady diet of rewards, consequences, and lots of patience will gradually introduce your child to responsible behavior over a period of several years.

- On specific occasions (with some children, on a regular basis), however, the issue will be willful defiance. This may begin surprisingly early (between fifteen and eighteen months of age), may continue through adolescence, or may become relatively rare by the grade-school years.

  Willful defiance takes place when your child (1) knows and clearly understands what you want (or don't want) to happen, (2) is capable of doing what you want, and (3) refuses to do so.

  Whether passive or "in your face," a child's defiance is asking several questions: Do Mom and Dad really mean business? What's going to happen if I don't do what they want? Are they tough enough to make me? Who's really in charge here?

  When confronted with such a situation, act clearly and decisively, meeting the challenge head-on. Not only must your child not have his way, but his attitude about what he has done must be turned around as well. When the conflict is over, you should be on the same team once again. You don't need to be harsh or hostile, but you must not back down. If you do not establish your right to lead early in the game (by the age of two or three at the latest), your ability to influence or control your child later on will be seriously compromised.

  At times it may be difficult to tell whether your child is being defiant or irresponsible. Did he hear you? Did he understand clearly what you wanted? Can he actually accomplish it? Failing to get straight As is not defiance. But refusing to shut off the TV and sit down with the books after being told to do so probably is. When dealing with willful defiance, the child's attitude is the central issue. As Dr. James Dobson has noted in a memorable adage, "If he's looking for a fight, don't disappoint him." This doesn't refer to having a literal brawl with your child, of course, but rather to a consistent posture of standing your ground when your authority has clearly been challenged.

4. Accept the fact that conflict between parent and child is inevitable.

Whether dealing with a full-blown showdown or managing a series of minor irritations, it is impossible to avoid conflict with your child at some point. Effective, loving parenting is characterized not by the absence of conflict but by the resolution of conflicts in ways that maintain both your leadership and your child's dignity.

5. Love and concern for the child's best interests must be your final guide.

The effort required to give good discipline is a continuous expression of love, and that love may take you in some unexpected directions. It may lead you to allow a child to suffer some consequences for his irresponsibility, even when you might easily bail him out. If he repeatedly forgets to take his lunch to school, letting him feel hunger for a couple of hours (rather than running the wayward sack over to the school office every day) will change his behavior far more than reminding him sixteen times over the breakfast table. You may both hurt while the consequence is playing out, but the final outcome—a learning experience with long-term benefits—will serve his best interests.

On the other hand, love may also lead you to overlook the specifics of a child's transgression based on his intent. If he makes a mess in the kitchen while trying to fix breakfast for you, the motive of the heart should overshadow whatever has been spilled on the counter and floor. (He can, of course, be asked cheerfully to participate in the cleanup chores—another good learning experience.)

Love will also cause you to examine your own motives as you deal with different child-rearing situations. Are you responding harshly to whining because you're tired or overwhelmed? Are you giving in to demands and tantrums from a two-year-old because you were the victim of excessive punishment as a child and don't want to overreact? If you're upset over her messy room, are you concerned about her attitude toward her possessions or what your relatives will think if they see it? If you feel that your motives are unclear and your actions unpredictable, spend some time with an older parent whose child-rearing results you respect, or meet with your pastor or a counselor to discuss what has been taking place.

6. Stay on your knees.

If you think you've got parenting figured out because your firstborn was a compliant, relentlessly pleasant child, cheer up. You will probably be blessed with a miniature tornado next time around, and whatever you did with Number One won't begin to manage Number Two. Similarly, if you've read books (including this one) and feel you've got the discipline situation figured out and reduced to a formula, brace yourself—something thoroughly humbling will probably cross your path in the near future. There is only one Parent who completely understands all sons and daughters on the face of the earth, and seeking His wisdom on a daily basis should be a priority for all who train and nurture children.

Top Ten Ground Rules of Discipline

Here are some building blocks, the brick and mortar of the process of training children.

1. Keep your primary goals in mind.

If you plan to take the assignment of training children seriously, it is important to have a firm grip on your basic goals. What are you trying to accomplish? The following, listed in order of increasing sophistication, should be on your child-rearing agenda.

Keeping the child safe. Many limits you place on your child, beginning as soon as he can move himself from point A to point B, will be designed to keep him from harm. Early in his explorations he will have no idea whether an object in his world is friend or foe. He should not find out primarily through painful trial and error. As the months and years pass, he should gain an increasingly sophisticated understanding of cause and effect as well as consequences.

Preventing harm to others.

Preventing damage to property (whether the child's or someone else's).

Teaching respect for those in legitimate positions of authority. This must begin with you, the parent, and later extend to other designated caregivers. Soon after her first birthday, your child will make clear that she wants to know who's in charge here. If you haven't established your authority and your right to lead very early, you will be in for a bumpy ride later on. Establishing your authority does not mean that you need to be harsh, vindictive, or dictatorial. Instead, you are preparing her for the reality that *everyone* at various times of life must submit to someone else.

Eventually a child's respect must encompass teachers, coaches, law-enforcement officers, employers, and so on. Ultimately, she must also learn to recognize God's authority over her life—and understand that this authority is motivated by love and a boundless desire for her (the child's) well-being. Whether you realize it or not, your child's concept of God will be affected to a significant degree by her experiences with you during her years at home.

Teaching internal controls for actions and words. The ability and willingness to delay gratification are not programmed into children, who usually want what they want when they want it, which is *now*. Learning to wait one's turn and to put off the reward until the work is done isn't merely an exercise for toddlers and grade-schoolers. This training received in childhood has ample application to adult life as well, in arenas as diverse as education (plowing through years of coursework to earn a degree), finances (waiting to buy something until one can afford it), and sexuality (delaying the pleasure of intercourse for the wedding night).

Furthermore, what comes "out of the mouths of babes" (as well as older children) often isn't particularly delicate or thoughtful. While not enforcing a repressive notion of children being seen but not heard, one of your most important projects over the years will be teaching your child to engage the mind before putting the tongue in gear.

Teaching basic civility. Manners, politeness, and general decorum are not inborn behaviors in children. Not only should saying please and thank you and following other details of civilized life be taught at an early age and repeated until they become automatic, but as a child passes through the grade-school years, the *attitudes* of respect and selflessness that underlie the habits will become habits as well. Ideally, both the attitudes and the behaviors will be modeled consistently at home—but this does not guarantee that your example will be followed, and specific instruction will usually be necessary.

Preventing negative behavior patterns and more serious long-term consequences. Selfishness, dishonesty, disrespect, poor impulse control, aggression, and destructiveness are annoying and disruptive in a four-year-old. In a fourteen-year-old they can lead to devastating or even lethal outcomes, not only for a teenager but for his family and an ever-widening circle of people who must deal with the consequences of his words and actions.

Teaching internalized values. Honesty, responsibility, compassion, perseverance, loyalty, self-discipline, courage, and faith are admirable qualities in a grade-schooler. In an adult they lead to a life of productivity and service. People demonstrating these qualities often emerge as leaders in their circles of influence.

2. Discipline should be appropriate for the child's age and capabilities.

A baby under the age of seven months is unable to act in a self-conscious manner or to carry out more than a handful of specific acts. Thus, efforts to make baby "mind" at this age are futile and ill-advised. If she cries or wiggles during a diaper change, there is no point in attempting to discipline her to do otherwise. If she develops a world-class episode of colic, she isn't doing it to ruin your day, assert her independence, or challenge your authority. She doesn't feel right, and crying is the only way she can express that discomfort. However, some shaping of behavior (such as reversing day and night sleep patterns by stimulating her during the day) is possible at an early age, as discussed in earlier chapters of the book.

> *It is easier to build strong children than to repair broken men.*
>
> Frederick Douglass, nineteenth-century orator, writer, and abolitionist leader

Between a baby's eighth and fifteenth months, some limit setting must begin as a baby becomes more mobile. However, as detailed in chapters 7 and 8, *an intense desire to explore her surroundings is normal, and her fierce determination should not be interpreted as defiance.* She may crawl toward the same plant fifteen times, not because she is trying to take charge, but because it looks terribly interesting and her memory is very short. The primary methods to utilize at this age are baby-proofing and distraction, which are preferable to a steady diet of No's! from parents and older children.

After fifteen months, episodes of true clashing of wills are likely to begin. She will not only be more mobile but increasingly capable of actions that can be annoying, damaging, or dangerous. Her improving memory prevents distraction from being effective in turning her attention away from the things you want her to avoid. And while she is also capable of understanding simple directions, overt defiance and negativism are also likely to be displayed.

During these months (up to about age three), your expectations for behavior that your child can control should focus on her safety, as well as on preventing her from harming people or damaging the world around her. Specific goals for her should include coming when called, responding to simple directions (such as not touching or manipulating things that are off-limits), and not hitting or biting anyone—including you.

On the other hand, you cannot expect a child this age to sit still for long periods of time (such as in church or at a movie), to be affectionate with someone (a visiting relative, for example) on cue, or to show much interest in formal learning activities. It is futile to force a child this age (or any other) to consume whatever food you have placed before her. Remember that you determine what kinds of food are on the plate; she determines how much she'll eat.

As your child progresses into grade school, your expectations will become more sophisticated, encompassing both moral behavior and increased levels of responsibility. Be careful, however, about imposing consequences upon a child for physical or intellectual shortcomings that are beyond her control (see sidebar "Behaviors That Should Not Normally Be Subject to Punishment" below).

3. Constantly praise what your child does right.

Praise and positive feedback are a critical cornerstone for training children. The positive things you say to a child should normally outnumber the negative by a wide margin. This may seem difficult when you're dealing with a toddler who is constantly into everything throughout the house or with an adolescent for whom you feel time is running short for corrective action at home. But at both ends of childhood, and in between as well, actively watch for and applaud behaviors that are praiseworthy. ("I really liked the way you helped your brother put away his toys.") As part of an effort to accentuate the positive, let her overhear you when you compliment one of her accomplishments or a virtuous behavior to a friend or relative. The well-worn advice to "praise in public, criticize in private" is particularly applicable to children, who can be profoundly affected

BEHAVIORS THAT SHOULD NOT NORMALLY BE SUBJECT TO PUNISHMENT

- *Normal exploratory behavior in infants and toddlers* (as discussed in chapters 7 and 8).
- *Toilet training.* It will happen when she's ready.
- *Bed-wetting.* This is a physiological event that is not under conscious control and will rarely (if ever) respond to rewards and punishment (see "bed-wetting," Reference Section, page 629).
- *Speech problems.* These need professional assessment, and a lot of work may be needed at home, but delayed or garbled speech is not a character-development issue.
- *Accidents.* An older child can be involved with cleanup, repair, and restitution, especially if carelessness was involved.
- *Irritability and negativity specifically related to illness or extreme fatigue.*
- *Report cards that fall short of perfection.* Children should not be punished for failing to bring home straight As, but you can set up appropriate ground rules for the effort a child puts forth at home, such as doing homework before fun and games. If a child's school performance is falling short of her capability, the problem may be a need for more self-discipline, but specific learning problems may be involved as well.
- *Attention deficit/hyperactivity disorder (ADHD) problems.* A child with ADHD may have a great deal of difficulty with impulse control and learning from mistakes, even when she wants to do the right thing. However, among many other things (including perhaps medication), she still needs discipline and training to make progress and survive in the world. Parenting a child with ADHD is an art and a true test of one's patience and stamina. (See "Attention Deficit/Hyperactivity Disorder" on page 379).
- *Performance in sports.* Dropping the ball in center field or failing to make a team shouldn't provoke disciplinary measures at home. In fact, parental support and encouragement at such times are extremely important. ■

by what they hear said about themselves in the presence of others. Remember also that saying complimentary things about her appearance ("I just love your curly hair") may be nice during a cuddle session, but this won't necessarily improve her behavior.

Rewards and special privileges are perfectly appropriate ways to bring about desirable results, especially in situations where you are trying to increase effort or responsible behavior. For example, many parents set up systems in which points are awarded for activities such as getting out of bed on time, keeping a room clean, or taking out the trash. When a certain number of points are accumulated, an appropriate reward (such as a trip to the park or a small toy) is given. A variation on the theme (especially for children with a shorter attention span) involves offering a treat that will begin as soon as one or more tasks are completed. ("When everyone's toys are picked up, the back porch is swept, the animals fed, and dishes put away, we can all go out for frozen yogurt.") Or money may be offered for completing extra work such as weeding the yard. And, yes, it's okay to offer a reasonable premium for a certain number of As or Bs on the report card, especially if this inspires a child to put forth more effort on schoolwork.

Some parents might argue that rewarding children is merely bribing them for things they should do anyway. It's true that you should not use rewards on a nonstop basis, especially for nonnegotiable behavior such as brushing teeth or coming when called. But few adults go to work every day purely out of the goodness of their hearts, and a paycheck is as concrete a reward for you as anything you might concoct for your child. There is nothing wrong with allowing a child to strive toward tangible goals as long as they are not fostering overt greed or materialism.

4. Limits and expectations must be defined clearly by parents and understood by their children.

For discipline to be effective, especially during the early years, a child needs to know and understand what you want and what will happen if he doesn't comply. By the time he arrives at the preschool years or soon thereafter, he should be able to repeat back to you both the limit and the consequence of breaking it. If he misbehaves but truly appears not to have known that what he did was wrong, an explanation is more appropriate than punishment. (However, if a mess was made or damage done, he should take part in the cleanup and restoration process.)

When discussing consequences, don't make threats that are outright lies. ("If you do that again, the police will come and take you away," or "If you don't stop that, the doctor will give you a shot!") A child who has been told that an immunization or any other medical treatment is a punishment is not only misinformed but may come to resent the doctor or nurse as well. Cooperation during future visits may be jeopardized, and the child might become reluctant to say something about an important symptom for fear of being "punished" by the doctor again.

Furthermore, don't issue a warning involving a consequence you are not actually willing to carry out. "If you don't stop arguing, we're going to cancel our trip to the lake!" is either an excessive or an idle threat, especially if the trip has been planned for six months, with reservations and a deposit already mailed. After several grandiose warnings that never come true, your children will catch on and not pay attention to you. But if you're truly willing to blow an entire vacation over an argument in the backseat, you need to reconsider whether your punishment really fits the crime.

How many rules and regulations you actually spell out will depend on your child. He should learn that the basic moral principles you have taught him apply to the world at large and not just to his immediate family. But you may have to make these connections explicit. For example, even if it seems self-evident to you, you may have to make it clear that the statement "Don't take things that don't belong to you" includes what is in the neighbor's garage as well as what is in his sister's toy chest.

As you begin to increase a child's responsibilities at home, your expectations will generally need to become more detailed. It probably won't occur to him to hang his shirts in the closet rather than throw them on the floor, for example, so if you want him to do this (and he's capable), he will need specific directions.

One fundamental expectation deserves special mention: Your child should learn to follow your directions whether or not you decide to give reasons and explanations. If you find yourself haggling and debating with your child every time you ask or tell him to do something, it's time to tighten the reins. First, present a plainspoken declaration of your right to lead. ("I'm the parent, you're the child, and what I say goes. Period!") Next, warn him that further arguing will lead to unpleasant consequences.

Remember, however, that while you have the right to expect your child's obedience, you also have the responsibility to lead in a manner that is reasonable and has his best interests at heart. Like adults, children and adolescents care passionately about what is fair, and they become agitated when consequences seem to appear out of thin air. The New Testament warns parents not to exasperate their children, and a steady stream of arbitrary or unjust punishments will not only exasperate them but reap a bitter harvest years later.

You will need to exercise particular wisdom in situations where you really didn't give specific directions, even if you feel they shouldn't have been necessary. He might insist that "Nobody said I couldn't jump off the roof!" and you might feel justified in retorting with equal fervor (as you head for the emergency room to treat his twisted ankle), "You should have known better!" But these frustrating episodes can actually be rich opportunities to teach broad principles (looking before leaping, thinking before acting), which will be more effective than merely generating more detailed rules.

5. Consequences must occur consistently and in a timely manner.

Ideally, your child should respond to any specific direction you give ("Please pick up your toys now") without delay, distraction, or argument. In reality, many parents would faint if their child actually obeyed them right away, without some fussing or complaint. But this goal can be achieved if the following principles are put into action:

When appropriate, give a little advance notice if you intend to interrupt something your child is doing. ("Tyrone, in ten minutes I want you to head upstairs and start your bath. I'll set the buzzer so you'll know when it's time." Or "Monique, when your video is finished, I need you to set the table.") Make sure your directions are understood.

If and when your child doesn't do what you have asked, take action and explain why. ("I see you're still sitting here twenty minutes after I told you to start your bath. Tyrone, it's very important that you do exactly as I tell you. To help you remember next time, you're going to bed a half hour early tonight." "Monique, I let you finish your video, but you didn't set the table when it was done. I respected what you were doing, but it's very important that you respect me by following my directions. I want you to set the table now, and to help you remember to do what I ask, you're not going to watch any videos for a day.")

You don't have to get angry or raise your voice. You don't have to complain or make threats. Just take appropriate action, making sure that what you do will be meaningful but not harsh and that you will follow through with the action. If Monique shrugs and says she wasn't going to watch any videos tomorrow anyway, extend the ban for as many days as needed to get her attention.

Make certain that your response to a child's misbehavior is timely. A toddler will not remember what you were upset about an hour ago, and an older child should not be kept in suspense all day waiting for some undefined but worrisome punishment to be delivered.

Be sure to enforce your rules and limits *consistently*. Not only should your children know that you will back up your words with action every time, but they should also know that your response won't waver to any great degree. The same transgression shouldn't bring about a soft reminder one night and a harsh punishment the next. On-again, off-again discipline is confusing, and it generates disobedience and unhealthy fear. In a two-parent family, both parents should strive to dispense consequences in a similar manner. "Wait till your father gets home" is a phrase you should never have to use, because Mom and Dad should deliver the goods with equal conviction.

All of these principles are important because most children become experts at the game called "What happens if . . . ?" They spend a lot of time observing cause and effect, and can usually predict with some accuracy when parental action is likely to occur. In many families, the odds depend upon which parent is playing the game, what else is going on, time of day, tone of voice, and numerous other factors. If a child hears a lot of talk about what he should or shouldn't do but little of it is backed up with action, he will probably pay little attention (unless he is extremely sensitive to tone of voice or verbal disapproval alone). The bottom line is that if and when your child challenges your leadership (whether actively or passively), you must respond with action—calmly, respectfully, quickly, decisively, and consistently.

6. The consequence should be appropriate for the transgression.

In most situations, words are all the response you will need. For toddlers and small children, a disapproving look and a tone of voice that says you mean business will often promptly change behavior or even bring tears and the need for comfort. Remember that what you say should be appropriate for the age-group. For the toddler, simple statements such as "Don't touch the stove," especially when accompanied by physically lifting him away from it, are appropriate. For older children, reaffirming the reasons for your limits is worthwhile as well. And if you make it a point to sound pleasant and relaxed most of the time, your more serious tone of voice will be far more effective when you choose to use it.

Withholding a privilege can be effective from toddlerhood through adolescence. If your toddler bangs a toy against the coffee table despite your clear direction to stop, put the toy away for a while. If you've told your first grader to put his bike in the garage but it remains on the front lawn all night, a day without it will help remind him next time. If your adolescent has ignored specific instructions about being home by a certain hour, a week without phone or driving privileges can be a meaningful way to get her attention.

Time-out can be useful with toddlers, preschoolers, and early grade-school children, especially when emotions need to cool down. This involves isolating the child in a playpen, in his room, or simply on a chair—without toys or other entertainment—for a specified period of time. Usually one minute of time-out per year of age is appropriate, although if the child hasn't calmed down, more time may be necessary. This approach is usually effective—assuming, of course, that the child is willing to cooperate. If he refuses to stay on the chair or starts trashing his room during a time-out, more direct physical intervention may be necessary.

Restitution is an important principle of discipline that can and should be used, especially with older children and adolescents. If your child makes a mess, he cleans it up. If he causes someone else's property to be damaged or destroyed, whether directly or through passive negligence, he participates in the repair and restoration. He may have to work to repay all or part of the costs involved.

Not all acts of restitution necessarily involve property. If your daughter lies to someone, for example, she should confess to that person. If she has broken a promise or failed to honor a commitment, she will need to apologize to the persons involved. These acts of humility are often far more difficult—but also more character building—than enduring any time-out or loss of privilege.

Allowing consequences to play out is a potentially powerful approach to discipline, especially during the school-age years. The basic principle is this: Look at childhood mistakes as learning opportunities, and avoid rushing in to rescue your child from natural consequences (provided, of course, they are merely unpleasant and not potentially dangerous). For example:

- If he leaves his bike on the front lawn and someone steals it, don't replace it immediately. He'll be more careful with the next bicycle he owns.
- If she forgets to bring home her permission slip for the field trip, let her miss it. She won't forget the next time.
- If he plays roughly and carelessly with his new toy and breaks it, don't go straight to the store to buy a new one. Let him mourn the loss and talk with him about taking better care of his possessions in the future.
- If she dawdles every morning and then misses the school bus, let her deal with the fallout from the unexcused absence.

Your motivation should not be anger or spite, and your tone should not be "I told you so," "Now you'll listen to me," or "That'll teach you!" If anything, this process should be painful for you; you should provide emotional support and comfort while you resist the urge to bail your child out. Whatever you choose to teach during one of these episodes need not come with a flood of reprimands because he has already felt the sting of wrongdoing.

Why should you and your child endure these unpleasant experiences, especially when it is often within your capability to end them quickly and easily? Because what he learns from an uncomfortable episode as a child may save him from a disastrous or even lethal miscalculation as an adolescent. A child who is allowed to become an expert on consequences will be more likely to think through the outcomes of his actions later on when the stakes are higher. Going without his lunch won't kill him, but getting involved with illegal drugs or premarital sex might. Furthermore, if he is repeatedly spared the consequences of his misbehavior throughout childhood and adolescence, he may never learn self-control or exercise good judgment as an adult.

Physical punishment (specifically, disciplinary spanking) is a tool that can be useful in specific circumstances. However, some voices in our culture condemn all spanking, based on claims that it teaches violence, perpetuates abuse, damages a child's dignity, and doesn't change behavior. These criticisms are valid for abusive forms of corporal punishment such as slapping, kicking, beating, and in cases of spanking that is excessive or inappropriate (such as when it arises out of anger and frustration), or when it causes injury.

But when utilized with appropriate guidelines, spanking can and should be neither abusive nor damaging to a child's physical or emotional well-being. With toddlers and preschoolers, a controlled swat on the behind may be appropriate to bring a confrontation to a timely conclusion. A disciplinary spanking should be administered only in response to an episode of willful defiance characterized by a clear, appropriate parental directive that the child understands and is capable of following; a direct challenge from the child, especially one given in a disrespectful or hostile tone; or persistent and blatant refusal to cooperate.

In such situations, attempts to reason with a hotly defiant toddler or to "share your feelings" with a disrespectful preschooler are likely to be futile. Allowing a child to call you names, spit at you, throw objects, take a swing at you, or damage your home is inappropriate and unhealthy, does not help him "get it out of his system," and virtually guarantees more of the same destructive and obnoxious behavior in the future. And if the conflict continues to boil or escalate, your anger and frustration may reach a flash point at which hurtful words or actions are unleashed.

Any physical action you take in such circumstances should not be an outpouring of anger or an act of revenge, but rather a tactic to turn your child's behavior around and bring the rebellion to a swift conclusion. A spanking of one to three quick swats should provide a brief, superficial sting to the buttocks or the back of the upper thighs. It should be just hard enough to get the child's attention, bring on some tears, and break through the defiance.

Many parents wonder whether a disciplinary spanking should be administered with a neutral object or with the palm of a hand. One might argue that a child should not experience the touch of a parent's hand as a painful event and that a mother's or father's hands should be used exclusively for holding, caressing, or comforting. Furthermore, if a spanking is administered with a neutral object—a thin flexible switch, for example—a brief time will elapse while it is located, decreasing the likelihood of lashing out impulsively in the heat of the moment.

On the other hand (no pun intended), any object that extends more than a few inches from the hand can gain surprising momentum during a spanking, especially when the wrist is in motion at the same time. Since a neutral object, unlike the hand, cannot "feel" the force of its impact, it may be difficult to know whether a spanking is producing an appropriate superficial sting or much more severe pain.

The bottom line is this: Whether the hand or a neutral object is used in a spanking, it should not cause bruising or other damage to the skin. (You should try your method of choice on your own skin first.) Unfortunately, some misguided or abusive parents utilize fearsome hardware during spankings—razor straps, heavy belts, belt buckles, canes, or worse—that virtually guarantee injury to the child. This type of punishment, as well as face slapping, punching, hair pulling, or any other form of violence, is completely inappropriate and has no place in the rearing of a child.

A disciplinary spanking should be carried out in private, between parent and child (and not in front of the rest of the world or wide-eyed siblings). It must be followed by reconciliation, comforting, reassurance, and simple teaching about how to avoid such

Parental warmth after discipline is essential to demonstrate that it is the behavior— not the child himself—that the parent rejects.

The New Dare to Discipline
By Dr. James Dobson

an episode in the future. *You should not need to take this course of action more than a few times during your child's life.* Once you have established clearly that you are in charge, many (if not most) defiant episodes can be settled using other measures such as verbal reprimands, time-outs, or restriction of privileges. If you have a particularly strong-willed child, however, more than a few disciplinary spankings may be necessary. But if you find yourself taking this type of action on a daily or weekly basis, you should reevaluate your basic approach to discipline. Perhaps you are taking too harsh a response to childish irresponsibility or not communicating clearly to the child what you expect. Or it is possible that for various reasons your child is not capable of understanding or following your directives. If spankings have become a frequent occurrence in your home, in order to prevent physical, emotional, or even spiritual damage to your child, you should consider seeking alternative approaches and other help from a counselor or pastor who shares your basic values and views on child rearing.

Disciplinary spanking should *not* be carried out

- if you feel extremely angry, highly stressed, or emotionally unstable;
- if you were abused as a child, unless you have worked through your past hurts (and the issue of corporal punishment of your own children) with a professional counselor;
- if you are not clear about the difference between childish irresponsibility and willful defiance, either in general or in the specific situation at hand;
- if both parents are not in agreement about its appropriate use;
- after a child reaches the age of ten (and should occur infrequently after the age of five or six);
- by anyone other than a child's parent, except under specific circumstances (such as a prolonged period of care by another person in the parent's absence) in which explicit permission and ground rules have been laid down.

7. A unified approach to discipline, carried out regardless of who is in charge of a child at any given time, should be a firm parental goal.

If other caregivers are involved in your child's upbringing, they should understand your viewpoint and techniques of training and discipline. If a child's mother and father are divorced, every effort should be made to maintain the same standards in each parent's household. Without such unity, children will learn to play one parent or caregiver against the other. ("Mom said no, so let's ask Dad.")

An honest disagreement about principles and practices should not be discussed in front of the children. Under no circumstances (except an imminent threat to a child's life or health) should one parent openly contradict or overrule the instructions of the other. This is not only disrespectful, but it also undermines the other parent's authority. If necessary in the heat of the moment, parents should call a time-out and discuss their issues behind closed doors before taking further action.

8. Don't restrict teaching of values to times of confrontation.

In many families, the only time moral principles are discussed is during corrective action resulting from an episode of wrongdoing. But this will tend to leave children with a stunted or even repressive sense of values. Be on the lookout for "teachable moments," those conversations during which you can give your child a broader and deeper understanding of right and wrong. Chapter 10 (pages 337–340) contains a number of helpful suggestions.

9. When appropriate, allow your child to make choices that will give her a growing sense of competence and individuality.

During the preschool years, this can involve simple decisions such as which pajamas she wants to wear or which story she wants to hear at bedtime. As the years pass, the range and significance of the options should increase—which summer camp to attend, which musical instrument to play. The gradual granting of increased independence and responsibility, which is one of the fine arts of parenting, is discussed in more depth in chapter 13.

Don't offer choices or begin haggling over issues for which there should be no negotiating, such as sitting in the car seat, bathing, or visiting the doctor.

10. Remember that children learn a great deal about appropriate behavior from what they see modeled by the adults in their lives.

You can talk about virtues and work diligently to instill values in your children, but like water seeking its own level, their moral sensibilities aren't likely to rise above whatever goes on in front of them at home. At least for the first several years of life, you as a parent are their authority on just about everything. Your words and actions provide hundreds of little vignettes that can teach them about responsibility, kindness, honesty, faith, and perseverance—or the opposite of these virtues. The beginning of wisdom in providing training and discipline for your children is an honest, ongoing appraisal of your own life and values. No matter how busy or tired you might feel, don't shrink from this important and worthwhile process.

Child Abuse and Neglect

In 1960 when the term *battered child syndrome* was first introduced into the medical literature, it was estimated that fewer than 750 children were significantly abused every year in the United States. Fourteen years later, about 60,000 incidents of child abuse were reported. That number soared to 1.1 million in 1980 and to 3.9 million in 1995. Investigation by child-protection agencies substantiated nearly one million of these reports. By 2004 these numbers had decreased to 3 million reports of possible mistreatment, of which 872,000 were substantiated. These statistics suggest that about 1.2 percent of children in the United States are abused every year, and of these nearly 1,500 die as a result of their mistreatment. More than 80 percent of these deaths involve children under the age of four.[1] (Tragically, the number of deaths every year has gradually increased since 1995, even while the overall number of cases of mistreatment has shown a modest decrease.)

This dramatic increase in the number of reported cases of child abuse over the past three decades is partly the result of increased awareness of the problem combined with mandatory reporting requirements for health-care professionals, teachers, and others who work with children. In addition, the breakdown of families, the escalation of violence in many communities, and most important, the overall deterioration of moral values (including loss of respect for all human life) in our culture undoubtedly play a significant role as well.

There is but one small bit of comfort to be found amidst these alarming statistics and trends: While without question all parents make mistakes and fall short of perfection—including saying or doing things that they later regret and might even apologize for—the vast majority do not repeatedly act in a way that could be considered abusive, and likewise the vast majority of children are not victims of abuse. Unfortunately, however, when mistreatment does occur, the abuser most often is a parent, relative, or someone who has an ongoing relationship with the child. It is uncommon for a child to be harmed by a total stranger.

Without a doubt the most sobering aspect of abuse statistics is that they represent large numbers of individual babies and children—with names, faces, voices, desires, and needs—who have suffered intense and often horrifying pain, usually at the hands of those who should have been nurturing and protecting them. What is equally troubling is the enormous damage that child abuse produces: deep physical and emotional wounds (which may not heal for years, if they ever do), tortured memories, distorted relationships, and the likelihood that history will repeat itself when the abused children grow up and have their own children. Those who mistreat children—whether out of ignorance, irresponsibility, uncontrolled emotions, or actual intent and planning—cannot begin to understand the extent of these repercussions.

There are four basic types of child abuse: physical, sexual, and emotional abuse, and neglect. Of the confirmed instances of abuse, over 60 percent involve some form of neglect, 17 percent involve physical abuse, and nearly 10 percent involve sexual abuse. (About 15 percent involve other types of maltreatment such as abandonment or threats of harm.) Neglect is more readily recognized in children under four years of age, who are unable to provide for their most basic needs. And while physical abuse can occur in children of all ages, life-threatening and fatal injuries are seen more commonly in children under age three. All forms of abuse can occur individually or (worse) more than one type can be inflicted on the same child. Emotional abuse can be assumed to exist when any other type of abuse is present.

Physical Abuse

Physical abuse is perhaps the easiest form of abuse to recognize, but its definition varies among doctors, health professionals, parents, and states. Spanking a child one time on the buttocks, for example, when done in a controlled and loving fashion, may be an appropriate form of discipline to one parent but perceived as abuse by another.

Physical abuse often occurs when a parent (or other adult) who is stressed and upset strikes out at a child in anger and frustration. Adults who are at higher risk for this type of behavior include those who

- were abused themselves as children;
- have relationships with other adults (often their spouse) in which physical violence recurs;
- are stressed by financial, employment, or marital problems;
- are isolated from other adults who might provide emotional support, companionship, accountability, or a break in child-care responsibilities;
- have limited knowledge of the normal behavior of infants and children and highly unrealistic expectations of what is required to care for them properly;
- have a limited repertoire of responses when a child is disruptive or disobedient; or
- use alcohol and drugs to the extent that their inhibitions are reduced and their judgment is impaired.

In addition, children with the following problems and characteristics are at higher risk of being abused:

- babies who are irritable or demanding—sensitive to the environment, easily aroused, and slow to calm;
- premature infants;

- children with behavioral or learning problems, such as attention deficit/hyperactivity disorder (ADHD), which may create a particular risk when the child is very hyperactive (see the Special Concerns section "Attention Deficit/Hyperactivity Disorder," page 379); and
- children with mental retardation.

Physical abuse often results in distinct patterns of injuries that are not typical for everyday childhood accidents. For example, marks or bruises over the back, buttocks, abdomen, or cheeks might indicate abuse because these areas of the body aren't usually injured during normal childhood activity. Skin markings or welts in the shape of a hand, belt, rope, or buckle could be signs of intentional injury. Unusual fractures (especially in infants), bite marks, and symmetrical or patterned burns are often identified in emergency rooms or physicians' offices as possible signs of abuse. Health-care professionals (including doctors and dentists), teachers, and counselors are required by law to report even a remote suspicion of abuse to local child-protection services. While not under legal obligation to do so in most states, neighbors or family members may at times have to consider the difficult decision of bringing their concerns to the attention of the appropriate community agency.

Unfortunately, some accidental bumps and bruises might be mistaken for abuse. For example, toddlers and active children often bang their shins and fall on their foreheads during normal play and may have bruises in those areas. A false accusation of child abuse can be a devastating experience for parents; therefore, adults who care for children in any setting must be knowledgeable about normal patterns of injury versus those inflicted by abuse and must not make accusations lightly. On the other hand, it would be more harmful (or even fatal) for a child to experience ongoing physical battering merely because those who were concerned about him were afraid to take appropriate action to protect him.

Remember that it is not the job of the person reporting a suspicion of abuse to be absolutely certain that harm is being inflicted. Uncovering the truth about a child's injuries can be extremely difficult, and those who work in child-protection agencies must often make very tough decisions, weighing the potential risk to the child against the trauma that can result from taking action when in fact no wrongdoing took place. A judicious blend of common sense, compassion for all concerned, and courage to intervene when necessary is required of anyone who must deal with child abuse.

Sexual Abuse

Sexual abuse is so psychologically complex for the victim that its true incidence is difficult to ascertain. Shame and embarrassment heavily shroud this form of abuse, and many victims fail to report it. According to a 1993 report, professionals believe that between one in three and one in four women suffered some form of sexual abuse during childhood. The rates reported for men are generally lower (from 3 to 24 percent), and most professionals estimate that anywhere from one in ten to one in six men experienced sexual abuse as children.[3] (The inconsistencies between various studies in estimating rates of sexual victimization reflect a host of factors, including interview techniques, types of questions utilized, the specific populations under consideration, and the researchers' definition of abuse.) The report noted that victimization of boys was probably underreported, for a variety of reasons. It would be reasonable to suspect that, since 1993, increasing publicity regarding sexual abuse of boys would increase the likelihood of such events being reported. Sadly, it is also unlikely that sexual abuse has declined significantly since this report was published.

It is important to understand that sexual abuse can take a variety of forms. The common denominator is that a child or adolescent is used in some way for the sexual stimulation of another person who is an adult or at least significantly older than the victim or someone who holds power or control over the victim. **Sexual contact** involves any form of physical touch that is intended to provoke sexual arousal of the abuser or the victim. This can include:

- direct genital contact with the victim, including penetrative intercourse (vaginal, anal, or oral), whether or not overpowering force is used;
- fondling, rubbing, touching, or manipulating genitals or breasts, including simulated intercourse; and
- kissing or touching clothed or unclothed areas of the victim's body for sexual stimulation or arousal.

Sexual interactions do not involve direct physical touch and may be more difficult for the victim to interpret, but they are no less abusive. These can include a number of scenarios:

- Visual interactions in which the perpetrator deliberately watches a naked child or adolescent or exposes the victim to sexual imagery—whether pornographic literature or videos, or an exhibition of his or her own body—to obtain sexual arousal. Very often exposing a child to pornographic material is intended to desensitize the child to more overt sexual contact.
- Verbal interactions in which inappropriate sexual or suggestive comments are made about the child or adolescent, usually in a degrading or seductive manner.
- Psychological interactions in which a child or adolescent becomes a confidant in an adult's highly personal or even sexual matters. In such cases a child may become a surrogate spouse or partner with whom the abuser shares deep and intimate secrets that violate appropriate boundaries between adult and child.

While some of the situations listed above might sound less severe than others, *every form of sexual exploitation is destructive and degrading, an assault on the body and soul of the victim.* Even in situations where a child or adolescent is seduced into apparent compliance with ongoing sexual activity, this is never a victimless crime. The consequences are not only damaging physically—involving at least pain and at worst injuries and possible exposure to sexually transmitted infection—but emotionally and spiritually as well. Children who are sexually abused are at risk later in life for various forms of self-destructive behavior, distorted or impaired long-term relationships (including difficulty with marital commitment and sexuality), addictions, and overall feelings of shame and worthlessness.

Sexual abuse occurs at all socioeconomic levels. As with physical abuse, instances of sexual abuse involving a total stranger are far less common than those in which the perpetrator is someone the child knows—in a worst-case scenario, one of his own parents. Risk factors for the child include the absence of the natural father at home, parental discord, a poor relationship with one or both parents, a parent who was sexually abused as a child, and general lack of supervision. However, even a child who is raised by attentive parents in an intact family might be victimized by a relative, a neighbor, a caregiver, or an adult in a position of authority over him, such as a camp counselor or a youth leader. This violation of a child's trust by someone in a close relationship—a person who is supposed to be looking after his welfare and protecting him from harm—is extremely damaging to a child's basic understanding of the world. One of the saddest assignments of parenting is to warn a child about the possible risks "out there" and to help him become streetwise about the dangers he might encounter as he grows up and becomes more independent. Being sexually abused by someone who isn't "out there" but who instead is in a child's circle of trusted family, friends, or acquaintances sends a very powerful message to the abused: *There isn't any place in the world that is safe, and you can't trust anyone.* This mind-set is a major mental and emotional handicap, and years of counseling could be required to overcome it.

Children who have been sexually abused can be difficult to identify since most are too afraid or embarrassed to disclose mistreatment. The power of secrecy is profound, particularly when the abuser is a family member. Often the perpetrator seduces a child into silence ("This is our little secret") or threatens the child or a member of the child's family with emotional or bodily harm if anyone finds out what has happened.

There are several signs of sexual abuse that parents might look for:

- Sexual knowledge or speech that is not appropriate for the child's age (excluding normal bathroom fascination and humor in the early grades).
- Overtly sexual behavior or demonstrations. While children fantasize frequently, the content of normal fantasy does not include adult sexual acts.
- Disturbed sleep and nightmares that are more frequent than usual.
- Refusal or extreme reluctance to go to a particular place or spend time with a particular person.
- Fear of being left alone.
- Physical complaints such as abdominal pain or headaches.

Sexual abuse is so abhorrent for children as well as parents that denial of its existence by either party is not only common but often doggedly persistent. Often mothers fail to recognize it in their daughters. Even when the abuser is not a family member, parents might not believe a child's story or, while acknowledging the abuse, may downplay its effects on the child. One of the most devastating scenarios for a child or adolescent is to be subjected to ongoing abuse because everyone looks the other way instead of coming to his rescue.

In many cases, the accuracy of a younger child's testimony regarding sexual abuse is called into question or even flatly challenged. However, in light of their concrete thinking patterns, it is almost impossible for young children to concoct sexual scenarios about which they should have little or no knowledge unless the events have actually occurred. In fact, since sexual abuse embodies tremendous shame, even children with physical signs of abuse frequently deny its occurrence. *Parents must be strong enough to listen carefully, face the fact that abuse may indeed have occurred, and then support their child or adolescent through its aftermath.* This includes the process of physical evaluation (which can be highly threatening and uncomfortable for a child, even in the best of hands), as well as appropriate psychological and spiritual counseling, which will need to extend for months or possibly years to repair the damage.

It is also critical to take appropriate action to protect the child from the perpetrator. Aside from the obvious step of ensuring that the abuser does not have further access to the child, appropriate legal action should be taken. There may, however, be considerable reluctance to put a child through the trauma of interrogation by police, testimony in court, and so forth, especially if the abuser is known to the family. But it is also critical that the child knows that this violation is not going to be ignored or taken lightly. Furthermore, taking action could prevent other children from being victimized by the same perpetrator.

Neglect

Neglect is a more passive but no less devastating form of abuse. *More than one-third of all child-abuse deaths result from neglect.*[4] Caring for infants and children is a time-consuming and labor-intensive responsibility, and some parents (or other caregivers) are unable or unwilling to put forth the effort necessary to carry out this task. In neglect's most severe forms, a child's basic needs for food, clothing, shelter, and nurturing are not met, resulting in a syndrome known to health-care workers as **failure to thrive**. (You should be aware that the term *failure to thrive* encompasses problems arising from a variety of situations, including—but not limited to—abuse and neglect.) Infants and children living in such circumstances exhibit diminished subcutaneous fat, poor growth, and inadequate weight gain. While any child could suffer neglect, children are at greatest risk if born to mothers with a history of substance abuse or to those living in situations where parents or other caregivers are overwhelmed by chaotic lifestyles, intense emotional turmoil, and scarce resources. If the neglected child's plight is not discovered so that corrective action can be taken, delays in growth and development—physical, psychological, and spiritual—can have significant long-term repercussions.

Other forms of neglect are no less significant. A child who lives in an unsanitary environment, who is infrequently bathed, or who rarely receives medical care will be at risk for a variety of infections. Lack of adequate supervision, especially for toddlers, puts children in harm's way for injuries related to accidents, contact with hazardous materials, and even trauma inflicted by other children. Indifference to a child's education, while not immediately life-threatening, can seriously hinder his future quality of life.

Emotional Abuse and Neglect

Emotional abuse, which accompanies all other forms of abuse, can be difficult to define, since psychological coping mechanisms vary in children. Technically, emotional abuse is any parental behavior that is harmful to the emotional well-being of a child. Verbal attacks and emotional abandonment are perhaps the most common forms of this abuse, leaving a child starving for attention, love, and affirmation. In order to develop and thrive, infants and children need not only physical sustenance and safety but also ongoing emotional nurturing. Such nurturing is not optional but a basic ingredient of well-being. Parents must acknowledge and accept their God-given responsibility for meeting a child's emotional needs for love, security, and affirmation. Failing to satisfy the deep emotional needs of a child could result in psychological instability (manifested as severe anger outbursts and depression), developmental delays and retardation, and physical failure to thrive.

Emotional abuse of children takes various forms:

- **Harsh, degrading language:** "You are such an idiot," "I'm sick of you," "You little jerk," and other insults that can't be printed here burn into the memory and emotions of a child for years, if not for a lifetime. The effect is magnified when these insults are hurled in the presence of other family members. Verbal abuse scars the mind and heart.
- **Inconsistency:** The child never knows whether to expect hugs or harassment from one day (or hour) to the next.
- **Indifference:** One or both parents are too busy, overwhelmed, tired, or disinterested to pay attention to the child, show affection, or set consistent limits.
- **Authoritarianism:** Every detail of a child's behavior is sternly micromanaged, stressing pure obedience in the name of "discipline" or even "raising godly children." Little or no allowance is made for childish mistakes or exploration.
- **Nonstop criticism/unwillingness to give praise or approval:** This is the fraternal twin of authoritarianism, causing a child to believe that whatever he does is never good enough, no matter how hard he tries.

What Can Be Done?

The response to any situation in which children are abused or neglected must involve the following components:

The problem must be recognized and acknowledged.

A number of signs and symptoms that might be observed in a child or adolescent who has been abused have been listed earlier in this section. Many of these (such as depression) are not specific for abuse, although they could represent a general response to a traumatic event. A few, such as the presence of a sexually transmitted infection, provide airtight proof that abuse has taken place.

When worrisome findings or behaviors are observed in one's own child—or in certain instances, someone else's—a parent or other responsible adult may have to ask, at an appropriate time, some nonthreatening, open-ended questions: "You've looked kind of sad since the campout last weekend. Can we talk about it?" "That's an interesting mark on your tummy—can you tell me how you got it?" "Is there anything that bothers you about going over to Uncle John and Aunt Mary's?" The response most often will be reasonable, but if it sounds evasive or doesn't ring true, you may need to probe a little more specifically: "Did something happen last weekend that upset you?" "Has anyone touched you in a way that made you feel bad or uncomfortable?"

Attentive and compassionate listening, and not interrogation, is extremely important when such sensitive questions are being raised. Above all, make sure the child understands that you will not become angry with her over what she tells you. *Even more critical is the reassurance that any abuse that has taken place, especially sexual molestation, is not her fault.* Victims of abuse are often burdened with the idea that they were responsible for whatever happened to them, that they are "bad" or "dirty," and that their parents will reject or punish them if they tell what happened.

If in fact you hear some unpleasant or even horrifying details from a child, you will need to remain calm and focus on both comforting her and making her feel safe. Try to avoid venting any strong emotions of your own (especially anger over what has happened) in a way that might bring more discomfort to the child. However, you will want to talk in private with a mature, trustworthy individual in order to process what has happened, pray about it, and make appropriate decisions regarding the next steps to be taken. Even if you are not under legal obligation to report abuse, if you suspect that a child you know is being victimized or neglected, seek input from a trained counselor, your pastor, or the nearest child-protection service.

The child must be protected from further harm.

In some cases, this may require taking the child out of the home, at least temporarily, either because it is clear that he is in immediate danger there or because concerns have been raised that are so serious that his safety must be ensured while the situation is investigated. Such an action can be traumatic for all concerned, even for the child who has been abused at home, but in most cases the ultimate goal of those who must make this type of decision is to keep families together, not break them apart.

If the abusing individual does not live at home, usually it is less difficult—but no less important—to see that the child is protected from further risk. This usually will involve keeping him away from any situations in which abuse may have taken place. Your commitment to his security should be made abundantly clear, especially if any threat has been made by the abuser.

If a child's basic needs are not being met at home, decisions regarding his future must be tailored to the individual family. Obviously, if a neglected child has significant medical problems, dealing with those will be the first order of business. Ideally, multiple resources will be brought to bear on the situation. Perhaps members of the extended family can take care of the child while other individuals or organizations work with the parent(s) to stabilize the home. In many cases, families that are very distressed or barely getting by will derive great benefit from community volunteer groups, including local churches, which can provide more multifaceted support. In a best-case scenario, this includes not only help with material needs but also ongoing interactions with individuals who can teach basic parenting skills, encourage, troubleshoot, and if needed, exhort the parents toward more constructive and stable lifestyles.

The abuser's behavior must change, and he or she must be prevented from harming anyone else.

Dealing with the person(s) alleged or proven to be abusing a child is a difficult, emotional process, which to a large degree will (and should) be managed by child-protection and law-enforcement personnel. In many cases, physical abuse occurs when someone whose parenting skills are limited and whose personal problems are overwhelming lashes out at a child in the heat of the moment. Very often there was no premeditated intention to do harm, and the primary need is for assistance in resolving problems at home, learning different coping skills, or gaining a new and basic understanding of handling infants and children. Depression, anxiety, or substance-abuse problems might need to be addressed, and ongoing accountability will be critical.

In cases of sexual abuse, the action taken will depend greatly on the circumstances and the age of the perpetrator. A young adolescent who discovered some pornographic material and then acted out his fantasies with a child may be extremely remorseful and more in need of rehabilitation than imprisonment. A career pedophile, on the other hand, is someone from whom society and its children must be protected at all costs.

With rare exception, confronting a perpetrator is extraordinarily difficult, especially if the individual is a relative, family friend, or someone who has been in a position of responsibility and trust. On many occasions, raising the issue of abuse will be met with adamant denial on the part of both perpetrator and victim, especially if the child is fearful of repercussions. Parents who have been abusing their children virtually always know that their actions are wrong, but fear of losing their children and shame in facing their own behavior may prevent them from seeking help. Breaking through the denial is necessary for restoration of physical, emotional, and spiritual health. Loving friends or family members who recognize abuse may be able to convince and reassure the parent involved that restorative help is available and critically important.

If you yourself have abused your own or someone else's children or have had some close calls in which you felt an impulse to harm a child, it is urgently important that you deal with this problem. You will need to broach the subject with a responsible adult to whom you have ongoing accountability, such as your pastor, your physician, or a counselor. The process of acknowledging any wrongdoing to God and to those who have been harmed, owning up to its painful consequences, understanding its origins, and preventing recurrences will not happen overnight. Be prepared for a long and probably difficult process, but also be encouraged by the fact that no one is beyond hope. No matter what has happened, no matter how much pain must be processed, it is possible—one step at a time—to learn to function in a more healthy and loving way. But it is vitally important that you not attempt such a difficult journey alone. If you are confronting and dealing with your own abusive behavior, allow trustworthy people to come alongside you, both for support and accountability.

Sexual Identity in Childhood

During the first several months of life, a baby's gender is signaled to the outside world primarily by the way he or she is dressed, and possibly by the way the hair is fixed (assuming there is enough to fix). As the toddler becomes a preschooler and then enters the school-age years, indicators of maleness or femaleness begin to encompass more than clothing and hairstyles.

During these early years, nearly every parent sends a multitude of messages and cues that suggest, or even explicitly state, what it means to be a boy or a girl. At the same time, parents begin to look for behavior patterns that suggest their child has accepted his or her sexual identity. Considerable worry can develop if one or both parents start to wonder whether their child is getting the picture about what it means to be male or female. They may think, *My boy likes to play store and draw pictures all day, and he can't throw a ball three feet—what kind of sissy is he turning into? My girl plays football better than the boys next door and never wants to wear a dress—is she ever going to settle down and become more feminine?* Beneath such questions runs an anxious concern, especially regarding the older child: *Is this behavior an indication that my child is not going to have normal relationships with the opposite sex later in life?* What parents may or may not realize, however, is that what shapes healthy identification with one's sex as male or female is not merely the kind of toys children are given to play with or even specific efforts to direct them toward masculine or feminine pursuits. The process involves a number of factors as well as deeper currents in a child's life.

There is not absolute agreement among child-development experts regarding the factors that establish a child's gender identity and ultimate sexual orientation. This section does not set out to define the subject of homosexuality versus heterosexuality in any comprehensive fashion. But there are certain factors that are fairly easy to recognize and assess, and parents who want to bring up children who have a healthy acceptance of their sex can make some basic additions to their parenting awareness and skills in this area.

Every human is born with what might be called a "father vacuum" and a "mother vacuum"—an explicit need for attention and approval from a loving adult of each sex.

If children grow up with an abundance of love (expressed both verbally and physically), positive attention, and discipline from both a father and a mother, they will develop a basic sense of trust, self-worth, and a healthy comfort with their sex. Our sexual identity is established in early childhood, especially between the ages of two and six. Quality time spent with affirming adults of both sexes is particularly crucial for a child during those years.

What happens if one of those vacuums isn't filled? While we may think of a vacuum in terms of a parent's physical absence, many children who develop gender-identity problems have significant male and female adults in their lives, but one or both of those adults are absent emotionally, if not abusive emotionally or physically. Much damage to a child's identity can be inflicted by ongoing rejection and criticism from the parent of the same sex. This is particularly true if the negativity focuses harshly on the child's expression of sexual identity.

For example, suppose that Shawn is a physically slight and shy six-year-old in a family where manliness is embodied in contact sports and aggressiveness. He wants to look at books rather than wrestle, draw rather than throw a ball, and dress up his stuffed animals rather than bang his toy trucks into his blocks. His father, who lettered in varsity football and continues to enjoy an informal scrimmage in the vacant lot across the street, envisions throwing passes to a strapping son and daydreams about someday watching him score a key touchdown in the city play-offs. Shawn's younger brother, Bret, loves rough-and-tumble play and at the age of four already seems to have a head start on athletic skills.

As Dad sizes up his sons, he has a very important decision to make. He could apply a narrow grid of expectations to Shawn and drown him in negativity. He could constantly make fun of the "little girlie" things Shawn likes to do. He could repeatedly compare Shawn unfavorably to Bret: "Why can't you be like your brother?" Dad could withdraw and ignore his older son altogether. In this situation, Shawn's identity as a boy would be challenged and berated. Later in life, there may be an increased risk that he could have difficulty sorting out his sexual impulses, since these might become mixed with unfulfilled longings for a father he never really knew.

But there is a more positive way for Dad to respond to his son. While still enjoying Bret's budding physical prowess, Dad could also get involved in Shawn's world of books, drawings, and stuffed animals, making it clear to his son that these are also "cool things for guys to do." In this case, Shawn will become secure with the idea that he is definitely male and, at the same time, will not have to spend years of his life seeking masculine love and approval.

This example illustrates a very important principle: Children should be affirmed as male and female as they are, even if their form of expression doesn't fit whatever their parents might have envisioned as a truly masculine boy or feminine girl. Even if it requires considerable parental effort and self-control, the child must be protected from relentless criticism, especially about something so sensitive. This is a particularly important assignment for the parent who is the same sex as the child, because it is likely that persistent negative or even hostile input from that parent will create a craving for attention and affection from an adult of the same sex. If this intense need eventually finds fulfillment in a same-sex relationship that includes intimate physical contact, a long-term homosexual orientation may develop.

There are limits to unquestioning acceptance of a child's behavior, whether it relates to sexual identity or anything else, and appropriate course corrections may be necessary from time to time. If a boy has decided to see how he might look in a dress and makeup, for example, parents can and should calmly set house rules about attire, just as they do about other everyday activities. If a daughter's interests don't mesh with those of other girls in the neighborhood, she may need help finding some friends with whom she can share common pursuits. If a child's behavior or mannerisms are so eccentric that they alienate or draw fire from others, especially in areas involving sexual identity, it is definitely appropriate to initiate changes to prevent the child from developing an ongoing sense that he or she is different from, and perhaps not accepted by, others. (This painful sense of being marginalized during childhood can play a role in the development of a homosexual identity later in life.) Just as in every other area of shaping and molding a child's behavior, this should be done without browbeating or sarcasm.

Although sexual abuse certainly doesn't lead to a same-sex orientation all or even most of the time, it may contribute to the process. If, for example, a young boy has one or more sexual experiences with an older boy or man, he may derive some physical pleasure from these activities and thus decide early on that he is homosexual. He will probably not understand that sexual response can be automatic and that the presence of physical pleasure does not mean that a certain act establishes his sexual identity. In another scenario, a girl who is sexually abused by one or more men might avoid relationships with males later in life and then eventually turn to other women for emotional and physical intimacy. Sexual (or physical or emotional) abuse that breaks down any child's trust in people of the same or opposite sex can have a very damaging impact on that child's understanding of sexuality.

Single parents have reason to be concerned that their children interact during those early, critical years with responsible, loving adults of both sexes. What if a boy who is being reared by a single mother has very little interaction with adult males during the years from age two to six? If his craving for male attention remains unfilled, circumstances and interactions (including sexual molestation) at critical moments in his life could lead to a "sexualizing" of these needs, where their fulfillment becomes associated with intimate physical contact with another male. Or an insecure sense of masculinity might push him toward heterosexual promiscuity as a means of proving himself.

This does not mean that every boy raised by a single mother is destined for turbulence over his sexual expression. In most cases he will receive enough attention from one or more significant males that will help fill the vacuum and secure his identity as a boy during those early, formative years. Among boys raised by single mothers, positive male role models are also very important for their civilizing effects: keeping unruly behavior in check, instilling respect for Mom and others in the family and neighborhood, encouraging consistent efforts at school, and so forth. Developing a deep personal relationship both with God and with mature heterosexual males in the family, at his local church, or elsewhere can help a boy secure not only his identity (including its sexual component) but also his understanding of right and wrong. In minority communities where a significant percentage of children are raised by single mothers, extended families and church communities often play a prominent role in supplying positive male role models.

What about the more unusual situation of a two- to six-year-old girl who is raised by a single father and who spends very little quality time with a female authority figure? She may be at risk for sexual-identity issues similar to those of her male counterpart who is raised without a father figure. Her deep need for female attention might draw her toward a lesbian relationship later in life or result in multiple heterosexual encounters to overcome a need to prove her femininity to herself. Indeed, if her experiences with men are particularly unsatisfying or even hurtful—a likely possibility if they involved casual sex—this could increase the odds that she will seek a physically intimate and more fulfilling relationship with a woman.

A healthy relationship between a young child and the parent or a loving adult of the opposite sex is no less important, but in different ways. A two- to six-year-old female with an attentive mother but an absent or emotionally distant father will usually have a normal sexual identity, but she may crave male attention. If the vacuum left from the lack of a father's love (or adequate male substitutes) remains unfilled as she grows up, her desire for emotional intimacy may leave her vulnerable to sexual advances from males in high school. Similar dynamics with regard to sexual identity and relationships with the opposite sex may arise when a boy is raised by an attentive father but an absent or emotionally distant mother.

More extreme cases in which a child has a definite and persistent unwillingness, even intellectually, to accept his or her sexual identity ("I am not a boy; I don't want to be a boy") are uncommon and need formal evaluation by a professional who is qualified to deal with behavioral and identity issues in children. Some of these situations arise when one or both parents have strongly desired a baby of the opposite sex from the one who was born. There is a risk in such situations that the child will be given all sorts of input and cues, some more overt than others, that in essence push him or her toward fulfilling the role of the sex that the parents desired. In extreme situations, a parent may actually bring up and identify the child as a member of the opposite sex—for example, consistently dressing a boy in girl's clothing for at least the first few years of life. While few parents attempt to meet their own needs in such a drastic and inappropriate manner, it is important for parents to recognize and deal with any such longings so that mixed or negative messages about sexual identity are not broadcast to a child—especially during the critical years between ages two and six.

In summary, the development of sexual identity and its later expression is a complex process that can be directed and redirected in a variety of ways. Like so many other aspects of child rearing, there are no simple formulas that can guarantee a healthy outcome in this area. Nevertheless, three principles mentioned in this section bear repeating. In essence they are exhortations to cherish each child as a unique gift from God. Implementing these principles will contribute to a stable sexual identity for your child and greatly benefit his or her general well-being.

Whether brought up in a one- or two-parent home, a child needs loving and affirming attention from both male and female adults. This is particularly important in early childhood (especially between the ages of two and six), but it is never too late for a child, or even an adolescent, to begin fulfilling this need. If his own mother or father cannot carry out this assignment, relatives, friends, or fellow church members should reach out in love to help meet that need.

While allowing for appropriate course corrections, the worth of children should be affirmed based on who the children are, not on what others think they should be. Parents should be careful not to send messages of rejection if their children don't seem to fit certain expectations of masculinity and femininity.

A child must be fully accepted and cherished as a boy or a girl, as determined by his or her physical sex, even if one or both parents had hoped for a child of the opposite sex.

Two-Year-Olds: Movers and Shakers

"Give me an army of two-year-olds, and I can conquer the world."

—*Bill Cosby*

Although you have probably heard the phrase "terrible twos" more often than you care to remember, the birthday cake with two candles on it shouldn't create a feeling of impending doom. True, your two-year-old may be working through the negativism of his "first adolescence" in all its defiant glory. Yes, you will have days when he runs headlong away from you when you call him, then later clings to you like Velcro when you want to leave him with a trusted caregiver for an hour. And, yes, your two-year-old is bigger, stronger, and faster than he was six months ago, and he is probably turbo-charged with energy much of the day. And to be sure, if you have a new baby who is starting to be more mobile and is becoming a bigger blip on your two-year-old's radar screen, you can count on some fireworks erupting between them.

But while you have your work cut out for you in many respects, you will also have the privilege of watching some incredible developments in language, thinking, and creativity unfold during this twelve-month period. The transition from infant to child will be completed by the third birthday, and with this transition will come the joy of having more complex interactions and sustained companionship with him.

As has been stressed already (and will be repeated throughout this book), during the next twelve months it is extremely important that your child know how deeply committed you are to him, how much you truly love him, and how secure his home base really is. At the same time, he must also know that you are in charge and that the limits you set down will be enforced consistently. As the year progresses, you will be able to help him understand the reasoning behind a number of the rules you have made, especially those that have to do with his safety. Giving him some whys won't be a sign of weakness; what you say will still go, whether or not he buys your logic. Instead, these explanations will begin to build an internal moral foundation that should become a mighty fortress as the years pass. (This process is described in the Special Concerns section "Principles of Discipline and Training," page 259.)

Physical Developments

A weight gain of about four pounds (1.8 kg) and the addition of two-and-a-half to three-and-a-half inches (about 6½ to 9 cm) in height can be expected this year. A popular notion holds that your child will have reached half of his adult height by the age of two. While you may get a general idea of his ultimate altitude by doubling his height at twenty-four months, don't start buying his high school wardrobe quite yet. Differences in nutritional and hormonal patterns may hand you a surprise during the teen years, especially if the onset of puberty is either quite early or delayed.

The gradual change in the overall shape of your child's body that began last year will become more obvious. The size of his arms, legs, and upper body will increase much more than his head as he loses the top-heavy proportions of an infant. His posture will become more erect and stable, his abdomen less prominent, and his back straighter. Baby fat will continue to disappear, replaced by more grown-up contours.

His body movements, which are already perpetual, will also become much more sophisticated. By the third birthday he will be able to run, jump, climb up or down stairs while holding your hand or the rail, stand on one foot (if you demonstrate), and do any number of things with his hands while walking. During the course of this year he will discover the pleasure of maneuvering up and down a small slide, kicking a ball, and pedaling a small tricycle.

As his capacity for vigorous activity continues to increase, you will want to find a pleasant and safe outdoor environment where he can discharge some of his boundless energy every day. But whether in your own yard, a greenbelt, or a local park, you must continuously keep track of his activities and explorations and not merely turn him loose without supervision. Indeed, he will be delighted if you join him in whatever tumbling, chasing, or piggyback pursuits he enjoys.

As during his first months of crawling and toddling, his judgment at this age will be no match for his physical capabilities. This is especially true around bodies of water such as spas and swimming pools, which must be securely gated or otherwise inaccessible. *Never* underestimate the ability of your two-year-old to climb onto, into, or under whatever hazardous place he can find.

Along with his full-body activities, his coordination of hand, wrist, and finger movements will also improve. Given a pencil or crayon, he will be happy to scribble at age two and will add circular motions to his artistic repertoire by age three, even attempting to represent some object on the page. Be sure to ask him what it is and be prepared for some wonderful and unique explanations. Write down what he says on the back of his masterpiece, along with the date. After a decade or so passes, these small treasures will spark sweet memories.

Your child will learn to turn the pages of a book one at a time, a skill he will enjoy demonstrating (along with more focused attention) during story time. New abilities with grip and wrist motion will allow him to turn doorknobs and handles, as well as to unscrew lids—and the tops of medicine bottles—by the end of this year. He will also begin to enjoy stacking blocks or even use them to build little structures such as towers or corrals. He will probably derive equal if not greater pleasure out of knocking these creations over, sometimes with wild abandon. Some guidance and ground rules about the proper handling of building blocks and similar toys, including respect for what playmates or siblings may be creating with them, will not only prevent damage from flying objects but also preserve peace in the playroom.

Language: A Blossoming of Words

During the next twelve months, you can expect an enormous increase in the number of words your child can speak and understand. You should be aware, however, that normal children will vary significantly in the use of language at this age. Some will seem to pick up new vocabulary day by day, while others may say little for weeks, then surprise you with a complete and quite expressive sentence. As a general estimate, your child will arrive at her second birthday with the ability to use about fifty words, some of which will be connected in two-word sentences ("Doggy jump!"). She will, however, *understand* about three hundred words. By the third birthday, roughly one thousand words will be in her memory bank, and sentences of four to six words (including pronouns such as *I* or *you*) will be forthcoming.

Many parents become unnecessarily concerned about their child's progress in language skills when they compare notes with other parents. Remember that the child who seems to be a walking dictionary is not necessarily more intelligent or gifted than the one who speaks less frequently. Check with your child's health-care provider, however, if her speech seems garbled or unintelligible by two and a half years of age or if she persists in using grunts and gestures rather than words to express her desires. Potential problems such as hearing loss will need to be ruled out, and an assessment by a speech therapist can help clarify whether there is a problem with comprehension, expression, or both.

In addition to learning the meanings of hundreds of new words, your child will also begin to pick up other important information about how words are assembled and in what tone of voice they are used. Are your family's conversations calm and laced with respectful and soothing phrases, or do they sound like a cross between a barracks and a back alley? If you don't believe your child is tuned in to your language, wait until she repeats some choice comment she overheard last week—just when the pastor stops by for a visit.

Is your family's vocal volume roughly equal to that of a jet engine? If so, is it because everyone must sound off in order to be heard over the noise of the TV, radio, or CDs blaring in the background? Young children naturally tend to use "outdoor voices" whether they are playing in the backyard or sitting at the dinner table, and most will need to be reminded on more than one occasion to turn down the volume. But such training can be seriously undermined if the opposite is demonstrated every day by everyone else at home.

A more subtle but important aspect of communication with your two-year-old—and with older children as well—may be lost in the day-to-day business of living. Much of your day will be spent taking care of her basic needs, keeping her out of harm's way, and picking up whatever is strewn in her wake. In the process, most of your conversations with her will gravitate toward imperatives: "Don't touch the . . . ," "Watch out for the . . . ," "Get down from the . . . ," "Eat your . . . ," or even "Good girl!"

As necessary as these communications are (especially the positive statements), your child will blossom when you show interest in what she is doing or thinking. "Tell me about your cars" or "What do you think that bird is trying to do?" or "Look at all these ants on the sidewalk—I wonder where they're going" are the kinds of comments that tell your two-year-old she is interesting and important. As her ability to express herself becomes more sophisticated, her responses to these overtures from you will become some of your most cherished memories. Her mind is a fascinating place, and your genuine interest in what is going on inside of it should be cultivated and exercised from now on.

Sleeping

Two-year-olds generally need nine to thirteen hours of sleep, most of which (eleven hours or thereabouts) occur during the night, with about a two-hour nap at midday. Some will still do best with two shorter naps, while others will regularly fight nap time with a vengeance. How long you continue a daytime sleep routine will depend upon its impact on your child. If he resists but eventually falls asleep for an hour or two, most likely a nap is worth maintaining. Similarly, if he turns into a three-foot-tall tyrant by the end of the day whenever he skips his nap, you should overrule his objections to a siesta. The time to phase out naps—whether this year or later—will arrive when he can regularly make it through the entire day without having a prolonged attitude meltdown.

Your more important assignment will be to maintain a bedtime routine in the face of increasing resistance, which in some children can become impressive. Some of the turbulence you may encounter at bedtime or during the night can arise from the following issues:

It's not his idea. The recurring cry for many two-year-olds will continue to be a heartfelt rendition of Frank Sinatra's theme song "My Way." If the all-important question "Who's in charge here?" has yet to be settled, bedtime can be one of the great battlegrounds in a contest of wills between you and your child. You will certainly want to make sure that bedtime is a calm, relaxing, reassuring time of day and that other concerns are dealt with. But ultimately someone will have to decide when it's bedtime, and it shouldn't be your two-year-old.

Separation anxiety. As independent as he may want to be, he may not feel that he's gotten quite enough time and attention by the end of the day. Or he may be unsettled about being away from you, even in the familiar surroundings of your home. Often this can be resolved by making sure that the bedtime routine isn't rushed; by providing security/comfort objects (a favorite toy or blanket); by playing quiet, soothing music in his room; or by leaving the door to his room open—provided that other sounds in the home won't keep him awake. If he hears the family having noisy fun without him, he will have little interest in lying down and closing his eyes.

Other fears. Your child is reaching an age at which he may become worried about scary sounds he hears, funny shapes in the closet, or darkness itself. A night-light in his room or light from the next room coming through an open doorway is likely to be a necessary

BEDTIME CASSETTES

An alternative to quiet music at bedtime is a cassette tape of a parent or grandparent singing or reading favorite stories. You can create a "library" of these by turning on a portable recorder while you sing or read to your child. If you capture some of his cooing and comments, these tapes will become precious keepsakes after he is grown. One drawback: If the cassette player won't reverse itself, your child may become unhappy if he isn't asleep by the end of the tape. Like any routine, if he becomes used to the tapes he may eventually have a difficult time falling asleep without them. ■

fixture at this age and for a number of years to come. Unexpected loud noises, such as a catfight outside his window, a siren passing nearby, or a booming thunderstorm, may frighten a small child and require some hands-on comforting.

Your two-year-old may also be unsettled about what went on during the day. Noisy arguments between parents are alarming, even when he can't understand their content. A move to new living quarters, a new baby in the house, the first trip to a preschool or day-care facility, or changes in family routines related to one or both parents' job schedules may also rock his sense of security. Ongoing overtures for attention at bedtime may signal a need for more (or more reassuring) attention during the daylight hours.

Night terrors. These unpleasant events, which affect up to 2 to 4 percent of children (more commonly boys), scare the daylights out of everyone who sees them. During the middle of the night a confused, wild-eyed child will suddenly begin screaming, kicking, thrashing, sweating, moaning, and jabbering incoherently. His heart will be pounding and his breathing rapid—and so will yours. He may climb out of bed, stumble around and injure himself, and if he is older, try to run out of the house. What is especially unsettling during a night terror is that your child won't respond to you or even seem to know you. When you attempt to calm him, he may thrash more violently and try to push you away.

Despite all of the wild activity, children do not actually awaken during a night terror. They are instead having a disordered arousal from deep (non-REM) sleep. (See chapter 5, page 151, for a brief review of REM and non-REM sleep.) The first episode occurs between the ages of two and four years, and other family members may have done the same thing during their toddler years.

Your job during a night terror is to sit tight through the interminable ten to thirty minutes, provide soothing reassurance that you're there and that he's okay, hold him if he'll let you, and most of all prevent him from hurting himself. You may also need to calm down any older children who have been awakened by the commotion and are witnessing this wild event. *Don't leave him alone* because there is a very real risk of injury, and *don't try to wake him up*. He is actually in a state of sleep that does not readily progress to wakefulness, and shaking or speaking forcefully to him ("Wake up! Wake up!") will only compound his (and your) agitation. Furthermore, if you succeed in bringing him to full consciousness, he will be unhappy and irritable and may have difficulty going back to sleep. Instead, if you sit tight and stay cool, you will be surprised at how quickly the night terror ends once it has run its course. Your child will suddenly fall back to sleep, and in the morning he will have no memory of the previous night's uproar. You, on the other hand, may stare at the ceiling for a while as your adrenaline surge calms down.

Your child may have only one night terror, or you may have to endure many episodes before he outgrows them. Identifying a cause may be difficult, although it is possible that a sudden pain, such as a cramp in the abdomen, during the wrong phase of sleep may set off a night terror. In rare cases, night terrors may be frequent enough to require preventive medication prescribed by a physician.

Nightmares. These are different from night terrors in all respects. They are scary dreams, occurring during active (REM) sleep late in the night or very early in the morning. In contrast to the bug-eyed thrashing of the night terror, a child who cries out after a nightmare will be wide-awake, aware, and responsive to your presence and comfort. Instead of the sudden return to sleep that follows a night terror, a nightmare may leave a child unwilling or unable to fall back to sleep.

Whether or not he can tell you about the dream will depend upon his age and vocabulary. Even if he can't fill you in on the details, it's safe to assume that whatever he experienced was frightening and that his need for comfort is genuine. In particular he will need your reassurance that the dream was not real, a difficult concept to grasp at this age. A few moments of prayer can also help impart the idea that Jesus is truly in charge and looking after your child whether he's asleep or awake. Be sure, however, that you are not contributing to the problem by reciting "Now I Lay Me Down to Sleep." This poem's infamous lines "If I should die before I wake, I pray the Lord my soul to take" are not only alarming and inappropriate for children (and adults) but have no basis in Scripture or anywhere else.

How you deal with nightmares will depend on your perception of what is going on. A child who suddenly awakens at 4 a.m. crying and frightened will need conversation and cuddling. When he was younger, you may have worked diligently to end routine nighttime awakenings by holding back on "room service" during the wee hours (see chapter 7, page 213). But after a real nightmare, this approach should be set aside.

Rarely you may find it expedient to let him fall asleep in your bed if he won't calm down any other way. However, if he repeatedly wanders into the family room a half hour after bedtime and calmly announces that he "had a bad dream" or crawls into your bed night after night using "nightmare" as the password, he may be trying to change the bedtime ground rules, and a more businesslike approach will be needed.

Unlike night terrors, nightmares are influenced far more by daytime input. The old adage about turning off the scary movie because "it might give you nightmares" is certainly appropriate for small children, who cannot readily distinguish reality from fantasy. Because television, videos, DVDs, and video games can bring hair-raising images before your toddler's undiscerning eyes, you will need to exercise nonstop vigilance in this area. Even films such as *Pinocchio* or *Snow White*, widely considered to be childhood classics, contain sequences that could definitely scare a toddler.

New sleeping quarters. One of the important transitions most two-year-olds must navigate is the move from crib to "real bed." This will become necessary when the side rail of his crib reaches to less than three-quarters of his standing height (usually at about thirty-six inches), since the risk of scaling the rail and falling out increases after this point. The arrival of a younger sibling may also prompt the move.

The move to a bed can be a happy occasion, an indication that he is a "big boy" and no longer a baby. If he is unhappy about leaving the crib, affirming how grown-up he is may help change his opinion. You may help him gain more enthusiasm for moving to a bed if you let him help pick it out (assuming you are shopping for one) or at least choose a set of fun sheets and pillowcases to adorn his new sleeping quarters.

One potential drawback of a bed is that it allows your toddler to get up and come calling if he doesn't want to stay put. A more unsettling possibility is that your toddler may decide to wander around the house—or even go outside—when everyone is asleep. You may be able to limit these nighttime explorations (and certainly prevent accidental falls from bed) by installing a simple safety rail. However, a determined toddler can easily climb around the rail and get out of bed. For this reason, if size and circumstances permit, it may be wise to maintain the crib until he is closer to three years of age and possesses a little more wisdom and training. If you aren't already doing so, keep all doors and windows locked.

Bedtime confrontations

All the factors just described can add up to bedtime confrontations. If your toddler is no longer in a crib, not feeling the least bit sleepy, unhappy about missing out on grown-up company, worried about bad dreams, or in a challenging mood, he may try to get up several times after he's been tucked in. Another drink of water, another trip to the potty if he's toilet trained, curiosity, boredom, interesting aromas from someone's late snack, a "tummy ache," a claim of a "bad dream" (probably bogus if he just went to bed), or anything else he might think of may all be reasons he feels compelled to exit his bed and his room.

As in every other area in which you are shaping your child's behavior, a consistent response—loving but firm—will be necessary. Once he has been through the bedtime routine, any further interactions should be calm, brief, and businesslike. "It's time for bed" should be your monotonous response, and his return to bed should be enforced without any further fun, games, food, or ceremony. The problems come when there's a lot of variation at bedtime, or if one or both parents feel guilty about the kind of interactions they've had with him during the day. But the time to remedy the need for more quality time with your two-year-old shouldn't be at 11 p.m. If you give in and let him fall asleep on the couch or agree to a snack or another story, be prepared for more of the same tomorrow night.

If your two-year-old is a late-night or early-morning explorer, you may need to install a barricade (the same type of folding gate used to keep toddlers off the stairs) across his exit route. Otherwise, you may awaken to find him finger painting on the walls, dumping flour on the floor, or worse—turning on appliances, leaning precariously over the toilet bowl, or perhaps checking out the garage.

Finally, if you have been co-sleeping with your child, now is a good time to end this practice. When you decide that moving day has arrived, carry out the transition with some advance notice. Talk about how great it is to have "your own bed" or "your own room." If possible, let him help you prepare the new sleeping place. At this age, he most likely would like to have a say in the choice of his bed, if you're buying one, or at least in the decor of the new surroundings—sheets, pillowcases, night-light, or even wallpaper if you feel ambitious. Some parents graduate their toddler to a futon or sleeping bag near their bed and then gradually move it closer to the ultimate destination. And most of all, reassure him that snuggle times aren't over.

You will also need to decide what to do if your toddler occasionally slips into your bed in the middle of the night. If you feel too weary to escort him back to his room or you don't mind the extra sleeper when you're already conked out, you may choose not to make this an issue. But if you decide that your bed is off-limits except by special invitation, enforce your policy consistently, no matter how tired you might feel. One exception to consider is that of designating some special snuggle times—for example, on weekend mornings.

Feeding: Foods and Snacks

Many of the recommendations about foods and snacks presented in chapter 7 (page 204) apply to your two-year-old as well, and reviewing them now would be a good idea. The variations on the basic themes are as follows:

Offer a few more calories. As was the case a year ago, your two-year-old does not need a huge number of calories to grow and fuel her full-throttle engine. Roughly 1,200 to

1,400 calories per day—which won't seem like much—will do, spread out over three meals and one or two snacks. Don't bother trying to count or regulate these calories, by the way, unless your child has an unusual medical problem that requires nutritional oversight by a registered dietitian. You may hear conflicting advice about the percentage of fat calories that your two-year-old should consume every day (advisories range from 25 to 40 percent), and as with calories, trying to regulate that percentage every day will probably drive both you and your child crazy. Unless a risky metabolic problem (such as an inherited tendency to develop very high cholesterol levels and heart disease at an early age) has been diagnosed, a restricted-fat diet is neither necessary nor appropriate in this age-group because of the importance of dietary fat for the developing brain.

What matters now (and for years to come) is that you provide a variety of high-quality foods for everyone in your family, including your two-year-old. Your job is to prepare and make them available at appropriate times of the day, and her job is to decide how much of them she wants to eat. (For more information about what is considered "high quality" and what isn't, see "Some ABCs of Good Nutrition" on page 771.)

One quantity you will want to track is milk intake, which at this age should be at least sixteen ounces and not more than thirty-two ounces per day, in order to supply enough calcium for growing bones without interfering with her appetite for other types of food. Between one and three years of age, your toddler needs about 500 mg of calcium per day; eight ounces (one cup) of milk supplies about 300 mg. (If your child won't drink or doesn't tolerate milk, you will need to offer and encourage other high-calcium foods such as cheese, yogurt, leafy green vegetables, and perhaps calcium-containing orange juice.) At this age, you can offer any form of milk from whole to skim, and your best bet is to pick one concentration for the entire family to use. (Usually one or 2 percent offers the most agreeable compromise between calories and taste.) Remember that fat content doesn't affect the amount of calcium in milk.

Avoid bringing up a junkaholic or a food hermit. Over the next year and thereafter, your child will be exposed to a whole new world of commercial food products with more sugar, salt, and fat than she should eat on a regular basis. She will probably like at least some of these concoctions, and her inclinations will be supported by clever ads on TV (if you let her watch the tube) and colorful packages at the store. In light of this reality, you will need to avoid two extremes.

First, don't let her sway your food-preparation choices by persistent requests or demands for Chocolate Frosted Gonzo Flakes, Cheddar-Ecstasy Dip Chips, or Super-Zapper Sodas. Stick with the basics when you buy and serve foods, and then stand your ground. On the other hand, don't become a dietary diehard, a purist who won't allow your child to go anywhere that doesn't serve food that is hand-grown, organically fertilized, homemade, unrefined, and 100 percent free of sugar. Your child can't live in a nutritional glass bubble, and it won't kill her if she has a couple of french fries or some birthday cake at a friend's party.

Utensils will be under better control, but not all foods are safe. During this year your child will master the use of both spoon and fork, relieving you completely of the duty of transferring food from her plate to her mouth; she will become adept at using a cup with one hand. However, she still isn't free from the risk of choking on the same foods that were hazardous last year: seeds, nuts, grapes, popcorn, celery, and little hard candies. Hot dogs and carrots should also be off-limits unless cut into bite-size pieces.

Avoid mealtime power struggles. If there is one arena in which a two-year-old has nearly as much autonomy as she would like, it is in eating. If she won't swallow it, you can't make her, and you shouldn't try. There are more important battles to win.

For the next several months, you may wonder if your child is getting enough to eat, because often she may refuse to consume foods you place in front of her. But a child at this age may be an eager eater at only one meal a day. If she doesn't take much at lunch, she'll probably make up for it at dinner or the following day. Don't ruin a meal by nagging, bribing, or punishing a toddler who isn't interested in food.

Don't be extorted into preparing a separate toddler meal containing food that is different from everyone else's. Your job is to serve your two-year-old modest servings of wholesome foods that cover the gamut of the major food groups. Your child's job is to decide how much she'll actually eat. If she begins to push you for something else, hold the line. She won't starve.

If you are truly worried about your child's nutritional well-being, write down what she eats for a few days and then take this list to her physician. A check of height and weight and a brief exam will usually clear the air. A child who is in trouble medically usually shows other signs of illness: fever, diarrhea, lethargy, or poor weight gain, for example. A child who doesn't eat much but is otherwise very active is most likely getting enough food.

Toilet Skills and Phasing Out Diapers

For many families, seeing a child graduate to a diaper-free lifestyle is as important a milestone as his unassisted first steps across the room. Like walking, toilet skills can't and won't happen until your child is good and ready. But unlike standing up and stepping out, the sequence of steps needed to send urine and stool from child to toilet isn't programmed into a toddler's brain. It needs to be taught by someone—usually one or both parents, although in large families older children sometimes teach the younger quite effectively.

When is it time to start this process? Some kids begin to master toilet skills between eighteen and twenty-four months of age, but it is uncommon for children to be diaper free during the day by age two. The majority can be trained by thirty-six months, but for some children, daytime control may not be accomplished until the fourth birthday. Staying dry through the night may occur at the same time, but more often (for physiological reasons) dry mornings may not arrive until several months or even years later. Most children will learn to control bladder and bowel at the same time. However, for some, bowel control is easier to achieve, while for others, bowel control may lag several months behind.

Aside from his age, you should be on the lookout for indications that your child is ready to learn bladder and bowel control:

- He demonstrates some awareness that elimination (especially of stool) is going on. When a bowel movement is on its way, he may squat, grunt, grimace, or try to manipulate his diaper. Afterward he may be more insistent about getting cleaned up.
- The time between wet diapers is increasing. This indicates that a specific spinal-cord reflex, which automatically empties an infant's bladder whenever a certain amount of urine accumulates, is now being inhibited by signals from the brain. *No amount of training can speed up this neurological development.*

- He is able to understand and carry out two or three simple commands in sequence.
- He tries to imitate some of the things you do every day. You will want to take advantage of this normal behavior of two-year-olds during the toilet-training process.
- He is not embroiled in negativism. If his favorite word is still *no* and you're still neck deep in a daily struggle with him over who's in charge, this is not the best time to start a venture that requires as much cooperation as using the toilet.

In addition to your two-year-old being ready to learn, you must be ready to teach. While you undoubtedly would have been thrilled to see the last diaper disappear yesterday, be prepared to offer some patient, persistent, but relaxed attention to this project for as long as three to six months. This means that you should not be working under time pressure. All too often potty training turns into a do-or-die crash course because one or both parents want their toddler in a preschool or day-care setting where diapers are off-limits. If you feel that somehow time is of the essence and find yourself impatient over your toddler's bathroom progress and exasperated when he has an accident, you may need to take a deep breath and reconsider your priorities.

If patience is not your virtue, you may want to start training later rather than sooner, when your child will have better comprehension, be more cooperative, and have fewer accidents. If you tend to be more laid-back, you may be able to try your luck with a younger trainee. You may find it easier to begin when the weather is warmer and there are fewer layers of clothing to worry about.

Once you feel that everyone is ready for the first day of potty school, you can begin a series of steps that will work most of the time. These may be stretched out over a period of several weeks or, for adventurous families with an agreeable toddler, compressed into a few days. Be prepared to adapt, revise, and adjust as you see fit. Above all, make sure you praise every step he takes in the right direction and don't show disappointment, dismay, or anger if he doesn't quite get what you're driving at. Punishment or harsh reprimands are counterproductive in teaching a child to use the toilet and should not be used.

Start talking about the process in an upbeat way. You will need to choose your vocabulary for these conversations with a little caution, since any particularly colorful words you use may be broadcast by your child in public, usually when least expected. Most families manage quite well with terms such as "pee," "peepee," or "tinkle" for urine and "poop" or "poopoo" for stool, with "going potty" designating the process of eliminating either. In most settings these terms won't raise any eyebrows but will communicate a child's needs with reasonable precision.

While you're changing a diaper, mention that soon he won't need diapers anymore and that he'll be using a potty just like Mom and Dad and his older siblings. You may want to read a children's book about becoming potty trained (there are a number on the market) if you find it appropriate.

Let him become familiar with the sight of his own potty seat. If you buy one, let him help you pick it out. At the outset, a toddler-size seat that allows him to push against the floor while having a bowel movement is preferable to one that attaches to the big toilet but requires him to dangle his feet. You can make this item a familiar sight in the bathroom, although for safety reasons, your toddler should not be spending time there by himself if he has just turned two. As an alternative, it can be part of the furniture in his room for a while before he begins to use it.

Invite him to sit on the potty-chair. If he's willing, let him take this "test drive" without his pants and diaper on. If he's wary and reluctant, let him sit on it while still dressed. If you don't mind the temporary intrusion on your own bathroom time, you might have him sit on his throne while you sit on yours. For the sake of orienting him to some ground rules for modesty in the family, this part of the process would best be done with the parent of the same gender. Sharing potty time should be skipped if either parent (or the toddler) is uncomfortable with the idea.

A quick story might make the process more interesting to him. After he has done this several times and appears comfortable with it, have him sit on the toilet *without* his pants or diaper on. You don't need to prolong this exercise, but make it pleasant.

Let him see you empty stool from a soiled diaper into the receptacle of his potty-chair, while you explain that soon he will let his own "poop" drop in without the diaper. You may want to demonstrate how you flush his product down the toilet—but then again you may not, because your progress may become sidetracked by riddles of the universe ("Where does it go?"), deep concerns, or utter fascination with the loud noise and rushing rapids. Or (believe it or not) toddlers have been known to resist the idea that "part of them" suddenly just disappeared before their wondering eyes.

When you're ready to go for it, put him in loose pants that are easy to remove (or if you're feeling adventurous and can confine him to floors that are easy to wash, let him go bare). Watch for his telltale signs that a stool is coming 'round the bend, being especially vigilant thirty to sixty minutes after his biggest meal of the day. This takes advantage of the **gastrocolic reflex**, through which the stomach notifies the colon to get things moving because more digested food is on the way.

If you're not getting any obvious signals, place him on his potty every hour or two and encourage him to do his business. Take your time, look relaxed, chitchat, or even read part of a story if you'd like. If he succeeds, give him lots of praise. If he doesn't, don't worry about it—and don't become aggravated if he goes right after you get him off his potty. If he seems completely clueless about the whole project or you find yourself getting increasingly frustrated, go back to diapers for a while and try again later. Usually urine will be released at the same time as stool, so both boys and girls typically learn to pass urine while sitting down. Sometime later, after control is well established, a boy can be shown (usually by Dad or an older brother) how to void while standing up.

Even though he has succeeded several times, you can continue to give him potty prompts during the day: when he gets up, after meals, before naps, on your way out the door, before bedtime—basically every couple of hours throughout the day. As he becomes more adept at this process and you are changing fewer moist or dirty diapers, you can graduate to training pants during the day and eventually during naps as well. If you so desire and both of you are ready, he can move to a kid-size training seat on the big toilet. When using this equipment, it will be easier for him to push during a bowel movement if you place a small stool under his feet.

Remember to instill some hygienic routines as part of your training program. Little girls should be taught to wipe from front to back for both urine and stool, in order to reduce the risk of bladder infections. Washing hands with soap after using the potty should become a habit. When your son uses public facilities, show him what he can and can't touch, and how to use the faucet/soap/paper towels/hand dryers after he has done his business.

Eventually he will use the potty at bedtime and wake up dry the next day, then triumphantly empty his bladder into the potty or big toilet. Give him lots of praise when this happens, but don't be discouraged if history doesn't repeat itself with total consistency.

The time it will take before you can count on dry diapers and then dry sheets every morning will vary enormously among children. For some, a combination of very deep sleep, weak inhibition of the bladder reflex, and other physiological factors will delay nighttime bladder control for years. Getting him up at night to stagger into the bathroom and use the potty in a dead sleep will not hasten the process. *Do not reprimand, humiliate, or punish a child who has trouble in this area because it is completely out of his control.* Not only will such measures fail to bring about the desired results, but they burden a child with needless shame, frustration, and ultimately resentment. Indeed, punishing him for wetting the bed is about as fair as punishing him when it rains outside during the night (see "bed-wetting" in Reference Section, page 629).

Toilet troubleshooting

Despite everyone's best intentions, your student in Toilet Training 101 may not follow the curriculum you've set forth. Some possible glitches include the following:

"He just doesn't get it" or "He just isn't interested." He probably isn't ready. Take a deep breath, back off, and don't appear disappointed or angry with him. "That's okay, we'll try the potty again later on" is a lot better than "Aren't you ever going to get rid of those diapers?" This is a developmental and physiological issue, not one involving laziness, lack of intelligence, disobedience, or contest of wills. It's important that your child—and you—not feel like a failure over toilet training.

Make sure the problem isn't your own time pressure, perhaps manifested by non-stop nudging about "getting rid of those diapers." You need not worry that he's going to enter first grade in diapers, no matter what the in-laws or neighbors say. However, if you have been working with your child for a few months and you're not getting anywhere or he's reached his third birthday with no control in sight, talk this over with his physician.

"He was doing well for quite a while, but now he's back to wetting or soiling his pants." There are a number of possible causes for bathroom backsliding. Has there been a significant change in his life? A move to a new house or even a new room can rock his boat enough to disrupt the plumbing control. Even more challenging is the arrival of a new baby, who may suddenly become the center of attention. He may have come to the conclusion that doing what the baby does is a good way to recapture adult interest. Take some time with him—perhaps at bedtime or during an outing to get a special treat—to sound him out. Is he worried about something or someone? You may be surprised by his answer, and the time you spend with him might solve the problem.

Another possibility is that he is becoming so engrossed in play (especially with new toys or neighborhood cohorts) that he ignores nature's call until the last second—and then it's too late to get to the toilet. You may need to reinstitute some reminders about using the bathroom throughout the course of the day.

A possibility that is less likely but should not be overlooked is a bladder infection. Because their urine travels a shorter distance from the bladder to the outside world, this type of infection is more common in little girls. Clues that might suggest this problem include vague complaints of discomfort in the lower abdomen, an unusual and unpleasant odor arising from the urine, unexplained fever, or the appearance of urine in the underwear. The classic adult symptoms such as burning, stinging, and the need to void frequently are not commonly expressed by children. If you can't figure out why your toilet-trained child suddenly isn't making the grade, consider having her urine checked at the doctor's office.

Sometimes soiling his pants is a sign that he is constipated, with liquid stool leaking around a solid plug that is stuck in his rectum. Read on.

"He complained that his bowel movements were hurting, and now he won't go at all." Take some irritation of the anal area, combine with stool that's a little firm, add a touch of apprehension about all of this toilet business, and you have a recipe for full-blown toddler constipation. If that last bowel movement was painful, you can guarantee that he won't be interested in trying again. What may turn this common scenario into an ordeal is mounting pressure from all directions. He is getting more uncomfortable, especially after he eats, because the colon is squeezing down on increasingly hard and bulky stool. He is hearing from you that he needs to sit on the potty and let the "poopoo" out so he'll feel better. He wants to, but he doesn't, and to top things off, he needs for it to be his idea.

To break the mounting tension, you will want to help the next few stools exit as painlessly as possible. A little lubricating jelly gently applied to his anal area two or three times during the day and perhaps some anti-inflammatory ointment prescribed by his doctor (if there is local irritation that needs to be calmed down) will make the passage of stool less risky for him. You will have to sell him on the idea, however, before he tries again.

In order to "prime the pump" and start the bowels moving, you might consider letting him use diapers again for a few days, especially if he's a new convert to using the potty. The diaper may seem a safer place to let the poop come out, but let him know that he'll be able to use the potty again soon (see "constipation" in Reference Section, page 648).

"We know he's ready to use the toilet—in fact, he's done it a few times—but he refuses to cooperate, and we know he's not constipated." Make sure there aren't any unexpected reasons for his resistance. You might take him step-by-step through the motions by playacting with a stuffed animal who "needs to learn to go potty" and see if he'll talk to you about what the animal is thinking. Perhaps he is worried about falling into the big toilet and being flushed away. Or maybe he saw a commercial or cartoon in which some creature came out of the toilet. Whatever it is, don't laugh at him, but calmly separate worry from reality.

If there are indications that "all systems are go" but he won't—and the problem appears to be flat-out balking—you may want to give him a friendly nudge in the right direction. When he comes to you wanting to have his diaper changed, for example, take your sweet time before you attend to this chore, and when you do, make it cool and businesslike. On the other hand, if his diaper has been dry after a few hours, make a pleasant fuss about it and exclaim how grown-up it would be to use the potty and not need diapers anymore. It may help to offer a pleasant incentive (some stickers, new underwear, or an outing he would enjoy, for example) in exchange for a designated period of daytime potty cooperation.

Care of the Teeth

Between eighteen and thirty months of age, all twenty of the **primary ("baby") teeth** (see illustration on page A5) will have arrived. Although they will all be replaced, **secondary (permanent) teeth** (see illustration on page A5) won't appear for a few more years, so primary teeth deserve attention and care. (If a tooth becomes injured, see a dentist immediately. Sometimes it is possible to save damaged teeth.) Their biggest enemy will be decay, or **caries**, which affects many children by the age of three. If damage from caries is severe enough to cause the loss of any primary teeth, proper alignment of the permanent teeth may be affected later on.

There are four ways to reduce the likelihood of decay.

Check with your child's health-care provider about the use of fluoride. This decay-retarding substance may already be present in your local water supply, or it may be given in the form of an oral supplement, with or without vitamins. It is important that your child not receive too much fluoride, however, because it can cause discoloration of teeth.

Have your child checked regularly by a dentist who sees children (pedodontist). Ideally he will have had his first visit by the age of twelve months. If he hasn't yet seen a dentist by his second birthday, it's definitely time to make an appointment. Special preventive measures such as topical fluoride treatment or sealants may be recommended, and you can also check about the use of supplemental fluoride.

Your toddler won't be adept at handling a toothbrush, so you will need to do the honors with a soft brush at least once a day, usually at bedtime. To remove any plaque, which can start the process of decay, take enough time to brush both front and back of all the teeth. This process may go more smoothly if the child's head is leaning against you or resting on your lap. If she doesn't like toothpaste, just use water. If you use fluoride-containing toothpaste, do so sparingly, because it is likely that some will be swallowed, and a surprising amount of fluoride can be absorbed this way. A pea-sized amount of toothpaste is all that should be used. There is enough fluoride in a strip of toothpaste covering the length of the bristles to cause eventual discoloration of a child's teeth if a substantial amount is swallowed regularly. An alternative is to use a fluoride-free toothpaste until your child is old enough to rinse and spit after brushing.

Finally, don't let your toddler become hooked on foods that will provide a playground for destructive bacteria. Gummy candy, dried fruit, toffee, or caramel, which leave residue stuck on teeth for hours, are not only bad for teeth but also present a risk of choking incidents at this age. Keep these items away from your two-year-old.

Safety Concerns: Special Cautions for Your Two-Year-Old

Your two-year-old is as intensely curious about the world around her as she was last year, but her methods of gathering and processing information are now more sophisticated. At this point she should be moving well beyond random touching, grabbing, banging, and gumming everything in sight. Instead, her efforts will become more focused and purposeful as she spends more time manipulating objects with her mind as well as her hands.

As this year progresses, she will be able to switch toys on and off; put together simple puzzles; and match objects by size, shape, and color. Her expanding memory will allow her to understand both time sequences ("This happens before that") and cause-and-effect relationships ("If I push this, it falls over") and to apply them to new situations. This does not, unfortunately, give you much breathing room for safety concerns, especially at the beginning of this year. While she can understand more sophisticated prohibitions ("Don't chase your ball into the street"), her impulse control and judgment have a long way to grow. She also is unlikely to comprehend the ultimate risks of violating your warnings. To make matters worse, if she's in a limit-challenging mood, she may decide to create a contest over one of your safety rules. Therefore, constant vigilance must be maintained throughout the next several months and years, with particular attention to the following areas:

Traffic hazards. Because she can run more swiftly and dart into the nearest street, she must be monitored at all times when she is in an area where there are no barriers separating her from traffic. Also, be watchful of your child in parking lots.

Harmful substances. Medications must remain completely inaccessible, especially if they happen to be liquid and pleasantly flavored. Not only is she more skillful with the use of her hands, but her pretending games or imitation—new and important behaviors at this age—may include scenarios of playing doctor or taking medicines to get well. As we noted in the previous chapter, the use of ipecac to induce vomiting after an accidental ingestion is no longer recommended. (See page 224.) Instead, if you suspect that your toddler has swallowed a toxic substance, do the following:

- Call the toll-free number for the U.S. Poison Control Center at **1-800-222-1222** for advice if she doesn't appear ill.
- Call **911** immediately if she is unconscious, breathing erratically, or having convulsions. If she has stopped breathing, you must begin CPR while someone calls 911.

Car-seat struggles. She may become more vocal in protesting the use of her car seat, or she may actually figure out how to get out of it at some choice moment. Don't give an inch on your insistence that the seat be used for every ride in the car, no matter how short.

Dangerous "grown-up toys." Never underestimate her ingenuity in getting her hands on appliances, tools, or other hardware that she has seen you use. Imitation may come into play here as well.

The bathtub. She is still too young to be left in a tub unsupervised. The physical prowess that now makes shallow water seem less hazardous also enables her to turn on the faucet, leading to a possible scalding injury or an overflowing tub. (Lowering the temperature of your water heater below 120°F [49°C] will reduce the risk of scalding. See sidebar "Preventing Hot-Water Burns" on page 200.) She might also decide to see what happens when she jumps up and down in the water—and in so doing, slip and fall. For more on preventing accidents in the tub, see the sidebar on the next page.

Water hazards. Nonstop watchfulness is an absolute necessity whenever your two-year-old is near a swimming pool or any other body of water. Curiosity is abundant and caution scarce at this age, and a child can make a beeline toward a body of water in just a few moments while you are distracted with something else. If you have a pool at home, it is essential that a childproof fence—at least four feet high, not climbable, and equipped with a self-closing and self-latching gate—surrounds it. A spa or hot tub must be covered when not in use. If your child is playing in water, she must be observed by a responsible individual—ideally by someone who is in the water with her—at all times. Do not rely on inner tubes, water wings, or other flotation devices to keep your child safe.

Sibling skirmishes. Be on the lookout for impending aggression toward siblings, both older and younger. Whether or not your two-year-old is the one who initiates the conflict, her ability to inflict damage is ever increasing.

Special concerns: imitations and attitudes

One of the fascinating developments of a two-year-old's emerging intellect is the capacity for imitation, role-playing, and make-believe. Watch her be a mommy to one of her dolls or pretend to drive her toy car around the carpet or collect some of her animals into a miniature zoo, and you can learn a lot about what she's thinking.

A normal and important component of this phase is imitating parents, especially the one of the same gender. Listen to her give an exhortation to her favorite stuffed animal, and you may hear words, phrases, and even vocal inflections that sound amaz-

PREVENTING BATH-TIME COMPLICATIONS

Normally you would expect the only result of a bath to be a clean and pleasant-smelling child. However, occasionally bath time may play a role in provoking vaginal irritation and discharge as well as bladder infections in young girls. Irritation at the tip of the urethra—the small tube through which urine passes—may also be a bath-time-related problem in boys. The culprit very often is bubble bath, soap, or shampoo in the bathwater. Some simple preventive maneuvers include the following:

- Avoid bubble baths altogether.
- Keep bath times relatively short—fifteen minutes or less.
- If a child wants to play around in the bath for a while, let her do so before any soap or shampoo enters the water. As soon as the cleansing and hair washing are done, get her out.
- The genital area is sensitive and should be washed with water alone, not soap.

Remember—if a child is having problems with recurrent urinary tract infections or ongoing vaginal discharge, a thorough medical evaluation should be undertaken. Other measures may be recommended, including emptying the bladder immediately after exiting the tub (if the child is toilet trained) or switching to showers (see "urinary tract care and concerns" in Reference Section, page 731). ■

ingly familiar. You may even see a little mirror of yourself in a young child's stride or in her hand gestures. This imitation is, in fact, normal and healthy—provided, of course, that what your child sees is worth copying. Remember that the little computer is always on, and now the data going into the memory banks isn't just the names of objects around the house. Character traits that are on display at home—whether respect, courtesy, stability, and love, or their opposites—are all being watched and assimilated, no matter who is modeling them.

Parents often wonder whether they should try to influence the type of role-playing their child carries out. In bygone generations some might have fussed and fumed, usually in vain, if Johnny played house and Susie pretended to be a train engineer. Today some cultural forces push parents and preschools—with equal fervor and futility—to keep children "gender neutral" in their play roles. In fact, at this age kids will gravitate toward the types of toys and play activities they find interesting, no matter what you do. Later on, however, there may be some potential concerns regarding play patterns and sexual identity (see the Special Concerns section "Sexual Identity in Childhood" on page 287).

You should monitor more closely the *attitudes* that are being manifested in the pretending. Are you generally seeing and hearing pleasant themes and variations on your family's activities and interests? Or are you noticing some disturbing trends, focused more on violence and destruction? If you don't like what you're seeing, you may want to take stock of the material to which your two-year-old is exposed.

This is the time to become particularly attentive to the role of television in your child's life, not to mention your own. A year ago your walking baby didn't show much sustained interest in the tube. But two-year-olds can become captivated by the stories and images they see on the flickering screen, and by age three, they can become TV addicts. Furthermore, a huge variation exists in the quality and appropriateness of network and cable programming geared toward children. While you may find material that is nourishing to your child's mind and heart, far too much children's TV is deplorable—violent, occultic, manipulative, dumb, and dumber. As noted earlier in the discussion of nightmares, many classic films for children are far too intense for two- or three-year-olds. Without being paranoid or overly legalistic, now is the time to get a firm grip on what you allow into your home and your child's mind.

Social Developments: Interactions with Other Children

One obvious setting in which you will want to keep track of your two-year-old's playing and pretending is in the company of other children. Remember that as a one-year-old it would have been unusual for your child to engage in interactive play with another toddler her age. They might have played alongside one another, noting any potential threats to their possessions (which for each included everything in the room), but cooperative ventures would have been rare indeed.

As she passes her second birthday and moves toward her third, however, the possibility for more cooperative, interactive play with peers definitely increases. Ideally this will include situations in which she sets the pace ("Let's play with this now . . .") and others in which she follows another child's lead. Whether or not she can strike a healthy balance between leading and following other children will depend, in part, on the flavor of her relationships at home. If she is consistently loved and respected, she will be more likely to feel confident and friendly with other children and content to interact with them in a variety of ways. But if she has received the messages that she isn't worth much and that the world in which she lives is dangerous and unpredictable, she may shy away from dealing with other children or may be easily bullied. In the same way, seeing the adults at home overpowering others with loud voices and threatening actions may inspire her to adopt a similar, aggressive approach to her peers or younger children.

If she believes that she rules the world (or at least everyone who crosses her path), her interactions with peers will probably be stormy, unless the others are willing to play servants while she continues her starring role as Queen of Everything. But when she has learned about meaningful limits and knows that she can't get her way through whining, yelling, hitting, grabbing, or other negative behaviors, she'll be less likely to try these out on other children.

But no matter how flawlessly she has been reared, the virtue of sharing with peers—or anyone else—will probably *not* become part of your child's repertoire until sometime around the third birthday. Sharing is still not an easy concept to grasp at this

SUGGESTIONS FOR TAMING THOSE VIDEO SCREENS

In chapter 7 (see page 194) we broached the question of whether or not infants and toddlers should spend time watching "educational" DVDs. As your toddler grows into his preschool and school-age years, you will have more complicated issues to address regarding his relationship to video screens of all kinds—TVs, computer monitors, handheld units, game players, and beyond. We'll take a much more detailed look at managing media of all types in a segment called "Monitoring the input to mind and heart" in chapter 11, beginning on page 368. You're welcome to take a look at that material, especially if you have older children at home, but for now, here are a few key considerations for your toddler. For the sake of simplicity, we'll use the generic term *TV* to refer to any and all types of electronic screens that a child might be interested in watching.

- Decide what, when, and how long your child will watch TV. Specifically:
  (a) Set definite limits on time and content.
  (b) Monitor what's going on, and be prepared to remove your toddler from the viewing area (or shut the program off) if things are getting too intense.
  (c) Talk to your child about what she just watched. Even a program with elements or a message you don't like can be a teaching springboard if you put your spin on its content. ("That boy didn't speak very nicely to his mom, did he?")

- Be discerning about children's programs that you may have bought or borrowed on DVD or videocassette. Watch them yourself before showing them to your child. While many worthwhile stories utilize fantasy or supernatural elements, some G-rated cartoons contain messages that may undermine or contradict the spiritual values you cherish and teach at home. You may also be surprised at the intensity and violence of many vintage cartoons that you watched when you were growing up and that are now age for a number of reasons: The inborn, primitive self-centeredness of infancy and toddlerhood doesn't wane easily; patience is in short supply at age two; and it takes awhile to grasp the idea that something given up now can be retrieved later.

While you shouldn't let your two-year-old act like a playroom tyrant, you may not see any lightbulbs go on while you give an inspirational message about being unselfish or invoke the famous admonition, "How would *you* feel if someone did that to you?"

When you intervene in a squabble over a toy or book, you can divert the combatants' attention to something else or demonstrate the concept of taking short turns (five minutes or less) by using a little timer: "Jared can have the book until the buzzer goes off, and then Samantha gets to look at it." In this way she can experience sharing (however reluctantly) and even make it a habit of sorts, under your direction. Save your oration about the virtues of sharing until next year, when she can better understand what you're talking about and retain the basic idea.

What about nursery schools and play groups? Don't feel pressured to enroll your child in preschool to give her an academic "head start." Child-development experts

being recycled on DVD. Don't assume that if it was good enough for you, it's okay for your own children.

- Be even more discerning about video games. Even though a toddler won't have much luck manipulating the controls, she may watch with rapt attention while the older kids battle monsters, space aliens, or other humans—and she may view some grisly and disturbing images.

- Don't get into the habit of using the TV as an electronic babysitter. After a long day it is extremely tempting to park the kids in front of the screen so you can pick up the clutter, get a meal started, or simply put your feet up for a few minutes. If you need a time-out, put on a specific DVD or videocassette you know to be worthwhile or at least search for wholesome children's programming. But don't leave the TV on for hours on end or allow older children to channel surf, because you will lose control of those powerful images and sounds entering the minds of the most important people in your life.

- Ask yourself periodically whether television viewing is replacing conversation in your family. Consider declaring your home a "TV-free zone" one or more evenings every week in order to encourage reading, games, or other activities. Don't allow the TV to become a routine guest (or intruder) at any family meal.

- If you are having trouble controlling the broadcast material coming into your home, consider disconnecting the cable or antenna and relying strictly on DVDs or videocassettes that you buy or rent, choosing material based on quality, age appropriateness, and family-friendly values.

- If TV watching is getting out of control and the tube is exerting far more influence in your family's life than you feel is appropriate, consider as a last resort giving the television a new home for a while—unplugged in the garage. ■

generally agree that formal schooling at this age rarely brings about any long-term educational benefit. Burton L. White, for example, in his classic work *The First Three Years of Life*, notes that "no nursery school curriculum yet devised has been shown to bestow any lasting educational advantage on children, not even superiority in social adjustment."[1] Furthermore, you should also resist any push to start her in a preschool because "she needs to learn to socialize." Most children won't get much out of structured socializing until they are at least two-and-a-half years of age, at which time there are two basic reasons to consider this option:

1. If she's ready, your child will probably enjoy it.
2. If you're ready, you'll probably enjoy a short break in your child-care routines during the week.

Under normal circumstances, the foundations for healthy, productive interactions with others will be laid at home and in low-key, informal play with friends under your supervision. As it is, children at this age tend to play one-on-one rather than in true group activities, and yours can learn how to get along with others quite nicely without attending any structured program for toddlers.

If you and your child are ready and willing to try preschool or play-group experiences, look ahead to the next chapter (page 336) for suggestions and cautions.

If you are bringing up a young Mozart or a prodigy in some other area, special programs to encourage her skill may be appropriate. But be careful of highly regimented training or undue pressure to perform that can rob her of her childhood.

If your child's physician or a consultant has identified learning problems or delays in development, early intervention may help prepare her for her formal school years. The form this might take, of course, will vary greatly, depending upon the type and severity of the problem, the programs available in your area, and your own resources. Most states have instituted programs to provide special help for children as young as three (or in some locations, during infancy); the professional who counsels you should be able to make an appropriate recommendation.

Dealing with a two-year-old's emotions

Many parents approach this period of their child's life with a mixture of eager expectancy and dread. There's a real person emerging here, and it's exciting to see how he's going to develop. But in reflecting on the nonstop activity and the limit testing that went on during the previous year, you may be less than enthusiastic about the prospect of both perpetual motion and perpetual *e*-motion.

Like the adolescent, the two-year-old is undergoing major changes in his body and mind; he is still learning about the limits of his power and independence, and he tends to *feel* intensely about nearly everything. If he likes something, he can be ecstatic about it. If he loses or breaks it, the world might as well be coming to an end. If some task or toy frustrates him, he may fly into a rage. If he wants something and you won't let him have it, you may be shocked by the intensity of his reaction.

You might be reassured (or dismayed) to know that this is not only common but is, in fact, a warm-up for similar events—with a much bigger child—ten to twelve years from now. Even if you were consistent in contending with his negativism last year and have established a clear understanding that you care deeply about him but you are in

Children are incredibly vulnerable to rejection, ridicule, criticism, and anger at home, and they deserve to grow up in an environment of safety, acceptance, and warmth.

The New Dare
to Discipline
By Dr. James Dobson

charge, you still need to be prepared for some flare-ups. If he is still entrenched in a major power struggle with you as he passes his second birthday, you should make it a top priority to set up your boundaries in love—and concrete.

One of the arts of parenting a two-year-old is finding the right balance in responding to this changing emotional weather. Obviously, when he's cheerful or happily excited, you can for the most part enjoy the moment with him. Your only caution to him may be a reminder to contain his exuberance if it's getting a little rowdy, especially indoors. But when he's upset or you see a storm broiling on the near horizon, you'll have to make some judgment calls about the causes and effects and what course to take. Some examples:

If it's the end of a long, active day and he's becoming increasingly irritable (and irritating), getting him fed and to bed will probably do the most good.

If he's trying to do something that's beyond him and the frustration is mounting, your job will be to provide a good-natured reality check. If the project looks to you like it's impossible for him—stacking fifteen blocks one upon the other, for example—put it away and tell him "you'll do better with this later." It won't be the last time you offer this advice.

If he's having a hard time getting along with a younger sibling, don't be shocked. If a new baby has arrived, we hope your two-year-old has been well prepared (see chapter 4, page 112). However, don't expect him to buy the idea that "we have so much love for you that we wanted to share it with your baby sister."

A better approach would be to let him know that the new baby does need lots of attention, but that as an older child he has some special privileges. Make sure that he gets his own time with each parent without the baby in the vicinity. Otherwise, if he observes that the baby is getting all the adult attention, logic will dictate that he should act like the baby (or act up in general) in order to get some attention of his own. Also avoid constantly sending him messages that say the newcomer is more important ("Be quiet! You'll wake the baby!" or "I can't help you right now—the baby needs me"). Of course, he must be taught what is okay and what isn't in touching or handling a new baby: no poking eyes and ears, shaking, or any rough treatment.

As the novelty wears off and the new baby becomes part of the furniture, she will eventually be of less concern to your two-year-old until she starts crawling, toddling, grabbing his stuff, or even grabbing *him*. It is nearly impossible for a two-year-old to handle this intrusion on his space and possessions without some friction. Plan on several episodes in which you hear yelling and crying from another room, find one or both children in tears, and then have no idea who did what to whom. (Don't always assume that the older has attacked the younger. Some young toddlers can really dish it out to older siblings.) You may have to break up a few skirmishes without justice being served because you won't have enough evidence to arrive at a verdict. Comfort the wounded, separate the combatants, and perhaps remove an object of contention for a while. If consequences are due, be sure they are delivered to the guilty party.

Don't cave in to emotional outbursts that are clearly designed to manipulate you or change a decision you've made. Many young parents have been held hostage by a two-year-old who throws a tantrum in the grocery store when he can't have a cookie or who whines long enough to wear down their resistance. Once you've drawn your line ("We're not buying a toy today"), don't budge, and don't allow requests, begging, or demands to continue. In a firm, calm voice, eyeball-to-eyeball, take your stand: "I've said no and I mean it—don't say anything more about it."

However, as he progresses toward his third birthday, it will give your toddler great satisfaction if you allow him to make some simple decisions. "Do you want the red or the blue shoes today?" "Would you like to visit the park or the pet shop?" Remember that you will be gradually releasing control over to him during the next several years and that giving him appropriate (and not terribly taxing) choices will serve to remind both of you of this reality.

Dealing with a full-blown tantrum. When actually faced with one of these episodes, you will need to determine what works best for you and your child. This will depend to some extent on the cause. If it appears that the blowup has been brought on by factors such as fatigue, hunger, lack of sleep, or perhaps too much stimulation for one day—for example, an outburst occurs at the end of a long afternoon at an amusement park—you should try not only to deal with the spectacle in front of you but also to look for ways to cool off what is fueling it. (This may be easier said than done, especially in the heat of the moment.) Depending upon your assessment, calm but firm measures such as getting him to a quiet place or putting him down for a nap may be helpful. If your child's emotional fuse always seems to get short under specific circumstances—perhaps at a certain time of day such as late afternoon or before a meal or at the end of a long car ride—you may want to adjust activities to reduce the likelihood of a repeat performance.

If the tantrum is born out of frustration with a toy or game whose proper use is beyond him, your best bet is to put the offending object away and try to distract your toddler with something else. But if the angry outburst is primarily an attempt to influence you to do something or to change your mind, you must be firm in your resolve never to allow any decision to be altered by a tantrum. If you give an inch, you can plan on many repeat performances.

Whatever is provoking and fueling a tantrum—whether physical factors beyond your child's control, the frustrations and conflicts of toddlerhood, or a deliberate attempt to manipulate the nearest adult—you still have to deal with it. Some have argued that a tantrum needs an audience and that ignoring it will therefore serve to remove fuel from the fire. If the outburst is at home and you can walk away, this approach may work. Make it clear that you will talk to him when he quiets down and not before. A variation on this theme suggests isolating the tantrum thrower in his room until he calms down.

But sometimes ignoring the tantrum won't be appropriate. If he is sounding off in the church foyer, turning away will prolong a disturbance that is disruptive to others. In this case, bodily removal to a quiet, private area followed by a more direct intervention is appropriate. If he is clearly trying to manipulate or goad you, a judicious swat or two on the behind followed by a calm explanation of how the problem can be avoided in the future will be more likely to bring the incident to a conclusion (see the Special Concerns section "Principles of Discipline and Training" on page 259 for more information on discipline). On the other hand, if he is beside himself, flailing wildly and out of control, containing him in a bear hug until he calms down may be more appropriate. Whatever action you take, you must not allow the threat or eruption of a tantrum to torpedo your plans, whether in church, a restaurant, the mall, or anywhere else.

Another situation in which you cannot ignore a tantrum thrower is when he is causing damage. You might put him in his room to cool down, but what if he starts kicking the door or smashing the furniture? Or what if he delivers a swift kick to the dog or yanks his sister's hair? Once again, some form of direct intervention will be necessary. Trying to have a rational conversation in such situations is fruitless, negotiating is inappropriate, and asking or pleading for him to stop is disastrous. Protection of people and property and swift action to bring the episode to a close (including administration of consequences) take the highest priority. Discussions should begin only when the child is back under control.

If your two-year-old suddenly seems to be having tantrums more frequently with little or no provocation, consider having his health-care provider take a look at him to rule out a medical problem.

Another less dramatic but equally important form of emotional output is the verbal insult or disrespectful gesture. If you have a disagreement with your two-year-old and he lets fly with a choice comment such as "I hate you!" or "You're a doodoo-head," you should not punish him the *first* time. At this age he does not fully grasp the power of language, and it's your job to provide his first lessons. Sit him down, lock eyes with him, and explain clearly why such statements will be off-limits from now on. Let him know that it hurts you if he says he hates you, and that you will not allow him to call you names like "doodoo-head" or "dummy." The same should go for sticking out his tongue or aiming other disrespectful gestures in your direction.

Your two-year-old needs to begin learning the ABC's of what is, in fact, a sophisticated skill: how to express anger appropriately. Right now, virtually all of your input on this subject will be focused on what not to do—not to hit, bite, kick, throw or destroy things, launch a tantrum, or spew insults. When he is a little older, you can give him a basic but critically important message: *The way to express anger is in words that are not disrespectful to another person.*

It will take him years—perhaps his entire life—to learn not only how to control his impulses (both physical and verbal) when he is upset but also how to say the right words at the right time and in the right way when he needs to vent his anger. For example, he needs to learn that it is appropriate to tell another person that "I'm angry with you" or "I'm angry about what you said/did," rather than use hurtful words such as "I hate you." If this is a problem area in your own life or perhaps in your entire family, by all means get some counseling and go to work on it, because your child will learn far more (for good or ill) from your example than from your admonitions about what he should or shouldn't do.

Health Concerns: Medical Visits

Beginning at age two, routine medical checkups will take place every year. Whether or not your two-year-old will remain calm or combative during the exam will depend on her temperament and her memory. One way to ease her apprehension is to bring a favorite stuffed animal or doll. Not only will this serve as a little piece of familiar landscape in a strange environment, but the doctor, physician assistant, or nurse practitioner may be willing to "examine" the toy along with your child. This will show her what's coming and provide some reassurance as well ("Minnie's heart sounds fine; now let's check yours"). If she wants to sit on your lap for the exam, let her. By next year, she'll probably be eager to climb up on the table by herself.

Remember to be completely straightforward about any shots or other procedures that your child may not like. If something is going to hurt, don't say it won't or your child won't believe you next time. She should know that it's okay to cry but that she needs to hold still. *Never say that the doctor is going to give her a shot if she doesn't behave.* It is vital that your child understand that medical procedures will never be done as a punishment but only because you and the doctor care about her.

Parental Maintenance: Fatigue, Relationships, and the Meaning of Life

This year you will wonder at times why God didn't install roller skates on parents' feet, and you will perhaps wish you could get a transfusion of your child's energy. Indeed, ongoing fatigue is often an unwelcome companion during the eventful years of bringing up young children.

This energy deficit is particularly common among mothers of toddlers. For whether or not she stays at home with her young children, and whether or not she has a supportive husband who shares in the work of child rearing, much of the responsibility for caring and nurturing a young child will tend to fall on Mom. Furthermore, if there is a new baby in the family, Mom will be recuperating from the physical changes of pregnancy and childbirth and, quite likely, nursing as well. In this case, her need for stamina may seem even more profound.

The following comments about fatigue are therefore directed to mothers. They are, however, in no way intended to overlook the importance of fathers in rearing

SUGGESTIONS FOR FATHERS OF SMALL CHILDREN: HOW TO HELP YOUR WIFE AT HOME

- As demanding as your day may be, never harbor the delusion that rearing children at home isn't real work. If you need convincing, send your wife away on a retreat and take full charge of your children for a weekend. Note how utterly relieved you feel when she returns.
- When you arrive home after your long, tiring day, remember that your wife has had an equally long, tiring day. She needs, most of all, two things:
  (a) adult conversation, including expressions of appreciation for what she has been doing, and
  (b) an adult pair of hands to pitch in, take charge of one or more children, wrangle dirty diapers or other debris, or begin any other activity that will lighten her load.
- Do not expect to be taken care of like another child in the house. Pick up your own clothes and toys.
- Don't expect much sexual response if your wife is exhausted and you haven't done much to lighten her load during the course of the entire evening. Remember that sex begins in the kitchen—with meaningful conversation, compliments, acts of kindness, and some elbow grease applied to helping reduce her to-do list.
- Get involved in or even take over the process of getting your kids ready for bed. As they get older, you will hear thoughts and questions at bedtime that won't be expressed at any other time of the day. Be ready to listen and be amazed.

small children, nor to slight those fathers who are carrying the primary child-care load, whether married or single. We hope they, too, will find this material useful.

Mothers who stay at home with one or more kids under the age of three may find themselves suffering from lack of sleep, lack of adult conversation, and (most important) lack of recognition for the job being done. All of these can sap huge amounts of energy from the most talented, motivated, and dedicated moms.

If you are in this position, you may begin to suspect that the only milestones in your life are those achieved by your children and that you are a fool for staying home while your childless friends are busy earning advanced degrees or accomplishing great things in their glamorous careers.

If you feel that there is no end to your day's work and that life has been reduced to an endless, draining, and monotonous routine, wake up and smell the coffee, because life is not passing you by. On the contrary, you are at the center of the action. You are shaping and molding the very core—the attitudes, the faith, the future—of one or more young lives. *Very few careers offer anything resembling this opportunity and none to the depth that is possible as a parent.* Believe it or not, your friends who are navigating the freeways by the dawn's early light may actually envy you.

This is a time to renew your fascination with your child and to remind yourself that you have him on loan for but a few short years. An attitude of deep thanksgiving—even in the midst of toys strewn all over the house, piles of laundry yet to be done, crayon marks on the walls, and little hands frequently pulling at your sleeve—is not only appropriate but invigorating.

- Maintain the habit of a regular date night—a meal (fancy or otherwise), a concert, a walk, whatever your imagination and budget can manage—in which the focus is conversation and companionship. Make it a point to keep your wife current on your day's activities and find out about hers.

- If your hours at work seem to be getting longer, take an honest stock of your attitude. Do you really need to work through dinner every night? Is that trip necessary? Are you listening to the siren song that says your career is a lot more fulfilling than the tasks awaiting you at home? Think again, long and hard, if your hours are gradually turning your wife into a single parent. And if you are going to be later than expected on any given day, be sure to let her know.

- Take her away for a romantic weekend, or even dinner and an overnight stay, at a pleasant location where her daily responsibilities are temporarily suspended. (With planning and creativity, this need not be expensive.) Another worthwhile activity is a marriage-enrichment weekend such as a FamilyLife conference, which can serve as a therapeutic time-out and an opportunity to renew and deepen your commitment to one another. (Check http://www.familylife.com or call 1-800-FL-Today for more information about these weekends.)

- Call her during the day to touch base, offer an encouraging word, or simply say "I love you."

- Flowers and gifts for no particular reason speak volumes. ▪

While it may seem as if the current responsibilities will last forever, there will in fact be many years ahead to pursue education and career, if that's your calling. Who said that you had to check your mind at the door of the maternity ward or that your reading must forever be limited to *The Runaway Bunny* or *The Cat in the Hat*? There is no law against ongoing learning while children are young, whether through informal study or more formal courses (even one at a time) taken at a local college or other continuing-education resource.

The arrival of your child's second birthday is also an important time to take stock of the parental state of the union. Is there still a strong sense of teamwork, shared goals, communication, and intimacy? Or are Mom and Dad moving through the months on different tracks, which may be parallel but more likely are diverging? Without taking deliberate steps to maintain your marriage, drifting in different directions is all too easy. Both husband and wife must take part in keeping their marriage fresh and strong.

As important as it is to maintain communication within your marriage, your spouse may not be able to meet all your needs in this area. Regular times of grown-up conversation with other adults of the same gender who share your values can help keep the demands of each day in perspective.

Time-outs for personal refreshment—not just for running errands but for exercise, coffee with a friend, an unscheduled afternoon out, or time to be alone with God—are both legitimate and necessary. Track down the best babysitters in your area and reward them well. If cash is short, consider utilizing a babysitting co-op with people you know well, where child care is swapped among several people on a barter system. If you are blessed with loving grandparents nearby, give them the opportunity to spoil the kids for a few hours (or even overnight) while you take a break.

SUGGESTIONS FOR STAY-AT-HOME MOTHERS OF SMALL CHILDREN: HOW TO HELP YOUR HUSBAND FEEL HAPPY AT HOME

- Let him know that you're happy to see him. Don't greet him with a laundry list of complaints or "honey-do's" before he has crossed the threshold. Start the evening's agenda with a heartfelt embrace. Give him a few moments to unwind if possible.
- Don't neglect your own grooming and appearance. Like it or not, even the most committed and principled male is still affected by what he sees. A fashion statement isn't necessary, but freshening up before the evening arrives will make more of an impact than you might realize.
- If you are overdue for time alone with your husband, you can take the initiative to clear a night, arrange child care, and make some plans. You don't have to wait for him to get the ball rolling.
- Do you know what's happening at his workplace? He'll be affirmed if you're as interested in his day's events as you would like him to be in yours.
- While you don't want to be faking or participating with teeth firmly gritted, remember that your husband is strongly affirmed by a positive sexual response from you, just as you are by thoughtful gestures from him throughout the day. He will feel loved and honored in his own household when you initiate sex, especially if he realizes that you've had to plan carefully for intimate time with him at the end of a very busy, tiring day. ■

Mothers who work outside of the home, whether single or married, face additional generators of pressure and fatigue. Fulfilling the responsibilities of a job requires that the demands and details of parenting be carried out during fewer hours—often at the end of a workday when a great deal of energy has already been expended. You may feel guilt ridden over the time you have to be away at work or concerned about the adequacy of your day-care arrangements ("Are they doing as good a job as I would?"). Worries over income, especially for single moms, may add to the burden.

All these issues might tempt you to abandon reasonable limits that your child needs or to spend money you don't have to make up for any shortages in your time and attention. Whatever you do, don't allow a child to play the guilt card in order to get his way or con you into buying something for him. *Remember that consistency in expressing love and enforcing reasonable limits is far more valuable to your child in the long run than a lot of material goods.*

If both parents work outside of the home, cooperation, communication, and sharing responsibilities will be even more important. The suggestions already listed for homes in which one parent (usually the mother) is at home definitely apply to you as well, with slight modification.

Single parents have the challenging and important job of being both mother and father to their children and creating an environment for them that is safe and stable. If you are a single parent, you may at times wonder whether you can really carry out all these obligations adequately, especially if hours are long and income is limited. The answer is that you can, especially if you stay with the basics: love and limits for your children, lots of prayer, and a little help from your friends. As mentioned in previous chapters, you should maintain and tap into your support team (family, friends, church groups, pregnancy resource centers) for ongoing camaraderie, attitude adjustment, troubleshooting, and adult conversation. Maintain a stable attitude with your children, and in future years they will rise up and bless you, marveling at what you accomplished without a mate. (For some helpful resources, check the materials listed under "Single Parenting" in the Additional Resources section, beginning on page 868.)

Three- and Four-Year-Olds: Windows of Opportunity

An extraordinary period awaits you during the next several months as baby days and toddlerhood become more distant memories. For a number of reasons, the two years leading to the fifth birthday are a unique and critical period during which you can shape the entire gamut of your child's attitudes and understanding. Developments in his intellect and speech will enable you to communicate with him in much more sophisticated ways. He will still be intensely curious about the world around him and is now better equipped to learn about it. More important, he will also want to understand how *you* see things both great and small and what is important to you. Whether the topic is animals, trucks, the color of the sky, or the attributes of God, he will be all ears (even though his mouth may seem to be in perpetual motion) and deeply concerned about what you think.

This wide-eyed openness will not last forever. While you will greatly influence his thinking throughout childhood, during the coming months you will have an important window of opportunity to lay foundations that will affect the rest of his life. No one can do this job perfectly; therefore generous doses of humility and much time in prayer are definitely in order for this phase of parenting.

Physical Developments

During the next twenty-four months, your child's growth should maintain a steady, if not spectacular, pace. You can expect gains of two and a half to three inches (6.3 to 7.6 cm) and four to five pounds (1.8 to 2.3 kg) each year. He will continue his gradual physical transition from toddler to child: More baby fat will disappear, his abdomen will no longer protrude, and his arms and legs will slim down to the point of looking almost scrawny. Don't be too concerned if his limbs look a bit delicate, since muscle development will catch up in due time. Indeed, if a chunky look persists well past the third birthday, ask his health-care provider to check how he's doing on the height and weight chart. (By the way, the flat foot you saw when he was a toddler should be developing an arch.)

Your child's medical checkups at ages three and four will probably be rather uneventful, but he shouldn't skip them. Aside from checking growth and developmental milestones and giving a head-to-toe exam, his health-care provider may recommend giving him his DTaP (diphtheria/tetanus/pertussis) and polio boosters if he has passed his fourth birthday. He will probably also receive his second dose of MMR (measles/mumps/rubella) vaccine between ages four and six. Yearly influenza vaccines and a series of immunizations to protect against hepatitis A may also be recommended during these visits. (For more information about all of these immunizations and the infections they prevent, see the section "Immunizations—Which Ones, Why, and When?" beginning on page 739.)

The third birthday is a good time to begin recording your child's growth milestones in a way that everyone in the family can follow. A poster marked with numbers to measure height can be attached to the wall of his room, or you can even make some marks on the back of his door if you're careful not to wash them off or paint over them. You can enlist your child's eager cooperation by making the measuring process a special event twice a year—on each birthday and then six months later. Make sure that his feet are flat on the floor, he is standing straight, and his head isn't tilted up or down. Mark the spot using a ruler or other flat surface that rests across the top of his head and is perpendicular to the surface you're using. As he grows, he will take special pleasure in seeing how much he has changed from year to year.

His walking, running, and jumping movements should become increasingly smooth and will be joined by tiptoeing, hopping, spinning, and standing on one foot. By age four he will also climb up and down stairs without holding a rail or your hand. He will enjoy pedaling a tricycle and throwing a ball, although his ability to catch a ball with any reliability will develop somewhat later. He will, however, be thrilled if he succeeds in snagging any soft object that you gently toss right to him. If you take him to a local park, he will relish his time on small-scale swings, slides, tunnels, climbing gear, and sandboxes.

Although he won't careen randomly from one place to another as he did as a toddler, don't be surprised when he decides to charge ahead of you in the park, church, mall—or at the end of the sidewalk. At this age enthusiasm and the desire for independence are far more abundant than are wisdom and judgment. Keep your eyes peeled and a good grip on your child's hand when you are approaching traffic, playing near a pool, or walking through a crowd.

Car seats are still necessary for children this age; keep in mind that *adult seat belts are not designed for children in this age-group.* Every time your child rides in a car, he should be secured in a child safety seat with a full harness. When he reaches the weight limit of the seat (typically forty pounds, or 18.2 kg), he can graduate to a booster seat. He won't be ready for regular lap and shoulder belts until he is about eight years old, or at least four feet nine inches tall (fifty-seven inches, or 145 cm).

You may have to deal with peer pressure for the first time as your child's social skills and interests in other children begin to blossom. A child who normally is cautious about taking risks may suddenly decide he wants to climb on, jump off, or crawl under something that is off-limits—in response to the tempting, teasing, encouragement, or example of other children. As a result, during the coming months you will need to begin teaching your child, in very simple terms, the "why" of your rules, along with the "what and where" (or more often the "what not" and "where not").

There are qualities in your special youngster that may not have been seen before. Find them. Cultivate them. And then give God time to make something beautiful in his little life!

Parenting Isn't
for Cowards
By Dr. James Dobson

At this age it is likely that he will push you a little or even wear you out with "Why . . . ?" questions. This isn't necessarily an attempt to start an argument but more likely a sign of growth and simple curiosity about the "whys" in his world—including your limits and ground rules. Try to use the reason "Because I'm the mom, that's why!" sparingly. You are now building your child's value system, precept upon precept, as well as his ability to link actions with consequences. At this age, he is beginning to understand and is capable of appreciating the reasons for your rules. Take advantage of his openness by explaining them whenever you can.

His accomplishments with hands and fingers over the next two years will please him and you as well. When drawing with a pencil or crayon, he will begin to use a more sophisticated grip, with thumb on one side and fingers on the other, rather than grasping with his fist. Watch for his first wonderful drawing of a person—with arms and legs extending directly from the head. After he turns four, his "people pictures" will begin to include details such as facial features (eyes, nose, ears) and eventually a body to which the arms and legs are attached. When not creating his own images on paper, he may enjoy tracing or reproducing geometric shapes.

Budding three- and four-year-old artists also delight in using brushes, clay, paste, and finger paints—materials that are much more fun for everyone if clothes, furniture, and carpets aren't in jeopardy. Wearing grubby clothes and setting up shop in the yard (or laying down lots of newspaper indoors) is a good idea. Kid-safe, blunt-ended scissors are also a big hit with this age-group, but be sure everyone is clear on what is to be cut and what is to be left alone. Finding your bank statement converted into tiny geometric shapes or having little sister's locks shorn can be a jarring experience at the end of a long day. A less messy but surprisingly satisfying activity for many preschoolers is "painting" the front steps or a corner of the back patio using a brush and a can of water.

Whatever arts and crafts your child works with, be sure to relax, enjoy, and most of all show interest in what he is producing. Groaning over the messy hands and clothes, trying to "correct" what he creates, or plunging headlong into lessons for the genius-in-the-making are less worthwhile at this age than asking some open-ended questions ("What's happening in the house you drew?"). You'll have plenty of time to get him involved in formal training in later years if he really has a knack for a particular craft.

Your child will also develop new skills manipulating other types of objects: jigsaw puzzles with a few pieces, fasteners and buttons for his own or his toys' clothes, and building blocks, among other things. Meals should generate less cleanup as he becomes more adept at using his fork and spoon. Since some accidents and spills are inevitable, you may want to wait another couple of years before adding glassware to his dining equipment.

Feeding: Speaking of Mealtimes . . .

During the coming months, your child will continue to show wide variations in her desire for food. A ravenous appetite one day followed by picking and dawdling sessions the next won't be at all unusual. Just as when she was two, your job will be to provide an appropriate mix of healthy options; her job will be to decide how much of each (within reason) she will consume. If you need a calorie estimate of her needs, figure about forty calories per pound (or about ninety calories per kilogram) per day. A child weighing thirty-five pounds (about 16 kg), for example, will consume about fourteen hundred calories per day, spread over three meals and two snacks. Between 25 and 35 percent of the total calories should be in the form of fats. Milk should be kept to a maximum of sixteen ounces (about 475 ml) per day. Vitamin supplements are not necessary at this age, but if you have any concerns, check with your doctor.

In the coming months, you will want to pay more attention to the patterns of your child's food intake than to the details of what she eats at any particular meal. Specifically, keep the following in mind:

Emphasize variety and freshness. The average North American supermarket contains a dazzling selection of vegetables, fruits, grains, and meats—available in any season. Children should be exposed to this rich diversity at an early age, whether or not they partake of it. In general, fresh foods are more nutritionally intact than frozen items (though not by much), and both fresh and frozen foods are better nutritionally than canned foods. Dishes prepared using raw ingredients are more likely to be more wholesome and economical than prepackaged microwave concoctions—although time pressures for many families have made meals from scratch increasingly uncommon.

Resist the encroachment of sugary, salty, fatty, and otherwise low-quality enticements. Your child may be getting the good stuff at home, but advertising and slick packaging are working desperately to woo her taste buds in other directions. A few trips to the local Burger Ecstasy franchise or a bowl of Double-Cocoa Frosted Mega-Flakes at a friend's house may create a long-term enthusiastic customer. At this point, you have control over what lands on her plate, a responsibility and opportunity that will not last long. Do what you can to mold her tastes, and don't let her manipulate you into buying products that are short on nutritional value.

Don't allow food to become an accompaniment to a whole gamut of other activities. Eating is a good thing to do when she's hungry or when the family sits down together for a meal. Period. It should not become a cure for boredom, a pacifier for a stubbed toe, or a bribe for doing something you want.

Don't turn meals into power struggles. If you provide a wholesome selection of foods at a meal and she isn't interested, don't fight over it, make it the main subject of conversation, or force her to sit for hours at the table until she eats it. Put her plate in the refrigerator, and take it out again when she's hungry. Don't be badgered into preparing something specifically for her at every meal, and don't allow her to become stuck in a rut of three or four foods that are "the only things she ever eats." She won't starve if you hold your ground.

While busy schedules may rule out formal dining three times a day, at least one meal a day should pull the family around the table at the same time. Dinner is most often the choice, but for many children breakfast is the biggest meal of the day, and socializing at that time may be more productive than at other times. For some families, one or two meals per week—perhaps Saturday breakfast or Sunday dinner after church—serve as the special time everyone can come together. At such times, the atmosphere should be relaxed and inviting. The TV should be off, phones taken off the hook, cell phones silenced, and conversation geared to draw everyone into this important event.

A preschooler is old enough to learn some basic table manners: keeping the volume of her voice reasonable, chewing with her mouth closed, saying please and thank you, using a napkin, and waiting until everyone is seated and a blessing is offered before beginning to eat. If she is done with her meal and conversation among the adults is extending beyond her interest and attention span, don't insist that she sit indefinitely.

But before she gets up, she should ask to be excused. After she departs, don't let her crawl around under the table with the family pets.

Graduate-Level Potty Skills

By the third birthday or soon thereafter, it is likely that your child will be well versed in the basics of using the toilet. If you are still working through this process, review the previous chapter, beginning on page 301.

Your next assignment in this area will be to teach the skills necessary for solo trips to the toilet, which will be desirable if preschool is on the horizon and necessary for kindergarten. These skills include:

- Learning how to get clothes and underwear out of the way and then reassembled afterward. Obviously, easy-on, easy-off garments are desirable. Boys at this age are still a little young for zippers, which have a way of getting stuck or (worse) accidentally pinching the penis when zipped up.
- Learning how to wipe clean after a bowel movement. Girls need to be taught to wipe front to back to reduce the risk of moving bacteria from the anus to the opening of the vagina and bladder, where the bacteria can gain access to the bladder and start an infection.
- Learning to finish the job by flushing and then washing hands with soap.
- For little boys, learning to urinate standing up.
- Learning to use restrooms out of the house. You'll need to give directions during visits to public facilities, pointing out things of interest such as the appropriate gender sign on the restroom door, the flush handle (if it's different from the ones at home), faucets/paper towels/hand dryers, and so on. (Even after these skills are well established, you should continue to escort your child on any trip to a public restroom. At this age he is by no means ready to handle a chance encounter with someone whose behavior might be inappropriate or abusive.)

Your child may not be waking up dry in the morning at this point. In fact, by the age of five, at least 10 to 20 percent of children occasionally or regularly wet the bed. For some children this problem persists for years, and often in such cases there is a family history of this problem. *Rewards, (or worse) reprimands, humiliation, and punishment have no place in dealing with bed-wetting because the problem is one of physiological maturity and is completely out of a child's control.* The best solution in nearly all cases is patience, continued use of diapers or training pants to contain the nocturnal flood, a lot of reassurance, and a few more birthdays (see "bed-wetting" in Reference Section, page 629).

If your child has been dry through the night for a number of months and then begins to lose bladder control, a physical problem such as a bladder infection or an emotional upheaval such as a move or a new sibling might be the cause. A visit to the doctor would be a good idea if this occurs.

Private Parts and Decent Exposure

During or before toddler days, your child undoubtedly discovered that touching the genital area felt good, and you may have been dismayed to see little hands exploring inside the diaper zone (whether clean or otherwise) on a number of occasions. This type of exploration and ongoing curiosity about body parts is common and quite normal in young children. Questions about where they (or their siblings) came from are part of the same package. When it comes to dealing with such sensitive areas and topics, you have a number of important assignments:

Make it clear that you are the prime source of information about these matters—and not the kid next door or some other unreliable source. Be levelheaded, honest, calm, and straightforward when you name body parts and explain what they do. Using actual terms (penis and vagina) and not more colorful vocabulary may save some embarrassment later on if your child happens to make a public pronouncement. This information by itself doesn't jeopardize your child's innocence.

Instill respect for the body your child has been given, the Creator who made it, and the functions it performs. This means that you should not communicate a sense of shame or repulsion about any part of your child's (or your own) anatomy. It also means that you need to teach what, where, when, and how it is appropriate to touch or talk about these areas.

Your child needs to know that these are things to discuss at home with Mom and/or Dad and not with other kids in the neighborhood. If you discover him and a playmate checking out each other's pelvic area, don't panic. This is also normal curiosity at work, and he just needs a brushup on the ground rules. Remind him that these areas of his body are just for himself, his parents, and his doctor to see, and not other people. Tell your child that if someone else tries to touch those areas, he should protest noisily, get away, and tell you as soon as possible. He must know that you will not be angry or upset with him if this should happen.

If a child makes comments, gestures, or body movements that suggest exposure to or experience with sexual activity, further evaluation will be needed. Other signs of possible sexual abuse include age-inappropriate sexual behavior or demonstrations, depression, disturbed sleep, fear of being left alone, or pain on urination (see Special Concerns "Child Abuse and Neglect," page 277, for more information on sexual abuse). You will need to review what you have seen and heard with your physician, who will investigate and/or refer you to an appropriate professional for further evaluation.

Release information on a need-to-know basis. Your child does not need to hear everything about reproduction in one sitting and will be overwhelmed (or bored) if you try to explain too much at once.

Respond forthrightly with a minimum of fluster when your child cuts loose with offensive language that he didn't hear from you. Our culture is flooded with off-color messages and images that degrade the beauty and wonder of sexuality, and you will not be able to keep your child completely insulated from such negative input. As a result, he may pick up some R-rated expressions in the neighborhood, even at this young age. (Be sure, by the way, that what you say or the language you allow in your home isn't in any way inspiring this unpleasant verbiage.)

If this occurs, stay calm. It is unlikely that he even understands what he just said, as a simple quiz ("Do you know what that means?") will often confirm. He is far more likely to be interested in the power of words to create a stir than in actually expressing some specific sexual or crude sentiment. Without sounding alarmed or flustered, explain that the words he just used are not ones that you use in your family and that he needs to stop saying them in your home or anywhere else. You should emphasize that such words and expressions put down other people and can make them feel upset or even afraid.

If your child's new expressions include casual or inappropriate use of the words *God* or *Jesus*, a simple explanation about the importance of respecting those names will be needed as well.

Once you have stated your case, be sure to take appropriate action if you hear a repeat performance. If he persists after one or two reminders, let him know that a consequence will follow next time, and then carry it out if needed. If your child begins using harsh or obscene language, you need to not only retrain his vocabulary quickly and decisively but also have a frank conversation with whomever you determine to be the source.

Sleeping Routines and Monster Patrol

Most three- and four-year-olds will sleep about twelve hours each night. A daytime nap may continue to be part of your child's routine, but don't be surprised when it is phased out during the next several months. If you are struggling with your child over bedtime, read again the section on sleep in the previous chapter (page 296). This is also a good time to review the management of nightmares (and their less common counterparts, night terrors) described in that same section.

Remember that bedtime should be early because your child needs the sleep and you need time with other children, your spouse, or yourself. During the middle of summer, this can be a challenge. The sun may still be shining, and all sorts of activity may still be going on outside at what is normally bedtime. You will need to decide how much to bend your routines to match the seasons, or perhaps invest in heavy window shades if you need to darken your child's room at this time of year. You may also need to exercise sensible flexibility to accommodate family work schedules.

The activities that surround getting tucked in should become a familiar and quieting routine. At this age, bedtime can be a delightful, enlightening experience. You can introduce your child to some wonderful stories, including books with several chapters that can create eager anticipation for the next night's installment ("I wonder what's going to happen to Pooh and Piglet tonight. Better get ready for bed so we can find out!"). Your child's desire to keep the lights on and you in the room as long as possible will usually cause her to be remarkably transparent and receptive.

Expect to hear some of her private thoughts ("I think I know what Buster is saying when he barks . . .") or to tackle some riddles of the universe ("Where is heaven?"). Without being manipulated *too* much, allow enough slack in your day so you can relax during these wide-eyed sessions. You will probably have many more opportunities at bedtime to talk about God and the values you care about than during family devotions or even at church, Sunday school, or other formal religious teaching sessions. The lyrics of the following song illustrate the importance of spending quality time with your child:

TAKE THE TIME

It's nine-fifteen, and bedtime took too long, once again—
Another drink, another glass of water, and then
The questions come, the hands hold tight, and the eyes are opened wide,
And something in me whispers, "Now's the time."

"Mommy, why did Muffy die? Daddy, where's the sun?"
"Are there cats in heaven? And why did Jesus come?"
And though a whole day's dishes wait, and bills are piled high,
Something in me whispers, "Take the time."

Take the time, while they're right here by your side,
Take the time, while their arms are opened wide.
Teach them how to love the Lord with all their heart and mind.
Oh, they're only home a season, take the time.

Riding off to Narnia upon a lion's back,
Chubby fingers close the book and add it to the stack.
"Aslan didn't kill the witch—oh Dad, why did he die?"
And something in me whispers, "Now's the time."

Her baseball game's tomorrow, but so's my interview.
How can I play Scrabble, when there's so much to do?
Little faces plead with me to put my work aside,
And something in me whispers, "Take the time."

Take the time, while they're right here by your side,
Take the time, while their arms are opened wide.
Teach them how to love the Lord with all their heart and mind.
Oh, they're only home a season, take the time.

For one day they'll want to spend time alone.
One day they'll need to be on their own.
Next week their hugs may not seem quite the same—
Oh Lord, may they honor Your name.

It's nine-fifteen, and bedtime took too long, once again—
Another drink, another glass of water, and then
The questions come, the hands hold tight, and the eyes are opened wide,
And something in me whispers, "Take the time."

Take the time, while they're right here by your side,
Take the time, while their arms are opened wide.
Teach them how to love the Lord with all their heart and mind.
Oh, they're only home a season, take the time.
    —1985, Paul and Teri Reisser

You will also need to deal with some childhood fears when it's time to tuck in. Monsters in the closet, under the bed, or outside the window may need to be banished. Be sure to ask what your child has in mind—is the creature something from a book or video, or perhaps a tall tale spun by an insensitive adolescent next door? Are we talking about space aliens, Brothers Grimm concoctions, or something from the nightly news that is in fact a reality somewhere in the world or the community? Are there tensions at home creating a need for reassurance?

Very often the beast in question doesn't exist except in someone's imagination. In this case it can be tempting to give a lighthearted, direct inspection ("I don't see any monsters in your closet—just a lot of junk!"), but you may leave the impression that there are monsters or aliens running around *somewhere*—they just don't happen to be here at the moment. For these fears, more decisive reality checks are important ("Bigfoot isn't under your bed or anywhere else").

When the issue is burglars or other villains who actually *do* exist out there, you will need to be more specific about the safeguards in your home: You are present (or if you are going out, someone you trust will be there), the doors are locked, and perhaps you have a dog or an alarm system that adds to your home's security. In addition, remind your child that God is keeping watch over her twenty-four hours a day. What your child really wants is reassurance and confidence that things are under control.

If a fearful bedtime resistance persists or escalates, take time to find out if something else is bothering her. Did your child see a disturbing image on TV or a video? Did she hear an argument the other night? Did something else frighten her? Once you have spent time exploring the problem, it's okay to make some minor adjustments to reduce the anxiety level: leaving a light on in the hallway or the door open a little wider, for example. But don't get pulled into more elaborate or manipulative routines, such as her insisting on falling asleep in your bed or on the living-room floor when she claims that she's afraid of something. She needs to know that she will be just as safe and sound in her own bed as anywhere else.

Language: Mastering the Mother Tongue

Your child arrived at his third birthday with a vocabulary of about five hundred to one thousand words. During the next two years, you can anticipate a dramatic increase to about twenty-five hundred words. At age three, these will be gathered into sentences of five or six words, and from here on the assembly of words into phrases and sentences will gradually become more sophisticated.

Watch and listen carefully, and you will witness a miracle.

As he has grown from baby to toddler, you have heard your child's babbling, his mimicry, his one- or two-word exclamations, and his first simple statements. And you have seen how much more he could understand than what he could say. In the coming years, your child will be revealing his ideas, his rhymes and music, his fantasies, his questions, and his fears. Language will be a window into his soul and spirit—and the most obvious evidence that you are dealing with a unique human being.

Whether he is very verbal or more conservative with his narrations, don't let your brain slip into neutral when he is chirping away about anything and everything. Listen, learn, and marvel. At the same time, you can help him develop this most incredible gift of speech.

He will soon be using personal pronouns (*I, you, he, she*), and you can speed up his process of sorting them out by using them correctly yourself. As natural as it may seem to refer to yourself and your child in the third person ("Mommy wants Andrew to get into the tub"), this is the time to begin using the words *I* and *you* instead. When he mixes them up ("Me want a cookie"), be careful that your correction doesn't create further confusion. (If you say, "You mean, '*I want a cookie*,'" he may think that you want one too. A correction such as "Andrew, you should say, '*I want a cookie*'" would work better.)

Pronouns won't be the only verbal mistakes you will hear. Other mispronunciations will be abundant, although you (or anyone else) should be able to understand what he is trying to say. Your friends should not need an interpreter when he speaks; if he is truly unintelligible at this age, he should have a formal speech evaluation.

At times his comments may remind you more of Tweety Bird ("Da kitty went up da twee!") than the King's English, and you will have to decide how many times per day (or hour) you will want to offer corrections. Some friendly input in response to his most obvious mistakes can help move his speech in the right direction. But badgering him or correcting every last syllable will exasperate him while he's trying to get the hang of this complex new skill.

The best approach is to spend plenty of time speaking clearly to him. Just as you avoided using endless baby talk when he was starting to vocalize, in general you should not parrot back his creative pronunciations, no matter how cute they might be. Write them down as a keepsake in his baby book, and then persist in using words and sentences properly.

One common language glitch at this age is stuttering or stammering, which may cause some concern when you first hear it. Before you call a speech therapist, however, understand that one in twenty preschool children manifests this on a temporary basis, especially when tired, excited, or upset. Boys are three times more likely to stutter than girls. This may be a case of too many words in the assembly line between the thought and the actual expression. The opening syllable or even the first couple of words in a sentence may trip repeatedly on the tongue before moving on to the rest of the thought. "Um" or "uh" may show up midword or midsentence if he loses track of where the idea was going.

Don't worry about this if it occurs on an occasional basis over a month or so. Avoid showing impatience or disapproval while he's trying to get through his sentence. Also, don't try to fish the words out for him, complete his thoughts, or add any pressure to the situation. If anything, his stuttering may be a signal that the speed and pitch of everyone's conversation at home needs to calm down a bit. Normally this situation will resolve itself. However, if your child is having an ongoing problem getting his sentences launched, looks tense, twitches and grimaces, or is definitely upset by his stuttering, he should be evaluated by a speech therapist.

Other things you can do to help your child's language blossom include:

Read to her and with her. Don't limit storytelling to bedtime. Go to the library regularly and help her fall in love with books. Have her sit next to you while you read so she can study the pictures and watch the words as you say them. Don't be in a rush to get to the last page. If she wants to linger over a picture and point out a few highlights, by all means, stop and enjoy the scenery.

The object here is not to produce a four-year-old who is ready to enter high school. Driving and drilling for early academic achievement may actually backfire, especially if she begins to feel pushed and anxious about her progress in learning letters or words. Reading at this age should forge emotional bonds—not only to books but also to *you*. This lasting benefit, by the way, cannot happen in front of a TV screen.

Listen. This is a skill you may have to learn (or relearn), especially if you feel as though all you do is listen to chattering throughout the day. At least once each day—and much more often if possible—consciously stop, look, and listen to what your preschooler has

Provide your children with many interesting books and materials, read to them and answer their questions.

The New Dare
to Discipline
By Dr. James Dobson

to say. Lock eyes, uncross your arms, and acknowledge what you hear ("Wow! That's pretty exciting! What else happened?") as if you were sitting with a friend over a cup of coffee. This simple activity is one of the most important ways to validate your child's identity and significance, and its impact will last throughout his lifetime.

Carry on conversations. This flows from taking the time to listen to your child but adds the dimension of a thoughtful exchange. Decades ago one of the most successful television programs was Art Linkletter's *House Party*, and its most popular segment was called "Kids Say the Darndest Things." Linkletter simply conversed with children in a calm and friendly manner and was rewarded with responses that were incredibly candid and funny. His skill was in showing interest in children, without worrying for those few minutes whether they had clean hands or tidy rooms. He didn't correct, rebuke, scold, or exhort, and what he heard in return was extraordinary.

As a parent, your job is to be concerned about the daily welfare and training of your child. You can't run your home like a TV talk show, but for a few minutes each day, try settling back and simply talking with your child, even pretending for a moment that you are interviewing her. You may be surprised when you hear what's on her mind. And if you show that what she says is worthy of your attention, it is likely that she will return the favor. While you're creating some sweet memories (both for you and for her), her language skills will grow by leaps and bounds.

Try to answer questions. You'll hear them from dawn till dusk, and if you can give a simple but meaningful answer, not a mumbled "I dunno" or a disinterested shrug, your child will learn language, information, and values. Your child's questions will also provide you with priceless opportunities to talk with him about God. Okay, so you don't know exactly why the grass is green or how airplanes fly, or you may become frustrated when your brilliant response is met with a sudden change in his train of thought, as if he paid no attention to what you said. But he does care very much what you think about life and the world, a state that won't last forever. All through the first years of your child's life, the little computer is on all the time, waiting eagerly for someone to provide input. No one is better qualified than you.

Social Developments: Mind, Heart, and Relationships

Language is not the only territory your preschooler will be striving to explore and master. At this point he is sorting out not only words but reality itself. He is now well past the basic "see-touch-taste-drop" method of exploration that served him in his toddler days. By age three or shortly thereafter, he has come to understand that he is an individual separate from you. By now he should know—without any doubt whatsoever—that he is deeply loved and respected, that his welfare is your highest priority, and that he doesn't rule either the universe or your family. (The Special Concerns section "Principles of Discipline and Training: Balancing Love and Limits," beginning on page 259, can help you in this important aspect of your parenting.)

With this foundation firmly established, your child is free to launch out into the world and learn about it with curiosity and confidence rather than with fear and trembling. Taking part in conversations within the family, asking questions, and falling in love with books are important basic components of his exploring process. Other components include:

Mimicry and imitation. This was mentioned already in the previous chapter on two-year-olds, and it becomes more obvious (and potentially more fun, if you're patient) during the preschool years. If you are working in the garden, he'll want to dig and rake along with you. If you're sorting laundry, he may be surprisingly good at finding the matching socks. If you're painting or pounding nails, guess who will want his own brush or hammer. If you're setting the table, he is quite capable of learning what goes where and eventually can carry out this everyday task on his own.

Try not to look at his efforts to participate as a hassle that will bog you down. Rather, see them as giving you an opportunity to chat with him during everyday activities and giving him practice in some basic skills in the process. Not only does he need your praise and affirmation for wanting to help, but it is healthy for him to experience the act of serving someone else, even if his attention span is rather short.

Don't forget that imitation can include negative behaviors as well. If you hit your finger with a hammer, guess who will learn some new words if you don't watch how you react. If you use harsh or unkind words when there's a disagreement, guess who is learning a nonproductive way to solve problems. If you slam your fist on the table when you become frustrated, guess who will be scared or do the same thing when he feels the same way.

What may be a little frustrating during this stage of your child's life is that you may hear him mimic the words and tone of voice that you use when you're blowing off steam, yet not see a whole lot of evidence that he is imitating your positive role modeling. Mom and Dad may speak to one another with consistent respect and kindness—a worthy goal, by the way, whether or not children are in the room—yet hear a blistering exchange between brother and sister over a toy that each wants. *Where did that come from?* you might wonder.

Before you become discouraged, keep two facts in mind. First, your child really *is* taking in the flavor of your habits and conversations at home. They form the foundation of his expectations and assumptions about life: what he is used to, what he considers normal, what he will carry with him throughout his life (including the family he starts himself in another twenty or thirty years). Believe it or not, your attitudes are being caught.

Second, a healthy and wholesome family environment does not override the core of self-centeredness that is present in every human being from birth. The manifestations of willfulness and negativity that you saw in your child as a toddler and a two-year-old probably have been contained by now, but they sprang from deep roots that never completely disappear. Therefore, you need to not only demonstrate virtues but teach them as well, including "lab exercises" when appropriate. Saying please and thank you (and later understanding a depth of meaning in these words), waiting one's turn, and telling the truth need to not only be observed but also talked about and practiced on an ongoing basis.

Role-playing and fantasy. This staple activity of childhood will get into full swing during the preschool years. Whether in your home, at a play group, or among other children in the neighborhood, you can bet the children will play variations on "let's pretend" with great fervor. Your child will undoubtedly try everything from copying domestic roles (the traditional "playing house") to trying out occupations (bus driver, nurse, airline pilot), setting up play situations (store, airport, hospital, church), or assuming the roles of characters (human and otherwise) he has seen in books or videos. Costumes and props will be imagined and constructed from things at hand, although toy manufacturers have been eagerly supplying ready-made accessories for generations.

In general, this is not only normal but healthy. Pretending to be Moses or Cinderella, setting up a store or a ranch on the back patio, and devising their own adventures will exercise language and the imagination far more than staring at a TV screen. Children can learn to plan, solve problems, and cooperate with one another during these projects. For the most part, you can not only encourage these activities but also capture some of them on video for future enjoyment (and a little watery-eyed nostalgia). In fact, your child(ren) will be ecstatic if you occasionally enter into the adventure yourself for a while. If you happen to see a procession of kings and queens in the hallway, you might enjoy serving lunch as a dignified servant, using your hammiest British accent. If your child announces that she is a world-famous doctor, tell her you have a symptom or two and see what she diagnoses.

You can generally allow these make-believe sessions to proceed with a minimum of parental intrusion, but keep your eyes and ears open for a few situations that might need some revision of the script:

- *Inappropriate characters.* While someone may want to play Captain Hook or Goliath to round out the characters in a make-believe story, role-playing options shouldn't include serial killers, vampires, or other relentless evildoers. Suggest more heroic or more neutral characters.

- *Destructive scenarios.* Action and conflict drive many adventures, from knights in armor to Wild West and outer-space fantasies. But if your child's pretend characters do nothing but ninja-kick, wave laser sabers, fire toy guns, and generally inflict make-believe (if not real) damage, you may want to suggest some less violent alternatives. If he is allowed to watch TV, he's probably reenacting some rough (and dumb) stuff from the tube. Do everyone a favor and muzzle the electronic beast (see chapter 11, page 368).

- *Toxic fantasy.* This is a tough call in some cases because fantasy elements of many stories (such as C. S. Lewis's *Chronicles of Narnia*) can serve to convey some very positive values. But role-playing that involves "pretend" occult practices (such as séances or Ouija boards) or elaborate spell casting could whet young appetites for more hazardous practices later on.

- *Hurt feelings.* When the pretending is orchestrated by older children, younger or less popular participants may become stuck with roles no one else wants or receive lots of "make-believe" abuse that starts to feel like the real thing. If you see that someone regularly seems to be getting the short end of the stick, suggest alternative casting as well as caution about the kinds of things that are said, even when pretending.

- *Too much of a good thing.* Preschoolers can become so enthused about pretending to be Superman or Pocahontas that they may not want the game to end, or they may try to use their character to gain power or attention. When your call to get into the tub is met with a resounding refusal ("X-wing pilots don't need baths!"), you'll have to decide whether to have your way by playing along ("Your bath orders come directly from your squadron leader!") or by calling for an intermission.

- *Early adolescence.* Little girls love to play "lady dress up" with old hats, costume jewelry, and gloves. However, if your four-year-old insists on putting on nail polish and frilly dresses for every occasion or becomes overly infatuated with the teenage social life of a popular doll, you might encourage her to broaden her horizons.

Making friends. Unlike the parallel play of younger children—in which "playing together" means playing side by side without actually interacting except to squabble over a mutually favored toy—preschoolers are usually ready for some genuine cooperative play. The concepts of sharing and taking turns can now be understood and usually put into action, but reminders and supervision will still be necessary.

Some children enter a bossy phase during this period, which can make things unpleasant for younger or less assertive children in their vicinity. If your child begins to sound like a miniature dictator, take her aside for a gentle reminder about basic kindness and manners. Also be sure to give her lots of praise when she plays well with other children. Specific information helps: "I like the way you let Megan have the ball so nicely when she asked for it."

Along with the make-believe and role-playing activities, your child will begin enjoying a variety of interactions with other children. These might include simple games, puzzles, and assorted play "projects" such as creating buildings, roads, and unidentified objects with blocks and other construction toys.

Before long, your child will enjoy inviting a friend over for playtime or a meal and will most likely receive a similar invitation in return. You will, of course, already have some idea of the ground rules of the other family, and vice versa, before this "cultural exchange" takes place. Obviously, your child can't live in a glass bubble, but it would be desirable if the basic standards and values you hold dear aren't undermined by playmates at this young age. If she brings home words or attitudes from a friend's house that rub you the wrong way, talk to her about what you find troublesome, and then see if you can influence the other child and her family in a

WHAT TO LOOK FOR IN A PRESCHOOL OR PLAYGROUP

As in any situation in which you leave your child in someone else's care, your primary concern for a potential preschool experience will be that it is safe, beneficial for your child, and basically enjoyable. To improve the likelihood of this happening, consider the following:

- What is the basic outlook/worldview of the school? Do the teachers and administrators share your values, or will what you teach at home be undermined by the day's events at school?
- Do the teachers have special training in working with small children? How long have the teachers been employed there? (A high turnover rate of staff should raise some concerns. If teachers don't stay long, there may be a worrisome reason.)
- How many children will be assigned to each teacher? In general, the smaller the classes or groups are, the better.
- Are the facilities safe and sound? Are staff members trained to handle an emergency? Is there a reasonable level of cleanliness? If the school accepts children who are not toilet trained, are the changing areas adequately separated from other activities, especially food handling?
- Is the school endowed with an adequate supply of toys, games, crafts, and other equipment? Does the day's schedule include free playtime as well as structured activities?

more positive direction. If you can't make any headway with a playmate who is having a negative impact on your child, you may need to direct your child's attention to other children.

Where can you find prospective companions for your preschooler? If your circle of friends or immediate neighborhood doesn't include any families with children the same age, check the ranks of your church. Assuming child care is provided, you might see if she hits it off with someone while you're attending the service.

You may wish to enroll your child in a preschool or other structured playgroup for a specified amount of time each week. While the term *preschooler* is used widely (including in this chapter) as a synonym for three- and four-year-old children, whether your child actually attends preschool is completely up to you. This experience is not a requirement for future academic achievement or necessary for proper social development. If she's ready, she'll enjoy it, and you may find the break in child care a welcome change of pace during the week.

Keeping the faith. Some parents have bought into the idea that their child's spiritual development is such a personal matter that no attempt should be made to influence the direction the child chooses. This is a serious mistake. While your child must ultimately decide on her own whether or not she will begin and nurture a relationship with God, you have not only an opportunity but a responsibility to teach and demonstrate the spiritual principles that are the foundation of your family life (see chapter 14, "Passing the Baton," page 585).

- What is the school's policy regarding children who are ill? Do you notice kids with runny noses and hacking coughs running around with the others? If sick children are not sent home, you might see a dramatic increase in the number of colds and other illnesses your child develops.
- What is the school's approach to discipline? What measures will be taken if your child misbehaves? Do you agree with them?
- Does your child know any of the children in the school? Sometimes a familiar face can make a transition into an unfamiliar environment much easier for your child.
- Does the staff have any problem if you drop in to see how things are going? Do they encourage parents to be involved with the school? Think twice if a school is resistant to parental visits or participation, which should be welcomed. A school and a child's parents should be teammates, not competitors.
- Do you know other families who use the school? Some candid input from graduates of the facility can be very useful when you are deciding whether or not to send your child there.
- Do you sense a real heart for children among the administrators and teachers? Fancy learning programs are far less important at this age than a genuine interest in your child's well-being. ■

So how do you communicate spiritual truths and moral values to a three- or four-year-old? Can she conceive of an infinite God or understand theology or sit through a religious service? Both Old and New Testaments address this quite plainly:

> Hear, O Israel: The Lord our God, the Lord is one. Love the Lord your God with all your heart and with all your soul and with all your strength. These commandments that I give you today are to be upon your hearts. Impress them on your children. Talk about them when you sit at home and when you walk along the road, when you lie down and when you get up. Tie them as symbols on your hands and bind them on your foreheads. Write them on the doorframes of your houses and on your gates. *(Deuteronomy 6:4-9)*

> Jesus called the children to him and said, "Let the little children come to me, and do not hinder them, for the kingdom of God belongs to such as these. I tell you the truth, anyone who will not receive the kingdom of God like a little child will never enter it." *(Luke 18:16-17)*

First, we are to talk to our children about God as we go about our daily business. As important as regular observances can and should be, spiritual matters shouldn't be confined to a specified religious time slot once a week. Conversations about God should be as routine and natural as those about any other subject. Our children should see us

WHAT ABOUT SANTA?

The minute Halloween is over, a certain jolly face and rotund red form begins to appear everywhere as the cultural (and highly commercial) symbol of yuletide cheer. For many families, he is the subject of long-standing and cherished traditions, while others find it unsettling or even offensive that stories of his supersonic Christmas Eve visitations seem to overshadow the celebration of Jesus' birth. Whatever opinion you might hold, there's virtually no escaping him or the inevitable question that arises in homes with young children: What do we tell the kids about Santa?

Some parents go to great lengths to convince the kids that St. Nick is the real deal and that he will reward good behavior abundantly on December 25. But what happens after the inevitable revelation that Mom and Dad were advancing a hoax, perhaps an elaborate one at that? When it comes time to teach about the life of the One who walked on water—including the wondrous and miraculous events surrounding his birth—why should little ones believe those stories any more than the tales of the flying reindeer? On the other hand, is it necessary to debunk Santa and the gang from the get-go? What's wrong with a little innocent fun at the end of the year?

Here's an illustration that might help with this dilemma: When you take a toddler or preschooler to a theme park, what usually happens when a familiar character pops into view? "Look, Ella, there's Mickey!" Ella says hello, gives Mickey a hug, and poses for a picture. It's all part of the day's fun and creates some sweet memories. You probably don't feel the need to conclude the visit with a disclaimer:

pray about the issues of our lives, give thanks for our food (and everything else), and acknowledge God's leadership in our decisions. In dealing with more formal teaching or family devotions, simple stories will communicate volumes to preschoolers. The Scriptures are filled with them, and Jesus often told stories to get His point across.

Second, small children appear uniquely qualified to understand intimacy with God in ways that may elude them later in life. Perhaps it is their utter trust in their earthly parents (which can be expanded to include a heavenly Father) or their lack of cynicism or their openness or their uninhibited joy and enthusiasm for the objects of their love that draw them to the God they cannot see. Whatever else parents and the other adults who care for children do, they must not hinder children from trusting in God, which seems to come naturally to them.

One important job for parents who care about the spiritual lives of their preschoolers is to help them distinguish not only right from wrong but truth from fantasy. This means that you will have to make some careful decisions about dealing with a few popular traditions in our culture. The crux of the matter is this: If your child is going to take you seriously when you talk about the God who made heaven and earth, you don't have the luxury of deliberately bending the truth (or tying it in knots) in other matters. Whatever else you do, never mislead your child when she asks you point-blank for the facts about mythical personalities or anything else.

On a day-to-day basis, you will also have a responsibility to help your preschooler understand the difference between truth and make-believe in her own life. At an age

"Now, Ella, you need to understand that that really wasn't Mickey, but rather a well-trained young adult in an elaborate costume who is being paid an hourly wage to meet and greet visitors." On the other hand, you might need to offer a little explanation if she becomes obsessed with the idea that it really *was* Mickey that she met and that he is going to come to her birthday party next week because she asked him and he didn't say no. Furthermore, you wouldn't want to announce that Mickey is bringing all the gifts to her party, that he knows what she's doing every minute of the day, and that pleasing him is the primary reason why she should mind Mom and Dad.

You get the point. It's possible to have some fun with the idea of Santa without going to the extremes of becoming a sour Scrooge or promoting the bogus doctrine that "He sees you when you're sleeping, he knows when you're awake." If your child is excited about saying hello to Santa in the mall and the line's not too long, you can both enjoy the visit and perhaps even bring home a photo as a souvenir. But be careful about making St. Nick the center of gravity at Christmas by avoiding such things as:

- Giving him credit for all of the gifts under the tree
- Giving him the responsibility for your children's moral training (including threats of Santa being a no-show if they don't behave)
- Lying to your child when she specifically asks whether Santa is real or make-believe
- Focusing so much on the North Pole crew that the baby in the manger becomes an afterthought ∎

when there is so much to learn about the world and so much imagination at work in your child's head, the boundaries between reality and fantasy will wear thin at times. If you hear a breathless report that there are giant spiders crawling around her room, and it appears that her main interest is in gathering attention or reassurance, explain what can go wrong if she makes up alarming stories. A brief recounting of the fate of the boy who cried wolf may be in order.

If she tells a whopper of a tale to explain why her dollhouse is now caved in on one side ("A big gorilla climbed through my window and jumped on it!"), you will need to coax the truth out with some finesse. In particular, she must understand that telling a lie to escape punishment is far more of a concern than the actual misdeed itself. The first offense in this area should be treated more with explanation than with punishment, but repeated episodes will require specific and meaningful consequences. Otherwise a habit of lying will eventually undermine every relationship in her life.

You cannot afford to demonstrate any "white lies" of your own. If your child hears you say, "Tell him I'm not here" when an obnoxious caller is on the phone, for example, whatever you are trying to teach about truth and lies will be wasted breath.

This is an appropriate time to present your child with her own Bible (age appropriate and containing lots of pictures), which can provide a rich source of input and topics for conversation. Tell her stories of Old and New Testament heroes, and above all, talk about the life and deeds of Jesus again and again. Should your preschooler memorize Scripture? Some are able to commit Bible verses to memory quite easily before their fifth birthday, and for these children the words will be "hidden in their hearts" for the rest of their lives. For others, attempts to memorize are like pulling teeth, and if you force the issue, you may create a distaste for Scripture rivaling that for their least favorite foods.

A more effective way to hide the Word in a child's heart when she doesn't memorize easily is to use songs. Many tapes, CDs, and videos communicate spiritual principles and Scripture verses to children (and their parents) through music. The best of these not only teach and entertain but leave both parent and child humming uplifting tunes—sometimes for years to come. Few investments pay such rich dividends.

Ages Five through Eleven:
Life Lessons

Check the books lining the shelves of the child-care section of the library and you'll see a crateload of titles dealing with birth and infancy and nearly as many devoted to toddlers and preschoolers. Just down the aisle you'll find another impressive collection dealing with teenagers. What happened to those in-between years? You might ask the same questions of this book. It took us ten chapters to arrive at the fifth birthday, but after this chapter we move on to a lengthy discussion about adolescence. Doesn't anything happen between preschool and junior high?

Actually, plenty is going on: physical growth, maturing emotions, the acquisition of a host of intellectual and physical skills, the shaping of moral values, and, yes, the gradual approach to that eventful transition to adulthood known as adolescence. All of these changes are important and need plenty of parental guidance, prayer, and input. This is not time for Mom and Dad to put their parenting skills on autopilot as their child cruises through the elementary grades. Indeed, the attention you give your child during these years may significantly reduce the stress and difficulties of adolescence.

Many themes recur without major variations between the ages of five and eleven. Relationships with family and friends, and school, sports, and other group activities dominate the landscape. Parents usually don't feel they are climbing as steep and slippery a learning curve, or breathlessly wonder what's coming around the next bend, as they do during a child's infancy and teen years. The child's emotional weather tends to be calmer. The tides of toddler rebellion subside somewhat, and truces are usually forged in any conflict between the generations.

There are, of course, exceptions. You may feel that the first five years were wonderful but that you have now entered a time of turmoil. Perhaps you have been dealing with a strong-willed child whose "terrible twos" have persisted and developed into "fighting fives" or "struggling sixes." Even if your child's grade-school years prove to be smooth sailing, you will probably encounter some turbulence before your parenting assignment is over.

But these years should be deeply gratifying, a time to enhance and deepen your relationship with your son or daughter—who will not remain a child for long. While you may have thought you would never see your child graduate from infancy and toddlerhood, the grade-school years pass with incredible speed. Keep your eyes, ears, and heart open so you don't arrive at your child's high school graduation wondering where these years went.

Growth and Development

Changes in size and shape occur at a predictable rate from year to year for most children between the ages of five and eleven. And yes, growth really does take place in spurts rather than in a slow and steady climb. Both boys and girls typically gain two inches (5 cm) in height and six to seven pounds (2.7 to 3.2 kg) each year. This may vary, of course. Your child's doctor will continue to mark her progress on a growth chart to confirm that she is maintaining appropriate rates of growth and weight gain from year to year. As mentioned in previous chapters, you can get a rough idea of your child's eventual adult height from the growth curve on her medical chart.

One development that might catch you off guard during this period is the beginning of **puberty**. You might not suspect that your fifth grader is poised at the dawn of her reproductive years, but the first event of this process for girls—the appearance of breast buds—occurs, on average, at age ten. This could happen as early as age eight, or it may wait until thirteen. The first menstrual period, which signals that the intricate hormonal interplay between central nervous system, ovaries, and uterus has completed its first cycle, typically takes place about two years after the appearance of breast buds. In boys, the onset of puberty occurs, on average, a year later than in girls.

The stages of this remarkable process will be reviewed in detail in chapter 12 (see pages 442–444). You might want to look over that information now if your child is approaching the age at which pubertal changes might begin. Ideally, you will not only be prepared to answer questions about these important events when they occur but will anticipate their arrival so they and many other concerns can be discussed ahead of time. Some suggestions for preparing your child for adolescence will be discussed later in this chapter.

Sometimes the timing of birth dates and growth spurts will place children of noticeably different sizes in the same grade-school classroom. Children can become quite self-conscious if they are the tallest or shortest among their peers. They can also be incredibly unkind to one another over differences in body size or shape. If your child is clearly at the extreme for his age in either height or weight, keep track of his emotional well-being as well as his growth chart while he progresses through school. If he is accumulating a collection of unflattering nicknames ("Moose," "Shrimp," "Beanpole") you should definitely intervene, because the impact of this verbal assault on his emotions and spirit can be profound. The overweight child is particularly vulnerable to scorn and rejection. Likewise, you must not allow any nicknames for your child that have remotely negative connotations to take root in your family. What you or his siblings might consider playful and harmless fun could painfully chip away at his sense of worth for months on end and shape his image of himself for years to come.

Your response to any significant variations from average height or weight will depend on the particular problem. Discussions with a doctor, dietitian, teacher, and even school principal may be in order, along with evaluations of home structure, hormonal status, food intake, and progress in school, if appropriate. For example, a short child, especially a boy, without a treatable medical problem may do better if he delays starting school for a year so he is on more even terms (height-wise) with his classmates. But if height really doesn't bother him and he is on equal terms emotionally and intellectually with the taller classmates, it might cause more harm to hold him back. If being grouped with younger students were to stigmatize him as "slow" or "dumb," the impact could be more negative than being shorter than everyone else. As you consider various options, be sure to bring your child into the decision-making process.

An obviously overweight child may need ongoing supervision of food choices and specific measures to increase his physical activity. If your child is overweight, or if his health-care provider raises a concern that his weight is excessive for his height, you will need to address this issue with both tact and diligence. Consultation with a qualified dietitian is definitely advisable because weight loss in children isn't a simple matter of "just eat less." Food choices must take into account ongoing growth, the child's likes and dislikes, family eating patterns, and long-term planning. At times parent and child may have different ideas about what an ideal weight should be, or a preadolescent may be so worried about body image as to be at risk for an eating disorder in the near future. If there are emotional undercurrents and unrealistic expectations relating to food and appearance, a dietitian can serve as a professional source of reliable information, as well as a neutral party to help sort out any disagreements within the family. Once a dietary course is set, a child may need some ongoing supervision of food choices and perhaps encouragement toward appropriate physical activity.

Classmates may need some exhortation, either as a group or individually, regarding the way they treat others who are different. If you learn that your child has been making cutting comments about another child's appearance, seize the opportunity for friendly but firm discussion about the importance of respect for others' feelings. Above all, your child will need ongoing reassurance that you are on his team, that you care about his problem, and that you will be a steadfast ally while it is being solved. (Three Special Concerns sections address these issues in more detail: "The Overweight Child and Teenager," page 387; "Eating Disorders," page 401; and "Bullying: Neither Right nor a Rite of Passage," page 501.)

Food and Nutrition

Despite the significant change in your child's body size and weight in the coming years, your role in fueling that growth will be remarkably similar to what it was during the past few years: providing a variety of wholesome foods from the major food groups. Your child's job will be to decide how much of it to eat. Keep in mind that appetites will vary greatly from meal to meal and day to day. Your best overall check of adequate intake will be tracking your child's weight over time.

Your biggest nutritional challenge during these years will be to stem the cultural tide of fast foods, soft drinks, candy bars, and salty snacks that compete with better-quality foods. As she grows older and more independent, your child may have more access to junk foods through contact with friends, increased mobility on her bicycle, and some allowance money burning a hole in her pocket. And at this age she is still likely to be influenced by clever advertisements designed to mold her nutritional preferences.

Your other major difficulty will be in fostering regularity of eating habits. If your child has an early school bus to catch, breakfast may be lost in a blur as she runs out the door. If you don't make her lunch, she may choose cafeteria food based more on taste preference than nutritional content. If she has all kinds of activities after school and you have a full agenda as well, dinner may be a survival-of-the-fittest exercise, with the refrigerator serving as the hunting ground. Even with complex activity schedules, for the sake of communication and cohesiveness it's still beneficial to gather the family for a meal together at least two or three times per week, if not more often. Whether you are a whiz in the kitchen or prefer to occupy it as little as possible, plan on plugging away at the following during the next several years:

Don't skip breakfast. She doesn't need a three-egg omelet and a rose on the table, but she does need some reasonable fuel to start the day. Cereal, toast, and juice can be prepared with a minimum of fuss and will launch the day properly.

If you don't pack her lunch, find out what's on the menu at the school cafeteria and guide her choices. If you make her lunch, get her involved in the process and make sure she's eating it. Kids are notorious for swapping or ignoring foods they don't really want, so why waste your money and time on things she won't consume?

Continue leading the charge for less fat, more whole grains, less sugar, more fruits and vegetables, and less salt in your family's everyday food choices. (For more information on this topic, see "Some ABCs of Good Nutrition," beginning on page 771.)

Check with your child's doctor about vitamin supplements. Truly picky and erratic eaters may need them, but most children in this age-group do not.

Make sure your child receives two to three servings of calcium-rich foods daily.

DOES YOUR CHILD NEED A TB TEST?

A century ago, one in five people in the United States had active tuberculosis (TB), which was the leading cause of death at that time.[1] By the mid-1950s, the rate of new cases of TB had dropped 75 percent, but for the next few decades, infants and children were routinely tested to detect exposure to the bacteria that causes this condition. The reason: If TB is treated while in a latent state, progression to active and more damaging (or lethal) disease is much less likely. However, active TB in children has become increasingly rare. In 2004, only 961 children under the age of fourteen were diagnosed with this disease in the United States, and this represented a 40 percent drop from the number diagnosed in 1993.[2] As a result, when children in low-risk populations are tested for TB, more than half who have positive tests will in fact be uninfected—in what is called a **false positive** test—and as a result, may be given unnecessary treatment.

Most experts now recommend a **targeted** approach, selectively screening children who are at higher risk of exposure to TB. These risk factors include (but aren't limited to):

- Contact with another person who has confirmed or suspected tuberculosis.
- Immigration from or recent travel within areas where there is a high prevalence of tuberculosis. These areas include Asia, Africa, Latin America and the Caribbean, the Middle East, the former Soviet Union, and Eastern

Medical Checkups and Immunizations

Your child's checkups at ages three and four were probably uneventful, at least from the child's perspective. At five, however, school is on the horizon, and specific screening and immunization updates are due. Find out about local school entrance requirements and your health-care provider's routine for this exam, because a little preparation may soften some of the "sticker shock." You don't have to go into the gory details, but you might mention that this is a special visit and that the doctor is going to make sure that your child is ready for school.

Aside from the normal height, weight, vision, and hearing screening, and a head-to-toe exam, what else may happen?

- A **urinalysis**. A number of problems can be detected by an evaluation of urine, so make sure your child doesn't urinate just prior to the visit.
- A **blood test** (usually by finger stick) to check for anemia.
- A number of **immunizations**, including diphtheria/tetanus/pertussis (DTaP), polio, varicella, and measles/mumps/rubella (MMR) updates, and possibly others as well. (See "Immunizations—Which Ones, Why, and When?" beginning on page 739 for detailed information about these and other vaccinations.)
- A **skin test for tuberculosis**. This may be given if required by the school or if your child is (or has been) at risk for exposure to this infection. (See sidebar "Does Your Child Need a TB Test?") The test may have been done at a previous checkup, but if so, your child may not remember it. The small prick on the forearm must be checked by the doctor if a firm bump develops at the site of the injection after

Europe. (Low-risk areas include Western Europe, Canada, Australia, and New Zealand.)
- Living in a household with an individual who has a positive TB skin test or has recently emigrated from a high-prevalence area. (The individual with the positive skin test isn't necessarily a source of infection for the child, but this situation may indicate that the child is at risk of exposure from another source.)[3]

Even if your child doesn't have one or more of these risk factors for exposure to TB, his school may require a skin test for entry. In addition, other local concerns (such as an outbreak of TB in or near your community) might result in recommendations for routine screening.

The test (known as the Mantoux test) involves a small prick of the forearm skin and the injection of a tiny amount of material that will be recognized by his immune system if he has had contact with the bacteria that cause TB. *The test is not dangerous and cannot cause tuberculosis.* A positive reaction involves a small area of both redness and increased thickening of the skin (known as **induration**) that develops over two or three days. This may result in further testing (such as a chest X-ray) and other measures. Remember that a local reaction may represent a false positive response, and a careful evaluation of the entire situation (including your child's risk for exposure to tuberculosis) by your child's physician or an infectious-disease specialist will be in order if this occurs. ■

forty-eight to seventy-two hours. A local reaction may indicate that your child has had contact with the bacteria that cause tuberculosis, although he may not have an active infection. Further testing will usually be necessary.

Many five-year-olds have heard unpleasant things about shots, so plan on meeting some resistance when the moment arrives. Don't be tempted to pass on this part of the visit because you don't want to cause him pain (or perhaps because you're dreading the loud protests and vigorous resistance that occurred last time). While waving off the immunizations might feel like a compassionate decision if you assume that he isn't likely to be exposed to any of these infections, think again.

First, your local school district will require that immunizations be current. More important, just because he has reached this age without having contracted any of these illnesses doesn't mean he is out of the woods. Measles epidemics still break out from time to time and can cause serious complications. The bacteria that cause tetanus most likely reside in the soil outside your back door. And whooping cough (pertussis, the *P* in DTaP), while not nearly as risky at age five as during infancy, can produce an extremely annoying and persistent cough. For these and many other infections, an ounce of vaccine prevention is worth far more than several pounds of misery and expensive treatment.

Let your child know that the shot will help him stay well, that you know it will hurt and may even ache for a day or two afterward, and that he can say ouch and even cry—as long as he holds still. If he can't or won't, you may have to take charge and hold him (or at least his arm) steady for the person giving the injection. Stay calm but firm. If you look apprehensive, upset, or guilty, the procedure will be much harder for everyone. When the visit is over and if he has been reasonably cooperative, you may want to do something that he enjoys to honor the occasion.

After your child reaches age five, his physician will want to see him for routine checkups annually or every other year, depending on a variety of considerations. *Quick exams for camp or sports, especially those done assembly-line style on large groups of children, should not substitute for more comprehensive physicals by your regular health-care provider.* His vision will be screened as part of some or all of these checkups, and if there is any concern, a visit to an ophthalmologist may be recommended. A formal eye exam would be wise if your child is squinting, complaining of blurry vision, having difficulty seeing the chalkboard at school, or bringing objects close to his face in order to see them (see "eye care and concerns" in Reference Section, page 660). Dental checkups should be carried out at least every twelve months or as recommended by your child's dentist.

In addition to the immunizations that are commonly given at age five, several others may be recommended at various times during the grade-school years. These may include vaccines against:

- **Meningococcus**, a type of bacteria that can cause a fast-moving and often fatal infection (frequently including an intense form of **meningitis**, or inflammation of the tissue that covers the brain and spinal canal). For years, an immunization to protect against meningococcus was advised for college freshmen living in dormitories and for military recruits, but now it is recommended that all children receive this vaccine as part of their eleven- or twelve-year checkup. (Teenagers can and should receive this vaccine if they have not yet been immunized.)
- **Hepatitis A and B.** If your child has not been immunized against either of these viruses that cause inflammation of the liver, ask your doctor about starting the two-dose series for A or three-dose series for B. The hepatitis B vaccine for all

infants has been advised for many years, whereas routine hepatitis A vaccination at age one or later is a more recent recommendation.

Because hepatitis A is transmitted through contaminated food and water, vaccination is especially important for both children and adults if your family travels extensively, especially to rural or impoverished areas of foreign countries.

- **Chickenpox (varicella).** If your child has never had chickenpox or the vaccine, two doses, at least three months apart, will prevent the disease or reduce its severity if it should occur. Remember, chickenpox tends to be more severe, and at times dangerous, in teenagers or adults.
- **Influenza.** This virus makes an annual appearance in most communities during the winter, provoking fever, aches, and coughing that are often more intense than a garden-variety upper respiratory infection. While most children recover from influenza after a few days of rest, fluids, and acetaminophen or ibuprofen, those with significant medical problems such as heart disease, diabetes, chronic respiratory disturbances (especially asthma), sickle cell disease, and HIV infection may suffer severe complications.

  These children normally are given the influenza vaccine each year in the fall. Because new strains of this virus appear annually, a new vaccine must be prepared every year (see "influenza" in Reference Section, page 689).
- **Human papillomavirus (HPV).** HPV is the most common sexually transmitted infection in the United States, with some 20 million Americans infected. Most of these infections do not cause symptoms, and they clear without medical treatment. However, some who are infected develop growths known as **genital warts**.

  Of greater concern is the association of certain strains of HPV—typically *not* those that cause genital warts—with cancer of the cervix (the opening of the uterus), vulva (the external female genital area), anus, and penis. Cancer of the cervix is diagnosed in more than ten thousand women, and kills more than thirty-five hundred, in the United States every year.

  A vaccine that can help prevent infection with the types of HPV most commonly associated with cancer is now available and targeted for eleven- to twelve-year-old girls. (It may be given as early as age nine.) While the thought of giving a school-age child a vaccine to protect against a sexually transmitted virus might be unsettling to parents, there are a number of good reasons to consider doing so. We will discuss these and look at more detailed information about all of the immunizations listed in this segment in "Immunizations—Which Ones, Why, and When?" beginning on page 739.

Common Symptoms and Health Concerns

Not all of your child's medical visits will be for routine checkups. Certain common problems, both acute and chronic, are worth mentioning briefly. (Most of these are reviewed in detail in the Reference Section of this book.)

- **Headaches.** A little effort may be needed to separate the annoying but harmless ones from those that need medical attention.
  - (a) Tension-type headaches, the most frequent in children and adults, have a typical pattern of pain across the forehead, often accompanied by a feeling of tightness around the head and/or neck like a rubber band. These may be a

physical response to hunger, stress, worry, or even mild dehydration (as might occur after playing hard on a hot day) and usually respond to simple treatment: acetaminophen, a snack if the child is hungry, a brief rest in a quiet environment, perhaps some fluids and a cool washcloth across the forehead.

(b) Migraine headaches typically involve more severe, throbbing pain on one or both sides of the head and are often accompanied by nausea and vomiting. A migraine in children often improves dramatically after throwing up. Many children are able to tell when a headache is about to begin, and a prompt dose of a nonprescription pain reliever may stop or relieve it. (Check with your child's physician.)

(c) Headaches caused by colds and sinus infections are usually accompanied by a runny nose, congestion, and pressure in the face. Decongestants may help relieve this discomfort, and your child's doctor may prescribe antibiotics if a sinus infection appears likely.

(d) Headaches frequently accompany any illness that generates a fever, such as a sore throat, upper-respiratory infection, or chickenpox. The headache will typically wax and wane with the temperature. If the pain is severe and relentless, and especially if it is accompanied by a stiff neck or change in behavior such as confusion or marked drowsiness, a medical evaluation should be carried out immediately to rule out a more serious infection such as meningitis.

- **Colds, ear infections, and other upper-respiratory infections** will typically occur less frequently now, but they will be easier to diagnose and treat because your school-age child is better able to describe his symptoms.

(a) More than one hundred types of viruses can cause **colds**, with the characteristic runny nose, scratchy throat, and hacking cough. Rest, fluids, a cold-mist humidifier, and seven to ten days (or less) for the immune system to banish the invaders are usually all the treatment needed. Over-the-counter remedies may—or may not—ease some of these symptoms for a few hours. Despite decades of availability without prescription, the effectiveness and safety of these concoctions in children has not been fully evaluated, and professional organizations generally discourage their use. Nevertheless, if one of them helps your child feel better, you may use it as needed in the appropriate dose. (Common ingredients found in these medications are listed in "colds" in Reference Section, page 643.)

Acetaminophen or ibuprofen can help reduce aches, pains, and fever. Remember that the reason for reducing your child's fever is comfort, not medical necessity, except in rare circumstances (see Special Concerns "When Your Child Has a Fever," page 241). Antibiotics are useless in treating a cold, but your child's physician may prescribe them if bacteria complicate the picture. Signs that bacteria could be part of the problem include symptoms persisting ten to fourteen days or longer, the appearance of discolored (yellow or green) drainage from the nose or phlegm from the chest for more than a few days, or fever that begins or worsens after several days of illness.

(b) **Ear infections** occur less often because bacteria must travel a longer distance through the eustachian tubes now than when your child was an infant and toddler. An infection can cause persistent and sometimes severe pain and may—or may not—be treated with antibiotics, depending on the specifics of the illness, the physical exam, and the clinical judgment of the physician. Because fluid can accumulate in the middle-ear space during and after an infection, a follow-up visit to check both the ear and hearing may be recommended. Intense, continuous ear pain may also be caused by an infection in the outer ear canal or even by inflammation in the throat. Any ongoing ear pain should be checked as soon as possible.

During a cold, your child may complain of intermittent ear pain that may disappear when she swallows or yawns. She probably has a congested eustachian tube. Time and possibly decongestants should resolve the problem, but the ear(s) should be checked by your doctor if the pain is severe, if fever is present, or if there is any hearing loss or drainage from the ear. Occasionally, irritation of the joint where the jawbone connects with the skull produces what seems to be an earache. A medical checkup will be necessary to determine what is wrong.

(c) **Sore throats** are generally caused by viruses, although postnasal drainage down the throat during a cold can provoke discomfort. In a limited number of sore throats, the culprit is a type of bacteria known as **group A streptococci** that can generate an illness commonly known as "strep throat." If your child's throat is sore, inflamed, and accompanied by fever and headache, the doctor may do a strep test and/or a throat culture. If the test is positive, antibiotics will be necessary.

If your child is prone to **allergies** and/or **asthma**, you will probably know it well before she reaches her fifth birthday. Nevertheless, some children who have had little trouble with the nose or chest may start to sniff, sneeze, or cough on an ongoing basis, raising concerns that "He's sick all the time" or "She's had a cold for two months." These symptoms are often caused by newly developed allergies. Reactive airways that twitch and spasm sometimes provoke frequent coughing or overt wheezing, especially after exercise. Because allergies are often provoked by specific environmental factors (for example, house dust and mold), they can often be treated more effectively after you and your physician or an allergist have done some detective work. If symptoms are frequent or continuous, it's a good idea to seek medical assistance for managing allergies rather than relying strictly on over-the-counter antihistamines or decongestant-antihistamine combinations. Helpful approaches for dealing with allergies are discussed in "allergies in children" in Reference Section, page 612.

- **Abdominal pains** (stomachaches) will be felt occasionally by nearly every child, but in some they are a more frequent complaint (see sidebar on page 352). Sorting out the source of abdominal discomfort, whether a new event or an ongoing problem, will require some investigation at home and possibly in the doctor's office. For more information about common patterns of pain in this area and their possible causes, also see "abdominal pain" in Reference Section, page 605.

- **Orthopaedic (bone and joint) problems** are common in school-age children. As kids in this age-group develop greater body weight and stronger muscles and then throw themselves enthusiastically into neighborhood games or organized sports, opportunities to sustain sprains, strains, or fractures increase dramatically. Depending upon your child's enthusiasm for rough-and-tumble play, you may become well acquainted with a local orthopaedist during these years. Safety precautions for outdoor activities will follow later in this chapter (also see "Safety: Outdoors" in the Emergency section, page 848).

Another orthopaedic concern is pain in an arm or leg, the pelvis, back, or some other area of bone or muscle for no apparent reason. In general, bone/muscle/joint discomforts that need medical attention include:

- Pain that persists in one specific area for more than a day or two
- Pain that is intense enough to interfere with normal activities
- Pain associated with local redness, swelling, tenderness, or inability to move a joint through its normal range of motion
- Limping or refusal to walk or run because of pain
- Fever, nausea, rash, or other generalized symptoms associated with any of the above

THE RIDDLE OF RECURRENT ABDOMINAL PAIN

"My stomach hurts . . ."

Most parents cringe when they hear this complaint—especially when they've heard it before, usually on a school morning when the car pool is a block away. Is this pain real, or is it a ploy to stay home from school? Does it require a trip to the emergency room, the doctor's office, or simply back to bed? If you let your child stay home, are you being manipulated? What if you make her go to school and something is really wrong?

Recurrent abdominal pain is a common and vexing problem among school-age children. The good news is that the vast majority of these episodes are not caused by diseases such as infection, cancer, inflammation, or structural abnormalities that need to be repaired. The bad news is that the most common form of recurring discomfort, known as **functional abdominal pain**, is very real and can be quite disruptive to a child and her family. Current research suggests that functional abdominal pain arises from abnormalities in the communication between the central nervous system and the **enteric nervous system** (or **ENS**, also called the "gut brain" or the "little brain in the gut"), a complex network of nerves supplying the entire digestive tract. One explanation is that children with this problem may have an increased sensitivity to pain within the bowel—so sensitive in fact that normal changes in pressure within the bowel may be perceived as uncomfortable. Whether this arises from a malfunction within the enteric nervous system, the central nervous system, or both—or even a complex interaction between the two—is uncertain.

Functional abdominal pain may be sharp or dull, high or low in the abdomen, widely spread or somewhat localized. After one to three hours, the pain typically disappears. Various subtypes have been defined based on location and pattern. When functional pain is felt primarily in the upper abdomen, it is called **functional dyspepsia**. When associated with alterations in bowel movements (looser, more constipated, or a combination of these), it is known as **irritable bowel syndrome**. The term **abdominal migraine** refers to paroxysms of pain associated with nausea, vomiting, and paleness, especially when there is a family history of migraine headaches.[4]

While these episodes may interfere with a variety of daytime activities, they rarely

The last three items above should be evaluated as soon as possible to avoid serious complications such as destruction of a joint or uncontrolled infection. These symptoms could indicate that serious trouble is brewing, including inflammation or infection of a bone or joint, an unsuspected fracture, or even a destructive process including the very rare instance of a tumor involving a bone or soft tissue.

It's not uncommon for children in this age-group to mention occasionally that a leg or some other area hurts. If none of the above red flags are present, a wait-and-see approach is reasonable. Usually the pain will calm down on its own within a short time and be forgotten. Some particularly vigorous play, for example, can cause overuse injuries such as a minor muscle strain or irritation where a muscle attaches to bone (**tendonitis**). Temporary aching in one or both legs late in the day or during the night awaken the child from sleep. Very often there appears to be no obvious relationship to food or time of day, and there are no other signs of illness such as fever, weight loss, persistent diarrhea, or blood in the stool. (Indeed, if any of these symptoms are present, the problem cannot be assumed to be functional abdominal pain.)

In many cases, the pains seem to be related to stress, whether of the everyday variety or from more significant events such as harassment by a school-yard bully, uncertainty generated by a stormy parental relationship, or more serious forms of emotional, physical, or sexual abuse. A medical evaluation may need to be accompanied by some sensitive questions about what currently resides within a child's worry zone. While you should not assume that these discomforts are imaginary or manufactured to escape responsibility, judgment will be needed to gauge a child's tolerance to pain in general and the severity of these pains in particular.

If diagnosing functional abdominal pain is a challenge, treatment is an art. Reassurance, passage of time, mild pain relievers, stool softeners, and some troubleshooting of the issues of life should be on the agenda. You should pay particular attention to the impact of school on the pain, and vice versa. Is there a problem with a particular teacher, subject, or classmate? Is harassment occurring on a frequent basis? Has the pain resulted in repeated absences that are in turn provoking more stress about keeping up with schoolwork? Some patient, gentle, but persistent questioning may be needed, especially if your child seems evasive or reluctant to discuss certain topics.

If recurring episodes of abdominal pain are particularly disruptive, and especially if there is uncertainty about the diagnosis, your child's physician might recommend an evaluation by a specialist. Remember that your child will need more immediate medical evaluation if an episode of abdominal pain

- is severe and sudden;
- doesn't let up after a few hours;
- is accompanied by repeated episodes of vomiting and/or diarrhea;
- is associated with fever over 100.4°F (38°C);
- is accompanied by other symptoms such as headache or listlessness;
- begins in or shifts to the upper or lower right side of the abdomen; or
- is associated with blood in the stool. ■

has traditionally been called **growing pains**, although the cause is uncertain. No specific treatment is needed other than your TLC, perhaps accompanied by gentle massage, heat, stretching, and acetaminophen or ibuprofen.

Physical Fitness and Sports

Your child may have seemed like a perpetual-motion machine during his toddler and preschool years, and perhaps you looked forward to when he would slow down a little. Now you may be facing a very different problem. As a child grows and his attention span increases, so does the lure of activities in which minds are engaged but bodies sit still. TV, video games, and computers can captivate children even before they set foot in preschool, and for many the grip of those electronic devices never loosens. Add to that the demands of school attendance, studying, and homework, not to mention time spent in conversations with friends (whether face-to-face or via phone, cell, or computer), and far too many of our youngest citizens exit childhood and adolescence overweight and underactive. Unfortunately, any bad habits forged in your home over the years (beginning in preschool) are likely to continue well into adulthood.

How can you launch your children into a healthy trajectory for this important aspect of their lives? Basically in the same ways you promote any value that you care about: by modeling it yourself, by doing it with them, and by encouraging them to do it on their own.

Children love daily routine activities of the simplest kind. You can turn the routine chores of living into times of warmth and closeness if you give a little thought to them.

Dr. Dobson Answers
Your Questions about
Raising Children

1. Modeling physical activity. You may be convinced that your offspring are hard of hearing when it comes to heeding your advice. But children and teenagers actually care a great deal about consistency and integrity, and they will rarely take to heart any input from you that implies "Do as I say, not as I do." Throughout this book you will frequently encounter a warning to be careful how you behave, because your sons and daughters are likely to imitate it. (Children who see their parents smoking, for example, will be more inclined to try tobacco products—and other harmful chemicals—than those who do not.)

You can't keep your body in shape by exercising once a month. Maintaining physical fitness requires a routine and a measure of self-discipline, and hopefully your children will have the opportunity to see you doing what needs to be done, in season and out of season. Should you decide to buy fitness equipment to use at home—a treadmill or a set of free weights, for example—not only will you have the flexibility to exercise at times that suit you, but your children will also be more likely to see you in action. Indeed, when they are old enough to use such equipment safely, you can let them try it as well. But by all means don't let your investment gather dust for weeks on end in your bedroom or the garage. Doing so will waste not only your money but also untold numbers of teachable moments.

You can increase your amount of physical activity in many ways other than participating in designated exercise sessions. If you get in the habit of doing a number of these, not only will you burn extra calories and improve your muscle tone, but you will also set an example for other family members to follow. Some possibilities:

- Take the stairs instead of the elevator or escalator.

- Don't search for that hotly contested parking space near the entrance to the mall. Deliberately park some distance away (where there are plenty of spaces) and walk.
- If you have to run an errand that isn't too far away, walk or ride a bike. If possible, have one or more of your kids join you.
- Do your own yard work (or at least some of it), and involve your kids in these tasks as much as possible.
- When socializing with other families, consider options beyond merely talking and eating. Try walking or hiking together, or playing recreational sports such as tennis.
- If you're going to limit the amount of time your kids spend staring at the television, playing video games, or using the computer for recreation—definitely a wise idea, as we will discuss shortly—you should impose similar limits on yourself.

SHOULD KIDS STRENGTH TRAIN?

Nearly all advisories about physical fitness in children and adolescents—including the ones in this book—emphasize aerobic exercise such as walking, running, or cycling. While the idea of children pumping iron may seem a little odd, organizations such as the American College of Sports Medicine and the American Academy of Pediatrics have suggested that strength training can make a worthwhile contribution to overall fitness in a child or adolescent, with the following provisions:

- Children who are old enough to participate in organized sports programs can also potentially participate in strength training, assuming that they can follow directions and use appropriate equipment safely. Children should not participate in competitive weight lifting or bodybuilding until they have attained full physical maturity.
- The purpose of strength training should be to improve overall fitness, in conjunction with aerobic exercise. If the goal is to improve performance in a particular sport, practicing and mastering the specific skills for that sport are more likely to be beneficial. A child should not start strength training for the purpose of building muscles like Popeye (he won't), clobbering a neighborhood rival, or satisfying some other need for recognition or superiority.
- As with adult strength training for general fitness, children and adolescents can learn basic exercises for eight to ten muscle groups, doing a set of eight to fifteen repetitions for each group, two or three times per week. They should start with a low resistance and an emphasis on proper technique and safety. Weight is added in small increments only when all eight to fifteen repetitions can be performed without strain and with good technique.
- A medical evaluation should be considered before a child or young adolescent begins a strength-training program. If there is any pain, dizziness, or other symptoms in connection with this (or any other) type of physical activity, a physician should be consulted before the activity is resumed.
- Adult supervision, proper training in the use of equipment, safety precautions, and appropriate expectations are essential. ∎

2. Doing physical activities as a family. Role modeling is great, but you will definitely get more mileage by involving your kids in activities you do together. Not only does everyone reap physical benefits, but also the potential for bonding, communication, and pure fun is virtually unlimited. Young children rarely turn down an opportunity to play a physical game with one or both parents. For older children and adolescents, these activities can play a huge role in establishing their identity as a member of your family. Consider the following:

- As soon as your children are old enough, have them join you when you walk or jog. Little ones can be pushed in a stroller or carriage. (Some models are specifically geared for greater distances and speed.) Older children who can't keep up with your walking or jogging pace can tag along on a scooter or bicycle.
- Let your children try recreational sports they can enjoy throughout the rest of their lives. Nearly every child enjoys learning to play catch. Tennis, golf, and skiing (both downhill and cross-country) can be enjoyable family pastimes if you have the resources to participate in them. Backyard games—badminton, volleyball, and even informal softball tournaments (using toy balls and plastic bats that can't cause any damage or injury)—can introduce children to sports that they may take more seriously later on. Remember that if you're going to teach these games to your kids, the object is to have fun and create cherished memories. Impatience, anger, or taking the outcome of a game a bit too seriously can spoil what should be a pleasant experience.
- When you go to the beach or a park, don't just bring blankets and food. Sporting goods and variety stores sell all sorts of nifty flying objects (such as plastic disks of various shapes and sizes), as well as ingenious toys that swat or fling balls back and forth, which are fun and challenging for all ages. Playing with them has the added benefit of generating a lot of muscle motion.
- Plan vacations that include walking, hiking, swimming, and other physical pursuits, rather than merely sitting (in a car or tour bus) or hanging out at a hotel.

3. Encouraging your kids' physical activity. Aside from your own example and your participation in physical activities with your kids, there are a number of ways to increase the likelihood that your offspring will move their muscles on their own:

- For *many* reasons, it is wise to limit your kids to two hours per day (or less) of TV, video games, or recreational computer activities. Without outside limits, some children and adolescents will spend most of their waking hours in these passive, frequently mind-numbing, and at times flatly negative pursuits.
- Children who have just arrived home from school should have some time for physical activity rather than plowing directly into homework.
- When buying birthday or Christmas presents, think about gifts that will encourage physical activity. A tennis racket or a baseball glove may not have the immediate appeal of a new computer game, but in the long run it will nearly always prove to be a better investment.
- Encourage your child's participation in school physical-education classes and programs, even if it isn't her strong suit. If she's having trouble keeping up, take an active role in helping her improve her performance. Comments such as "Oh well, it's just PE" may convey an attitude that exercise is a waste of time.

At age five or six, some children enter organized team sports programs, especially soccer and T-ball (or later Little League baseball). Others become active in individual competitive sports such as swimming, gymnastics, or skating. In some families, children become involved in archery, bowling, sailing, or horseback riding. There are few athletic or physical skills that children cannot begin to learn during these years, with these exceptions:

- Collision sports such as football or hockey should be postponed until age fourteen unless they are specifically noncontact forms of these games. Sports with a potential for physical contact such as soccer or basketball may be intimidating for children under age eight. A child who is young or who is smaller or less aggressive than his fellow players may find these activities too intense.
- Because of its potential for causing damage to the brain, boxing should be avoided completely.
- Exercise caution and discernment if your child wants to join a martial-arts program. Martial-arts classes for children and adolescents are more popular than ever, and they can help build confidence as well as skills in self-protection. But some guidelines are in order. Make sure that the emphasis is on building balance, coordination, and restraint, not on thrashing an opponent—you don't want *your* child to become the neighborhood bully. Check out the safety guidelines in the classes. For example, breaking boards should not be part of the curriculum before the age of twelve because of the risk of damage to bones, tendons, and ligaments in the hands and feet. Also watch out for any religious or mystical component that might be incompatible with your faith.

Participation in sports and competition can have many benefits for children: developing strength and coordination, acquiring self-discipline, learning cooperation and sportsmanship, and building friendships. But these activities also have the potential to cause physical injury, generate considerable stress or permanent emotional scars, and nourish a host of negative attitudes, including elitism, hostility, and an obsession with winning. To maintain balance and build positive experiences through sports, revisit the following questions on a regular basis:

- Is your child really interested in this activity? You may have loved Little League, but your child may prefer soccer.
- Is your child physically and emotionally ready to practice and compete in the sport?
- Is the proper protective equipment available and used at all times?
- Do the coaches and trainers enjoy working with children, including the least skilled? Are they focused on the right attitudes and values, or do they appear driven to win at all costs? Are they competent?
- Do you have the resources and time to support your child through the tryouts, practices, and events?
- How heavily is your child's—or your own—self-concept dependent on his success? Does the emotional weather at your home rise and fall with the fortunes of the team or your child's ranking at the last swim meet?
- Are positive values being taught and modeled by all concerned? Is unsportsmanlike conduct tolerated? Are parents who watch the events behaving themselves?
- Are we having fun yet? The vast majority of children will not become professional athletes or Olympic contenders, so the experiences of sports and competition should be enjoyed, not endured. If the sport becomes a thorn in your child's side or constantly drains him of energy and joy, reconsider goals and priorities.

Music, Dance, Art, Clubs, and Other Pursuits

Between their fifth and twelfth birthdays, many children begin to play musical instruments, start dance lessons, or join scouting or other programs that offer a variety of valuable experiences. As with athletic programs, your child will take to some of these more fervently than to others, and the benefits and costs of each should be evaluated on a regular basis. Pay particular attention to your child's level of interest, enjoyment, progress, and commitment, as well as to any signs of stress or distress.

In general, this should be a time for a child to sample a variety of activities and interests. What does she do well? Where does she fit in? She may not be a whiz with a ball and glove, but she may have a knack with a trombone or a special touch with animals. Finding her niche(s) in life will require trying a number of activities on for size. Some will fit better than others, and she needs to be able to see what works for her without the threat of rebuke or humiliation—although some activities that you consider central to your family's identity, such as attending church, will not be open for negotiation.

If you are bringing up a child with unusual gifts, whether in athletics, music, or some other arena, the training and discipline required for her to develop her fullest potential may be demanding for everyone in the family. Focused and prolonged practices, unusual schedules, and intense competition will need to be balanced against the other needs of a growing child, including friendships, play, and a broad-based education. (This issue is presented with considerable insight in the 1993 film *Searching for Bobby Fischer*,

WHEN IS IT OKAY TO QUIT?

Your daughter begged you to let her begin gymnastics classes, but now her muscles are sore, and it's clear that it is hard work—much harder than she thought it would be. Furthermore, she's not as good as the other girls, and more than a couple of times she's landed with a painful thud on the mat. She's had enough, but you've spent a couple of hundred dollars for a class that will continue for another six weeks. Do you let her bail out or make her continue to the bitter end—perhaps quoting the adage that "winners never quit and quitters never win"?

The answer will depend on your child and her track record. If she has a habit of making enthusiastic false starts and rarely bringing any project to completion, she will probably benefit from the experience of struggling to complete the course she started. This reality therapy will be especially important if you have funded the classes after she promised to finish them. In this case, being true to her word is the issue rather than the classes themselves.

When the activity in question is something that other family members enjoy together, such as skiing or skating, some positive encouragement to struggle through the learning process in order to enjoy a lifelong payoff would be appropriate.

If she has been consistently involved in other long-term activities but is clearly miserable in this one, you may want to let her quietly retire. Make sure the problem isn't a mismatch of a child and coach or a mistaken entry into a group that is too advanced. At times a change of venue, trainer, or team can make a significant difference. However, if the activity proves to be a dead end, don't berate her for it. Allowing her to maintain her dignity will accomplish far more than any trophy on the family shelf. ■

a true story of a child with extraordinary skill in chess. Parents of children who possess unusual gifts would benefit from watching this film on DVD and thinking carefully about the importance of developing character along with talent.)

The other potential pitfall during these important years is the problem of "too much of a lot of good things." Some children who are involved in school, Little League, music/dance lessons, Scouts, and church activities have calendars that make a corporate president look like a slacker. If two or more children in the same family are in this busy loop, juggling schedules, transportation, and phone calls can crowd out such basic activities as sharing a meal together or attending the same church service. It may become necessary to evaluate the impact of a child's commitments on the family as a whole and not merely on the child herself.

As with team sports activities, in artistic, social, and even church group settings there is always the potential for cliques, unhealthy comparisons, and excessive emotional pressure that can be especially harmful for younger or shyer children. Pay attention to your child's response to her extracurricular activities. If she is gifted or interested in a particular pursuit, she will probably not only thrive but also survive the occasional bad day, tedious meeting, less-than-stellar performance, or spat with her cohorts. But take heed if you see ongoing crying, complaints, withdrawal, or even aggression. A good way to keep tabs on these activities is to get involved yourself where you can—perhaps serving as a chaperone, assistant, snack provider, or even occasional teacher of something you do well.

Earlier we listed some questions to keep in mind in order to promote balance and positive experiences with sports. A similar list applies to other group activities:

- Is your child truly interested in this activity? You may have been an Eagle Scout, but she might hate camping and hiking. Piano may be your forte, but she might prefer the electric guitar.
- Are the adults in charge responsible, competent, caring toward children, and acceptable as role models? Do they promote and demonstrate moral and ethical behavior? Are they more worried about how well a performance or a project turns out or about making sure that everyone involved has a positive growing experience?
- Are the attitudes of the other children involved in the group having a positive or negative impact on your child? Is there general acceptance of everyone as one of the gang, or do cliques and pecking orders abound?
- Do you have the time and resources to support your child through the meetings, rehearsals, performances, excursions, fund-raisers, or other components of the group? (The schedules involved in some performing-arts activities can become daunting as curtain time draws near.)
- Is your child's, or your own, self-concept strongly dependent upon her abilities, acceptance, and accomplishments in one or more activities? If she doesn't get a solo or a part in the play, do the storm clouds roll in?
- Last but not least, is everyone enjoying the activity or merely enduring it? Is it enhancing your family's life and providing some cherished memories or sapping energy and joy from child and parent alike?

Physical Safety, Indoors and Out

During the next several years, your child will generally not require the type of nonstop surveillance that was necessary to keep her safe as a toddler and preschooler. However, you will now have the responsibility and privilege of teaching your child habits that will increase the likelihood that she remains safe and healthy. The following areas are particularly important:

Automobiles and other machines that have wheels and motors. Automobile accidents are the most common cause of death in this age-group, so make sure that each person in the car wears a seat belt/shoulder harness or is fastened into a car/booster seat appropriate for her age and size, even if you're going just a few blocks. The rule must be that the car doesn't move until everyone is properly secured and that the car stops if someone unfastens her belt. Period. Remember that she'll be in a child safety seat with a full harness until she reaches the weight limit of the seat (typically 40 pounds, or 18.2 kg), at which time she can graduate to a booster seat. She won't be ready for regular lap and shoulder belts until she is eight years old, or at least four feet nine inches (57 inches, or 145 cm) tall. This limitation may have an impact on carpooling opportunities. When she is ready to use a seat belt, teach her to buckle up whenever she rides in someone else's car, even if that person's rules are more lax than yours.

In addition, practice these safety guidelines:

- Children under twelve years of age should not sit in the front seat of a car that has a passenger-side air bag, according to the National Highway Traffic Safety Administration (NHTSA). Even in a low-speed accident, the sudden inflation of an air bag (which moves at about 200 mph) can injure or even kill a child.
- Never allow your child to ride in the cargo area of a station wagon, van, or truck. She may find the novelty exciting, but in an accident, she could be thrown from the vehicle or crushed.

WHEN IS YOUR CHILD READY FOR AN ADULT SEAT BELT?

The shoulder/lap belt combination in your car has been designed to restrain an adult in the event of a collision. But the legs and bodies of most children under age eight are not long enough to allow for a proper fit of a safety belt. Furthermore, a lap belt may ride up from the pelvis onto the abdomen of a small child who can't sit still or straight, and this could cause serious internal injuries during a collision. As a result, the National Highway Traffic Safety Administration (NHTSA) recommends that children remain in booster seats until they are eight years old, or at least four feet nine inches (fifty-seven inches, or 145 cm) tall. (Very few children eight years or younger are likely to be fifty-seven inches tall, by the way—this is the average height of an eleven-year-old.)

In order to graduate from the booster seat to a regular shoulder/lap belt, your child must be tall enough to sit without slouching, with her feet flat on the floor, knees comfortably bent over the edge of the seat, and back against the seat. The lap belt must be able to fit low and tight across the upper thighs (not the abdomen), and the shoulder strap should rest across the chest and over the shoulder. The shoulder strap should never rest under her arm or behind her back.

An important note: During this transitional phase from booster seat to adult shoulder/lap belt, your child may fit properly in the restraint system of one vehicle but not another. Check your child's fit in every vehicle she rides in. When in doubt, use a properly secured booster seat. ■

- Don't let preteen children operate motorcycles, motorbikes, all-terrain vehicles (ATVs), or off-road vehicles. Preteens lack the coordination and judgment to drive these vehicles without risking accident and injury.
- Don't give your child driving lessons out on a deserted stretch of country road or in your quiet neighborhood. Let her learn when and where it's legal and after she's had the appropriate driver-training class.
- Be wary of allowing your child to ride as a passenger on any open vehicle such as Uncle John's motorcycle or the neighbor's dune buggy. Helmets are a must, and the operator should be mature and prudent, without any inclination to show off or give your child a high-velocity thrill. Be a party pooper proudly and fervently for the sake of your child's safety.

Bicycles, skateboards, scooters, roller skates, and in-line skates. The right equipment and the right habits can prevent falls, bruises, fractures, head injuries, or worse.

- Make sure that the bicycle is the right size for your child. The balls of your child's feet should touch the ground when he sits on the seat. When he stands, there should be an inch of clearance between the center bar and his crotch. Don't be tempted to buy a bike that is too big for him so he can grow into it, because he will have trouble controlling it. Hand brakes should be used only when his hands are strong enough to use them effectively.
- No one (including Mom or Dad) rides a bike or uses a scooter without a properly fitting helmet that meets the standards of the U.S. Consumer Product Safety Commission (CPSC). A sticker inside the helmet should provide this information. Critical injuries to the skull and brain can occur during a bicycle accident, and research shows that wearing a helmet can reduce the risk of sustaining a head injury by 85 percent and the risk of brain injury by up to 88 percent. As your child grows, the helmet will need to be sized upward accordingly and replaced if it is damaged in a crash.
- Although a bicycle helmet might seem like a natural choice for protecting a skateboarder's head, the dynamics of skateboarding are a bit different from those of cycling. Skateboarders tend to fall more frequently than cyclists, and they travel at lower speeds. For that reason, skateboarding helmets are designed to withstand a greater number of hits at a somewhat lower impact intensity. When shopping for a skateboarding helmet, look for a sticker indicating that it meets skateboarding standards (ASTM F-1492 standard). Some manufacturers make multisport helmets that meet or exceed standards for both bicycling and skateboarding.
- Skateboarders should wear elbow pads, knee pads, and protective gloves or wrist braces that can help prevent abrasions and even the occasional broken bone that occur with spills. They should also wear shoes with nonskid soles.
- Teach your child the rules of the road, stressing that he has the same responsibilities as the operator of any other vehicle. Riding in the street should be a privilege reserved for those over six years old who can demonstrate that they have full control of the bicycle and understand how to maneuver it properly, whether or not cars are in the vicinity. Darting in and out of driveways, ignoring traffic signs and signals, riding on the wrong side of the road, or showing off with tricks or stunts (such as riding two on a bike) should be corrected immediately, and if necessary, a temporary restriction of riding privileges should occur if there are repeat performances.

- Children should not ride bicycles, skateboards, scooters, or skates at night. Skateboarders and in-line or roller skaters should stay out of the street and avoid homemade ramps and jumps. They should avoid riding in pedestrian crowds and should never hitch rides on car bumpers.
- Anyone who rides a skateboard *will* fall, and when this happens it's almost instinctive to extend the arms in order to break the fall. However, slamming the palms on a hard surface can cause fractures of the hands or wrists (especially if one isn't wearing protective gear). Children should be taught that when riding a skateboard it is wiser to try to absorb the impact of a fall by landing on the fleshier, more padded parts of the body and then rolling. Bending the knees if a fall appears imminent may also help, since there will be less distance to fall.
- Because young children generally lack well-developed judgment skills with regard to safety, traffic, or their own abilities, the American Academy of Pediatrics recommends that children under ten not be allowed to skateboard without adult supervision.
- Children younger than eight should use scooters only with adult supervision. Because of the speeds they can achieve, children twelve and under should not ride motorized scooters at all.

Pedestrians. Not all of the risks in traffic belong to those on wheels.

- Teach your child how to use crosswalks and interpret traffic and pedestrian signals. Show her how to look both ways and double-check before crossing the street, even when the signal says she has the right-of-way. Supervise her street crossing until she is at least seven.
- Talk to your child until you're blue in the face, if needed, about darting into the street. Remind her that the ball she is trying to save from being run over can always be replaced, but she cannot.

Bodies of water. With or without swimming lessons, your child is not ready to use a pool or enter any other body of water without adult supervision. No adult, no swimming. When supervising kids who are swimming, avoid distractions (reading, talking on the telephone, etc.) that take your attention away from them. If using a public pool, do so at times when a lifeguard is on duty. Don't overestimate your child's ability or endurance in water. Drowning is the second most common cause of death in this age-group, so everyone who supervises children by the pool, including relatives and babysitters, should know first aid and CPR. Your local Red Cross can provide information about training classes in your area.

- Your backyard pool should be surrounded by a fence that is at least four feet (1.22 m) high, not climbable, and equipped with a self-closing and self-latching gate. Entry access should be locked if an adult is not present.
- Gate alarms, pool alarms, and automatic pool covers can also reduce the risk of accidents. Pool alarms sound whenever someone or something enters the water; these alarms can be set to sound inside the house as well. Automatic pool covers consist of tarpaulin-like material that can extend over a swimming pool in a matter of seconds and can support the weight of one or more adults. When considering a pool cover as a safety device, look for one that meets standards set by ASTM International. An important note: A solar pool cover is a thin covering designed to reduce heat loss and evaporation—but it is *not* appropriate as a safety measure.

- Keep safety equipment such as personal flotation devices (PFDs), life preservers, and shepherd's hooks close to the pool. A telephone should also be kept near the pool in case of emergency. Remove toys from the pool after everyone is out to keep little ones from accidentally falling into the water while reaching for a toy.
- Floating toys or rubber rafts do not provide adequate flotation safety for a child who cannot swim. If the toys were to deflate or overturn, he would drown.
- Teach your child always to swim with a buddy, never alone. Let him know that horseplay, shoving others into the water, and jumping on others are strictly forbidden.
- Don't allow your child to swim in a river or canal. If he wants to wade into the water at the beach, wade with him and stay close by. If there's any undertow, get out and play in the sand instead. Your child must understand that rivers, lakes, and oceans do not behave like a backyard pool, and they should be treated with the utmost respect.
- No one should dive without knowing how to do so safely (hands striking the water first, not the head) and knowing how deep the water is. Diving should take place only from a true diving board at a pool full of water. Diving off a dock or platform at a lake could lead to a disastrous head or neck injury if the water is not sufficiently deep.
- When in a boat, every child under thirteen years of age should wear a personal flotation device, and one should also be available for each older passenger. Parents should consider wearing one as well, not only for their own safety, but also to model this behavior for their children. In addition, a harness (which attaches the child to Mom or Dad) may be appropriate to limit the explorations of children under the age of five.
- No one should swim during an electrical storm.

Fire hazards and firearms. The bottom line is to separate your child from things that burn, ignite, explode, or discharge.

- Make sure that your home has properly installed and functioning smoke detectors protecting every area in which people sleep. There must be at least one on each floor of a multistory dwelling. Replace the batteries every six months. Consider getting a carbon monoxide detector as well. If anyone in your home has a significant hearing impairment, you should purchase smoke detectors equipped with a strobe light and a wireless transmitter that activates a vibrator placed under the pillow or mattress.
- Teach your child what to do in case of a fire (see sidebar on page 364).
- Never underestimate your child's fascination with things that burn. School-age children can be incredibly creative with matches or leftover Fourth of July fireworks. Tell your child in no uncertain terms that playing with fire in any way is strictly off-limits and that he should steer clear of—and report—other children who are doing so.
- Think very carefully before bringing or keeping guns in the home. Children rarely have a sense of their destructive power or a grip on the fact that real people who are shot don't just get up and walk away (or show up unscathed in the next episode), as TV and movie characters sometimes do. If you own one or more guns, the unloaded weapon(s) should be under lock and key and the

ASTM International, formed in 1898 as the American Society for Testing and Materials, is a voluntary organization (now with members in more than one hundred countries) that develops technical standards for materials, products, systems, and services.

ammunition locked elsewhere. Talk to your child candidly about the real dangers of firearms, and make it clear that under no circumstances is he to handle any gun—yours or anyone else's—on his own. Furthermore, if another child appears to have a real gun, your child should get away immediately and notify you or the nearest responsible adult.

Promoting Emotional, Moral, and Spiritual Health

As a baby, toddler, and preschooler, your child needed—and demanded—your attention. When she was a hungry newborn, no one could sit still while she was crying at

FIRE-SAFETY PREPARATIONS FOR YOUR CHILDREN

We hope you will never have to deal with a major fire in your home, but some basic preparations will prevent panic, injury, or even a tragic loss of life if one should occur. Some details to cover with your children include:

- How to use 911 and other emergency numbers.
- Escape routes—ideally there should be two—from every room. (Important: Are there any potential barriers to a quick exit, such as a sticky window, that need to be addressed?)
- Staying low to the ground when smoke is present.
- Avoiding opening any doors that are hot to the touch.
- How to escape through a window (including the use of a chain ladder if needed).
- How pets will be evacuated. (Children must be taught that they are not to jeopardize their own escape from a fire while trying to find and remove a frightened and potentially uncooperative animal.)
- What firefighters look like in their full gear. (Children might be frightened by the bulky shapes with face masks and axes or other tools and run away from them.)
- Getting help from neighbors.
- Meeting in a designated place after escape.

After you have reviewed these details, practice them by holding a number of family "fire drills" until everyone's response appears to be brisk and consistent. Then hold one more drill late at night, after everyone has gone to sleep (pick a weekend night for this), to be sure that family members can awaken and respond appropriately.

While you are talking about your family's response to a fire, you should also go over contingency plans for any possible natural disaster (such as an earthquake, flood, tornado, or hurricane) that might occur where you live. Include instructions as to whom you or your children might contact in case communications are disrupted. (It may be easier to get in touch with a relative across the country, whether using cell phones or landlines, who could serve as a communication dispatcher for the family.) ■

full volume. As a toddler, when she wanted something, most likely everyone heard about it—over and over—until she got a response.

But your school-age child won't behave this way. She won't be coming to you a hundred times a day needing a little problem solved or looking for a hug. As she becomes more involved with school, friends, and various activities outside the home, you may begin thinking of her as self-sufficient and no longer needing the time and attention you provided during her first five years of life. But she still needs your ongoing attention, input, and guidance. She cannot and should not play the role of her own parent. In addition, she also deeply craves your ongoing acceptance and affirmation. If she can't get these from you, she'll seek attention elsewhere, and those who might give it to her may have agendas radically different from yours.

This can be a hazardous time in a family's development. During a child's school years, parents often become deeply embroiled in their own career development or other pursuits. But if one or both parents are careening through the workweek with schedules and deadlines bearing down relentlessly every day as well as on weekends, who will have time to play a game of Scrabble or talk about a problem? If parental energy is consumed by achievement and acquisition, who will have the interest to sort through this week's math problems or walk up the beach and chat about what makes people tick?

Right now, your child's eyes and ears and heart are likely to be as open to your input as they will ever be in her life. Once she begins adolescence, this will probably not still be the case—at least for a while. As these next few years pass, therefore, you will need to create some margin in your life, some reserve of time and energy, so you can *be there*—both physically and emotionally—for your school-age child.

What specific areas of her life should you be paying attention to?

Instilling basic moral values

During the next few years, your child will need to make an important transition. She will need to shift from being good because you told her so to becoming civilized and virtuous on her own. Whatever you choose to call it—internalizing values, assimilating moral principles, buying into what you've told her, developing good habits, or as Scripture describes it, having the law written on the heart—encouraging this process is the most important responsibility of your parenting career. Of course, no one will be 100 percent successful at it because no one will ever arrive at moral perfection. But while recognizing everyone's limitations, you will want to track your child's progress in acquiring a number of important assets:

- An active, meaningful faith in God that is applied to everyday life experiences and influences attitudes and decisions.
- Respect for others within and outside the family, regardless of age, race, gender, appearance, or behavior.
- Submission to those who are in proper authority, beginning with parents and extending to teachers, coaches, law-enforcement officials—and ultimately to God Himself.
- Respect for the property and possessions of others, while at the same time understanding that happiness ultimately does not arise from the material things a person might acquire.
- A commitment to honesty and integrity, with a consistent, internalized habit of telling the truth.

- Self-control, self-discipline, and an understanding of the importance of delaying gratification while working toward future goals.
- Refraining from using language that is offensive, obscene, or profane.

Obviously your child will not develop these virtues overnight. She may do the right thing repeatedly out of obedience to you, but growing in wisdom and exercising moral values is a lifelong project, and most values are understood more clearly through example and modeling. She will learn a lot about faith when she hears you pray, about respect for property when she sees you pay for something you accidentally broke, and about relationships when she sees you apologize when you've done something

WHAT IF YOU AND YOUR CHILD ARE PERPETUALLY IN TURBULENT WATERS?

All this talk of spending time to share affirmation and values with your school-age child may sound like so much hot air if you are still embroiled in a nonstop trench war. Are you dealing with a son or daughter who is constantly irritable, negative, or disruptive? Do you spend most of your time simply trying to maintain some semblance of order? Are your requests or directives routinely met with passive indifference or outright rebellion? Do you feel a major sense of relief when you get away from your child for a while?

If so, some basic evaluations and course corrections are in order. Among other things, you may be dealing with one or all of the following:

- *A medical problem.* Many chronic conditions (for example, allergies, recurrent headaches, sinusitis, or anemia) can cause a child to feel poorly enough to provoke ongoing irritability. Acute illnesses (such as the flu) or injuries (especially a blow to the head) can do the same. In either case there are usually more specific symptoms or a series of events that would suggest a medical problem. Nonetheless, a review of the situation by your child's physician can help determine whether a medical problem is responsible for your child's behavior.
- *Medication and drugs.* Antihistamines or decongestant-antihistamine combinations may cause irritability, although usually the connection between the drug and the mood change is readily apparent. Drugs which themselves are intended to change behavior (for example, Ritalin or Dexedrine for attention deficit/hyperactivity disorder) can sometimes backfire and worsen negative behavior. Illicit drugs and inhalant abuse now penetrate the school-age population in many parts of the country, and their effect on behavior can be very significant. (See the Special Concerns section on drug abuse on page 545.) If you are concerned about a possible connection between your child's mood and medication or drugs—whether prescribed, over the counter, or bought on the street—a physician's evaluation is essential.
- *A neurochemical disturbance* such as attention deficit/hyperactivity disorder (see Special Concerns "Attention Deficit/Hyperactivity Disorder" on page 379).
- *A significant emotional disturbance.* Children can suffer clinical depression, for

wrong. She will be all ears as you respond to annoying situations and people, and like it or not, she will likely model your language and attitudes when she's faced with similar circumstances. She may not understand or appreciate how hard you work to provide food, clothing, shelter, and other necessities and niceties of life. But when you demonstrate courage, kindness, appreciation, and charity, your actions will be deeply embedded in her memory.

Most of these interactions can't be planned or crammed into a few minutes of "quality time" every day. Many opportunities to teach or demonstrate moral values may catch you off guard and will be gone in the blink of an eye. In order to seize the moment, you have to be there to do the seizing.

example. (See "Recognizing Depression and Preventing Suicide in Children and Adolescents," beginning on page 571.)

- *An innately strong-willed child* who is going to challenge your leadership until the day he sets out on his own as a young adult.
- *A problem with consistent limit setting* during the first few years of life—perhaps brought on by parental turmoil, burnout, illness, or divorce—which now needs to be corrected.
- *Abuse*—by other children or by an adult in your child's life. Children who have been abused emotionally, physically, or sexually will often demonstrate drastic changes in their behavior around other people, even those they love and trust. Withdrawal and ongoing hostility could be signs of a problem in this area.
- *Your own behavior as a parent.* Could your words, attitudes, or actions be contributing to your child's current behavior? Is your parenting style either excessively controlling or overly permissive? Are your responses to him unpredictable and disrespectful of his feelings? Is he getting enough of your time and attention, or could his negativity actually be a cry for more of it? A wise parent will periodically carry out prayerful self-examination, and a significant behavior problem in a child is certainly an appropriate occasion for this task.

Your problem-solving approach will depend on your child and the resources available to you. An evaluation by your child's physician would be a good start, and if appropriate, a referral for family counseling with someone who shares your values might be the next step. Personal reflection and prayer, consultation with your pastor, and support from a group of parents with children of similar ages would be wise as well. Repair work in relationships takes time, and you can expect this project to continue for a number of months.

The Special Concerns section "Principles of Discipline and Training: Balancing Love and Limits" (page 259) outlines the basics of balancing love and meaningful limits. In addition, specific books that deal in more depth with problems of childhood behavior include:

The New Dare to Discipline and *The New Strong-Willed Child* by Dr. James Dobson (Wheaton, Ill.: Tyndale House Publishers, 1992 and 2004, respectively).

Making Children Mind without Losing Yours by Dr. Kevin Leman (Grand Rapids: Fleming H. Revell Company, second edition, 2000). ■

Monitoring the input to mind and heart

In the mid-1950s, television had no more than twelve channels, the content of movies was constrained by a code of strictly enforced values, the top ten songs on the radio dealt with "moons and Junes," and the most provocative game in the toy store was Monopoly. Today, material containing crude language, intense violence (including scenes of mutilation and torture), casual nudity, explicit sex, and general disrespect for life and traditional values is readily accessible to anyone, including children. Network television's "family hour" programs routinely explore themes that would have knocked the first generation of viewers out of their chairs. A couple of clicks of the remote control or the mouse can deliver hard-core pornography to your TV screen or your child's computer monitor. A number of electronic games not only include this type of content but also offer children and teenagers vicarious participation in antisocial and criminal activity. Even more troubling has been the explosive growth of Internet sites that allow children to expose themselves to a vast audience, both verbally and visually, in ways that are highly inappropriate.

Whatever is true, whatever is noble, whatever is right, whatever is pure, whatever is lovely, whatever is admirable—if anything is excellent or praiseworthy— think about such things.

Philippians 4:8

Words and images that are jarring, value eroding, discouraging, and generally inappropriate for kids of all ages (not to mention grown-ups) can flood a home unless parents and other responsible adults take deliberate defensive measures. And even if you are careful about the types of things you allow your children to see and do, parents of friends may not be as vigilant about the images flickering on their TV screens as you are. School-age children are intensely curious about "adult" matters and consider it a badge of honor to have had a look at something you've declared off-limits. And while violent or sexually explicit sights and sounds create strong and disturbing memories, repeated exposure has a desensitizing effect that can warp attitudes and erode respect for the human body—and life itself. Unless you cut your family off from civilization altogether, you will need to be perpetually vigilant about the material your child sees and hears, and you should be prepared to deal with whatever leaks past your defenses. More important, you need to do this in a way that prepares your children to make mature, informed decisions about their listening and viewing habits after they leave home. They won't watch *Sesame Street* reruns forever.

When dealing with TV, movies, DVDs, video games, and the Internet, you have several options:

- A simple but rather austere approach: no TV, movies, DVDs, video games, or Internet. If everyone will go with this flow and you can provide plenty of other forms of stimulation (such as reading, music, games played between human beings, and good, old-fashioned, interesting conversation), you may bring up the smartest and most literate kids in town. But if you take too rigid an approach, including strict social restrictions to maintain your rules, sooner or later rebellion is inevitable. It is likely that your child will secretly seek and find some rotting forbidden fruit and ingest it without your knowledge or input. Also, Internet access is increasingly important for students completing research projects—not to mention for adults completing routine functions in most jobs and homes. Unplugging the computer is becoming about as realistic as refusing to ride in an automobile.
- At the other extreme, a hang-loose, anything-goes mentality abdicates important responsibilities. Some parents become so intimidated by the swarm of media mosquitoes that they shrug their shoulders and don't bother to put up any protective netting. This is about as irresponsible as turning children loose to play with power tools or caustic chemicals in the garage.

- Somewhere in between lies a limited-access approach, which demands time and energy but is potentially rewarding. In this case, the various media are regarded as neutral tools through which either positive or negative material may flow. Specific standards must be set for your family as well as for individual members, based on age and maturity. Viewing should be planned and limited, both in time and content. Previewing and choosing material that children may watch is an important part of the process. Most worthwhile are the opportunities to discuss what has just been seen and to teach some critical thinking. What take-home lessons were depicted? What positive values were portrayed? If negative material was present, what was wrong with it?

With respect to TV and DVDs, there are a number of good reasons to limit the amount of time children spend staring at flickering images, even when the material is entirely wholesome:

- TV and DVD watching is mentally passive. Images, sounds, and ideas (including sales pitches) are actively pouring into your child's mind, while thinking, reasoning, imagining, or creating—and homework—come to a screeching halt.
- TV and DVD watching is physically passive. Young viewers who sit for hours are not running, climbing, cycling, or moving muscles in any meaningful way. Obesity and poor physical fitness are common among avid TV users.
- Watching video screens can become the centerpiece of family life. Group staring can replace talking, working, playing, eating, or praying together.

To prevent the tube from taking over your child's world, set specific ground rules for everyone:

- Establish how much, when (after homework and other responsibilities are done), and what will be viewed.
- Make use of videocassette recorders, DVD players and recorders, and time-shifting technologies (such as TiVo and others). Material can be recorded, rented, purchased, or even borrowed from the library, allowing you more control over content and scheduling.
- Before a DVD (whether bought, rented, or borrowed) slips into your player, do some homework. There's a lot more to the content of a film or TV program than you can discover from its rating and the thumbnail information that might accompany it.
- Think carefully before subscribing to a cable or satellite service that includes access to unedited films. You'll not only be more likely to waste hours watching something obnoxious that just happens to be on, but your child may become acquainted with objectionable material when you aren't around.
- Think *very* carefully before installing a TV in your child's room. Not only will you lose control of your child's viewing activity, but you'll also increase his potential for isolating himself from the normal flow of family life.
- Don't let a video screen babysit your child for hours on end.

TV won't be the only potential media hazard in your child's path during the next few years. You will need to be vigilant in a number of other areas as well:

- Be sure to check reviews carefully before taking your child to a **movie**. While you can click off objectionable TV images, motion pictures on big screens have a greater sensual impact, especially now that most theaters have bone-rattling sound systems. Remember that even films with the PG rating may contain material that can jolt a child's mind for months. And even movies geared to children may contain supernatural or occultic themes that can collide with your family's faith, or subtle messages that can undermine values you have been teaching.

Whether a film proves to be a wonderful experience or ninety minutes of nails on the chalkboard, talk to your child about it. What made it good or awful? Were any values taught? Was this a cautionary tale, and if so, what lessons were on display? *Plugged In* magazine, published by Focus on the Family, is an extremely useful resource for evaluating films in current release and on DVD, as well as tracking trends on television. Reviews of current films are posted online almost immediately after the movies are released, and an extended library of reviews is maintained at http://www.pluggedinonline.com.

- **Video games** (whether played on a home computer or on a dedicated game system) are enormously popular with all age-groups and can consume vast amounts of time and money. Whatever platform you might have available at home, *everyone* needs specific limits on the time spent playing them. Kids aren't the only ones who become hooked on electronic games. Adults can also spend hundreds of hours playing solitaire or become hopelessly entrenched in complex virtual worlds where they interact with thousands of other players on the Internet. (Believe it or not, marriages have been threatened or even broken apart when one partner becomes so immersed in an online game that he or she neglected basic responsibilities at home.) Even if you have a good grip on the time factor, be careful about the content of games you or your kids buy, borrow, or rent. While many are good, clean fun, some consist of nonstop fighting, and a few contain harsh language, vivid images of carnage and sex, or overtly antisocial themes. Sometimes these show up at advanced or deeper levels of the game, so once again you need to read up on the current electronic fare.

- While you might think of **fantasy/role-playing games** as a healthy alternative to TV and video, beware of those in the Dungeons and Dragons genre. Older children can become deeply enmeshed in one or more roles they assume in these games, spending huge amounts of time in complex scenarios that often are pervaded by destructive supernatural themes and violence.

- Few parents would object to seeing their child engrossed in **books**. Indeed, introducing children to classic tales such as *Charlotte's Web, The Secret Garden,* or *The Chronicles of Narnia* can be one of the great joys of parenting. That being said, some popular book franchises geared to young readers contain material that may be of dubious value or even objectionable.

For example, a series of more than eighty paperback horror stories for kids, Goosebumps, often written in first person, has exposed millions of young readers to jarring imagery and grotesque, disturbing situations. A number of so-called "chick-lit" novels are long on sex, drugs, alcohol, and social cruelty, and short on values and consequences. While ostensibly geared to women in their twenties and thirties, many become the hot ticket among young adolescents or even the preteen set.

Three excellent resources for families who want to watch and discuss movies together are *Movie Nights, Movie Nights for Teens,* and *Movie Nights for Kids.* Each provides commentary and discussion questions on twenty-five films—the first two books are geared toward teenagers, focusing on films such as *Remember the Titans* and *The Lord of the Rings,* while the third is intended for younger viewers, covering films such as *Babe* and *The Black Stallion.* All three books are available from Focus on the Family at www.family.org or 800-A-FAMILY.

According to BBC News, as of 2004 more than 20 million people worldwide have played Dungeons and Dragons since it was created in 1974, spending more than one billion dollars on equipment and books for the game. An estimated 3 million people play the game in the United States every month.[5]

Many parents have welcomed the Harry Potter series as engrossing stories that engage children in reading, while others who are uncomfortable with the characters' involvement in witchcraft and spell-casting have steered their children away from them. While there has been honest disagreement among committed Christians about the merits and liabilities of the Harry Potter books, parents who are open to their children reading them should be aware that the stories have become more complex and emotionally intense as the series has progressed. Bottom line: Be mindful of the content of the books your kids are devouring. Reading these books yourself will give you the most accurate take on their content and tone, and would provide some great topics for conversation.

- You must supervise your child's use of the **Internet** as carefully, if not more so, as his film, video, or TV viewing. *Don't leave him alone in his room for hours on end sitting with a computer that has an Internet connection.* You might be pleased to think that your budding genius is becoming proficient with modern communications technology, but he could be tapping into extraordinarily explicit and perverse sexual material, antisocial and violent text and images, and Web sites where verbal and visual interactions can become highly inappropriate. *Make it clear that your child should not give his name, address, phone number, or any other personal information to someone online or agree to go somewhere to meet any new "friends" with whom he might have communicated on the Internet.* (Pedophiles and other criminals are well aware that the World Wide Web can serve as their own personal web for ensnaring unsuspecting prey.) Most online services have mechanisms that allow you to limit your child's access to certain areas, and you can also install software designed to serve as an electronic watchdog that will block inappropriate material, though with variable degrees of success. Because these tools are imperfect you would be wise to require that all your child's online activities take place only when you are home and only on a computer you can directly monitor.

> Harry Potter is the best-selling children's book series of all time, with over 300 million copies sold worldwide. This is much higher than the total estimated sales of books by Dr. Seuss (about 200 million worldwide).[6]

Sex education: the faculty (you)

For decades, movies and sitcoms have presented a caricature of the sweaty-palmed, birds-and-bees conversation in which Dad stammers through a convoluted description of sex to a preadolescent child—who, it turns out, knows all of the details already. The humor arises from the tension most parents feel about discussing sex with their kids. ("What if we tell him too much?" "Will this rob him of his innocence?" "What if he starts asking about what *we* do?")

What isn't so funny is the reality that too many children learn about sex from everyone but their parents. Playground slang and obscenity, a distorted description of intercourse from the tough kid up the street, or worst of all, a look at some pornographic material on cable TV or the Internet often provides a child's first jarring glimpse of sex. What should be seen as the most beautiful, meaningful, and private communication between a married couple becomes a freak-show curiosity. "Mom and Dad did *that*? More than once?!"

Efforts by public schools to correct misinformation from the street and lack of information from home often leave out a critical ingredient: the moral framework within which the facts about reproduction should be presented. Without an ethical context, sex education becomes little more than basic training in anatomy, physiology, infectious diseases, and contraception.

Many churches have made laudable efforts to teach biblical principles of sexuality to their youth groups. But these important concepts are not always accompanied by accurate medical information or refusal skills. Furthermore, youth-group presentations usually begin late in the game (i.e., during the teen years) and rarely involve an ongoing dialogue about this subject.

The best place for a child to learn about sexuality is at home from those who care most about him. Anyone can teach the basic facts about reproduction in an hour or two (or they can be read in any of several reference books), but you are in the best position to put this information in the proper context and give it the right perspective over a period of years. There are no cut-and-dried formulas for carrying out this assignment, but keep the following principles in mind:

Giving a child facts about reproduction, including details about intercourse, does not rob him of innocence. Innocence is a function of attitude, not information. A school-age child who understands the specifics of sex, while seeing it as an act that, in the proper context, both expresses love and begins new life, retains his innocence. But a child who knows very little about sex can already have a corrupt mind-set if he has been exposed to it in a degrading, mocking, or abusive context.

If you feel squeamish or inhibited about broaching this subject with your child, reflect for a moment about your own attitudes. Do you harbor any feelings that sexual activity, even within the context of marriage, is somehow base or something that God really doesn't approve of? If you realize that this is an issue for you, some conversations with your pastor, a counselor, or both may be in order. Hopefully these discussions, and perhaps a reading of the Song of Solomon and other Bible passages, will alleviate any uneasiness you might harbor regarding God's attitude toward sexuality. Books that are reliable, informative, and honoring to sex, marriage, and the Creator of both can also be very helpful. Two good examples are *The Gift of Sex: A Guide to Sexual Fulfillment* by Dr. Clifford and Joyce Penner (W Publishing Group, revised edition 2003) and *Intended for Pleasure* by Dr. Ed and Gaye Wheat (Revell, third edition, 1997). But for many people uneasiness about sex may be rooted in life experiences, especially if they involve sexual abuse experienced during childhood, adolescence, or even adulthood. It is never too late to address such issues with an individual who has training and experience in this area and can help you work toward healing.

Don't wait to tell your child everything you know about sex during a single, intense marathon session. Doing so risks either waiting until it's too late or dumping more in the child's lap than he can process. Instead, information should be released gradually during many conversations over a period of several years. (The same principle applies to any other area of life—faith, values, responsibilities, relationships, handling money, and so on—in which you intend to offer guidance to your child. These subjects are too important to be confined to a single conversation.)

In many instances, you will be giving information on a need-to-know basis. Your five-year-old is probably going to want to know how the baby inside Aunt Susie is going to get out. But your child may not think to ask how the baby got there, and you don't need to broach the subject at that time. On the other hand, if you haven't yet had any discussions about reproduction with your ten-year-old, you will need to take the initiative to start some conversations. She has already heard all sorts of things on the playground and needs to hear from more reputable and mature sources.

What if your child asks you questions you can't answer? Be honest, and then do some research. You gain far more stature in your child's eyes by showing candor than by bluffing. You may not have a detailed knowledge of the intricacies of the menstrual cycle or the developmental stages of puberty, but you're never too old to learn. You could brush up on some of these topics by reading the sections in the next chapter regarding adolescent growth and development (see page 442).

Sex education: the curriculum

As you ponder the process of communicating to your school-age child about sex, remember that the primary message you need to give him—more important in the long run than the specific facts and figures—is the importance of respect:

- Respect for the body each of us has been given and for the Creator of that body.
- Respect for the wonder of reproduction.
- Respect for privacy in sexual matters, not only his own, but parents', friends', and others'.
- Respect for his future and an understanding that sexual activity can have a profound effect on his health and happiness for the rest of his life.
- Respect for marriage as the appropriate context for sexual expression.

Think in terms of a gradual and relaxed release of information to your child: During the preschool years, begin with the basic naming of body parts and a general understanding of where babies come from, and before puberty begins, progress to full disclosure of the reproductive process.

Young children should know the correct names of their body parts (usually learned during bath time) and gain a basic sense of privacy and modesty for the "bathing suit" areas of the body. While understanding that their genitals are not "bad" or "dirty," they should also know that they are not intended for public display. Now that diaper days are over, your child should learn that the genital area should be touched only by the child himself, a doctor or nurse during an exam, or a parent for a specific reason. Tell your child that if someone else tries to touch those areas, he should protest noisily, get away, and tell you as soon as possible. He must know that you will not be angry or upset with him if this should happen.

It is extremely likely that before age five, and possibly later as well, your child will engage in some form of genital show-and-tell with a sibling or another small child. If and when you discover this in progress, your response should not be overblown. Don't tell him that you are shocked and terribly ashamed of him, but instead clearly reinforce the privacy rule and remind him about respect for himself and the other child. The same should happen if your child streaks through the house or yard when others are present or exposes himself to someone else to get a reaction. More significant consequences should follow, of course, if you have talked to him about this behavior but he repeats it anyway. Here, however, the issue is obedience more than the specific act itself.

At some point he may barge into the bathroom when you're in the shower or even wander into the bedroom at a highly inopportune time. Again, don't overreact, but calmly ask him to leave. Later let him know that there is nothing bad about what he saw, but that it is meant to be private and that he should knock on the door first before coming into your room. Incidentally, once the toddler years have passed, grown-ups should abide by a dress code when the kids are at home: If you're not wearing enough to be seen by adult houseguests, you're not wearing enough to be seen by your children.

Along with learning the names and addresses of body parts, younger children will also be interested in the big picture of reproduction. Questions will undoubtedly come up if you are expecting a new baby in your family, and this event can provide a nice long window of opportunity to talk about the entire process of pregnancy and birth. With or without a nine-month object lesson at home, a straightforward explanation that a baby grows inside the mother and that at the right time he or she comes into the world through the mother's vagina will satisfy the need-to-know concerns for many children through the first or second grade.

Some will want to know more: How could the baby get through that small hole? Does it hurt to have a baby? Does Daddy help the baby come out? Matter-of-fact answers can alleviate a lot of concern: Yes, it is uncomfortable when the baby is born, but a doctor helps the baby come out and can give medicine to help the mother feel better. Moms who are going to have babies go to special classes, usually with the dads, so they'll be ready when the time comes.

Eventually, one way or another, the Big Question will come up: Why and how does a baby start to grow inside a mother? (Another common scenario: Once your child is old enough to appreciate a reading of the Christmas story, you may need to explain what a virgin is.) You should avoid mythology (storks) or pseudotheology ("God sends the baby to the mother") or misleading euphemisms ("The mother and father sleep together, and then the baby begins to grow inside the mother"). Some parents talk about mothers and fathers having a very special kind of hug, just for the two of them, which starts the baby growing, but even that explanation may be unclear. Indeed, all of these explanations suggest that pregnancy is a random or unpredictable event.

Only you can judge the readiness of your child, but in most cases when the question needs to be answered, offer a very simple but straightforward explanation. You can talk about how a mother makes a tiny egg inside her body every month, and if there is some sperm from the father to join with the egg at the right time, a baby will begin to grow.

When you get more specific about the process that brings the man's sperm and the woman's egg together, remember to stress context: A man and woman who are married and love each other very much have a special time, just for the two of them, when they get very close to each other—in fact, so close that the man inserts his penis into the woman's vagina. After a while he releases his sperm inside her. Younger children will usually find this idea rather strange, and you can stress that when the man and woman love each other very much, they feel very good while this is going on.

You will need to supply a name for this activity: *Having sex* is probably the most direct without being vulgar; *making love* is a little vague; and *sexual intercourse* is rather clinical, although children should know that this is the term they'll be hearing later in life. Throughout, stress how good sex is—provided it occurs at the right time, with the right person, and in the context of marriage.

Sooner or later, you will also need to talk about situations in which single adults are pregnant or raising children without a partner. You may be having these conversations with your children as a single parent. Children will need to know that some people have sex even though they are not married and that a baby may begin to grow inside a mother as a result. Or they may be married when the baby starts to grow but not married later on.

Whether you will want or need to delve more deeply into the complexities of adult life will depend upon your situation and the age of your child. A young child is going to be more concerned about basic information and his own security with you, whether married or single. A child approaching puberty will probably need more details: What happens when a single woman becomes pregnant? Do they all have their babies? Why do some mothers and fathers split up?

These may be emotional questions to tackle, especially if you have been involved in a divorce or are rearing one or more children on your own for whatever reason. But without condemning others or justifying irresponsibility, this can be an appropriate time to talk about the fact that sexual activity should not be taken lightly. You may want to mention that the Designer of human beings laid down some rules about sex for good reason—not to be a killjoy but to maximize our enjoyment of it and to prevent painful consequences. Sex experienced within those boundaries—between one man and one woman, maintained within a marriage relationship to which both are committed for the rest of their lives—is not only right but the safest and most pleasurable.

Preparation for the onset of puberty

As your child approaches puberty, you are going to have to shift gears from talking about sex in general to more specific briefings on his or her own sexuality. Whether you make this a specific discussion or include it as part of a more extensive explanation of what lies ahead during the adolescent years, you will want your child to be ready for the physical changes that are about to take place.

Girls need to know about breast development, new hair growth, and the reproductive cycle. The first menstrual period should be viewed in a positive light, as a passage into adulthood rather than a burden or a "curse of women." Some parents honor the occasion by taking their daughter to dinner at a nice restaurant or presenting her with a special gift. This event is usually the final stage of pubertal development. If you and your daughter stay in communication about the changes she is experiencing, you can usually anticipate and discuss what she can do if her first period begins when she's away from home.

Similarly, boys should be aware that changes are on the horizon, such as deepening of the voice, enlargement of the genitals, and new hair growth. They should also know about the likelihood that they will have an unexpected emission of seminal fluid during the night (the "wet dream"), and that this is not a sign of disease or moral failure.

Parents will need to discuss with their child the increasing interest in the opposite sex. The boy or girl will also need to be prepared to deal with attention from the opposite sex if and when it occurs. This is an important time to review specific guidelines, and perhaps a little street wisdom, about relationships and physical contact. While reinforcing the importance of saving sex for marriage, what will you say about other kinds of affectionate touching?

Your preadolescent child will most likely wonder if you're going overboard in broaching this subject. "Dad, I'm not going to jump into bed with people, okay? What's the big deal?" But he or she must understand that we are all designed in such a way that physical contact, once started, naturally progresses to increasing intimacy. Indeed, sex is like a car that begins rolling down a hill. At first the hill is nearly flat, but then it becomes progressively steeper. The farther you go, the harder it is to stop. That in itself isn't bad or wrong but simply the way we're made. Since the right time to have sex will be some years away, it will be important to make sure that the car doesn't roll very far before the wedding night. This means that your child will want to have a clear idea what his or her boundaries are, and how to maintain them effectively, well before the first socializing with the opposite sex begins.

At some point (probably more than once) during these years, you will need to deal with the subject of **masturbation**. As children approach adolescence, you will have to make a judgment call on what to say about the significance of self-stimulation after puberty arrives. It is extremely likely that masturbation leading to sexual climax will occur at some point, especially for a male. If he is racked with guilt about it and repeatedly vows never to let it happen again, he will probably expend a lot of energy feeling like a moral failure and worrying unnecessarily about his spiritual welfare.

But when masturbation becomes a routine and frequent habit, especially when accompanied by vivid sexual fantasies or, worse, the viewing of pornography, it can be damaging to sexual and emotional health. In essence, a young man may have hundreds of sexual experiences associated with unrealistic or overtly distorted imagery, reinforced with the extreme pleasure of sexual release. At the very least, when he marries, his real-life sexual partner may seem disappointing by comparison, and his physical and emotional bonding with her may be impaired. This problem will be more significant if there have been many actual sexual partners before the wedding night. At worst, he may come in contact with violent or degrading images and associate his own sexual release with them.

Your approach to this issue will need to be both tactful and realistic. *A bottom line worth stressing is that masturbation should not play a major role in your child's life, either as a source of relentless guilt or as a frequent and persistent habit that displaces healthy sexual relations in the future.* If it happens once in a while, it happens. But it should not be pursued as a form of recreation, especially while viewing sexually provocative material, and it should never be allowed to occur with other people.

Who should deliver these messages to your growing child? In many families, everyone will feel more comfortable if mothers talk with daughters and fathers with sons. It may be more fruitful in the long run, however, if both parents participate in many of the discussions of sexuality, where mother and father can each offer specific perspectives, and one can pick up the thread if the other draws a blank in a particular area. This also solidifies the notion that sex is a matter for couples who are committed to one another and provides your child with two sources of appropriate information rather than one. In single-parent families in which the child is of the opposite sex from the parent, a trusted friend, relative, or youth pastor may need to fill in some gaps in sensitive areas.

While it may be useful to have both parents involved in discussions of sexuality, it will usually not be wise to talk to more than one child at once. This is especially important when you are dealing with your child's own sexuality rather than with less personal topics. A ten-year-old girl who is learning about very personal changes that will be taking place in her body should not have a wisecracking eight-year-old brother in the room. If necessary, take her to a place where you can ensure privacy before you bring up these subjects.

Preparing for Adolescence: Painting the Big Picture

While discussions about your child's sexuality can help ease the arrival of puberty, there is much more to the upcoming adolescent years than surging hormones. Many children enter the preteen and teen years unprepared for the gamut of changes and challenges that await them. As a result, a grade-schooler may enter adolescence happy and well-adjusted and within a few short years emerge battered, bruised, and thoroughly discouraged—along with the rest of the family.

Your school-age child is likely to be much more interested now in what you have to say than she will be later. Once she enters the adolescent years, it may seem as if she has temporarily changed the frequency of her mental tuner so she won't receive your broadcasts. While you may now feel as though you've got her number, in a few years you might hear a busy signal.

Years ago, Apollo astronauts would pass behind the moon as part of their normal flight plan. But during those tense minutes, communication between the spacecraft and mission control would be impossible. When they emerged from the dark side of the moon, contact would resume. You may face a dark-side-of-the-moon experience in the coming years, during which a cool head and lots of prayer will be needed while you wait for your child to emerge from the other side. But you may avert or shorten it by walking your child through the trajectory called adolescence before the rocket takes off.

Ideally, you should plan on having a series of conversations with your prepubertal child, at age nine or ten for a girl, and perhaps a year or two later for a boy. Some parents plan a special weekend away from home, perhaps in the mountains or at a pleasant hotel, in order to have some undistracted, one-on-one time during which these discussions can take place. If possible, both parents should be involved in this process. If you are a single parent, don't feel that you can't deal with most (if not all) of the topics involved in this preadolescent briefing. As was mentioned in the previous section on sexuality, if you feel uneasy talking about the physical transition to adulthood with your prepubertal child of the opposite gender, you may want to enlist a trusted friend, a relative, or your youth pastor to help with this particular topic.

Before you embark on this series of discussions, you may want to brush up on information about this upcoming period of your child's life. Feel free, though, to mine your own memories for illustrations and recollections about how you felt when you were growing up. If you know any cautionary tales about people who made some unwise decisions, don't hesitate to tell them. Your child will probably remember such stories long after these conversations are over and may even pass them on to her children.

To gather additional details for this task, you may want to read ahead in this book to the chapters regarding adolescence. Another excellent resource is Dr. James Dobson's book and CD/tape series entitled *Preparing for Adolescence*, which is directed specifically toward the child who is about to embark on this voyage toward adulthood. Some parents have found it helpful to listen to the tapes with their children and then discuss them, while others digest the materials on their own and adapt them to their own child's specific needs and personality.

During this preparation, you will want to talk about the following subjects, among others:

The physical changes that will be taking place in the near future. Along with hormonal and sexual developments, there will be rapid growth of bone and muscle, although the timing and rates may vary greatly among children. As a result, an eighth-grade gym class may contain skinny boys with alto voices who are competing and taking showers with peers who are hairy, muscular, and highly intimidating. Remind your child that, whatever his particular timing might be, the transition to adulthood will indeed take place.

The emotional weather forecast. The transition from childhood to adulthood is usually marked by times of intense emotions, especially during the early teen years. When things are going well, she may feel ecstatic. When there is a problem, the world will seem to be coming to an end. Relationships with her peers may swing wildly from love to hate and back again—within the same day.

The valley of the shadow of lack of confidence. Your child needs to know that all who pass through this period feel unsure of themselves. This goes for the most popular, attractive, athletic, intelligent students as well—they all desperately crave acceptance and approval. It also holds true for the tough, mean, sarcastic types who make everyone else miserable.

The herd instinct. Because everyone wants desperately to be accepted and avoid ridicule during adolescence, the opinions of peers can carry incredible and sometimes ridiculous weight. Your child must understand the importance of standing her ground, even in the face of intense pressure, when she is being pushed to say or do something she knows to be wrong. The obvious areas to stress are those that might threaten life and health: smoking, drinking, illegal drugs, sex, breaking the law. But a few seemingly less dangerous concessions to peer pressure can also set long-term negative habits in motion. Under the influence of a poorly chosen friend, your child might sample the following:

- Music with antisocial or amoral lyrics
- Films, DVDs, or Internet sites with violent or pornographic content
- Occultic or death-oriented games
- Obscene, profane, or simply disrespectful language
- Counterproductive attitudes about school, church, and family

Explain to your child that anyone who might pull her in any of these directions simply does not have her best interests in mind. Getting into something that violates the standards you have set at home in order to impress a friend or win someone's approval is like throwing her most prized possession down the toilet.

As will be discussed in the following chapters, you will need to pick your battles in the area of conformity to the crowd. If peer standards call for everyone to wear white socks and sneakers, and anyone who wears dark socks and dress shoes is declared a geek, let her wear the official footwear. Within reason, she shouldn't have to suffer ridicule in areas that do not involve ethical or moral standards.

The process of picking a husband or wife. What kind of person will your child be looking for? You will want to spend some time with this one, stressing the importance of shared faith and values, character, and the ease of making conversation with anyone who may become a marital partner. Good looks and the buzz of romantic chemistry are nice frosting on the cake, but they aren't enough to serve as the foundation for a lifelong journey. Remind your child that you will be praying for that special person, whoever he or she might be. If you haven't done this before, now is a good time to start.

Reassure your child that these growing pains will not last forever. Remind her also that, in contrast to the fluctuations of her emotions, the whims of the peer group, and whatever is "hot" and "not" during the coming years, some things will last: your love for her, her place in your family, and above all, the care and involvement of God in her life.

Attention Deficit/ Hyperactivity Disorder (ADHD)

He is the toddler in perpetual motion, his throttle wide-open every waking moment of the day (and a good deal of the night). He runs, jumps, climbs, opens, closes, pushes, shoves, and bulldozes over playmates, who seem nearly comatose by comparison.

He is the five-year-old whose kindergarten checkup is the major challenge of his doctor's afternoon. If the appointment is delayed for only a few minutes, he will rapidly investigate every surface and piece of equipment within reach. Despite his haggard mother's valiant efforts, permanent alterations of the room's contents are likely.

She is the third grader who fidgets, squirms, and taps her fingers through most of the school day. Anything and everything—the hair ribbons adorning the girl in front of her, the birds in the tree outside the classroom window, the sound of a passing truck, and a thousand other sights and sounds—distract her from whatever the teacher wants her to do. She can't seem to listen to directions, finish any assignment, or cooperate in any game. Her list of friends is as short as her attention span.

He is the young adult who dropped out of school, just lost his job, and can't maintain a relationship. His fuse is short (and he has a few scars to show for it), his moods are unpredictable, his apartment is a mess, and his calendar is empty. Depression and anger are his constant companions; drug and alcohol abuse could be waiting in the wings.

These vignettes illustrate variations on the theme called **attention deficit/ hyperactivity disorder (ADHD)**, which is estimated to affect at least 3 to 5 percent of American children. (This includes approximately 2 million school-age children, nearly one per classroom.) Boys with ADHD outnumber girls at least four to one. No statistics can remotely estimate the depths of frustration, disappointment, resentment, and guilt that the parents of these children feel, at least at times. Despite a common belief that this problem disappears during adolescence, it usually doesn't go away, and millions of adults are probably affected as well. However, with help (and medication, when appropriate), adolescents and adults can learn to cope and live successfully with this condition.

Common Features of ADHD

Inattention and distractibility. An ADHD child has great difficulty staying focused on any task that requires continuous attention, especially schoolwork. He may daydream or become distracted by any sight or sound in his vicinity. Completing an assignment may require much effort, but he is likely to misplace the final product between home and school. He cannot remember a sequence of directions: "Take out the trash, feed the bird, and pick up your clothes before you take your bath" might result in one or at most two of the commands being completed. The others will be forgotten or jumbled.

Hyperactivity. While difficulty with attention may not be apparent until the child enters school, hyperactivity makes an impact on everyone in his world from the time he is very young. Some parents are aware that "something is different" from the first days of life with their demanding baby, who later turns into a turbocharged toddler. Most parents of small children wish they could acquire some of the energy of their offspring, but the hyperactive child is in a different league, living every day at top speed. Many children with ADHD also have volatile emotions. Whether they are joyful or angry—sometimes over what seems to be a trivial issue—everyone in earshot will hear about it. Just as rapidly, these feelings seem to pass as the child forgets the episode and moves on to something else.

Impulsiveness. The child with ADHD often has little patience. He cannot wait his turn, stand in line, follow directions, or keep his hands off whatever he isn't supposed to touch. He talks before he thinks, acts before he analyzes, and leaps before he looks. As a result, he may suffer more than a few battle wounds and fractures.

Professionals who deal with this problem now divide ADHD into three subtypes based on these features:

- The **predominantly hyperactive-impulsive type**, in which the child does not show significant degrees of inattention.
- The **predominantly inattentive type**, in which the child does not show significant hyperactive-impulsive behavior. (This is sometimes called ADD, although the initials ADHD are now widely used to encompass the entire spectrum of the problem.)
- The **combined type**, in which both inattentive and hyperactive-impulsive behaviors are observed.

ADHD has been given many names over the years, including Minimal Brain Dysfunction and Hyperkinetic Reaction of Childhood. It has been attributed to every cause imaginable: brain damage, birth trauma, poor parenting, lack of discipline, food additives, sugar, and pure willfulness. The best understanding presently is that the primary basis for ADHD is neurochemical, a subtle inherited malfunction of the intricate passing of messages between cells in the brain. (A genetic component is suggested by research showing that about 25 percent of close relatives of children with ADHD also have this disorder, whereas about 5 percent of the general population is affected.[1]) So far, no specific medical finding, blood test, or X-ray is sensitive enough to detect the abnormality, although a doctor's evaluation is important in ruling out other causes of the troublesome behavior.

The child with ADHD exhibits difficulties in many areas of life (home, school, playground), but not always to the same degree, and parents may be confused and frustrated by some of the inconsistencies. Certain activities—usually ones that are highly intense such as video games—can hold his interest, at times to a striking degree. In some one-on-one situations, he may act quite normal. This variability is actually very typical of ADHD, but it gives the definite impression that the child's lack of attention is simple laziness or that his impulsivity is willful defiance.

One of the greatest challenges of parenting an ADHD child is discerning how much of a particular behavior arises from biology and how much from conscious decisions. As the child grows older, the causes may blend. For example, extreme difficulty with schoolwork, which requires prolonged concentration and mental effort, leads to dislike and then eventually to refusal to participate at all. Repeated rejection by others because of behavior he cannot control may push him toward more deliberately destructive acts.

Diagnosing ADHD

If you believe your child might have ADHD, it is very important to seek input from a qualified professional—better yet, from a team of professionals. Do not ignore the problems you see and assume that "he just needs more discipline" or that "he'll grow out of it"—because he probably won't. The diagnosis of ADHD should be made with a careful evaluation. Other learning disabilities, medical conditions, or problems at home may be causing the disruptive behavior.

The person who evaluates your child should be a properly licensed physician (usually a pediatrician, although family practitioners, neurologists, and psychiatrists who are experienced with ADHD may be involved) and/or a psychologist, social worker, or education specialist with training in ADHD and its management. Input from parents and school personnel, observation of the child, medical tests (if necessary), certain behavior-rating scales, tests of attention-related skills, and other measures may all be used, depending upon the evaluator's preference and experience.

Your child's doctor or teacher may suggest one or more preferred consultants. Local support groups such as Children and Adults with Attention-Deficit/Hyperactivity Disorder (CHADD) can offer recommendations as well. (CHADD's Web site is http://www.chadd.org.) Your school district is obligated by law to provide assessment services as its resources allow, even if your child is not enrolled in public school. The obvious advantage of this route is that it's affordable, especially if ADHD evaluation isn't covered under your health insurance or if you are uninsured. But as is the case with some public services, you may have to wait several months for the evaluation to be done.

Helping the ADHD Child: First Steps

Managing a child with ADHD requires participation from the entire family. Each member—including Grandpa and Grandma—needs to become educated about this problem, just as they would if a child had diabetes, asthma, or any other significant chronic condition. Input from the professional(s) involved and from books, tapes, and local support groups can be extremely helpful. The nonprofit organization CHADD provides a variety of services, including printed information (fact sheets, newsletters, educational materials for parents and teachers) and local chapters where parents—and adults with ADHD—can vent, support one another, and share ideas.

Parents of a child with ADHD must be unified and cooperative. The survival of your marriage will require your conscious decision to create a flexible team and firm support. If you are a single parent with an ADHD child, you will need to marshal all the support you can find—from relatives, friends, members of your church, even coworkers—to give yourself some breathing room. In all cases, prayers to God for wisdom and patience should be a vital part of each day.

The following can help restore and maintain order at home:

The ADHD child needs structure and consistency. A predictable routine every day, with specific times for meals, chores, homework, bathing, and bedtime, creates a stable framework for his life. The ADHD child most often *wants* to do what is right. External structure helps move him in the right direction.

House rules and expectations for behavior should be explicit, understandable, and—very important—achievable. It would be unrealistic to expect a child with ADHD to sit quietly through a full-length sermon, go on an extended shopping trip, or dine in a formal restaurant without some difficulty—or total disaster.

Give instructions simply and clearly; avoid giving a chain of directions. A half hour after making a seemingly simple statement such as "Put the LEGOs away, let the dog out, and get your coat," you may find the ADHD child playing with another toy he spotted while putting away the LEGOs. The dog and the coat will have been long forgotten. If you have more than one thing you want him to do, tell him one step at a time.

Enforce rules and limits consistently and predictably, with consequences appropriate for the violation. For example, if he charges into a busy street on his bicycle despite being warned not to do so, bike-riding privileges should be suspended for a day. If he knowingly mistreats a toy and it falls apart, don't repair or replace it right away. If he has become too excited or aggressive playing with other children, give him a time-out in an uninteresting spot.

Remember, the child with ADHD may not seem to "get the picture," and he may actually repeat the behavior for which you just punished him. *It is important to make him suffer consistent consequences each time but not to yield to extremes: either giving up, which forfeits your right to be in charge, or reacting with increasingly harsh punishments.* As with all children, pick your battles carefully. Behaviors that put him or others at risk or are overtly destructive need your decisive response. But if you go to the mat with him over every minor annoyance, you'll be exhausted—and thoroughly depressed—every day.

Offer praise and encouragement. The child with ADHD needs to know he is loved and accepted as an important member of the family, especially because his disruptive behavior, difficulties with schoolwork, and lack of success in other areas such as games and sports will generate negative feedback from several directions. He needs to know that you and others are on his team and always will be.

When he does what he's told, accomplishes a task, plays well with another child, or makes progress at school, praise him. A special time of ten or fifteen minutes every day with one or both parents can allow some positive attention to be focused on him regularly.

Helpful Approach at School

The demands of school are nearly always at odds with the natural bent of the child with ADHD. Often it is one or more problems in the classroom that bring the issue to a head. Many children are first diagnosed with ADHD as a result of a teacher's observations.

Some adjustments are usually necessary to prevent school from being the site of endless defeat, embarrassment, and disruption. Smaller, calmer, more structured classrooms are preferable to larger, more chaotic environments. Sitting at the front of the class where there are fewer distractions and closer supervision can be helpful. Giving her brief physical tasks, such as passing out papers or erasing the blackboard, will provide acceptable ways for her to get up and move around the room during the day.

In a best-case scenario, the teacher will be aware of her diagnosis and be sympathetic, tolerant, and willing to provide frequent, tactful reminders about assignments and appropriate behavior. Small-group and even individual instruction can be helpful. Just as in the home, the child with ADHD will need praise for her accomplishments and areas of strength to balance the negative feedback that invariably and frequently comes her way.

In the real world, not all of these helpful features will be readily available in the classroom. Parents may want to become advocates for special services for their child, which by law are to be provided by the local school district for those with educational handicaps, including ADHD. Advice from the professional who made the diagnosis or from a local support group might be necessary to guide parents in finding help within the system.

For some ADHD children, home schooling provides an environment that is more structured and conducive to learning. Taking this route obviously requires a fair amount of parental planning and effort, but it could pay off in the long run if it allows the child to complete her primary education more efficiently and with her self-esteem intact.

ADHD and Medication

Children with ADHD are likely to respond favorably to medication. This can be a sensitive subject for parents who worry about their child being "drugged" or controlled by mind-altering medications. But the appropriate prescription, adjusted by a physician attentive to the child's needs and schedule, can be very beneficial. Medication is only one component of a total approach to ADHD, not a magical quick fix for all the problems children have with this disorder. A major study of school-age children conducted by the National Institute of Mental Health—the Multimodal Treatment Study of Children with Attention Deficit Hyperactivity Disorder or (MTA)—found that medication was more effective than behavioral treatment (or no treatment at all), and that the best results were obtained from a combination of medication and behavioral approaches.[2]

Medications for ADHD might be likened to eyeglasses that correct blurry vision. While the glasses allow the child to see letters more clearly, they will not teach him to read. Similarly, medications for ADHD do not exert some mystical power over the child but merely enhance his own efforts to control himself and deal more effectively with daily events. Children under the age of five, however, are less likely to respond well to medical treatment and are more likely to experience adverse side effects.

The medications that bring about positive changes are not sedatives and do not directly affect intellect or perception. Oddly enough, most ADHD medications are classified as stimulants, which would seem to be the last thing a hyperactive child needs.

But rather than provoke turbocharged behavior, they most likely help normalize certain neurotransmitters (the chemical messengers within the brain). This causes increased attention span, better impulse control, less disruptive behavior at home and school, and more stable emotions.

The most commonly prescribed medications are **methylphenidate** (Ritalin, Concerta, and others), **dextroamphetamine** (Dexedrine and Adderall, a combination of dextroamphetamine and amphetamine), and various antidepressants. While methylphenidate and dextroamphetamine/amphetamine are designated by the FDA as controlled substances, ADHD children do not become addicted to these medications, nor do they show any increased risk for substance abuse later in life. The specific choice and dosage must be determined for each child, usually by trial in which a low dose is started, behavior observed, and appropriate adjustments made. Feedback from the child himself, as well as from parents and teachers, is important in this process. Often the effects are obvious within an hour, although the final medication routine could take a few weeks to sort out.

Over the years, hundreds of studies have shown few problems with long-term side effects of these drugs with normal use. Some children will experience loss of appetite or difficulty sleeping, but changes in dose, timing, or type of medication will usually resolve these symptoms. Others may experience a "rebound" effect, in which disruptive behaviors or mood swings occur as a given dose wears off. Adjustments can usually minimize this effect. In addition, the product labels for drugs containing amphetamine or dextroamphetamine carry a warning about the potential for cardiovascular side effects if these drugs are misused.

Because of concerns over the effects of these medications on a child's long-term growth, many physicians have advocated drug "holidays" on weekends and during the summer. However, a child's ultimate height and weight rarely appear to be affected, and some children benefit from medication every day.

Atomoxetine (Strattera) was introduced in 2003 as the first nonstimulant medication approved by the FDA for treating ADHD. (It was originally studied as an antidepressant, but found to be more effective in treating ADHD.) It has been approved for use in children six and over, as well as in adults and adolescents. Because a small percentage (0.4 percent) of children and adolescents taking atomoxetine have been reported to experience suicidal thoughts early in treatment, a child or teen should be watched carefully for unusual behavior or suicidal thoughts if this drug is prescribed.

Since ADHD usually continues to be a problem during the teen years and into adulthood, it is likely that medications will play a role later in life. (About 80 percent of children who respond to medication for ADHD will continue to need it as teenagers, and more than 50 percent will benefit from medication as adults.[3]) Each child's needs and responses must therefore be carefully considered over a period of years, not merely for a few months.

Diet, Sugar, and Food Additives

Over the past several decades, a number of individuals have proposed that sugar, dairy products, preservatives, and artificial colors and flavors in foods trigger or aggravate ADHD symptoms. The most widely publicized theory has been from pediatric allergist Dr. Benjamin Feingold, who claimed in the mid-1970s that at least 50 percent of hyperactive behavior was caused by artificial colors and flavors. The Feingold diet thus involved the scrupulous avoidance of these items. Based on some success in individual cases, Dr. Feingold took his theory to the public, and his diet became the nutritional bulwark for thousands of parents of ADHD children. But subsequent controlled studies in larger numbers of children failed to support his claims. Similarly, a common belief that eating refined sugar triggers hyperactive behavior has not held up in large-scale studies.

It is quite possible that some children show a deterioration of behavior when they eat certain foods. If this happens consistently, those foods should be avoided. But proving cause-and-effect relationships can be very difficult, and some caution and skepticism are in order to prevent a child from becoming a food cripple who isn't allowed to eat anything but a handful of "safe" items.

Because a child with ADHD can create such havoc in a family, the desire for a magic formula to make the problem go away can become overwhelming. Several fringe therapies (e.g., the use of megavitamins) have attracted parents desperate for a cure, but the likelihood that these therapies will create lasting success without other measures being taken is remote.

ADHD Resources

Children and Adults with Attention Deficit/Hyperactivity Disorder (CHADD), 8181 Professional Place, Suite 150, Landover, MD 20785. Toll-free number for ADHD information: 800-233-4050. Web site: http://www.chadd.org

Why ADHD Doesn't Mean Disaster by Dennis Swanberg, Diane Passno, and Walt Larimore (Tyndale, revised 2006)

You and Your A.D.D. Child by Paul Warren and Jody Capehart (Thomas Nelson, 1995)

Help! My Child is Struggling in School by Grant Martin and Bill Maier (Focus on the Family/Tyndale, 2006)

The Overweight Child and Teenager

While millions of children worldwide suffer from a chronic lack of adequate food to sustain normal growth and development, the most common nutritional disorder among children and adolescents in the United States is an excess of body fat. In many ways, this is not surprising. When food is both abundant and tasty, it's easy to eat much more than we need to relieve hunger, and also to seek food for a host of reasons that have little to do with appetite. Eating can easily become a routine response to excitement, boredom, anger, and depression, and food is a welcome companion for virtually any form of relaxation, entertainment, or social gathering.

This ongoing input of calories often results in consequences that are unpleasant but very predictable, especially when we understand that our bodies are designed primarily for surviving the ebb and flow of an unstable food supply. When more food arrives than is immediately needed, the body's intricate biochemical processes see to it that leftovers are stored as fat for use during the next famine. If a famine never arrives, the excess fat becomes a permanent resident and continues to accumulate.

Modern technology has provided us not only an abundance of food, but also a multitude of labor-saving devices and beguiling passive entertainments that promote much more sitting and watching than active muscle motion. Because of this, many grade-school children and adolescents have moved from the perpetual motion of their toddler years to a sedentary lifestyle that does not maintain even a modest level of regular exercise. The excessive body fat that often results is a serious problem, with ongoing physical and emotional consequences for millions of kids and teenagers. Indeed, there has been a dramatic increase in the number of young people who are overweight over the past forty years. Before we take a look at the unpleasant statistics, however, we need to understand the terms and definitions used by the Centers for Disease Control and Prevention (CDC) to describe the weight of children and adolescents.

Is Your Child or Teenager Overweight?

In chapter 1, we introduced the **body mass index** (**BMI**), a number calculated for adults based on height and weight, without reference to age or sex. We use this number to get a general idea of one's weight status—underweight, normal, overweight, or obese—and this can serve as a useful tool both for individual assessment and for research. In children and adolescents, however, the significance of a given BMI is much more dependent on age and sex than it is in adults. Not only does the normal amount of body fat differ between boys and girls, it also changes as they grow and mature. As a result, the CDC has established specific charts of **BMI-for-age** for both boys and girls. (Note that these are not the same as the height and weight charts that your health care provider utilizes as a part of every well-baby or well-child checkup. You can find both types of charts later in this book, starting on page 788.)

For children and adolescents from two to twenty years of age, the charts show a series of curved lines, each of which represents a certain **percentile** rank. Given a child's height and weight, a BMI can be calculated using the same formula as for adults:

$$BMI = \frac{\text{weight in kilograms}}{(\text{height in meters})^2} \qquad\qquad BMI = \frac{\text{weight in pounds}}{(\text{height in inches})^2} \times 703$$

If you don't have a calculator handy, you can find BMI calculators on several Web sites, such as http://nhlbisupport.com/bmi/bmicalc.htm or http://www.cdc.gov/nccdphp/dnpa/bmi/index.htm.

But the similarity ends there. One must determine the percentile rank for that BMI by looking at the appropriate chart for the child's age. If the child's BMI falls on the 50th percentile curve, it means that half of the children at his age have a higher BMI, while half have a lower one. A BMI at the 95th percentile rank means that 95 percent of the children at that age have a lower BMI. As an example, a five-year-old boy with a BMI of 18 would fall on the 95th percentile curve, and this would raise concerns about his weight. But the same BMI for a twelve-year-old boy falls on the 50th percentile curve, indicating a normal combination of height and weight. We have included BMI-for-age charts on pages 792–793.

Currently the CDC uses the term *overweight* rather than *obese* when referring to excessive weight in children and teenagers, and it uses these two categories:

- Being **at risk for overweight** means that the BMI lands between the 85th and 95th percentiles for age and sex.
- Being **overweight** means that the BMI is more than the 95th percentile for age and sex.

Over the past thirty years, the prevalence of this problem among children and teenagers has increased dramatically. Altogether, about 9 million young Americans—children between the ages of six and nineteen—are overweight. Among children ages two to five and adolescents ages twelve to nineteen, the percentage who are overweight more than doubled over the past three decades. For children ages six to eleven, that percentage more than tripled. According to the 2003–2004 National Health and Nutrition Examination Survey (NHANES), which was conducted by CDC's National Center for Health Statistics, nearly 19 percent of children age six through eleven and more than 17 percent of adolescents (age twelve through nineteen) are overweight.[1]

What Are the Consequences of Being Overweight?

For young people, the fallout from excessive weight involves three major types of issues:

1. Immediate and ongoing health risks. Most of us are aware that excessive weight is associated with a number of important medical problems in adults. But the potential health consequences of being overweight are no less serious for children and teenagers. These include:

- **Insulin resistance and type 2 diabetes.** As we describe in more detail in the Reference Section (see "diabetes mellitus," page 651), diabetes involves a rise in the level of blood glucose (often called blood sugar) with a host of potentially serious short- and long-term consequences. Type 1 diabetes, brought about by a shortage of the hormone *insulin*, is less common but most often affects children and young adults. The more common type 2 (often called *adult onset*) diabetes involves abnormalities in the body's response to insulin (known as *insulin resistance*) and is typically seen later in life, often accompanying excessive weight. One alarming aspect of the obesity epidemic in the young is the increasing presence of blood glucose problems normally seen in older adults. An estimated 25 percent of overweight children and adolescents have insulin resistance, and 4 percent have type 2 diabetes.[2]
- **Fatty liver disease** involves the accumulation of fat within the liver, which may lead to inflammation and in some cases progressive damage. As many as 75 percent of obese adults and as many as 25 to 50 percent of overweight children and adolescents may have this problem.[3]
- **Orthopedic problems**, including sore muscles and joints (especially knees), fractures, and difficulties with mobility are, not surprisingly, more common among those who are overweight.
- **Sleep apnea** involves intermittent obstruction of the airway by soft tissue in the neck during sleep, manifested by snoring and pauses in breathing that disrupt sleep. This can cause a number of problems, not the least of which is daytime drowsiness and poor school performance. (In children, sleep apnea may be aggravated by enlarged tonsils.)
- **Gastroesophageal reflux disease** (or **GERD**) involves a backflow of stomach acid into the esophagus (the tube that carries food from mouth to stomach), causing irritation and discomfort commonly experienced as heartburn.

Another sobering statistic: Sixty percent of overweight children between the ages of five and ten already have at least one risk factor for cardiovascular disease, such as an elevation of cholesterol, triglycerides, or blood pressure. Twenty-five percent have two or more of these risk factors.[4]

2. Long-term weight problems. The amount of fat in your body reflects both the *size* and the *number* of fat cells, and the number of cells increases most dramatically during late childhood and early adolescence. The overweight child gains more of these cells than his lean counterpart and may begin his teen years with as many fat cells as an adult. When weight is lost, fat cells shrink in size but not in number, and people with more cells regain any lost fat more quickly. As a result, the overweight child or early teen is more likely to become an overweight adult who has difficulty maintaining any weight loss. Furthermore, those who are able to control their weight later in life are still more likely to develop coronary artery disease and arthritis, compared to adults who were not overweight as children or teens.[5] This is a key reason for dealing thoughtfully and carefully with a child's weight problem.

3. Emotional and social risks. For the overweight child or adolescent, whose culture at school (or down the block) rarely overflows with human kindness, every day can be a brutal gauntlet of insults, snubbing, and loneliness. *This ongoing assault on the heart and spirit may have lifelong consequences,* and preventing or limiting them is one of the most important reasons for parents to take an active role in their children's nutritional health.

Why Are So Many Kids Overweight?

The short answer to this question is the same for young and old alike: Over an extended period of time, more calories are going in than are being used, and the body responds by storing the extra fuel as fat.

Obviously, the long answer is more complex, with a number of factors affecting how a person gains or loses weight. As you read through this list, keep in mind an important fact: *The impact of each of these varies considerably from person to person.* For some, genetics is a driving force. These people gravitate toward being thin or overweight no matter what they eat. Others are affected more by family traditions, the culture in which they live, or behaviors such as eating to calm emotions. Most overweight people are affected by a combination of the following:

Heredity. Your child's genetic code affects his shape, size, hormone patterns, metabolic rate, regulation of hunger and fat storage, and numerous other biochemical characteristics, including many that have yet to be discovered. It is well-known that adopted children tend to follow the weight patterns of their biological parents rather than their adoptive parents, and that identical twins are more likely than fraternal twins to weigh the same, even if they are reared in different families. Genes certainly determine how susceptible we are to becoming overweight if we eat and behave in a certain way, but they don't cause it.

Activity level. Many experts state that lack of exercise among both adults and children plays a major role in our current obesity epidemic. When they're not asleep, infants, toddlers, and preschoolers younger than two or three years old normally move around *a lot*. Unfortunately, for too many children this level of activity doesn't last. One important reason is the abundance of irresistible opportunities to sit (or lie down) in front of a video display: dozens of cable channels, movies on DVD, extremely elaborate electronic games, and the virtually limitless domain of the Internet. Children become fascinated by video images at a very early age, and time spent watching a screen is time when very little physical activity is going on.

Another reason for decreased activity lies in the fact that over the past few decades physical education has been phased out of the normal school day in many school districts, especially during the high school years. Furthermore, for too many children and adolescents who haven't developed much athletic prowess or team sports skills, PE can be an ordeal rather than an enjoyable class in which they develop habits that maintain fitness for life.

Family eating habits. Children inherit not only genetic tendencies to gain or lose weight from their families but also *patterns* of eating, including favorite foods, recipes, portion sizes, and occasions for having a meal. For some families, any get-together is an occasion for lots of food to appear, and not partaking enthusiastically is considered impolite (or a sign of illness). Because of busy schedules, long workdays, time pressure, and general fatigue, regular home-cooked meals during which family members sit down and talk with one another have become somewhat of a rarity, a fading memory from the days of *Ozzie and Harriet.* We are not better off as a result, for two reasons.

First, meals can and should be a time of sharing (indeed, of intimacy), mutual encouragement, and bonding as a family, not to mention learning about wholesome foods. Second, we have become overly dependent on prepackaged, processed convenience foods or—worse—on trips to the nearest fast-food restaurant, where the fare is cheap, tasty, highly satisfying, and habit forming.

Culture. Unless you have brought up your children in rather strict isolation from our culture, the kinds of foods that have been the most popular and heavily promoted for the past several decades are generally high in calories and low in nutrients. Whether sold at the supermarket, convenience store, or fast-food outlet, these types of foods are marketed aggressively to children, who readily become regular (and sometimes compulsive) customers. While some manufacturers and fast-food franchises are making changes for the better, the abundance of products laden with fat, added sugars, salt, and processed grains has been identified by a number of experts as a "toxic food environment." Another important component of our food culture is **portion sizes**. For the past few decades, Americans have been exposed to supersize portions, especially in fast-food restaurants and convenience stores, and many restaurants serve entrées in quantities large enough to satisfy two people with a fair amount left over.

Socializing and emotions. Sharing a meal is a wonderful way to interact with family, friends, and strangers. Food also soothes basic physical and emotional discomforts from the moment we leave the womb. Thus, for children and adults alike, eating becomes more than just a way to relieve hunger. It is an accompaniment to celebration and sorrow, socializing and solitude, excitement and boredom, working and relaxing, studying and goofing off, and especially to watching anything—TV, a movie, a sports event, you name it. For many, certain items—known famously as comfort foods—become a means for coping with anything, whether it be a bad day, the normal bumps in life's road, or a major crisis.

How Can You Help Prevent Your Child or Teenager from Becoming Overweight?

In a way this is like asking, "How can I help prevent my child or teenager from becoming a smoker or a drug user?" Certainly there are defensive measures to consider, but accentuating the positive and becoming a role model of healthy eating and physical activity is definitely preferable. You may feel as though you don't have a chance against the billions of dollars of advertising spent by the food and restaurant industry to influence what your child or teenager eats. But your child's bedroom isn't located in a fast-food restaurant, and soft drinks don't sneak into your home during the night.

You have the opportunity and responsibility to decide what foods show up on your table, what drinks chill within your refrigerator, and where your child will have his or her first restaurant experiences.

As with so many other dimensions of parenting, you will need to avoid extremes. You cannot afford to sit back and let marketers and media determine what your family will eat. If nothing else, America's epidemic of obesity, cardiovascular disease, and diabetes should serve as convincing evidence that nutritional "business as usual" isn't an option. Nor can you become an uptight, repressive food dictator with a delusion that you can force your kids to eat exactly what you put in front of them, and nothing more or less. If that's your expectation, you can look forward to a lot of conflict, tears, frustration, and disordered eating patterns once your children are out of your immediate control. You will also increase the likelihood that your child will be overweight. Recent research has suggested that children whose parents are either too permissive or too authoritarian are more likely to be overweight by the first grade, compared with children whose parents set clear boundaries while showing respect for their opinions.[6]

With those general thoughts in mind, here are some specific age-related recommendations. (We have mentioned a number of these elsewhere in this book, but they bear repeating.)

During infancy. In chapter 4 we presented many reasons to encourage breastfeeding infants, and one worth repeating is that it has a modest protective effect against the development of obesity. One possible reason is that the nursing baby normally is fed according to his own hunger cues; he sucks and swallows when he's hungry and stops when he is full. The sensation of fullness is affected not only by the quantity of breast milk he consumes, but also by changes in the fat content of the milk during the course of a feeding. A baby drinking from a bottle doesn't receive any cues from the content of the formula, and the person holding the bottle may be tempted to continue the feeding session until the bottle is empty. This might lead to overfeeding, at least with some infants.

Remember also that juices should not be substituted for breast milk or formula, and that infants younger than six months should not receive juice at all. There are several reasons for this (and for limiting juice intake in older babies and young children), one of which is to limit their exposure to sweet tastes that could lead to an appetite for sweets later in life. *Soft drinks have no place in the diet of an infant or young child.*

Among older infants, toddlers, and preschoolers. This is an important period of life for developing eating habits, healthy or otherwise. It is also the time during which children and parents may have more than a few "food fights." Your job is to give your child many opportunities to try a variety of nutritious foods in modest quantities. By her first birthday, if not before, these can be small portions of whatever the family is eating (which hopefully is of good quality). Your child's job is to eat what she wants from what you offer and to stop when she's no longer hungry. *Attempting to force young children, or for that matter older ones, to eat food they don't want is an exercise in futility and frustration.*

Whatever you do, don't force a child to sit for hours until he finishes every last morsel on the plate. Showdowns over membership in the "clean plate club" are not only miserable and pointless, but also a potential setup for overeating later in life. One of the great challenges of weight management is to learn to listen to hunger as a cue to eat and its absence as a cue to stop. Young children do this instinctively, but by the age of five, they're more likely to respond to external cues (what's on the plate, and what will happen if they don't eat it) than to internal ones (*Am I hungry or not?*). The last thing you want to do is attach a lot of guilt and shame to leaving food on a plate. Many overweight adults feel compelled to eat everything placed before them because of an irrational argument they heard repeatedly during childhood: "Don't waste food; children are starving in Africa." Aside from the fact that cleaning a plate in North America doesn't feed anyone on the other side of the planet, it's important to ask which destination is better for food that can't be saved and served another day: the trash can or the fat cells of a person who is overweight?

As much as possible, keep your young child away from the fatty, salty, or sugary foods that are aggressively marketed to kids through colorful packaging and TV ads. Fast-food franchises have been spectacularly successful at gaining young customers with kids meals, toys, play areas, highly recognizable characters, tie-ins with animated films, and food items that appeal to their palates. The marketers' goal is to build intense brand loyalty and lots of repeat business that first involves your money, and later your children's. What you need to build instead is attachment to the basics—whole grains, fruits, vegetables, lean meats, and so forth. Be careful and conservative about purchasing packaged and processed food items that your preschooler asks (and asks and asks and asks) for in the store, especially those that are geared to young eyes and appetites.

One more caution: Avoid using food to manipulate a child's behavior. If you respond with food to every sign or sound of displeasure from your child (especially when he can't tell you what's bothering him), you may unintentionally teach him to calm himself by eating. Depriving children of food as a punishment—"I heard you and your sister fighting; you're going to bed without your supper!"—or using it to reward their behavior—"If you're good while we're shopping, you'll get ice cream!"—can attach all kinds of unnecessary emotional baggage to eating. There are already plenty of emotional ties to food: It satisfies hunger, first and foremost; it provides pleasant sensations of taste, smell, and texture; and it can be associated with times of closeness, connection, and acceptance with family and friends. What small children (and older ones too) do *not* need is to attach their acceptance or worth to the foods that are offered to or withheld from them.

And finally, these are the years when you need to establish limits and expectations regarding TV and video viewing. Current recommendations for prevention and management of excessive weight in childhood call for limiting "screen time" to two hours or less every day. While your toddler won't hound you to watch hours of TV (as he may do when he's older), you may be tempted to use TV and video programs as extended diversions for your child while you try to get other tasks done. Remember, he probably will not become *less* attached to sitting and watching as he gets older, so be very careful about habits you set in place for him at a young age.

Among older children and adolescents. Here is where the rubber meets the road, so to speak, because your children or teenagers will be eating more often away from home—at school, with friends, and on their own. Many kids and teenagers bolt out the door without thinking about breakfast. But depending on the policies of your local school district, the offerings on campus (whether in the cafeteria or from vending machines) may range from healthy to mediocre to genuine junk. Unfortunately, in order to supplement sagging revenues, many public schools have made deals with soft drink, snack, and even fast-food companies to offer their products to the captive audience showing up every day for classes. In high schools that allow students to leave campus for lunch, the only source of a relatively fast meal may be—you guessed it—a local fast-food franchise.

If your children and teens are involved in extracurricular activities, their schedules—and yours—may get so complicated that restaurants, fast-food chains, and pizza deliveries become your family's primary food suppliers. Furthermore, interest in computers, the Internet, and video games goes into high gear at this age, not to mention awareness of TV programs and movies that *everyone* seems to be watching. The amount of time spent staring at screens can increase exponentially as a result.

All of these developments have the potential to contribute to obesity or, at the very least, a less-than-ideal intake of nutrients. In order to stem this tide, some deliberate steps will be necessary. Ideally, many of these should already be well established as part of your family's culture while your children are growing up.

- Establish several family meals as predictable events every week. This will take some effort, but older children and teens can and should be involved in the planning, shopping, preparation, serving, and cleanup. Kids are not going to get this type of hands-on experience at school, and they need to know more about cooking than how to operate the microwave. Ideally these should be times to introduce and reinforce the value of such staple items as vegetables, fruits, lean meats, and whole grains, as well as some adventurous recipes to complement the old favorites.
- While you're planning the family's sit-down meals, think through with your kids what they're going to do about breakfast and lunch. Skipping meals (especially breakfast) is common among teenagers but definitely *not* recommended by nutrition experts. You don't need to set up a breakfast buffet every day, but a simple start—juice, fruit, and some cereal (preferably not the presweetened, empty-calorie variety) beats the no-food or grab-a-doughnut approach. While bringing lunch from home also requires some planning, you can usually get more value, both in nutrition and cost, from food items you and your kids assemble than from the cafeteria and vending machines at school. If your children are going to buy lunch at school, do you have any idea what's being served?
- Keep fresh fruits and vegetables available as snacks. (Nuts can be great snacks as well, but remember they are calorie dense. Kids need to learn that a small handful of these constitutes a serving.)
- Phase out the soft drinks and other flavored, sweetened beverages at home. According to the Institute of Medicine, by age fourteen, more than 30 percent of girls and 50 percent of boys are drinking three or more eight-ounce servings of sweetened soft drinks—roughly three hundred calories' worth—every day. If all of these are excess calories—that is, calories beyond the number needed for normal metabolism and daily activities—they will result in more than thirty pounds of weight gain over the course of a year.
- Limit recreational screen time—TV, videos, and electronic games, as well as computer and Internet activities (including chat rooms) that aren't connected with homework or other productive pursuits—to two hours per day or less. This isn't just a recommendation for the kids, by the way. A profusion of network and cable TV channels beckons adults to sit for hours at a time after work and on weekends. Parents are just as vulnerable as kids to pouring many more hours—including several during the night that would be better spent sleeping—into computer games and the limitless realms of the Internet.
- Encourage all kinds of physical activity. Model it yourself, and brainstorm with your kids about games and activities, whether in the yard or as a family outing, that get everyone moving instead of sitting. (See "Physical Fitness and Sports," beginning on page 354.)

What Should You Do If Your Child or Teenager Is Overweight?

This is an emotionally charged issue for both parents and kids, and you would be wise to think, pray, and proceed with caution as you address it. The wrong attitude and approach can generate a great deal of pain, shame, guilt, anger, and divisiveness among family members who desperately need to be on the same team. In particular, *beware of putting a child or teenager on a "diet"—especially one that involves a significant number of food restrictions—without consulting a professional who is knowledgeable in this area.*

At the outset of making a plan, examine these basic questions and then revisit them periodically:

Is your child actually overweight? This may sound like a silly question, but an informed answer usually involves three steps that should be carried out by your child's physician or a dietitian. First, height and weight need to be measured accurately. Second, a body mass index (BMI) should be calculated and then compared to percentile ranks for the child's age and gender, as described earlier in this section. Finally, the current height and weight should be compared with other measurements recorded on your child's growth chart, which ideally has been set up and maintained at the doctor's office during checkups. This is a form on which height and weight are plotted in relation to percentile curves that provide a comparison of height and weight with those of other children or adolescents of the same age and gender. (If you have moved, or your child has seen more than one physician, you may have to collect height and weight information at different ages from more than one source.)

It's important to note whether your child's weight and height patterns have been following a certain percentile over a period of years or if there has been a recent change. For example, if her weight has been at the 50th percentile for years (that is, where 50 percent of children of the same age and gender are heavier and 50 percent are lighter) and then over a few months it has shifted to the 90th percentile, you might need to consider what was going on during that period of time to cause such a shift. (Was there a move? a change in schools? some turbulence between parents?) On the other hand, a look at the growth chart may demonstrate that a child or adolescent has always been on the large size (often reflecting similar patterns in other family members), and that she is merely following a predictable height and weight trajectory.

Whose issue is this? (Part 1) Are you primarily intent on maintaining or protecting your child's health and emotional well-being as he grows up and moves into adulthood? If so, good for you. Or are you at some level embarrassed by your child's appearance? Are you afraid that his weight problem may reflect badly on your parenting job? Do you have difficulty speaking to or showing approval for your child because of his weight? Are some of your dreams in jeopardy because your child or teenager isn't turning out the way you hoped? If the answer to one or more of these questions is yes, you may be at risk for broadcasting all sorts of critical messages. You may also find yourself owning your child's problem more than he does, thus preventing him from assuming his share of responsibility (and virtually guaranteeing that whatever you have in mind as a solution won't work).

Whose issue is this? (Part 2) Is your child or adolescent concerned about her weight, even though she looks perfectly fine to you? At any given time, a significant percentage of adolescents are attempting some sort of diet, often based on unrealistic ideals of physical beauty tied to being thin. A variation on this theme involves a dedicated dancer or athlete who becomes alarmed over gaining a few pounds, which may in fact be tied to normal development. It's tempting to brush these situations off as adolescent drama, but kids have been known to take drastic (or even dangerous) measures to correct what they perceive to be a threat to their performance. We will discuss these issues in the next Special Concerns section, "Eating Disorders," beginning on page 401.

Assuming that there is a definite problem with your child's weight and its physical and emotional consequences, there are several action items to consider and a number of pitfalls to avoid if at all possible. Remember that the measures we discussed above for preventing children from becoming overweight also apply here—indeed, we'll repeat a couple of them for good measure.

1. Get professional input. Ideally this should include two evaluations. One should be done by your child's physician to clarify whether there is a weight problem (and to what degree) and to determine if any other health issues might be present (such as elevated blood pressure, cholesterol, or glucose). The other person to have on your team if at all possible is a registered dietitian who works with children and adolescents. The kind of help you should seek from the dietitian is *not* a lecture about overeating and a highly restricted diet for your child, but rather information for the entire family as well as some positive engagement with and encouragement for the child (see below). If you are dealing with a teenager, a lot of other emotional and social undercurrents will likely need to be addressed. Unrealistic expectations about weight, body image, and dieting may call for some gentle reality checks. A dietitian who works with adolescents should be well aware of these issues and adept at gaining the confidence of a teenager so that they can be discussed in a candid but nonjudgmental way. (It may be appropriate, by the way, to allow for some one-on-one time between the dietitian and your child or teenager.) You need to be open to the possibility that the weight problem is the tip of an emotional iceberg. If the dietitian identifies some personal and family issues that would best be addressed by a qualified counselor, don't ignore this advice.

2. Do not make a specific restrictive diet the focus of your efforts, except under unusual circumstances involving professional supervision. This orientation to attitude and daily habits is essential for overweight children and adolescents, who respond far better to behavioral change than to diets. Earlier in this section we mentioned that attempting to force a child to eat food items or quantities that he doesn't want is a miserable exercise in futility. The same is true with attempts to force a child to adhere to a strict diet plan, *especially* if it involves spending a lot of time being hungry. Hunger is unpleasant for all of us, and for a child it is particularly unsettling. Even if you are able to enforce this type of approach for a few days at a time, you can count on your child to figure out how to get around it. Everyone will lose in the process—the child will overeat in order to compensate (or retaliate) for the ordeal, and you will be at odds with him in an important arena where you should be allies.

3. At all costs, avoid nagging, name-calling, insults, or other negativity as a tactic to "encourage" weight loss. If she is truly overweight, your child is almost certainly receiving a heart-wrenching amount of negativity from her peers and perhaps from some thoughtless adults as well. *It is particularly crucial that she understands that her worth* *as God's child and yours—and His and your love for her—do not change based on what she weighs.* This also means that you'll need to impose a moratorium on wisecracks from other family members (especially brothers and sisters) about her weight. In fact, it's a good idea to think twice before making critical remarks about *anyone's* weight problem, because your overweight child will likely apply that sentiment to herself as well.

4. Accentuate the positive. The changes in eating habits that you'll be encouraging for your overweight child or adolescent are *good* for him, in every sense of the word. They are not a punishment or a sign of failure or stupidity. What you are promoting is not endless deprivation but learning to truly enjoy eating. Indeed, there are far more intriguing foods and flavors awaiting those who get out of the burger/fries/soft drink rut. Go out of your way to praise good eating decisions rather than focusing on blocking bad ones.

5. Everyone in the family should be eating from the same meal plan, which can be healthy without being austere. What's good and healthy for the overweight person(s) should be good and healthy—and pleasant as well—for everyone else in the family. Giving one person a plate of broccoli and carrot sticks while the others are having burgers and fries will guarantee resentment and failure.

You'll want to emphasize these types of foods:

- Fresh vegetables and fruits.
- Whole-grain cereals and breads. Try whole-grain pasta, but if it's not to your liking, try slightly undercooked regular pasta (al dente style), which is absorbed more slowly.
- Lean cuts of meat in modest (palm-sized) portions—preferably grilled, baked, or broiled. Steer clear of the deep-fried stuff.
- Water or milk instead of soft drinks or sweetened juice-flavored drinks.

6. As with adults, gradual changes in eating habits (and thus weight) are more likely to succeed than drastic commando tactics. If everyone in the family is *really* ready to jettison soft drinks, high-calorie fat/sweet snacks, and frequent trips to fast-food restaurants, great. If not, it may be better to phase these items out and introduce better choices over time.

7. While you can't ultimately force an overweight child or teenager to watch what he eats, you can take a number of steps to encourage better habits.

- As much as possible, make three meals and two snacks predictable events every day. The object of these is to satisfy hunger and enjoy pleasant food, but also to learn (or relearn) to recognize when the hunger is gone as a cue to stop.
- Encourage (and model) eating slowly, which may take a lot of patience. To avoid constant verbal nagging, you may want to create signals to remind your child to slow down. A silent maneuver such as a referee's time-out gesture might serve this purpose, with an understanding that you're reminding him to put his utensils down, chew and swallow his bite of food, and then silently count to ten before picking up the fork again. (You could even do a subtle version of this in a restaurant so as not to embarrass him.)

We noted earlier that consuming three 8-ounce soft drinks daily could potentially lead to a weight gain of as much as thirty pounds every year if these were excess calories—that is, calories beyond the number needed for normal metabolism and daily activities. Conversely, phasing out a daily intake of soft drinks or sweetened juice drinks may by itself lead to loss of excessive weight. The heaviest third of teenagers who participated in one research study lost about one pound per month by substituting water or diet soft drinks for sugar-sweetened drinks—without any other change in diet or increase in physical activity.

- As part of the "take your time while eating" campaign, you can certainly encourage your kids to enjoy their food—but this involves paying attention to it while they're eating. This means, among other things, that you should phase out meals in front of the TV, and by all means don't let it play in the background while you're sharing a meal. (You may of course make an exception for a "TV dinner" on an unusual occasion in which everyone in the family has an interest in the program being televised.)
- If providing predictable meals and snacks means you don't intend for your overweight child or teenager to be hungry, it also means that random eating can be ended. You'll want to remove open boxes, bags, and bowls of snack foods that cue this type of mindless munching, especially while doing other activities. Don't allow food to be taken, scattered, and stashed all over the house.
- Encourage physical activity in which everyone in the family participates—hiking, biking, gardening, backyard games, and so on. As much as possible, lead by example and encourage kids to join you.
- Set a family policy limiting recreational time spent in front of TV, computer, or electronic-game screens. Two hours per day should be the maximum as a

THE STOPLIGHT DIET

One teaching tool used by many pediatricians and dietitians to give children a feel for foods to eat and foods to avoid is the Stoplight Diet. This simple approach, devised in the 1970s by University of Buffalo psychologist and childhood obesity expert Dr. Leonard Epstein, links various types of foods with the colors of a traffic light:

- "Red" foods are high in calories and low in nutritional yield, and should be avoided as much as possible. These include items such as (you guessed it) cookies, candy, soft drinks, doughnuts, fried foods, and sugary cereals.
- "Yellow" foods are moderate in calories and nutritional yield, and should be eaten in moderate portions. These include starchy foods (such as bread, low-fiber cereal, pasta, rice, muffins, crackers) as well as cheese, butter, and eggs.
- "Green" foods are low in calories and high in nutritional yield, so *go right ahead*. These include vegetables and fruits, whole-grain cereals, lean meats, and low- or nonfat dairy products.

Think of this as a way to prioritize the foods you and your children will eat, perhaps setting a goal to limit "red" foods to once a day. (Make sure your kids understand that the categories aren't related to the actual color of the food.) Your approach should have a light touch to it. Have a little family fun together as you try to figure out which foods in the fridge and cupboards belong in which category and plant some appropriately colored stickers on them as a reminder. You might even change the emphasis from the stoplight—what should be avoided—to the "go light."

The point isn't to create a rigid and legalistic system for your family, but rather to help children (especially preteens) get a handle on the foods that will serve them well throughout life. If you're interested in using the stoplight approach in more detail, check your local library for *The Stoplight Diet for Children* by Leonard Epstein and Sally Squires. ■

general rule (with exceptions for special events, of course), and everyone in the family should abide by these limits.

It will take some time, attention, prayer, and a fair amount of trial and error to figure out the strategies that will work for your child and your family. If you don't seem to be making any progress, by all means regroup with the dietitian (or schedule your first visit, if you haven't done this yet) and figure out what's working and what isn't. Ditto if your efforts to help an overweight child or teenager (and improve the family eating habits) are deteriorating into a lot of arguing and hard feelings. The dietitian will no doubt have many ideas for you to adapt to your own situation, and they may be more meaningful after you've tried a few things already.

Remember that, as with training and molding your children in any area, there is no surefire, detailed plan that works for everyone. There are, however, some fundamental goals and principles (as outlined above) that should give you a basic sense of direction as you work out the specifics for your own family. If you are struggling with your children over food-related issues, two books by childhood nutrition expert Ellyn Satter may prove very helpful: *Child of Mine: Feeding with Love and Good Sense* (Bull Publishing, revised in 2000) addresses in great detail the feeding of infants, toddlers, and preschoolers; and *How to Get Your Kid to Eat—but Not Too Much* (Bull Publishing, 1987) deals with eating issues from birth through adolescence. Another excellent resource focused specifically on the overweight child is *SuperSized Kids: How to Rescue Your Child from the Obesity Threat* by Walt Larimore, MD (Warner Books, 2006).

What about Diet Pills or Even Bariatric Surgery for Children and Teenagers?

Prescription diet medications currently on the market offer very limited (if any) help in weight loss for adults, and nonprescription pills, supplements, and other concoctions sold as cures for obesity serve only to lighten the wallets of those who put their hope in them. *These are not appropriate for children,* and are as unlikely to produce significant results in overweight adolescents as in adults. Prescription medications for weight loss should be considered *only* after careful evaluation of the situation by a dietitian and a physician who have special expertise in their use by this age-group.

Likewise, some bariatric surgery centers are now carrying out gastric banding and bypass procedures on adolescents with severe weight problems. In properly selected teenagers with significant, long-standing obesity (especially when medical complications have developed)—those who have failed ongoing supervised weight-loss efforts, who have reached their adult height, and who have been carefully screened (medically and psychologically)—this type of procedure may be health- and even life-preserving. It should only be carried out by surgeons who are highly experienced in performing this surgery on adolescents in the setting of a comprehensive program, most likely in a university or major medical center. If your adolescent is contemplating this type of procedure, ask your primary-care physician (who should be involved in this discussion) for a referral to a qualified bariatric surgeon. You can also check the Web site of the American Society for Bariatric Surgery (ASBS) at http://www.asbs.org to obtain names of members in your area, or contact the ASBS at 100 SW 75th Street, Suite 201, Gainesville, FL 32607 or 352-331-4900.

Eating Disorders

While excessive body fat is a continuing physical and emotional problem for millions of children and adolescents, powerful cultural forces provoke behaviors that pose even more serious threats to the young. We are saturated night and day with powerful images of beautiful, shapely, impossibly sleek women or buff, tight-muscled masculinity. This leads many, especially prepubertal and adolescent girls, into dangerous thinking: *If only I could look like* that, *my problems would be over.* Often this fantasy fuels a deeply felt desire for physical perfection that collides rudely with the imperfect appearance of a very real body seen in the mirror.

The conflict can lead not only to erratic eating habits and dieting, which are not without some risks, but also to the more severely disordered eating patterns known as **bulimia** and **anorexia nervosa**. These eating disorders arise from a complex interaction of anxiety, depression, issues of life, and concern over body image that converge into compulsive and often highly dangerous behaviors that can rob an adolescent of health or life itself.

Because eating disorders are not routinely reported by physicians and counselors to government or professional associations, estimates of the number of people affected vary widely: from five to as many as ten million Americans may manifest an eating disorder at any given time.[1] Of these, 90 percent are women, and most are between the ages of twelve and thirty-five. Recent research suggests that eating disorders are less common in non-Western countries, but their presence appears to be increasing.[2] Athletes, models, dancers, and others in the entertainment industry are at particular risk, usually because of intense concern over maintaining a particular, often unrealistic, appearance or level of performance.

Anorexia nervosa

Anorexia nervosa is a condition of self-imposed starvation that eventually leads to a body weight at least 15 percent below the expected level for an individual's age and height. Affecting as many as one in one hundred girls and young women, it is characterized by an extreme fear of—or antagonism to—gaining weight and a striking disturbance of body image: The anorexic who appears grossly emaciated will look in the mirror and see herself as overweight. This distorted perception typically is stubbornly resistant to feedback from families, friends, and health professionals, even in the face of serious physical and medical consequences.

As more weight is lost, the fear of gaining weight intensifies rather than diminishes, leading to nonstop preoccupation with eating and weight. Behaviors seen in what is called obsessive-compulsive disorder often attend this anorexia as well. What little food is eaten will usually be derived only from "safe" low-calorie sources, often measured out in precise quantities and then consumed in an exacting, almost ritualistic manner. Food might be cut into tiny pieces and then arranged and rearranged on the plate to give the impression that some of it has been eaten. Anorexics may obsess over the number of calories they consume from medication or even from licking a postage stamp. Often they carefully monitor body measurements such as upper arm circumference. The fervor with which calories are restricted is frequently applied to burning them as well, and an anorexic individual will sometimes exercise vigorously for hours every day. Other efforts to rid the body of calories may include "purging" behaviors, such as self-induced vomiting, which are seen more commonly in bulimia nervosa (see below).

It should come as no surprise that medical consequences, most arising from the body's attempt to conserve energy, become more serious as starvation and weight loss continue. With loss of fat and circulating estrogen, the intricate hormonal interplay of a woman's monthly cycle shuts down. (The absence of three consecutive menstrual periods is one of the diagnostic criteria for anorexia nervosa.) This, combined with an ongoing inadequate intake of nutrients and calcium, leads to loss of bone density, which can cause stress fractures, especially during intense exercise.

Starvation leads to reduced capacity of the stomach, delays in its emptying of food, and constipation, all of which may be falsely interpreted by the anorexic as weight gain. Dry skin, thinning of the scalp hair, and development of a fine hair growth on the body called **lanugo** typically occur. Loss of fat stores and metabolic energy conservation lead to a lower body temperature, often causing the anorexic individual to wear more layers of clothing to keep warm. (Wearing extra clothing may also be a strategy to hide changes in body weight during medical checkups.) More serious complications arise in the heart, which typically slows its contraction rate and decreases in size in response to efforts to conserve energy. Heart rhythm might become irregular, sometimes to a degree that is life threatening, especially in the presence of purging behavior that can deplete the body of potassium.

For all these reasons, anorexia nervosa should be considered a very serious condition with lethal risks. At least 5 percent—some sources say as high as 20 percent—of anorexics die from starvation, cardiac arrest, or suicide, giving this disorder the dubious distinction of having one of the highest death rates of any mental health condition. (The higher death rates are observed among those with a long duration of anorexia, more severe weight loss, poor family support, and multiple relapses despite treatment.)

Bulimia nervosa

Bulimia nervosa is characterized by behavior known as **bingeing** and **purging**, which may continue for decades. During a binge, an individual quickly consumes an enormous amount of food containing many thousands of calories, often without even chewing or tasting it. The resulting physical and emotional discomfort will then provoke a purge, usually involving self-induced vomiting. Bulimics often use laxatives and diuretics (medications that increase urine output), sometimes in dangerous quantities, in a misguided belief that the medication will somehow help rid the body of the food that isn't lost through vomiting. The bingeing and purging cycles may occur a few times a week or, in severe cases, several times daily.

Bulimia is more common than anorexia, affecting an estimated one to 3 percent of women in Western countries at some time in life, but it frequently goes undetected because most episodes take place in secret and typically do not lead to significant weight loss. (However, some individuals with anorexia may engage in binge-and-purge behaviors.) Nevertheless, bulimia can have many serious medical consequences. The repeated exposure of teeth to stomach acid (during vomiting) erodes enamel, causes a yellowish discoloration, and sometimes leads to decay. The throat and esophagus may become chronically inflamed, and the salivary glands—especially the parotid glands that lie directly in front of the ears—can become enlarged in response to continuing episodes of vomiting. Repeated use of laxatives often leads to severe constipation, while heavy diuretic use may have an adverse effect on kidney function.

Potentially dangerous disturbances in heart rhythm can arise from the repeated loss of potassium from vomiting, as well as from excessive ingestion of diuretics and laxatives. Other equally serious (but fortunately uncommon) events include bleeding and even rupture of the esophagus or stomach from frequent vomiting. Food aspirated into the airway during vomiting can cause choking or pneumonia.

More recently the concept of **binge-eating disorder**, which some experts consider to be a form of bulimia (but others characterize as an obesity disorder), has received increasing attention among those who study eating disorders. There is not a consensus at this time as to a precise definition, or whether binge eating should even be formally classified as a behavior disorder, but some believe that it is in fact the *most* common eating disorder. Binge-eating disorder involves repeated episodes (lasting at least two hours) of eating excessive amounts of food, but without the purging and exercising behaviors seen with bulimia. Binge eaters often eat alone, consume their food quickly until they experience discomfort or pain, and are aware that their eating is out of control. Depression, anxiety, and frequent unsuccessful dieting attempts are common. Because they are not vomiting or using diuretics and laxatives to counter their excessive food intake, binge eaters are not prone to the medical complications of bulimia. Not surprisingly, however, most (though not all) binge eaters are overweight, although the converse is not true: Most overweight people are not binge eaters.

What Causes Eating Disorders?

What influences cause such seemingly unrewarding and even dangerous behaviors? While each case is unique, potential contributing factors include the following:

- *Personality and psychological factors.* A typical profile of an anorexia patient is a perfectionist, high-achieving, adolescent female. She may be seen as a compliant, "good" girl by her parents (one or both of whom might be perfectionists also), and she usually does not rebel or even have much of a social or dating life. While excelling in many areas, she may berate herself over any performance that falls short of perfection. Some researchers theorize that refusing to eat may serve as a form of rebellion or that it may represent one area of her life over which she can exercise total control. Bulimics, on the other hand, are less predictable in personality and attributes, although alcohol or drug abuse may be a concurrent issue. In nearly all individuals with either type of eating disorder, anxiety and depression play a significant role.

- *Biochemical factors.* Chemical messengers in the brain called *neurotransmitters* are known to be associated with mood, emotional stability, appetite, and sleep. Many people are genetically vulnerable to changes in neurotransmitter levels, which can lead to overt depression and anxiety disorders, as well as a condition called **obsessive-compulsive disorder (OCD)**—performing certain repetitive acts or ritualistic behavior to relieve anxiety. Neurotransmitter imbalances appear to play a role in the origin of eating disorders, and many features of anorexia bear a striking resemblance to those of OCD.
- *Cultural factors.* In developed countries, advertisements, films, videos, and TV programs continually display images of bodily perfection, especially for females. Those who are shapely, sleek, and most of all *thin* are seen as successful, sophisticated, desirable, and apparently free of emotional or personal pain. A vulnerable individual who desperately desires these attributes but cannot attain them through normal means may engage in unhealthy and extreme behaviors.
- *The "pro-ana"/"pro-mia" subculture.* Some people with eating disorders (especially adolescents) have been known to share "tricks of the trade" with one another. But a more disturbing development over the past several years has been the emergence of Web sites proclaiming anorexia and bulimia to be positive lifestyles and not disorders. Posting "Thin Commandments" (such as "Being thin is more important than being healthy" and "Being thin and not eating are signs of true willpower and success"), bingeing and purging tips, and "thinspiration" stories, these sites offer an unsettling look into the mind-set of those who are not interested in "recovering" from their ongoing behavior. One researcher has aptly summarized the key ideas of pro-ana Web site content as "strength, will, achievement, fulfillment; eating disorders are portrayed as a means of achieving perfection and of forming an elite, a group of humans who have successfully 'mastered' or 'governed' their bodies."[3]

Because eating disorders can put health and even life in serious jeopardy, they should be taken very seriously. Initiating treatment can be difficult for the bulimic, who hides so much of her disordered behavior, and for the anorexic, who may stubbornly deny that she needs help and undermine (or vigorously oppose) therapeutic efforts.

In order to be effective, treatment must address a variety of issues and will often require a team approach. A thorough medical evaluation is extremely important and will sometimes reveal a variety of problems that need attention. Counseling will be needed on a long-term basis and should involve the entire family. Antidepressant medication that normalizes neurotransmitter levels can help stabilize mood, relieve depression, and reduce the obsessive component of anorexia. A dietitian should also be involved to provide nutritional input and accountability. Pastoral counseling (ideally by someone who has some familiarity with eating disorders) can help address issues of guilt and shame, as well as critical worldview and spiritual issues, especially for those who see their eating behavior as a means of achieving self-mastery and perfection. In severe cases of anorexia, hospitalization and medically supervised refeeding may be necessary to prevent a fatal outcome.

How parents can help

It is impossible to predict who might develop an eating disorder, but it *is* possible for parents to reduce an adolescent's risk in the following ways:

Beware of perfectionism, especially in regard to a child's weight or physical appearance. Your child must understand that her worth and your acceptance of her are not based on physical beauty or perfect performance but are, in fact, unconditional. If you have difficulty expressing this idea to your child or adolescent, you might need to address this issue in counseling on your own.

Beware of demands on an adolescent to "make weight" for an athletic team, slim down for a cheerleading or dance team, or in some other way subject the body to stringent dietary restrictions for any reason.

Help your child understand that body shape and build have a strong genetic basis and that few women are capable of attaining cover-girl status, even with intense effort.

Eliminate from your own and your family's conversations jokes or other demeaning comments about the appearance of others.

Point out to your children how advertising and other media put forth images of beauty and body image that are out of reach for nearly everyone.

Be a good role model in your own eating and exercise habits, and be careful about openly criticizing your own body appearance.

Focus on relationships and building emotional intimacy in your family, rather than on food-related issues. Be aware of the purposes beyond relieving hunger that food might be serving in your home. Is it used for comfort or reward? Is it used to relieve boredom? Be careful not to use food as a substitute for hugs and saying "I love you."

Education Issues

The human capacity to receive information, store it, process it, retrieve it, alter it, and then apply it to new situations is a profoundly complex process and a unique gift from God. It should inspire awe whether we are beholding an infant's recognition of a face, a school-age child's first comprehension of a multiplication table, or a college student's completion of a senior thesis. Developing this capacity to its fullest is a lifelong project, but it is particularly important during childhood and adolescence. The benefits of doing so for individuals and for society at large have long been recognized, leading to mandates for compulsory education in most developed countries.

The educational process does not suddenly begin when a child reaches the age of five and enters kindergarten.
Vast amounts of information about the world and how it works are assimilated during the first several months of life through an infant's interactions within his family. The infant examines objects with his eyes, hands, and mouth, bangs them together, and drops them on the floor while observing what happens. The toddler eagerly explores any place his wobbly legs will take him. Preschoolers are persistently curious about how (and why) things work as they do and are eager for input from adults and other siblings.

Parents can encourage all of these learning processes and, in so doing, prepare their children for formal education in very simple ways:

Interact constantly with your child during the early years in ways that are appropriate to his age. Talk to your baby a lot, even before he is using words himself, so that he can hear and learn words and phrases. Ask him about what he sees and hears when he is old enough to communicate with you. Let him watch you carry out simple tasks in your home, and talk about what you are doing. (Let him help you, if possible.) Don't delegate this responsibility to the television or other forms of passive entertainment. Your child needs input from people, not electronic devices.

Read to your child and instill in him a love of books, starting at a very early age. A child who is just forming his first words can benefit from sitting on a lap, looking at the pretty pictures in a book, and hearing the soothing words that accompany them. Toddlers and preschoolers become enthralled with stories and want to hear favorites dozens or even hundreds of times. Even a child who is an excellent reader benefits from hearing stories read aloud at home, especially when they inspire interesting conversations. (Actually, this delightful activity can continue long after the kids are completely grown.)

Take your youngster places. Young children love to explore, and virtually any outing you devise can be turned into an adventure. Help him fall in love with the local library. Let him become acquainted with zoos, museums, and other types of exhibits. Take him to an airport, a train station, a harbor, a dairy farm, or a factory where they make something interesting. Let him hear live music or watch a parade from the curbside rather than through the narrow window of a TV screen. You might learn a few things yourself during these outings.

Once the process of formal education begins, parents must remain active participants and not mere bystanders.

It is a major miscalculation to assume that you can drop your child at the schoolhouse door at the age of five and expect others to take over the total responsibility of educating him for the next thirteen years. You must play an active, ongoing role in selecting the school; tracking his progress; and encouraging, coaching, and troubleshooting when problems arise. No school "owns" your child while he is on their grounds, and any school your child attends is accountable to you—not the other way around. You may even choose to provide some or most of your child's education at home. Whatever approaches you and your child follow, remember that you should be in charge and that you are ultimately responsible for the outcome.

What Type of School Setting Should a Child Attend?

The answer is *whatever works best for him and the family.* Your child may thrive in the public-school system, at a private school, or in a home-school program from the first day of kindergarten through senior high graduation. For some children and teenagers, the best approach involves spending varying amounts of time in different educational settings. Input from friends, relatives, and others in your community can help you clarify your options, but you should not be pressured into an educational decision that doesn't best fit your child's needs and your capabilities. Remember also that what works best for one child may be very different from what works for another within the same family.

Public schools are attended by the majority of children between the ages of five and eighteen.

Advantages of public schools include:

- They are available without tuition in every community. (If the nearest facility is some distance from your home, transportation is normally available at no or minimal cost.)
- They are likely to have resources, equipment, and programs that are difficult to duplicate in other settings.
- In many communities public schools maintain a commitment to excellence and achievement that can help a child reach his fullest potential.

Disadvantages of public schools (which vary greatly between school districts and individual facilities) may include the following:

- Large class sizes might minimize individual attention to a child's particular needs or strengths.
- Social environments in some schools are disruptive to learning, oppressive, or even dangerous.
- Formal prayer and religious teaching are not allowed in the public-school classrooms.
- Some schools or teachers may promote agendas that contradict values taught at home. (For example, teaching about sexuality may stress condoms and contraception while ignoring or minimizing the importance of responsibility, abstinence, and connecting sexuality to a value system.)

If your child attends public school, there are several things you as parents can do to help him achieve successful learning there:

- Get involved with the school in a supportive way. Take part in school functions and, if possible, become a classroom volunteer. Join the local parent-teacher organization (PTO) for your child's school. Make friends with the teachers and administrators, pray for them, and let them know how much you appreciate what they are doing. They have an incredibly challenging and often stressful job, and they would appreciate any words of praise. Assume that you and the school's faculty are on the same team, unless ongoing problems convince you otherwise. A great way to support your child is through a mothers' prayer group such as Moms in Touch International (800-949-MOMS or http://www.momsintouch.org).
- Talk to your child on a regular basis about what is going on at school. Keep track of the materials your child is bringing home, not only to make sure she is keeping up on her schoolwork, but also to note any trends or issues in the curriculum about which you might have concerns.
- If your child is having run-ins with teachers or other students, gather all the information you can before arriving at any conclusions. If it does appear that your child is being treated unfairly by a teacher or harassed by other students, you will need to lend her some assistance. But if *your child* is acting up in class and causing problems for the teacher or other students, the school might need you to back their efforts to maintain order.
- If you disagree with something that is being taught or promoted at school, deal with your concerns in a gracious, stepwise approach. Make sure your facts are straight. (Perhaps your child didn't give you the "big picture," or she misunderstood what was being said.) Talk about your concerns with the teacher or appropriate administrator without making emotional accusations or threatening to take your issue "all the way to the school board." They've got enough problems on their hands without being browbeaten or bullied. If you feel there is a need for a significant change in the curriculum, your best bet is to join forces with other like-minded parents and work for change within the system. For example, you might volunteer for special committees appointed by the school district (such as the curriculum committee) or even run for a seat on the school board. If you hear about legislation under consideration at the state or local level that would undermine or marginalize values you care about, by all means speak out: write letters, call your representatives, and let your voice be heard. (Just be sure to do your homework. Nothing downgrades

credibility like a passionate response to the wrong information.) Remember: The school—and all the agencies that govern it— are ultimately accountable to you. Just be careful that the measures you take to rectify a wrongheaded agenda, however egregious, generate light and positive results rather than just a lot of heat.

Private schools may range from new and limited operations to well-endowed academies with histories stretching back for centuries. There are several advantages of a private school:

- In most cases private schools have smaller classes; this allows for more individual attention for each child.

THE CHARTER SCHOOL ALTERNATIVE

Since the charter school movement began in the early 1990s, more than 3,600 have been organized in the United States, serving over one million students from kindergarten through twelfth grade. Currently forty states and the District of Columbia have enacted laws that allow the formation of charter schools.

Charter schools are public schools that often have the look and feel of private schools. Each school is "chartered" by a board (consisting mainly of parents and community leaders) that governs it independently from the local public school board. The charter is a contract that holds the school accountable for its overall performance and outlines its educational mission, vision, and goals.

Because charter schools operate independently from local school boards, they manage their own budgets, select their own curricula, and can more easily take innovative approaches to the educational process. Some of these have included uniform codes, same-sex classrooms, and intensive programs aimed at developing character and ethical decision-making skills. Charter schools may focus on certain academic priorities or serve special populations. For example, many charter schools take a rigorous college preparatory approach; others may concentrate on the visual and performing arts or the sciences; still others are chartered specifically to address the needs of "at-risk" students who might have difficulty succeeding in traditional academic environments.

Charter schools not only offer academic options that may not be available in local public schools, but by offering an educational choice they often place competitive pressure on local schools. Many experts believe this type of competition can raise the performance of traditional public schools that could potentially lose students to nearby charter schools.

Because charter schools are public schools, they do not charge tuition fees. Charter schools utilize state and district educational dollars, although in many states their funding is lower than that of comparable schools in their district. They also do not receive district funds to buy or build facilities. In addition, most states allow charter schools to hire teachers who have not earned formal credentials. This provision might cause concern for some, but in fact it eases the way for individuals who have accrued "real world" experiences in other career fields to become teachers and share valuable information and life lessons.

- Academic standards are sometimes higher and more rigorously encouraged than in public-school settings.
- There is likely to be stronger control over the social and classroom environment.
- Private schools are free to include religious teaching as part of the curriculum as well as prayer and promotion of moral values that support those taught at home. In Christian academies, teachers can help students integrate a biblical worldview into any and all areas of study.

The disadvantages of private schools include:

- Unless your state has a voucher system in place, it could cost a significant amount of money for tuition and other fees for private education. This may well be worth

Charter schools are not without their critics. Some complain that charter schools divert essential funds from other local public schools. Others point to studies that suggest that charter schools do not perform as well as traditional public schools. But supporters argue that charter schools deal with less bureaucracy and red tape than traditional public schools, and thus utilize educational funds more efficiently. They also assert that studies comparing charter schools unfavorably to public schools contain serious flaws, such as the use of improper comparison groups and inadequate controlling for factors such as poverty.

Not every child is a candidate for a charter school. If you are thinking about sending your child to an existing charter school in your community, do some investigation. Contact a member of the charter school's board or check the school's Web site to review its mission and goals. Schedule a visit to the school to observe how it functions, and ask questions. What is the school's guiding philosophy? How is student progress assessed? If your child has a special interest (such as playing in an orchestra or participating in a particular sport), is that type of program available? Likewise, ask about the financial condition of the school. In addition to state or district funding, is the school receiving grants to assist with operating costs or capital expenses such as classroom computers?

Note that a particular charter school's educational mission might not fit your child. If a local charter school focuses, for example, on music and the performing arts and your child has no interest or aptitude for either, you may be setting her up for difficulties that she would not encounter at a traditional public school. Also, because charter schools rely heavily on parental involvement and often request or require parents to volunteer at the school for a set number of hours, you will need to determine whether you are willing and able to make this type of commitment.

To find out more about charter schools, the laws that allow and govern their formation in your state, and information about the process of starting one, visit http://www.uscharterschools.org. Additional information can be found at the Web site of the Center for Education Reform (http://www.edreform.com). ■

the extra effort, but for many families the extra expense is simply beyond the reach of the family budget.

- The school may have limited resources for programs such as athletics, the arts, or science (for example, laboratory facilities).
- The school may not be equipped to deal with children who have special needs or learning disabilities.

If your child is going to attend private school, all of the parental recommendations noted earlier for public schools apply. In addition, parents can do the following:

- Find out if the school is properly accredited and learn about the teachers who are on staff. What kind of credentials do they hold? Is there a high turnover rate (a bad sign), or do the teachers tend to stay at the school for a number of years?
- Ask about the school's curriculum and approach to academics. Will your child learn basic reading, writing, and mathematical skills? Can he move forward at a faster rate if he is capable? Will he get extra help if he needs it?
- Find out about the school's approach to discipline and maintaining order in the classroom. What are the policies and procedures if a child misbehaves?
- If the school is church-based or has commitments to teaching biblical content and values, how is this carried out? Are special assemblies or class time devoted to this task?

Home schooling has gained considerable momentum over the past several years, and it is definitely not a "fringe" approach to education.

According to the National Center for Education Statistics, between 1999 and 2003 the number of children and adolescents who are home schooled in the United States increased from 850,000 to 1,096,000, or from 1.7 to 2.2 percent of those in kindergarten through twelfth grade.[1] There are several advantages to home schooling:

- Parents can educate their children within the context of the family and all of the security, love, and guidance it affords.
- Home schooling provides maximal flexibility. The content, pace, approach, and style of the curriculum can be adjusted to each child's ability. In addition, home-schooling families can schedule the educational process according to the family's needs, rather than adhere to a fixed academic calendar.
- Home-schooled children have been found in general to learn as well as, if not more quickly and efficiently than, their counterparts in more structured settings.
- While home schooling is most widely carried out among children in elementary and middle-school grades, curricula are available for all age-groups through high school.
- Parents can freely integrate values and faith into their child's curriculum.

Disadvantages of home schooling include:

- Home schooling is a significant undertaking for one or (ideally) both parents, and someone needs to be home to do it. A great amount of time and effort is needed to obtain curriculum, map out the activities and assignments, review work and progress, and so forth. If both parents must work outside the home, or if a single parent is supporting the family, the demands of earning a living will make home schooling extremely difficult.

- Parents involved in home schooling may have to consider and possibly adjust their parenting style when they are functioning as teachers. Low-key, less demanding parents sometimes have difficulty being assertive about imposing assignments and deadlines. Those who are prone to be more controlling and impatient may exasperate their children with excessive structure and workloads.
- Curricula for adolescents (especially in languages, math, and science) might reach a level of complexity that exceeds a parent's education, comprehension, or resources. Outside help will be needed in these situations.
- As with private schools, resources and facilities for certain activities or special needs may not be available within the local home-school community.

If you are planning to become involved in home schooling, there are several things you can do:

- Get in touch with (and possibly join) a local home-school association or support group. In some communities these are highly organized, offering not only information about local and state educational requirements but also an impressive array of activities and guidance regarding curriculum. Some home-school groups organize special classes (for example, in science, math, or languages), field trips, athletic teams, and graduation ceremonies.
- Don't try to reinvent the wheel (unless you really want to). A variety of curricula are available for all age-groups that can provide you with a basic outline and study materials for virtually any subject.
- Be patient and flexible. Part of the advantage of the home-school environment is that you do not need to stay locked into a particular approach if it isn't working for you and your child.

What If Your Child Isn't Doing Well in School?

Every parent dreads the prospect of discovering that his child is falling behind or utterly failing in one or more subjects in school. Whether the news is delivered by a teacher or suspected when a child is having difficulty in a home-school environment, it is very important to work diligently to find out what is (or isn't) going wrong and then seek to correct it or at least make improvements as soon as possible. The emotional distress of falling behind, of feeling overwhelmed, or of being singled out as "stupid" or a "retard" can be devastating to a child and can start him on a downhill spiral with disastrous consequences. The child who decides that school isn't for him and isn't worth the hassle will "check out," first emotionally and then literally, charting his first steps on a course toward low-paying, unskilled labor or even unemployability because of inadequate job skills. In a worst-case scenario, the frustrated child or adolescent will find others who share his lack of regard for school, increasing his risk for destructive or even criminal activity.

Because learning is such a complex process, simple answers and quick fixes for such problems are rarely, if ever, available. Furthermore, any number of conditions may interfere with school performance, and in some children more than one factor may be involved.

A problem with vision or hearing. The eyes and ears are the primary entry points for information that the brain must receive and process. If a child cannot see or hear adequately, the demands of school will eventually overwhelm his ability to compensate for these deficits. Usually both vision and hearing are evaluated at a child's five-year medical checkup, but gradual changes might take place over a period of years. Periodical checkups are important and should be scheduled.

Emotional or personal turmoil. A child who is besieged by personal issues (such as parental divorce, frequent moves, or loneliness) may be too distracted to attend to school-related tasks. If anxiety and depression interfere with concentration and memory, your child may need specific medical intervention as well as counseling (see the Special Concerns section, "Recognizing Depression and Preventing Suicide in Children and Adolescents," page 571).

Attention deficit/hyperactivity disorder (ADHD). This important condition is discussed in detail in the Special Concerns section beginning on page 379.

Learning disabilities. These are disorders of the complex mechanisms in the brain that are responsible for processing written or spoken material. Nearly 3 million school-age children in public schools (about 5 percent) have been classified as having learning disabilities and receive some type of special-education support. (This number does not include children in private schools or who are home schooled.)[2] Children with learning disabilities by definition have normal or above-average intelligence yet have significant problems with one or more of the following activities: reading, writing, listening, speaking, concentration, or performing mathematical computations. (This does not mean, incidentally, that all children with problems in a particular subject area have a learning disability.)

In most cases, the reason for a learning disability is unknown. Heredity may play a role, manifested by learning disabilities that run in a family. However, these difficulties are sometimes associated with prematurity, exposure to toxins (such as alcohol or illicit drugs) prior to birth, infections of the central nervous system, or head injuries. Another contributing factor in some children is a lack of appropriate stimulation during the early years of life, resulting from extremely impoverished or chaotic conditions at home.

A child's medical history might provide clues to the origin of a learning disability, but frequently risk factors and early signs of trouble are not detected during routine physical exams. While a physician's evaluation can be helpful in ruling out other problems, the diagnosis of a learning disability usually requires specific educational and neurodevelopmental testing by a professional who is experienced in this field. Once the problem is identified, treatment could involve a variety of approaches, including new learning strategies, speech therapy, specialized instruction, and curriculum modifications. Coping with a learning disability will require ongoing effort by the child and coaching by professionals and parents for many months or possibly years.

Alternative or unconventional solutions such as dietary modification, megavitamins, special eyeglasses, eye exercises, or "vision training" have failed to pass scientific muster. Resorting to such methods that offer the tantalizing hope of a "cure" for the learning disability will only delay the assistance the child truly needs and may also cost significant sums of money.

Chronic illness. Usually the presence of a chronic illness is already known to the child's parents and physician, and special efforts must be made to minimize absences and their impact on educational progress.

Mental retardation. Significant retardation is usually diagnosed during infancy or the preschool years, but milder forms may not be apparent until a child begins having difficulty in the early grades of school. Appropriate testing by a qualified psychologist can identify this problem, which should be managed in such a way as to maximize the child's educational potential.

Miscellaneous factors. These could include motivational difficulties, learning styles that do not accommodate well to standard classroom activities, and issues of personality and temperament that conflict with school activities.

Helping a child who is having difficulty at school will require both parents and professionals working with the child as a supportive team. If there are family issues at home causing significant anxiety or distraction, counseling may be needed to sort them out and regain equilibrium. A physician's evaluation related to this specific problem is a wise idea. Testing and guidance from an educational psychologist, a developmental expert, and/or a special-education teacher will probably be necessary. Sometimes a child needs help with the basic tasks of setting up a work environment at home: turning off the TV, sitting down in a quiet spot, pulling his materials together, and getting started. This can be done gently but firmly through parental guidance.

In general, parents of a child who is having difficulty in school will need to protect him from ridicule, praise the things he does well, and provide ongoing encouragement and exhortation to do the work that needs to get done. Having a learning disability or other difficulty does not mean that a child can't be challenged in a positive way to work on his basic skills and in so doing improve his prospects for the future.

Divorce and Its Effect on Children

"What God has joined together, let no man put asunder."

In spite of this solemn admonition that concludes most wedding ceremonies, more than 40 percent of all marriages are eventually "put asunder" in the United States, which currently has one of the highest divorce rates in the industrialized world.

Not too many decades ago, couples having significant marital conflict frequently saw children as a reason to stay together. Many would postpone divorce and strive to maintain the appearance of normalcy at home until their children were grown and gone. But in the wake of many cultural shifts that began in the 1960s and 1970s, children have come to be seen as beneficiaries of divorce and less often as an obstacle to it: "The children will be better off if we're not arguing/we're not in a loveless marriage." In other words, "Everyone will be better off if we go our separate ways."

The Pain Inflicted by Divorce

After more than three decades of widespread dissolution of marriages, research suggests that, in general, children of divorce are *not* as well off as those who grow up in intact families. Children from divorced homes are more likely to have problems with physical and emotional health, experience academic and behavioral difficulties in school, engage in risky behaviors—alcohol, drugs, and sexual activity—as teens, and even be incarcerated for committing a crime.

Author and researcher Judith Wallerstein reported in *Second Chances: Men, Women, and Children a Decade after Divorce* that in a study of sixty families divorced between 1971 and 1981, ten years after the breakup of their parents the children felt "less protected, less cared for, less comforted" and still had "vivid, gut-wrenching memories of their parents' separation." A comprehensive analysis known as the California Children of Divorce Study found that more than a third of the children studied were dealing with moderate to severe depression five years after their parents' divorce. According to Wallerstein, almost all of the adolescent girls in the study "confronted issues of love, commitment, and marriage with anxiety, sometimes with very great concern about betrayal, abandonment, and not being loved."[1] In a subsequent book, *The Unexpected Legacy of Divorce*, Wallerstein details how children of divorced parents continue to suffer emotional and relational fallout from this event well into their adult lives.[2]

Recent research also suggests that parental divorce may have long-term physical consequences for children. A seventy-year longevity study reported in the *American Journal of Public Health* in 1995 indicated that individuals who were younger than twenty-one years of age when their parents divorced were likely to have a shorter life span than those whose families remained intact.

Even when Mom and Dad's relationship has ongoing conflicts, from a child's perspective the breakup of the family is the end of life as she knows it. Depending upon the age and personality of the child, several immediate and long-term reactions are virtually inevitable, even when the divorce is amicable. These are likely to include fear, insecurity, sadness (in some cases overt depression), anger, and guilt. Younger children are particularly vulnerable to the idea that they were somehow at fault and that "Mommy and Daddy wouldn't have split up if I had been better." Older children and adolescents are often as angry as they are sad; in some cases they act out that anger, especially if the divorce is going to force them to move or cause some other significant change in their normal activities.

Divorce has such serious consequences for all concerned, especially children, that it should be considered an extreme measure. Sometimes there may be no alternative, such as in a marriage that has been severely damaged by repeated and unrepentant infidelity. A partner cannot be forced to stay in a marriage if he or she has decided to leave it—no matter how fervently the other partner desires to repair the relationship and prevent divorce.

A commitment to avoid divorce at all cost does not mean that all marital partners should drift silently through years of discontent without taking appropriate action when needed. In many ways a marriage is like a house—it needs a solid foundation, ongoing maintenance, intermittent repair, and perhaps major remodeling. Too many couples look at a marriage that needs a lot of repairs and conclude—often too quickly—that it can't be fixed, that they want to move out, or that they never wanted to live there in the first place. But when one or more children have grown up in this family and see it as the center of their world, the process of leaving it is traumatic.

A detailed look at the process of marriage mending is beyond the scope of this book, but numerous resources—including books, seminars, support groups, and couples' retreats—are available to help with this task. Most important, a couple whose marriage is in trouble should enlist the help of a counselor whom they trust and with whom they can work over a period of months or years if necessary. This process should also include a spiritual inventory. If both husband and wife have committed their lives to Christ, each should seek to submit to Him daily and consciously place the marriage under His authority. If one or both have not yet established a personal relationship with Christ, there can be no more crucial time to do so than during major marital reconstruction.

Additional accountability to a pastor, other couples (especially those who have built solid marriages over some years), or even mature relatives, assuming they are not contributing to the problem, may be necessary. In a society that seeks a quick fix for everything from excessive weight to misbehaving children, making a commitment to an arduous process of restoring a marriage—especially when the possibility of a satisfying finished product seems hopelessly out of reach—may require both a leap of faith and a lot of small steps. But when we consider the damage that divorce inflicts upon children, this effort should become a couple's first priority. Ending the marriage should be considered only as the very last resort.

What If Divorce Is Already in Progress?

If a divorce is indeed going to take place, now is a crucial time for you to put your children's welfare ahead of your own emotions. *The divorce process itself can be brutal for children if parents do not make very deliberate choices about their behavior—especially in regard to legal matters.* The following basic decisions can help keep the damage to a minimum.

Settle as many issues as you can outside the courtroom.

The adversarial nature of legal proceedings and the determination of attorneys to deliver the best outcome for their clients can bring out the worst in people, especially if there are many unresolved conflicts between the parents. One or both members of a divorcing couple may feel justified in attacking and blaming the other for what has happened or even taking revenge in a public courtroom for hurts that have been suffered. You owe it to your children to resolve as many issues as you can without turning the process into an endless nightmare of fights and name-calling, lawsuits and countersuits, and meetings with lawyers and judges.

Not only is this type of open warfare between Mom and Dad traumatic for their children to watch, but it ultimately imposes a major financial burden on a family already beset with a great deal of stress. Do you really want to spend your children's college funds on unnecessary and avoidable legal fees? No matter how much hurt a spouse may have inflicted, it is unwise to finance your retaliation with your children's (and your) future. When decisions have been reached by mutual agreement, expensive enforcement procedures are less likely to be needed later.

A competent professional mediator or a divorce attorney who places a high priority on fairness and maintaining civility in family relationships may be able to help a couple come to an agreement without the pain and cost of a bruising legal battle. If a spouse is determined to "play dirty" in court, you will probably have no choice but to defend yourself—but don't assume that your only resource is to "fight fire with fire." Your children will likely be burned in the process.

Do not ask your children to take sides.

When you feel you have been wronged by your estranged spouse, it is natural to want those closest to you to sympathize with your cause. But you must consider very carefully what is appropriate for your children to hear about your difficulties with the other parent. Even if it is clear that you have not been treated respectfully or fairly, telling your children all about your spouse's misdeeds may help you feel better for a while, but it could be devastating for them.

If you are going through a divorce, your children are already struggling with how to relate to both parents in a situation that feels very unnatural and threatening to them. It is inappropriate—and blatantly unfair—for them to be called upon to choose sides, to relay messages between warring parents, or to hear unpleasant details that are neither their responsibility nor under their control.

Children are born with the need and desire to love both parents. It is not your prerogative to isolate them from their other parent's love, even when that person has hurt you. In some situations it will be necessary for children to have limited (or no) access to a parent whose lifestyle is unhealthy or dangerous. Even then, however, in many cases the children may be able to maintain a relationship within certain boundaries.

Do not allow your conflicts with a spouse to interfere with your responsibility for the children.

A skillful attorney might be able to win a settlement that is more favorable to one party than it is fair. But a loving parent may have to consider relinquishing a few "points" in the divorce negotiations if doing so means that the children will receive better care and resources adequate to meet their needs.

A frightening number of otherwise reasonable adults become neglectful after a divorce settlement, and in doing so, act in a way that defies God's principles for caring for their families. If you owe child support, it is important—and right—to pay it when due. Furthermore, you need to make certain that your child's medical needs are properly met, even if doing so involves contributing more than is required of you. Your former spouse may be struggling to pay bills and provide a decent home for your children. Strive to be helpful and supportive in such a situation rather than add to the problem.

Do not turn to your children for emotional support.

As vulnerable as you may feel while your marriage is ending, it is your responsibility to be the emotional anchor for your children—and not the other way around. While you can't avoid allowing them to see your sadness or even anger at times, you will need to make extra efforts to provide stability for your children at a time when their world feels very unsafe to them. Providing stability will include repeated reassurances that the divorce is not their fault and ongoing confirmation that they are still loved by both parents.

Above all, it is not their job to take care of you or become your confidant, even if they appear to be adjusting well to the divorce. Make every effort to find the emotional support you need through relationships with other adults.

What If Divorce Has Already Taken Place?

Even when a marriage has ended, it is critical to remember that parenting responsibilities have *not* ended. In the best situations, children of divorced parents should be able to continue a meaningful relationship with both mother and father, even if one has primary custody and the other's contact is more limited.

In reality, this does not always occur. One parent may abandon the other (and the children), move away, adopt a destructive lifestyle, or behave in an abusive manner. In such cases the other parent will need to carry on alone but supported by other adults who can help fill some of the gaps left by the parent who is gone.

Maintain a civil and cooperative relationship with your former spouse.

Assuming that both parents remain involved with the children, every effort should be made to agree upon policies that affect the children. Curfews, spending money, after-school jobs, trips, driving privileges, and disciplinary measures should be handled in a similar manner in both households. This can occur, of course, only if the parents cooperate. Unfortunately, it only takes one parent to create conflict for a child by making new rules, abandoning the old ones, or disregarding the other parent's concerns or wishes. Parents may consider seeking the help of a counselor to help them arrive at appropriate mutual guidelines.

Help your child work through her emotions about life after divorce.
Children will need help processing the emotions that are an inevitable response to the divorce, as unpleasant as those feelings may be. Don't hesitate to connect your child with an appropriate resource—a counselor, youth pastor, or a trusted relative—who can help her sort through her feelings.

Ongoing insecurity and sadness may cause a child to become overly dependent upon (or even clingy with) the parent who is providing the majority of the care. The parent might even reciprocate, allowing a child to assume the role of a confidant or surrogate spouse. This may extend as far as allowing (or even inviting) a child past toddlerhood to sleep in the same bedroom (or bed) with the parent, which is detrimental to the emotional health of both. As hard as it may be in the emotional storms that follow divorce, it is important for a parent to *remain* a parent—loving, affirming, compassionate, but also setting and maintaining appropriate limits for the child and boundaries for their relationship.

Keep discipline and order intact.
Children need structure when life is stable and going well; in the wake of a parental breakup, the security of loving boundaries is more important than ever. Parents are often tempted to "ease up" on children in the interest of relieving sadness or guilt. But abandoning your house rules and failing to take appropriate action when your child misbehaves will only compound the problem.

You may find it especially difficult to maintain discipline if the other parent becomes lax, because the children will be more than willing to point out the differences during a time of conflict ("Dad doesn't make us go to bed this early"). If at all possible, meet with your former spouse and attempt to establish consistent disciplinary policies. If the other person remains lackadaisical or inconsistent in this area, don't lower your own standards—but don't try to overcompensate by becoming more strict.

Take care of yourself.
Because of the significant physical and emotional consequences following divorce, men and women who have undergone this process should be mindful not only of their child's well-being but also of their own health. Basic self-care—a sensible diet, regular exercise, adequate sleep, and a balance of work and recreation—is a starting point. To this should be added the support of a network of friends, involvement in a church (if possible, one that has an active ministry for divorced individuals), and above all, a day-by-day walk with God, who is the ultimate source of life and health.

What about Remarriage and Blended Families?

More than 40 percent of all marriages are actually remarriages for one or both parties, and approximately one in three Americans is a stepparent, stepchild, stepsibling, or in some way a member of a stepfamily. Half of all Americans will be part of a stepfamily at some point in their life. The formation of a new marital partnership in which children from one or both prior relationships come together under the same roof is no small undertaking. Idealized, "Brady Bunch" interactions are a sitcom fantasy, and in the worst situations conflicts between stepsiblings or between children and stepparents can undermine the remarriage or destroy it completely.

At the same time, there is the potential for building a new family that is loving and productive. This is possible with time, patience, and a lot of communication. Some principles to keep in mind include the following:

Remarriage should be preceded by effective counseling to prevent history from repeating itself.

Why did the previous marriage(s) fail? Was there anything that could or should have been done to prevent it? What understanding of God and moral values is each member bringing to this new partnership? What about goals, priorities, and expectations? What are the child-rearing styles of each parent? Does one tend to be more permissive or more authoritarian than the other? Will each person plan to discipline the other's children, and if so, how? All of these questions, and many more, need to be addressed in detail before wedding plans are made.

Beware of sexual involvement during this exploratory process. Not only can it cloud your judgment, but it will send any older children or adolescents at home a mixed message ("Sex outside of marriage is okay for me but not for you"). Sexual entanglement outside of marriage is as bad an idea for adults as it is for adolescents (see Special Concerns "A Parent's Guide to Teen Sexuality," page 509).

The transition from acquaintance/friend to marriage partner and co-parent of someone else's children cannot be made overnight.

Depending upon their ages and experiences, children may manifest intense—and at times contradictory—responses to the prospect of Mom or Dad (or both) getting involved with a new partner. The idea of having a "whole family" again can be appealing, especially if it seems to be making the child's own parent happy. But there will also be anxiety or even agitation over a potential competitor for the parent's affection and attention. Becoming friendly with a new adult in the parent's life might bring up confusing feelings of divided allegiance—*If I like Mom's new boyfriend, does that mean that I'm not being loyal to Dad?* Children of divorce often maintain a fantasy that Mom and Dad will get together again, and remarriage to someone else will end that dream abruptly. Thus, another adult in the parent's life may be greeted by responses that are cool, if not hostile, from the children who are watching developments with great interest and concern.

The plot thickens when remarriage brings into focus the lines of authority. Should the new stepparent be giving out orders or disciplining the partner's children? What happens when the child has a conflict with the stepparent and comes to the natural parent for support and comfort? All of these potential complications should be anticipated and talked over before a remarriage takes place. Even when this is done, the nuts and bolts of daily life will create new issues that must be worked through over many months.

At the outset, it is often best for each parent to handle disciplinary matters for his or her own children, while serving as backup and support for whatever the other parent decides to do. A stepparent's sudden application of rules that the children have not been used to can lead to serious conflict. Each parent can learn something from the other, and in doing so, strengthen his or her own child-rearing skills. A unified parental front in a blended family is every bit as important as in an intact family.

When children from two different families are combined through remarriage, be prepared for some turbulence.

During the initial "getting to know you" process, sweetness and light may prevail. But some degree of conflict is inevitable. For example, a child who has to share his room with a new stepsibling may resent the sudden lack of privacy and will probably be very territorial about his possessions. Issues will arise over who uses the bathroom when, who picks up what, or who does which jobs around the house. Be sure that the house rules, assignments of chores, administration of consequences, and granting of privileges are carried out in ways that are scrupulously fair and open to respectful discussion. Children become extremely indignant if they feel there is favoritism or injustice from either parent.

Be prepared to seek counseling when two families become one.

Given the number of potential conflicts within a blended family, you would be wise to see a counselor to expedite problem solving and troubleshooting. Depending on the damage incurred by the loss of the original family, whether through divorce or death, children in particular may need help adjusting to a new family. This should never be seen as strictly the child's problem but as an issue for the entire family. Family counseling can provide a safe forum in which every family member can share and be heard and, in turn, hear how the others feel.

You, as parents, will need outside support as well. A church family or local support group might provide this, but don't hesitate to see a counselor or pastor for more focused aid if you need it.

Conflict within the Family—Parental Disagreements and Sibling Rivalry

Conflict between parents and their children is inevitable. The toddler's foot-stomping negativity, the preschooler's refusal to pick up his toys, the schoolchild's disinterest in homework and chores, and the adolescent's adamant declarations of independence from parental restrictions are but a few variations on this universal theme. But conflicts within families are not limited to differences of opinion (or pitched battles) between parents and children. Parents normally disagree with one another about any number of concerns, even in the most harmonious marriages. Furthermore, if they have more than one child, strife between offspring is so common that it has achieved a well-worn title: sibling rivalry. Thus for any family the question isn't so much *whether* discord will arise, but *how to manage it* in a way that will build up rather than tear down relationships.

A variety of age-specific suggestions for handling conflicts between parents and children are set forth throughout the chapters and Special Concerns sections of this book (see particularly "Principles of Discipline and Training," page 259). This section is concerned primarily with conflicts between members of the same generation—between parents or between children.

When Mom and Dad Disagree

It is a sad fact that *few people have the opportunity to observe their parents resolve a conflict in a positive and mutually satisfying manner.* Instead, disagreements within a marriage all too often deteriorate into one of several unhealthy scenarios:

- *Suppression.* Fear of conflict causes husband and wife (or both) to allow issues to smolder and simmer—sometimes for years—into a stew of resentment. There may not be any fireworks in the home, but there's not much happiness either.
- *Repression.* One person dominates the other, winning every conflict through physical or verbal intimidation.

- *Guerrilla warfare.* Conflicts are manifested through quick jabs—indirect put-downs, subtle insults, sly sarcastic comments—that chip away at the other person without ever dealing with any issues directly.
- *Character assassination.* One person is subjected to name-calling, harsh remarks about appearance or intelligence, or ongoing scorn for his or her opinions or motives by the other. Continuing direct assaults on an individual's identity and value create wounds that can take years to heal, and such behavior indicates that the relationship is in serious trouble.
- *Dredging up past grievances.* This tactic is manifested by counterproductive phrases such as "You *always* do this" or "Here we go again" or "This is just like that time when . . ." It is virtually impossible to settle the present issue when baggage from the past is continually dragged out of the closet.
- *All-out war.* Yelling, abusive language, shoving, and hitting are clear signs that the marriage is seriously damaged.

Children who have repeatedly observed one or more of these destructive responses to conflict are likely to be ill equipped to manage disagreements that will inevitably arise in their own marriages. Unhealthy patterns may thus be perpetuated—either duplicating what was demonstrated by the older generation or perhaps moving toward opposite extremes. For example, someone who has lived through many intense and painful arguments may decide to ignore or sidestep issues to avoid the threat of an unpleasant altercation. But his course of inaction can allow anger and resentment to fester for years, leading ultimately to a sour—or dead—marriage.

If parents hope to demonstrate healthy conflict resolution for their children, they will need to practice—both before and after children are born. Some couples will have broached this subject during premarital counseling. Virtually every marriage could benefit from working on it in more formal settings—in small groups organized through churches (assuming they are properly led), in couples' communication classes, or in private counseling. While it is not possible to detail in this book all of the principles involved in settling disagreements in marriage, the following basic concepts can serve as a foundation for parents who desire to work on this important area.

Mutual respect is an absolute necessity. Without respect on both sides, any relationship will ultimately deteriorate or become destructive. With mutual respect, it is possible to have an intense disagreement with another person without causing damage to a relationship or those who are affected by it. Respect acknowledges the ultimate worth of the other person—as established by God and not by any other attributes or accomplishments—and affirms that worth in attitudes, words, and actions.

If parents do not respect one another or if respect flows only in one direction, attempts to resolve issues are likely to be unsuccessful or hurtful. This fundamental problem must be addressed—usually in a counseling setting—if a marriage is going to survive and thrive through the years of raising children and beyond.

When a disagreement arises, conversation should focus on the issue and not the person. If Mom feels she needs more help with the kids in the evening, it isn't productive to begin the discussion with the statement "You care more about that TV than your own children!" If Dad is getting worried about the family budget, he won't get very far by saying, "All you ever do is spend the money I work so hard to bring home!" Once the issue is defined ("How do we care for the kids when we're both tired?" or "How can we keep better track of our finances?"), the focus can shift toward generating and evaluating a potential solution.

When an issue needs to be discussed, pick an appropriate time and place. Not at the end of the day when energy is low and fuses may be short; not right before bed; not when anger is at a fever pitch; not when there isn't time to work through it; not when the TV is on, the phone is ringing, the kids are crying, and the dog is barking. If it is clear that an issue needs to be addressed, it's quite all right for either person to call a time-out and say, "This isn't a good time to discuss this" or "I don't feel like talking about it right now"—as long as a specific time is set to talk about it in the very near future. The best time to talk is when both parties are rested, focused, and attentive. It's helpful to work through an issue in a place that is relatively free of distractions and interruptions. This may be a particular room, somewhere out in the yard, or a place away from home. Many couples do their best negotiating at a coffee shop or on a long walk.

Pray together before discussing the issue. Laying the issue before God can help keep it in perspective and reinforce your common ground. Be careful not to use this prayer time unfairly to express your viewpoint or claim God's backing for your side of the conflict. Prayer should be an exercise in humility, not a power play.

Each person must be able to express his or her viewpoint fully, without interruption. A key element of respect is listening carefully to what the other person is saying, without thinking about one's own response. One technique that encourages attentive listening involves picking an object (such as a pen) and stipulating that whoever holds it is entitled to speak without any interruption. The other person cannot say a word until the pen is passed, and the pen will not be passed until the person receiving it can summarize what was just said to the speaker's satisfaction—without argument, rebuttal, or editorial comment. If the listener doesn't get it right, the pen doesn't pass. This approach may at first seem awkward and ritualistic, but it is surprisingly effective at improving listening skills.

Get in the habit of checking frequently to be sure that you understand what the other person is saying. "I hear you saying that . . ."

Avoid "you" statements—especially those containing the words *always*, *never*, *should*, or *shouldn't*. Replace them with statements that express your own feelings. "You never spend any time at home anymore!" essentially demands a rebuttal ("That's not true!"). In contrast, "It seems as if the kids and I are spending more evenings by ourselves than ever before, and it makes me feel lonely" is a straightforward observation and an expression of a genuine feeling. Similarly, a statement such as "You shouldn't make commitments for both of us without talking to me first!" is likely to provoke a defensive response. The one way in which a "you" statement can legitimately enter a conversation is in this form: "When you say (or do)____, I feel____." (For example, "When you make commitments for both of us without talking to me first, I feel as if my opinion doesn't count.") This type of statement can help one person understand how specific words or actions are affecting the other person.

Avoid "why" questions—especially those (once again) containing the words *always* or *never*. "Why do you always leave the back door open?" can be answered in only one of two ways: defensively ("I don't either!") or sarcastically ("Because I'm an idiot!") "Why" questions immediately and automatically turn a discussion into a battle.

Avoid dragging events from the distant past into the current issue. Comments such as "Here we go again!" or "This is just what you did on our vacation five years ago, when you . . ." are likely to derail any productive resolution of the issue at hand. If current problems are indeed related to grievances from the past, then those specific concerns need to be discussed and resolved.

Name-calling and other forms of insults are disrespectful and should be banned from all conversations within a family (or anywhere else). Verbal insults live in everyone's memory long after apologies have been made. One of the most powerful lessons your children can learn from you is how to disagree or be angry with a person without labeling, name-calling, or insulting them in other ways. Remember that body language (sighing, rolling the eyes, etc.), gestures, and tone of voice can communicate disrespect as powerfully as the most explicit insult.

The discussion of an issue should eventually arrive at a point of exploring possible courses of action. "What can I do to help you not feel so tired at the end of the day?" or "How can we make Sunday morning less hectic?" It may help to list a number of possibilities and then talk through the pros and cons of each one.

Realize that on a number of issues you may have to "agree to disagree," and that in doing so, the other person's viewpoint is not to be subject to constant ridicule. This will mean compromising in some cases. There is usually, however, some solution that will allow for each person's needs to be met.

If your discussions of issues frequently deteriorate into shouting matches or glum stalemates, get some help. It takes courage and maturity to go to a counselor, or to a mature couple whom you know to be experienced in conflict resolution, in order to determine what goes wrong when disagreements arise in your home. Constructive suggestions from an unbiased third party, if acted upon consistently, can drastically improve the quality and outcome of these conversations.

Should You Have Disagreements in Front of the Children?

Parental modeling of respectful disagreements can be a powerful and useful life lesson for children to observe, provided that a few cautions are kept in mind:

Consider your audience. The children should be old enough to comprehend what you are talking about and emotionally mature enough to grasp the concept that you can disagree with someone whom you deeply love and respect. Preschoolers and early-grade-school children can become terrified by the thought that Mom and Dad don't like each other and may misinterpret a spirited parental exchange as the unraveling of their world. They probably should rarely, if ever, witness a serious parental disagreement. Older children and adolescents, on the other hand, can benefit from seeing how two mature people can settle an issue in a positive way.

Play by the rules. If kids are going to watch or listen, you should be well versed in healthy conflict resolution, resolve to keep the tone of conversation respectful, and strive to come to a positive resolution of the issue.

Consider demonstrating how you settled an issue. If you have had a particularly fruitful conversation about a problem, think about reenacting it for your children to show how you dealt with it. You might even demonstrate some right and wrong ways to deal with an issue—especially if your children are having some problems in this area themselves.

Beware of voicing a disagreement in front of a child who is the subject of the disagreement. Parents should be united, even if they are not in total agreement, when dealing with basic issues of child rearing—especially those relating to limits and discipline. A child must never get the idea that if Mommy says no, he can go talk to Daddy, or that one parent will veto the other's disciplinary measures. However, with some concerns that are not fundamentally important, an older child might benefit from hearing different viewpoints, as long as they are expressed appropriately. (For example, the pros and cons of going to a summer camp or joining an athletic team could be an excellent topic for discussion among child and parents, even if there is not total agreement about the best decision.)

Declare a cease-fire, if necessary. If your discussion is deteriorating into a shouting match and children are within earshot, *call it off* until you can continue in private—after you have cooled down. It is devastating—and inappropriate—for children to hear their parents yelling, insulting one another, or being physically aggressive. If your disagreement reaches this level, you should not only isolate it from your children but seek counseling as soon as possible.

When Siblings Engage in Combat

This section does not begin with the word *if* because siblings *will* have conflicts—sometimes with shocking ferocity. In some families the nonstop bickering and pummeling that goes on in the backseat of the car, at the kitchen table, around the TV set, or in any other location where two or more children are gathered is enough to cause mothers and fathers to want to turn in their resignation from parenthood. This is particularly exasperating when the parents have not modeled antagonistic or harsh behavior. *Where does all this awful hostility come from? Where did we go wrong?*

What generates so much conflict between brothers and sisters? With rare exception, it is not the result of poor parenting. Much of it is an expression of basic human nature. There is nothing in the human genetic code that spontaneously brings forth from children concern for the rights and needs of others—including their closest family members. This (and nearly all other values) must be taught and modeled by parents, relatives, teachers, and other civilizing influences as children grow up.

A number of other factors may contribute to sibling combat. Recognizing them and working to reduce their impact can go a long way toward maintaining peace in your home.

Desire for parental attention. *There's only so much of Mom or Dad to go around—how do I know that I'm still loved and important?* This isn't merely the unspoken question of a toddler when a new baby comes home. Regardless of the number and the ages involved, if there is more than one child in the nest there may be some serious concerns about (and competition for) a parent's attention. Ironically, in some cases children may instigate a fight merely to get an adult involved with them—even when the consequences are unpleasant. But even if the attention-seeking behavior is annoying, the basic questions are the same: *Who cares about me? Am I significant to anyone? Does what I think or do really matter?*

To avoid endless guilt, you need to acknowledge that you have limits—that you can't be all things to one child, let alone many. Nevertheless, amid all the basic responsibilities of daily living, maintaining a home, generating income, and pursuing church, educational, or community projects, *some time and energy must be available for individual attention to each child on a regular basis.* If your schedule is particularly busy, you should consider setting a regular date with each child, during which he will have your undivided attention. This need not be elaborate; a walk in the park or an outing for an ice-cream cone can be a memorable occasion, provided that the parent isn't distracted by thoughts about all the other things that need to be done at home.

Comparisons. When two children first meet, comparisons are an immediate and normal occurrence: Who is older, bigger, and faster? If there is a disagreement, who is tougher? What toys does one have that the other doesn't? Depending on the situation, these questions may be minor points of interest that do not affect a budding friendship, or they may prove to be a source of major conflict.

Within the close quarters of a family, comparisons between children will be an inevitable daily reality and may become a source of ongoing friction. What happens if one child is a prodigy in school and her brother has learning disabilities? What if one is gifted in sports and another literally can't get to first base? What if the first two children are relatively compliant but the third has a will of steel and a limitless capacity to tell everyone where to get off?

Parents of more than one child will regularly have to exercise a delicate responsibility: recognizing and praising each child's unique skills, strengths, and accomplishments without implying that one sibling is somehow better than another. In some cases, you may have to look a lot harder to find what is praiseworthy, but it is that child who will most need your affirmation. Whatever you do, avoid negative comparisons such as "Why can't you throw a ball like your brother?" or "You'll go a lot farther in life if you buckle down to your schoolwork like your sister does!" These kinds of comments are virtually guaranteed to stir resentment.

Invasion of privacy. While sharing is a virtue that should be encouraged during and after the preschool years, no child—or adult—appreciates having his possessions pawed through, broken, strewn on the floor, or taken to places unknown. This often becomes a point of contention when a child becomes mobile and begins exploring (and trashing) the fascinating toys belonging to older siblings. It is quite appropriate to help an older child safeguard his belongings when there is a toddler on the loose, perhaps by providing closet or shelf space for him that is inaccessible to the younger child, keeping the older child's bedroom door closed, or limiting the range of the toddler's explorations. Unfortunately, older children and adolescents can also thoughtlessly raid a sibling's (or a parent's) possessions, often provoking surprisingly harsh responses.

You need to caution your children about becoming overly attached to and emotional about their possessions. But you also need to instill in them a healthy respect for the possessions of others, especially within your own home.

Oppression. Older children can be merciless in their physical and emotional torment of younger siblings, and parents must be prepared to intervene when this type of behavior is going on. But sometimes younger children can harass and irritate older siblings, and they should not be given free rein to do so simply because they are smaller.

Injustice. "He did it!" and "She started it!" are common "not guilty" pleas of siblings who are asked to account for a mess, a broken toy (or window), or a fight. Many times you will have to sort out who did what to whom, and at times you will need the wisdom of Solomon to dispense justice in the face of conflicting testimony or inconclusive evidence. While children may fervently seek to escape punishment, they care desperately about fairness. Don't play favorites. The fact that one child is normally more compliant than another doesn't mean that he isn't capable of instigating wrongdoing.

In addition to your efforts to minimize these hot spots for sibling rivalry, here are a few more general principles to keep in mind:

Don't get pulled into every conflict. Sometimes children will start an uproar in a misguided attempt to gain adult attention. Ignoring their efforts will reduce the odds of a repeat performance. Even if that isn't their motivation, in some situations it's reasonable to give children a chance to sort out their own conflicts.

Don't let conflicts get out of hand. If the children are not arriving at an appropriate solution, if someone is being bullied, or if insults (or fists) are flying, call a time-out for tempers to cool down.

Repeatedly teach the principle of mutual respect and its implications. Just as marital conflicts must be settled within a framework of mutual respect, so also must disagreements between children. This is the basis for curbing insults and not allowing arguments to escalate into physical combat.

Administer disciplinary measures privately. The embarrassment of being disciplined in front of other people—especially other children who may secretly take pleasure in watching the punishment—is both painful and counterproductive and more likely to lead to resentment than improved behavior.

Discourage tattling. If one child tells you about the misdeeds of another, the second child's behavior must be dealt with, assuming that the story is true. But if the first child seems smug or gleeful while reporting to you what his sibling did, or if he appears to gloat over the other child's discipline, he needs to be reprimanded too. The issue isn't that he reported the wrongdoing; at times such information may prevent an accident or injury. What you want to discourage is the attitude of tattling that derives satisfaction or pleasure from another's "crime and punishment."

Remember that "this too will surely pass." It is often difficult to believe that children who have squabbled so intensely for so many years can actually have civilized relationships later in life. Yet in the vast majority of cases, a child's passage into adolescence and adulthood ends sibling warfare and replaces it with pleasant camaraderie, deepening friendship, and (most surprisingly) fervent loyalty.

Helping Children Cope with Death

Death is a reality not easily grasped by children (or, for that matter, by adults). Between the ages of three and five your child will begin to realize that nothing lives forever, and from then on you can expect him to have many questions, fantasies, and fears about death. He may or may not express these directly, but as he grows through the preschool years and beyond, he will certainly be aware of them. In a variety of ways through the course of childhood and adolescence, he will need to work through his concerns and adjust his understanding of life so that it encompasses and eventually comes to terms with death.

In many ways, talking to a child about this subject poses many of the same problems as talking about sexuality. Both topics are very important matters of the human condition, but they are sensitive, emotional, and difficult to broach with children. Furthermore, most children receive a great many impressions, ideas, and messages—often grossly inaccurate or wrongheaded—about both topics from the media, their friends, and conversations they happen to overhear. Just as a child's knowledge and attitudes about sexuality should not be left to develop by chance, neither should those related to dying and death. The same principles of "decent exposure" described in chapter 11 (see page 372) apply to both of these topics.

Tell the truth.

Misrepresentations or lies about anything, including death, ultimately cause far more harm than good. Tact and gentleness are important, of course, but they should not stray into the realm of fantasy or falsehood. Statements such as "Grandpa went away on a long trip" may sound soothing at the moment, but they will cause problems later as your child attempts to get a grip on what actually happened. *It is very important for a child to know that you will not mislead him, even if the facts aren't comfortable for either of you.* This also means that you will need to prepare him if a loved one is seriously ill or near death. Secrets and hushed conversations do more to raise a child's anxiety than a candid appraisal of the situation expressed in simple terms he can understand.

Provide information on a need-to-know basis.

While telling the truth is imperative, your child's ability to deal with the explicit details of illness or death will definitely depend on his age and maturity. Your preschooler doesn't need to know the pathological details about cancer or the gruesome details of the injuries sustained in an auto accident, especially when it involves someone he has known and loved. On the other hand, a high school student might not be satisfied with generalities, and more specific information would be appropriate.

Be aware of your child's concerns related to death, and address them accordingly.

While every child approaches this subject with a unique set of experiences, some conceptions and concerns are common in particular age-groups. When discussing death with a child, it is very important to understand what she is thinking about, a process that may require gentle questioning, open ears, patience, and the willingness to respond respectfully to whatever you hear.

Younger children (roughly ages three through six) are still in the process of sorting out real versus make-believe, and their understanding of death may include a variety of fantasies or magical beliefs. For example, they may have seen a TV or movie actor die and then show up the next week in another show. Many children have watched E.T. die and then come back to life, and cartoon characters routinely survive severe pummelings. These exposures can cause children to have difficulty understanding the *finality* of physical death, the fact that someone who has died won't come back sometime later.

Younger children may also have problems with cause-and-effect relationships related to death. A child may conclude that something she did, said, or merely thought caused a loved one's death. She may feel terrible guilt and even believe that she can or should do something to bring that person back. Or she might make some frightening connections related to the circumstances of the death. For example, if Grandpa developed a bad cough and then died a week later, someone else's cough could cause a lot of concern: *Daddy has a cough—is he going to die too?*

Older children (ages seven through twelve) are more likely to grasp the realities of death, but as a result they may also be very prone to worry excessively about those they love. If Mom is a half hour late getting home from choir rehearsal, dire images might come to mind: *What if she had an accident? What would I do without her?*

Adolescents dealing with the death of a loved one or perhaps a classmate whose life has been lost to accident or illness will undoubtedly have a variety of strong feelings to sort through. *What if that had been me? How can I go on without_____?* They will need to talk, to be heard and taken seriously, and probably to be held and comforted at some point.

Remember that your child's ideas and attitudes about death are likely to mirror yours.

If you are very anxious about death—as evidenced perhaps by how quickly you attempt to dismiss it or by your reluctance to feel or express grief—your child will pick up on these cues and may well join in your fear. But when the inevitable occasions arise, if you model an open, honest grief that is coupled with your faith, she is likely to adopt that approach.

Death of a Pet

Whenever your family acquires a pet, whether a fifty-cent goldfish or an expensive thoroughbred, you can count on two realities: (1) Your child will form an attachment to it, whether or not you do, and (2) except in unusual circumstances, the pet's life expectancy will be shorter than your child's passage into adulthood.

Depending on the type of animal and the age of the child, it is quite likely that your child will think of a pet as a family member. This is especially true if the pet has been in your home from the time your child was an infant or toddler. Activities and experiences with a pet, especially one that is very affectionate, can become an integral part of a child's earliest recollections and often carry deep emotions. The death of a beloved pet can thus represent a major loss to a child or adolescent.

Do not be surprised if your child becomes upset over the death of even a hamster or a bird. And if the pet was cuddly and deeply loved, the response will probably be much more emotional. A parent's immediate impulse may be to try to make the hurt go away, either by downplaying the loss ("C'mon, Evan, it was only a *cat*, for Pete's sake!") or by replacing the departed pet as quickly as possible. But it is important to give your child a chance to grieve, to cry and sob and say how much he misses the pet. (The same process will nearly always occur, by the way, when a pet is lost or runs away and does not return home.)

Very often the loss of a pet will be the first time a child is confronted at close range with the reality of death. As emotional as this will be, it presents an opportunity not only to comfort but also to walk your child through the process of dealing with the loss of a loved one. Depending on the age of the child(ren) involved, if the pet is going to be sorely missed, you may want to set aside a brief time to acknowledge his passing, either in conversation around the kitchen table or in a brief "memorial service," perhaps in the backyard. This will not only validate everyone's feelings about the pet but also allow them to remember and give thanks for the good times everyone had while he was alive. It provides an opportunity to interact with your child about this difficult subject and especially correct (gently) any misconceptions or fantasies about what happens when an animal—or a human—dies.

It is likely, in the course of your conversations, that your child will ask where the pet is now. Don't worry about being too precise with your theology when talking to younger children. They can be reminded how Jesus taught that not even a sparrow can fall to the ground without God knowing about it—and that God certainly knows about the death of your family pet. If your child asks if the pet is in heaven, be truthful and say that the Bible doesn't tell you—but that it does say quite a bit about the importance of *our* being with God after we die. You might take a few moments to pray together, thanking God for the time the pet was part of your family, and to talk to your child about the most important aspects of your faith.

Death of a Family Member

The death of a family member—especially a grandparent, a brother or sister, and most of all a parent—is a grievous blow to a child of any age. A very young child (before the age of about two and a half) may not feel or be able to verbalize his response the way an older child will, but it will affect his life nonetheless. To best help a child deal with that emotional blow, maintaining heart-to-heart communication is the overriding principle from which all else follows.

Be aware of components—not stages—of grief.

You may have heard about the stages of grief: denial, anger, bargaining, depression, and acceptance, or some variant of these. But the idea that grief unfolds in fixed stages is oversimplified. More commonly, the emotions of grief will vacillate rather wildly from one component to another. In some children, one of these elements may predominate for a long time, or more than one may coexist. When acceptance is experienced, it is rarely fixed and permanent. Rather, as the storm slowly abates, moments of acceptance will eventually extend for longer periods of time. Only after considerable time has passed and a measure of healing has occurred does acceptance of the loss predominate.

Stay with your child.

How do you relate to your child as she experiences a seemingly unending storm of terrible—and terrifying—feelings? The most important point is to comfort her in her grief but not to squelch or discount those feelings. This will never be easy, especially when you are dealing with intense emotions of your own. While there are no formulas for this process, the following are a few examples of a child's various expressions of grief at the death of her mother, and her father's comforting responses. These could apply to a variety of situations.

- *Anger:* "I hate her, I hate her! Why did she have to go?"
- *Response:* "We all get mad when people leave us when we don't want them to. I do too. But Mom wanted to stay with you so much. She just couldn't."
- *Denial:* "I know that Mom is just going to come back after she has a rest."
- *Response:* "You know, sometimes I feel as though Mom is just in another room, and that I'll walk through the door and there she'll be. It hurts so much when she isn't."
- *Bargaining:* "Daddy, if I promise to be really, really good and stop hitting Jimmy, maybe Mommy will come back."
- *Response:* "Sweetheart, you didn't do anything wrong that made Mommy die."

The most natural expression of our loving concern is to try to make the hurt go away as quickly as possible. But grief is a process that will be measured in months rather than in hours or days. This is especially true if a parent has died, because his or her absence will continue to be felt throughout childhood. Indeed, complete healing of this emotional wound may not come until well after a child has reached adulthood.

Try to recognize disguised reactions.

Children will often react to death in ways that serve to protect them against their terrible feelings of loss. Some of these reactions include:

Indifference. A child may become listless and emotionless, displaying a degree of indifference to her loss that seems inappropriate. Children who suffered a major loss (for example, one or both parents) may go through the funeral this way, without tears and seemingly intent on returning to their usual activities as quickly as possible—yet without relish. This may even aggravate other family members: *Doesn't she care about what has happened?* If your child reacts this way, it is important not to try to jolt her into a more "genuine" reaction. Instead, make yourself available to her, spending lots of time together in an atmosphere of caring. Don't pressure her. In time, she will most likely open up and collapse in your arms, pouring out grief that was not apparent immediately after the death occurred.

Acting out. Sometimes instead of talking about their grief, anger, and depression, children will become agitated and irritable, seeming to look for opportunities to misbehave or lash out. While this might appear both insensitive and disrespectful, it may in fact be much easier for a child to do battle with someone else than to deal with the terrible pain that is bottled up inside. While you will need to enforce appropriate rules and limits as consistently as ever, redouble your efforts to initiate nonthreatening conversations during which you can ask some questions. Sometimes you will see with great clarity how a particular misbehavior is directly tied to an unexpressed feeling of loss. Use these moments to take your child aside and explain how you also feel angry at times because of this death, and that you'd like to lash out as well. Perhaps you won't get an immediate acknowledgment, but more often than not you'll see tears begin to well up—and the behavior improve.

Depression. A child may develop a clinical depression after a parent or other loved one dies. A depression, as opposed to normal grief, is manifested in some or all of these ways:

- Unusually persistent and severe grief, showing little or no sign of resolution after a few months and interfering with the child's ability to carry out normal activities.
- Difficulty falling or staying asleep, or the opposite—persistent oversleeping.
- Change in appetite, with unusual weight loss or gain.
- Suicidal thoughts.
- Expressed feelings of hopelessness about the future.
- Withdrawal from normal activities.
- Inability to experience and express pleasure in any activity.
- A sudden change in friends or, in adolescents, drug abuse or sexual activity.

Since normal grief and clinical depression often are so similar in appearance, you may need the counsel of your pastor or a professional to help sort things out. Formal intervention—which could include counseling and, when appropriate, the use of medication—may be necessary and should not be withheld or delayed out of a mistaken notion that "she's young—she'll get over it." Depression is a very real and potentially dangerous disturbance among children and adolescents and should not be ignored (see Special Concerns "Recognizing Depression and Preventing Suicide in Children and Adolescents," page 571).

What about Faith in the Face of Death?

Few events in life bring spiritual concerns into focus as powerfully as the death of a friend or loved one, an event that forces those left behind to face the reality that everyone's life on earth must eventually come to an end. For better or worse, the role that your faith plays in the days and weeks that follow the death of a loved one can have a profound impact on your child. Your child should see God's love and care manifested in you and many others during this intense and difficult experience. The following suggestions might help bring this about:

Think carefully about how you describe God's role in death.
A few generations ago, children and adults alike were surrounded by the cultural and religious beliefs that God routinely struck people down, either as punishment or for no apparent reason ("The Lord gave, and the Lord hath taken away"). Today we are more likely to hear about a God who kills with kindness—"God loved Jenny so much

that He wanted her to be with Him, so He took her to heaven." It is certainly wise to have a healthy respect for God as the One who holds our lives in His hands, and it is very comforting to know that God has welcomed the loved one who has just died. But a child might be reluctant to draw near to Him if she believes that He can hardly wait for her to die—whether as judgment for one or more transgressions or as an act of love. *(If God loved Jenny so much that she died, does that mean that I'm going to die because God loves me?)* Pay attention to the messages you and others give your child about God, and don't hesitate to check in with her to see how these ideas have affected her.

Be honest when you don't have all the answers.

Often it isn't possible to make sense out of a particular death. The question "Why would God let this happen?" has for centuries challenged young and old alike whenever illness or accident ends young and apparently innocent lives. The risk in such situations is to offer shallow or pat answers or in bitterness and frustration to reach the devastating conclusion that God either "isn't there" or "doesn't care." What parent and child need to grasp is that God does indeed care very deeply for each of us, but that we aren't always going to be allowed complete (or even partial) understanding of every event that occurs during our lifetime. (This important concept is discussed in detail in Dr. James Dobson's book *When God Doesn't Make Sense*.)

Don't underestimate your child's ability and willingness to trust in God during difficult times.

Children typically desire and understand intimacy with God in ways that may elude adults, especially during a crisis. Quite simply, if they believe in you and trust in your love, so too will they believe in God and trust in His love. In the emotional upheaval of your own grief, be careful not to hinder a child from finding comfort in God, which often will come naturally to a child.

The Adolescent Years, Part One:
Bodies in Motion

Adolescence: The period of physical and psychological development from the onset of puberty to maturity. (From the Latin *adolescere*: "to grow up.")

Between the twelfth and twenty-first birthdays, your child will undergo rapid and intense physical, psychological, and social changes, and at the end of this period she will no longer be a child. Just as you probably approached the "terrible twos" (sometimes called the "first adolescence") with a combination of eager anticipation and a little apprehension, you may now have a similar mix of positive expectation and growing concern as the "real thing" arrives. Without a doubt, adjustments and challenges are ahead for everyone in the family.

Indeed, the years to come may at times feel like a canoe trip down a mountain river. The scenery is constantly changing; the ride is always interesting and often pleasant; but choppy waters, roaring rapids, and an occasional waterfall may await you around the next bend. Your job will be to stabilize the family canoe as much as possible, and by all means prevent it from turning over before your adolescent reaches the calmer waters of adulthood. Dr. James Dobson has aptly stated that "parenting isn't for cowards," and the coming years may well serve up the greatest tests of your parental fortitude.

It won't be all trials and turbulence. These are highly rewarding years for many families, full of accomplishments, commitments to worthwhile causes, and experiences that weren't possible when the children were younger. You can't expect your two-year-old to appreciate a basketball game, a performance of *Les Miserables*, or a great sermon, but your sixteen-year-old can share these experiences with you and be as interested or enthralled as any adult.

This chapter will focus on the physical aspects of this remarkable transformation from child to adult, while emotions, relationships, and other growing pains will be discussed in the chapter to follow. Both chapters will begin with a survey of normal development and then review potential pitfalls, preventive measures, and positive goals for parents and their rapidly growing children. Fasten your seat belt, hold on tight, and enjoy the ride.

Physical Growth and Development

From a physical standpoint, the main event of adolescence is puberty, which serves as the physiological bridge between childhood and adulthood.

> *Puberty*: The stage of maturation in which an individual becomes physiologically capable of sexual reproduction. (From the Latin *puber*: "adult.")

Rapid growth and body changes during these years are to a large degree brought about by interactions between several **hormones**, biochemical compounds that are created in one part of the body and sent via the bloodstream to have a specific effect somewhere else. These chemical messages provoke an impressive number and variety of responses throughout the body. All of the hormones and the glands that secrete them are collectively known as the **endocrine system**. Not all hormones, however, are related to reproduction. Thyroid hormone, for example, plays an important role in the body's metabolic rate. Insulin, secreted by the pancreas, escorts glucose (or blood sugar) into the cells that need and use this basic fuel. Growth hormone, as its name implies, is necessary for the attainment of normal adult height.

Speaking of growth hormone, a major growth spurt is one hallmark of adolescence, usually occurring between the ages of ten and fourteen in girls, and twelve and sixteen in boys. (Perhaps "spurt" isn't the most accurate term for this event, which actually lasts between two and three years.) The rate of growth can vary, but it tends to be the fastest during spring and summer. Weight increases as well, and bones progress through their final stages of maturation. In addition, the percentage of body fat increases in girls and decreases in boys.

Pubertal development in boys

A number of marvelous changes take place as a boy's body grows into that of a man's. Male sexual development usually begins between the ages of ten and thirteen (the average age is eleven or twelve), and the process is usually completed in about three years, although it can range anywhere from two to five years. The timing and speed of bodily changes can vary greatly between boys of the same age, and the slow developer may need extra encouragement and continued reassurance that he will eventually reach the goal of manhood. A boy should be checked by his physician, however, if he begins to show pubertal changes before age nine or has none of these developments under way by age fourteen.

The first physical sign of puberty in boys is enlargement in the size of the testicles and thinning of the scrotum. Hair appears on the face, chest, under the arms, and in the genital area. His voice starts to deepen, although it may pass through an awkward phase of breaking, especially when he is excited or nervous.

The testicles begin manufacturing sperm, which are transported through a structure called the epididymis (one of which sits adjacent to each testicle) and then onward to the penis through a pair of flexible tubes called the vas deferens. The prostate begins to produce seminal fluid, which carries sperm out of the body during ejaculation. The newly functioning sexual equipment will at times unexpectedly carry out its functions during the middle of the night in what is called a nocturnal emission or "wet dream," a normal event that an uninformed adolescent might find alarming. Along the same lines, boys may be concerned or embarrassed by unexpected erections, which can occur at very inopportune times (for example, just prior to giving a report in front of a class). Neither of these should be interpreted as a sign of impending moral failure. In fact, it's best to brief your son about these normal events before puberty arrives so he's not taken by surprise.

If you are a single mother who feels uncomfortable discussing these matters with your son, consider seeking help from an adult male who not only shares your values but has enough rapport to talk with him about these topics.

Some boys develop a small, button-sized nodule of breast tissue directly under the nipple. This is a common response to changing hormones, although it may cause a minor panic when first discovered ("Is this a tumor?" "Am I going to develop breasts like a woman?"). This area may become a little tender but should return to normal within twelve to eighteen months. If you have any questions, or if breast tissue appears to be increasing in size (a phenomenon known as **gynecomastia**), have it checked by your son's doctor.

Pubertal development in girls

While pubertal development and the reproductive process are relatively straightforward in boys, the changes that take place as a girl progresses to womanhood are in many ways much more complex. (As you will see, they also take quite a bit longer to explain.) Not only does she undergo significant changes in her outward appearance, but inside her body a delicate interplay of hormones eventually leads to a momentous occasion: her first menstrual period (also called **menarche**), announcing her potential to reproduce.

The first visible sign of puberty in girls is the development of **breast buds**, which usually appear about two years before the first menstrual period. Each breast bud is a small, flat, firm buttonlike nodule that develops directly under the areola (the pigmented area that surrounds the nipple). This tissue eventually softens as the breasts enlarge. Occasionally a bud will develop on one side before the other, which might lead to the mistaken impression that a tumor is growing. But the passage of time and (if necessary) a doctor's examination will confirm that this growth is in fact normal.

As the breasts continue to develop, hair begins to grow under the arms, on the legs, and in the genital area. The contour of the hips becomes fuller, and the internal reproductive organs grow and mature. Glands within the vagina produce a clear or milky secretion, which may appear several months before the onset of menstrual bleeding. Finally, at the conclusion of an intricate sequence of hormonal events, the first menstrual flow arrives. This typically occurs around twelve or thirteen years of age, with a range between nine and sixteen. As with boys, girls who begin this process earlier or later than average will need some information and reassurance. In general, a girl should be checked by her physician if she develops breast buds before age eight or has her first period before age nine. At the opposite end of the spectrum, the absence of pubertal changes by thirteen or menstrual periods by sixteen should trigger a medical evaluation.

For many adolescents (and their parents), the menstrual cycle is a complex mystery or even a source of some anxiety. While this event may not be a routine topic of conversation over Sunday dinner, you might want to refresh your memory or learn about it for the first time well before the first stirrings of puberty in your offspring. Your daughter(s) at some point will have questions and concerns about the monthly flow: What is normal and what isn't? How often should this occur? What if there's a lot, very little, or none at all? What about cramping?

While the menstrual flow will be the focus of your adolescent's attention, it is only a single event in an elaborate process that prepares her physically each month for the possibility of bearing a child. It is therefore both practical and wise for you and your daughter(s) to understand the basics of a woman's reproductive cycle.

Furthermore, a boy also should acquire some basic information about the female reproductive cycle in the course of learning how to treat the women in his life with care and respect. How and when he gains this information, however, will depend both on timing and his maturity level. In order to protect boundaries of modesty (and prevent potential embarrassment), be careful about what is said and who is listening when discussing what is going on inside the body of your teenager. Generic comments ("When a woman is having her menstrual period . . .") are more appropriate than naming names ("When Jessica is having her menstrual period . . ."). When in doubt, conversations about such matters with adolescents, who are likely to be extremely self-conscious, will feel safer if carried out in private or at least with boys and girls separately.

A single father who feels out of his element discussing the female reproductive cycle with his adolescent daughter may want to request help from a woman who is mature, is comfortable communicating this information to adolescents, and holds similar values regarding sexuality.

The Menstrual Cycle

In case your memories of health-education or childbirth classes are a little fuzzy, the following section is a primer on the menstrual cycle. If your adolescent is ready and interested, she or he may read along.

What goes on during the menstrual cycle?

Under normal circumstances, each month a woman's body performs a three-act play entitled *Preparing for a Baby*. What you are about to read is a summary of the essential characters and plot. (As with many other aspects of human physiology, there are thousands of other details that will not be spelled out here and thousands more yet to be discovered. The design of this process is indeed exquisite.)

The main characters in the play are:

- The **hypothalamus**: a multifaceted structure at the base of the brain that regulates basic bodily functions such as temperature and appetite. It also serves as the prime mover in the reproductive cycle.
- The **pituitary**: a small, punching-bag-shaped structure that appears to dangle from the brain directly below the hypothalamus. It has been called the "master gland" because it gives orders to many other organs. But it also takes important cues from the hypothalamus.
- The **ovaries**: a matched pair of organs in the female pelvis that serve two critical functions—releasing one or more eggs (or ova) each month and secreting the hormones **estrogen** and **progesterone**. At birth the ovaries contain about 2 million eggs, a woman's lifetime supply. During childhood, the vast majority of these gradually disappear, and by the time a girl reaches puberty, only about 300,000 will be left. During her reproductive years, she will release between three hundred and five hundred eggs; the rest will die and disappear.
- The **uterus**: a pear-shaped organ consisting primarily of muscle and containing a cavity where a baby grows during pregnancy. This cavity is lined with delicate tissue called **endometrium**, which changes remarkably in response to estrogen and progesterone produced by the ovaries. The uterus, also called the womb,

is located at the top of the vagina and positioned in the middle of the pelvis between the bladder and the rectum.

- The **fallopian tubes**: a pair of tubes, about four to five inches (10 to 13 cm) long, attached to the upper corners of the uterus and extending toward each ovary. Their job is to serve as a meeting place for egg and sperm and then to transport a fertilized egg to the uterus.

Act I: Preparing an egg for launch (the follicular phase). The hypothalamus begins the monthly reproductive cycle by sending a message called **gonadotropin-releasing hormone** to the pituitary gland, which lies directly below it. The message says, in effect, "Send out the hormone that prepares an egg to be released by the ovary." The pituitary responds by secreting into the bloodstream another biochemical message known as **follicle-stimulating hormone (FSH)**, which prepares an egg to be released by the ovary. Each egg within an ovary is covered with a thin sheet of cells, and the term **follicle** (which literally means "little bag") refers to the entire package of egg and cells together. Under the influence of FSH, eight to ten follicles begin to grow and "ripen." Usually only one becomes dominant and progresses to full maturity.

This follicular phase of the cycle lasts about two weeks, during which the dominant follicle fills with fluid and enlarges to about three-quarters of an inch (2 cm). The egg contained within it will soon be released from the ovary. At the same time, this follicle secretes increasing amounts of estrogen, which (among other things) stimulates the lining of the uterus to proliferate and thicken. This is the first stage of preparation of the uterus for the arrival of a fertilized egg.

Act II: The egg is released (ovulation). As in Act I, this part of the story also begins in the hypothalamus. In response to rising levels of estrogen, the hypothalamus signals the pituitary to release a brief but intense surge of luteinizing hormone (LH) into the bloodstream. This hormone sets off a chain reaction in the ovary. The dominant follicle enlarges, its outer wall becomes thin, and finally it ruptures, releasing egg and fluid. This mini-eruption called ovulation takes only a few minutes and occurs between twenty-four and forty hours after the peak of the LH surge. Sometimes a tiny amount of blood oozes from the ovary as well. This may irritate the lining of the abdomen, producing a discomfort known as mittelschmerz (German for "middle pain," because it occurs about halfway through the cycle).

Act III: The voyage of the egg and the preparation of the uterus (the luteal phase). The egg is not left to its own devices once it is set free from the ovary. At the end of each fallopian tube are structures called **fimbriae** (Latin for "fingers"), whose delicate tentacles move over the area of the ovary. As soon as ovulation takes place, the fimbriae gently escort the egg into the tube, where it begins a journey toward the uterus. The cells that line the fallopian tube have microscopic hairlike projections called **cilia**, which move in a synchronized pattern and set up a one-way current through the tube. If sperm are present in the outer portion of the tube, and one of them is successful in penetrating the egg, fertilization takes place and a new life begins. The fertilized egg will incubate in the tube for about three days before arriving at its destination, the cavity of the uterus, where it floats for about three more days before implanting. Around the seventh day it "rests," so to speak, implanting in the cavity of the uterus. If the egg is not fertilized, it will live only twelve to twenty-four hours and then disintegrate or pass through the tube and uterus into the vagina. (Since sperm live for forty-eight to seventy-two hours, there are three or four days in each cycle during which intercourse could lead to conception.)

Meanwhile, much activity takes place in the ovary after ovulation. The newly vacated follicle has another job to do: prepare the uterus to accept and nourish a fertilized egg should one arrive. The follicle turns into a gland called the **corpus luteum** (literally "yellow body" because cells lining the inside of the follicle develop a yellowish color), which secretes estrogen and, more important, progesterone. This hormone, which dominates this **luteal phase** of the cycle, promotes growth and maturation of the uterine lining. This layer of tissue eventually doubles in thickness and becomes stocked with nutrients. Progesterone not only prepares the uterine "nursery" for a new arrival

PADS OR TAMPONS?

From the very first to the final reproductive cycle, either tampons or external pads may be used to absorb menstrual flow. Each has its specific advantages and disadvantages.

External pads may be more comfortable for a young adolescent who feels uneasy about inserting a foreign object into her vagina. However, pads may cause heat and moisture to be retained around the external genital area (especially in hot or humid climates) and increase the likelihood of local irritation or infection.

Tampons allow more freedom of activity (especially for vigorous exercise or swimming) and less chance of contributing to external irritation. Some parents may worry about tampons causing damage inside or at the opening of the vagina. However, inserting a tampon does not tear the hymen (the ring of soft tissue just inside the labia at the entrance to the vagina), although difficulty inserting tampons may be the first indication of an abnormality of this structure. Very rarely, small vaginal ulcerations may result from improper tampon insertion.

Of more concern is the association of tampon use with **toxic shock syndrome (TSS)**, a condition caused by a toxin produced by *Staphylococcus aureus* bacteria. A number of cases in the early 1980s occurred in connection with a particular type of tampon that appeared to foster the growth of staphylococci in the vagina and irritate the vaginal lining. This tampon was taken off the market, but subsequent evidence has indicated that the primary risk factors for the development of TSS are the amount of time a tampon is left in place near the opening of the vagina and the size/absorbency of the tampon.

Most of the symptoms of this problem are nonspecific: fever, chills, headache, muscle aches, vomiting, diarrhea, and faintness (caused by a drop in blood pressure). A more specific sign is a sunburnlike rash on the palms and soles. When severe, toxic shock syndrome is treated in the hospital with large doses of antibiotics as well as fluids given intravenously to maintain blood pressure. The development of flulike symptoms and light-headedness—feeling faint or actually passing out, especially associated with standing up or other changes in position— may be very significant if they occur during a menstrual period. These symptoms should be evaluated by a physician *as soon as possible*.

Fortunately, TSS is rare. (Some *Staphylococcus aureus* or streptococcal bacterial infections may provoke TSS in situations that do not involve tampon use, and thus but also relaxes the muscles of the uterus, decreasing the chance of contractions that might accidentally expel its guest. Progesterone also temporarily stops the preparation of any other eggs within the ovaries.

If a fertilized egg successfully implants and continues its growth within the uterus, it secretes a hormone called **human chorionic gonadotropin (HCG)**, which sends an important message to the corpus luteum: "Keep the hormones flowing!" The corpus luteum obliges and for nine or ten weeks continues to provide the hormone support that allows the uterus to nourish the baby growing inside. After ten weeks, the **placenta** (the complex organ that connects the baby to the inner lining of the uterus) takes over the job of manufacturing progesterone, and the corpus luteum retires from active duty.

may occur in either males or females.) Most physicians feel that tampons are safe for both adolescents and older women, although fifteen- to nineteen-year-olds are at the most risk for developing toxic shock syndrome from tampon use. Simple precautions can markedly reduce this risk:

- First, and most important, don't leave a tampon in place for more than six hours.
- Follow the manufacturer's instructions closely.
- Insert (and remove) a tampon carefully.
- Store tampons in a clean, dry place.
- Wash hands before inserting or removing tampons.
- Use tampons with the least absorbency necessary to control the flow. Tampons are now graded for absorbency as follows:
  (a) Junior
  (b) Regular
  (c) Super
  (d) Super plus (not recommended for use by adolescents)

  Less absorbent tampons are smaller and less likely to irritate the lining of the vagina. If a tampon is difficult to remove, shreds, doesn't need to be changed for several hours and/or is associated with vaginal dryness, a smaller size should be used.

  Consider alternating tampons and pads during the same menstrual period. (For example, use tampons during the day—changing them every few hours—and pads at night.)

Occasionally a tampon may disappear into the vagina, where it may turn sideways and cannot be located by the wearer. This is not a dangerous situation: A lost tampon cannot injure the uterus or enter the abdomen. Also, the anatomy of the vagina is such that a tampon that disappears is not at all likely to cause the type of local tissue irritation or injury that could lead to toxic shock syndrome.

However, if left behind for more than a day or two, a stray tampon may generate a powerful odor and discharge. Fortunately a doctor or nurse practitioner can retrieve it without much difficulty. An adolescent (or older woman) who is concerned that her tampon may have disappeared into the vagina should be checked, especially if she notices a discharge or odor. ■

If there is no fertilization, no pregnancy, and no HCG, the corpus luteum degenerates. Progesterone and estrogen levels fall, resulting in spasm of the blood vessels that supply the lining of the uterus. Deprived of the nutrients it needs to survive, the lining dies and passes from the uterus, along with blood and mucus, in what is called the menstrual flow (also referred to as the period or **menses**).

While the menstrual period might seem to be the end of the story, the first day of flow is actually counted as day one of a woman's reproductive cycle. For while the flow is taking place, the three-act play is starting over again as a new set of follicles begins to ripen in the ovaries. This "circle of life" will thus normally continue month after month throughout the reproductive years until menopause unless it is interrupted by pregnancy or a medical condition that interferes with this cycle.

What is normal during menstrual periods?

The words *menstrual* and *menses* are derived from the Latin word for "month," which refers to the approximate frequency of this event. A typical cycle lasts from twenty-seven to thirty-five days, although for some women normal menses occur as frequently as every twenty-one days or as infrequently as every forty-five days. Most of the variability arises during the first (follicular) phase leading up to ovulation. Assuming that a pregnancy does not begin, the luteal phase (from ovulation to menses) is nearly always fourteen days, with little variation.

For a year or two after her first menstrual period, an adolescent's cycles may be irregular because of **anovulatory cycles**, meaning an egg is not released. If ovulation does not take place, the cycle will remain stuck in the first (follicular) phase. Estrogen will continue to stimulate the lining of the uterus until some of it becomes so thick that it outgrows its blood supply. The shedding of this tissue resembles a menstrual period, but it is unpredictable and usually occurs with very little cramping. When ovulation finally takes place, the lining of the uterus will mature and then be shed all at once if a pregnancy has not started.

After a girl's first menstrual period, several months may pass before her endocrine system matures to the point of producing regular ovulation. During this time it is not unusual for her to skip two or three months between cycles. Since cramping doesn't normally occur unless ovulation has taken place, menstrual pains may not be noticed for months (or even one or two years) after the first cycle.

Menstrual flow normally lasts three to six days, although very short (one-day) or longer (seven- or eight-day) periods may be normal for some women. One to three ounces (about 30 to 90 ml) of blood is usually lost during each cycle, although more or less than this amount may be a regular occurrence without any ill effects.

Virtually all normal activities can be continued during a menstrual period. Bathing or showering is not only safe but also advisable in order to minimize any unpleasant odor. Feminine hygiene sprays and deodorant pads and tampons may irritate delicate tissue, and douching is unnecessary and should be avoided. Any persistent drainage that is discolored, itchy, painful, or foul-smelling should be evaluated by a physician.

What can go wrong with menstrual periods?

Menstrual cramps (the medical term is dysmenorrhea) most often are a by-product of the normal breakdown of the lining of the uterus (endometrium) at the end of a cycle. Chemicals called **prostaglandins** are released into the bloodstream by the endometrium, often with unpleasant effects. The most obvious response is a series of contractions of the muscles of the uterus, which may actually be as forceful as contractions during labor. During a strong contraction, blood may be inhibited from circulating through all of the uterine muscle, which, like any other muscle temporarily deprived of oxygen, will sound off with genuine pain. Prostaglandins may affect other parts of the body during a menstrual period, causing diarrhea, nausea, headaches, and difficulty with concentration. One bit of good news in connection with menstrual cramps is that they do *not* predict what level of pain a woman will feel later in life during childbirth. In other words, a teenager with severe menstrual cramps is not necessarily going to have equally severe labor pains.

Menstrual cramps can be relieved in a variety of ways:

- Heating pads or warm baths are often helpful, for reasons that are unclear. (These may increase blood flow within the pelvis, improving the supply of oxygen to uterine muscle.)
- Exercise and good general physical condition are often helpful in reducing cramps. Walking is a good exercise during this (or, for that matter, any) time of the month.
- Specific prostaglandin-inhibiting medications work well for many adolescents and older women alike. These were formulated to reduce the pain and inflammation of arthritis but were found also to have a significant effect on menstrual cramps. Several are now available without prescription: ibuprofen (Advil, Motrin, Nuprin, and other brands), naproxen (Aleve), and ketoprofen (Orudis and others). These anti-inflammatory drugs should be taken with food to decrease the chance of stomach irritation. They are most effective if they are taken at the first sign of cramping and then continued on a regular basis (rather than "here and there" in response to pain) until the cramps stop. Your daughter's physician may recommend one of these medications (sometimes with a dosage schedule different from what is written on the package) or prescribe one of several anti-inflammatory medications. Individual responses vary. If one type doesn't work well, another may seem like a miracle.
- Other pain-relief medications that may be helpful include:
  (a) Acetaminophen (Tylenol and others), which does not inhibit prostaglandins but can be quite effective nonetheless. Some women have found that alternating medications is helpful—for example, starting with ibuprofen, using acetaminophen for the next dose a few hours later, then switching back, and so on.
  (b) Midol has been marketed for decades as a treatment for discomforts associated with menstruation. Traditionally, it has included acetaminophen, caffeine, and the antihistamine pyrilamine, which not only may be mildly sedating but also may have a modest diuretic effect (to reduce fluid retention). Today, Midol is a product line with several different formulations. Some of these substitute an anti-inflammatory drug (ibuprofen or naproxen) for acetaminophen. Some Midol products also contain pamabrom, another mild diuretic. If you plan to buy one of these products *check the label* to be sure that its ingredients are not duplicating those found in other non-prescription remedies you already might be using.
  (c) Stronger pain relievers may be prescribed by a physician if the discomfort of menstrual cramps cannot be controlled by other measures.

If menstrual cramps are disruptive and unresponsive to home remedies and non-prescription medications, it is important that they be evaluated medically. Abnormalities of the cervix (the opening of the uterus) or the uterus itself, or a syndrome called endometriosis (in which tissue that normally lines the uterus grows in other parts of the body, usually in the pelvis) can on rare occasions be the cause of significant menstrual pain in an adolescent. If the medical examination is normal, a physician may prescribe one or both of the following types of medications:

- Diuretics decrease fluid retention but do not directly relieve cramps; however, discomfort may be less annoying if any fluid retention is relieved (see the section on premenstrual syndrome later in this chapter, page 452).
- Birth control pills (oral contraceptives) may be helpful in reducing or eliminating significant cramps that are not adequately controlled by other means. In fact, for many adolescents this may be the only type of medication that is helpful in reducing severe cramps that regularly interfere with normal activity. Each four-week cycle of pills provides three weeks of estrogen and progesterone in a specified amount. This prevents the LH surge and ovulation, and also usually results in less proliferation of the lining of the uterus than occurs during a normal cycle. During the fourth week, no hormones are present in the pills, so during this time the lining is shed as in a normal cycle. However, the smaller amount of tissue involved usually generates less cramping. A variation on this approach, known as continuous oral contraception, extends the length of each cycle beyond twenty-eight days in order to reduce the number of menstrual periods.

A decision to use birth control pills should not be made casually. A medical evaluation to rule out other causes of pain may be necessary. (Indeed, if severe menstrual cramps continue while a woman is taking oral contraceptives, she should be reevaluated by her physician. Endometriosis is a definite possibility if this occurs.) Nausea, headaches, bloating, and/or worsening of acne are unpleasant side effects experienced by some users. (Note, however, that certain oral contraceptives can also improve acne.) The pills must be taken consistently each day to be effective.

In addition, the use of birth control pills may raise another concern: Could taking them for menstrual cramps (or any other therapeutic purpose) indirectly lower your adolescent's resistance to sexual activity? If you don't know the answer to this question, now is the time for candid conversation about sexuality. It would be unfortunate to withhold a treatment that might reduce debilitating pain because of a parent's vague mistrust of an adolescent who is actually fervently committed to remaining abstinent. Furthermore, the decision to postpone sex until marriage should be built on a strong, multilayered foundation. If the absence of contraceptives is the only reason a teenager is avoiding intercourse, she needs to hear and understand many more reasons. (See the Special Concerns section "A Parent's Guide to Teen Sexuality," page 509, for more information on this important topic.)

Irregular menstrual periods may be a cause for concern if they are

- too rare, occurring every three or four months after more than a year has passed since the first period;
- too frequent, with bleeding or spotting occurring throughout the month;
- too long, lasting more than seven or eight consecutive days;
- too heavy, soaking through more than six to eight pads or tampons per day.

For any of these problems, a medical evaluation is usually indicated to discover the underlying cause. In many instances the diagnosis will be anovulatory cycles resulting from an immature endocrine system. But other physical or even emotional events can also interfere with the complex interaction of hormones that brings about the monthly cycle. These include:

- *Medical disorders.* These could include malfunctions of the endocrine system (including pituitary, adrenal, or thyroid glands) or abnormalities of the ovaries, uterus, or vagina.
- *Significant changes in weight.* Obese adolescents can generate enough estrogen in their fat cells to impact the lining of the uterus. At the opposite extreme, stringent diets or the severe reduction of food intake seen with anorexia will effectively shut down the menstrual cycle (see the Special Concerns section "Eating Disorders," page 401).
- *Extreme levels of exercise.* Female athletes with demanding training programs may have infrequent periods, or their cycles may stop altogether.
- *Stress.* Stormy emotional weather is no stranger to the adolescent years, and personal upheavals can cause a teenager to miss one or more periods.
- *Pregnancy.* In some cases an unexpected absence of menstrual cycles indicates that an unplanned pregnancy has begun.

It is important that extremes in menstrual flow (whether too much or too little) be evaluated. Not only may the underlying cause have great significance, but the menstrual irregularity could also have damaging consequences of its own. For example:

- Very frequent or heavy bleeding may outstrip an adolescent's ability to replenish red blood cells. Iron deficiency can develop when there is an inadequate amount of iron in the diet to keep up with what is being lost in menstrual blood flow each month. This not only can cause ongoing fatigue and poor concentration in school but may also lead to anemia—a shortage of red blood cells (which are also smaller and contain less of the oxygen-carrying molecule hemoglobin) that can result in light-headedness or even fainting episodes.
- Absence of menstrual periods related to a continual failure to ovulate may result in months or years of nonstop estrogen stimulation of the uterus. Without the maturing effect of progesterone, the lining of the uterus may be at increased risk for developing precancerous abnormalities. This scenario is one of the concerns for women (young and older) with **polycystic ovary syndrome**, a metabolic disturbance usually characterized by infrequent menstrual periods as well as excessive weight and body hair.
- Adolescents whose cycles stop because of weight loss or intense physical training (or both) may suffer an irreversible loss of bone density, known as **osteoporosis**. Normally a problem faced by women much later in life (typically well after menopause), osteoporosis can lead to disabling fractures of the spine, hips, wrists, and other bones.

It is impossible to state a single course of action that will resolve all the various forms of menstrual irregularity. However, if there appears to be no underlying disturbance that needs specific treatment and the problem is determined to be irregular ovulation, a doctor may recommend hormonal treatment to regulate the cycle. This may take the form of progesterone, which can be given at a defined time each month to bring on a menstrual period. As an alternative, birth control pills may be recommended to restore some order by overriding a woman's own cycle and establishing one that is more predictable. As mentioned earlier, the decision to use this type of medication in an adolescent must be made with particular care and discernment.

PMS and PMDD. Most women experience some degree of discomfort that may occur for a day or two prior to menstruation or may extend over the entire two-week period following ovulation. Mild physical or emotional distress during this time, sometimes called premenstrual tension, is very common. But 20 to 40 percent of women experience symptoms severe enough to disrupt normal activities. This is commonly called **premenstrual syndrome**, or **PMS**.

A specific cause for PMS has not been identified, but the effects are all too familiar for many women, including adolescents. Physical symptoms can include bloating and fullness in the abdomen, fluid retention (with tightness of rings and shoes), headaches, breast tenderness, backache, fatigue, and dizziness. More dramatic are the emotional symptoms: irritability, anxiety, depression, poor concentration, insomnia, difficulty making decisions, and unusual food cravings. These can occur in various combinations and levels of severity. The most striking feature is usually the instability and intensity of negative emotions, which can send other family members running for cover. Some teenagers and older women feel like Dr. Jekyll and Ms. Hyde—calm and rational for the first two weeks of the cycle and out of control for the second two weeks, with dramatic improvement once the menstrual flow is under way. Between 3 and 5 percent of women have premenstrual emotional storms severe enough to cause significant disturbances at home, school, or work, a condition designated in recent years as **premenstrual dysphoric disorder**, or **PMDD**.

A few decades ago PMS was considered primarily a psychological event, an "adjustment reaction" to reproductive issues or life in general. This is no longer the case. PMS should be taken as seriously as any other physical issue. While no quick-fix remedies or lifetime cures exist for PMS, a number of measures can help your adolescent (and others at home) reduce its impact:

- *Make sure the emotional and physical symptoms are, in fact, PMS.* Adolescent emotions are often intense and variable, and other life issues (involving school, friends, etc.) may be at the heart of the problem. If there is any question, symptoms can be charted on a calendar, along with menstrual periods, for two or three months. You should see an improvement for at least a week following menses. Symptoms that continue well after a period is over or throughout the cycle involve something other than (or in addition to) PMS, including depression. Keep in mind that PMS or PMDD can be superimposed on an ongoing depression, and turbulent emotions can take a marked turn for the worse—even including suicidal thoughts—during the week or two prior to menses. Anyone whose thinking turns to self-harm, even if it occurs only during certain times of the month, should be evaluated and treated immediately. (For more information about this important topic, see the Special Concerns section "Recognizing Depression and Preventing Suicide in Children and Adolescents," beginning on page 571.)
- *Keep the lines of communication open and plan ahead.* A teenager whose cycle is well established will be able to predict when the more troublesome days are coming. This may give others at home a little advance "storm warning," and they will be able to respond with an extra measure of TLC or at least a little slack. This is particularly important if more than one person at home has difficulty with PMS, since the collision of two unstable moods can be quite unpleasant. If your

daughter is currently irritable because of the time of the month and a change for the better is likely in the immediate future, you would be wise to postpone any conversations about emotionally charged issues for a few days if possible. At the same time, while it is important to acknowledge the reality of PMS symptoms, they shouldn't be allowed to become a blanket excuse for blatant disrespect, acting out, or abandonment of all responsibilities.

- *Encourage sensible eating and exercise.* Frequent, smaller meals may help prevent bloating, and avoiding salt can reduce fluid retention. Caffeine may increase irritability, so decaffeinated drinks (and medications) are more appropriate. All-around physical conditioning through the entire month can improve general well-being and play a major role in helping a woman navigate more smoothly to the end of a cycle.

In addition, a variety of remedies, nutritional supplements, and medications have been recommended at one time or another for this problem. Some have a more consistent track record (and better scientific support) than others, and your adolescent should consider getting advice from her physician before trying any of these. Keep in mind that megadoses of any vitamin or mineral—quantities that greatly exceed RDAs (recommended daily allowances)—are not recommended for this condition. Ultimately the bottom line for any PMS treatment is an honest assessment of the effectiveness, safety, and side effects for the individual taking it.

- *Nonprescription medications* such as acetaminophen or ibuprofen to reduce aches and pains may be of some help.
- *Calcium* (1,200 mg per day) and *magnesium* (200 mg per day) supplementation have both been shown to reduce symptoms of PMS (especially physical discomforts) by 40 to 50 percent. Improvements may not be noticed, however, until two or three cycles have passed while taking supplementation.
- *Vitamin E* supplementation (usually at 400 international units [or IU] per day, but no more than that) has shown mixed results in research studies on PMS.
- *Vitamin B_6*, which has long been advocated as a remedy for PMS symptoms, has performed poorly in controlled studies and probably has limited usefulness at best. If numbness or tingling of the hands or feet occur while taking this vitamin, it should be discontinued.
- A number of *herbal preparations*, such as evening primrose oil, have been advocated for one or more symptoms of PMS, but research studies investigating such claims have yielded mixed results. While the scientific jury is out, keep in mind that the Food and Drug Administration (FDA) does not certify herbal preparations for safety and effectiveness.
- *Prescription medications* that are most widely used for PMS fall into three basic categories. Obviously, the use of any of these will require evaluation and follow-up by a physician.
  (a) *Diuretics.* For many women, much of the discomfort from PMS arises from bloating and fluid retention, so the use of a mild diuretic (or "water pill") to maintain normal fluid levels during the second half of each cycle can be effective.
  (b) *Antidepressants.* Many PMS symptoms, and certainly those of PMDD, essentially duplicate those seen in depression. Some women with severe PMS fight milder forms of the same emotional symptoms throughout the entire

month. It now appears that the fundamental physiological problem in PMS involves changes in the levels of biological messengers in the brain known as neurotransmitters. New research has shown significant reduction in PMS symptoms with a specific family of antidepressants called selective serotonin reuptake inhibitors (or SSRIs), such as fluoxetine (Prozac or Sarafem), sertraline (Zoloft), paroxetine (Paxil), and others. Often doses lower than those needed to treat depression are effective in reducing PMS/PMDD symptoms, and many women obtain satisfactory results by taking one of these medications on an intermittent basis, typically seven to ten days each month. While these drugs are safe and well-tolerated for the vast majority of those who use them, and definitely *not* habit-forming, individual responses and side effects can vary considerably—especially in adolescents. Before your daughter starts a prescription (or takes samples from the office), it is essential to have a careful discussion with her health-care provider about the potential benefits and problems associated with SSRIs. It is particularly important to report any *increase* in irritability or agitation in a teenager who is taking this type of medication. (See page 576 for more information about SSRIs and other antidepressant medications.)

(c) *Hormonal manipulations* have been utilized with variable success, although they are not commonly prescribed for adolescents with PMS. Women who take supplemental progesterone during the second half of the menstrual cycle may report marked improvement, a worsening of symptoms (especially depression), or no effect at all. Hormonal preparations should be utilized in adolescents only after thoughtful consideration of the pros and cons by patient, parent, and physician.

Medical Exams and Evaluations during Adolescence

During the next few years, your teenager will probably need medical input on a number of occasions. Screening exams for sports, camp, and general health assessment will need to be done. Injuries arising from sports or other vigorous activities may need attention. Problems related to menstruation may require medical evaluation and intervention. In addition, a variety of symptoms and emotional concerns may arise during these years.

Adolescent health-care guidelines recommend yearly visits to the doctor for assessment, screening, and guidance, even if there have been evaluations during the year for other medical problems. Quick exams for camp or sports, especially those done assembly-line style on large groups of adolescents, should not substitute for more comprehensive physicals by your regular health-care provider. If there are special health problems, more frequent exams may be necessary. Most doctors will talk with parent and teen together during the visit, but part of the time will be spent without the parent present. This is usually done in order to increase the likelihood that the doctor is receiving accurate information, with an assumption that many teenagers might feel uncomfortable answering sensitive questions in front of their parents. It is customary during this time alone for a physician to assure the young patient of the confidentiality of their conversation. (When abuse is suspected, however, the health-care provider must notify the appropriate local social-service agency. In addition, if there appears to be an imminent threat of suicide, referral to a qualified counselor, psychiatrist, or mental-health facility will be necessary.) *It is therefore extremely important that you consider carefully who is going to provide health care for your adolescent.*

In an ideal situation, you will be dealing with someone

- who is medically competent;
- whom your teenager trusts and can talk with comfortably;
- who knows you and your family;
- whom *you* trust, and who shares your basic values.

The last qualification is particularly significant because of the near certainty that your teenager will eventually be in a one-on-one situation with the physician. Your son or daughter may feel more comfortable discussing sensitive topics with a doctor than with you, even if you have an extremely close and honest relationship. You will want to be certain that the advice and counsel given behind closed doors, especially regarding sexual behavior, will not contradict or undermine principles you have been teaching at home. During these critical years, everyone needs to be on the same team.

Although adolescents usually have an interest in discussing a variety of topics with their doctors, they may feel embarrassed to broach certain subjects. The physician should have the interest (and time) to ask some probing questions and then offer sound input based on the response. (There is no guarantee, of course, that a teenager will tell "the whole truth and nothing but," even when confidentiality is assured.) Along with questions about past history and any current symptoms, specific topics that are usually on the physician's agenda (if not on the patient's) include:

- Growth and development. Younger adolescents are particularly concerned about whether they are normal, especially if pubertal changes are taking place earlier or later than in their peers.
- Physical safety, including the use of seat belts, bicycle or motorcycle helmets, and appropriate sports equipment.
- Current dietary practices. Are they healthy, erratic, or extreme in any way?
- Immunization history and updates.
- Exercise and sleep. Is there enough of each?
- Tobacco use.
- Alcohol and drug use.
- Sexual activity.
- Relationships at home and school.
- The emotional weather. Are there any signs of depression?
- Sexual or other physical abuse. A physician who is attentive to an adolescent's physical well-being and demeanor may be the first to detect signs of abuse. By law the physician is required to report any concerns about abuse to the appropriate local social-service or law-enforcement agency.

In addition to the usual elements of a medical exam (ears, throat, neck, chest, heart, abdomen), a few other areas are important:

- Blood pressure. While not common in adolescents, hypertension (elevated blood pressure) must be evaluated further if it is detected.
- The spine. Special attention is given to scoliosis, a sideways curvature of the spine. There are specific guidelines regarding the degree of curvature that help determine whether treatment is needed, and if so, what methods might be appropriate.

- The groin area should be checked for hernias (primarily in boys).
- The testes should be checked for appropriate development and for any masses. Testicular cancer is unique for its prevalence among young men, and teenagers should get in the habit of a brief monthly self-check for unusual growths in this area.
- The breasts in both sexes.

When should a girl receive her first internal pelvic exam? Most medical authorities recommend that this be done

- if there is a symptom or concern about disease: vaginal discharge, pelvic pain, or other symptoms in this area normally cannot be diagnosed by history alone;
- if a girl has become sexually active;
- if she is going to be married in the near future;
- if she is in her late teens or at the latest by age twenty-one, even when there are no specific concerns;
- if she is going to start on birth control pills for any reason.

No adolescent (or any older woman) is excited about having a pelvic exam, especially if there is discomfort in this area to start with. It is important that whoever does the exam explain step-by-step what is going to happen and then talk her through it while it is being done. She should be reassured that it is normal to feel nervous and awkward and that while the exam is not particularly comfortable, it shouldn't be extremely painful either. Both patient and parent should understand that a pelvic exam does not terminate a girl's virginity. Sexual morality is not violated by a medical procedure whose purpose is to help assess, diagnose, and treat a physical problem.

A young girl should feel free to tell her physician when and where it hurts and know that the exam will be modified if she is having a lot of pain. Many teenagers feel more comfortable if the exam is done by a physician they know and trust, regardless of gender, while others specifically prefer that it be done by a female health-care provider. In either case, the examiner should be accompanied by a female attendant.

Normally during a pelvic exam, the external genitals are briefly inspected, and then a speculum (the "duckbill" instrument) is gently inserted. A narrow speculum should be available for younger patients, and this should pass through the hymen (the ring of soft tissue just inside the labia at the entrance to the vagina) without tearing it. The vaginal walls will be checked, and a Pap test (smear) is normally done. This painless test collects cells from the cervix (the opening of the uterus) to check for abnormalities that might indicate an increased risk for developing cancer in this area (or, in rare cases in this age-group, the actual presence of cancer). Using a wooden or plastic spatula, the outer surface is scraped, and then a swab or thin brush is used to collect material from the opening of the cervix. These specimens may be spread on microscope slides or placed in a liquid preparation before being placed on a slide. The latter approach, called a "thin prep" Pap, is more likely to remove extraneous debris from the specimen and spread the cells more evenly.

However it is prepared, the slide is read by a specially trained technologist and/or a pathologist—a physician who, among other things, is an expert at identifying abnor-

The Pap smear was named for Greek-born physician George Papanicolaou (1883–1962), who in the 1920s began to identify cancer cells in human vaginal and cervical smears. Formally validated as a screening technique in the 1940s, the Pap smear has been credited with saving thousands of lives by detecting cervical cancer at an earlier, treatable stage.

malities in cells. (Some laboratories use computerized equipment to scan Pap tests for abnormal cells. This approach may be used as a backup check on smears read as normal by a technologist, or even as the primary check, with humans evaluating any specimens identified as abnormal.) The specimen will be interpreted as normal, highly likely to be cancer, or abnormal to some degree that does not yet appear cancerous. With thin prep Pap tests, it is also possible to identify specific types of the human papillomavirus (HPV) that are associated with cancer of the cervix, and even to diagnose two other sexually transmitted infections: gonorrhea and chlamydia. The action taken in response to an abnormal Pap test will depend on several factors, including the severity of the changes that are observed. (For more information about HPV and its relationship to cancer of the cervix, see the Special Concerns section "Sexually Transmitted Infections [STIs] among Adolescents," page 539.)

HEALTH PROBLEMS, HYPOCHONDRIA, OR CRIES FOR HELP?

You may at times become frustrated by ongoing physical complaints from your adolescent, especially those that sound very compelling in the morning and seem to evaporate by midafternoon or weekends. How do you know whether to offer TLC and bed rest or to escort him out to the bus stop despite his complaints? The answer isn't always easy. More than once you may struggle with guilt after discovering he *was* sick after you overruled his protests and sent him to school. On other occasions, you may be compassionate in the morning, then feel like you've been had when he takes off on his bike at the end of the day.

If symptoms are frequent, ask your health-care provider to help sort things out. To get the most out of this consultation, spend time before the visit talking over the problem with your teenager, listing the problems (fatigue, headaches) and their characteristics (how often, how long, what helps, what makes it worse).

While you're at it, try to get a feel for the social weather at school, in the neighborhood, or at church. Questions with no obvious right or wrong answer ("Who do you like to hang around with?" or "What's your least favorite class?") may open the window to some current events and possibly tip you off about pressures that might be contributing to the symptoms.

Ultimately, your teen's doctor will need to ask questions, including, perhaps, a little gentle probing into the issues of the patient's daily life. If the medical evaluation uncovers a specific diagnosis, be sure that both you and your adolescent understand what should be done about it—including the parameters for going to school versus staying home. If the problem doesn't appear to be an ongoing physical illness, all of you together should develop a game plan for dealing with mornings when he doesn't feel well and agree on the ground rules for school attendance.

If you do indeed uncover personal issues that are contributing to physical symptoms, don't back away from working toward solutions. Whether it's a hard-nosed teacher, local bullies, an acute absence of friendships, or some other emotion-jarring problem, your teenager needs to know that you're on his team and that you weren't born yesterday. Making progress in one or more of these areas will usually go a long way toward shortening his symptom list. ■

Then the examiner will insert one or two fingers into the vagina while the other hand gently presses on the lower abdomen. Much information can be obtained from this simple maneuver, including the size of the uterus and ovaries and the location and intensity of any tenderness. A rectal examination may also be done at this time.

Some additional tests may be done during a basic physical exam. These could include:

- Vision and hearing screening
- Urinalysis
- Blood tests, especially:
  (a) a blood count to check for anemia (especially in girls)
  (b) cholesterol and other circulating fat molecules (called lipids) if there is a history of elevated cholesterol or heart attack before age fifty-five in one or more family members
- A screening test for tuberculosis (TB) may be put on the arm if there is a risk of prior exposure to this infection, or if required for school or college entrance. (For more information about TB skin testing, see "Does Your Child Need a TB Test?" on page 346.)

A number of immunization updates are usually given during the adolescent years, including:

- A tetanus and diphtheria booster should be given ten years following the last injection, which in most cases will have been at four or five years of age. For most adolescents this will be a newer formulation (called Tdap) that includes a booster immunization against whooping cough (pertussis). (The combination given to infants and children up to six years of age is the more familiar DTaP.) This is typically given at a fourteen- or fifteen-year-old checkup, unless an injury prior to this age required an earlier booster. Remind your adolescent that tetanus immunization is normally repeated every ten years for the rest of his life. A booster may be given after five years if he sustains a wound that results from a puncture, crush injury, burn, or frostbite, or one that is contaminated with dirt, feces, or saliva. In addition, some physicians give a tetanus booster if five years have elapsed since the last one and the adolescent is going on a wilderness expedition or to a foreign country where vaccine might not be available.
- Meningococcus vaccine should be given if it was not included during an earlier visit (at age eleven or twelve).
- Measles/mumps/rubella (MMR) vaccine should be given if your adolescent has had only one injection thus far. It is unwise to count on a single immunization during infancy to protect against these infections throughout adolescence and adulthood. (Many colleges now require proof of two doses of MMR prior to entrance.)
- Hepatitis A and/or B vaccines should be given if one or both series has not been completed already. Most adolescents have received a hepatitis B series during infancy or prior to admission to kindergarten. Routine vaccination against hepatitis A is a more recent recommendation, but it is particularly important for your teen to complete a series of two doses if she is planning to travel extensively, especially to rural or impoverished areas of foreign countries.
- If your adolescent has never had chickenpox (varicella) and has not been previously immunized against it, vaccination against this virus would be advisable,

especially because infections in teenagers and adults tend to be more severe than in younger children. Two doses of varicella vaccine are recommended, separated by at least four weeks. If your child previously had one dose of vaccine, now is the time for a booster. Varicella vaccine may be given at the same time as an MMR and/or Tdap injection. However, if varicella and MMR are not given simultaneously, an interval of at least a month should separate the two.

- The influenza virus makes an annual appearance in most communities during the winter, provoking fever, aches, and coughing that are often more intense than a garden-variety upper-respiratory infection. While most adolescents recover from influenza after a few days of rest, fluids, and acetaminophen for their aches and pains, those with significant medical problems such as heart disease, diabetes, or chronic respiratory disturbances (especially asthma) may suffer severe complications. These individuals normally are given the influenza vaccine each year in the fall. Because new strains of this virus appear annually, a new vaccine must be prepared each year.

- As was discussed in the previous chapter, a vaccine that can help prevent infection with the types of human papillomavirus (HPV) most commonly associated with several types of cancer (most notably cancer of the cervix) is now available and targeted for eleven- to twelve-year-old girls. (See page 349.) If your adolescent has not yet received this vaccine, it may be offered during a routine visit.

A more detailed look at all of these vaccinations can be found in "Immunizations—Which Ones, Why, and When?" beginning on page 739. You should check with the doctor's office if you have any questions about the advisability of these immunizations. This is particularly important if your adolescent has a significant medical issue, especially one that affects the function of the immune system (for example, leukemia, symptomatic HIV disease, pregnancy, or a cancer under treatment with chemotherapy). In addition, be sure to inquire about precautions or potential side effects of any vaccine that he or she might be given.

Taking On the Tough Topics: Sex and Substances

If parenting an adolescent required only providing guidance through growing pains, schoolwork, mood swings, and preparations for independence, the assignment would still be challenging. But unfortunately we live in an unsettled day and age, a time when various unhealthy choices are often more accessible to teenagers than ever before.

Indeed, the next several miles on your adolescent's highway of life contain several potential road hazards, including premarital sexual activity and its consequences, alcohol, tobacco, and drug use. In many places, no guardrails exist, and steep cliffs await those who swerve a short distance off course. To make matters worse, seductive billboards along the way proclaim that veering toward those cliffs is exciting and pleasurable and that everyone else is doing it.

Like it or not, you don't have the luxury of sending your adolescent off on a journey into adulthood without warning him about destructive detours and deadly cliffs. He should be hearing some of the same advisories from responsible adults at school, church, or within your family, but you can't count on them to do this job for you. You may need to muster enough courage to tell him about poor decisions that turned out costly in your own life. At some point, you may have to help him navigate back from a bumpy side road or even pull him out of a ditch.

We all hope that your adolescent will, like many others, avoid these hazards and their consequences. In order to encourage healthy choices and offer effective help when it's needed, you would be wise to be well informed about these important topics. They are discussed in detail in the following Special Concerns sections, and we encourage you to read them carefully:

- "A Parent's Guide to Teen Sexuality," page 509
- "Sexually Transmitted Infections (STIs) among Adolescents," page 539
- "Tobacco, Alcohol, and Drug Abuse—Resisting the Epidemic," page 545

While knowledge of these topics is very important, it will be of little value if not utilized in ways that will help mold attitudes and decisions. Finding the best approaches to talking with your adolescent(s) about sensitive subjects requires forethought and patience. The following ideas can help you lay the groundwork for this task.

Talking to Teens about Risks: Nine Basic Principles

1. It's easier to talk about sensitive or difficult subjects if you have good rapport with your child about the easier ones. Time spent building relationships during the preteen years usually pays major dividends later on.

2. Parents often worry that if they discuss certain topics (especially sex) in any detail, it will "give the kids ideas." Here's a late news flash: The kids *already* have plenty of ideas, and now they need to hear your viewpoint about them. However, they probably won't ask you, so you need to take the initiative.

3. Warnings about behaviors that threaten life and limb will be more effective if they aren't diluted by nagging about less serious matters. Accentuate the positive, and what you say about the negative will carry more weight.

4. Don't expect to communicate your values in a few marathon sessions. Brief but potent teachable moments crop up regularly throughout childhood and adolescence. Seizing these opportunities requires spending enough time with a child to allow them to take place.

5. It's easier for an adolescent to stay away from the dangerous detours if the main highway is clearly marked, well lit, attractive, and enjoyable. Encourage and support healthy goals, commitments, friends, and activities—all of which are strong deterrents to destructive behaviors.

6. Your actions will reinforce (or invalidate) your words. The misguided commandment "Do what I say, not what I do" has never worked and never will. However, this doesn't mean that mistakes, miscalculations, and reckless behavior in your past invalidate what you say today. Some parents worry that they can't legitimately warn their kids not to do what they did as teenagers. Heartfelt confessions, cautionary tales, and lessons learned at the University of Hard Knocks can have a profound impact on young listeners. As long as you're not setting a hypocritical double standard ("It's okay for me but not for you"), don't be afraid to share what you've learned the hard way.

7. Don't shift into "lecture gear" very often, if at all. Your teenager's desire for independence and his heartfelt need to be treated like an adult (even if his behavior suggests otherwise) will cause eyes to glaze and attention to drift if you launch into a six-point sermon on the evils of _____. If you feel strongly about these issues (and you should), say what's on your heart without beating the point into the ground.

One way to communicate your view indirectly but effectively is through cassette tapes or CDs. You might bring one or more prerecorded messages on a car trip and play them at an appropriate time, perhaps mentioning that they're interesting but not necessarily announcing that you want your adolescent to pay close attention. It helps, of course, if the speaker is engrossing and your teenager isn't plugged into his own portable music device.

8. Don't give up if your efforts to broach tough topics aren't greeted with enthusiasm. Even when your tone is open and inviting, you may find that a lively conversation is harder to start than a campfire on a cold, windy night. Your thoughts may be expressed honestly, tactfully, and eloquently, but you still may not get rapt attention from your intended audience. Be patient, don't express frustration, and don't be afraid to try again later. If your spouse has any helpful suggestions about improving your delivery of the messages you care about, listen carefully and act accordingly.

9. While you state your principles about sex, drugs, and other important matters with consistency, conviction, and clarity, your adolescent also must understand that he can come to you when he has a problem. If your teenager is convinced that "Mom and Dad will kill me if they find out about _____," you will be the last to find out about it. But if he knows you, like God, are "a refuge and strength, a help in time of trouble," you will be able to help him contain the damage if he makes an unwise decision. And indirectly, you may show him the attributes of God, his ultimate refuge and strength.

The Adolescent Years, Part Two: Hearts and Minds in Motion

For centuries teenagers have routinely challenged and at times exasperated their parents. Public and private turmoil about what to do about the younger generation is not unique to our moment in history, nor are most of the fundamental concerns that a child will encounter during her eventful passage into adulthood. This chapter will deal with many aspects of that important process, along with a number of parenting attitudes and strategies that can help an adolescent navigate through it in a positive and productive way.

When your child was a newborn, coping with short nights of sleep, dirty diapers, and crying spells may have hampered your ability to marvel at the incredible little person before you. When she was a turbocharged and at times defiant toddler, the nonstop effort required to keep her (and your home) safe and sound may not have given you much time to appreciate her rapidly developing abilities. Similarly, when your adolescent experiences normal growing pains and emotional turbulence (and possibly a crisis or two) during the coming years, it may be all too easy to lose sight of a number of very encouraging and gratifying developments.

Yes, there will be a lot of problems to solve, arriving in all shapes and sizes (often when you least expect them). You will need to guide, monitor, and sometimes intervene to keep the cultural wolves a respectable distance from your teenager's door. You may have to put out some fires or even an occasional four-alarm blaze. Hopefully, through it all you will be able to recognize and appreciate in your adolescent many of the positive attributes that are common in this age-group. How and when these qualities will be expressed will vary with each individual, but be on the lookout for them—and be sure to express your appreciation when they show up:

- Energy and enthusiasm
- Idealism
- Concern for the needs of others—often coupled with a willingness to offer help in ways that adults might find risky or "unrealistic"
- A desire for meaningful relationships

- A sense of humor that can be witty and insightful
- A concern for fairness and justice
- An interest in other cultures and countries
- Development of new skills in athletics, the arts, crafts, the use of tools, writing, and speaking—often with extraordinary achievements
- Curiosity—not only about the way things work in the world but *why*
- Willingness to commit to worthwhile causes and to back up that commitment with specific actions
- Ability (and attention span) to appreciate sophisticated music, drama, films, and artwork
- A deep desire for a relationship with God and a willingness to make a lifelong commitment to serve Him

Despite the relatively few years separating one generation from the next, most adults seem to have amnesia about their own adolescence. Parents who have already "been there, done that" may have difficulty recalling how they felt and thought between the ages of twelve and twenty-one. As you read through the stages of adolescent development in the next few pages, try to recall what you were experiencing during those years. Whether your effort brings fond memories, a lot of pain, or merely a sigh of relief that you don't have to go through that again, you will connect more smoothly with your teenager(s) if you can remember what it's like to walk a mile in their sneakers.

Since many important differences exist between a twelve-year-old seventh grader and a college student, it is helpful to divide the adolescent years into three developmental phases:

- Early adolescence—ages twelve through fourteen (junior high/middle school)
- Middle adolescence—ages fifteen through seventeen (senior high)
- Late adolescence—ages eighteen through twenty-one (college/vocation)

Each adolescent's life will run on a unique track, of course, and all sorts of variations on the basic themes occur during each phase. Some junior high students may appear intellectually and emotionally ready for college, while some college students behave as though junior high were still in session. Some thirteen-year-olds are immune to the opinions of their peers, and some twenty-one-year-olds' convictions change with each day's companions. But some familiar trends and behaviors about each of the three phases are generally recognizable.

Throughout these years, a number of important developmental tasks are under way:

The task of achieving independence from parents

With rare exception, adolescents develop a powerful drive to become independent, to be in charge of their daily affairs and their future. As a result, bucking the limits, challenging authority, and resisting constraints imposed at home and at school are pretty much par for the course. Just as in the first adolescence of toddler days, the extent of willfulness and the lack of good judgment can at times be spectacular. And while it may sometimes seem outrageous, some degree of struggling against parental control is a normal and necessary part of growing up.

Your job in helping your adolescent complete this task is to release your grip in a controlled and reasonable manner. You still have the right and responsibility to make house rules. But when you impose (and defend) them, you need to do so calmly and respectfully. "Because I'm the Mom, that's why!" may have worked with your two-year-old, but it will rarely be appropriate anymore. Few things exasperate and discourage a teenager more than being treated like an immature child, even if it may seem appropriate (to you) at the time.

Even more important is linking your adolescent's blossoming independence to the realities and responsibilities of adult life. He will need hundreds of age-appropriate reality checks before he leaves your nest, and you are in the best position to provide them. (See chapter 14, "Passing the Baton.")

The task of accepting and respecting one's body

Your adolescent is (or soon will be) in the midst of intense physical changes, especially during the early years of this period. Virtually all systems in the body are involved, but those affected by new surges of hormones will generate the most attention and concern. Three issues will dominate the landscape:

> *A boy becomes an adult three years before his parents think he does, and about two years after he thinks he does.*
>
> General Lewis B. Hershey

"What's happening to me?" If your adolescent has not received some advance warning about the changes of puberty, a friendly and factual huddle about this subject will be most reassuring. (Review chapter 12, pages 442–444.) Even if your teenager already appears quite mature physically, the impact of hormones and rapid growth on emotions, energy, and various parts of the body may not be clear to her—or you. Your input and, if needed, her physician's can calm many concerns.

"Do I like this body?" Adolescents are keenly interested, at times seemingly obsessed, with body image—both their own and everyone else's. As a result, comparisons with others are always in progress. Whoever holds the winning ticket in the physical sweepstakes—the most attractive features, the knockout figure, the well-sculpted muscles, the athletic prowess—will nearly always reign supreme where teens gather. But even those who would seem destined to appear on a future cover of *People* magazine will struggle with doubts about their appearance and worthiness.

No matter how well assembled your teenager might appear to you and others, from her perspective someone will always seem to have a better package. Negative comparisons with that person—sometimes amazingly unrealistic—are likely. And an adolescent with an obvious physical deficit may be cruelly taunted by peers and develop a lifelong preoccupation with appearance. Accepting one's body and taking appropriate care of it are important tasks to be accomplished during this transition to adulthood.

Your job here is a delicate one. Your teenager will need generous doses of reassurance that worth is not dependent on appearance, even when the culture around her says otherwise. You will have to endure the fact that any positive comments you make about looks, temperament, accomplishments, or inherent value may not be met with expressions of thanks. It may appear that what you say doesn't count, but it does—in a big way.

One challenge for parents will be to find the fine line between making constructive suggestions and being a nag. Your adolescent's preoccupation with looks may not necessarily translate into specific actions to improve them or to appear pleasing to adults. In fact, at times the opposite will be true. The current "dress code" at junior high, for example, may decree an extremely casual, semi-unkempt look in order to appear "normal." As will be discussed later, within limits, generational differences in clothing and hairstyles may not be worth a family battle.

But sometimes you may need to take the initiative. If he suffers from acne, he'll need your help and some professional input to bring the blemishes under control. If she is clueless about clothes, Mom or a savvy relative may need to help rehabilitate the wardrobe, a project that does not need to be expensive. If weight is a problem, tactful efforts to move the scale in the right direction may improve your adolescent's self-image and general health. These efforts should be positive, stressing healthy foods and activities for everyone in the family without focusing all the attention on one person. If there is a major problem related to food—whether an unhealthy obsession with thinness, or weight that is far above the norm for an adolescent's height—professional help should be sought from a physician, dietitian, counselor, or all of the above. (See the Special Concerns section "The Overweight Child and Teenager" on page 387 or the Special Concerns "Eating Disorders" on page 401.)

"Will I respect this body?" Whether or not they are comfortable with their physical appearance, adolescents must decide how they will care for themselves. Lifestyle and habits established at this age may continue well into adulthood, and it is never too early to establish a healthy respect for their one and only body. Prudent eating habits can be modeled and encouraged, and you can also point out that exercise isn't merely something to be endured during PE class but is also worth pursuing (in moderation) for its own sake. Unfortunately, some teenagers who harbor a mistaken belief that "nothing can happen to me" choose to engage in substance abuse, sexual misadventures, and other risk-taking behaviors that could establish long-standing negative habits or leave permanent physical (not to mention emotional) scars.

Your work in this arena should have begun years ago, and if this took place, your child's concept of respect for his body will have roots dating from the preschool years. Even so, reasonable vigilance, good role modeling, and forthright and open conversations about risky behavior will need to be on your agenda until your adolescent has completed the transition to full independence. (Risky activities involving the body will be discussed in the important Special Concerns sections that follow this chapter, and some tips for broaching them ended the last chapter. If you have a teenager at home, or a child who will be one in the near future, you would be wise to review this material if you haven't done so already.)

The task of establishing healthy peer relationships

The impact of peers on adolescents cannot be underestimated. The right people crossing their path at critical times can reinforce positive values and enhance the entire process of growing up. The wrong individuals can escort them into extremely negative detours or suck the life out of them.

Your job is to pray with utter abandon for the friends your adolescent will make over the next several years. Without being too pushy about it, make every effort to make friends with your teenager's friends. If your home is the most teen friendly in the neighborhood, chances are the troops will gather under your roof or in your backyard and respond to your influence in the process.

Because peers can play such a serious role for good or ill in your teen's life, you will need to be forthright and directive about where and with whom his time is spent—especially in the early years. If the drama club, 4-H, Scouts, or athletic teams provide a consistently healthy niche, by all means encourage them. But if a new "friend" who manifests an abundance of toxic language and behavior enters your adolescent's life, don't hesitate to take some defensive measures. This may include insisting that they spend time together only under your roof with an adult on the premises (and no closed bedroom doors). If it becomes apparent that your teenager is being swayed toward destructive habits, however, reasonable measures to keep them separated will be necessary.

If your church has a strong and active youth group, do everything you can to support it and your teen's involvement in it. But if your youth group has gone stale or has become a clique zone, find another one. The program should honor your family's faith and values, of course, but should also accept all comers, build positive identities, and be fun as it promotes spiritual growth.

The task of developing a coherent identity

Whether they are National Merit Scholars or total nonconformists (or both), adolescents are fervently searching for a clear sense of identity. Whatever the guise or getup, the questions they continually ask boil down to these: *Who cares about me?* and *What can I do that has any significance?*

If the answers are "my God, my family, and my close friends" and "impact the world in a positive way," your main task—and it usually will be a pleasant one—will be serving as cheerleader and sounding board as your son or daughter finds the best track on which to run.

If the answers are "my friends (and hardly anyone else)" and "have fun (and hardly anything else)," the ultimate outcome could be more unpredictable. Most adolescents with this mind-set eventually grow up and find a productive niche, while some stay in this shallow, meandering rut well into adulthood. Some also drift into drug use or sexual activity in their search for the next diversion—and ultimately pay dearly for it.

For the teenager whose answers are "no one" and "nothing," if different answers are nowhere on the horizon, the consequences may be more serious: depression, acting out, even suicidal behavior (see the Special Concerns Section, "Recognizing Depression and Preventing Suicide in Children and Adolescents," on page 571).

Obviously, it is important that your child enter adolescence with some clear and positive answers to the questions of caring and significance. During the coming seasons, he will probably ask them often and in many different ways—some of which may catch you way off guard. Even if he has lost his bearings or abandoned common sense, you will still need to communicate that your love and his significance are unshakable. As in earlier years of childhood, you will need to enforce limits and help him make some course corrections until he is on his own. But he must always know that your fundamental love for him will never change, regardless of grades, clothes, a messy room, dented fenders, or more serious issues.

The task of discovering personal gifts, interests, and passions

One of the most important and life-enhancing aspects of adolescence is the process of looking at a variety of activities and interests. If her childhood interests in Scouts and piano lessons don't continue into the teen years, don't count your time spent in those activities as wasted. She may want to explore drama or gymnastics for a while, and they may become her new passions—or she may discover that the piano really is her true love after all. Your encouragement for her to find and develop her strengths and perhaps to overcome what she (and you) might have considered her weaknesses will pay off in many ways. Not only might she find a niche of true excellence and accomplishment, but all of these activities—even the ones that don't pan out as permanent interests—will broaden her fund of knowledge and experience. Furthermore, your support during these efforts will repeatedly affirm her value.

This is also a time during which many young people develop and hone a social conscience. Altruism often peaks during the teen years, and she may find considerable satisfaction in helping others solve problems and in volunteering to serve in worthy causes. Teenagers can be surprisingly empathetic to the suffering of others, and they may go to great lengths of energy and time to lend someone a helping hand. You will obviously want to encourage selfless and sacrificial behavior—at times you may find your own conscience stirred by your adolescent's willingness to love the unlovely.

Above all, love each other deeply, because love covers over a multitude of sins.

1 Peter 4:8

You should model practical concern for the needs of others and at the same time offer guidance as to the parameters of your teen's involvement. For example, your daughter might want to rescue a friend from an abusive family situation by inviting her to stay at your home. Perhaps you are able to offer a safe haven—certainly an honorable and meaningful action—but you will also need to walk your daughter through some of the realities and details that may not have occurred to her in the rush to help. If you have a particularly generous and tenderhearted teen at home, you will have to pass along a little street wisdom to help prevent her charitable instincts from being soured by encounters with users and abusers who might take advantage of her.

The task of developing a worldview

The adolescent years are a crucial period in an individual's development of a worldview—the basic (and often unspoken) assumptions that govern attitudes, decisions, and actions. Young people often make decisions during their teens that will set a course for the rest of their lives. Many make permanent spiritual commitments at church, camp, or other events and continue to mature in their faith as the years pass. But these are also years during which fundamental questions about God and the universe are asked, and parents may find their own beliefs (or lack thereof) held up for inspection.

Many teens feel the need to chart a different spiritual course from their parents during these years, a development that can make parents feel very uneasy. *What if he turns away from God and all we have taught him over the years?* Before you lose too much sleep over this question, remember that your child must eventually make his own decision whether or not to follow God. You can't do it for him. In fact, to some degree an examination of what he has heard as a child is a healthy process because he must understand eventually how his faith applies to adult situations and problems.

Your primary job will be to keep your *own* relationship with God thriving—which should include meaningful time in prayer for your child(ren) on an ongoing basis. Spiritual vitality that consistently manifests genuine joy, peace, and other positive expressions will ultimately communicate more to your adolescent than a lot of clever (or convoluted) answers to his questions. In matters of faith (and in other arenas as well), teenagers are particularly responsive to honesty and integrity and turned off with equal fervor by hypocrisy.

If his need to assert his independence from you spills into the spiritual realm, you may need to entrust his growth in this area to other adults (or even peers) who can positively influence his view of God, faith, and the world in general. Youth leaders, teachers, young couples or single adults, or other friends of the family can often "stand in the gap" for you in this area. Do what you can to encourage these contacts and interactions (without being pushy about it) and then leave the results in God's hands.

Early Adolescence: Life in the Trenches

Take an informal poll of one hundred adults about what years of their lives they would never want to repeat, and you will probably hear "junior high" or "middle school" most often. All too frequently, a relatively well-adjusted, good-natured child enters the sixth or seventh grade and two or three years later emerges emotionally (if not physically) battered and bruised. What turns these years into such a war zone?

First, the tides of puberty are likely to be flowing at full speed. Among other things, these generate much concern and self-consciousness about physical changes that are (or aren't yet) under way. Such worries are intensified by the marked variations in development at this age. Within the same class will be skinny thirteen-year-old boys with squeaky voices and hairy hulks who appear qualified for the defensive line of the high school football team. Similarly, flat-chested girls who have yet to experience their first menstrual cycle are mingling with fully developed counterparts who could pass for women several years older. The inevitable comparisons and insecurities can become more acute at the end of gym class if many classmates shower together.

Second, wide mood swings and strong emotional responses to the ups and downs of life are the order of the day. Physical and hormonal components contribute to this stormy weather in both sexes, although the biochemistry of the monthly cycle can accentuate the mood swings in girls.

Like the two-year-old, the young adolescent experiences life in extremes. If she gets a friendly smile from a guy she thinks is cute, everything is coming up roses. If he finishes last in the fifty-yard dash, the whole world stinks. Today two girls declare their undying friendship; tomorrow they announce they hate each other. Last summer he campaigned passionately for a new guitar; today it gathers dust in his room.

Emotional reactions to life's twists and turns, even in a stable home environment, can provoke physical responses as well, especially headaches, abdominal pains, and fatigue. While any of these may be caused by the daily strain of growing up, they should be evaluated by a physician if persistent or disruptive. Insomnia, withdrawal from activities that were once enjoyed, irritability, and a marked change in appetite could signal full-blown depression, a more significant problem that should be taken seriously and treated appropriately. (For more information, see the Special Concerns section, "Recognizing Depression and Preventing Suicide in Children and Adolescents," on page 571.)

In addition to these physical and emotional upheavals among individual adolescents, bringing many of them together (as occurs every school day) creates a social stew containing large doses of these volatile ingredients:

- An intense need for acceptance by peers.
- An equally intense concern about looking dumb, clumsy, or at all different from the surrounding herd of other early adolescents—who themselves are intensely concerned about looking dumb, clumsy, or at all different from everyone else.
- An ongoing struggle with self-confidence or overt feelings of inferiority, even among those who are the most attractive and talented (or tough and hostile).
- A surprising—and at times shocking—intolerance for anyone who looks or behaves a little unlike everyone else.

- A limitless capacity for creative (and often obscene) insults, put-downs, and jokes directed at nearly everyone—but especially the one who is different. This is particularly and sometimes painfully obvious in group settings. Kids who are quite civilized one-on-one or who pledge their allegiance to virtue and values at their Sunday-night youth group can unleash a torrent of crude slurs during a slumber party or a school-yard basketball game. In some cases, nonstop verbal harassment can escalate to physical confrontations or violence.

Consequently, school represents more than classroom activities and homework for many adolescents. It can be a daily social gauntlet—unpleasant at best, a barbaric ordeal at worst—requiring every ounce of effort and energy just to complete the round-trip back to home base. As a result, if *any* physical symptom is present when the alarm clock goes off—a headache, a minor cold, too little sleep the night before, some menstrual cramping—you may encounter major resistance when you try to pry your junior higher out of bed (see sidebar, page 457).

While you might expect your young adolescent to come to you for aid and comfort or to take cover from the daily shellings at school, the opposite may take place. The budding (or broiling) urge for independence, combined with mood swings, extreme self-consciousness, and intolerance for anything that strikes them as "stupid" or "lame," may begin to drive an alarming wedge into your relationship.

This is the age at which kids may decide that their parents are hopelessly naive, out of touch with reality, or terribly short on intelligence. Your adolescent may avoid sitting with you at church. You may hear criticism of your clothes, musical tastes, and opinions. And don't even think about wearing that slightly weird hat or doing something a little unusual (such as humming your favorite tune a little too loud) in a public place—especially the mall. You may be strongly rebuked for this "embarrassing" display, especially if (heaven forbid) someone she remotely knows might possibly see it. Her concern, of course, will not be for your reputation but hers.

The right to criticize must be earned, even if the advice is constructive in nature. . . . You are obligated first to demonstrate your own respect for your child as a person.

Dr. Dobson Answers
Your Questions

This apparent detachment from you and the family may extend to cutting other moorings to the past. One day your son may suddenly pack up his action figures, shove his baseball cards into a drawer, and insist that you replace the race-car wallpaper that was painstakingly installed in his bedroom just a few years ago. Your daughter's dolls and figurines may suffer a similar fate. Some adolescents also choose this time to abandon cute childhood nicknames in favor of more grown-up-sounding names. Don't be alarmed, and certainly don't smirk or ridicule, if you are told one day that Suzie wants to be called Susan or that Skipper is now Jonathan. Such sudden announcements that childhood is over may catch you off guard, provoking a lump in your throat or even a few tears. But welcome the transition as best you can. Pack up the toys and memorabilia they don't want, and save them for their own children.

During this period, early adolescents typically form and maintain strong same-sex friendships, even as interest in members of the opposite sex is growing more intense. Infatuations and crushes are to be expected, but intense romances and dating are not good at this age for a number of reasons.

As already mentioned, friends and peers can play a major role in reinforcing or undermining the values that matter to you. You may become frustrated by the fact that a classmate's half-baked opinions seem to matter more than all the common sense you've imparted over the years. But choose wisely if you decide to intervene because the more you complain about her newfound friends, the more vigorously she may defend them. Some streetwise vigilance, ongoing prayer, and evenhanded but candid conversations about who's hot and who's not on the current friendship list (and why) should be regular agenda items for your busy week.

While the value of your parental stock may seem to be falling by the hour, you may be surprised (and perhaps a little hurt) to see your adolescent form a powerful attachment to another adult. A teacher, choir director, favorite aunt, coach, or youth leader can become the object of intense admiration and attention. This common turn of events can be a blessing if the object of this affection is an ally who shares your values and goals and who moves her in positive directions. But someone with a less constructive agenda can have a significant negative impact.

Middle Adolescence: Peace and War

For many adolescents and their parents, senior high brings a breath of fresh air after the suffocating social environment of junior high. By now the most significant transitions and transformations of puberty are well under way or completed for nearly everyone. The apprehensive question "What's happening to me?" is replaced by the more reflective "So that's what was happening." Physical attributes and attractiveness are still major concerns, but obvious differences in development among members of this age-group are far less common.

Opposite-sex relationships are likely to move beyond crushes and awkward non-conversations into friendships and romances that can displace the same-sex and group camaraderie of the past. The issue of appropriate expressions of physical affection should be candidly broached. If you brought up this topic a couple of years ago, it may well have seemed like a philosophical question. But when real-life relationships are involved, it becomes a very practical one.

While peer influence remains strong, many of the extreme, often ridiculous herd instincts of two or three years ago have begun to fade. No longer does everyone need to look, dress, and talk exactly alike to avoid nonstop ridicule. In fact, many adolescents now pride themselves on their tolerance and acceptance of all manner of eccentricities among their cohorts. (This does not necessarily extend to adults, however.)

Teens in this age bracket tend to find at least one group they identify with and that provides friendships, fun, and a sense of identity. Church and service organizations, athletics, performing arts (music, drama, dance, film), academics, and even political/social activism will bring kindred spirits together. Idealism may flourish during these years, and commitments made to God and basic values can be fervent and life-changing. If you share one or more of these interests, you can cement deep and satisfying bonds with your teenager.

For many families, however, these years bring a crescendo of conflict. The urge for independence that provokes detachment and verbal criticism from junior highers can deteriorate into a Grand Canyon–sized rift or all-out war at this age. Now, however, you're not dealing with a foot-stomping two-year-old or a misbehaving grade-school child. He may no longer be intimidated by your size or stern look. In order to demonstrate his separation from your influence, he may undergo extreme alterations of appearance, including weird haircuts and hair colors, body piercing, tattoos, and clothing that looks like it came from another planet. If you have a major blowup over some issue, he may take off for parts unknown. He may have access to transportation (his own or someone else's) and may be able to crash temporarily at a friend's place if things aren't going well at yours.

Furthermore, adolescents at this age are capable of carrying out acts with far more serious consequences. Their quest for self-determination or their outright rebellion can be combined and energized by an unspoken belief in their own power and immortality. As a result, risky behavior involving alcohol, drugs, and motor vehicles, as well as other physical feats of daring and stupidity, are more likely now. If the social niche that satisfies a teen's longings for identity happens to be a gang, crime and violence may enter the equation. Furthermore, intense sexual drives, sensual imagery in films and music, peer pressure, and increased opportunities for intimacy markedly increase the risk for sexual encounters—often with disastrous results. These can indeed be the times that try parents' souls.

For the vast majority of teens, a rebellious phase will eventually end. Only a small percentage will doggedly continue in antisocial and self-destructive paths. Usually a combination of maturing emotions, stabilizing identity, and unpleasant consequences

DEALING WITH BEHAVIOR MELTDOWN

What do you do when a child declares war on your family, the neighborhood, or the entire civilized world? Without question, one teenager who goes off the deep end can rock a lot of boats in the community. Social workers, doctors, lawyers, police, and clergy may all be in the loop, while Mom and Dad endure an avalanche of pain, frustration, guilt, and expense.

If you find yourself embroiled in a civil war at home or confronted by a teenager who is making some dangerously bad decisions, you need to keep these principles in mind:

Take the bull by the horns. Don't tolerate flagrant disrespect, destruction of your home or other property, criminal activity, or abuse from one of your children. Drastic action may be necessary to keep this type of behavior from tearing your family to shreds. You may need to enlist help from a number of allies, including other parents, counselors, your pastor, your adolescent's physician, and the police. If more conservative measures aren't working, you may need to consider informing him that he cannot remain under your roof if these acts continue. Living at home would then become a privilege to be earned on your terms, with some critical minimum requirements: no drugs, no booze, no stealing, no sex, and no verbal or physical abuse of anyone in the family.

And that's just the beginning. Most states require that parents supply their children younger than eighteen with the following necessities: food, shelter, a mattress on the floor, two changes of clothes, and medical care. Everything else is optional and can be considered additional privileges to be earned by appropriate behavior. A car, phone, CD collection, computer, MP3 player, the closet full of clothes, the decorations on the wall, even the door to the room can be removed from a minor's possession until further notice. This may sound harsh, but too many parents who wring their hands over a teenager's wild behavior are also paying all brings an unruly adolescent to his or her senses. As the years pass and the school of life dishes out hard lessons and reality checks, parents seem to gain intelligence in the eyes of their maturing offspring. In a few decades many of today's rebels will be asking their parents for advice about their own teenagers' uprisings. If you have been tearing your hair out over an adolescent's behavior, don't despair; more likely than not, within a few years you and your grown child will be back on the same team.

Late Adolescence: The Art of De-Parenting

The conclusion of the teen years and the beginning of the twenties often bring stability to a number of areas but also raise new issues. Physical appearance is rarely the ongoing concern that dominated early adolescence, and efforts to improve looks will not only be more common but generally more productive. Direct peer-group manipulation of opinions and actions will be less obvious, although attitudes about the issues of life are not likely to be set in concrete.

Your advice and values will be more readily accepted, acknowledged, or at least tolerated by your older adolescent. By now your offspring will probably be wiser, and

of the prodigal's bills. Cutting the supply line for a while can be an effective way to restore order. If at all possible it would be wise to work with a counselor who is experienced in adolescent issues (and who knows your state's laws regarding the "bare necessities" you must provide) when taking decisive steps like these.

If he breaks the law and is arrested, depending on the circumstances you may need to choose not to bail him out, as painful as this decision would be. In doing so you would have but one purpose: allowing him to experience the brunt of his bad decisions and to come to his senses.

Don't live with false guilt. Perhaps you have made mistakes (who hasn't?) in raising your prodigal offspring. But even those who work diligently to "train a child in the way he should go" (to quote Solomon in the book of Proverbs) can find themselves in the midst of a parent's nightmare. Each child is an independent being with a free will who decides if he will proceed in the "way he should go" or "turn from it." Even this famous verse is not an ironclad guarantee but a statement of the way things generally happen.

Don't underestimate the depth of your adolescent's emotions. Serious problems are not "just a phase he's going through," and often disruptive behavior on a child's part is the manifestation of real suffering and inner turmoil. Also, as we will discuss in the Special Concerns section beginning on page 571, sometimes serious emotional and behavioral issues arise from conditions with underlying biochemical disturbances that are responsive to medical treatment (including anxiety disorders, depression, bipolar disorder, and even schizophrenia). By all means seek professional help, including psychiatric consultation if necessary.

Pray without ceasing, and don't give up. Even if you have to allow your child to reap the bitter harvest of his choices, continue praying for his safety and return to sanity. More often than not, even the most die-hard prodigals eventually get tired of the pigsty and trudge home. ■

perhaps sadder as well. While active rebellion is likely to subside as the twenties arrive, some consequences of unwise behavior during the past few years may not go entirely away. Hopefully, however, your teenager will arrive at this final phase without having made any difficult detours, or at least without obtaining any serious or painful scars. Whether the past few years have been smooth sailing or stormy weather, the dawn of independent adult life now looms on the horizon. Your parenting job isn't over until you have escorted your grown child across this threshold into the world of grown-up rights and responsibilities. In a real sense, you will work yourself out of a full-time job.

This process includes a number of transitions that may prove as challenging for you as for your teenager. You must progress

- from parent to caring friend and confidant;
- from gravy train to career guide;

WHAT IF YOUR GROWN CHILD DOESN'T LEAVE THE NEST?

For all their chomping at the bit, when the moment of truth arrives, many adolescents aren't so eager or willing to leave Mom and Dad. If a grown child remains at home after the age of twenty-one or so, two important principles should be observed.

First, the arrangement must be mutually agreeable. It's one thing to let the kids know the porch light will always be on, but they also need to know that having a key to the door is a privilege, not an eternal right.

Second, and more important, the relationship between parent and adult child must be redefined. This means that you will need to insist subtly (and sometimes not so subtly) that she function as an adult. She must treat you and your property with respect, assume responsibility for her own expenses and perhaps some household expenses, do her own laundry, and clean up her messes. In other words, she must live in your house more or less with the status of an adult boarder. Treating her as though she were still in junior high school will stifle her emotional maturity and ultimately frustrate everyone under your roof.

But requiring that she take on adult responsibilities at home also means you can no longer be in charge of her decisions. You can't set curfews, tell her what to wear, or pass judgment on her friend(s). You do have the right, however, to ask—not insist—that she keep you posted on her whereabouts as a matter of common courtesy.

You also have the right—and responsibility—to set and enforce codes of conduct under your roof. If your postadolescent offspring is making bad decisions about smoking, drinking, sex, or disorderly conduct, you can insist she do it elsewhere. You are under no obligation to facilitate self-destructive or antisocial behavior.

If house rules are respected and there is a deliberate shift from a parenting to a "benevolent landlord" mode, the situation can be both pleasant and mutually beneficial. You might even develop a nice, grown-up friendship with your child— something that usually requires not only time but a little physical distance between you. ■

There isn't a child who hasn't gone out into the brave new world who eventually doesn't return to the old homestead carrying a bundle of dirty clothes.

Art Buchwald,
humor columnist

- from being in charge to giving friendly advice—if asked;
- from bailing out and mopping up to allowing some consequences to be suffered.

As in all previous parenting tasks, extremes should be avoided. Give a teenager too much independence too early, and she may suffer serious harm on the campus of the school of hard knocks. But hold the reins too tight for too long, and you may endure one of these equally painful scenarios:

- A strong-willed young adult who literally tears herself out of your sphere of influence, leaving gaping emotional wounds.
- A compliant "good girl" who never learns how to make her own decisions or earn her own way in the world.
- A rebellious and reckless adolescent/young adult who repeatedly gets into hot water and is always promptly bailed out by concerned and caring parents. Remember that the father of the Prodigal Son didn't rescue him from the pigpen. The son had to suffer the consequences of his foolishness and then come to his senses by himself.
- The adult child who hangs out at the happy homestead long after her formal education has come to an end and sees no urgency in seeking her own means of support.

There are a number of reasons parents might feel reluctant to release their grown children to stand on their wobbly feet:

- The world seems a lot more treacherous than it was a generation ago. Parents who deeply desire that their children maintain spiritual commitments and ethical standards into adulthood are genuinely concerned about turning them loose into a culture that has lost its moral compass.
- The prolonged educational process required for many careers can keep young adults in a state of dependence on their parents for years. If you're paying those college bills and perhaps offering room and board (or more) during a graduate program, it is difficult not to keep some strings attached along the way.
- The costs of living independently—a place to live, transportation, food, clothing—can be awfully steep, keeping kids in the nest long after they are grown. Young married couples who are struggling to make ends meet may even be tempted (or forced) to move back in with Mom and Dad.
- A child with a significant physical, intellectual, or psychiatric handicap may need parenting well into the twenties or beyond. Even in these difficult situations, however, it is healthy to release as much responsibility and foster as much independence as possible.
- Parents may have invested so much of their lives into their children's formative years that the dawning of adulthood strikes them with apprehension or even dread: "What will we do when they're gone?!"

This difficult task of letting go can be accomplished by keeping the big picture in mind from the moment you hear that first cry in the delivery room. Your child is priceless, but she is only on loan to you for a season. Furthermore, while she can't do anything for herself as a newborn, from that time forward you will be involved in the ongoing process of transferring more responsibilities and decisions to her. Your two-year-old should be feeding herself, your five-year-old tying her own shoes, and your eight-year-old picking out what to wear to school—even though you can do it more neatly, quickly, or skillfully.

As the adolescent years pass, your teenager needs to hear repeatedly that you will always love her (whatever paths she chooses) but that your parenting role will be coming to an end much sooner than she realizes. Your public-service announcements are as important for the strong-willed fifteen-year-old who is stomping her feet and demanding more freedom ("I'm not a child anymore!") as they are for the laid-back eighteen-year-old who needs to know that the free meal ticket won't be issued forever. The responsibilities you transfer will become more complex—driving a car, balancing a checkbook, and (scariest of all) picking a spouse, among many others. But by walking step-by-step with your adolescent through these processes, your final release will seem like a small step rather than a plunge off a cliff.

Parental Survival Skills

Without a doubt, the adolescent years are a crucial and eventful period—not only for your child but for you as well. Working through it successfully requires wisdom, finesse, attention to detail, and above all, prayer. Prayer is particularly important because you cannot predict the future or know for certain how your children will respond to the challenges and opportunities that cross their paths.

It is inevitable that we will make mistakes. We will miss important signals from our children about their desires and needs, and we will overreact to other signals based on our desires and needs. We may at times become too distracted, tired, overcommitted, or swamped with other responsibilities to do much more than attempt to put out fires. For the single parent raising one or more teenagers, every aspect of this job may seem overwhelming. With all that is on the line at this critical time, we dare not float through these years without coming before God every day, seeking His wisdom in the face of our inadequacies.

With that important perspective in mind, here are some basic principles that can serve as guideposts for your teen-rearing efforts. The exact paths that you and your family travel will be uniquely your own.

Know thyself.

Among the things you most want for your adolescent in the coming months and years are good health, success in school, meaningful friendships, a positive impact in the community, spiritual vitality, and a loving spouse. Your teenager probably would agree with most of these, at least in principle. But when it comes to the details and the means of accomplishing these goals, you can count on differences of opinion, and plenty of them. Furthermore, it is likely that your basic assumptions about what matters in life and what doesn't will be challenged, sometimes vigorously, during the process of rearing a teenager. How you react will probably be driven by your own needs and desires as much as by any consideration of what's best for your child.

The familiar phrase "Know thyself" is no empty cliché when you are parenting adolescents. As one or more of your children approach the teen years, you need to take stock of a few important issues of your own:

Where are you looking for fulfillment and contentment? Do these rise or fall with your adolescent's appearance, grades, social life, performance in sports, or other accomplishments? If things don't go well in one of these areas, how much will this rock your boat and why? Are you more concerned about his well-being and future—or your own? Has your sense of significance been built upon the rock of a solid relationship with your Creator or on the shifting sand of your teenager's performance or opinion of you?

The answers will affect whether you can accept and appreciate your teenager on a day-to-day basis, warts and all, or whether there will always be another hurdle he must clear to earn your favor. It is not your teenager's responsibility to enhance your image in the community, duplicate your successes, atone for your failures, or provide you with vicarious pleasures.

Equally important, your feet will need to be firmly planted on solid emotional ground if and when your adolescent enters a phase of annoying negativity. If you begin to sense that your viewpoints or your company is at the moment no longer valued, you will need the internal strength to ward off pangs of rejection or a flush of resentment. Recognizing that this is a common adolescent phase will help. You may find some comfort in the following wry observation by Mark Twain:

> When I was a boy of fourteen, my father was so ignorant I could hardly stand to have the old man around. But when I got to be twenty-one, I was astonished at how much the old man had learned in seven years.

Above all, knowing that your worth doesn't hinge on the ebb and flow of teenage opinion will help you avoid angry reactions (which can create a much more serious rift in your relationship), while allowing you to deal forthrightly with any disrespectful behavior or comments.

Does your life have any margin? Is your calendar jammed? Are you physically, emotionally, and financially spent most of the time? Do you have any spare time or energy to deal with a problem at school or an adolescent crisis (there will be plenty of them) or simply to get to your teenager's performance in the school play?

Many parents arrive at midlife neck-deep in responsibilities and commitments— just as their kids are entering and passing through adolescence. The burden doesn't suddenly arrive on the doorstep one day, of course. It gradually accrues over the years as the career track accelerates, monthly expenses (and debt) mount, and volunteer positions at church and in the community expand. At the same time, parents may find themselves taking care of *their* parents, whose health or faculties may be failing. All of these cares and concerns can be so overwhelming that a teenager's anxiety about a weekend date or an overdue homework assignment may seem trivial.

Retreating from a marginless, stressful, chronically tiring lifestyle requires a number of conscious decisions, and perhaps some sacrifices, from everyone at home. But it also is a powerful act of love, especially when it allows for more time and energy to be spent on building relationships within the family. *Years from now, your grown children will not care nearly as much about your accomplishments, career track, or net worth as they will about the quality of the relationship they had with you while growing up.*

Are you invested too heavily in your growing children? Are they the intellectual and emotional center of your life? Will there be a gaping hole in your life when the last young adult leaves the nest? Many parents—especially moms who have poured themselves without reservation into their children's lives—underestimate how emotional the process of letting go will be. Feelings of abandonment and depression may arrive unexpectedly as the last child departs. In some situations, one or both parents become inappropriately embroiled in the details of a grown child's life.

While your children must be a priority in your life, remember that the two of you became a family before you had any babies, and that basic unit will continue after they are grown and gone. Maintaining your marriage, lifelong learning, and worthwhile projects are as important for parents as for kids.

Are you nurturing your marriage? As you approach your child(ren)'s adolescent years, are you still on the same team as your spouse? Do you build one another up in front of the kids, or do you unleash verbal attacks for all to witness?

An intact, stable marriage in which affection and mutual respect are openly demonstrated is a valuable asset for raising teenagers. Adolescents learn volumes about relationships from watching interactions at home. When the teen weather is stormy, a united parental front will be very important in restoring calm and maintaining limits. There will be many occasions when one parent can help quiet a conflict between a teenager and the other parent—not by contradicting his or her mate but by supporting and reaffirming him or her. If either partner believes that the marriage needs a tune-up, both should by all means set aside whatever time is necessary to work with a counselor or pastor.

Are you thinking about walking out on your marriage? Do you think that this would be a good time to escape and start over, now that the kids are older and can "handle it better"?

Think again. With all the physical, emotional, and developmental changes of adolescence in full swing, losing a parent to divorce at this time is a major blow. No matter how skillfully you may offer reassurances that "things will be okay—in fact, probably better" or pledge your undying love and interest in your child's life, with very rare exceptions a divorce will create a profound sense of loss and insecurity. All hands are needed on deck during these important years. If your marriage is in a preterminal condition, find a good counselor, roll up your sleeves, and get to work repairing it. The exception to this scenario occurs when it is necessary to escape from a spouse whose behavior is continuously abusive and destructive. Even then, separation may provoke a crisis that brings about the first steps toward change and ultimate reconciliation. But by no means should you allow yourself or a child (of any age) to be subjected to harassment, violence, or molestation.

If you are bringing up one or more adolescents as a single parent, are you maintaining a healthy balance between love and limits? Are you overcompensating for the demands on your time, any lack of resources, or perhaps guilt over your marital situation by being too permissive or overly strict? Do you have a relative or good friend you can call upon to lend a hand when conflicts arise?

Rearing teenagers is a major undertaking for two parents and a far tougher assignment if you are on your own. Without the balance provided by another adult, you may find yourself drifting toward one or another extreme in your parenting style. You may need to be particularly careful about becoming so emotionally attached to your child that he or she becomes a surrogate spouse. This state of affairs is unhealthy for both of you.

If at all possible, enlist another mature person (such as a relative or perhaps a member of a support group) to spend time with your teenager. Someone who knows you and your child(ren) well can be particularly helpful in providing another vantage point if you reach an impasse with an adolescent.

Are you modeling behavior that you don't want your teen to imitate? If you are a smoker, don't be surprised if your daughter becomes one also. If you use alcohol on a regular basis, especially as a means to blow off steam or "party hearty," your son may very well follow in your footsteps. If you believe that adolescent sex is no big deal as long as everyone is "protected," or if you carry on sexual relationships outside marriage, don't expect your teenager to remain sexually abstinent.

The adage about actions speaking louder than words is the gospel truth with teenagers. If you're going to talk the talk about health and morals, be prepared to walk the walk as well.

Show genuine interest and respect.

Adolescents despise being treated like little kids. They hate being talked down to. They bristle when orders are dished out and there's no room for discussion. They shut down if they try to express a heartfelt thought and no one listens or someone ridicules it. More often than not, their tempers flare and their feelings are hurt because of the way something is said—disrespectfully—rather than because of the actual issue.

In other words, they are just like adults.

Even though your teenager may be light-years away from grown-up maturity and responsibilities, you will build strong bonds and smooth your path over the next few years by talking to her as you would to another adult you respect. This, like anything else in life that is worthwhile, takes time and energy. Specific ways to build and maintain a relationship with your teenager include the following:

Take her out for a meal, one-on-one, on a regular basis—monthly at least, and more often if possible. Ask questions about what she's interested in, and listen carefully to what she says. The cuisine doesn't have to be expensive. What you're buying is more than food—it's undistracted, uninterrupted *time* to find out what your adolescent is thinking about. (You don't need to wait until the teen years to start this tradition, by the way.) For extra credit, stroll with her through her favorite mall or other shopping destination. Pay attention to what she likes, and you'll always have plenty of ideas for birthday or Christmas gifts.

> *Fathers, do not exasperate your children; instead, bring them up in the training and instruction of the Lord.*
>
> Ephesians 6:4

Take advantage of common interests. Does he love to ski? Take some time off work and head for the nearest mountain that has snow and ski trails on it. Is she an avid movie- or theatergoer? Go with her and talk about what you've seen. Is he crazy about baseball? Take him out to a ball game, and be sure to show up to watch if he's on a team. Does she enjoy chess, Scrabble, or other games? Become a willing (but not too aggressive) opponent.

Ask your teen's opinions about things going on in the world, your community, and your family. If she says something that isn't exactly well-informed, don't jump in and "straighten her out." You can gently guide her in the right direction during the natural flow of conversation without making her feel like an idiot after opening up about her views. When she wants to talk, put down the paper, turn off the TV, look her in the eyes, and pay attention.

Find things to praise—even when there's always much more that you might criticize—and do it often.

If you commit a genuine offense—whether a stray comment that is sarcastic or hurtful, an action that causes your teenager genuine embarrassment or pain, or some other error in judgment—have the courage to apologize. If there has been an argument and both you and your adolescent have said things you regret, you may need to be the first one to admit that you were wrong. You will not lose face by doing so—instead you will gain great respect (although you may not hear about it until a few years have passed).

At unexpected times, express satisfaction or outright joy that she is your daughter or he is your son. If you have trouble with this, ask yourself why. It could be that you are breaking new ground here, modeling unconditional acceptance that wasn't explicitly stated when you were growing up.

THE IMPORTANCE OF OPPOSITE-GENDER RELATIONSHIPS

In many families fathers have more interests in common with sons, and mothers with daughters. But the importance of nurturing father-daughter and mother-son relationships cannot be overstated.

The tendency in father-son and mother-daughter relationships is for the parent to compare (with some anxiety) the progress of the child to memories of his or her own adolescence. Thoughts such as *He's not doing as well as I was at this age* or *I don't want her to make the same mistakes I did while growing up* can cloud your appreciation of your teenager's uniqueness and your enjoyment of his or her company. Since Dad was never a girl and Mom never a boy, these ongoing comparisons and concerns aren't as likely in opposite-gender relationships.

For a girl, Dad is usually the man in her life for many years. How he treats her will affect her relationships with men throughout her teenage and adult years. She will be looking to him for affection, respect, and affirmation of her femininity and will usually expect the same type of treatment from the males in her life later on. If she has lived with neglect, criticism, and abuse, she may spend years enduring the same from men who are self-centered, irresponsible, and predatory. But if she has been treated with courtesy and respect, she isn't likely to tolerate men who treat her otherwise.

For a variety of reasons, mothers and daughters may butt heads more often during the adolescent years than at other times in their lives. A father's input can help de-escalate conflicts and build Mom's image in the mind of his frustrated daughter.

Mothers can also have a unique relationship with their sons who are nearly grown. While Dad can and should instill standards for behavior with members of the opposite sex, Mom can usually better serve as an adviser regarding matters of the heart. If a son is struggling with a relationship that is tying his emotions in knots, a woman's perspective can offer both insight and comfort. ■

Know who (besides you) and what is influencing your teenager.

While you as the parent have the primary assignment in shaping your adolescent's journey to adulthood, many other people, institutions, and social forces will have supporting roles. But not all of them will have your teenager's best interests at heart.

Two generations ago the general drift of our culture encouraged basic virtues: honesty, responsibility, sobriety, and the expression of sex within marriage, among others. If a teenager used drugs, was promiscuous, or openly defied authority, he was considered a juvenile delinquent. Today that is no longer the case. Even a casual look at the music, videos, and films geared to adolescents is a harrowing experience. Themes of casual or predatory sex, drug use, extreme violence, death, and despair are not only commercially successful but are readily accessible in virtually any home via cable, DVD rentals, or the Internet. And even public-service and educational messages created for teenagers in the interest of health and safety assume that premarital sex (hetero or otherwise) is the norm, and that condoms should be present and accounted for in every wallet or purse.

These voices, and those of many of your teen's peers and even educators, sing a lethal siren song every day of the week: "No standards or values are absolute. Anything goes. You are the center of your moral universe."

Unless your family lives in an extremely isolated area, it is virtually impossible to keep these harmful messages and influences away from your adolescent. In fact, a child who is kept in a social vacuum for eighteen years and then suddenly leaves for college, the job market, or the military won't know what hit him when he gets a taste of what's out on the street. You can and should, therefore, keep your eyes open and be prepared to talk about whomever and whatever you think might be having a negative impact on your teenager's mind and emotions. Specifically, you should note:

Friends. The importance of peers has already been described, especially for early and middle adolescents. As much as you can, get to know and even make friends with your teenager's friends. Listen to what they have to say. An adolescent who likes and respects you will be less likely to encourage your own teenager to disregard your opinions. You may be able to smooth out a conflict between one of your teen's friends and his parents. You might even learn a thing or two about your own child. As you get to know your teen's friends, you can also pray for them.

If you can't connect and it appears that one or more friends are pulling your teenager in directions that are destructive or dangerous, you may have to take the social bull by the horns. Calmly, rationally, and carefully present your concerns. Very often your teenager may be relieved to have a reason to disengage from one or more relationships. In a *worst-case* scenario, you may have to insist that one or more friends are off-limits, which will probably generate a fair amount of protest. Obviously you can't patrol the corridors at school, but you need to make it clear that freedom and privileges will be seriously restricted if she refuses to cooperate. Keep in mind that this plan of action should be reserved for situations in which your child's health and welfare are clearly on the line—not for isolating your teenager from friends whom you find merely annoying.

Music. With a few exceptions, contemporary music plays a prominent and intense role in the life and thought processes of adolescents; this has been true for generations. Today, however, this is not particularly good news.

Over the years, most parents have complained about the music their kids enjoy. During the 1950s and early 1960s, the content of most popular music focused on teen romance, the joys of surfing, and an occasional novelty item such as the "Purple People Eater" or "Alley Oop." Obviously, these songs were hardly masterpieces, and many of them celebrated unrealistic or even silly notions about love and relationships. However, their shortcomings pale in comparison to the malignant tide that rolled into the Top 40 during the late 1960s, when drugs and rebellion began to be celebrated more openly.

Pop music now runs the gamut from upbeat and even thoughtful (though often mixed with a fair amount of flexible morality) to vivid expressions of obscenity, brutal violence (including rape), sexual anarchy, death, and despair. In between lies a lot of angst, heartache, and emotional turbulence. In bygone days, rebellion was at least supposed to be fun. Now it's often glum or even murderous. Sophisticated videos that accompany rock hits often add a visual punch to the audio assault.

A "Parental Advisory" label is designed to alert adults that a CD contains "strong language or depictions of violence, sex, or substance abuse," and that "parental discretion is advised." How effectively it limits access of this material to adolescent ears and minds is debatable. The program is entirely voluntary: The Parental Advisory label is affixed to the product at the discretion of the artist and the company releasing the recording. Some companies release edited versions of recordings that have been given Parental Advisory labels. These display an Edited notice that indicates the content has been toned down, though with no guarantee that it is entirely family friendly. Certain stores—Wal-Mart and Sam's Club are notable examples—will not carry recordings with Parental Advisory labels, although they may sell certain edited editions. Others will not sell Parental Advisory–labeled CDs to anyone under eighteen. But where there's an adolescent will there's a technological way, and if a teenager really wants to hear the latest output from his favorite artist (whose name alone might raise a few eyebrows), virtually anything can be downloaded from the Internet or swapped among friends.

Depending on your teenager's musical tastes, at some point you and he may need to face the music, so to speak. There is simply no way that relentlessly negative and destructive lyrics can pound into anyone's mind without making an impact. The issue, by the way, is *content*, not style. Some music that is grating to your ears may actually contain lyrics that challenge the listener to a better lifestyle or tell a cautionary tale.

If you hear something that turns you off throbbing through the walls or leaking through earbuds or headphones, call for a joint listening session. Get the liner notes if possible (and a magnifying glass to read them), or download the lyrics from the Internet, then review the music together with your teenager. Talk about what the lyrics are saying and how he feels when he listens to them. You may hear an argument that "I just like the beat and the music. I don't listen to the words." Don't buy it. More often than not, he can recite the lyrics from memory.

You'll need courage to separate your adolescent from music that is toxic, an open mind to endure the stuff that isn't, and wisdom to know the difference. You should also be prepared to suggest alternatives. For families with Christian commitments, there is a thriving world of contemporary music available in a breadth of styles—including pop, rock, rap, metal, and alternative—that specifically (if noisily) promotes positive values. In addition, a little research will uncover secular music that, while not including overtly biblical phrases or themes, combines high-quality musicianship with family-friendly themes. Parents who want to stay abreast of the music scene without directly wading through it should consider subscribing to *Plugged In*, an informative magazine that analyzes current offerings with particular attention to content and values (or lack thereof). *Plugged In* is available from Focus on the Family, Colorado Springs, Colorado (1-800-A-FAMILY), but even more useful is its extensive Internet archive of album reviews at http://www.pluggedinonline.com. At the *Plugged In* Web site, you and your teenager can subscribe to a free weekly e-mail that will help keep you informed about current events in pop culture.

Movies, TV, and videos. If you haven't read it recently, review the material in chapter 11 entitled "Monitoring the input to mind and heart" (page 368). As your teenager grows older, you will need to reassess your ground rules for managing these media. You still have a responsibility to oversee the viewing choices in your home, but you may not be able to govern what she watches at a friend's house. Ideally, ongoing conversations about the content of films and TV programs have already instilled some standards and accountability. If you've nurtured a healthy regard for quality and values, she will feel uneasy if she is exposed to trash and stupidity.

Conflicts may arise when "everyone" has seen a certain R-rated film, and she wants to go too (at the ripe old age of fourteen) or watch it on DVD, cable, or a computer download. You will need to set and maintain your own family's standards, but at some point you may want to introduce her to more grown-up subject matter under your supervision. Do some homework and read the write-ups (especially in family-oriented magazines). Sometimes an otherwise excellent film receives an R rating for a brief spurt of bad language or for one or two quick sequences with violent or sexual content that can be bypassed using the fast-forward button on the remote control. Likewise, a film bearing the milder PG or PG-13 rating may actually be loaded with obnoxious and offensive material. As with music, an excellent resource for detailed information about a film's content is *Plugged In* magazine or its extensive Internet archive of reviews of films (whether in current release or on DVD) at http://www.pluggedinonline.com.

Whatever you and your teenager see, talk about tone and content. Is this film or program selling a viewpoint, and if so, what is it? If something struck you as offensive, why? Was there a positive message involved? What was it? Before she's finally living on her own, she's going to need to acquire enough discernment to find the wheat and avoid the chaff. Otherwise, while you may succeed in keeping every scrap of offensive material off her mental radar screen during her high school years, she's eventually going to be exposed to it later on—but without your preparation or guidance.

Video games, the Internet, and online social networks. Content issues and the potential for massive time investments (and losses) playing electronic games are discussed in chapter 11. We also raise concerns there about unrestricted and unsupervised Internet access (see page 371). Social networking Web sites such as MySpace.com have grown explosively over the past few years, creating vast new opportunities for online teen interactions but also posing some serious concerns about content and safety. We will discuss these in more detail in the Special Concerns section "Safety in Cyberspace," beginning on page 497.

Literature and nonliterature. While you want to encourage reading as an alternative to TV watching, pay attention to the material your adolescent brings home from the library or bookstore. Much of what lands on current best-seller lists is truly pulp fiction, laced with vivid scenes of horror, violence, and sex that are far more explicit than the content of most R-rated films. Even the so-called romance novels, whose covers are emblazoned with bare-chested hulks looming over bodice-busting sirens, generally contain an abundance of vivid and immoral sexual material. If your teenager is engrossed in a steady diet of books focused on bloodletting, body counts, and bawdy situations, offer some alternatives of better content and quality. (Perhaps you should also evaluate what books are on your own nightstand.)

Pornography. A more dangerous influence, one that encompasses a variety of media, including books, magazines, and videos, is pornography. A few decades ago someone who wanted to see a "skin flick" had to travel across town and sneak into a seedy theater where no one would recognize him. Since then, an explosion of new technologies has given pornography access to nearly every home. Most cable services offer not only un-edited feature films and sexually explicit original programming on premium channels such as HBO and Showtime, but there are also a number of subscription and pay-per-view channels whose programming consists entirely of sexual material. Nearly every video store has a back room full of hard-core stuff available to rent for a few dollars per night. Most major hotel chains offer pay-per-view movies in every room—including a selection of explicit and idiotic "adult" films. Now the Internet has become a lawless Dodge City in which an adolescent—or an adult—is just a couple of mouse clicks away from a world of extraordinarily harsh and perverse material. Consider the following disturbing statistics:

- The estimated number of pornographic Web sites is 4.2 million (or 12 percent of the total), containing more than 370 million pages. Fewer than 15 million pages of Internet pornography existed in 1998; the number has increased more than twentyfold since that year.
- Twelve- to seventeen-year-olds are one of the largest consumer groups for Internet pornography.
- Nine out of ten children and teenagers between the ages of eight and sixteen have viewed Internet pornography, most often accidentally while doing homework online. (A common scenario is that a neutral word entered into an Internet search engine links to a pornography site.)[1]

While some—especially those who advocate unrestricted access to anything by anyone—might characterize pornography as harmless (if mindless) entertainment, this material in fact has significant effects on attitudes and behavior. The blessings of sex—intimacy, bonding, sensitivity, commitment, sense of relationship, and reproduction—are not merely absent from pornography. They are routinely trampled by its unbridled promiscuity, shallowness, excesses (including violence), and utter stupidity. This might be dismissed as mere bad taste and lack of imagination were it not for a host of destructive effects, especially among the young. Research has revealed the following trends among those with ongoing exposure to pornography:

- The emotional discomfort or disgust on first exposures disappears and eventually gives way to overt enjoyment.
- Habituation—like that seen with an addicting drug, where increased doses are required to have an effect—and boredom with depictions of "routine" male-female sex lead to an increased preference for material showing group sex, sadomasochistic practices, and sex with animals.
- Pornography fosters beliefs that premarital and nonmarital promiscuity is normal and healthy, and that "repression" of unrestrained sexual activity is unhealthy.

- Among men, prolonged exposure to pornography tends to promote callousness (sexual and otherwise) toward women, erode attitudes toward marriage, and decrease satisfaction with a spouse's appearance and sexual performance.
- Ongoing exposure to pornography is associated with an increased likelihood of antisocial and criminal behaviors, including sex with prostitutes, date and stranger rape, domestic violence, and incest.[2]

Because pornography is so readily accessible in our culture, the sad reality is that you will need to talk about it with your child before and during adolescence, just as you will need to have an ongoing dialogue about other matters relating to sexuality. (If you choose to back away from this parental assignment, remember that many other sources of misinformation will readily fill the void.) If you're having this conversation for the first time with a high school student, keep in mind that *he has probably already taken at least a cursory look at pornographic material,* especially if he has spent any amount of time on the Internet—even if you are fastidious about what you allow into your home. Many parents find out about this intrusion accidentally, perhaps stumbling onto some sexually provocative or even hard-core material while cleaning out a teen's closet, turning his mattress, or checking the history and cookie files on his computer, which can tell you the Web sites he has been visiting. (We'll look at parental oversight of the computer and cyberspace in the Special Concerns section "Safety in Cyberspace," beginning on page 497.) Whether your conversation is planned or provoked by a discovery that he's been looking at unsavory material, keep the following in mind:

Remember and acknowledge that he is curious about sexuality—just as you were—and that this is normal. If he has made a commitment to keep his mind and body unpolluted, great—but he's still curious. However, he needs to understand that pornography is the worst source of information about this subject, that it exploits women, that it can be both addictive and progressive, and that it is very offensive.

Avoid extremes. If you shrug off involvement with pornography as harmless "boys will be boys" entertainment, you're missing both the importance of the issue and the opportunity to instill some key values. If you preach a forty-five-minute sermon, especially one that includes a lot of exclamations of shock and shame, you'll drive him into secrecy rather than inspire accountability.

The best approach is to be calm, straightforward, and matter-of-fact, but very clear about your principles. Indeed, the tone of your conversation can have a serious impact on your ability to broach some critical topics: If he has been looking at pornography, how long and how often has it occurred? Is he a habitual user? Has he been trying to break free of it? You won't find out if you approach this topic with verbal guns blazing.

Someone struggling with pornography will need more than a single discussion to overcome this compulsion. Entrenched behavior that has strong reinforcement rarely disappears easily. Confronting the problem, becoming educated about it, accepting responsibility for one's actions, taking practical steps to limit exposure to provocative material, and maintaining accountability with others who are willing to exercise tough love are all part of the process. Some resources you might consider include:

- *Every Young Man's Battle* (2003) and *Every Man's Battle* (2000) by Steve Arterburn and Fred Stoeker with Mike Yorkey (WaterBrook).
- *Help! Someone I Know Has a Problem with Porn* by Jim Vigorito (Focus on the Family, 2006).
- Focus on the Family's TroubledWith.com Web site includes the section "Pornography and Cybersex," offering practical information and useful links.

- A number of topics related to sexuality, including pornography, sexual addiction, and raising children with healthy attitudes toward sexuality, are discussed at http://www.pureintimacy.org.

By the way, there are many households in which an adolescent isn't the only person struggling with pornography. If Dad (or perhaps an older sibling) has been dealing with this issue, everyone needs to be on the same page. A double standard on this or any other behavioral question is unacceptable. In addition, depending on the status of family communications, some candid and transparent conversation could establish a bond and an environment of accountability that would go a long way toward a permanent household ban on this noxious product.

If you learn that your teenager has been delving into more malignant pornographic realms such as homosexuality, violence, or material involving children, you will need to go a step further and get him involved in counseling with a qualified individual who shares your basic views on sexuality.

School and its curriculum. It goes without saying that your teenager's schoolwork should include the basics: reading, writing, math, history, and so forth. In general, it's reasonable to assume that your local schools are staffed by men and women who take their job seriously and have their students' best interests at heart. If your teenager is having problems understanding the material or getting the work done, you will want to review some basic strategies that are set forth in the Special Concerns section, "Education Issues," on page 407.

But what if the problem isn't academics, but personality or ideology? What if a particular teacher seems to have it in for your son or daughter, or a class appears to be pushing a political or social agenda that disagrees with yours? What if the family-life or sex-education unit is contradicting the basic values you have been teaching at home? And, more important, what if your adolescent is subjected to ridicule for expressing a contrary point of view?

Once again, a calm but purposeful approach is in order. You shouldn't abandon your teenager to fend completely for herself. But you should avoid charging into any situation at school with righteous indignation and verbal guns blazing.

First, get all the facts. Find out what "My teacher doesn't like me!" really means. What exactly was said? Is there a pattern? Can you get some written material from the class to look at? Is it possible that your teenager is primarily at fault because of disrespectful or inattentive behavior? It may help to talk to someone else in the same class to get confirmation that a problem really does exist.

You may be able to coach your adolescent through the situation by suggesting ways to de-escalate a conflict (including apologizing, if necessary). If the problem involves a clash of viewpoints, it may in fact be character building for her to deal with differences of opinion in an open forum. In this case you may choose to help her review the facts to bolster her viewpoint or find someone who can provide the input she needs. Remember—it won't hurt her to think through and defend what she believes.

Think carefully before you demand or choose to have her opt out of a controversial activity. This may seem a noble gesture on your part, but it might generate a lot of unnecessary ridicule from peers. For example, if a teacher or speaker gives a skewed presentation on sexual behavior (stressing condom use over abstinence), it may be appropriate for your teen to hear it—and then have an open discussion and review at home afterward. This may also be a starting point for you to influence the future curriculum in a more positive direction. On the other hand, if you have advance warning that extremely offensive material is going to be used, exercise the opt-out choice—and then work diligently to change what happens next year.

If it looks as though the situation is out of hand (for example, your teenager is obviously upset, developing physical symptoms, or doesn't want to go to school because of the pressure) or the deck is stacked (points and grades in the class appear to depend on agreement with a teacher's ideology), you'll need to enter the arena.

Schedule an appointment with the teacher to get his or her perspective on the situation. Ask an open question: "Teresa seems to be having some problems in your class. What can we do to smooth things out?" If you begin with "Why are you picking on my daughter?" or "You're out of line, and I'm taking this all the way to the school board!" there won't be any discussion at all.

Perhaps you haven't gotten the whole story. Maybe some evenhanded give-and-take on controversial issues has been encouraged, and your teenager didn't present her views very well. If so, building bridges rather than lighting fires would be a better course of action.

If, however, it is clear that certain beliefs and viewpoints aren't welcome or are subject to ridicule in the class, and friendly persuasion isn't making any headway, you may have to pursue your teenager's right to a hassle-free education. A meeting of other like-minded parents with the teacher in question, a conference with the principal, and if necessary a transfer to another class may be appropriate. Your bottom line should not be a tirade that "This school is leading our youth down the road to ruin," but rather the simple notion that school should be a neutral ground for mastering basic material, not pushing a specific social or political agenda.

You can't spend all your time and energy trying to fend off potentially negative influences in your adolescent's life. Aside from your own input, you will also want to identify several allies who can encourage your teenager to move in positive directions. These might include:

- A relative (aunt, uncle, cousin, grandparent, or even a much older sibling) who shares your values. Someone older than your teenager but younger than you may connect well and not seem so "old-fashioned."
- A teacher, coach, youth pastor, or other person in an authority role who also deals effectively and constructively with areas that adolescents care about.
- A physician, nurse, physician assistant, or counselor who has professional expertise and supports your value system. Someone with stature and authority can have a major impact on your teenager, especially if that person has known him for a number of years. Since health exams—and potentially sensitive discussions—will be on the agenda during the next few years, find out if the physician, physician assistant, or nurse practitioner who may be involved is committed to the standards that you promote within your family.
- A positive peer group. Even one friend who shares your adolescent's values can help him resist a negative tide of peer pressure. A thriving church group can take him well beyond merely holding his ground and involve him in making a positive impact among his peers and in your community.

Your modern teenager is not about to listen to advice from an old person, defined as a person who remembers when there was no Velcro.

Humorist Dave Barry

Some things that bother you may not be worth a major conflict with your teenager. Think carefully before starting a war over the following:

- A mess in his own room (unless the health department pays a visit)
- Length of hair
- Earrings (for either gender)
- Style of music
- Sound level of music
- Choice of everyday clothing
- Fast food
- Sleeping in when there's not a specific need to arise for school or work
- How, when, and where homework is done—as long as it is getting done

On the other hand, there are a number of areas (some related to the list above) in which you will need to state your case and hold your ground, or at least have some family summit conferences to resolve your differences:

- A mess that is not confined to his room. If you are constantly gathering up your teenager's stuff from every room, it's time for retraining. Let everyone know that you have resigned from unpaid janitorial duties. Furthermore, after one or two reminders, valuables will be confiscated for an unspecified period, and trash may end up in the owner's bed. You can declare your intentions humorously, of course, but be sure to follow through.
- Extreme alterations of hair. A heart-to-heart talk is in order if your adolescent plans to adopt a totally bizarre hairstyle (such as giant green spikes) that will blatantly announce to the world, "I don't care what anybody thinks of me!" Important issues of acceptance and rejection lie below the surface of outlaw or alien appearances and deserve thoughtful exploration rather than ridicule.
- Tattoos. Despite a rising acceptance of "body art" in many circles, your adolescent needs to know that it is extremely unwise to do *anything* with permanent physical consequences when his life is in a state of flux. This is particularly important if he seems intent on embedding negative or offensive images in his skin. It will cost him a lot of money and discomfort if he wants them removed later on, which is likely. He should also be aware that serious viral infections such as hepatitis B, hepatitis C, or HIV, as well as bacterial skin infections, can be spread by contaminated tattoo needles. A makeshift "tattoo parlor" in a friend's garage should be avoided. Tell him that he can have all the tattoos he wants—after he is eighteen and living on his own. By then his interest in body alterations may well have passed.
- Body piercing. Aggressive body piercing (nose, tongue, navel, etc.) should be discouraged, perhaps with a reminder about respecting one's body and resisting peer pressure. As with tattoos, serious viral infections can be spread if contaminated instruments are used during piercing. In addition, if a bacterial infection arises around any embedded hardware, it will need to be removed—a process that can be quite uncomfortable.
- Content of music, as was discussed earlier in this chapter.
- Sound level of music. If your adolescent's music is keeping everyone at home (or the entire neighborhood) awake at night, or if you can hear it across the room when he's wearing headphones or earbuds, you will need to insist that the volume come down. Ongoing exposure to extremely loud noise can cause permanent hearing loss.

- Choice of everyday clothing. If garments contain images or words that are violent or offensive, they don't belong on your adolescent. You will also need to veto female attire that is blatantly sexually provocative.
- Extremes in food choices—either excessive or limited in variety or amount. Obesity in adolescence is not only a social issue but may set in motion lifelong health problems. Anorexia and bulimia are obsessions with food that can have very serious consequences as well. In a nutshell, being extremely overweight tends to create medical trouble later in life; anorexia can be lethal in a few months. Both deserve focused attention and help from your health-care provider, a dietitian, and a counselor who is experienced with these issues. Anorexia may require psychiatric hospitalization because it can be very difficult to treat. (See Special Concerns, page 401.)
- Toxic friends, as was discussed earlier. (See pages 468–469 and 483.)
- Tobacco, alcohol, and street drug use, as is discussed in Special Concerns, beginning on page 545.
- Sexual activity—see chapter 11 and accompanying Special Concerns, pages 509 and 539.
- Disappearing. In any home it is a common courtesy—and may be critically important in an emergency—for family members who live under the same roof to be notified of each other's whereabouts. Your teenager needs to understand that this doesn't mean you're treating him like a child. It is childish and irresponsible to take off for hours at a time—especially at night—without keeping the home front posted. If he's going to be at a friend's house for the evening, it's not unreasonable for you to get a name and number. If he's going to go somewhere else, you need to know the destination.

  As he progresses through high school, let him know that you intend to give him more latitude about the time he is expected home if he is trustworthy in this area. Remind him that this expectation applies to everyone in your home, parents included.
- Disrespectful comments and actions. Much has been said earlier about treating your adolescent with respect. The same should be expected of his behavior toward you. This does not mean that he isn't allowed to disagree with you or even become angry. In fact, there may be times when he becomes quite upset with you—and perhaps for good reason. He needs to know that you are willing to hear his point of view on anything, even if he is angry, as long as he says it respectfully.

  Occasionally a comment uttered in the heat of battle, a roll of the eyes, or a door that closes a little too hard will strike you as inappropriate. It may not have been deliberate, but you need to let him know how it came across and suggest other ways for him to make his case.

  If you are definitely on the receiving end of sarcastic or even abusive language—or you hear it being dished out to your spouse—you need to immediately end the conversation. Calmly explain that the issue now is no longer whatever you were talking about but the unacceptable way in which the ideas are being expressed. You may get a blank stare, and you may need to spell out what you found objectionable. If there is an appropriate retraction, you can proceed—and you will have provided an object lesson for your adolescent in how to handle issues later in life.

  If your teenager will not back away from comments that are out of line or if the problem escalates, more drastic action will be necessary (see sidebar, page 474). ∎

- The parent of one of your teenager's friends. Someone who doesn't have an emotional stake in your adolescent but shares your views on morals and behavior may be able to serve as a positive sounding board for topics that your teenager doesn't feel comfortable discussing with you.
- Films, DVDs, or music with positive, affirming, or redemptive messages.

You should make every effort, without being too pushy or manipulative, to connect your adolescent with any and all of these resources. But remember, if your efforts are too blatant, your teenager may resist merely because it isn't his idea.

Pick your battles carefully.

Differences of opinion with a growing adolescent on a variety of subjects are inevitable. Even the teenager who is compliant and agreeable will lock horns with you eventually—or become expert at quieter ways to demonstrate her opinions. When you are challenged on a rule at home or you see or hear your teenager doing something you don't like, you'll need to heed these principles:

To quote the apostle Paul, "Do not exasperate your children" (Ephesians 6:4). If you choose to comment, nag, or nudge about *everything* she does that isn't up to your standards, be prepared for several years of misery. Yes, she needs your guidance. The choices she makes now can have significant consequences, and she still has lots of room for improvement. But if she hears about her deficits constantly, she will become frustrated and eventually hostile. And guess who she won't want to talk to if there's a *real* problem. If all the nitpicky stuff arouses nonstop criticism at home, she can only imagine what will happen in response to a major mistake.

> *Don't subject your [teen] to perpetual threats and finger-wagging accusations and insulting indictments. And most important, don't nag her endlessly.*
>
> The New
> Strong-Willed Child
> By Dr. James Dobson

Think through your rules. Ask yourself regularly, "Why am I making this rule?" Does it truly have an impact on your adolescent's well-being? Or does it merely reflect the way things were done when you were growing up?

Don't be afraid to negotiate in some areas. If your teenager respectfully suggests an alternative to a rule or restriction you've imposed, listen carefully. If it's reasonable, seriously consider letting the decision go her way. You will gain some major points and demonstrate that you are truly listening rather than reacting.

Do go to the mat when necessary. There will be issues regarding health, safety, moral principles, and attitude that will require you to state your case and hold your ground. You must still be friendly. You can discuss the reasons and suggest alternatives. You can remind your teenager that her total independence is not too many years away, but for now you're still in charge in a few key areas. You must reinforce your love for her and treat her with respect. But even though you may risk a temporary decline in popularity, when it's time to take a stand, don't shirk your duty.

Teach and release responsibilities.

The importance of escorting your adolescent into the realm of adult independence and responsibilities has already been discussed at length. With rare exception he will be very eager to have as much of the first and as little of the second as possible. Ideally he should be experiencing similar amounts of each. Keep in mind that this includes an introduction to many of the mundane tasks you take for granted every week.

Does he want his own car? If you help him obtain one, he needs to be involved in the whole package. What does the registration cost? What about the insurance? How about maintenance? The use of an automobile should rarely be unconditional. Reasonable school performance, trustworthiness, and probably some contribution to expenses (perhaps the insurance, the upkeep, or even saving up for a percentage of the whole purchase) should be part of the bargain. If he gets a ticket, he's going to have to pay for it. Let him look over the registration bill every year as well. This isn't much fun, but he'll have to do it eventually when he's out of your nest.

Another useful reality check is escorting your teenager on a guided tour of your monthly bills. Let him see what you pay for mortgage, taxes, utilities, and the other things he takes for granted every month. Better yet, let him fill out the checks and the register with you during a bill-paying session. He'll learn about a few significant nuts and bolts of everyday life and save you some time as well. Help him open his own checking account, and show him how to balance it every month.

It also should go without saying that everyone at home should have specified duties in maintaining household cleanliness and order. Be sure to hand out age-appropriate housekeeping assignments (which may be daily, weekly, or both), with the understanding that the children should do their chores automatically without requiring nonstop nagging and reminders. If you hear whining about this being an imposition, slave labor, etc., remind the complainer that this is merely the way civilized, responsible grown-ups live.

If your adolescent's behavior causes any harm or damage, whether accidental or otherwise, make sure he participates in the restitution and repairs. If you automatically bail him out of every consequence, you will succeed only in perpetuating childish irresponsibility. Indeed, one of the most significant parting gifts you can provide for a grown child is a practical, working knowledge of consequences. Adulthood often involves asking sober questions about a future course of action: "If I do _____, what is likely to happen? What things might go wrong with my plans? What do I need to do to prepare for the possibilities?"

When he has a red-hot idea for an activity or a project, enjoy his enthusiasm but also coach him through the potential problems he may not have thought about. You can do this without raining on all of his parades. At times he may think you're a party pooper for bringing up the negatives, but reassure him that you're only doing so because he's almost an adult—and that's what adults do.

Go to bat when necessary.

While you want your adolescent to become increasingly self-reliant as the years pass, there will be times when a problem simply overwhelms her. If it looks like she's going down for the count, don't sit on the sidelines.

School problems, whether academic or ideological, have already been mentioned as an area where you may have to take part in the conflict. A more common situation in which she may need help is in dealing with harassment, especially in junior high. The social swamp at this age breeds amazing verbal and physical abuse, and your young adolescent may not be up for the battle—especially if she displays any vulnerability. Always ask about hassles from other kids if she repeatedly looks distressed, depressed, haggard, or literally beat up. A little persistence may be needed to get to the core of the problem (and the name of the perpetrator) because kids in this age-group desperately fear ridicule or reprisals.

The solution to harassment is not preparing your son for a fistfight after school. Instead, swift and decisive (but nonviolent) action from one or more adults normally is quite effective. We will look at the important problem of bullying, and a number of options for responding to it, in the Special Concerns section "Bullying—Neither Right nor a Rite of Passage" that begins on page 501.

A less dangerous (but still very painful) situation that may require your strong arm around slumped shoulders is loneliness or repeated rejection by peers. If your adolescent can't seem to make or keep any friends, don't shrug and tell her that she'll get over it. She may not. Try to find out what's going wrong, and help her make whatever changes are necessary to alter this course.

If she needs to work on grooming, lend a hand (or find someone who can). If you overhear her talking to others in a way that is an obvious turnoff, coach her on conversational skills. Encourage her to invite a friend over for an evening or a special outing. Work with her to find a niche in the community where healthy friendships can develop. And if all else fails, go out of your way to be her best friend until other candidates cross her path.

There will be times when you won't be able to be all things for your adolescent, and other supportive adults in your child's life may need to lend support. Single adults, church youth workers, neighbors, and relatives can fill in a number of gaps and provide a rich, meaningful influence for years to come. Try to keep your son or daughter in contact with different types of people who might have a positive impact. (You might invite them to be guests around your dinner table, for example.)

Keep them busy, within reason.

Without jamming his schedule to the gills, encourage worthwhile activities—a job, church-related projects, sports, performing arts—to add structure to the hours that aren't involved in education. As long as he's not overcommitted and exhausted, these can make his life more well-rounded, add to his social network, and (usually) reduce the risk of his getting into trouble.

Stay on your knees.

This section on parental survival skills began with this admonition, and it is worth repeating. You are not omniscient, omnipotent, or omnipresent. (That is, you can't know everything, do everything, or be everywhere.) But your adolescent's Creator is. Talking to Him regularly about your young adult in the making will therefore help you maintain your perspective, sanity, and strength. These times of prayer can also be opportunities to acknowledge and thank God for the incredible growth and changes that you are witnessing as your child approaches adulthood.

A Final Thought: Looking Ahead

As you invest your time and energy into shaping the life of your adolescent, keep the ultimate goal—the prize at the end of this marathon called parenting—firmly in mind. Picture the baby you introduced to the world not too many years ago living as a responsible, self-sufficient, productive, and morally integrated adult. Imagine walking and talking together, swapping ideas and insights over a cup of coffee, enjoying a concert or a film (perhaps with your child paying for your ticket!), fighting back tears as he or she stands at the wedding altar, and ultimately watching your child start a family.

In the midst of raging hormones and overdue homework assignments, this may seem like an impossible fantasy. But your child will indeed reach adulthood, and we anticipate that, through all of the sweat, tears, and laughter, you will emerge as friends and allies.

Few rewards in your life will be more satisfying.

Safety in Cyberspace

When the first edition of this book was prepared in the mid-1990s, the Internet was a fascinating but relatively new entity. To get online, most families were using sluggish dial-up services that could tie up their phone lines for hours, and most personal interactions consisted of e-mails and scattershot conversations in chat rooms set up by providers such as America Online. At that time, we advised parents to warn their kids about giving personal information and agreeing to meet "friends" they might encounter in chat rooms. Those warnings are still valid, but over the past decade new technologies have changed the landscape—and the land mines—in cyberspace with breathtaking speed.

Today high-speed, often wireless, Internet connections have displaced clunky, noisy modems, and the Internet is not only accessible via personal computers, but also through cell phones, personal digital assistants (PDAs), and video-game consoles. Kids and adults can transmit not just words but also digital photos, music, and video images instantaneously. Chat rooms have given way to instant messaging, text messaging, Web logs (or "blogs"), and social networking Web sites such as MySpace.com that have acquired tens of millions of users within months of their creation. All of these can provide wonderful, diverse, and efficient ways to communicate—but like every new technology, they can be misused or overused. They can also serve as sophisticated tools for predators.

As the use of new technologies continues to explode, busy parents may feel so bewildered by the gadgets and associated vocabulary used by their kids that they may make a major mistake: buying computers, cell phones, and other electronic devices for them without supervising how they are used. In the brave new world of cyber technologies, that could prove to be a terrible mistake.

Throughout this book we have encouraged parents to engage in ongoing conversations with their children about topics that can have a serious impact on their lives: friends, school, sexuality, healthy choices, safety, and above all the way they embrace

God and the values that will give their lives depth and stability. Proper use of the Internet and other electronic technologies (including whatever may appear after this book is published) is as important as any of these and thus deserves to be the subject of intentional and thoughtful conversations. (The fact that these are conversations, by the way, means that *listening* to your kids is an important part of the process, even while you are laying down the house rules.) Here are some basic topics that you'll want to discuss as a family:

Potential Benefits of the Internet and Other Communication Technologies

Education. Vast resources are now available online both for school projects and personal learning. Many teachers and college professors post information and reading assignments on the Internet.

Information and assistance. News, weather, traffic reports, directions, phone numbers, local events, health information, help with relational problems, support groups, "how to" advice for almost anything—you name it, you can find it on the Web.

Enrichment and entertainment. Music, books (both written and audio), radio stations, sermons, commentary on a host of subjects, video clips, films, and much more are available online. The Internet supplies or hosts thousands of games, some of which are of the solitaire genre while others involve hundreds or even thousands of people simultaneously around the world.

Communication. E-mail, instant messaging, cellular calls and text messages, and other technologies allow us to contact one another at a moment's notice, share information and pictures with family and friends around the world, express our views on important topics, and ask for prayer. Web logs ("blogs") can provide lively, thought-provoking, and often highly meaningful exchanges between individuals on a host of subjects. Your church probably has a Web site that serves many of these purposes.

Potential Risks of the Internet

Inappropriate content. We have noted elsewhere that pornography abounds on the Internet and is often viewed accidentally by children and adolescents who are looking for something else. (See page 486.) Violence, hate speech, and other highly objectionable material can be accessed, intentionally or otherwise, with a couple of mouse clicks.

Inaccurate content. Not everything on the Internet is gospel truth. Misinformation abounds on all sorts of topics, and separating the wheat from the chaff online (or anywhere else) is an important life skill for kids and adults alike.

Too much time in front of a screen. Interactive games, Web surfing, blogging, and other pursuits on the Internet can consume vast amounts of time that might be better spent elsewhere. One of many concerns related to teens spending hours engrossed in social networking sites, text messaging, and other forms of electronic interactions is that these are not face-to-face (or at least voice-to-voice) conversations. The nuances of inflection and facial expression—important elements of building relationships—are absent online, as are their restraining effects on inflammatory comments.

Careless dissemination of images and statements. A twist on the oft-repeated ad slogan for Las Vegas should serve as a note of caution about the Internet: "What happens in cyberspace stays in cyberspace . . . indefinitely." Children and teenagers have unwisely posted provocative images of themselves and their friends, sensitive information about themselves and their families, and thoughts about their lives that would be more appropriately written in a journal that is locked in a desk drawer. Instead, this material can be read and passed around the world within seconds, *and it can't be taken back*. Some teens and college students have learned—to their chagrin—that teachers, employers, and even law enforcement personnel have accessed embarrassing material, sometimes with very unpleasant results.

Abuse. One of the ugliest realities of the Internet is the ease with which gossip, rumors, harsh accusations, and unbridled hate can be spewed in any direction. Adolescents, and especially younger teens, are notorious for their capacity to gang up on an unpopular peer and make his life miserable. This type of abuse can be magnified online, because many feel free to make harsh and obscene comments that they wouldn't dare express in person. Cyberbullying is a real phenomenon, and too many kids have been victimized by it.

Predators. Criminals who seek children and adolescents for sexual exploitation and other more horrifying fates have become expert at making the World Wide Web a literal one, entangling their prey through a number of clever ruses. They may patiently gather information about a potential target, pose as another child or teen, feign interest and sympathy, attempt to arrange innocent-sounding get-togethers, or even show up unannounced at the home of an unsuspecting victim about whom they have learned a great deal over time.

Expectations and Limits to Establish and Enforce

Appropriate purposes. The Internet can and should be used for education, information, edification, civilized entertainment, and straightforward communications with relatives and friends that they (and you) know are okay, subject to reasonable time limits and other restraints. Porn, violence, obscenity, and involvement with games or other online pursuits that becomes obsessive should be off-limits.

Appropriate time limits. Reasonable restrictions on recreational computer/Internet activity (two hours or less per day, for example) should be discussed and implemented.

No release of personal information. You need to be very explicit about this one. Information such as their name, address, phone, school or church attended, and information about family members must never be given out in a blog, instant message, chat room, or anywhere else. What kids may not realize is that predators can piece together a surprising amount of information from casual remarks or photos that are posted online. Needless to say, it is also inappropriate to release anyone else's personal information into cyberspace.

No tolerance for online abuse, bullying, or potential predators. Your child or teen needs to understand the importance of telling you if she receives any hostile or inappropriate content, including requests for personal information or a meeting. Any attempt to solicit a child to meet for sexual activity, or sending a child unsolicited obscene material online, is a criminal act that should be reported to law enforcement. (For more information, check http://www.cybertipline.com, a Web site operated by the National Center for Missing and Exploited Children.)

No posting of comments or photos that are provocative, highly personal, or abusive. If your child or teenager would be uncomfortable having you, her pastor, teacher, employer, or future spouse see what she intends to send from her computer into cyberspace, *it shouldn't be sent.*

This last restriction, along with the other limits we have listed, has an important corollary that may be hotly contested, especially by an adolescent:

No privacy when it comes to cellular and online communications. In other words, you reserve the right to know *everything* that enters and leaves your child's or teenager's computer. You should seriously consider implementing a house rule that online activity occurs only out in the open, where anyone can see what's on-screen, and not in a bedroom or behind closed doors. If you allow your adolescent to establish a profile on a networking site such as MySpace, you must be allowed access to it—and you should visit it often. (She should set the profile so that it can be accessed only by people she knows and to whom she has given permission to view it.) If you hear the objection, "But this is private stuff between me and my friends," you will need to revisit a critical reality check: By definition, anything that is posted online is no longer private. Even if only one or two people are meant to read it, they can easily pass it along to hundreds of others.

If you are concerned about the traffic coming and going into your teen's computer, you may want to install monitoring software that silently relays to you the content of every incoming and outgoing communication. (This is not the same, by the way, as filtering software that can limit to some degree access to inappropriate material.) If you decide to install monitoring software in your adolescent's computer, you should be open about it and make clear that any attempt to inactivate it will lead to immediate loss of computer privileges. If she knows that her computer is being monitored, she's likely to be more careful about what she says and where she goes online—and that's the whole point. By the way, if she has a cell phone you should also review your monthly bill to keep track of the numbers she has called and those that have called her.

A final thought bears repeating: Your efforts to keep your kids out of harm's way on the Internet may meet with considerable resistance. Don't be surprised if their reaction to your expectations and limits implies that you're out of touch, a snoop, or worse. Listen to their concerns, but make sure they understand what's at stake, and don't compromise their safety. If they don't like your rules, remind them that all of these technologies are optional and that using them is a privilege, not a right. Hopefully you won't need to resort to an ultimatum, but don't ever forget that until they're grown and gone, you're responsible for their safety, you're the parent, and you're in charge.

Bullying—Neither Right nor a Rite of Passage

Many parents assume that a few scuffles with other kids are par for the course during childhood, and that dealing with a bully or two builds character, especially if a son or daughter learns to stand up to the offender (with or without a punch or two being thrown in the process). These themes have driven crowd-pleasing movies such as *The Karate Kid* and *Back to the Future*, but what happens off the silver screen is another story. In everyday life bullying is abusive, ugly, and disturbingly common, with profound and sometimes lethal consequences. Indeed, its physical and emotional impact on children is now being addressed as a serious health issue by professional organizations such as the American Academy of Family Physicians and the American Medical Association, as well as by governmental agencies. The U.S. Health Resources and Services Administration, for example, has launched a formal campaign and Web site called Stop Bullying Now (http://stopbullyingnow.hrsa.gov).

What Is Bullying, and How Bad Is This Problem?

To be specific, bullying involves ongoing aggressive behavior intended to cause harm or distress in a relationship where there is an imbalance of power, physical or otherwise. Bullying is literally "as old as sin" and can occur at any stage of life, but it is particularly common—and destructive—during childhood and adolescence. Sadly but not surprisingly, the targets of bullying are often those who are poorly equipped to deal with it: the small, the weak, those who look or act a little different from the crowd, and those who have difficulty making and keeping friends. Bullying goes well beyond the usual horseplay, verbal and otherwise, of childhood and adolescence. It is essentially child abuse perpetrated by peers, and it may take a variety of forms:

- *Verbal*. Insults, name-calling, racial or ethnic slurs. These are experienced equally by boys and girls, and represent the most common form of bullying.
- *Physical*. Hitting, kicking, shoving, or other direct bodily injury, as well as destruction of property. Boys are more likely to be physically bullied by other boys.

- *Social*. Spreading gossip and rumors (often sexually related), exclusion, or outright isolation. These are more common forms of bullying among girls.
- *Electronic*. "Cyberbullying" on the Internet or through other electronic devices such as text messaging on cell phones.[1]

Statistics about bullying are based primarily on survey data, which have typically found that at any given time between 20 and 30 percent of students are involved, either as perpetrators, victims, or both.[2] For example, one national survey of more than fifteen thousand adolescents in the sixth through tenth grade found that 11 percent reported being bullied, 13 percent admitted to bullying others, and another 6 percent said they both bullied others and had been the targets of bullying themselves.[3] Bullying is ubiquitous: It is not restricted to any particular geographic location, community setting (urban, suburban, or rural), ethnic group, or socioeconomic status. It is more common at school—in the classroom, hallway, playground, or lunchroom—than on the way to or from school.

Unfortunately, statistics only dimly reflect the pain endured by victims of bullying. Aside from any physical injuries they might sustain, they are also more likely to suffer from anxiety, depression, and physical complaints such as headaches, abdominal pain, and fatigue. Needless to say, reluctance to go to school (or wherever the bullying is taking place) is a common manifestation and may result in numerous missed days of school. *When a child or adolescent is experiencing frequent school absences, especially due to physical complaints for which a medical evaluation reveals no specific cause, victimization by bullying should be considered as a possible—or likely—cause.* Unfortunately, all too often a child or teen will be reluctant to report what has happened to parents or school officials—even if asked directly—because of a conviction that nothing can be done about it, lack of confidence that teachers or administrators will take effective action, and (most importantly) fear of retaliation.

Even more worrisome is the connection between bullying and violence, by both the perpetrator and victim. Children and teens who bully are more likely to be involved or injured in fights, and to steal, vandalize, smoke, use alcohol, drop out of school, and carry a weapon. Furthermore, those who have been repeatedly victimized may decide to seek spectacular and tragic revenge. In 2002, the United States Secret Service and the United States Department of Education evaluated thirty-seven mass school shootings that had occurred between 1974 and 2000. Of the forty-one attackers involved, three out of four had felt persecuted and bullied prior to the incident.[4]

What can be done about bullying? Preventing, detecting, and responding to bullying require involvement of parents, schools, churches, and (when necessary) law enforcement.

Strategies to Prevent Bullying

Parents have the primary responsibility for training, instilling, and modeling values in their children, including respect for other people, regardless of age, appearance, or other characteristics. Bullying, at its core, is an expression of disrespect. Thus the atmosphere at home should be one in which abusive speech or actions, whether directed at others within or outside of the family, are clearly understood to be unacceptable for everyone—children and adults alike. More specifically, parents should impress on their school-age and adolescent children that they are not to participate in bullying, whether as individuals or in a group, and that they should report bullying to an adult (teacher, administrator, or parent), whether they themselves or someone else is the target. Furthermore, when possible, they should understand that coming to the assistance of someone who is being bullied is not only appropriate, but an act of courage.

Schools are responsible for providing a safe environment for all who attend, including a schoolwide culture in which bullying is definitely not acceptable. This goes well beyond cracking down on individual bullies. It requires an ongoing, comprehensive effort involving students, teachers, administrators, and support staff that is designed to increase awareness of bullying, improve adult supervision, and generate rules and a social climate that clearly discourage bullying. The staff and teachers must also provide protection from all forms of bullying. A number of recommendations for implementing this type of program, if one isn't already in place at your child's school, can be found at the Health Resources and Services Administration (HRSA) Web site http://stopbullyingnow.hrsa.gov in the section "What Adults Can Do."

Churches should clearly teach young and old alike that bullying directly contradicts the life and teaching of Jesus Christ. It was He, after all, who sought out the outcasts and powerless and who taught the critical importance of helping "the least of these." Furthermore, church youth groups can be a learning laboratory for accepting and welcoming everyone—including those who aren't particularly attractive or popular in school. Unfortunately *this does not happen automatically* among children and teens—even those who have been raised in church—so youth and student leaders alike must continually strive to keep their gatherings a welcoming, clique-free zone.

Strategies to Deal with Bullying

Be aware of the following indicators that may indicate a child is being harassed:

- Injuries—unexplained bruises, cuts, or scratches
- Torn, damaged, or missing clothing or other belongings
- Anxiety, tearfulness, moodiness, and resistance to going to school
- Ongoing physical symptoms—especially headaches, stomachaches, or fatigue—that are invoked as a reason to stay home

If you are suspicious, ask questions that express your interest and concern: "How are things going at school? Is anything—or anyone—giving you a hard time?" Your child may be reluctant to reveal what has happened, and you may need to exercise some persistence to find out. If bullying has indeed occurred, make sure he understands that you take it very seriously, that you intend to take appropriate action, and that keeping silent will only allow the bully to continue what he is doing. You will need to get as much information as possible: who, when, where, and what happened. If there have been witnesses to the bullying, gather information from them as well.

Assuming that this has happened at school, make an appointment as soon as possible with the principal or administrator who is designated to handle this type of problem. Most likely this person will be ready and willing to put the heat on anyone who is involved in bullying, but he or she will need specifics. Tell the story but also provide information in writing, and be sure to take note of the response to your concern. You may want to arrange a meeting with the perpetrator and one or both of his parents in a school official's office. Your posture should be calm, but resolute: Look the bully in the eye and make it abundantly clear that even one further episode will bring disastrous consequences and that you expect his parents to cooperate.

If the harassment continues and the principal or parents of the perpetrator appear unwilling to take appropriate action, they should be put on notice that the problem may be taken to a higher level of school administration, an attorney, the police, or all of the above. If the problem involves risks of extreme violence or gang activity, you will need to seek advice from law-enforcement personnel. In a worst-case scenario, a change of school (or home schooling) may be necessary to bring your child or adolescent through this situation in one piece. *Do whatever it takes (within the bounds of the law) to protect your child's safety and self-respect.*

What If Your Child Is Accused of Bullying?

Whatever you do, don't shrug it off (*Hey, boys will be boys*) or deny that there's a problem. Get the facts. You should get your child's side of the story, but also diligently seek input both from school officials and from whomever else was involved, including the victim(s) of the bullying. If the evidence (or your child's or teen's own admission) points to involvement in bullying, you will need to have a number of serious conversations:

- You must make it clear not only that this behavior is unacceptable, but that if continued, it will lead to serious consequences imposed by you, the school, and possibly the law.
- You will need to contact the parents of the victim(s) involved to apologize and express your determination to prevent further episodes. As a gesture of integrity and courage, you might want to arrange a meeting with the other family at an appropriate location so that a formal apology can be made by your child, as well as an offer of restitution for any expenses (involving medical care or property damage) related to the incident(s).
- If others have been involved in bullying—perpetrators often act in groups—you should take the lead in contacting their parents to encourage corrective and restorative action.
- If your child or teen has been involved in multiple bullying incidents, you should arrange for him to undergo counseling, both for evaluation and prevention of further episodes. Other issues—depression, drug use, impulse control, and even prior victimization (since some bullies have been bullied themselves)—may need to be addressed. *This is a family issue*, so be prepared to participate in some important discussions in the counselor's office yourself.

Suggested resources you might find useful include:

Help! My Child is Being Bullied by Bill Maier (Focus on the Family, 2006).

No More Victims by Frank Peretti (Thomas Nelson, 2001).

No More Bullies: For Those Who Wound or Are Wounded by Frank Peretti (Thomas Nelson, 2003).

The HRSA Web site http://stopbullyingnow.hrsa.gov contains numerous resources for kids, parents, and educators.

The National Youth Violence Prevention Resource Center Web site http://www.safeyouth.org is a portal of entry for information on a broad range of topics related to violence committed by and against the young.

The Teenage Driver

Driving is one of the most momentous steps that a teenager will take toward personal independence. Being able to drive provides mobility, the gratification of not having to rely on parents or friends for a ride, and a definite sense of prestige (even if the vehicle involved is the family fixer-upper). Like every other new freedom that beckons the adolescent moving toward adulthood, there are a number of risks—and responsibilities—that must be acknowledged and addressed. Because of the safety issues that accompany taking the wheel for the first time, new drivers and their parents should prepare for this next phase of life with the utmost diligence.

If you're a little apprehensive about your teenager becoming a driver, your concerns are not unfounded. (The fact that automobile insurance rates are greatly increased for adolescent drivers—especially for males—is no accident.) Motor-vehicle accidents are the leading cause of death of young people ages fifteen through twenty-four, killing more than ten thousand teens and young adults in America each year.[1] Every year nearly seven thousand fatal automobile crashes involve young drivers (age sixteen to twenty), and more than 450,000 cause nonfatal injury. More than three thousand young drivers die every year.[2] Though this age-group comprises less than 7 percent of the driving population, it accounts for 14 percent of vehicle-related fatalities. Over the past decade, over sixty-eight thousand teens have died in car crashes.[3]

Inexperience is a major risk factor for teens involved in accidents. Driving is, after all, an amazingly complex task. New drivers must learn to control their vehicle and its speed, while at the same time detecting and responding to hazardous driving conditions and emergency situations. The vast majority of teens are not lacking in the motor skills and coordination necessary to be an excellent driver. (Indeed, they're probably better equipped in this regard than Mom and Dad.) But what isn't fully developed is their judgment, decision-making ability, or a healthy respect for the unexpected—and their own mortality.

Indeed, an important factor contributing to accidents involving teens is their willingness to engage in risky behaviors. Speeding is a factor in about 30 percent of all traffic fatalities, and putting pedal to the metal is a major temptation for teenage drivers—

especially males.[4] Alcohol is involved in more than a third of all traffic deaths for young people ages sixteen through twenty.[5] One survey found that almost 10 percent of high school students reported driving after drinking alcohol, and more than 28 percent of teens had ridden with a driver who had been drinking.[6]

Teenagers love to hang out and drive around with their friends, but for a sixteen-year-old driver the likelihood of having a fatal accident increases nearly 40 percent when one nonadult passenger is present, nearly 90 percent with two, and nearly 300 percent with three or more young riders.[7] More than half of all deaths in crashes involving sixteen- and seventeen-year-old drivers occur when there is at least one passenger younger than twenty (and no adult) in the car.[8] More than 10 percent of high school students report that they never or hardly ever use a safety belt when riding in a car driven by someone else.[9] All of these behaviors increase the odds of a teenager being involved, injured, and/or killed in an automobile accident.

After reading such discouraging information, some parents may vow never to let their children sit behind the wheel of a car until they are in their twenties and living on their own. Aside from being unrealistic, such a mind-set is counterproductive and insulting to teens who really want to learn to drive safely. A more constructive outlook is to view the adolescent years as a time when adults can teach safe driving habits and influence a young driver's behavior for life, imparting skills and knowledge that will perhaps save lives many years in the future. Becoming an expert driver requires years of experience, and overseeing the first few years of that experience is a wonderful, though at times ulcer-generating, privilege.

As a parent you can pass on a wealth of driving wisdom in many ways. First, be patient with your teen. His learning to drive may be nerve-racking for you, but it's much more so for him. (Giving all instructions calmly and clearly will help.) Second, as with other behaviors they want their children to adopt, parents must model safe driving habits. For better or worse, children will imitate their parents. Also, parents should not only learn the traffic laws for their state but also be prepared to enforce additional limits and expectations based on their adolescent's attitude and skill.

Recognizing that driver-education courses by themselves are not a complete preparation for novice motorists, a number of states have instituted graduated driver licensing for teens. Such a system is designed to phase teens into full driving privileges by allowing them to mature and develop their driving skills in steps. Each state's system is different, but the typical graduated-licensing model involves three stages. Beginners must remain in the first two stages for a minimum amount of time, demonstrating a mastery of basic skills under less-challenging driving conditions. (For example, the stage-one teenage driver might not be allowed to drive after dark, while in stage two he might be allowed to drive at night, but only with adult supervision.) Even if your state has not yet enacted graduated licensing, you may wish to grant your teen's driving privileges in a similar manner, which allows him to acquire the experience he needs while reducing some of the risks. For example, you might require that your teen driver be accompanied by a parent or other responsible licensed adult driver at all times for a set period of time. You may also wish to set specific ground rules, such as limiting the number of passengers he may have in the car or restricting driving to daylight hours, until he has demonstrated responsible driving behavior for a number of weeks or months.

Always require your teen to buckle up before the engine is started, whether driving or riding. (This is an area where your example speaks louder than your words.) Your adolescent should never drive if he is drowsy. Additionally, while there are many good reasons for him to abstain from alcohol and drugs, don't fail to drive home the message that drinking kills thousands of people every year—many of them teens. Not only should your teenager never drink and drive, but he should also never get into a car if the driver has been drinking. And no matter how strongly you might feel about the use of alcohol, let your adolescent know that he can *always* call you for a ride in order to avoid being in a car with an intoxicated driver—whether himself or someone else.

Unfortunately, no matter how calmly and rationally you explain the conditions you are placing on your teen, he may see these restrictions as unreasonable. If he protests your limitations, stand your ground. And if you see unsafe driving patterns or habits that your adolescent refuses to correct, don't let him have the keys. The first commandment for would-be drivers to learn (and burn deep in their consciousness) is that driving is a privilege, not a right. Your first priority is not to win a popularity contest. It's to keep him (and others on the road) alive and well while he learns to operate an automobile safely and skillfully.

A Parent's Guide to Teen Sexuality

PART ONE: PRESERVING THE GIFT

This section will focus repeatedly on an important principle: It is appropriate, wise, and potentially lifesaving to teach your kids to wait until marriage to become sexually active.

God designed sex to bring new life into existence, to generate a powerful bond between a husband and wife, and to be intensely pleasurable. It is a wonderful, extraordinary, and powerful gift that deserves to be treated with great and abiding respect. In the context of a permanent and public commitment, it can be savored, explored, and nurtured without guilt or fear of serious consequences. But at the wrong time with the wrong person, sex can bring disappointment and disease, as well as derail life plans and purposes.

Your adolescent, who is curious about and highly interested in sex, needs a clearheaded understanding of its benefits and risks in order to make a serious commitment to remain sexually pure until marriage. Maintaining such a commitment won't always be easy.

Why is it so challenging to preserve the gift of sex for marriage?

Inner drives. Normal adolescents—even yours—have sexual interests and feelings. No one passes through the teen (or adult) years devoid of sexual urges before suddenly switching them on as soon as the minister says, "I now pronounce you man and wife." Just like anyone else, teens deeply need love and affirmation. As a result, they can become emotionally and sexually attracted to others around them and drawn toward physical intimacy. But they also enter adolescence with a sense of modesty that tends to inhibit sexual exploration.

These realities were clearly recognized just a few generations ago, when modesty was encouraged and more formal boundaries were set between unmarried members of the opposite sex. Today many would call such efforts stuffy, inhibited, and puritanical. But our ancestors were in many ways more "streetwise" about adolescent sexuality and made it somewhat easier for their sons and daughters to resist sexual pressure. Our culture, on the other hand, practically drowns them in temptation.

Provocative images and messages. Sex sells everything from beer to burgers, from cars to chewing gum. Images that tantalize young men are everywhere: in department-store lingerie ads, in the *Sports Illustrated* swimsuit edition, and on covers of magazines in the supermarket checkout line.

More explicit sexual content is readily available on mainstream or pay-per-view cable television channels, or on the millions of commercial porn Web sites that are but a few mouse clicks away from the home page of their favorite search engine. Messages, photos, and videos with provocative or explicit sexual messages also show up in blog sites, e-mails, text messages, and online social networking realms such as MySpace.com. These images also speak powerfully to young women: *This is what guys want.*

Even in the "safe" confines of the classroom, a teenager's natural modesty is often dismantled during explicit presentations about sexual matters in mixed company.

Seductive messages. A half century ago, Western societies generally supported the concept that marriage was the appropriate arena for sexual activity. During the late 1960s, a cultural upheaval sometimes called the sexual revolution assaulted traditional expectations for sexual behavior. Virtually all popular media (movies, TV, DVDs, music) as well as educational, health-care, and governmental organizations were affected by this moral free fall. As a result, by the time your child arrives at puberty, he or she will have heard the following destructive messages many, many times and in a variety of ways:

Four Fantasies of the Sexual Revolution

1. Sex is okay any way and with anyone (even someone you just met a few minutes ago), as long as there is mutual consent, no one gets pregnant (unless she wants to), and no one gets hurt.

2. Sex is usual and customary if you are attracted to someone.

3. Sex unrelated to marriage is normal, natural, expected, and inevitable, so carry a condom and know how to use it correctly.

4. If you are postponing sex until marriage, you must be incredibly unattractive, socially inept, or fanatically committed to some type of prudish or fundamentalist religion.

Hearing "anything goes" and "everyone's doing it" over and over can be difficult for teenagers to ignore. Under the assault of these messages, even those who are committed to preserving sex for marriage may begin to feel as if they are completely out of step and needlessly missing out on one of life's greatest pleasures.

Lack of supervision. Because of fragmented families, complex parental work schedules, easier access to transportation, and at times carelessness among adults who should know better, adolescents today are more likely to find opportunities to be alone together for long stretches of time. In such circumstances, even teens who have made a commitment to wait for sex until their wedding night can find it much more difficult to keep their promises to God, to themselves, and to their future spouse. (A small number of parents actually allow their teenage children to engage in sexual activity at home, based on the foolish notion that this makes "safe sex" more likely.)

Overbearing, overprotective supervision. Adolescents who are smothered in a controlled, micromanaged, suspicious environment are strong candidates for rebellion once the opportunity arises. When restraints are tightly enforced in an atmosphere of ongoing mistrust, kids may be tempted to become sexually involved simply to "get it over with," to see what all the fuss is about, and to assert their independence. Ironically, a big (and dangerous) rebellion may represent an effort to break loose from an overabundance of trivial constraints. As will be discussed later in this section, parents can set appropriate boundaries while still entrusting adolescents with increasing responsibility to manage themselves and their sexuality.

Peer pressure. This ever-present influence comes in four powerful forms. If two or more of these are present at the same time, resistance to premarital sexual activity may be worn down quickly:

A general sense that "everyone is doing it except me." Movies, TV, videos, and popular music nurture this idea. Conversations with friends or even offhanded comments overheard between strangers may bring the idea closer to home. Your child's school health-education presentation will confirm the suspicion if it emphasizes contraception and condom use but barely mentions abstinence. The weight of this evidence may lead a young person to conclude, "These professionals know more about this than I do. I must be the only seventeen-year-old in town who hasn't had sex."

Apparent widespread acceptance of casual, recreational, or "disposable" sexual contact. If teenagers of the 1960s saw themselves as pushing against outmoded and puritanical restraints imposed on previous generations, their children seem bent on obliterating those restraints altogether. For example, many of today's adolescents do not consider oral sex to be sex—a fanciful notion that can have disastrous consequences—or they consider it to be less intimate or meaningful than intercourse (see sidebar "Oral Sex Is Sex" on page 512). While at parties, many adolescents and college students have experienced "hooking up"—a spontaneous physical (usually sexual) encounter disconnected from any relationship or, for that matter, meaning (see sidebar "The Painful Hook in 'Hooking Up'" on page 514). The term *friends with benefits* and a variety of far more crude variations are commonly used for individuals who have sex (in various forms) without any expectation from the relationship, romantic or otherwise. All of these reflect a naive but all too common notion that sex can be experienced not only without physical consequences but also without any relationship or emotional fallout.

Personal comments from friends and acquaintances, such as:

- "You've been with him for six months and haven't slept together yet? What's wrong?"
- "Hey, guys, check out Jason, the last American virgin!"
- "Did you do it/score/get lucky last night?"

Direct pressure from another person who wants a sexual experience, or an invitation from a willing potential partner. Come-ons, smooth talk, whining, haggling, and outright coercion by men who want sex with a woman are timeworn negative behaviors. A young woman's resistance to them may be lowered by a need for closeness and acceptance, and the mistaken belief that physical intimacy will secure a man's love.

In recent years a turnabout has become common: A young man is informed by his girlfriend (or a new acquaintance) that she wants to have sex with him. Personal convictions that sex is intended for marriage will be put to the ultimate test in a situation like this, especially if some physical contact is already under way. His moral code and all the admonitions he has heard may suddenly seem terribly abstract, while the intense pleasure that is his for the taking is very real. Which will prevail?

Lack of reasons (and desire) to wait. Some adolescents are determined to have sex, regardless of the risks. Others are unshakably committed to the goal that their first and only sex partner will be their spouse. In between these opposite poles live a large number of teenagers who keep an informal mental tally of reasons for and against premarital sex. Inner longings and external pressure pull them toward it, while standards taught at home and church, medical warnings, and commonsense restraints put on the brakes.

For many teenagers (even those who intend to abstain until marriage), decisions about sex tend to be made based on the drift of this internal "vote count." When the moment of truth arrives, the tally may be close—or a landslide in the wrong direction.

ORAL SEX IS SEX

While oral sex—contact between one person's mouth or tongue and another person's genitals—isn't typically a topic of polite conversation, it became a frequent subject for newscasters and talk-show hosts during the high-profile political scandals of the 1990s. These discussions revealed that a surprising number of people don't perceive oral sex as sex, a view that is often accompanied by a dangerous—and wrong—belief that it isn't particularly risky. This belief is especially common among teenagers. In a study of twelve- to fifteen-year-olds, one in six reported having tried oral sex, and many of these denied ever having vaginal intercourse.[1] A more recent study from the National Center for Health Statistics found that more than 50 percent of the fifteen- to nineteen-year-olds surveyed had engaged in some form of oral sex (giving, receiving, or both). The same survey found that 10 percent of females and 12 percent of males in this age-group have had oral sex but not vaginal intercourse.[2] Not surprisingly, alcohol and drug use increase the likelihood that a teenager will try oral sex.[3]

Some adolescent girls who practice oral sex consider themselves to be virgins or sexually abstinent. Health-care providers or counselors who are attempting to obtain an accurate sexual history from teenagers must routinely ask not only "Are you sexually active?" but also "Are you giving or receiving oral sex?" It is not uncommon for a teenager or young adult to answer no to the first question and yes to the second. Even significant numbers of college students—as many as one in three in one study—consider practicing oral sex to be compatible with a sexually abstinent lifestyle.[4] This idea is both emotionally and morally naive, and it may be medically misinformed as well if it assumes that oral sex is risk free. While it is true that pregnancy will not result from oral sex, a number of sexually transmitted infections can be transmitted through oral-genital contact, including syphilis, gonorrhea, herpes simplex virus, HPV, chlamydia, and even HIV. The potential consequences can range from a sore throat (from gonorrhea) or hoarseness (from HPV) to serious systemic illness (syphilis) and even death (HIV/AIDS). Estimates of the number of HIV cases that result from oral sex range from one to 7 percent.[5] ■

It may even result in an approach—what some call **serial monogamy**—that attempts to reconcile what are in fact incompatible positions: "I'll be careful with my health and emotions by having sex with only one person at any given time." Adolescents with a shaky or negative self-concept may be particularly vulnerable to sexual involvement if they think it might win approval from someone whom they perceive to be attractive or popular.

Therefore, without being overbearing or obsessive, make an effort to have ongoing dialogues with your teenager about the many compelling reasons to postpone sex until the wedding night. (It goes without saying that you should be talking to your teenager about many things besides areas of concern and danger. If your communication is smooth in other less-volatile areas, it will likely flow more easily with a sensitive topic such as sexuality.) The following list of reasons to wait may help you formulate and express your thoughts during these important conversations.

Reason to wait #1: The moral high ground

Despite the rising tide of sexual anarchy in our society, a great many people still believe the words *right* and *wrong* apply to sexual behavior. Even someone with a casual exposure to traditional Judeo-Christian values should pick up an important message: The Designer of sex cares a lot about when it's done and with whom. Sex outside of marriage can be dangerous to one's physical, emotional, and spiritual health. Even for those who do not follow specific religious precepts, basic decency and concern for the well-being of others should curtail the vast majority of sexual adventures, which so often are loaded with selfish agendas.

Unfortunately, some adolescents who have had ongoing church experiences and explicit teaching about sexual morality may still become involved with premarital sex, which does nothing for spiritual growth. Intimacy with God on Sunday morning (or any other day) will be seriously impaired when physical intimacy the night before has clearly violated the boundaries set forth in the Scriptures.

We need to issue an important reminder at this point: Biblical teachings on sex extend far beyond the words *no* and *don't*. Indeed, there is much more to be gained from adhering to God's prescription for sex beyond avoiding disease, emotional pain, and spiritual derailment (although these are certainly good reasons). Like everything else in life, sexuality is most enjoyable and satisfying when one follows the "owner's manual," a fact that is worth emphasizing to teenagers during any discussion of this topic.

Reason to wait #2: Sex is how babies get started

Each year nearly 750,000 American teenagers become pregnant, and approximately three in ten of these pregnancies end in abortion. (Approximately 10 to 15 percent of teen pregnancies end in miscarriage.) The vast majority of the pregnancies are unplanned, and a sizable percentage begin even though a contraceptive is used. Eight out of ten teenage mothers are unmarried (as opposed to fewer than three in ten in 1970). Altogether, one out of three adolescent girls will become pregnant at least once before the age of twenty.[6]

These statistics do not begin to communicate the profound effects of a pregnancy on a young woman's life. Whatever the circumstances of the sexual encounter that began it, a pregnancy cannot be ignored, and whatever is done about it will have a permanent impact on the young mother's life. Once she becomes pregnant, she will never be the same. Only two outcomes are possible: The baby will be born, or the baby will die before birth, whether through deliberate abortion or spontaneous abortion (miscarriage).

Neither of these events is easy to deal with. There's no quick fix where human life is concerned, no way to "rewind the tape" and start over as though nothing happened.

If an unmarried teenager bears and brings up her child, her life (and probably the lives of other family members) will be affected for years to come. She must deal with the many challenges that all new mothers face, but nearly always with some additional difficulties. Her educational plans are likely to be postponed or significantly rearranged. Only three out of ten adolescents seventeen and under who bear a child will earn a high school diploma. Seven out of ten adolescent mothers drop out of high school, and more than 80 percent of single mothers eighteen and younger eventually become dependent on welfare.[7] Unless she has considerable help and support, a teenage mother will risk difficulties with parenting, difficulty in a future marriage relationship, and more unplanned pregnancies.

In some cases, one or both of the mother's parents choose to take on primary care of their grandchild. (On occasion, the father's parents may assume this responsibility.) This situation can serve to forge new bonds in the extended family, allowing the baby to grow up loved and nurtured in his family of origin, while his mother manages part of his care and continues her schooling or vocation. But the added strain of such arrangements can take a significant toll on a family, and some families are simply too dysfunctional or lacking in material resources to provide adequate care for a new baby.

If a young mother gives up her child for adoption—an act of considerable courage—she will help bring about what is often a relatively positive combination of outcomes.

THE PAINFUL HOOK IN "HOOKING UP"

For most adults, the phrase *hooking up* refers to something one does with stereo equipment or cable TV. If you overhear teenagers talking about hooking up with someone, you might innocently believe that they mean meeting someone or getting together with friends.

Wrong. Ask your adolescent or college-attending offspring (or anyone at random in your church's youth group), and you'll hear the current definition: a spontaneous, nonconversational, usually emotionless, apparently meaningless, and definitely commitmentless physical encounter, typically at a social gathering where alcohol or other intoxicants serve as catalysts.

Lest anyone misconstrue the meaning of the term *physical*, novelist/satirist Tom Wolfe offered a colorful definition in his essay "Hooking Up." Comparing contemporary vocabulary to the passé baseball analogy in which "first base" once designated an embrace or kiss, and a "home run" meant having sexual intercourse, he notes: "In the era of hooking up, 'first base' meant deep kissing ('tonsil hockey'), groping and fondling; 'second base' meant oral sex; 'third base' meant going all the way; and 'home plate' meant learning each other's names."[8]

One might presume that enthusiasm for hooking up would be limited to males, given their propensity to seek nonrelational sexual release through pornography, prostitution, and other such pursuits. After all, aren't young women the ones who have traditionally desired a relationship, respect, and at least some romance as a prelude to a physical encounter? Have times changed so radically that a willingness to disconnect sex and communication now broadly and boldly crosses gender lines?

Her baby will be reared by people who are usually better prepared to provide the time, attention, and resources. She in turn can move on with her education and social life. But even this solution will not exempt her from pain. She will never forget her baby, and she may experience a sense of loss, sometimes profound, for the rest of her life.

We noted earlier in this book that in recent decades **open adoption**, in which there is some degree of interaction between the birth mother (or both birth parents) and the adoptive family, has become more common. In many cases, the birth mother actually selects who will rear her child from a number of potential candidates presented by an adoption agency. The couple may then become involved with the birth mother through an extended period of her pregnancy, and one or both adoptive parents might even attend the birth of the baby. Such a relationship can be fulfilling for all concerned, but it is not without potential pitfalls. It is critical that the relationship between the adoptive parents and the birth mother—and everyone's expectations regarding the amount of contact between mother and adoptive family once the baby is born—be carefully discussed and clarified before the birth (see the Special Concerns section "The Adopted Child," starting on page 77.)

Women with unplanned pregnancies often feel a burning need to find a solution as quickly as possible. They may find the options of bringing up or giving up a baby for adoption highly uncomfortable, at least at first. Furthermore, for a teenager, a nine-month detour from normal activities may seem like an eternity. These and other factors (especially pressure from a boyfriend or parents) may lead to the conclusion

The answer appears to be "Yes, but . . ." Research conducted by the Institute for American Values' Courtship Research Team, led by University of Texas sociology professor Norval Glenn, found considerable ambivalence among college women about this phenomenon. Among one thousand undergraduates surveyed regarding dating and courtship attitudes, 40 percent said they had experienced at least one hookup, and one in ten had done so more than six times. In describing how they felt the day after, many used both positive and negative adjectives: More than 60 percent of those who said the episode made them feel "desirable" also said they felt "awkward."

In-depth interviews carried out with sixty-two women on eleven different campuses elicited a common thread not only of awkwardness, especially confusion over "what comes next" and whether the hookup would lead to something else (i.e., a real relationship), but also of vulnerability, regret, and hurt feelings.[9] Commenting on the study's findings, Nancy Pfotenhauer, president of the Independent Women's Forum, which funded the research, notes that "young women are trying more and more to act like men, but the problem is they don't react like men."[10]

Interestingly, the Institute for American Values' report, which covered a number of dating and mating issues among college students, actually bemoans the loss of a "culture of courtship"—the "set of social norms and expectations that once helped young people find the pathway to marriage." It also calls on older adults, including parents, college administrators, and other cultural leaders, to take a meaningful role in correcting this deficit: "The virtual disappearance of adult participation in, or even awareness of, how today's young people find and marry one another should be seen as a major social problem, and should end." ■

that abortion is the only viable alternative. It may appear to offer a quick resolution, fewer personal complications, far less financial cost compared to having a baby, and usually confidentiality as well. (Many teenagers obtain abortions without parental involvement or consent.)

But abortion is not a completely risk-free procedure. Damage to the uterus that could jeopardize future pregnancies (or even require major surgical repair), infection, bleeding, future infertility, and even more serious events (including death) are possible complications, though rare. Furthermore, even if an abortion is performed without any apparent hitch, a different type of pain may develop months or years later. Because they want so desperately for the crisis to go away, many women will undergo an abortion even though they are knowingly violating their own moral standards. Many come to realize later in life that a human being—a son or a daughter, not a shapeless wad of tissue—was destroyed through abortion. For these and other reasons, many women live with significant, long-term regrets after an abortion, especially if they have difficulty becoming pregnant later in life.[11]

As with many issues related to crisis pregnancies, a pregnancy resource center (which in your community may be called a crisis pregnancy center, pregnancy care center, or women's resource center) may offer support for women who are dealing with the emotional aftermath of an abortion. (You can also obtain help from organizations such as Care Net [800-395-HELP or http://www.optionline .org].)

Reason to wait #3: Sexually transmitted infections (STIs)

Forty years ago the typical high school health-education class discussed two types of sexually transmitted infections (STIs): syphilis and gonorrhea. They were described as potentially hazardous but nothing a little penicillin couldn't handle. But the sexual playground that opened during the late 1960s has resulted in an ongoing STI epidemic populated with exotic, dangerous, and often incurable infections.

More than twenty significant diseases can be transmitted skin to skin or by exchange of body fluids during sexual activity. Some are fatal, a few are relatively harmless, and many have long-term physical and emotional consequences. A few can be successfully treated with antibiotics—but without creating any long-term immunity. As a result, infections such as gonorrhea and chlamydia can be acquired over and over by the same individual. (For more information on STIs and teens, see the Special Concerns section on page 539.)

Reason to wait #4: The risk of infertility

An estimated 10 to 15 percent of couples (about 6.1 million people) have difficulty conceiving, and more than a million couples seek treatment for infertility each year in the United States. Statistics cannot begin to reflect the intense distress this problem creates in a couple's life. Dealing with infertility can be complicated, time-consuming, stressful, and expensive—when the process of starting a pregnancy is designed to be pleasurable and free. Unfortunately, a significant number (but not all) of these infertility problems arise as a consequence of sexually transmitted infections and thus could have been avoided if both husband and wife had postponed sex until marriage. (For more information on the impact of STIs on women and unborn children, see the Special Concerns section on page 73.)

A note on terminology: Any infection acquired as a result of sexual contact was once called *venereal disease (VD)*, a quaint reference to the Roman goddess of love, Venus. The term was eclipsed a few decades ago by the more clinically precise term *sexually transmitted disease (STD)*. The recognition that an individual can be infected with a sexually transmitted organism without manifesting disease has recently led to the use of the more encompassing term *sexually transmitted infection (STI)*, which we use throughout this book. In other books and articles you may see *STD* and *STI* used interchangeably, but *STD* now refers specifically to disease that manifests as a consequence of a sexually transmitted infection.

Reason to wait #5: "Safe(r) sex" isn't

In spite of a relentless worldwide epidemic of sexually transmitted infections (not to mention unplanned pregnancies), many people—among them, health-care professionals, government-agency workers, and educators—have been unwilling to give serious consideration to a self-evident truth: These problems and the heartaches accompanying them could be eliminated if adolescents (and single adults) would postpone sex, find and marry one partner, and remain mutually faithful for life. This idea has been widely downplayed as unrealistic by an influential cadre of individuals and institutions that, in response to the AIDS epidemic, began promulgating the notion of "safe sex." When it became clear that only sex exclusively within marriage was truly safe, the concept was redubbed "safer sex."

Presentations that promote safer sex (including those geared to adolescents) typically give a brief nod to abstinence from nonmarital sex before presenting three faulty propositions:

Myths of safer sex

Myth 1: *If I limit the number of partners with whom I have sex, I'll be safe.* It is true that having fewer partners means fewer chances for exposure to disease. But it only takes one contact to become pregnant or to acquire a significant or lethal infection.

Myth 2: *If I know something about a potential partner's sexual history and I avoid having sex with someone who has had many partners, I'll be safe.* This sounds reasonable, but in fact taking a sexual history is tricky, even in a doctor's office. A prospective partner is often not willing to tell the truth if it means a pleasurable evening might be called off as a result. It is virtually impossible to discover the sexual history of the prospective partner's previous partners, or those partners' partners, and so on. From an infectious-disease standpoint, one has sex not with just one person but with all of that individual's previous sexual contacts, and all of their contacts' contacts, and so on. Furthermore, a significant number of people who are infected with STIs have no symptoms and do not know they are infected.

Myth 3: *If we use a condom every time, I'll be safe.* True, using a condom correctly (a multistep procedure) during each act of intercourse will reduce the risk of pregnancy and some STIs. But condoms are not a terribly effective form of birth control, with failure rates commonly estimated at 15 percent during the first year of typical use.[12] This means that out of one hundred women who are sexually active, ten to fifteen will be pregnant within a year if condoms are the only form of contraception used. *Among adolescents, these failure rates are generally higher* for a variety of reasons. Not only are teens more likely to forget or mismanage some of the fine points of proper condom use (including having one available in the first place) during the heat of the moment, many teenagers, and older men as well, simply resist wearing them.

Even if used correctly and consistently, condoms can break, leak, or fall off during intercourse. And while the risk for condom breakage and slippage during a single sexual act may be quite small (one to 4 percent in most studies), the cumulative risk when condoms are used as a long-term prevention strategy is significant.[13] These failure rates are even more alarming if one remembers that intercourse can lead to pregnancy on only a few days each month, while STIs can be transmitted *every day of every month.*

Scientific evidence shows that condoms are far from 100 percent protective, but rather they reduce the transmission of STIs to a variable degree—and with some infections, not much at all. Consistent condom use—that is, use with *every* sexual encounter—has been shown to reduce the risk of transmitting HIV about 85 percent.[14] For gonorrhea, herpes, syphilis, and chlamydia, consistent use reduces the risk of transmission by about 50 percent at best.[15] One reason for this incomplete protection is that a number of infections such as syphilis, herpes, and especially human papillomavirus (HPV) are often spread through contact between skin surfaces that a condom does not cover. The majority of research on condoms and HPV transmission suggest that the level of protection offered by condoms against the spread of HPV is modest at best.[16]

"Safe sex" and "safer sex" presentations send a paradoxical message. We tell kids and adults alike that there is no such thing as safe smoking, and no one would say that using filtered cigarettes constitutes "safer smoking." Our messages about the hazards of drinking and driving or riding with an intoxicated driver are unequivocal, and we don't give lessons in "safer driving while under the influence." We don't explain how to survive an auto accident when you haven't buckled up. But when it comes to sex, we essentially tell teenagers, "We know you can't control yourself, so be sure to put on a condom and hope for the best. And by the way, we won't mention that for many STIs condoms aren't terribly effective, because full disclosure would erode your confidence in them, and then you wouldn't bother to use them."

Reason to wait #6: To preserve the value of sex

Advocating that sex be kept within the boundaries of marriage is not based on notions that intercourse is "dirty" or "unholy" but on a true appreciation for sex as God's fine art. If the original *Mona Lisa* were entrusted to you for a month, you wouldn't leave it in your backyard, use it as a TV tray, or line a birdcage with it. Similarly, sex deserves more respect than our culture gives it.

- What truly devalues sex is the idea that intercourse is no more meaningful than a good meal or a drive in a fast car.
- What stifles sexual satisfaction is casual copulation with little or no emotional involvement.
- What people miss in nonmarital sex is the opportunity for enjoyment far greater than the immediate sensual experience.

While movies and television often portray casual sex as the epitome of sensual excitement, a healthy, long-term marital relationship is actually the best setting for satisfying sexual experiences. Not surprisingly, a landmark study—the 1992 National Health and Social Life Survey (NHSLS), summarized in the book *Sex in America: A Definitive Survey*—found that those who reported the most physical and emotional satisfaction with sex were married couples.[17] It isn't difficult to understand why this should be the case. The security of commitment can free both husband and wife to relax rather than "perform," and their familiarity over a period of years allows them to please and excite one another with ever-increasing expertise and finesse. In a growing and deepening marriage relationship, sexuality can encompass far more than the superficial, bumper-sticker mentality of merely "doing it." Sex becomes a comfort, a natural stimulant (or relaxant), a playground, a special means of communication, and a bridge that can connect individuals to one another after a difficult day or season. Short-term relationships provide few if any of these benefits, and those involved in casual sex cannot approach (or in some cases even comprehend) them.

Reason to wait #7: To prevent distorted relationships

Adding sex to a nonmarital relationship, especially when adolescents are involved, is like throwing a one-thousand-pound weight into a rowboat. The center of gravity drastically shifts, forward motion becomes difficult, and the whole thing may eventually sink. Sex never enhances a teenage romance but almost always overwhelms and stifles it. Arguments, secrecy, stress, and guilt usually replace laughter, discovery, and meaningful conversation.

Indeed, sex has a way of wrecking good relationships and keeping bad ones going long after they should have ended. After a sexual relationship is broken off, there is likely to be a sense of loss (sometimes severe), regret, and awkwardness whenever the other person is encountered. Condoms can't prevent a broken heart, and antibiotics can't cure one.

When one or both partners have had prior sexual experience, what's to guarantee that tonight's coupling isn't just another notch on the belt? Trust has become so foreign to the sexual playground that the phrase "trust me" has become the caricature come-on, the phrase uttered by the predator who hopes the intended prey is too dumb not to burst out laughing. Additionally, prior sexual experiences create memories that may interfere with bonding and sexual intimacy in a future marital relationship. Compare this with the experience of two people who have waited until marriage to initiate their sexual experience. For them the wedding night can be a wonderful time of discovery and bonding, and whatever they might lack in technique can be learned pleasantly enough at their own pace.

Reason to wait #8: To avoid devaluing one's sexuality and identity

An important warning for adolescent females: In the sexual revolution, women have been—and still are—the big losers:

- The woman virtually always pays a far bigger price than her partner when an unwanted pregnancy occurs.
- With the exception of syphilis and AIDS, many sexually transmitted infections have more serious consequences in women.
- When women accept the "playboy" philosophy of "sex as recreation," they trade a number of sexual encounters for nothing. No ongoing relationship, no security, no commitments, no love, and possibly no children in the future (if they acquire a pelvic infection from a partner).

But there is another critical arena in which far too many women have reaped a bitter harvest from seeds sown during the sexual revolution: the devaluation of their sexuality and their very identity. For a woman, the ability to enjoy an uninhibited and healthy sexual response requires that her sexual experiences begin in a setting of complete trust, respect, and love. But this nurturing context is very uncommon when sexual activity first occurs in a nonmarital relationship, even if she is feeling desperately "in love" with someone. Instead, all too often adolescent sex occurs in the setting of immature, predatory, or even abusive relationships.

The consequences from such encounters can be devastating. One consequence may be a strong sense of having been used, violated, and devalued. Instead of learning from experience and resolving not to be burned again, a sexually experienced adolescent—especially one for whom sex has not been entirely voluntary—is likely to think, *What does it matter now? I might as well just go ahead the next time.* Without specific counseling to counteract this mentality, resistance to continuing sexual activity may be seriously weakened. (This devaluation of both sexuality and self, while generally more common and profound in girls, certainly occurs in boys too. Girls and boys alike can also be emotionally devastated by the breakup of one or more relationships that involve sexual intimacy.)

Another likely consequence of early nonmarital sexual experiences is that a young woman's sense of self-worth may become linked to her sexual usefulness to others. Ironically, even though she may look and act sexually sophisticated, her ability to *respond* sexually is almost certain to be compromised—an issue that may come home to roost if and when she marries. Rather than being enjoyed in an uncomplicated way, sex is more likely to be experienced as a complex and often contradictory mixture of functions: as currency and power in a relationship or as a source of anxiety over a partner's approval. (Men who have engaged in sex with one or more partners may also bring a lot of emotional and physical baggage into a marriage. If they have experienced sex with partners who have had a variety of agendas and lovemaking techniques, they may harbor any number of unrealistic expectations.)

What Can Parents Do to Reduce the Risk of Premarital Adolescent Sex?

Plenty. First, reread "Talking to Teens about Risks: Nine Basic Principles" (page 460). Then seriously consider the following measures (all are long-term projects):

Be aware of the specific risk factors for teen sex.

Alcohol and drug use. Aside from reflecting problem attitudes (rebellion, poor self-concept, invulnerability) that make sex more likely, intoxication also clouds judgment and weakens resistance to sexual overtures.

A steady boyfriend or girlfriend. Strong attachments and feelings of exclusivity invite nature to take its course, especially when physical expressions of affection begin early in the relationship. *This is a particular risk in a situation where the boy is more than two or three years older than the girl.* Ideally, a take-it-slow approach to relationships can be encouraged and set in motion through conversations both before and during the adolescent years. (This process is discussed at length later in this section.) If a teen romance appears to be getting hot and heavy and a lot of physical contact is already displayed, you will have a more delicate task. You will need to speak with both boy and girl diplomatically but candidly about the physical process they are setting in motion. If you're too easygoing about it, you will do little to discourage further progress down the road toward intimacy. On the other hand, if you come down too hard, you may drive the young lovers closer together, emotionally and physically. Forbidding further contact (which is much easier said than done) should be reserved for situations in which it is clear that the relationship is damaging, dangerous, or abusive.

Little parental monitoring. Adolescents aren't likely to remove clothing and get horizontal if parents are in the next room. Leaving them alone for hours at a time or not requiring accountability is a setup for sex.

A parental belief that adolescent sex is appropriate. If you think nonmarital sex is okay, your adolescent will too and will act on that belief.

A parental belief that adolescent sex is inevitable. Many parents who disapprove of teen sex have also concluded that it is as certain as death and taxes. Their approach to this subject thus can sound like double-talk: "Don't do it, but in case you do, be sure to use a condom." A few take their daughters to doctors or family-planning clinics to obtain birth control pills—*even if they have not become sexually active*. But in sexual matters, the venerable motto "Be prepared" communicates not merely precaution but expectation: "I know you're going to do it." Adolescents will get that message loud and clear and are likely to act accordingly.

Low grade point average/low attachment to school. While school performance is affected by a variety of factors, a basic desire to do well in school reflects (among other things) a more hopeful outlook on the future and a willingness to put off immediate gratification for long-term goals. Teen sex, on the contrary, is a here-and-now event, usually reflecting ignorance of or little regard for consequences. This doesn't mean, of course, that every scholar is a bulwark of morality or that all who are not academically oriented are destined to be promiscuous. What ultimately matters is a person's commitment to basic values such as responsibility, respect for self and others, and concern about the effect of today's decisions on the future.

A history of physical or sexual abuse. These acts against children and adolescents violate their bodies, minds, and hearts. Sexual abuse creates a grossly distorted view of sexual behavior, destroys boundaries, and drives a deep sense of worthlessness into the emotions. Whether the abuse occurred in the distant or recent past, adolescents with this history need ongoing support, counseling, and prayer to help them develop healthy attitudes about sex and about themselves.

Frequent family relocations. Moving is generally stressful for both parents and adolescents (especially if the kids resent the decision). This can erode parental authority and distract parents from involvement with their children. Bonds to social supports such as church groups that help prevent sexual activity are severed by multiple moves. Loneliness and loss of friendships may lead some teenagers to use sexual activity as a means to gain social acceptance. These issues should be considered by parents who are thinking about a possible relocation.

Only one parent in the household. Parenting was meant to be a team effort, and some risks will naturally increase when one parent is left to do all the protecting and monitoring alone. Some studies do indicate that adolescents living with a single parent are more likely to become sexually active than those living with both parents. Work and household demands can prevent single parents from being as involved and attentive as they need and want to be. And the divorce and desertion that sometimes lead to a one-parent home can make teens uncertain about the value of marriage as the setting for sexual activity and about the role of sexuality in parental relationships.

This increased risk does not mean that adolescent sex is inevitable in single-parent families. But it does place an additional responsibility on single parents to send their teenagers clear and consistent messages about sexuality. And it is one more reason for single parents to enlist as much support as they can.

Understand the specific factors that lower the risk for teen sex.

- Religious commitment. Studies have shown that this consistently lowers the likelihood of adolescent sexual behavior.
- Educational accomplishment/commitment to school.
- Friends who have a similar commitment to abstinence.
- Presence of both parents in the home, especially the biological father. Positive involvement of a father with his teenage offspring has been shown to be an effective deterrent to early sexual activity.
- Parental and community values that support and clearly promote sexual abstinence until marriage.
- A host of other interesting activities and passions. Adolescents who have other burning interests—such as earning academic honors; starting on a certain career path; traveling abroad; participating in ministry; or excelling in music, drama, sports, or other areas—will be less likely to allow premature sexual involvement to derail their plans and dreams. If they belong to a stimulating family that serves as a launching pad for fulfilling and fun activities, they will be less vulnerable to the boredom, purposelessness, and impaired self-concept that can sweep an adolescent toward unhealthy relationships.

Be a role model for the kinds of relationships you want your kids to develop with members of the opposite sex.

Parents should make every effort to keep their marriage intact and to nourish, enrich, and celebrate it, demonstrating respect and affection for each other on an ongoing basis. This gives adolescents a sense of security and a strong attachment to your values.

Fathers have a particularly important role to play. A boy who sees his father treat his mother with physical and verbal courtesies (which may range from fine points such as opening doors for her to broader strokes such as regularly seeking her opinions and advice, and listening to and praising her) and is taught to do likewise will be more likely to carry this behavior and attitude into his own relationships with women. Girls who are consistently affirmed, cherished, and treated respectfully by their fathers aren't as likely to begin a desperate search for male affection that could lead to sexual involvement. Furthermore, they will expect appropriate behavior from the other men in their lives.

Single parents who are bringing up teenagers must repeatedly affirm them and create as stable a home life as possible. Values concerning nonmarital sex should be practiced as well as preached. A sexually active single parent or one who has a live-in partner is proclaiming in no uncertain terms that this activity is all right for teenagers as well.

Do your best to give your teen(s) a strong, positive sense of identity.

Teenagers who feel incomplete, inadequate, and unappreciated are more likely to seek comfort in a sexual relationship. But those with a life rich in relationships, family traditions, activities, interests, and—most of all—consistent love and affirmation are less likely to embark on a desperate search for fulfillment that could lead to unwise sexual decisions. Those who see their future as promising are more likely to protect themselves from physical or emotional damage arising from sexual activity. Those who have a healthy, productive faith in God are more likely to have deeply rooted reasons to respect and preserve the gift of sex and to respect rather than exploit others.

Create a special occasion to talk about abstaining from sex until marriage.

Early in your child's adolescence, plan a special evening (or a weekend away from home) during which the importance of preserving sex for marriage is the central focus. This time, shared by the teen and both parents, could culminate in the presentation of a special token—a necklace, ring, or key, for example—that symbolizes commitment to an abstinent lifestyle. It can be very meaningful if this item is carried or worn by your adolescent for years and then presented to his or her marriage partner on their wedding night.

If your adolescent has already had sexual experiences, make it clear that it is never too late to make a commitment to reserve sex for marriage.

This important concept is called "secondary virginity" and should be strongly encouraged among adolescents who have been sexually active. Some churches and parachurch organizations have formal programs organized specifically to promote the decision to remain sexually abstinent until marriage.

Continue sending healthy messages about sexuality throughout your son's or daughter's adolescent years.

The best time to build a solid foundation for healthy sexuality is before puberty (see chapter 11, page 375, for more details). But even if you've never discussed the subject directly, you still send all kinds of signals about your attitudes over the course of time.

- Your adolescent needs to know you are comfortable with the subject. If you seem embarrassed, flustered, ashamed, or unapproachable whenever the topic comes up, your teenager will look elsewhere for input.
- Don't hesitate to broach the subject yourself. Adolescents are reluctant to bring up sexual subjects with their parents, and your chances of having one or more conversations may be nil unless you take the initiative. Remember that the facts of sexuality are morally neutral. Anyone (even you) can teach them, but you have the opportunity to put the proper perspective on the subject.
- Be careful how you talk about someone else's sexual issues. News of a crisis pregnancy in another family can provide a powerful teachable moment, for good or ill. If you give a clear signal that the nonmarital sex was wrong but respond with compassion (and prayer) for the people involved, you make it clear that you can be approached if anyone at home has a problem. But if your response sounds something like "Don't you ever do something as stupid/shameful/evil as this," you could block potentially critical communication in the future. Pregnancy resource centers routinely find that many of their most difficult clients are the daughters of good, moral, upright, churchgoing parents. "I can't tell Mom and Dad—it'll kill them (or they'll kill me)" is a common refrain as these girls head for an abortion clinic.

Talk about healthy and unhealthy relationships, and train your adolescent to avoid situations that increase the likelihood of a sexual incident.

Make them streetwise about the general course of relationships, dating, risky situations, and the ugly reality of date rape.

Encourage supervised, structured, nonpressuring group activities with the opposite sex as opposed to single dating situations, especially for adolescents in junior high and early high school. The object should be to learn how to talk and have fun without romantic expectations or sexual pressure. Group activities such as a church picnic or youth-group outing are generally healthier than dances or other situations in which pairing up is necessary.

Talk to your adolescent about the qualities that ultimately matter in a relationship with a person of the opposite sex. Shared values (especially spiritual orientation), mutual respect, easy conversation, and enjoyment of everyday activities count far more heavily in the long run than good looks, money, popularity, or intense romantic attraction. Indeed, the best romances and marriages often come from relaxed friendships that progress gradually, with lots of conversations about everything under the sun. Accordingly, dating activities should be seen as experiences that are pleasant, enriching, and relaxing, not times of perpetual emotion.

Talk to your adolescent about unhealthy relationships, and have the courage to speak honestly if you see one developing in one or more of the following ways:

- Relationships that ride a roller coaster of emotions—where two people are madly in love one day, fight like cats and dogs the next, and then cry and make up over and over—distract and drain a couple's time and energy and wear out everyone else for miles around. They are also a setup for sexual involvement, as the passionate fight often concludes with equally passionate reconciliation (what many couples refer to as "make-up sex"). This type of turbulent relationship is likely to turn into an even stormier marriage.

HOW MUCH TOUCH IS OKAY? GUIDELINES FOR TEENAGERS ON DATES AND OTHER OCCASIONS

Establish clear and unequivocal respect for your body, your life, and your future. Decide *before* the conversation, *before* the date, *before* the relationship gets more serious that physical intimacy is reserved for your wedding night.

Respecting yourself (and the person you're with) means setting your own limits for physical contact. Stick to them, and be ready to defend them if necessary. Sexual pressure can become a major problem if you are unclear about your boundaries, if you are afraid of rejection, or if you are worried about being called a prude because you won't go past a certain point.

Physical contact—even something as simple as holding hands—may be interpreted in ways you don't intend. What to you means "I like you" or "I think you're okay" might be received as "I'm madly in love with you" or "I want to go further." It's better to express how you feel in words, rather than through unclear and potentially powerful physical messages.

Remember that the events that lead to sex are progressive. Think of a car gaining momentum as it coasts down a steep hill. Once a given level of intimacy has been reached, it is very difficult to back up to a more conservative one. It is also more difficult to defend a boundary in the heat of the moment.

- Relationships in which one person is intensely needy for the other, and thus clingy and smothering, are parasitic and draining. For example, the woeful refrain, "I'd kill myself if you ever left me" puts inappropriate and unhealthy pressure on the other person.
- Relationships that have ongoing verbal disrespect in one or both directions are doomed.
- Relationships in which physical abuse occurs must be terminated immediately.

An important note: Unhealthy relationships carry a significant risk for sexual involvement.

Talk to your adolescent about physical demonstrations of affection. This is a natural desire when two people like each other, but how much (and how far) is okay? What about handling the desire—or some pressure—to push physical boundaries? You can lay down rules and regulations, but your adolescent needs a rationale for making good decisions without you. Here are some ideas that may help your teenager.

Set up your expectations and ground rules about dating in advance—well before your teenager asks if he or she can go out with someone.

Each family will have to set its own standards, but extremes are best avoided. Rigid parental control through high school and beyond (including selecting a limited number of "acceptable" candidates for courtship) stifles growth and independence and virtually guarantees rebellion. But a lax, anything-goes approach without parental guidelines is like handing the car keys to someone who has had no driver's training.

Think seriously about adopting a stepwise approach, especially for your adolescent's first socializing experiences with the opposite sex. Many parents have a policy

You are much better off setting very conservative limits for expressing affection (holding hands and perhaps a brief embrace or kiss) and progressing slowly, both emotionally and physically, in a relationship. This isn't old-fashioned but smart and realistic. More intense kissing, lying down together, touching personal areas, and increasing the amount of skin-to-skin contact sets off increasingly intense responses that are designed to lead to sexual intercourse—even when neither person intended this conclusion.

If you're not sure whether what you're doing physically is appropriate, ask yourself if you would be comfortable doing it in front of either set of parents, your pastor, or your future spouse. Remember that the person you are with now will probably not be the person you will marry. Would you feel comfortable having that person watch what you're doing?

If resisting physical intimacy is becoming more difficult, don't tempt fate. Stay away from situations where the two of you are alone together. Deliberately plan to be around other people or in places where nothing can happen. (It's difficult to have sex at a coffee shop.) Don't lie down on the sofa together to watch a video, and don't watch movies or videos with overt sexual content. Don't banter sexually provocative comments back and forth on the assumption that talk is safer than sex. Remember that your most important sexual organ is your mind, and where it goes your body will follow. (In some school sex-education programs, erotic conversations are actually recommended as an alternative to intercourse. Perhaps this idea works—on another planet.) ■

that if someone wants to spend time with their son or daughter under age eighteen, the first step is spending an evening at home with the family or joining in a family activity such as dinner and a movie or a ball game. This gives everyone a chance to get acquainted and broadcasts an important message: "The one you want to spend time with is deeply cherished by a family to whom you are accountable. We are happy to welcome you aboard, but nothing less than respectful and honorable behavior will do." Your expectation should be to make friends with the person, not to carry out a third-degree interrogation. In fact, you may develop a friendship that lasts long after your son or daughter has become interested in someone else. If anyone refuses or is extremely reluctant to spend time with the family in this way, however, consider it a red flag—and put further socializing with this person on hold.

If the first step goes well, group dating can be a good way to continue this process, assuming the other people involved are trustworthy. Many parents give the green light to single dating at age sixteen if there is ongoing evidence of maturity and responsibility and if the relationship appears basically healthy. Whenever this activity begins, you have the right and responsibility to know specifics *every* time, including the intended companion(s), the activity and its location, who's providing transportation, etc. Have a clear agreement about the expected time to arrive home. Whatever time you set, talk about the importance of letting you know if they're going to be home later than

PROTECTING YOURSELF FROM DATE RAPE

- You are much better off dating someone you know fairly well rather than someone who is a casual or chance acquaintance.
- In general, multicouple or group activities are less risky (and more fun) than single dates.
- Single dates—especially the first time with someone—should take place in public places. An invitation to a play or a sporting event is by far preferable to "Come to my place to watch a video." Be especially leery of the suggestion that it would be nice "to go someplace private to talk." Enjoyable and meaningful conversation can happen anyplace where two people can hear each other's voices.
- Consider accepting a blind date only if the person carries a strong endorsement from someone you trust. Even then, this should not be a single date.
- Bring your own money. Paying your own way in the early stages of a relationship can help establish your independence. Even if your date picks up the tab, you might need cash for transportation home if things get out of hand.
- Stay sober. Alcohol and drugs cloud judgment and put you off guard and off balance.
- Never leave a restaurant, party, or other get-together with someone you just met.
- Trust your instincts. If you don't feel right about the way the date is progressing, bail out. A little awkwardness is far better than a sexual assault. You should have an understanding with your parents (or another trusted individual) that you can call at any time for a ride home.
- Avoid situations in which you do not feel on equal footing with your

planned. *Consistency and reliability about keeping you posted should be a bigger issue than abiding by an absolute time limit.*

While they may complain outwardly about some of these ground rules, most adolescents will feel more secure when you are appropriately involved in the socializing/dating process. This should extend beyond setting limits to offering some encouragement as well, such as quietly providing a little extra cash to help enhance a special occasion. Even more important is making it abundantly clear that your teenager can call you anytime, day or night, from anywhere, if any help is needed—including a ride home from a date that has gone sour.

Talk candidly to your daughter(s) about the unpleasant topic of date rape and how best to avoid it.

The odds are at least one in six that a woman will be coerced into unwanted sex at some point in her life. In four out of five cases, the rapist is someone the woman knows—a fellow student, a business acquaintance, a neighbor, or (all too often) a date.

For your part, aside from issuing specific recommendations and warnings (see sidebar below), set some policies that will reduce the risk of a sexual catastrophe. First, veto any dating relationship between your adolescent daughter and someone who is more than two or three years older. The majority of teenage pregnancies involve

companion. If you feel unequal, intimidated, awestruck, or indebted to your date in some way, your willingness to assert yourself may be weakened or delayed. Unhealthy situations include relationships with men more than two or three years older than you, an employer, a teacher, or someone to whom you or your family owes a debt.

- Beware of expensive gifts and lavish dates. Too many guys still carry the Neanderthal notion that picking up the tab for a nice evening entitles them to a sexual thank-you. If your date presents that message, don't hesitate to straighten him out. Declining a present that appears to have strings attached is a healthy way to set boundaries.

- Look out for the control freak, someone who insists on his way and ignores your likes and dislikes. If he shows contempt for your tastes in restaurants, movies, and music, he may also have little regard for your physical boundaries.

- Beware of the person who tries to isolate you from your other friends and your family or who constantly bad-mouths them. If he is extremely possessive and wants you all to himself, chances are he will eventually want all of you sexually as well.

- Steer clear of guys who tell raunchy jokes, listen to sexually explicit music, enjoy pornography, or make degrading comments about women. These men have a diseased attitude about women and sexuality, and they don't belong in your life.

- Don't waste your time with anyone who won't accept your limits; who begs, pleads, and haggles for physical contact; or who trots out worn and pathetic lines such as "If you loved me, you'd do it" or "Trust me." Anyone who pressures you for sexual favors is a loser and an abuser and most certainly doesn't love you. ■

relationships with men in their twenties or older. Object vigorously to her dating anyone who might have a position of authority or leverage over some part of her life, such as an employer, teacher, family friend, or business associate of yours. These situations are a setup for potential date rape.

Talk explicitly to your son(s) about respect for members of the opposite sex and about sexual responsibility.
Your mission is to embed some very important values deeply into his mind and heart, not only for the teen years but for the rest of his life:

- *Never become a sexual predator.* A male who specifically sets out to maneuver women into sexual encounters might be called a playboy, red-hot lover, or Don Juan, but he's basically a jerk. If and when you see this behavior depicted in a movie or TV program or displayed by someone you know, let your son know that this is no way to treat any woman.
- *Never push a woman's physical boundaries.* If she says no to anything, even holding hands, that statement is final and not to be questioned.
- *Respect and maintain a woman's body, integrity, and future, even if she is inviting intimacy.* Without question one of the most difficult challenges for a healthy teenage male is to hold his ground when a desirable female flashes a bright and explicit green light. *Talk through this situation, including what he might say and how to walk away from this situation immediately.* It is important that he not be flustered or embarrassed and that he be able to decline the invitation in a way that expresses a desire to protect each person's health and future.
- Approach any activity or relationship with the opposite sex with the intention of enhancing the other person's life rather than leaving a wake of regrets. Thinking in terms of protecting the other person's long-term well-being instead of merely satisfying immediate needs or desires is a sign of maturity. Some thoughtful conversations between parents and sons can help establish these grown-up attitudes.

PART TWO: SEXUAL CRISIS SITUATIONS

What if—despite your best intentions, careful conversations, and earnest efforts—your adolescent slips, slides, plunges headlong, or is coerced into sexual experiences long before his or her wedding night? How will you respond?

As unpleasant as it might seem, it is important to think about the possibilities ahead of time. Parents would be wise to spend some time alone together (or single parents, with a trusted and mature friend) talking through these difficult and emotional "What if . . . ?" questions.

What If You Discover Your Adolescent Is Sexually Active?

Many contemporary resources for parents of teenagers make the wrong assumption that premarital sex is inevitable and recommend that parents help their kids make "mature" sexual decisions—by which they mean wearing condoms and taking other contraceptive precautions. Some parents respond by bringing their teenage (or even preteen) daughters to a doctor or a family-planning clinic for various birth-control measures and insisting that no one goes out for the evening without a supply of condoms.

These actions may seem responsible and open-minded to some parents, but giving tacit approval to teenage sex is foolhardy for many reasons: the risks of STIs, distorted relationships, damaged identities, and disrupted marital bonding later in life, not to mention the moral issues involved.

For a reality check, consider whether a responsible parent would carry out this sort of damage control in response to other risky adolescent behaviors:

- If your twelve-year-old started smoking, would you teach him to buy low-nicotine brands?
- If your fourteen-year-old wanted to move out of your home and get an apartment with a bunch of adolescent friends, would you pay the rent?
- If your sixteen-year-old began downing six-packs every weekend, would you include a few inebriated practice sessions as part of her driver's training?
- If your eighteen-year-old decided to try IV drugs, would you supply sterile syringes and make sure he understood sterile injection techniques?

Each response would theoretically reduce risks but would also enable and promote misguided decisions.

If facilitating adolescent sex is a bad idea, so is ignoring it. Equally unproductive is blowing up, finger-wagging, lecturing, or name-calling. This is a significant family problem deserving a loving and thoughtful response. The goal is to contain the damage and coach your adolescent toward more healthy and rational decisions. Therefore:

Think before you react. It is normal to feel upset and disappointed, and you will probably need a couple of days to settle down. Setting a time to talk about what has happened may be more appropriate than risking a more volatile, spur-of-the-moment confrontation. Ultimately, emotions should fuel appropriate action rather than ongoing angry outbursts.

Ask open-ended questions ("Can you tell me about your relationship with _____ ?") rather than judgmental ones ("How could you have done this?" or "What in the world were you thinking?"). *Listen* to the whole story (or as much as you are given) before offering your viewpoint. Eye rolling, crossed arms, finger drumming, and editorial comments will shut off communication in a hurry.

Put the emphasis on the big picture. You want your son or daughter to have a long life, good health, meaningful relationships, and freedom from unnecessary turmoil. Premarital sexual activity jeopardizes all of those goals. Be prepared to explain why. If you aren't convinced, review the reasons to postpone sexual involvement outlined on pages 513–520. Based on your broader range of experience and knowledge, you must tackle one of the most important jobs of parenting—opening young eyes to life's many consequences.

Don't tear down your teenager's sense of worth with comments such as "I am so ashamed of you" or "How could you act like such a jerk/tramp/lowlife?" This kind of rejection and judgment is what drives a lot of adolescents to sexual activity. A strong sense of identity and a conviction that one's future is worth protecting are deterrents to reckless or immoral behavior.

Stress the importance of new beginnings. Many teens who have been sexually active are willing to commit to secondary virginity, postponing any further sexual relationships until marriage. Actively encourage such a decision. Otherwise the feeling that "it doesn't matter anymore" may lead to more bad decisions.

Get medical input. A doctor's evaluation should be on the agenda to check for STIs (and for girls, to obtain a Pap test or perhaps a pregnancy test). *Choose your provider carefully.* Your adolescent is less likely to choose abstinence if he or she has a doctor who feels that teens can't control their sexual urges and who therefore emphasizes methods of contraception.

Strongly consider getting your son or daughter (and yourself) into counseling. A counselor whom you trust may be able to talk more candidly to your son or daughter about sexuality while promoting the decision to remain abstinent. Sexual activity may be a symptom of more basic problems that need ongoing work. Be prepared to put in time with the counselor yourself to deal with the causes and effects of this problem within your family.

Be prepared to take action appropriate for the situation and the age of your adolescent. Sexual activity in the elementary or middle-school grades deserves a highly concerted effort from parents, physicians, counselors, and others (a trusted youth-group leader at church, for example) to deal with the behavior and with underlying issues. A sexually active twelve- or thirteen-year-old has experienced a serious breach of physical and emotional boundaries, and considerable work will be needed to repair the damage.

You may need to have one or more candid conversations with your adolescent's partner(s) and possibly with the parents of the other individual(s) as well. More often than not, this will lead to one or more relationships being terminated and implementation of much tighter supervision and accountability. Parental schedules may need to be rearranged. If the situation involves an adult having sexual contact with a young adolescent, legal action may be necessary. (At the very least, an adult's sexual activity with a minor must be reported as required by law. Any indications of coercion and abuse must also be reported.)

Sexual activity in high school is no less significant, but the response (including medical and counseling input) should represent more of a parent-directed collaboration between the adolescent and the teachers, counselors, and physicians involved in his or her life. This does not mean abandoning efforts to curtail sexual contact but using strategies that stress a mature assessment of consequences. Dating and other socializing patterns that may have increased the chances for intimacy should be reassessed and restructured.

After the age of eighteen, as has been discussed in more detail in chapter 13, you are essentially dealing with a young adult. This will necessarily modify your approach because your position of authority has changed somewhat, especially if your son or daughter is beyond adolescence. However, you can and should offer your input and concerns, and you have the right to stipulate what behavior is appropriate under your roof. If you are still paying the bills for an older adolescent or young adult, you have the right to decide whether such support will continue if it is helping finance a lifestyle that runs counter to your basic values.

What If Your Adolescent Daughter Becomes Pregnant?

Before considering how you might respond to the news that your unmarried teenager is pregnant, take a brief tour of the emotions and thought processes that are likely to be swirling through her mind and heart.

Your daughter's experience

Fear is an overriding emotion in nearly every teen pregnancy. "I can't tell my parents. They'll kill me!" "How can I finish school when I'm pregnant?" "My boyfriend will take off if I don't have an abortion." The adolescent with a crisis pregnancy probably sees nothing but loss on the horizon—loss of love, time, education, and physical health. Fear of one or more of these losses propels most of her other responses.

Denial is common, especially during the early weeks of pregnancy when the only indication might be one or more missed periods, a little fatigue, possibly some nausea, or even a positive pregnancy test. The longing for things to be "the way they were" may delay acknowledging the problem and seeking appropriate help for weeks or even months.

Ambivalence about being pregnant may cause fluctuating emotions. One day the only solution may appear to be an abortion, while the next the prospect of a cuddly baby may seem appealing. Time spent with a friend's crying newborn may jolt the emotions in yet another direction. Indecision and apparent lack of direction in such an overwhelming situation are common.

Guilt. When a pregnancy results from the violation of moral values held since childhood, an adolescent will usually feel ashamed and worthless. Her growing abdomen becomes a constant reminder of her failure.

Pressure to have an abortion. This may come from several directions. A teenager may be weighing what appears to be a dismal future of hardship and remorse against a quick and relatively inexpensive procedure. "No one needs to know, and I can get on with my life." A boyfriend (who may be dealing with his own fear and guilt, along with concerns about future financial responsibilities) may exert considerable pressure to abort, even offering to pay the bill. He may also threaten to bail out of the relationship if the pregnancy continues. Some parents, worried about their daughter's future or perhaps their own reputation in the community (or even the prospect of being responsible for the actual child rearing), may also find abortion attractive.

The "cuddly doll" mentality. Some unmarried teenage girls see their pregnancy unrealistically as an escape from a difficult and unpleasant home situation. They may envision a baby as a snuggly companion who will require roughly the same amount of care as a new puppy, not realizing the amount of energy a newborn will take from her without giving much in return (especially during the first few weeks). Teens with this mind-set need to adjust their expectations of child rearing—not to drive them to abort but to help them make more appropriate plans. If adoption is not chosen as a solution, some careful groundwork should be laid to prevent serious disappointment and even the mother's abuse of the baby.

Your experience as parent(s)

If a pregnancy is an upheaval for a teenager, it is also no picnic for her parents. Discovering that your adolescent daughter is pregnant is a trial like few others, and reactions—fear for her future, denial, guilt—may parallel hers with equal intensity. Parents are likely to feel anger in a number of directions—anger toward their daughter for being careless, not taking their advice, not using good judgment, and disobeying both them and God. They may be angry with the boy (or man) involved, who has violated their trust and their daughter's well-being. They may be angry with themselves for any number of reasons: They were too narrow or too permissive, too busy or too tired to tune in to their daughter's world for the past several months—*and now look what has happened.*

Anger is such a classic parental response that the daughter may try to keep her pregnancy a secret. In fact, many states allow minors to obtain abortions without parental consent or knowledge, based on the presumption that the mother or father may be so disruptive and unreasonable that the teenage daughter can better deal with her pregnancy without them.

Your most difficult (and character-building) task is to show how much you really love your daughter, even though you don't approve of what she has done. The classical Chinese symbol for the word *crisis* has special meaning in this situation. It consists of two symbols: one representing *danger*, the other, *opportunity*. The danger is that your response to the pregnancy may open wounds in your family that will take years to heal, if they ever do. Your opportunity is rising to the occasion in such a way as to earn your daughter's lifelong respect and gratitude.

Your mission is to remain calm when panic is in the air and to be more concerned about her embarrassment than your own, which may be enormous. It is to be comforting when you feel like saying, "I told you so!" It is to help organize everyone's conflicting impulses into a thoughtful plan in which the family can work as a team. It is to guide the baby's father into responsible participation if he is willing, when you would just as soon enlist him in the Marines for a tour of duty in a faraway country. Most of all, it is to channel your intense feelings into productive outlets—through planning, prayer, vigorous exercise, and blowing off steam to a tolerant friend rather than at your child.

Your daughter will need help, and lots of it, but not a total rescue. She must make a fast transition to adulthood, a state about which you know a great deal more than she does. You must resist the temptation to throw her out or keep her stuck in childish irresponsibility by making all of her decisions. She needs to face all the tough decisions and demands of pregnancy, but with you at her side as a confident ally.

You may have one very critical decision of your own to make. What role do you intend to take in the child's upbringing? If the mother-to-be is very young, you may see another parenting job on the horizon and perhaps resent the idea. Or you may be excited about having the nest occupied for several more years. Your feelings on this issue need to be sorted out, and your course of action planned accordingly.

In the midst of your family's deliberations, be sure ample consideration is given to adoption. A pregnant teenager may be torn by the thought, *If I had the baby, I couldn't handle giving her away.* But adoption can provide a livable solution for all parties involved. The baby is raised by a couple who intensely desire to be parents, and the birth mother can pick up and move on to complete her education and career goals, postponing her own parenting until she is ready.

You will also need to address the question of abortion. Many voices will be calling your daughter to the abortion clinic, claiming this simple procedure will bring the crisis to a swift and straightforward resolution. Some parents may be tempted to give this option serious consideration for similar reasons. But before lending encouragement to ending the pregnancy this way, return to the first chapter in this book and read the description of the first weeks of life after conception.

Abortion is not a procedure like an appendectomy that eradicates a piece of diseased tissue. It ends a human life that is designed to develop in a continuous process from conception through birth and beyond. Because this life is unseen for now, its identity and significance may pale in comparison to the problems and concerns of the moment. That developing person, whose life is in the hands of her mother and those influencing her, cannot speak for herself. Like it or not, even under the most trying circumstances, that new person is not better off dead.

Your daughter should consider making an appointment with a local pregnancy resource center in order to sort through the issues, gather information, and consider her options in a compassionate setting. (As we noted earlier, in your community this may be called a crisis pregnancy center, pregnancy care center, or women's resource center.) Even if she has strong opinions about what her course of action should be, one of these centers can be an extremely valuable resource. Services available typically include a realistic assessment of the long-range impact of each option, ongoing counseling support, assistance with medical and other referrals, and maternity clothes and baby supplies. Many also provide some on-site medical services such as prenatal screening exams. All of these services are normally provided at no charge. (For the name and location of a pregnancy resource center in your area, contact Care Net at 800-395-HELP or on the Internet at http://www.optionline.org.)

It is important that capable and compassionate medical care be maintained throughout the pregnancy. Many pregnant teens delay or avoid seeking appropriate care for a variety of reasons. This is unfortunate because adolescents have higher rates of complications related to pregnancy and childbirth compared with older women. Most of these problems can be significantly reduced (or at least anticipated) with consistent prenatal visits and appropriate medical follow-up.

What If Your Adolescent Son Is Involved in a Pregnancy?

If your son has had a sexual relationship from which a pregnancy has resulted, remember that he will probably be experiencing many of the same emotions as his girlfriend, including fear, guilt, and ambivalence. In addition, he will feel considerable conflict and confusion over the role he should play.

Usually the relationship with the mother-to-be has not, until this point, involved any long-range plans. Now he must make a decision about the level of commitment he intends to assume, and the issues are significant. What does he owe this young woman? Can he walk away from this situation? Should he make a lifelong commitment to her because of this unplanned pregnancy?

He does not bear the biological consequences, of course, and the mother of the baby has the legal right to have an abortion or carry the pregnancy to term with or without his input. This may leave him with the impression that he has no control over the unplanned pregnancy and therefore no responsibility for it. As his parents, you are one step further removed from the situation and may have similar questions about the role you should play.

Above all, your son will need encouragement and guidance to assume the appropriate level of responsibility for his role in the pregnancy. He should not be allowed to abandon his girlfriend with a cavalier, hit-and-run attitude. "It's her problem now" or "She should have protected herself" or even "She should just get an abortion" are shallow and disrespectful responses to a serious situation. Pushing for a quick marriage may seem honorable but is probably unwise. Teenage matrimony carries with it very short odds of long-term success, and the combination of immaturity, lack of resources, and the intense demands of a newborn baby will usually strain an adolescent relationship to the breaking point.

In a best-case scenario, the families of both participants will cooperate to find a productive balance among several tasks: facing the consequences of the sexual relationship, accountability of adolescents to the adults in both families, short- and long-term planning, and mature decision making.

Your son will need encouragement to acknowledge his responsibility to the girl's family and to accept with humility their response, whether it is measured or angry. All of you may have to face the possibility that the other family will choose to deal with the pregnancy on their own, even if you are willing to participate in the process. And if that decision includes forbidding your son to have further contact with someone about whom he cares very deeply, he will have to find the strength to abide by the other parents' wishes. If he is allowed to continue their relationship and support her when the going gets tough, clear ground rules (including abstaining from sexual contact) will need to be established and respected.

Having a pregnant girlfriend is tough and painful. But it also can be an opportunity for your son to mature, to find out what he is made of. In the long run, the pregnant adolescent girl isn't the only one who has to make important choices.

What If Your Adolescent Isn't Sure of His or Her Sexual Orientation?

Few parenting concerns during adolescence generate as much emotional turbulence as the possibility that one's child might have a homosexual orientation. For many parents, especially those deeply committed to traditional values, the thought of a child becoming involved in homosexual relationships raises unsettling moral questions. For some, reactions to homosexuality extend into the darker emotions of hatred and loathing.

In contrast, many influential voices in media, government, and health care promote the unproven notion that sexual orientation is inborn and unchangeable. In their view, if your child is destined to be attracted to members of the same sex, nothing can or should be done about it other than to accept it. Gay and lesbian activists proclaim that adolescents who feel same-sex inclinations should explore, embrace, and celebrate their homosexual identity and that their parents should celebrate it along with them.

The vast majority of parents, while neither hating homosexual individuals nor applauding homosexuality, deeply desire to see their adolescents eventually bear and rear children. They anticipate the joys of watching the next generation's courtships, marriages, and family life. Therefore, contemplating a child's involvement in homosexual acts and in unconventional relationships for decades into the future is enough to provoke considerable concern, if not ongoing insomnia.

What should you do if your adolescent's sexual orientation is uncertain or if he or she has had one or more homosexual experiences?

Don't assume that characteristics that fall outside your gender expectations indicate homosexual tendencies. A boy who has a slight build and prefers painting over pitching or fabrics over football may disappoint a father who envisioned bringing up a burly, athletic hero. A daughter who isn't shapely or petite and who excels at basketball rather than ballet may not fulfill a mother's expectations of magazine-cover femininity. But both need unconditional affirmation of their worth from parents who accept and encourage their particular strengths as appropriate.

What may drive a teenager toward same-gender sexuality is ongoing rejection from parents or peers. Cutting remarks about a child's or teenager's size, shape, or other attributes merely reinforce the idea that "I'm different from everyone else." If genuine acceptance is eventually offered by someone with a homosexual orientation, the teenager may conclude that "I'm different, so that must mean I'm gay—and furthermore, I've always been this way."

Remember that adolescents may feel transient confusion about sexual identity, especially if they have had a sexual experience with someone of the same gender. Whether as a phase of rebellion and experimentation or as the result of sexual abuse in childhood, a child or adolescent may have one or more same-sex encounters, which may raise questions about his or her ultimate sexual destination. It is therefore important for children and teens who have had such experiences to receive appropriate counseling that (among other things) will clarify the fact that these events have not destined them to a lifelong homosexual orientation.

If you discover that your child has had one or more homosexual encounters, whether coerced or voluntary, you need to remain his strongest ally. A child or young adolescent who has suffered sexual abuse needs to know that what happened was not his fault and that you are not in any way ashamed of him. He will need comfort, reassurance that his physical boundaries are now secure, and time to sort out his experiences, both with you (which will be very uncomfortable) and with a professional counselor. It is crucial that the damage done by an abuser to a child's sexual identity and sense of self-worth be contained.

If the activities involved one or more peers and were not the result of coercion, your response should parallel what was outlined in connection with premarital heterosexual activity (see page 528). You will need to make a particular effort to maintain a balance between taking a clear stand for moral principles and demonstrating that you and your adolescent are still on the same team. Harsh expressions of revulsion and condemnation are counterproductive, will probably confirm an adolescent's feelings of alienation, and may very well provoke more of the same behavior. At the same time, a resigned and passive nonresponse ("Nothing can be done about this, so I might as well get used to it") squanders an opportunity to bring about change. As with other early and midadolescent sexual activity, conversation and counseling with someone who shares your values is in order.

If your older adolescent moves into adulthood and becomes overtly involved in a homosexual lifestyle, your balancing act will become even more delicate—but no different from the approach you must take to any other of your grown child's choices that you find ill-advised or contrary to your values. It is possible and necessary—but at times also very difficult—to express love and acceptance without condoning the behavior. You have the right and responsibility to insist that sexual activity be off-limits under your roof. But decisions about a number of other situations will be tough. For example, should your adult offspring's homosexual lover be included at the family Thanksgiving dinner?

You must commit to patience, prayer, and perseverance. You may shed rivers of tears, but you must not allow animosity or bitterness to take root in your emotions. Most of all, you will need generous amounts of wisdom, because you may be the only voice expressing love while encouraging your child to begin the difficult process of disengaging from ongoing homosexual behavior. Two resources that you may find very helpful are Love Won Out (http://www.lovewonout.com) and Exodus International (http://www.exodus-international.org).

What If Your Daughter Is the Victim of a Sexual Assault?

In the sidebar on page 526, several recommendations were made that could reduce an adolescent's risk of date rape. But even when appropriate precautions have been taken, it is possible that your daughter will be the victim of a sexual assault. The odds are at least one in six that she will experience unwanted sex at some point in her life. As unpleasant as it may be to discuss this topic, she should know what (and what not) to do if this occurs, whether the attacker is an acquaintance or a stranger.

First, she should get to a safe place as quickly as possible and then contact a family member and the police *immediately*. In the emotional aftermath of an assault, the urge to deny what has happened may cause a victim to wait days or weeks to report it. But doing so reduces her credibility and makes prosecution of the attacker more difficult. Reporting the assault right away can help her regain a sense of control, obtain proper medical care, and guarantee personal safety. Furthermore, it is important that all physical evidence of the attack be preserved. She should not shower, bathe, douche, or even change clothes, even though it is normal to feel an overwhelming urge to rid herself of every trace of the attack.

Because of embarrassment, fear of reprisal, or apprehension over dealing with police, doctors, and attorneys, the majority of sexual assaults go unreported. The attacker has assumed that he could have his way without any consequences, and he must not be allowed that unjust satisfaction. He has committed a serious crime and deserves punishment for it. Furthermore, most rapists are repeat offenders, and taking action may help prevent someone else from being assaulted.

The officers who take the report will need to ask about specific details of the rape that may be painful to answer but are necessary for proper documentation of the crime. It is important that your daughter be completely honest and candid about what happened, even if she feels that she made a mistake or even violated her own moral standards prior to the rape. If her story changes later on, the case against the attacker will be weakened.

The police will advise that a medical evaluation be carried out, even if your daughter does not believe she was injured. A thorough examination is necessary to assess her physical condition, to collect important evidence, and to provide counseling regarding the possibility of pregnancy or sexually transmitted infection. This should be done in a hospital emergency room where the physicians and staff are equipped to deal with rape victims or in a rape treatment center (assuming that its services include appropriate medical evaluations).

As with the police report, parts of this examination will be difficult and uncomfortable, especially if she has not had a pelvic exam before. But cooperation with the physician and nurses is important, and the temporary discomfort will be worth the long-term benefits of proper medical care.

Finally, your daughter should receive counseling from an individual who is qualified to deal with the impact of the rape experience on her life. This event cannot be ignored and will not be forgotten. She will need both time and support to recover from the physical, emotional, and spiritual aftereffects of a sexual assault. Many powerful emotions must be sorted out, including guilt or mistaken feelings of blame.

It is important that your own anger and frustration not boil over and cause more damage. This is not the time for comments such as "I told you so" or "How could you have let this happen?" Even if your daughter used extremely poor judgment or flatly disobeyed your explicit instructions, she in no way "asked for" or deserved a sexual assault. She will need your help to rebuild her sense of dignity and worth. Without this important repair work, she will be vulnerable to sexual pressure and abuse in the future.

What If Your Son Is the Victim of a Sexual Assault?

The vast majority of information and advisories regarding rape are directed toward women, who are most commonly—but not always—the victims of sexual assault. In a less frequent (but no less serious) situation, an adolescent or young adult male may be the sexual target of one or more other men. Should this happen to your son, you will need to muster all the same strength and support you would offer a daughter who had been attacked.

In particular, it is critical that appropriate medical assessment, evidence collection, preventive measures for sexually transmitted infections, and counseling be provided in a timely fashion, just as in the case of a female victim. If possible, the perpetrator(s) should be identified, arrested, and prosecuted. Even if a parent learns about an assault months or years after it took place, medical care and counseling should be provided. It is particularly important that such an event not be allowed to confuse an adolescent's sense of sexual identity or integrity.

SPECIAL CONCERNS

Sexually Transmitted Infections (STIs) among Adolescents

In the United States, 19 million people are newly infected with STIs each year, and *nearly half of these occur in people between the ages of fifteen and twenty-four,* even though they comprise less than 25 percent of the sexually active population.[1] The direct lifetime medical costs for dealing with STIs in this age-group has been estimated to be about $6.5 billion for all cases acquired in a given year—a figure that does not take into account nonmedical costs (such as time lost at school or work) and equally if not more significant, the physical and emotional discomfort that can accompany these infections.[2]

When STIs are discussed in health-education classes and public-service messages geared to teenagers, the emphasis is on preventing the transmission of HIV/AIDS. As serious as this epidemic is, a number of other significant predators should not be ignored.

Chlamydia infection has risen from obscurity in the 1970s to become the most common bacterial STI in the United States. While more than nine hundred thousand cases are reported every year, experts estimate that the actual number of cases is more than three times that many. Half of the cases in females occur in fifteen- to nineteen-year-olds.[3] Assuming it is detected—which may not always occur because symptoms may be subtle or nonexistent—a chlamydia infection normally responds to antibiotics. (Half of men and three out of four women who have a chlamydia infection experience no symptoms.)[4] In men chlamydia can cause a discharge from the penis that tends to be more watery and less profuse than with gonorrhea. Pain with the passage of urine is also less severe. In women chlamydia may produce vague pelvic discomfort, pain with urination, or no symptoms. Whether or not symptoms are present, chlamydia can infect and damage a woman's reproductive organs and create a significant risk of infertility later in life. A single teenage sexual encounter that transmits chlamydia (or gonorrhea—see below) may cause untold emotional pain and major medical bills years later if a woman is unable to bear children.

Gonorrhea is a bacterial infection that is estimated to affect well over six hundred thousand Americans each year. (Typically 330,000 to 350,000 cases are reported to public-health officials annually, but experts believe these figures represent only about half of the actual infections.)[5] Symptoms in males tend to be dramatic: a thick discharge from the penis accompanied by significant pain during the passage of urine. Many infected women have no symptoms, while others experience problems ranging in severity from mild discharge to abscesses in the pelvis requiring surgical treatment. In some cases extensive scarring of a woman's tubes may occur. Depending upon the extent of damage, infertility may result.

Once uniformly responsive to penicillin, gonorrhea now must be treated with other antibiotics.

Syphilis is caused by a spiral-shaped organism known as a spirochete. It is usually curable with penicillin, but resistant strains are now emerging. The initial sign of infection is a single painless ulcer, or **chancre**, which appears in the genital area (or wherever the initial point of contact was made). The chancre heals in two to six weeks without treatment and may even go unnoticed by the infected individual. A secondary phase occurs in six weeks to six months, producing a mild (and nonspecific) rash or more serious changes in various parts of the body. If untreated, a third stage may develop years later, with life-threatening heart disease and central nervous system disturbances, even insanity. Syphilis can be detected by a blood test. If the initial screen is positive, additional tests will be necessary to confirm the diagnosis and determine the proper course of treatment.

Herpes simplex virus (HSV) is notorious for a property it shares with a number of other viral organisms: Once it enters a person's body, it has the capacity for reoccurrence, although the manifestations of this prolonged infection may vary considerably from person to person. HSV type 1 typically causes cold sores or fever blisters around the mouth or nose, although it can also cause genital infections through oral-genital contact. HSV type 2 is most commonly spread by genital sexual contact.

The first outbreak of genital herpes is usually the worst, with an irritating, sometimes painful, cluster of blisters that gradually crust and fade over ten to fourteen days.

PELVIC INFLAMMATORY DISEASE

Pelvic inflammatory disease (PID), in which one or more sexually transmitted organisms invade the uterus, fallopian tubes, ovaries, pelvis, or all of these, is diagnosed in more than one million women in the United States each year.[6] At least 10 to 12 percent of women become infertile after a single significant episode of PID, usually because of scarring of the fallopian tubes. This number increases to about 25 percent after a second episode, and 50 percent after a third.[7] Altogether, an estimated one hundred thousand women become infertile every year because of PID. Damage to the fallopian tubes resulting from PID is also linked to a large proportion of ectopic pregnancies—that is, pregnancies that begin outside the uterus.

Women younger than twenty-one are particularly susceptible to STIs in general and PID in particular because the cervix (the opening of the uterus) in this age-group is more likely to be covered by a lining of cells that are more fragile, produce more mucus, and are more easily invaded by sexually transmitted organisms. Later, in a woman's twenties (or after having a baby) the cervix is likely to be covered by cells that are tougher and more resistant to infection. ■

Men usually see an eruption on the penis, although they may not realize its significance because it resolves without treatment. Women are frequently unaware of the infection, but some suffer extreme discomfort in the genital area. The virus is commonly transmitted through the skin or mucous membranes *even when no blisters are present*. This undoubtedly contributes to its high prevalence. About one in five sexually active single people are infected, and it is estimated that more than one million people acquire this virus every year in the United States.[8]

Ninety percent of those infected with HSV-2 have another outbreak within a year following the initial infection. Recurrent outbreaks may take place over months or years, although their frequency and severity tend to decrease with the passage of time. Stress, intercourse, or other local irritation of the genital area (even from tight clothing) may trigger recurrences, which often cause concern and consternation in a subsequent relationship. For many, the primary discomfort from a herpes infection is psychological, arising from the knowledge that this virus can never be eradicated and that any future sexual partner will probably become infected as well.

Antiviral medications such as **acyclovir** (Zovirax), **valacyclovir** (Valtrex), and **famciclovir** (Famvir) can limit the severity of the first or subsequent herpes outbreaks, assuming they are started at the outset of the eruption. When taken daily, they can also reduce the frequency of recurrences; valacyclovir (Valtrex) has also been shown to reduce transmission of the virus that can occur even when no outbreak is present. Of course, ongoing daily treatment can become expensive on a long-term basis.

Herpes outbreaks are rarely life-threatening for adults. Unfortunately the same cannot be said for newborns. As we described in chapter 1, a baby born to a mother with HSV can be infected during vaginal delivery if there is a herpes outbreak in the mother's genital area. The risk of transfer is much higher (33 to 50 percent) if this is the mother's first outbreak rather than a recurrence (about 3 percent). One to 2 percent of pregnant women with recurrent HSV infection could transmit the virus at the time of delivery without any visible outbreak.[9] For the newborn, an HSV infection can be disastrous. In more than half of these infants, the disease will affect the central nervous system or multiple organs, resulting in serious long-term consequences or even death (see page 74).

Several types of the **human papillomavirus (HPV)** cause **genital warts**, while others are associated with cellular abnormalities that can lead to **cancer of the cervix**. Every year more than 6 million people are newly infected with HPV, making this the most common viral STI in the United States. Nearly three out of four new HPV infections occur in people between the ages of fifteen and twenty-four.[10] One recent study of sexually active eighteen- to twenty-two-year-old females found that 50 percent were infected with HPV.[11] Like herpes and many other STIs, HPV can be transmitted by an individual who has no visible signs of disease. Furthermore, research indicates that consistent use of condoms offers only partial protection against HPV transmission and its potential complications (genital warts and cervical cancer).[12]

Many who are infected with HPV never have any problem with it, and in 70 to 90 percent of women, HPV infections clear up within twelve to twenty-four months of detection.[13] However, some types of the virus can cause soft, wartlike growths in the genital area. Small growths (which are the most common) respond to topical chemical treatment, but some can become quite large in size, requiring laser or other methods to remove them.

Of greater concern is that some types of HPV have been clearly demonstrated to be the underlying cause of most cervical cancer and are also implicated in cancers of the vulva, vagina, anus, and penis. While cancer due to HPV in males is rare, cancer of the cervix causes more than 3,500 deaths each year. This cancer risk is specifically increased by early onset of sexual activity and contact with multiple partners, as well as by young age (under thirty to forty years of age) and tobacco use. Any woman who has been or is sexually active should have regular Pap tests to detect early changes in the cervix, which can be treated before they develop into a cancerous growth. An important recent advance in prevention is the development of a vaccine to induce immunity against a number of types of HPV that are associated with cervical cancer. We discuss this vaccination in the "Immunizations—Which Ones, Why, and When?" section, beginning on page 748.

Acquired immune deficiency syndrome (AIDS) is caused by the **human immunodeficiency virus (HIV)**. The virus is transmitted through semen, vaginal secretions, blood, and breast milk. Most HIV infections are transmitted during sexual contact (in all forms—heterosexual or homosexual, vaginal, oral, or anal), through accidental injection of infected blood, through contaminated needles, or by transfer from infected mother to baby during pregnancy. A small number of cases in infants have been attributed to nursing from an infected mother. Some early cases of HIV resulted from transfusions of blood from infected donors, but revised blood-bank procedures and scrupulous screening of donors have reduced the likelihood of this happening to less than one in one hundred thousand.

At highest risk for this disease are people who have many sexual partners (especially male homosexuals) and those who are intravenous drug users. But HIV infections are not limited to those with high-risk lifestyles. *The virus can be transmitted during a single sexual encounter,* even to someone having sex for the first time. For a variety of reasons, the rate of new HIV infections has been steadily rising among heterosexuals, especially adolescents.

After causing an initial flulike illness, HIV multiplies quietly within the immune system for years. The infected individual may feel perfectly well during this period but will be capable of transmitting the disease to others. Eventually the virus destroys the competence of the immune system, resulting in full-blown AIDS. Without adequate defenses, the body becomes vulnerable to a variety of devastating infections and some forms of cancer.

Screening tests for HIV detect a person's antibody response to the virus, not the virus itself. Once HIV enters the body, it will take a minimum of three weeks, and in some cases many months, to generate a detectable antibody response. An infected individual whose blood tests remain negative for HIV can still transmit the virus to others.

Hepatitis B is a viral infection of the liver transmitted through the same mechanisms as HIV. The majority of cases in adults resolve completely following a flulike illness with fever, nausea, and jaundice (a yellow discoloration of skin caused by a buildup of a compound called bilirubin, which an inflamed liver does not process normally). However, between 2 and 6 percent develop a chronic infection that can lead to cirrhosis (scarring) or even cancer of the liver. (Infants and children are less likely to experience an acute illness with hepatitis B, but 30 percent of those one to five years of age and 90 percent of infants, including those who are infected at birth, develop the chronic form of the infection and are at risk for long-term complications.)

Chronic carriers—there are about 1.25 million in the United States—can transmit the virus to sexual partners or, if they give birth, to their baby during pregnancy or delivery. Most infected newborns become chronic carriers as well and risk developing long-term complications if not treated.

Hepatitis B is one of two STIs for which a reliable vaccine has been developed. Because efforts to vaccinate those at highest risk did not substantially reduce the number of new cases, and because many cases of hepatitis B occur in people who do not have a history of risky behavior, current recommendations call for immunizing all infants, children, and adolescents against this virus.

In the midst of an enchanted evening at a secluded rendezvous, with romance in the air and hormones in high gear, it's easy to forget (or ignore) the unpleasant facts about STIs—including how prevalent they are. In most instances, an infected sexual partner will show absolutely no evidence of any illness. He or she may be a wonderful, intelligent person—dressed for success, impeccably groomed, attractive, and well mannered—but still capable of transmitting an organism that can impair health or threaten life itself. In other words, there is no way to look at a potential partner and determine if sex with that person might be safe or not. Furthermore, as is discussed in the section entitled "'Reason to wait #5: 'Safe(r) sex' isn't" (page 517), the "protection" offered by condoms is far from foolproof. When dealing with these diseases, the only sex that is safe takes place within an exclusive relationship with an uninfected life partner.

Tobacco, Alcohol, and Drug Abuse—Resisting the Epidemic

Not too many generations ago, our ancestors regularly watched in horror as bubonic plague, diphtheria, smallpox, and other lethal epidemics swept through their towns and families, taking rich and poor alike to the grave. Today, the consumption of alcohol, tobacco, and a host of addicting drugs has become a modern-day plague ravaging many of our youngest citizens.

Like the scourges of old, the drug epidemic spreads without regard to economic, racial, geographic, educational, religious, or family boundaries. More recently, it has become particularly aggressive among preteen children, dipping freely into the primary grades for new consumers. While all of us should work and pray toward ending this blight in our nation and our communities, we must ultimately be concerned about preventing it from moving across our own doorsteps.

No child whom you bring into the world will automatically be immune from the drug epidemic. Therefore you must work diligently over the years to "drug proof" your children. This project involves various tasks that cannot be tackled haphazardly. First, you must understand what draws kids toward drugs. You also need basic information about the substances that are currently available in your neighborhood. You should become familiar with the signs that a drug problem might be developing in your home. Finally and most important, you must be prepared to take long-term preventive measures and to respond appropriately if one or more of the toxins should breach your family's defenses.

Why Do Kids Start (and Continue) Using Drugs?

Four factors set the stage for adolescent drug use:

- *Attitudes of parents* toward tobacco, alcohol, and other substances. Children learn what they live. Smoking, drinking, and other drug-related behaviors among parents will usually be duplicated by their children.

- *Attractiveness of drugs.* Smoking and drinking are widely promoted as habits enjoyed by sophisticated, fun-loving, attractive, and sexy people—what most adolescents long to become. Illegal drugs are "advertised" by those using them in an adolescent's peer group.
- *The high induced by drugs.* If drug use wasn't pleasurable, it would be relatively easy to keep kids and harmful substances separated. But the reality is that many kids enjoy the way they feel on drugs—at least for a while.
- *Availability of drugs.* Finding drugs is not difficult for children and adolescents in most communities, but tougher local standards can help keep drugs out of less-determined hands.

Once the stage is set, the following factors exert a more direct influence on who will and who won't try drugs. The consequences of early experiences (whether pleasant or disagreeable), the drug used, and one's genetic predisposition will determine whether a problem is nipped in the bud or blossoms into addiction.

Peer pressure. Peers play a huge role at each stage of a child's or adolescent's drug experience—whether resisting them, experimenting, becoming a user, or confronting withdrawal and recovery. The need for peer acceptance is especially strong during the early adolescent years and can override (or at least seriously challenge) the most earnest commitments. "Just say no" may not mean a whole lot when smoking, drinking, or taking drugs determines who is included in highly esteemed ranks of the inner circle.

There are three important implications to the association between peers and drug use:

- *It is important that kids find their niche in the right peer group(s),* among friends who are not only committed to positive values (including drug-free lifestyles) but who are also involved in worthwhile and enjoyable pursuits.
- *You may have to intervene if your adolescent (especially in the early teen years) is hanging out with the wrong crowd.* This is discussed in detail in chapter 13 (see page 468).
- *Children and adolescents with a healthy, stable identity and an appropriate sense of independence will be more resistant to peer pressure.* This will be discussed later beginning on page 565.

Curiosity. Unless your family lives in total isolation, your child will be aware of smoking, alcohol, and drug use well before adolescence from discussions at school, watching TV and movies, or direct observation. Some curiosity is inevitable: *What do these things feel like?* Whether this leads to sampling and whether an experiment progresses to addiction will depend on the individual's mind-set and physical response.

Thrill seeking. This desire for excitement is in all of us to some degree and propels us toward all kinds of activities: skydiving, roller coasters, movies (where sights and sounds are "bigger than life"), fireworks displays, sporting events, and so on. Some of these are more risky than others, but none require chemical alteration of the senses to be satisfying. Unfortunately, many children and adolescents seek drug experiences to produce thrills that normal consciousness can't duplicate.

Rebellion. Wayward children may engage in smoking, alcohol, and drug use as a show of "independence" from family norms and values.

Escape from life/relief from pain. This is often the driving force in drug use. If everyday life seems boring, meaningless, oppressive, or painful (physically or emotionally), alcohol and drugs may appear to offer a powerful time-out. The strongest resistance to drug abuse therefore arises from an ongoing sense of joy and contentment that transcends circumstances. These attitudes are usually acquired, not inborn. Early positive experiences in the family and an active, wide-awake relationship with God play the most important roles in molding such attitudes.

The "Gateway" Drugs: Tobacco, Alcohol, Marijuana, and Inhalants

Few children and adolescents start a career of drug use by snorting cocaine or injecting heroin. The path usually begins with products from the corner store—tobacco, alcohol, or household products that are inhaled—or with marijuana, which some mistakenly consider safe.

Tobacco—the smoking gun

No drug habit has a greater negative impact on our national health than tobacco, which is implicated in more than four hundred thousand deaths in the United States each year. The list of disorders caused or aggravated by tobacco is staggering. Among these diseases are cancers of the lung, mouth, vocal cords, and other organs; chronic lung disease; asthma; ulcers; and clogging of the vessels that supply blood to the heart and other organs, causing heart attacks, strokes, amputations, and premature deaths. Babies and children who breathe smokers' exhaust at home are at risk for respiratory infections, asthma, and sudden infant death syndrome (SIDS).

The vast majority of diseases related to tobacco take their toll later in life after subjects have had years of exposure. So why is adolescent tobacco use such a major concern?

Nicotine is extremely addictive. A typical cigarette contains only about one milligram (mg) of nicotine but sends it directly from the lungs into the bloodstream with remarkable efficiency, rivaling that of an injection directly into the veins. (A dose of 60 mg of nicotine, if consumed all at once, would be lethal.) Each cigarette delivers several hits of nicotine that stimulate receptors in the brain, producing a unique combination of relaxation and alertness. Furthermore, as habitual smokers can attest, withdrawal is associated with unpleasant physical and psychological symptoms. The result is a physiological reward pattern that frequently becomes a compulsion—*especially when smoking begins at an early age.*

Almost every long-term smoker picks up the habit during adolescence. One-third of all smokers first light up by the age of fourteen, and more than 90 percent of adult smokers initiated their habit before the age of twenty-one. As of 2005, 23 percent of high school students identified themselves as current smokers, although rates had slowly declined since 1997. Among ninth graders, the smoking rate was nearly 20 percent; for twelfth graders, it was 28 percent. More than six thousand adolescents try a first cigarette *every day* in the United States, and of these, about half will become regular smokers. That represents more than one million new smokers every year.[1] The Centers for Disease Control and Prevention estimates that more than 6.4 million children alive today will die prematurely because of a decision to try smoking before they reach adulthood. One alarming trend among teenagers is the rising popularity of inexpensive fruit- and candy-flavored cigarettes called **bidis** and clove-containing cigarettes called **kreteks**. (See sidebar on the next page.)

A huge amount of money is spent every year to make smoking appear glamorous and exciting. The tobacco industry's annual multibillion-dollar advertising budget is supposedly intended to encourage adults to switch brands, but the cartoon characters, sexy young couples, macho men, and liberated women in cigarette ads have clearly been shown to influence children and adolescents. Heavy visibility of these ads at sporting and cultural events also sends definite signals that tobacco is hot stuff. Warnings issued in health-education class pale in comparison.

Cigarettes keep very bad company. Smoking is associated with significantly poorer school performance and a higher likelihood of sexual activity. Because the use of alcohol and marijuana is significantly greater among adolescent smokers, tobacco is identified as a "gateway" drug—one that increases the odds that a teen will begin using even more dangerous substances. It is the last of these points that should sound the alarm for parents of adolescent smokers. If your teenager is smoking cigarettes, he is eleven times more likely to be using illicit drugs and sixteen times more likely to be drinking heavily than his nonsmoking counterparts.[2]

Smokeless (chewing and snuffing) tobacco, which has been made highly visible (and glamorized to some degree) by users who are professional athletes, is not a safe alternative to cigarettes. The only good news about the use of smokeless tobacco among adolescents is that it has been decreasing following a peak in the mid-1990s. As of 2003, two major national surveys have shown an overall rate of smokeless tobacco use of 11 percent among ninth- to twelfth-grade boys, down from about 20 percent twelve to seventeen years earlier. (Rates for girls in this age-group have generally re-

WHAT ARE BIDIS AND KRETEKS?

Ever heard of a bidi? In India, 70 percent of tobacco is sold in the form of these small, inexpensive sweet-tasting cigarettes that are rolled in leaves rather than paper. With flavors such as chocolate, vanilla, fruit, and root beer, an exotic appearance resembling a marijuana joint, and the popular misconception that they are "additive free" and somehow safer than regular cigarettes, bidis have caught on with teenagers, especially in urban areas where they can be easily purchased in ethnic grocery stores, tobacco emporiums, and "head shops." (Your average grocery or convenience store probably doesn't sell them, but that merely adds to their mystique.)

The Centers for Disease Control and Prevention estimates that 2 to 5 percent of teenagers—up to 40 percent in some cities—have tried bidis at least once. Yet in spite of their candy flavoring and lower tobacco content, bidis actually pump more tar, nicotine, and carbon monoxide into young bodies than conventional cigarettes, both filtered and unfiltered. As a result, they pose a higher risk for causing tobacco addiction and long-term health consequences.

Kreteks are Indonesian cigarettes containing two-thirds tobacco and one-third clove, sold with or without filters, and typically wrapped in brown paper or even corn husk. In some American cities, they are more popular than bidis. Unfortunately, they also come loaded with two to three times the nicotine of a regular cigarette. ■

mained at 2 percent or less.)[3] Usage rates are even higher in many Native American populations. Chewing tobacco is clearly associated with damage to the gingiva (the soft tissues surrounding the teeth) and with aggressive cancers of the mouth. Furthermore, both chewing and snuffing deliver powerful jolts of nicotine. A typical dose of snuff contains more than twice the amount of nicotine in a cigarette, while a wad of chewing tobacco contains fifteen times that amount. Needless to say, addiction to these substances is very common, as are withdrawal symptoms when use is stopped.

Alcohol—the most dangerous gateway drug

Alcohol use by those under twenty-one is illegal in all fifty states for several good reasons. Alcohol causes more deaths among adolescents than any other illicit substance. It is involved in approximately half of all automobile crashes involving teenagers (the leading cause of death in this age-group), and it frequently plays a role in adolescent deaths from other causes, including homicides, suicides, drownings, and motorcycle and bicycle accidents. It is also linked to two out of three sexual assaults and date rapes, and it plays a prominent role in high-risk sex among the young.

The fact that putting alcohol into a young body frequently leads to reckless, dangerous, violent, and lethal outcomes is not breaking news. Recent research, however, has added an ominous new concern: Underage alcohol use may damage both the hippocampus, an area of the brain involved in memory and learning, and the prefrontal area, which undergoes major changes during adolescence and plays a role in shaping behavior and personality as an adult.[4] The human brain undergoes important transformations during adolescence and is more vulnerable to damage from alcohol before age twenty-one than at any time later in life. The underage drinker who is "sowing wild oats" may in fact be reaping long-term—or even lifelong—problems with learning and relationships.

A number of underage drinkers develop full-blown alcohol addiction and struggle with it for years. Ironically, the person who prides himself on the ability to "hold his liquor" is at the greatest risk for alcoholism. If large quantities of alcohol must be consumed to produce intoxication, he is demonstrating a tolerance for alcohol—something all alcoholics have in common—and addiction is likely to develop. Tolerance of alcohol and the risk of addiction are thought to be genetically predisposed and usually run in families. *Adolescents with family members who have had alcohol-abuse problems must be warned that they are at higher risk for becoming addicted to alcohol if they ever start drinking.*

Marijuana—inhaled intellectual impairment

Baby boomers who experimented with marijuana during the 1960s before abandoning drugs for the responsibilities of adult life (especially parenthood) may not be terribly concerned about this drug. But what adolescents and young adults are smoking today bears little resemblance to what flower children were inhaling three decades ago. The average batch of marijuana in the 1960s contained 0.2 percent delta-9-tetrahydrocannabinol (THC for short), its main mood-altering chemical. Today's vintage contains an average of 3 percent THC, or fifteen times the old concentration, along with four hundred other assorted chemicals.

What is it? A shredded mix of various parts (leaves, stems, seeds, flowers) of the hemp plant *Cannabis sativa*. Hashish (the Arabic word for hemp) is the sticky resin of the female plant flowers, containing an average of 3.6 percent THC (or as much as 28 percent). Marijuana is the most commonly used illegal drug in the United States.

What are some of its street names? *Pot, grass, weed, herb,* and *Mary Jane,* among others. Some strains of marijuana have been given "brand" names such as Texas tea, Maui wowie, and bubble gum. A marijuana cigarette is a joint, a water pipe used to smoke marijuana a bong, and a marijuana cigar a blunt. A blunt smoked while downing a forty-ounce bottle of malt liquor is called a B-40.

How is it used? Marijuana is most commonly smoked, whether rolled into a cigarette, packed into a pipe, or stuffed into a cigar from which tobacco has been removed. Crack cocaine or other dangerous drugs may be added to the mix to be smoked, with or without the user's knowledge, sometimes with unpleasant results. Marijuana can also be added to foods or drinks (or even brewed as tea), though much more THC is delivered to the brain when the drug is inhaled. When smoked, its effects are felt almost immediately and typically last one to three hours. In food or drink, effects are delayed by thirty to sixty minutes but may last as long as four hours.

What's the attraction? Marijuana users are seeking a sense of euphoria, a relaxed high, which may be accompanied by an increased sensitivity to sights, sounds, and smells. Time may seem to pass more slowly, and minor goings-on or conversations among friends may seem extremely interesting or funny. Increased thirst or hunger ("the munchies") is common. After the drug effect has worn off, the user may feel sleepy or even depressed. Depending on the preparation, additives, and mind-set of the user, unpleasant emotions such as anxiety, paranoia, or even panic can also occur. The presence of other drugs in the mix may cause unexpected and even serious reactions.

What are the health risks? The casual attitudes about marijuana in our culture and the media over the past few decades would suggest that this is basically a harmless

Those unfamiliar with the illicit drug culture will have a jaw-dropping experience at any Web site that offers a dictionary of street or slang names for these substances. More impressive (and alarming) than the multiplicity of creative names is the number of ways in which hazardous drugs are combined. An extensive collection can be found at the Office of National Drug Control Policy site entitled "Street Terms: Drugs and the Drug Trade" (www .whitehousedrugpolicy.gov/ streetterms/default.asp).

SOBERING STATISTICS ABOUT UNDERAGE DRINKING

- Approximately 11 million children and adolescents younger than twenty-one drink, and half of these do so to excess. Twenty percent of twelve- to twenty-year-olds report binge-drinking episodes (in which they consume at least four to five drinks at a time).[5]
- The average age for a first drink among boys is eleven, and for girls, thirteen.[6]
- It is estimated that the average American child will see one hundred thousand beer advertisements before the age of eighteen.[7]
- Youth between the ages of twelve and twenty drink nearly 20 percent of all alcohol consumed in the United States. Over 90 percent of this alcohol is consumed in the form of binge drinks.[8]
- More than 66 percent of ninth graders and eight out of ten twelfth graders have tried alcohol at least once. One in three ninth graders and half of all twelfth graders have used alcohol within a given month.[9]
- More alcoholic products that specifically appeal to kids are hitting the marketplace. Wine coolers are increasingly popular with younger drinkers, as are a new wave of alcoholic concoctions billed as "thirst quenchers," often containing lemon or other fruit flavors. ■

diversion. But the contrary is true: Marijuana smoke is more irritating to the mouth, throat, airway, and lungs than tobacco smoke, and it contains 50 to 70 percent more cancer-provoking hydrocarbons. The tendency to inhale deeply and hold one's breath while smoking aggravates this tendency. Long-term marijuana smokers, like their tobacco-puffing counterparts, are thus at higher risk not only for developing chronic lung disease but also cancer of the upper respiratory tract and lungs.

What about other consequences? Marijuana's greatest drawback, especially in light of its widespread use among the young, is that it impairs intellectual function—concentration, memory, and judgment—as well as motor skills. During the teen years, a child

COLLEGE DRINKING—A NOT-SO-VENERABLE TRADITION

> Landlord, fill the flowing bowl until it doth run over,
> For tonight we'll merry, merry be, tomorrow we'll be sober.
> *Traditional college drinking song*

Keggers, beer busts, T.G.s, frat-house parties, spring-break revels, and drinking songs (often set to four-part harmony) are an age-old tradition on college campuses, seemingly as much a part of the campus landscape as ivy-covered buildings and football games. But recently the destructive effects of student intoxication have become a matter of national concern. According to a sobering report published in April 2002 by a special federal task force of the National Advisory Council on Alcohol Abuse and Alcoholism, *every year* among American college students eighteen to twenty-four years of age:

- 500,000 are unintentionally injured under the influence of alcohol, and of these, 1,400 die.
- 600,000 are assaulted by another student who has been drinking.
- 400,000 have unprotected sex, and 100,000 report being too intoxicated to remember whether or not they consented to have sex.
- 70,000 are victims of a sexual assault or date rape involving alcohol.
- 150,000 develop a health problem related to alcohol.
- At least one percent report having attempted suicide because of drinking or drug abuse.
- More than 10 percent report damaging property while intoxicated.
- 2.1 million report driving while under the influence of alcohol.
- More then 100,000 are arrested for an alcohol-related offense (including driving under the influence).
- More than 30 percent would meet diagnostic criteria for alcohol abuse, and more than 5 percent would be classified as alcohol dependent, based upon questionnaire responses about their drinking habits.[10]

The report, entitled "A Call to Action: Changing the Culture of Drinking at U.S. Colleges," recommends a coordinated effort by college administrators, parents, student leadership, and communities surrounding college and university campuses to bring about significant changes in the drinking habits of students. ■

should be learning how to think and act more maturely, but frequent marijuana use can derail that process. Short-term fallout can include injuries and death from motor-vehicle accidents or other trauma, as well as sexual misadventures resulting from loss of inhibition and rational thinking. A number of research studies also have demonstrated that impairment of memory, learning, and concentration continues for days or weeks after the immediate effects of the drug wear off.

Long-term users are known for an amotivational syndrome in which goals and

PRESCRIPTION AND NONPRESCRIPTION DRUG ABUSE

Tobacco, alcohol, and illegal drugs aren't the only potential chemical traps that can snare adolescents and children. Many seek mind-altering experiences from the family medicine cabinet, sometimes with shocking—and at times lethal—abandon. A 2005 national study of more than 7,300 teenagers carried out by the Partnership for a Drug-Free America found that nearly one in five reported misusing one or more prescription drugs to get high, and one in ten reported abusing nonprescription cough syrup for the same reason.[11]

The most widely abused prescription drugs are:

- **Opiates**—painkillers related to morphine, most commonly **hydrocodone** (Vicodin, Lortab, Norco, and other brands and generics) and **oxycodone** (Percodan, Percocet, OxyContin, and other brands). OxyContin, a potent timed-release medication intended for serious chronic pain problems (such as those associated with cancer), has been abused by adolescents who may crush pills designed to be taken whole—thus allowing a sudden and potentially dangerous rush of medication into the bloodstream.

- **Anxiety-reducing drugs**—also called **anxiolytic** drugs, or the more familiar but less specific term **tranquilizers**. Most of these are in the family known as **benzodiazepines**, which, when used properly, are effective for controlling acute or chronic anxiety. In an overdose, especially when combined with other sedating drugs or alcohol, they can cause dramatic and sometimes fatal suppression of one's drive to breathe. Widely used benzodiazepines include alprazolam (Xanax), lorazepam (Ativan), clonazepam (Klonopin), and diazepam (Valium).

- **Stimulants**—medications that are widely used to treat attention deficit/hyperactivity disorder (ADHD), primarily variations on **methylphenidate** (Ritalin, Concerta, Metadate, and others) and **dextroamphetamine** (Dexedrine, Adderall, and others). When prescribed for the right individual and carefully monitored, these medications can be very useful, but some adolescents share them with (or sell them to) friends. Taking an excessive dose of a stimulant (especially when combined with other drugs such as those found in decongestant cold tablets) could provoke a variety of dangerous medical complications, including an irregular heart rhythm, elevated blood pressure, or lethal seizures.

Currently, the most widely abused nonprescription medication is **dextromethorphan**, a cough suppressant (often denoted by the letters *DM* in a self-discipline (especially in school and work performance) literally go up in smoke. One study demonstrated lower scores on standardized verbal and mathematical tests among twelfth-grade marijuana smokers compared to their nonsmoking peers, even though the two groups had performed equally well during the fourth grade. Other research has associated marijuana use with overall poorer job performance, including increased tardiness, absenteeism, accidents, and workers' compensation claims.

Finally, marijuana keeps very bad company. For adolescents and young adults alike

product's name) found in more than 120 different preparations and intended to relieve cough and cold symptoms. When taken in the appropriate amounts (as found on the product packaging or as prescribed by a physician), dextromethorphan has no psychological effects. At much higher doses, however—what abusers call "robodosing" or "robotripping," a slang reference to the familiar cough syrup Robitussin—dextromethorphan can cause alterations in consciousness that can range from euphoric to highly unpleasant. (Some of these effects may be altered by other substances in the particular dextromethorphan-containing medication that is being abused, or by alcohol and other drugs taken at the same time.)

Why are so many adolescents abusing these particular medications? Earlier in this chapter, we listed several reasons why kids use tobacco, alcohol, and drugs: an attempt to achieve a pleasurable altered state of consciousness or to self-medicate, or because of curiosity, thrill seeking, peer pressure, and so on. (See "Why Do Kids Start (and Continue) Using Drugs?" beginning on page 545.) All of these reasons apply to the abuse of "legal" drugs as well, but there are two additional reasons worth noting.

First, these drugs are readily available—from friends, the family medicine cabinet, the local pharmacy, the "cold and cough" aisle at the supermarket, or even their own legitimate prescriptions (such as a stimulant used to treat ADHD or a painkiller prescribed after a medical or dental procedure). Second, they are mistakenly assumed to be safe, in any quantity or combination, because they are legal medications. The study by the Partnership for a Drug-Free America found that 40 percent of those surveyed believe prescription medications (even if not actually prescribed by a physician) to be "much safer" than illegal drugs, and nearly 30 percent believe that prescription pain relievers aren't addictive.[12]

What can parents do to prevent abuse of legal drugs? The drug-proofing strategies described later in this section (see page 564) certainly apply here. In addition, while talking to your kids about tobacco, alcohol, and illegal drugs, you might also include some serious family "public service announcements" about the dangers of misusing prescription and nonprescription drugs. Also, think carefully about where your family's medications are stored—all drugs should be out of plain sight, perhaps hidden or even kept in a locked drawer. Parents should also keep careful tabs on the status of any commonly abused drugs that have been acquired by *anyone* in the family for a legitimate purpose. In particular, if your child or teenager is taking medications for ADHD, anxiety, or pain relief, with rare exception you should be the one dispensing them on a day-to-day basis. Even if you can count on your own son or daughter using them responsibly, it's important for you to protect friends who might be tempted by a prescription bottle sitting on the counter. ■

it can be a gateway drug, introducing them to the harrowing world of illegal drugs and the criminals who produce and distribute them.

While marijuana is not widely perceived as highly addictive, some long-term users will continue to smoke it compulsively even though it is clearly having a negative impact on school, work, and relationships. Long-term regular users who quit may experience anxiety, irritability, and sleeplessness.

Inhalants—cheap (and dangerous) thrills

More than a thousand different products that can be purchased at the supermarket, hardware store, or hobby shop—or that are simply sitting in the garage—can end up in the hands, lungs, and brain of a child or adolescent who is looking for an inexpensive intoxication, with potentially disastrous results.

What are they? Three types of products are inhaled by young thrill seekers:

- **Solvents** or solvent-containing products, such as paint thinner, lacquers, degreasers, model glue, contact cement, gasoline, felt-tip marker fluid, and dozens of other volatile products. These can have mind-altering effects if inhaled deeply.
- **Aerosols** that contain solvents and propellants, such as hair sprays, deodorants, and spray paint.
- **Gases** present in household products such as whipping-cream dispensers, butane lighters, and propane tanks.

Inhalant use typically starts in childhood or early adolescence. The age of peak use is typically twelve to fourteen, with first experiences occurring as early as six to eight years of age.

What are some of their street names? These include *air blast* and *poor man's pot*. Inhalant use is known as bagging or glading.

How are they used? Solvents, gases, or aerosols are either inhaled through the nose (sniffing) or the mouth (huffing), either directly from the container, from plastic bags containing the fumes and held over the mouth and nose, or from a cloth that has been sprayed or saturated with the material.

What's the attraction? Depending upon the substance used, several deep aspirations bring on a sense of euphoria—frequently with hallucinations—as well as stimulation and loss of inhibition, which may lead to other high-risk behavior. Drowsiness and sleep may follow.

What are the health risks? Given the huge variety of toxins that are being abused through inhalation, it should come as little surprise that a host of serious medical consequences have been observed. A number of products can be lethal during or after a single use. One disastrous consequence known as **sudden sniffing death syndrome** can occur in a previously healthy user, especially when butane, propane, and aerosols are inhaled. (This may result from an increased sensitivity of the heart muscle, and it is possible that an abrupt adrenaline surge in response to being startled can provoke a lethal irregular heart rhythm.) Users can also die by asphyxiation when the inhaled substance interferes with oxygen exchange within the lungs, or by suffocation from a plastic bag pulled over the head.

The most serious by-product of chronic inhalant use is permanent damage to the brain and nervous system, causing loss of intellectual function and coordination. Depending upon chemical structure and the number and intensity of exposures, inhaled substances can also damage the tissues of other internal organs. Toluene, for example, found in glue, spray paint, and gasoline, can cause brain damage (including actual loss of tissue), disturbances of gait (walking) and coordination, vision and hearing loss, and injury to the liver or kidney.

What about other consequences? Like other drug users, inhalant abusers may display erratic behavior, poor self-care, and declining school performance. Parents may notice specific clues such as the aroma of the inhalant (which can persist in the breath for several hours), stains and odors in clothes, and an unusual stash of products (such as gasoline or aerosol cans) in a child's room. An adult who discovers children or adolescents in the act of inhaling should avoid surprise tactics or a sudden confrontation that might cause a startle reflex, since this could precipitate a dangerous heart-rhythm disturbance.

Beyond the Gateway—Dead-End Drugs

Beyond these gateway substances lies a dark world of more powerful drugs that assault bodies and minds more quickly and savagely.

Club drugs—the death of the party

A number of unrelated substances have been grouped under this title because they are used by teenagers and young adults at dance clubs and bars, particularly at raves and trances—all-night dance parties held in clubs, warehouses, or even outdoors, for groups ranging from a few hundred to several thousand. While rave and trance culture is focused primarily on the driving music and the physical and emotional release of dancing for hours with an exuberant crowd, many who attend try to enhance the experience with one or more drugs, sometimes with disastrous results.

The most common club drugs include MDMA (Ecstasy), Rohypnol, gamma hydroxybutyrate (GHB), ketamine, and the not-so-golden oldie of the 1960s, LSD. Methamphetamine, a relative of MDMA that has been an abused drug for many years, often shows up at the rave scene as well. Obviously, this cast of characters is subject to change without notice. To complicate matters, club drugs are often combined with one another, with alcohol, and with other drugs. The exact ingredients lurking in the concoctions for sale at the all-night party, not to mention the presence of possible adulterants, are highly unpredictable—and so is the range of possible effects. Teens and young adults who have had an earful of warnings about "hard stuff" such as heroin and cocaine may feel that club drugs are a safer bet. But the odds are much worse than they imagine, and losing the bet can have far-reaching consequences. Those interested in staying current on this phenomenon may get updates at http://www.clubdrugs.org/, a service of the National Institute on Drug Abuse.

MDMA (Ecstasy)—love and brain damage

What is it? MDMA is a synthetic drug with a chemical structure resembling both methamphetamine (a stimulant) and mescaline (a hallucinogen). Originally intended to be an appetite suppressant, MDMA was used in psychotherapy during the 1970s to help individuals open up and discuss their emotions. This practice was discontinued in the mid-1980s when researchers found that MDMA causes brain damage in animals.

What are some of its street names? *Ecstasy* is the most widely used name. Others include *XTC, E, hug drug, love drug*, and *disco biscuit*.

How is it used? MDMA is nearly always swallowed as a pill, although more adventurous (and foolhardy) individuals may crush pills and then snort the powder or inject a solution containing it. Occasionally MDMA is taken in suppository form.

What's the attraction? This drug supplies a lot of energy to dance the night away. Users may feel relaxed, a sense of increased awareness, and deep feelings of love and empathy for others who share the experience with them. (Some users refer to MDMA as an "entactogen," in honor of its supposed enhancement of social interactions.) While it does not cause florid hallucinations, MDMA can alter one's perception of time.

What are the health risks? Like other stimulants, MDMA can raise the pulse and blood pressure, and may interfere with temperature regulation. In hot, stuffy, tightly packed club settings, the combination of MDMA and the ongoing intense exertion of dancing can lead to **hyperthermia**, a marked increase in body temperature that in turn can cause muscle breakdown, kidney failure, and other catastrophic effects. Also, as is typical with stimulants, MDMA use can provoke anxiety, headache, irritability, depression, insomnia, and paranoia—just the opposite of the good feelings that are its primary appeal. Users may also experience significant depression as a withdrawal effect just two days after the last dose.

Perhaps the most worrisome aspect of MDMA use is the finding that it causes long-term brain damage in animals and produces changes in brain scans (using positron emission tomography) in humans. Some research suggests MDMA users score more poorly on memory tests than their nonusing counterparts, but whether such changes are permanent is unknown.

Rohypnol and gamma hydroxybutyrate (GHB)—predator tools

Both of these have become notoriously known as date-rape drugs. Accounts of sexual predators using them to incapacitate victims led Congress to pass the Drug-Induced Rape Prevention and Punishment Act of 1996, increasing federal penalties for the use of any controlled substance in a sexual assault.

What are they? Rohypnol was originally introduced as a sleeping aid in Europe in the 1970s, but it was found to cause short-term loss of memory and profound drowsiness, especially when mixed with alcohol. It has never been approved for use in the United States, but it is produced and legally available in Europe and Latin America.

Until the early 1990s, **gamma hydroxybutyrate (GHB)** was sold in health-food stores and touted as an aid for weight reduction and bodybuilding. It is in fact a central nervous system depressant, especially when mixed with alcohol.

What are some of their street names? Rohypnol is called *roofies, rope, ropies, forget-me drug*, and most blunt, *date-rape drug*. GHB also goes by the names *liquid ecstasy, G, soap, goop*, and variations on its initials, such as *Georgia home boy* and *grievous bodily harm*.

How are they used? Both drugs are taken orally: Rohypnol is taken as a pill or ground into powder; GHB, as a powder or liquid. They are both colorless, tasteless, and odorless.

What's the attraction? When taken voluntarily, Rohypnol is used to induce sleep and GHB is used to create a sense of relaxed euphoria (usually mixed with alcohol). But more often sexual predators slip one of these drugs into an unsuspecting victim's drink. Rohypnol causes a rapid onset of deep sleep and amnesia for whatever happens during the next few hours—and thus serves as a rapist's best friend. It obliterates the victim's ability to resist or remember who did what. Similarly, when slipped into a victim's drink, GHB can incapacitate a victim against resisting a sexual assault.

What are the health risks? Long-term users of Rohypnol are likely to develop physical and psychological dependence, and may have withdrawal symptoms (including an increased risk for seizures) when the drug is stopped. Depending on dose and other drugs being taken, GHB's sedative effects can be extreme, leading to unconsciousness, coma, and even death. By far the most grievous damage related to these drugs, however, is the fallout from a sexual assault: physical and emotional trauma, as well as the possibility of pregnancy or a sexually transmitted infection.

LSD—checking out of reality

LSD (lysergic acid diethylamide) was first synthesized in 1938 by Swiss pharmaceutical chemist Albert Hofmann, who was looking for medical remedies among variations on lysergic acid, a compound derived from a fungus called ergot. One day he accidentally swallowed a tiny amount of this chemical and was startled when objects all around him appeared distorted, grotesque, and threatening. Far from finding this an entertaining or enlightening experience, he was terrified that he could not stop "these demonic transformations of the outer world" and "the dissolution of my ego."[13] He recovered, and for a while the drug was considered a possible candidate for treating schizophrenia.

In the early 1960s, Harvard professors Timothy Leary (who coined the phrase "Tune in, turn on, drop out") and Richard Alpert (later to become New Age philosopher Ram Dass) helped put LSD on the cultural map, after which it became a countercultural icon of the turbulent 1960s and early 1970s. Long after bell-bottoms and psychedelic artwork became faded relics, LSD has continued to find new consumers among the children of baby boomers, especially in the rave culture.

What is it? LSD is known as a hallucinogen, with properties similar to drugs such as mescaline (found in the cactus peyote, for example). These have been used for centuries in many cultures to induce visions and departures from reality, often in pursuit of religious or mystical experiences. Uncontaminated LSD is an odorless and colorless powder, sold as small tablets (called microdots) or more commonly dissolved and applied to absorbent paper, which is then cut into quarter-inch individual doses.

What are some of its street names? *Acid, dots, Lucy in the Sky with Diamonds, window pane, Elvis,* and *mellow yellow* are a few of its slang names.

What's the attraction? Depending upon the dose, setting, and other (usually unpredictable) variables, LSD produces both hallucinations and changes (especially increased intensity) in colors, sounds, and smells that can feel both pleasant and fascinating. Users are often intrigued by synesthesia—the blending of sensations in which a person "hears" colors and "sees" sounds. Some claim to have profound insights into themselves, the universe, and God while under the influence of LSD and other hallucinogens. With repeated use of LSD, tolerance can develop, such that higher doses may be needed to produce the same effect. This disappears after stopping the drug for several days, and ongoing use of LSD is not associated with physical withdrawal symptoms or overt addiction.

What are the health risks? Like its discoverer Albert Hofmann, LSD users may experience more than they bargained for when the drug induces a "bad trip," which can generate profound anxiety, panic, confusion, despair, or even self-destructive behavior. Helping and supporting such a person through the mental and emotional turbulence may keep friends, family, or health-care providers occupied for several hours until the drug wears off. If the LSD was taken with one or more other drugs—for example, a Frisco special is the combination of heroin, cocaine, and LSD—all bets are off and more elaborate medical or psychological care may be needed.

What about other consequences? Two long-term problems may plague LSD users for years after their last dose: The first, and most serious, is a **drug-induced psychosis**, a persistent mental disorder involving not only mood disturbances (including both mania and depression) but also disorganized and irrational thinking, as well as recurrent hallucinations. The second is the so-called LSD flashback, now more formally known as **hallucinogen persisting perception disorder**, or **HPPD**. This is usually a replay of one or more of the visual disturbances that the user experienced on LSD, which occurs spontaneously and often repeatedly for years.

Dissociative drugs—ketamine and phencyclidine (PCP)

What is it? Ketamine and its older and more toxic sibling PCP (which is not a common rave drug) are medications originally developed as anesthetics for both humans and animals. As it wears off, PCP causes so many problems, especially delirium and severe agitation, that it is only used in veterinary medicine. Ketamine, introduced in 1963 to replace PCP, is used for both humans and animals, although 90 percent of sales are to veterinarians.

What are some of their street names? Ketamine is known as *K, Vitamin K, Special K, cat Valium,* and *jet.* PCP is referred to as *angel* with various names attached (*angel dust, angel hair, angel mist,* etc.), as well as *super weed, super grass* (when mixed with marijuana), *zombie, hog, rocket fuel,* and *trank.*

How is it used? Ketamine comes in a liquid form that can be directly injected or evaporated into powder that is swallowed, snorted, or smoked. PCP is taken as a pill or ground into powder to be snorted or smoked (after being sprinkled on tobacco, marijuana, or even parsley).

What's the attraction? Both of these drugs produce a sense of detachment from reality, as if the user is floating or is out of the body altogether. Ketamine's effects are shorter, milder, and less likely to be violent than PCP's.

What are the health risks? PCP is notable for its unpredictable and often violent side effects. Elevations in pulse, blood pressure, and temperature occur at all doses, and a large dose can cause seizures, stroke, extreme elevations of body temperature (hyperthermia), coma, and death. Involuntary and uncoordinated muscle contractions can be so intense as to cause breakdown of muscle fibers or even bone fractures. PCP's behavioral effects are its most dreaded calling card, however. Users may experience not only detachment but also overt hallucinations, fear (or outright panic), paranoia, a sense of invulnerability, and decreased awareness of pain. A nightmare (and a highly dangerous problem) for law-enforcement or emergency-department personnel is to be confronted with a disoriented, agitated, violent PCP user who seemingly has superhuman strength and no apparent sense of pain.

Ketamine, as noted above, is less likely to induce the unpredictable and severe behavioral reactions seen with PCP, although it can generate most of the other medical side effects, especially at higher doses. An unpleasant and frightening sense of complete sensory detachment caused by ketamine has been dubbed the K-hole.

What about other consequences? Because ketamine is tasteless and can induce temporary memory loss, it is also part of the sexual predator's bag of evil tricks.

Methamphetamine—speed trap

What is it? A derivative of amphetamine and chemically similar in some respects to MDMA, methamphetamine is a potent central nervous system stimulant. When first synthesized, it was used as a nasal decongestant and asthma treatment. Today it is still prescribed occasionally to treat narcolepsy (a disorder in which an individual suddenly falls asleep without warning) and ADHD. Unfortunately, it is relatively easy to manufacture in home "laboratories" using store-bought ingredients, making it the most commonly synthesized illegal drug in the United States.

What are some of its street names? These include *speed, meth, poor man's cocaine, ice, crank, crystal,* and many others.

How is it used? Methamphetamine is taken in tablet form, dissolved in water or alcohol, smoked, snorted, or injected. Yaba, a tablet containing methamphetamine and caffeine, has been popular in Southeast Asia and has begun to appear in Asian communities on the West Coast.

What's the attraction? Like other stimulants, methamphetamine creates a temporary feeling of increased energy and well-being, as well as a decrease in appetite. Taken orally, its effects are noticeable within a half hour or less, and the pleasurable response may last for several hours. Smoking or injecting it, on the other hand, produces a more intense rush within a few minutes. Many of the drug's effects last for the better part of a day, but the pleasurable component fades well before that. This, and the inevitable tolerance that develops (that is, more drug is needed to produce the same effect), may induce methamphetamine users to go on binges to try to maintain their drug-induced high.

What are the health risks? Methamphetamine stimulates not only the nervous system but also the rest of the body, raising the pulse rate (and the likelihood of irregular heart rhythms), blood pressure, and body temperature. Heart attack, stroke, hyperthermia (dangerously elevated body temperature), seizures, and death are all possible consequences. Users who inject methamphetamine, like users of any drug shot into a vein, run the risk of acquiring HIV/AIDS and hepatitis B or C from shared needles or other equipment, not to mention bacterial infections of the skin, bone, or heart.

Long-term use is likely not only to lead to addiction but also to induce long-term, or even permanent, changes in the central nervous system. (Some evidence suggests that damage to nerve endings in the brain may occur after a single dose.) Intense emotional and behavioral turbulence—agitation, anxiety, insomnia, and violent behavior—are not uncommon. Psychosis, with delusions, hallucinations, and paranoia (including homicidal or suicidal thoughts), can result.

What happens when a user quits? Depression, fatigue, anxiety, and an intense craving for another dose occur. Methamphetamine users may embark on a desperate run in order to override their tolerance for the drug, injecting large quantities every few hours over several days in a sleepless binge.

Cocaine—a fast track downhill

What is it? Cocaine, the most powerful stimulant occurring in nature, is one of the most addictive drugs on the street and in many ways the most dangerous. Coca leaves, the source of cocaine, grow in the highlands of the Andes in South America, primarily in Colombia, Bolivia, and Peru. They have been chewed for thousands of years for their stimulant and hunger-reducing effects. In the late 1800s pure cocaine hydrochloride was extracted from coca leaves and found to be useful in medical procedures involving the nose and eyes because of its ability to reduce pain and constrict blood vessels. It was also incorporated into hundreds of patent medicines, tonics, cigarettes, and wines. In crack cocaine (also called freebase), the hydrochloride has been removed, creating a form of the drug that can be smoked. The crackling sound that occurs when cocaine is heated during this preparation gives the final product its name.

The *coca* bush bears no relation to the tropical *cacao* tree, from which we obtain chocolate and cocoa. While some people consider themselves "chocoholics," these everyday temptations have nothing in common with cocaine.

What are its street names? *Coke, blow, nose candy, C* (and numerous words that begin with this letter: *Cecil, Charlie, coconut*), and *snow* are just some of the dozens of street names.

How is it used? Cocaine is nearly always inhaled (snorted), entering the bloodstream via the inner linings of the nose; injected into a vein; or smoked. When inhaled, its high lasts about ten to fifteen minutes—much shorter than that seen with methamphetamine. When injected or smoked, the effects are felt immediately but may last only a few minutes. Cocaine is also injected along with heroin (a combination known as a speedball, among other names), smoked with tobacco or marijuana, or combined with virtually any other mind-altering drug. Powdered cocaine may be diluted with cornstarch, talcum, or sugar.

What's the attraction? Dopamine, one of several important chemical messengers between nerve cells, plays an important role in the activation of certain areas in the brain associated with pleasure. Cocaine causes a temporary pileup of dopamine in these areas, resulting in a sense of energy and euphoria well beyond anything a person has experienced before. This may be accompanied by increased alertness; mental focus; sensitivity to light, sound, and touch; and a decreased need for food and sleep. Because tolerance to cocaine can develop rapidly, a person's first experience with this drug may be the most intense, especially if it's smoked or injected. The desire to repeat this ecstatic event again and again is frequently overwhelming, but many users never experience as much pleasure as they did with their first dose.

What are the health risks? There are many, and they're serious.

- Cocaine's powerful jolt to the central nervous system also triggers a rapid heart rate, constricted blood vessels, and elevated blood pressure. Even in young, well-conditioned bodies, these events can cause stroke, seizures, or cardiac arrest. Cocaine precipitates more emergency-room visits than any other illegal drug.
- All of cocaine's routes of entry into the body pose unique hazards. Snorting cocaine up the nose can lead to destruction of the septum (the structure separating the two nasal passages) and eventual collapse of the bridge of the nose. Injecting cocaine into the veins can transmit dangerous microorganisms, including the viruses that cause hepatitis and AIDS, when needles or syringes are shared with other users. Allergic reactions to injected cocaine or to one of the additives mixed with it can be severe or even fatal.

- When cocaine and alcohol are used at the same time (not an uncommon event), the liver may convert them to a compound called **cocaethylene**, which is more toxic than either drug alone. According to the National Institute on Drug Abuse, cocaine and alcohol are the two drugs that, when used together, are most likely to result in death.
- Multiple doses of cocaine taken in a binge—often involving increasing doses because tolerance has resulted in a diminishing effect—can lead to increasing restlessness, paranoia, or psychosis, complete with delusions and hallucinations.

What happens when a user quits? When the drug wears off, cocaine users become anxious, irritable, depressed, and desperate for the next dose. Bigger and more frequent doses are needed to produce the desired effect, and the progression from first use to desperate addiction can be rapid. (With crack, addiction frequently begins with the first dose.) Money becomes important solely as a means to obtaining more cocaine, and huge sums may be spent, borrowed, or stolen to buy it. Exchanges of sex for drugs enhance the spread of HIV/AIDS, hepatitis, and other infections.

Heroin—no way to live

What is it? Heroin is the most highly addictive narcotic and the scourge of any individual, family, or neighborhood affected by it. Though by no means the most widely used illegal drug, heroin generates medical problems, crime, and general chaos that more than make up for its smaller number of users. A derivative of morphine, heroin was first synthesized in 1874 and, like cocaine, was widely used by physicians at the turn of the century before its powerful potential for addiction was recognized.

What are some of its street names? *Horse, smack, Big H, Dr. Feelgood,* and *thunder* are a few, but there are many more, including names for combinations of heroin and other drugs.

How is it used? For decades heroin has most commonly been taken by direct injection into a vein. Because of increasing supplies of purer and cheaper heroin, however, more users now smoke or sniff it.

What's the attraction? When injected directly into a vein, heroin proceeds within seconds to the brain, where it is converted to morphine and binds to special sites called **opioid receptors**. The result is an immediate rush that first-time users find overwhelmingly pleasurable. When sniffed or smoked, this occurs more slowly (over ten to fifteen minutes) and with less intensity (but no less potential for addiction). After the initial euphoria, users will feel relaxed and sedated for hours—and then want to find another dose.

What are the health risks? As with cocaine, there are many, and they are serious, especially for the user who is injecting it.

- Veins that are repeatedly invaded by needles and nonsterile materials become scarred, and bacteria accidentally shot into the bloodstream can infect heart valves, bone, and other tissues.
- Heroin sold on the street doesn't go through quality control. Dealer profits are increased when the drug is diluted (or "cut") with other substances such as sugar, cornstarch, powdered milk, other illegal drugs, or even strychnine (which is

often used as a rodent poison). Some of these materials do not dissolve in the blood and may obstruct small arteries, leading to tissue damage in vital organs such as the lungs, liver, kidney, or brain. These damaged areas are in turn more vulnerable to bacteria introduced during injections.

- Sharing needles and other paraphernalia is a highly efficient means of spreading life-threatening (and life-ending) viral infections, including HIV/AIDS and hepatitis B and C. The National Institute on Drug Abuse estimates that one-third of all HIV infections and half of hepatitis C infections are transmitted this way. These then can be spread to sexual partners and from infected mothers to their babies.

- The chaotic lifestyle, poor self-care, malnutrition, and general squalor that characterize the lives of hard-core addicts set them up for even more infections, such as tuberculosis, pneumonia, and skin ulcers.

- Heroin users rapidly develop tolerance—bigger doses are needed to bring about a pleasurable effect—and physical dependence, such that without a steady supply of the drug, the user experiences an unpleasant withdrawal within several hours.

- Variations in the quantity and purity of heroin can result in a user getting a much bigger dose than expected. Heroin overdose puts the brain into a stupor or flat-out unconsciousness and depresses respirations. If the dose is big enough, and especially if the user has ingested other sedating drugs (such as alcohol), any injection could lead to the morgue.

What about other consequences? Like cocaine, heroin can rapidly draw a user into a full-time pursuit of the next dose and the funds necessary to acquire it. Wages (if there is a job), savings, and possessions are likely to be consumed by this addiction. Theft, dealing one or more drugs, prostitution, or simply trading sex for the next dose often becomes part of a grim way of life.

What happens when a user quits? With increasing tolerance leading to bigger doses of heroin, physical dependence is virtually inevitable. Once this hook is set, the user will begin to feel uncomfortable within a few hours of the last dose. If no drug is forthcoming, by twenty-four to forty-eight hours life becomes a miserable mix of sweats, cramps, shaking, nausea, vomiting, and diarrhea. For most users these symptoms subside within a week, and as rotten as they may feel, an adult in reasonable health will survive this ordeal even without any medical support. (This may not be the case, however, for the unborn child of a pregnant woman undergoing withdrawal.) Unfortunately, a user may crave this drug and stumble back into its enslaving grip months after withdrawal symptoms have completely disappeared.

What Are the Stages of Involvement in Substance Abuse?

Experts in adolescent substance-abuse problems have identified a common progression of alcohol- and drug-related behaviors that moves from bad to worse. While it is not a foregone conclusion that everyone who experiments with drugs will progress to the worst stages of involvement, a child can already have incurred a lot of damage before parents or others notice that something is wrong. Secretive adolescent behavior and skillful lying, combined with parental denial ("No one in our family could have a drug problem!"), may delay identification of the problem. While paranoia and daily inquisitions around the breakfast table are counterproductive, wise parents will keep their eyes and ears open and promptly take action if they see any signs that a problem may be developing.

Stage one: Experimentation—entering the drug gateway

Characteristics:
- Use is occasional, sporadic, often unplanned—weekends, summer nights, someone's unsupervised party.
- Use is precipitated by peer pressure, curiosity, thrill seeking, desire to look and feel grown-up.
- Gateway drugs are usually used—cigarettes, alcohol, marijuana, possibly inhalants.
- A drug high is easier to experience because tolerance has not developed.

Parents may notice:
- Tobacco or alcohol on the breath or intoxicated behavior.
- Little change in normal behavior between episodes of drug use.

Stage two: More regular drug use—leaving the land of the living

Characteristics:
- Alcohol and other drugs are used not only on weekends but also on weekdays, not only with friends but when alone.
- Quantities of alcohol and drugs increase as tolerance develops; hangovers become more common.
- Blackouts may occur—periods of time in which drugs or alcohol prevent normal memories from forming; "What happened last night?" becomes a frequent question.
- More time and attention are focused on when the next drug experience will occur.
- Fellow drinkers or drug users become preferred companions.

Parents may notice:
- Son or daughter will be out of the house later at night, overnight, or all weekend.
- School performance worsens—unexplained school absences.
- Outside activities such as sports are dropped.
- Decreased contact with friends who don't use drugs.
- Disappearance of money or other valuables.
- Child withdraws from the family, is increasingly sullen and hostile.
- User is caught in one or many lies.

Stage three: Waist-deep in the mire of addiction—and sinking

Characteristics:
- Alcohol and drugs become the primary focus of attention.
- Becoming high is a daily event.
- There is a use of harder, more dangerous drugs.
- More money is spent each week on drugs; theft or dealing may become part of drug-seeking behavior.
- Adolescent displays increasing social isolation; no contact with non-drug-using friends; more drug use in isolation rather than socially.

Parents may notice the behaviors listed above, plus:

- Escalation of conflicts at home.
- Loss of nearly all control of the adolescent.
- Possible discovery of a stash of drugs at home.
- Arrest(s) for possession of drugs or dealing them, or for driving under the influence.

Stage four: Drowning in addiction
Characteristics:

- Constant state of intoxication; being high is routine, even at school or job (if they attend at all).
- Blackouts increase in frequency.
- Physical appearance deteriorates—weight loss, infections, poor self-care.
- Injectable drugs are possibly used.
- Involvement in casual sexual relationships (at times in exchange for drugs).
- User will likely be involved with theft, dealing, and other criminal activity.
- Guilt, self-hatred, and thoughts of suicide increase.
- Adolescent abandons any apparent interest in spiritual matters.

Parents are likely to be dealing with:

- Complete loss of control over adolescent's behavior; escalation of conflict, possibly to the point of violence.
- Ongoing denial by user that drugs are a problem.
- Increasing problems with the law and time spent with police, attorneys, hearings, court officials, etc.
- Negative effects on other siblings because the family is preoccupied or overwhelmed by consequences of drug user's behavior.

This descent into drug hell is a nightmare that no parent envisions while rocking a newborn baby or escorting an eager five-year-old to kindergarten. But it can happen in any neighborhood, church, or family, even when parents have provided a stable and loving home environment. In fact, it is often in such homes that a drug problem goes undetected until it has reached an advanced and dangerous stage. "This can't be happening, not in my house!" But if it does, parental guilt, anger, and depression can undermine the responses necessary to restore order.

What Can Parents Do to Reduce Their Child's Risk of Developing a Substance-Abuse Problem?

Drug abuse is so widespread in our culture that you cannot expect to isolate your child from exposure to it. However, as with diseases caused by bacteria and viruses, you can institute infection-control measures. Specifically, take steps to reduce the likelihood of contact with drugs, and build your child's immunity to using them. These measures should be ongoing, deliberate, and proactive.

Model behavior you want your children to follow.
When it comes to drugs, two adages are worth noting: "Children learn what they live" and "What parents allow in moderation their children will do in excess." While not absolute truths, these maxims reflect the reality that kids are looking to their parents

for cues as to what is acceptable behavior, while at the same time developing the discernment required to understand what moderation is all about.

If you smoke, your offspring probably will do likewise. But it's never too late to quit, and your decision to give up cigarettes will make an important statement to all the members of your family—especially if you are willing to hold yourself accountable to them.

If you consume alcohol at home, what role does it play in your life? Does it flow freely on a daily basis? Do you need a drink to unwind at the end of the day? Is it a necessary ingredient at every party or family get-together? If so, your children will get the picture that alcohol is a painkiller, tension reliever, and the life of the party, and they will likely use it in a similar fashion. For their sake (and yours), take whatever steps are necessary to live without alcohol.

If you drink modestly—an occasional glass of wine with dinner, a beer every other week, a few sips of champagne at a wedding—think carefully about alcohol's role in your family. Many parents decide to abstain while rearing their children in order to send an unambiguous message to steer clear of it. Others feel that modeling modest use of alcohol without intoxication (while speaking clearly against underage drinking, drunkenness, driving under the influence, and other irresponsible behaviors) equips children and teenagers to make sensible decisions later in life.

Each family must weigh the options carefully and set its own standards. But if you or any blood relatives have a history of alcohol addiction (or any problem caused by drinking), make your home an alcohol-free zone and warn your adolescent that he or she may have a genetic predisposition toward alcoholism.

Also think about the impact of your family's habits on visitors or guests, including your teenager's friends. What might be perfectly harmless for you could prompt someone who has a potential for alcohol addiction to make a bad decision. All things considered, nothing is lost and much can be gained by abstaining.

What about your medicine cabinet? If you are stressed, upset, or uncomfortable, are *d-r-u-g-s* the way you usually spell *r-e-l-i-e-f*? Have you accumulated a collection of prescription medications that you appear to utilize freely when the going gets tough? Kids aren't blind. If they see the adults around them frequently taking "legitimate" drugs to dull their pain, why can't they use their own drugs of choice to do the same?

Even when medications have been prescribed appropriately, overuse and even addiction is possible with certain types of drugs. If you have a chronic condition for which habit-forming medications have been prescribed, you would be wise not only to model responsible use but also to demonstrate when possible your commitment to find other types of treatment (for example, physical therapy, exercise, or counseling) that might be appropriate. Note: The appropriate use of antidepressants to treat the biochemistry of mood disorders does *not* represent a potential abuse situation. These medications are neither addicting nor habit-forming and are not sold on the street to create an artificial drug high (see Special Concerns, page 576).

Finally, if you use marijuana and other street drugs, whether for recreational purposes or because of an addiction problem, you are putting the parental stamp of approval not only on the drugs but also on breaking the law. For your own and your family's sake, seek help immediately and bring this dangerous behavior to an end.

Build identity and attitudes that are resistant to drug use.

This is an ongoing project, beginning during the first years of your child's life. Specifically:

- Create an environment that consistently balances love and limits. Children and teenagers who know they are loved unconditionally are less likely to seek "pain relief" through drugs, and those who have learned to live within appropriate boundaries will have better impulse control and self-discipline.

- Instill respect and awe for the God-given gift of a body and mind—even one that isn't perfect.
- Help children and adolescents become students of consequences—not only in connection with drugs but with other behaviors as well. Talk about good and bad choices and the logic behind them. "Just say no" is an appropriate motto for kids to learn, but understanding why it is wrong to use harmful substances will build more solid resistance.
- Build a positive sense of identity with your family. This means not only openly affirming and appreciating each member but putting forth the time and effort for shared experiences that are meaningful and fun. A strong feeling of belonging to a loving family builds accountability ("Our family doesn't use drugs") and helps prevent loneliness, which can be a setup for a drug experience.
- Encourage church-related activities (including family devotions) that build a meaningful, personal faith. Reliance on God should be the cornerstone of drug-treatment programs, and it makes no sense to leave the spiritual dimension out of the prevention process. A vibrant faith reinforces the concept that the future is worth protecting, stabilizes the emotions during turbulent years, and provides a healthy response to the aches and pains of life. In addition, an awareness of God's presence and a desire not to dishonor Him can be strong deterrents to destructive behavior.

Begin talking early about smoking, alcohol, and drugs.

Because experimentation with drugs and alcohol commonly begins during the grade-school years, start appropriate countermeasures in very young children. A five-year-old may not be ready for a lecture about the physiology of cocaine addiction, but you should be ready to offer commentary when you and your child see someone smoking or drinking, whether in real life or in a movie or TV program. If intoxication is portrayed as humorous (as in the pink-elephant sequence in the movie *Dumbo*, for example), don't be shy about setting the record straight.

Keep talking about smoking, alcohol, and drugs as opportunities arise.

Make an effort to stay one step ahead of your child's or adolescent's knowledge of the drug scene. If you hear about an athlete, rock star, or celebrity who uses drugs, be certain that everyone in the family understands that no amount of fame or fortune excuses this behavior. If a famous person is dealing with the consequences of drug use (such as being dropped from a team or suffering medical or legal consequences), make sure your kids hear the cautionary tale. If you become aware of a person (whether a celebrity or not) who is taking positive steps to deal with a drug or alcohol problem, be sure to acknowledge and praise that effort.

Be aware of current trends in your community, and look for local meetings or lectures where abuse problems are being discussed. Find out what's going on—not only from the experts but from your kids and their friends. If you hear that someone is smoking, drinking, inhaling, or injecting drugs, talk about it. What are they using? What consequences are likely? Why is it wrong? What help do they need?

All this assumes that you are available to have these conversations. Be careful, because the time when you may be the busiest with career or other responsibilities may also be the time when one or more adolescents at home most need your input. If you're too overworked, overcommitted, and overtired to keep tabs on the home front, you may wake up one day to find a major drug problem on your doorstep.

Don't allow your child or adolescent to go to a party, sleepover, or other activity that isn't supervised by someone you trust.

Don't blindly assume that the presence of a grown-up guarantees a safe environment. Get to know your kid's friends' parents, not just your kid's friends. Make certain your child knows you will pick him up anytime, anywhere—no questions asked—if he finds himself in a situation where alcohol or drugs are being used. And be sure to praise him for a wise and mature decision if he calls.

Have the courage to curtail your child's or adolescent's contact with drug users.

The epidemic of drug abuse spreads person to person. Whether a recent acquaintance or a long-term bosom buddy, if one (or more) of your teenager's friends is known to be actively using alcohol or drugs, you must impose restrictions on the relationship. You might, for example, stipulate that your adolescent can spend time with that person only in your home—without any closed doors and when you are around.

However, even with these limits in place, you will need to keep track of who is influencing whom. If your family is reaching out to a troubled adolescent and helping to move him toward healthier decisions, keep up the good work. But if there is any sign that the drug-using friend is pulling your teenager toward his lifestyle, declare a quarantine immediately. If your teenager feels called to help a friend climb out of a drug quagmire, don't let him try it alone. Work as a team to direct that person toward a recovery program.

Create significant consequences to discourage alcohol and drug use.

Teenagers may not be scared by facts, figures, and gory details. Even the most ominous warnings may not override an adolescent's belief in his own immortality, especially when other compelling emotions such as the need for peer acceptance are operating at full throttle.

You may improve the odds by making it clear that you consider the use of cigarettes, alcohol, or illegal drugs a very serious matter. Judgment regarding punishments fitting crimes will be necessary, of course. If your adolescent confesses that he tried a cigarette or a beer at a party and expresses an appropriate resolve to avoid a repeat performance, heart-to-heart conversation and encouragement would be far more appropriate than summarily grounding him for six months.

But if your warnings repeatedly go unheeded, you will need to establish and enforce some meaningful consequences. Loss of driving, dating, or even phone privileges for an extended period of time may be in order. You can make the bitter pill less threatening by pointing out the following:

- He can easily avoid the penalty by staying clear of drugs and the people who use them.
- Consistent responsible behavior leads to more privileges and independence. Irresponsible behavior leads to decreased independence and more parental control.

- The drastic consequence can be used as a reason to get away from a bad situation. If a friend starts to exert pressure to smoke, drink, or use drugs, he can say, "Sorry, but I don't want to be stuck without transportation for the next six months."

What If a Problem Has Already Developed?

Even in families that are close-knit, hold strong values, and practice ongoing drug proofing, there are no guarantees that substance abuse won't affect one or more of your children. The problems may range from a brief encounter with cigarettes to an episode of intoxication (perhaps with legal consequences) or may even involve addiction. As you begin to cope with the chemical intruder(s) in your home, keep the following principles in mind:

For more ideas and resources for preventing drug abuse during childhood and adolescence, check Focus on the Family's program "How to Drug Proof Your Kids" at www .drugproofyourkids.com.

Don't deny or ignore the problem.

If you do, it is likely to continue to worsen until your family life is turned inside out. Take the bull by the horns—but be sure to find out exactly how big and ugly the bull is. The marijuana cigarette you discovered may be a onetime experiment—or the tip of an iceberg. Talk to your child or adolescent about it—but also talk to siblings, friends, and anyone else who knows what he's up to. You may not like what you hear, but it's better to get the hard truth now than a ghastly surprise later.

Don't wallow in false guilt.

Most parents assume a great deal of self-blame when a drug problem erupts in their home. If you do carry some responsibility for what has happened (whether you know about it immediately or find out later on), face up to it, confess it to God and your family, and then get on with the task of helping your child. But remember that your child or adolescent must deal with his own responsibility as well.

Seek help from people experienced with treating drug problems.

Talk to your physician and pastor. They should be part of your team, even if in a supporting role. It is likely that you will receive a referral to a professional who is experienced in organizing a family intervention. This may include educational sessions, individual and family counseling, medical treatment, and long-term follow-up. When the user's behavior is out of control and he is unwilling to acknowledge the problem, a carefully planned confrontation by family members and others affected may need to be carried out under the supervision of an experienced counselor. The goal is to convince the drug user in a firm but loving way of the need for change—*now*. The confrontation should include specific alternatives for the type of treatment he will undergo and a clear-cut "or else . . ." if he is not willing to cooperate.

Be prepared to make difficult, "tough love" decisions.

If you have a drug-dependent adolescent who will not submit to treatment and insists on continuing drug use and other destructive actions, you will need to take the stomach-churning step of informing him that he cannot continue to live in your home while carrying on this behavior. This will be necessary not only to motivate him to change but to prevent his drug-induced turbulence from destroying the rest of your family.

If you must take this drastic step, it would be helpful to present him with one or more options. These might include entering an inpatient drug-treatment center, half-way house, boot-camp program, or youth home, or staying with a relative or another family who is willing to accept him for a defined period of time. More ominous possibilities may need to be discussed as well, such as making him a ward of the court or even turning him over to the police if he has been involved in criminal activity. If you continue to shield him from the consequences of his behavior or bail him out when his drugs get him into trouble, he will not change, and you will be left with deep-seated anger and frustration.

Don't look for or expect quick-fix solutions.

It is normal to wish for a single intervention that will make a drug problem go away. But one conversation, counseling session, prayer time, or trip to the doctor won't be enough. Think in terms of a comprehensive response encompassing specific treatment and counseling and the gamut of your child's life—home, school, friends, and church.

Remember the father of the Prodigal Son.

"Tough love" means allowing the consequences of bad decisions to be fully experienced by the one who is making them. It also means that he knows your love for him is so deep and secure that it will never die. Never give up hope, never stop praying, and never slam the door on reconciliation and restoration when he comes to his senses.

Recognizing Depression and Preventing Suicide in Children and Adolescents

Depression—As Common As the Common Cold

Depression is by far the most common and important emotional health problem in America. In terms of its frequency among the population, depression could be compared to the common cold. But the similarity ends there.

- The sneezing and hacking of a cold is readily apparent to the person who has it, as well as to everyone around her. But depression can be manifested in a bewildering array of symptoms, many of them physical, but it may not be recognized by the affected individual or those closest to her.
- Cold viruses are usually vanquished by the immune system within one or two weeks, while untreated depression can continue for months or even years.
- Cold remedies are simple to use and readily obtained at the nearest supermarket. But appropriate treatment of depression is a prolonged process that nearly always involves one or more professionals and sometimes carefully chosen medication.
- A person with a cold isn't considered defective or weak-willed or in need of "getting her act together." But depression is a diagnosis no one wants to acknowledge or accept because of the stigma associated with having a mental disorder.
- While colds never have a fatal outcome except in the most physically frail individuals, depression can lead to the sudden and tragic ending of a life that would most likely have continued for many more years.

All of the difficulties and heartaches arising from depression apply not only to adults but also to children and adolescents, often with greater intensity. According to the American Academy of Child and Adolescent Psychiatry, at any given time, 5 percent of children and adolescents suffer from depression—not a brief case of "the blues" or a temporary mood swing—and that number may be conservative.[1] What is more disturbing is that depression kills the young more frequently than it does adults. Suicide is the third leading cause of death in children between the ages of ten and fourteen, and it's also the third leading cause of death among those between the ages of fifteen and twenty-four, claiming the lives of nearly four thousand teenagers every year in the United States. The number may actually be higher, because many accidents (such as drug overdoses, drownings, or fatal automobile crashes involving a lone teenage driver) may in fact be suicides. According to the National Mental Health Association, since 1960 the suicide rate among fifteen- to twenty-four-year-olds has nearly tripled.[2]

The 2005 Youth Risk Behavior Surveillance by the Centers for Disease Control and Prevention noted that about 16 percent of the high school students surveyed had considered suicide, 13 percent had made a specific suicide plan, and over 8 percent had made a suicide attempt.[3] Females attempt suicide three times more frequently than males. However, because young males are more likely to utilize violent methods (such as leaping from an overpass or using a gun), their suicide attempts are four times more likely to be fatal than those of females.[4]

What Is Depression?

In our culture the term *depression* is applied to a broad spectrum of situations in which a person feels unhappy. Here, however, we are dealing specifically with what is called **clinical** or **major depression**—not a temporary emotional slump, such as after watching a sad movie or receiving a traffic ticket or even after a day in which one thing after another goes sour. Clinical depression involves a *persistent*—lasting two weeks or longer—and usually *disruptive* disturbance of mood and often affects other bodily functions as well. As we list the common characteristics of depression, it is important to note that these may manifest themselves quite differently in children and adolescents compared with adults. In fact, because the behaviors provoked by depression are frequently confused with the normal emotional and physical upheavals of growing up, at one time it was erroneously assumed that this condition occurred rarely, if at all, before adulthood. In each symptom category we will mention some of the unique variations seen in young people who are depressed.

Persistent sadness and/or irritability

Most parents complain at some point, if not frequently, that their teenager has a "lousy attitude." As described in chapter 13, it isn't at all unusual for adolescents to experience emotions and mood swings that seem out of proportion to the circumstances. But the depressed child or teenager seems to be in a perpetual slump.

Unfortunately, you won't hear a young person say, "In case you haven't noticed, I've been depressed for the past several weeks." Instead, you may see one—or more likely several—of the following distress signals that might appear disconnected:

- Continued overt sadness or moping; frequent episodes of crying.
- A loss of enthusiasm or interest in things that were once favorite activities.
- Increasing withdrawal and isolation from family and friends.
- Poor school performance: plummeting grades, loss of interest in schoolwork, and frequent absences.
- Outbursts of anger, arguing, disrespectful comments, or blatant hostility toward everyone at home.
- Repeated complaints about being bored or tired.
- Overt acting out: drug or alcohol use, running away, sexual activity, fighting, vandalism, or other antisocial activity.

This does not mean, of course, that all negative attitudes and actions are manifestations of depression. In previous chapters we have discussed a variety of parental "survival skills" for dealing with the emotional weather in childhood and adolescence, and you may want to review that material if you are encountering turbulence. (See "What If You and Your Child Are Perpetually in Turbulent Waters?" on page 366, as well as chapter 13 beginning on page 478.) But parents who are confronted with persistent disturbances in emotions and behavior should consider the possibility of depression and, more importantly, seek input from a qualified counselor, physician, or both.

Painful thoughts

If we compare depression to a very long, sad song, the mood disturbance just described is the mournful or agitated music. But accompanying the unhappy melody are painful lyrics—words that express, over and over again, a view of life that is anything but upbeat.

People who have experienced both depression and bodily injuries (for example, a major fracture) usually will confirm that physical pain is easier to manage than emotional pain. Usually one can expect physical pain to resolve or at least become tolerable. But no such hopeful expectation accompanies painful thoughts, which can roll into the mind like waves from an ocean that extends to a limitless, bleak horizon.

Painful thoughts, like a disturbed mood, can have several manifestations:

- *Relentless introspection.* Adolescents tend to be highly self-conscious during the normal (and necessary) process of establishing their identity during their transition into adulthood. But depression magnifies and warps this natural introspection into a mental inquisition. The inward gaze not only becomes a relentless stare, but it focuses exclusively on shortcomings. It can also move into some dangerous territory: "Wouldn't I and everyone else be better off if I weren't here? Why does it matter at this point whether I live or die?"

- *Negative self-concept.* Physical appearance, intelligence, competence, acceptance, and general worth are all subject to relentless and exaggerated criticism. This is not a healthy examination of areas that need improvement, nor repentance for wrongdoing that might lead to improvements in attitude and behavior. Instead, unrealistic self-reproach for whatever isn't going well in life—or at the opposite extreme spreading blame to everyone else—is likely to dominate a depressed child's or adolescent's thoughts and interfere with positive changes.

  A depressed teenager slumps into a lunchroom chair and moans, "I'm fat. I'm never gonna get a date. I'm stupid. I'll never pass algebra. I feel miserable. I'm never going to feel good again." Her friends, if they bother to hang around to listen to this litany of woe, may argue with her. "You're not stupid. Stop talking that way." If she persists in her lament, they may become fed up and agree with her, if only to end her complaints: "Okay, so you're fat and stupid. C'mon, we're gonna be late for class." Her parents might unwittingly make a similar mistake in trying to bolster her spirits: "What are you talking about? You look fine to us, and you're smart. That's enough of this negative talk!" Such responses only build feelings of rejection and a conviction that "no one understands me."

  This state of affairs will be drastically worsened for those who have been subjected to emotional, physical, or sexual abuse during childhood or adolescence. Whether these assaults attack the heart ("You're so stupid!" "Why can't you be like _____ ?") or the body, they create a sense of worthlessness that supplies powerful fuel for an ongoing depression.

- *Anxiety.* Persistent worry, whether focused on a specific issue or a free-floating apprehension that encompasses most daily activities, frequently accompanies depression. While a modest level of concern is not only normal but in fact necessary to motivate appropriate precautions for everyday activities, the anxiety associated with depression is disabling and actually interferes with effective responses to life's challenges.
- *Hopelessness.* This is particularly troublesome for children and adolescents, not only because they may feel emotions so strongly, but also because they haven't lived long enough to understand the ebb and flow of life's problems and pleasures. Most adults facing a crisis will think back to the last twenty-seven crises they have already lived through and will have gained enough perspective to know that this current trial will probably pass as well. But when young people collide with a crisis (or at least what appears to be one from their perspective), they usually have far fewer experiences with which to compare it and a limited fund of responses. If they can't see a satisfactory route past the current problem, it is no wonder they might begin to think that their life "is over" or "not worth living." This dark view of life isn't helped by some powerful voices in adolescent popular culture (especially in music) that focus on rage, alienation, despair, and death.

Physical symptoms

Physiological responses in the body routinely accompany emotional events, and so it should come as little surprise that physical symptoms are often associated with depression. Common problems include:

- *Insomnia and other sleep disturbances.* Difficulty falling asleep at night, awakening too early in the morning, and fitful sleep in between are very common in depressed individuals. This may be accompanied by a desire to sleep during the day. Some people experience **hypersomnia** (sleeping for excessively long periods of time), in which sleep seems to serve as an escape from the misery of waking hours. An important sign that depression is improving is the normalization of sleeping patterns.
- *Appetite changes.* Loss of appetite and weight or nonstop hunger and weight gain are common during depression. Such changes can complicate an adolescent's normal concerns about appearance.
- *Physiological problems.* Depressed individuals often have a variety of physical complaints. Fatigue is almost universally present. Headaches, dizziness, nausea, abdominal cramps, episodes of shortness of breath, and heart palpitations are not at all unusual. Sometimes poor concentration, unusual pain patterns, or altered sensations in various parts of the body will raise concerns about a serious medical disorder. Very often an evaluation for an assortment of symptoms will uncover no evidence of an underlying disease but will lead an attentive physician to suspect depression. The absence of a serious diagnosis may bring a sigh of relief to a young patient (and most certainly to his parents) but can also cause dismay. "Are you saying all of this is in my [my child's] head?" is a typical response. In fact, the symptoms are very real and a predictable component of depression. When depression improves with treatment, so do the physical symptoms.

Delusional thinking

Very rarely, a severe case of depression will also involve delusional thinking, in which the individual's beliefs and sensory experiences do not match with reality. She may hear voices or have hallucinations. She may believe that others are trying to harm her or entertain grandiose ideas about her identity or purpose in life. This is not merely a depression but a **psychosis**, a serious disorder of neurochemical function in the brain that must be addressed immediately by a professional and treated with appropriate medication. (Hospitalization is often required at the outset.) Many psychotic individuals require lifelong medication to prevent a relapse.

Why Do Children and Adolescents Become Depressed?

A complex blend of genetic, biochemical, personal, family, and spiritual factors can interact to cause depression. These include:

- *Genetics and biochemistry.* Many if not most cases appear linked to imbalances (for lack of a better word) in chemical messengers within the brain known as **neurotransmitters**. These compounds move in and out of the microscopic gaps between **neurons** (nerve cells) throughout the nervous system, allowing for interaction between cells in a rapid and extraordinarily complex manner. There are many different neurotransmitters, but those that are prominently linked to mood include **serotonin**, **norepinephrine**, and **dopamine**.

  Disturbances in the regulation or balance of these compounds between neurons in certain areas of the brain are associated with mood disturbances. Exactly how they affect mood, why they become abnormal, and to what degree they are the cause versus the result of the mood problem remain tantalizing questions. But their importance is confirmed by the dramatic effect of medications that adjust neurotransmitter levels for people with anxiety or depressive disorders. (More on them later.)

  Very often the vulnerability to a neurotransmitter disturbance appears to have a genetic origin, such that the same type of mood disturbance will appear in multiple members and generations of the same family. This appears to be biologically driven, and not merely the result of parenting patterns or children imitating behaviors they see in a parent. It can also account for an individual becoming depressed for no apparent reason, or struggling with depression throughout life.

- *Personal and family events.* A child who is brought up in an atmosphere of love, stability, encouragement, and consistent boundaries will usually see his world differently and interact with it more successfully than one who has lived with abuse, indifference, or chaos. For many individuals, depression is deeply rooted in early childhood experiences that taught them that the world is a dangerous place where no one can be trusted.

- *Recent stresses and reversals.* One or more major losses or traumatic events can set off a depressive episode (often referred to as a **reactive depression**) that is more prolonged and profound than the normal grieving process. Examples of such stressful events are a severe illness or death of a parent or other loved one (even a pet); parental separation, divorce, or remarriage; a move from a familiar home; one or more episodes of physical or sexual abuse; a natural disaster; war or violence in the community; difficulty or failure in school or an athletic pursuit; the breakup of a close friendship or romantic relationship; or a severe or chronic illness.

ANTIDEPRESSANTS IN CHILDREN AND ADOLESCENTS

The most widely used antidepressants in both adults and children are called **selective serotonin reuptake inhibitors** (or **SSRI**s). Introduced in the late 1980s, this class of medication revolutionized the medical treatment of mood disorders because of markedly improved safety profiles, fewer side effects, and effectiveness for both major depression and a broad spectrum of anxiety disorders. They have also been helpful for many women with significant premenstrual distress. SSRIs currently available include fluoxetine (Prozac—the first of these on the market), sertraline (Zoloft), paroxetine (Paxil), fluvoxamine (Luvox), citalopram (Celexa), and escitalopram (Lexapro). Venlaxafine (Effexor) and duloxetine (Cymbalta) affect two neurotransmitters, serotonin and norepinephrine.

While all of these medications have been used widely to treat depression and anxiety syndromes in adults, only fluoxetine (Prozac) has been formally approved by the Food and Drug Administration (FDA) for treating major depression in children and adolescents. (Fluoxetine, sertraline, and fluvoxamine have also been approved for treating a form of chronic anxiety known as **obsessive-compulsive disorder** in this age-group.) One reason for the limited spectrum of antidepressants sanctioned by the FDA for children and adolescents is that there are far fewer controlled studies of the effects of these drugs on young people compared to that those that have been done on adults. Nevertheless, experienced practitioners have successfully utilized a variety of antidepressants to treat depression in younger patients—but they also have been aware that some children and adolescents can become more irritable, anxious, or even agitated when started on these medications.

In 2004, after combining the results of twenty-four studies encompassing nine medications and more than 4,400 children and teens treated for a number of psychiatric conditions, the FDA found that 4 percent of these young patients manifested suicidal thoughts or behavior—though *no* suicides resulted—during the first few months on medication, compared with 2 percent taking a placebo (a pill that has no physical effects). As a result, since October 2004 the FDA has required that prescribing information for *all* forms of antidepressants carry a "black box" warning, the strongest caution that the FDA gives to practitioners, about the increased risk of suicidal thinking and behavior.

There are several reasons why some children and adolescents might feel more agitated or even suicidal when first given antidepressants:

- A small percentage of depressed adults actually have **bipolar disorder** (previously known as **manic-depressive disorder**), and when first treated with antidepressants they often feel more anxious and agitated. Among children presenting with depression for the first time, a higher percentage have bipolar disorder and may thus react unfavorably to antidepressants.
- Some who are treated for depression will feel more energetic before their

- *Personal and family faith.* A meaningful relationship with God and a sense of His love and involvement in an individual's life can have a significant stabilizing effect on mood and behavior. An ongoing personal commitment to God and

sad mood lifts. But a person who is both depressed and energetic may decided to "do something"—especially an impulsive, self-destructive act.
- Some people respond to antidepressants with **akathesia**—an unpleasant sensation that one cannot hold still physically or mentally, especially when a medication is started or a dose is increased. Children may be more prone to this side effect.
- Some antidepressants are associated with unpleasant sensations, such as anxiety and irritability, when one or more doses are missed. Fluoxetine (Prozac) has a long duration of action and is uncommonly associated with this effect.

Given these concerns, one might wonder whether antidepressants should ever be given to children or teenagers. While it is inappropriate to use these medications without careful evaluation and follow-up, it would also be very unwise for a parent to refuse this type of treatment for a young person who truly needs it. Antidepressants can be helpful—even lifesaving—and safe when given with appropriate precautions and proper supervision:

- Make sure both you and your child/adolescent have a basic understanding of what the medication is supposed to do and how it is to be taken. *Do not change or drop doses without talking with the prescribing physician (or if he is unavailable, the person covering for him).*
- You would be wise to arrange for counseling for your child or teenager while medication is being used. (One important study involving over four hundred adolescents with major depression—the Treatment of Adolescents with Depressions Study, or TADS—found that the combination of fluoxetine and counseling was more effective than either the counseling or medication by itself.)[5] Talking regularly with a professional who works with young people can identify stressors, clarify issues at home and school, improve coping skills, and serve as an additional safety net when the going gets tough.
- Keep checking in with your child or teen about how she is feeling. Make sure that she understands she can and should tell you if she is having suicidal thoughts or other bothersome symptoms while taking medication.

The FDA recommends that a child or adolescent who is starting an antidepressant be followed closely by the prescribing physician: A typical approach might be a weekly contact (in person or by telephone) for the first month, then every other week (preferably in person) for the second month, then monthly (or more frequently if needed) thereafter.[6] It is very important that both child and parent report any side effects or changes in behavior—*especially* if these involve increasing anxiety or irritability—as well as any self-destructive thoughts or actions. ■

positive connections with others who are caring and like-minded in faith serve to build a child's emotional world on a firm foundation, such that it will not crumble when the inevitable strains and storms of life arrive. Unfortunately, some religious situations involving intense legalism or an atmosphere of continuing condemnation can contribute to anxiety and depression.

What Can Be Done about Depression?

A parent's role in dealing with depression can be broken down into three key tasks:

Be alert for signs of depression.

These have already been listed, but it bears emphasizing that *parents are often caught off guard by their child's or adolescent's depression.* This disorder can occur even in the most stable home where children have been reared by devoted parents who provide consistent love and limits. Remember that for many individuals depression is caused primarily by a biochemical imbalance in the brain and not by bad parenting or a personal crisis. Don't assume that "it can't happen in our home," because in doing so you might ignore or write off as a "bad attitude" significant changes in mood or behavior that desperately need your attention.

If you suspect that your child or adolescent might be depressed or suicidal (see page 572), seek appropriate help immediately.

Depression is not a character weakness or a sign of parental failure. It is as important and *treatable* a problem as diabetes or asthma, and like those conditions, it can lead to serious consequences—including death—if it is ignored. The approaches to this problem include:

First and foremost, listen carefully to your child or adolescent, and take his feelings and problems seriously. Expressions of worry or a sad mood should never be met with indifference or (worse) a shallow rebuff ("You'll get over it" or "Snap out of it!"). Sit down, shut off the TV, look your child in the eye, and really listen—without judging, rebuking, or trivializing it. It might help enormously if you can say honestly that you (or others you know and respect) have struggled with some of the same feelings.

Get a physician's evaluation. Usually a number of physical symptoms such as fatigue or headaches will need to be assessed, and rarely a specific disorder (for example, an abnormal level of thyroid hormone) will be responsible for the entire gamut of emotional and physical complaints.

Get counseling with a qualified individual about the issues of life, including past problems, family interactions, stressful situations, and other concerns. This should be carried out with someone who is trained to do this type of work with young people and who also shares your basic values. Do not assume that a depression can be "straightened out" in one or two counseling sessions. Normally several weeks (sometimes months) of work will be necessary. Be prepared to become involved yourself at some point in the process. No depression occurs in a vacuum, and family dynamics very often are part of both the problem and the solution.

Be willing to consider medication. This can play an important role in the treatment of depression. **Antidepressants** can normalize disturbances in neurotransmitter function and are neither addictive nor an "escape from reality." On the contrary, more often than not they allow the individual to tackle life issues more effectively, and they greatly accelerate the recovery process. The decision to use one or more of these medications will involve a careful discussion with a physician who is well versed in their use in children and adolescents. (See sidebar "Antidepressants in Children and Adolescents" on page 576.) This will either be a psychiatrist who cares for this age-group or a primary-care physician (a pediatrician or family practitioner) who is experienced in prescribing antidepressants for young people and monitoring progress and any side effects. Assuming that positive results are obtained, it is common to continue medication on a maintenance basis for a number of months. (The neurochemistry of depression is not like a streptococcal throat infection that can be resolved with ten days of treatment.)

Be aware of the types of input your child or adolescent is receiving when his emotions are stormy. We've already mentioned the dark themes emanating from some corners of popular culture. If the music pounding through his headphones is feeding his brain a steady stream of rage and pessimism, a moratorium on this material would be in order. (Indeed, this would be wise even if he *isn't* depressed.)

But what about those speaking directly to him? Is he being ridiculed, bullied, or isolated at school? Are his interactions fueling self-destructive thoughts? It is possible to find *anything* on the Internet—including irresponsible individuals and Web sites that encourage your child or adolescent to commit suicide. Calmly but persistently talk with him, talk with his friends, and yes, even look through his room and check his computer when he's at school. Your responsibility for his life and health override any considerations of privacy.

Be willing to consider hospitalization. In severe cases, where the emotions have been extremely unstable or there has been suicidal behavior, hospitalization will usually be recommended in order to initiate treatment and ensure safety. The type of program utilized will vary considerably, depending on community resources, health insurance benefits, and the needs of the depressed individual.

Continue to support and pray for your depressed child. She needs to know that you are there for her and that you do not think of her as "crazy" or a colossal failure for having this problem. Prayer serves as an acknowledgment by parent and child that God alone has a complete understanding of this complex situation. Counseling and medication may serve as useful tools, but they are best used under His guidance.

Be on the lookout for risks of suicide and signs of suicidal behavior.

Many of the unique features of depression among young people also increase their risk of suicide. In particular, the intensity of their emotions and a shortage of life experiences that might allow them to imagine a hopeful future beyond an immediate crisis may give rise to self-destructive behavior, especially on an impulsive basis. In order to reduce the chance of a tragic loss of life, be aware not only of the signs of depression, which have already been listed, but also of the following risks and warning signs:

- *A previous suicide attempt.* This is considered the most significant predictor of a future suicide; between 30 and 40 percent of adolescents who commit suicide have attempted it at least once in the past.
- *A family history of suicide.* Compared to their nonsuicidal peers, teenagers who kill themselves are more likely than their peers to have a history of a family member who has committed suicide.
- *Expressions of intense guilt or hopelessness.*

- *Threatening, talking, or joking about suicide.* It is important to have a heart-to-heart conversation with any child or adolescent who makes comments such as "I would be better off dead" or "Nothing matters anymore." Find out what is going on in his life and how he is feeling, and make it clear that you are committed to obtaining whatever help he might need to work through his problems. Broaching the subject of suicide does not encourage it but rather increases the likelihood that a successful intervention can be started.
- *"Cleaning house."* You should be very concerned and should investigate immediately if a child or adolescent—whether your own or a member of someone else's family—begins to give away clothing, entire CD collections, or other favorite possessions. This is a common behavior among young people who are planning suicide.
- *A gun in the home.* Among young people, more suicides are carried out using firearms than by any other method—more than 60 percent of teens who kill themselves use a gun. If anyone in your family—especially a teenager—is having a problem with depression, remove all guns from the home and keep them out.
- *Alcohol or drug abuse.* One frightening aspect of substance abuse is that it can trigger erratic, self-destructive behavior for which little or no warning was given. A mild depression can suddenly plummet to suicidal intensity with the help of drugs or alcohol. Because of the unpredictable actions of chemicals on the system, a number of deaths occur among youngsters who did not intend to hurt themselves.
- *Suicide among other adolescents in your community.* Occasionally one or more suicides in a community or school precipitate a disastrous "cluster" of self-destructive behavior among local teens.
- *A sudden, major loss or humiliation.* All of the stressful life events that were listed earlier in this section—such as the death of a loved one, parental separation, or failure on an important test—not only can provoke a depressive episode but can also precipitate an unexpected suicide attempt.

If you feel that there is any possibility of a self-destructive act by your child, it is important that you not only express your concern but also *seek help immediately*. You may want to contact your child's or adolescent's physician for advice or referral. If anyone in your family has dealt with a counselor, this individual may be the appropriate initial contact. An evaluation at the nearest emergency department may be necessary. Many communities have a mental-health center that offers on-the-spot assessment of an individual's suicide risk or even an assessment team that will come to your home. *Stay with your child or adolescent* (or make certain that he or she remains in the company of a responsible adult) until you have reasonable assurance from a qualified individual and a clear commitment from your son or daughter that suicide is not going to be attempted. In situations where assurance cannot be obtained, the suicidal individual may need to be hospitalized for safety, further assessment, and the initiation of treatment. You will also need to take appropriate safety precautions, including removing any guns from the home and controlling access to medications.

What If a Child or Teenager Attempts Suicide?

Fortunately, the vast majority of suicide attempts by children and adolescents are unsuccessful. Some of these result in significant medical problems, while many are considered gestures or cries for help. *Any deliberate self-destructive act, whether planned or impulsive, should be taken very seriously, regardless of the severity of the outcome.* An evaluation at an emergency room should be carried out; subsequent hospitalization for medical treatment or observation is not uncommon.

After any medical problems have been resolved, a formal assessment by a qualified professional is mandatory. The course of action to be taken will depend upon a number of factors and may range from ongoing counseling while the child or adolescent remains at home to a formal treatment program in a psychiatric hospital setting. The latter approach is usually chosen both to ensure safety and to begin intensive treatment. While the details of treatment that might be used in such settings are beyond the scope of this book, it is important for parents to understand and approve of the approaches that will be used and to play an active role in their child's or adolescent's recovery process. As upset or guilty as you might feel under such circumstances, this is the time to draw close to your child who is in such pain and not to communicate shock and dismay ("How could you do such a thing?"). Above all, she will need loving and optimistic people on her team, and it will help immensely if her parents are at the top of the roster.

Passing the Baton: Instilling Values and Virtues in the Next Generation

If we were to attempt to summarize the scope of a parent's career in a single sentence, we might start with the following job description: a twenty-year process of nurturing and guiding a precious human being from the utter helplessness of infancy to the independence and maturity of adulthood. Here's another of way of putting it: One of your primary goals as a parent is to work yourself out of a job.

No matter how old your child grows, it is likely that you will always feel like a parent—but your role of guidance and authority has a very definite time limit and must eventually end. You should experience a major payoff when this occurs: Instead of having a dependent child for the rest of your life, you will have an adult friend whose company and conversation you will savor and who can help *you* grow as an individual.

One of the most important tasks of parenting will be working with your child, step-by-step, through this gradual release. Each child's pathway toward independence and each parent's willingness to grant it will be unique, and the process will not always be smooth. Judging your child's readiness for new freedoms and responsibilities is one of parenting's fine arts and should be shaped by awareness of her strengths and weaknesses, collaboration with your spouse (or a trusted adult if you are a single parent), soul-searching, and prayer.

But there's another dimension to this task beyond escorting your child from infancy to adulthood, one that all too easily can become lost amidst daily routines and responsibilities—especially when the pace of life quickens to a pace we might refer to as "routine panic." Keep in mind that, with rare exception, your child is going to live many years as an independent adult. *I can't wait,* you might be thinking, but you also need to ask yourself, *What values will my child carry with her as she makes that inevitable exit from my direct guidance and supervision?*

The question isn't if she'll have values, but which ones, and who will shape them? Will those values reflect what you say and (more importantly) what you do, day in and day out? Will they be molded by the precepts of Scripture and the life and teachings of Jesus? Will she borrow them from her friends or the music she listens to or the

TV shows she watches? If you are not intentional about and attentive to this critical assignment, any number of other influences will mold her values—and the result may be a far cry from what you would have intended.

It is critical not to underestimate the importance of this aspect of your parenting assignment. Children are, for a season, entrusted by their Creator, the perfect parent, to human fathers and mothers who are anything but perfect. Whether you are a single father/mother or a married couple, it is important to remember that your child is definitely a gift to you, and that you are a gift to your child. Your acceptance, attention, values, and role modeling will have a profound influence on the person he or she becomes.

Passing the baton: What will your children carry with them into adulthood?

In one very significant respect, parenting is like a relay race: One generation completes a very long lap and then passes a crucial baton to the runners in the next generation. In an Olympic relay, the gold medal usually hinges on the skill with which the baton is passed between the runners. If the baton is fumbled, the runner will still arrive at the finish line but probably with some disappointment over the final result.

Parents, grandparents, and others who are responsible for rearing the citizens of the next generation must repeatedly ask themselves some critical questions: Will this child carry with him into adulthood the values that are truly important? Will these values play a significant role in his life, his career, and his own family? Will they be passed on to his own children?

MAKING MEMORIES

There are many simple things you can do as a parent to build memories and enhance special occasions with your child. However, when schedules are jammed with activities, some of life's simplest but most satisfying pleasures may be lost. Taking the time to create special memories can help cement a wonderful relationship with your children.

Below are some ideas that have been successful memory builders for many families. This is merely a list to help stimulate your own creative juices. Use these or add your own ideas to the list, but don't let years pass without creating some special times that your children will cherish and perhaps pass on to their own children.

Give the gift of time to your children.

- Schedule time with each of your children and make these "dates" as important on your calendar as any other commitment.
- If you are running errands, take one of the kids along and talk about what she finds interesting—her favorite game, toy, or book, for example.
- Make a special occasion of taking your child to work with you, and in so doing share this part of your life with him.

Record your thoughts, hopes, and dreams for your child in letters and journals.

- Letters can be written while you are pregnant and then given to your child later in life.

Jesus asked a question that has given pause to men and women for two thousand years: "What good will it be for a man if he gains the whole world, yet forfeits his soul?" (Matthew 16:26). A similar question should be pondered regularly by parents: "What good is it if I achieve all my aspirations but my children reject the values I care about?"

The Basic Goals

As a parent you have been entrusted by God to help mold your child's character, values, and spirituality, while preparing her for such practical matters as choosing a career, handling finances, and finding a spouse. This is a tall order, but the important assignment of preparing your child for the future can indeed be accomplished—one small step at a time.

The first step is to define what your specific goals should be. This chapter is intended to help with that process by serving as a basic road map, one that can be reviewed every year to gauge whether your race is still on course and your baton ready to be passed. You may find the length and breadth of this endeavor daunting. *How can I instill all of my values and virtues in my children? I'm still trying to develop them in my own life!* If you realize that you can't accomplish all of these goals perfectly and that you can't be an infallible guide to life for your child (because you're still figuring out a few things yourself),

Children can't grow without taking risks. Toddlers can't walk initially without falling down. . . . And, ultimately, an adolescent can't enter young adulthood until we release him from our protective custody.

Dr. Dobson Answers Your Questions

- Letters can be written for special occasions, such as a graduation from elementary school, public profession of faith, special birthday, first day of school, or first date.
- Letters can be written to celebrate a success or to console after a discouragement.
- Even after the baton is passed, letters can be beautiful gifts at occasions such as engagements, weddings, births, achievements, and even failures.

Put special notes in your child's lunch box or on her pillow. Tell your child how much she means to you.

Take special family vacations. Follow the Santa Fe Trail if your family is into history. Scout out baseball stadiums. Go rafting. Or spend time at home camping in the backyard.

Make holidays special. Start new traditions, or re-create old ones.

On your child's thirteenth birthday, take a moment or an entire evening to celebrate the transition to adolescence. Consider presenting her with a special gift (for example, a ring, a necklace, or a "faith, hope, and love" charm) that can serve as a symbol of commitment to preserving the gift of sex for her wedding night.

When your son or daughter is ready to leave the nest for college or another destination, write a "release" letter (see page 603). ∎

congratulations! Acknowledging this fact is the beginning of parental wisdom. You can be certain that God knew your shortcomings before entrusting you with a child, and you would be wise to seek His counsel on a regular basis.

As you think about these concepts, you may experience misgivings or even remorse. You probably haven't cherished every moment with your child (few parents do), and it's likely that at some point (if not many times) you may have felt burdened with—or even resentful of—the demands of parenting. Perhaps your children are already in the midst of stormy adolescence or are grown and gone, and you are painfully aware that you have not exactly been the world's best cheerleader, teacher, or coach. But it is never too late to make course corrections—and amends—as a parent. Even if your children are already grown, what you have learned (sometimes the hard way) can still benefit *their* children. What ultimately matters is that you ask for forgiveness where it is needed and then move forward, providing input and support that is appropriate for their current stage of life.

The following pages will focus on five key areas of your child's life: spiritual growth, character development, handling finances, choosing a vocation, and preparing for marriage.

Spiritual Growth

It is a sad fact that some children who have been taken regularly to Sunday school and church will grow up to ignore God and reject the values their parents taught (or *thought* they had taught) at home. To their utter dismay, Mom and Dad learn too late that this training just didn't "take," and they wonder what went wrong.

The Old Testament story of Eli is an example. The devoted priest failed to influence the behavior of his own boys; both sons became profane and evil young men. Samuel—one of the greatest men in the Bible—witnessed Eli's parental mistakes and yet proceeded to lose his children too! The message the Bible communicates is loud and clear: Devotion to God is not inherited. God does not guarantee that our children will follow Him simply because we do. The reason, of course, is that every child must eventually decide *on his or her own* whether to follow, ignore, or reject God. If parents could lock in a child's commitment to God—if it were in fact impossible for the child to say no—then the child's love for God would not be love at all but the meaningless response of a preprogrammed machine.

Nevertheless, the fact that parents cannot preordain their child's faith does not mean that they shouldn't attempt to encourage it in a healthy way and to pray daily for his spiritual growth. Parents are admonished in the book of Proverbs to "train a child in the way he should go"—which means, among other things, that parents need some specific ideas about what that "way" should be. It is appropriate and desirable for a child to be exposed to a carefully conceived and systematic program of spiritual training. Yet many parents approach this project in a haphazard manner or yield to the all too common "let the pros do it" mentality that hands over this responsibility to a child's Sunday school teacher or youth-group leader. But as influential and dedicated as these people might be, your child normally won't spend more than a few hours a week with them, at most.

At the beginning of the Special Concerns section entitled "Principles of Discipline and Training" (page 259), we offered the following definition of discipline: "Training and instruction that is intended to produce a specific pattern of behavior, character development, and moral or mental improvement." This encompasses much more than the common concept of discipline as mere correction (or punishment) for wrongdoing. Similarly, a child's acquisition of spiritual values encompasses far more than learning some Bible stories, singing songs about Jesus, or bowing his head for a few moments before taking the first bite of dinner, as meaningful as these activities might be. Indeed, spiritual values cannot and should not be isolated from the definition of discipline above. If they don't affect behavior, develop character, and bring about moral and mental improvement, they are little more than sanctified hot air.

Whether or not you've already read the section on training and discipline, now would be a good time to look through it, paying specific attention to the application of many of its principles to transmitting spiritual values. A number of these are summarized in the sidebar "How Do You Encourage Character Growth and Spiritual Development?" on page 596. In addition, here are several "food for thought" questions to stimulate some reflection, prayer, and conversation about this important topic:

Do you have a clear understanding of your beliefs about God and your relationship with Him? While many mothers and fathers have spent years cultivating a living, growing, and well-articulated faith, others arrive at parenthood with little or no sense of God's role in their lives, except perhaps for some religious teachings and experiences dimly remembered from childhood. Some sense that their children should go to Sunday school or receive some type of religious training, even if they themselves don't buy into those teachings. The plot thickens when Mom and Dad are not on the same page, or even in the same book, spiritually speaking: What should the kids be taught, and by whom? Obviously, the more unified parents are on this important subject, and the earlier these questions are addressed, the better—but it's never too late. Communicating regularly with your spouse about your individual and mutual spiritual journeys isn't just for Sunday morning, but a vital topic for everyday conversation. If you are a single parent or are married to someone who is disinterested in this subject, by all means find a pastor, mature friend, or counselor who is willing to talk with you about it. Another option would be to read a book such as *The Purpose-Driven Life* by Rick Warren as an individual, a couple, or in a small-group study. This book provides a straightforward, back-to-basics approach to beginning, maintaining, and maturing one's relationship with God.

Are you deliberate about praying regularly for each of your children? This is the most important component of the whole process of transmitting spiritual values (not to mention the rest of your parenting assignment). One of the biggest mistakes we could ever make would be to assume that we can dial in a child's or teenager's decision to commit her life to Jesus Christ and then serve Him wholeheartedly. Acknowledging our lack of control over our child's physical and spiritual future, and our dependence on the One who holds it, is the beginning of wisdom. Find a time or occasion every day—perhaps as you are arising in the morning or settling in for a night's sleep—to bring each child before God and to be transparent with Him about your joys and concerns for this young life that He has entrusted to you. Along with a daily commitment to pray about each child, consider setting aside a day every week or month for more concerted and detailed prayer, perhaps in the context of time spent alone or even fasting. If at all possible, record your prayers, thoughts, and observations in a journal. Years from now these will be a priceless and powerful legacy for your children to read.

How do you sort out the input and advice that you get? Most parents hear plenty of opinions about child rearing from relatives and friends, books and magazines, TV and radio programs, church, and the Internet. You may hear fewer specific advisories about teaching spiritual values to children, however, unless someone in your life is passionate about this subject. Indeed, you may have to seek it out, and we've included a few good resources at the end of this segment. But as you evaluate various ideas, think and pray about which of them might work best in your own family. As with discipline, a commitment to the overall spiritual direction you are seeking for your children (and yourself) is more important than a "cookbook," formula-based approach. You must be prepared to improvise and make adjustments based on the age and temperament of each child, and to accept the fact that what seems to have an impact with one may not with another. At the same time, you must also remember that spiritual growth often involves seeds that may be planted now without bearing obvious fruit for many months or even years, often after they have been watered by a loving parent's persistent prayer.

Are you aware of the impact of your own childhood experiences on your approach to spiritual matters in your own home? If family devotions were the low point of your week (for whatever reason) as a child, you may mistakenly assume that they can't be successful in your own family. If your parents were noncommittal or disinterested in spiritual matters, you might find yourself gravitating to the opposite extreme of trying to micromanage your child's faith. Or if your spiritual upbringing was steeped in legalism that emphasized "rules and regs" rather than a loving relationship with God, you may be tempted to take a hands-off approach that assumes your kids can figure out their faith without your input. Every family is a unique civilization with its own history, traditions, and patterns of everyday living—including the ways in which God is discussed and honored. The spiritual traditions with which you grew up may serve as a wonderful foundation for your own family to build upon or may include baggage you want to throw overboard so that you can start afresh with your own children.

What kind of emotional attraction—or baggage—does your everyday family life attach to your spiritual values? This question is a corollary to the one we just asked. Is your home a place where love, safety, sanity, good humor, kindness, and appropriate limits are continually in residence? Or is it a place where anger, arguments, chaos, bitterness, and extremes of discipline (whether authoritarian or permissive) are the (dis)order of the day? Obviously no family is perfect, but keep in mind that the soil of the young heart in which you sow spiritual seeds will be strongly affected by the prevailing emotional weather at home. Many prodigals who spend months or years wandering away from God during adolescence or young adulthood are drawn back toward the faith they were taught during childhood because of their emotional ties to family and home. And sadly, too many would-be disciples have become long-term prodigals because they were desperate to escape a painful home environment that included a lot of empty or even toxic religious talk.

A tough but critical question for Dad: Are you aware of the powerful role you play in your child's *emotional* understanding of God's character? Whatever the breadth and depth of our grasp of biblical teaching, it can be challenging to hear about our heavenly Father without evoking some memories and emotions associated with our earthly one. If Dad is a perfectionist or unpredictable or emotionally disconnected or prone to fearsome outbursts of temper, guess what may come to mind (and heart) when the kids hear about their Father in heaven. Likewise, guess what they are likely to take to heart about God if Dad has consistently provided love, compassion, guidance, and security.

How are you handling tough questions, especially as your children are passing through adolescence? We mentioned in the Special Concerns section about discipline that there are times when it is appropriate to answer a young child's "why" questions with "Because I said so" or "I'm the Mom, that's why!" As they get older, however, they should be learning the reasons and rationale behind your rules and (hopefully) internalizing your values. But when it comes to spiritual matters, some parents with strong convictions talk to their teenagers as though they were two-year-olds. If your middle schooler asks why it's wrong to have sex outside of marriage, "Because the Bible says so" is a correct answer, but helping her understand many of the reasons *why* the Bible takes this stand will provide additional conviction for her to make wise decisions about sexuality. Similarly, if she asks some probing questions about God, the Bible, or troubling events—"Why would God allow so many people to die in that earthquake last week?"—you would be wise to avoid giving pat answers or shutting down the conversation because you're not comfortable with the direction it seems to be going. Having strong convictions and a solid grasp of the Scriptures doesn't mean that complex issues must be reduced to simplistic formulas, or that you must have the answer to everything, or that you can't have some respectful and productive dialogue with someone whose beliefs don't exactly match your own—especially when that person is one of your children.

Are spiritual values compartmentalized into limited, segregated, and perhaps ceremonial time slots? In chapter 10 we broached the subject of teaching moral and spiritual values to preschoolers by citing a critical passage from the Old Testament, which bears repeating here:

> Hear, O Israel: The LORD our God, the LORD is one. Love the LORD
> your God with all your heart and with all your soul and with all your
> strength. These commandments that I give you today are to be upon
> your hearts. Impress them on your children. Talk about them when you
> sit at home and when you walk along the road, when you lie down and
> when you get up. Tie them as symbols on your hands and bind them
> on your foreheads. Write them on the doorframes of your houses and
> on your gates. *(Deuteronomy 6:4-9)*

It's certainly appropriate to designate special times of the day or week—mealtime grace, bedtime prayers, Sunday school, church services, family devotions—when God is to be the center of attention. These can indeed play a formative role in your child's life. But what about soccer practices, rides to school, mealtime conversations, or browsing at the video store—what Deuteronomy so wonderfully summarizes as sitting at home, walking along the road, lying down, and getting up? You may not be able offer a Bible verse that applies to math homework, but your patience while helping your daughter complete a tough assignment may serve as a profound illustration of that particular fruit of the Spirit (see Galatians 5:22-23).

As you consider how you might encourage your child to develop spiritual sensitivity and maturity, it's important for you to have some clearly defined goals in mind. Below is a checklist for parents, a set of targets that apply to both childhood and adulthood. Some of these involve subject matter or require a level of maturity beyond that of young children. But you can still gently and consistently urge them toward these targets during their impressionable early years. Your three-year-old probably can't read the Bible herself, for example, but she can look and listen as you read Bible stories to her from an illustrated version. These concepts provide the foundation upon which both grown-up faith and biblical knowledge will be built. They should be taught deliberately and affirmed to children in a manner appropriate for their age.

Concept I: Loving God

One of the teachers of the law came and heard them debating. Noticing that Jesus had given them a good answer, he asked him, "Of all the commandments, which is the most important?"

"The most important one," answered Jesus, "is this: 'Hear, O Israel, the Lord our God, the Lord is one. Love the Lord your God with all your heart and with all your soul and with all your mind and with all your strength.'"

(Mark 12:28-30)

- Is your child learning of God's love through the love, tenderness, and mercy of his parents?
- Is he learning to talk about the Lord Jesus and include Him in his thoughts and plans as part of his everyday experiences?
- Is he learning to turn to God for help whenever he is frightened, anxious, or lonely?
- Is he learning to read the Bible?
- Is he learning to pray?
- Is he learning the meaning of faith and trust?
- Does he understand that God loved him so much that He sent His Son to die for him?
- Is he learning that loving and serving God is the ultimate source of joy and freedom in life?

Concept II: Loving others

"The second is this: 'Love your neighbor as yourself.' There is no commandment greater than these." *(Mark 12:31)*

- Is she learning to understand and empathize with others?
- Is she learning not to be selfish and demanding?
- Is she learning to share?
- Is she learning not to gossip and criticize others?
- Is she learning to serve others?

Concept III: Following God's rules

Fear God and keep his commandments, for this is the whole duty of man.

(Ecclesiastes 12:13)

In addition to loving God and loving neighbors:

- Is he learning to honor God's name and not to misuse it?
- Is he learning that one day of the week—the Sabbath—is to be set apart from normal activities and dedicated to God?
- Is he learning to honor and respect his parents?
- Is he learning to value human life at all ages—from conception to advanced age—without regard to appearance, race, physical condition, or mental capacity?
- Is he learning to respect the gift of sex and the importance of preserving sexual experiences for marriage?
- Is he learning to respect the possessions of others: neither stealing nor borrowing without permission, and making restitution if he damages another person's property?
- Is he learning to be truthful and honest?
- Is he learning the ultimate insignificance of material goods?

Concept IV: Following God's direction

Teach me to do your will, for you are my God. *(Psalm 143:10)*

- Is she learning that her primary purpose on earth is to serve the Lord?
- Is she learning to obey her parents as preparation for later obedience to God?
- Is she learning to behave properly in church?
- Is she learning a healthy appreciation for God's justice as well as His love?
- Is she learning that there are people in many types of benevolent authority roles—caregivers, teachers, coaches, police, youth leaders—to whom she must submit?
- Is she learning the meaning of sin and its inevitable consequences?

Concept V: Acquiring self-control

The fruit of the Spirit is love, joy, peace, patience, kindness, goodness, faithfulness, gentleness and self-control. *(Galatians 5:22-23)*

- Is he learning to control his impulses?
- Is he learning to take proper care of the body that God has given him?
- Is he learning to work and carry responsibility?
- Is he learning to tolerate minor frustration?
- Is he learning to memorize and quote Scripture?
- Is he learning to give a portion of his allowance (and other money) to God?

Concept VI: Acquiring an appropriate self-concept

Everyone who exalts himself will be humbled, and he who humbles himself will be exalted. *(Luke 14:11)*

- Is she learning a sense of appreciation?
- Is she learning to thank God for the good things in life?
- Is she learning to forgive and forget?
- Is she learning the vast difference between self-worth and egotistical pride?
- Is she learning to bow in reverence before the God of the universe? ■

Some additional resources that you may find helpful include:

The Focus on the Family *Parents' Guide to the Spiritual Growth of Children*, edited by John Trent, Rick Osborne, and Kurt Bruner (Tyndale, 2003)

Teaching Kids about God: An Age-by-Age Plan for Parents of Children from Birth to Age Twelve, edited by John Trent, Rick Osborne, and Kurt Bruner (Tyndale, 2003)

The Focus on the Family *Parents' Guide to the Spiritual Mentoring of Teens*, edited by Joe White and Jim Weidmann (Tyndale, 2001)

801 Questions Kids Ask about God, edited by Anisa Baker (Focus on the Family Publishers, 2000)

The Family Compass, by Kurt and Olivia Bruner (Chariot Victor, 1999)

Character Development

As we noted previously, the development of positive, stable character traits should flow directly from spiritual growth. If a person's religious activities and affirmations don't have any consistent impact on behavior, then his faith is shallow, false, or self-deluding.

> What good is it, my brothers, if a man claims to have faith but has no
> deeds? Can such faith save him? Suppose a brother or sister is without
> clothes and daily food. If one of you says to him, "Go, I wish you well;
> keep warm and well fed," but does nothing about his physical needs,
> what good is it? In the same way, faith by itself, if it is not accompanied
> by action, is dead. *(James 2:14-17)*

Similarly, attempts to train a child to be "good" will have only limited success if the child does not have an understanding of God's love and justice, the need for genuine repentance, and the importance of ongoing submission to God's leadership. A child can make all the right spiritual noises and toe the line when you're watching—but what happens when no one is looking, or when he's tempted to compromise?

Spiritual maturity and virtuous character traits that persist into adulthood will not develop during random lectures crammed into a few minutes every month. Parents need to plan ahead, focusing on the values they intend to instill. They must also take advantage of unscheduled "teachable moments," when a situation naturally lends itself to a discussion about positive (or negative) behavior. However this important task is carried out, the following are some important character traits, listed alphabetically, on which to focus.

Courage is frequently portrayed in movies and cartoons as the primary requirement for superheroes embroiled in daring exploits. But children need to understand that courage is also important for everyday life, both now and in the future. Indeed, one who learns courage as a child is more likely to be secure as an adult. Courage encompasses several elements:

- Daring to attempt difficult but worthy projects
- Saying *no* to the pressure of the crowd

- Remaining true to convictions, even when they are unpopular or inconvenient
- Being outgoing and friendly, even when it's uncomfortable

Courage can also apply to more stressful situations:

- Applying resources in creative ways when faced with overwhelming odds
- Following difficult instructions in the face of danger
- Confronting an opponent in an honorable way, confident that what is morally right will ultimately succeed

Determination can help your child avoid becoming a pessimist. This trait helps a child:

- Realize that present struggles are essential for future achievement
- Break down a seemingly impossible task by concentrating on achievable goals
- Expend whatever energy is necessary to complete a project
- Reject any distraction that will hinder the completion of a task
- Prepare to handle hardships that lie ahead, whether the task is spiritual, physical, emotional, or relational

Fidelity and chastity are rarely taught within our culture (by movies, television programs, popular music, etc.) and not as often by educators, coaches, or even church leaders as they were a generation ago. Therefore it is important that your children hear clearly from you about the benefits of reserving sexual activity for marriage. Children also need to grasp the serious potential consequences of sexual immorality: sexually transmitted infections and diseases, infertility, crisis pregnancies, and a broken heart (see the Special Concerns section, "A Parent's Guide to Teen Sexuality," on page 509).

Honesty is not always rewarded in our culture, but it is a bedrock virtue. Without it, all of your child's most important relationships will be compromised and unstable. Children should be taught that truthfulness is critical when dealing with:

- Family members, friends, and acquaintances
- School
- Organizations, including future employers
- Governmental agencies
- God

Dishonesty must be discouraged in all its forms, whether it be outright lying to another individual, misrepresenting to an employer what one has (or hasn't) done, cheating on a test, plagiarizing, or doctoring an income tax return.

My son, if your heart is wise, then my heart will be glad; my inmost being will rejoice when your lips speak what is right.

Proverbs 23:15-16

Humility arises from an honest assessment of one's own strengths and weaknesses, such that boasting is not necessary to gain acceptance or to feel contentment. Humility also involves submission to duly constituted authority, obedience to the law, and fairness in work and play. Most important, humility will keep your child on his knees in prayer.

Kindness and friendliness should be presented to a child as admirable and far superior to being "tough." Children need to be taught that it is usually better to understand than to confront, and that gentleness—especially toward those who are younger or weaker—is in fact a sign of strength. *Do not allow your child to become a bully.*

Love in many ways encompasses and surpasses other virtues, as stated by the apostle Paul nearly two thousand years ago:

> Love is patient, love is kind. It does not envy, it does not boast, it is not proud. It is not rude, it is not self-seeking, it is not easily angered, it keeps no record of wrongs. Love does not delight in evil but rejoices with the truth. It always protects, always trusts, always hopes, always perseveres.
> *(1 Corinthians 13:4-7)*

Children should be taught—and shown—how to love their friends, neighbors, and even adversaries.

Loyalty and dependability are traits needed for success in many arenas of life. A person who is flighty and cannot honor a commitment is unlikely to find true happiness or success. Your children need to learn the importance of loyalty to family, employer,

HOW DO YOU ENCOURAGE CHARACTER GROWTH AND SPIRITUAL DEVELOPMENT?

The answer hinges on the little word *time*. These traits mature over many years as parents leave enough *time* in their busy lives to spend enough *time* with their children to talk about these subjects many, many *times*.

With enough time, you can encourage spiritual growth and character development in the following ways:

- *Be your child's primary role model.* Let him see the values you care about enacted every day in front of him. "Do as I say, not as I do" is a recipe for moral failure.
- *When you have done or said something that was mistaken, inappropriate, or just plain wrong, admit it.* Have the courage to apologize for what went wrong, and then explain why it was wrong. You will gain great respect from your children for doing so, and they won't forget what you say in these moments.
- *Read or tell stories that illustrate the values you care about.* The Bible is full of them. So is other literature, including dozens of passages that have been compiled by William J. Bennett in anthologies such as *The Book of Virtues*, *The Moral Compass*, and *The Children's Book of Virtues*.
- *Seize the teachable moment.* When a situation arises in which a moral example (good or bad) is before you, talk to your child about it. *This should not be limited to times during which you are correcting misbehavior.* It might occur, for example, while watching a video, a ball game, an erratic driver on the freeway, or another child's tantrum in the mall.
- *Praise your child—in front of others, whenever possible—when he does what is right.* When correcting him or administering disciplinary measures, do so in private.
- *Pray specifically for your child's spiritual and character development.* ■

country, church, school, and other organizations and institutions to which they will eventually make commitments. If a child learns to be reliable and stand by his word, he will be trusted and see opportunities open before him throughout life.

Orderliness and cleanliness may or may not be "next to godliness," but they can increase a person's chances of success in many areas of life. While no one has ever died of dirty-room syndrome, a child who can learn to keep his possessions organized and in order will eventually be able to use his resources to their greatest efficiency. Personal cleanliness and good grooming speak of self-respect and project an important message to others: I care enough about those around me to try to appear basically pleasant.

Respect is a critical commodity in human relationships, whether within families, organizations, or entire nations. It has largely been lost in our culture, and it desperately needs to be regained. It encompasses basic courtesy, politeness, and manners toward others—and much more. While children and teenagers should receive basic training in polite speech and manners, these can also be a facade that masks contempt for the other person. True respect encompasses not just speech but core attitudes and behavior toward virtually everything—life, property, parents, those in proper authority, friends, strangers, the beliefs and rights of others, nature, and most of all God. While disrespectful behavior may reflect ignorance or at worst selfish and destructive attitudes, too many children have lost respect for their own body and mind long before they arrive at adulthood. While parents want (and should receive) respect from their children, they must also remember that respect in all of its dimensions should be modeled every day at home.

Self-discipline and moderation are rare but valuable traits in a culture that claims that you can—and should—have it all. Children need to understand that, even if it is possible for them to do so, it is not necessary or wise to "have it all." Exercising self-discipline over physical, emotional, and financial desires can prevent illness, debt, and burnout later in life. Children should be taught the importance of the following:

- Controlling personal appetites
- Knowing the limits of body and mind
- Balancing work and recreation
- Avoiding the dangers of extreme, unbalanced viewpoints
- Engaging the brain before putting the tongue in gear

Unselfishness and sensitivity are universally appreciated and respected. A child who is more concerned about others than himself will be seen as mature beyond his years and can benefit himself and others.

Managing Finances

Teaching children how to manage money can be one of the greatest benefits parents provide for them before they leave home. Before you attempt to teach your child about money, however, determine how you are doing with your own finances. Do you set goals? Are you out of debt? Do you have long- and short-term savings? Have you begun investing in a college-education fund or your retirement? If so, you're definitely making wise decisions.

On the other hand, do you live from paycheck to paycheck? Do you have trouble keeping track of how much money is in your checking account? Is there always "too much month at the end of the money"? Are you an impulse buyer? Do you depend on your credit cards to make ends meet? If this is the case, before you start teaching your child how to manage money, you need to get your spending habits in order.

Whether you are a financial wizard or still struggling to balance your checkbook, the most important lesson your child needs to learn about money is that *God owns it all*. God is the creator and ultimate owner of every resource, and He has entrusted you to be a wise steward of whatever He has loaned to you.

It is important to realize that children begin shaping their views about money at an early age. Unfortunately, many families deal with this important topic haphazardly, offering their children little specific guidance while presuming that they can learn the nuts and bolts of money management when they're older. But if you wait until your kids are ready to leave the nest before you begin to broach this subject, they may enter adulthood at a serious disadvantage when it comes to handling their finances wisely.

As a starting point, formulate coherent policies within your family for the following three issues. Keep in mind that there are several possible approaches and reasonable viewpoints for each issue.

Unpaid responsibilities. Each child over age five (some would say as young as three or four) should have certain jobs at home to do regularly without any specific pay.

WHEN YOU PAY YOUR CHILD FOR WORK

- *Be clear about what you want done and what you are offering.* Also be sure to let your child know if there is a time frame involved ("I need this done by four o'clock").
- *Make sure that your child is capable of accomplishing the task.* If you tend to be a perfectionist, be careful that the standards you set for the work you want done aren't beyond your child's reach. On the other hand, don't make the mistake of lowering your expectations if your child is in fact capable of performing the task.
- *When possible, give your child some on-the-job training.* Your child may be more open to learn how to use tools properly, for example, if the job helps earn money to buy something she wants.
- *Pay only for jobs that are completed.* Remind your children that you as a parent aren't paid a salary unless you go to work every day, work all day, and perform your duties completely.
- *Pay for quality work.* If your child didn't do his best, you're only penalizing him by paying for laziness. Teach your child to strive to do a job right the first time.
- *Pay fairly within your budget, but don't overpay merely because you can afford it.* Even if you have a bountiful income, it doesn't make sense to pay your child fifty dollars for taking out the trash or doing the dishes. This only sets unrealistic expectations for the future. Pay according to the job description.
- *Reward extra effort.* If your child goes out of her way to do an outstanding job, reward her both emotionally and financially. ∎

These might involve tasks related to her own possessions (e.g., cleaning up her room or helping with her laundry) as well as chores done for the good of the entire family (setting the table or feeding the dog). Obviously, the duration and complexity of the assignments should be appropriate for each child's age and capabilities. A child should learn that it is usual and customary for everyone in the family to pitch in and work for the common good without expecting a reward every time.

Allowances. Parents and financial advisors alike hold all sorts of divergent opinions about this subject. Some feel that giving a child a weekly allowance teaches her to expect a "free lunch," while others see it as part of a parent's appropriate expression of provision for a child. (Parents normally don't charge their grade-school children monthly rent or leave a food bill in their lunch box, for example, yet no one sees this as contributing to an expectation of free room and board throughout life.)

If you choose to give your child a weekly or monthly allowance, you should state clearly any guidelines you might have for the money you provide. For example, is the entire amount meant to be "mad money" for fun activities, or do you want your child to allocate amounts for certain expenses (such as school lunches), savings, and giving? As your child enters adolescence, you would be wise to give her the responsibility of managing funds designated for expenses such as clothing.

Opportunities to earn money. Both you and your child will benefit if she seeks opportunities to earn extra money in exchange for the satisfactory completion of a specific task (see sidebar, page 598).

In addition to setting basic policies about money and work, consider implementing the following ideas regarding money management:

Use visual reinforcement, especially for young children. Children love to track their progress visually. Keep a chart of your child's responsibilities; use colored stars or stickers to indicate jobs she has completed. This provides an opportunity for you to praise your child for her accomplishments, which will motivate her for the next task.

Teach children to share their resources. As you provide money for your children, teach them the rewards of giving to others. Talk to them about the importance of giving back to God (who, don't forget, owns everything) by contributing regularly to church and other ministries. Encourage them by your own example.

Teach children to save. Even during the preschool years, it's not too early to teach your child to save for the future. As she gets older, she can also learn "the magic of compounding"—how money accumulates over time when left in an account that earns interest.

When your child becomes an adolescent, in addition to continuing the above principles, you need to begin releasing her from your financial supply line and preparing her to earn a living. Consider how you might teach these financial skills:

Budgeting. This will be important whether her future income is modest or abundant. Beginning at sixteen or seventeen, your adolescent should be allowed to make most of her own financial decisions. You may choose to provide her with a monthly allowance to be budgeted among several items such as clothing, toiletries, and other personal supplies you used to buy. Help her set up a budget, but she must also be given the freedom to fail—and in the process learn valuable lessons. For example, if she blows her entire clothing budget in the first six months of the year, she will have to forgo desirable purchases later on. Allocating cash between basic necessities, entertainment, savings, and giving to church and other worthy causes is a concept most teens do not understand without some guidance. But if you teach your child budgeting principles now, she'll benefit for a lifetime.

Managing a checking account. Your adolescent should be given the opportunity to use and maintain her own checking account under your supervision. It is vitally important that you teach an older teenager how to balance a checkbook monthly. Many parents obtain a credit card (with a very modest spending limit) for an older child—perhaps in the senior year of high school—to train her to use it properly. Two warnings she must receive: (1) Never buy anything with a card that she would not have purchased with cash, and (2) pay off the total amount on the credit card each month without fail.

Personal expenses: Spending and bargain hunting. Your adolescent, whether living at home or away at college, should begin to deal with the amazing ability of "miscellaneous expenses" to derail her budget. Teach her to use self-control in her spending through your example. Show her where to shop and help her learn to seek the best values for her limited supply of dollars.

Career Preparation

Children begin thinking about "what I want to be when I grow up" early in life, as they play with their friends and watch their parent(s) go off to work every day. An ideal time to start career preparation is during the preteen years. Take the time to expose your children to a variety of occupations. If your son is interested in medicine, for example, let him spend time talking to his physician about the demands and rewards of this profession. The same approach can be taken for virtually any type of career that might interest your child.

Guiding and equipping your adolescent with skills to be gainfully employed is a major responsibility, one that must begin before he leaves home. The following are some ideas that might help in this process.

Equip your adolescent to discover his strengths and weaknesses.
- Expose him to job opportunities that fit his personality.
- Don't project your expectations on your child. Not all children follow in their parents' footsteps. If you're an accountant but your child has difficulty with math, don't push her into a career that would make her miserable. If you're an attorney but your son wants to be an artist, don't try to make him fit his artistic "square peg" temperament into the "round hole" demands of a legal career.
- Help your child discover his natural, God-given talents. During your child's formative years, he will excel in some areas and fail at others. Help him develop his strengths and identify possible career opportunities that might match them.

Equip your adolescent to think of vocation and career in spiritual terms.

- He is uniquely designed by God (see Psalm 139:13-14).
- He has been given specific talents for a purpose (see Romans 12:6-8).
- He must develop his God-given talents and strive for excellence (see Proverbs 22:29).
- Work is a stage for his higher calling (see Matthew 5:16).

Equip your adolescent to obtain guidance in the pursuit of education, training, and possible career fields.

You should be able to get some help in this area from the local school's professional guidance counselor.

- Identify your adolescent's likes and dislikes and expose her to fields she is interested in.
- Discover natural talents before college or vocational training. Work with your child (for example, by becoming involved with her in science class or in arts and crafts). Before spending thousands of dollars on college or vocational training, help your child find the path on which she is most likely to excel.
- Teach your child to pray for God's guidance and seek what He would have her do for a career.

Finally, consider seeking career-testing services that may help your older adolescent determine what career options fit her personality. These tests often help young adults hone in on their special talents, if they have not already done so, and they can also confirm whether a certain career choice is a logical path. Adolescents who are somewhat aimless might find that the test results point them in one or more specific directions. Others who are endowed with a number of definite interests might benefit from tests that help them focus on their areas of greatest strength. This might spare at least some from changing majors one or more times during college, which could prove both expensive and time-consuming.

Preparation for Marriage

One of your most important goals when passing the baton to your children is to prepare them for marriage. If you have a strong and vibrant marriage, it is important to share with your children the principles upon which you have built and maintained this relationship. But if your marriage is less than ideal or you have experienced a divorce, lessons you have learned the hard way can still benefit your children, assuming that you are willing to be candid and transparent about your experience.

At a time when more than 40 percent of marriages will end in divorce, parents face a formidable job educating their children about selecting a husband or a wife for life. Because we are a mobile society, children from stable and loving homes often select partners with different backgrounds, customs, goals, interests, and beliefs. This does not mean that they cannot succeed in marriage, but in such cases both parties must enter the relationship with their eyes open and a willingness to work through their differences.

Early adolescence is a good time to begin discussing with your children characteristics and traits to seek in a future wife or husband. You may want to give them a list of twenty or thirty of these qualities and have them rank in order the ones they think are the most important. Quite often children will discover that their mental image of their "dream partner"—frequently a fantasy derived from movies and television shows—does not match with this ranking. It might be helpful to have your children save this list (or make a copy) and review it annually.

Also early in adolescence—perhaps on a special birthday such as the thirteenth—encourage your children to begin praying for their future spouses. As parents, you should be doing the same if you haven't started already. Toward the end of high school, however, give your adolescents some books that explore the process of selecting a partner and building a strong marriage. You would be wise to read them yourself and set aside some time to discuss them with your children. One excellent book is *Saving Your Marriage before It Starts* by Drs. Les and Leslie Parrott (Zondervan, 1995). Another is Dr. James Dobson's *Love for a Lifetime* (Multnomah, 2004).

You should specifically talk about some basic principles for building a relationship that will culminate in a permanent and satisfying marriage. The following is by no means a complete list of the ideas you'll want to communicate to each child, but it's a good place to start.

- Decide ahead of time that you will pursue a serious relationship *only* with someone who very closely shares your spiritual views and who also actively cultivates his or her own relationship with God. You don't want to marry someone whose faith is dead in the water or who is going along for the spiritual ride merely to please you.
- The person you marry should be one with whom conversation flows freely and easily—in both directions. Beware of relationships in which one person does most or all of the talking or in which you run out of things to talk about.
- As we discussed earlier in the Special Concerns section "A Parent's Guide to Teen Sexuality," decide ahead of time what boundaries will be set in the relationship for expressing affection. (They should be very modest—see page 524.) Beware of moving too fast physically or of continuing a relationship in which one person doesn't respect the other's boundaries in this area.
- Decide ahead of time that you're going to save your first sexual encounter for your wedding night. Doing so will prevent sex from becoming the center of gravity in the relationship, enhance the romance and anticipation of your wedding, and contribute to a powerful emotional bond in your marriage.
- Beware of relationships in which there is a lot of "drama"—intense cycles of arguing followed by passionate making up (which can easily lead to sexual involvement).
- Dating experiences can be fun but artificial. Spend a lot of time doing ordinary things with someone you're considering marrying.
- Don't move too quickly toward marriage. All too often the old adage "Marry in haste, repent at leisure" proves to be true.
- Don't marry too young. At eighteen you may feel passionate about someone who will bore you to tears when you're twenty-five.
- Don't marry primarily to please someone else (for example, your parents) or out of pressure or guilt.
- Your passion for the other person should arise out of a clear-eyed understanding and acceptance of his or her strengths and weaknesses.
- Don't enter marriage with the expectation that the other person is going to meet all of your needs or be the ultimate source of satisfaction in your life. Jesus said, "I am the bread of life. He who comes to me will never go hungry, and he who

believes in me will never be thirsty" (John 6:35). Only He—not your spouse-to-be—is qualified to make that claim.

- Don't make the terrible mistake of assuming that you'll straighten out the other person's flaws after you are married. If you can't live with a person as he or she is now, you won't want to live with him or her in the future.

- Beware of entering a serious relationship if you are dealing with ongoing depression, anxiety, or an addiction to alcohol or drugs. Your judgment may be seriously impaired, and the relationship will probably look very different when you have recovered. Similarly, don't make the serious mistake of entering a relationship or marriage to "rescue" someone with a major psychological or addiction problem.

- An impending marriage should be a time of great anticipation and celebration. If you are getting red flags or overt disapproval from one or both sets of parents, trusted friends, your pastor, or a counselor who knows you, proceed with extreme caution. If you need to take more time to sort things out before you get married, by all means do so.

Encourage adolescents or young adults to obtain counseling before an official engagement is announced, even if they are certain that they have found the "love of their life." Offer to pay for counseling if it is not furnished by your church. Many inventories are available to help pastors and counselors uncover any potential problem areas. The *Prepare* inventory, for example, identifies both strengths and weaknesses of each potential spouse and can predict which marriages are likely to succeed and which are at higher risk for divorce.

Inform your children that, even when married, they need to work on this relationship for a lifetime. If you have grown children who are married, volunteer to pay for them to attend a marriage enrichment experience such as a Weekend to Remember conference presented by FamilyLife (http://www.familylife.com or 800-FL-TODAY) or a Love and Respect Marriage Conference (http://www.loveandrespect.com or 616-459-9190). You might offer to babysit their children if needed—and you might even consider attending such a conference yourself.

Finally, *warn your children once more about becoming sexually involved before marriage.* Among other things, premarital sex might lead them to marry the wrong people and rob them of a satisfying lifelong marriage. Children of divorce might be tempted to cohabit prior to marriage in hopes of avoiding their parents' mistakes. But statistics from a variety of sources indicate that cohabitants have a greater chance of divorce than those who wait until marriage to live together. An excellent resource for anyone contemplating cohabitation prior to (or instead of) marriage is *Before You Live Together* by David Gudgel (Regal, 2003).

The most important thing you can do for your children to help them develop a healthy concept of marriage is to allow them to see you loving, cherishing, and respecting your partner. If you are not married, allow your children to spend time with one or more families in which a nurturing, respectful marital relationship is modeled.

The Finishing Touch: Releasing Your Grown Child

In reality, you have been slowly releasing your child since birth. If he or she marries in the future, you will once again have to release your now-grown child—this time to become one flesh with a spouse. There will also come a time when you must pass the baton to your child. Of course, you will be a parent for life, but your role must change to that of a coach and friend, encouraging your grown child's progress—and perhaps later on watching your grandchildren take the baton to begin their lap.

I have no greater joy than to hear that my children are walking in the truth.

3 John 1:4

But ready or not, shortly after your son or daughter graduates from high school, your formal job of parenting should be completed, and he or she will need to be released. *The fact that you are doing so should be specifically conveyed to your grown child,* either verbally or in writing or perhaps both. The advantage of a letter is that it allows you time to organize your thoughts, it conveys a sense of permanence, and it allows your young adult to reread this important letter in the future.

Whether expressed in spoken or written words, your message of release may be communicated to a young adult who has given you a great deal more joy than grief and about whose future you feel confident. Or you may have to express sorrow and honest concern about your grown child's future health, safety, and financial stability. (Such a letter might have been written by the father of the Prodigal Son as the son was leaving home.) Regardless of the circumstances, however, the release must be given.

The specific wording of this conversation and/or letter will be different for each parent, but (among other things) it should communicate the following:

- Your job is done.
- You acknowledge that you have not been a perfect parent.
- You hope and pray that he will forgive you for your failings.
- You will continue to pray for him.
- If one day God allows him to marry and have children of his own, you hope that he will build on the positive traits of his parents and grandparents, avoid your mistakes, and improve in areas where you were weak.
- Whatever the future holds for him, you will always love him.
- You hope that he will hold fast to the values that you care about and teach them to his own children.
- He should hold fast to his faith or strongly consider beginning his relationship with God if he has not done so already.

Reference Section

A | **abdominal pain** A child who complains that her stomach hurts could have any number of things wrong, ranging in severity from cramping caused by anxiety or constipation to a full-blown medical emergency. Very often the reason isn't obvious, and identifying the source of pain may require investigation by both parent and physician. This is particularly true for infants and toddlers, who can communicate very little, if any, specific information about their discomfort.

This section is not intended as a definitive explanation of all the causes of abdominal pain in children. Instead, we have provided a series of questions to help you narrow down the possible causes when your child complains of abdominal pain. If you need to call your child's doctor, the information you gather using these questions will make your conversation or office visit far more productive.

Where is the pain?
Pinning down the location of pain is sometimes easier said than done. When asked where it hurts, a child might make a broad gesture over the entire abdomen. Ask her to point to where it hurts the most or to trace the location if it hurts over a wide area.

Pain caused by cramping of the large or small intestine is usually felt over a broad area or will seem to the child to be centered at the navel (belly button). But if a specific area is inflamed, the pain will tend to be focused in one location. The usual pattern in **appendicitis**, for example, starts with cramping in the upper abdomen or around the navel and then gradually shifts to the lower-right abdomen as the appendix becomes more inflamed. If a child has **hepatitis** (a viral infection of the liver), pain will be in the upper-right side of the abdomen. Pain in the upper-middle abdomen, especially a burning sensation, frequently involves irritation of the stomach (**gastritis**).

In preteen and adolescent girls, pain in the lower half of the abdomen can be more difficult to sort out because it could involve the reproductive organs (uterus, fallopian tubes, and ovaries) or the urinary tract. If the pain comes in cycles, it may be related to menses, ovulation (the release of an egg from an ovary), or the formation of an ovarian cyst. (See "The Menstrual Cycle" in chapter 12, beginning on page 444, for more information about what happens—and what can go wrong—during an adolescent girl's monthly cycle.) If she needs to urinate often and has a burning sensation when urine is passed, a **bladder infection** is likely. This and most lower abdominal pain—especially in girls—needs a doctor's evaluation and treatment.

How long has the pain been present?

A pain that ends within ten or fifteen minutes usually involves a **spasm** (an intense contraction) of some part of the intestine. Many children, especially during the preschool and elementary-school years, will complain about a stomachache. This will usually disappear within a half hour or so. (Often a brief rest will help.) Constipation can also cause this type of pain; checking how often your child has a bowel movement may provide you with helpful information.

School anxiety can cause stomachaches that begin on Monday morning and miraculously disappear on weekends. Gentle questioning about progress at school—and, if needed, some trouble-shooting about classwork or problems with other students—might help reduce both the anxiety about school and the weekday abdominal pain.

While pains such as these are not likely to be caused by serious disease, episodes that disrupt your child's activities or occur repeatedly over several weeks should be evaluated by a physician. If pain continues for more than an hour, especially if a child is obviously uncomfortable, call your child's physician.

Is there nausea and vomiting?

Nausea and vomiting can be caused by many types of problems in the abdomen. Often **gastroenteritis** (stomach flu) causes cramping or even constant pain, but vomiting is a more dramatic symptom. If your child vomits repeatedly, contact your doctor because ongoing fluid loss can lead to dehydration—especially in infants and small children. Listlessness, dry mouth, doughy skin texture, decreased production of urine (fewer wet diapers in infants), and in more extreme cases, sunken eyes, are symptoms of severe dehydration that should be evaluated immediately (see "vomiting").

Is there diarrhea or constipation?

Diarrhea is often caused by an infection and is usually accompanied by cramping pains. A variety of viruses, bacteria, and parasites can cause diarrhea, and special tests may be needed to identify the organism that is involved (see "diarrhea"). While less common than infection as a cause of diarrhea in children, **inflammatory bowel disease** can cause both diarrhea and bouts of abdominal pain. The sudden onset of vomiting and diarrhea together is typical of gastroenteritis, a viral illness that often settles down after twelve to twenty-four hours. This combination, however, can cause dehydration more quickly than either symptom alone. If diarrhea is the only problem and your child is alert and taking liquids satisfactorily, a call to the doctor's office can usually wait until office hours.

Constipation may also lead to cramping pains, often provoked by a meal and relieved by a bowel movement. When food enters the stomach, a reflex message is sent to the colon to contract and move the stool so it can be eliminated. Over time, stool can accumulate if the amount leaving the colon is less than the amount entering. If a day or two passes without a bowel movement—an event not uncommon in older children—the backup can become substantial. Furthermore, as the colon extracts water from stool, the contents tend to become harder with each passing day. When the stomach becomes full (especially after a large meal), the firm reflex squeeze of colon against a resistant collection of stool can produce major pain. If your child's doctor suspects that this is the cause of recurrent abdominal pain, simple measures to evacuate excess stool (such as increased fluid and fiber intake—see "constipation") can produce dramatic improvement.

Is there fever?

If abdominal pain is accompanied by an oral temperature over 99.4°F (37.4°C) or rectal temperature over 100.4°F (38°C), inflammation is nearly always present, likely involving an infection by bacteria or a virus. Your child's doctor should be contacted for further directions, which will depend upon the other symptoms.

Is the pain affected by eating?

Pain in the upper abdomen that is relieved by small amounts of food or milk may be caused by inflammation of the stomach, which is aggravated by stomach acid and neutralized by some foods. While ongoing stomach irritation caused by acid (**peptic ulcer disease**) is uncommon in small children, it can definitely occur in older children and teenagers. In adolescents a history of burning discomfort that is worse when the stomach is empty but relieved by food or antacid suggests this possibility. In younger children the symptoms may be more vague. In general, if abdominal pain is severe, food should be withheld until you have contacted your child's physician.

In some situations, specific foods provoke abdominal pain. For example, children who cannot digest **lactose**—the sugar found in milk—may develop abdominal pain and diarrhea after eating dairy products. In **celiac disease**, gluten—a protein found in wheat, rye, and barley—provokes an immune reaction that damages the lining of the intestines and leads to foul-smelling diarrhea, cramping pain, irritability, and weight loss over a prolonged period of time. Because there is no immediate cause-and-effect relationship between a particular meal and the symptoms, the connection will not appear obvious. After other possible causes of these symptoms have been ruled out, your doctor may recommend a blood test that detects a specific type of protein, and possibly a procedure in which a small amount of tissue is taken from the lining of the small intestine for microscopic evaluation. If the diagnosis is celiac disease, your child will need a gluten-free diet; you can obtain more information from the physician who makes the diagnosis or from a dietitian.

How old is the child?

Certain problems are more specific to the young infant. **Colic**, for example, usually occurs in babies under three months of age. While a universal cause for this disturbance is not known with certainty, the classic theory holds that contractions in the intestines provoke pain and intense crying, pulling up of the legs, and often passing of gas. While not medically serious, the infant's crying can easily frustrate and discourage any parent. *If the baby has a fever or is vomiting, the problem is more serious than colic, and a doctor should be contacted.* Strategies for dealing with colic are outlined in detail in chapter 5.

Intussusception is an unusual event in which a segment of the intestine telescopes into another, producing a blockage. Although infrequent, this is still the most common cause of obstruction of a child's intestine between the age of three months and six years, and it is seen most often between five and ten months of age. The pain from this condition is severe and even more relentless than the pain from colic. An X-ray procedure known as a **barium enema**, during which a thick liquid visible on an X-ray is introduced into the rectum, is usually necessary to make the diagnosis. (In some facilities, air is used rather than barium.) Very often this procedure solves the problem, pushing the displaced segment of intestine back where it belongs.

In older children, there are more possible causes of abdominal pain, but the child is usually able to communicate more detailed complaints. In addition to the conditions mentioned earlier (appendicitis, gastroenteritis, constipation), abdominal pain could be caused by the following:

- **Urinary tract infection.** In adults the discomfort of a urinary tract infection depends on its location. A bladder infection (**cystitis**) will cause stinging, burning, and the frequent need to urinate. A kidney infection (**pyelonephritis**) will cause fever and midback pain on one side of the body. In children specific symptoms are frequently absent; vague abdominal discomfort may be the only complaint. In a young child, especially a girl, a high fever and vague abdominal pain should always be evaluated for a possible kidney infection (see "urinary tract care and concerns").

- **Strep throat.** Even though the typical symptoms of a streptococcal infection of the throat are fever, headache, and sore throat, in some children abdominal pain or vomiting is also present. If your doctor suspects strep throat, a straightforward test from a throat swab can help make the diagnosis (see "sore throat").

- **Mesenteric adenitis.** This condition involves inflammation and swelling of lymph nodes located inside the abdomen. (Often lymph nodes in the neck are swollen and tender as well.) Because many of these nodes are found near the appendix, the pain they generate is often difficult to distinguish from that caused by appendicitis. However, unlike appendicitis, mesenteric adenitis resolves without specific treatment. (See "appendicitis," as well as the comments about appendicitis earlier in this section.)

- **Pneumonia.** Even though infections of the lung rarely involve the intestinal tract, in some children pneumonia may cause abdominal pain.
- **Reproductive-organ disorders.** In adolescent girls, a number of problems involving the uterus and ovaries can produce abdominal pain, which is usually felt in the pelvic area. These disorders include such diverse conditions as infections (especially **sexually transmitted infections**, or **STIs**), **ectopic pregnancy** (a pregnancy beginning to develop in the wrong location, most commonly the fallopian tube), ovarian cysts, pain related to ovulation (**mittelschmerz**), **menstrual cramps**, and **endometriosis** (a condition in which the type of tissue that lines the inside of the uterus is also present in other parts of the body—most commonly on the outer surfaces of the uterus, ovaries, fallopian tubes, intestine, and/or bladder). For an adolescent girl, a doctor's evaluation of the pelvis will be extremely important, and further studies (such as an ultrasound examination) may be needed to help make the diagnosis. (Detailed information about these conditions is provided in chapter 12.)
- **Functional and stress-related pain**, especially in older children and adolescents, can cause abdominal discomfort in several locations, sometimes with baffling patterns. (See "The Riddle of Recurrent Abdominal Pain," beginning on page 352.)

abscess A collection of pus that usually results from the "walling off" of an infectious process that serves to limit its spread. An abscess can occur almost anywhere in the body—on or beneath the skin, within the abdomen, near the tonsils, and elsewhere. An abscess at or near the surface of the body will form an area of swelling that is warm, tender, and quite painful. An abscess can occur at any age, and it nearly always will be treated with surgical drainage (which often provides immediate relief) as well as antibiotics.

acetaminophen (Tylenol and other brands, as well as generic forms) The nonprescription drug most frequently given to children in the United States. It helps reduce fever, aches, pains, and headaches in a variety of situations, including colds, sore throats, flu-like illnesses, and minor bumps and scrapes. It is also commonly used to relieve discomfort that may follow immunizations. It has no specific effect on cold symptoms such as a runny nose or a cough, although many manufacturers combine it with other ingredients to create cold/cough syrups or tablets that are intended to relieve multiple symptoms.

This medication can be given to infants as young as two months of age. However, if a baby under three months of age has a fever of 100.4°F (38°C) or more taken rectally, acetaminophen should not be given without first contacting your child's doctor (see the Special Concerns section "When Your Child Has a Fever," page 241, and chapter 4, pages 135–136).

Acetaminophen may be given every four hours, with a maximum of five doses per day (see dosage chart). It comes in various forms, including drops, syrups, chewable tablets, suppositories, and adult-dose tablets. *Be sure to read the label carefully* to ensure that you have the right strength for your child. The dosage should be based on current weight—not age. Typical doses are listed in the chart on the next page.

Overdose warning

When taken properly, acetaminophen is safe, and allergic reactions to it are unusual. *But an overdose can produce serious—and occasionally fatal—liver damage.* The toxic dose is about 65 mg per pound (0.45 kg) of body weight—about ten times a single recommended dose. For a twenty-two-pound (10 kg) one-year-old, this would be as little as a tablespoon (15 ml) of the pediatric drops, eighteen of the 80 mg chewable tablets, or three adult extra-strength 500 mg tablets.

The severity of the overdose problem might not be apparent for three or four days. Within the first twenty-four hours after ingestion, symptoms that might occur (such as vague abdominal discomfort or mild lethargy) are not specific. (After a very large ingestion, however, altered consciousness or coma may be present.) Between twenty-four and forty-eight hours after the overdose, the child typically improves and may not have any symptoms at all. After forty-eight hours, any liver damage will become apparent and may cause nausea, vomiting, confusion, or even coma.

ACETAMINOPHEN Medicine for fever or pain relief		
WEIGHT	**TYPE**	**DOSE** (dosage form)
10–11 lbs 4.5–5 kg	drops (80 mg/0.8 ml)	½ dropper (0.4 ml)
12–17 lbs 5.5–7.5 kg	drops (80 mg/0.8 ml) syrup (160 mg/5 ml)	1 dropper (0.8 ml) ½ tsp (2.5 ml)
18–23 lbs 8–10.5 kg	drops (80 mg/0.8 ml) syrup (160 mg/5 ml) chewable tablets (80 mg)	1½ dropper (1.2 ml) ¾ tsp (3.75 ml) 1½ tablets
24–35 lbs 11–16 kg	drops (80 mg/0.8 ml) syrup (160 mg/5 ml) chewable tablets (80 mg) chewable tablets (160 mg)	2 droppers (1.6 ml) 1 tsp (5 ml) 2 tablets 1 tablet
36–47 lbs 16.5–21.5 kg	drops (80 mg/0.8 ml) syrup (160 mg/5 ml) chewable tablets (80 mg) chewable tablets (160 mg)	3 droppers (2.4 ml) 1½ tsp (7.5 ml) 3 tablets 1½ tablets
48–59 lbs 22–27 kg	syrup (160 mg/5 ml) chewable tablets (80 mg) chewable tablets (160 mg)	2 tsp (10 ml) 4 tablets 2 tablets
60–71 lbs 27.5–32 kg	syrup (160 mg/5 ml) chewable tablets (80 mg) chewable tablets (160 mg) adult tablets (325 mg)	2½ tsp (12.5 ml) 5 tablets 2½ tablets 1 tablet
72–95 lbs 32.5–43 kg	syrup (160 mg/5 ml) chewable tablets (80 mg) chewable tablets (160 mg) adult tablets (325 mg)	3 tsp (15 ml) 6 tablets 3 tablets 1 to 1½ tablets
96+ lbs 43.5+ kg	syrup (160 mg/5 ml) chewable tablets (80 mg) chewable tablets (160 mg) adult tablets (325 mg)	4 tsp (20 ml) 8 tablets 4 tablets 2 tablets

Abbreviations: mg=milligrams ml=milliliter tsp=teaspoon
1 dropper = 0.8 ml   1 tsp = 5 ml

Note: Since acetaminophen pediatric products (such as Children's Tylenol) are available without a prescription, parents are warned on the package label to consult a physician for use by children under 2 years or for use longer than 10 days and to consult a physician or poison control center immediately in case of accidental overdosage.

One dose (based on child's weight) may be given every 4 to 6 hours. Do not exceed 5 doses in 24 hours.

To be effective, the antidote (a drug called **N-acetylcysteine**, or Mucomyst) should be given within eight hours of ingestion. *If you suspect that your child has taken too much acetaminophen, contact your doctor or local poison control center immediately or go to the nearest emergency room—even if your child does not appear ill.* If there is any doubt as to how much the child has actually swallowed, a blood test can determine whether there is a risk of liver damage, and treatment can be started immediately.

Since acetaminophen is commonly given to young children, most liquid and chewable preparations have a pleasant taste, so keeping the supply out of a child's reach is extremely important.

acne Pimples, pustules, and the occasionally more serious cysts and scars of acne occur primarily during the teen years, when a child's self-consciousness is very often at an all-time high. Nearly 80 percent of adolescents experience acne to some degree. Girls tend to be affected at an earlier age, but acne occurs in boys more frequently and with greater severity. While in most cases acne eventually clears up on its own, it should be treated and not ignored because some of the physical and emotional scars it leaves can last many years.

Acne originates in areas of the skin where there are large numbers of rudimentary hairs combined with large **sebaceous glands**, so named because they secrete a thick, oily material called **sebum**. The majority of these glands are present on the face, chest, upper back, and shoulders.

Causes
The hormonal surges of puberty stimulate the production of sebum, which normally passes uneventfully to the surface of the skin. Sometimes, however, the channels leading from the sebaceous glands to the skin become blocked by dead cells. Sebum then accumulates into a visible bump commonly known as a pimple or **whitehead**. If the enlarging mass of sebum pushes outward to the skin surface, oxidation—not dirt—darkens the fatty materials, forming a **comedone** (or **blackhead**).

Bacteria on the skin surface gain access to the buildup of sebum and multiply, releasing chemical by-products that not only irritate the skin but also attract white blood cells. The resulting inflammatory reaction produces more prominent irritated bumps called **pustules** or the larger (and more damaging) **acne cysts**, which in severe cases can leave disfiguring scars.

Factors that worsen acne
Why some teenagers develop a major acne problem while others are spared is not always clear,

but a number of factors are known to aggravate acne:

- Tight-fitting clothing or headgear. Wet suits, helmets, headbands, and bras that rub skin may provoke changes in the skin area directly below them.
- Picking or scratching pimples and pustules.
- Hot, humid environments that cause heavy perspiration.
- Some girls have a flare-up of acne before their menstrual periods, in response to hormonal fluctuations that may cause the outlet of the sebaceous glands to become more obstructed.
- Medications, including **isoniazid** (used to treat tuberculosis), **phenytoin** and **barbiturates** (used to control epilepsy), and **steroids** (whether forms prescribed by a physician or **androgens** used inappropriately by athletes to build muscles) may worsen acne. Some birth control pills improve it, while others will aggravate it.
- Oils and dyes in cosmetics and hair sprays can plug the sebaceous glands, so water-based products are better for people who are prone to acne. *Note: The impact of these factors on any given teenager's skin will vary a great deal.*

Effect of dirt, diet, and sunlight

Acne is not caused by dirt on the skin, and aggressive scrubbing (especially with abrasive materials) can actually make it worse. A mild, unscented soap should be used daily to remove oils from the skin surface.

The role of diet in acne has proven to be more of a legend than reality. Despite persistent beliefs that greasy or sweet foods turn directly into pimples, dietary changes in fact have not been proven to cause or cure acne in the general population. One analysis of data from a major study that has followed the health status of more than 47,000 nurses suggested an association between consumption of milk and an increased likelihood of developing acne. (The association was based on a survey evaluating food consumption between the ages of thirteen and eighteen, as recalled by nurses who reported having acne.) Possible reasons for this could include the presence of whey proteins or hormones in milk, but it should be noted that this study does not prove that drinking milk causes acne or, more importantly, that avoiding milk will prevent it. The same study, incidentally, did not find any association between the consumption of soft drinks, french fries, pizza, or chocolate with developing acne.[1] However, anyone who notices a consistent relationship between a particular food and worsening of acne should consider avoiding that food.

While some individuals feel that exposure to sunlight helps their acne, this has not in fact been proven to be true. Ongoing exposure to the ultraviolet rays in sunlight can damage skin and increase the risk of developing skin cancer later in life. Furthermore, a number of acne treatments increase the skin's sensitivity to sunlight. Deliberate sun exposure therefore is not recommended as a method for dealing with acne.

Treatment

Medications commonly used for acne treatment include the following:

- **Benzoyl peroxide** kills the skin bacteria that cause inflammation and helps open the ducts through which sebum passes to the skin surface. It is available without a prescription in 2.5, 5, and 10 percent strengths in several forms. Liquids and creams are better for dry skin, while gel forms are more helpful for oily skin. Benzoyl peroxide can be applied once or twice daily after washing the affected area with mild soap and water. It will improve the majority of acne cases if used consistently. If using benzoyl peroxide for one or two months doesn't help, a doctor should be consulted. A family physician or pediatrician can manage most cases of acne, but for more severe outbreaks, a dermatologist may be needed.
- **Topical retinoids** include **tretinoin** (such as Retin-A), **tazarotene** (Tazorac), and **adapalene** (Differin), all in a variety of forms and strengths. These medications are very effective in unplugging pores and even causing blackheads to be expelled from the skin. This can be alarming at first because the new appearance of comedones on the surface will suggest that the medication is making the acne worse. But this effect is only temporary. Retinoids typically cause some redness and peeling of the skin.

Skin treated with retinoids may be more sensitive to sunburn or reactions provoked by sunlight, so avoiding the sun or using a strong sunscreen is important. Adapalene is generally regarded as less irritating to skin, and tazarotene as more irritating, than tretinoin.

- Antibiotics applied topically or taken orally sometimes help by reducing the population of bacteria on the skin. Topical antibiotics such as **erythromycin** or **clindamycin** are often used concurrently with benzoyl peroxide, and they may be combined into a single preparation. Oral forms of **tetracycline** or erythromycin are particularly helpful when inflammation is intense. (Tetracycline and similar drugs cannot be given to pregnant women or children younger than eight because these drugs discolor the teeth of a developing fetus or a child.)

- **Isotretinoin** (Accutane), an extremely potent derivative of vitamin A, is used in the most severe cases of acne. Isotretinoin acts essentially like an enhanced version of tretinoin, and 85 percent of even the worst cases of acne will show a dramatic and prolonged (or even permanent) response to treatment over a four- to five-month period.

  This drug has a number of potential side effects, including dry skin, itching, and changes in liver function. While a direct cause-and-effect relationship has not been proven, concerns have been raised over a possible association between the use of isotretinoin and depression, and any changes in mood while taking this drug should be discussed with the prescribing physician. Most important, it can cause severe deformities in a developing fetus if taken during pregnancy. This risk is considered so serious that isotretinoin's prescribing guidelines state that a female who might become pregnant must use two forms of contraception during the course of treatment (and for one month after it is completed). She must also have two negative pregnancy tests prior to starting this drug and must continue monthly pregnancy tests while taking it.

- **Azelaic acid** (Azelex) is a topical medication that is unrelated to the others listed above. Derived from cereal grains, it inhibits skin bacteria, decreases the sebum that blocks pores, and reduces inflammation. It is applied twice daily to skin that has just been washed and should be continued for four weeks before deciding whether or not it is helpful.

- Certain oral contraceptive preparations may be helpful in treating acne, especially in women who have conditions, such as **polycystic ovary syndrome**, that are associated with excessive production of hormones known as androgens.

Whatever approach is taken, it is important to remember that (1) treatment can only control acne, not cure it (for most people, this problem will fade away before adulthood); and (2) once treatment is started, it may take several weeks before there is a noticeable change.

For the teenager who is agonizing over the latest crop of facial bumps, this news may bring little comfort. Parents (and a physician, when appropriate) will need to be empathetic and supportive. Sometimes support will involve a gentle reminder to be consistent with treatment.

adenoids Tissue located at the back of the nasal cavity, just above the throat. As part of the immune system, this tissue helps defend against viruses and bacteria entering the body through the nose. Like the tonsils found in the throat, adenoids may swell as they participate in fighting an infection. In some children this swelling can contribute to ongoing problems such as stuffy nose, mouth breathing, snoring, sore throat, and repeated ear infections. If symptoms and/or infections related to ear infections are persistent and disruptive, your child's physician may recommend a consultation with an ENT (ear, nose, and throat) specialist to consider removing the adenoids surgically. (Very often the tonsils in the throat are causing ongoing problems as well, and the tonsils and adenoids are removed at the same time.)

allergen Any compound or material that can provoke an allergic reaction. Common allergens are grass, weed, and tree pollens; mold spores; dust mites; animal products such as **dander** (skin scales) or saliva; insect venoms or other substances derived from animals that can gain entry to the human body; and substances such as foods, drugs, or other chemicals with which a person comes in contact (see "allergies in children").

allergies in children Allergic disorders are extremely common in children and very diverse in their manifestations. These may involve the eyes (**allergic conjunctivitis**), the nose (**allergic rhinitis**), the skin (**atopic dermatitis**), the airways (**asthma**), the gastrointestinal tract (**food allergies**), or even the entire body (**anaphylaxis**).

An allergic reaction is the expression of an interaction between an agent called an **allergen**, which comes from the outside world, with **antibodies**, which are created by an individual's immune system. The most common allergens are grass, weed, and tree pollens; mold spores; dust mites; animal products such as dander (skin scales) or saliva; insect venoms or other substances derived from animals that can gain entry into the human body; and a variety of substances such as foods, drugs, or other chemicals with which a person comes in contact.

When allergens come in contact with antibodies, a variety of compounds may be released. These in turn can produce several types of reactions, including runny nose, sneezing, wheezing, hives, eczema, upset stomach, and in severe cases, shocklike reactions. Some allergic events, such as the response to receiving the wrong type of blood in a transfusion, are common to all people. Most of the reactions that will be reviewed here, however, are the so-called **atopic disorders**—those that affect smaller numbers of individuals who are unusually sensitive to specific substances.

The tendency to develop allergies is frequently inherited. If both parents have allergies, their child has a 60 to 75 percent chance of developing an allergic disorder. If only one parent has an allergic syndrome, the percentage drops to between 25 and 50 percent. If neither parent has allergies, a child has less than a 10 percent chance of developing an allergic disorder. Children with allergies do not necessarily manifest the same reactions as their allergic parents. For example, a father with hay fever and a mother with allergic eczema might have a child whose primary problem is asthma. Allergic reactions to specific substances—for example, hives in response to penicillin—are not routinely passed from one generation to another.

And when both parent and child have allergies, the responses in the child may be either milder or more severe than those of the parents.

The pattern of allergic reactions may change during childhood, as in the following examples:

- A baby might develop eczema before her first birthday, resolve it by the age of three, and then develop hay fever and asthma during her school years.
- Food allergies are usually outgrown, with the exception of reactions to peanuts and shellfish.
- Ragweed allergy may not develop until a child has lived through at least one ragweed season.
- A child might not be allergic to a pet at first, but later she might manifest a reaction because her immune system has become increasingly sensitized through repeated exposure to the animal.

In general, nobody can accurately predict whether a child will outgrow one or more allergies, but in many cases the reaction becomes less severe with the passage of time.

Symptoms
Allergic reactions can occur in so many ways that they are frequently confused with other problems or illnesses. For example, clear, watery drainage from the nose accompanied by sneezing and itching may suggest a cold, but in fact any or all of these symptoms could be allergic in origin. At the same time, allergies can predispose a child to frequent colds and ear infections. Even without allergies, infants and toddlers can have as many as six to ten colds every year in their first two years and three to four a year during their third and fourth years. When allergic symptoms are also present, it can seem impossible to tell where one problem leaves off and the other begins. Thus, if a child's cold lasts more than two weeks or if she always seems to have a cold, allergies could be the reason.

Parents often think that a child's sniffing, nose rubbing, snoring, and mouth breathing are simply bad habits, but they could be signs of allergic activity. Constant mouth breathing caused by nasal congestion could even interfere with the proper alignment of a child's teeth.

Repeated throat clearing, especially when a child awakens in the morning, may be the result of allergies that cause the nose to swell and fill with mucus. The mucus drips into the throat, causing the child to clear it. The throat can in turn become irritated, and a child might complain repeatedly of a sore throat. Distinguishing an allergic sore throat from one caused by an infection can at times be quite difficult.

Coughing is another common allergic symptom. It can arise from postnasal drainage into the throat or from spasm of the airway. If this spasm is more intense, wheezing could result. If coughing persists for more than a few weeks and is worse at night and aggravated by smoke, exercise, or cold air, asthma is a possible diagnosis.

Frequent headaches, especially in the forehead or face near the nose, may arise from pressure caused by allergic swelling in the nose. Allergic eye symptoms can include redness, itching, watery discharge, and swelling. Dark circles under the eyes are sometimes called allergic shiners, but these may have other causes as well.

Many types of skin rashes are manifestations of allergies. **Eczema** is a patchy rash that is dry, slightly reddened, and very itchy. **Contact dermatitis** is an irritation of skin caused by an allergic reaction to a substance that comes in direct contact with the skin. Eruptions resulting from exposure to poison ivy, oak, or sumac are dramatic examples of contact dermatitis. **Hives**—the medical term is **urticaria**—are a generalized allergic response involving raised, reddened, irregular itchy patches of skin that may blanch (turn white) when pressure is applied. They may vary from dime-size to much larger areas of skin, and they change size and location. Hives are sometimes associated with itchy swelling of the face, eyes, lips, hands, feet, and genitalia.

Evaluation

A doctor will use two primary tools to arrive at a diagnosis of allergies: the patient's history and a physical examination. In the vast majority of cases, the history alone will suggest the diagnosis. Results of the physical exam are also helpful. Only in a small percentage of cases is laboratory testing needed to clarify the diagnosis of an allergy. (Several tests might be necessary to determine the allergens to which a child is reacting.)

Since the history is so important, prior to a medical evaluation it would be helpful to think back over the past few months (or years) to recall specific details of your child's symptoms: When did the problem first start? How often does it bother her? What time of the day (or year) is it worse? Are symptoms more severe at home, outside, inside, in the city, out in the country, at the coast, or at high altitudes? Do the symptoms change with physical events or environmental factors such as cold, heat, dampness, exercise, or exposure to cigarette smoke? Have specific medications been used? Which of these has been most effective? Sometimes a diary can help you recall specific reactions, symptoms, and seasonal responses your child has experienced. Details about your child's environment, especially her bedroom, could be helpful. Stuffed toys, pillows, the furnace and its filter, knickknacks and blinds (which collect dust), and trees outside the window are all potential sources of allergens.

During the physical exam, the doctor will look for various signs of allergic activity. These might include pale and swollen mucous membranes, clear drainage from the nose, a crease across the nose, or perhaps dark circles below the eyes. Wheezing or coughing would of course be significant but may not necessarily occur during a scheduled office visit. The skin will be checked for evidence of eczema, including scratch marks and areas of thickening and redness, especially behind the knees, in the creases of the arms, and on the wrists.

Tests for allergies

While your child's history and physical examination provide evidence that she has an allergic disorder, they may or may not provide clues to the specific allergens that are provoking the reactions. This information can be very useful in suggesting whether or not changes in the home environment would reduce or eliminate allergic symptoms. It might also provide the basis for a form of treatment known as **immunotherapy**, or **hyposensitization**, discussed later in this section (see also "immunotherapy").

If your child's symptoms are particularly bothersome or persistent, unresponsive to medications, or severe (for example, wheezing episodes requiring repeated medical intervention), the physician or allergist might recommend **skin tests** to help identify what might be triggering these allergic responses. The testing involves scratching or pricking the skin on the back in several places and exposing these areas to substances that might provoke an allergic reaction. If your child is sensitive to a particular substance, a local reaction (redness and itching) will develop within several minutes. Occasionally certain substances may be injected directly into the outer layer of the skin, a process called **intradermal testing**. This is usually done when the child's history raises suspicions that one or more substances might be involved in her allergies but prick tests using those substances are negative. In general, skin tests are more useful in detecting allergies to airborne materials such as pollen, dust mites, and animal dander, and less reliable for allergies to foods.

Another option is the measurement of **immunoglobulin E (IgE)**, a specific antibody produced when an allergen enters the body. Blood tests can determine elevated levels of immunoglobulin E as well as the amount of antibody that has been produced against specific allergens such as grass, animal dander, or ragweed.

Common allergic syndromes

ALLERGIC RHINITIS An allergic reaction involving the lining of the nose is the most common of the atopic disorders, presumably because the nose is so often the first point of contact with airborne allergens. Symptoms occur with equal frequency among girls and boys and include a watery discharge and stuffiness of the nose, reddened lining of the lower eyelids, frequent clearing of the throat, mouth breathing, snoring, and the "allergic salute"—an upward wiping of the nose with the palm of the hand. Many such wipes may result in the appearance of a line across the nose known as an allergic crease. There is often a history of repeated nosebleeds, headaches, earaches, dizziness, a nasal tone to the voice, and dark circles under the eyes.

There are two primary types of allergic rhinitis. **Perennial allergic rhinitis** causes symptoms throughout the year but especially during winter months, when children spend more time indoors and have ongoing exposure to house dust or any indoor pets. **Seasonal allergic rhinitis**, more commonly known as **hay fever**, is brought on primarily by plant pollens that may be blown for miles by winds. While the seasons and local flora vary from region to region, troublesome pollens are typically produced by trees in the late winter and early spring, grasses in the spring and early summer, and weeds (especially ragweed) in the late summer and fall. Molds may also cause seasonal nasal allergy symptoms. Irritants such as dry air, tobacco smoke, pollution, rapid weather changes, humidity, cosmetics, and perfumes can also trigger episodes of allergic rhinitis.

The treatment of allergic rhinitis will depend upon the frequency and severity of the symptoms.

- **Antihistamines** interfere with the action of **histamines**, which are biochemical mediators in many (but not all) allergic reactions. In a best-case scenario, an antihistamine will reduce congestion, dripping, and sneezing for a few hours. However, with the older (or first-generation) antihistamines, including **diphenhydramine** (Benadryl) and **chlorpheniramine** (Chlor-Trimeton), side effects—especially drowsiness—can limit the usefulness of these medications. In some cases a trial-and-error approach is needed to find the best preparation for a particular child. The newer (or second-generation) antihistamines last longer (twelve to twenty-four hours) and are less likely to cause drowsiness. **Loratadine** (Claritin and generic forms) is available over the counter, while **fexofenadine** (Allegra), **cetirizine** (Zyrtec), and **desloratadine** (Clarinex) require a prescription and may be more expensive. Your child's physician can guide you to an appropriate antihistamine for your child with allergic rhinitis.
- **Decongestants** can shrink swollen membranes within the nose and ease breathing through congested nasal passages. As with antihistamines, effectiveness varies in children, and irritability is a potential side effect.

- **Decongestant nasal drops and sprays** can be bought without prescription and may temporarily relieve congestion associated with allergic rhinitis. Local side effects can include stinging, burning, irritation, nosebleeds, and sneezing. When used regularly for more than a few days, "rebound" nasal congestion (which can be worse than the rhinitis) may develop each time the medication wears off. If used at all, decongestant nasal drops or sprays should be limited to occasional treatment of severe and disruptive congestion (for example, when it interferes with sleep).
- **Corticosteroid nasal sprays** may be prescribed for long-term use in a child who has extended bouts of allergic rhinitis. These do not provide immediate relief but may reduce the allergic activity within the nose for extended periods of time, without side effects such as sedation or irritability. To be effective, they should be used consistently on a daily basis.
- **Cromolyn nasal spray** is available without prescription. It helps prevent the release of histamines. Like corticosteroid sprays, it does not provide immediate relief and must be used regularly on an ongoing basis to prevent allergic rhinitis.
- **Immunotherapy** (or **hyposensitization**), more commonly known as allergy shots, is a type of immunization in which small amounts of allergen are injected into the child at regular intervals and at gradually increasing doses. Eventually antibodies develop that can reduce or prevent the allergic response to the allergen. Typically the injections must be given regularly (usually weekly) for at least one to two years. If they are effective, the interval between them is gradually increased. Immunotherapy can be particularly helpful in treating allergic rhinitis caused by allergens that cannot be easily avoided, such as airborne pollens, and in situations where environmental measures and other medical treatments have not been effective.

ASTHMA A condition characterized by intermittent and reversible narrowing of the airways, producing bouts of coughing, wheezing, and difficulty breathing. Inflammation within the airways results in swelling, increased mucus secretion, and spasmodic contractions that are experienced as wheezing. Treating this underlying inflammation is as important in controlling asthma as stopping the wheezing episode itself. (The characteristics, prevention, and treatment of asthma are described in detail on page 624.)

SKIN DISEASES There are three major forms of skin diseases caused by allergies.

Infantile eczema (also known as **atopic dermatitis**) is considered an allergic disorder for the following reasons:

- Many infants with this syndrome also develop allergic rhinitis and asthma later in life.
- In many cases the rash appears to be an allergic response to certain foods, especially egg white, milk, wheat, soy, fish, and (among older children) peanuts. However, inhaling or direct skin contact with other allergens such as dust mites may also be involved.
- Infants and children with eczema are very prone to itching; the ongoing scratching that results plays an important role in perpetuating the rash. (Eczema has sometimes been called "the itch that rashes.")

Eczema usually develops when the child is two to six months old and may wax and wane over the next several months, often disappearing completely by the age of three. In some individuals this condition persists into later childhood or even adulthood. The rash of eczema is patchy, dry, slightly reddened, and very itchy. Intense scratching of the affected skin may lead to oozing, deep scratch marks called **excoriations**, bleeding, and infection. Irritation of the skin from chronic scratching may cause the formation of thickened plaques, a process called **lichenification**. During infancy, eczema often appears on the cheeks, scalp, neck, back of the arms, front of the legs, and the upper body. In an older child, the rash is commonly seen in the creases of the knees, elbows, neck, wrists, and face.

While foods and other allergens play a role in eczema, environmental factors also affect the skin. Cold, dry air causes the skin to become dry and scaly, while a hot, humid climate induces sweating, which may increase scratching. Skin irritants such as rough clothing, soaps, detergents, and fabric softeners can also worsen eczema.

A number of measures can help an infant or child with eczema. Try to maintain a stable temperature and humidity within the home. A child's skin should be protected from excessive dryness, which provokes itching and scratching. Because prolonged contact with water (especially very hot water) may actually dry the skin, use comfortably warm water for baths or showers and keep them short. Use a nonirritating brand of soap and pat lubricating oil on the affected skin while the skin is still damp. Moisturizing skin creams and softeners should be applied daily. Cotton clothing is preferable to wool, silk, and nylon. Clothes should be washed with a mild detergent and rinsed twice.

Check with your child's physician for recommendations regarding appropriate soaps and skin moisturizers for your child's age and skin condition. The physician may also recommend that a topical steroid preparation be applied to the most severely affected areas of skin. These can dramatically improve local inflammation and itching, but they should be used only as directed. Time limitations on the use of steroids—and the selection of the mildest form that will improve the rash—will help prevent steroid-induced local skin changes. An antihistamine such as diphenhydramine may help prevent scratching at night, and keeping fingernails short will help prevent further irritation. Specific foods that are clearly linked to a child's eczema eruptions can be avoided, but determining which ones might actually be involved is usually not easy. Severe dietary restrictions are unlikely to help eczema. If you are concerned about the number of foods that may be provoking a child's rashes, he should be evaluated by an allergist.

Contact dermatitis occurs when a substance that touches the skin causes a local allergic reaction. The most familiar form of contact dermatitis is the eruption caused by poison ivy, oak, or sumac. Other potential causes of contact dermatitis include cosmetics, soaps, detergents, perfumes, dyes used in fabrics, rubber, metal (especially nickel, sometimes a component of jewelry or wristwatch casings), topical medications, and compounds used in the preparation of leather. Several days of exposure might be needed to provoke a reaction, but once a child is sensitized, a rash could appear within twenty-four to forty-eight hours after contact.

Usually the shape and distribution of the rash will suggest contact dermatitis to a parent or physician. Treatment involves, first and foremost, avoiding the irritating substances. A local eruption will usually respond to a topical steroid preparation, but in more extensive outbreaks (such as with poison oak or ivy) oral steroids may be prescribed for several days. Antihistamines such as diphenhydramine sometimes help reduce itching.

Hives (also called **urticaria**) are a generalized allergic response involving raised, reddened, irregular itchy patches of skin that may blanch (turn white) when pressure is applied. They vary from dime-size to much larger areas of skin, and they constantly change size and location. When hives affect the deeper layers of the skin, the eruption is called **angioedema**, a change that can develop anywhere on the body but most commonly affects the mouth, eyes, tongue, genitals, and extremities.

Hives can last from minutes to days and may even recur in crops for weeks and months. An impressive number of allergens cause hives, and identifying the specific agent is sometimes quite difficult. Some possible causes or triggers of hives include the following:

- Foods such as milk, eggs, peanuts, berries, shellfish, and nuts
- Medications such as penicillin, sulfa drugs, and aspirin
- A variety of infections, including those caused by viruses (such as hepatitis or infectious mononucleosis), bacteria, fungi, and parasites
- Inhaled substances such as pollens, dust, and animal dander
- Physical events such as exposure to cold, heat, local pressure, vibration, and exercise
- Insect bites

If hives are a recurring problem or last for more than a few days, keeping track of foods, symptoms, or other events (including where the child has been) preceding their arrival could be useful. Skin testing is occasionally helpful. If there is a clear relationship to a specific food or drug, the provoking agent should be avoided. (The child's doctor and any others who care for him in the future should be notified of a suspected drug reaction.) In most cases, hives can be controlled with antihistamines such as diphenhydramine, cetirizine, or hydroxyzine (Atarax). Unless there is an underlying disease causing them, hives do not lead to other problems and will disappear without complications.

When hives are associated with sudden and dramatic swelling (especially around the face), difficulty breathing, or feeling faint, the child should be taken to the nearest emergency facility immediately. *If a child has had an extremely severe reaction to a particular drug, always remind the physician whenever any prescription is written, and as an extra safeguard mention the reaction to the pharmacist when having it filled.* If a child has ever had an immediate and serious allergic reaction, ask the physician about obtaining a kit containing injectable **epinephrine** (adrenaline) for emergency use.

FOOD ALLERGIES Various symptoms and syndromes are commonly attributed to foods, but true food allergy is relatively uncommon. Many genuine reactions to food, such as **lactose intolerance**, do not directly involve the immune system, and many behaviors (such as fatigue or hyperactivity) are provoked neither by food nor by allergy. Certain types of foods—milk, eggs, shellfish, peanuts, tree nuts (such as cashews and walnuts), fish, soy, and wheat—are responsible for the vast majority of allergic reactions and may be involved in eczema, hives, or more serious reactions. In some children certain foods consistently provoke vomiting, diarrhea, bloating, or crampy pain; whether or not the reaction is truly allergic or occurs on some other basis, the particular food in question should be avoided.

Food allergies (or other forms of intolerance) can be difficult to identify conclusively since foods are highly complex substances and the relationship between food and reaction may not be clearcut. Keeping a diary of both foods and symptoms sometimes helps. Skin testing helps in some cases, but reactions in the skin do not always correlate with responses to foods. A blood test that detects antibodies to specific food allergens may be helpful

but, like skin testing, results must be interpreted in light of the child's history and symptoms. For many children a diagnosis can be made using an elimination diet; a child is first given simple foods that are unlikely to cause a reaction, and then others are added gradually. An elimination diet should be supervised by a physician or dietitian to reduce the risk of nutritional deficiencies.

BITES OR STINGS These may result in local or more widespread allergic reactions. An **immediate hypersensitivity** reaction (usually resulting from venom produced by bees, wasps, hornets, or fire ants) may be severe, involving hives, wheezing, and a rapid drop in blood pressure known as **anaphylaxis** (see "Emergency Care," pages 798–799). This is a medical emergency, and rapid treatment with epinephrine, intravenous fluids, and other measures will be necessary. These insects should not only be avoided in the future, but treatment kits containing an injection of epinephrine should be available at home, in the car, or in the gear taken on camping trips or other outings. Immunotherapy (allergy shots) may be recommended to prevent this type of reaction.

The more common **delayed hypersensitivity** reaction produces dramatic local swelling around the site of the bite or sting, but this occurs over one or two days and is accompanied more by itching than by pain. Antihistamines will reduce the swelling and itching, or a short course of oral steroids may be prescribed to resolve the reaction more quickly. Fortunately, someone who has this type of response is not destined to develop the more severe immediate hypersensitivity reaction in the future.

Special note: Reducing a child's exposure to common household allergens

Dust mites are tiny, insectlike creatures that thrive in carpets, upholstered furniture, and bedding, especially when the air at home is warm and well humidified. The waste products of these microscopic animals can provoke a variety of allergic reactions, even after they have died. Encasing mattresses and pillows in special plastic covers can significantly reduce your child's exposure to dust mites. Treating carpets with mite-killing chemicals every few months may be necessary as well.

Molds thrive in warm, moist environments. A basement, especially if it has had any seepage or flooding; damp, dark closet spaces; or even a leaky toilet that invites mold to grow in the carpet surrounding it can breed these organisms. If your child definitely has a mold allergy, keeping the humidity at home less than 30 percent, using an air conditioner or dehumidifier, and monitoring your progress with a humidity gauge can be very helpful. Bathrooms, which obviously become warm and moist regularly, frequently harbor mold. Regular cleaning of tiles, bathtub, shower curtain or stall, walls, and ceilings with a mold-killing solution (such as a mix of equal parts bleach and water, or a commercial spray) is a tedious but important job. Carpet should be taken out of the bathroom because water spilled from a shower or bathtub or a leaky toilet invites mold to grow both within and beneath the carpet.

Allergens are abundant in animal dander and may cause many different allergy problems. Dealing with pets in your home may become a highly emotional issue if animals are causing a child to have significant symptoms. An allergy evaluation might be necessary to settle the question of sensitivity, and if a pet is part of the problem, it will need to be kept outdoors. If symptoms are severe enough, the pet must be removed completely from the home for the sake of your child's health.

Every child deserves to live in a smoke-free environment, and for an allergic child, exposure to tobacco smoke can be a hazard both to health and to life itself. Smoking should not be allowed in the home or any other environment (such as a car) in which an allergic child is present.

alpha-fetoprotein (AFP) One of the two major proteins that circulate in the blood of the developing fetus. A small amount of this protein finds its way into the mother's bloodstream. The level of AFP in the mother's blood normally rises gradually during the first twenty weeks of pregnancy, and it can be measured as a screen for certain fetal abnormalities such as neural tube defects (see "Maternal blood tests: alpha-fetoprotein, beta-HCG, and estriol," beginning on page 90, for more information).

altitude-related illness In order to function at altitudes higher than a few thousand feet above sea level, the human body must make several adjustments to compensate for the reduced availability of oxygen, especially when exertion takes place. People who begin strenuous exercise in the mountains without first becoming acclimatized may become very uncomfortable or in some cases seriously ill. Some individuals have difficulty even without exerting themselves.

Acute mountain sickness can begin a few hours or days after arrival at altitudes over 6,500 feet. Headache, loss of appetite, nausea, and fatigue are its primary symptoms. Irregular breathing patterns during sleep may cause frequent awakening, but with time, sleep patterns return to normal. More severe cases are evidenced by changes in consciousness, **cyanosis** (a bluish discoloration of the skin, the area beneath the nails, and the lips), and a staggering gait.

Rapid ascent to higher altitudes (usually over 8,000 feet) followed by heavy exertion can lead to a serious disorder in which fluid leaks from small blood vessels into the air sacs of the lungs. Shortness of breath, cough, rapid heart rate, and fatigue develop over one to three days, and a characteristic gurgling sound may be heard if one listens to the chest. If untreated, this condition, known as **pulmonary edema**, can progress to cyanosis, changes in consciousness, coma, collapse of the cardiopulmonary (heart and lung) system, and even death.

Mild mountain sickness will usually improve with rest, increased fluids, and mild pain relievers for headache. A physician might prescribe the drug **acetazolamide** (Diamox) to help reduce symptoms. People who are more severely ill must be escorted or carried to a lower altitude as soon as possible. Improvement begins after the victim descends a thousand feet or more and receives oxygen by mask. *Never let the victim descend alone.* A thorough evaluation by a physician is mandatory before returning to a high altitude.

The most effective measure to prevent altitude-related illness is to allow enough time—two to four days, if necessary—for a child to become accustomed to the reduced oxygen concentration before beginning strenuous activities at a higher altitude. Increasing fluid intake will help, as will a high-carbohydrate diet. Teenagers or adults who have experienced acute mountain sickness (or worse) in the past may benefit from taking acetazolamide on the day of ascent and for two days after arrival. Teenagers involved in rock climbing or other mountain activities should be warned not to ignore symptoms because of peer pressure or a misguided desire to tough it out when they feel sick. Assume any illness at high altitude to be mountain sickness or one of its more serious variations until proven otherwise, and treat it accordingly.

amblyopia A visual impairment (sometimes called lazy eye) that can develop when an infant or young child experiences double vision from misalignment of the eyes (strabismus). Amblyopia can also arise when one eye is affected with more nearsightedness, farsightedness, or astigmatism than the other. Visual impairment occurs when the child's brain suppresses incoming information from one eye, which is otherwise normal. (See "eye care and concerns.")

amenorrhea Absence of menstrual periods.

amniocentesis A prenatal testing procedure in which fluid is withdrawn from the amniotic sac surrounding the fetus by placing a needle through the abdominal wall and into the uterus. An analysis of the fluid can detect chromosomal abnormalities such as Down syndrome. This procedure is sometimes done late in pregnancy in situations where a need to induce labor must be weighed against the possibility that the baby's lungs will not be mature enough to function normally once out of the womb. (See page 92.)

anal problems By far the most alarming anal problem in infants and children is bleeding, and the most common cause of bleeding in this area is a **fissure**, a crack or tear in the sensitive skin of the anal opening. Fissures are nearly always caused by the passage of a hard stool, although scratching or sometimes irritation from cleansers in baby wipes can promote the formation of fissures. Typically the blood appears as a streak on the stool, and it may not be present the next time the bowels move. If blood actually flows after a stool, it will usually stop on its own in five to ten minutes.

Treatment involves eliminating any underlying cause of the fissure, if possible, since nearly all will heal on their own if they are not continually irritated. If stools are hard, increased amounts of fluid, dietary fiber (from fruit, vegetables, and bran), a mild stool softener, or even mineral oil may be helpful, depending upon the age of the child (see "constipation"). Multiple fissures and inflamed tissues may improve with warm soaks and the use of a mild cortisone cream. If there are other contributing factors such as infection or pinworms (see below), these should be treated. Your child's health-care provider should give you input in the diagnosis and management of this problem.

Hemorrhoids are dilated veins in the anal area that can bleed, itch, or clot. They are extremely uncommon in infants and children, and if discovered, a cause should be sought. While prolonged constipation and straining may be the cause, abnormalities in the venous system, which returns blood to the heart, must be considered.

Anal itching can be caused by irritated skin, a fissure, soaps and cleansers, or **pinworms**. If you discover your child intensely scratching this area during the night, pinworms might be the cause (see "pinworms"). A local infection involving the common yeast *Candida albicans* can be treated with antifungal cream. Occasionally a child with a bacterial infection in the nose will accidentally transfer the bacteria to the anal area. In this case, antibiotics will eradicate the eruption.

anaphylaxis The most severe form of an allergic reaction. An allergen such as venom from a bee sting, medication, or food can set off a life-threatening reaction that may involve severe difficulty in breathing, a drop in blood pressure (known as **anaphylactic shock**), hives, and severe abdominal pain. *This is an emergency requiring immediate medical care* and then follow-up with an allergist or immunologist to review the likely cause(s) of the reaction, prevention, and treatment of any recurrences (see "Emergency Care," page 799).

anemia An abnormally low concentration of red blood cells, which are needed to carry oxygen to all tissues. Red blood cells are so vital to life that they are produced continually throughout the body in tissue called **marrow**, which lies protected within the bones of the skeleton. Red cells circulate within the bloodstream for about four months and then are removed by specialized tissues that recycle their contents. Anemia occurs when the production of red cells cannot keep pace with their loss or destruction. This condition is detected by a blood test that shows a low level of **hemoglobin**, the protein within red cells that transports oxygen, or by a low **hematocrit**, the percentage of whole blood that consists of red cells.

The significance and consequences of anemia will depend on a number of the following factors:

- The severity of anemia—whether the blood count is mildly or significantly reduced
- How quickly the anemia has developed
- The age and general condition of the infant or child
- The presence of other medical problems

The most common cause of anemia is **iron deficiency**, which results in a reduced production of hemoglobin. Deficiencies in vitamins and folic acid, which are much less common, can also cause a decreased production of red cells, along with other medical complications. Some forms of anemia, such as **sickle cell disease**, arise from a change in the shape or rigidity of red cells, which leads to more rapid destruction.

The causes of anemia are numerous and may reflect minor or serious problems. It is important to diagnose anemia correctly and to determine the underlying cause, prescribe appropriate dietary or medical treatment, measure the result of that intervention, and prevent recurrences.

anterior fontanelle (see illustration on page 63) The diamond-shaped soft spot near the front of a newborn's skull, where the bones have not yet grown together. This will be replaced with solid bone by eighteen months of age. The tough fibrous membrane covering the fontanelle is not easily injured, and parents need not fear touching

or stroking this area when washing or combing a baby's hair.

antibiotic A drug that takes a specific action against one or several types of bacteria. Unlike viruses, which multiply only within the cells they invade, bacteria can live and reproduce on their own. Most bacteria are harmless to humans, but some are capable of damaging tissues, producing toxins that interfere with normal body functions, and even overwhelming the immune system—sometimes resulting in death.

Many antibiotics work by interfering with the multiplication of bacteria, while others kill them outright. Antibiotics do not interfere with the immune system but supplement the body's own defenses. Without an intact immune system, even the most potent antibiotics are likely to be ineffective.

Use of antibiotics
Antibiotics can be effective in fighting infections under the following conditions:

THE INFECTION MUST BE CAUSED OR AGGRAVATED BY BACTERIA. *This means that infections such as the common cold, influenza, most cases of the stomach flu, croup, and the majority of sore throats will not respond to antibiotics, because they are caused by viruses.* Antibiotics are designed to affect specific structures and functions of bacteria that are not present in viruses, and thus viruses are not affected by antibiotics. Skin problems such as ringworm or *Candida* (yeast) infections cannot be cured by antibiotics; specific antifungal medications can help resolve them.

Antibiotics can be beneficial in treating a variety of infections, including:

- Wound and skin infections, especially when pain, swelling, redness, and tenderness arise from a cut or scrape.
- Infections of the throat (**pharyngitis**) or tonsils (**tonsillitis**), if streptococcus or other disease-causing bacteria are involved. A throat swab for quick antibody testing or culture is necessary to make an accurate diagnosis of streptococcal infection. *The majority of sore throats, however, are caused by viruses and will disappear on their own.* If symptoms last more than a few days or if fever

is persistent, contact your child's physician (see "sore throat").

- Certain upper-respiratory infections, such as **sinusitis**, **bronchitis** (infection involving the bronchial tubes that carry air into the lungs), and **otitis media** (infection involving the middle ear, the space behind the ear drum). The decision to use antibiotics in a given case will depend on the history, physical findings, and judgment of the prescribing physician. Note that the common cold is a viral infection that will not respond to antibiotics. (See "bronchitis," "colds," "ear infections," and "sinusitis" for more information on these specific infections.)
- **Otitis externa** (swimmer's ear), an infection of the skin and soft tissue that line the ear canal. This is usually treated with antibiotic drops and sometimes with oral antibiotics as well. (See "ear infections.")
- **Pneumonia**, infection of the lung tissue itself (as opposed to the bronchial tubes). An exam and (with rare exception) an X-ray are needed to make this diagnosis. A variety of organisms (including viruses) can cause pneumonia, and in some cases blood tests and cultures may be utilized to clarify the diagnosis and guide treatment.
- **Urinary tract infections**, which involve the bladder or kidneys. These are usually caused by bacteria and should be treated with antibiotics. Cultures may be necessary to find the right medication. Follow-up is essential after a child is treated for a bladder or kidney infection because of the possibility of an underlying problem in the anatomy or the function of the urinary tract (see "urinary tract care and concerns").
- The presence of a fever over 100.4°F (38°C), taken rectally, in an infant younger than three months may indicate a serious bacterial infection. A thorough evaluation will probably be necessary to make the correct diagnosis.

THE BACTERIA CAUSING THE PROBLEM MUST BE SENSITIVE TO THE ANTIBIOTIC. Not only must the antibiotic have the ability to affect the specific type of bacteria, but it must be effective in treating the particular strain of the bacteria.

Many infections can be treated based on what is known about the bacteria that usually cause them. In serious, stubborn, or recurrent infections, however, a culture of the organisms and an evaluation of their sensitivity to various antibiotics are necessary to guide further treatment.

THE ANTIBIOTIC MUST BE CAPABLE OF REACHING AN EFFECTIVE THERAPEUTIC LEVEL AT THE SITE OF THE INFECTION. Some antibiotics, for example, cannot be used to treat meningitis because they do not readily pass from the bloodstream into the central nervous system.

THE ANTIBIOTIC MUST BE APPROPRIATE FOR THE CHILD'S AGE-GROUP. Tetracyclines, for example, should not be given to a pregnant woman or to children younger than eight years of age, since these drugs may cause permanent discoloration of developing teeth.

THE DOSE, TIMING, AND RELATIONSHIP TO MEALS SHOULD BE ACCURATE. Obviously, it is up to the doctor to make an appropriate choice of antibiotic for your child's infection, but it is also important that you follow all the directions. Before you leave the pharmacy or the doctor's office, be sure that you understand the following:

- How much is to be given? Infants, toddlers, and school-age children will probably be taking liquid forms. A well-marked measuring device (such as an oral syringe) is more accurate than a kitchen spoon. If doses are given in terms of teaspoons, remember these equivalents:

  1 tsp = 5 cc or ml
  ½ tsp = 2.5 cc or ml
  ¼ tsp = 1.25 cc or ml
  1 cc (cubic centimeter) = 1 ml (milliliter)

- How often? Some antibiotics have convenient dosage routines of once or twice daily, but others must be given more often.
- With or without food? Some antibiotics must be taken on a full stomach to avoid nausea, while others won't be absorbed very well unless the stomach is empty.
- How long? This will depend on the type of infection and the antibiotic being used. Often a

prescription must be continued for ten days or longer to bring the infection under control and prevent a recurrence. Be sure to complete the full course of antibiotic that has been prescribed—*regardless of how much the symptoms decrease or disappear.* (If an allergic reaction or other side effect is taking place, however, stop the antibiotic and contact your child's physician.)

- If the antibiotic is liquid, should it be refrigerated or left at room temperature? Some liquid preparations tend to dehydrate over the course of treatment (especially when kept in the refrigerator), but this can be minimized by placing the container in a resealable plastic bag.

- Is a follow-up appointment needed? A recheck may be recommended by your doctor, even if things are going well. For example, if ear infections have been a problem, a follow-up on the appearance and functioning of the ear will be important. If your child has had any type of urinary tract infection, the urine may be rechecked to ensure that bacteria are no longer present.

Special note: How to get the medicine down

Giving the proper doses of an antibiotic (or any other medication) at the right time can be challenging when the patient is an infant or toddler, especially if he isn't cooperating. Some ideas that may help this process include the following:

- Most liquid antibiotics are formulated in fruity flavors that are usually palatable to children. If the taste isn't appealing to your child, check with the pharmacist about disguising the flavor in food or liquid such as applesauce, juice, or (for an older child) peanut butter.

- Use the most effective delivery device for your child's mouth. For infants, calibrated droppers usually work the best; the medication can be inserted a little at a time into the space between the cheek and the gums. An alternative is to put a nipple (without bottle attached) into the baby's mouth and put the medication into the back of the nipple, or add the antibiotic to a small amount of juice or other liquid in a bottle. For toddlers and older children, most pharmacies or doctors' offices can supply a child-size spoon whose handle is a calibrated tube that measures the precise amount of medication.

- If an infant spits up immediately after taking an antibiotic, it is usually appropriate to try again. (This is not necessarily true for other types of medications.) If you are not sure about whether or not to do this, or if your child is vomiting and cannot keep the antibiotic down, contact the physician for further directions.

- An older child can be rewarded for taking medicine pleasantly—perhaps with a gold star on a chart after each dose and a modest prize when the entire course of treatment is done. However, he must understand that the antibiotic must be taken whether he cares for it or not, and you won't debate with him over every dose.

- If your child has a particular preference (such as chewable medications rather than liquid) or if he is able to swallow tablets, let the doctor know at the time the prescription is written.

Using antibiotics appropriately and effectively

- Don't assume that every infection has to be treated with antibiotics. If your doctor feels that your child's illness is caused by a virus, don't insist that antibiotics be given "just in case."

- Don't give one child's antibiotic to another, even if the illnesses seem very similar, without checking with the doctor first.

- Don't assume that if a little is good, more is better.

- Finish the full prescription.

- If cost is a concern, ask your doctor if there is a generic form of the medication that would be appropriate.

What about allergic reactions and side effects?

If you think an antibiotic may be causing a problem, contact your child's physician for further advice and clarification as to whether this might be an allergic reaction, a side effect, or something else entirely. Allergic reactions are a response of a child's immune system to a specific substance and are usually manifested as a rash or more serious conditions such as hives, swelling of face or tongue, or wheezing. If an allergic reaction to a drug has occurred, it is very likely that it will occur again—often more severely—if the same drug is given in the future. Antibiotics most commonly involved in true allergic reactions are derivatives of sulfa drugs (used most often to treat urinary infections) and certain forms of penicillin. Allergic reactions to specific drugs are not routinely passed from one generation to another. If one parent is allergic to penicillin, for example, this does not necessarily mean that the child will be.

Side effects, in contrast, are not brought about by the immune system and will not necessarily occur every time the same medication is given. A common side effect of some antibiotics is nausea, especially with **erythromycin** and its various derivatives, such as **clarithromycin** (Biaxin). Diarrhea can also be caused by any antibiotic that alters the normal assortment of bacteria in the colon.

It may be difficult to decide whether a problem is an allergic reaction or a side effect or whether it was caused by the antibiotic, the infection, an interaction between the two, or something entirely unrelated. Amoxicillin, for example, frequently provokes rashes if it is taken during certain types of viral infections (especially infectious mononucleosis) but not during subsequent uses. (Note: Amoxicillin is not prescribed specifically to treat viral infections, but it may be added if there appears to be a bacterial complication.) In this case the reaction is not a true allergic response, and the antibiotic can be used in the future. If it is unclear whether or not an antibiotic caused a particular problem, the drug (and others similar to it) may have to be used with caution, if at all, in the future.

Your child's physician will record in the child's medical chart any reaction to a drug, and you should add this information to your child's health record at home as well. If you have phoned your child's physician about a reaction, remind him or her about it during your next office visit to ensure that it has been noted in the chart.

antibody A specialized protein that participates in the body's immune response to specific microscopic organisms (such as bacteria or viruses) or to foreign substances. A large number of specific antibodies have been identified and categorized into subclasses that are associated with diverse protective functions. Some antibodies, for example, appear immediately in response to a specific infection, while others participate in long-term immunological "memory" that can protect against future infections by the same organism. In some situations an antibody response may cause mild or severe symptoms, as in allergic reactions, or it may cause inflammation or damage to normal tissue, as in autoimmune disorders such as rheumatoid arthritis.

antigen Any molecular structure, whether existing independently or as a component of an organism (such as a virus) or a cell, that brings about an immunological response (see "allergen").

Apgar score A scoring system on a scale from zero to ten that assesses the condition of a newborn at birth based on heart rate, breathing, reflexes, muscle tone, and color. Newborns are scored at one, five, and ten minutes after birth (see page 61).

apnea A temporary cessation of breathing.

appendicitis An acute inflammation of the appendix, a narrow, worm-shaped structure positioned near the junction of the small and large intestines in the lower-right corner (called a quadrant) of the abdomen. Appendicitis is the most common reason for abdominal surgery in children.

The first symptom is usually cramping pain in the upper-middle abdomen that gradually moves downward and to the right while becoming more constant as the inflammation intensifies. Loss of appetite, nausea, and vomiting commonly occur as well. Appendicitis has several different pain patterns, especially in children. Sometimes younger children do not pay attention to (or are unable to describe) the shift in location of pain from one area to the other, especially when they are not feeling well. Older children may be more cooperative and better able to describe the location and characteristics of the pain.

Fever may develop as infection and inflammation of the appendix become more severe. If the appendix is not removed, it will likely rupture. The infection contained within it can then spread into the abdominal cavity, resulting in inflammation of the inner lining of the abdomen—a condition called **peritonitis**. When this occurs, pain worsens and the child becomes increasingly ill.

In children with appendicitis, the time from the first symptom (typically cramping pain or nausea) to rupture of the appendix is usually less than thirty-six hours. Because the symptoms of appendicitis are much more difficult to identify in children younger than two years of age, the likelihood of rupture in this age-group is almost 100 percent. The frequency of rupture is much lower among older children because they can usually communicate their symptoms more clearly, allowing for an earlier diagnosis.

No single test can establish or exclude appendicitis 100 percent of the time. The diagnosis is made by evaluating the child's history, a physical examination, laboratory results, and usually some form of imaging (ultrasound or CT scan). If your child's doctor or an emergency-room physician suspects appendicitis, a surgeon will be consulted. In some areas, most often in rural settings, family physicians perform appendectomies, in which case a surgeon would not be called. If the surgeon agrees with the diagnosis, surgery is performed as soon as possible in an attempt to remove the appendix before it ruptures. This can prevent a much more severe illness, prolonged antibiotic treatment in the hospital, and longer postoperative recovery. If the doctor feels that the appendix has already ruptured, the operation might be delayed for a number of hours to allow for the administration of antibiotics and intravenous fluids. If the surgeon is not sure of the diagnosis, he or she may observe the child for a period of time.

Sometimes surgery for suspected appendicitis reveals a normal appendix. This is not evidence of bad medical judgment, however, because other conditions can mimic the pain of appendicitis. One common example is a condition called **mesenteric adenitis**, in which lymph nodes inside the abdomen (especially near the appendix) become enlarged, inflamed, and painful, in a manner strikingly similar to an inflamed appendix. Even if a normal appendix is found, it will be removed for three reasons: (1) The appendix has no proven function of importance to human health; (2) if it is left in the patient, it could become infected at

some time in the future; and (3) if the appendix is left in and the patient's memory of the original surgery is faulty, a doctor evaluating any future problems would see the scar and could mistakenly assume that the appendix was removed—leading to a potentially disastrous misdiagnosis.

If the appendix has not ruptured, the child will usually leave the hospital in one to three days. If it has ruptured, hospitalization normally continues for several days to continue intravenous antibiotics and fluids. Usually normal activities can be resumed as soon as they are tolerated, with the exception of contact sports, which might cause pain in the event of a direct blow to the incision.

arthritis See "Musculoskeletal Problems in Children," page 761.

ascariasis An infection caused by a large roundworm (ranging from five to fourteen inches in length) that is the most common human intestinal parasite worldwide. It is found most frequently in young children in tropical or subtropical climates, primarily in underdeveloped countries. Ascariasis is uncommon in the United States. It is commonly transmitted by eating food that has been grown in soil contaminated by human feces. Symptoms, if present, may include vague abdominal discomfort, loss of appetite, or diarrhea. The diagnosis is made by examining a stool sample for microscopic-size eggs or by seeing adult worms passed in a bowel movement.

asthma An inflammatory disorder of the airways, characterized by a tendency of the muscles surrounding both large and small airways to undergo spasmodic contractions, resulting in coughing, wheezing, or both. The events that trigger wheezing vary from person to person but can include illness (especially colds, bronchitis, and sinusitis), exercise, emotional upset, as well as exposure to smoke, dust, pollen, mold, air pollution, animal dander, cockroach infestation, perfumes, colognes, or even certain foods. Some girls may wheeze during the days prior to their menstrual periods. Wheezing may also be provoked by certain medications, such as aspirin. An important characteristic of asthma is that this spasm or constriction is reversible; with medication or time, the airway will return to normal.

As noted above, inflammation is an important component of asthma. Even when not in spasm, the inner lining of an asthmatic child's airways may be chronically inflamed, accompanied by swelling, increased mucus production, and large numbers of inflammatory cells. Treating the wheezing while ignoring the inflammation will usually result only in temporary improvement. Asthma is often called **reactive airway disease** because the airways react (or overreact) to a variety of stimuli. However, experts note that there are individuals who manifest reactive airways on one or more occasions for any number of reasons, but they do not in fact have asthma.

Asthma may be an occasional annoyance or a disruptive, frightening, and at times life-threatening illness. It is the most common chronic illness among children: As many as 10 percent of girls and 15 percent of boys will be affected at least once by this problem. Roughly four out of five children with asthma will have had their first episode before entering school; asthma causes more days of missed school and places more limits on activity than any other chronic childhood condition.

While the majority of children with asthma have occasional episodes that can be treated relatively easily, some develop severe and persistent symptoms that can be very stressful for everyone in the family. Usually the more seriously afflicted children have a family history of asthma and allergic disease and show signs of trouble during their first year of life. At least half of all asthmatic children become symptom free eventually, at least in part because their airways enlarge as they grow. As more sophisticated treatments have become available, deaths from asthma have decreased over the past few years and are rare among children.[2] Nevertheless, because uncontrolled asthma can be lethal, *treating this disease diligently should be a very high priority in any family in which one or more children are affected.*

Symptoms
A dry, tight cough that occurs for no apparent reason or in patterns (such as during the night or after exertion) may be an early—and in some cases the only—sign of asthma. In more intense episodes, overt wheezing may be audible from across the room. Some sounds that resemble wheezing, however, can actually arise from upper-airway infections such as croup, and a physician's evaluation will be necessary to make the distinction.

If the airways are particularly tight, the child may show more obvious signs of distress: rapid respirations, labored breathing with minimal exertion or when at rest, and noticeable use of muscles in the rib cage and neck with each breath. In severe cases, he may be unable to walk or talk, the skin may be pale or even dusky, and abdominal pain or even vomiting may occur. A child who is extremely short of breath should be seen by a physician immediately or taken to an emergency room.

Depending on the severity of the symptoms and the patterns of wheezing your child is showing, a variety of tests may be performed. Your child's doctor may ask you to obtain a **peak flow meter**, which measures the maximum rate of airflow your child can generate at a given time and can be used as a guide to adjust medications. This simple test can be extremely useful in keeping track of your child's progress on a day-to-day (or hour-to-hour) basis. A chest X-ray may be needed to rule out an underlying infection. Allergy testing may be appropriate to determine what is triggering wheezing episodes.

Prevention
This will depend to some degree on the specific triggers that provoke the airways to twitch and tighten. Some of these triggers will be clear-cut and others less obvious.

Dealing with furry and feathered pets in your home may become a highly emotional issue if animals are causing your child repeated bouts of breathlessness. An allergy evaluation might be needed to settle the question of sensitivity, and if a pet is indeed part of the problem, it may have to be kept outside. If symptoms are severe enough, the pet must be removed completely from the home for the sake of your child's health.

Dust mites are tiny, insectlike creatures that thrive in carpets, upholstered furniture, and bedding, especially when the air is warm and humid.

The waste products of these microscopic animals can provoke all sorts of allergic reactions, including wheezing, even after the mites have died. Encasing mattresses and pillows in special plastic covers can significantly reduce your child's exposure to dust mites. Treatment of carpets with mite-killing chemicals every few months may be necessary. In some situations, it might be best for you to remove carpeting altogether.

Molds also thrive in warm, moist environments. A basement, especially if it has had any seepage or flooding; damp, dark closet spaces; or even a leaky toilet that invites mold to grow in the carpet surrounding it could breed these organisms and perpetuate asthma. Unfortunately, the humidifier you might have purchased to make your baby more comfortable can become a source of mold if it isn't cleaned and the water changed frequently.

If your child definitely has a mold allergy, keeping the humidity at home at less than 30 percent, using an air conditioner or dehumidifier, and monitoring your progress with a humidity gauge can be very helpful. Bathrooms, which obviously become warm and moist regularly, frequently harbor mold. Regular cleaning of tiles, bathtub, shower curtain or stall, walls, and ceilings with a mold-killing solution (such as an equal mixture of bleach and water or a commercial spray solution) is a tedious but important job. Carpet should be taken out of the bathroom because water spilled from a shower or bathtub or a leaky toilet invites mold to grow both within and beneath the carpet.

Every child deserves to live in a smoke-free environment, and for an asthmatic child, smoke exposure can be a hazard both to health and to life itself. Any form of tobacco smoke—including residual particles left on clothes or hair after smoking outside—will provoke and perpetuate wheezing; smoking should not be allowed in the home or any other environment (such as a car) in which an asthmatic child is present. In addition, if a child is sensitive to other environmental triggers, such as paint fumes, perfume, aerosol sprays, or even air pollution, any and all reasonable efforts to minimize exposure to these should be taken in order to prevent asthma attacks.

Reactions to pollens that appear at different times of the year (or year-round) may be more difficult to prevent because these particles are so tiny and can be blown for miles by the wind.

For the severely affected child, an evaluation by an allergist might be wise. The allergist can offer guidance regarding preventive measures, and when appropriate, treat with **immunotherapy** (allergy shots), which will cut down the child's reaction to specific triggers, especially pollens, that you can't easily control.

Treatment

A child of any age with asthma needs a team of attentive parents and health-care providers on his side. *Good rapport among all concerned is essential.* The specific approaches used for your child will depend upon the frequency and severity of the asthma episodes and the triggers that set them off. Treatment may be needed sporadically or year-round. *The most important intervention for asthma may be daily medication that prevents wheezing, not the sporadic treatment of flare-ups.*

Several types of medications are prescribed to treat asthma, but patients (or the parents of young children) must clearly understand their specific functions and when and how they should be used.

A family of medications called **bronchodilators**—such as **albuterol** (Proventil or Ventolin) or **levalbuterol** (Xopenex)—immediately relieve wheezing and usually maintain improved airflow for four to six hours. These are usually taken through **metered dose inhalers (MDIs)**, which dispense measured bursts of medication. For very young children as well as older children with more severe asthma, a **home nebulizer device** may be more appropriate. This converts liquid medication into an aerosol form that is easily inhaled using a face mask or mouthpiece. Because bronchodilators are distantly related to adrenaline, they may cause tremors or rapid heart rate, especially if taken more often than prescribed. These symptoms are more likely if the pill or syrup forms are used rather than an inhaler, and they are uncommon with levalbuterol. Because bronchodilators help asthmatic children feel much better right away, they are frequently overused. Repeated doses of this type of medication may cause enough temporary relief to delay more definitive care while the overall situation is actually deteriorating. If your child is using the bronchodilator four or five times a day regularly, his asthma is very likely out of control, and you should see his doctor as soon as possible to discuss additional treatment. *Do not buy and use over-the-counter asthma inhalers as a substitute for proper medical care and supervision.*

Corticosteroids in various forms more directly quiet down the inflammation that underlies the reactive airway response. Your child's doctor might prescribe a brief course of oral steroids to bring an intense wheezing episode under rapid control. Long-term oral corticosteroid treatment can cause a number of significant side effects, but inhaled corticosteroids pose far fewer risks and are very effective—indeed, they are a mainstay of asthma management. *Using a corticosteroid inhaler daily for weeks or months to prevent wheezing will generally be safer than intermittent doses of bronchodilators to stop acute asthma attacks.* **Budesonide** (Pulmicort), **beclomethasone** (QVAR), **fluticasone** (Flovent), **mometasone** (Asmanex), and **triamcinolone** (Azmacort) are examples of corticosteroid inhalers that may be employed to prevent asthma in a child or adolescent. One preparation, Advair, combines fluticasone with the long-acting bronchodilator salmeterol.

Leukotriene inhibitors—such as **montelukast** (Singulair) and **zafirlukast** (Accolate)—may help prevent asthma attacks and are usually very well tolerated by children and adults alike.

Cromolyn (Intal and other brands) is another option for long-term prevention, especially for a child with exercise-induced wheezing or a strong allergic component to his asthma. This medication is given by inhaler. While it is not as potent as a steroid, cromolyn can help prevent or minimize wheezing in a child who is already stabilized.

All inhalers are usually more effective in children if **spacers** such as the AeroChamber or InspirEase are used with them. A spacer is purchased separately (or provided by the physician), and the inhaler canister is inserted into it prior to each use. (One steroid product, Azmacort, comes with a built-in spacer.) These devices eliminate the need for precise coordination of the child's deep inhalation and the actuation (firing the puff) of the inhaler. Spacers also prevent larger droplets of the medication from being deposited in the mouth and throat and improve the overall delivery of the drug to the lower airways. If your child is going to use a bronchodilator and a steroid or cromolyn inhaler at the same time, the bronchodilator should be given first because it will open up the airways and allow better distribution of the other medication. Holding the breath for a few seconds after inhaling a puff will help more of it arrive at its destination. If you are confused about the operation of an inhaler or a spacer device, don't leave the pharmacy or doctor's office until you understand exactly what to do with whatever device you have been given, since your child's ability to breathe may depend on it. As noted above, for very young children or those with more severe symptoms, a home nebulizer may be recommended both for bronchodilator and inhaled corticosteroid treatments.

Theophylline has been used to treat asthma for many years and may be helpful for some children, though it is more often for maintenance than for acute care. Usually given in liquid, tablet, or powdered form (which is stirred into food such as cereal or applesauce), most theophylline given today is in timed-release forms that last for eight to twelve hours. Side effects can include nausea, vomiting, and jitteriness. Checking blood levels will usually be necessary to confirm that the right dose is being given.

Antibiotics may be needed at some point to treat a bacterial infection of the bronchial tubes or the sinuses. If your asthmatic child has a cold, check with the doctor before giving a decongestant or antihistamine formula. Some of these—especially certain antihistamines that can cause bronchial mucus to thicken—may interfere with the action of other medications.

Because so many medications are potentially helpful in treating wheezing, you may become concerned about the number of drugs your asthmatic child is taking. But if wheezing is intense, chronic, or difficult to control, a number of different medications may indeed be needed, and it is extremely important that you (and your child, if he's old enough) understand the purpose, dose, timing, and precautions for every medicine he is going to use. You should have written directions in your hand before you leave the doctor's office or pharmacy as well as an invitation to call back if you have questions. You should know whom to call and where to go in case the problem increases after office hours, since asthma has a tendency to worsen during the night.

Remain vigilant with maintenance medications (such as an inhaled corticosteroid) even when your child seems to be doing better—the fact that wheezing episodes are less frequent is a sign that these are working, and they should be continued unless you are specifically instructed to do otherwise. *One of the most common reasons for an unexpected trip to the emergency room to treat an asthma attack is failure to continue one or more maintenance medications.*

You and your child's doctor should discuss the basic goals of therapy, which should not be limited merely to stopping acute wheezing episodes but should address preventing them as well. You may also need to learn how to use a peak flow meter, which will give everyone a better feel for how your child is doing. Ultimately, your child should be able to sleep through the night, feel normal during the day, and enjoy reasonable strenuous activity without coughing or wheezing. He should not think of himself as the sick kid who can't play ball or participate in sports because of his condition. Bronchodilators and cromolyn each have the capacity to reduce or prevent exercise-induced wheezing. A child or adolescent who coughs or wheezes during vigorous exercise may have less difficulty breathing and better endurance if one of these inhalers is used about a half hour before the activity begins.

astigmatism An egg-shaped curvature of the cornea that prevents the eye from focusing correctly, resulting in blurry vision. This can usually be corrected through eyeglasses, contact lenses, or surgery.

athlete's foot A common skin infection caused by a type of fungus called a **dermatophyte** (literally "skin plant"). It can live only in the outermost layer of skin, where there are no living cells. Warm and humid conditions increase the likelihood of infection, as do shoes (especially those made of rubber or nylon) that do not allow the skin to dry or cool. Athlete's foot is more likely to occur after puberty.

The fungus itself does not penetrate into the skin, but substances generated by the fungus seep into the deeper (live) skin layers and provoke an allergic response. This commonly appears as a mild, scaly rash between the toes that may spread to the skin on the top or the sole of the foot. More intense reactions can occur, with bumps, blisters, burning, and itching.

A variety of antifungal creams, ointments, lotions, powders, and aerosols (many are nonprescription) are effective in treating athlete's foot. Creams are often used because they are less greasy and easier to apply. A mild cortisone cream may also be used for a few days to relieve itching and irritation. A rapid improvement in symptoms does not mean that the fungus has been eradicated. Most antifungal medications must be continued every day for three to four weeks to bring about a cure. If symptoms do not improve after a week of treatment, the eruption should be evaluated by a doctor.

Unfortunately, someone with a healed case of athlete's foot is not immune to getting it again, and new contact with the fungus can restart the infection. Keeping the feet as clean and dry as possible can help prevent recurrences.

autism An extremely complex neurological disorder with varying symptoms and signs. Among the most notable symptoms are nondeveloped or poorly developed verbal and nonverbal communication skills: abnormalities in speech patterns, impaired ability to sustain a conversation, abnormal social play, lack of empathy, and an inability to make friends. Autistic children often have a compulsive adherence to routines and rituals, and they usually lack interest in their peers.

The professional assistance provided for an autistic child will depend on various factors, including behavior and functional level, the availability of consultants and facilities in a given area, and the resources and stability of the family. Several professionals—physicians, psychologists, developmental specialists, speech therapists, and teachers—as well as ongoing programs, both in and out of the home, may be involved in the process of helping the autistic child reach her full potential.

B

bacteria Microscopic single-cell organisms that are present in nearly every environment, including the human body. Unlike viruses, which can multiply only by taking control of the genetic equipment of cells they invade, bacteria are capable of reproducing by fission (or dividing) under all kinds of conditions—within and on the surface of living (and dead) animals and plants, in bodies of water, in the soil, in food, or virtually anywhere else. They are not necessarily harmful. In fact, the human skin, nose, mouth, intestinal tract, and vagina are colonized by more than two hundred species of bacteria, whose number and type vary with age, sex, diet, and nutritional status. Many of these play a variety of beneficial roles, such as preventing harmful microorganisms from gaining a foothold on or in the body, as well as stimulating immunological responses against more harmful bacteria.

Other bacteria, however, cause disease by generating toxins that damage tissue or disrupt normal body functions. Sometimes the body's immune response to invading bacteria is damaging in itself. Illnesses caused by bacteria include many forms of pneumonia, tuberculosis, strep throat, sinusitis, whooping cough (pertussis), bladder and kidney infections, abscesses, gonorrhea, syphilis, and many others. The development of antibiotics that can selectively disable or kill bacteria without destroying normal cells was one of the most important breakthroughs of the twentieth century (see "antibiotic").

bad breath See "halitosis."

bed-wetting (enuresis) Gaining consistent control of bladder and bowel functions during daytime hours is a significant milestone for a toddler or preschooler. For many children, keeping the bed dry at night is a more elusive goal, one that might not be reached until quite a bit later in life. Children who still wet the bed at night well into their grade-school years too often take an emotional beating (and in some sad cases a physical beating) because of this problem—*which is not under their conscious control.* One of the greatest problems faced by bed-wetting children is a parent with unrealistic expectations that every child should be completely dry, day and night, by the

age of three. To deal with bed-wetting effectively and supportively, it is important to understand some basic realities of nighttime bladder function in children.

Definition

Enuresis is the involuntary passage of urine into the bed or clothes at least once or twice per month in a child who is at least five years of age. Although involuntary wetting may occur during the day, this discussion will be limited to nighttime enuresis.

A child with **primary enuresis** has never remained consistently dry through the night for more than six to twelve months. A child with **secondary enuresis** has achieved consistent nighttime bladder control for six to twelve months and then for some reason loses it.

Causes

Only about one percent of children with enuresis will be found upon medical examination to have an underlying disease or disorder such as a urinary tract infection, diabetes, significant constipation, a congenital abnormality of the urinary tract, or a disturbance in the central nervous system. When evaluating persistent bed-wetting, a child's physician will consider these physical possibilities (which usually have other manifestations) and carry out appropriate studies if necessary.

In the other 99 percent of children with enuresis, the problem may involve one or more of the following, but clinicians are not in complete agreement about the relative importance of each of these factors:

• *Delayed maturation.* During infancy, the bladder automatically empties six to eight times per day when a certain volume of urine is present. As a child matures, this emptying reflex is inhibited (held in check) by the central nervous system so that he can hold larger amounts of urine and eventually release it voluntarily. In general, control is achieved earlier by girls than by boys. By the age of three, most children can consistently postpone urinating during waking hours. However, the ability of a child's central nervous system to inhibit emptying of the bladder during sleep may lag behind daytime control by months or even years. By the age of five, as many as 10 to 20 percent of children are not consistently dry in the morning.

- *Small functional bladder capacity.* A normal child can usually voluntarily hold urine in an amount of ounces equal to his age in years plus two. (A six-year-old child, for example, should be able to hold about eight ounces, or about 240 ml, of urine.) If a child cannot hold at least the same number of ounces as his age, this decreased capacity may contribute to enuresis.

- *Increased formation of urine during the night.* A hormone called **vasopressin**, which is produced by the pituitary gland, reduces urine production by the kidneys. An increased amount of this hormone is normally secreted during the night, cutting the rate of urine production in half. Some bed wetters apparently do not secrete more vasopressin during the night and produce more urine than their non-bed-wetting peers. A similar result may occur, regardless of vasopressin levels, if a child consumes liquids before going to bed.

- *Difficulty awakening when the bladder is full.* While the general patterns of sleep are similar in both bed-wetting and non-bed-wetting children, many parents observe that their child with enuresis will "sleep through anything" and seems very difficult to awaken during the night.

- *A family history of enuresis.* Since so many of the factors contributing to bed-wetting have an inherent physiological basis, it should not be surprising that this problem often runs in families. Enuresis is seven times more common in children whose fathers were bed wetters and five times more common if the mother had this problem. If both parents were bed wetters, the likelihood that their child will have enuresis is greater than 75 percent, compared to roughly 40 percent if one parent was a bed wetter and 15 percent if neither parent was a bed wetter.

Evaluation

If your child is wetting the bed repeatedly after his fifth or sixth birthday, an evaluation by your child's physician is a reasonable first step. (Very often this problem can be addressed during a routine checkup.) A careful history will be taken and a physical examination performed, along with any appropriate laboratory studies (such as a urinalysis). A culture of the urine will be taken if there is concern about an infection. In most cases elaborate diagnostic tests are not needed. But if the initial assessment raises concerns about the structure or function of the urinary tract, your child's physician will want to evaluate further.

If a child develops secondary enuresis—that is, he has been consistently dry in the morning for more than six months and then begins wetting the bed again—a specific explanation should be sought. Situations that are stressful to a young child (such as a move or a new baby in the house) very often play a role, although a medical problem such as a bladder infection or diabetes might also be manifested in this way.

Management

First and foremost, remember that for the vast majority of children, enuresis will eventually resolve on its own as the central nervous system matures. (Each year after the age of six, 15 percent of children who still have enuresis will spontaneously stop wetting at night.) *Enuresis is not a sign of disobedience or weakness of character.* The child who wets the bed is already embarrassed and uncomfortable about it; ridicule or punishment for bed-wetting, including teasing by siblings, is cruel, unjust, and ineffective. Not only will it cause additional emotional problems, but it might actually delay the resolution of enuresis.

Unless an underlying medical problem has been discovered by your child's physician, it is unrealistic to expect the doctor to provide a specific treatment that will cure enuresis overnight. Steps can be taken to eventually achieve one of two satisfactory goals: Your child holds his urine through the night and then voids into the toilet or potty-chair in the morning, or your child awakens during the night when his bladder is full and voids into the toilet or potty-chair.

The following measures may help a child with enuresis:

- Encourage fluid intake during the day and discourage drinking liquids after the evening meal or within two hours of bedtime. If your child wants a drink before bed, limit intake to one or two ounces (30 or 60 ml).

- Have your child empty his bladder just before he goes to bed.
- Encourage your child to get up during the night to urinate. A child who feels that his only goal is to delay emptying his bladder until morning may fail repeatedly. Giving verbal cues before bed ("Try to get up and use the toilet if your bladder feels full"), leaving the light on in the bathroom, or providing a potty-chair near the bed can help.
- To a degree that is appropriate for his age, let him participate in the cleanup process when his pajamas and bed are wet. *This should be presented not as punishment but as a matter-of-fact routine.* This can include rinsing out his pajamas and underwear and taking a quick bath or shower in the morning if he smells of urine. Sheets can be left open to air-dry but should be washed if they have a disagreeable odor. A dry towel placed under the child's bottom may help reduce the amount of laundry. A school-age child who wakes up wet during the night can change his own pajamas and place a dry towel over the wet area of the sheet. (Dry pajamas and towels should be made readily available in his room.)
- Protect the mattress with a plastic cover.
- Offer praise and perhaps a smiley-face sticker on the calendar when he has a dry night or gets up to use the toilet.
- Avoid expressing dissatisfaction, dismay, or anger when he is wet in the morning.

Bed-wetting alarms

These devices might be helpful for a child with enuresis who is eight or older (or in younger bed wetters if they are highly motivated) and who has not succeeded with other methods. Unlike the older pad-and-bell systems, the newer alarms are compact, portable, and relatively simple to use. (Retail prices range from about $70 to $120.) (Beware of aggressively advertised, expensive programs that promise to "cure" bed-wetting. Helping your child accomplish this goal may be labor-intensive, but it shouldn't be expensive.) A sensor attached to the child's underwear will cause the device to buzz or vibrate against the skin like a pager when very small amounts of urine are released. The child should be encouraged to wake up as quickly as possible when the alarm goes off, get to the toilet, and empty any remaining urine. Over a period of several weeks, most children begin to associate the full bladder with the alarm-awakening process, and then with awakening before the alarm goes off. Medical studies have demonstrated an overall success rate of about 70 percent of cases in which these alarm systems are used; they are most effective when both parent and child are motivated to use them every night for two to three months.

Difficulties may arise if the child does not readily awaken to the noise or vibration. Parents should be prepared to get up when the alarm sounds, gently rouse the child, and have *him* turn off the alarm and use the toilet after he is definitely awake. Patience and persistence on everyone's part will be needed to condition the child's central nervous system to awaken, first to the alarm and eventually to the full bladder.

For those who want to try a less high-tech approach, a regular alarm (bell, buzzer, or radio) can be set to go off three or four hours after the child goes to bed. The alarm should be out of his reach so he must get up to turn it off. He should be encouraged to proceed from alarm to toilet to empty his bladder before returning to bed. The timing of this wake-up call will have to be determined by trial and error, of course, and will depend upon the hour that bed-wetting most commonly takes place. As with the bed-wetting alarms, this approach will require more effort if the child is extremely difficult to awaken during the night.

Drugs to stop bed-wetting

Two medications have been recognized as potentially helpful in controlling bed-wetting. The use of either requires a doctor's prescription and a thorough understanding of potential benefits, risks, and proper use. Consider these important points before using either of these drugs:

- They are best suited for children who are at least eight years old and for whom other methods have not been consistently successful.
- In many cases they provide temporary assistance rather than a permanent cure. Enuresis often resumes when a medication is discontinued

(especially if done abruptly) unless other training methods have been utilized as well. Long-term use of medication might be considered in specific situations—for example, an older child or adolescent with persistent enuresis—depending upon the underlying cause.

- They can be very helpful for the child who wants to participate in activities such as campouts or sleepovers with friends or relatives without worrying about wetting the bed or sleeping bag.
- Either drug should be tried at home to check for effectiveness or side effects before being used on an overnight outing.

Imipramine (Tofranil and other brands) increases the bladder's functional capacity and reduces its tendency to empty spontaneously. It is inexpensive and usually tolerated well when given in the proper dose, although it can cause anxiety and insomnia. The major problem with this drug, however, is its toxicity in case of an accidental overdose, which can lead to seizures, coma, or fatal heart-rhythm disturbances. For this reason, if your child is taking imipramine for enuresis, *never give a larger dose than the doctor has recommended, and be sure the bottle is not accessible to any other child at home.*

Desmopressin (DDAVP) acts like the pituitary hormone vasopressin (described in the earlier section regarding causes of enuresis), reducing the amount of urine produced during the night. It is safe and relatively easy to take (it comes as a tablet or as a nasal spray), but results obtained with it are inconsistent, and enuresis commonly recurs when the drug is discontinued. It is also expensive—well over seventy-five dollars per month, compared with about five dollars per month for generic imipramine. When it works, desmopressin can be particularly useful for the older child or adolescent who needs some protection from bed-wetting during an overnight outing as well as minimal risk of unwanted side effects.

Another type of medication known as an **anticholinergic agent**—for example, **oxybutynin chloride** (Ditropan) or **tolterodine** (Detrol)—may sometimes be prescribed for older children or adolescents with bed-wetting.

In summary, bed-wetting can be a great source of ongoing distress and discouragement for a child. It is therefore very important that a child understands these points:

- He will eventually grow out of this problem.
- He is not the only child who has ever dealt with bed-wetting. (Perhaps Mom, Dad, or other relatives had enuresis as well. If so, letting him know this will provide some reassurance.)
- His parents, siblings, and physician are all on his team.
- There may be some effort involved (appropriate for his age) in dealing with the wet pajamas and sheets and in bringing bed-wetting under control, but his participation is not a punishment.

Bell's palsy A sudden and usually temporary weakness affecting one side of the face. This condition is seen more commonly among adolescents and adults than children. Movement of the mouth and eyelids (including the ability to close the eye) is most commonly affected. Bell's palsy often follows a viral illness, but many times the underlying cause is unknown. Most cases begin to improve within a week or two, and the vast majority resolve within two months. However, about 10 percent of people with Bell's palsy experience some persistent lack of symmetry of facial muscles, and 5 percent have significant long-term problems. A child or adolescent who develops weakness of facial muscles should be evaluated by a physician as soon as possible, both to establish the diagnosis and to begin appropriate treatment. Anti-inflammatory and antiviral medications may be prescribed, although their effectiveness remains uncertain. In addition, specific measures may be recommended to protect the cornea, which can become dry because of incomplete closure of the eyelids during blinking.

benign A term used to indicate that a condition is relatively mild or not likely to cause serious consequences. It is most commonly applied to a tumor that is not cancerous. (In contrast, a tumor that invades other tissue or spreads to other parts of the body is referred to as malignant.)

bilirubin A by-product of the breakdown of red blood cells, which normally circulate in the bloodstream for about four months until they literally wear out. The liver processes and excretes bilirubin. If the liver is diseased, as in hepatitis, or immature, as in newborns, the level of bilirubin in the bloodstream may become high enough to cause a yellow-orange discoloration of the skin known as **jaundice**.

Before birth a baby's bilirubin is largely managed through the mother's circulation. After birth it takes a newborn's liver a few days to take over this process, so the level of bilirubin in the baby's bloodstream will increase by a modest amount. If a significant backlog develops, the baby's skin will take on a yellow-orange hue, beginning with the head and gradually spreading toward the legs. Whether or not jaundice is significant will depend upon several factors, including the actual level of bilirubin, how soon and how fast it has risen, the suspected cause, and whether the baby is full-term or premature. In some instances, extremely high bilirubin levels can damage the central nervous system, especially in the premature infant. If you notice your new baby's skin color changing to bright yellow-orange, contact your baby's doctor.

If there is any concern, the baby's physician will order blood tests to check the bilirubin level, and if needed, other studies will be done to look for underlying causes. Sometimes high levels of bilirubin result from a difference between a mother's blood type and that of her newborn. For example, if the mother's blood type is O and the baby's is A or B, some anti-A or anti-B antibodies from the mother may cross the placenta into the baby's circulation before birth. These antibodies can destroy many of the newborn's red cells, leading to a high bilirubin level shortly after birth.

A more severe form of this process used to occur commonly in connection with a protein known as the **Rh factor**, which is either present on the surface of blood cells (making a person Rh-positive) or absent (Rh-negative). In the past whenever a mother with Rh-negative blood gave birth to an infant who was Rh-positive, the mother's immune system would become sensitized to the Rh factor. If she had another pregnancy with an Rh-positive baby, her Rh antibodies would cross the placenta and destroy significant numbers of the new baby's red cells. Babies born under these conditions were often jaundiced at birth and became quite ill, requiring immediate transfusions of antibody-free blood. Today Rh incompatibility problems are avoided by giving Rh-negative mothers a shot (called RhoGAM) that prevents her immune system from developing Rh antibodies.

In most cases a newborn's jaundice is the by-product of normal physiological processes and is not caused by an Rh or blood-type incompatibility or other problems (such as infection). This so-called **physiologic jaundice** will eventually resolve on its own within ten to fourteen days.

In some situations (depending on various factors), the baby's doctor will recommend one or more of the following measures to help lower a bilirubin level that has become significantly elevated:

- Treat any underlying cause (such as an infection), if present.
- Increase the baby's fluid intake by feeding her more often.
- Expose the baby to *indirect* sunlight for periods of twenty to thirty minutes—dressing her in only a diaper in a sunlit room *where the sun does not shine directly on her sensitive skin.* Since indirect sunlight has only a modest effect on clearing bilirubin, don't use this approach unless you are sure that your baby won't become too hot or too cold.
- Sometimes an enzyme found in the mother's milk interferes to a modest degree with the clearing of bilirubin. Your physician may ask you to stop breastfeeding for a short time and use formula until the problem improves, after which nursing can resume. In such a case, it is important that you continue to express milk to maintain your supply. This should not be an occasion to stop nursing altogether. Some healthy breastfed infants will have a slight orange hue for weeks.
- A treatment called **phototherapy** may be utilized if the bilirubin level needs to be treated. Under a physician's direction, the baby lies under a special intense blue light while wearing eyeshades like a sunbather at the beach. In addition or as an alternative, a baby can lie on a thin plastic light source called a BiliBlanket.

Whether carried out in a hospital or at home (using equipment provided by a home-health agency), phototherapy usually reduces bilirubin gradually within two or three days, if not sooner.

A newborn whose jaundice resolves and then reappears should be checked by a physician, as should an older infant or child who appears jaundiced for the first time. The skin of some older infants who are taking solids and regularly enjoy carrots and other yellow vegetables may actually develop a slight orange hue, which is harmless and has nothing to do with bilirubin. This does not cause the whites of the eyes to become yellow. A more obvious yellow coloration of skin (as well as the whites of the eyes) in a child may indicate that the liver is inflamed or (far less common) that the drainage of bile from the liver is obstructed.

birthmarks Birthmarks occur where there is an overabundance of a particular component of normal skin, such as tiny blood vessels (capillaries) or pigment cells. The cause of this local condition is unknown.

The flat, pink birthmarks commonly seen on the forehead, eyelids, back of the neck, and above the bridge of the nose are called **capillary hemangiomas**, also known as stork bites or salmon patches. These are seen in about 50 percent of newborns. Eyelid patches will disappear by three to six months of age, while those on the neck will fade but may last for years.

Areas of dark or bluish gray pigmentation known as **Mongolian spots** are common on the low back and buttocks of dark-skinned newborns, although these marks may be found in all racial and ethnic groups. These marks vary greatly in size and shape and usually disappear by two to three years of age.

A more permanent type of birthmark is the **café au lait spot**, a light brown flat patch that can occur anywhere on the body. Some may be present at birth, but others may appear later in life. While these markings are benign, the presence of six or more of them measuring more than five-eighths of an inch (16 mm) in diameter may indicate a more serious problem known as **neurofibromatosis** (see "neurofibromatosis").

One or more dark brown, black, or blue-black spots known as **nevi**, which contain large numbers of pigmented cells, may be seen at birth in about one in one hundred Caucasian infants. While the vast majority of these spots never cause any trouble, on rare occasion (usually in adolescence or even later in adulthood), one or more may transform into a dangerous type of skin cancer called a **malignant melanoma**. You should become familiar with the appearance of any nevi on your child's skin and watch in particular for any of the following warning signs: significant change in size; crusting, oozing, or bleeding; the development of an irregular border or color pattern; and change from a flat to a raised or rough contour. Should any of these changes develop, ask your child's doctor or a dermatologist to examine the area.

A more troublesome (but also uncommon) birthmark is the **giant pigmented nevus**, an irregular, raised dark brown patch more than four inches (10 cm) in diameter. When this covers a large area of the lower trunk, it is called a bathing trunk nevus. At a microscopic level this is structurally similar to common moles (or **junctional nevi**), which become more common and widespread over the skin later in life. Unfortunately, giant pigmented nevi are much more likely than the smaller congenital pigmented nevi to transform into malignant melanomas. This change can occur during infancy or at any time later in life. For this reason a consultation with a dermatologist or plastic surgeon may be recommended at an early age.

blood poisoning Nonmedical term for the serious condition known as **septicemia**, in which a significant number of microorganisms (usually bacteria) are present in the bloodstream.

blood pressure The pressure of the circulating blood within the arteries is dependent on the strength of the heart's contraction, the elasticity of the walls of the arteries, and the volume of blood in an individual's body. Blood pressure is expressed as two numbers: the **systolic** pressure, which occurs at the peak of the heart's contraction, and the **diastolic** (or minimum) pressure in the blood vessels, which occurs when the heart is filling up with blood, preparing for the next beat.

High blood pressure (also called **hypertension**, which is no reflection on one's emotional state) is not unusual in adults and is a risk factor for coronary artery disease and stroke. Even though it is much less common in children, your physician will begin measuring your child's blood pressure routinely at age three. Persistent high blood pressure in children should be investigated to find the cause.

body odors

Before puberty

Parents are usually aware of subtle (or at times strong) aromas emanating from their baby or young child during a typical day. Occasionally you may notice an unfamiliar odor that could indicate a specific problem.

Bad breath (**halitosis**) usually indicates that an infection is present somewhere—in the gums, throat, tonsils, adenoids, or sinuses. A child with nasal congestion who breathes through the mouth or a child with a chronic cough may also have bad breath. A trip to the doctor's office will probably be necessary to find and treat the cause.

An *extremely* foul odor emanating from a small child's face, worsening by the day and not improved by toothbrushing or bathing, is probably the result of an object that has been stuffed up the nose. Thick, discolored drainage from one nostril may be a more prominent symptom than the smell. A wad of paper, a pencil eraser, a piece of foam from the couch, a pea or bean, or a small body part from a stuffed animal are among the possibilities. In most cases, your child's doctor will be able to extract the foreign object with narrow forceps, but be prepared to help hold your child still while the object is removed.

A similar but less common scenario may occur if your daughter inserts a small object into her vagina. A strong odor from the genital area, with or without discharge, should be checked by her doctor. A bacterial infection can also generate a disagreeable odor that won't clear with simple bathing and will need medical attention.

Smelly feet can occur in a child of any age who wears poorly ventilated shoes. Heat, sweat, and bacteria are the main ingredients, and treatment isn't particularly complicated: Have the child wear well-ventilated footwear or sandals, or let her go barefoot. Clean socks and a daily bath or shower will certainly help. Foot powder sprinkled into shoes may absorb some of the perspiration and help curb the aroma.

A sick child sometimes gives off unusual odors. An oddly sweet aroma (or one that resembles nail polish) can be caused by compounds called **ketones**, which accumulate when a child hasn't been eating because of stomach upset. Rarely this smell heralds the onset of diabetes, but if this is the case, the child will have other symptoms: thirst, frequent urination, weight loss, and increasing listlessness. *This situation needs immediate medical attention* (see "diabetes mellitus").

Unusual odors such as a maple-syrup or sweaty-feet smell in an infant who isn't wearing shoes may indicate metabolic disorders that are often serious but fortunately are extremely rare. Usually other features of these diseases—failure to gain weight, lethargy, seizures, and delayed development, among others—will signal that something is drastically wrong well before anyone is concerned about unusual smells.

After puberty

With the onset of puberty comes a different set of odor problems. Sebaceous glands on the neck and upper body, under the arms, and in the genital area begin to produce material called **sebum**. Skin bacteria acting on this substance can generate very disagreeable body odor after one or two days. Interestingly, the watery perspiration that appears during exercise or stress has no odor at all.

Teenagers can fall into two extremes in dealing with body odors. Some are overly concerned about the social consequences of body odor and go to extremes using antiperspirants (which can irritate the skin under the arms), aftershave, cologne, vaginal douches, foot powders, or other products they have seen advertised in magazines or on TV. Other teens may need prompting to take care of even the most basic hygiene.

In dealing with adolescent odor issues, moderation and common sense should prevail. Daily showering or bathing, regularly using shampoo (every day for some teens), wearing clean socks and underwear each day, brushing teeth after meals, and laundering or dry-cleaning clothes—in other words, basic self-care—will prevent most body-odor problems.

Girls who have begun menstruating may worry about odor arising from this monthly event and may be tempted to use "hygienic" measures such as douches or feminine sprays. Menstrual flow itself is not malodorous. Simple measures such as daily bathing or showering, changing saturated pads, or (most important) not leaving a tampon in the vagina for more than six hours will prevent or minimize unpleasant odors. Feminine-hygiene sprays can irritate delicate tissue, and douching is unnecessary to maintain cleanliness. Any persistent drainage that is discolored, itchy, painful, or foul smelling could indicate the presence of an infection (or, rarely, a lost tampon). This should not be treated by douching but should be evaluated by a physician.

botulism (see also "foodborne illness") A rare but extremely dangerous form of food poisoning. It is caused by a toxin produced by the bacterium *Clostridium botulinum*, which may grow in improperly canned food. (Home-canned foods are the most common source of botulism.) **Infant botulism** may occur in babies younger than one year of age and is most commonly caused by the ingestion of honey contaminated with the spores.

breath-holding spells These are frightening but common events that occur in about 5 percent of children, typically beginning between about six months and two years of age. There is a history of breath holding among parents or siblings in about one out of four families in which it occurs.

There are two types of breath-holding episodes. In the more common **cyanotic** type, crying occurs after a physical or emotional incident that provokes fear, anger, or frustration. Normally most young children who suddenly become upset will release a long, continuous cry that finally ends just in time to take a big gasp of air, and then they cry out again. The breath holder extends her cry so long that she doesn't quite make it to the breath she needs. She suddenly becomes stiff, arches her back, and turns blue in the face. She may lose consciousness for about fifteen seconds

(which can seem much longer to the first-time observer) and make brief jerking movements of the arms and legs that resemble (but are not) a brief seizure. Finally she will take a breath. When the episode is over she will be fully awake and aware, not confused or unresponsive as would be the case after a seizure.

The second type is the **pallid** breath-holding spell, in which the child becomes pale in response to a sudden painful stimulus (for example, getting her finger caught in a door or having blood drawn at the doctor's office). Aside from the child being pale rather than blue, this episode looks similar to the cyanotic breath-holding spell.

These spells ultimately arise from a brief lack of oxygen available to the brain. Although they are very dramatic and may appear life-threatening, breath-holding spells end spontaneously. They do not cause brain damage, nor are they a form of epilepsy. However, they can be very stressful to a parent or caregiver, especially if he or she has never seen one.

Once you have observed one or more breath-holding spells and know how they end, you can be calmer when one occurs in the future. While the term *breath-holding spell* implies that this event might be purposeful, be aware that it is not a performance or a deliberate, premeditated act. Nevertheless, don't let the potential of one of these spells become an indirect form of manipulation by your child. Some parents may give in to a child's demands to avoid seeing another spell ("We can't let Johnny get too upset or he might turn blue again"). This is both unwise and unnecessary. If your child becomes upset over reasonable limits or appropriate disciplinary measures and has a breath-holding spell as a result, you should not feel guilty or alarmed. Stick to your principles. Ninety percent of breath-holders stop having these episodes on their own by the age of six, and by age seven or eight, breath-holding episodes should stop altogether.

breech birth The delivery of a baby feet or buttocks first rather than headfirst.

bronchiolitis An acute respiratory illness that most commonly affects young infants, especially those between two and six months of age, although it can be seen in children as old as two. The viruses that cause this infection not only irritate the nose and upper airway (as seen in a typical cold), but they also provoke inflammation and narrowing of very small airways known as **bronchioles**. (This is a different illness from **bronchitis**, which affects the larger airways.)

Bronchiolitis is a seasonal illness, usually seen between November and April. While any of a number of viruses (including influenza) could be the cause, the **respiratory syncytial virus (RSV)** is usually involved. RSV is such an extraordinarily contagious virus that virtually all children have been infected with it by the age of two. Only about one in three develop lower-airway problems such as bronchiolitis or pneumonia, while the rest have more routine colds. Breastfed infants are less likely to develop bronchiolitis than those who have been exclusively bottle-fed. Other risk factors for developing bronchiolitis include prematurity, exposure to tobacco smoke, underlying disease of the heart or lungs, or exposure to many children, as occurs in a nursery or day-care setting.

Bronchiolitis usually begins with typical cold symptoms—a runny nose, cough, and low-grade fever—for one to three days. Then comes a deeper, raspy cough, followed by more rapid, shallow, and noisy breathing (or in some cases wheezing), depending on the severity of infection. Infants with bronchiolitis frequently lack interest in feeding and often become restless and agitated.

For most infants, bronchiolitis resolves on its own over seven to ten days without special medication or hospitalization. The most important thing you can do for your child is to watch her activity, feeding, and breathing patterns. Calming and comforting her as much as possible can help, since fussing and crying can aggravate any breathing difficulty. Using a cool-mist humidifier and encouraging her to take liquids will help her clear secretions and prevent dehydration. Because of the extra effort needed to breathe, she may nurse or take formula more slowly. Over-the-counter decongestants or cough mixtures are not usually recommended for infants with bronchiolitis, and antibiotics will not alter its course, although they may be used if a secondary bacterial infection develops. Oral **bronchodilators** (medications that

help open the airway) may be prescribed by your child's doctor.

You should call your infant's physician during a respiratory illness if she appears to be having difficulty breathing, which may be manifested by rapid respirations (forty or more times per minute), retracting (visible pulling inward) of the spaces between the ribs with each breath, or a pale or bluish color (especially around the lips or fingertips). A temperature of 100.4°F (38°C) or more in an infant younger than three months of age, or the inability to keep fluids down because of vomiting in a child or infant of any age, would also be reasons to call the doctor for further advice.

Occasionally an infant with more severe bronchiolitis will need to be hospitalized. Oxygen and supplemental fluids are usually given, and inhaled bronchodilators may be considered as well.

A child with RSV sheds a large amount of virus from the secretions of the nose and upper airway, and these viruses (like many others) are easily passed from person to person by hands and inanimate objects. If you are caring for a baby or child with a runny nose and cough, remember to wash your hands after you have handled her (or anything she has touched or gummed) to reduce the risk of spreading the virus to other children. Infants and toddlers are contagious for two to three days before their symptoms begin and for one to two weeks after.

A baby with chronic medical problems who might have more difficulty with bronchiolitis might best be kept away from groups of small children (such as day care or the church nursery) during the winter and early spring, especially when RSV or influenza is known to be present in your community. Check with your baby's health-care provider for specific advice.

For most infants and children, there are no lasting effects of bronchiolitis, but those who have had it are more likely to develop asthma later in life. It is unknown whether damage to the airways from RSV makes them more prone to wheezing or whether children who are destined to become asthmatic simply have more trouble with RSV.

bronchitis Inflammation of the passages of the lungs known as the **bronchial tubes**. In the vast majority of cases, bronchitis in children is

B

a component of an upper-respiratory infection caused by a virus—the same type of virus that causes runny nose, scratchy throat, and perhaps a fever. Because bacteria are rarely the cause of bronchitis in children and adolescents, antibiotics are unlikely to be of any help with this type of illness. However, coughing often persists for many days after the acute illness has ended, disturbing child and parents alike and raising diagnostic issues for the health care provider: Is this ongoing cough caused by inflammation in the bronchial tubes that was stirred up by the virus and is taking some time to resolve? Or could it be caused by something else, such as pneumonia, allergy, tobacco smoke in the home, wheezing, a sinus infection, or even whooping cough? Even after a child is carefully evaluated by a health-care provider, the cause may not be obvious, so some patience on everyone's part may be needed. Needless to say, if coughing continues for more than seven to ten days (especially if it is frequent) or if a child manifests any difficulty breathing prior to that time, she should be seen by a physician.

bruxism Grinding or clenching of the teeth. See "teeth care and concerns" (page 726) for more information.

bursa A fluid-filled sac, found in various locations in the body, where there is potential for friction to develop between two adjacent structures, such as a tendon and a bone. Typically a bursa is positioned to allow these structures to move freely in relation to each other. If a bursa becomes inflamed (a condition called **bursitis**), local pain, swelling, tenderness, and difficulty moving the affected area may result.

C   **cancer** Cancer is frightening for adults and even more frightening when discovered in an infant or child. Fortunately, in children cancer is not only frequently treatable but also often curable.

Cancer is not a single disease but a collection of different syndromes that have a common theme: the uncontrolled multiplication of a particular type of cell. Because there are many types of cells, each having a different function and behavior,

there are also many types of cancers. **Tumor** and **neoplasm** (literally, "new tissue") refer to abnormal growths, which may be further divided into **benign** and **malignant** subcategories. Benign (or "good") tumors arise in one place and stay there. They range in size from tiny warts (which are technically benign tumors caused by a virus) to rather bulky growths that may require extensive surgery to remove.

Malignant tumors not only grow at their point of origin but also tend to invade and disrupt surrounding tissue. (The term *cancer* is applied specifically to malignant tumors.) Worse, malignant cells may enter the lymphatic system. This system consists of tiny vessels that collect fluid from every part of the body and route it back into the bloodstream. Collections of cells known as **lymph nodes**, which assist in the body's immune response, are also found throughout the system. Unfortunately, cancer cells arising from a particular organ may invade nearby lymph nodes. When cancer enters the lymphatic system or the bloodstream, it can spread to other parts of the body. This process is called **metastasis**; a tumor that has spread to a place distant from its point of origin is **metastatic**. Tumor cells multiply and spread so extensively that they disrupt normal body functions, eventually resulting in illness or even death.

Much research has been done to understand why certain cells rebel and override the normal processes that regulate their growth. Multiple factors may be involved, including genetic vulnerability, environmental exposure (for example, to radiation), and infection with certain viruses. It is usually not possible to determine why a particular individual has developed cancer at a young (or older) age.

The most common forms of cancer in children are actually not solid tumors but **leukemias**, in which certain types of white blood cells appear in the circulation in enormous numbers. These cells not only can interfere with normal immune function but also can overrun the bone marrow, where normal blood cells are produced. Many cases of childhood leukemias are very responsive to medical therapy. Other common childhood tumors arise in the lymph tissue (**lymphomas**), kidneys, and central nervous system. Each type of cancer has its own characteristic patterns of growth, spread, symptom production, and response to treatment. (The most common adult cancers, which arise in the lung, breast, colon, or prostate gland, are very unusual in children.)

Symptoms that might suggest that a child has cancer are often vague or elusive and may not be evident until abnormal cells are disrupting normal body functions. These might include persistent fever, unexplained weight loss, fatigue, headache, or abdominal pain that is localized in one area. It is important to remember that such symptoms are not specific for cancer (or anything else) and should not lead to an immediate concern that a child has cancer. Occasionally a malignancy is discovered during a routine checkup when a doctor notices an unusual mass in the abdomen or perhaps skin changes that raise concerns over abnormalities in the blood.

The diagnosis of a tumor and identification of its particular cell type will require a formal medical evaluation and usually several tests and procedures. Some studies (such as blood tests) are relatively simple, while others, such as X-rays, CT scans, or even surgical removal of tissue for diagnosis (**biopsy**) can be much more involved. Treatment options will depend upon the type of tumor, the extent of its spread, its cellular characteristics, the age of the child, and the experience of the physician. While detailed explanations of treatments such as radiation or chemotherapy are beyond the scope of this book, it is important that both parent and child (if the child is old enough) understand at each step what is going on, what the options might be, and what the benefits and potential risks of any proposed therapy are. Because of the anxiety and family disruption that childhood cancer can bring, a parent might not grasp all the information being presented and may need further explanations later. *Do not hesitate to ask for as much information as you need, as often as you need it, when dealing with a problem of this significance.*

Because medical treatments for cancer can be frightening to the child and the parents, the temptation to abandon standard therapy in favor of alternative or unconventional therapies is sometimes strong. But the search for such an approach could delay treatments that have proven response rates and much stronger validation from scientific research. Your child will be much better served by your emotional support and prayer in combination with timely administration of well-studied therapy.

candidiasis An infection caused by organisms called *Candida* (a type of fungus). Candidiasis most commonly involves the species *Candida albicans* and occurs either on the skin surface or within the mouth or vagina. These so-called yeast infections are not uncommon in infants, appearing either as oral **candidiasis** (or **thrush**) or as **candidal diaper dermatitis**. Occasionally oral candidiasis is seen in children and adolescents who are using a steroid inhaler to treat asthma. This side effect may be avoided by rinsing out the mouth with water after each use of the inhaler.

Thrush appears as a white film or patches on the tongue, inner surfaces of the cheeks, or roof of the mouth. It may be confused with milk coating the mouth, but leftover milk can be scraped off easily with a cotton swab. Thrush is not harmful, but it can be a persistent annoyance, especially when *Candida* transferred to the mother's breast causes a local eruption on her skin. Thrush can be treated with an oral antifungal solution such as **nystatin**, which the baby's physician will prescribe. Antifungal creams may also be applied to the areola and the nipple of breastfeeding mothers. Usually infant and mother are treated concurrently for several days to prevent the infection from being transferred back and forth between them. To prevent reinfection, nursing pads should be changed after every feeding. If the baby is bottle-feeding or using a pacifier, the rubber nipples and pacifiers should be boiled every day until the infection clears. (Soaking these items overnight in a mixture of two tablespoons (30 ml) of vinegar in a quart (liter) of water is an alternative to boiling.)

Candidal diaper dermatitis is intensely red, often with small extensions or "satellites" around the edges of the rash. This can be treated with an antifungal cream recommended by the baby's physician, as well as with other basic measures (see sidebar, page 146).

Candida vaginal infections can occur in postpubertal girls and adult women. These infections typically are manifested by an itchy vaginal

C

irritation and discharge that contains white clumps resembling cottage cheese curds. The diagnosis can usually be established without difficulty in the physician's office and treated with one of several vaginal preparations (in cream or suppository form) or with oral medication. In some cases a yeast infection may occur in a child or adolescent after a course of antibiotics, since these drugs can temporarily reduce the population of oral or vaginal bacteria that normally help inhibit the growth of *Candida*. If yeast infections occur repeatedly, a search for a possible underlying cause may be carried out.

In recent years a small number of practitioners have claimed that a great variety of symptoms, such as chronic fatigue, headaches, weight gain, depression, and intestinal disturbances, can be linked to the presence of *Candida albicans* in the body. These assertions have not been validated by medical research and are not widely accepted in the health-care community.

canker sores See "mouth care and concerns."

caries Decay or death of teeth or adjacent bone tissue. See also "teeth care and concerns."

cataract A clouding or loss of transparency of the lens of the eye. Cataracts may be present at birth, or they may occur later in childhood, either as a result of an eye injury or as a component of certain conditions such as diabetes or Down syndrome.

cat scratch disease A bacterial infection with two components:

- A small, pimplelike eruption, usually on the arm or leg, where a child has had a recent cat scratch or bite. The eruption typically develops three to ten days after the encounter with the cat.
- Ten to thirty days later, a tender swelling of nearby lymph nodes (collections of cells that play an active role in the body's immune response). These lymph nodes can become quite large, sometimes measuring two inches in diameter. They are usually noticed in the armpit if the scratch was on the hand, in the groin if the leg or foot was involved, or in the neck if a cat

scratched the child's face. Mild headache, loss of appetite, abdominal pain (without vomiting or diarrhea), low-grade fever, and fatigue may occur along with the swollen lymph nodes.

Cat scratch disease is a benign infection and will resolve on its own in about two months. In some cases, an antibiotic may be prescribed, especially if the infected child has impaired immunity (as might occur, for example, with an HIV/AIDS infection or during chemotherapy).

Over 35 million homes in the United States have one or more cats; as a result this illness is fairly common (more than twenty thousand cases per year), though fortunately not contagious between humans. If you intend to keep one or more cats as a pet, you should teach your children how to approach, handle, and play with cats. In particular, children need to know that any rough play with a cat—and sometimes merely a gentle overture—can result in an unexpected clawing.

cellulitis A bacterial infection of the deep layer of skin (and at times the soft tissue directly beneath it), producing local redness, heat, swelling, and tenderness to the touch. Cellulitis should be treated with oral or (in severe cases) injectable antibiotics.

cerebral palsy A group of disorders involving posture and muscle tone resulting from a defect or localized damage in the developing brain. The symptoms will usually become evident within the first year or two of life. It is neither hereditary nor progressive, and its manifestations do not necessarily include mental retardation. The impairments of cerebral palsy can vary greatly in severity, and the cause may or may not be identifiable.

cerumen Brownish or yellowish waxlike (or in some children, dry and granular) material secreted within the external ear canal. Also called **earwax**.

chalazion A round, painless (or slightly uncomfortable) swelling on the upper or lower eyelid, resulting from chronic inflammation of one of the glands (known as **meibomian glands**) that lubricate the inner surface of the eyelid (see also "eye care and concerns").

chickenpox (varicella) A common childhood viral illness characterized by the eruption of multiple red bumps, each with a small fluid-filled central blister.

New "crops" of pox erupt for three to five days. Gradually the blisters become crusted, form tiny scabs, and disappear, usually without leaving a scar. The rash is most prominent on the chest, abdomen, and face, but might cover the entire body, including the scalp, genital area, and inside the mouth. In some children only a few scattered bumps will be visible, while other children are covered from head to toe. Adolescents or adults who develop chickenpox sometimes have a more severe case than do their younger counterparts. Fever may or may not be present. Itching is common and at times can be intense.

The incubation period for chickenpox can range from eleven to twenty-one days, but most often the time from exposure to onset of symptoms is fourteen to sixteen days. A child with chickenpox is contagious one or two days before the rash erupts and continues to be so until all the blisters have crusted. This will occur five to seven days after the rash first appears. Children should be kept out of school for about a week.

An expectant mother who has never had chickenpox or is uncertain about her immunity to it should avoid exposure to this infection, especially during the first half of her pregnancy. If she becomes ill during the first twelve weeks of pregnancy, there is a 0.4 percent risk—or a one in 250 chance—that her baby will develop **congenital varicella syndrome**, which may include any of several defects of eyes, heart, and limbs. If the infection occurs between thirteen and twenty weeks of the pregnancy, the risk of congenital varicella syndrome is about 2 percent. (See chapter 1, page 22 for more information.)

Most infants and children who develop chickenpox recover without any major problem. A few scars may remain, especially in areas where scabs have been repeatedly picked or scratched off. In some cases, bacteria such as streptococci or staphylococci infect a number of pox lesions. A child

who suddenly worsens four or five days into the chickenpox outbreak, especially if fever recurs, should be seen by a physician to check for this complication.

Pneumonia is a rare but potentially serious complication of chickenpox. If a child develops a cough, shortness of breath, and rapid respirations during or shortly after chickenpox, contact a doctor as soon as possible. **Reye's syndrome**, a rare but potentially fatal illness affecting brain and liver, has been linked to the use of aspirin during chickenpox and other acute viral infections. *Aspirin should not be used to treat fever or aches for anyone, child or adult, who has chickenpox* (see "Reye's syndrome"). Persistent vomiting or a significant change in alertness or orientation could indicate this rare complication.

For most children and adolescents with chickenpox, treatment is supportive: rest, fluids, acetaminophen for fever and aches, and antihistamines such as diphenhydramine (Benadryl and other brands or generic preparation) as needed to relieve itching. Cool baths and calamine lotion also may relieve itching. These measures, along with gentle parental reminders and trimming the fingernails, can help a child resist the urge to scratch and pick at the blisters and scabs, minimizing the risk of scarring. If sores are present in the mouth, cool liquids (other than citrus or tomato juices, which may sting) and soft foods will be easier for your child to swallow than other foods.

There are specific measures for treatment and prevention of chickenpox:

- The prescription medication **acyclovir** (Zovirax) is sometimes given to reduce the severity of the illness. To be effective it must be started within twenty-four hours of the onset of the eruption.
- **Varicella-zoster immune globulin (VZIG)** contains antibodies to the chickenpox virus. It is used in specific and very uncommon situations where immediate (although temporary) protection is needed. These situations might include a person with a severely impaired immune system who is exposed to chickenpox or a newborn whose mother develops this illness between five days before and two days after delivery. In the latter case, the newborn will be

at risk for a more intense infection because of the immaturity of the immune system at this age combined with a lack of antibody protection from the mother.

- **Chickenpox vaccine** (Varivax) induces the body's immune system to create antibodies against the virus and can provide long-term protection. It is now recommended for all children aged twelve to eighteen months, as well as older children and adults who have never had chickenpox or the vaccine. (See "Immunizations—Which Ones, Why, and When?" page 747.)

cholesterol A fatty substance that is necessary for the formation and maintenance of the complex membranes that surround every cell in our body. It is also a component of **bile**, the liquid formed by the liver that helps disperse fat molecules in the intestine so that they can be absorbed. High levels of circulating cholesterol are associated with an increased risk of developing fatty plaques within blood vessels, a process that in many people begins very early in life. The gradual thickening of these plaques, which is called **atherosclerosis**, can lead to partial or even complete obstruction of blood vessels. When one or more of the **coronary arteries** that supply blood to the heart become blocked, the muscle supplied by that artery will die. This is known as a **myocardial infarction**— often called a **heart attack**—and is frequently fatal. Coronary artery disease is one of the leading causes of death in the United States and other developed countries.

About 85 percent of the cholesterol in our body—in fact, all that we can possibly use—is generated internally, mostly by the liver, in quantities affected dramatically both by genetics and weight. The rest comes from animal sources in our diet: meats (especially the so-called organ meats, such as liver and kidney), eggs, fish, and dairy products.

HDL, LDL, and triglycerides

Cholesterol belongs to the family of nutrients called **lipids**—we usually refer to them as fats— that are, among other things, generally not soluble in water. Blood is essentially a water-based liquid, and if cholesterol molecules were released directly into the bloodstream, they would clump together and not disperse to all of the cells that need them. Instead, cholesterol molecules, as well as other lipid molecules such as the **triglycerides**, are escorted through the bloodstream by carrier proteins that *are* water/blood soluble. These proteins and various combinations of lipid molecules are packaged together to form **lipoproteins**, which researchers have sorted into categories based on their density. Two of these— the **low-density lipoproteins** (or **LDL**) and the **high-density lipoproteins** (or **HDL**)—are particularly important to health.

LDL packages are larger, lighter, and loaded with more cholesterol. They also have a tendency to deposit cholesterol in the walls of arteries, contributing to the buildup of blood-blocking plaque. HDL packages, on the other hand, are smaller and heavier, and carry more protein and less cholesterol than LDL. More important, they help "clean up the mess" left by LDL, removing some of the excess cholesterol and other lipids from tissues and bringing them back to the liver. An abundance of research has shown that higher levels of cholesterol carried by LDL are associated with a greater likelihood of developing atherosclerotic disease congesting your arteries. Conversely, higher levels of cholesterol carried by HDL are associated with greater protection from this problem.

Should cholesterol be checked in children and teenagers?

It is widely accepted medical practice to check the blood cholesterol level in adults as part of general health screening and to utilize diet, exercise, and in some cases medication to reduce it if needed. What about children? Presently cholesterol screening is not a part of routine medical checkups in children, but it should be considered in those two years and older who are at risk for having elevated blood cholesterol levels. These include children or teenagers who:

- Have one or more parent who has a cholesterol level greater than 240 mg/dL (see next page).
- Have a parent or grandparent who has had known coronary artery disease before the age of fifty-five.

- Are overweight or obese. (See "The Overweight Child and Teenager," beginning on page 387.)

In the United States, the most widely followed guidelines for assessing and treating cholesterol are those issued by the National Cholesterol Education Program (NCEP) of the National Heart, Lung and Blood Institute, one of twenty-seven institutes and centers within the National Institutes of Health (NIH). The NCEP's Expert Panel on Blood Cholesterol in Children and Adolescents has recommended the following cholesterol and triglyceride levels for children two to nineteen years of age:[3]

Category	Total Cholesterol (mg/dL)	LDL Cholesterol (mg/dL)
Acceptable	less than 170	less than 110
Borderline	170–199	110–129
High	200 or greater	130 or greater

In addition HDL cholesterol levels should be greater than or equal to 35 mg/dL and triglycerides should be less than or equal to 150 mg/dL. (Like many common blood tests, the levels of cholesterol and its various components are most commonly expressed in mg/dL, or milligrams per deciliter of serum. A deciliter is a tenth of a liter, or 100 milliliters—a little over three ounces. Serum is the liquid that is left when the red cells are removed from blood. Fortunately, only a small amount of blood is needed to test for cholesterol.)

If a child's or adolescent's cholesterol levels are in the borderline or high range, a variety of measures to reduce it may be recommended:

- Weight loss, if appropriate. (See "The Overweight Child and Teenager," page 395).
- Regular exercise—at least thirty minutes per day.
- Reducing the quantities of cholesterol, saturated fats, and trans fats in the diet. (See "Some ABCs of Good Nutrition," beginning on page 771.)

The cholesterol levels will be monitored over time. In certain cases—such as children with family histories of significant coronary artery disease, especially when it occurs among adults in their thirties or forties—cholesterol-lowering medications may be recommended for those ten or older whose cholesterol levels have not improved with lifestyle changes. These issues should be reviewed carefully with the child's physician, who may recommend additional consultation with a dietitian or a pediatric cardiologist (a heart specialist who cares for children and adolescents).

circumcision See chapter 3, page 70.

clavicle Collarbone.

colds (upper-respiratory infection, or URI)

The most common acute illness in children, especially among infants and toddlers. Most are caused by one of a large assortment of viruses. (There are, for example, more than one hundred types of the rhinovirus, which is but one of many viruses that can cause a cold.) Some URIs are caused by bacteria, but more often these organisms are secondary invaders that infect specific locations, such as the ears or sinuses, during or shortly after a cold caused by a virus. Colds tend to be relatively uncommon during the first several weeks of a baby's life because an infant derives some protection against many viruses from antibodies transferred from the mother prior to birth. Breastfed babies also receive protection from antibodies in their mother's milk. Eventually infants must begin developing their own immunity through exposure to the numerous viruses (and occasional bacteria) that cause URIs.

After about six months of age it is common for infants and toddlers to have six to ten colds every year. Some exasperated parents come to the doctor with small children who seem to have joined the Bug of the Month Club or whose colds seemingly overlap into nonstop illness lasting several months. Some of these situations may involve a child with allergies, which can cause a runny nose or cough to continue even when acute infections have resolved. However, an allergy is difficult to diagnose before the age of two. A careful medical evaluation is usually necessary to sort out the reasons for nonstop symptoms.

The frequency of colds is directly influenced by the opportunities for exposure to viruses—more specifically, exposure to other children (and adults) who are carrying and spreading the viruses. Children in day care or who are members of large families tend to have more frequent URIs. Colds can occur year-round, although they are more common during winter months—not directly as a result of frigid weather but as an indirect result of people gathering indoors during those months.

Symptoms

The familiar discomforts of a runny nose, sneezing, a dry hacking cough, and a low-grade fever (lower than 101.4°F, or 38.6°C) are the most common symptoms in children and adults. Mild irritation of the **conjunctiva**—the membrane that covers the surface of the eyeball and the inner eyelids—and increased tearing may also be present. Infants may show signs of irritability.

The nasal drainage typically is clear and watery at first and then may become thicker and discolored (yellow or green). Usually it returns to a clear, thin consistency as the cold resolves. In an infant, mucus blocking the nasal passages could cause difficulty with nursing. Profuse or persistent discolored drainage may be an indication that a bacterial infection is present.

If present, fever tends to occur early in the illness and usually lasts for a few hours or up to three days. A fever that recurs after being gone for more than twenty-four hours may indicate that a secondary infection has developed. Infants younger than three months may have no fever at all. In this age-group a rectal temperature higher than 100.4°F (38°C) is significant and should prompt a call to your baby's physician. (See the Special Concerns section "When Your Child Has a Fever," page 241, for further information.)

Additional cold symptoms may include a dry, scratchy throat, headache, tiredness, or loss of appetite. When the throat is sore, lymph nodes in the neck may enlarge and become tender. An infection of the throat with Group A beta-hemolytic streptococcus—more commonly known as strep throat—is a specific bacterial illness that should be treated with appropriate antibiotics (see "sore throat").

Treatment

Since most colds are caused by viruses, they are usually self-limited; that is, they go away by themselves within two to seven days, although some symptoms may last as long as two weeks. *Unless there is specific evidence that bacteria are involved, antibiotics will not help a cold resolve more quickly.* The best approach is to provide supportive care and observe your child for any complications. Adequate or increased fluid intake (water or juice) might help keep drainage from becoming thick and difficult to clear. In infants, feedings (breast milk or formula) can be maintained or even increased in frequency. Solids may be continued if your child is interested in them, but don't force the issue. Appetite sometimes decreases during a cold (especially when the body's temperature is elevated), and it is not uncommon for an infant or child to lose a little weight during a cold.

Acetaminophen (Tylenol and other brands) can be given as often as every four hours to reduce fever if your child appears uncomfortable. As an alternative, **ibuprofen** (Children's Motrin, Children's Advil, and other brands) can be given every six to eight hours to reduce fever; in some children, this appears to be more effective. Dosage charts for acetaminophen and ibuprofen may be found on pages 609 and 688. (Aspirin should not be used during an acute illness because of its reported link with a rare but serious disorder of the liver and brain called Reye's syndrome.) Irritability will typically improve and activity will increase as the fever resolves.

Decongestants such as pseudoephedrine and phenylephrine may—or may not—reduce nasal congestion and help your child feel more comfortable. Their effectiveness varies widely with the particular child and illness. (Because of illegal conversion of pseudoephedrine into the dangerous stimulant methamphetamine, cold remedies containing pseudoephedrine are usually kept "behind the counter" and sold in limited quantities.) Similarly, antihistamines such as diphenhydramine or chlorpheniramine may also be useful in keeping the nose dry, especially when allergies are involved. These and other antihistamines often cause sleepiness. In babies and children younger than two years of age, side effects can be more unpredictable, so it is wise to contact your child's doctor before using these medications. In very young infants, the use of saline nose drops and suctioning the nose with a bulb syringe is recommended to allow easier breathing. Some recent research has suggested that decongestants and antihistamines are unlikely to relieve cold symptoms in infants and young children.

Decongestant nose drops, which directly shrink the lining of the nose, are sometimes helpful in older children who are very congested, especially when this symptom interferes with sleep. These drops should be used only for short periods of time. If used regularly for more than two or three consecutive days, the drops may not only lose their effectiveness but may create a rebound effect, in which the nose becomes even more congested when the last dose wears off.

If coughing is disruptive, especially at night, a cough syrup containing **guaifenesin** (an expectorant that tends to loosen secretions) or **dextromethorphan** (a cough suppressant) may provide a few hours of relief. If a nonprescription preparation is not effective, your child's doctor may prescribe a stronger formulation after seeing your child. (Dextromethorphan taken in excessive doses has become a drug of abuse. See "Prescription and Nonprescription Drug Abuse," page 552.)

Potential complications

While most colds resolve without any great difficulty within seven to ten days, in some instances bacteria infect certain areas of the body during a cold, resulting in more serious or prolonged illness. Potential secondary bacterial infections (sometimes called superinfections because they are superimposed on the viral infection) can include:

- **Otitis media**—infection of the middle ear (the space behind the eardrum), usually manifested as pain or fever (see "ear infections").
- **Sinusitis**—infection of one or more of the air-filled cavities within the head, usually manifested as localized headache or persistent discolored (yellow or green) drainage from the nose (see "sinusitis").
- **Conjunctivitis**—infection of the linings of one or both eyes (known as the **conjunctivae**), causing irritation, redness, crusting, and discolored drainage (see "conjunctivitis").
- **Pneumonia**—infection of a localized or widespread area in one or both lungs, manifested as fever, fatigue, coughing (mild or frequent and

intense), and in severe cases rapid or labored breathing. (Note: Pneumonia only rarely arises in connection with a cold. Most pneumonias develop suddenly and spontaneously without prior symptoms.)

Prevention

No available vaccine will prevent infants and children from developing colds, so the most effective preventive measures are those that separate the child from viruses. Particular care should be taken to limit the exposure of infants younger than three months of age to people with colds because a baby's immune system is less effective at fighting infection during the first several weeks of life. Infants in this age-group should spend little if any time in day-care settings, nurseries, and crowded public areas.

When one infant or child at home has a cold, frequent hand washing is perhaps the best way to reduce the risk of passing the infection to others, since viruses are often spread by direct touch. Infected droplets from the nose or chest may be present on a child's skin (especially if hands have contacted nose or mouth), or the droplets may become airborne during sneezing and coughing, eventually landing on clothes, toys, or other objects. When another child or adult touches any of these items (or the infected child himself), the virus can be picked up on the fingers and unwittingly introduced into an uninfected person's mouth, nose, or eyes if hands have not been washed.

Over the years there has been considerable discussion about the role of **vitamin C (ascorbic acid)** in cold prevention and treatment. While medical evidence does not suggest that vitamin C will prevent a cold, it may reduce the intensity or duration of symptoms. Using vitamin C for this purpose in children is not an established medical practice. Doses in great excess of the recommended daily allowance (RDA) are not advisable. Check dosage guidelines with your child's physician before using supplemental vitamin C.

When to call the doctor

Most colds can be managed at home without any specific input from or examination by your child's physician. However, there are a few exceptions to this general rule. Call your child's doctor, regardless of the hour, if any of the following conditions are present:

- A baby younger than three months of age has a fever of 100.4°F (38°C) or higher (taken rectally).
- Your infant or child appears unusually listless and unresponsive or is extremely irritable and won't stop crying despite your efforts to comfort her.
- Your infant or child appears to have difficulty breathing (beyond that produced by a stuffy nose). This would be manifested by noisy, labored breaths and in some cases by visible inward movement of the spaces between the ribs.

You should call your child's doctor during office hours in situations such as these:

- A cold lasts more than seven to ten days.
- Nasal drainage is persistently thick and discolored.
- Your older child complains of significant ear or throat pain.
- Your older infant or child has a fever over 102°F (39°C) for more than twenty-four hours.
- A cough persists for more than a few days or disrupts sleep and cannot be controlled using nonprescription cough syrup.

colic A particularly distressing pattern of crying that occurs in some infants between two weeks and three months of age. Several explanations for colic have been proposed (such as spasms of the bowel, a reaction to milk, a problem interacting with parents), but a universal cause has not been determined.

Infants with colic generally cry inconsolably for three or more hours, usually at the same time of day—most frequently between 6 and 10 p.m. During episodes of colic, the baby may draw his legs up, pass gas, thrash around, and generally appear extremely uncomfortable (which he probably is). When extended for hours, this can be very disruptive to a family, especially when it occurs with the first child.

Treatment
If your baby has prolonged crying spells, it is important to have him checked by his physician to rule out any medical problem. If he is in the age-group, his crying pattern is typical for colic, and he is developing and gaining weight appropriately and not suffering from an acute or chronic illness, the physician will probably diagnose colic. If so, your primary agenda during these episodes should be simply to comfort your baby as much as possible. Simple strategies can help, including gentle rocking (not jiggling too quickly), stroking the skin, singing or humming, wrapping him in a blanket, keeping the environment soothing and quiet, feeding him if he's hungry, or giving him a pacifier.

Remember that you are not a failure if you cannot quickly end the colic episode. Your goal is to be available to your baby and to survive the crying season the best you can. If you begin to feel frustrated or angry with your baby, it is very important that you not shake, swat, or otherwise physically harm him. If you are by yourself, lay him in the crib and let him cry for fifteen or twenty minutes while you take a breather and calm down. This will not harm him, and he may be more responsive to your comforting measures when you pick him up again. If your spouse, another relative, or a good friend is with you, let that person relieve you for a while.

Chapter 5 (see "Crybabies: What Happens When the Tears Won't Stop?"on page 159) contains an expanded discussion about colic and the various measures that might help comfort a distressed infant.

colitis Inflammation of the lining of the large intestine that may result from an infection (usually bacterial or parasitic) or may occur without an identifiable cause. The severity, duration, complications, and treatment of colitis vary considerably and will depend in part on the underlying cause. Manifestations commonly include abdominal cramping and frequent loose stools containing mucus and blood. A child with these symptoms should be evaluated and diagnosed so appropriate treatment can begin.

computerized tomography (CT or CAT scan) A type of X-ray study that provides cross-sectional views of an area of the body. When first introduced during the early 1970s, CT scanning was a dramatic breakthrough in medical diagnosis because it provided cross-sectional images of the body with unprecedented detail. However, in order to prevent distortion of those images, patients had to lie very still for extended periods of time. As computers have become more powerful, scans using newer techniques can be performed very rapidly—often in a minute or less. CT scanning is widely used for diagnosing tumors, fractures in complex structures (such as the skull and spine), certain types of infections, and other problems in which disease causes changes in the shape and size of internal structures. A CT scan is not painful. Depending on the area being evaluated, a small amount of a liquid called a **contrast material** may be injected into the vein or taken orally so that various structures can be seen more clearly.

congestion A general term indicating the presence of abnormal fluid, mucus, or other material anywhere in the respiratory tract.

Congestion is a component in a number of illnesses. All of these syndromes have different causes, implications, and treatments. An infant with a stuffy nose, for example, will not need the same level of attention as one with noisy, rapid, labored breathing. When you call your doctor and mention your child's congestion, it will help greatly if you can be specific about the location of the problem and any other symptoms, such as fever, cough, wheezing, abnormal breathing patterns, or even something you can't quite pin down. Your observation that "she just doesn't look right" may be very important information, especially in an infant less than three months old.

For more detailed information about problems related to congestion, see the following topics:

asthma, page 624
bronchiolitis, page 636
bronchitis, page 637
colds, page 643
croup, page 649
epiglottitis, page 660
laryngitis, page 692
pneumonia, page 707

conjunctivitis (pinkeye) Inflammation of the thin lining (**conjunctiva**) that covers the white of the eyeball and the inner surface of the eyelids.

Conjunctivitis may be caused by viral or bacterial infection, an allergic reaction, or chemical or physical irritants that come in contact with the eye. The most common symptoms of conjunctivitis are watering eyes, itching or irritation, and a diffuse pink or bloodshot appearance. In some cases there is puffiness of the eyelids or mild sensitivity to light. *Pain and extreme sensitivity to light are rarely seen in conjunctivitis and usually indicate a more serious problem.* If your child persistently complains that his eye hurts, he should be evaluated by his primary-care physician or an ophthalmologist as soon as possible.

Newborns can develop a **reactive conjunctivitis** from medicines that are put into the eyes at birth to prevent infection. During the first year of life, babies may also develop conjunctivitis because of obstruction of a tear duct, which prevents proper drainage of tears from the eye. Low-grade infection might persist until the tear duct opens spontaneously or (uncommonly) is probed and opened by an ophthalmologist.

In toddlers and older children conjunctivitis may accompany a bacterial or viral infection of the upper-respiratory tract. Hands that have wiped runny noses often touch the eyes too, transferring the infection to one or both.

Conjunctivitis caused by bacteria usually produces a thick discharge that gathers on the lids. In the morning the eyelids may appear crusty or even stuck together. A warm, wet washcloth will remove the crust and unstick the lids. (Be sure to launder the washcloth before using it again to prevent spreading the bacteria to others.)

Bacterial conjunctivitis will usually respond to antibiotic drops or ointment within a few days. As you might suspect, instilling medicine into the eye(s) of a toddler or preschooler can be a major challenge. In fact, two adults may be needed— one to restrain the child's head and body and the other to apply the medication. The best method is to gently pull the lower lid downward and place a drop or small amount of ointment into the outer corner of the eye.

Conjunctivitis caused by viruses tends to be accompanied by a more watery drainage than with bacterial infections, but in some cases the redness and swelling can be very intense. In severe cases an ophthalmologist may prescribe drops that calm the inflammation, but the medication won't stop the infection, which will run its course in ten to fourteen days. As with all viral infections, antibiotics will have no effect on this form of conjunctivitis.

The bacteria or viruses that cause conjunctivitis can be quite contagious through direct contact: Little hands rub infected eyes, then touch toys or other children, whose fingers then touch other eyes and noses, including their own. Toddlers and smaller children with these infections should be kept out of day-care or nursery situations until the problem is calmed down or at least until treatment is well under way. (Check with your child's physician.) You and any other caregivers should wash hands frequently when dealing with a child who has infectious conjunctivitis.

Allergic conjunctivitis is usually provoked by seasonal airborne pollens such as trees or grasses in the spring, or weeds (especially ragweed) in the late summer. It often causes more itching and less inflammation than bacterial or viral conjunctivitis, and the drainage is invariably watery. In addition, nasal symptoms such as dripping and sneezing are likely. Any oral antihistamines used to treat nasal allergy may also improve allergic conjunctivitis, but in some cases your child's doctor might also prescribe antihistamine or anti-inflammatory eye drops.

constipation Constipation is present if any of the following occurs on a regular basis:

- Passing stool is painful.
- Stools are passed with difficulty or aren't passed at all, despite long straining efforts.
- Stools are passed fewer than two times per week, with the following exceptions: It is common for breastfed infants older than six to eight weeks to pass painless, large, soft bowel movements as infrequently as once a week. Infants younger than six months of age may strain to pass hard bowel movements, but the passage of stool occurs without pain. Occasionally an older child will pass a stool every three or four days without discomfort, although this is not usually felt to represent normal bowel function.

In addition, the following signs of constipation may be present:

- Small, hard, pebblelike stools

- Blood streaks on the stool or toilet paper when bowel movements are firm
- Resistance—even overt expressions of fear—when sitting on the toilet is suggested
- Soiling the pants with stool (called **encopresis**)
- Abdominal cramps and bloating, sometimes with loss of appetite

Causes

Among children older than one year of age, the vast majority (more than 90 percent) of constipation problems are *functional*—that is, brought on by one or more of the following situations:

- *A diet that is short on fiber,* especially if it contains large amounts of dairy products. Fruits, vegetables, beans, whole-grain breads, and bran cereals help keep stools soft and easier to pass.
- *Resisting the urge to use the toilet.* An active child who is engrossed in play with friends or who is embarrassed about using the toilet at school or another location where privacy may not be available may ignore or resist the signal from the colon that a bowel movement is imminent. Eventually the urge will disappear, but the stool waiting to be eliminated will not.
- *A painful bowel movement,* usually arising from a small tear at the anal opening called a fissure. Normally children do not want to repeat a painful experience and may not grasp the concept that bowel movements are not optional.
- *Certain medications* such as codeine-containing cough syrups, methylphenidate (Ritalin), and iron supplements may also contribute to constipation.

One or more of these factors—especially a painful bowel movement—can lead to an ever-enlarging wad of stool developing in the colon segments (the **sigmoid** and **rectum**), which are the last stop before release to the outside. The situation is compounded by the colon's continuous extracting of moisture from stool that isn't moving, causing it to become increasingly firm and difficult to pass. Eventually the final segments of colon become so distended that it becomes difficult for the anal sphincter to do its normal job of holding back stool, and small amounts may pass involuntarily and soil the child's underwear. Occasionally liquid stool will leak past the large, hardened stool, creating the paradox of diarrhea that is actually caused by constipation.

Evaluation and treatment

Constipation that is accompanied by abdominal distention, failure to gain weight, vomiting, or fever should be evaluated by a physician sooner rather than later—especially when it occurs in an infant younger than four months of age. In a toddler or older child, if constipation is ongoing—especially if it's associated with painful bowel movements, soiling, fear of using the toilet, or abdominal pain—your child's doctor should examine her to rule out any disorder that might require specific medical treatment. In some situations, removal of an impacted stool may be necessary (often through pediatric-size enemas), and your child's doctor will give you specific directions for doing so.

Continued home treatment of constipation will depend upon the child's age and dietary patterns. The following are general guidelines only and should not override any specific directions given by your child's physician.

Breastfed infants who are not yet taking solids rarely develop true constipation (and may not have a bowel movement for five to seven days), and additional water or juices are unnecessary unless specifically recommended by the physician. If a breastfeeding mother is taking medication that is constipating (such as codeine), alternative medications may need to be considered.

For bottle-fed infants younger than four months of age, usually juices (white grape, pear, and possibly prune) or Maltsupex (a barley extract) may be utilized twice daily, but you would be wise to contact your baby's physician for further input. Solids are not needed by infants younger than four months of age and might actually contribute to constipation. If one or more solids have been initiated in an infant this age who is now constipated, it may be prudent to withhold them until she has passed the four-month mark.

For infants older than four months of age who are on solids, add juices and Maltsupex as noted above and offer foods rich in fiber, such as cereal, fruits (pears, peaches, apricots), and vegetables (peas or spinach), twice daily. Avoid applesauce, rice cereal, bananas, and carrots, which tend to be constipating.

For children who are eating table foods, adding foods containing higher levels of fiber or bran (oatmeal, bran cereals, whole wheat bread) and serving fruits or vegetables twice per day will often relieve constipation. Decrease constipating foods such as bananas, cooked carrots, applesauce, and dairy products (milk, ice cream, cheese).

Stool softeners such as Maltsupex (a barley extract), psyllium-seed derivatives (such as Metamucil or Citrucel), or mineral oil are sometimes beneficial, although approval from your child's physician would be wise before using any of these agents. You should also talk to the doctor before using any oral laxatives, such as milk of magnesia, or when considering the use of enemas.

A child refusing to use the toilet because of a painful anal fissure will probably need some local treatment along with stool-softening efforts. A fifteen- to twenty-minute bath two or three times daily, mild (0.5 or 1.0 percent) **cortisone** cream, or a topical anesthetic (2.5 percent **lidocaine** ointment) might ease the pain so a child can resume bowel movements without fear. Needless to say, a constipated toddler who is fighting use of the toilet is not a good candidate for toilet training. Postpone this project until she is pain free and stools are moving more freely.

Call the doctor in the event of any of the following:

- Recurrent or persistent rectal bleeding occurs. (An occasional, tiny dab of blood on the toilet tissue after a hard stool is not likely to indicate a major problem.)
- Constipation is accompanied by abdominal pain.
- Constipation persists despite dietary changes.
- Definite rectal pain or a visible anal fissure is noted.

cornea The outermost transparent layer of the central colored part of the eye. Trauma to this structure causes intense pain.

croup A variety of infections that involve the **larynx** (vocal cords) and **trachea** (the upper airway just below the larynx). When these structures become inflamed and irritated, they provoke a barking cough, noisy respirations, and in some cases labored breathing. Croup is most commonly seen among children younger than five, and it can be particularly difficult for a child under the age of three.

The most common version of this problem, and the one for which the term *croup* is normally reserved, is **viral croup** (also called **laryngotracheobronchitis**, indicating that the larynx, trachea, and bronchial tubes are involved). This is caused most often by the **parainfluenza virus** and generally occurs in epidemics during the fall and early winter. If your child has croup, it is very likely that other children in your community have it as well. The illness usually lasts three to five days but may extend as long as a week.

Symptoms

Croup begins like a typical cold in a child between the ages of six months and three years. She then develops a seal-like barking cough that progresses to noisy congested breathing called **stridor**. Fever may occur, and acetaminophen may be given to reduce it and make the child more comfortable.

Croup frequently begins in the middle of the night. It can develop within a few hours after your child goes to bed. She may awaken frightened and distressed, with symptoms worsening when she is crying and agitated. As the illness progresses, the ongoing coughing and increased effort needed to breathe may cause her to lose interest in food or fluids and become mildly dehydrated. In more severe cases, she will appear to gasp for air when at rest.

Treatment

First, try to calm your child, because croup symptoms will worsen if she is upset. (This is one situation where it is appropriate to try to keep her happy, or at least comfortable, at all costs.) If she is breathing rapidly and noisily, appears to gasp for air even when at rest (that is, sitting quietly or lying down), or develops a bluish color around the lips, nose, or fingernails take her *immediately* to the nearest emergency room. She may improve dramatically on the ride over, but make sure she is evaluated anyway.

If she is not gasping when at rest, a time-honored home treatment for croup is steam, since moisture relieves congestion and opens the airways. The best way to create steam is to turn on a hot shower in your bathroom, close the door, and wait for the room to become foggy.

You can sit or stand with your child in the steam for fifteen to twenty minutes. As an alternative, bundle her up and take her outside. Often the cool night air, especially when it is moist or foggy, will dramatically improve breathing.

If you don't see much improvement after fifteen to twenty minutes, call the doctor (or take the child to the nearest emergency room if she appears to be getting worse). The doctor will want to know how rapidly your child is breathing (count the number of breaths in a minute before you call), whether the spaces between her ribs are moving in and out with each breath, and her general appearance.

If she improves, put a humidifier in her room while she sleeps. Because this cycle may repeat itself, it would be wise for you to stay with your child to monitor her breathing throughout the night. If your child relaxes and sleeps through the night, she probably won't need additional treatment except for steam and fluids. Over-the-counter cold and cough medicines are not particularly helpful for treating viral croup. Antibiotics are not effective unless a medical evaluation indicates that the symptoms are being caused by bacteria (see below). In some cases the doctor will recommend a short course of steroids, which decreases the severity of the symptoms in some children.

Severe croup might be treated in the emergency room (or in some offices) using a medication called **racemic epinephrine**, given as an inhaled aerosol. This usually helps the child breathe more easily for two or three hours. Some children with croup are sent home after one treatment and observation, while others who are more severely affected will be admitted to the hospital for further care, including frequent breathing treatments and oxygen as needed.

Other illnesses with croup symptoms
Bacterial tracheitis is an uncommon complication of viral croup in which bacteria invade the

upper airway. A typical scenario is that of a child who develops symptoms of viral croup but fails to improve or actually worsens despite standard treatment. This infection is sometimes seen in children who are older than those who usually have viral croup. The child with bacterial tracheitis usually appears very ill, with high fever and increasingly severe shortness of breath. *Prompt medical care is very important,* because the upper airway can become so inflamed and swollen that the child is unable to obtain an adequate amount of air.

Epiglottitis is a rapidly progressive and very dangerous infection of the **epiglottis**, the soft tissue flap that covers and protects the airway whenever your child swallows. A child who has been well will rapidly develop a high fever and an extremely sore throat. Within a few hours she will be unable to swallow and may lean forward and actually drool rather than swallow. *This condition is a medical emergency because the swollen epiglottis can suddenly block the airway, leading to suffocation.* Fortunately, this disease has become extremely uncommon because most children are now routinely immunized against *Haemophilus influenzae* type B, the bacteria that cause epiglottitis.

One final reminder: Whether croup symptoms involve the more common viral syndrome or the serious bacterial infections, all can significantly affect your child's ability to breathe—sometimes with rapid changes in her condition. *If you are at all uncomfortable with your child's breathing pattern (or her general appearance) during one of these illnesses, don't hesitate to take her to the nearest emergency medical facility, regardless of the time of day or night.* If her breathing appears significantly compromised and you don't feel you can transport her safely, call 911 to request emergency paramedic evaluation and transfer.

CT scan See "computerized tomography."

culture A laboratory test in which a small sample of body fluid (such as urine or blood) or other tissue is evaluated for the presence of microorganisms that might be causing an infection. The sample is introduced into material called a culture medium, which enhances the growth of certain types of bacteria, viruses, or fungi. The choice of culture medium will vary depending upon the organism(s) suspected to be present.

cyanosis Bluish discoloration of skin caused by lack of oxygen in the blood.

cystic fibrosis An inherited disease characterized by abnormalities in the secretions of glands in many parts of the body. The respiratory tract, the pancreas, and the sweat glands of the skin are most commonly affected. Mucus secreted in the airways is abnormally thick and more difficult to clear, resulting in frequent and often serious respiratory infections. Deficiencies in pancreatic enzymes can cause inadequate absorption of nutrients (especially fats and protein), leading to slow growth and poor weight gain. Increased concentrations of salt in sweat may actually cause a parent to notice a salty taste when kissing a child with this disorder. There is no cure for cystic fibrosis, although advances in medical management have increased the life expectancy of children born with this disease. Treatment objectives include preventing and treating respiratory infections, supplementing digestive enzymes, and replacing salt lost through the skin.

cystitis Inflammation of the bladder. The term is commonly used to refer to a bladder infection.

D **dacryocystitis** Inflammation of the tear (or **lacrimal**) sac located just below the inner corner of the eye, adjacent to the nose. This infection usually results from the blockage of the duct that carries tears from the lacrimal sac into the nose (see "eye care and concerns").

dehydration See "diarrhea" and "vomiting."

diabetes mellitus A disorder in which there is an impairment in the transfer of **glucose** (blood sugar) from the bloodstream into the body's cells. Glucose serves as a primary energy source for cells throughout the body and the exclusive fuel for the brain and central nervous system, which cannot function without a steady supply. Glucose molecules do not simply float through the blood and then ooze into the nearest cell. They must be escorted inside by **insulin**, which serves somewhat like a key that opens the door to the cell, allowing glucose to enter. Insulin is created by special cells (called **beta cells**) scattered throughout the pancreas, a large organ tucked behind the stomach in the upper abdomen. Normally after a meal the level of glucose in the blood rises, and the pancreas responds by sending enough insulin "keys" into the bloodstream to open the cellular "locks." As glucose enters cells throughout the body, the blood glucose level goes down again. Diabetes occurs when there aren't enough keys or when the locks don't work properly.

Type 1 diabetes—previously called **juvenile onset** or **insulin-dependent** diabetes—affects only 5 to 10 percent of diabetics, usually children and young adults. In type 1 diabetes, the insulin-producing beta cells in the pancreas are destroyed by what is called an **autoimmune** process. This is a "friendly fire" scenario in which the immune system mistakenly attacks normal tissue. What sets off this self-destruction is unclear, although many researchers suspect that genetic vulnerability interacting with some type of environmental event, such as a viral infection, is to blame. While it may take a while (perhaps years in some cases) to deplete the beta cells, once symptoms appear they are usually dramatic. As blood glucose levels soar and cells are starved of the fuel they need, a number of metabolic consequences kick into high gear.

Normally the kidneys prevent glucose in the blood from appearing in the urine. When blood levels reach a critical level, however, glucose begins to spill into the urine, drawing extra water with it. This leads to the classic symptom of excessive urine flow, and with it an intense thirst. Because so much fuel is literally going to waste, weight loss is common, despite (at first) an increase in appetite. Unless the correct diagnosis is made and treatment started, the hapless individual—all too often a child—eventually develops a dangerous mix of severe dehydration, increased acidity of the blood, and other serious abnormalities that together are known as **diabetic ketoacidosis**. If this metabolic runaway train is not stopped, coma and death are inevitable.

Before the early 1920s the diagnosis of diabetes in a young person was nearly always a death sentence. But in 1922, Toronto researchers Frederick Grant Banting and Charles Best successfully treated a dying fourteen-year-old diabetic with animal pancreatic extracts containing insulin. The discovery of insulin won the Nobel Prize in 1923, and soon thereafter this compound became available to patients all over the world. Because it is broken down in the digestive tract, insulin must be injected under the skin (or, in an emergency, into a vein). Various short- and long-acting forms are available, and many type 1 diabetics now use a sophisticated electronic pump that gradually releases insulin throughout the day.

Type 2 diabetes—previously called **adult onset** or **non-insulin-dependent** diabetes—represents 90 to 95 percent of cases of this disorder. As its prior names suggest, type 2 diabetes usually occurs later in life—usually after age forty, and most commonly after age fifty-five—and does not arise from a shortage of insulin. (An alarming development in recent years, however, has been an increasing number of cases of type 2 diabetes among younger adults and even children. This has been linked to the increasing presence of obesity among young people.) Instead, there are plenty of keys (insulin) available to open the biochemical locks at the surface of the cells, but the locks don't work properly, a problem called **insulin resistance**. Glucose thus has greater difficulty entering the cells that need it, and higher levels gradually appear in the bloodstream. At first the pancreas responds by sending out more keys, but eventually it can "burn out," and production of insulin may fall, aggravating the problem. Unlike type 1 diabetics, those with type 2 do not need insulin to survive, although in some cases it may be prescribed when other efforts are unsuccessful.

Diabetes may first be discovered during a routine exam when glucose is detected in a child's urine; during an evaluation for symptoms such as weight loss, increased hunger, or abnormal thirst; or during an acute and unexpected deterioration of a child's overall condition—usually an episode of diabetic ketoacidosis requiring intensive medical care. Once diabetes is identified and stabilized, a comprehensive care plan will be needed. This will involve the combined skills of a physician, a dietitian, and frequently a specially trained diabetes educator. *This disease cannot be treated casually; it requires detailed understanding of dietary principles, monitoring of blood sugar using a glucose meter and test strips at home, and proper use of insulin to control day-to-day glucose levels.* Such detailed care is necessary for two reasons. First, it is important to prevent the immediate and sometimes dangerous problems that arise from extremely high or low levels of glucose. (Low blood sugar, or **hypoglycemia**, can result from a mismatch of insulin, food, and activity at a given point in time.) Second, ongoing elevation of blood glucose (or **hyperglycemia**) may not be high enough to cause acute symptoms but can nevertheless contribute to long-term disease in many organs or organ systems, including the eyes, kidneys, nervous system, or blood vessels. These potential complications and strategies to avoid them are normally explained in detail during diabetic-instruction sessions.

Depending upon age and maturity level, the child should gradually be given increasing responsibility for managing his diabetes. Continued education and troubleshooting by one or more experienced health-care providers will be necessary. Often emotional support is important for the child or adolescent who feels "stuck" with this disease. Despite all the extra effort involved in carrying out his everyday routines, the diabetic child should not be restricted from participating in normal activities, including team sports and other athletic pursuits. It may be necessary to remind him from time to time that, with proper self-care (including diet and exercise) and attention to the details of managing glucose, he should be able to live a long and healthy life.

diaphragm The respiratory muscle that separates the chest from the abdomen.

diarrhea A common event in infancy and childhood, normally understood as a condition in which bowel movements (or stools) are looser than normal, occur too frequently, or both. In fact, the significance of a child's stool pattern will depend on two basic considerations.

First, *what is normal for the age-group and for the particular infant or child?* A normal breastfed newborn will have as many as six to ten watery stools per day, which can vary in color from yellow to green to brown. Bottle-fed infants tend to have stools that are less watery and more mushy. After a few weeks a breastfed baby may absorb nutrients so efficiently that a stool is passed no more often than every few days. An older child may pass a stool every two or three days, or two or three times a day, on a routine basis without any problem. Some infants and children vary their pattern from week to week without any particular sign of trouble.

Second, and more important, *is the stool pattern causing any problems?* These problems could range from merely annoying to life threatening and include the following:

- Irritation of the skin around the anus or over the entire diaper area
- Cramps or other discomfort
- Ongoing soiling of clothing, bedding, furniture, and carpeting
- Fluid losses serious enough to cause dehydration and, in severe cases, death

Increased frequency or volume of stools can occur for three reasons, any or all of which could apply to a given case of diarrhea:

- The intestinal tract is moving food more rapidly.
- Some or most of the food or fluids, as well as the substantial amount of liquid produced every day by the intestine, are not being absorbed normally.
- The intestine is secreting more fluid than usual.

To understand what might be happening to your child whose stools are more loose and frequent than you (or she) would like, it is helpful to think in terms of three basic types of diarrhea: acute diarrhea, chronic nonspecific diarrhea, and chronic diarrhea related to a pathological condition.

Acute diarrhea is usually infectious and accompanied by other signs of illness such as fever, nausea, or vomiting, and possibly dehydration if the infant's or child's intake of fluids is not keeping up with losses. Around the world, acute diarrhea causes an estimated 2 million deaths among children under the age of five every year. In developed nations such as the United States, severe diarrhea leading to death is far less common (about three cases annually in the same age-group). The average American child has one or two episodes per year by the age of five. Diarrheal illness in children leads to about 1.5 million visits to doctors' offices, clinics, and emergency rooms, as well as two hundred thousand hospitalizations every year in the United States.

A variety of viruses and bacteria can cause acute infectious diarrhea (which is often referred to as **gastroenteritis** when nausea and vomiting occur). The most common offender is the **rotavirus**, which is seen most often among children between six months and two years of age. Bacteria that are transmitted in contaminated food (see "foodborne illness") or in unsanitary or crowded living conditions are also common causes of acute diarrhea, as are parasites such as *Giardia lamblia*, which may contaminate water supplies. Occasionally an acute illness somewhere else in the body (for example, an ear infection) or medications (especially antibiotics) will provoke diarrhea.

Since acute diarrheal episodes will usually resolve without antibiotics, in most situations your greatest concern will be keeping track of the infant's or child's fluid intake and watching out for dehydration. When fluid losses are mild, you will see some increased thirst and a modest decrease in urine output (fewer wet diapers). If these occur, call your child's physician for advice, which may include a recommendation for a direct evaluation.

If the dehydration becomes more severe, an infant or child will manifest a number of the following signs:

- Constant thirst (in an older child who can express this need)
- Dry mouth and lips
- Fewer tears when crying
- No urine production for eight to twelve hours, indicating that the kidneys are conserving fluids
- Sunken eyes
- A sunken fontanelle (the soft spot in the skull, which is most readily felt during the first six months of life)
- Skin texture that is no longer elastic but more like bread dough

- Persistent fussing in an infant, especially if it is more of a whine than a vigorous cry

With rare exception, these signs indicate a need for urgent evaluation.

Even more serious dehydration (with fluid losses of more than 10 percent of the child's normal body weight) will be suggested by the following symptoms:

- Cool and/or mottled skin
- Rapid, thready pulse
- Rapid respirations
- Moaning or grunting, or a weak, feeble cry
- Marked listlessness, with lack of interest in play or feeding, little response to being handled, and (in an infant) markedly reduced movements of arms and legs

A baby or young child with these symptoms is likely to be in serious trouble and should be evaluated immediately, usually in an emergency-room setting.

Other indications that medical evaluation should be sought sooner rather than later include:

- Bloody diarrhea, which may indicate that a significant bacterial infection or **colitis** (inflammation of the colon) is present
- Loose stools that are accompanied by vomiting and/or a temperature over 100.4°F (38°C), taken rectally, in an infant younger than three months of age
- Diarrhea that is accompanied by significant pain in the abdomen

Your child's doctor will give you specific advice for preventing or correcting dehydration, which will depend to some degree on the age of your child and the severity of the problem. Traditional treatment of diarrhea attempted to put the bowel "at rest" for a day or two while the infection ran its course. This involved giving the infant or child one or more forms of clear liquids—water, soft drinks, clear soup, clear juice, etc.—which are supposed to be absorbed more easily when the bowel is inflamed or damaged by infection. *However, recent research has indicated that for a variety of reasons these liquids are not very effective and in some cases may make the diarrhea worse.*

One of the most significant advances in medical care during the last few decades has been the discovery of an extraordinarily effective and inexpensive treatment for acute infectious diarrhea. Research into the physiology of the small intestine led to the development of a variety of **oral rehydration solutions (ORS)**, which cooperate effectively with the body's mechanisms for absorbing fluid. These solutions contain specified amounts of sodium, potassium, and glucose mixed in water, can be safely used in infants and children of all ages, and are effective in treating both mild and severe dehydration.

Premixed ORS is available at drugstores in products such as Pedialyte, Rehydralyte, and Infalyte. This type of solution—not the traditional clear liquids—is better suited to treat acute diarrhea, especially in infants and toddlers under two years of age. ORS may be given by bottle, spoon, or even dropper, sometimes in frequent, very small amounts (especially if nausea and vomiting are present). Your child's doctor can recommend the type and minimum quantity of fluid you should give your child. If the rehydrating solution isn't flavored, its taste can be improved by adding one tablespoon (15 ml) of Jell-O powder to one tablespoon of boiling water and then adding this mixture to an eight-ounce (about 240 ml) bottle of the solution.

Breastfed infants may continue nursing throughout an acute diarrheal illness. Infants who are formula-fed may also continue without stopping, although the physician might recommend switching temporarily to a formula that is lactose free and/or not made from cow's milk. Diluting formula to half- or quarter-strength has often been recommended in the past, but more recent research has shown that this is unnecessary and may in fact delay recovery.[4] Children who have been taking other foods may continue doing so, although foods containing a lot of simple sugars (candy, soft drinks, fruit juices) might cause more water to enter the bowel and worsen diarrhea. Complex carbohydrates such as rice, bread, and potatoes are a better choice. Bananas and applesauce contain pectin, which may help thicken loose stools. Avoiding fatty foods during a diarrheal illness has often been recommended, although these are an important source of calories in young children, and they may slow bowel activity. In general, recent research suggests that withholding food does not shorten the duration of diarrhea and may actually lengthen it, because the lining of the intestine needs fuel to repair its damage.

Depending upon the duration and severity of the diarrhea, your child's physician may order stool tests to determine whether a specific, treatable bacteria or parasite is present. If this is found to be the case, appropriate antibiotic therapy may be recommended. Nonprescription products such as Kaopectate, which thicken stool, and drugs such as **loperamide** (Imodium), which reduce the frequency of bowel movements, are not recommended for young children.

Chronic nonspecific diarrhea is a common problem in which a child has ongoing loose stools that are not severe enough to cause dehydration, nor are they associated with weight loss, developmental problems, or other disease activity. They can vary greatly from day to day or week to week and may be associated with stress, an acute illness, a move, dietary changes, or nothing in particular. Throughout this process, the child does not appear ill.

A medical evaluation should be done if an unusual pattern of loose stools continues for more than three weeks in a child who does not otherwise appear ill. If no specific cause is found and the child is otherwise doing well, the diarrhea will eventually resolve on its own. Recent research indicates that many cases of chronic nonspecific diarrhea may be caused by excessive intake of fruit juices, especially apple juice. And surprisingly, children on very low-fat diets may also have this problem. While maintaining conservative dietary habits regarding fat is important as a lifelong goal, younger children have a somewhat higher nutritional requirement for fat than adults do, and stringent restrictions on this (or any other) food group are not advisable. Your child's physician or a dietitian can give you further advice on this subject (see "Some ABCs of Good Nutrition," page 771).

Chronic diarrhea related to a pathological condition (for example, a parasitic infection or a specific defect in absorption) will usually be manifested by a failure to gain weight as well as other signs of illness, such as fever. During a medical exam for ongoing diarrhea, a number of these conditions will be considered and appropriate tests done to determine if one of them might be the cause.

diphtheria An infectious childhood disease that causes sore throat, fever, and in many cases the formation of a thick, gray covering in the nose, throat, and airway. Before immunizations were developed for this disease, it was one of the leading causes of death in children. Diphtheria vaccine is now routinely combined with tetanus immunization, and because of widespread vaccination efforts, this infection is rarely seen in the United States today. (See "Immunizations—Which Ones, Why, and When?" page 740.)

diplopia Double vision. See "eye care and concerns."

dislocation An injury in which the relationship between bones on either side of a joint is disrupted.

diuresis Increased elimination of urine.

dorsal Toward the back.

Down syndrome One of the most common genetic birth defects, occurring in roughly one in eight hundred to one thousand live births (or about four thousand per year in the United States). Normally every cell in the human body contains twenty-three pairs of chromosomes, with one set of twenty-three chromosomes contributed by each parent. Down syndrome occurs when part or all of an extra twenty-first chromosome is present in some or all of a person's cells. The most common scenario, in which an entire third twenty-first chromosome is present in all of the cells, is also known as **trisomy 21**. Maternal age is the only risk factor that has been identified for having a child with Down syndrome. The risk for this occurring in a twenty-five-year-old woman is about one in 1,250. At age thirty, it is one in one thousand; at thirty-five, one in four hundred; at forty, one in one hundred; and at forty-five, one in thirty. Neverthe-

less, 80 percent of infants with Down syndrome are born to women younger than thirty-five.

Down syndrome encompasses a number of physical and developmental characteristics, including:

- Mental retardation that most commonly is mild to moderate, typically with delays both in language and motor development. In addition, an estimated one in four adults with Down syndrome over age thirty-five develop signs and symptoms of a dementia similar to Alzheimer's disease.
- Short stature
- Upward slanting of the eyes, flattening of the nose, a small mouth, and a short neck
- Small hands with short fingers
- Decreased muscle tone. Infants with Down syndrome are often described as floppy.

In addition, those with Down syndrome are at risk for a number of health problems:

- Heart defects of varying severity affect about half of those with Down syndrome, and they may require medical or surgical treatment.
- More than half are affected by defects in vision or hearing.
- One in ten children with Down syndrome has abnormalities of the intestinal tract that will require surgical correction.
- Children with Down syndrome have a lower resistance to respiratory infections—colds, ear infections, bronchitis, and pneumonia.
- Children with Down syndrome have a fifteen- to twentyfold increased risk of developing leukemia.

A century ago, children with Down syndrome were not expected to live to adulthood. Today advances in health care have increased their life expectancy to at least the midfifties. Of equal importance has been the recognition that infant development, early intervention, and special-education programs can help them develop to their fullest potential. Opportunities for inclusion in regular classrooms, participation in sports and other community activities, gainful employment, and independent living as adults are available to an ever-growing number of people with Down syndrome. Organizations such as the National Down Syndrome Society (http://www.ndss.org) and many others offer support and encouragement to individuals with Down syndrome and their families. Without question, rearing a child with Down syndrome presents unique challenges—and opportunities—to his parents, siblings, extended family, physician, community, and church. But, like all children (and their parents), he is cherished by God, and his life is worth living to its fullest possible capacity.

A final thought: For many women the news that a child has Down syndrome comes before birth as the result of prenatal testing, often creating considerable pressure to terminate the pregnancy. If you or someone you know is facing this highly emotional dilemma, we would encourage a review of the Special Concerns section dealing with birth defects, and in particular the last two segments entitled "How Do You Decide Whether or Not to Have Amniocentesis or Chorionic Villus Sampling?" and "What If the Results of Prenatal Screening or Diagnostic Tests Are Abnormal?" (see pages 95 and 97).

dysentery Any of several intestinal disorders characterized by inflammation and manifested by abdominal cramping and frequent, usually bloody stools. Certain types of bacteria and parasites are the most common causes of dysentery (see "diarrhea" and "foodborne illness").

dysmenorrhea Painful menstruation (menstrual cramps).

dyspepsia Indigestion.

dyspnea Difficult or labored breathing.

E

ear infections Ear infections can involve any of the following three areas (illustrated on page A4):

- **Outer ear**—the part of the ear you can see and the ear canal that extends to the eardrum
- **Middle ear**—space behind the eardrum that contains the tiny bones that conduct sound from the eardrum to the inner ear
- **Inner ear**—the balance center, located deep within the bony skull

Infection of the outer ear: otitis externa

More commonly known as swimmer's ear, **otitis externa (OE)** is common among school-age children, especially during the summer when swimming and water sports are in full swing. Bacteria invade the skin and soft tissue that line the ear canal, causing inflammation and swelling.

SYMPTOMS In mild cases a little irritation and itching will be noticed. But more commonly the child with OE will complain of nonstop pain—which can be very severe—in and around the ear. Discomfort may increase when the child chews. Even the gentlest tug on the earlobe will provoke pain. In some cases swelling and debris in the ear canal can be severe enough to cause a slight temporary decrease in hearing. A small amount of drainage may develop as the infection progresses.

CAUSES Water remaining in the ear canal after swimming can serve as a reservoir for bacterial growth and make the skin surface more vulnerable to bacterial invasion. Wax buildup contributes to this process by blocking the natural drainage of water from the canal. A second major cause is trauma to the canal from overzealous attempts to clean the ear using cotton swabs or other objects. Occasionally chronic drainage from a perforated eardrum will result in OE.

TREATMENT Even if your child's history and complaints strongly suggest OE, a physician should confirm the diagnosis. If a large amount of wax and debris is present, the doctor will need to remove it. The infection is usually treated with eardrops that contain antibiotics to kill bacteria, and cortisone to reduce swelling. The doctor may carefully place a soft "wick" in the ear canal to prolong the contact of the drops with the infected surface. In severe cases, or when diabetes or an immune deficiency is present, oral antibiotics may be prescribed as well. Swimming should be avoided until the infection has cleared.

Adequate pain control is important. Acetaminophen or ibuprofen and a warm compress placed over the ear can provide temporary relief, but your child may also need stronger prescription pain medication.

PREVENTION If excessive wax buildup is a recurrent problem (this often runs in families and is not a reflection of inadequate hygiene), your child's physician may need to remove this material periodically. The doctor might also suggest wax-clearing measures—other than rigorous use of cotton swabs—to try at home. In some cases, the use of soft, molded earplugs when swimming is beneficial. Another approach is to instill a bacteria-inhibiting preparation (such as a mixture of equal parts white vinegar and alcohol) into the ear canal after swimming.

Infection of the middle ear: otitis media

Otitis media (OM) is the most common acute illness, other than the common cold, in children younger than three years of age. Seventy-five percent of all children will experience at least one episode of OM.

SYMPTOMS Typically an infant develops a cold, becomes irritable, cries persistently, sleeps fitfully (if at all), and loses her appetite; fever may or may not be present. Tugging at one or both ears is not a reliable indicator of an ear infection. An older child will complain specifically and continuously of ear pain. At times fluid trapped behind the eardrum will build up enough pressure to rupture it. When this occurs, thick, discolored material (usually yellow or green) will drain from the ear—a reliable sign that an infection is present and a definite reason to contact the child's physician. Spontaneous perforation of the eardrum, which relieves pressure and results in a dramatic reduction of pain, usually heals in seven to fourteen days as the infection resolves. (Before antibiotics were developed, deliberate incision of the eardrum with a tiny scalpel to drain the middle ear was the only specific treatment available for severe otitis media.)

CAUSES The underlying problem in most cases of OM is a malfunction of one or both **eustachian tubes**, the small passages that connect each middle ear to an area at the back of the nose, just above the **palate** (roof of the mouth). Normally the eustachian tubes drain secretions from the middle-ear cavities and prevent infected material from entering them. In infants and young children the tubes are shorter, narrower, and more nearly horizontal. As a result, any acute viral infection (specifically a cold) can disrupt eustachian-tube function more easily. Fluid collects in the middle ear, allowing bacteria also present in the nose to gain access to the ear. If an infection develops, inflammation and even more fluid in the middle ear increase pressure on the eardrum, causing pain and irritability.

A number of factors increase the risk of otitis media:

- Recurrent upper-respiratory infections (which can be a problem among children in day-care settings).
- Exposure to cigarette smoke at home.
- Chronic nasal allergy.
- Enlarged adenoids.
- Drinking from a bottle while lying flat.
- An inherited tendency for otitis media based on the shape and characteristics of the eustachian tube and middle ear. Typically, one or both parents will have had ear infections during childhood.

TREATMENT If your infant or child has the symptoms described above, she should be evaluated by a physician. If otitis media is diagnosed, antibiotics will nearly always be prescribed if she is younger than two years of age, but for an older child the doctor may choose to treat with pain measures only.[5] *It is important that your child take all the medication as prescribed and that any recommended follow-up be carried out.* Usually symptoms will improve significantly within a day or two. **Acetaminophen** (Tylenol and other brands) or **ibuprofen** (Children's Motrin and other brands) can help relieve pain. (See dosage charts for acetaminophen and ibuprofen on pages 609 and 688.) Decongestants have not been shown to have a significant impact on OM, and drops (whether oil, pain relievers, or antibiotics) should be placed in your child's ear only if prescribed by the physician.

POSSIBLE COMPLICATIONS
- Persistence of fluid (called **effusion**) in the middle ear that interferes with the conduction of sound. This can result in significant hear-

ing loss, a particularly important problem in young children because it can delay language development. In older children, hearing problems caused by chronic middle-ear effusion can contribute to school and behavior problems.

- Perforation of the eardrum, as already mentioned. Occasionally this will fail to heal on its own, which can result in ongoing or intermittent drainage along with mild to moderate hearing loss.
- **Mastoiditis**, an infection of the honeycombed, bony mastoid air cells directly behind the ear. Although mastoiditis can take place in any age-group, it is unusual before the age of two (see "mastoiditis").

All of these complications require appropriate care by your child's primary-care physician and in some cases by an ear, nose, and throat (ENT) specialist. If there have been repeated bouts of otitis media and/or persistent fluid in the middle ear (especially with hearing loss), the physician may recommend a minor operation called a **tympanostomy**, during which a small **ventilating tube** is placed in the eardrum. The initial procedure drains the fluid and improves hearing. The tube then continues to equalize pressure between the middle ear and the outside atmosphere, preventing the reaccumulation of fluid and usually reducing the number and duration of subsequent ear infections. (The insertion of ventilating tubes is the second most common surgical procedure performed on children under the age of five.)

When dealing with otitis media, you should call your child's doctor if any of the following occur:

- Your child's pain or elevated temperature persists after forty-eight to seventy-two hours, whether or not antibiotics have been started.
- Your child has persistent drainage from the ear canal.
- Your child becomes increasingly ill.
- Your child develops a stiff neck, severe headache, nausea, or vomiting.

Inflammation of the inner ear: labyrinthitis
Inflammation involving the inner ear (**labyrinthitis**) is uncommon in children and is also somewhat difficult to diagnose because it is not possible to see this area during an examination. More commonly seen in older children, labyrinthitis is characterized by sudden dizziness (**vertigo**). There may also be nausea and vomiting.

CAUSES AND TREATMENT While labyrinthitis occasionally arises as a complication of otitis media, in most cases it is probably viral in origin; antibiotics are not helpful unless otitis media is present. Labyrinthitis normally resolves on its own within a few weeks. However, this type of illness should be evaluated by your child's physician to rule out any other causes of vertigo and, if necessary, to begin medication to relieve symptoms.

eclampsia A serious condition occurring late in pregnancy or within twenty-four hours after delivery, characterized by convulsions (without any underlying seizure disorder). The cause is unknown. Increased blood pressure, water retention, and excessive loss of protein in the urine—a combination of symptoms referred to as **preeclampsia**—are usually observed beforehand, enabling the physician to take therapeutic measures in an effort to prevent eclampsia from occurring.

ectopic pregnancy A pregnancy that occurs outside the uterus, most commonly in a fallopian tube.

eczema (atopic dermatitis) See "allergies in children."

edema A diffuse abnormal accumulation of fluid within a particular tissue (for example, the lungs) or part of the body (such as the legs).

effusion A localized abnormal collection of fluid.

embolism The sudden blockage of an artery or vein by a clot or other obstructing material (such as fat, a tumor, or an air bubble) that has been carried through the bloodstream from another part of the body.

emesis Vomiting.

encephalitis Inflammation of brain tissue, usually caused by a virus.

encopresis Fecal soiling or leakage that is not due to illness or physical defect and occurs past the age of normal toilet training.

endocarditis An inflammation of the internal lining of the heart, usually caused by an infection.

endometriosis A condition in which the type of tissue (**endometrium**) that lines the inside of the uterus is also present in other parts of a woman's body—most commonly on the outer surfaces of the uterus, ovaries, fallopian tubes, intestine, or bladder. Like its counterpart within the uterus, this tissue builds up each month in response to the normal hormonal cycle and bleeds at the end of that cycle. Blood accumulated in one or more abnormal locations can irritate the surrounding tissue, causing considerable pain as well as scarring that can lead to infertility.

enema A liquid preparation inserted into the rectum for the purpose of bringing about a bowel movement.

epiglottitis A life-threatening, rapidly progressive infection of the epiglottis, the leaf-shaped plate of elastic cartilage at the root of the tongue. In a typical case, a child who has previously been well will rapidly develop a high fever and an extremely sore throat. Within a few hours she will be unable to swallow and might lean forward and actually drool rather than swallow. *This condition is a medical emergency because the swollen epiglottis can suddenly block the airway, leading to suffocation.* Even a simple examination with a tongue depressor can precipitate closure of the airway. A child who manifests these symptoms should be taken immediately to the nearest emergency department.

Fortunately epiglottitis has become uncommon because most children are now routinely immunized against *Haemophilus influenzae* type B, the bacteria that cause it.

epinephrine A hormone (also known as **adrenaline**) secreted by the adrenal glands that prepares the body to respond to stress. Among its many physiologic effects, epinephrine raises blood pressure, increases heart rate, raises the output of the heart, and elevates the level of glucose (blood sugar) in the bloodstream. It has been synthesized for medical use and is commonly given as an emergency treatment for severe allergic reactions.

esophagus The hollow structure that transports food from the throat to the stomach.

eustachian tube The narrow tube that connects the middle ear to the back of the nose and allows equalization of pressure between the middle ear and the outside world. The "popping" in the ears experienced when driving up or down a mountain or flying in an airplane arises from movement of air through the eustachian tubes as the outside air pressure changes. If one or both tubes are obstructed (as may occur during a cold), a change in altitude may lead to uncomfortable pressure in the affected ear. Decongestant medication or nose drops may be recommended to help relieve the obstruction and resulting pressure discomfort.

exanthem A skin rash accompanied by an acute infection (for example, measles).

expectorant A compound included in many cough and cold preparations intended to loosen secretions and allow them to be cleared more easily from the respiratory passages.

eye care and concerns The eye is a marvel of engineering. Each eye is a compact but exquisitely sensitive biological camera that focuses images of the external world onto the **retina**, a ten-layer cellular membrane directly connected to the brain through the **optic nerve**. Before arriving at the retina (located at the back of the eyeball), light must pass through these parts of the eye:

- The **cornea**, a clear, highly sensitive structure that forms a domelike covering over the **iris**, whose pigment gives the eye its color.

- The **pupil**, the small black circular aperture (opening) in the center of the iris. The pupil dilates or constricts in response to the amount of light striking the eye.
- The **lens**, placed directly behind the iris, which focuses light on the retina.
- The **vitreous humor**, clear, gelatinous material that fills the eyeball.

(See illustration on page A4.) Vision disturbances can arise from abnormalities in the shape, function, or clarity of these structures.

Other important structures of the eyes are the **sclera**, the white surface of the eyeball; the **conjunctiva**, a membrane that covers the sclera and the inner surface of the eyelid; the **lacrimal gland**, which produces tears; and the **nasolacrimal duct**, through which tears travel from the inner corner of the eye into the nose.

Early developments

Even though a baby's eyes are not fully developed at birth, the intricate process of collecting visual information begins as soon as a newborn can open her eyes. The retina is not fully functional during the first few months, and the brain needs time to assemble visual images into meaningful patterns. Nevertheless, during the first few weeks of life a baby will gaze intently at objects eight to fifteen inches from her face. She prefers to study plain, high-contrast, black-and-white images such as stripes, checks, or spirals, or a simple drawing of a face. But a newborn's favorite subject to scrutinize will be a person's face, about a foot away from hers. She will not respond directly to a smile for the first few weeks.

The iris in a light-skinned newborn contains little pigment and is usually blue gray or blue brown. The final color of a baby's eyes won't be known for at least six months or longer, during which time pigment gradually forms. The iris is brown from birth in most dark-skinned infants. The lacrimal gland does not become fully functional for about four weeks, so a crying newborn makes few tears. The sclera is relatively thin at birth and may have a slightly bluish tinge because of the dark color of the tissue lying just beneath it. A rise in **bilirubin** level shortly after birth may cause the sclera to appear yellow (see "bilirubin").

By two or three months of age a baby will be able to coordinate her eye movements to stay locked on an interesting visual target that passes through a semicircle in front of her. She will also be interested in more complex shapes and patterns and will be able to hold her head steady enough to fixate on simple, high-contrast objects hung over her crib. By three months of age her depth of vision will have increased so that she will recognize you halfway across a room. Responses to color also develop over the first several weeks. At first a newborn will pay attention to objects with bright, strongly contrasting colors. It will take a few months before her color vision has matured enough to distinguish a full palette of colors and shades.

All babies cross their eyes briefly as they develop their tracking skills. However, an infant who does not follow a face by the age of three months or whose eyes frequently wander or cross after five or six months may have a vision problem that should be addressed by the pediatrician or family doctor. The primary-care doctor will examine the eyes and, if appropriate, refer the patient to an ophthalmologist for evaluation. (Ideally this would be a **pediatric ophthalmologist**—a physician who specializes in children's eye problems—although many ophthalmologists deal with patients of all ages.)

By six months of age an infant is normally able to focus on people or objects several feet away and follow movement in all directions. **Visual acuity**, or the ability to see objects, will improve from approximately 20/400 at birth to about 20/80. (The numbers used to express visual acuity are based on the ability to identify letters at a certain distance. A visual acuity of 20/80 means that the smallest letters a person can identify twenty feet [6 meters] away could be read by someone with normal [20/20] vision at a distance of eighty feet [24 meters]. Obviously infants cannot identify letters, but their visual acuity measured by other methods is still expressed in the 20/__ format.) A six-month-old will also show interest in more complex patterns and subtle shades of color.

By seven or eight months, a baby's visual capabilities will mature to the point that she can focus on people and objects across the room, though not quite with the same clarity she sees something directly in front of her. The average one-year-old can see well enough to spy small objects across the room or planes flying overhead, and by the age of two a child's visual acuity may approach 20/30 or 20/20, although this can be difficult to establish objectively. A child age two or older who squints a lot or brings objects close to her face to see them should have a formal eye exam, as should a child who is old enough to complain specifically of blurry vision or difficulty seeing the blackboard at school.

Routine infant and childhood exams include a brief check of the eyes: the clarity of each cornea, appearance of the eyelids, and responses of the pupils. Beginning at six months, the infant's ability to gaze at and follow an object, as well as the alignment of the eyes, will also be assessed. (Sometimes alignment can be difficult to judge because the skin adjacent to a baby's nose may partially cover the inner portion of the sclera, giving a misleading impression that one or both eyes are crossed.) Children as young as three can be screened for visual acuity using an appropriate eye chart or other testing methods that the child can comprehend.

Common eye problems during infancy

Blocked tear duct (nasolacrimal duct obstruction). The nasolacrimal duct normally drains tears into the nose after they have entered small openings in the inner corner of each eye. Between 6 and 10 percent of infants are born with an obstruction of this duct. Within a few days or weeks after birth, tears will accumulate in and overflow from the affected eye. The small lacrimal sac located just above the obstructed duct may become infected, causing a constant backflow of discolored mucus into the eye. This usually bothers parents more than the baby, but more severe signs of infection, such as inflammation and swelling, may develop in the inner corner of the eye.

If the baby's primary-care physician diagnoses this problem, he or she might recommend warm soaks and massage of the tear duct up to six times per day. This is done by pressing the tip of a finger against the baby's nose just above the lacrimal sac (in the area where the upper and lower eyelids come together) and pushing downward toward the nasolacrimal duct. The pressure exerted against the obstruction may gradually open the drainage system. Antibiotic drops or ointment may be prescribed if an infection is present.

More than 90 percent of obstructed nasolacrimal ducts will open before the first birthday. If the problem does not resolve spontaneously, a probing, which involves placing a thin wire probe through the obstructed area, can be done in the office (or hospital) between three and nine months of age.

Strabismus is a misalignment of the eye. An eye may turn inward (esotropia), outward (exotropia), up (hypertropia), or down (hypotropia). Strabismus occurs in 4 percent of infants. Since eye movements are not fully coordinated until the child is three to six months old, temporary deviations in any direction before the age of three months usually do not require specific treatment. However, persistent deviation after the age of six months should be checked by the baby's physician, and usually the physician will refer the patient to an ophthalmologist. Appropriate treatment of strabismus is important because misalignment of the eyes causes ongoing double vision (called **diplopia**), causing the infant's brain to suppress information arriving from one eye or the other. This results in an impairment of vision called **amblyopia**, which develops in 2 to 3 percent of individuals. Depending on the extent of the strabismus, correction may require the use of special glasses or even muscle surgery on one or both eyes. The operation, usually done on an outpatient basis, modifies the attachment position of one or more of the muscles that control eye movements.

Common eye problems in childhood

By far the most common vision disorders in children are **refractive errors**, in which the retina does not receive a perfectly focused image. These affect 20 percent of children by the age of sixteen. Since genetic factors play a role in these disturbances, other family members may have similar problems. There are several types of refractive errors:

- **Myopia (nearsightedness)**—distant objects are out of focus. This condition usually develops as the eyeball grows and becomes longer than is ideal for focusing images on the retina. Normally myopia is not seen until a child is five to ten years of age, and it may become more pronounced during adolescence and early adulthood. A nearsighted child may squint because this helps bring distant objects into focus.

- **Hyperopia (farsightedness)**—distant objects are more easily brought into focus than those that are close. This condition is present to a mild degree in most newborns, a consequence of the smaller size of a baby's eye. Normal alterations in the shape of the newborn's lens and cornea compensate for hyperopia early in infancy. Farsightedness may actually become more pronounced during the first few years of life, but a child's eye has a greater capacity than an adult's to adjust the shape of the lens (a process called **accommodation**), which effectively brings a close object into focus. However, hours of this effort can cause eyestrain, headaches, and crossed eyes.
- **Astigmatism** is an abnormality in which the cornea is more egg-shaped than round, producing blurry or distorted vision. Squinting may improve a child's focus when astigmatism is present, but a severe distortion can cause eyestrain and headaches.

Refractive errors can be corrected with glasses or contact lenses. Mild hyperopia is usually not treated. Children who are highly active should use shatterproof lenses. Youngsters involved in sports can wear an elastic strap that attaches to the glasses and extends around the back of the head to keep them in place and prevent loss or damage.

Eye trauma, ranging from a scratch on the cornea to a severe injury that causes permanent visual impairment or loss, is not uncommon in childhood. According to the U.S. Public Health Service, more than eight hundred thousand eye injuries occur every year in the United States among children and adolescents younger than eighteen, and of these the vast majority are preventable. (Injuries due to darts, BB guns, and firecrackers are all too common. See "Emergency Care," page 822.)

A **corneal abrasion** is a scratch in the cornea's outer cell layers, often caused by a seemingly minimal incident such as being brushed by a leaf or twig. Since the cornea is very sensitive, the pain of an abrasion is usually intense. After the eye is examined by a doctor or ophthalmologist, an antibiotic is usually placed on the eye and a patch applied to prevent the eyelid from opening and closing over the injury. The antibiotic helps prevent secondary infection that could lead to more serious damage of the cornea. The surface of the cornea normally heals completely within twenty-four to forty-eight hours.

Sometimes trauma will cause internal bleeding of the eye, resulting in extreme pain and clouded vision. When blood appears in the clear space behind the cornea (a condition called a **hyphema**), the child should be taken immediately to an ophthalmologist or emergency room. To prevent further bleeding, the child must be kept at strict bed rest for up to five days. Enforcement of this low level of activity is critical. If the blood is not absorbed, an operation might be needed to remove it. A hyphema can cause scarring of the eye, which can in turn produce **glaucoma** (increased pressure within the eye). Further eye exams may be conducted to ensure that no additional damage has occurred.

If the eyeball has been penetrated or cut open, the child should be taken directly to the emergency room for immediate evaluation. If fluid is oozing from the eye, the child should be transferred while lying flat on her back so that additional fluid will not escape from the eye. A simple shield such as a small paper cup should be held over the eye (but without exerting pressure) to protect it.

A chemical injury to the eye, especially from an alkaline substance such as drain cleaner, can be very damaging and difficult to treat. It is important to flush any such material out of the eye with prolonged irrigation. Immediately place the child's face under a water faucet or hose and rinse the eye. Then promptly see an ophthalmologist or go to a hospital.

A foreign object (such as a piece of dirt) in the eye will cause irritation, pain, and tearing. Sometimes a parent can locate the foreign body under the upper or lower eyelid and gently remove it. If the object's size or location or the child's discomfort prevents removal at home, the child's doctor or an ophthalmologist should be contacted.

Usually an anesthetic drop will be placed in the eye so the foreign body can be removed without pain.

Eye infections can be caused by viruses, bacteria, or fungal agents. Common symptoms of an eye infection are redness, tearing, watery or mucous drainage, and mild sensitivity to light. *Significant pain in one or both eyes, with or without sensitivity to light, should not be ignored.* In such cases, the child should be examined by a physician or ophthalmologist, not only to relieve the discomfort but to treat conditions that might damage the eye if left alone.

Any virus or bacteria that infects the nose or throat can find its way into the linings of one or both eyes (or conjunctivae). Infections here, known as **conjunctivitis**, produce a reddish discoloration and thick, discolored drainage. When this material dries overnight, the eyelids may stick together with crusty debris, which you will need to remove gently with a warm, wet washcloth. Your child's doctor will normally prescribe antibiotic drops or ointment for a few days. If the infection is caused by a virus (such as the common **adenovirus**, which is usually accompanied by an upper-respiratory infection, fever, and sore throat), symptoms may not resolve for several weeks. Careful hand washing is a must for anyone handling a baby with conjunctivitis because the organisms involved can spread to others via contaminated fingers (see "conjunctivitis").

Various forms of the **herpes virus** can on rare occasion cause problems on the surface of (or deeper within) the eye. **Chickenpox (varicella)** occasionally causes conjunctivitis if the virus forms one or more small blisters (similar to those on the skin surface) on the conjunctiva of the eye. These normally resolve without damage. A reappearance of the chickenpox virus later in life, known as **herpes zoster** or **shingles**, can also involve the cornea. In addition, the **herpes simplex virus**, which causes common cold sores of the lips, may affect the eye. Treatment of any herpes infection involving the eye will require an ophthalmologist to relieve discomfort and prevent rare complications that can cause scarring and long-term visual impairment.

Allergies can cause itchy and runny eyes, a condition known as **allergic conjunctivitis**, which often responds to antihistamines. In some cases eyedrops containing antihistamines or other anti-inflammatory substances can help reduce symptoms, although they do not provide a cure. Thick mucus, crusting, and pain are not a part of this problem, and causes other than allergy should be considered. In more severe allergic reactions, swelling of the conjunctival membrane occurs, producing a bubble on the surface of the eye or inner lids. This can look frightening, but it resolves without harming the eye.

Problems with the eyelids and the iris

The eyelids can be the site of both inflammation and infection. **Blepharitis** is a chronic condition that causes swelling and redness of the eyelids and a scaling of dandruff-like material from the eyelashes. Often blepharitis is caused by bacteria called **staphylococci**, but it may also be related to an inflammatory condition called **seborrhea**. Treatment involves removing the crust with a moist cotton swab (which may be dipped in baby shampoo diluted with an equal amount of water). Antibiotic ointment may also be useful.

A **hordeolum**, better known as a **sty**, is a staphylococcal infection of a gland in the eyelid. This usually begins as a tiny red spot that grows into a pustule, which will eventually drain. Warm compresses may be applied three or four times a day, and antibiotic drops can be helpful. Inflammation of a different type of gland in the eyelid leads to a small lump called a **chalazion**. Warm soaks are also helpful, although this condition may take up to three months to resolve. Rarely, a chalazion will not disappear, and surgical removal under anesthesia becomes necessary. The persistence of blepharitis or a chalazion is often discouraging to parents, but most children will outgrow these problems.

As mentioned earlier, persistent pain in the eye, especially when discomfort is aggravated by light, should be evaluated as soon as possible. One condition that may cause this combination of symptoms is **iritis**, or inflammation of the iris. Frequently this is accompanied by redness of the sclera, which may give the misleading impression that a child has the more common conjunctivitis (pinkeye). But iritis must be treated quite differently to relieve pain and prevent scarring of the iris and other related structures. In children, iritis is often associated with medical conditions that affect other parts of the body (most commonly **juvenile rheumatoid arthritis**), and further evaluation to search for one of these disorders will probably be recommended.

For help with eye problems, contact your child's physician during daytime hours if your child experiences any of the following:

- Repeated episodes of eyes crossing, wandering, or failing to align after the age of three months, or persistent misalignment of the eyes at any age
- Mild itching, discharge, or irritation of one or both eyes
- Blurred vision or difficulty focusing (unless this is sudden and accompanied by other symptoms such as headache, in which case the physician should be contacted immediately)
- Squinting when looking at objects in the distance
- Repeatedly bringing objects very close to the eyes to see them

Contact your child's physician *immediately* in the following situations:

- Your child complains of persistent and significant pain in or around the eye.
- Your child is struck in the eye by any object, especially if there is ongoing pain or visible damage.
- Your child accidentally gets any chemical substance in one or both eyes (irrigating the eyes with water should begin *before* you call the physician).

Basic eye safety and reminders

- Never stare at the sun, even when most of it is blocked during an eclipse, because of the risk of permanent ultraviolet damage to the retina.
- When spending extended hours playing on a sunny beach or in the snow, dark glasses that block ultraviolet light (which is reflected from sand or snow) can prevent a painful corneal burn.
- Always wear protective goggles when working with home or garden tools or in science labs where chemicals might splash into the eye.

- Protective eyewear should be worn at all times when playing racquetball or squash.
- Never aim flying toys (such as paper planes) at anyone's face.
- Playing with fireworks—especially those that fly, explode, or spew sparks—poses a significant risk to the eyes and is not an appropriate activity for children.
- Darts and BB guns are high-risk toys.

F **failure to thrive** A medical term designating a perceptible decrease in the rate of growth and/or a persistent failure to gain weight (or actual weight loss) in an infant or child who previously has been developing normally. Possible causes include difficulty with nursing, inadequate or inappropriate food intake, a medical problem that interferes with the proper ingestion or utilization of food, chronic disease (such as cystic fibrosis or diabetes), an ongoing infection, or in some cases social or emotional issues at home.

One of the many reasons routine checkups are important during infancy and childhood is that they provide an ongoing record of height and weight measurements, which may be the first indicators of failure to thrive. If these measurements raise any concerns, the physician may review a child's health history and dietary habits, carry out a physical examination, and possibly order other tests to help identify the cause. If no specific medical illness can be identified, it may be necessary to assess whether interactions within the family might be affecting the child's food intake or digestion.

fainting A relatively sudden and usually brief loss of consciousness caused by a temporary reduction in flow of blood to the brain. See "Emergency Care," page 823.

femur (Also called the thighbone.) The bone extending from the pelvis to the knee. The femur is the longest and largest bone in the body.

fetal alcohol spectrum disorders A number of irreversible problems observed in a baby exposed to alcohol before birth. The most extreme manifestation of these is **fetal alcohol syndrome (FAS)**, which was first described in the late 1960s.

Occurring in about one out of every thousand births, it is considered one of the leading causes of preventable birth defects and mental retardation. Common features of fetal alcohol syndrome include:

1. *Poor growth* before or after birth, with weight, height, and head circumference smaller than 90 percent of other newborns.
2. *Abnormalities of central nervous system function.* Of these, mental retardation is the most significant, seen in more than 80 percent of affected children. Fetal alcohol syndrome is one of the leading causes of mental retardation in the United States. Other problems include irritability during infancy, hyperactivity during childhood, and delays in development. In some infants, jitteriness soon after birth is the direct result of alcohol withdrawal. Abnormalities in the central nervous system caused by alcohol may also affect development of bones and joints.
3. *Various defects of the face, eyes, and ears.* These are often more apparent during infancy and may become less obvious as the child grows into adulthood. Symptoms may include incomplete development of the facial bones, a thin upper lip, a short nose, prominence of the vertical skin fold on each side of the nose, and drooping upper eyelids. Various visual disturbances may be present as well, including incomplete development of the optic nerve, misalignment of the eyes, nearsightedness, and astigmatism. Varying degrees of hearing loss are common in infants with this syndrome. These abnormalities frequently lead to delays in language development.
4. *Other birth defects* occur in infants with this syndrome, including a variety of congenital abnormalities of the heart (affecting approximately 30 percent) and the urinary tract (affecting about 10 percent).

While there is no cure for fetal alcohol syndrome, infants who have it can be helped to reach their fullest potential. Particular attention should be paid to the child's vision and hearing, to detect and treat problems that could impair normal development. Infants and children with fetal alcohol syndrome are also prone to develop ear infections and persistent fluid behind the eardrums, which should be treated to prevent hearing loss. Cavities in the teeth are more common in these children, so conscientious dental care is important. As these children approach school age, educational testing and special programs should be sought for them.

For every child with FAS, it is estimated that there are three or more who have some but not all of its manifestations. These tend to fall into two specific subgroups: Those with **alcohol-related neurodevelopmental disorder (ARND)** primarily manifest mental and behavioral disturbances, while those with **alcohol-related birth defects (ARBD)** have problems with one or more body structures, such as the heart, kidneys, or bones.

Fetal alcohol syndrome occurs most often among infants born to women who chronically abuse alcohol (typically consuming four or more drinks daily), but ARND and ARBD can occur when mothers drink much less. Some research has suggested that babies born to women who have had as little as one drink per week during pregnancy may be at higher risk for behavior problems later in life.[6] Furthermore, fetal alcohol spectrum disorders can occur in a child whose mother drank at *any* stage of her pregnancy. Birth defects (such as heart abnormalities) are more likely to arise from alcohol consumption during the first three months of pregnancy; growth disturbances can occur when a mother drinks during the last few months; and adverse effects on the brain can result from a mother's alcohol use at any time while pregnant.[7]

Here's an important bottom line regarding alcohol and pregnancy:

- There is no amount of alcohol that can be considered safe for a woman to drink during pregnancy.
- There is no time during pregnancy when consuming alcohol can be considered safe for the developing baby.
- It is wise for a woman to abstain or to consume no more than two alcoholic drinks per week if she is not yet pregnant but might become so in the near future.

fever See the Special Concerns section "When Your Child Has a Fever," page 241.

fibula The smaller of the two bones that extend from the knee to the foot. It is located closer to the lateral, or outside, part of the leg, and it does not bear weight.

fissure A slit or groove, which may be normal or abnormal, in tissue. Fissures often occur at a junction of skin and mucous membrane, such as at the anal opening.

flat feet (see illustration on page 763) A condition in which the normal arch of the foot is flattened. (See "Musculoskeletal Problems in Children," page 763.)

flatulence Excessive production and passing of gas from the intestines.

fluorescein An orange-red dye used to detect certain types of abnormalities within the eye or to identify an injury on its surface.

fluorosis A discoloration of the teeth, usually appearing as lacy white lines or specks, caused by excessive ingestion of fluoride. Supplemental fluoride helps strengthen the outer tooth enamel and may be present in the local water supply, in vitamin supplements, or in fluorinated toothpaste. Fluorosis sometimes develops if a child who drinks tap water is also given fluoride supplements exceeding the amount recommended for the area he lives in, based on the fluoride concentration in the local water supply. Some children also swallow toothpaste when brushing their teeth. There is enough fluoride in the amount of toothpaste that covers the bristles of a toothbrush to cause eventual discoloration of a child's teeth if a substantial amount is swallowed regularly (see also "teeth care and concerns").

folliculitis Inflammation of one or more follicles (tiny sacs or glands in the skin), typically as a result of bacterial infection. This occurs most often in hair follicles and in sebaceous glands, especially in the neck, thighs, buttocks, or armpits.

fontanelle See "anterior fontanelle."

food poisoning See "foodborne illness."

foodborne illness A general term for a variety of illnesses arising from an infection or, less commonly, an actual toxin in something we eat or drink. More than 250 specific types of foodborne illness have been described. This is not the same as food allergy or intolerance, in which a person reacts to a constituent of a food that otherwise is tolerated by most people. Foodborne illness often provokes a combination of intestinal symptoms: nausea, vomiting, abdominal cramps, and diarrhea. Headache or fever may also occur, depending on the organism involved (usually some type of bacteria). One foodborne illness—**botulism**—affects the central nervous system and is sometimes life threatening.

Very often foodborne illness looks and feels like common viral **gastroenteritis** (so-called "stomach flu"), and the only clue that food is the cause may be the simultaneous eruption of similar symptoms among family members or friends, especially if these people recently shared a meal or ate at the same restaurant. Unfortunately, food contaminated by bacteria does not necessarily look, smell, or taste any different from uncontaminated food, so this type of illness usually catches its victims by surprise.

Severe foodborne illnesses such as cholera and typhoid fever have been known to ravage many parts of the world, especially after a disaster such as a flood or earthquake. In North America we are blessed with widespread standards of sanitation, waste disposal, and food preparation that allow us to eat just about anywhere—at restaurants or at our own kitchen table—without worrying about contracting a major intestinal upset. Yet the Centers for Disease Control and Prevention estimates that every year in the United States approximately 76 million cases of foodborne illness are reported, requiring 325,000 hospital admissions and causing 5,000 deaths. It is impossible to know exactly how many actual cases of foodborne infection occur every year because many consist of acute bouts of vomiting and/or diarrhea from which a person recovers without specific treatment, without a diagnosis, and without the illness being reported.

As you might imagine, the most serious problems tend to arise among the very young, the very old, or those with compromised immunity.

Staphylococcal food poisoning is the most common and often the most unpleasant food-related illness; fortunately it is the most short-lived. Staphylococci (or staph) are best known for causing skin infections such as boils and impetigo. Someone with an infected wound or sore on the hands might introduce staph into food. If the food is warm—not hot or cold but about 100°F (38°C)—the bacteria will multiply and produce a toxin that is resistant to cooking. (This is an important reason why warm foods should not sit for long periods of time. They should either be kept hot or refrigerated immediately.)

Symptoms of staphylococcal food poisoning begin abruptly, less than six hours after the meal, and set off a combination of intense vomiting (usually the worst symptom), diarrhea, and severe abdominal cramps. The illness ends within twenty-four hours without specific treatment.

Campylobacter bacteria colonize wild, domestic, and farm animals, especially poultry. Undercooked chicken, turkey, and waterfowl are common food sources for this bacteria, along with raw (unpasteurized) milk.

Campylobacter infections begin with flu-like symptoms: high fever and headache, nausea, vomiting, and abdominal cramps. Then comes diarrhea: frequent (up to twenty stools per day), usually watery, mucous (containing mucus), or even bloody. Usually the illness subsides on its own, but relapses are possible. If a stool test identifies campylobacter as the cause of illness, appropriate antibiotic treatment will shorten the duration of the symptoms as well as reduce the shedding of bacteria, which might infect someone else. (Outbreaks in day-care centers have been reported.)

Salmonella are bacteria that can cause not only food poisoning but more serious, widespread infections (especially in newborns and infants), as well as typhoid fever. While typhoid is far less common in North America than in developing countries, about forty thousand cases of foodborne *Salmonella* infections are reported every year in the United States.[8] (Many more cases are not diagnosed or reported.) Animals, especially fowl and reptiles, are carriers of many *Salmonella*

species but do not transmit the specific form that causes typhoid (see also "typhoid fever").

Meats, dairy products (including ice cream), undercooked eggs, and contaminated egg products used in other foods (such as custards and mayonnaise) can contain *Salmonella*. One or two days after ingestion, fever, vomiting, and diarrhea begin. Older children may complain of a headache and abdominal cramps. If all goes well, symptoms resolve in a few days without treatment. In fact, a child who is stable and showing no other signs of trouble probably should not be given antibiotics for *Salmonella* infection because these drugs may prolong the time that the bacteria remain in the intestinal tract.

Of all the bacteria that cause food poisoning, *Salmonella* is the most likely to enter the bloodstream (although this is rare) and infect bones, kidneys, heart, lungs, or joints. *Salmonella* can also cause meningitis if it infects the linings around the brain and spinal cord.

Since a *Salmonella* infection that spreads throughout the body can be a serious problem, infants younger than three months of age and children with chronic medical problems (such as sickle-cell disease, immune deficiency, or heart or kidney disease)—all of whom are more vulnerable to this complication—should be treated with appropriate antibiotics if this bacteria is found in their stool. Young infants or children who are severely ill with *Salmonella* infection will require treatment in the hospital with intravenous fluids and antibiotics.

Salmonella is known for its capacity to remain in the intestinal tract for weeks or even months after the acute symptoms are gone. The child in this carrier state won't be ill but can spread the bacteria to others, even after receiving antibiotics. Careful hand washing by adult caregivers and by the child herself (if she's old enough) is extremely important in the wake of a *Salmonella* infection.

E. coli normally live in the intestinal tract of humans without causing disease, but some strains are associated with a variety of diarrhea syndromes. A common form is the mild but annoying **traveler's diarrhea**, which normally resolves on its own. Other forms are more serious and are accompanied by fever, cramping, and bloody diarrhea. (*E. coli* species are also commonly involved in urinary tract infections, and in infants they may cause meningitis or other serious illness. Most of these occur independently of the diarrhea syndromes discussed here.) One subtype can cause a serious combination of kidney failure, anemia, and clotting problems known as **hemolytic uremic syndrome** (see page 681). This particular bacteria and other dangerous forms of *E. coli* are known to contaminate ground beef and other foods.

Two distinct types of infections are caused by species of the bacteria called *Clostridium. Clostridium perfringens* resides in soil, sewage, and the intestines of humans and animals. It is best known for contaminating food produced in large quantities, such as that cooked in restaurants, institutional kitchens, or school cafeterias, where food may sit for hours slightly warm or at room temperature. Stews, casseroles, and gravies are particularly prone to transmitting this organism. Symptoms are unpleasant—abrupt onset of vomiting and explosive diarrhea—but normally resolve without specific treatment within a few days.

Clostridium botulinum is another story. This bacterium produces a potent toxin that causes **botulism**, but only under conditions in which there is no oxygen plus the right mix of chemicals. This contamination can occur within improperly canned foods, such as corn, beets, peas, and green beans, as well as in honey contaminated with *Clostridium botulinum* spores. Unlike other food poisonings, botulism affects the central nervous system. After an eight- to thirty-six-hour incubation, fatigue and headache begin, followed by visual symptoms (droopy eyelids, double vision, dilated pupils). A few hours later, swallowing and speech may be affected. Paralysis can develop, and if muscles necessary for breathing are affected, respiratory failure and death could follow.

Infant botulism often occurs when babies under twelve months of age are given contaminated honey. They become constipated and lethargic with a weak suck and cry, floppy muscle tone, and in some cases sudden failure to breathe (apnea).

A specific antitoxin can be given with some success once the diagnosis is made, but long-term supportive care, including intravenous or tube feeding and respiratory support using a ventilator, might be necessary for several weeks. Botulism is less likely to be fatal in children than in adults, and eventually symptoms resolve completely. But without a doubt, this is an illness that you want your child to avoid.

Treatment

If your child suddenly begins vomiting and having diarrhea, no one will be able to say whether foodborne infection, viral gastroenteritis, or some other illness is the problem—unless of course other family members have the same symptoms and your doctor has made a specific diagnosis. If your child has a persistent high fever with diarrhea, the doctor may check stool cultures (or perform other lab tests) to find a treatable bacterial infection, especially if the diarrhea is bloody. While no single antibiotic is appropriate for any and all acute infections of the intestinal tract, some types of food poisoning will respond to the properly chosen antibiotic. In any case, your primary tasks will be the following:

PREVENT DEHYDRATION. If fluids lost through vomiting or diarrhea are not replenished, infants can become dehydrated within several hours, and an older child after one or two days. Talk to your child's physician for specific directions, which will depend upon the child's age, general health, and the intensity of the illness. Be alert for signs of significant fluid loss that may need more aggressive medical care: decreased urine output (fewer than six wet diapers per day in an infant), fewer tears, dry mouth, and—most important—worsening listlessness (see "vomiting" and "diarrhea").

KEEP THE CHILD COMFORTABLE. For this type of illness, you will be offering compassion and acetaminophen—and not much more. Medications that stop diarrhea (such as Imodium or Lomotil) should not be given to infants and toddlers under two years of age, and they should be given to older children only with your doctor's recommendation. While they might reduce the number of stools, they never cure the underlying disease. In some cases these medications prolong the stay of pathogenic bacteria in the intestine. In addition, they can mislead everyone about your child's condition, because fluids lost into the bowel may continue to accumulate while not appearing as stool. In other words, your child could become dehydrated without any visible fluid loss.

Similarly, medications that treat vomiting should be used sparingly and only as explicitly prescribed by your child's health-care provider for that specific child's current illness. Antiemetic medications (drugs that control vomiting) tend to sedate small children, which can be problematic if you're concerned about worsening dehydration.

WATCH FOR SIGNS OF TROUBLE BEYOND THE INTESTINAL TRACT. Weakness, confusion, complaints of difficulty swallowing, or significant localized pain somewhere other than the abdomen should be reported to your child's physician. If your child's health is deteriorating and you cannot contact the doctor, take him to the nearest emergency room.

Prevention

The three primary ways that foods become contaminated are (1) improper preparation, (2) inadequate cooking, and (3) improper storage.

The foods most likely to become contaminated by unsavory organisms (usually bacteria) are perishables, especially meat and other animal products, fresh fruits, and vegetables. Foodborne illness often occurs because of factors such as these:

- Hands aren't washed enough
- Fruits and vegetables aren't washed enough
- Meats aren't cooked long enough
- Stored foods aren't kept cold enough

Here's a top ten list of dos and don'ts to reduce your risk of getting sick from food and drink:

1. Wash your hands with soap and water before you prepare food—especially if you're going to handle meat, poultry, fish, shellfish, or eggs. If you use the toilet, play with a pet, or change a diaper during the course of preparing food, *wash your hands again*. If *you* have diarrhea or some other intestinal illness, play it safe and let someone else prepare the food.
2. Everyone in the family should wash hands before eating.

3. Wash your utensils, cutting board, and other surfaces with hot, soapy water after you have prepared food (especially meat, dairy, and egg products). This helps prevent cross-contamination, in which organisms from one food are accidentally transferred to another. Also, avoid using wooden cutting boards for meat. Pores in the wood can harbor dangerous bacteria.
4. Keep your raw meats, poultry, fish, and shellfish out of contact with other foods. (This is another measure to prevent cross-contamination.) Ideally, these various animal products should be bagged separately at the grocery store, kept in sealed bags or containers so that their juices don't drip onto other foods or surfaces, prepared on separate cutting boards, and placed on different plates.
5. Wash raw fruits and vegetables in running water before eating them—especially those that are not going to be cooked. Once they're washed, don't put them back into the original package or container.
6. Cook your meat, poultry, and eggs thoroughly. Because contaminated food can look and smell normal, experts recommend the use of a food thermometer to help you gauge what's hot enough—140° to 180°F (60° to 82°C), depending on the food—and what's not. The U.S. Department of Agriculture recommends that the following *internal* temperatures be reached in order to kill potentially harmful bacteria:

   - Beef, veal, and lamb: 145°F (63°C) for medium rare (the rarest you should allow), 160°F (71°C) for medium, and 170°F (77°C) for well-done. Fresh pork: The same, except it should not be eaten medium rare.
   - Poultry: 180°F (82°C) for whole birds, legs, wings, and thighs; 170°F (77°C) for breasts.
   - Ground meat: 160°F (71°C) for ground beef, pork, veal, and lamb; 165°F (74°C) for ground poultry.
   - Ham: 160°F (71°C) if fresh, 140°F (60°C) if previously cooked.
   - Fish and shellfish: 145°F (63°C) for at least fifteen seconds.
   - Egg dishes: 160°F (71°C); cook eggs until the yolks are firm.

- Casseroles, stews, and leftovers: 165°F (74°C).

7. Room temperature isn't good for perishables, but bacteria love it. Put your perishables in the refrigerator or freezer within two hours of purchase or preparation (and within one hour if you're having a heat wave and room temperature is 90°F, or 32°C, or more). This includes the doggie bag from the restaurant containing the food you—or your dog—want to enjoy the next day.

   - Make sure your refrigerator maintains a temperature of less than 40°F (4°C) and your freezer less than 0°F (-18°C).
   - Fresh beef, veal, lamb, or pork should go in the freezer if you're not going to eat it within three to five days.
   - Ground meat, fish, shellfish, and poultry should go in the freezer if you're not going to use it within two days.
   - Don't let prepared perishables sit at room temperature for more than two hours. If you're having a get-together where food needs to be available for a longer time, keep the hot foods hot with a warming tray or chafing dish, and keep the cold foods on ice.
   - Thaw your frozen meat in the refrigerator or microwave, not on the kitchen counter. At room temperature the outer portions can become hospitable to bacteria long before the center portion has thawed.
   - Marinate meat in the refrigerator, not at room temperature.
   - Toss refrigerated leftovers after four days.
   - When in doubt, throw it out.

8. Think twice before you eat, or serve your family, any of the following:

   - Raw, rare, or undercooked meat, poultry, fish, and shellfish. (Raw oysters and clams are well-known for transmitting **norovirus**, one of the two types of viruses that can cause **acute gastroenteritis**—a miserable but usually brief illness notable for repeated episodes of vomiting and diarrhea over one or two days.)
   - Unpasteurized (raw) milk, even when it's "certified," as well as products made from unpasteurized milk.
   - Raw sprouts, such as alfalfa, clover, or radishes. (Raw sprouts themselves are a healthful food, but they have been associated with outbreaks of illness caused by *E. coli* and *Salmonella*. They're grown in a humid environment, and they can harbor bacteria if they are exposed to water or harvesting equipment that is contaminated.)
   - Uncooked eggs or foods containing them.
   - Uncooked hot dogs or other lunch meats.

9. Never give honey, which may contain *Clostridium botulinum*, to a baby younger than age one.

10. Use reasonable caution when traveling. If you are visiting a foreign country where you are not certain of the cleanliness of food preparation, stay away from salads and food sold by street vendors. Avoid water or ice unless you are certain that it came from a purified source.

foreskin A free fold of skin, also known as the **prepuce**, that covers the head of the penis. The foreskin is removed when a boy is circumcised. (See "genital care and concerns.")

frenulum A fold of skin or membrane that limits the movement of a body part by attaching it to an adjacent nonmovable structure. (An example is the attachment of the tongue to the base of the mouth.)

G **galactosemia** An inherited metabolic disorder characterized by an enzyme defect, present at birth, that prevents the body from breaking down galactose, a sugar derived from lactose (milk sugar). If not detected and treated very early in life, accumulation of galactose in the liver and kidneys can damage these organs, and accumulation in the brain can lead to mental retardation. Newborns are routinely screened for this condition; when detected, a galactose-free diet can prevent these consequences.

gallbladder A sac, resembling a deflated balloon, that collects and concentrates bile secreted by the liver. Bile is a gold brown to greenish yellow liquid that serves several functions in the digestion and absorption of food. When food is eaten, the gallbladder contracts, releasing bile into the intestine to help digest it. In a small number of children (and more often in adults), hereditary and metabolic factors may lead to the formation of gallstones, which can range in size from tiny sandlike grains to an inch or more in diameter. If gallstones are present, contraction of the gallbladder may cause abdominal pain, often located in the upper-middle or right abdomen. Pain often occurs after a large meal (but not always), especially if it contains a lot of fat. If gallstones provoke abdominal discomfort, treatment in most cases is surgical removal of the gallbladder.

gamma globulin A type of protein, present in the plasma (fluid portion) of human blood, that contains antibodies against many potentially harmful viral and bacterial organisms.

ganglion cyst A cystic swelling on the sheath of a tendon, usually on the back of the wrist.

gastritis Inflammation of the stomach lining.

gastroenteritis Inflammation of the stomach and intestinal tract, usually resulting from an acute viral or bacterial infection. Sometimes called **stomach flu** (though unrelated to influenza), gastroenteritis typically causes vomiting and diarrhea, often beginning abruptly and accompanied by abdominal cramps. Most viral gastroenteritis resolves within one or two days, but in some cases it leads to dehydration, especially among infants and young children (see also "vomiting" and "diarrhea").

generic A term designating a specific type of medication without reference to a brand name. For example, the drug ibuprofen is available in several generic preparations as well as in the brand-name forms Advil, Motrin, and Nuprin. Generic preparations are generally less expensive and theoretically contain the same medication as their brand-name counterparts. However, variations in manufacturing techniques may result in differences in both effectiveness and side effects between generic and brand-name versions of the same medication.

genital care and concerns Under normal circumstances, a newborn's genitals not only clearly identify the baby as male or female at the time of birth, but they will show very few distinct changes until puberty a number of years later. (Genital developments during puberty are described in detail in chapter 12, page 442.) The baby girl's genital area—specifically the **labia**, or lips at the opening of the vagina—may appear swollen. In addition, a little mucus or even a small amount of blood may drain from the vagina during the first few days of life. Both are caused by sudden changes in hormone levels after birth and will disappear within several days without treatment. When the labia are gently spread apart, the hymen, a thin membrane that surrounds the opening of the vagina, will be visible.

Occasionally the labia will partially or completely grow together during the first or second year of life. Sometimes ongoing irritation of the labia from diaper rash or detergents will contribute to this condition, which is called **labial adhesions**. Normally no symptoms are present, but if the labia begin to obstruct the flow of urine, the child will be at risk for urinary tract infection. If you notice that your daughter's labia appear stuck together, tell her doctor. The physician may be able to pull them apart with gentle manipulation. If this cannot be done, a small amount of estrogen cream (obtained by prescription) can be applied to the edges of the labia for several days until they can be separated. Estrogen cream can also be used if adhesions form repeatedly. Eventually a combination of physical growth and the body's own internal estrogen production will end this problem.

The **scrotum** of a newborn baby boy may appear puffy or swollen, a condition that normally resolves within a few days. Usually the **testes** (or **testicles**) will have arrived in the scrotum after their short but important journey from within the abdomen to the scrotal sac during the final weeks of pregnancy. If the boy is born at full term (forty weeks), both testes should be easily felt in the scrotum, although they might move around inside the scrotum and may be felt as high up as the crease at the top of the thigh. This is normal as long as both testes can be felt in the scrotum most of the time.

Basic care and hygiene

If your son has not been circumcised, you need only bathe his genitals in soap and water along with the rest of the diaper area. At birth, the foreskin is firmly attached to the penis and cannot be retracted (pulled back). In fact, trying to do so can damage the sensitive tissues underneath. As your son grows, the foreskin will gradually separate from the head of the penis, and eventually it can be retracted. Once this has occurred, parents can begin gently pulling the foreskin back during bathing to clean the end of the penis. As your son grows older, he can do this himself as part of his normal bathing. Do not use cotton swabs to clean beneath a foreskin that will not retract. By one year of age, 50 percent of boys have foreskins that can be pulled back, and by five years of age 90 percent of boys have retractable foreskins.

If your son has been circumcised using a device called a Gomco clamp, a thin dressing such as gauze with Vaseline will be used to cover the tip of his penis. If the dressing becomes stuck to the penis, it can be soaked off with warm water. The edge of the circumcision may look quite yellow while it is healing. This appearance is sometimes confused with an infection. If you have any questions, call your physician. Many circumcisions are done with a Plastibell, and the baby will leave the hospital with the Plastibell still on his penis. The plastic ring should gradually fall off within a few days. If it does not or if you notice that the skin around it is becoming red, call your baby's physician.

No special care is needed for the genitals of infant girls. Tub baths, along with routine diaper changes, are sufficient. Occasionally spread her thighs and labia apart to wipe gently in the creases with warm water. (See chapter 5, page 147, for further details about bathing infants.)

Even when you change your baby's diaper frequently and keep the area clean, diaper rash may still develop. The first thing you might notice is redness or small bumps on the skin covered by the diaper. Usually the skin in the creases or skin folds is not affected. The most common cause of diaper rash is prolonged contact with a wet or soiled diaper, because chemicals in the urine and stool can irritate a baby's sensitive skin. Babies are more likely to develop diaper rash when they begin sleeping through the night, when they begin eating solid foods (probably due to the increased acids that are excreted), and when they have diarrhea. Other causes of diaper rash include chemical or fragrance irritants in baby wipes, detergents used to wash diapers, or soaps used during bathing. Some babies will even react to the material used in a specific brand of disposable diapers. Sometimes rashes are the result of a yeast infection (*Candida*) or, less commonly, bacteria. Yeast infections tend to cause a more intensely red irritation, often with small extensions or satellites around the edges of the rash.

Several measures can help prevent or heal diaper rash:

- Change the diaper as soon as possible after it becomes wet or soiled. Once a rash develops, ongoing contact with urine and stool can irritate it further.
- Try to eliminate other types of irritants. Change to fragrance- and alcohol-free wipes. If you wash your own cloth diapers, use soap and hot water rather than detergent, and double rinse. If using disposable diapers, try another brand.
- Let your baby's bottom air-dry after it is cleaned; leave it open to the air for a while before putting on a new diaper.
- Ointments such as Desitin or A and D can have a soothing effect. If the rash is severe, your baby's doctor may prescribe a mild cortisone cream to use for a few days. If yeast appears to be involved, an antifungal cream, either alone or blended with cortisone, will usually calm the rash within a few days.

Infections involving the genital area occur less frequently among older children. Uncircumcised boys occasionally develop an infection under the foreskin, manifested by local pain, swelling, and discharge. This should be evaluated and treated by a physician. Irritation at the tip of the **urethra** (the small tube through which urine passes) can also be a bath-time-related problem in boys as well as girls (see next page).

Prepubertal girls sometimes develop irritation of the vagina and external genitalia (**vulva**), most commonly caused by prolonged exposure to bubble bath, soap, or shampoo in bathwater. Some simple preventive maneuvers include the following:

- Avoid bubble baths altogether.
- Keep bath times relatively short—fifteen minutes or less.
- If a child wants to play in the bath, let her do so before any soap or shampoo enters the water. As soon as her body and hair are washed, get her out.

If a prepubertal girl develops a distinct vaginal discharge, she should be seen by her physician. Occasionally during self-exploration a toddler or preschooler will insert a small object (such as a bead or a small wad of tissue) into her own vagina, or another child may insert an object into her vagina. This will cause a bacterial infection if not removed, but attempts to do so should not be made at home. Bacterial infections may also occur without a foreign object present. The doctor may collect a small amount of discharge on a sterile cotton swab to do a culture to identify the organism. Vaginal yeast infection is not typically seen before puberty. Using a nonprescription vaginal yeast remedy is not an appropriate substitute for a medical evaluation when a vaginal discharge is present in a prepubertal girl. If you are concerned about sexual abuse, it is imperative that the physician be notified because this will significantly alter what tests are carried out, the treatment plan, and the follow-up (see the Special Concerns section "Child Abuse and Neglect," page 277).

Among adolescents who have had intercourse even once, any unusual discharge from the vagina or penis must be evaluated for sexually transmitted infections (see the Special Concerns section "Sexually Transmitted Infections [STIs] among Adolescents," page 539).

Specific genital problems in boys

HYDROCELE (see page 65) As the testes move from the abdomen to the scrotum during fetal development, they take with them a covering from the abdominal contents called the **processus vag-**inalis. This covering produces a small amount of liquid that is normally undetectable. Sometimes, however, more fluid accumulates around one or both testes, forming a **hydrocele**.

A hydrocele will cause the scrotum to look larger and feel boggy to the touch, but it does not cause pain. (A flashlight beam placed directly behind the scrotum will cause the scrotum to glow red if this extra fluid is present.) A hydrocele on one or both sides of the scrotum may be present at birth, but if the genitalia are otherwise normally formed and both testes can be easily felt, no treatment is necessary. The fluid will gradually be absorbed, and in most cases, the hydrocele will disappear by one year of age.

A hydrocele can also develop later in life. Trauma, infection, tumor, and other illnesses can cause fluid to collect in the scrotum, but most often the cause is unknown. If your son has never had a hydrocele and you notice swelling in his scrotum, he should be evaluated by his physician, who may refer him to a general surgeon, pediatric surgeon, or urologist for further assessment.

VARICOCELE A **varicocele** is a dilation of the veins that drain the testes. This abnormality feels like a soft "bag of worms" above the testicle and occurs more commonly on the left side. It can cause a feeling of pressure in the scrotum, but it rarely produces pain unless it becomes quite large. A varicocele associated with a difference in size between testicles might impair fertility in the future. Surgery may be recommended in such cases, or in cases where ongoing pain is a problem.

TESTICULAR TORSION The testes usually are firmly attached to the scrotal wall, so the testes cannot twist or rotate inside the scrotum. In some boys, however, the testes do not have normal attachments and are free to twist or turn. (Unfortunately, this cannot be diagnosed during a routine checkup.) When this happens, the blood supply to the testes is constricted and may be cut off, causing intense pain.

Testicular torsion (or twisting) can occur at any age, but the vast majority of cases are seen in teenagers. It usually causes sudden, severe pain in the scrotum, most often on one side only. Some boys may also experience nausea, vomiting, or severe right-sided abdominal pain similar to that occurring with appendicitis.

Testicular torsion is a surgical emergency because the cells of the testes cannot survive without a constant supply of blood. Boys who have testicular torsion should be treated within a few hours of the onset of pain so that the normal functions of the cells within the testes (specifically, sperm and hormone production later in life) may be preserved. Even with appropriate and rapid treatment, it is possible that the testes may not function totally normally after torsion.

ORCHITIS AND EPIDIDYMITIS **Orchitis** is an inflammation of the testes, usually occurring in adolescents and young adults as a rare complication of a viral infection such as mumps or infectious mononucleosis. (Mumps was the most common cause of orchitis before widespread vaccinations drastically reduced the number of cases.) Orchitis is manifested by swelling and tenderness of the testes and is sometimes accompanied by fever. A physician should confirm the diagnosis. Treatment of orchitis is usually limited to bed rest and appropriate pain medication.

Epididymitis is an inflammation of the **epididymis**, the tube that carries sperm from the testes to the urethra, and it can occur at any age. Symptoms of epididymitis include pain and swelling in the scrotum, usually with marked tenderness just above the testicle. Viral and bacterial infections, as well as trauma, can cause epididymitis. In sexually active teens, infection with gonorrhea or chlamydia may cause the inflammation. Treatment for epididymitis will depend to some degree upon the cause, which is sometimes difficult to determine. Bed rest may be necessary, along with appropriate pain relief.

UNDESCENDED TESTES (see illustration on page 65) Testes are formed early in fetal development (beginning at six weeks gestation) and initially are located in the abdomen, close to the kidneys. During the second trimester of the baby's development, the testes gradually move lower in the abdomen. By the twenty-eighth week of gestation, they begin migrating toward the scrotum through a tube called the **inguinal canal**. The movement of either testicle from the abdomen into the scrotum can be obstructed anywhere along its normal path, and if it fails to progress into the scrotum by the time of birth, it is said to be undescended.

Among normal, healthy newborn boys, 3 to 4 percent will have one (unilateral) or two (bilateral) undescended testes. In these infants the scrotum may appear small and underdeveloped. Infants who are born prematurely, twin boys, and infants with spina bifida are more likely to have undescended testes. In most infants the undescended testicle(s) will move into the scrotum by the first birthday.

Sometimes a testicle that has descended normally will intermittently move into the upper end of the scrotum or even into the inguinal canal. This so-called retractile testicle may at times be difficult to feel—especially when the infant or child is cold, excited, or afraid. When the child is in warm water, which usually relaxes the muscles of the scrotal sac, the retractile testicle will usually drift (or can be gently maneuvered) downward into the scrotum, where it can be felt more easily.

If one or both testes cannot be felt by the first birthday, the child's physician may recommend an evaluation by a urologist or pediatric surgeon. To clarify the testes' location, an imaging study may be done or a **laparoscopy** advised. During a laparoscopy, performed under general anesthesia, a narrow scope is introduced into the abdomen through a small incision, allowing the urologist or surgeon to view the abdominal contents and locate the testes. This information can help plan future surgery, should it prove necessary.

For two reasons, evaluation and treatment are usually recommended if the testicle hasn't descended by the first birthday, or the second birthday at the latest. First, there is a slight increase in the risk of developing cancer in a testicle that remains undescended. Second, testes remaining in the warmer environment of the abdomen may become less capable of producing healthy sperm and might contribute to infertility problems later in life.

germ A term once commonly applied to any microorganism that can cause disease. This term no longer appears in medical literature.

Giardia A protozoal (one-celled animal) parasite that commonly causes intestinal infection. Symptoms include abdominal cramps, bloating, and foul-smelling diarrhea, which may extend over weeks or even months. *Giardia* infection is most commonly acquired by drinking contaminated water from streams, lakes, or, less often, city water supplies. The infection may also be spread through contaminated food. Because this parasite is present in stool, it may spread person to person among those in close contact with an infected individual, primarily when hands are not washed adequately. *Giardia* infection is usually diagnosed through evaluation of stool specimens, and it is treated with specific antibiotics.

gland An organ containing specialized cells that manufacture and release specific substances. Glands are classified into two primary types. Endocrine glands secrete biochemical compounds directly into the bloodstream; these chemical messengers affect one or more areas elsewhere in the body. The thyroid, the adrenal glands, and the gonads (testes and ovaries) are examples of endocrine glands. Exocrine glands excrete substances through a duct to a nearby location, which may be within or on the surface of the body. Examples of exocrine glands are sweat and salivary glands. The pancreas has both endocrine and exocrine functions because it secretes insulin directly into the bloodstream while manufacturing and releasing digestive enzymes via the pancreatic duct into the small intestine.

glaucoma A condition characterized by increased pressure within the eye. While adults are at greater risk for developing glaucoma, one in ten thousand infants born in the United States has glaucoma, and half of children who develop **hyphema**—blood behind the cornea resulting from blunt trauma to the eyeball—are at risk for developing glaucoma.[9] Signs and symptoms of glaucoma in young children may include unusually large eyes, excessive tearing, and/or cloudiness of the eyes. Older children may have symptoms such as headaches, eye pain, difficulty adjusting to the dark, frequent blinking, and chronically red eyes. If your child displays one or more of these symptoms, his eyes

should be checked by an ophthalmologist. Glaucoma can cause blindness if left untreated.

glomerulonephritis Inflammation of the filtering units (glomeruli) of the kidneys. Glomerulonephritis may be manifested by fluid retention, diminished urine output, and elevated blood pressure. Loss of red blood cells from the kidneys into the urine may occur, causing reddish brown or tea-colored urine. The long-term outcome of this condition will depend upon its type and severity.

glucose The simple sugar that serves as the primary fuel for biochemical reactions within the cells of the human body.

goiter Enlargement of the thyroid gland that is chronic, diffuse, and noncancerous. Various metabolic and inflammatory conditions can cause a goiter, which is visible as a swollen area on the front of the neck.

groin The area of the body where the lower abdomen and upper thigh meet.

Guillain-Barré syndrome A nonhereditary, noncontagious, potentially life-threatening syndrome that occasionally follows a viral illness. This condition primarily affects motor nerves and causes weakness and sometimes paralysis starting in the legs and moving upward to the upper body, including the arms and the respiratory muscles. In spite of its frightening and sometimes severe manifestations, Guillain-Barré syndrome resolves spontaneously and completely in most individuals within three weeks.

H ***Haemophilus influenzae*** A family of bacteria that can cause significant disease in infants and children. *Haemophilus influenzae* type A causes ear infections, and type B causes several life-threatening diseases including pneumonia, epiglottitis, and meningitis. Before the introduction of an effective vaccine for *Haemophilus influenzae* type B (Hib), this organism was the leading cause of serious bacterial infections (especially meningitis) among children younger than five. With widespread use of Hib immunization among infants beginning in the early 1980s, cases of serious disease caused by this bacteria have declined by more than 99 percent in the United States.

halitosis Bad or foul-smelling breath. Halitosis can indicate that an infection is in progress in the gums, throat, tonsils, adenoids, or sinuses. Viral colds, sinus infections, tonsillitis, dental caries (tooth decay), poor oral hygiene, and even lung infections are common causes. A child with nasal congestion who breathes through his mouth or a child with a chronic cough may have bad breath. A trip to the doctor's office might be necessary to find and treat the cause of unusually intense or persistent halitosis. (See also "body odors.")

hallucination A false perception involving any of the five senses, resulting from a disturbance in central nervous system function. In young children, transient visual hallucinations might occur during a high fever. In older children or adolescents, visual hallucinations are more commonly associated with the ingestion of a drug, whether an accidental overdose of a legitimate medication or the purposeful use of an illegal hallucinogenic drug. Recurrent auditory hallucinations are more characteristic of schizophrenia. A person (usually an adolescent) afflicted with schizophrenia might believe that he hears accusing or commanding voices, to which he may react with panic, self-protection, obedience, or even suicide.

Any hallucinatory sights, sounds, or other perceptions described by a child or adolescent should be discussed with your physician and appropriately evaluated.

hamstring The tendon located at the back of the knee and thigh; also a group of muscles in the back of the leg commonly referred to as the hamstring muscles. A strain of these muscles is called a pulled hamstring.

hand, foot, and mouth disease An annoying but self-limited illness caused by certain strains of the coxsackie virus. It affects infants, toddlers, or preschool children, most commonly occurring during summer and fall, although it may be seen throughout the year.

After an incubation period of three to six days, ulcers appear on the tongue and the mucous membranes inside the mouth. Small blisters may also develop on the palms of the hands, on the soles of the feet, and occasionally on the buttocks. Discomfort from the mouth, tongue, and throat is usually more pronounced than that coming from the hands and feet. Fever sometimes accompanies this illness.

Hand, foot, and mouth disease will clear up on its own in five to seven days. Creams, ointments, or any other topical medications will not help the healing process. Antibiotics are unnecessary and should not be used unless a secondary infection is present. Analgesic medications such as acetaminophen or ibuprofen may be used for pain. It is important to keep your child hydrated and nourished. Avoid spicy foods and acidic fluids that may irritate the mouth.

Because this infection can be transmitted from one person to another through oral secretions, your child should stay home from day care or school until the illness has run its course.

headache One of the most common problems seen by physicians who care for children. Very often headaches arise from infections such as colds or flu-like viral illnesses; occasionally they follow an accidental blow to the head. Unless the illness or injury is severe, these acute headaches will resolve within a few days, if not more quickly. By age fifteen as many as 50 to 75 percent of children (in all socioeconomic and ethnic groups) experience headaches, often recurrent, that do not have an obvious immediate cause. Fortunately, only a very small percentage of these are a symptom of a serious disorder.

Most childhood headaches can be managed with relatively simple measures at home, but your child's physician should be consulted if they recur or if any headache is severe or prolonged for more than twenty-four hours.

Whenever a child is seen by a doctor for headache, an accurate assessment of the history and pattern of pain is extremely important. If your child complains about headaches, try to get a feel for the following characteristics (perhaps write them down for future reference if you need to seek medical help):

H

- How long has the headache been a problem?
- How often does it occur? Once a week or once a month? Daily?
- How long does it last? A few minutes? Several hours? A few days?
- Is there a pattern during the day? Is the headache in the morning, afternoon, evening, or all day long?
- Where does the head hurt? One side or both? Front or back?
- Does the head throb or pound, or is the pain more constant?
- Does the neck move easily, or is it tight or stiff?
- Is the pain increased by light, sound, body movement, or exertion?
- Are there other symptoms, such as nausea, vomiting, abdominal cramps, or irritability? Is the child's skin cold and clammy?
- Does anything happen before the headache, such as visual changes (sparkling, flickering, blurring, or loss of vision), weakness of some part of the body, or dizziness?
- Does anything seem to provoke the headache?
- Does anything in particular help the headache go away?

It may not be easy to gather this information, especially if your child is very young and can't express what he is feeling. When headaches occur regularly, keeping notes can be very helpful as you, your child, and your child's doctor work to find the problem. Occasionally specific tests will be needed to rule out unusual causes of headaches.

Headaches caused by acute illness

Headaches associated with an acute infection will normally be accompanied by other symptoms such as fever, body aches, runny nose, sore throat, or cough. Very often the pain will wax and wane as fever rises and falls. Sinus infections sometimes produce pain localized above or behind one or both eyes, in the area of the cheekbone, or above the upper teeth. Typically this is accompanied by nasal drainage or postnasal drip that may continue for several days if not treated.

Headaches related to an acute illness can be treated with acetaminophen (Tylenol and other brands) or ibuprofen (Children's Motrin and other brands) in doses appropriate for your child's weight. (See acetaminophen and ibuprofen dosage charts on pages 609 and 688.) *Aspirin should not be used because of its association with Reye's syndrome (a rare but serious disorder of the brain and liver) when taken during viral infections.* Other measures to relieve symptoms may also be appropriate, depending upon the illness (see "colds," "sore throat," and the Special Concerns section "When Your Child Has a Fever," page 241).

If your child has a headache during an acute illness, you should contact your physician in the following situations:

- the headache is severe or unresponsive to treatment;
- your child complains of pain, stiffness, or difficulty moving the neck;
- pain is localized (on one side or in one area of the head);
- the headache continues for more than twenty-four hours;
- your child is confused, listless, or difficult to arouse.

Headaches caused by injury

Headache frequently follows an accident in which the head is struck, whether after a fall at home or on the playground, a spill from a bicycle, a collision during an athletic activity, or a more serious accident. If there are no obvious cuts, bumps, or bruises that need attention, you can observe your child afterward for any changes in alertness and arousability. He may feel sleepy or even nauseated during the first few hours, and headache might occur as well. Since you need to keep track of your child's headache status after a blow to the head, don't give any pain relievers stronger than acetaminophen or ibuprofen unless specifically directed to do so by your child's physician. (Aspirin should not be used at all because it can increase the risk of bleeding.) You should contact your child's doctor after a head injury in the following situations:

- your child lost consciousness or shows signs of disorientation, confusion, loss of memory, or other behavioral change immediately after the accident;

- crying continues without letting up for more than fifteen minutes after the injury;
- the headache is progressively worsening;
- vomiting occurs more than one or two times;
- your child becomes increasingly difficult to arouse;
- your child displays any behavior that concerns you.

Recurrent headaches

Recurrent headaches will normally require a physician's evaluation to identify their cause or causes—some individuals have more than one type of headache—and a careful history can identify distinguishing characteristics.

Tension-type headache (also called **muscle-contraction headache** or **stress headache**) is a common form of recurrent headache in children. One of these can last from thirty minutes to several days or even weeks. Unlike migraine headaches (see below), no nausea, vomiting, or light sensitivity is present. This headache usually creates a viselike pressure located all over the head, is constant (not pulsating with the heartbeat), and is not worsened by exertion. A tension headache usually does not interfere with sleep or awaken the child during the night.

Assuming that your child has been diagnosed as having tension headaches, you should attempt to identify any underlying stress or other psychosocial issues. This may or may not be a straightforward assignment. Children might not always express their feelings or may be reluctant to reveal the problems or cares they are facing. Open-ended discussion ("Tell me about how school is going") may provide some clues, although occasionally a more specific query ("Is there any particular person who is giving you a hard time right now?") will elicit more information.

It will take time and patience, but both parent and physician may need to explore concerns about school, friends (or enemies), or relationships within the family. Certainly major upheavals such as the death of a loved one, a move, or a family problem (especially the parents' separation or divorce) could play a role. It is common for children with tension headaches to also display symptoms of depression.

Sometimes the causes of a tension headache are more straightforward. Skipping a meal or eating erratically in general, getting too little sleep, getting overheated, or simply being worn out at the end of a long day can bring on headaches, sometimes daily. Some children routinely come home from school with a headache and simply need some quiet time to bring it under control. A simple combination of a light snack followed by a fifteen- or twenty-minute rest, perhaps with a cool washcloth across the forehead and calming music, may work wonders. An over-the-counter pain reliever (acetaminophen or ibuprofen) sometimes helps, but these medications should be used sparingly. Multiple doses on a daily basis can actually perpetuate headaches. Efforts to control the pace of life, combined with exercise and more stable eating and sleeping patterns, can also be effective.

Migraine headaches affect up to 3 percent of children between the ages of three and seven, and about 5 to 10 percent of children between the ages of seven and eleven. As many as 20 percent of adolescents may experience migraine headaches.[10] In children, this type of headache is evenly distributed between genders, but after age fifteen it is three times more common in females. As many as 90 percent of patients with migraine headaches have a strong family history of this condition.

The pain of migraine headaches is usually more intense than tension-type headaches and may last between two and seventy-two hours. Many people mistakenly believe that the term *migraine* designates any intense headache. The word actually is a French variation of the term *hemicrania*, which literally means "half of the head." Migraines commonly but not always occur on one side of the head. What characterizes migraines is not merely their intensity, but any of the following specific and unique features:

- The headache is often located on one side of the head.
- Pain typically pulsates with the heartbeat.
- Headaches are worsened by physical activity.
- Nausea and/or vomiting are common; even abdominal pain may occur.
- There is sensitivity to light and/or loud noise.

- The headache may be preceded by an **aura**—a specific disturbance in the nervous system that lasts several minutes or longer and nearly always disappears as the headache arrives. The most common auras are visual: sparkling or shimmering light patterns, blurred vision, or even loss of part of the visual field. More unusual auras involve transient loss of sensation or weakness over part of the body, difficulty speaking, confusion, or dizziness. (Some children feel fatigued or irritable for hours or even days prior to a migraine, but this is not the same as an aura.)
- The headache is nearly always relieved by sleep. In many children with migraine headaches, there is marked improvement after vomiting.
- Between migraine episodes—even those that are severe—the child feels perfectly well.

The mechanism of migraines has traditionally been assumed to involve changes in blood vessels within the head, with constriction bringing about the aura, if one is present, followed by a reflex dilation or widening that produces the pounding headache. More recent research suggests that migraines may also involve a disorder of chemical messengers within the brain known as neurotransmitters.

Even if your child has most or all of the typical symptoms of a migraine headache, the diagnosis should be established by a physician. This will involve a physical examination plus a discussion of the child's medical and family history. Usually other studies will not be needed unless the headache pattern is very unusual. It is important for both you and your child to understand that these headaches, even when very uncomfortable, are not dangerous. The mechanism that causes them does not damage the brain, and in two out of three children who experience migraines, the headaches subside or disappear altogether later in life. (Migraines that begin late in the teen years, however, are more likely to continue into adulthood.)

Like tension headaches, migraines can be triggered by a variety of events, including stress, erratic eating or sleeping patterns, exertion, the menstrual cycle, or a bump on the head. Specific foods (for example, nuts, chocolate, cola drinks, hot dogs, spicy meats, and foods containing monosodium glutamate) set off migraines in some children. Keeping track of the events leading up to these headaches may help you and your child identify and perhaps avoid such situations.

Migraine headaches in children are often surprisingly responsive to over-the-counter pain relievers such as acetaminophen or ibuprofen, especially if given early in the episode. Your child's doctor will review these options with you and consider other medications if necessary. Very often a process of becoming calm and relaxed (in some cases achieved simply by resting in a dark, quiet room) will reduce migraine pain, especially if the child can fall asleep for a while.

Other possible but less common causes of recurrent headaches
- Withdrawal from continued use of caffeinated foods and beverages.
- Sinus infections, which can produce acute headaches as already described, can continue for weeks and cause persistent headaches. (Note that most so-called "sinus headaches" are in fact migraine headaches in which pain is experienced in the face.)
- Problems with vision that might cause squinting or straining are worth investigating, especially if headaches develop while the child is reading or doing schoolwork. A complete eye evaluation is worthwhile, whether or not it uncovers a cause for headaches.
- Dental problems or inflammation of the jaw (**temporomandibular**) joint, or **TMJ**, are rare causes of headaches, which tend to be localized to the ear, face, jaw, or temple. TMJ pain can be aggravated by grinding the teeth during the day or night. It may begin after trauma to the face, or it can occur without any clear cause.
- Brain tumor—the diagnosis parents fear most when a child has recurrent headaches—is actually extremely uncommon. Headaches associated with a tumor tend to be persistent, relentless, and progressively more intense over several days or weeks. They may awaken a child from sleep or cause recurrent vomiting.
- Carbon monoxide exposure, usually from a leak in a gas furnace, can produce ongoing headaches. A clue to this possibility is the presence of headaches in other family members at the same time, especially if accompanied by nausea

and vomiting. *If everyone in a home simultaneously develops severe headache and nausea, evacuate the house, call the gas company or fire department, and seek medical attention immediately.*

Special note: Final cautions on headaches

Call your child's doctor in these situations:

- your child develops a sudden headache that she complains is the worst she's ever had;
- a headache is unresponsive to your doctor's recommended treatment;
- the headache is accompanied by abnormal weakness, difficulty with coordination, or unusual body or eye movements;
- headaches develop in the middle of the night or upon awakening;
- your child's level of alertness or consciousness changes with the headache.

heartburn A burning sensation in the chest arising from irritation of the esophagus (the hollow structure that transports food from the throat to the stomach). Heartburn is an uncommon complaint in children. In adolescents (and adults) it is often caused by **reflux** (backflow) of acid from the stomach into the esophagus and may be aggravated by large meals, spicy foods, alcohol, chocolate, tobacco use, stress, or lying down less than an hour after eating.

A particularly intense burning sensation in the chest may occur if a medication (especially erythromycin or tetracycline, which may be used by an adolescent to treat acne) is swallowed immediately before lying down at bedtime without taking enough fluid to carry it into the stomach. If a tablet or capsule remains in contact with the lining of the esophagus for a prolonged period of time, severe pain may develop during the night or in the morning. This discomfort will resolve within a day or two, although a doctor's evaluation may be necessary to confirm the diagnosis.

heat exhaustion/heatstroke See "Emergency Care," page 831.

hemangioma A reddish purple birthmark caused by an abnormal distribution of newly formed blood vessels in the skin. The shape and size may vary. Treatment is rarely needed because most cases spontaneously disappear by two or three years of age.

hematoma (see "Emergency Care," page 834) A localized collection of blood that has escaped from one or more damaged blood vessels. (The term literally means "blood mass.") A hematoma can form in soft tissue (such as below the skin or in a muscle) or within a specific area of the body (such as inside the skull). A hematoma near the surface of the body will feel like a smooth nodule. In contrast, blood that forms the discoloration of a black-and-blue bruise is usually spread diffusely through soft tissue and not necessarily collected into a hematoma.

hematuria Blood in the urine. See "urinary tract care and concerns," page 733.

hemiplegia Paralysis of one side of the body.

hemoglobin The protein within red blood cells that binds to oxygen, thus allowing red cells to deliver oxygen to every cell in the body.

hemolysis The destruction or breakdown of red blood cells.

hemolytic uremic syndrome A rare disorder characterized by damage to small blood vessels, especially within the kidneys, resulting in three significant problems:

- Acute kidney failure
- Anemia caused by destruction of red blood cells within the damaged blood vessels
- Low levels of platelets, the microscopic, disclike bodies (smaller than red cells) in the blood that are important in the normal clotting process

The cause of this disorder is uncertain, but a combination of factors, including genetics, a disturbance in immune function, and a precipitating infection (especially an intestinal illness caused by a certain strain of *E. coli* bacteria) is probably involved. Children under age two are most commonly affected. Initial symptoms typically include vomiting, diarrhea (which eventually becomes bloody), and abdominal pain, followed by decreased urine output. Significant fluid imbalances caused by kidney failure and intestinal fluid losses require intensive medical care, but more than 85 percent of children survive the acute phase and regain normal kidney function.[11]

hemophilia An inherited bleeding disorder, seen predominantly in males, caused by an inability to produce certain clotting factors. Manifestations of hemophilia vary greatly, depending upon the severity of the clotting defect. Infants and children with severe hemophilia are prone to frequent, spontaneous bleeding into skin, muscles, joints, and internal organs. Recurrent bleeding into joints, especially knees and elbows, can lead to a potentially crippling arthritis. In milder cases, excessive bleeding may occur only after injury or surgery.

hemorrhage Bleeding.

hemorrhoid A dilated vein in the anal or rectal area. Hemorrhoids vary in size and may cause itching, local pain from inflammation, or bleeding.

hemostasis Control of bleeding.

hepatitis Inflammation of the liver, nearly always caused by a viral infection. (Inflammation of the liver caused by drugs or toxic substances may also be called hepatitis, but most commonly the term indicates an infectious origin.) Depending upon the type of virus involved and the individual's response to it, the inflammation may go undetected or, at the other extreme, produce profound illness. A child or adolescent with clinically significant hepatitis will typically experience fever, flu-like symptoms, fatigue, jaundice (yellow orange skin and yellow color in the white area of the eyes), light or gray stools, and dark urine.

Many forms of viral hepatitis have been identified, and undoubtedly more will be discovered. Of these, A and B are by far the most common.

Hepatitis A (previously called **infectious hepatitis**) is transmitted through contaminated food or water and is often acquired during foreign travel. The time from exposure to onset of symptoms is usually fifteen to forty days. The illness usually begins with five to ten days of nonspecific flu-like symptoms, which may be followed by jaundice. Typically symptoms are mild (or even nonexistent) among children under six, while older children and adolescents are more likely to develop overt symptoms, including jaundice. Children without symptoms who can transmit the virus are a potentially significant source of hepatitis A infection in a community; not only do they shed virus (in stool) longer than adults, but they may be careless about hygienic habits as well. In the vast majority of cases, this infection resolves without complications in about one or two months, with rest as the primary treatment. Severe illness (or death) resulting from hepatitis A is extremely uncommon.

People who have ongoing close contact with the infected person may benefit from an injection of immune (gamma) globulin given within one or two weeks after exposure. This provides temporary protection that may prevent or minimize the impact of infection. Equally if not more important is good hygiene, including frequent hand washing, especially after any contact with stool from an infected individual. Children and infants may shed the virus in stool for several weeks after the illness has begun.

People who are planning to travel to high-risk areas (especially in developing countries) should consider obtaining specific hepatitis A vaccine, which is safe and nearly always effective, at least four weeks prior to departure. In addition, the American Academy of Pediatrics now recommends routine hepatitis A vaccination for all toddlers, with the first dose given between the ages of one and two. Older children are also candidates for the vaccine if they live in areas with increased rates of hepatitis A infection.[12]

Hepatitis B (formerly called **serum hepatitis**) is transmitted in ways similar to those that spread HIV/AIDS:

- From an infected mother to her baby before or at the time of birth.
- Through shared needles during intravenous drug use or through improperly cleaned tattoo needles that have been in contact with an infected person.

- Through contaminated blood products during transfusion. (Careful screening of donors and blood products has virtually eliminated this type of transmission.)
- Through an accidental needle stick of a health-care worker who is drawing or processing blood from an infected person.
- Through sexual contact with an infected individual.
- In as many as one in three cases, the source of the infection is unknown.

The incubation period for hepatitis B is longer—50 to 150 days—than for hepatitis A. Among adults and children over five, about 70 percent of infected individuals develop nonspecific flu-like symptoms such as fever, nausea, vomiting, and fatigue. In some cases, jaundice (a yellow discoloration of the skin and eyes) may be the first sign that the infection is present. Rarely, severe or life-threatening illness occurs at the outset. For the vast majority of these individuals, the infection resolves in about two weeks without any specific treatment or long-term problems. However, between 2 and 6 percent of infected persons develop a chronic form of the infection that later poses a risk for scarring (**cirrhosis**) or even cancer of the liver. In addition, those with chronic hepatitis B can transmit the virus through sexual contact or to a baby during pregnancy or delivery. They must never donate blood because even a tiny amount of it can infect another person.

While adults infected with hepatitis B are likely to experience an acute illness and then recover, infants and children tend to have a different course. Acute symptoms are less common among the young, but they are much more likely to develop a chronic infection. Among infants and children infected with hepatitis B, 30 percent of those one to five years of age and 90 percent of infants (including those who are infected at birth) develop the chronic form of the infection and are at risk for long-term complications.

Newborn hepatitis B infection can be prevented if an injection of hepatitis B immune globulin (HBIG) is given within twelve hours after birth. To anticipate births at which this treatment might be necessary, pregnant women are now screened for hepatitis B virus as part of routine prenatal care. Furthermore, a vaccine that is both safe and highly effective in preventing this infection has been available in the United States since 1986.[13] Because of the significant number of new cases of hepatitis B that continue to occur each year and its potential for causing serious long-term consequences, universal immunization of all children against this virus has been recommended since 1991, and in many states it is required for school entry. The vaccine may be given at any age, starting at birth, and involves three injections—the second given one month after the first, and the third injection at least four months after the second.

In the past, **hepatitis C** was usually acquired from transfusions, but since blood products are now routinely screened for evidence of hepatitis C infection, the risk for acquiring the virus from a transfusion is now extremely low—less than one in a million. The majority of cases now arise from the use of illegal intravenous drugs. Hepatitis C can also be transmitted during sex, by sharing razors or other personal items with an infected individual, from equipment used during body piercing or tattooing that has been contaminated with the blood of an infected person, from workplace contact with infected blood (as could occur in a health-care worker), and by transmission from infected mother to her newborn infant.

In a minority of cases, hepatitis C causes acute symptoms such as fever, fatigue, and jaundice. It is more likely to cause no immediate illness but to smolder for years as a chronic infection. At least 80 percent of infected adults develop chronic infection, 20 to 30 percent develop cirrhosis of the liver, and between one and 5 percent develop liver cancer. Less is known about the long-term outcome in children. Very often the first indication of a prior hepatitis C infection is an abnormal blood test found during a routine physical later in life or, more often, noted among the screening tests done when an adolescent or young adult donates blood. Whenever such abnormalities are found, the donated blood is never given to a patient, and the potential donor is notified of his or her results so that further evaluation can be carried out.

hernia (see page 65) The protrusion of an organ or tissue through an opening in an adjacent body structure. This term is applied most commonly to defects in the abdominal wall, especially in the groin (**inguinal hernia**; see illustration on page 65) or at the navel (**umbilical hernia**). A small segment of intestine may push into one of these defects, forming a visible bulge that may be more obvious during crying or coughing, but may disappear when the child lies down. Inguinal hernias are normally repaired surgically to prevent the defect and its associated bulge from gradually enlarging. If a segment of intestine becomes trapped (incarcerated) in the hernia, local pain and tenderness will develop, and immediate evaluation by a physician is necessary. Umbilical hernias normally resolve on their own without surgery (see "umbilical hernia").

hiccup Involuntary spasm of the diaphragm.

hirsutism Excessive growth of body or facial hair, especially in women.

HIV infection/AIDS The immune system is a wondrously complex and efficient mechanism that continuously defends us from a formidable number of microscopic enemies. Most of its functions are carried out silently as would-be invaders are identified and destroyed before they multiply enough to cause any symptoms. Even when defenses are temporarily overcome, in the vast majority of cases the immune system mobilizes enough reinforcements to contain and eventually overcome the infection. Many infections provoke a complex biochemical "memory" called immunity, which helps prevent future invasions by the same organism.

One vital component of the immune system is the population of white cells called **lymphocytes** that play an important role in defending against viruses, fungi, parasites, and certain bacteria. A subgroup called **helper T cells** is necessary for the normal function of all lymphocytes. It is these cells that are gradually destroyed by the **human immunodeficiency virus**, or **HIV**, which results in a gradual deterioration of immune function. Eventually the affected individual develops unusual infections or severe cases of common infections, at which point he is said to have **AIDS**, or **acquired immune deficiency syndrome.**

HIV gains access to an uninfected person primarily through events in which blood or certain body fluids pass from one individual to another, including:

- *From an infected mother to her baby*, through contact with the mother's blood either before or at the time of birth. The majority of children with HIV/AIDS have acquired the disease this way. A pregnant woman infected with HIV has a 25 to 35 percent risk of transmitting the virus to her baby if no preventive treatment is given. However, medical treatment can decrease the likelihood of transmitting the virus to her baby to less than 2 percent; therefore, *it is now widely recommended that every expectant mother be tested for HIV as part of routine prenatal care.*
- *From the breast milk of an HIV-infected mother to her baby.* Infants born to mothers with HIV should be fed formula because breastfeeding carries a 10 to 14 percent risk of transmitting the virus to the baby.
- *Through sexual contact with an infected individual.*
- *Through shared needles during intravenous drug use*, or, much less commonly, through improperly cleaned tattoo needles that have been in contact with an infected person.
- *Through contaminated blood products during a transfusion.* Careful screening of donors and blood products has virtually eliminated this type of transmission.
- *Through an accidental needle stick of a health-care worker who is drawing or processing blood from an infected person.* This is also an extremely rare cause of HIV/AIDS transmission.

It is important to note that HIV is not transmitted through everyday interactions—holding hands, hugging, sharing a meal, or other routine activities. It does not pass through the air. Tears, saliva, urine, and stool from an infected individual have not been proven to transmit HIV unless they are contaminated with blood. If blood—or body fluids that might contain it—from an HIV-infected individual must be handled or cleaned up, latex gloves should be worn to prevent direct contact with skin. The virus can be neutralized by a disinfectant such as a 10-percent bleach solution.

Initial contact with HIV may produce a mild flu-like illness or no symptoms at all. For many months or years thereafter, there may be no unusual symptoms or signs of disease, but during this time the virus gradually destroys the T-cell population. The virus can be transmitted to others even while the affected person feels perfectly well. Eventually full-blown AIDS develops, during which a variety of infections become recurrent and disabling problems. These can include unusual pneumonias, chronic diarrhea, abscesses, bone and joint infections, unusually severe episodes of candidiasis or chickenpox, and central nervous system infections. The lymph nodes, spleen, and liver commonly become enlarged. An unusual form of cancer known as **Kaposi's sarcoma** may develop. HIV also causes damage within the central nervous system. In infants and children, this can result in delays in physical, intellectual, and behavioral development or in the loss of abilities that had previously been present. Inevitably death results from a combination of one or more infections or other complications.

Among infants who are infected with HIV at birth, about one in five will develop AIDS-related illness by one year of age, and most of these will die from overwhelming infection by the age of four. The rest have a slower rate of disease progression and may not develop AIDS until later in childhood or even adolescence. HIV that is acquired later in life (most often through sexual contact or intravenous drug use) tends to progress more slowly toward AIDS, and a number of years may pass before any evidence of the disease is apparent.

HIV infection is diagnosed through a blood test that detects the presence of specific antibodies against the virus. If they are present, the individual is said to be HIV positive. Additional medical evaluation and ongoing follow-up are very important, even if no symptoms are present, in order to monitor the infected individual's immune status and general medical condition.

Management of HIV/AIDS is focused on four basic areas:

- *Slowing the virus's proliferation and its damage to the immune system.* While there is presently no cure for HIV infection, research continues to discover new treatment options that can help contain or slow the disease's progress. Because these medication regimes are constantly revised based on new research findings, they will not be described here. However, the physician(s) involved in the child's or adolescent's care will review the current options, including benefits, risks, and costs. Treatment protocols may require careful attention to proper dosing and timing of multiple medications to obtain the best results.

- *Reducing risk of infection.* Children with HIV will normally receive routine immunizations, including DTaP (diphtheria/tetanus/pertussis), MMR (measles/mumps/rubella), IPV (inactivated polio), *Haemophilus influenzae* type B and influenza vaccines. Prudent efforts should be made to minimize the child's exposure to people who have common infections such as colds, stomach flu, or cold sores (herpes simplex virus infections), or more unusual diseases such as tuberculosis while at the same time not isolating him. Ongoing use of antibiotics that prevent certain infections may be recommended for those with significantly reduced levels of helper T cells.

- *Treating infections that arise as a result of impaired immunity.* This can become a major challenge as AIDS progresses and more serious and complicated infections develop. Expert input from specialists, especially in infectious disease, will most likely be necessary.

- *General support.* Adequate nutrition, regular exercise, and attentive dental care for the infected individual, as well as continued emotional, social, and spiritual support for both patient and family, are all very important in the process of living with HIV. In many cases, one or both parents of an HIV-infected child have HIV and/or AIDS, complicating the process of providing care. Meeting the needs of both patient and family will usually require tapping into the resources of the extended family, local church, and community at large. It is very important that HIV-positive children, adolescents, and adults not be cut off from these sources of support, especially out of misguided fear of contracting this infection from casual contact. As deemed appropriate by their physicians, HIV-infected children should be allowed to attend school and activities with other children. Like those with diabetes, asthma, cancer, and other chronic conditions, their life experiences should not be entirely defined by their medical condition.

Special note: Who should be told about a child's HIV infection?

Despite more widespread public knowledge about HIV, for many reasons it is not easy to tell other people that one's child has this infection. Fear of negative reactions and uneasiness about disclosing the manner in which the virus was acquired (especially if one or both parents are also infected) can make discussing this disease an emotionally charged issue for many people. For this reason, revealing the diagnosis to just anyone may not be in the child's (or parent's) best interest. A child's doctor and other health-care providers who deal with HIV infection on a regular basis can provide valuable input on this subject. In general, the individuals who should be aware of the diagnosis are those who will be providing some form of care for the child, including:

- Physicians, dentists, nurses, and other health-care workers who will be involved in medical treatment, whether on a short- or long-term basis
- Caregivers, whether at home or in a day-care environment
- Teachers
- Relatives who are involved with the child on a regular basis

Relatives and friends who are not directly involved in the child's care may be made aware of the diagnosis if they are known to be trustworthy and supportive. Last but not least, the child himself should be informed about his condition in a manner compatible with his age and maturity. For younger children, basic facts can be explained on a need-to-know basis. An older child or adolescent will need more detailed information about his condition, its treatment, and his future prospects. In many ways, this subject should be approached the same as any other difficult topic: with respect for the child's need for truth, tempered by compassion and love, while avoiding secrets and misinformation.

hives (urticaria) A generalized allergic response characterized by multiple raised, reddened, irregular patches of skin (often called welts). The patches are itchy, vary greatly in size, and continually change in size and location (see also "allergies in children").

hoarseness A rough or raspy quality of the voice brought about by conditions that alter the normal anatomy or function of the vocal cords. The following are the most common causes in children:

- **Laryngitis**, or inflammation of the vocal cords. Usually laryngitis is a component of a viral upper-respiratory infection and is accompanied by coughing and runny nose.
- In **croup**, hoarseness is accompanied by a barking cough and in more severe cases by labored breathing (see "croup"). Sometimes the child's voice will be reduced to a whisper. With rare exception, as the infection resolves, the voice will gradually return to normal over one to two weeks.
- Overuse of the vocal cords, from continual loud talking and yelling. Among teenagers, this sometimes occurs following overzealous cheering at sporting events or concerts. Persistent abuse of the vocal cords could lead to thickening or the development of nodules on them, which could perpetuate hoarseness. Speech therapy may be necessary to help a child or adolescent change vocal patterns that are causing this problem.

Less common causes of hoarseness in children include the following:

- The presence of one or more **papillomas**, warty growths on the vocal cords caused by the **human papillomavirus (HPV)**. This virus can be acquired during birth if a child's mother has a genital HPV infection, although hoarseness is typically not noted until two to four years of age.
- **Vocal cord paralysis**, which usually results from injury to nerves in the neck that control movement of the vocal cords. This can occur at birth or from trauma or surgery.

H

Acute hoarseness, whether brought on by infection or by overuse of the vocal cords, will normally resolve on its own if the voice is allowed to rest for a few days by limiting the amount of speaking. (Whispering does not actually rest the vocal cords.) Any acute hoarseness associated with difficulty in breathing, especially when bursts of harsh coughing leave a child gasping for air, should be evaluated by a physician. If a child is clearly in distress, she should be taken to an emergency center *immediately*.

If hoarseness continues for more than a few weeks, the child's doctor should be contacted. In some cases, an ear, nose, and throat (ENT) specialist will be asked to evaluate the problem, especially if there is concern about a possible abnormality of the vocal cords.

homeopathy System of alternative medicine based on the theory that certain diseases can be treated or cured by giving extremely small doses of substances (chemicals, minerals, or even poisons) that in larger quantities would produce the symptoms of the disease being treated. Homeopathy's theory of disease causation and treatment is not recognized as valid in the mainstream scientific community, and the effectiveness of homeopathic treatments remains controversial.

hordeolum (also called a **sty**) A bacterial infection of sebaceous glands in the eyelid (see also "eye care and concerns").

humerus The bone of the upper arm that extends from the shoulder to the elbow.

hydrocele A painless swelling of the scrotum caused by accumulation of fluid in the space surrounding one or both testes (see also "genital care and concerns").

hydrocephalus An abnormal increase in the amount of fluid (specifically called **cerebrospinal fluid**, or **CSF**) that normally circulates within the central nervous system and cushions the brain within the skull. During infancy, hydrocephalus is associated with unusual enlargement of the head. It is often associated with congenital abnormalities.

hymen A thin membrane that surrounds the opening of the vagina.

hyperglycemia High blood sugar.

hyperventilation A pattern of deep breathing (whether rapid or slow) that results in exhaling an excessive amount of carbon dioxide. This in turn can cause changes in the body's internal acid-base balance, which in turn leads to light-headedness, weakness, numbness, and tingling of the fingers and mouth, all of which may provoke even more anxiety and heavy breathing. Usually hyperventilation arises from emotional stress. The person with this problem (usually an older child or adolescent) experiences a compelling hunger for air, often described as a feeling that the air isn't going all the way into his lungs. Hyperventilation is sometimes accompanied by tightness in the chest, a racing heart, anxiety, or panic.

Any child or adolescent who complains of shortness of breath or appears to be breathing more rapidly or deeply than usual should be evaluated by a physician to rule out a medical disorder. If hyperventilation is diagnosed, the child will be instructed to breathe more slowly. This will normalize his acid-base balance and improve his sense of well-being within a few minutes. While cupping a paper bag over the mouth and "rebreathing" exhaled air has been a time-honored approach to this problem, it is no longer recommended. (If the problem is in fact an inadequate level of oxygen, rebreathing exhaled air will worsen the situation.) If hyperventilation episodes are recurrent and disruptive, counseling or even medication may be necessary to control the underlying causes.

hypoglycemia Low blood sugar.

hyposensitization See "immunotherapy."

hypospadias Abnormal position of the opening of the urethra on the underside of the penis.

hypoxia Condition in which an inadequate supply of oxygen is delivered to the tissues.

ibuprofen (generics and brand names such as Motrin and Advil) An anti-inflammatory medication, available without prescription, that may be helpful in reducing fever and relieving minor pain. It may be given to infants as young as six months of age, with dosing based on weight (see chart). Higher doses may be utilized for reducing fever greater than 102.5°F (39.2°C). Ibuprofen is available in a variety of dosage forms and may be given every six to eight hours as needed. It should not be given to children with kidney disease, asthma, nasal polyps, or dehydration unless specific direction to do so has been given by a physician who is aware that one or more of these conditions are present. Rarely, ibuprofen can cause a serious allergic reaction, especially in children who are known to be allergic to aspirin. It can also provoke bleeding from the stomach, especially in a child who has had stomach ulcers or bleeding problems in the past. The Food and Drug Administration recommends that ibuprofen not be given to an infant or child for a period longer than ten days unless specifically instructed to do so by a physician.

Ibuprofen is available in a variety of forms for infants and children, including concentrated infant drops, liquid suspension, chewable tablets, and caplets. Be sure to follow the directions provided with the preparation you are using. The dosage chart on this page provides recommendations for various ibuprofen formulations.

idiopathic Arising from an unknown cause.

IM Abbreviation for **intramuscular**, literally meaning "within muscle." This word and its abbreviation are normally applied to injections given directly into muscle.

immunity Resistance to a potential disease-causing organism. Immunity may be inherited, acquired from contact with the organism, induced through immunization, or passed temporarily to a newborn from the mother.

immunotherapy (hyposensitization) A form of treatment for allergies and commonly known as allergy shots. It is a series of immunizations designed to reduce or eliminate an individual's allergic response to a particular substance (called an allergen). Small

IBUPROFEN Medicine for fever or pain relief		
WEIGHT	**TYPE**	**DOSE** (dosage form)
12–17 lbs 5.5–7.5 kg	drops (50 mg/1.25 ml)	1 dropper (0.8 ml)
18–23 lbs 8–10.5 kg	drops (50 mg/1.25 ml) liquid (100 mg/5 ml) chewable tablets (50 mg)	1½ dropper (1.2 ml) ¾ tsp (3.75 ml) 1½ tablets
24–35 lbs 11–16 kg	drops (50 mg/1.25 ml) liquid (100 mg/5 ml) chewable tablets (50 mg) chewable tablets (100 mg)	2 droppers (1.6 ml) 1 tsp (5 ml) 2 tablets 1 tablet
36–47 lbs 16.5–21.5 kg	drops (50 mg/1.25 ml) liquid (100 mg/5 ml) chewable tablets (50 mg) chewable tablets (100 mg)	3 droppers (2.4 ml) 1½ tsp (7.5 ml) 3 tablets 1½ tablets
48–59 lbs 22–27 kg	liquid (100 mg/5 ml) chewable tablets (50 mg) chewable tablets (100 mg)	2 tsp (10 ml) 4 tablets 2 tablets
60–71 lbs 27.5–32 kg	liquid (100 mg/5 ml) chewable tablets (50 mg) chewable tablets (100 mg)	2½ tsp (12.5 ml) 5 tablets 2½ tablets
72–95 lbs 32.5–43 kg	liquid (100 mg/5 ml) chewable tablets (50 mg) chewable tablets (100 mg) adult tablets (200 mg)	3 tsp (15 ml) 6 tablets 3 tablets 1½ tablets
96+ lbs 43.5+ kg	liquid (100 mg/5 ml) chewable tablets (50 mg) chewable tablets (100 mg) adult tablets (200 mg)	4 tsp (20 ml) 8 tablets 4 tablets 2 tablets

Abbreviations: mg=milligrams ml=milliliter tsp=teaspoon
1 dropper = 0.8 ml   1 tsp = 5 ml

Note: Since ibuprofen pediatric products (such as Children's Advil and Motrin) are available without a prescription, parents are warned on the package label to consult a physician for use by children under 2 years or for use longer than 10 days and to consult a physician or poison control center immediately in case of accidental overdosage.

Give the correct dosage for your child's weight every 6 to 8 hours. Do not exceed 4 doses in 24 hours.

amounts of selected allergens are injected into a person at regular intervals and in gradually increasing doses. The injections are usually given weekly for at least one to two years. If they are effective, the interval between them is gradually increased. Immunotherapy can be especially helpful in treating allergic nasal congestion caused by allergens such as airborne pollens, which cannot be easily avoided. (See also "allergies in children.")

impetigo A bacterial skin infection, usually caused by common strains of *Streptococcus* or *Staphylococcus*, in which an irregular, honey-colored, crusted eruption spreads over the face and/or upper body. The affected child usually has no pain, itching, or other signs of acute illness (such as fever). In a less common type of impetigo caused by certain strains of *Staphylococcus*, the eruption appears as large blisters containing a discolored, puslike material.

Impetigo responds rapidly—often as quickly as it appeared—to topical and/or oral antibiotics, which are normally continued for one week. Crusts can be gently soaked off with a warm, wet washcloth, and the areas beneath them cleansed with soap and water. Because the bacteria that cause impetigo can easily spread by direct touch, the child's fingernails should be kept short and her hands washed frequently with antibacterial soap. She should be kept away from group-care situations until the infection has resolved.

incontinence Uncontrollable or involuntary loss of urine and/or stool.

induration A localized hardening of skin or other tissue.

inflammation The response of body tissue to injury or infection, usually identifiable by local redness, swelling, pain, and warmth.

influenza Better known as **flu**; an acute infection that frequently occurs in epidemics or occasionally in worldwide outbreaks known as pandemics. Three types of influenza virus, known simply as types A, B, and C, have been identified; types A and B are responsible for nearly all epidemics. Unfortunately, each of the three types has a number of different strains, and the virus undergoes subtle biochemical changes on an ongoing basis. As a result, someone who catches the flu or is vaccinated this year usually will not be immune during next year's outbreak. That is why those who need flu shots must get a new one each year. Influenza is typically seen in the United States and Canada in the fall and winter, usually involving strains that have been identified a few months earlier in Asia. These outbreaks develop quickly, spread rapidly, and may involve sizable numbers of people in a given community. While complications and mortality are uncommon in healthy individuals, influenza can be serious for children who have chronic illnesses.

Symptoms
Influenza is characterized by the sudden onset of chills, fever, muscle aches, headache, lack of appetite, and a dry cough. Nausea, vomiting, and abdominal pain sometimes occur in younger children but are less common in adolescents and adults. (Acute gastroenteritis, often called stomach flu, is an entirely different type of infection.) In some children, influenza can appear to be a simple respiratory-tract infection or an illness with fever but without any cold or cough. Influenza does not cause a rash or intense inflammation of the throat (pharyngitis). If bacteria become involved as secondary invaders, complications such as bronchitis, sinusitis, middle-ear infection, or pneumonia may develop.

Flu is spread via respiratory secretions that become airborne with coughing or are passed person to person by unwashed hands. A child or adult is most contagious for a period extending from twenty-four hours before the onset of symptoms through the time they show signs of resolving. The incubation period (the time from exposure to onset of symptoms) is one to three days.

Treatment
Treatment of influenza is usually focused on relief of symptoms. **Acetaminophen** (Tylenol and other brands) or **ibuprofen** (Children's Motrin and other brands) can be used to relieve fever and aches, but aspirin should be completely avoided because of the risk of Reye's syndrome (see "Reye's syndrome"). (Acetaminophen and ibuprofen dosage charts can be found on pages 609 and 688.) The child should drink a lot of fluids. (There is usually not much appetite for solids until symptoms begin to abate.) Until the fever, aches, and cough have calmed down for twenty-four hours, the child should remain at home and rest. Antibiotics will have no effect on the course of the illness, although they can be helpful if secondary bacterial infections develop.

Two drugs, **amantadine** and **rimantadine**, may reduce the severity of symptoms if given within the first forty-eight hours of the onset of a type A influenza virus infection. (The type of virus involved in a local epidemic may be identified by the local health department.) They can also prevent influenza from spreading to other family members. These drugs are not routinely given to children, since influenza normally resolves without treatment in two to five days. Your child's doctor can advise you whether one of these medications might be helpful or necessary.

A flu vaccine is developed each year and given every fall, and it is recommended for all children between the ages of six months and five years because they are at greater risk for complications from this infection. It should also be given to infants and children older than six months who have chronic conditions such as heart disease, asthma, kidney failure, and disorders of the immune system. For children with these and other long-term medical problems, influenza can be a much more serious, even fatal, illness. Other family members in the home of a high-risk child, as well as caregivers of children younger than six months of age, should be vaccinated as well.

Some parents may choose to vaccinate older children who do not have chronic illnesses to minimize the risk of their missing school or other important activities. For healthy children older than five and nonpregnant adults younger than fifty who are reluctant to have an injection, a flu vaccine in the form of a nasal spray is available.

intussusception A condition in which one segment of the intestine telescopes into another, usually causing an obstruction and abdominal pain (see also "abdominal pain").

iron A mineral necessary for the production of hemoglobin, the protein within red blood cells that transports life-sustaining oxygen throughout the body. Without adequate amounts of iron, an infant or child can develop iron-deficiency **anemia**, characterized by small red blood cells containing abnormally small amounts of hemoglobin. Depending upon the severity of the anemia, the child may appear pale and be irritable and easily fatigued. (Children who are iron deficient sometimes display a behavior called **pica**, in which they feel compelled to eat ice, clay, or dirt.) Prolonged anemia can interfere with growth. In addition, iron deficiency can have adverse effects on a child's behavior, intellectual development, and school performance.

Normal infants are born with enough iron to prevent deficiency throughout the first few months of life, even if dietary iron intake is inadequate. After the age of six months, however, consistent iron intake is necessary to prevent anemia. Breast milk normally provides enough iron for a growing infant, while bottle-fed infants should receive iron-fortified formula. Cow's milk should not be given to infants younger than twelve months of age because what little iron it contains is poorly absorbed by children. Cow's milk may irritate the intestinal tract and cause small amounts of blood loss when given to infants before their first birthday. Once a baby is eating solid food, iron-enriched cereals should be a regular part of the diet. Green and yellow vegetables, potatoes, red meat, and egg yolks also supply iron.

If iron deficiency is diagnosed in an infant or child during routine screening or an evaluation for another problem, the physician will look for possible causes. Before age two, inadequate dietary iron intake is the most common explanation. In children older than two, a possible chronic loss of blood (usually from the intestinal tract) may need to be investigated. In addition, an appropriate iron supplement (drops, liquid, or tablets) will be recommended, with the amount determined by the child's weight and the severity of the anemia. It is important to follow the directions carefully because inadequate dosing can delay the resolution of anemia, while excessive doses can be toxic. Taking the iron supplement with milk might interfere with absorption of the iron, but vitamin C will enhance it. (For a child older than twelve months of age, orange juice is a useful accompaniment to the iron.) *Keep iron supplements away from young children; accidental ingestion of iron preparations is one of the most common and serious types of poisoning in children under five.*

The physician who is treating the iron deficiency will eventually request a follow-up blood test (which usually can be performed as a simple finger-stick) to confirm that the problem is resolving.

J **jaundice** See "bilirubin."

jock itch (tinea cruris) A fungal skin infection of the groin, inner thighs, and in some cases the lower abdomen. It is more common in adolescent males, especially during hot weather, and is characterized by a pink, scaly, itchy rash. Jock itch can be treated with nonprescription antifungal cream, powder, or spray for several days. Keeping the affected areas clean and dry improves this condition and can help prevent recurrences. Daily showering or bathing followed by careful drying, wearing loose-fitting cotton underwear, and washing shorts and athletic supporters after each use aids recovery and prevention.

jugular Having to do with the neck or throat. The term is used most often in connection with the large veins in the neck.

juvenile rheumatoid arthritis See "Musculoskeletal Problems in Children," page 761.

K **Kawasaki disease** (also called **mucocutaneous lymph node syndrome**) An illness that most commonly affects children of Asian descent under age five. Most cases occur between the ages of two and five, and it is rare in children older than eight. The cause is unknown, but it is clearly not contagious. Kawasaki disease is characterized by a fever (typically over 103°F, or 39°C) that rises and falls repeatedly for five or more days, followed by a cluster of at least four of the following symptoms:

- Enlarged lymph nodes in the neck
- Inflammation in and around the mouth—a rough, "strawberry" tongue, redness of the mouth and throat, and cracking and peeling of the lips
- Swelling (**edema**) of the hands and feet, with peeling skin as the disease progresses
- Redness of the membranes over the eyes, but without pus
- A diffuse rash over the upper body and possibly the arms and legs

Fever may continue for ten to fourteen days, during or after which a number of heart abnormalities may develop in 15 to 25 percent of untreated cases. The most serious of these is damage to the coronary arteries, which supply blood to heart muscle. However, prompt treatment can reduce the likelihood of this potentially serious complication.

Treatment of Kawasaki disease includes a single dose of intravenous immune (gamma) globulin and high doses of aspirin. Depending on the course of the illness, aspirin may be continued for a prolonged period of time. This is one of the few situations in which aspirin is given to a small child with a fever. In viral illnesses such as chickenpox and influenza, aspirin is to be avoided because of the risk of Reye's syndrome (see "Reye's syndrome"). Follow-up by a pediatric heart specialist is important to be certain that no abnormalities of the heart are present.

keloid An excessive formation of scar tissue where a wound (traumatic or surgical) has healed. Keloid formation is more common in dark-skinned individuals. A keloid may enlarge over months or even years. Local injections of cortisone into the scar tissue may help decrease its size.

knock-knee (see illustration on page 766) A common deformity of the legs seen in children after the age of two, in which the knees are unusually close together when the child is standing or walking. Normal alignment of the knees typically takes place by the age of eight. (See "Musculoskeletal Problems in Children," page 766.)

kyphosis (see illustration on page 770) An excessive backward curvature of the upper (thoracic) spine, resulting in a humpback or rounded appearance when viewed from the side.

L **labia** Lip-shaped structures or outer folds that protect the female genitalia.

labyrinth The fluid-filled chambers in the inner ear.

laceration (see "Emergency Care," page 835) A cut or tear in the skin.

lacrimation The secretion and discharge of tears.

lactose Type of sugar found in breast milk, cow's milk, and most nonsoy infant formulas.

lactose intolerance The inability to digest lactose, one of the two most common sugars in the human diet and the primary sugar in cow's milk. Variable amounts of it are found in many products that are derived from milk, such as cheese, ice cream, and yogurt. Lactose intolerance occurs when there is a deficiency of the enzyme lactase, which is necessary to convert lactose into simpler sugars that can be absorbed into the bloodstream. An affected person who consumes foods containing lactose may develop bloating, cramping, diarrhea, increased bowel gas, and general abdominal discomfort. This type of reaction to lactose may be a lifelong tendency or a temporary problem. Lactose intolerance is very common in both African-Americans and Asians after the age of five. Because lactase is found in the outer cell layer of the small intestine, it may also be lost temporarily during infections or other disorders that damage the intestinal lining. After a child has had gastroenteritis (stomach flu), intestinal lactase may be reduced for days or even weeks; it is sometimes recommended that milk products be avoided for several days after a child has had this type of infection.

Avoidance of foods containing lactose will prevent symptoms in a child with lactose intolerance. In addition, nonprescription lactase preparations (such as Lactaid) may be added to milk products or taken with lactose-containing foods to prevent symptoms.

laryngitis Inflammation of the vocal cords, characterized primarily by hoarseness or even a temporary complete loss of the voice. Most cases of laryngitis are caused by viruses and are commonly associated with a dry cough. With rare exception, the voice returns to normal in one to two weeks without specific treatment (see also "hoarseness").

laryngomalacia The most common cause of stridor or noisy breathing in infants. It usually starts several days after birth and generally does not affect the health of the child but is often worrisome to parents. Laryngomalacia is thought to be due to the incoordination or flaccidity (looseness) of the laryngeal tissue. This condition usually resolves by one year of age, and surgical intervention is rarely required. An infant with ongoing noisy breathing should be evaluated by an ear, nose, and throat (ENT) specialist and followed until the symptoms resolve.

lateral A term indicating a position away from the midline of the body. For example, the ear is lateral to the cheek, and on each foot the little toe is lateral to the big toe.

lavage The washing out of an organ, such as the stomach or bowel.

lead poisoning Depending upon the amount of lead ingested and the time span during which it enters the body, lead poisoning can cause many symptoms: weakness, irritability, weight loss, vomiting, personality changes, staggering gait, constipation, headache, and abdominal pain. In extreme cases, mental retardation, convulsions, and coma develop. More commonly, small amounts of lead are continually ingested and may not cause obvious symptoms in early childhood but sometimes become evident later in the form of learning disorders. Young children—especially toddlers who are prone to put everything they find into their mouths—are at risk of lead poisoning if they live in homes or apartments built prior to 1978. (In that year, federal regulations reduced the amount of lead that could be added to house paint.) Paint chips and flakes on windowsills, paint peeling from walls, and dust-size particles can be picked up by exploring hands and swallowed.

The level of lead in the bloodstream can be screened during an evaluation for the above symptoms. In some neighborhoods where a significant percentage of homes are older, such screening might be part of a routine checkup. Based on the result of this screening, the child may be treated with a medication (known as a **chelating agent**) that binds to the lead and increases its rate of elimination from the body.

An obvious means of preventing further exposure to lead is to repaint old houses and furniture after first removing the lead-containing paint. Sanding or scraping old paint can generate dust that contains lead, however, so care must be taken to avoid exposing the family to this material. This job is best done by workers who are experienced in removing lead-containing paint.

lens (see illustration on page A4) The transparent body of the eye, located just behind the iris, that focuses light on the retina (see also "eye care and concerns").

lesion A nonspecific term that refers to a wound, injury, or pathological change in any tissue, especially the skin.

lethargy Lack of energy; a feeling of tiredness or listlessness.

leukemia A form of cancer involving uncontrolled production of immature white blood cells. Depending on the type of cells involved, there can be a number of significant consequences:

- The increased numbers of abnormal cells in the bone marrow interfere with the production of red blood cells (which carry oxygen) and platelets (which begin the clotting process if blood vessels are damaged), as well as other types of white cells. This can cause anemia (a low number of red cells), as well as bruising and clotting abnormalities.
- The immature white cells do not carry out immune functions as well as their normal counterparts, resulting in susceptibility to infection.
- The abnormal white cells may proliferate in other tissues, such as those in the central nervous system.

Leukemia can cause a variety of symptoms, including recurrent fever, lymph-node enlargement, joint swelling, unusual bruising, fatigue, and irritability. The disease is usually detected when a blood count reveals significant abnormali-

ties, including an extremely high white cell count. Further studies are then necessary to clarify the type and extent of the leukemia.

Acute lymphoblastic leukemia (ALL) is the most common form, accounting for about one out of every four cases of all cancers occurring before the age of fifteen. About 2,500 children are affected every year in the United States, and of those, 85 percent are diagnosed between the ages of two and ten. The good news about this type of leukemia is that with chemotherapy, the overall cure rate is 80 percent, with the best results obtained among children one to ten years of age, and a poorer prognosis for infants younger than one year of age.[14] Other forms of leukemia may be more difficult to treat and bring into remission. Some cases respond to more sophisticated treatments, such as bone-marrow transplantation.

leukopenia A reduction in the number of leukocytes (white blood cells) in the blood.

lice (pediculosis) One of the most aggravating health problems faced by parents is dealing with head lice in their children. If you or perhaps a school nurse has discovered one or more of these tiny, wingless parasites in your child's hair, you need not panic or feel embarrassed. This common infestation affects millions of children each year.

Three different kinds of lice live on the human body: head lice, body lice, and pubic or "crab" lice.

Head lice, which commonly infect people (especially in childhood), are about the size of a sesame seed. They live on the scalp, biting and sucking small amounts of blood, and cannot survive more than a few hours away from a human host. Since they cannot fly or jump from person to person, they are usually passed by sharing clothing, combs, or hairbrushes, or sometimes by cuddling with someone who has lice. They are not found on dogs, cats, or other pets.

Head lice hatch from eggs called **nits**, which are tiny, grayish white, and teardrop shaped. Nits are attached to the hair by a gluelike substance produced by the female louse. They will not wash out or blow away but must be combed out or picked out of the hair with tweezers. (This tedious process gives us the term *nit-picking*.) Nits hatch in about a week to produce mature lice, which then lay more eggs.

Detection of lice

The most common symptom of infestation with head lice is itching caused by their bites. Intense scratching of the infested area may lead to a secondary bacterial infection if the child's hands are contaminated. A child who repeatedly scratches the head should be checked for lice, especially if there is a known epidemic in the school or neighborhood.

Lice, which are grayish in color, can be difficult to locate because they move surprisingly fast and tend to shy away from light. The nits, which are lighter, are easier to see. Using a magnifying glass in natural light, look for small, grayish white eggs firmly attached to the hair shafts near the scalp. Nits can sometimes be mistaken for dandruff flakes, but since they are firmly anchored to hair, they do not brush away.

Treatment

Lice can be safely and effectively treated by shampooing the hair with agents that destroy both lice and nits. Two effective nonprescription treatments for head lice are permethrin cream rinse (Nix) and pyrethrin shampoo (RID). As an alternative, one-percent lindane is available only by prescription. Because central nervous system toxicity from absorption of lindane through the skin has been reported in infants, it is not recommended for use on infants or toddlers, nor on pregnant women or nursing mothers. It should be left on the skin for only five minutes and then thoroughly rinsed. Lindane shampoo should be applied once when the head lice are identified, then reapplied in seven to ten days to ensure that all nits are destroyed.

An effective way to remove nits is to use a ten-minute pretreatment of the hair with a one-to-one mixture of water and white vinegar followed by regular shampooing. This will help loosen nits from hair shafts and make their removal easier.

Bedding, blankets, or clothing that has been in contact with your child during the forty-eight hours prior to discovery of the lice should be dry-cleaned or washed in hot water (130°F, or 54°C) for twenty minutes. Hair accessories should be soaked in hot water. If an item cannot be washed (for example, a stuffed animal), it may be put in the dryer on a hot setting for thirty minutes (which will kill the lice) or sealed in a plastic bag and left alone for two weeks (which will cause the lice to die out).

Head lice can infest anyone, rich or poor, even in immaculate homes. Even after appropriate measures have been taken to eliminate lice, they can appear later because of reexposure. This can be extremely frustrating and demoralizing, especially after a lot of time and effort have been spent shampooing, nit-picking, and cleaning. To avoid reinfestation, all affected family members must be treated, and all infested children in a school or camp should be excluded from playing with others until they are nit free. To end a local epidemic, a coordinated effort to check all children will be needed.

Body lice and **pubic lice** are less common in the pediatric age-group. Body lice are more commonly associated with crowded living conditions with limited access to laundry facilities. The lice might be found in the seams of children's underwear rather than directly on the skin. Body lice can be eradicated by washing clothes in boiling water and then applying a hot iron to the seams. In adolescents and adults, pubic lice are usually discovered crawling among the pubic hairs and may have been transmitted during sexual activity. They can be eliminated by topical application of the same medication used to treat head lice.

ligament Strong but flexible fibrous bands that are attached to adjacent bones to keep them in proper alignment. A sudden and forceful twisting motion can stretch or tear a ligament, resulting in a sprain. (See "Musculoskeletal Problems in Children," page 759.)

lipoma A benign growth of fatty tissue.

lockjaw The common term for **tetanus**, which (among other symptoms) can cause spasm of the muscles involved in chewing and can make it difficult for the victim to open his mouth (see "tetanus").

lordosis An excessive forward curvature of the lower (lumbar) spine, resulting in a swayback appearance when viewed from the side.

lumbar A term referring to the lower part of the back located between the ribs and the pelvis.

Lyme disease The most common disease spread by tick bites. More than twenty thousand cases are now reported annually in the United States. It is caused by a corkscrew-shaped bacterium called a spirochete, carried by the pinhead-size deer tick (also known as the black-legged tick) and the related Western black-legged tick. In the United States, Lyme disease is seen most commonly in the upper East Coast and upper Midwest states, as well as in the Pacific Northwest, but cases have been reported in every state. (The disease was named for the town of Lyme, Connecticut, where an unusual cluster of children with arthritis in 1975 first led to its discovery.)

The ticks that carry the Lyme disease bacteria have a prolonged life cycle (two years) involving large mammals, including deer and humans, as well as rodents and birds. The bacteria are normally transmitted when the ticks are at the nymph stage (midway between larvae and adults). Nymphs are so small that they may not be noticed when they attach to the skin. They are more active in the summer, increasing the odds of contact with campers and hikers. The spirochetes are not transmitted through contaminated food or water, or by insects such as mosquitoes or fleas, nor can they be caught from another person with Lyme disease.

Nymphs (or less commonly, adult ticks) are picked up when animals or humans brush against shrubs or grasses that harbor them. The ticks cannot fly or jump but can crawl and eventually attach anywhere on the body, favoring hidden areas such as the groin, armpits, and scalp. Once the tick's head is embedded in a person's skin, it begins a long process of sucking the blood. This process can take days, during which the body of the tick slowly enlarges. The spirochetes that cause Lyme disease are normally not transmitted until the tick has been feeding for about thirty-six to forty-eight hours.

Symptoms

In 80 percent of the people who have been infected with the Lyme disease spirochete, a telltale rash will develop in three days to a month (but typically within one to two weeks) after the tick bit the individual. This rash, called **erythema migrans** (literally, "migrating red"), typically has the appearance of a bull's-eye that appears at the site of the bite and then slowly expands. Other smaller lesions may also occur. The rash does not itch, is not painful, and lasts for about three to five weeks. Flu-like symptoms (such as chills and fever, headache, fatigue, and pains in muscles and joints) sometimes occur in the early stages of the disease. Any rash that develops within forty-eight hours of a tick bite is not likely to be Lyme disease but rather an allergic reaction to the bite.

When Lyme disease goes untreated, some people will progress to a second stage in two to twelve weeks, during which a stiff neck, facial-nerve paralysis, abnormalities of heart rhythm, and weakness or numbness of extremities develop. The final stage occurs six weeks to two years after the tick bite. Symptoms primarily involve painful, swollen joints (arthritis)—especially of the knees—which may become chronic in 10 percent of children who are untreated.

Similarity to other diagnoses

Lyme disease can be difficult to identify because the symptoms are either vague or similar to those of other disorders. In addition, many people will not have seen or felt the tiny deer tick that transmitted it, and one in four will not have the distinctive circular rash. The spirochete that causes Lyme disease is difficult to culture from blood or body tissue. Blood tests might be utilized to identify antibodies the body has produced against the spirochete, but the antibodies may not be detectable within the first few weeks of infection. To confuse matters further, someone with vague symptoms of fatigue and joint aches might show a positive antibody response to the Lyme disease spirochete but in fact have another type of infection.

Ultimately, a combination of history, symptoms, exam, and laboratory findings will lead a physician to suspect Lyme disease.

L

Treatment

In its early stages Lyme disease is treated with two to three weeks of antibiotics, usually **amoxicillin**, **cefuroxime**, or a tetracycline derivative called **doxycycline**. (Doxycycline should not be given to children younger than eight because it can cause staining of the teeth, nor should it be taken by pregnant women.) If not treated until the later stages, more prolonged treatment with antibiotics may be necessary.

Prevention

Appropriate clothing—especially light-colored slacks tucked into boots—as well as insect repellents and frequent tick checks are necessary to avoid transmission of the disease. (See "ticks" for additional measures to reduce the likelihood of tick bites.)

lymphadenopathy Swollen lymph nodes.

lymph nodes Small collections of cells that assist in the body's immune response. They are found throughout the lymphatic system, which is composed of tiny vessels that collect fluid from every part of the body and route it back to the bloodstream. Lymph nodes are commonly enlarged when reacting to an infection, such as when the nodes in the neck become swollen and tender in response to a sore throat. They may also become enlarged when invaded by cancer cells, a rare event in children and adolescents. Lymph nodes are frequently but inaccurately called lymph glands.

M

macula (of the eye) (see illustration on page A4) Central part of the retina responsible for detailed vision.

macule (of the skin) General term for a discolored flat spot on the skin.

magnetic resonance imaging (MRI) A type of imaging study that utilizes a strong magnetic field to create detailed cross-sectional views of an area of the body. An MRI study is not painful and does not involve X-ray exposure.

malaria A tropical infectious disease caused by a parasite that is carried and transmitted by mosquitoes. Malaria remains a major health problem in developing countries, killing more than eight hundred thousand children under age five worldwide every year. Travelers to foreign countries where malaria may be present (especially Africa, Asia, Central and South America) should check with their physicians and/or local public-health departments for advice regarding preventive medication, which should be started prior to departure.

malignancy Cancer.

malleolus Either of the rounded, prominent ends of the bones of the lower leg (the tibia and fibula) that protrude on each side of the ankle.

malocclusion Failure of the upper and lower teeth to align properly when a person bites down or chews.

malunion Failure of the pieces of a broken bone to heal in proper alignment.

mandible The lower jaw.

marrow The soft tissue that fills the central cavities within bones. Red and white blood cells are produced continuously within bone marrow, as are platelets (the tiny, disclike structures within the blood that participate in the clotting process).

mastitis Inflammation of the breast tissue, usually caused by a bacterial infection.

mastoiditis An infection of the honeycombed, bony **mastoid air cells** located just behind the ears. Over the past few decades, the availability of antibiotics (and surgical procedures when needed) has greatly reduced the frequency and severity of serious complications, including mastoiditis, which can arise from middle-ear infections (see "ear infections").

Although mastoiditis can take place at any age, it is unusual before the age of two, since the mastoid air cells usually have not started to develop until that age.

Symptoms

The child who develops mastoiditis typically has been fighting an ear infection that has not improved over a two-week period. He is still feverish and has persistent pain and a red, inflamed eardrum. He also develops a characteristic swelling and tenderness behind the ear, typically displaced outward and downward.

Just as mastoiditis can be a complication of otitis media, **meningitis** may complicate mastoiditis in some cases. Fever, severe headache, and stiff neck will typically be present, and a lumbar puncture (spinal tap) will be needed to make this diagnosis (see "meningitis"). A small percentage of children with mastoiditis will develop an intense, localized, pus-forming infection called an **abscess** in the brain. This is manifested by persistent headache, fever, and confusion, and it is diagnosed using computerized tomography (CT) or magnetic resonance imaging (MRI).

Treatment

When acute mastoiditis is diagnosed, a child will usually be hospitalized for further evaluation, intravenous antibiotics, and when necessary, surgery to drain the infected area. Once therapy has begun, the child should be free of pain in four or five days. After discharge from the hospital, oral antibiotics will probably be continued for an additional four to six weeks.

masturbation Self-stimulation of the genitalia for sexual gratification. (For information about discussing this topic and other aspects of sexuality with children, see chapter 10, page 327, and chapter 11, page 375.)

maxilla The irregularly shaped bone that forms the upper jaw, the hard palate, part of the nasal cavity, and the floor of the eyeball. The upper teeth are implanted in the maxilla.

measles (rubeola) A highly contagious viral infection that begins with high fever and malaise (lethargy or fatigue), followed by a harsh cough, intense runny nose, and watery, inflamed eyes. Severe conjunctivitis may be present along with sensitivity to light. White specks on a red base, known as **Koplik's spots**, may develop on the inside of the cheek. Finally, a rash begins near the hairline and progresses downward, disappearing from the face as it involves the arms and legs. The rash disappears within six days, after which the affected skin may peel.

Secondary bacterial infections of lungs, ears, sinuses, and lymph nodes, or respiratory complications such as wheezing, croup, or pneumonia may occur in as many as 15 percent of cases. A rare but much more serious inflammation of brain tissue known as **measles encephalitis** occurs in one out of a thousand cases, and half of those affected may suffer severe neurologic consequences or even death.

Fortunately, measles is far less common now than it was a half century ago because of the widespread use of measles vaccine, which is typically given as part of the MMR (measles/mumps/rubella) combination. The first dose of MMR is usually given when the child is twelve to fifteen months of age and a second dose between the ages of four and six. Sporadic outbreaks of measles have occurred in areas where significant numbers of children have not been vaccinated or have not received a second dose of MMR (see also "rubella").

melanin Brownish black pigment that gives color to hair, eyes, and skin.

meninges The membrane that covers and protects the brain and spinal cord.

meningitis An inflammation of the membranes that cover the brain and spinal cord, usually caused by a viral or bacterial infection. This condition can develop at any age, although young infants are particularly vulnerable.

BACTERIAL MENINGITIS The most serious form of this illness may lead to such complications as impairments in hearing and/or vision, mental retardation, and seizures. The bacteria that most commonly cause meningitis during childhood are pneumococcus and meningococcus. Some strains of meningococcus are quite contagious, so those who have had household and day-care contact with a child or adolescent who develops meningococcal meningitis are usually given a preventive antibiotic. For many years *Haemophilus influenzae* was the most common cause of childhood bacterial meningitis, but the vaccine now routinely given during infancy has drastically reduced the number of cases involving this organism. Routine vaccination of infants against pneumococcus has been recommended since 2000. In addition, one dose of vaccine against meningococcus is now recommended during adolescence, and it may be given as early as the eleven- or twelve-year-old checkup.

Symptoms

A child with meningitis will commonly have dramatic symptoms: headache, irritability, lethargy, stiff neck, vomiting, and sensitivity to light (**photophobia**). An infant or toddler with meningitis may have only a fever and possibly a seizure. Distinguishing a harmless **febrile convulsion** (that is, a seizure caused by fever) from one caused by meningitis may not be easy. *In infants younger than three months of age, the signs of meningitis may be much less obvious.* A fever, poor feeding, and perhaps an episode or two of vomiting might be the only signs of this serious infection. An infant this age with a fever over 100.4°F (38°C), taken rectally, should be evaluated thoroughly by a physician.

If your doctor is concerned about the possibility of meningitis, it is likely that he or she will order blood tests and perform a **lumbar puncture (spinal tap)**. Parents often believe that this procedure is extremely painful or dangerous, especially on a tiny baby, but this is not so. To make the proper diagnosis, a small amount of the fluid that surrounds the spinal cord must be extracted and sent to the laboratory for a variety of tests, including bacterial culture. Your doctor will explain the procedure to you in detail if it needs to be done.

Treatment

Bacterial meningitis is a serious condition. To prevent significant complications or even death, intravenous antibiotics are usually given for one to two weeks. When it is uncertain whether or not the infection is bacterial, antibiotics are started and continued for forty-eight to seventy-two hours until the results of spinal tap and blood cultures become available.

VIRAL MENINGITIS (also called **aseptic meningitis**) This type of meningitis is more common in the summer and fall and resolves without antibiotics. Frequently patients do not need hospitalization once the diagnosis is clear.

meniscus Crescent-shaped cartilage tissue found within the knee joint, which serves as a cushion between the two bones (the femur and the tibia) that form the knee.

menorrhagia Heavy bleeding during menstruation.

metatarsal A term referring to the five long bones in each foot that are adjacent to and form a joint with each of the toes.

microcephaly Having an abnormally small head.

milia Small white bumps that appear on the face of up to 50 percent of newborns. These tiny cysts arise from structures known as sebaceous glands whose ducts are temporarily blocked. The glands are not infected, and milia will disappear without treatment during the first two months of life.

miliaria (heat rash, prickly heat) Rash caused by blocked sweat glands. The small, white, fluid-filled bumps can occur in infants who are dressed too heavily, especially in a warm humid environment. The rash will disappear when the infant is placed in dry, cooler surroundings or dressed in lighter clothing.

mittelschmerz Pelvic pain that occurs approximately two weeks prior to a menstrual cycle. The pain arises from the release of an ovum (egg) from one of the ovaries (see chapter 12, page 445). The word is German for "middle pain," referring to the fact that it occurs about halfway through the cycle.

mole A pigmented spot or bump on the skin.

molluscum contagiosum A common, somewhat contagious skin condition caused by a virus.

The rash is characterized by small, discrete, pearly white or skin-colored, dome-shaped papules with sunken tops from which a plug of cheesy material can easily be expressed. They are found most commonly on the face, neck, and thighs. It is a self-limited disease but can persist for months.

mononucleosis (mono) Acute, infectious viral illness that occurs most commonly during adolescence. (For consistency, throughout this book we refer to this illness as **infectious mononucleosis**.) The vast majority of cases are caused by the **Epstein-Barr virus (EBV)**, which infects virtually all individuals by the time they reach adulthood. In most people, however, infection with EBV occurs during childhood, when it either goes unnoticed or causes symptoms identical to those of other common illnesses. If the first encounter with this virus occurs after puberty, the results are often much more dramatic.

Symptoms

After a prolonged incubation period of thirty to fifty days, the virus may cause fatigue, headache, and a low-grade fever for a few days, followed by a severe sore throat, higher fever, and marked enlargement of lymph nodes in the neck. Tonsils sometimes become very inflamed, with swelling, redness, and white patches (called **exudate**). Nausea and even vomiting might also occur. This phase of the illness may last for one or two weeks, and the fatigue, quite a bit longer. During this time the spleen might enlarge, causing vague upper-left abdominal discomfort.

If your adolescent (or younger child) has these symptoms, contact his doctor. A blood count and a more specific test for infectious mononucleosis can help confirm the diagnosis, although these tend to be more accurate if the illness has been under way for a few days. The doctor may swab the throat to check for infection with **group A beta-hemolytic streptococcus** (strep throat), which may occur at the same time and cause similar symptoms; this will normally be treated with antibiotics. There is no antibiotic that treats EBV specifically.

Treatment

Infectious mononucleosis will usually run its course with treatment consisting only of comfort measures: rest, liquids, acetaminophen or ibuprofen for pain relief and fever reduction as needed, and more rest. Do not give aspirin, because it has been linked to a rare but serious disorder called Reye's syndrome when given during acute viral infections (see "Reye's syndrome"). More intensive medical intervention could become necessary to manage two uncommon complications:

- Swelling of tonsils so severe that swallowing or even breathing is difficult.
- Rupture of an enlarged spleen, a rare event that is manifested by sudden and persistent pain in the upper-left abdomen. This may in some cases be the first manifestation of mono. If rupture is diagnosed, the spleen is removed or repaired surgically to prevent significant blood loss.

Short- and long-term outlook for someone with infectious mononucleosis

Light activities may resume as tolerated after the fever and sore throat resolve, but several more days or even weeks of fatigue could limit participation in school or other pursuits. Contact sports or rough-and-tumble play should be avoided for three or four weeks to reduce the risk of rupturing the spleen. (However, in half the cases in which the spleen ruptures, there has been no trauma to the abdomen.) Your teenager's physician will provide more specifics about returning to athletic activities.

Because of the striking fatigue associated with infectious mononucleosis, there was at one time speculation that EBV might be the cause of long-term chronic fatigue in teenagers and adults. The diagnosis of chronic Epstein-Barr syndrome was in fact given to many people suffering from fatigue, but further research has not validated the existence of this disease. Only very rarely does an individual have persistent symptoms that can be attributed to ongoing active mononucleosis, usually involving a disturbance in immune response. In general, anyone who has disabling fatigue for more than a few weeks, whether or not it is preceded by infectious mononucleosis, should be evaluated for other possibilities. (This statement applies to fatigue affecting light, everyday activities. For athletes, stamina and conditioning may be hampered much longer; peak performance

M

may not be restored for many months following infectious mononucleosis.)

Prevention

EBV is known to be transmitted through saliva (thus earning its popular distinction as the "kissing disease"), but it is actually not highly contagious. Only those who have never been infected with EBV by the time they reach puberty are at risk for infectious mononucleosis. (A large number of people acquire EBV during childhood without developing major symptoms and are thus immune without knowing it.) As a result, widespread epidemics of infectious mononucleosis do not take place. Nevertheless, if you have someone at home with this illness, others should avoid sharing utensils or anything else that would bring them into contact with the infected person's saliva (including mouth-to-mouth kissing). Unfortunately, unless a person had infectious mononucleosis that was confirmed by a physician, there is no way to be certain of one's immunity to it without doing expensive antibody tests.

motion sickness Nausea, sometimes accompanied by vomiting, that develops in susceptible individuals during automobile, airplane, train, or boat travel, as well as on certain types of amusement-park rides. This common problem can often be alleviated in a grade-school child or adolescent by teaching him to focus on the horizon rather than reading or watching objects that are at close range while in a moving vehicle. Providing adequate fresh air in the car can also be helpful.

Sitting in the front seat can reduce motion sickness, but for safety reasons this approach should be restricted to children over twelve years of age who can be properly secured with both lap and shoulder belts. *(In general, children are safer in the backseat, and if the car is equipped with a passenger-side air bag, no child younger than twelve should ride in the front seat.)* **Dimenhydrinate** (Dramamine) sometimes reduces motion sickness if taken prior to a long auto trip or before an airplane or boat ride.

mouth care and concerns The mouth serves as the entrance for a baby's life-sustaining nourishment and the exit for her cries and laughter, and later in life for her speech. It is bordered by

the mandible (lower jawbone) and the maxilla (upper jawbone). Structures contained within the mouth include the tongue, soft palate and hard palate (roof of the mouth). At birth, the muscles surrounding the mouth are remarkably strong, allowing babies to suck firmly enough to acquire adequate nutrition.

Mouth infections

As the point of entry for food and often other objects (none of which are sterile), the mouth is continually exposed to a variety of bacteria, viruses, and other microscopic organisms. In fact, the mouth is continuously colonized by enormous numbers of bacteria, but as long as the tissues (especially the gums and teeth) are healthy, these bacteria normally do not cause problems. A significant exception is a human bite to another person (or oneself), which creates a contaminated wound if the skin is broken. In such cases, the bite wound should be evaluated by a physician to ensure that it is properly cleansed. Antibiotics are usually prescribed.

Bad breath

Bad breath can occur in children of all ages but is more common in older children with a full set of teeth. If your child has bad breath, make sure she is brushing and flossing her teeth often and regularly. Bad breath can be a sign of infection in the throat, tonsils, adenoids, gums, or sinuses. If brushing alone doesn't help, a trip to the doctor's or dentist's office will probably be necessary to find and treat the cause.

Candida

Known commonly as **thrush**, this infection is caused by the common yeast *Candida albicans*. It is seen most often in newborns. Thrush appears as a white film over the tongue, inner surfaces of the cheeks, or roof of the mouth. It may be confused with milk coating, but unlike thrush, milk can be easily dabbed off with a cotton swab. Thrush is not harmful, although *Candida* transferred to a mother's breast may cause a local eruption of her skin.

Thrush can be treated with an antifungal solution such as nystatin, which your physician will prescribe. You can use an ordinary cotton swab or a device known as a toothette (which looks like a lollipop stick with a small sponge on the end) to apply the medication. Dip the toothette in the solution and gently scrub the affected areas inside the mouth. If you don't scrub, the thrush will still resolve with repeated applications of the medicine, but the process may take longer. Be patient, because even with diligent efforts, the infection might not disappear for weeks. (Don't worry if your baby swallows some of the nystatin, because it is not harmful.)

Some oral *Candida* infections don't clear with nystatin, or they return in spite of repeated treatments. An alternative treatment is one percent gentian violet, a dye that can be purchased from the pharmacist without prescription. Gentian violet is applied with a cotton swab to the inside of your baby's cheeks twice daily for three days. Though harmless, it can stain everything in sight a vivid purple unless you are very careful with the swabs.

Canker sores

Also known as **aphthous ulcers**, these small, painful sores appear inside the mouth, either singly or a few at a time. They may occur on the gums, inner surfaces of lips or cheeks, tongue, palate, and in the throat. They have a well-defined, depressed whitish center surrounded by redness. They may arise during an acute illness, although no specific virus or bacteria is known to cause them, or they may form in an area that has been traumatized (such as where the inner surface of a lip or cheek has been accidentally bitten). They tend to recur throughout the lifetime of susceptible individuals.

The sores are usually preceded by burning, itching, or pain for a day or so before they actually appear in the mouth. They can be painful enough to interfere with eating; avoid foods that are hot, spicy, and acidic (such as citrus fruits and tomatoes). Cold foods, particularly liquids, are usually better tolerated.

There is no specific cure for canker sores, which will eventually disappear without treatment in ten to fourteen days. Over-the-counter analgesics, including **acetaminophen** (Tylenol and other brands) and **ibuprofen** (Children's Motrin, Children's Advil, or other brands) may relieve some of the discomfort. (Dosage charts for acetaminophen and ibuprofen may be found on pages 609 and 688.) Check with your child's physician about topical medications. If the sores persist for more than fifteen days, the child should be seen by a physician.

Hand, foot, and mouth disease

See "hand, foot, and mouth disease" beginning on page 677.

Other mouth problems

Newborns can be born with a condition historically referred to as **tongue-tie**, in which the **frenulum**—the piece of tissue connecting the tongue to the floor of the mouth—extends too far forward. Parents may notice a dimple on the tip of the tongue as the child grows. Doctors used to snip the frenulum at birth, but this is an uncommon procedure now. Most children with this condition suffer no significant consequences. However, if tongue-tie seems to cause feeding or speech difficulties, you should talk to your child's physician about treatment options.

About one in one thousand children is born with **cleft lip** or **cleft palate** (or both), a defect in the development of the central part of the lip or palate (roof of the mouth). The cause of these conditions is unknown, but it occurs during weeks seven to twelve of pregnancy, when the middle of the mouth fails to form properly. It is seen more commonly among Native American and Asian infants and least frequently in African-Americans.

Cleft lip and palate are not life-threatening conditions, although their appearance may provoke anxiety or other negative responses in adults or older siblings. The bonding process between parent and child may be impaired as a result, but it is very important that these infants receive all the cuddling, cooing, and other signs of affection that babies need to thrive. (It is equally important not to overcompensate by becoming overly attentive to the child with the defect, and in so doing, deprive other children at home of the time and attention they need.) While some infants with this problem are able to breastfeed easily, others have sucking difficulty and require a specialized soft nipple. Depending upon the extent of the problem and the timing of surgical repair (see below), speech development and socialization may be affected.

Because of the breadth of problems associated with cleft lip and palate, caring for an infant with this condition usually requires an experienced medical team consisting of a plastic surgeon, ENT (ear, nose, and throat) specialist, pediatrician, dentist, orthodontist, nutritionist, and speech therapist. A psychologist or social worker can help the family work through emotional and practical issues, both before and after the corrective process. The good news about cleft lip and palate problems is that they are surgically correctable, a process that may begin as early as four months or as late as eighteen months of age.

Future siblings of a child with cleft lip or palate are at higher risk of being affected. If the parents are normal and no other siblings have it, the risk of cleft lip or palate occurring again is about 2 percent. If either parent or another sibling is affected, the future risk could be as high as 7 percent, and if both a parent and a sibling are affected, the risk is 10 to 17 percent. Children with this condition may have associated problems, such as congenital heart disease and spinal abnormalities. If your child has a cleft palate, don't be alarmed if your pediatrician orders extra tests to ensure that he does not have other medical conditions.

Teeth

The care of the teeth and common dental problems in children are discussed in "teeth care and concerns."

MRI See "magnetic resonance imaging."

mumps A childhood viral infection of the **parotid (salivary) glands** located in front of the ears. Before the availability of mumps vaccine in 1967, about two hundred thousand cases and twenty to thirty deaths from mumps occurred every year in the United States. While the disease is now very uncommon in the United States, a few hundred cases are reported every year, and mumps remains common in many parts of the world.

The disease typically involves swelling and soreness of the parotid glands, along with fever and fatigue, which in most cases resolves without treatment over two or three weeks. Complica-

tions of mumps are uncommon but more serious. These can include inflammation of one or both testicles (orchitis) that can lead to sterility; meningitis; inflammation of brain tissue (encephalitis); inflammation of the pancreas (pancreatitis) that manifests as pain in the upper abdomen, nausea, and vomiting; and hearing loss in one or both ears. Children are routinely immunized against mumps in the combination MMR vaccine given at twelve to fifteen months of age, with a second dose typically given between the ages of four and six. (See "Immunizations—Which Ones, Why, and When?" beginning on page 745.)

muscular dystrophy A group of more than thirty forms of inherited disease that lead to progressive degeneration and weakness of muscles that control voluntary movements and respiration. The various muscular dystrophies differ greatly in severity, time of onset (early versus later in life), rate of progression, muscles affected, and overall outcome. The most common form, known as **Duchenne muscular dystrophy**, primarily affects boys, manifests itself between the ages of three and five, and usually leads to an inability to walk by late childhood. While there is no specific cure for any of the muscular dystrophies, a variety of approaches—including medications for some forms of the disease, braces and other supportive devices, physical therapy, and in more severe cases ventilator care—play an important role in maximizing functional ability and prolonging life.

myalgia Muscle pain.

myopia Nearsightedness; the inability to see distant objects clearly (see also "eye care and concerns").

myositis Inflammation of one or more muscle groups, resulting in pain, tenderness, and/or weakness.

N **nail care and concerns** Because an infant's fingernails grow quickly and may accidentally scratch the face, they should be gently trimmed once or twice a week using infant nail clippers. Toenails, which do not grow as quickly and can't cause any injury, need only be trimmed once or twice a month.

The hands of a young child are constantly exploring the world around him, and thus both fingers and fingernails are at risk for a variety of injuries. If a child is barefoot much of the time, toenails could occasionally be injured as well. If a nail becomes cracked without rough edges, no special care is needed. If a nail is nearly torn off, however, use clippers or scissors cleansed with rubbing alcohol to cut off the loose fragment. Each day soak the hand or foot for twenty minutes in a solution of warm salt water (½ tsp [2.5 ml] salt in two cups [about 480 ml] water), then apply antibiotic ointment and a small adhesive bandage. Within about a week, the raw nail bed will be covered with new skin, and this routine can be stopped. A new nail will eventually grow out.

Occasionally a crushing injury (as occurs when a finger is caught in a closing door) will cause bleeding under a fingernail. This will be manifested by a deep blue discoloration of the nail and a great deal of pain. This injury should be seen by the child's physician, who may use a special tool to poke a hole in the nail to release the blood and relieve pain immediately. If the nail bed is cut as the result of a crush injury, it may need to be sutured (stitched) under local anesthesia.

Nail-biting is a common self-comforting, unconscious habit among children. Attempts to stop it through nagging, ridicule, or punishment will cause more harm than good. A child who wants to break the habit can be assisted in a variety of ways:

- Offer a reward for a certain number of days or weeks of no nail-biting.
- Devise a simple, nonjudgmental signal (such as saying the child's name in a friendly tone and pointing to your hand) that you can use when you see him biting his nails.
- Bitter-tasting solutions (such as Control-It! or Thum) painted on the nails may serve as a reminder to keep fingers out of the mouth.

An infection of the soft tissue at the junction of the cuticle and the fingernail is called a **paronychia**. This usually involves common staphy-

lococcal or streptococcal bacteria, although the herpes virus can also cause this problem. The infection usually arises from a break in the skin resulting from thumb sucking or chewing or pulling on a cuticle. Occasionally pus will drain from the red, tender, swollen tissue. If a pus pocket is clearly visible, your child's doctor might lance it, which will relieve pressure and reduce pain. The doctor might recommend ten- or fifteen-minute soaks in a solution of a little antibacterial soap in six to eight ounces (about 180 to 240 ml) of warm water, along with the application of an antibiotic ointment. In more severe cases, oral antibiotics might be prescribed.

Ingrown toenails, caused by improper cutting of the toenails or wearing tight shoes, occur when the nail becomes embedded in the flesh. To prevent them, always cut toenails straight across rather than curving them down on the sides. If an ingrown nail develops, soak the foot daily in a solution of soap and water as described above. Massage the swollen part of the toe away from the nail. Frequently ingrown toenails (especially on the big toe) become infected, causing pain, redness, and swelling where the nail joins the infected skin. While gentle cleansing and warm soaks may help to some extent, your child's doctor might recommend antibiotics and/or removal of the segment of nail that has become embedded in the skin. (A local anesthetic is given to numb the toe before this is done.)

narcolepsy A disorder characterized by profound difficulty maintaining wakefulness during the day, regardless of surrounding activity or noise. Increasing sleep at night does not improve this condition, which begins after puberty in the majority of cases but may be seen as early as three years of age. Narcolepsy can be highly disruptive to normal activities but can be treated on a long-term basis with central nervous system stimulants.

nausea Queasiness or unpleasant sensation in the stomach that makes a person feel like vomiting.

nebulizer A device used to administer medication in an aerosol form through a face mask.

neoplasm A tumor.

neuralgia Pain along the course of a nerve.

neuritis Swelling or inflammation of a nerve.

neurofibromatosis An inherited disorder characterized by soft, fibrous tumors that may be found over the entire body. Associated areas of brownish skin pigmentation are called **café au lait spots**.

neuroma A benign tumor growth that arises from a nerve.

neutrophil A type of white blood cell that is specifically associated with the body's immune response.

nevus A birthmark or a mole. See "birthmarks."

nocturia Urination at night.

node A collection of lymph tissue. See "lymph nodes."

nonunion The failure of the broken ends of a fractured bone to reunite.

nosebleed (epistaxis) See "Emergency Care," page 828.

N

O

occiput The lower portion of the back of the head where it merges with the neck.

ocular Having to do with the eyes.

orifice Entrance or exit of a body cavity (such as the mouth).

osteoma A tumor arising from bone tissue.

osteomalacia Softening of the bone due to a calcium or vitamin D deficiency or kidney disease.

osteomyelitis A serious bacterial infection of bone. Treatment involves a prolonged antibiotic regimen and in some cases splinting of the affected area. Surgical intervention is sometimes necessary to remove pus and diseased tissue.

osteoporosis Abnormal loss of bone density. This condition is normally associated with postmenopausal women, but it can also occur among adolescent females who have stopped menstruating because of severe weight loss (as in anorexia nervosa) or extreme levels of exercise (see the Special Concerns section "Eating Disorders," page 401).

otitis externa Inflammation or infection of the outer ear canal; commonly called swimmer's ear (see "ear infections").

otitis media Inflammation or infection of the middle ear (see "ear infections").

P

palate The roof of the mouth.

pallor Pale appearance of the skin.

palpate To feel with the fingers.

palpitation The sensation that the heart is beating too rapidly, irregularly, or strongly.

papilloma A wart.

papule A small, solid, raised skin lesion.

paraplegia Paralysis of the legs and lower part of the body, with impairment of both motion and sensation.

parasite An organism that lives on or within another living creature (called the host) and draws nourishment from its host's body.

parenteral A term applied to medications or fluids that are injected into a vein, muscle, or fatty layer below the skin rather than given by mouth or suppository.

paresis Partial paralysis or weakness of a specific muscle.

paresthesia Abnormal burning, prickling, or tingling ("pins and needles") sensation on the skin.

paroxysm A sudden attack (such as coughing).

patella The kneecap.

peptic ulcer A crater resulting from digestion (by stomach acid and the enzyme pepsin) of a localized area of the tissue that lines the stomach or first segment of the small intestine. This can also be associated with a bacterial infection.

perforation A hole or breakthrough in the membrane or wall of an organ.

pericarditis Inflammation of the sac that surrounds the heart.

periosteum The tough fibrous tissue that covers bone.

peripheral Located at or near the surface or an outward part of the body.

pertussis (whooping cough) A highly contagious bacterial infection that primarily affected infants and children before the introduction of an effective vaccine in the 1940s. The disease has not been eradicated in the United States, and the majority of cases now occur among people ten years of age and older. However, the most serious complications, including death, occur primarily among infected infants younger than one year of age.

Pertussis typically begins with symptoms that are indistinguishable from those of a common cold, such as runny nose, low-grade fever, and fatigue. After one or two weeks, however, the individual develops a persistent and aggravating cough. Among infants and younger children, the cough tends to occur in paroxysms—rapid, intense bursts of coughing during a single expiration, followed by a gasping, whooping sound with the inhalation of the next breath. (You can hear a recording of an infant with this cough by clicking on "Pertussis Cough" at the Web site http://www.immunizationed.org. The sound is unforgettable.)

Paroxysms of coughing may continue for one to six weeks and can lead to vomiting, dehydration, weight loss, seizures, and pneumonia, the most common cause of death related to this disease. Infants younger than six months of age (especially those under four weeks) may not develop the coughing paroxysms, but they often become seriously ill nonetheless. Unless a physician has a very high degree of suspicion that this disease is present (as may occur when a child develops symptoms after exposure to a known case of it), pertussis is rarely diagnosed before the paroxysms of coughing begin—at which point treatment is primarily supportive while the infection runs its course. Antibiotics do not shorten the duration of the illness once this stage has been reached, but they can help reduce transmission to others.

Widespread pertussis immunizations among infants and young children—pertussis is the *P* in the DTaP immunizations—reduced the number of cases in the United States from more than 120,000 per year in 1960 to 1,730 in 1980. However, the number of cases steadily rose to more than 7,800 in 2000, and then dramatically increased to more than 25,000 in 2004. One reason for this increase in reported cases may be an increasing awareness among physicians that pertussis is "alive and well" in the United States and can cause persistent, disruptive coughing in all age-groups, including adults. Thus, more cases are being diagnosed and reported. Another reason for this shift is that the pertussis vaccine does not provide lifelong immunity—indeed, immunity begins to decline within four to twelve years after vaccination, which until recently was not given after the age of six. Since 2005, the pertussis vaccine in combination with diphtheria and tetanus (the Tdap combination) has been available for adolescents and adults younger than sixty-five.[15]

petechiae Flat, purple to red, pinhead-size spots that appear in the skin or mucous membranes as a result of leakage of blood from tiny blood vessels.

phlegm Mucus produced in the lungs, especially during an infection.

photophobia An abnormal intolerance of light.

pigeon toes (intoeing) (see illustration on page 766) A minor abnormality in which the leg or foot is rotated, causing the foot or toes to point inward. (See "Musculoskeletal Problems in Children," page 766.)

pinna The fleshy, projecting part of the ear on the outside of the head.

pinworms The most common type of parasitic worm that infects children in developed countries. While certainly annoying, they are essentially harmless. Pinworms are white or gray, thin, and one-quarter to one-half inch (6 to 12 mm) long. They may easily be mistaken for a vegetable fiber or a piece of lint—until they move.

Their thirty-five-day life cycle begins when eggs are unknowingly swallowed. Pinworms hatch in the small intestine and migrate to the colon (large intestine). After mating, the females move to the anal area to lay their eggs on the surrounding skin, usually late in the evening. While this is taking place, children may awaken with itching (or in girls, pain in the genital area). The eggs around the anus are picked up when a child scratches this area and may be returned to the body when he sucks on a finger or puts his hands in his mouth. The eggs can also be transferred to toys or other objects, where they may be picked up by someone else. Pinworm eggs can survive outside a human body for approximately two weeks.

If you notice your child frequently scratching his anal area or if your young girl has pain in the genital area (which may increase with passing urine), check for pinworms. You may be able to spot them if you check your child's anal area with a flashlight a few hours after the child has gone to bed or in the early morning. If you suspect that your child has pinworms but don't see them, contact your doctor, who may ask you to collect a specimen using clear cellophane tape. You can press the sticky side of the tape against your child's anus a few hours after bedtime or in the early morning and apply it to a glass slide the doctor may give you. Your doctor will then examine the slide under a microscope for pinworm eggs to confirm your suspicions.

Pinworms can be treated relatively easily with a single dose of an oral prescription medication called **mebendazole** (Vermox). This is sometimes repeated a week or two later. Your doctor may recommend that the entire family be treated.

Pinworm eggs are so tiny—invisible to the naked eye—and so easily spread that it can be difficult to make your home completely worm free. You can reduce your child's chances of reinfection by taking the following steps:

- Remind him to wash his hands after using the bathroom, or do it for him if necessary, and keep his fingernails short and clean.
- Regularly clean his toys and any surfaces he has touched.

You may also want to wash your child's clothes and bedding or clean his room to prevent reinfection or the spread of pinworms to the rest of the family. But if the worms return even after a thorough cleaning, don't despair. Ask your doctor for another round of pinworm medication (this time treating the entire family if it wasn't done before), keep everyone's hands as clean as possible, and eventually you will be rid of these unwelcome parasites.

pityriasis rosea A common, benign skin eruption that most often occurs between the ages of ten and thirty-five, although it can appear at any age. The cause is thought to be a virus, but this condition is not contagious. The rash tends to occur more often during the colder months. About 20 percent of those with pityriasis rosea may have coldlike symptoms: fatigue, headache, sore throat, and fever.

Most cases begin with the sudden appearance of what is called a **herald patch**, usually on the upper body or the neck. This patch is typically oval, usually one to two inches (2.5 to 5 cm) long, slightly raised, and may be reddish purple in color. More eruptions develop over a period extending from a few days to several weeks. These patches are smaller than the herald patch and are typically located on the upper body, neck, and upper portions of the arms and legs. The patches have a wrinkled, tissuelike scale, and their oval shapes tend to lie parallel to skin creases. This is most noticeable on the back, where the rash will vaguely resemble a Christmas tree—a pattern that is classic for pityriasis rosea.

The rash, which may be accompanied by itching, disappears after a few weeks without any specific treatment. An oral antihistamine such as **diphenhydramine** (Benadryl) may provide some relief if itching is a problem. Moisturizing lotion is sometimes soothing. While the rash is essentially harmless, sometimes the patches may leave behind a darker coloration of the skin. This is called **postinflammatory hyperpigmentation** and is especially prevalent in African-Americans.

placebo A substance that has no biological effect on the body. Placebos are used in research studies to evaluate the effectiveness and side effects of a drug.

plantar Referring to the bottom of the foot.

plasma The fluid portion of human blood.

platelets The tiny, disclike structures in the blood that participate in the clotting process.

plumbism Chronic lead poisoning (see "lead poisoning").

pneumonia Infection of a localized or widespread area in one or both lungs, manifested as fever, fatigue, coughing (mild or frequent and intense), and in severe cases rapid or labored breathing.

pneumothorax The presence of air or gas in the pleural cavity (the space between the lungs and chest wall), which may compress the lungs and cause difficulty breathing.

poison ivy/poison oak/poison sumac The most common causes of allergic contact dermatitis among both children and adults. When the leaves of these plants are broken or crushed, they release an oily substance that can provoke a significant allergic response in many (but not all) people. When this substance penetrates the skin, it stimulates the immune system to respond more

vigorously to it in the future. The person becomes sensitized to the plant so that the next time it touches her skin, an intense, itchy inflammation of the skin (dermatitis) erupts at the point of contact. This rash is an internal response of the allergic individual and is not contagious. (However, if the oil from one of these plants has not been washed from the infected person's skin or clothing, it can be transferred accidentally to someone else by direct contact. This can give the misleading impression that a plant dermatitis is contagious.) Despite their dangerous-sounding names, these plants do not contain any poisons or toxins that directly damage skin.

Reactions to one of these plants will vary from person to person and will depend on the size of the exposed area and the thickness of the skin involved. Thick-skinned areas such as the palms and soles tend to suffer little reaction, while thin-skinned areas such as the forearm and face develop a rash more quickly and severely.

In the sensitized person, a skin rash will break out within a few hours of new contact with the plant. Itching is common and often intense, and blisters may form on the involved areas. There is often an oozing of yellowish liquid, which can become crusted. If the plant comes in contact with eyelids or with male genitalia, it may provoke marked swelling in these areas. Areas exposed to less of the plant allergen may respond several days later, giving the misleading impression that the eruption is spreading. In the absence of complications or continued exposure, the eruption rarely lasts longer than ten days.

Because it takes about ten minutes for the plant allergen to penetrate the skin, rinsing the affected area with water immediately after exposure may prevent initial sensitization or an allergic response. *Don't use soap, which removes protective oils from the skin and may increase the allergen's penetration.*

Once the rash develops, nothing will reduce its duration. However, if the area of skin involved is relatively small, early application of a steroid cream can reduce the severity of the dermatitis. One percent hydrocortisone cream (nonprescription) may be used, or a stronger preparation may be prescribed by a physician. If the rash is widespread, the doctor may prescribe oral steroids. When used as directed for several days,

P

this medication can help calm an intense allergic response.

Cool, moist compresses and calamine lotion can reduce itching and irritation. Oral antihistamines such as **diphenhydramine** (Benadryl) can reduce itching, and their sedative effect may promote sleeping.

polio An acute viral infection of the central nervous system that has serious complications, such as muscle paralysis and the inability to breathe. Polio has been eradicated in the United States through widespread immunizations. (For more detailed information about this disease and the vaccine that prevents it, see "Polio" in "Immunizations—Which Ones, Why, and When?" beginning on page 743.)

polydactyly An abnormality in which one or more extra fingers or toes are present.

polyp A growth arising from a mucous membrane, such as the inner surface of the nose or the lining of the colon (large intestine).

prolapse Displacement (usually downward) of an organ or other body part from its original anatomical position.

proteinuria Protein in the urine.

ptosis Drooping of the upper eyelid.

pubis The lower front portion of the pelvis.

pupil (see illustration on page A4) The opening in the center of the iris of the eye.

purpura A hemorrhage into the skin that looks like a bruise.

purulent Containing or consisting of pus.

pustule A small nodule, cyst, or blister that contains pus.

pyloric stenosis A condition occurring during early infancy in which the muscle surrounding the pylorus, the outlet of the stomach, thickens such that the channel through which food must pass to enter the small intestine becomes extremely narrowed or obstructed. When breast milk or formula enters the stomach but cannot pass any farther, the infant may begin spitting up, but eventually this will become projectile vomiting, in which milk is literally ejected several inches (or even feet) from the baby's mouth. The infant might not appear distressed and may even be eager to feed again after this occurs.

Pyloric stenosis manifests itself between two weeks and three months of age, and it is more frequently seen in firstborn males. If untreated, it will lead to malnourishment and dehydration. The diagnosis is made through a combination of the baby's history, physician's examination, and laboratory and certain imaging tests. (The most commonly used are ultrasound or **barium swallow**, in which the infant swallows a small amount of chalky substance that allows visualization of the stomach on an X-ray.) If pyloric stenosis is diagnosed, the infant will usually require intravenous fluids to restore hydration and electrolytes to normal, after which a relatively straightforward surgical procedure can correct this condition.

Q **quadriceps** The four thigh muscles that meet at the tendon below the kneecap.

quadriplegia Paralysis and impaired sensation of both the arms and legs.

R **rabies** (see "Emergency Care," page 800) A viral illness affecting the central nervous system that is virtually always fatal. Rabies is transmitted to humans through the bite of an infected animal, most commonly wild animals such as bats, foxes, skunks, and raccoons. Transmission by domestic dogs and cats is extremely uncommon, and the disease is not spread by mice, rats, gerbils, or hamsters acquired from pet shops.

rectum The last segment of the large intestine. The rectum carries stool to the outside of the body through an opening called the anus.

reflux A backflow of liquid caused by a valve or sphincter failing to close.

retina (see illustration on page A4) The cellular membrane covering the back inner surface of the eyeball. The retina contains the light-sensing cones and rods that are necessary for vision and connects directly to the brain via the optic nerve.

Reye's syndrome A rare but potentially fatal illness of preschool and school-age children. A number of organs may suffer damage, but the brain and liver are typically the most severely affected. The most worrisome feature of this disease is **edema** (increased fluid) within the brain, which can cause a dangerous increase in pressure within the skull. At least 70 percent of children diagnosed with Reye's syndrome survive, but they may have neurological defects, depending upon the severity of the illness. The likelihood of recovery improves when this disorder is recognized and treated early in its course. Younger children appear to be at greatest risk; very rarely has Reye's syndrome been reported in adults.

Symptoms
This syndrome is usually preceded by a viral infection such as chickenpox or influenza. The exact cause is unknown, but it is believed to be associated with taking aspirin or products containing aspirin during the infection.

The following is a typical scenario of Reye's syndrome:

1. A child has the chickenpox, flu, or other viral illness, during which she receives a product containing aspirin to reduce fever and aches.
2. At first she seems to improve, but five to seven days after the beginning of the illness, she begins to vomit repeatedly.
3. After the vomiting ceases, she becomes listless, inattentive, irritable, and delirious.
4. As the disease progresses, the child may become confused, and within a few hours seizures and a deep coma may develop.

Treatment
It is important that you seek medical attention immediately if your child displays the above symptoms, especially listlessness or confusion that follows vomiting. If Reye's syndrome is suspected, blood tests and a spinal tap will usually be necessary to make the correct diagnosis. Treatment is supportive and requires admission to a hospital equipped to deal with life-threatening situations involving increased pressure within the skull and abnormalities of liver function. (This may be a regional medical center or children's hospital rather than a community hospital.)

Prevention
No one understands why Reye's syndrome affects some children and not others. Over the past several years, physicians and other health resources have warned parents not to give aspirin to their children during viral infections or, for that matter, most other acute conditions, and this has decreased the number of reported cases of this disease. *If your child develops a fever and/or aches during an illness, you should use acetaminophen or ibuprofen instead of aspirin to relieve it.* Check the label of any product you give your child during an acute illness to be sure that it does not contain aspirin. The label of aspirin-containing products should include a specific warning about Reye's syndrome.

rheumatic fever A serious but uncommon disease in which an infection involving bacteria known as Group A beta-hemolytic streptococcus provokes an exaggerated response by the immune system, which in turn attacks the heart, joints, and other tissues.

Rheumatic fever is more common in winter and spring. In general, children between the ages of six and fifteen are most susceptible to it. This disease has become extremely uncommon in North America over the past several decades, occurring in less than one in one hundred thousand people every year, probably because fewer streptococcal infections go untreated. The disease is still common, however, in developing countries.

Rheumatic fever involves many systems and tissues, and distinguishing it from other conditions can be difficult. The American Heart Association has developed criteria that help determine if an illness is in fact rheumatic fever. Usually finding two of the following symptoms (or one, along

R

with other evidence) is necessary to make this diagnosis:

- *Heart disease*. Rheumatic heart disease, the most serious component of rheumatic fever, occurs in one-half to two-thirds of all cases. The most significant problem is damage to one or more heart valves, although the heart muscle is frequently affected (**myocarditis**), as is the fibrous covering of the heart (**pericarditis**).
- *Arthritis*. Pain, swelling, redness, and tenderness occur in multiple joints, either simultaneously or in a migratory fashion (literally appearing to move around to different parts of the body). Arthritis results in limitation of motion of joints and the inability to support weight.
- *Rash*. Called **erythema marginatum**, this characteristic rash has an elevated, reddened margin. It typically appears only in severe cases of rheumatic fever.
- *Sydenham's chorea*. This neurological disturbance (once called **St. Vitus' dance**) is characterized by involuntary facial grimacing, clumsiness, abnormal movements of the extremities, and irritability.
- *Lumps under the skin*. These nodules, which are not tender to the touch, occur on the arms, legs, or skull, usually only in severe cases.

Other findings that support the diagnosis of rheumatic fever include a persistent fever above 101.4°F (38.6°C), joint pain without signs of inflammation or swelling, an abnormal electrocardiogram, or the history of a previous episode of rheumatic fever. In about 80 percent of cases, there will be clinical or lab evidence of a recent streptococcal infection.

All the signs of rheumatic fever, including arthritis, chorea, and skin rash, will eventually disappear, but effects of damage to one or more heart valves may last a lifetime. Severely affected valves, which do not close properly during the heart's normal cycle of contracting and then refilling with blood, may cause congestive heart failure, a condition in which a child's heart cannot keep up with the demands of exertion or even quiet activities. In such cases, valve replacement may be necessary.

Children who develop rheumatic fever must be treated with antibiotics to prevent any future streptococcal infection and regular doses of aspirin for two to six weeks to reduce arthritis and fever. This is one of the few instances where aspirin is used to treat a child with an acute illness involving fever. Rarely, cortisone is used in cases with severe heart involvement. Additional medications will be required to control heart failure if it occurs.

rheumatoid arthritis, juvenile See "Musculoskeletal Problems in Children," page 761.

Rh factor An antigen (a substance that can produce an immune response) present on the surface of red blood cells in some individuals. When present, the person is said to be Rh-positive. Rh status is routinely determined when blood is donated and will be appropriately matched (along with blood type) to that of the recipient. In the past, differences in Rh status between an Rh-negative mother and her Rh-positive baby led to significant jaundice in some newborns (see "bilirubin").

rhinitis Inflammation or swelling of the mucous membranes of the nose.

rhinorrhea A runny nose.

ringworm A common and easily treated skin infection caused by a fungus called a **dermatophyte** (literally, "skin plant"), which invades only the outermost layer of skin. This condition is not caused by worms.

Ringworm is mildly contagious through direct contact. Poor hygiene increases the likelihood of infection, but anyone who comes in contact with the fungus can become infected. House pets such as cats and dogs can pass dermatophytes to children via direct contact with skin.

Ringworm usually begins as one or more small, round, somewhat itchy, scaly, reddish spots that gradually increase in size. As each spot grows, its center usually begins to clear while the outer rim becomes raised. (The circular shape of the eruption and the wormlike appearance of the outer rim are the inspiration for its name.)

R

Your child's doctor can often diagnose ring-worm simply by its appearance. He may scan the skin with an ultraviolet light, since areas infected by some dermatophytes may glow slightly, or she may gently take scrapings from the affected skin and look for signs of the fungus under a microscope.

Once the diagnosis is made, ringworm can usually be treated with over-the-counter or pre-scription antifungal creams. Depending upon the type used, the cream should be applied for two to three weeks to be effective. In severe cases, oral medications may be prescribed. Skin-to-skin contact with infected individuals or pets should be minimized to avoid spreading the infection.

Rocky Mountain spotted fever A potentially fatal tick-borne infectious disease that is rarely found in the Rockies. Rather, it is prevalent in the tick-infested woods in the mid-Atlantic and southern states. It is characterized by a rash, low-grade fever, headache, muscle aches, nausea, and vomiting beginning approximately seven days following a tick bite.

roseola A viral illness most commonly seen in children younger than two years of age. It is characterized by an average of three to five days of high fever—ranging from 103°F to 105°F (39.4°C to 40.6°C) and occasionally as high as 106°F (41.1°C)—accompanied by very few spe-cific symptoms. A mild runny nose, an occasional cough, a little drowsiness, and at times irritability may be noted, but overall the child with roseola does not appear as ill as the temperature might lead you to expect. In fact, a child may seem to be in surprisingly good spirits. After the temperature abruptly returns to normal, a rash appears. Fine red spots or bumps first appear on the upper body and then spread to the upper arms and neck, with little involvement of the face and legs. The rash fades quickly.

If your child experiences a high fever for more than twenty-four hours, check with his physician, who may want to evaluate him. Typically there will be no findings from examination or labora-tory tests (such as a blood count or urinalysis) to suggest a specific treatable cause of the fever. Supportive measures, including acetaminophen (Tylenol and other brands) to reduce fever, extra fluids, and light clothing, are the only necessary treatment. Since roseola is caused by a virus, an-tibiotics will not affect its course. The illness is contagious until the fever has disappeared.

Roseola is not considered dangerous, although the high fevers it often generates can be worri-some to parents. Remember that with very rare exception the main purpose of cooling measures is to keep the child comfortable. If he is responsive and appears relatively content, the fever can be left to run its course.

In some children with roseola, a rapid upswing of temperature may provoke a more serious ill-ness. Aggressive cooling measures for a child who already has a high fever will do little to prevent febrile seizures. (For more information about fe-ver and febrile seizures, see the Special Concerns section "When Your Child Has a Fever," page 241, and "seizures.")

rubella (German measles or three-day measles) A mild viral illness that lasts three to four days and is characterized by a widespread rash of pink-red spots that begin on the face and move rapidly down the body. Mild fever, head-ache, stuffy nose, and enlargement of lymph nodes both behind the ears and at the back of the neck and skull are common features. Young women with rubella often have aching joints. The infection normally resolves uneventfully, but if a woman has rubella in early pregnancy, her baby may develop significant congenital abnormalities (see chapter 1, page 22).

During the last widespread outbreak in the United States, which occurred in 1963–1964, 12 million people developed rubella. Among these were thousands of pregnant women, and as a result, eleven thousand fetuses died and twenty thousand babies were born with signifi-cant rubella-related defects. Widespread use of rubella vaccine, first licensed in 1969, has vir-tually eliminated both the disease and its birth defects in the United States. (Rubella is the *R* in the MMR vaccine, typically given between twelve and fifteen months of age and again between four and six years.) However, rubella remains com-mon in many parts of the world, and routine im-munization of infants and children is still very important. (For more detailed information about this disease and the vaccine that prevents it, see "Measles, Mumps, and Rubella" in "Immunizations—Which Ones, Why, and When?" beginning on page 745.)

S scabies Scabies has been described by physicians for more than two thousand years and was the first infection in humans for which a responsible organism was specifically identified. The cause of scabies is a tiny, eight-legged arthropod called a mite, which carries out its life cycle on and within human skin. Female mites are twice the size of males but are only about three-tenths of a millimeter long and barely visible to the naked eye. They cannot hop or fly, and thus transmission from one person to another nearly always involves skin-to-skin contact. The female mite burrows below the skin in a meandering pattern, laying a few eggs each day. After two to four weeks, she dies. Her eggs hatch, and new mite larvae grow, molt, and eventually emerge on the skin surface. The itching and rash of scabies don't begin until ten to thirty days after the first mites crawl under the skin, since itching is actually an allergic reaction to the mites, their eggs, and their waste products.

Scabies infections are more common in crowded living conditions where there is greater opportunity for skin-to-skin transmission. They tend to be worse among those who cannot bathe very often, in which case hundreds or even thousands of mites may infest one individual. (Normally, fewer than fifteen active mites are enough to cause symptoms.)

Symptoms

If your child or anyone in your family experiences intense itching, especially at night, you should suspect scabies. In older children, numerous itchy, fluid-filled bumps may be visible next to a reddish burrow track on the hands, feet, face, elbows, waist, wrists, or genitalia. In younger children, the bumps appear more often on the upper half of the body.

Unfortunately, burrow tracks aren't always evident without a close look at certain areas such as the spaces between the fingers or the toes. The severe itching provokes equally intense scratching, which may damage skin. The skin in turn may become infected by bacteria. As a result, scabies can look like nearly any other skin disease, a problem that could delay the correct diagnosis.

Treatment

If your child's doctor suspects scabies, he or she will examine the rash and may gently scrape the skin of the affected area to check it for mites or eggs. If mites are found or if the rash is highly suspicious even when mites are not visible, one of the antiscabies medications (usually **permethrin** or **lindane**) will be prescribed. The medication is usually a lotion. It must be applied to the entire body, left on for a number of hours, and then rinsed off. Your child should shower and wash his body and hair completely when rinsing. Since scabies is so contagious, it is likely that your doctor will choose to treat everyone in your household so your child does not become reinfected.

It is important to follow your doctor's directions precisely. Concerns have been raised about the possibility that lindane might cause seizures in children, and thus this medication should be avoided in children with preexistent epilepsy. It is also not recommended for use in infants and toddlers nor in pregnant women or nursing mothers. In addition to the antiscabies medication, your doctor may prescribe anti-itch medication (such as cortisone cream or calamine lotion). Antibiotics may be needed if any areas of skin have become infected with bacteria.

Once the first round of medication is applied, your child is no longer contagious. However, the rash will continue to be visible and itchy for up to four weeks. *You should not repeatedly treat your child with antiscabies medication to stop the itching.* If the itching does not go away after a month, it is possible that your child has become reinfected, but you should not use another round of medication until specifically told to do so by your child's doctor.

Since scabies is transferred through close contact, it is important to treat anyone who has had repeated direct contact with your child. In a few cases, mites are spread indirectly via clothing and linens, so wash these items in hot water after everyone has received treatment.

scarlet fever A striking red rash caused by a toxin produced by some strains of streptococci. Children who are sensitive to the toxin will develop scarlet fever during a streptococcal throat infection (strep throat). Scarlet fever is more common in children between the ages of three and twelve. Along with sore throat, the child may have headache, nausea, and high fever. Within forty-eight hours, a fine red rash appears on the neck and face, then spreads to the chest and abdomen. The rash often feels like coarse sandpaper and begins to fade after a few days, but it often peels like a sunburn. Scarlet fever is treated with supportive measures (rest, liquids, acetaminophen) and antibiotics if streptococcal infection is confirmed, usually by checking a throat swab for this organism. (See "sore throat," page 720.)

schizophrenia A hereditary mental disorder characterized by a significant disturbance in thought processes. Symptoms may include random and illogical speech, hallucinations (usually auditory), delusions, and withdrawal into internal fantasy. Schizophrenia is rare before the age of fifteen but affects one percent of adults. It is usually first manifested during the late teens and early twenties in males, and later in life (midtwenties to early thirties) in females. Treatment includes the long-term use of medications that can significantly help normalize thought patterns, and efforts to teach and maintain social and learning skills.

sclera (see illustration on page A4) The white covering of the eyeball.

scrotum The skin-covered sac that contains the testes.

sebaceous cyst A saclike nodule that arises from a sebaceous gland.

sebaceous glands Glands in the skin that release sebum (an oily substance) through the hair follicles.

seborrhea Excessive production of sebum, usually resulting in an oily or scaly face and scalp.

seizures If your infant or child is having a seizure now, see "Emergency Care," page 833.

A **seizure** is a sudden abnormal surge of electrical activity in the brain, with manifestations that may range from subtle lapses in attention to terrifying convulsions. The word *seizure* is well chosen; during an episode, it seems as if the affected child's thoughts and activity have been abruptly seized or taken over by a hostile force.

Each of us has a seizure threshold. Given the right (or wrong) set of circumstances—an infection or tumor involving the brain, a low level of sodium in the bloodstream, or a sudden withdrawal from certain types of medications—anyone can have a seizure. But some people, particularly in childhood, are much more vulnerable to this disturbance.

A seizure is a specific event. When seizures occur more than once without an immediate precipitating cause (such as a fever or injury), the condition is called **epilepsy**. The term *epilepsy* (derived from a Greek word meaning "seizure") is synonymous with the term **seizure disorder**. Epilepsy is not truly a disease but rather a complex of symptoms arising from disordered brain function, which itself may have a variety of pathological causes. In about 60 percent of diagnosed epileptics, no specific cause for the seizures is ever found, and the condition is referred to as **idiopathic epilepsy**. (*Idiopathic* is a medical term used when the cause of a condition is unknown.)

There are different kinds of seizures, each with characteristic behavioral patterns and usually specific brain-wave abnormalities that accompany it. It will be important for your child's doctor to classify the seizures accurately because the type will often dictate which treatment approach (usually one of the antiepileptic or anticonvulsant medications) is appropriate to control the problem. Details of a given episode can help distinguish a true seizure from events and behaviors that are not seizures.

In the more common **generalized seizures** (sometimes identified by the older term **grand mal**), there is an abrupt loss of consciousness. The individual falls to the floor with both stiffness and jerky movements. Uncontrolled jaw movements may cause injury to the tongue. Loss of control of the autonomic nervous system may cause the seizure victim to urinate or have a bowel movement.

This type of seizure may be preceded by an **aura**, an odd sensation such as tingling or a strange aroma that no one else can smell, which the child may come to recognize before subsequent episodes. After the seizure, there is nearly always a prolonged state, referred to as the **postictal phase**, during which the child sleeps, is very sluggish, or has transient weakness of an arm or leg.

A generalized seizure is without a doubt extremely dramatic. Children who see one of their classmates suddenly writhing on the floor may literally panic. Parents who first observe their child in the throes of a full-blown convulsion are usually horrified and may be convinced that he is going to die before their eyes. But the seizure itself is not dangerous unless it involves situations such as these:

- Food or vomited material is aspirated into the airway during the episode.
- It occurs in a situation where sudden loss of consciousness would be dangerous, such as while swimming or driving a car.
- It is extremely prolonged (more than thirty minutes).

If a single seizure (or multiple seizures without full recovery) lasts more than thirty minutes, a child is said to be in **status epilepticus**. This frightening situation occurs more commonly in children younger than five years of age. If not brought under control, status epilepticus can have serious consequences (including brain damage or even death); emergency medical assessment and treatment are very important.

Absence seizures (also called **petit mal**) are momentary lapses of awareness with no recollection of the event after it happens. The child may stop and stare for a few seconds. In some cases there may be brief jerks or fluttering of the eyelids. Absence seizures may occur frequently and be so brief that they escape detection. All children occasionally stare or daydream, but they can be aroused or spoken to during the lapse. In a true absence seizure, the child will be out of contact and cannot recall the event after it ends.

Myoclonic seizures are jerking or rhythmic muscle contractions involving a few (or many) muscle groups and are sometimes accompanied by a fall. **Complex partial seizures** (previously known as **psychomotor** or **temporal lobe seizures**) begin with an aura that may involve a vague sensation of fear, an odd and usually unpleasant taste or smell, or hallucinations. Then comes the seizure, which may involve a minute or more of blank staring, chewing, or swallowing movements, or perhaps purposeless activity, followed by a period of confusion.

In **akinetic seizures** (also called **drop attacks**), the child falls but does not shake or become stiff. Physical injuries (such as cuts on the head or face) occur more frequently as a direct consequence of this type of seizure than from any other.

Febrile seizures

Febrile seizures are a type of generalized seizure precipitated by a fever. Because there is a specific reason for febrile seizures, they are not considered a form of epilepsy. They are estimated to occur in 2 to 5 percent of children between the ages of four months and five years. The majority take place between six months and three years of age, with a peak incidence between fourteen and eighteen months. They become less common after age three and are very unusual after age five.

The setting for a febrile seizure is most commonly an upper-respiratory infection, although other situations that induce a fever may provoke it as well. The seizures often begin early in an illness, usually during the rapid upswing of a fever (which doctors refer to as a temperature spike). In fact, an infant or child whom you find hot and cranky with a temperature of 104°F (40°C) *is not likely to have a seizure in the immediate future, since he has already arrived at the high temperature without incident.*

Febrile convulsions normally last less than five minutes (which may seem like an eternity), although rarely they continue as long as fifteen minutes. During one of these episodes, typically a child's eyes will roll backward, then he will stiffen and rhythmically shake both arms and both legs.

S

After the seizure subsides, he will still have a fever, but other than experiencing a little sleepiness, he should feel and act relatively normal.

If your child experiences febrile convulsions, first and foremost you should try to stay calm and let the seizure run its course. Panicky efforts to stop the seizure or otherwise help your child may do more harm than good.

After the seizure is over and while your child is resting, take his temperature rectally, then call your doctor and describe what happened. If this is your child's first seizure, he should be evaluated in the office or the emergency room. Further tests may be necessary, depending upon his age, his appearance when examined, and other features of his illness. It will be very important to determine whether this episode was a febrile seizure or a manifestation of a more significant problem. In infants and children under the age of two, there may be particular concern about the possibility of meningitis.

If your child has had a febrile convulsion, he has a 20 to 40 percent chance of having at least one similar episode before the age of five. But only 2 to 4 percent of children who have a febrile convulsion will continue to have seizures that are not related to fevers during late childhood or adulthood. Children who are at risk for this long-term seizure problem are those whose febrile convulsion was more complex in some way—for example, lasting more than fifteen minutes, involving only one side of the body, or occurring more than once in a day—or those for whom there is a family history of seizures.

It is important to understand that febrile seizures are not actually harmful to a child, even though they can be very upsetting to the parents. Repeated episodes do not damage the brain or cause behavior or learning problems later in life, and parents need not live in terror every time their child has a fever. For this reason, children with febrile seizures are typically not given ongoing anticonvulsant medications to reduce the likelihood of recurrences. However, after the first occurrence and evaluation, it is a good idea to notify the doctor whenever one takes place. During an illness in which fever is present (or might occur), it is reasonable to give acetaminophen every four to six hours or ibuprofen every six to eight hours to a child who has had a febrile seizure in the past, although this may or may not be a successful measure in preventing one of these episodes.

Four important and reassuring facts about seizures

- A seizure is a complex neurological symptom, not a disease in and of itself. It is also *not an indication of an emotional or spiritual disturbance.* If your child witnesses someone else having a seizure, he may be frightened, especially if he knows the person. Explain to him what has happened and reassure him that he does not need to be afraid of that individual.

- With the rare exception of an extremely prolonged (more than thirty minutes), uncontrolled seizure, these episodes do not cause brain damage or mental retardation. While it is true that some children who are mentally retarded or who have brain abnormalities may have convulsions, an underlying condition is likely to be the cause of both the retardation and the seizures.

- The vast majority of children with a history of convulsions have normal intelligence and should not be put in special-education classes merely because they have seizures. Most epileptic children will be completely normal except for a few minutes (if that much) during a given year.

- Most people who have seizures during childhood will not continue to have them for the rest of their lives.

Diagnosis and treatment

If your baby or child appears to have had a seizure, it will be important for the physician to know as accurately as possible what actually took place, determine whether any underlying problem(s) provoked the episode, and decide whether further studies should be done and/or medications given. Some important elements of the medical evaluation will include the following:

- *The history.* What actually happened? Did the episode begin gradually or suddenly? Was the whole body or only a limited area (such as a twitching arm or leg) involved? How long did it last? (Keep track of the time because seizures always seem to last longer than their true duration.) Did the child lose consciousness? If so, how quickly did he return to normal? If he is old enough to describe what happened, did he notice anything before the episode? Did he lose control of urinary or bowel functions? Did he bite his tongue or sustain any other injury? Was he ill at the time, or was there any injury (such as a blow to the head) prior to the episode? It may be difficult to keep track of such details during an event as terrifying as a seizure, but all of this information is extremely important for the physician who is evaluating the problem. It will be necessary to decide whether a seizure has actually taken place. (See "Special note: Was that a seizure?" at the end of this section.)

- *Physical examination*. This may not be terribly revealing if the episode in question happened last week. But immediately after a lapse in consciousness or a febrile convulsion in an infant, a physical exam might offer important clues to the diagnosis.
- *Laboratory tests*. The physician may request that certain blood tests be performed to rule out a metabolic cause for the seizure or to help evaluate any infection that might be in progress.
- *A lumbar puncture (spinal tap)*. This may be recommended if there is any question that a seizure might involve an infection in the central nervous system, most commonly meningitis. It is more likely to be requested in infants and children under two years of age who have had their first febrile seizure, especially when they are younger than three months of age. In this age-group, a fever and a seizure may be the only indications that meningitis is present. While it might sound frightening and dangerous, a lumbar puncture is not a highly risky procedure, even in an infant.
- *An electroencephalogram (EEG)*. This study of electrical activity in the brain is a very helpful tool in the investigation of a seizure disorder. It can be particularly useful in distinguishing true convulsions from certain behavioral or physical abnormalities (such as those mentioned on page 717 in "Special note: Was that a seizure?"). Unfortunately, at times the EEG

can appear normal in a child who in fact has a seizure disorder. The most important use of the EEG, however, is to identify characteristic brain-wave patterns that, when correlated with the child's symptoms during a seizure, allow the physician to classify the seizure disorder. This helps determine which medication(s) will be most effective in controlling the seizures. An EEG involves attaching electrodes to the scalp but does not deliver any electrical shock and is not painful. In some cases the child may be sedated for the procedure, while in others he will be studied after he has been kept awake all night (a tactic that increases the odds of seeing abnormal activity).

- *CT, MRI, or other imaging of the brain*. This may be needed if there is a history or evidence of trauma to the head or any concern about other physical abnormalities within the brain that might be causing seizures.

Not all of the tests just described will necessarily be done as part of an evaluation of possible seizure activity. After a classic febrile seizure, for example, a child may simply be observed for a while in the doctor's office or emergency room and then sent home. Depending upon the entire picture, however, some or all of these studies may need to be done.

If the diagnosis of a particular type of recurrent seizure disorder is confirmed, it is likely that the physician will recommend that one or more anticonvulsant medications be given over a period of time. These drugs will decrease the likelihood of further seizures or eliminate them altogether, hopefully without interfering with normal activities or school performance. Febrile convulsions are an exception to this approach and normally are not treated with ongoing preventive medication.

Details regarding specific drugs and their potential side effects should be carefully reviewed with the prescribing physician. *It is very important to take the medications consistently as they have been prescribed.* Some children may require periodic blood tests to confirm that drug levels are appropriate and that certain adverse effects are not taking place. All these measures may seem burdensome for children and parents alike, but haphazard use of these medications may allow more seizures to occur or increase the risk of side effects. If your child is taking one or more anticonvulsant medications that you feel are adversely affecting his life (such as causing excessive drowsiness or poor school performance), you should not change the dose or discontinue any drug without discussing the problem with his physician.

Occasionally seizures that are disruptive and not adequately controlled with medication may be improved with surgery. Extensive evaluation and highly technical procedures are required for this type of treatment, which typically is carried out by a team of specialists at a regional children's hospital.

Epilepsy and lifestyle

Most children with epilepsy can lead normal lives and participate in most activities, including sports. Some physicians prefer to exclude children with convulsive disorders from collision sports such as football and hockey. However, unless seizures have resulted from head trauma or tended to occur following blows to the head, it is likely that most children can compete while wearing protective headgear. (Boxing is not recommended as an athletic activity for *any* child because of its potential for causing damage to the brain. It is definitely not appropriate for a child with a seizure disorder.)

Children with well-controlled seizures may swim, but when doing so, they should utilize a buddy system with someone else in the pool. High diving, rock climbing or tree climbing, and scuba diving are activities that should be off-limits to a person with a history of seizures.

Some convulsions can be provoked by flickering light patterns, and children with this tendency may experience a flare-up of seizures if they spend long periods of time playing video games. Loss of sleep, erratic eating habits, and alcohol use—behaviors that sometimes occur during adolescence—are also risky for the person with epilepsy and should definitely be avoided.

Of great concern for the teenager with a history of seizures is whether driving will be allowed. Laws vary from state to state, but most require evidence of an extended seizure-free period (such as two years) before a learner's permit or driver's license will be granted. Medications that are being taken to prevent seizures should not impair the teenager's ability to operate a car safely. It is important for parents to follow these guidelines explicitly. Failing to report an adolescent's recent seizure activity because of fear of losing driving privileges could be a major, if not fatal, mistake. These regulations exist for your child's protection as well as for the safety of everyone else on the road.

Special note: Was that a seizure?

Many unusual or even frightening behaviors in infants or children may appear to be seizures but are in fact other types of episodes. Some of the more common of these include:

- *A fainting episode.* Usually a child or adolescent who is about to faint feels dizzy, weak, or light-headed beforehand. Several circumstances could precede the episode: a hot and/or crowded environment, lack of fresh air, hunger, an acute illness, an emotional incident, or a medical procedure such as having blood drawn. Sweating, paleness, and a slow heartbeat are usually present also. Most important, the episode resolves quickly when the individual lies down, elevates the feet, and breathes fresh air. On the other hand, after a generalized seizure there is a prolonged time during which the individual is first unconscious and then dazed and confused.

- *Shuddering or shivering episodes in infants.* These may occur frequently but without any apparent change in consciousness. Often there is a history of tremors among family members.

- *Breath-holding spells.* These incidents are frightening but harmless and are invariably brought on by physical or emotional incidents that provoke fear, anger, or frustration. They occur most commonly in children six months to three years of age. During the spell, the child may stiffen, make jerking movements of the arms and legs that resemble a brief seizure, and appear pale or blue in the face. Finally he will take a breath and very quickly regain color and responsiveness, after which there may be a brief period of inactivity or even sleep. When the episode

S

is over, he will be fully awake and aware, not confused or unresponsive as seen after a seizure (see "breath-holding spells").

- *Night terrors.* During the early hours of sleep, a child may display intense crying, thrashing, sweating, and no apparent recognition of his parents. After several minutes, he falls back to sleep and has no memory of the episode the following morning (see chapter 9, page 297).
- *Tics or Tourette syndrome.* These are syndromes of involuntary muscle jerks, grunts, or vocalizations, which may worsen under stress. They are notable for being stereotyped—that is, they are the same over and over (see "tics" and "Tourette syndrome").
- *Staring episodes.* A parent or teacher may notice that a child is so preoccupied that he seems temporarily unresponsive as he stares into space. Distinguishing this from a petit mal seizure may be difficult.

When in doubt about any of these behaviors or any other situation in which an infant or child shows sudden unusual body movements or changes in consciousness, a medical evaluation is in order. Carefully describing the event to the physician is the first and in many ways the most important step in arriving at a diagnosis.

sepsis A life-threatening condition involving the presence of large numbers of microorganisms (usually bacteria) in the bloodstream.

septum A thin dividing wall within or between parts of the body.

serum The liquid portion of blood that does not contain blood cells or the protein fibrinogen, which is involved in clotting.

sickle cell disease A worldwide health problem that primarily affects people of African descent but also occurs in people of Mediterranean, Asian, and Central and South American heritage. About one in five hundred black children is affected, and one in twelve carry the gene for this disease. Carriers are said to have **sickle cell trait** and may at times have mild symptoms of the disease.

The underlying problem in sickle cell disease is a slight but critical change in **hemoglobin**, the oxygen-carrying protein within red blood cells. Under certain conditions, "sickle" hemoglobin aggregates into elongated crystals that distort the shape of red cells. These crescent- or sickle-shaped cells do not survive as long as normal, round red cells do, leading to chronic anemia. This aspect of the disease led to its being called **sickle cell anemia** in the past, but this term does not adequately convey the wide variety of medical problems that can result from this condition. These irregular cells can also obstruct small blood vessels, causing repeated episodes of severe pain, especially in the abdomen, bones, and joints. Damage or functional problems involving bone, spleen, kidneys, lungs, or other organs may occur. In addition, children with sickle cell disease are at significant risk of serious infections from certain types of bacteria.

Sickle cell disease is normally not manifested at birth, and the first symptoms typically do not appear until the latter part of the first year of life. However, infants with this problem can be identified by blood screening after birth. Appropriate immunizations and daily preventive doses of penicillin during the first five years of life can help prevent a variety of infections.

While these basic measures substantially reduce the risk of serious disease and mortality during childhood, there is no specific treatment that will normalize the sickle hemoglobin. Therefore, a thorough understanding of this disorder by parents and other family members, and ongoing comprehensive medical care—including treatment of pain crises, anemia, infections, and other complications—will be necessary to protect the life and health of a child born with sickle cell disease.

sinusitis Inflammation of one or more of the air-filled cavities within the head, which is sometimes a complication of an upper-respiratory infection or allergic rhinitis (see "colds" and "allergies in children"). Any of several types of bacteria may be involved in this process, and these organisms may be difficult to eradicate if there is poor drainage from the affected area(s).

The most common symptom of sinusitis is persistent nasal drainage or postnasal drip for more than ten days. The drainage is often discolored and may be accompanied by low-grade temperature, coughing, and/or bad breath. Specific sinuses sometimes generate localized symptoms. The **ethmoidal sinuses**—the only sinus cavities developed at birth—may produce pain behind one or both eyes if infected. Infected **maxillary sinuses**, located between the eyes and the upper teeth, produce facial pain or aching in the upper molar teeth. Maxillary sinusitis usually does not occur before the first birthday. **Frontal sinusitis**, which is rare before the age of ten, typically produces pain above one or both eyebrows.

Treatment of sinusitis usually requires at least ten to fourteen days of oral antibiotics. Additional measures such as decongestants, antihistamines, and/or prescription nasal sprays containing cortisone may be recommended by the physician, depending on the specific conditions of the infection. In rare cases, severe sinusitis or complications such as **periorbital cellulitis** (an infection of the soft tissue surrounding the eye) require hospitalization for intravenous antibiotics and close observation.

Chronic or recurrent sinusitis is caused or aggravated by a variety of factors, including allergies, anatomical abnormalities, and immunity disorders. Evaluation by an allergist or ENT (ear, nose, and throat) specialist will be recommended in some cases.

sitz bath A bath taken to relieve rectal or vaginal discomfort; only the lower body is immersed.

smallpox An acute, highly contagious viral illness that was characterized by an extensive eruption of tiny nodules that subsequently formed pus-filled blisters. Victims were often left with hundreds of pitted scars or pockmarks. Because of worldwide vaccination efforts, this disease has been completely eradicated. The last case in the United States occurred in 1949, and vaccination against this disease ended in 1972. However, because of concerns that smallpox might be utilized as a biological weapon, old vaccine has been stockpiled and continues to be available (and new vaccines are being developed) in the event of a terrorist incident involving this organism.[16]

snoring A harsh noise produced by vibration of the soft palate and uvula of a sleeping child who is breathing predominantly through the mouth. Not all noisy breathing is snoring. Nasal congestion and wheezing, for example, also generate sounds during sleep, but these are often heard during waking hours as well.

Snoring occurs for a number of reasons, most of which are not causes for concern. One of the most common causes is relaxation of the muscles and tissues in the back of the mouth, which allows them to vibrate while the child is inhaling or exhaling. Since the position of the head affects the vibration of these structures, simply moving the child can reduce or eliminate the snoring. This type of snoring can occur whether a child is breathing through the mouth or the nose.

Children with nasal congestion, whether caused by upper-respiratory infection or allergy, will breathe through the mouth at night and thus be more likely to snore. Over-the-counter decongestants and antihistamines are often not effective in children, but if one of these preparations helps a child breathe more easily through the nose, a bedtime dose could help alleviate the snoring. Unfortunately, decongestants (such as **phenylephrine** or **pseudoephedrine**) sometimes have a stimulant effect and actually interfere with sleep. While antihistamines (such as **diphenhydramine** or **chlorpheniramine**) usually make children drowsy, occasionally these drugs cause an increase in activity. You may want to give a test dose during the day to see how your child responds.

If a child's tonsils are unusually large (hypertrophied), they may actually touch each other in the back of the mouth. This can cause not only loud snoring during sleep but also short periods of **apnea**, or cessation of breathing, lasting for several seconds. If your child has a pattern of continuous loud snoring and episodes of apnea, have her checked by your primary-care physician or an ENT (ear, nose, and throat) specialist. Tonsils or adenoids large enough to cause snoring and obstruct breathing at night can lead to more serious problems involving the heart and lungs. Tonsillectomy or adenoidectomy may be necessary to correct this condition.

S

sore throat In most cases a sore throat results from inflammation of the **oropharynx**—the area at the back of your child's mouth that is directly visible when the doctor examines it with a light and tongue depressor. Inflammation of this area is called **pharyngitis**, and if the tonsils are involved, the illness is called **tonsillitis**. Most acute sore throats are caused by viruses and are often associated with postnasal drainage from colds. A small percentage (about 10 percent) of all sore throats are caused by the bacteria known as group A beta-hemolytic streptococci. These infections are commonly called **strep throats**. Chronic throat pain may also be caused by allergy.

Viral sore throat

Most acute sore throats are caused by viruses, usually in the setting of a cold. Throat discomfort tends to be scratchy or raw rather than severely painful and is but one of several complaints, including runny nose, cough, aches, and fever. These symptoms will normally resolve on their own—without antibiotic treatment—in three to five days, although occasionally they may last as long as one to two weeks. If you are concerned about the severity or duration of your child's sore throat, don't hesitate to seek advice from her physician.

Some special forms of viral sore throat include:

- **Acute infectious mononucleosis**. This illness is seen primarily among teenagers and is often more prolonged and severe than the sore throat associated with a cold. The tonsils are inflamed, with swelling, redness, and white patches called **exudate**; lymph nodes (or "glands") in the neck are usually swollen and tender as well (see "mononucleosis").
- Coxsackie virus can cause **herpangina**, an illness in which painful blisters form in the throat and on the palate. This virus also causes **hand, foot, and mouth disease** (see page 677), in which small blisters appear in the mouth and on the tongue as well as on the palms and soles. Both of these infections, while quite uncomfortable, resolve without treatment.
- Herpes simplex, the virus that causes **cold sores** (fever blisters) on the lips, may erupt in the mouth or throat with a cluster of painful sores that resemble tiny blisters. These occur in approximately one percent of children having their first encounter with the herpes virus and will disappear within a week without specific treatment. The herpes virus is known for causing recurrent eruptions, but these will occur only in the form of the more familiar cold sores on the lips.

Strep throat

Streptococcal sore throats are usually more severe and focused. Children have more difficulty swallowing, and there is an absence of typical cold symptoms (such as runny nose, cough, or low-grade fever). A sudden onset with high fever and swollen neck glands is not unusual. The tonsils may be inflamed, with swelling, redness, and white patches of pus (called **exudate**). Occasionally abdominal pain, vomiting, rash, and headache are also present. Strep throat is unusual in children younger than three years of age. In this age-group, streptococcus more commonly causes chronic nasal infections with thick, discolored drainage.

When a child or adolescent develops an uncomfortable sore throat, it is important to determine whether or not streptococcus is the cause, especially when fever is present. This may be done in the doctor's office or another laboratory by gently swabbing the throat with a cotton swab and performing a rapid strep test, throat culture, or both. If strep is identified, your child's doctor will prescribe an appropriate antibiotic. In most cases this will need to be continued for ten days, although some newer antibiotics require shorter courses.

Whatever medication is prescribed, *follow the directions and give your child the entire course of medication, which may extend for a few days after she feels well*. Failure to do so might result in a recurrence of illness. Proper treatment tends to shorten the course of the illness and prevents more serious complications. It may also reduce the spread of streptococcal infection to other people and allow an earlier return to school or day care. Most physicians feel that after twenty-four hours of antibiotic therapy, a child will no longer be contagious.

Occasionally streptococcal infections are accompanied by a sandpaper-textured rash. This

S

syndrome, known as **scarlet fever**, is treated in the same manner as the more common strep throat and will be equally responsive to antibiotics (see "scarlet fever").

Allergen-induced sore throat

Many children develop seasonal allergic complaints, especially in the spring or fall. Swollen nasal passages often lead to frequent mouth breathing. When accompanied by postnasal drip, this results in a sore throat, especially upon awakening. The child with this type of sore throat is not acutely ill and will lack fever and swollen lymph nodes in the neck. Specific treatment options can be reviewed with your child's physician (see "allergies in children").

Less common causes of sore throat

CANKER SORES (aphthous ulcers) When one or more of these develop toward the back of the mouth, a child will complain of an intense sore throat. Other signs of illness are typically absent. Canker sores do not require antibiotic treatment and gradually resolve over several days (see "mouth care and concerns").

ACUTE EPIGLOTTITIS Fortunately, this disease has become uncommon because most children are now routinely immunized against *Haemophilus influenzae* type B, the bacteria that causes it (see "epiglottitis").

LARYNGITIS/TRACHEITIS When the larynx (vocal cords) and/or the airway just beyond it are inflamed, a child may complain of sore throat. Usually she will point to the midportion or lower neck when asked where she feels uncomfortable. Hoarseness and coughing (often with a barking quality) are usually present also. If your child is very uncomfortable or has noisy or labored breathing, call her physician.

Home treatment for sore throat

Whatever might be the cause of your child's sore throat, much if not all of your treatment at home will involve measures to keep her comfortable and prevent the spread of the infection to others:

- Rest. When the child is feeling better and the fever has subsided for at least twenty-four hours, the worst has probably passed.
- Give liquids of all kinds, either chilled or warm. But avoid acidic juices (orange, lemon, tomato), which may cause a stinging sensation in an inflamed throat.
- Offer her soft foods that won't irritate the throat.
- Gargling with warm saltwater every few hours may be soothing, if your child is old enough to cooperate. (Mix about a half teaspoon [2.5 ml] of salt in four ounces [about 120 ml] of water.)
- Acetaminophen (Tylenol and other brands) or ibuprofen (Children's Motrin and other brands) in doses appropriate for your child's weight can be very helpful in relieving throat pain, fever, headaches, and body aches. (Acetaminophen and ibuprofen dosage charts may be found on pages 609 and 688.) *Aspirin should not be used to treat sore throats or other acute childhood infections because of its link to Reye's syndrome, a serious illness affecting both brain and liver tissue (see "Reye's syndrome").*
- Prevent others from sharing your sick child's toothbrush or silverware. Encourage her to wash her hands frequently during the day, and wash your own hands after handling your child to reduce the risk of spreading the infection.
- *Don't treat your child with any leftover antibiotics unless specifically instructed to do so by her doctor.* Most sore throats do not respond to antibiotics, and diagnostic tests for strep throat may not be valid if an antibiotic has been taken beforehand. If you feel that your child needs specific treatment for a sore throat, call her doctor for further advice.

Some symptoms require a doctor's examination; contact your physician if your child has any of the following complaints:

- A sandpaper-textured rash
- Drooling or difficulty swallowing
- Severe pain
- Persistent fever higher than 102°F (39°C)
- Sudden onset of severe symptoms

- Sore throat lasting more than three to five days, especially if fever is present

spasm An involuntary contraction of a muscle that is more prolonged than a twitch.

sphincter A circular-shaped muscle that constricts a passage within the body (such as the junction between the esophagus and the stomach) or an opening leading to the outside of the body (such as the anus). Depending upon its location, a sphincter may open automatically as part of a specific function (such as passing swallowed food into the stomach), or it may be under voluntary control.

sputum Mucus secreted by the respiratory tract; phlegm.

steroid abuse Competitive athletes and bodybuilders of both sexes may be tempted to boost their physical prowess by using **anabolic steroids**. These compounds are chemically distinct from the **corticosteroids** (such as prednisone) prescribed by physicians to treat allergic reactions, asthma, and many other conditions. While some forms of anabolic steroids are available to treat specific medical problems, prescribing them for athletic or bodybuilding purposes is illegal.

Anabolic steroids are readily available to adolescents through underground sources. Abusers of these drugs may "stack" them (take more than one type at once) or utilize "pyramiding" (increasing the dose, sometimes to massive levels, over time). Their effects include rapid muscle growth, increased strength, and endurance for longer and more vigorous workouts. In the long run there are numerous drawbacks for both men and women.

Male users may develop acne, reduction in size and function of the testicles, impotence, purplish skin marks called **striae**, and male-pattern baldness. Women risk developing a permanently low-pitched voice, thinning hair around the temples, enlargement of the clitoris, striae, and increased facial hair. Adolescent users may retard their growth or end it prematurely, resulting in a shorter stature than they would have otherwise attained. All users risk liver disease, elevated blood pressure, and heart disease. In addition, aggressive behavior, impaired judgment, abuse of alcohol and other drugs, and in some cases significant psychiatric disturbances, including psychosis (losing touch with reality), may be associated with the use of anabolic steroids.

School programs are now more actively addressing the issues surrounding steroid abuse. Adolescent steroid abuse should be taken as seriously as any other illicit drug problem. A medical evaluation and ongoing counseling should be carried out to address dependence, withdrawal symptoms, and the underlying causes of this drug-seeking behavior.

steroids A group of compounds that are biochemically related but have several physiologic effects. Because **anabolic steroids** build muscle mass, they may be used—inappropriately and illegally—by athletes and bodybuilders, but these steroids have numerous adverse reactions (see "steroid abuse").

Corticosteroids, which inhibit the body's inflammatory response, may be prescribed by physicians for several therapeutic purposes. Potential uses of systemic corticosteroids (which are taken by mouth or injection) include the treatment of severe allergic reactions, acute asthma attacks, and widespread poison oak or poison ivy. Corticosteroids are also prescribed in cream, lotion, or ointment for certain types of skin eruptions; in nasal inhalers for allergic rhinitis (see "allergies in children"); and in oral inhalers for controlling or preventing asthma (see "asthma"). Steroids can have multiple side effects associated with long-term usage. Short-term usage (less than two weeks) usually has no significant side effects.

stomatitis Inflammation of the inner surface of the mouth.

strabismus Misalignment of the eyes. For example, one may go up or down, or move in or out in respect to the other. (See "eye care and concerns.")

strawberry hemangioma A bright red benign skin growth consisting of newly formed

capillaries (tiny blood vessels) whose color and surface texture suggest a strawberry. In some cases this marking is present at birth, while in others it appears during the first month of life. All typically grow rapidly over the next few months. They usually undergo a significant reduction in size between the second and third years of life, and the vast majority disappear by the age of nine. Consequently, this growth may appear unsightly for several months or even years, but surgical removal is rarely needed.

strep throat See "sore throat."

stridor Harsh, raspy breathing usually caused by the narrowing of the larynx or trachea.

sty An infection of the sebaceous glands on the edge of the eyelid (see "eye care and concerns").

subluxation Incomplete or partial dislocation of a bone.

subungual Under the nail.

sudden infant death syndrome (SIDS) The sudden, unexplained death of an infant. This syndrome is discussed in detail in the sidebar on pages 154.

suppository A bullet-shaped preparation that is placed in either the vagina or the rectum, allowing medication to be absorbed through the mucous membranes into the bloodstream.

suture A surgical stitch.

syncope Loss of consciousness. Medical term for a fainting episode, or passing out. (See "Fainting" in the Emergency Care section, beginning on page 823.)

T

tachycardia A rapid heart rate.

tachypnea A rapid rate of breathing.

teeth care and concerns (See also "Emergency Care," page 819.)

The debut of teeth

One of the memorable milestones in parenting is seeing the first white nubbin poking though a pink gum line, nearly always between six and ten months of age. This is the first of the **primary (temporary) teeth**, which allow children to chew and speak until the **secondary (permanent) teeth** appear.

Between six and nine months of age (or in some infants, as late as fifteen months), the lower **central incisors** (middle teeth), the upper **central** and **lateral incisors** (the teeth to the side of the middle teeth), and the lower lateral incisors will erupt—usually in that order. Between twelve and sixteen months, look for the first top and bottom **molars** (jaw teeth used for chewing), along with the lower **cuspids** (the pointed teeth on the sides). Between eighteen and thirty months, all of the primary teeth will be in place, with the appearance of the upper cuspids and the upper and lower second molars. (See page A5 for diagrams of the teeth and mouth.)

Many babies experience discomfort with the eruption of teeth. They drool more than usual and may try to gum the nearest firm object. Contrary to popular belief, teething does *not* generate a temperature over 100.4°F (38°C), taken rectally. (A baby or toddler with a higher fever should be assumed to have another problem.) Rubbing a finger against the gum through which the tooth is erupting sometimes helps; some infants prefer teething rings. Acetaminophen (Tylenol and other brands) can help, but topical preparations that are supposed to numb the gums usually do not provide dramatic relief because they don't remain in place very long.

The general order and appearance of the permanent teeth are as follows:

Ages 4 to 6	Primary teeth begin to fall out and be replaced by permanent teeth
Ages 6 to 8	Arrival of upper first molars, lower central incisors, lower first molars, and upper and lower central incisors
Ages 8 to 10	Lateral (side) incisors erupt on the top; lower cuspids appear

Ages 10 to 13	Upper first and second bicuspids, lower first and second bicuspids, second molars appearing on the upper and lower gums
Ages 17 to 22	Wisdom teeth

The timing of tooth eruption can vary greatly from child to child.

Dental care in the young child

Dental care at home can begin before the first teeth erupt. Infants begin collecting plaque on their gum pads even before the teeth break through them. The gums can be gently cleaned of breast milk or formula residue and other food debris using a clean washcloth moistened only with water. After the first teeth have erupted, a small, soft toothbrush may be used. Teeth should be brushed within five or ten minutes after a meal. You can use a very small dab (pea-size or less) of fluoride toothpaste, but if a young child objects, this can be postponed until he is older. When he is using a fluoride toothpaste regularly, be sure that only a small amount is placed on the brush. Fluoride helps strengthen the outer enamel, but there is enough in the amount of toothpaste that covers the bristles of a toothbrush to cause eventual discoloration of a child's teeth if he swallows the toothpaste regularly.

Continue to supervise toothbrushing as your child matures: He starts, you finish. Many parents allow their toddlers to do the majority of the brushing, but if your child insists that he wants to "do it himself," find creative ways to encourage him to let you help. You should continue this supervision through seven to ten years of age, until you are convinced that your child is adequately brushing all of his teeth.

Fluoride taken by mouth is important to the development of strong teeth. To determine whether your child is receiving an adequate amount, find out how much is present in your water supply. If you are breastfeeding, you should discuss with your baby's doctor whether or not fluoride supplementation is necessary. Children drinking tap water containing fluoride in a concentration of 0.6 parts per million (ppm) do not need any supplementation. If you have a private

well, call your local water or health department, which may offer free fluoride-level testing. For areas in which the water supply contains less fluoride, the American Academy of Pediatrics recommends that fluoride be supplemented each day according to the following schedule:

DAILY FLUORIDE
SUPPLEMENT

Ages	WATER FLUORIDE CONTENT		
	0 ppm–0.3 ppm	0.3 ppm–0.6 ppm	>0.6 ppm
6 mo–3 yrs	0.25 mg	0	0
3–6 yrs	0.5 mg	0.25 mg	0
6–16 yrs	1.0 mg	0.5 mg	0

First trip to the dentist

The American Academy of Pediatric Dentistry recommends a dental check once the first teeth come in (but no later than the first birthday), followed by dental checkups and cleaning every six months. You may wish to utilize a pediatric dentist, who will be well prepared to work on younger patients and will often have an office setting that is inviting and relaxing for children.

The welfare of the primary teeth should not be ignored merely because they will eventually be replaced by permanent teeth. If primary teeth become damaged or decayed or lost prematurely, the alignment of the permanent teeth could be adversely affected.

Dental caries (tooth decay)

Statistics compiled by the Centers for Disease Control and Prevention and the National Institute of Dental and Craniofacial Research indicate that about 40 percent of children ages two to eleven have dental caries in their primary teeth, and a similar percentage of children and adolescents six to nineteen years of age have dental caries in their permanent teeth.[17]

The development of a cavity requires the following ingredients:

- Cariogenic (cavity-producing) bacteria, which can produce tooth-eroding acid.
- Accumulation of plaque on the surface of one or more teeth, which provides a place for bacteria to grow.

T

- Prolonged contact between the teeth and carbohydrate food materials (especially simple sugars found in sweets).
- A susceptible tooth surface. While any surface can be the site of a cavity, pits and fissures in the teeth are particularly vulnerable.

Much of the pain, inconvenience, and cost resulting from dental caries is preventable through a combination of everyday measures at home and regular screening and appropriate intervention at the dentist's office:

- Regular brushing at home and periodic cleaning by a dentist or dental hygienist to remove accumulated plaque.
- Fluoride, whether as a supplement or as an ingredient in toothpaste, strengthens enamel and reduces bacterial activity.
- Avoid contact of sugars with teeth for prolonged periods of time (see "Special Note: Reducing fuel for tooth decay," below).
- Along with cleaning, appropriate screening, X-rays, and any necessary repair work, your child's dentist may recommend the use of sealants—thin plastic coverings for the molars that effectively prevent the formation of plaque and cavities.

Special note: Reducing fuel for tooth decay

While sugary foods have traditionally been associated with dental caries, the primary issue is how long these simple carbohydrates remain in contact with the teeth. Particularly troublesome situations to avoid include:

BOTTLE CARIES These cavities of the upper front teeth develop when babies repeatedly fall asleep with a bottle of formula, milk, or juice in the mouth, allowing the liquid to bathe the teeth. Once bottle caries appear, a pediatric dental specialist may be needed to correct the problem.

The best way to prevent this condition is to resist the temptation to put a fussy baby to bed with a bottle. If a baby has already become used to a bedtime bottle and parents are not ready to deal with the unhappy response to an abrupt withdrawal, a little water in the bottle is safer than milk or juice. Even when a child is in an upright position, the simple carbohydrates in juices sucked from a bottle tend to remain in contact with the teeth longer than when they are sipped from a cup. Therefore, hold off on juices until he can drink from a cup, and work toward weaning him off bottles altogether by the age of fifteen months (see chapter 8, page 229).

FOODS THAT ARE BOTH SWEET AND STICKY The regular consumption of chewy, sticky candies and other sweet concoctions that are not easily removed from the teeth increases the odds of decay.

EATING SWEET FOODS BETWEEN MEALS Unless a child brushes after every snack, these foods will remain in contact with teeth for prolonged periods of time.

Discoloration of the teeth

A variety of situations can lead to discoloration of the teeth:

- Trauma to the pulp (soft tissue that fills the center of the tooth) may result in a grayish discoloration.
- Ingestion of excessive fluoride may cause a whitish discoloration (**fluorosis**). Larger amounts may create a mottled or dotted appearance.
- Tetracycline antibiotics and their derivatives (including minocycline and doxycycline) can cause brown staining of the teeth in children if given to them before the age of eight or if taken by their mothers during pregnancy.

Injuries to the teeth

About one in three children will suffer an injury to the primary teeth by the age of five, and one in four children will have an injury to the permanent teeth by the age of twelve, most commonly as a result of falls, bicycle and motor-vehicle accidents, fights, and sporting events. Dental fractures, tooth loss (avulsion), and gum lacerations comprise the majority of injuries. Because these are often associated with other more serious injuries (such as blows to the head), the significance of tooth injuries can be overlooked. Besides damage to the tooth itself, periodontal tissues can be damaged and need attention as well.

To minimize the likelihood of dental injuries, each child who participates in contact sports should wear a mouth protector. Children with protruding teeth should have them properly aligned. Those with neuromuscular disorders should wear the appropriate headgear if their condition causes frequent falls. Using seat belts can also prevent dental injuries resulting from car accidents.

See also "Emergency Care," page 819.

Bruxism (teeth grinding)

An estimated 30 percent of children clench or grind their teeth at some time in life, very often during sleep and most commonly before the age of five. However, grinding may also occur during late adolescence or adulthood. Though the exact causes of bruxism are unclear, it may be a response to misalignment of the upper and lower teeth, the discomfort of teething, or stress. Usually grinding resolves on its own by the age of ten without causing any harm to a child's teeth or jaw, although it may be alarming or annoying to those who happen to hear it.

In some cases teeth grinding or clenching may cause headache or generate pain in the jaw or ear. (The ear pain is actually arising from the jaw or temporomandibular joint, also called the TMJ for short, and not the ear itself.) If occurring for extended periods of time, especially during sleep, grinding can also wear down tooth enamel or cause other damage. If you notice that your child is clenching or grinding his teeth, schedule a dental checkup. If there is a problem with alignment or evidence of damage, your dentist can recommend appropriate treatment options. These might include an evaluation by an orthodontist (see below) or the use of a special mouthpiece (somewhat like the mouth guard worn by football players) to protect the teeth from grinding during the night. It may also be helpful to ask your child whether anything has been bothering or upsetting him.

Orthodontics

Occlusion of the teeth (the way they come together when the mouth is closed) is important not only for cosmetic purposes but also for speech and eating. If your child has an **overbite** (the upper teeth protrude in front of the lower teeth), an **underbite** (the lower teeth protrude in front of the upper teeth), or a **crossbite** (upper teeth over the bottom teeth on one side, and vice versa on the other), and the misalignment significantly impairs speech or appearance, ask your dentist to refer you to an **orthodontist**—a dentist who specializes in correcting the alignment of the teeth and the bite.

Since orthodontic practice now focuses on preventive care, many appliances can be used to mold the bones of the mouth while they are still forming (between ages seven and twelve). But even if your child has passed puberty and is well into his teens, corrective orthodontics can still be done effectively.

temporal Referring to the side of the head.

tendon The tough, white fibrous tissue connecting muscle to bone.

tendonitis Inflammation or swelling of a tendon.

tetanus A serious and frequently fatal disease of the central nervous system caused by a potent toxin produced by bacteria known as *Clostridium tetani*. In an unvaccinated individual, the toxin may be produced in a wound (especially a puncture) that has been contaminated by soil containing spores of this bacteria. After an incubation of four to fourteen days (or longer), severe muscle spasms develop throughout the body. (The stiffness and spasms commonly seen in the neck and jaw muscles led to tetanus receiving the nickname lockjaw.)

Because of widespread vaccination, less than one hundred cases of tetanus occur in the United States every year, of which about 10 percent are fatal. Worldwide, between five hundred thousand and one million cases occur annually, and roughly 45 percent are fatal.[18] A startling number of these deaths occur among newborn infants and their mothers. According to UNICEF, about two hundred thousand newborns and thirty thousand women in other countries die every year from tetanus, primarily in impoverished areas where unsanitary birthing practices (such as cutting the umbilical cord with unsterile instruments or using contaminated dressings) are common. Vaccination would prevent the maternal deaths, while clean delivery and cord care practices would spare the infants from this disease.

Tetanus immunization is typically given to infants at two, four, and six months of age, with boosters at fifteen to eighteen months and four to six years. Thereafter, boosters are recommended every ten years, or after five years if a person sustains a wound significantly contaminated by dirt or other debris (especially animal manure). (See "Immunizations—Which Ones, Why and When?" on page 741 for more information about tetanus immunization.)

thrush See "candidiasis."

thumb-sucking All infants are born with a sucking reflex; it is both satisfying and necessary for survival. Ultrasound studies have shown babies sucking their thumb before birth; after birth it is quite normal for babies to suck their fingers, thumbs, and even toes! The majority of children give up thumb-sucking on their own as they pass through infancy and toddlerhood. However, experts generally agree that thumb-sucking that continues during and after the arrival of permanent teeth may cause problems with proper tooth alignment. (This will depend to some degree on the vigor with which sucking takes place.) Also, children who continue thumb-sucking after entering school may be targets of merciless teasing.

Since thumb-sucking is an unconscious self-comforting measure, it should not be treated as a punishable offense. (Bad-tasting products once marketed as a deterrent to thumb-sucking are no longer available.) You may wish to devise a simple, nonjudgmental signal (such as a wink or saying the child's name in a friendly tone and then pointing to your hand) that can serve as a reminder to stop when you see her sucking her thumb. Rewards for a certain number of hours or days spent without thumb-sucking may be effective. Many children who can control this habit during the day continue to suck at night, however. If there is a concern about the effects of thumb-sucking on the teeth of an older child, a pediatric dentist can evaluate the situation and may recommend additional measures (such as a dental appliance worn at night that makes thumb-sucking less comfortable).

thyroid An important endocrine gland located at the front of the neck. Thyroid hormone, which is manufactured and released into the circulatory system by this gland, plays a key role in setting the body's basic metabolic rate.

The thyroid gland occasionally becomes either overactive or underactive. **Hyperthyroidism** is a condition in which excessive amounts of thyroid hormone circulate in the bloodstream. Symptoms can include tremors, anxiety, rapid heart rate, weight loss, weakness, and sweatiness. Hyperthyroidism may occur when a portion of the thyroid gland produces excessive hormone. It may also develop when an inflammatory or infectious process damages the gland, causing injured cells to release thyroid hormone into the bloodstream. Treatment of hyperthyroidism will depend upon the underlying cause. Medication may be given to minimize the symptoms or to reduce the gland's output. More involved measures, such as radioactive iodine that effectively terminates the thyroid's activity, may be needed in rare cases.

Hypothyroidism is a condition in which too little thyroid hormone is in circulation. In infants, hypothyroidism is a serious problem that usually leads to mental retardation and developmental delays if not treated. Because hypothyroidism often does not cause any symptoms in the newborn, screening tests are done at birth in an effort to detect this problem and treat it as early as possible. In older children and adolescents, hypothyroidism may be manifested by delayed growth, intolerance to cold, constipation, brittle hair, sluggishness, and a lack of menstrual periods. When supplemental thyroid hormone is taken in appropriate doses, these symptoms gradually resolve.

tibia The larger of the two bones of the lower leg.

ticks (see illustration on page 805) Insects that can attach themselves to the skin of birds or mammals, including humans, and feed off their blood for many hours. Usually tick bites are neither painful nor itchy, so a child or adult is unaware of their presence. The amount of blood ticks remove is not significant, but many species can transmit microscopic organisms that cause serious human illnesses.

Ticks vary greatly in size and are usually brown or black. The tiny deer tick that can transmit Lyme disease is the size of a pinhead. Wood or dog ticks, which carry the organisms that cause Rocky Mountain spotted fever, may grow to half an inch (1.3 cm) in diameter. Ticks cannot jump or fly, so they come in contact with humans only when a person brushes against grass, bushes, or other objects where ticks are present.

Once on the skin, a tick can crawl to any part of the body, although many prefer hidden areas such as the groin or armpit. A tick firmly attaches its head deeply into the skin, and its body gradually swells as it feeds. Diseases carried by ticks are not transmitted until the ticks have been attached for approximately twenty-four hours.

Prevention

If you live or vacation in a tick-infested area, there are several precautions you can take. Dress your child in light-colored clothing (which will make a tick easy to spot), and if possible cover his entire body. If he is wearing long pants, tuck them into socks and use insect repellent on the shoes and socks.

While outside, use a buddy system in which two people check each other for ticks. After returning from outdoor excursions, inspect every family member (including infants) thoroughly. Since ticks tend to hide in hairy places, be sure to check the scalp.

If your child plays outdoors alone, teach him to identify ticks, and make sure he comes to you immediately for removal if he finds one. If you discover a tick attached to your child or any family member, don't be alarmed, but carefully remove it as soon as possible (see below). Remember that disease transmission is unlikely if the tick has been attached for less than twenty-four hours.

Removal of ticks

Ticks must be removed gently and completely. Do not squeeze, crush, or squash ticks that are on your child's body. Instead, use a pair of tweezers to pull the tick off with a gentle, outward mo-

tion. Do not twist while pulling because this may cause the head to break off and remain within the skin. If you don't have tweezers, use your fingertip—covered with tissue or a latex glove if available—and some thread. Place the thread around the tick and pull gently. If the head remains under the skin, use a sterilized needle to remove it as you would a splinter or sliver. Applying rubbing alcohol, fingernail polish, or petroleum jelly to the tick is not likely to cause it to release its grip.

Once the tick is removed, wash the area thoroughly with soap and water.

Call your doctor in the following situations:

- You can't remove the tick completely.
- A fever or rash develops a week or so after the tick has been removed.
- You think your child has been bitten by a deer tick, especially if it remained attached for more than twenty-four hours.

tics Quick, repetitive, but involuntary movements of specific muscle groups that are estimated to occur at some point in as many as one in five children by the age of ten. Tics are often hereditary. Common tics include grimaces, twitches, eye blinking, and squinting. Twisting or flinging movements of the extremities can occur. Vocal tics such as throat sounds or other noises are less common. Boys are more commonly affected than girls, and the behavior may be more obvious during periods of excitement or fatigue. However, tics disappear during sleep.

In most cases, tics gradually resolve without specific treatment over a period of a few weeks to a few months. For some individuals, however, they can be an ongoing or even lifelong problem. If tics are persistent, severe, or disruptive, neurological or psychiatric evaluation may be appropriate, and sometimes medication is recommended.

tinea versicolor A rather common fungal skin infection that produces patches of flaking skin with varying colors ranging from white to salmon to brown; they are located primarily over the neck, upper chest, back, and upper arms.

tinnitus A noise heard in the ear and described as a ringing, buzzing, or clicking sound.

tonsils Paired structures located in the back of the throat that are composed primarily of lymph tissue and are strategically placed to serve as a defense against infection. Unfortunately, they themselves can become acutely or chronically infected, a condition called **tonsillitis**. While any number of viruses or bacteria can cause tonsillitis, two of the most important types of infection are **streptococcal tonsillitis** and **infectious mononucleosis** (see "sore throat" and "mononucleosis").

In previous generations, **tonsillectomy** (removal of the tonsils) was an extremely common surgical procedure, but it is done much less frequently today. Reasons for tonsillectomy that are widely accepted at this time include:

- Severe, persistent enlargement of the tonsils causing repeated difficulty with swallowing, sometimes accompanied by drooling and noisy breathing. The tonsils may appear to touch each other in the back of the mouth (see "sore throat").
- Recurrent infections of the tonsils. Typical criteria are two or three infections in three months, or six infections in six months.
- Recurrent **peritonsillar abscess**, a severe infection involving the soft tissue adjacent to one of the tonsils. This infection not only causes serious illness but also indicates that infection has spread behind the tonsil into the neck.
- Suspected tumor of a tonsil, which is an extremely rare situation.
- Severe snoring accompanied by multiple episodes of **apnea** (more than ten seconds of interrupted breathing) during the night. This condition disrupts sleep and is associated with both daytime drowsiness and worsening school performance.

Tourette syndrome (see also "seizures") A chronic disorder characterized by a variety of muscular and vocal tics: quick, involuntary, repetitive movements of the face, arms, or legs, or sounds such as grunts, sudden exclamations (sometimes using vulgar language), or other noises. Like other forms of tics, Tourette syndrome is hereditary. In most cases it is first manifested between the ages of seven and ten. Stress, excitement, or fatigue may aggravate symptoms. Whether or not tics may be made more severe by stimulants such as **methylphenidate** (Ritalin) or **dextroamphetamine** (Dexedrine), medications frequently prescribed for **attention deficit/hyperactivity disorder (ADHD)** has been the subject of ongoing research and review. This is a point of some concern, since ADHD often coexists with Tourette syndrome. If tics are persistent, severe, or disruptive, neurological or psychiatric evaluation may be appropriate, and one or more specific medications may be recommended.

toxin A substance produced by a living organism (such as an animal, plant, or bacteria) that is poisonous to another organism.

triceps The muscle used to extend or straighten the forearm.

trisomy Presence of an extra chromosome in addition to the usual pair.

tuberculosis (TB) An infectious disease caused by the bacteria known as *Mycobacterium tuberculosis*. One hundred years ago tuberculosis was the leading cause of death in the United States, killing more than sixty thousand people every year. Effective antibiotics as well as public-health measures and effective screening procedures led to a gradual decline in the number of TB cases and the deaths they caused. That trend changed after 1986, as the number of cases in the United States began to rise again, often involving strains that have developed resistance to drugs that were previously effective. Renewed public-health efforts have led to a decline in cases since 1992, but as of 2004, fourteen thousand new cases are still reported in the United States every year. Worldwide, TB is a scourge: About 1.7 million people die of this infection every year, and as many as one in three people in the world are infected. Southeast Asia and sub-Saharan Africa have been hardest hit by this infection, fueled in part by the spread of HIV/AIDS.[19]

Those at greatest risk for TB include certain ethnic minorities; people from areas of the world where TB is prevalent, especially Asia, Africa, and Latin America; indigent and homeless people; individuals infected with HIV; long-term abusers of drugs and alcohol; the aged; migrant workers; people who live or work in facilities such as prisons, immigration centers, and nursing homes; and health-care workers who care for TB patients. The most common risk factor for a child becoming infected with TB is household exposure to an infected adult.

In a child whose general health and immune function are intact, contact with TB bacteria usually does not lead to active disease. The bacteria is typically inhaled into the lungs and then literally walled off by an immune response that prevents future activity, often for the rest of the child's life. This condition is often called **latent TB**, and it is not contagious. The only evidence that the exposure took place may be a positive response to a skin test applied to the forearm as a screening test, most commonly (but not always) done during a checkup prior to entering kindergarten. (See "Does Your Child Need a TB Test?" on page 346.)

If the test is positive, a chest X-ray will normally be done to confirm that active TB is not in progress. If active disease is not present, usually the child will be given prophylactic (preventive) antibiotics for six to nine months to prevent disease in the future. If active infection is under way, additional long-term drug therapy will be necessary to contain it. Both of these measures are necessary to prevent much more severe or even fatal consequences, such as diffuse and severe disease throughout one or both lungs, involvement of other tissues such as the bones or kidneys, or even meningitis.

Turner syndrome A female genetic disorder caused by having only a single X chromosome rather than the usual pair of X chromosomes. It is characterized by a small jaw, a high-arched palate, the appearance of widely spaced nipples, and a deformity of the forearms that causes the palms to face outward. In infants, swelling of the hands and feet, loose skin folds at the nape of the neck, and significantly low birth weight and decreased length are common. In adults, it is characterized by short stature.

typhoid fever A bacterial infection caused by a type of *Salmonella* (*Salmonella typhi*) and transmitted by contaminated water, milk, or foods (especially raw oysters and other shellfish). Symptoms include a prolonged fever, abdominal pain, diarrhea, and in some children, a rash with rose-colored spots. Intestinal bleeding and perforation are serious but relatively uncommon complications. Typhoid fever is treatable with appropriate antibiotics and supportive care. A vaccine is available for those planning travel to foreign countries where exposure to *Salmonella typhi* might occur.

U **ulcer** A sore on the skin or mucous membrane resulting from the destruction of surface tissue.

umbilical hernia A protrusion of abdominal contents (usually the intestines) through the **umbilicus** (belly button), caused by imperfect closure of the muscles of the abdominal wall where a natural widening was present before birth to accommodate the umbilical cord. The hernia appears as a soft swelling covered by skin that bulges from the umbilicus during crying, coughing, or straining. The swelling can be gently pushed back through the fibrous ring of the umbilicus.

Most umbilical hernias appear before a child is six months old, and they will disappear spontaneously by the age of twelve to eighteen months as the structures of the abdominal wall fuse together and close the defect. Surgery is rarely needed, but it may be considered if the hernia is persistent and still enlarging at the age of two, or if it remains in a child three to five years of age.

Surgery will be necessary on an emergency basis if a rare condition called **incarceration** develops: A small segment of intestine becomes caught in the hernia defect, producing significant pain and local swelling. Reduction of blood flow to intestinal tissue can cause significant damage if the incarcerated intestine is not released. Normally a repair of the hernia defect is also done during the emergency surgery.

ureter The narrow tube that carries urine from the kidneys to the bladder.

urethra The tube that carries urine from the bladder and out of the body.

urethritis An inflammation of the urethra.

URI Upper-respiratory infection. See "colds."

urinary tract care and concerns The kidneys produce urine and serve a number of important functions, including maintaining fluid balance and blood pressure and eliminating waste products. They are very complex and efficient filters of the blood, allowing unnecessary components to pass into the urine while returning 99 percent of the filtered fluid to the circulatory system. The kidneys adjust to the body's fluid needs. For example, a dehydrated individual will produce less urine, allowing the body to conserve water. The kidneys also adjust the salt and mineral composition of the blood. When a kidney is damaged, diseased, or receiving an inadequate supply of blood, it cannot carry out its filtering functions properly. When this occurs, certain components of blood such as protein, sugar, and red blood cells may leak into the urine.

Normally the clear yellow urine produced by each kidney flows continuously through a narrow, muscular tube called the **ureter** to the bladder, where it is stored until automatic or voluntary input from the nervous system causes it to be eliminated. This process involves simultaneous contraction of muscles within the bladder wall and relaxation of the muscle called the **sphincter** at the bladder's outlet.

The following are some common problems that can arise within the urinary tract.

Painful urination (dysuria)
Discomfort while passing urine can be caused by one of the following situations:

- Infection (see below)
- Irritation from something coming in direct contact with the genital area, such as bubble bath or other soapy material in the tub, laundry soap, creams, or lotions
- Trauma
- A foreign body in the vagina or urinary tract (see "genital care and concerns")

Any time your child complains of painful urination, or if you notice a distinctly abnormal color of the urine (especially a reddish tinge that could indicate that blood is present), contact your child's physician as soon as possible. If a child is having difficulty urinating because of pain, you can help by placing her in a bathtub of warm water and allowing her to urinate there.

Urinary tract infections
Urinary tract infections are common in children but may be difficult to diagnose because of the unpredictable and variable symptoms that accompany them. Infants with urinary tract infections may have fever, irritability, poor feeding, vomiting, or diarrhea. An older child may have the more familiar symptoms of frequent, burning urination but may also have abdominal pain, bloody or cloudy urine, or incontinence.

To diagnose a urinary tract infection (UTI) a doctor must have a urine sample. In younger children this may be obtained by placing a specially designed sterile plastic bag over the genitalia. When an uncontaminated specimen (such as in a very young infant with a fever) is needed, a catheter may be inserted directly into the infant's urethra, or the doctor may perform a **suprapubic tap**. In this procedure, urine is aspirated directly from the bladder through a thin needle inserted briefly through the infant's lower abdominal wall. Older children will normally be able to void into a sterile container after the genitalia are cleansed with an antiseptic solution.

Once the specimen is obtained, a urinalysis is performed. This will include an examination under the microscope to look for white and red blood cells as well as bacteria. If it appears that an infection is present, or if there is concern about infection even when the urine appears normal, a portion of the specimen will usually be sent to a laboratory for culture to confirm that bacteria are present in significant numbers. If so, the sensitivity of the bacteria to various antibiotics will also be evaluated to ensure that an appropriate medication is prescribed. Often an antibiotic is started while results of the culture are awaited.

A bacterial infection can occur virtually anywhere along the pathway of the urine flow. An infection involving the kidney is called

U

pyelonephritis and is a serious illness. Infection of the bladder, which is much more common but fortunately also far less serious, is called **cystitis**. **Urethritis** is an infection of the urethra (the tube through which urine exits the body) and is most often seen in sexually active adolescents, especially males with gonorrhea or chlamydia.

Urinary tract infections in infants are more common in boys, particularly those who are not circumcised. An infant younger than six months of age with a urinary infection is also more likely than an older child to have bacteria present in the bloodstream. Treatment may thus involve hospitalization for closer observation and intravenous antibiotics.

An infant who develops a urinary tract infection may have a malformation of one or both kidneys, ureters, or the bladder. After the infection has been treated, the physician may recommend that he undergo imaging of the urinary tract, which may involve an ultrasound of his kidneys, as well as a **voiding cystourethrogram (VCUG)**. A VCUG is performed by placing a catheter in the urethra, filling the bladder with water-soluble contrast, removing the catheter, and then watching the infant void while X-rays are taken. This allows the physician to evaluate the location, size, and shape of the bladder and to determine whether emptying the bladder is associated with a backward flow of urine (called **reflux**) through one or both ureters toward the kidneys. These results will help the doctor plan proper management, which may include prophylactic (preventive) antibiotics or possibly surgery if a malformation is found.

Urinary tract infections in older children may occur either in the bladder or the kidneys. A kidney infection is likely to cause a more severe illness with fever, nausea, vomiting, and abdominal or back pain on the same side as the infection. Bladder infections usually cause frequent or painful urination, a sense of urgency (the child feels the need to pass urine immediately), and bloody or cloudy urine. If the infection appears to involve the kidney and the child is definitely ill (especially if vomiting), it may be necessary to admit her to the hospital for intravenous antibiotics and fluid replacement. Infections in the bladder can usually be treated with oral antibiotics.

Girls who have their first urinary tract infection after the age of five are less likely to have underlying structural abnormalities. The decision to recommend ultrasound and X-ray examinations in this age-group will depend a great deal on the circumstances and severity of the infection. Many physicians feel that any boy who has a urinary tract infection, regardless of age (except for an adolescent with a sexually transmitted disease), should be evaluated to look for an underlying cause.

Recurrent urinary tract infections are occasionally seen among children, especially in girls, usually because of the relatively short distance from the female bladder to the outside. After she has been evaluated for any underlying problem that might predispose her to infection, it is important that a child with recurrent UTIs be followed carefully by her physician, since ongoing untreated infection could lead to kidney damage. In some cases, the physician may decide to prescribe a prophylactic antibiotic to prevent further infections. Usually this medication is taken only once a day and is not likely to cause any long-term problem.

Kidney disease

Changes in the characteristics or amount of urine may result from a disorder of the kidney itself or from a problem in the ureter or bladder. Decreased urine production may be caused specifically by dehydration, kidney disease, or obstruction to the flow of urine. There are many types of kidney diseases, but they cause only a limited number of symptoms:

- Decreased or (more rarely) increased urine production
- Passage of blood, which may be visible to the naked eye or detected only by chemical tests or microscopic examination
- Sugar (glucose) in the urine, which is virtually always associated with a high level of glucose in the blood (diabetes)
- Increased amounts of protein in the urine, which can usually be detected by a simple chemical test in the physician's office
- Swelling of the hands, ankles, feet, scrotum, or eyelids (called **edema**)

- Pain in the midback or flank area on one side of the body
- Fever, which may be a sign of infection within or adjacent to a kidney

Increased urine production (polyuria)

Increased urine production can be a normal response when a child drinks a lot of fluid, or it can indicate a more serious problem. Kidneys will produce an abnormal amount of urine for three basic reasons:

- Kidney damage prevents the kidneys from concentrating urine.
- The hormones that control the kidneys' concentrating abilities are not being produced or are not functioning properly.
- A disease such as diabetes causes a marked elevation of certain substances (especially glucose or blood sugar) in the bloodstream. When the concentration of glucose in blood exceeds a certain level, the kidney can no longer prevent some from spilling into the urine. This results in a higher volume of urine and can eventually lead to substantial fluid loss.

Blood in the urine (hematuria)

Seeing blood in the urine can be frightening for both parent and child. But not everything that makes the urine look red is blood. It is not uncommon to see a small amount of pinkish red, pastelike material in a newborn's diaper. This is usually caused by urate crystals that form in concentrated urine. If these are seen in a breastfed baby, it may be helpful to nurse more frequently. If you are bottle-feeding, consider giving a few ounces of additional water. Urate crystals will usually disappear by the second week of life.

Some foods such as beets and certain medications can cause a child's urine to change color. You should consult with your child's physician if this occurs.

Blood in an infant's diaper area may come from the urinary tract, from the vagina in little girls, or from the gastrointestinal tract. If you notice blood in the diaper, take the diaper with you to your physician.

Blood in the urine is sometimes clearly visible but at other times may be present in quantities so small that it can be detected only by a microscopic evaluation or a dipstick—a thin test strip that identifies a variety of substances in the urine. The following conditions cause red blood cells to be present in the urine, and it is important that the underlying cause be determined if at all possible:

- Urinary tract infection
- Trauma, including injury to the kidneys or genitalia
- Kidney diseases, including hereditary kidney problems, that leak small amounts of blood into the urine
- Kidney stones
- Blood-clotting problems
- Abnormalities of immune function
- Exposure to toxic substances
- Tumor, which in children nearly always involves the kidney rather than ureter, bladder, or external genitalia
- Vigorous exercise—running, jumping, etc.

Your physician will examine your child and ask questions to sort through these possibilities. A urine specimen will be evaluated. If a urinary tract infection does not appear to be the problem, the physician will probably do a careful evaluation of the genital area and order special blood and/or imaging tests (X-ray or ultrasound) to help determine the cause of the hematuria.

Obstruction

HYDRONEPHROSIS Malformations of any portion of the urinary system can occur during fetal development. The most common of these in both girls and boys is an obstruction that decreases or completely stops the flow of urine. The resulting increase in pressure causes swelling within the urinary tract. When one or both kidneys are involved, the condition is called **hydronephrosis** (literally, "water kidney"). Sometimes this type of obstruction can be diagnosed during pregnancy through an ultrasound. One of the first surgeries developed for preborn babies was the treatment of hydronephrosis, which involves removing the obstruction while the kidneys still have time to grow.

U

PERSISTENT URETHRAL VALVES In boys, the urine flows through the urethra inside the penis. During fetal development, small flaps of tissue called valves stop the flow of urine. Before the baby is born, these valves normally disappear, allowing urine to pass freely. If the flaps remain after birth, they can obstruct the urine flow and cause bladder distention. One clue that a baby may have urethral valves is that the urine stream is weak and dribbling rather than forceful. (Most parents of boys have been sprayed during diaper changes, an indication that the flow of urine is not obstructed.)

MEATAL STENOSIS The opening at the end of the penis through which urine passes is called the **meatus**. If the baby boy is circumcised at birth, the head of the penis (glans) is exposed to urine and stool in the diaper. The sensitive cells of the meatus may become irritated and heal with scar tissue, which can cause a narrowing known as **meatal stenosis**.

If the boy's urine stream appears narrowed—a thin, jetlike stream as if coming from a nozzle—or if it deviates to one side so much that he must deliberately aim his penis to keep the urine stream within the toilet bowl, he should be examined by a physician. If meatal stenosis is severe, a urologist may perform minor surgery to dilate the meatal opening.

urinary urgency The sensation of needing to urinate immediately.

urticaria (hives) A generalized allergic response involving raised, reddened, irregular itchy patches of skin that may blanch (turn white) when pressure is applied. They may vary from dime-size to much larger areas of skin, and they change size and location. Hives are sometimes associated with itchy swelling of the face, eyes, lips, hands, feet, and genitalia. (*Urticaria* comes from the Latin word for "nettle," the plant with stinging hairs.)

UTI Urinary tract infection.

uvula The fleshy mass that hangs down from the roof of the mouth at the back of the throat.

 vertigo A spinning sensation that often results in nausea.

viruses Small particles capable of reproducing themselves, but only within living cells. They cause many diseases, some common and some rare, such as colds, influenza, measles, mumps, chickenpox, herpes, AIDS, and rabies. At the present time there is no cure for a virus; antibiotics are totally ineffective. There are certain antiviral agents that can modify, shorten the course of, or even temporarily keep some viruses under control, but none can cure the body of a virus once it is present. Most viral infections spontaneously resolve on their own, but some, such as HIV infection, do not. Vaccines are available for a number of viruses (such as polio, hepatitis A and B, and measles, among many others) that will prevent or limit disease in a person who is exposed to them.

vitiligo A skin condition identified by patches of skin that don't contain pigment, thus appearing white.

vomiting The forceful ejection of stomach contents through the mouth. Vomiting is not the same as spitting up or regurgitating, when a small amount of previously swallowed material (usually breast milk or formula) reenters an infant's mouth without force. Spitting up is not uncommon during the first year of life because the sphincter (a ringlike muscle) between the esophagus and the stomach does not always close tightly or may remain open much of the time at this age. During the first year, the sphincter gradually matures and tightens, reducing the number of spitting-up episodes.

Forceful vomiting is always a significant symptom in an infant younger than three months of age. It may be related to milk-protein intolerance and could require formula substitution. It may also be a symptom of a partial or complete obstruction of the gastrointestinal tract. The most common such obstruction in infants is **pyloric stenosis**, a condition in which the muscles that line the segment of small intestine just beyond the stomach thicken and block the outlet of the stomach. The vomiting associated with this condition is so forceful that it is called **projectile vomit-**

ing. Additional symptoms include failure to gain weight and a general look of undernourishment. This condition is most common in firstborn boys. It requires surgical correction (see also chapter 4, page 140, and "pyloric stenosis").

The most common cause of vomiting in older infants and children is infection. Vomiting of this type is frequently accompanied by nausea, abdominal cramps, and in some cases fever. The infection may be in the stomach and bowel (**gastroenteritis**, or so-called "stomach flu"), in which there can be both diarrhea and vomiting. Vomiting is sometimes caused by stimulation of the brain's vomiting center by toxins that circulate as the result of infections elsewhere, such as in the throat, ear, or lung.

Sometimes vomiting is so forceful it produces a tear in the esophagus. In such instances there may be streaks of blood in the vomited material. *The presence of large amounts of vomited blood is a serious concern that should be evaluated by a physician immediately.*

The danger of dehydration

The main concern with repeated vomiting, especially if accompanied by diarrhea, is that an infant or young child may become dehydrated from fluid loss. When these losses are mild, increased thirst and a modest decrease in urine output (fewer wet diapers) will occur. If this happens, call your child's physician for advice, which may include a recommendation for a direct evaluation.

The following symptoms indicate more severe dehydration, and with rare exception, you should call for immediate evaluation:

- Constant thirst (in an older child who can express this need)
- Dry mouth and lips
- Fewer tears when crying
- No urine production for eight to twelve hours, indicating that the kidneys are conserving fluids
- Sunken eyes
- A sunken fontanelle (the soft spot in the skull, most readily felt during the first six months of life)

- Skin texture that is no longer elastic but more like bread dough
- Persistent fussing in an infant, especially if it is more of a whine than a vigorous cry

Even more serious dehydration (with fluid losses of more than 10 percent of the child's normal body weight) will be suggested by the presence of these symptoms:

- Cool and/or mottled skin
- Rapid, thready pulse
- Rapid respirations
- Moaning or grunting, or a weak, feeble cry
- Marked listlessness with lack of interest in play or feeding, little response to being handled, and (in an infant) markedly reduced movements of arms and legs

A baby or young child with these symptoms is likely to be in serious trouble and should be evaluated immediately, usually in an emergency-room setting.

Prevention and treatment of dehydration

Your child's doctor will give specific advice for preventing or correcting dehydration, which will depend to some degree on the age of your child and the severity of the problem. Usually some effort will be made to rest the bowel for a day or two while the infection runs its course. Traditionally this has involved giving the infant or child one or more forms of clear liquids—water, soft drinks, clear soup, clear juice—which are supposed to be absorbed more easily when the bowel is inflamed or damaged by infection. However, research into the physiology of the small intestine has led to the development of a variety of **oral rehydration solutions (ORS)**, which cooperate more effectively with the body's mechanisms for absorbing fluid. These solutions contain specified amounts of sodium, potassium, and glucose mixed in water; they can be safely used by infants and children of all ages; and they are effective in treating both mild and severe dehydration.

Premixed ORS is available at drugstores in products such as Pedialyte, Rehydralyte, and Infalyte. *It is this type of solution, not the traditional clear liquids, that is best suited to treat acute gastroenteritis, especially in children under two years of age.* ORS may be given by bottle, spoon, or even dropper, usually in small amounts given frequently. If the rehydrating solution isn't flavored, its taste can be improved by adding one tablespoon (15 ml) of Jell-O powder to one tablespoon of boiling water, and then adding this mixture to an eight-ounce (about 240 ml) bottle of the solution.

Your doctor will specifically recommend the type and minimum quantity of solution you should give to your child. A typical routine is to give a teaspoon to a tablespoon (5 to 15 ml), depending on the child's size, every ten minutes for an hour and then doubling the amount each hour if vomiting does not occur.

Breastfed infants can continue nursing, but with frequent and shorter feedings (such as ten minutes every hour or two, one side at a time). If vomiting persists in a nursing infant, the doctor may recommend using a rehydrating solution for a few hours.

In most cases of gastroenteritis, after eight hours without vomiting, foods such as rice cereal or applesauce for infants, or bread, rice, mashed potatoes, or crackers for older children can be eaten in small amounts. If vomiting recurs, solids should be ceased for an hour, and rehydrating fluid can be started again.

Vomiting accompanied by significant pain in the abdomen, whether generalized or localized, may indicate the presence of an acute medical problem such as appendicitis. Vomiting accompanied by intermittent abdominal pain and blood in the stool may indicate an obstruction or a bacterial infection. If vomiting and abdominal pain persist for more than a few hours, the child should be examined by a physician.

vulva External parts of the female reproductive tract surrounding the opening of the vagina.

W **warts** Small, benign skin tumors caused by various strains of the human papillomavirus. They are a common affliction of children and teenagers. The virus enters the skin through direct contact with another infected person or with a warm, moist surface (such as a locker-room floor) where infected skin has been shed.

Warts eventually disappear as the immune system recognizes and eliminates the virus, but this process may take many months or even years. If not treated, the virus—and the warts it causes—may spread from its initial location (usually the hands) to other parts of the body or (less commonly) to other people.

Warts come in three basic forms:

Common warts appear as round, firm bumps on the skin with a sharply defined margin and a slightly roughened surface. If picked or pared with a scalpel, they will bleed actively. Common warts are generally found on the hands (especially around the edges of fingernails) and occasionally on the legs (most frequently around the knees).

Plantar warts occur on the soles of the feet, virtually always over pressure points (particularly on the heel or ball of the foot). They can be bothersome or even painful, since a callus can build up around the wart and create uncomfortable pressure, which is particularly noticeable while walking or running.

Flat warts, which are flat-topped and flesh-colored, are seen most often on the backs of the hands or on the face, sometimes in small clusters or in a line.

Genital warts, which are also caused by strains of the human papillomavirus, behave and are treated differently from the other types of warts mentioned here. They are discussed in detail in the section on sexually transmitted infections on page 541.

While warts eventually go away on their own, removing them when possible to prevent them from spreading is wise. The method chosen will depend on the size and number of warts, their location, and the age (and level of cooperation) of the child. Whatever method is used, it is important to encourage your child *not* to pick or pull at the warts to prevent them from spreading.

Various weak acid formulations, available in both over-the-counter and prescription varieties that can be applied at home, are a slow but painless approach for both common and plantar warts. The medication will work best if the wart has first been pared down to remove the thick outer layer of dead skin. A physician can do this with a scalpel, or you can use an emery board at home (one not used for any other purpose, in order to prevent the virus from spreading). If the wart bleeds a little, don't pare any further but don't worry. This may actually allow white blood cells to interact with the wart virus and speed up the immune response.

The wart site is soaked in warm water for a few minutes, and then a drop of the acid solution (such as Duofilm) is applied onto the wart surface, allowed to dry into a film, and then covered for twenty-four hours. A variation of this is the **salicylic acid plaster**, which contains medicine and self-adhering covering in one package. These are usually left in place for eight hours out of the day. Either format will require six to twelve weeks of daily use.

For a more rapid response, your child's primary-care physician or a dermatologist may be able to destroy one or more warts directly. **Liquid nitrogen** applied directly to a wart with a cotton swab feels very cold and stings while the wart is being frozen, after which the area turns pink and aches for several hours. Eventually a dark blister will form, and the wart will peel away on its own. (Your child should be encouraged not to do this herself.) This method is appropriate for a few warts on areas of skin that aren't too sensitive (such as the back of the hand), but after the first experience, your child may balk at having freezing done repeatedly, especially if fingertips (where there is an abundance of nerve endings) are involved.

An even more direct approach in the doctor's office involves a shot of local anesthetic under the wart, followed by **curetting** (scraping the wart out of the skin with a sharp instrument), and then using an electrical instrument to **cauterize** the base. The dark crater that remains must be protected with a small dressing to prevent infection. Flat warts can be managed with topical medications (such as Retin-A) rather than acids, freezing, or burning. This is particularly important when they are present on the face.

whiplash An injury to the soft tissues of the neck or upper back caused by sudden, unintended bending of the neck.

Immunizations—Which Ones, Why, and When?

"Do I have to get a shot today?"

The prospect of being on the receiving end of an injection is a common cause for concern when children find out that they're headed for the doctor's office. If they're fighting a cold or a sore throat, the good news is that they're not likely to get a jolt of penicillin like Grandpa did so often fifty years ago. (The routine use of injectable antibiotics or a vitamin B shot as the treatment for everything and anything is thankfully a thing of the past.) But if the visit is for a checkup, an immunization could well be on the agenda. Although Grandpa may have ended up with a sore backside whenever he got sick, he certainly didn't have to endure nearly as many vaccinations as his grandchildren now receive.

"Does my baby get a shot today?" While an infant doesn't know what's coming at the end of the well-baby visit, Mom does, and sometimes she has mixed emotions: *I don't want Emily to get whooping cough or polio, but could these shots harm her? Why does she have to get so many? Could they overwhelm her young immune system? Are they really necessary?*

We are fortunate to live in a time when the vast majority of us don't have to worry about losing a child to the merciless choking of diphtheria or the painful spasms of tetanus. Furthermore, we are usually only dimly aware of the incredible surveillance and self-defense provided by our immune system, day in and day out. Indeed, it is only through the amazingly complex function of an intact immune system that we reap the benefits of vaccinations. How exactly do they work? And more importantly, why do we give so many of them to children who are already in good health? Aren't good hygiene and nutrition enough to protect our kids?

A Few Facts about Immunity and Vaccinations

Though we cannot isolate ourselves from every conceivable infectious agent, the human body has the ability to develop an immune response as a defense against potential invaders. Immunity to a disease is frequently acquired naturally, as when a child develops chickenpox and then is no longer susceptible to it, even if he is later exposed to others with the disease. Immunity can also be acquired artificially by purposefully introducing a weakened or killed **pathogen** (a disease-causing agent such as a virus or bacteria), or portions of the pathogen, into the body. Like a microbiologic wanted poster, this process primes the immune system to recognize and mount an efficient defense if the infectious agent makes an appearance.

The elaborate system that defends us from potentially harmful microorganisms has two basic divisions. **Innate immunity** is provided by organs, tissues, and cells that serve as a first line of defense against would-be invaders, though it is not specific against any particular type. For example, our skin is a component of our innate immunity in that it minimizes access of bacteria, viruses, and other microscopic assailants to our body.

Acquired immunity, on the other hand, is based on the responses of cells of the immune system to specific **antigens**. Antigens are large molecules present on the surface of all microorganisms (and on human cells as well) that are capable of eliciting two basic types of responses from the immune system. **B lymphocytes (B cells)** are stimulated to multiply and produce antibodies, proteins that bind specifically to particular antigens and allow other cells of the immune system to destroy them. **T lymphocytes (T cells)** directly attack the antigens or the cells on which they reside and also offer a measure of control to the immune response. Exposure to an antigen results in the creation of a pool of "memory" cells, B cells and T cells that, when challenged with the antigen again, can help mount a swift and robust response. This allows the immune system to rally a quicker, more powerful defense when a pathogen is encountered after an initial infection, and it is this mechanism that provides future immunity against an infectious disease once the disease has been contracted.

The body can encounter a pathogen or its antigens naturally (through infection) or through artificial means. Since intentional introduction of a dangerous pathogen is obviously unwise, scientists have devised ways to introduce weakened or killed forms of certain pathogens, small portions of them, or the toxins they produce. These preparations are called vaccines, and once introduced they can stimulate the immune system to recognize pathogens or their toxins in the future and destroy them before they cause full-blown disease.

Vaccination was first developed in 1796 by English physician Edward Jenner, who noted that milkmaids who had contracted cowpox (a mild disease passed from infected cows to humans) did not contract smallpox, a highly contagious and often deadly and disfiguring disease. When Jenner took some material from a cowpox sore and scratched it into the arms of patients, they became immune to smallpox. (The word *vaccine* derives from *vacca*, the Latin word for cow.)

We now know that the virus that causes cowpox contains antigens that are very similar to those of the smallpox virus. The initial challenge against the cowpox virus thus allowed the body to build an immune response that was also effective against the smallpox virus. Since Jenner's discovery, a host of other vaccines have dramatically reduced suffering and death caused by a number of diseases around the world—and in your neighborhood.

Diphtheria, tetanus, and pertussis (whooping cough)

Diphtheria is a serious bacterial infection in which a thick membrane forms in the nose, throat, or airway. (The term *diphtheria* comes from a Greek word meaning "leather"—a vivid reference to the thick membrane created by this disease.) The membrane attaches to underlying tissues, and attempting to remove it causes bleeding. Diphtheria bacteria within the membrane produce a toxin that can cause permanent damage to the heart, liver, kidneys, and nerve tissue. Of those who become ill with diphtheria, 5 to 10 percent die.

Only senior citizens are likely to have any memory of the misery and loss inflicted by diphtheria before a vaccine was developed in 1923. In 1921, 206,000 cases and 15,520 deaths were reported in the United States. While only two cases were reported in the United States in 2001, diphtheria is not uncommon in other parts of the world. In the former Soviet Union, a breakdown in public-health services (and specifically a lack of vaccination) led to an epidemic with more than 150,000 cases that claimed 5,000 lives between 1990 and 1999.

Tetanus results from a toxin produced by a specific type of bacteria that can enter the body through contaminated wounds, especially punctures. Tetanus can also occur following animal bites, burns, and abrasions, but it is not spread from person to person. The toxin causes painful, spasmodic contractions of muscles (which gave rise to the colloquial term *lockjaw* for this disease) and can lead to death. Tetanus is always a threat to someone who has never been immunized because the bacteria that cause it are ever-present in soil and on other materials, ready to populate a puncture wound and generate the toxin that causes an extremely unpleasant and often fatal illness.

Before childhood tetanus vaccination became routine in the late 1940s, five hundred to six hundred cases were reported in the United States every year. Currently about one-tenth of that number of tetanus cases occur in the United States every year, but 30 percent of these are fatal. Worldwide, between five hundred thousand and one million cases occur annually, and roughly 45 percent are fatal. A startling number of these deaths occur among newborn infants and their mothers. According to UNICEF, in other countries approximately two hundred thousand newborns and thirty thousand women die every year from tetanus, primarily in impoverished areas where unsanitary birthing practices (such as cutting the umbilical cord with unsterile instruments or using contaminated dressings) are common. Vaccination would prevent the maternal deaths, while clean delivery and cord care practices would spare the infants from this disease.

Pertussis (**whooping cough**) is a highly contagious bacterial infection that causes severe bouts of coughing, often to the point of choking, that can last for months. It is particularly severe in infants and small children and can lead to pneumonia and death, as well as long-term consequences such as brain damage, seizures, and mental retardation. (See "pertussis" in Reference Section, page 705.) Despite a dramatic reduction in the number of cases that occurred after an effective vaccine was introduced in the 1940s, the disease has not been eradicated in the United States, and the majority of cases now occur among people ten years of age and older. However, the most serious complications (including death) occur primarily among infected infants younger than one year of age. While modern medical care has reduced the death rate compared to that seen in prior generations, eighteen lives were lost in 2002—all among infants younger than one year of age.

Infants and adults alike can be effectively protected from diphtheria, tetanus, and pertussis through combined immunizations that are routinely started during infancy. The **DTaP (diphtheria/tetanus/acellular pertussis)** vaccine is normally given at two, four, and six months of age, with a booster at fifteen to eighteen months and again between four and six years old. (The fourth dose can be given as early as twelve months of age, provided that six months have passed since the previous dose.)

Until 2005, neither children older than six nor adults were given any additional pertussis booster. However, pertussis vaccine does not provide lifelong immunity—indeed, immunity begins to decline within four to twelve years after vaccination—and increasing numbers of cases among adolescents and adults have been identified in recent years. As a result, since 2005, pertussis vaccine in combination with diphtheria and tetanus—known as **Tdap**—has been available for adolescents and adults younger than sixty-five. A single dose Tdap should be given between the age of eleven and eighteen, unless a dose of **diphtheria/tetanus (Td)** booster has been given within the past five years. Adults ages nineteen to sixty-four should receive a single dose of Tdap unless a Td booster has been given within the previous ten years.

The *aP* in *DTaP* refers to the **acellular** form of the pertussis (whooping cough) vaccine, which contains only a part of the bacterium that is essential for an immune response. DTaP was licensed in 1991 for only the fourth and fifth childhood doses, and then in 1997 for all five immunizations against pertussis during infancy and childhood. It is considered safer and causes fewer reactions than the older DPT vaccine that contained the entire (killed) pertussis bacterium and caused the most side effects among all routine childhood immunizations.

DTaP can cause local soreness and fussiness after the injection, which may be treated with a dose of acetaminophen given at the time of the immunization or shortly thereafter. For babies weighing less than twelve pounds (5.4 kg), the appropriate amount is one-half a dropper (0.4 ml) of the standard infant solution (which contains 80 mg per 0.8 ml). For infants who are heavier than twelve pounds, a full dropper (0.8 ml) may be used. For doses in older children, see the chart on page 609. (Remember that acetaminophen doses are based on weight rather than age.) Fewer than one in one thousand infants will develop a persistent cry (lasting longer than three hours), and one in sixteen thousand may get a high fever (ranging as high as 105°F, or 41°C). Severe allergic reactions occur in fewer than one in one million immunizations. All things considered, these are reasonable risks to take in exchange for protection against three very disruptive and potentially lethal illnesses.

Haemophilus influenzae type B

Before the **Haemophilus influenzae type B (Hib) vaccine** became widely available, this bacteria caused more than twenty thousand serious infections among infants and children in the United States every year. Two out of three of these cases were meningitis (an infection of the membranes that enclose the brain and spinal cord), and the rest were a variety of other life-threatening diseases, including pneumonia, sepsis (bacterial invasion of the bloodstream), and epiglottitis (a highly dangerous inflammation of the flap that covers the airway when swallowing). *Haemophilus* B meningitis took the lives of six hundred children every year and left many more with neurological impairments, including seizures and mental retardation. Since the introduction of the vaccine in 1987, the annual incidence of serious *Haemophilus* B infection in the United States has dropped 98 percent. Indeed, before the vaccine was developed, pediatricians and family physicians routinely cared for infants and small children with *Haemophilus* B meningitis. Now the vast majority of physicians training in these specialties never see a case, while seasoned practitioners recollect (with no fondness whatsoever) the not-so-recent bygone days of lumbar punctures (spinal taps) in sick infants, intensive antibiotic regimens, and parents agonizing over their critically ill children.

The Hib vaccine is normally given at ages two, four, and six months, with a booster between twelve and fifteen months. For some forms of the vaccine, the six-month dose is not necessary. In some offices and clinics, the Hib vaccine may be given in a combination dose that includes DTaP or hepatitis B vaccine. About one in four children receiving the vaccine will experience local redness, swelling, or pain at the injection site, and about one in twenty may experience a fever over 101°F (38°C).

Hib normally is not given to children older than five, but it may be recommended for an older child or adolescent with certain health conditions that affect immune function, such as sickle cell disease, HIV/AIDS, absence of the spleen, or cancer that is being treated by chemotherapy.

Pneumococcus

Pneumococcal infection is a major cause of bacterial meningitis in the United States, although it has become much less common since vaccination has been more widely utilized. Pneumococcus can also cause ear infections (an estimated 5 million cases each year), pneumonia, and sepsis—a serious illness in which large numbers of the bacteria are present in the bloodstream. Children under two years of age are at the greatest risk for significant infection.

Unfortunately, many strains of pneumococcus have become resistant to antibiotics that were once effective in treating it. As a result, prevention of pneumococcal infection has become increasingly important, especially in young infants, who now routinely receive an immunization called the **pneumococcal conjugate vaccine** (**PCV**) at ages two, four, six, and twelve to fifteen months. This vaccine is also recommended for children between the ages of two and five years who have certain health conditions that affect immune function, such as sickle cell disease, HIV/AIDS, absence of the spleen, or other diseases or medications that are likely to impair immunity.

PCV is generally well tolerated. Infants and children given this vaccine may experience soreness or redness at the injection side, irritability, and decreased appetite. About one in three may get a fever of 100.4°F (38°C), and one in fifty, a temperature higher than 102.2°F (39°C).

Polio

Polio is a viral infection that primarily affects children younger than five and is spread from person to person via stool and saliva. The vast majority (95 percent) of those infected with polio have no symptoms, and those who experience discomfort have minor, nonspecific symptoms such as sore throat, low-grade fever, and nausea. About one percent of infected individuals develop stiffness in the neck, back, or legs, and one in two hundred cases leads to irreversible paralysis that may affect the legs or the muscles needed to breathe. Five to ten percent of those who are paralyzed die as a result of difficulty breathing.

Before the widespread availability of vaccine, paralytic polio affected between thirteen thousand and twenty thousand people (mostly children) every year in the United States. During the 1950s, many parents refused to let their children participate in activities such as swimming at public pools during hot summer months because of the fear that they would contract this disease and become permanently dependent on crutches, braces, and wheelchairs. Pictures of rows of children confined to iron lungs (canister-shaped respirators, developed in the 1930s, that assisted breathing) because of paralysis caused by polio were a familiar sight in newspapers and magazines.

The release and widespread use of the Salk (inactivated) polio vaccine in 1955 and then the Sabin oral vaccine in 1961 led to a dramatic reduction of cases in the United States. The Global Polio Eradication Initiative, launched in 1988, has yielded a dramatic reduction in polio cases around the world: from 350,000 in 125 countries in 1988 to 1,951 cases reported in 2005. The last case of polio caused by a naturally occurring (or "wild-type") virus in the western hemisphere was seen in 1991. As of 2006, polio was endemic in only four countries, but one infected individual can readily import the disease into a susceptible population. (Between 2003 and 2005, twenty-five countries that had been free of polio were reinfected through importation.) One international airline passenger could quickly reintroduce polio to North America if vaccination coverage in the United States and Canada were to dip too low.

Inactivated polio vaccine (**IPV**) is routinely given by injection to infants at two and four months, with a third dose between six and eighteen months and a fourth between four and six years of age. **Oral polio vaccine (OPV)** was used in the United States until 2000, when it was phased out because of concerns over the rare incidence of polio being caused by the vaccine. OPV, which is easier to administer, is still utilized in countries where polio caused by wild-type virus occurs. IPV cannot cause polio and has not been found to cause side effects or reactions, except occasional soreness at the site of injection.

Rotavirus

Rotavirus is an intestinal virus that infects virtually all children by the age of five. It is the most common cause of acute diarrhea in children, and it may cause vomiting and fever as well. Most cases are mild, but one in fifty of those infected will become significantly dehydrated. Every year in the United States, rotavirus infections result in more than four hundred thousand visits to physicians, two hundred thousand trips to the emergency room, fifty thousand hospital admissions, and twenty to sixty deaths, primarily among young children. In developing countries, rotavirus is a much more serious threat, causing roughly five hundred thousand deaths every year.

A vaccine against rotavirus, **RotaShield**, was released in 1998. However, after one million children were immunized, it was determined that about one in ten thousand children who had received it developed an unusual intestinal problem called **intussusception**, in which one segment of the intestine telescopes into another, usually causing an obstruction and abdominal pain. This problem, while rare, occurred three times more often among immunized children, and RotaShield was withdrawn by the manufacturer late in 1999.

A new vaccine, **RotaTeq**, was licensed in 2006 and has not been associated with an increased risk for intussusception after more than seventy thousand children have been immunized. RotaTeq is recommended as a routine infant immunization at two, four, and six months of age. The first dose should be given between six and twelve weeks of age, and all three doses should be given by thirty-two weeks. Unlike the DTaP, Hib, and pneumococcal vaccines that are normally given at this age, the rotavirus vaccine is given orally. (The vaccine is not recommended if an infant has already had intussusception, a very rare situation.) While it will not prevent diarrhea that is caused by other types of viruses and bacteria, this vaccine reduces the likelihood of rotavirus diarrhea by nearly 75 percent and the likelihood of severe rotavirus diarrhea by 98 percent.

Measles, mumps, and rubella

Measles (rubeola) is a viral infection that causes fever, severe coldlike symptoms, and a conspicuous red rash. In adults, measles symptoms are usually more severe. Complications from the disease can include diarrhea; secondary bacterial infections of the ears, sinuses, and lymph nodes; and respiratory problems such as wheezing, croup, or pneumonia. Encephalitis, an inflammation of the brain, occurs in one in one thousand cases, and measles is fatal in one to three out of one thousand cases.

Prior to the introduction and widespread distribution of an effective vaccine beginning in 1963, measles infected nearly everyone in the United States, and an average of 450 people died each year because of this infection. While the number of new measles cases reported in the United States in 2001 was under 120, with no reported deaths, in the same year there were 30 to 40 million new cases worldwide and a staggering 745,000 deaths. Because measles can be imported by individuals infected in countries where it is still common, ongoing vaccination of children is very important.

Mumps typically involves swelling and soreness of the parotid glands (salivary glands located in front of the ears), along with fever and fatigue, which in most cases resolves without treatment over two or three weeks. Complications of mumps are uncommon but more serious. These can include inflammation of one or both testicles (**orchitis**), which can lead to sterility; **meningitis**; inflammation of brain tissue (**encephalitis**); inflammation of the pancreas (**pancreatitis**), which manifests as pain in the upper abdomen, nausea, and vomiting; and hearing loss in one or both ears.

Before the availability of mumps vaccine in 1967, about two hundred thousand cases and twenty to thirty deaths occurred every year in the United States. While the disease is very uncommon in the United States, a few hundred cases are reported every year, and mumps remains common in many parts of the world.

Rubella (German measles) is sometimes referred to as **three-day measles**. Rubella is a viral infection that causes a distinct red rash and is less severe than measles except in one respect: If a woman contracts rubella while pregnant, especially during the first trimester, she is at a higher risk of having a miscarriage or delivering a child with **congenital rubella syndrome**, a combination of serious birth defects that may include deafness, blindness, and mental impairment. (See chapter 1, page 22.)

During the last widespread outbreak in the United States, which occurred in 1963–1964, 12 million people developed rubella. Among these were thousands of pregnant women, and as a result, eleven thousand fetuses died and twenty thousand babies were born with significant rubella-related defects. Widespread use of rubella vaccine, first licensed in 1969, has virtually eliminated both the disease and its birth defects in the United States.

Children are routinely immunized against measles, mumps, and rubella using the combination **MMR vaccine**, which is given at twelve to fifteen months, with a second dose typically between the ages of four and six. (The second dose can actually be given at any age, as long as at least twenty-eight days have passed since the first dose.) Most children who receive the MMR vaccine have no side effects from it. However, one in six may experience a fever, and one in twenty may develop a mild rash. A rare complication (one in thirty thousand) is a temporary reduction in the number of platelets, microscopic disclike structures in the blood that play an important role in the clotting process. A very low platelet count could result in bruising and/or excessive bleeding.

Hepatitis A and B

Many forms of viral hepatitis (inflammation of the liver) have been identified, and undoubtedly more will be discovered in the future. Of these, A and B are by far the most common, and these are the two types against which children and adults can be immunized.

Depending upon the type of virus involved and the individual's response to it, the inflammation may go undetected, or at the other extreme, it may produce profound illness. A child or adolescent with clinically significant hepatitis will typically experience fever, flu-like symptoms, fatigue, jaundice (yellow orange skin and yellow color in the white area of the eyes), light or gray stools, and dark urine.

Hepatitis A (previously called **infectious hepatitis**) is transmitted through contaminated food or water and is often acquired during foreign travel. The illness usually begins with five to ten days of nonspecific flu-like symptoms, which may be followed by jaundice. Typically symptoms are mild (or even nonexistent) among children under six, while older children and adolescents are more likely to develop overt symptoms, including jaundice. Children without symptoms who can transmit the virus are a potentially significant source of hepatitis A infection in a community; not only do they shed virus (in stool) longer than adults, often for several weeks, but they may be careless about hygienic habits as well. In the vast majority of cases, this infection resolves without complications in about one or two months, with rest as the primary treatment. Severe illness or death resulting from hepatitis A is extremely uncommon.

Hepatitis A vaccine, which is both safe and effective, is now recommended for all toddlers, with the first dose given between the ages of one and two, and the second dose six to twelve months later. Older children are also candidates for the vaccine if they live in areas with increased rates of hepatitis A infection.[1] People who are planning to travel to high-risk areas (especially in developing countries) should consider obtaining specific hepatitis A vaccine at least four weeks prior to departure.

Hepatitis B (formerly called **serum hepatitis**) is an infection of the liver caused by a virus that is most commonly transmitted in three ways: from an infected mother to her infant, through sexual contact with an infected person, or by exposure to infected blood. However, as many as one in three cases occur without a history of any of these events, which is one reason health officials recommend universal vaccination against this virus.

Fortunately, most people infected with hepatitis B recover without any long-term effects. In a small percentage of cases, however, the immediate illness can be severe enough to cause death. In others, prolonged active infection with the virus occurs, a process that can eventually lead to cirrhosis or even cancer of the liver. While hepatitis B is not a common childhood disease, children are at a higher risk for developing long-term complications if they become infected. Among adults infected with hepatitis B, between 2 and 6 percent will develop the chronic form of the disease. But among infants and children who become infected, 30 percent of those one to five years of age and 90 percent of infants (including those who are infected at birth) develop the chronic form of the infection and are at risk for long-term complications. (See "hepatitis" in Reference Section, page 682.)

Because of the significant number of new cases of hepatitis B that continue to occur each year, and because of its potential for causing serious long-term consequences, universal immunization of all children against this virus has been recommended since 1991, and in many states it is required for school entry. The vaccine may be given at any age, starting at birth, and involves three injections—the second given one month after the first, and the third injection at least four months after the second. Like hepatitis A vaccine, hepatitis B vaccine is very safe. Because of the way these vaccines are manufactured, *it is impossible to develop hepatitis or any other infection from either of these immunizations*. Occasionally a child or adult receiving the vaccine will experience a little soreness where the injection was given, and possibly a mild fever. Sometimes one or more hepatitis B immunizations may be given in a combination vaccine with *Haemophilus influenzae* type B, DTaP, or hepatitis A.

Chickenpox (varicella)

Chickenpox is caused by the varicella-zoster virus. The hallmark of the disease is an itchy rash consisting of small red spots that evolve into blisters. Chickenpox is usually a mild disease, but in rare instances it can involve the lungs or the brain, with potentially serious consequences, including death. (Bacteria can also infect skin through the blisters.) It may be tempting to think of chickenpox as an annoying but otherwise benign and inevitable childhood event. But prior to the introduction of the chickenpox vaccine, this infection affected 3 to 4 million people (mostly children) and caused eleven thousand hospital admissions and one hundred deaths every year in the United States. Furthermore, after a chickenpox infection some of the varicella-zoster virus can survive within nerve cells and then reactivate at a later date, causing a painful condition called **shingles**. This is characterized by the appearance of groups of blisters involving an area of skin supplied by one nerve root (and thus always only on one side of the body). The rash is accompanied by sharp, stabbing pains (called **neuralgia**), which in a small percentage of cases (usually in the elderly) may continue for months or even years.

Because of the discomfort, potential for serious complications, and disruption of school and work schedules that inevitably accompany this common infection, routine immunization against chickenpox at the age of twelve to eighteen months has been recommended since 1995. The vaccine is 85 to 90 percent effective at preventing chickenpox, and it is 100 percent effective at preventing severe disease. Because of reports of breakthrough infections (which are mild but still contagious) among children who have been immunized, as of 2006, a second dose is recommended between the ages of four and six. (Adolescents thirteen and older who have had neither the disease nor the vaccine can have two doses at least twenty-eight days apart.)

Because the recommended immunization schedule for chickenpox is now the same as that for the MMR (measles, mumps, and rubella) vaccine, a combination measles-mumps-rubella-chickenpox vaccine has been licensed. If separate MMR and chickenpox vaccines are to be given, they should either occur on the same day or one month apart. (The chickenpox vaccine is less effective if given between one and twenty-nine days after the MMR vaccine.)

Influenza

Better known simply as the flu, **influenza** is an acute infection that frequently occurs in epidemics or occasionally in worldwide outbreaks known as pandemics. Three types of influenza virus, known simply as types A, B, and C, have been identified; types A and B are responsible for nearly all epidemics. Unfortunately, each of the three types has a number of different strains, and the virus undergoes subtle biochemical changes on an ongoing basis. As a result, someone who catches the flu or is vaccinated this year usually will not be immune during next year's outbreak. That is why those who need flu shots must get a new one each year. Influenza is typically seen in the United States and Canada in the fall and winter, usually involving strains that have been identified a few months earlier in Asia. These outbreaks develop quickly, spread rapidly, and may involve sizable numbers of people in a given community.

The symptoms of influenza include the abrupt onset of fever, chills, sore throat, headache, and body aches. This is much more intense than the runny nose and a scratchy throat brought on by a cold. Some patients sum up their symptoms by saying, "It feels like I've just been hit by a truck." (The "stomach flu," an abrupt and unpleasant bout of nausea, vomiting, and diarrhea that mercifully lasts only a day or two in most cases, is nearly always **gastroenteritis**, an acute inflammation of the stomach and intestinal tract. This is usually caused by one of two types of virus—rotavirus and norovirus—that have nothing to do with influenza.) Aside from the misery it typically causes, influenza can also have serious or even deadly complications, including pneumonia, dehydration, and worsening of chronic conditions such as cardiovascular and lung diseases (including asthma). These complications are more likely to occur among young children, older adults, and those with weakened immunity.

Since the strains that are likely to cause trouble change from year to year (and new strains may appear as well), a new vaccine must be developed and millions of doses distributed on an annual basis—a phenomenal accomplishment that is often taken for granted as flu shots are distributed every fall and winter. **Influenza vaccine** is recommended for all children between the ages of six months and five years because they are at greater risk for complications from this infection. It should also be given to infants and children older than six months with chronic conditions such as heart disease, diabetes, chronic respiratory disturbances (especially asthma), sickle cell disease, kidney failure, and HIV infection, as well as other disorders of the immune system. For children with these and other long-term medical problems, influenza can be a much more serious or even fatal illness. Other family members in the home of a high-risk child, as well as caregivers for children younger than six months of age, should be vaccinated as well. Some parents may choose to vaccinate older children who *don't* have chronic illnesses to minimize the risk of their missing school or other important activities. For healthy children older than five and nonpregnant adults younger than fifty who are reluctant to have an injection, a flu vaccine in the form of a nasal spray is available.

Meningococcal infection

Meningococcus is a type of bacteria that can cause a fast-moving and often fatal infection (frequently including an intense form of **meningitis**, or inflammation of the tissue that covers the brain and spinal cord). More than 2,500 people develop a serious meningococcal infection in the United States every year. Of these, 10 to 15 percent die, and of those who survive, about 10 to 20 percent suffer significant long-term consequences.

For years, an immunization to protect against meningococcus was advised for military recruits and college freshmen living in dormitories. Now it is recommended for all preadolescents as part of their eleven- or twelve-year checkup. Teenagers can and should receive this vaccine if they have not yet been immunized.

Human papillomavirus (HPV)

HPV is the most common sexually transmitted infection in the United States, with some 20 million Americans infected. Most of these infections do not cause symptoms and disappear without medical treatment. However, some who are infected develop growths known as **genital warts**. Of greater concern is the association of certain strains of HPV—typically *not* those that cause genital warts—with cancer of the cervix (the opening of the uterus), vulva (the external female genital area), anus, and penis. Cancer of the cervix is diagnosed in more than ten thousand women, and kills more than 3,500, in the United States every year. **Gardasil**, a vaccine that can help prevent infection with the types of HPV most commonly associated with cancer (as well as types commonly associated with genital warts), is now available and targeted for eleven- to twelve-year-old girls. (It may be given as early as age nine.) The vaccine is given in a three-dose series, with the second and third doses given two and six months after the first. It can also be given to adolescents and young women thirteen to twenty-six years of age.

While the thought of giving your school-age child a vaccine to help protect against a sexually transmitted virus might be unsettling to parents, there are a number of good reasons to consider doing so:

- The immune response is more robust when the vaccine is given at a younger age.
- Girls in this age-group are not likely to have been exposed to HPV infection.
- Even if an adolescent girl or young woman makes and keeps a commitment to remain sexually abstinent until marriage, she cannot guarantee that the man she marries will have done so, nor can she determine whether or not he is carrying (and could transmit to her) one of the high-risk HPV viruses. Furthermore, if she were to be the victim of a sexual assault, the attacker could be carrying one or more of the high-risk viruses.
- The HPV immunization process presents an opportunity for parents to have candid, ongoing conversations about sexuality before the onset of adolescence. A girl receiving the vaccine should understand that it does not protect her against all strains of HPV or against other sexually transmitted organisms, and that reserving sexual activity for marriage is the healthiest decision she can make—physically, emotionally, and spiritually. For some detailed input and guidance regarding this important parenting task, see "Taking On the Tough Topics: Sex and Substances" (page 459) and the Special Concerns section "A Parent's Guide to Teen Sexuality" (page 509).

Weighing the Risks of Vaccination

As we have already noted, vaccinations sometimes cause unpleasant side effects, although the vast majority of these are minor. Low-grade fever, rash, irritability, and local reactions—redness, swelling, or soreness at the site of the injection—are the most common. The risks of more serious events, such as high fever and body aches, are much lower, and the chances of a life-threatening allergic reaction to an immunization are less than one in a million doses. Other severe but extremely rare occurrences after vaccination include:

- Long-term seizures and brain damage after receiving DTaP vaccine
- Encephalitis, deafness, and long-term seizures after receiving MMR vaccine
- Pneumonia after receiving varicella (chickenpox) vaccine

These devastating events are so rare that it is often difficult for experts to be sure whether or not they are caused by the vaccine.

Vaccine safety has been and continues to be a high priority for health-care professionals and regulatory agencies, and vaccines deemed to be unsafe or whose benefits are outweighed by their risks are removed from the recommended immunization schedule. For example, oral polio vaccine (OPV) contained a weakened but live form of the polio virus that in rare cases (one in 2.4 million) could actually cause polio. Today the chances of getting polio naturally are so low that the risks posed by OPV were regarded as unacceptably high by comparison, so this vaccine was taken off the market in the United States. Despite its higher cost, inactivated polio vaccine (IPV), which is given by injection, is the only form currently in use in the United States.

It should be noted that there are instances in which a health-care provider might postpone immunization of a child. If a child is given a vaccine while ill, for example, it might be difficult to determine whether subsequent symptoms, especially fever, are due to the vaccine or part of the natural history of the illness. Likewise, a severe illness might prevent a child from developing an adequate immune response to a vaccine, rendering it less effective than if the child were healthy. Also, some vaccines contain live but weakened viruses that are considered unsafe for children with suppressed immunity—such as those who have HIV/AIDS or are undergoing certain cancer chemotherapies.

Despite the dramatic effectiveness of vaccines in curbing the spread of serious diseases and saving lives over the past century (especially the past fifty years), some have strongly questioned their safety, especially in young infants. In response to horror stories—real or rumored—about vaccines and the opinions of naysayers—often with dubious credentials—disseminated on the Internet, some parents have concluded that immunizations represent a greater threat than the diseases they are designed to prevent, and they refuse to have their children immunized. This decision represents a serious miscalculation of the potential risk to the individual child, not to mention the community at large. Ironically, the success of widespread vaccination programs in the United States can give a false impression that the infections for which children are immunized no longer represent a threat. Hopefully a careful reading of the facts and figures provided earlier in this section will counter that conclusion.

What about individuals who have never been vaccinated and yet have never contracted measles, mumps, or other diseases for which immunizations are routinely given? The fact that these people remain disease free might seem to argue against the necessity of vaccination, but their good health would be better interpreted as evidence of the benefits of **herd immunity**, a phenomenon that provides a buffer of immunized individuals between infected persons and unvaccinated ones. For example, someone with an infectious disease may encounter many individuals in his community during the course of his or her infection. If most people in the community are immunized against the disease, the chance of it being spread throughout the community is lower than it would be if many people were not immunized. (Because tetanus is not spread from person to person, herd immunity offers no protective benefit for this disease in an unvaccinated individual.)

Herd immunity requires that a large number of people in the community be immunized. In regions where vaccination rates drop, herd immunity decreases and the incidence of disease rises. Pertussis (whooping cough), for example, is notorious for reappearing wherever vaccinations against it wane in popularity. In eight countries where immunization declined, cases of pertussis soared to ten to one hundred times the infection rate seen in other countries where vaccination rates remained stable. A well-publicized and sad example occurred in Japan in the 1970s, when concerns over the safety of the older pertussis vaccine caused the vaccination rate to drop from about 80 percent in 1974 to 20 percent by 1979. As a result, a pertussis epidemic occurred in 1979, resulting in thirteen thousand cases of whooping cough and forty-one deaths.

When vaccination rates subsequently climbed, the incidence of pertussis once again dropped.

Refusing immunizations thus not only puts the unvaccinated individual at risk but also increases the risk of disease for others in the community. This may be of special concern for individuals who, because of chronic illness or suppressed immunity, are not able to be vaccinated and therefore rely on herd immunity for protection. Furthermore, in many parts of the world, herd immunity to many dangerous infections has not been established, and thus it may be particularly risky for an unvaccinated child or adolescent to travel abroad.

Vaccine Safety Controversies

We have already noted that the vast majority of vaccine side effects are minor and that significant adverse events such as pneumonia or encephalitis occur very rarely. In recent years, however, other serious reactions have been attributed to vaccines, and those claims have caused many parents to decide against immunizing their children. Here are three specific controversies surrounding vaccines that have generated a great deal of concern:

- Does MMR cause autism?
- Does the mercury preservative used in some vaccines lead to learning or developmental disabilities?
- Do multiple vaccinations in a short time span overwork an infant's immune system and cause harm?

MMR and autism

In 1998, a team of British researchers published a preliminary report based on their examinations of twelve children, all of whom showed symptoms of both inflammatory bowel disease and developmental regression. Nine of these children were diagnosed with autism. From this report, the parents of these children concluded that there must have been a connection between the onset of these problems and their immunization with the MMR vaccine. The authors of this study suggested only the possibility of an association between the MMR vaccine and some cases of autism, and they clearly stated that there was not enough information to establish any definitive link. Nevertheless, their report received wide media attention, and the notion of a connection between MMR and autism has persisted, especially on the Internet, even after ten of the study's thirteen authors issued a statement in 2004 retracting their original interpretations and reaffirming that there is insufficient evidence to establish a causal link between autism and the vaccine.

Since the 1998 study was published, several other reports have investigated a possible connection between autism and the MMR vaccine, and so far no such association has been established. For example, researchers in the United Kingdom and the United States have found that increases in the number of newly diagnosed cases of autism had occurred in places where MMR coverage had remained relatively consistent over the same time frame, indicating that the vaccine was not a factor.

Reputable professional organizations such as the American Academy of Pediatrics and the Institute of Medicine have extensively and independently reviewed this and other research, and they have reached the same conclusion: The available evidence indicates no relationship between the MMR vaccine and autism.

Mercury

Since the 1930s, a mercury-containing preservative called **thimerosal** has been added to some vaccines to inhibit bacterial or fungal growth in the preparations. A number of parents of children with ADHD, speech or language delays, or neurological and developmental problems questioned whether vaccines containing thimerosal were responsible for these conditions.

In 1997, the Food and Drug Administration performed a comprehensive review of vaccines containing thimerosal and found that the amount of mercury a child might receive under existing recommended vaccine schedules was within acceptable FDA limits. However, depending on the vaccine formulation administered and the weight of the infant, it was determined that during the first six months of life, a child could possibly be exposed to a level of mercury higher than that recommended by the Environmental Protection Agency. As a precautionary measure, the Centers for Disease Control and Prevention and the American Academy of Pediatrics issued a joint statement (later affirmed by the American Academy of Family Physicians) calling upon vaccine manufacturers to eliminate or greatly reduce the amount of thimerosal used in vaccines.

Although data from several studies indicated that toxicity from thimerosal did not occur until the level of exposure reached one hundred or one thousand times that found in vaccines, it was nonetheless considered prudent to urge the reduction of mercury content to as low a level as possible. (It should be noted that thimerosal had never been used in many routine vaccines, including inactivated polio, MMR, varicella, and two common formulations of DTaP.) Today, with the exception of some influenza vaccines, all vaccines on the recommended childhood immunization schedule appear in either thimerosal-free or thimerosal-reduced forms (with only trace amounts of this compound). Influenza vaccines are also available in thimerosal-reduced forms.

Too many vaccines

Some parents have expressed concern that their infant's immune system might be weakened as a result of getting too many vaccines at one time. Currently, some vaccines are administered in combination (such as the MMR and DTaP vaccines), and infants often receive several vaccines during a single office visit. This means fewer office visits, which not only saves time and money for the parents but also is less traumatic for the child. Research indicates that this multiple vaccination strategy offers no increased risk of adverse reactions compared to the administration of single vaccinations over a course of many office visits.

Part of the concern over multiple immunizations is that it overloads a child's immune system. However, a child's immune system is capable of responding to antigens even before birth. Since an infant's immune system has never encountered some of the viruses or bacteria that cause serious diseases (and therefore cannot defend against them), it is important that immunizations be given at this time when children are most vulnerable.

The total number of immune challenges given during vaccinations is negligible. Over the entire recommended immunization schedule, the total number of immune challenges a child receives due to vaccines is just a fraction of the number of challenges he experiences every day. A viral respiratory infection introduces between four and ten antigens, while a case of strep throat can introduce between twenty-five and fifty. Furthermore, thousands of bacteria are present on a baby's skin and in a baby's intestinal tract, mouth, and nasal passages.

While some parents suggest that, just to be safe, children should receive only one vaccine per visit and that vaccines should be given one component at a time rather than in combination, most medical professionals and child-health advocates, including those in national leadership roles, disagree. Spreading immunizations over a longer period of time is cumbersome for parents and ultimately more unpleasant for the child. Furthermore, it decreases the likelihood that a child will stay up-to-date on his immunization schedule and may leave him vulnerable to disease during the intervals between vaccinations.

Some Final Comments about Childhood Immunization

The Advisory Committee on Immunization Practices (ACIP) is a panel of experts in the United States that recommends which immunizations should be given, and when, to children, adolescents, and adults. Because ACIP's recommendations (including guidelines on how to make up one or more missed immunizations) may change slightly from year to year, and because new combinations of vaccines become available periodically, you should review your child's (and your) immunization status with your own physician. To check the most current immunization recommendations, you can visit http://www.cdc.gov/nip/ACIP. You can also learn more about each immunization discussed in this section at the Centers for Disease Control and Prevention's vaccine information Web site (http://www.cdc.gov/nip/publications/vis/default.htm).

Finally, here are some additional recommendations:

- Keep your own immunization record for each child (and yourself), and update it every time a new vaccination is given.
- Be sure to report any significant reaction to a vaccine to your child's physician, and make note of it in your child's immunization record. This is particularly important if the immunization is one in a series that is going to involve additional doses in the future. Reactions that should be noted include fever over 102°F (39°C), a seizure or other significant changes in behavior following a vaccination, and especially a severe allergic reaction such as **anaphylaxis** that may involve severe difficulty in breathing, a drop in blood pressure, hives, and severe abdominal pain.
- Be sure to tell your child's physician if he is ill at the time of any proposed immunization(s). Many vaccines can be given if a child has a mild illness such as a cold, while some may be postponed, especially if the child is running a fever.

While virtually every credible health-care professional and infectious-disease expert agrees that it is in the best interest of children to be immunized in accordance with current schedules, it is the responsibility of parents or guardians to see that this task is actually carried out. If, after reading this section, you still have doubts about whether it is safe and appropriate to immunize your child, we strongly recommend that you confer with her doctor and make decisions carefully and prayerfully, based on sound information.

FIGURE 1. Recommended immunization schedule for persons aged 0–6 years — United States, 2007

Vaccine ▼ Age ▶	Birth	1 month	2 months	4 months	6 months	12 months	15 months	18 months	19–23 months	2–3 years	4–6 years
Hepatitis B[1]	HepB	HepB		See footnote 1		HepB				HepB Series	
Rotavirus[2]			Rota	Rota	Rota						
Diphtheria, Tetanus, Pertussis[3]			DTaP	DTaP	DTaP		DTaP				DTaP
Haemophilus influenzae type b[4]			Hib	Hib	Hib[4]	Hib			Hib		
Pneumococcal[5]			PCV	PCV	PCV	PCV				PCV PPV	
Inactivated Poliovirus			IPV	IPV		IPV					IPV
Influenza[6]						Influenza (Yearly)					
Measles, Mumps, Rubella[7]						MMR					MMR
Varicella[8]						Varicella					Varicella
Hepatitis A[9]						HepA (2 doses)				HepA Series	
Meningococcal[10]										MPSV4	

- ▢ Range of recommended ages
- ▢ Catch-up immunization
- ▢ Certain high-risk groups

This schedule indicates the recommended ages for routine administration of currently licensed childhood vaccines, as of December 1, 2006, for children aged 0–6 years. Additional information is available at http://www.cdc.gov/nip/recs/child-schedule.htm. Any dose not administered at the recommended age should be administered at any subsequent visit, when indicated and feasible. Additional vaccines may be licensed and recommended during the year. Licensed combination vaccines may be used whenever any components of the combination are indicated and other components of the vaccine are not contraindicated and if approved by the Food and Drug Administration for that dose of the series. Providers should consult the respective Advisory Committee on Immunization Practices statement for detailed recommendations. Clinically significant adverse events that follow immunization should be reported to the Vaccine Adverse Event Reporting System (VAERS). Guidance about how to obtain and complete a VAERS form is available at http://www.vaers.hhs.gov or by telephone, 800-822-7967.

1. **Hepatitis B vaccine (HepB).** *(Minimum age: birth)*
   At birth:
   - Administer monovalent HepB to all newborns before hospital discharge.
   - If mother is hepatitis surface antigen (HBsAg)-positive, administer HepB and 0.5 mL of hepatitis B immune globulin (HBIG) within 12 hours of birth.
   - If mother's HBsAg status is unknown, administer HepB within 12 hours of birth. Determine the HBsAg status as soon as possible and if HBsAg-positive, administer HBIG (no later than age 1 week).
   - If mother is HBsAg-negative, the birth dose can only be delayed with physician's order and mothers' negative HBsAg laboratory report documented in the infant's medical record.
   After the birth dose:
   - The HepB series should be completed with either monovalent HepB or a combination vaccine containing HepB. The second dose should be administered at age 1–2 months. The final dose should be administered at age ≥24 weeks. Infants born to HBsAg-positive mothers should be tested for HBsAg and antibody to HBsAg after completion of ≥3 doses of a licensed HepB series, at age 9–18 months (generally at the next well-child visit).
   4-month dose:
   - It is permissible to administer 4 doses of HepB when combination vaccines are administered after the birth dose. If monovalent HepB is used for doses after the birth dose, a dose at age 4 months is not needed.
2. **Rotavirus vaccine (Rota).** *(Minimum age: 6 weeks)*
   - Administer the first dose at age 6–12 weeks. Do not start the series later than age 12 weeks.
   - Administer the final dose in the series by age 32 weeks. Do not administer a dose later than age 32 weeks.
   - Data on safety and efficacy outside of these age ranges are insufficient.
3. **Diphtheria and tetanus toxoids and acellular pertussis vaccine (DTaP).** *(Minimum age: 6 weeks)*
   - The fourth dose of DTaP may be administered as early as age 12 months, provided 6 months have elapsed since the third dose.
   - Administer the final dose in the series at age 4–6 years.
4. **Haemophilus influenzae type b conjugate vaccine (Hib).** *(Minimum age: 6 weeks)*
   - If PRP-OMP (PedvaxHIB® or ComVax® [Merck]) is administered at ages 2 and 4 months, a dose at age 6 months is not required.
   - TriHiBit® (DTaP/Hib) combination products should not be used for primary immunization but can be used as boosters following any Hib vaccine in children aged ≥12 months.

5. **Pneumococcal vaccine.** *(Minimum age: 6 weeks for pneumococcal conjugate vaccine [PCV]; 2 years for pneumococcal polysaccharide vaccine [PPV])*
   - Administer PCV at ages 24–59 months in certain high-risk groups. Administer PPV to children aged ≥2 years in certain high-risk groups. See *MMWR* 2000;49(No. RR-9):1–35.
6. **Influenza vaccine.** *(Minimum age: 6 months for trivalent inactivated influenza vaccine [TIV]; 5 years for live, attenuated influenza vaccine [LAIV])*
   - All children aged 6–59 months and close contacts of all children aged 0–59 months are recommended to receive influenza vaccine.
   - Influenza vaccine is recommended annually for children aged ≥59 months with certain risk factors, health-care workers, and other persons (including household members) in close contact with persons in groups at high risk. See *MMWR* 2006;55(No. RR-10):1–41.
   - For healthy persons aged 5–49 years, LAIV may be used as an alternative to TIV.
   - Children receiving TIV should receive 0.25 mL if aged 6–35 months or 0.5 mL if aged ≥3 years.
   - Children aged <9 years who are receiving influenza vaccine for the first time should receive 2 doses (separated by ≥4 weeks for TIV and ≥6 weeks for LAIV).
7. **Measles, mumps, and rubella vaccine (MMR).** *(Minimum age: 12 months)*
   - Administer the second dose of MMR at age 4–6 years. MMR may be administered before age 4–6 years, provided ≥4 weeks have elapsed since the first dose and both doses are administered at age ≥12 months.
8. **Varicella vaccine.** *(Minimum age: 12 months)*
   - Administer the second dose of varicella vaccine at age 4–6 years. Varicella vaccine may be administered before age 4–6 years, provided that ≥3 months have elapsed since the first dose and both doses are administered at age ≥12 months. If second dose was administered ≥28 days following the first dose, the second dose does not need to be repeated.
9. **Hepatitis A vaccine (HepA).** *(Minimum age: 12 months)*
   - HepA is recommended for all children aged 1 year (i.e., aged 12–23 months). The 2 doses in the series should be administered at least 6 months apart.
   - Children not fully vaccinated by age 2 years can be vaccinated at subsequent visits.
   - HepA is recommended for certain other groups of children, including in areas where vaccination programs target older children. See *MMWR* 2006;55(No. RR-7):1–23.
10. **Meningococcal polysaccharide vaccine (MPSV4).** *(Minimum age: 2 years)*
    - Administer MPSV4 to children aged 2–10 years with terminal complement deficiencies or anatomic or functional asplenia and certain other high-risk groups. See *MMWR* 2005;54(No. RR-7):1–21.

The Recommended Immunization Schedules for Persons Aged 0–18 Years are approved by the Advisory Committee on Immunization Practices (http://www.cdc.gov/nip/acip), the American Academy of Pediatrics (http://www.aap.org), and the American Academy of Family Physicians (http://www.aafp.org).

FIGURE 2. Recommended immunization schedule for persons aged 7–18 years — United States, 2007

Vaccine ▼　　　　Age ►	7–10 years	11–12 YEARS	13–14 years	15 years	16–18 years
Tetanus, Diphtheria, Pertussis[1]	See footnote 1	Tdap	Tdap		
Human Papillomavirus[2]	See footnote 2	HPV (3 doses)	HPV Series		
Meningococcal[3]	MPSV4	MCV4		MCV4[3] MCV4	
Pneumococcal[4]		PPV			
Influenza[5]		Influenza (Yearly)			
Hepatitis A[6]		HepA Series			
Hepatitis B[7]		HepB Series			
Inactivated Poliovirus[8]		IVP Series			
Measles, Mumps, Rubella[9]		MMR Series			
Varicella[10]		Varicella Series			

Range of recommended ages

Catch-up immunization

Certain high-risk groups

This schedule indicates the recommended ages for routine administration of currently licensed childhood vaccines, as of December 1, 2006, for children aged 7–18 years. Additional information is available at http://www.cdc.gov/nip/recs/child-schedule.htm. Any dose not administered at the recommended age should be administered at any subsequent visit, when indicated and feasible. Additional vaccines may be licensed and recommended during the year. Licensed combination vaccines may be used whenever any components of the combination are indicated and other components of the vaccine are not contraindicated and if approved by the Food and Drug Administration for that dose of the series. Providers should consult the respective Advisory Committee on Immunization Practices statement for detailed recommendations. Clinically significant adverse events that follow immunization should be reported to the Vaccine Adverse Event Reporting System (VAERS). Guidance about how to obtain and complete a VAERS form is available at http://www.vaers.hhs.gov or by telephone, 800-822-7967.

1. **Tetanus and diphtheria toxoids and acellular pertussis vaccine (Tdap).** *(Minimum age: 10 years for BOOSTRIX® and 11 years for ADACEL™)*
   - Administer at age 11–12 years for those who have completed the recommended childhood DTP/DTaP vaccination series and have not received a tetanus and diphtheria toxoids vaccine (Td) booster dose.
   - Adolescents aged 13–18 years who missed the 11–12 year Td/Tdap booster dose should also receive a single dose of Tdap if they have completed the recommended childhood DTP/DTaP vaccination series.
2. **Human papillomavirus vaccine (HPV).** *(Minimum age: 9 years)*
   - Administer the first dose of the HPV vaccine series to females at age 11–12 years.
   - Administer the second dose 2 months after the first dose and the third dose 6 months after the first dose.
   - Administer the HPV vaccine series to females at age 13–18 years if not previously vaccinated.
3. **Meningococcal vaccine.** *(Minimum age: 11 years for meningococcal conjugate vaccine [MCV4]; 2 years for meningococcal polysaccharide vaccine [MPSV4])*
   - Administer MCV4 at age 11–12 years and to previously unvaccinated adolescents at high school entry (at approximately age 15 years).
   - Administer MCV4 to previously unvaccinated college freshmen living in dormitories; MPSV4 is an acceptable alternative.
   - Vaccination against invasive meningococcal disease is recommended for children and adolescents aged ≥2 years with terminal complement deficiencies or anatomic or functional asplenia and certain other high-risk groups. See *MMWR* 2005;54(No. RR-7):1–21. Use MPSV4 for children aged 2–10 years and MCV4 or MPSV4 for older children.
4. **Pneumococcal polysaccharide vaccine (PPV).** *(Minimum age: 2 years)*
   - Administer for certain high-risk groups. See *MMWR* 1997;46(No. RR-8):1–24, and *MMWR* 2000;49(No. RR-9):1–35.
5. **Influenza vaccine.** *(Minimum age: 6 months for trivalent inactivated influenza vaccine [TIV]; 5 years for live, attenuated influenza vaccine [LAIV])*
   - Influenza vaccine is recommended annually for persons with certain risk factors, health-care workers, and other persons (including household members) in close contact with persons in groups at high risk. See *MMWR* 2006;55 (No. RR-10):1–41.
   - For healthy persons aged 5–49 years, LAIV may be used as an alternative to TIV.
   - Children aged <9 years who are receiving influenza vaccine for the first time should receive 2 doses (separated by ≥4 weeks for TIV and ≥6 weeks for LAIV).

6. **Hepatitis A vaccine (HepA).** *(Minimum age: 12 months)*
   - The 2 doses in the series should be administered at least 6 months apart.
   - HepA is recommended for certain other groups of children, including in areas where vaccination programs target older children. See *MMWR* 2006;55 (No. RR-7):1–23.
7. **Hepatitis B vaccine (HepB).** *(Minimum age: birth)*
   - Administer the 3-dose series to those who were not previously vaccinated.
   - A 2-dose series of Recombivax HB® is licensed for children aged 11–15 years.
8. **Inactivated poliovirus vaccine (IPV).** *(Minimum age: 6 weeks)*
   - For children who received an all-IPV or all-oral poliovirus (OPV) series, a fourth dose is not necessary if the third dose was administered at age ≥4 years.
   - If both OPV and IPV were administered as part of a series, a total of 4 doses should be administered, regardless of the child's current age.
9. **Measles, mumps, and rubella vaccine (MMR).** *(Minimum age: 12 months)*
   - If not previously vaccinated, administer 2 doses of MMR during any visit, with ≥4 weeks between the doses.
10. **Varicella vaccine.** *(Minimum age: 12 months)*
   - Administer 2 doses of varicella vaccine to persons without evidence of immunity.
   - Administer 2 doses of varicella vaccine to persons aged ≤13 years at least 3 months apart. Do not repeat the second dose, if administered ≥28 days after the first dose.
   - Administer 2 doses of varicella vaccine to persons aged ≥13 years at least 4 weeks apart.

The Recommended Immunization Schedules for Persons Aged 0–18 Years are approved by the Advisory Committee on Immunization Practices (http://www.cdc.gov/nip/acip), the American Academy of Pediatrics (http://www.aap.org), and the American Academy of Family Physicians (http://www.aafp.org).

for children and adolescents who start late or who are more than 1 month behind

TABLE. Catch-up immunization schedule for persons aged 4 months–18 years who start late or who are ≥1 month behind — United States, 2007

The table below provides catch-up schedules and minimum intervals between doses for children whose vaccinations have been delayed. A vaccine series does not need to be restarted, regardless of the time that has elapsed between doses. Use the section appropriate for the child's age.

CATCH-UP SCHEDULE FOR PERSONS AGED 4 MONTHS–6 YEARS

Vaccine	Medium age for Dose 1	Minimum interval between doses			
		Dose 1 to Dose 2	Dose 2 to Dose 3	Dose 4 to Dose 5	
Hepatitis B[1]	Birth	4 weeks	8 weeks (and 16 weeks after first dose)		
Rotavirus[2]	6 weeks	4 weeks	4 weeks		
Diphtheria, Tetanus, Pertussis[3]	6 weeks	4 weeks	4 weeks	6 months	6 months[3]
Haemophilus influenzae type b[4]	6 weeks	4 weeks if first dose administered at age <12 months / 8 weeks (as final dose) if first dose administered at age 12–14 months / No further doses needed if first dose administered at age ≥15 months	4 weeks[4] if current age <12 months / 8 weeks (as final dose)[4] if current age ≥12 months and second dose administered at age <15 months / No further doses needed if previous dose administered at age ≥15 months	8 weeks (as final dose) This dose only necessary for children aged 12 months–5 years who received 3 doses before age 12 months	
Pneumococcal[5]	6 weeks	4 weeks if first dose administered at age <12 months and current age <24 months / 8 weeks (as final dose) if first dose administered at age ≥12 months or current age 24–59 months / No further doses needed for healthy children if first dose administered at age ≥24 months	4 weeks if current age <12 months / 8 weeks (as final dose) if current age ≥12 months / No further doses needed for healthy children if previous dose administered at age ≥24 months	8 weeks (as final dose) This dose only necessary for children aged 12 months–5 years who received 3 doses before age 12 months	
Inactivated Poliovirus[6]	6 weeks	4 weeks	4 weeks	4 weeks[6]	
Measles, Mumps, Rubella[7]	12 months	4 weeks			
Varicella[8]	12 months	3 months			
Hepatitis A[9]	12 months	6 months			

CATCH-UP SCHEDULE FOR PERSONS AGED 7–18 YEARS

Vaccine	Medium age for Dose 1	Dose 1 to Dose 2	Dose 2 to Dose 3	Dose 4 to Dose 5	
Tetanus, Diphtheria/ Tetanus, Diphtheria, Pertussis[10]	7 years[10]	4 weeks	8 weeks if first dose administered at age <12 months / 6 months if first dose administered at age ≥12 months	6 months if first dose administered at age <12 months	
Human Papillomavirus[11]	9 years	4 weeks	12 weeks		
Hepatitis A[9]	12 months	6 months			
Hepatitis B[1]	Birth	4 weeks	8 weeks (and 16 weeks after first dose)		
Inactivated Poliovirus[6]	6 weeks	4 weeks	4 weeks	4 weeks[6]	
Measles, Mumps, Rubella[7]	12 months	4 weeks			
Varicella[8]	12 months	4 weeks if first dose administered at age ≥13 years / 3 months if first dose administered at age <13 years			

1. Hepatitis B vaccine (HepB). *(Minimum age: birth)*
- Administer the 3-dose series to those who were not previously vaccinated.
- A 2-dose series of Recombivax HB® is licensed for children aged 11–15 years.

2. Rotavirus vaccine (Rota). *(Minimum age: 6 weeks)*
- Do not start the series later than age 12 weeks.
- Administer the final dose in the series by age 32 weeks. Do not administer a dose later than age 32 weeks.
- Data on safety and efficacy outside of these age ranges are insufficient.

3. Diphtheria and tetanus toxoids and acellular pertussis vaccine (DTaP). *(Minimum age: 6 weeks)*
- The fifth dose is not necessary if the fourth dose was administered at age ≥4 years.
- DTaP is not indicated for persons aged ≥7 years.

4. Haemophilus influenzae type b conjugate vaccine (Hib). *(Minimum age: 6 weeks)*
- Vaccine is not generally recommended for children aged ≥5 years.
- If current age <12 months and the first 2 doses were PRP-OMP (PedvaxHIB® or ComVax® [Merck]), the third (and final) dose should be administered at age 12–15 months and at least 8 weeks after the second dose.
- If first dose was administered at age 7–11 months, administer 2 doses separated by 4 weeks plus a booster at age 12–15 months.

5. Pneumococcal conjugate vaccine (PCV). *(Minimum age: 6 weeks)*
- Vaccine is not generally recommended for children aged ≥5 years.

6. Inactivated poliovirus vaccine (IPV). *(Minimum age: 6 weeks)*
- For children who received an all-IPV or all-oral poliovirus (OPV) series, a fourth dose is not necessary if third dose was administered at age ≥4 years.
- If both OPV and IPV were administered as part of a series, a total of 4 doses should be administered, regardless of the child's current age.

7. Measles, mumps, and rubella vaccine (MMR). *(Minimum age: 12 months)*
- The second dose of MMR is recommended routinely at age 4–6 years but may be administered earlier if desired.
- If not previously vaccinated, administer 2 doses of MMR during any visit with ≥4 weeks between the doses.

8. Varicella vaccine. *(Minimum age: 12 months)*
- The second dose of varicella vaccine is recommended routinely at age 4–6 years but may be administered earlier if desired.
- Do not repeat the second dose in persons aged <13 years if administered ≥28 days after the first dose.

9. Hepatitis A vaccine (HepA). *(Minimum age: 12 months)*
- HepA is recommended for certain groups of children, including in areas where vaccination programs target older children. See *MMWR* 2006;55(No. RR-7):1–23.

10. Tetanus and diphtheria toxoids vaccine (Td) and tetanus and diphtheria toxoids and acellular pertussis vaccine (Tdap). *(Minimum ages: 7 years for Td, 10 years for BOOSTRIX®, and 11 years for ADACEL™)*
- Tdap should be substituted for a single dose of Td in the primary catch-up series or as a booster if age appropriate; use Td for other doses.
- A 5-year interval from the last Td dose is encouraged when Tdap is used as a booster dose. A booster (fourth) dose is needed if any of the previous doses were administered at age <12 months. Refer to ACIP recommendations for further information. See *MMWR* 2006;55(No. RR-3).

11. Human papillomavirus vaccine (HPV). *(Minimum age: 9 years)*
- Administer the HPV vaccine series to females at age 13–18 years if not previously vaccinated.

Information about reporting reactions after immunization is available online at http://www.vaers.hhs.gov or by telephone via the 24-hour national toll-free information line 800-822-7967. Suspected cases of vaccine-preventable diseases should be reported to the state or local health department. Additional information, including precautions and contraindications for immunization, is available from the National Center for Immunization and Respiratory Diseases at http://www.cdc.gov/nip/default.htm or telephone, 800-CDC-INFO (800-232-4636).

Musculoskeletal Problems in Children

The human body is designed with an elaborate system of approximately seven hundred muscles and more than two hundred bones. Like all other components of the body, the musculoskeletal system functions very well most of the time, but problems can develop at any age.

This section is not intended as a comprehensive textbook of pediatric orthopaedics. Its purpose is to help you become somewhat familiar with the more common musculoskeletal problems of infancy, childhood, and adolescence. These will be divided into three major groupings: injuries (the most common); inflammatory and infectious diseases; and structural disorders, a number of which are congenital.

A note on medical terminology: **Orthopaedics** (a term derived from the Greek words for "straighten" and "child") is the surgical specialty that deals with the musculoskeletal system. **Orthopaedists** or **orthopaedic surgeons** have completed a number of years of training in this field following graduation from medical school. Among many other problems, orthopaedists care for fractures and other types of traumatic injury involving bones, joints, muscles, and the tissues that connect them. Physicians who specialize in the nonsurgical treatment of metabolic and inflammatory disorders of joints, bones, and muscles (for example, syndromes such as **rheumatoid arthritis**) are called **rheumatologists**.

Fractures, Sprains, Dislocations, Strains, and Tendonitis

A child's bones are generally much more flexible than an adult's. They are covered with a fairly thick layer of fibrous tissue called **periosteum**, which contributes to healing if a bone should fracture. At each end of long bones (such as the shinbone), there is an area known as the **growth plate**, where growth in the length and width of the bone takes place. The fastest-growing growth plates are the lower end of the **femur** (thighbone) and the upper end of the **tibia** (shinbone). Growth plates disappear completely during adolescence.

Fractures

As a child grows, gains weight, and becomes more mobile, falls and other accidents can exert enough stress on a bone to cause a **fracture**, or break. There are several types of fractures.

BONE ANATOMY

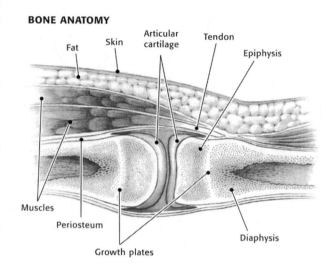

Fat · Skin · Articular cartilage · Tendon · Epiphysis · Muscles · Periosteum · Growth plates · Diaphysis

Nondisplaced fracture. Sometimes a bone breaks completely but the pieces are not separated. Many fractures in children can be subtle, and they may go unnoticed while the child continues to use the arm or leg. A common nondisplaced fracture in children is a torus or "buckle" fracture where the bone literally buckles rather than breaking all the way through. Depending upon the location of the fracture, it will be straightened if necessary and then immobilized in a splint or cast for a period of time recommended by the treating physician.

Greenstick fracture. If you have ever taken a fresh branch off a tree and tried to break it, you may have noticed that one side of the branch may break while the other side bends. The same phenomenon can occur in a child's bone; this is called a greenstick fracture. The treatment is the same as for a nondisplaced fracture.

Displaced fracture. This occurs when the bone breaks completely and the broken ends move away from one another. This will be treated in one of three ways:

In a **closed reduction**, the child is usually sedated or given a general anesthetic. In some instances, the physician may decide to inject local anesthetic directly into the fracture site. The doctor then attempts to move the broken pieces into proper alignment. If the procedure is successful, a cast or splint is applied for stabilization until the fracture heals.

Sometimes the broken ends of the bone can be brought together, but they are so unstable that they will not remain in proper alignment, even with a cast. In such cases **metal pins** are inserted into the bone to hold the pieces together. This is also done under anesthetic, and usually a splint or cast is applied afterward. Depending upon the location of the fracture, the pins will be left in place for a few weeks and then removed.

If the ends of the fractured bone cannot be brought together by a closed reduction, an **open reduction** will be performed to accomplish this goal. In this case, the surgeon has to make an incision in the region of the fracture to be able to see the bone ends directly. The alignment is corrected and is often held in place with pins or a plate and screws.

Open fracture. This injury, in which one end of a fractured bone protrudes through the skin, is an urgent situation. The wound should be covered and the child taken immediately to the nearest emergency room. Often, open fractures are contaminated with dirt, grass, clothing, etc. The surgeon will attempt to remove all of the debris to reduce the chance of infection. Antibiotics should be given. Usually the wound is not sutured together right away, but it may be closed later if there is no sign of infection.

Sometimes weeks after a child has suffered a fracture, the bone will appear crooked, even though the healing process is going well. Because bone is a living tissue, it not only heals but also undergoes **remodeling**, a process by which the growth plate and periosteum gradually correct the deformity. If an X-ray of the same bone is taken years later, it may be hard to tell that it was ever broken.

Remodeling cannot correct all deformities, however, and the ability of bones to remodel decreases as a child gets older. If a fracture involves the growth plate, a crooked and/or short limb occasionally results, and surgery may be required to correct this problem.

FRACTURES

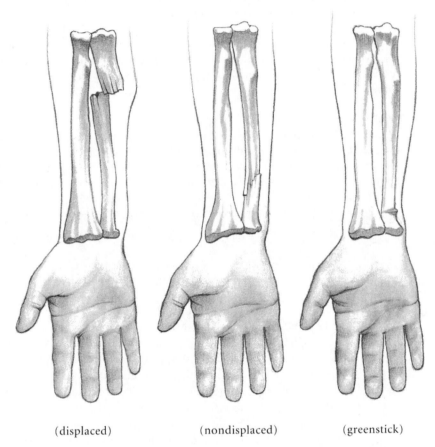

(displaced)   (nondisplaced)   (greenstick)

Sprains

To allow adjacent bones to move properly in relation to each other, the joint between them is bridged by strong but flexible fibrous bands called **ligaments** that help keep the bones in proper alignment. A sudden, forceful twisting motion can cause stretching or tearing of a ligament, better known as a **sprain.** This will typically produce pain when a child attempts to move or put weight on the affected area, as well as swelling and often a bluish discoloration. Since sprains are more common in adults than in children, and since it may be difficult to determine if a fracture is present merely by looking at an injured arm or leg, a child with these symptoms should be evaluated by a physician.

The simple acronym **RICE** can help you remember the steps to take following a sprain:

- **R**est the injured area.
- **I**ce or cold packs can decrease swelling and pain, but their contact with skin should be limited to twenty minutes, three to four times a day.
- **C**ompression, such as an elastic wrap around the affected area, can also reduce swelling and pain. This should not be so tight that it causes discomfort, numbness, or tingling.
- **E**levate the injured area as much as possible for twenty-four hours to help reduce uncomfortable swelling.

In addition, the affected area should be protected from further injury by minimizing movement (using a splint or crutches if necessary) until swelling and pain have resolved. You should seek medical input if there is no improvement in two or three days.

Dislocations

When a **dislocation** occurs, the relationship of the two bones that make up a joint is disrupted. For example, in a dislocation of the hip, the ball comes out of the socket. The areas most commonly affected are the shoulder, elbow, kneecap, and fingers. Frequently there is an associated fracture. Dislocations are best treated by a physi-

GENERAL FIRST-AID PRINCIPLES FOR BONE AND JOINT INJURIES

Some fractures are obvious, and others are suspected when significant pain, swelling, or discoloration follows an injury. If you know or suspect that your child has fractured a bone, do the following:

- Make sure he avoids putting pressure or weight on it.
- Gently splint the affected area to reduce pain and the risk of further damage. For an arm injury, a simple sling or a magazine held against the arm with an elastic wrap will usually be adequate. A leg may be splinted by carefully binding it to the other leg with a towel placed between them.
- Don't try to manipulate fractures or dislocations unless you are trained to do so and you are certain of the nature of the injury. Significant additional injury can occur through inappropriate movement of an injured limb.
- If possible, cover any open wounds to prevent further contamination.
- Don't give the child anything to eat or drink until the injuries have been evaluated and it is clear that surgery will not be needed.
- Take the child to the nearest emergency department for treatment.
- If the neck appears to be injured, it is very important that the child be moved only by people trained to deal with this type of injury. This is an emergency, and assistance should be sought immediately by calling 911. As much as possible, keep the child from moving while you wait. The transport team will carefully apply a neck brace and place the child on a spine board. ■

cian—not by untrained bystanders—and will likely require sedating medication or a general anesthetic to relax surrounding muscles before the bones are put back in their proper relationship. The injured area is usually protected for a few weeks and followed by a gradual return to normal activities. Shoulder and kneecap dislocations often occur repeatedly after the initial episode; sometimes surgery is needed to prevent further episodes.

A common dislocation in younger children is the so-called **nursemaid's elbow,** which occurs when a toddler or preschooler is tugged forcefully by one arm. Often the injury takes place when an adult is holding the hand of a child who trips while walking. The adult may actually pull upward in an effort to stop the fall. This causes the upper end of the **radius** (the shorter of the two bones in the forearm) to slip through a ring of fibrous tissue that normally holds it in place. Afterward the child's arm may hang limp at his side, and he will protest loudly if anyone attempts to move it. Often a doctor can resolve this type of dislocation with a simple maneuver. Normally this quickly resolves the pain, and soon afterward the child will begin using the arm again.

Strains

During vigorous exercise, muscles may be stretched or even torn, resulting in a **strain.** This will cause pain and tenderness of the muscle itself—for example, the front of the thigh following repetitive jumping or a day of skiing—rather than pain in a joint that a sprain would cause. Most strains can be treated at home with rest and a mild pain reliever (such as ibuprofen or acetaminophen). If the pain is severe or does not improve after forty-eight hours, the child should be evaluated by a physician. A child or adolescent who has had problems with strained muscles should be taught to do gentle stretching exercises prior to any strenuous exertion.

Tendonitis

Tendons are fibrous tissues that attach muscle to bone. Some tendons, such as those extending to the fingers, are quite long. Repetitive use of certain muscles may cause local inflammation known as **tendonitis** at or near the attachment site. If your child's doctor diagnoses this problem, avoidance of activities that provoke pain and possibly the use of anti-inflammatory medications such as ibuprofen may be recommended until the pain resolves.

Inflammatory Diseases

Arthritis

In **arthritis**, one or more joints become inflamed, resulting in local tenderness, swelling, redness, and pain with movement. Arthritis is much less common in children than in adults. Its occurrence is nearly always an acute condition and not the result of the long-term wear and tear that goes with aging.

Juvenile rheumatoid arthritis (JRA)

This is the most common cause of chronic arthritis in children. It generally occurs between the ages of three and six or early in puberty. (It is uncommon before the age of one or after the age of sixteen.) The symptoms of JRA may disappear in 50 percent of affected children. Generally the greater the number of joints involved, the more severe the disease. In JRA, for reasons not clearly understood, the child's own immune system begins to damage joints, and in some cases other tissues as well. There are a number of different forms of JRA:

- The **polyarticular** form involves five or more joints and is more common in girls than boys. Both small joints and large joints can be affected. There may be an associated low-grade fever.
- The **pauciarticular** form, which is more common, involves only one or two joints. It may also be associated with inflammation of structures within the eye, which can lead to glaucoma or cataracts.
- The **systemic** form involves not only joints but also other tissues such as the lungs or heart or the fibrous linings that surround them.

A combination of swelling and pain within one or more joints that lasts for at least six weeks and is accompanied by fever may lead a child's physician to consider this diagnosis and order laboratory tests. If JRA is diagnosed, treatment will focus on containing the inflammation for prolonged periods of time. **Nonsteroidal anti-inflammatory drugs** (**NSAIDs**), including ibuprofen (Advil and other brands) or naproxen (Aleve), are often the first line of treatment. Aspirin is not used routinely because of concerns that it might irritate the stomach and provoke bleeding, as well as its association with Reye's syndrome (see "Reye's syndrome" in Reference Section, page 709). However, in some children aspirin may prove to be an effective treatment. If JRA is not well controlled with an NSAID, the physician (nearly always a rheumatologist) might prescribe one or more **disease modifying antirheumatic drugs** (**DMARDs**), which over time can be very effective but require close monitoring for possible side effects. In some cases, **corticosteroids** or a newer class of drugs known as **biologic agents** may be deployed. **Physical therapy** is sometimes recommended to maintain muscle tone and range of motion in affected joints.

Lyme disease

This is the most common disease spread by tick bites. It is caused by bacteria carried by the pinhead-size deer tick. In untreated cases, arthritis may develop weeks or months after the initial infection. Symptoms primarily involve painful, swollen joints—especially of the knees. This arthritis is often transient, but it may become chronic in 10 percent of those who are untreated. (See "Lyme disease" in Reference Section, page 695.)

Transient synovitis

This inflammation occurs most commonly in the hip and much more frequently than septic arthritis (see below). The child may have all the symptoms of septic arthritis—especially a limp or an unwillingness to walk because of pain, and a slight fever—but she does not appear as ill as a child with septic arthritis. Medical evaluation will be necessary to make a diagnosis. If the physician is confident that the child does not have an infected joint, he or she may recommend rest, quiet activities, and ibuprofen.

Infectious Diseases

Septic arthritis

A bacterial infection of a joint, or **septic arthritis,** can be very serious and could potentially cause permanent, major damage if not detected early and treated appropriately. The hip and the knee are most commonly involved. The cause may be obvious (such as a puncture wound from a nail), but more often the source of the infection is unknown. Most likely bacteria are carried through the bloodstream and deposited in the lining of the joint. Septic arthritis may also begin when a bone infection (**osteomyelitis**) extends from a bone into a joint (see below).

Symptoms of septic arthritis vary, depending on the age of the child. In young infants, the only sign may be irritability until it becomes clear that the baby does not tolerate movement of the affected joint. A toddler might develop a limp and within a short time refuse to walk. She may appear quite ill with a high fever, and any attempt to move the joint produces severe pain. The school-age child might complain of pain in a joint after playing sports or other vigorous activity, and by the next day the affected joint is hot and swollen.

A child who has a hot, tender joint should be evaluated by a physician as soon as possible. If the diagnosis of septic arthritis is confirmed, the joint will need to be drained and washed out. This is usually done under general anesthesia in the operating room. The child will also need to be treated with antibiotics, which will first be given intravenously. After several days the antibiotic may be given orally.

Osteomyelitis

This bone infection may produce symptoms similar to those in septic arthritis. The child will be acutely ill and irritable, with fever and a sore, tender limb that she may refuse to use. The doctor may do special tests in addition to routine blood work to confirm the diagnosis and identify the specific bacteria causing the infection. Because X-rays taken early in the disease may appear completely normal, the physician may order other imaging procedures such as a CT scan, MRI, or bone scan (a study utilizing a tiny amount of radioactive material that selectively accumulates in bone that is inflamed or recently damaged). This may identify one or more areas of inflamed or damaged bone that cannot be visualized with standard X-rays. If an area of redness and swelling is visible, the physician may also attempt to aspirate a sample of infected material through a needle after numbing the area with local anesthesia.

When osteomyelitis is diagnosed, it will be treated with a prolonged course of intravenous antibiotics followed by a longer course of oral antibiotics. In some cases, surgical removal of infected material is necessary.

Structural Problems and Pain Syndromes of the Limbs

Flat feet

Parents are often concerned about the appearance of a child's feet and specifically whether **flat feet** might be present. When children begin walking, it appears that many have flat feet because of increased fat deposits in the arch. As a child grows, it becomes apparent that, in most instances, the feet are not flat at all; an arch becomes evident by age ten.

If a child is diagnosed with flat feet there is little justification for prescribing expensive "orthopaedic" shoes or custom-molded inserts, since there is no proof that they help to correct this condition.

FLAT FEET

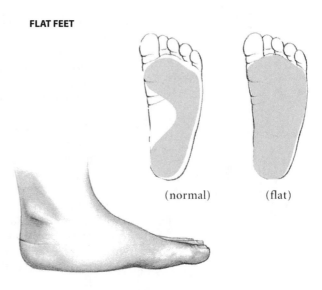

(normal) (flat)

Similarly, there is no evidence that high-top shoes are better than low-cut shoes for a child with flat feet.

However, children with flat feet may develop aching in their feet, particularly when they have been on them for much of the day. In such cases, it may be helpful to provide a support within the shoe. For some, a good pair of running shoes with an arch support already in place will be adequate. For others, a custom-molded insert may be helpful in providing relief. Surgery is needed only very rarely to treat flat feet and is usually reserved for severe cases that have not responded to simpler measures. Before agreeing to such surgery, a second and possibly even a third opinion should be sought. At least one of the consultants should be an orthopaedic surgeon with extensive experience in treating children's feet.

FLEXIBLE FLAT FOOT

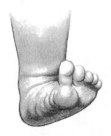

Flexible flatfoot (calcaneovalgus)

This is a common deformity found at birth. The top of the foot lies directly against the front of the leg. This occurs as a result of positioning within the uterus, and it may occur in one or both feet. Fortunately the deformity starts to correct spontaneously after delivery, and gentle stretching can help speed up the correction. While this will often correct itself without treatment or with gentle stretching alone, infants with a more significant deformity may be treated with splinting or casting. If the deformity is very rigid, the diagnosis may instead be a rare condition called **congenital vertical talus** that will require surgical intervention.

CURVED FOOT
(Metatarsus Adductus)

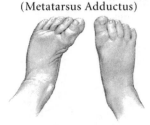

Curved foot (metatarsus adductus)

This deformity is common at birth and often mistakenly called clubfoot, but it does not have all the features of clubfoot and generally causes fewer problems. The curved shape of the foot spontaneously corrects itself by the first birthday in 85 to 90 percent of cases; thus, treatment is often reserved for more severe or persistent cases. Treatment usually involves stretching and casting or using special braces or shoes. In very few cases will the deformity persist or be severe enough to warrant surgery. Occasionally there is an association between metatarsus adductus and **developmental dislocation (dysplasia) of the hip** (see page 767).

CLUBFOOT

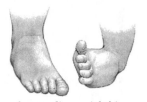

(normal)   (club)

Clubfoot (talipes equinovarus)

Clubfoot is a congenital deformity in which one or both feet are misshapen and twisted into an abnormal position. This deformity is easily recognized in newborns, and can vary considerably in severity and rigidity. In most cases the cause of clubfoot is unknown. The affected foot will be smaller than normal; the calf above the clubfoot will often be significantly smaller, and the entire leg slightly shorter than normal. These differences will continue throughout the child's growth process. Treatment should be started as soon as possible by a physician who has experience treating this condition. The initial treatment includes frequent stretching of the foot by the physician followed by the application of a cast. In some instances, the deformity will be corrected. However, some children will require a small procedure to lengthen a tight heel cord. This technique is usually referred to as the **Ponseti technique**. When the problem is sufficiently corrected, the cast will likely be replaced by a brace or special shoes for several months.

A small number of clubfeet are resistant to complete correction by this method. Such cases require a surgical procedure to release the tight structures and position the bones in the foot to a more normal relationship. An even smaller number of clubfeet will require further surgery as the child becomes older to correct persistent or recurrent deformity.

In the majority of cases, near-normal shape and function is achieved, and the child is able to fully participate in all activities.

High-arched foot (pes cavus)

HIGH ARCH

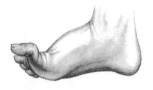

This condition, which is much less common than flat feet, may indicate the presence of an underlying disease. If your child's feet appear normal during childhood but develop high arches later in childhood or adolescence, have him assessed by a physician, who will look carefully for evidence of an underlying orthopaedic, neurologic, or neuromuscular problem.

Bunions (hallux valgus)

A **bunion** is a prominence (bump) that forms at the joint at the base of the big toe. The big toe itself is usually angled toward the second toe. The soft tissue over the bump thickens because of the pressure of the shoe. Bunions can occur on one or both feet in older children and adolescents. Often the appearance of the deformity and the pain that accompanies it bring an adolescent to the doctor. In some cases, finding shoes that are wide enough to fit comfortably is difficult. Occasionally, a **foot orthosis** (such as an arch support) may help slow down the deformity's development, but usually acceptable correction is achieved only through surgery. While surgery is successful much of the time, sometimes subsequent surgeries become necessary. If pain is tolerable and appropriate footwear can be found, it is best to postpone surgery as long as possible. There is a very high recurrence rate after surgery for this deformity in an adolescent. The likelihood of recurrence declines as the adolescent becomes an adult.

Heel pain

Often seen in very active children, heel pain probably represents an overuse syndrome. One of the most common causes is **Sever's disease**, which occurs where the Achilles tendon attaches to the heel bone. The heel is often quite tender to the touch at this site. In most instances, restricting activities that cause the greatest discomfort, developing an exercise program to stretch the heel cord, and adding heel cups inside the shoes are of greatest benefit. Icing the heel before and after activity can also help. Very rarely is it necessary to immobilize the leg in a cast. Surgery does not help this problem. In most cases, this condition disappears on its own in ten to twelve weeks.

Knee pain and disorders

Knee pain is a common complaint in children and adolescents. A number of conditions can cause this, including significant hip problems that produce pain near the knee. (See "Slipped capital femoral epiphysis," page 769.) Most often pain in the knee occurs during activity rather than when the knee is at rest.

Pain in the region of the kneecap is very common in teenage girls, although the underlying cause is often not clear. Frequently the best approach is to start a program of thigh-muscle (quadriceps) strengthening and hamstring-stretching exercises with occasional use of a nonsteroidal anti-inflammatory drug such as ibuprofen. Sometimes it's advisable to restrict participation in physical education and sports until the pain resolves.

An extremely tender area, often with an obvious bump, may be present about an inch below the kneecap where the large tendon from the kneecap attaches to the shinbone. This condition is known as **Osgood-Schlatter's disease** and is similar to Sever's disease of the heel. It is best treated by rest, application of ice packs, ibuprofen, thigh exercises, and in rare cases, immobilization. This condition usually resolves on its own as the child passes through adolescence.

A condition called **osteochondritis dissecans**, which produces a softening of bone under the cartilage, can cause pain deep within the knee. With restriction of running and jumping activities, this condition usually heals slowly on its own. Occasionally the affected area of bone and/or cartilage separates partially or completely from the rest of the bone and requires surgery.

BOWLEG (Genu Varum)

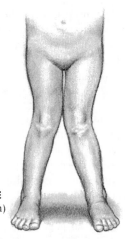

KNOCK-KNEE
(Genu Valgum)

If your child complains of a sore, swollen knee, has no history of injury or infection, and the symptoms persist for several weeks without improvement, he may have **juvenile rheumatoid arthritis** (see page 761).

As children grow, their legs usually progressively change in shape. Toddlers are most commonly quite **bowlegged**. Between the ages of two and six, children typically appear **knock-kneed**. After the age of five or six, the legs gradually become straighter, although they don't always correct completely.

If your child's legs seem excessively crooked and don't seem to be following the basic pattern described above, it is important that you consult your child's doctor. Occasionally, severe bowlegs or knock-knees are signs of underlying disease. Leg braces have not proven very effective in correcting these deformities, and surgery becomes necessary in some cases.

Intoeing, outtoeing, and toe-walking

A common reason for a child to be brought to an orthopaedic surgeon is to be evaluated for **intoeing** (a pigeon-toed appearance of the feet). The complaint most frequently expressed by parents is that the child seems to trip and fall a lot.

PIGEON TOES

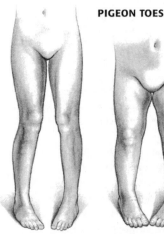

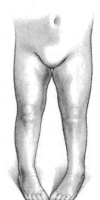

(internal femoral rotation)   (internal tibial rotation)

The source of intoeing varies. Younger children may have a curved deformity of their feet (**metatarsus adductus**; see page 764) that gives the appearance of intoeing. Children most commonly develop intoeing because they have a **torsion** (twist) in the **tibia** (shinbone) or the **femur** (thighbone), or sometimes both. Torsion of the tibia is usually responsible for intoeing in a child younger than age two or three. If the problem begins when the child is over age three, the location of the torsion is more often in the femur.

Most intoeing among children younger than eight will correct on its own without braces, casts, or surgery. A slight degree of persistent intoeing is not a serious problem. (Some of the fastest runners in the world have this condition.) There is no clear evidence that persistent intoeing leads to increased incidence of degenerative arthritis in the hip in adulthood. Several methods have been used in children to try to correct torsional problems, including wedges on the sides of the shoes, braces, various night splints, and casting. There is little evidence that any of these methods directly improves the degree of intoeing.

Many children "toe out" when they start to stand. In most children this condition will also correct itself in time. A persistent **outtoeing** deformity is much less common than intoeing. If the problem is severe, it may require corrective surgery.

A condition called the **miserable malalignment syndrome,** in which the thigh bone (femur) is turned inward and the shin bone (tibia) is turned outward, may result in significant knee problems. Surgery may be required to correct the malrotation.

Occasionally a child will continue **toe-walking** (walking on tiptoes, which is often seen when a toddler is learning to walk) through the first few years of life or even later into the school years. This usually results from one of the following:

- A persistent habit, which can be altered by having the child practice a normal gait
- Congenital tight heel cords, which may need gentle stretching
- Cerebral palsy, in which case other manifestations of this disorder will be present as well

If your child toe-walks all or most of the time after the age of three, your physician or an orthopaedist can evaluate her gait and recommend an appropriate approach for correcting it.

Growing pains

Children commonly experience growing pains. A typical scenario is that of a healthy five-year-old who is very active during the day and has no noticeable problems. He goes to bed but sometime later awakens, screaming about pain in one leg or occasionally in both. (The pain might develop before he falls asleep.) There is no history of injury, and the child is not sick. The parents do what they can—rubbing the leg, applying heat, giving him a warm bath or a pain reliever—and in thirty to sixty minutes the pain resolves and the child goes back to sleep. In the morning, it appears that nothing has happened. There is no pain, limp, or any other evidence of a problem. This may recur frequently, at which point the child is taken to the doctor, who can find absolutely nothing wrong with him. The physician says the child has **growing pains.**

Nobody really knows what causes these pains, nor does there appear to be any way to prevent them. The pain is reasonably short-lived, and there are no long-term consequences. The best advice is to be patient because the pains will eventually stop.

On the other hand, if a child screams with pain at night and then limps and complains of pain during the day, he needs to be evaluated by a physician.

Developmental dislocation (dysplasia) of the hip (DDH)

A physician may uncover some form of unstable hip in an infant shortly after birth. If the hip is completely out of place, it is **dislocated.** This is the most serious infant hip problem, and it should be diagnosed and treated as soon as possible. Generally a splint, harness, or cast will be required for several weeks, with frequent progress checks by the physician. In some instances, the hip cannot be maintained in the joint and surgery (open reduction) must be performed to stabilize the hip.

Sometimes the hip is in its proper position, but with a little pressure it can be moved out of joint and then back into place. This is called a **dislocatable hip**. If this is detected at birth, the physician may decide to use some form of splint, harness, or brace to hold the hips in the best position for healing. In most cases, the hip will eventually develop normally.

In other instances, the hip-joint socket is too shallow, in which case the hip is called **dysplastic**. A dysplastic hip can be extremely difficult to diagnose, however, even in the most experienced hands. It may become apparent only after the hip eventually dislocates. In milder forms, it may not become apparent for many years and then manifest itself as a painful hip with early arthritis.

The term **developmental dislocation (dysplasia) of the hip (DDH)** is now used to refer to this problem. DDH occurs more commonly among female infants and among babies born in the breech position. The left hip is more often affected than the right, but DDH can be present in both hips.

Some babies' hips will appear normal during the examination at birth but will later dislocate. You may notice when changing the baby's diaper that you cannot spread one leg as far as the other. This should be pointed out to the doctor. An X-ray or sonogram will probably be performed, and if a dislocated hip is found, treatment will begin.

SLIPPED CAPITAL FEMORAL EPIPHYSIS

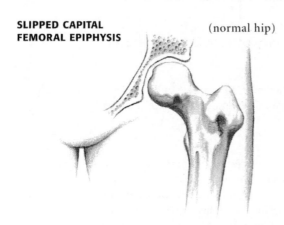

(normal hip)

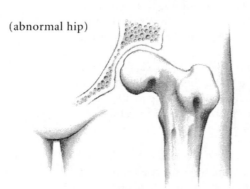

(abnormal hip)

Occasionally a dislocated hip will not be diagnosed until the child begins to walk. The child may be observed walking on tiptoes on one leg, which will appear shorter than the other. See a doctor immediately; an X-ray will probably be taken. The older the child is when the diagnosis is made, the more likely it is that surgery will be required to place the hip back in the socket.

Legg-Calvé-Perthes disease

This occurs in children as young as eighteen months and as old as fourteen years of age, with a peak incidence between ages four and eight. Boys are affected four or five times more often than girls. The condition develops when, for reasons that are uncertain, the blood supply to the ball-shaped head of the **femur** (thighbone) is interrupted. As a result, part or all of the head of the femur dies. At first there may be little or no indication of this. Over time, however, the hip will begin to hurt, causing the child to limp and decrease movement of the hip joint. An X-ray of the hip usually confirms the diagnosis.

While the body is removing the dead bone and replacing it with new live bone, the tissue at the head of the femur is somewhat soft and pliable. This tissue can become deformed, and if uncorrected, the deformity can become permanent as the soft tissue transforms to bone.

Once Legg-Calvé-Perthes disease is diagnosed, treatment focuses on keeping the ball of the femur positioned properly in the hip socket and moving the hip as much as possible to help mold the pliable tissue into the appropriate round shape. Casting, bracing, exercise, and surgery may be used.

Slipped capital femoral epiphysis

This most commonly occurs in overweight teenage boys, but it can occur in girls as well. The ball of the hip joint gradually slides off the neck of the **femur** (thighbone). The slip takes place through the growth plate. The child will begin to experience groin pain or sometimes knee pain, which worsens with activity. One foot may turn out more than the other when the child walks. Diagnosis and treatment must be carried out as early as possible. If there are delays, the ball of the hip may slide further off the neck, making the prognosis worse. Sometimes a fall causes further slippage, in which case pain is usually more severe. In either case, surgical treatment is necessary.

A final note about pain and limping

From time to time, a child may complain that an arm or leg hurts and then become absorbed in play without any apparent discomfort. If this happens, it is reasonable to wait and watch for further reports of pain. However, any complaint about pain in a particular area that lasts for more than a day or two should be investigated by a physician. In a child of any age, *a limp or unwillingness to walk because of leg pain may indicate a significant problem and should be reported to the doctor immediately.*

Problems Involving the Neck and Back

Torticollis is sometimes referred to as wryneck. The child's head is tilted to one side with the face turned slightly to the other side. When it occurs during infancy, torticollis is usually not visible at birth but appears a week or so later. The cause is not clear, but the problem is usually an excessive tightness in one of the neck muscles. The treatment is usually a careful stretching program. In many cases the deformity will be corrected with this treatment. If the problem is ignored until the child is older than one year, a stretching program is not likely to be effective, and surgery is usually necessary.

SCOLIOSIS

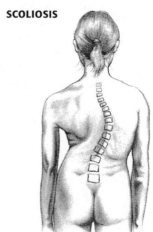

A similar condition may develop acutely in an older child, and it will typically disappear over a few days. Rest, local heat, pain relievers, and possibly physical therapy may be helpful once a physician has confirmed the diagnosis. There are a number of possible causes of this condition, including inflammation or infection in the neck and throat, as well as injury. It is important to have the child checked by a physician to make a diagnosis and initiate appropriate treatment.

Scoliosis is an abnormal curvature (usually sideways) of the spine, most commonly seen in adolescent girls but occasionally found in boys. The cause of this curvature is not known, but it seems to be associated with the growth spurt that takes place around puberty. Often the problem is picked up in school screening programs when the child bends forward at the hips while the examiner looks along the spine. If the ribs on one side appear higher than those on the other, scoliosis may be present. An X-ray is the best way to confirm the presence of a spinal curvature, from which the doctors can measure the degree of curvature.

Usually more than one curve is present. One of the curves is considered the main or primary curve, and the other is called the compensatory or secondary curve. If the primary curve is less than 25 degrees, the child is watched carefully, and an X-ray is usually taken every six months during the growth spurt. Curves greater than 25 degrees may require a brace to prevent the curve from worsening. (It is not intended to reduce the size of the curve.) Bracing is not always effective, however, and sometimes the curve continues to worsen. If the curve exceeds 40 to 50 degrees, surgery is usually recommended. The surgery is designed to decrease the size of the curve and fuse the spine to prevent the curve from increasing again. Steel rods are usually inserted along the spine to hold it straighter while the fusion becomes solid. After the fusion is solid (usually twelve months or more after surgery), the child can return to most activities.

KYPHOSIS

Kyphosis (round back) is an accentuation of the normal curvature of the upper (thoracic) spine. Usually this is first noted during early adolescence (between the ages of ten and fifteen) and often simply results from bad posture. More severe cases are associated with wedge-shaped vertebrae, a condition known as **Scheuermann's disease**. This is treated with an approach similar to that taken with scoliosis. If the deformity is less than 45 degrees, the child is taught specific exercises and watched carefully. If the curve is between 45 and 75 degrees, braces are used. Once the curve exceeds 75 degrees, surgery is usually needed to correct it.

Unlike back pain in adults, back pain in children normally should not be assumed to be the by-product of a mechanical strain (simple wear and tear) of ligaments and muscles, unless there is a particular injury that might explain it. *Ongoing back pain in a child or adolescent usually has a specific cause, such as inflammation, structural abnormality, infection, or (rarely) tumor, and it should be thoroughly assessed by a physician.*

One of the more common causes of back pain in children is **spondylolysis**, a bony defect in a vertebra that may allow it to slide forward onto the one below it (a condition called **spondylolisthesis**). Treatment is directed toward relieving symptoms and may include rest, anti-inflammatory medication, and perhaps bracing. If pain persists despite conservative treatment, or if the gradual slipping of one vertebra onto the other worsens, surgery may be necessary to stabilize that short segment of the spine.

Some ABCs of Good Nutrition

The capacity to eat and enjoy food is one of God's wonderful gifts to our physical bodies. Furthermore, we live in a nation blessed with a richer bounty and variety of foods for the average citizen than at any other time or place in history. One would think that deciding what to eat would be a straightforward task, or even a pleasant diversion from the normal routines of life. But we are bombarded every day with advice—half of which seems to contradict the other half—about what we should or shouldn't eat, drink, and take as supplements. This section is intended to help you make better-informed decisions about the foods you buy and prepare for yourself and your family.

If you stop and think about it, the utilization of food by our bodies is an incredible accomplishment. An enormous number and variety of substances that we chew and swallow, usually with some pleasure, are broken down into basic components that serve three general purposes:

- Provide a steady supply of fuel for thousands of mechanical, electrical, and chemical processes that go on twenty-four hours a day
- Build, maintain, and repair structures of incredibly diverse shapes, sizes, and constituents
- Protect to some degree against certain destructive processes

If you read chapter 1, you may recall that we considered what might happen if a new law mandated that you could own only one automobile in your lifetime, and that you couldn't ride in anyone else's vehicle. (See page 6.) How would you take care of your "one and only" car? What kind of fuel would you buy to fill its tank? Taking that analogy another step, consider for a moment that we that may buy the best fuel for our car, but that high-grade petroleum can still only power the engine and perhaps reduce some wear and tear. Imagine if a vehicle could take gasoline and other raw materials and then repair itself. Such a car exists only in the realm of fantasy. The fact that our bodies do all of this and more without our awareness, supervision, or understanding is truly mind-boggling.

There are six types of nutrients: **carbohydrates**, **fats**, **proteins**, **vitamins**, **minerals**, and **water**. The first three are called **macronutrients** because we use them in substantial quantities. They are also known as **energy-yielding nutrients** because they provide the fuel we need for all bodily functions. **Vitamins** and **minerals** are called **micronutrients** because of the tiny amounts we use. They do not provide any energy but play a number of important roles in releasing and regulating it.

A detailed review of the basic structure, function, and important roles of the various macro- and micronutrients cannot be covered here (For those who are interested, that information can be found in the Focus on the Family *Complete Guide to Family Health, Nutrition, and Fitness* [Tyndale, 2006]). Even with a solid understanding of the basic nutrients, it is important to remember that we eat food, not isolated biochemical compounds. Furthermore, the length and breadth of cuisines, preparation techniques, cultural variations, cost factors, and individual tastes are so enormous that no single book, let alone one section within a book, can possibly address all of the choices we have to make in setting our daily table.

Nevertheless, we must start somewhere, and so as a point of reference we'll begin with some basic recommendations known as **Dietary Reference Intakes (DRIs)** from the Institute of Medicine (IOM). (See sidebar "Where Do the Dietary Reference

WHERE DO THE DIETARY REFERENCE INTAKES COME FROM?

The most widely quoted source of advice on what we should or shouldn't eat is the **Institute of Medicine**, a component of the **National Academies**. The National Academies is a private, nonprofit organization chartered by Congress in 1863 with a mandate to advise the federal government on scientific matters and to promote the use of science and technology for the public welfare. Unlike the National Institutes of Health (NIH) and its various components, it is not an agency of the government.

The Institute of Medicine (IOM), chartered in 1970, is one of four components of the National Academies. The IOM is a private, nonprofit, nongovernment organization whose mission is to provide information and advice to citizens, professionals, corporations, and government regarding health and science policy. All of its work is done in committees composed of experts who volunteer their time. The IOM is organized into nine oversight boards, one of which is the **Food and Nutrition Board**, which was originally created in 1940.

For more than half a century, nutritional guidelines in the United States were based on standards from the Food and Nutrition Board called the **recommended daily allowances (RDAs)**, which were focused on a somewhat narrow but important goal: preventing nutritional deficiencies caused by inadequate amounts of specific essential nutrients. Recommended Daily Allowances (RDAs) were originally formulated for eight nutrients in 1941 at the request of the War Department (now the Department of Defense), which was concerned about the nutritional status of new recruits, soldiers in the field, and malnourished people who would be liberated by Allied troops. By 1989, the list of RDAs had expanded to twenty-seven nutrients. (The Canadian version of the RDA has been the **recommended nutrient intakes**, or **RNIs**.)

Intakes Come From?") After considering these standards, we'll look at some of their practical implications.

How much fuel? The total number of calories each member of your family needs each day depends on several factors: age, gender, height, weight, activity level, and to some degree genetics (which affects the efficiency of your individual metabolic engine). You can see the genetic factor at work when someone consistently eats large amounts of food without gaining weight, while another person of a similar age, build, and activity level has to eat far less to prevent weight gain.

The IOM has estimated the calorie needs for children and adults at various ages that are related to height, weight, and levels of physical activity. While the following list is not comprehensive, here are some approximate daily calorie goals to note:

- For children between two and six, some older adults, and many women: 1,600 calories.
- For the "average" adult: 2,000 calories. On nutrition labels, you will typically see this listed as the total number of daily calories.
- For older children, teenage girls, and active women: 2,200 calories.
- For teenage boys and active men: 2,800 calories.

More recently, however, new research and a broader vision of the role of nutrition in health have led to major revisions of these standards, which are now called the **dietary reference intakes (DRIs)**. These guidelines are intended not only for the prevention of specific nutritional deficiencies, but also for reducing the frequency and impact of important chronic health problems such as cardiovascular disease, cancer, and osteoporosis. The DRIs for a variety of nutrient groups have been released in a series of reports beginning in 1997.

The DRIs actually encompass four different guidelines:

- The familiar-sounding **RDA**—revised and now called the **recommended dietary allowance**, which specifically refers to the amount of a nutrient necessary to meet the nutritional needs of 97 to 98 percent of healthy people of a certain age and gender (including pregnant and nursing mothers). You will see RDAs listed on the nutrition labels of packaged foods.
- The **adequate intake (AI)**, which is basically an educated guess of the necessary amount of a specific nutrient based on observations and scientific findings when the available evidence is not conclusive enough to arrive at an RDA.
- The **estimated average requirement (EAR)** which is defined as the amount of a nutrient that will be adequate for half of the healthy members of a specific population. These EARs are used primarily as guidelines for groups and populations, rather than individuals. (You won't find EARs on nutrition labels.)
- The **tolerable upper intake level (UL)** applies to certain nutrients for which there can be "too much of a good thing." The UL is the highest daily intake of a nutrient that is not likely to have an adverse effect on the vast majority of individuals.

How much carbohydrates? The IOM recommends that 45 to 65 percent of total daily calories come from carbohydrates, or at least 130 grams for an adult, with no more than 25 percent of total daily calories from added sugars. Within those percentages, there is a lot of room for good and not-so-good choices, so we need to pay attention to the type and quality of the sources of these nutrients.

How much fiber? The IOM recommends the following amounts of dietary fiber:

- For children two and older: an amount in grams equal to their age plus five
- For adults up to age fifty: 38 grams for men and 25 grams for women
- For adults fifty-one and older: 30 grams for men and 21 grams for women

How much fat? The IOM recommends that 20 to 35 percent of total daily calories come from fat. For children, the percentage of total fat may be a little higher because of the need for fat in the developing central nervous system. Thus, among children four to eighteen years of age, 25 to 35 percent of daily calories may come from fat; for one- to three-year-olds, 30 to 40 percent.

How much protein? The IOM states its recommendation for daily protein intake as a range of 10 to 35 percent of total calories for adults, 10 to 30 percent for children ages four to eighteen, and 5 to 20 percent for children one to three years of age. An estimate based on a person's body weight is 8 grams of protein per 22 pounds of weight, or 0.8 grams per kilogram (2.2 pounds) for adults. For example, a woman weighing 150 pounds (68.1 kg) would need 56 grams of protein, which could be obtained by drinking two 8-ounce (roughly 250 ml) glasses of milk, having a slice of ham and cheese in a sandwich, and eating a three-ounce (85 g) portion of meat for dinner. Unlike many impoverished areas of the world, most Americans get plenty of protein. An average-size hamburger contains about 25 grams of protein, as does a cup (about 250 ml) of cottage cheese or a three-ounce portion of most types of meat (chicken, turkey, beef, lamb, or fish). An eight- to twelve-ounce (227 to 340 g) steak can supply an entire day's protein for a large adult.

Three Ways to Improve Your Family's Nutritional Habits

How do we translate all of these recommendations into actual decisions about the kinds of foods that we buy, prepare, order at a restaurant, and ultimately eat? How many of us actually calculate, or even have a rough idea, what percentage of our daily calories come from carbohydrates, fats, and proteins? And do these percentages tell the whole story of our nutritional health?

We could, of course, shrug our shoulders and proceed with business as usual: eat what and however much we like, guided by family traditions, taste buds, emotions, advertising, and convenience. In the United States, however, that approach has led to an epidemic of obesity and contributed to an increase in cardiovascular disease and diabetes. Some cancers and a number of other chronic diseases may also be the by-product of this approach. If we want to take some positive, proactive steps toward improving our personal and family nutrition, how might we proceed? There are three basic approaches. All three have merit, and you may find it worthwhile to pick and choose certain elements from each approach that work for you and your family.

1. Get a notebook and calculator, and study those food labels.

In the United States, the Food and Drug Administration (FDA) requires that packaged foods bear a **Nutrition Facts label** that includes pertinent information about what's inside. Even if you don't keep a running tally of your daily nutrient intake, you should pay attention to at least some of the information on the label.

Highlights include:

- *Serving size.* This number is important because all of the facts on the label are based on a serving size that the label assumes you will eat. The serving size may be obvious, such as the entire can of soda, but it is not always so clear. For example, the serving size for dry cereal is typically listed as one cup (about 240 ml), which may be a bit less than you pour into the bowl every morning. The label on a container of crackers or chips will list a certain number of these as a serving—but do we ever keep count when we're enjoying one of these snacks? Serving sizes for salad dressings are usually two tablespoons (30 ml), but you may be surprised how that compares to the typical dollop on that bowl of greens. Measuring the amount of the serving size—and the amount you actually use—for a number of your favorite foods can be an eye-opening experience.

- *Calories per serving.* All of the numbers on the label must be adjusted if you use more or less than the stated serving size.

- *Calories from fat.* Divide this number by the calories per serving and multiply by one hundred. You'll get the percentage of calories derived from fat, which may or may not be useful, depending on the type of food. The percentage of a food's calories derived from fat does not necessarily reflect its quality. Extra virgin olive oil is 100 percent fat, but it contains monounsaturated fatty acids that are beneficial to health.

- *Total fat, cholesterol, and quantities of saturated, monounsaturated, polyunsaturated, and trans fats are more useful numbers.* These are listed in grams and (for total fat, saturated fat, and cholesterol) as a **percent daily value (%DV)**. The percent daily value is not the percent of calories in the serving, nor the percent of total calories for the day, nor fat or saturated fat in the serving. Instead, it is the percent of the maximum recommended amount of these substances for a person eating two thousand calories per day. This number is intended to help you get a handle on how much of a contribution the particular food is making to what should be your daily maximum. At the bottom of the Nutrition Facts label is a listing of these recommendations, under a statement that begins "Percent Daily Values are based on a 2,000-calorie diet." The %DV listings are based on the assumption that we should keep our fat calories below

Nutrition Facts

Serving Size 1 Cup (228g)
Serving Per Container 2

Amount Per Serving

Calories 100	Calories from Fat 10

	% **Daily Value***
Total Fat 3g*	5%
Saturated Fat 1g	5%
Trans Fat 1.5g	
Cholesterol 0mg	0%
Sodium 188mg	5%
Total Carbohydrate 45g	15%
Dietary Fiber 4g	16%
Soluble Fiber 1g	
Sugars 20g	
Other Carbohydrates 21g	
Protein 5g	

Vitamin A	20%
Vitamin C	8%
Calcium	4%
Iron	15%
Vitamin D	20%
Vitamin E	25%
Thiamin	25%
Riboflavin	25%
Niacin	25%
Vitamin B6	100%
Folate	100%

a maximum of 25 percent and our saturated fats below 10 percent of the total number of calories we consume every day. For cholesterol, the assumption is that we should eat foods containing a total of 300 mg or less per day. Note that you will not find any %DV listings for mono- or polyunsaturated fats. This means that the FDA hasn't provided recommended daily intakes for these nutrients.

- *Total carbohydrate, dietary fiber, and sugars.* Of these, the most useful are the grams of fiber and sugars, since you want to get enough of the first and limit your intake of the second.
- *Protein.* The Nutrition Facts label includes grams of protein per serving but without an estimate of the percent daily value, because the recommended amount for an individual is based on his or her weight.
- *Other nutrients.* The amounts of vitamins and minerals contained in a serving of the food are listed under the main nutrients.

Few people are going to work through the laborious process of calculating the daily percentages of their various nutrients, a task that can be even more challenging if you are actually *cooking*—combining various ingredients to create a masterpiece in the kitchen—as opposed to eating prepackaged food. Nevertheless, you should know your way around the Nutrition Facts label because several of its statistics can help you make informed choices.

2. Follow the USDA Food Guide Pyramid.

For nearly a century, the United States Department of Agriculture (USDA) has published a series of guides that combine foods into various groups and then recommend that we eat a certain number of servings from each group each day. For example, the first set of guidelines released in 1916 listed five food groups: milk and meat, cereals, fruits and vegetables, fats and fat foods, and sugars and sugary foods. Over the years, the number of groups has expanded and contracted dramatically: Twelve food groups were identified in 1933, a "basic seven" in 1942, a "basic four" in 1956, and then back to five in 1979.

In 1980 the USDA and the U.S. Department of Health and Human Services (HHS) jointly published the first installment of the *Dietary Guidelines for Americans*, which has been updated every five years. The *Guidelines* represent what is called **federal nutrition policy**, affecting nutrition-assistance programs and education messages for the general public. In 1992 the USDA and HHS introduced the Food Guide Pyramid as a learning tool to help Americans visualize the recommended number of daily servings for five food groups as well as make better food choices.

For more than a decade, this original pyramid illustrated how we should eat more servings of some food groups and fewer of others. The base was occupied by the bread, cereal, rice, and pasta group because the USDA recommended six to eleven servings of foods from it every day. Vegetables, with three to five servings a day, shared the next level with fruits (two to four servings). The next level was shared by the milk and meat groups, each with two to three daily servings. At the apex of the pyramid were fats, oils, and sweets—not really food groups but rather the foods we were advised to "use sparingly."

With the publication of the 2005 edition of the *Dietary Guidelines for Americans*, the Food Guide Pyramid got a major overhaul (see pages A6–A7). The sections on the front of the new pyramid, representing the five basic food groups—grains, vegetables, fruits, milk, and meat and beans—are arranged vertically, and they only vaguely suggest that some groups might be emphasized over others. ("Meat and beans" includes meats, poultry, fish, eggs, nuts and seeds, as well as dry beans and peas.) In fact, the pyramid offers virtually no nutritional information but rather serves mainly as a symbol for the revised contents of the *Dietary Guidelines* and the new interactive Web site that supports it (http://www.mypyramid.gov). Significantly, the left side of the pyramid is drawn as a stairway that a stick-figure human appears to be climbing rapidly—a visual message about the importance of exercise.

Those who visit the Web site may explore several informative options:

- "MyPyramid Plan" invites you to enter your age, gender, and an estimate of daily physical activity. The site then provides a semi-individualized outline of the recommended daily intake of foods from the five basic categories, along with oils and an allowance for extra fats and sugar.
- "Inside the Pyramid" not only lists the foods in each of the five basic food groups but also offers photo illustrations. For each group, you can learn about recommended quantities, health benefits, and specific tips to maximize enjoyment and nutritional value.
- "MyPyramid Tracker" is a more ambitious option for those who want a detailed assessment of their eating and exercise habits. Users can enter detailed information about their daily food choices and receive feedback about the quality of their diets. They can also track their intake of specific food groups or nutrients over the course of a year. In addition, physical activity can be assessed and tracked for up to a year.
- "MyPyramid for Kids" includes games, posters, black and white diagrams to color and worksheets that encourage children to make healthy food and activity choices.

Unlike the original Food Guide Pyramid, the new version promotes exercise, emphasizes the benefits of whole grains, and makes an appropriate distinction between the healthier mono- and polyunsaturated fats and the less healthy saturated and trans fats. Overall, the interactive MyPyramid.gov Web site is a definite improvement over the old pyramid, provided one has access to a computer and the Internet. People without these electronic tools can obtain a copy of the 2005 *Dietary Guidelines for Americans* by calling the U.S. Government Printing Office toll-free at 866-512-1800.

3. Orient (or reorient) your eating habits around some basic principles.

Several practical conclusions are supported by a rising tide of research—and some common sense. For most people, it is more helpful to think along these lines than to spend hours calculating percentages of calories from different nutrients. Here are some ideas to consider:

Don't eat too much. While it may be stating the obvious, the freshest, most perfectly balanced, most exquisitely prepared food can still get you into trouble *if you eat too much of it.* If you are overweight, it is extremely unlikely that you will lose unwanted pounds without at some point addressing the portions of food that you are accustomed to eating.

The most dramatic illustration of the wisdom of not eating too much is the so-called French paradox. The French enjoy a traditional cuisine that is known for its rich, calorie-dense sauces, cheeses, pastries, and other delights. Yet only 7 percent of the French are obese, compared to 30 percent of Americans. One reason appears to be *portion size*. A group of researchers actually weighed servings of foods at similar types of restaurants in Paris and Philadelphia, including fast-food outlets and ice-cream parlors. They found that the average portion size in Paris was 25 percent smaller than its counterpart in the United States. The researchers also found that the French patrons at a Parisian McDonald's spent an average of twenty-two minutes enjoying their hamburger, *frites,* and *boisson,* compared to fourteen minutes for Americans consuming their burger, fries, and soft drink.

One additional observation: At a truly upscale restaurant, French or otherwise, the portions are usually quite small. With fine dining, it is assumed that you will take your time, savor every morsel—especially when it's costing you a bundle—and walk out feeling pleasantly satisfied rather than stuffed. At less-expensive restaurants that we're likely to visit on a more frequent basis, the portions are often colossal, and nearly every fast-food franchise offers you the option to buy supersize portions for a very modest bump in price. Avoid the temptation to get more for your money, because what you'll really get is more calories, saturated and trans fat, and sugar. Another way of looking at this principle is this: *Take your time and savor your food.* Put your fork down between bites, and enjoy the taste and texture of what you're eating. By doing so, you can have a longer, more enjoyable experience while consuming fewer calories.

A simple trick to reduce portion sizes at home is to serve your meals on smaller plates. Not only is there less room for oversized servings, but this also creates a minor optical illusion suggesting to the brain that "less is more." When dining out, you can conserve both cash and calories by splitting your meal with your companion (assuming that you can agree on the same one). If you're eating alone, plan on taking half of that huge entrée home. You won't offend your server, and you can enjoy it in a day or two.

Exercise on a regular basis—daily if possible. This section deals primarily with nutrition, but moving your muscles on a regular basis is extremely important to your overall health and will help prevent accumulation of any extra calories as fat.

Go easy on the added sugars. Contrary to the opinions found in a number of popular books over the past few decades, sugars aren't the cause of all disease, the root of all evil, or an imminent threat to world peace. But they are definitely a poor-quality fuel for our bodies, and the dramatic increase in their consumption in the United States and other developed countries has been a major step in the wrong direction.

The upper limit for added sugars suggested by the Institute of Medicine—25 percent of total calories—is rather generous. The current recommendation from the U.S. Department of Agriculture, on the other hand, calls for limiting the day's amount of added sugars to less than 10 percent of total calories. This translates to 24 grams (the equivalent of six teaspoons of table sugar) for sixteen hundred calories, 40 grams (ten teaspoons, or the amount in one twelve-ounce soft drink) for two thousand calories, and 56 grams (fourteen teaspoons) for twenty-four hundred calories. Remember that *this restriction doesn't apply to the sugars that occur naturally in foods such as fruit and milk.* You can tally the number of grams of sugar on any packaged product at the store by checking the Nutrition Facts label. Unfortunately, this does not distinguish between naturally occurring and added sugars. Often the nature of the product leaves little doubt: in a soft drink, you can be certain that all 40 or so grams of the sugar were added, while in an orange all of the 12 or more grams of sugar were there to start with. A cup of raw blueberries contains 14 grams of natural sugar, while a cup of frozen sweetened blueberries contains 45 grams of sugar, and the Nutrition Facts label doesn't tell you that 30 grams are added.

You can reduce your family's sugar intake in several ways:

- On packaged foods, check the ingredient list for added sugar, whether named directly or under one of its many aliases—brown sugar, sucrose, fructose, dextrose, corn syrup, high-fructose corn syrup, molasses, or honey. Try to avoid foods in which some form of added sugar is the first or second ingredient on the list.

  Limit the number of soft drinks and other sweetened drinks you—and especially your kids—consume every week. During the second half of the twentieth century, production of soft drinks in the United States increased ninefold, from an average of 60 twelve-ounce (about 360 ml) servings per person in 1942 to more than 575 in 1998—the equivalent of one and a half cans per day for every man, woman, and child in the country. Soft drinks now account for more than one-fourth of our national beverage consumption and about one-third of our added sugars.

  Even more eye-opening, but not surprising, is the consumption of soft drinks by the young: One out of five one- and two-year-old children drink an average of seven ounces (about 210 ml) of soft drinks every day. For teens, the number has soared to an average of nearly two and a half cans of soda per day for boys and more then one and a half per day for girls. This is roughly double the amount consumed during the late 1970s.

  While many factors contribute to obesity, surveys of eating habits in young people indicate that among those who are overweight, soft drinks tend to contribute a higher percentage of daily calories compared to those who are not overweight. Furthermore, an ongoing flow of sugary liquid over the teeth adds to the risk of tooth decay (although not as dramatically as candies and other sweet solids that stick to the teeth for longer periods).

  According to the USDA, in the late 1970s teenagers on average consumed twice as much milk as soft drinks. Two decades later, that number has reversed, and teenagers drink twice as much soda as milk. USDA nutritional surveys have indicated that among teenagers, only one in three boys and fewer than one in six girls is getting the recommended dietary allowance (RDA) for calcium. Recent research has also suggested that phosphoric acid in cola drinks interferes with the absorption of calcium and the building of bone mass. Furthermore, caffeine—an ingredient in six out of seven of the most popular soft drinks—increases daily loss of calcium in the urine. As a result, many health professionals are sounding the alarm about increased fracture rates among young people who regularly consume soft drinks, especially cola.

  While various fruit-flavored beverages may seem like a healthier alternative to soft drinks, most of these contain a small percentage of actual fruit juice—if any—and a lot of sugar. They are essentially soft drinks without the fizz. If you're not sure, check the label for the amount of juice—and the amount of sugar. For children, milk is a far better option (unless they are lactose intolerant) on a day-to-day basis.

- For your infants and children, don't view fruit juice as an appropriate substitute for breast milk, formula, or (after the first birthday) cow's milk. Those who come to favor juice over better sources of nutrition can develop diarrhea and gas, and they may become malnourished. Furthermore, young children who drink juice from bottles, cups, and boxes throughout the day are at risk for developing tooth decay. Here are some guidelines that allow children to enjoy fruit juice without becoming "juiceaholics" or damaging their teeth:

(a) Infants younger than six months of age should not be given fruit juices at all. Avoid feeding juice to any infant or toddler from a bottle; wait until he can take it from a cup.

(b) Limit juice intake to four to six ounces (about 120 to 180 ml) per day for children six and younger. Starting at age seven, you can set the limit at eight to twelve ounces (about 240 to 360 ml) per day.

(c) If he wants more than the daily limit, dilute juice with an equal amount of water.

(d) Don't allow an infant or child to go to sleep sucking on a bottle containing juice, milk, or any other liquid that contains sugar. This not only promotes tooth decay but can also increase the risk for developing an ear infection.

(e) Encourage children to eat whole fruit, which contains fewer calories and more fiber per serving than juice.

(f) Since citrus fruits may provoke allergic responses during the first year, consider withholding orange juice until after the first birthday. (Check with your baby's doctor.)

- Limit the intake of other major sources of sugar (and calories): cakes, pies, cookies, pastries, and candies. These foods won't kill anyone if eaten once in a while, but daily doses of them should be avoided. (They're also unfriendly to the teeth.) Fruit is a better option for a sweet snack or dessert.
- Check the sugar content of breakfast cereals, and choose brands that contain less than 8 grams per serving. (The Nutrition Facts label comes in handy here.)

Gravitate toward whole-grain foods rather than those made from refined or processed grains. Whole grains are better for you than those that have been "refined"—an ironic term for this process:

- Fiber, vitamins, and minerals are lost during refining and processing, though some are replaced. Whole-grain products contain a variety of useful compounds, including antioxidants, folic acid, B vitamins, iron, and vitamin E.
- A number of studies have shown a link between eating whole grains and a lower risk of developing cardiovascular disease, diabetes, and cancer.
- Dietary fiber has a number of health benefits, and whole-grain foods generally have a more generous supply.

How do you get more whole-grain foods into your daily food routine?

- Buy whole-grain bread or other baked products, including crackers. Check the ingredient list for whole wheat, whole oats, whole rye, whole barley, whole cornmeal, etc., or a combination of these in a multigrain product. The term *cracked wheat* is also a good sign, referring to whole wheat grains that have been cut or crushed, and *graham flour* refers to flour made from the entire wheat grain (also called the wheat berry). The term *wheat flour*, on the other hand, doesn't tell you whether you're dealing with whole wheat or a refined version.
- Similarly, buy cereals made from whole grains, and look for cereals that contain 5 grams or more of fiber per serving. As with baked products, check the ingredient list and look for one or more of the whole grains listed above as the first

ingredient. Note that oatmeal is a whole grain, but old-fashioned or steel-cut oats are less processed than instant versions. When selecting a cereal, its whole-grain status and fiber content should definitely be your first two considerations, with vitamin content ranking a distant third. Vitamins are merely added ingredients, and they don't improve the overall nutritional quality of the cereal itself. (You could add vitamins to a candy bar, but that doesn't make the contents of the candy any better for you.)

- Eat brown rather than white rice.
- When baking, try substituting whole wheat flour for a quarter to a half of the flour needed in the recipe.
- Look for pasta made from whole wheat or from a combination of whole wheat and refined flours.

Eat lots of vegetables and fruits. You've heard this from your mother, your health-education teacher, the American Dietetic Association, the government, and hopefully your doctor. Fruits and vegetables are supposed to be good for us—and they are—but they're nearly always the side dish rather than the main event at a meal. How many times have you picked up the menu at a restaurant and found a list of fruit and vegetable entrees? Since 1991, the 5 a Day for Better Health program, a joint project of several large federal agencies and private organizations, has been promoting the idea that we should eat five to nine servings of fruits and vegetables every day. But according to the Centers for Disease Control and Prevention's Behavioral Risk Factor Surveillance System telephone survey (the world's largest telephone survey), as of 2000, fewer than one in four Americans were actually following this advice, and one in three was consuming only one or two servings every day.

Why eat so many servings? Because Mom was right: An impressive and growing body of research supports her opinion that fruits and vegetables are good for you. Specifically, they can help reduce your risk of some significant health problems that you and your family definitely want to avoid, particularly cancer, heart disease and stroke, and vision loss from cataracts and macular degeneration.

Fruits and vegetables are amazingly complex. Nutritional science has identified a number of substances found in plants that do more than provide basic nutrients (carbohydrates, proteins, and fats) for fuel and building materials. Some of these, such as vitamins C and E, are familiar to us. Others, with tongue-twisting names such as carotenoids and isothiocyanates, belong to a diverse group of compounds called **phytochemicals**. These are not necessary for life or health as vitamins are, but many of them appear to have a protective effect against cancer and heart disease. Researchers have only scratched the surface of this biological treasure trove. Furthermore, because of complicated interactions between various substances in fruits and vegetables, the most diligent human effort to reproduce or extract some useful "essence" of a plant for a surefire supplement usually doesn't come close to delivering the goods that are readily available by eating the real thing.

Here are some practical suggestions for increasing your intake of these important foods:

- Try to eat a variety of **colors** every day. It appears that phytochemicals associated with different colors of fruits and vegetables provide a variety of health benefits. If you limit yourself to products bearing only one or two colors, you'll miss out.
- Add some frozen mixed vegetables to your favorite soup as you heat it.

- Spice up your salads with some pieces of fruit.
- While most of us are used to the typical meat/potato or grain/vegetable combination for a meal, try a second vegetable instead of potatoes, rice, or pasta.
- If you order a pizza for takeout or delivery to your home, order a salad with it or make one before it arrives. Or add another fruit or vegetable to balance out the meal.
- If the prospect of putting a salad together from scratch provokes you to reach for something simpler, like a box of macaroni, think about buying some precut salad mixes at the store. They're not as economical as using the separate ingredients—you're paying for the convenience, after all—but they may be worth it if they increase your family's consumption of greens.
- Encourage your family (and yourself) to munch on carrot or celery sticks instead of chips for appetizers or snacks.
- Keep some fresh fruit in a bowl in the kitchen or family room for a healthy snack.
- Add slices of fruit to your favorite cereal. Be adventurous with the types that you try.
- Serve fruit with dessert—or as dessert.
- For a treat on a hot day, think about fixing or buying a fruit smoothie rather than a milk shake.

When it comes to preparing vegetables and fruits for your meals, you have several options:

- If you enjoy your fruits and vegetables uncooked (but properly washed), eating them this way can allow you to benefit from phytochemicals that may be altered by cooking. Still, it's best to prepare them in ways that result in pleasant flavors and textures rather than curbing everyone's interest in these foods by insisting that they all be eaten raw.
- When you cook these foods, preserve the good stuff. Heating fresh or frozen vegetables in a pan of water allows some important nutrients to go down the drain when you pour off the excess water. Lightly steaming, microwaving, or stir-frying your vegetables—keeping them on the crisp rather than the mushy side—will preserve more nutrients, not to mention taste and texture. If you do cook your vegetables in water, think about using the liquid that's left behind in a soup or sauce rather than tossing it.
- Frozen vegetables and fruits usually run a close second to fresh produce in the nutrient and flavor department, and they may even have an advantage over their fresh counterparts that have been stored in such a way as to prevent ripening. Generally canned products rank a distant third to fresh or frozen. Not only is flavor and texture affected by the canning process, but a fair amount of salt and sugar may have been added as well. Canned fruit, for example, often floats in syrup. However, don't miss an important bottom line: Ultimately the best forms of fruits and vegetables are *those that you and your family will actually eat.*

Limit saturated fat, which is linked to higher cholesterol levels, to 10 percent or less of your total daily calories. For someone on a two-thousand-calorie diet, this means that six hundred calories would come from all fats combined (or about 65 grams of fat), and two hundred calories (about 22 grams) from saturated fat.

This is one situation in which the Nutrition Facts label displayed on many foods can be very helpful, since it lists not only the amount of saturated fat in the food, but also the percent daily value (%DV)—that is, the percentage of the total day's allotment, assuming that you're trying to take no more than 10 percent of your total daily calories from saturated fat. (Remember that most Nutrition Facts labels also assume that your total daily intake is either two thousand or twenty-five hundred calories.)

The most abundant sources of saturated fats are red meats, dairy products such as butter and ice cream, as well as tropical oils (such as palm and coconut). A mere tablespoon (15 ml) of butter, for example, contains 7 grams of saturated fat—about a third of the recommended daily amount for someone eating two thousand calories per day. Coconut oil is 92 percent saturated fat, while 50 percent of palm oil is saturated fat. Some practical ways to keep the saturated fats at a reasonable level include:

- Limit your meat intake to about six ounces (170 g) per day. Better yet, consider going "Mediterranean style" and eating red meat only a few times per month, and poultry and eggs only a few times per week.
- Choose leaner forms of beef. Avoid the marbled cuts, which means they are fat-laden. Look for ground round containing lower percentages of fat—10 percent or less if possible (although the leaner forms are more expensive).
- Roasting, baking, grilling, broiling, and stir-frying meat are preferable to frying it.
- Trim the fat from your beef and pork, and remove the skin from your chicken.
- When you buy tuna or other meats in a can, you're better off choosing those that are packed in water. If you get oil-packed meats, rinse them in warm water to remove the fat.
- If you're drinking whole milk, try switching to milk containing 2 percent fat. If you're used to 2 percent, try one percent. If the watery texture isn't a turnoff, try nonfat milk. All of these forms are clearly marked in the dairy case.
- You can also try low-fat or nonfat versions of cheese, yogurt, sour cream, and ice cream.
- Try low-fat or nonfat versions of your favorite salad dressings. Remember, the regular forms can deliver more than 150 calories in two tablespoons (30 ml).
- Before using butter—in whatever capacity—ask yourself whether olive oil would work just as well. It's a lot better for you.

Watch out for the trans fatty acids (or trans fats). These compounds raise the levels of circulating fats (specifically, the LDL or "bad" cholesterol and triglycerides) that are considered harmful to health. How much trans fatty acid is too much? No one knows, and thus far no professional organization or government agency has suggested a specific daily limit. While completely eliminating trans fatty acids from your diet is neither practical nor necessary, limiting them is definitely a good idea. Packaged foods now must list the amount of trans fats on their Nutrition Facts label, and many that have eliminated them (or never had them in the first place) now proudly advertise that fact. The FDA has estimated that by 2009, reduced consumption of trans fatty acids resulting from food labeling, as well as voluntary efforts by manufacturers to reduce the amounts of these compounds in foods, will prevent 600 to 1,200 heart attacks and save 250 to 500 lives every year.

Foods that contain trans fatty acids are hard to avoid without subjecting your family to a rather spartan diet. But some foods that contain unhealthy portions of these compounds deserve to be reduced from your family's table or eliminated altogether.

The FDA estimates that the typical American adult consumes nearly 6 grams of trans fats every day. Some trans fats occur naturally in animal products such as milk, cheese, butter, and red meats—the same foods that are rich in saturated fats. The vast majority, however, occur in products containing naturally occurring fats that have been processed in some way, usually involving partial hydrogenation. These include:

- *Stick margarine.* This spread contains nearly 3 grams of trans fat (and 2 grams of saturated fat) per tablespoon (15 ml). By contrast, butter contains a mere 0.3 grams of trans fat, but more than 7 grams of saturated fat per tablespoon. Some who have heard about the trans fat problem have dumped margarine and gone back to butter, but take note that tub margarine usually has much less of both trans and saturated fat. If you buy margarine, *read the labels* to find brands that have little or no trans fat.
- *Baked goods.* Perennial pleasures such as cakes, doughnuts, and cookies, aside from the sugar and very often the processed flour they contain, are also likely to have generous doses of trans fats. (A doughnut, for example, can pack 5 grams each of trans and saturated fat.) The same is true for packaged cake and baking mixes.
- *Chips and crackers.* A small bag of chips contains about 3 grams of trans fat. If it's fried or buttery in texture, you can assume trans fats are present.
- *Frozen treats.* Frozen pizzas, pies, potpies, waffles, and breaded whatevers (fish, shrimp, etc.) also contain trans fat.
- *Fast food.* Last but certainly not least are a few favorites of the franchises. The primary offenders are fried chicken and french fries. Their last moments prior to entering your digestive tract are spent in boiling hydrogenated oil, thus a medium serving may contain a whopping 14 grams of trans fat. (Many fast-food chains and other restaurants are now seeking to prepare their foods with less or no trans fats.)

Keep an eye on the cholesterol content of foods. The USDA recommends that adults limit their daily intake of cholesterol to 300 mg or less. The American Heart Association sets the upper limit at 200 mg, less than the amount in a single egg yolk. While the vast majority of the cholesterol in our blood is generated by the liver, our daily intake of saturated and trans fats can also significantly affect blood cholesterol levels.

The impact of the cholesterol that comes from our food, however, can be quite variable. For many people, eliminating or adding cholesterol in the diet has little impact on the amount circulating in the blood. For others, the effect is somewhat more significant. If you are trying to lower your cholesterol through dietary efforts, cutting back on saturated and trans fats will usually accomplish more than trying to limit cholesterol intake alone. Of course, a number of foods, such as red meats and cheese, contain generous amounts of both saturated fats and cholesterol, so limiting foods with saturated fats often will reduce the cholesterol as well.

Eggs, on the other hand, pose a nutritional dilemma. Each contains more than 200 mg of cholesterol (all of it in the yolk), but also some polyunsaturated fat, very little saturated fat (about 1.5 grams), and about 7 grams of high-quality protein. Thus far, no research has shown a clear relationship between eating eggs on a regular basis and developing coronary artery disease, and one could argue that an egg cooked using a little vegetable oil represents a more nutritious breakfast option than a doughnut full of trans fats or a few slices of white toast. Of course, eating the egg white without the yolk will eliminate the cholesterol, as will using a no-cholesterol egg substitute.

Get enough of the "good" fats. A type of fatty acid known as **monounsaturated fatty acids**, and in particular the **omega-6** and **omega-3 fatty acids**, are beneficial to life and health. Some tips on getting enough of these fats into your family's diet include:

- Become a regular user of olive oil, which contains more than 70 percent monounsaturated fatty acids. Buy the extra-virgin oil, which comes from the first pressing of the fruit. Among other things, you can dip bread in it (rather than using butter) and use it when you stir-fry or sauté vegetables or meat. When not in use, keep it in a dark cupboard.
- If you don't care for olive oil, try other vegetable oils that contain high percentages of monounsaturated fatty acids, including canola, peanut, and soybean oils. You may find canola oil more to your liking than olive oil for baking.
- Eat at least two servings of fish per week.
- Add nuts and seeds to your diet, especially as a substitute for less healthy snacks such as chips, or even as a source of protein. An ounce (28 g) of nuts, for example, contains 8 grams of protein, roughly the same amount as in a glass of milk. Watch out, however, because these are calorie-dense foods—an ounce of walnuts contains 160 calories—and it's easy to down a bowlful without realizing that you've just swallowed several hundred calories. Depending upon their preparation, nuts and seeds may also have a fair amount of added salt or sugar. Think handfuls: A serving size is an ounce (28 g), which is roughly fifteen to twenty cashews.
- Try avocado slices instead of cheese in your sandwiches.

Why Family Meals Should Be a Priority

While it is definitely wise to consider carefully *what* we eat, we also need a reminder about the importance of the *context* of our nourishment. We are not animals that graze in a field or gather at a trough; we do not inhale our food and then wander away. We are meant to be nourished at the table in more ways than merely transporting food from plate to stomach. Meals are a time for socializing, conversing, sharing, and celebrating. Family meals can be particularly powerful events in the lives of both children and adults. They can and should be the occasion to share the day's events, decompress, commiserate with and encourage one another, laugh, learn how to speak and listen politely, instill values, establish one's identity as a member of a family, welcome guests, and acknowledge God's provision on a day-to-day basis.

In a classic case of scientific research bearing witness to common sense, a study of more than five hundred adolescents in 1997 by the American Psychological Association found that those who ate dinner more often (five times per week) with their families at home were less likely to be depressed or involved in drug use, more likely to have better relationships with friends, and better motivated at school, compared with teenagers who ate with their families less often (three times per week).[1]

Family dinners are, unfortunately, an endangered species, threatened by overcommitment, crowded calendars, and electronic distractions such as TVs and phones. If you take away nothing else from this chapter, make a decision that shared family meals will become a priority in your home. As part of that process, consider the following:

- Set aside three nights per week if not more (perhaps including a "cook's day off" meal, such as after church on Sunday) that are designated for family meals. The expectation should be that all hands will be on deck, even young children, unless prior notice is given.
- After considering the ages and abilities of family members, establish routines that will spread the work around. The tasks involved in planning the menu, preparing the various components of the meal, and cleaning up can be rotated among the able-bodied family members who are living at home. Younger children can learn to set the table, and everybody should help clear it.
- Table manners, including such niceties as pulling out chairs for the ladies and waiting to eat until everyone is seated and grace has been said, can and should be encouraged.
- Televisions should be turned off and phones unanswered, taken off the hook, or in the case of cell phones, turned off. This is a time to talk to one another, unhindered by the yammering of the tube or the demands of whoever decides to dial your number.
- Without being too restrictive on the topics of conversation at the table, it is wise to address hot issues in the family at some other time. If mealtimes are a constant hotbed of bickering and animosity, no one is going to want to show up. Ideally the family table should be a place of warmth, respect, safety, genuine interest in what everyone has to say, and mutual support. If the kids are having a little trouble with this, some role modeling of respectful conversation from Mom and Dad will speak volumes. If no one seems to have much to say, ask a few open-ended questions such as "What was the highlight of your day?" or "What didn't go well today?"

Mealtimes can also provide opportunities to talk with your children about the foods they (and you) eat, and why some are definitely better than others. Learning by example at the table—sampling the foods you're discussing, and experiencing appropriate portion sizes —also speaks volumes and helps set patterns that will continue long after children have left home to live on their own.

A Final Thought: Giving Credit Where It's Due

Hopefully your mealtime routine, whether a quick bite on the way to work or Thanksgiving dinner with family and friends gathered together, includes at least a moment to thank the true "Father of the feast." We're so accustomed to a steady bounty of food, usually available at one of several supermarkets within a short drive of home, that it's all too easy to forget what must happen before the food we enjoy ever reaches our plate.

We of course appreciate those who have prepared our food. But we should never take for granted the productivity of our farmers year after year or the stable and efficient methods of distribution that set our national table with a spread that most of the world's citizens would consider a vision of paradise. We should also offer thanks every day to the Creator of the natural resources of our land, for seed and sun and rain that must converge at the right time and in the necessary amounts to produce huge amounts and varieties of crops.

We also need to stop, marvel, and give thanks for an incredibly complex phenomenon that is even more fundamental than the planting, harvesting, and distributing of food. In order for any of God's creatures to obtain any nourishment, energy must be captured from one source: the sun. Trees, plants, grasses, algae, and some bacteria do this every day on a monumental scale, in a process called photosynthesis. The biochemistry involved is well beyond the scope of this book, but we want to call attention to a crucial bottom line: Plants take the energy in sunlight and apply it to carbon dioxide and water to generate glucose, the basic carbohydrate fuel of both plants and animals. In exchange they return oxygen into the atmosphere. Humans and animals cannot survive without oxygen that the plant kingdom continually replenishes, and our metabolic engines in turn generate carbon dioxide that plants need for photosynthesis. All of the food consumed by animals and people—including meat—contains energy that was originally captured from the sun and stored by plants.

The complexity of this interdependent system is truly remarkable, and it becomes even more breathtaking when we consider the other factors, both colossal and intricate, that must interact perfectly for us to take our next breath. These include the size of our planet, its distance and orbit around the sun, the size and stability of that nearby star, the presence and composition of the earth's oceans, and so on. "The heavens declare the glory of God; the skies proclaim the work of his hands," wrote King David (Psalm 19:1). The marvelous processes that allow our body to function every day do likewise, and so should we who inhabit them.

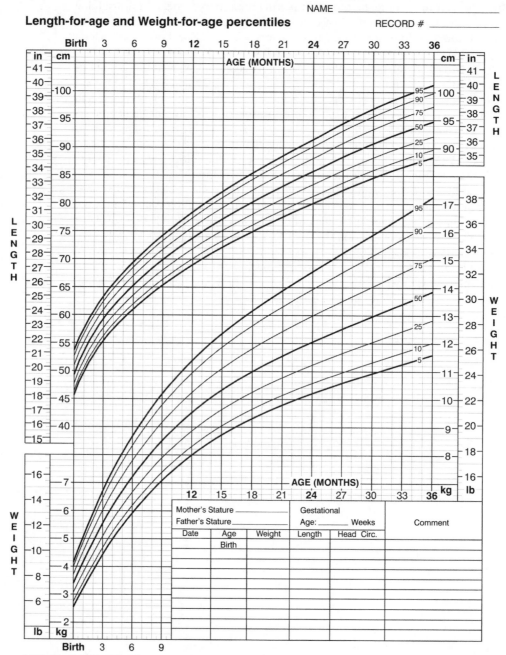

NAME _____

Length-for-age and Weight-for-age percentiles

RECORD # _____

AGE (MONTHS)

Birth 3 6 9 12 15 18 21 24 27 30 33 36

Mother's Stature _____

Father's Stature _____

Gestational Age: _____ Weeks

Comment

Date	Age	Weight	Length	Head Circ.	
	Birth				

Published May 30, 2000 (modified 4/20/01).
SOURCE: Developed by the National Center for Health Statistics in collaboration with
the National Center for Chronic Disease Prevention and Health Promotion (2000).
http://www.cdc.gov/growthcharts

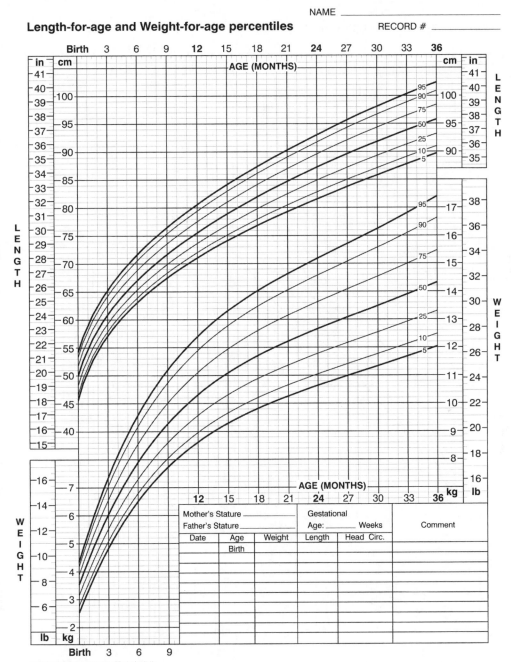

Length-for-age and Weight-for-age percentiles

NAME _____

RECORD # _____

Pubished May 30, 2000 (modified 4/20/01).
SOURCE: Developed by the National Center for Health Statistics in collaboration with
the National Center for Chronic Disease Prevention and Health Promotion (2000).
http://www.cdc.gov/growthcharts

Stature-for-age and Weight-for-age percentiles

NAME _____

RECORD # _____

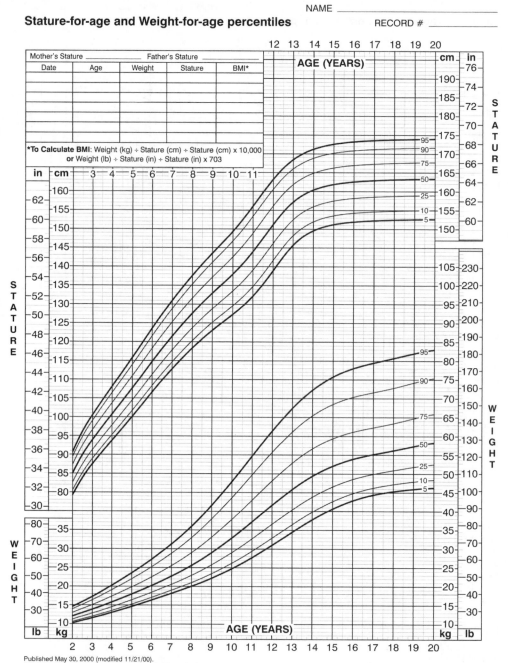

Mother's Stature _____ Father's Stature _____

Date	Age	Weight	Stature	BMI*

*To Calculate BMI: Weight (kg) ÷ Stature (cm) ÷ Stature (cm) x 10,000
or Weight (lb) ÷ Stature (in) ÷ Stature (in) x 703

AGE (YEARS)

Published May 30, 2000 (modified 11/21/00).
SOURCE: Developed by the National Center for Health Statistics in collaboration with
the National Center for Chronic Disease Prevention and Health Promotion (2000).
http://www.cdc.gov/growthcharts

Stature-for-age and Weight-for-age percentiles

NAME _____

RECORD # _____

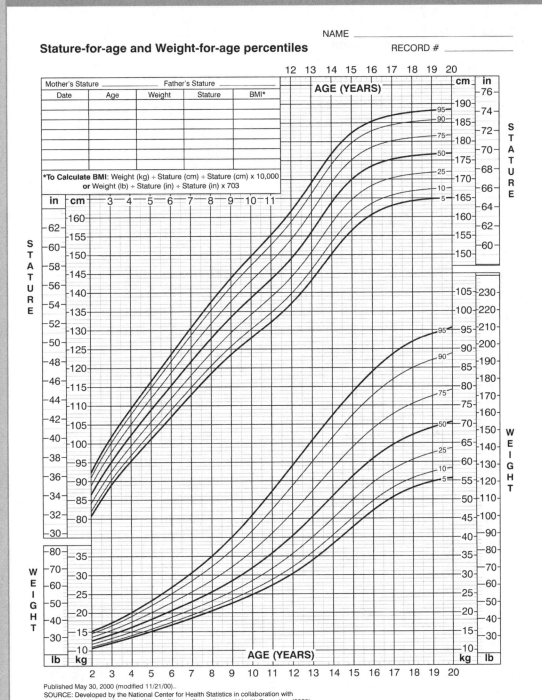

*To Calculate BMI: Weight (kg) ÷ Stature (cm) ÷ Stature (cm) x 10,000
or Weight (lb) ÷ Stature (in) ÷ Stature (in) x 703

Published May 30, 2000 (modified 11/21/00)..
SOURCE: Developed by the National Center for Health Statistics in collaboration with
the National Center for Chronic Disease Prevention and Health Promotion (2000).
http://www.cdc.gov/growthcharts

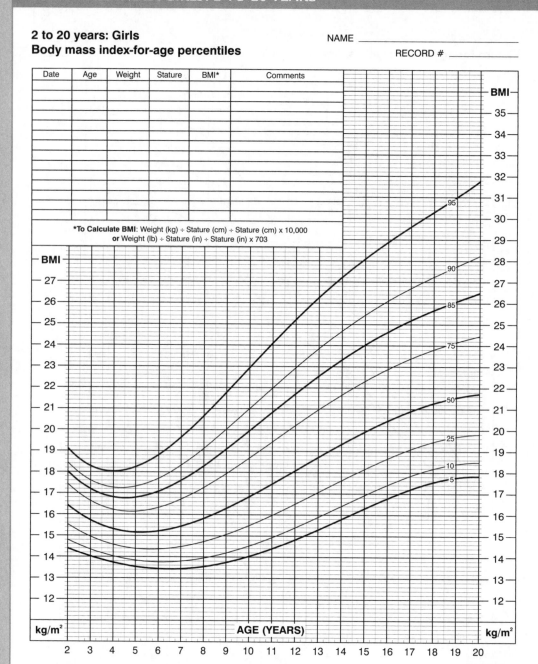

2 to 20 years: Girls
Body mass index-for-age percentiles

NAME _____

RECORD # _____

Date	Age	Weight	Stature	BMI*	Comments

*To Calculate BMI: Weight (kg) ÷ Stature (cm) ÷ Stature (cm) x 10,000
or Weight (lb) ÷ Stature (in) ÷ Stature (in) x 703

AGE (YEARS)

kg/m²

Published May 30, 2000 (modified 10/16/00).
SOURCE: Developed by the National Center for Health Statistics in collaboration with
the National Center for Chronic Disease Prevention and Health Promotion (2000).
http://www.cdc.gov/growthcharts

SAFER · HEALTHIER · PEOPLE™

2 to 20 years: Boys
Body mass index-for-age percentiles

NAME _____

RECORD # _____

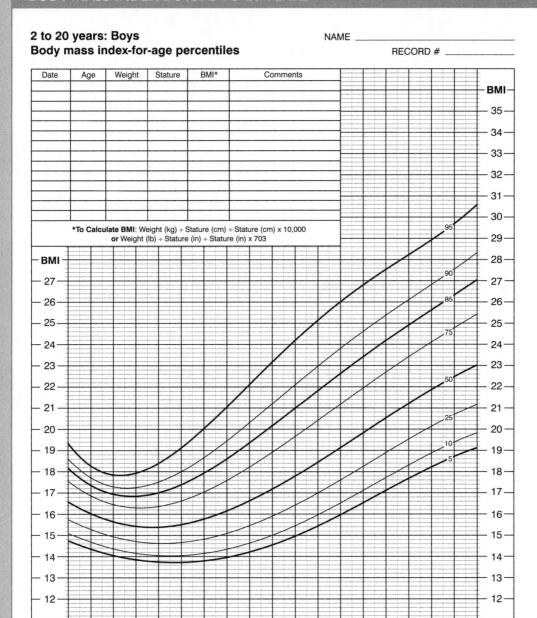

Date	Age	Weight	Stature	BMI*	Comments

*To Calculate BMI: Weight (kg) ÷ Stature (cm) ÷ Stature (cm) x 10,000
or Weight (lb) ÷ Stature (in) ÷ Stature (in) x 703

AGE (YEARS)

Published May 30, 2000 (modified 10/16/00).
SOURCE: Developed by the National Center for Health Statistics in collaboration with
the National Center for Chronic Disease Prevention and Health Promotion (2000).
http://www.cdc.gov/growthcharts

SAFER · HEALTHIER · PEOPLE™

Emergency Care

TABLE OF CONTENTS

IF YOU DIAL 911

- Tell the dispatcher that you have a medical emergency, and then state briefly what has happened (including the age of the child), where you are, and the phone number from which you are calling.
- *Stay on the line* so you can answer any questions the dispatcher might ask. He or she may also give you specific instructions for emergency care prior to the arrival of emergency personnel. Do not hang up until the dispatcher indicates it is time to do so. (He or she should hang up first.)
- If it is nighttime, turn on your outside lights—especially those that illuminate your address.
- If possible, have someone stand outside to direct the emergency personnel to the victim.

IF YOU DIAL 911 FROM A CELL PHONE

- The dispatcher cannot determine the exact location of your call. Therefore it is very important to *give the dispatcher the location of the emergency right away*.
- Give the dispatcher your wireless number so that it can be called back if you are disconnected.
- *Don't* program your cell phone to dial 911 when a particular button is pushed. This can result in an unintentional emergency call that could waste the time and resources of responders.

ITEMS FOR THE FIRST AID KIT

Prepare a first aid kit for each car and a smaller version for hiking or biking. Include the following items:

- Antiseptic wipes for cleaning cuts
- Antibacterial ointment
- Band-Aids
- Gauze pads and adhesive tape for larger scrapes
- Sunblock
- Instant cold pack
- Elastic bandage—three-inch width (7.5 cm)
- Acetaminophen (such as Children's Tylenol) or ibuprofen (such as Children's Advil or Children's Motrin)
- Tweezers
- Steri-Strips or butterfly closures
- Prepaid phone card or prepaid cell phone. (The phone should have a car charger or separate battery pack.)

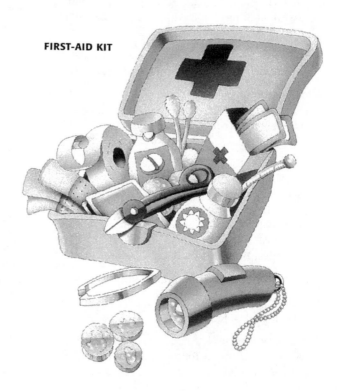

FIRST-AID KIT

- Appropriate thermometer for age of child. Know how to read it. (See "When Your Child Has a Fever," page 241.)
- Petroleum jelly (Vaseline).
- Antiseptic wipes.
- Band-Aids, gauze pads, and adhesive tape for cuts and scrapes.
- Steri-Strips or butterfly closures.
- Antibacterial ointment.
- Elastic bandages: two-inch width (5 cm) for children under twelve months; three-inch width (7.5 cm) for children ages one to five; four-inch width (10 cm) for children over age five.
- Popsicle sticks for finger splinting.
- Acetaminophen drops, liquid, or tablets (Tylenol or other brand), appropriate for age and weight (see dosage chart, page 609).
- Ibuprofen drops, liquid, or tablets (Children's Advil, Children's Motrin or other brand), appropriate for age and weight (see dosage chart, page 688).
- Instant cold packs (small plastic bags that become cold when squeezed to mix the chemicals inside them).
- Tweezers.

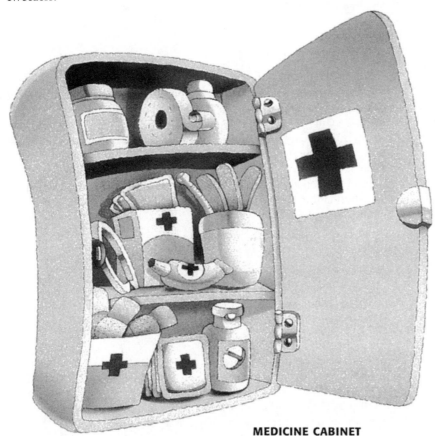

MEDICINE CABINET

Emergencies *(listed alphabetically)*

ALLERGIC REACTIONS See also "allergies in children," Reference Section, page 612

Generalized allergic reactions

Generalized allergic reactions can vary greatly in severity, from mild itching to life-threatening anaphylaxis, and may occur in response to any of these:

- Foods (especially nuts, eggs, shellfish, and berries)
- Medications
- Substances called contrast materials that are injected into the body during certain X-ray procedures
- Insect stings

Symptoms

of mild reactions
- Rash—typically scattered widely over the body. Raised, itchy welts called hives are a common manifestation of a generalized allergic reaction.
- Generalized itching.

Treatment

for mild reactions
- Use antihistamines—especially diphenhydramine (Benadryl and other brands), cetirizine (Zyrtec, a prescription drug), or clemastine (Tavist and other brands)—to help relieve itching, swelling, and hives.
- Have the child lie down if feeling light-headed.
- If you think the reaction involves a medication, withhold further doses until you consult your child's physician.
- When a drug reaction (of any kind—see page 800) has occurred, remind your child's doctor during the next office visit to ensure that the information about the reaction is recorded on the child's permanent medical record.

Symptoms

of moderate reactions
- All of the above and these:
- Swelling of the face, tongue, or throat
- Wheezing or coughing
- Light-headedness

Treatment

for moderate reactions
- All of the above. In addition, contact your child's physician immediately or go to the nearest emergency room.

Symptoms *of severe reactions (anaphylaxis or anaphylactic shock)*

In the more severe, life-threatening reaction known as anaphylaxis, these symptoms may develop very rapidly and be very intense. In addition to the above, the following may occur:

- Difficulty swallowing or breathing
- Nausea or vomiting
- Abdominal cramps
- Sudden drop in blood pressure, manifested by pale, clammy skin; altered consciousness or unconsciousness; and rapid, weak pulse

Anaphylaxis may lead to cardiac arrest and death if not treated promptly.

Treatment *for severe reactions (anaphylaxis, or any involving rapid swelling of face/throat/tongue or difficulty breathing)*

- Call 911.
- If the child has been bitten, stung, or has ingested a substance, any of which have caused severe reactions *in the past,* call 911 even before symptoms are evident.
- Try to keep yourself and your child calm.
- If the child is wheezing and has an inhaler available that is intended for acute treatment of wheezing—for example, albuterol or levalbuterol (Xopenex)—have him use it as directed.
- If the child has an emergency kit (such as EpiPen or Ana-Kit) containing syringes prefilled with epinephrine (adrenaline), follow the instructions for giving this injection.
- Check responsiveness and breathing. If necessary, begin CPR (see page 836).
- If the episode follows a bee sting, remove the stinger by scraping it off with a credit card or other flat object—*do not use tweezers, since this may squeeze more venom into the skin.*
- If the child feels faint, have him lie down on a flat surface, loosen any tight clothing, cover him with a blanket or a coat, and elevate his feet eight to twelve inches (about 20 to 30 cm) to help maintain his blood pressure.
- *Do not* elevate the head if there is a breathing problem; this may aggravate a blockage of the airway.
- After your child has had an anaphylactic reaction, talk to his doctor about obtaining emergency treatment kits containing an injection of epinephrine (such as EpiPen or Ana-Kit) that can partially or completely reverse the reaction. These should be available at home, in the car, and in the gear taken on camping trips or other outings. A visit with an allergist may be appropriate as well.
- A child who has had an anaphylactic reaction should wear a medical ID tag with this information, especially if he may need an emergency injection of epinephrine.

A child can have an allergic reaction to a substance that has never caused problems before, even with many prior contacts. If a reaction occurs, every reasonable effort should be made to prevent contact with that substance in the future because reactions that are initially mild can become more severe with further exposure.

ALLERGIC REACTION OR DRUG SIDE EFFECT?

Some children (and adults) experience side effects from over-the-counter (OTC) or prescription medications. Examples of common side effects are drowsiness with many antihistamines, nausea and/or diarrhea from certain antibiotics, and dry mouth from some forms of antidepressants. These reactions can vary considerably from person to person, and over time they can also change in a given individual using the same drug. Usually the potential side effects of a medication are listed on the label of an OTC drug. For prescription drugs, the physician will often review possible side effects, or the effects will be noted by the pharmacist when the prescription is filled.

Side effects are not the same as allergic reactions, which involve a specific response of the immune system. Distinguishing between side effects and allergic reactions is important: If a true allergic reaction has occurred, repeated doses of the same or a related drug might cause a more serious reaction in the future. By contrast, side effects may or may not occur if the drug is taken in the future. Sometimes a symptom that might seem like a drug reaction actually has no relationship to the medication, and the timing of its appearance is purely coincidental. Deciding whether or not a drug has caused a particular problem and whether it may be safely taken in the future can often be difficult and should be discussed with your child's physician.

BITES AND STINGS

Animal Bites

Treatment

If your child has been bitten by any animal, wild or domestic, do the following:

- Clean the wound at once with copious amounts of water and mild soap.
- If the wound is severe—with large tears or perforations—handle it as you would any large wound (see "Wounds and Wound Care," page 834).
- Contact your child's doctor as soon as possible. Many animal bites—even those that do not require sutures (stitches) to close them—should be treated with antibiotics, especially if they occur on the hands or fingers. Cats in particular have sharper, narrower teeth that tend to create deeper puncture wounds, which are more likely to become infected.
- A tetanus shot should be given within twenty-four hours of the bite if the child or adolescent has not had one in five years.

CONCERNS ABOUT RABIES

The major concern after the bite wound is treated is whether or not the child will need specific treatment to prevent rabies (a viral infection that is nearly always fatal). If the bite is from a wild animal and the animal has been caught, it will be killed and its brain examined microscopically for evidence of this disease. While awaiting the results of this examination—or more commonly, if the animal is not captured and its brain cannot be evaluated—a decision must be made whether or not to begin a rabies vaccination series. This will depend to a large degree on the type of animal involved and the circumstances of the bite.

In most parts of the United States, bites from wild rodents such as squirrels, rats, chipmunks, mice, and rabbits usually will not be treated with rabies vaccination. However, your child's doctor may consult the local public-health authority for specific advice. On the other hand, skunks, raccoons, opossums, bats, and all wild carnivores should always be considered potentially rabid (rabies carrying) and should never be touched, even in a park or other setting where they are accustomed to receiving food from human hands. A bite from one of these animals—especially if the animal was not provoked or defending itself—is more likely to raise concerns about rabies. Contact with bats is a particular concern because people who have contracted rabies from a bat often do not recall being bitten. Any direct contact with a bat—or even seeing a bat in your house—warrants immediate contact with a knowledgeable health-care provider and consideration of rabies vaccination.

Bites from domestic animals (dogs, cats, etc.) are more common but rarely cause rabies. If someone is bitten by a domestic animal, treat the wound as described above. The animal will usually be available for observation, and public-health officials may quarantine it for ten to fourteen days. If the animal appears normal at the end of the quarantine, no rabies vaccination is required. But if the animal becomes ill, it will be promptly sacrificed and its brain examined microscopically for rabies. Rabies treatment and vaccination should be started as soon as a quarantined animal is found to be ill, not delayed while awaiting results of the brain examination.

When purchased from pet stores, mice, rats, gerbils, and hamsters are not known to transmit rabies.

Wild animals that have been raised as pets—such as raccoons, skunks, foxes, wolves, ferrets, and small wildcats—can carry rabies even if they have appeared healthy in captivity for long periods. This is particularly true of skunks, which have had the rabies virus isolated from their saliva even when the skunk was born in captivity.

PREVENTING DOG BITES

- Before you get a dog, consider the breed and gender. Female dogs and neutered males are less likely to bite than unneutered males. Some breeds of dogs are more aggressive than others.
- Teach children how to treat a dog properly. Prodding, poking, and tail pulling may provoke a bite even from the most mild-mannered canine. This also can occur if a sleeping dog is jolted awake by a child or if a child tries to play with a dog who is eating. If you have one or more active toddlers who might not understand these ground rules, you might consider waiting until they are more mature before getting a dog.
- Don't leave infants or small children unattended with a dog.
- Obedience training for dogs—which should not involve harsh physical punishment—is a worthwhile investment. Teach children to use commands ("Down," "No," etc.) appropriately.
- When walking your dog, observe local leash laws. Do not let your dog approach a child it does not know.
- Do not let your child approach a strange dog.
- Teach your child to stand still and stay calm if approached by a strange dog. Running away may arouse a dog's instinct to chase and bite.
- Teach your children never to try to break up a dogfight.

Human Bites

These bites commonly become infected because they are likely to be heavily contaminated by bacteria, which are abundant in saliva. In addition, the victim may be reluctant to seek medical help because of legal concerns or embarrassment.

Treatment

Treatment for a human bite is the same as that outlined for animal bites. Human bite wounds are rarely sutured because of the contamination risk noted above. These wounds should be vigorously irrigated and then left open. Antibiotics are usually required for all but the most minor wounds.

Bee and Wasp Stings

Honeybees almost always leave the stinger (with attached venom sac) in the skin. This should be removed as quickly as possible by scraping the skin at the stinger base with a credit card or other flat object. Do not grasp the venom sac with fingers or tweezers because this will inject the venom remaining in the sac into the skin. Wasp stingers are smooth and do not remain in the skin.

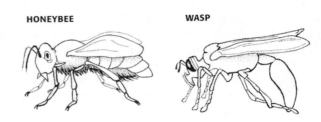

HONEYBEE   WASP

Symptoms

of immediate response to venom
- Pain, redness, and swelling at the sting site
- Itching, sometimes intense, which may occur twelve to twenty-four hours after the sting

Treatment

- Avoid scratching to reduce risk of infection.
- Apply ice to affected area.
- Elevate affected area.
- Nonprescription one-percent hydrocortisone cream or calamine lotion may be applied two or three times daily until local symptoms subside.

Symptoms

of delayed hypersensitivity reaction
- Significant swelling, usually beginning one or two days after the sting and spreading past one or more neighboring joints
- Mild itching
- Usually very mild pain, or no pain at all

Treatment

- Give an antihistamine such as diphenhydramine (Benadryl) to relieve itching and swelling.
- For more severe local reactions, contact your child's physician. Sometimes oral steroids (prednisone) are prescribed.
- Antibiotics are rarely necessary.

Symptoms   *of multiple stings*

A toxic reaction may occur when a person is stung multiple times, often ten or more. Symptoms include:

- Moderate swelling
- Vomiting
- Diarrhea
- Light-headedness

Treatment   Go to an emergency facility immediately or call 911. Severe symptoms can develop quickly, and the emergency room is better equipped to treat a serious reaction to bee or wasp venom.

Symptoms   *of life-threatening or anaphylactic reaction*

This reaction affects the entire body and can result from one or multiple stings. Initial symptoms occur shortly after the sting. For symptoms and treatment, see page 799.

PREVENTION

If your child has had a severe reaction to an insect sting in the past, talk to her doctor about obtaining emergency treatment kits containing an injection of epinephrine (such as EpiPen or Ana-Kit) that can partially or completely reverse a similar reaction in the future. These should be available at home, in the car, and in gear taken on camping trips or other outings. The child should wear a medical ID tag indicating that she is at risk for this type of reaction, especially if she may need an emergency injection of epinephrine. You might also want to see an allergist about giving your child immunotherapy injections to prevent this potentially life-threatening problem in the future. Even after completing an allergy-shot series, emergency kits containing epinephrine should still be available.

Spider Bites

In the continental United States and Canada, only the bites of brown recluse and black widow spiders inject venom that can cause serious problems. However, any spider bite can cause significant swelling.

Brown Recluse

Symptoms   Often a brown recluse bite is at first painless or causes only a brief stinging. Several hours later, pain begins around the site and can become severe. The involved area often has a red, white, and blue appearance: a wide area of reddened skin, within which is a smaller patch of white-appearing skin, and finally a central bluish

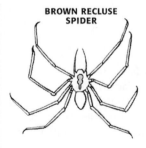

BROWN RECLUSE SPIDER

discoloration around the fang marks. The central bluish area usually forms an ulcer that may take weeks or months to heal and occasionally requires skin grafting. This procedure is generally done about two months after the bite because the graft may slough off if applied to the poisoned area too early. Other possible symptoms of brown recluse bites include fever, skin rash, nausea or vomiting, joint pain, and bloody urine.

Treatment

There is no specific treatment or antidote for brown recluse bites. A variety of treatments (such the use of corticosteroids) have been tried, though evidence for their effectiveness is inconclusive. Cleanse and elevate the wound. Antibiotics are occasionally prescribed, and a tetanus booster is given if needed. In general the best approach is a combination of effective pain relief and keeping the bite site clean and dry to prevent secondary infection.

PREVENTION

Brown recluse spiders prefer warm, dry, and abandoned locations—for example, vacant buildings, woodpiles or sheds, or seldom-used closets. The spider is brown with a violin-shaped marking on its back. They are active primarily at night and usually bite when trapped in clothing or shoes. Be careful when delving into closets and other spaces that have been undisturbed, and shake out clothes and shoes that have been stored awhile or that are kept in areas where brown recluse spiders have been seen. (Brown recluse spiders are generally found in the central Midwest southward to the Gulf of Mexico, but rarely west of the Rocky Mountains.)

Black Widow

Symptoms

A black widow bite is generally unnoticed at first but then becomes painful—often severely so—within fifteen minutes to four hours. Pain will usually reach a peak in two or three hours, but it can last up to forty-eight hours. Associated muscle spasms, which may be very severe, contribute to the pain. Usually only two tiny red spots are visible at the bite site, or no local reaction may be seen at all.

BLACK WIDOW

Treatment

The primary goal of treatment for a black widow bite is to relieve pain and muscle spasms. An antivenin is available, but it is generally reserved for severe cases, which are more commonly seen in young children.

PREVENTION

The black widow is a shy, coal black spider with a red or yellow hourglass marking on the underside of the abdomen. Only the female spider bites. She builds a chaotic, irregular-shaped web that is easy to recognize when compared to the highly symmetrical webs of other spiders. The black widow is found throughout the United States, preferring warm, dry environments, both indoors and out.

Tarantulas

These spiders attack only when handled roughly. Their bite can be painless or can cause a deep, throbbing discomfort that generally stops after about an hour. The only treatment needed is elevation and possibly a pain reliever, although most of the discomfort usually subsides before the medication takes effect.

Tick Bites See also "ticks," Reference Section, page 727

While tick bites are generally insignificant in and of themselves, some ticks transmit infections that can be serious, including Lyme disease (see "Lyme disease," Reference Section, page 695) and Rocky Mountain spotted fever (see "Rocky Mountain spotted fever," Reference Section, page 711). Generally most tick-borne diseases are transmitted only after the tick has remained attached to the skin for many hours. For example, transmission of Lyme disease is unusual if the tick remains attached less than twenty-four to forty-eight hours.

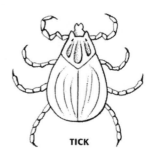

TICK

Another less-common tick-borne illness is tick paralysis, which usually afflicts children. Weakness and paralysis begin in the legs and progress upward with increasing severity as long as the tick is attached. Eventually difficulty with speech and swallowing and respiratory problems occur; rarely, death may result. Tick removal reverses this disorder (see "ticks," Reference Section, page 727).

Snakebites

Pit vipers—rattlesnakes, cottonmouths, and copperheads—inject venom through two hollow, needlelike fangs.

PIT VIPER

Coral snakes are also poisonous, but they are much less common than pit vipers. Unlike pit vipers, coral snakes do not have hollow fangs; instead they have short (less than one-eighth inch, or about 3 mm), rigid grooved pegs. Therefore, they must gnaw on their victim to inject venom.

If a child has been bitten by a snake, identifying the particular type is important but not critical. Even if the snake has been killed, the head should be preserved to make identification easier. Be very careful when handling dead poisonous snakes because their strike reflex can cause a venom-injecting bite up to an hour after they are killed.

CORAL SNAKE

Symptoms When a strike from a pit viper has injected venom, swelling or pain almost always occurs within thirty minutes. Anyone who has been bitten by one of these snakes should be en route to the hospital before this much time has elapsed.

Treatment   First aid for a snakebite victim is quite simple:

- Don't panic; keep the victim as calm as possible. Activity speeds the spread of venom.
- Splint the bitten body part and keep it slightly below the level of the heart if possible.
- Transport the victim to the nearest hospital immediately.
- There is almost no evidence that cutting the bite site and suctioning it will remove much venom. There is clear evidence that in untrained hands this practice can lead to tissue damage and infection. Suction devices that are designed to remove venom from a wound without incision are of modest (if any) benefit, and are definitely not a substitute for appropriate emergency medical care.
- The use of tourniquets is not recommended because they are difficult to apply correctly and can cut off blood supply to the affected limb.
- Remove any rings or other items that might constrict the affected area.
- Do not apply ice or cold packs to a snakebite.

The victim should be observed in the emergency department for at least four hours before a "dry strike" is diagnosed. Any symptoms of envenomation (venom injection) will be treated with antivenin, and the child will be admitted to the hospital. Antibiotics are frequently used even in dry strikes because these puncture wounds are easily infected. A tetanus booster is usually given if the victim has not had one in the past five years.

PREVENTION

Prevention of snakebites lies mainly in recognizing poisonous snakes and staying clear of them. Pit vipers are readily identified by their triangular or arrow-shaped heads and oblong pupils (like a cat's). All native North American snakes with oblong pupils are poisonous.

Coral snakes have round heads and bright red, black, and yellow bands around their body. They always have a black-tipped head, which has given rise to the warning "If the head is black, get back." About fifteen nonpoisonous snakes mimic the coral-snake color pattern, but the coral snake is unique in having its red bands next to yellow bands. If the red band is next to a black band, the snake is a non-poisonous mimic. (An easy way to remember the color patterns is this rhyme: "Red on yellow kills a fellow; red on black, venom lack." However, in some parts of the world, including Mexico, coral-snake color bands do not follow this pattern.)

Scorpion Stings

Scorpions inject venom through a single stinger in the tail. They rarely inject enough venom to be lethal, although small children and the elderly are at risk for severe reactions.

Symptoms   Immediate pain with minimal redness and swelling but increased sensitivity to touch at the injured area. In severe cases, muscular paralysis and respiratory failure can occur. Symptoms last for about four hours in most healthy individuals.

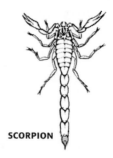

SCORPION

Treatment

First aid includes the application of ice to the injured area. Most patients with symptoms should see a doctor and will probably be observed for several hours. Oral pain medication is usually effective, but occasionally stronger pain-relief measures are necessary. A tetanus booster may be given if more than five years have passed since the last dose.

PREVENTION

In the United States scorpions are found almost exclusively in the Southwest and hibernate from about October through April. They feed at night and hide during the day—often in sleeping bags or boots. Stings can be prevented by shaking out sleeping bags or boots prior to using them. Scorpions also hide under rocks and on ledges, so caution is advisable when hiking or rock climbing.

Marine Animal Stings

Stingrays

Symptoms

A jagged wound that is immediately and intensely painful; the worst pain occurs after about an hour and then gradually subsides over a period of up to two days.

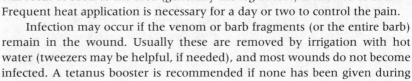

STINGRAY

Treatment

Stingray venom breaks down when warm but is stable when cool. First aid consists of applying hot water from the faucet—as hot as one can tolerate without causing a burn—to the affected area. This will promptly decrease the pain, but discomfort will recur as soon as the area (generally the leg or foot) is allowed to cool. Frequent heat application is necessary for a day or two to control the pain.

Infection may occur if the venom or barb fragments (or the entire barb) remain in the wound. Usually these are removed by irrigation with hot water (tweezers may be helpful, if needed), and most wounds do not become infected. A tetanus booster is recommended if none has been given during the previous five years.

PREVENTION

Stingrays partially submerge themselves in sandy shallow water in sheltered bays, lagoons, and river mouths. The animal's whiplike tail has several (one to four) barbs (spines) that are covered with a mucous venom. The tail reflexively whips upward when the ray is touched.

To prevent being stung, swimmers should shuffle—not step—when walking in shallow water. This disturbs the stingray, and it will flee before it is stepped on.

E

M

E

R

G

E

N

C

Y

Jellyfish and Fire Coral

These two marine animals have a tiny venom-containing capsule (nematocyst) on the outer surface of their tentacles or near the mouth. Contact with a swimmer causes the capsule to penetrate the skin and diffuse venom into it. The attached capsule can discharge repeatedly when it's exposed to water.

JELLYFISH

Symptoms

The nematocyst sting is generally quite painful but rarely causes serious medical problems. However, a person who is stung multiple times may develop symptoms such as vomiting, extreme weakness, bloody urine, or fainting.

Treatment

For treatment of a severe reaction resulting from multiple stings, go to an emergency facility for prompt medical attention.

Less severe stings can be managed at home. The best way to neutralize the nematocysts is to apply liberal amounts of a solution containing equal parts vinegar and water mixture for thirty minutes. Large tentacles should be removed using gloves. Remaining nematocysts can be removed by applying shaving foam and gently scraping the area with a dull instrument, such as the edge of a credit card.

Starfish

Starfish have thorny spines that are coated with a slimy venom. When the spines penetrate a victim's skin, the venom seeps into the wound.

STARFISH

Symptoms

Immediate, intense burning pain at the wound site. The venom rarely causes a more serious reaction.

Treatment

As with stingray venom, heat will hasten pain resolution.

Sea Urchins

These creatures have venom-bearing spines that are long, sharp, and brittle and can break off in the skin. Purple pigment from the spine can leach into skin and appear to be a retained spine fragment.

SEA URCHIN

Symptoms	Intense burning pain where the skin has been penetrated.

Treatment	If a spine fragment remains in the skin, it should be removed by a physician because unnecessary pain and further tissue damage can result from attempts to take it out without adequate local anesthetic. Immersion in hot water will decrease pain, as previously described for stingrays and starfish. X-rays may be needed to determine whether any spine fragments remain in the skin. Antibiotics and a tetanus booster will be given if necessary.

BLEEDING See also "Wounds and Wound Care," page 834

Bleeding can arise from two sources:

- veins, which carry a slow and steady supply of blood back to the heart, or
- arteries, which carry blood under higher pressure from the heart to the rest of the body.

An arterial injury is potentially more serious because blood escaping under pressure may be lost in large amounts in relatively little time. The amount of blood directly visible is not necessarily a reliable sign of the severity of an injury and may not reflect how much blood a person has lost. For example, some serious injuries do not bleed heavily or may bleed internally. Some minor wounds, such as scalp lacerations, may appear to bleed profusely, but in fact the amount of blood lost is relatively insignificant.

Treatment	• If possible, wear latex gloves or keep several layers of cloth or bandage between you and the blood. This is a good idea even if you have no reason to believe that the bleeding person has an infectious disease that could be transmitted through blood. • If time permits, wash your hands before tending a wound. This will help prevent infecting the wound with any bacteria on your hands. • If the wound is superficial, wash it gently with soap and water. • If there is severe external bleeding or evidence of major trauma, call 911. • Have the child lie down, and try to keep him (and yourself) calm. • Remove any loose debris from the wound. • Apply direct pressure to the wound using a sterile dressing or a clean cloth unless there is an eye injury, skull fracture, or an embedded object. In these cases do not apply direct pressure. • If an arm or a leg is bleeding, elevate it above the level of the heart unless movement causes increased pain or you suspect the arm or leg is fractured. • If direct pressure has stopped the bleeding but it starts again, reapply pressure. • If you must free your hands, apply a pressure bandage (see page 811). • If the wound is large enough to make direct pressure ineffective or if direct pressure has not stopped the bleeding after fifteen minutes, pressure-point bleeding control may be necessary (see page 811).

- If there is no indication of a neck, head, or back injury and the bleeding is severe, take steps to prevent shock (a severe drop in blood pressure). Signs of shock include bluish color of the fingernails or lips, clammy skin, pale skin color, weakness, confusion, and decreasing alertness. If one or more of these occur, be sure that someone has called 911. Lay the person flat, and if possible elevate the feet about twelve inches (about 30 cm). Cover the victim with a blanket or coat.
- *Do not* move a child who may have an injury to the head, neck, or back.
- *Do not* attempt to clean a large wound because this could aggravate bleeding that would otherwise slow down.
- *Do not* probe, explore, or pull any embedded or penetrating object out of a wound. Doing so could worsen bleeding and damage internal structures. This should be done only by a physician after appropriate evaluation.
- *Do not* apply ice directly to a wound.
- *Do not* use a tourniquet.
- *Do not* remove a dressing that becomes soaked with blood or attempt to peek at the wound to see if bleeding has stopped. These actions can disturb the wound surface and may actually increase bleeding. If necessary, add more dressings.

WRAPPING A WOUND

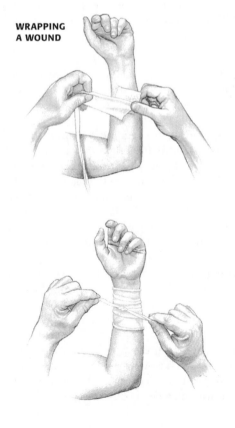

PRESSURE POINT BLEEDING CONTROL

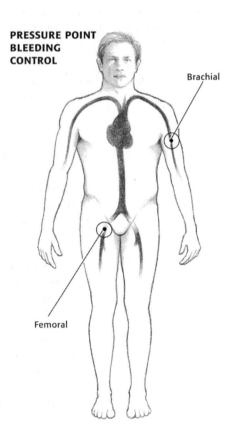

Brachial

Femoral

Even when bleeding is controlled, many wounds require medical attention, including the following:

- Gaping wounds
- Animal or human bites
- Wounds located directly over joints
- Wounds associated with a broken bone, loss of muscular function, or loss of sensation

Treatment

applying a pressure bandage

If you need to free your hands to move the child or attend to other injuries (whether or not the bleeding has stopped), a pressure bandage can be applied. This holds the dressings in place and maintains direct pressure on the wound.

1. Apply a dressing of sterile gauze to the wound (or a clean cloth if gauze is not available). Wrap long strips of cloth or a long bandage around the area where the wound is located to hold the dressing in place.
2. Cut or split the end of the bandage or cloth into two strips and tie these together to secure the bandage in place. The knot should be tied directly over the wound.
3. Make sure the pressure dressing is not too tight. It should be tight enough to maintain pressure on the wound, but not so tight that it prevents the tissue beyond the wound (that is, more distant from the heart) from receiving the blood it needs. If the area beyond the dressing is throbbing with pain or becoming blue and cold, the bandage should be loosened.

Treatment

pressure-point bleeding control

Important: If you need to use this technique, be sure that someone has called 911 and medical help is on the way.

This technique is used to control bleeding from an extremity, only when other methods have not worked. First try using direct pressure combined with elevation of the extremity. Pressure-point bleeding control is a last resort because areas of the body that are not bleeding will also have their blood flow reduced. Each arm or leg has a major artery supplying it. When bleeding cannot be controlled by other means, pressure on that specific artery can reduce blood flow. When this approach is accompanied by direct pressure to the wound and (if possible) elevation of the injured area, bleeding can usually be controlled.

When the bleeding is coming from the leg, the pressure point is over the femoral artery. If there are no suspected injuries to the head, neck, or spine and the child can be moved, place her on her back. Locate the femoral artery at the point where the leg and the groin meet, a little toward the groin side. Use the middle three fingers to feel for a pulse. Once the pulse has been located, apply firm pressure with the heel of the hand to compress the artery against the underlying bone.

When the bleeding is coming from the arm, the pressure point is over the brachial artery. This can be found at the middle of the inner aspect of the arm, just underneath the biceps muscle on the top of the arm. After you have found the pulse, use three or four fingers along the path of the artery to apply pressure and compress the artery against the underlying bone.

Remember: Elevation of the limb and direct pressure on the wound should be continued along with pressure-point bleeding control. When performed correctly, this technique will stop or significantly reduce major bleeding.

Bleeding without a Visible Wound

Symptoms

Bleeding can occur without visible wounds. Bleeding can be a significant symptom in these situations:

- Blood in the stool. This can be bright red, which indicates bleeding from a source at or near the anal opening, or a deep purplish black, which usually is more characteristic of blood lost from the upper intestinal tract.
- Blood in the urine. This may be bright red, which usually occurs with bleeding from the bladder or urethra (the tube through which urine exits the body) or a darker (tea) color, which suggests an origin within the kidney. Blood in the urine should be fully investigated by your child's doctor.
- Vomited blood. This may arise from bleeding within the stomach or esophagus (the passage between the throat and stomach). More commonly, in children and adolescents vomited blood arises from a nosebleed that drained down the throat rather than out the nose. An acute illness such as gastroenteritis (so-called stomach flu) may produce blood-tinged vomited material but not blood itself. In general, any vomiting of bright red material should prompt an immediate call to your child's physician.
- An abnormal amount or duration of menstrual bleeding. Note: Any vaginal bleeding in a young girl who has no other signs of puberty (such as breast development) is abnormal and should be evaluated.

Treatment

Any of the above situations calls for medical evaluation or consultation.

BONE AND JOINT INJURIES See also "Musculoskeletal Problems in Children," page 757

Fractures and Dislocations

A fracture (broken bone) occurs when enough force is applied to a bone to disrupt its structure and break it.

A dislocation occurs when the bones on either side of a joint move out of their normal alignment with one another. Either of the bones involved in a dislocation may also be fractured.

Symptoms

One or more of the following may indicate that a fracture or dislocation has taken place:

- Swelling
- Deformity
- Moderate to severe pain
- Localized tenderness
- Poor function or movement of the involved area

Treatment

- Avoid putting pressure or weight on the affected area.
- Stop any bleeding, as described in the previous section.
- Gently immobilize the injured area to reduce pain and prevent further damage. Elbows should be supported on a pillow, and suspected arm or shoulder injuries should be placed in a sling while the person is taken to the emergency room. A leg may be immobilized by carefully binding it to the other leg with a towel placed between them. Toes and fingers usually do not require splinting but should be protected until they're examined by a doctor.
- If the neck appears to be involved, the person should not be moved without a backboard and neck brace, which will normally be provided by an emergency transport team.
- Don't try to set or realign fractures or dislocations. Significant additional injury can occur through inappropriate movement of an injured limb.
- If possible, cover any open wounds to try to prevent further contamination.
- Take your child to his physician or the nearest emergency room for treatment.

Open Fractures

With this type of injury, one end of a fractured bone is protruding through the skin.

Treatment

Cover the wound (using a sterile dressing, if available) and take the person to an emergency facility immediately. Don't give the person anything to eat or drink because surgery will likely be required.

Sprains

In order for bones to move properly in relation to one another, the joint spaces between adjacent bones are bridged by strong but flexible fibrous bands called ligaments, which help keep the bones in proper alignment. A sudden and forceful twisting motion can cause a sprain—the stretching or tearing of a ligament.

Symptoms
- Pain when moving or putting weight on the affected joint
- Swelling and often a bluish discoloration

Since sprains are more common in adults than in children, and since it may be difficult to determine if a fracture is present merely by looking at an injured arm or leg, these symptoms should be evaluated by a physician.

Treatment
The simple acronym RICE can help you remember what to do following a sprain:

- **R**est the injured area.
- **I**ce or cold packs can decrease swelling and pain, but their contact with skin should be limited to twenty minutes out of every hour.
- **C**ompression, such as an elastic wrap around the affected area, can also reduce swelling and pain. This should not be so tight that it causes discomfort, numbness, or tingling.
- **E**levate the injured area as much as possible for twenty-four hours to help reduce uncomfortable swelling.

In addition, the affected area should be protected from further injury by minimizing movement (using a splint or crutches if necessary) until swelling and pain have resolved. You should seek medical input if there is no improvement in two or three days.

BURNS

The most widely used classification system for burns categorizes them according to size and depth. Since first aid treatment depends on a burn's severity, it is important to check the center of the wound. This is usually where the burn will be deepest, and its appearance will give an indication of the type of treatment the burn needs.

WHAT *NOT* TO DO FOR A BURN
- Do not open blisters. When sealed, they normally provide excellent protection for the underlying skin. However, in some situations a physician may rupture and remove the covering of a blister using a sterile technique, especially if infection is evident.
- Do not attempt to remove clothing that is stuck to a burn because this could peel away the skin.
- Do not use butter, antiseptic creams, or any other folk remedies on burns. These items may significantly slow the healing process and can actually cause or contribute to infection.

First-Degree (Superficial) Burns

These burns are the most common and the least severe. They can be caused by sun exposure or brief contact with hot water or a hot surface, such as the burner on a stove.

Symptoms

- Bright redness of the affected area, but no blisters
- Mild swelling
- Minor pain, because first-degree burns irritate nerve endings

Treatment

- Hold the affected area under cold running water for several minutes.
- Do not use ice, which might reduce the local blood supply.
- To soothe the pain, use a nonprescription pain reliever.

Second-Degree (Partial-Thickness) Burns

These are generally caused by contact with a hot liquid and occasionally by sun exposure.

Symptoms

Second-degree burns are characterized by blisters, which form because the burn penetrates more deeply into the skin, causing body fluids to be released.

Treatment

- Immediately submerge the burned area in cold water.
- Keep cold water in contact with the burn for at least five minutes or until medical help is given.
- If the burn is minor, treat it the same as a first-degree burn. A sterile, loose gauze dressing will reduce pain and protect the blister(s). When a blister eventually breaks and the fluid escapes, the affected area should be protected until it is dry. Your child's physician will probably want to check a second-degree burn (especially if the child is young) even if the area involved is small, and he or she will advise you about changing the dressing.
- If the burn is more widespread, apply cool, wet cloths to the affected areas and see a doctor immediately. A sizable burn will require medical follow-up, including regular dressing changes, topical medication if appropriate, adequate pain relief, and possibly antibiotics. A burn to the genitals, even if it appears to cover only a small area, should also be evaluated by a physician.
- Extensive partial-thickness burns can be serious or even fatal and may require specialized medical care. Very often this is carried out at a regional burn center.

Third-Degree (Full-Thickness) Burns

These are the most serious and, if extensive, can be fatal. All skin layers are destroyed, and the surface will usually appear charred or white. Paradoxically, full-thickness burns do not hurt as much as other burns because the nerve endings in the skin are no longer functioning.

Treatment   Do not attempt to treat this type of burn; get medical attention immediately.

Burns of varying size and depth can occur in the following ways:

Thermal Burns

Scalds, the most common thermal burns, are usually caused by contact with hot water. Exposing skin to water at 140°F (60°C) for three seconds or 156°F (69°C) for one second will result in a scald. (Coffee is usually about 180°F, or 82°C, when freshly brewed.) Immersion burns, such as those that might occur in a hot bathtub, involve longer contact and usually burn a wider area. Because grease or hot oil is around 400°F (204°C) and may not run off of skin as quickly as water does, it tends to cause deeper burns.

Flame or **flash** burns are the next most common thermal burns, and these result from fires or explosions. It is important to remove the person immediately from the heat source and take off burning or smoldering clothing. (Clothing that is not burning should not be removed.) A person with flash burns should be observed for wheezing or difficulties breathing.

Contact burns are often deep and are caused by touching hot surfaces such as curling irons, stoves, hot coals, etc.

Treatment   Treatment for any thermal burn includes immediate application of cool water, which will decrease pain and may reduce the extent of skin damage. Do not apply sprays, creams, or butter to this or any other type of burn.

Electrical Burns See also "Electric Shock," page 821

Electrical burns can cause more damage internally than might be suspected from the appearance of the skin surface.

Treatment
- Separate the victim from the electrical source. Do not touch the victim until it is certain that she is no longer in contact with the source of electricity.
- Check for responsiveness and breathing, and administer CPR if necessary (see page 836).
- Because of the possibility of internal damage, a person who has sustained an electrical burn should see a physician even if she does not feel any immediate discomfort.

Chemical Burns

Chemical burns are commonly caused by household cleansers and solvents. Alkali burns tend to be more serious than acid burns.

Treatment
- Carefully remove contaminated clothing.
- Flush the affected area thoroughly with water for at least fifteen minutes.
- Call your child's physician or take the child to the nearest emergency facility.

CARBON MONOXIDE POISONING

Carbon monoxide poisoning is likely to occur in situations such as the following:

- Wherever there is fire or smoke, especially in enclosed places
- In poorly ventilated rooms that are heated by wood-burning stoves or kerosene-type space heaters
- In homes or buildings with malfunctioning furnaces or heating systems
- In closed garages, or any closed structure, in which a gasoline engine is running
- In cars that have faulty exhaust systems

Symptoms

Early signs of carbon monoxide poisoning include:

- Headache
- Dizziness
- Distorted vision
- Mild difficulty breathing

Signs of more severe poisoning include:

- Intense headache
- Nausea and/or vomiting
- Reddening of the skin
- Sleepiness
- Poor coordination
- Unusual behavior
- Loss of consciousness

Carbon monoxide poisoning should be strongly suspected if several individuals in the same house develop these symptoms simultaneously.

Treatment

- Move everyone to fresh air immediately.
- If someone is unconscious, begin rescue breathing or CPR if necessary (see page 836).
- Whether there is one or many victims, seek medical evaluation as quickly as possible. If no one can drive or a victim is unconscious, call 911 for emergency treatment and transportation.
- After each person has received treatment, contact the local gas company or fire department so they can check for carbon monoxide in the building.
- The primary treatment for carbon monoxide poisoning is 100 percent oxygen given by mask for several hours.

Swallowed Objects

It is common for children to swallow nonfood objects, either deliberately or accidentally. Toddlers, who are prone to place small items into the mouth, are at particular risk for this type of accident. Fortunately, once the object passes through the esophagus (the tube that carries food from the throat to the stomach), it will usually progress through the rest of the intestinal tract without difficulty. As this occurs, the child will not show any signs of distress, except in rare cases where an odd-shaped and usually pointed object, such as a toothpick, becomes stuck or perforates the bowel.

Treatment

An X-ray may be done to try to confirm the object's location (although not all objects will be visible on an X-ray), and the child's stools may be examined for the next few days until the object passes. If the object is not found after four to seven days, a second X-ray may be performed. If the object is metallic, some emergency facilities use a metal detector to track its progress. Seek immediate medical attention if abdominal pain develops before the object has passed out of the child's body.

Symptoms

of object lodged in esophagus

A small percentage of swallowed objects become lodged in the esophagus. When this occurs, a mild pain will usually develop in the chest below the sternum (breastbone), along with increased salivation caused by the inability to swallow.

Treatment

- The child is likely to be frightened, so keep him as calm as possible.
- *Do not* attempt to force the object into the stomach by giving fluids or food.
- In most cases the object will pass into the stomach within ten minutes. But if pain or difficulty in swallowing persists, the child will need emergency medical attention.

An X-ray of the chest or abdomen will usually disclose the location of the object. A specialist may be consulted to perform an endoscopy. In this procedure, a narrow, flexible fiber-optic device, known as an endoscope, is passed into the sedated child's esophagus in an attempt to dislodge or remove the foreign body. If the consultant does not feel that the object can be removed safely using a flexible endoscope, the procedure may be done in the operating room using a rigid endoscope.

Treatment

for swallowing small batteries

If a child swallows a "button battery"—the small, round battery used in watches, hearing aids, and other electronic devices—see a doctor immediately. A button battery that does not pass through the esophagus must be removed (usually using an endoscope) because it can cause a serious local erosion or even a perforation within a matter of hours.

Avulsion (Loss of a Tooth)

Treatment

An avulsed tooth has been completely knocked out or torn away from the socket. If a permanent tooth is avulsed but is reimplanted within thirty minutes of the injury, it is very likely that the tooth will survive. (Primary or baby teeth cannot be successfully reimplanted.) If the delay exceeds two hours, however, the chances of success are poor. Therefore, the tooth must be replaced in its socket almost immediately.

If your child has lost a tooth, do the following:

- Find the tooth.
- Rinse the tooth in a bowl using tap water; do not touch the dental roots.
- Gently reinsert the tooth, making sure it is facing the right direction.
- Go directly to the dentist while gently holding the tooth in place. The child can gently bite down on moistened gauze (or, in a pinch, a wet tea bag) to help keep the tooth in position.

If the parent or child is unable (or afraid) to replace the tooth, place it in cow's milk, saliva, or salt water (a quarter teaspoon of salt in a quart of water) while seeking emergency dental care.

Displaced Tooth

A displaced tooth is one that has not been completely knocked out of the mouth but has been seriously dislodged—usually inward toward the tongue, as when the child has fallen on his face or been hit in the mouth.

Treatment

- Control bleeding with direct pressure and ice as long as this does not increase pain.
- Reposition the tooth, if possible, and gently hold it in place.
- Seek dental care immediately. Delaying treatment decreases the likelihood that the tooth will survive.

Loose Tooth

In this case, the tooth is loose but not displaced from its socket. The tooth can be moved backward and forward (or sometimes up and down).

Treatment

If your child's tooth becomes loose, do the following:

- Control bleeding if present.
- Try to avoid repeated movement of the tooth. Remind your child not to wiggle the loose tooth or chew food until you have spoken with the dentist.
- Contact a dentist as soon as possible for further advice.

Sensitive or Chipped Tooth

Minor injuries to the mouth or teeth often result in a chipped tooth or increased sensitivity to gentle tapping on the tooth—but the position of the tooth has not changed. In this situation, consult your dentist as soon as possible for further advice.

BEWARE OF OTHER INJURIES

Children with dental trauma often have other head and facial injuries. Appropriate medical treatment should be given in addition to any emergency dental care. A tetanus booster may be considered if one has not been given within the last five years. Do not use aspirin to control pain because it may prolong bleeding.

DROWNING

Treatment

- Prolonged lack of oxygen from being submerged under water leads to cardiac arrest, so it is important that rescue breathing or CPR (either mouth-to-mouth or mouth-to-nose ventilation) be started immediately (see page 836)—even in the water if necessary.
- Call 911 for medical assistance and a quick transfer to the nearest emergency center.
- If you know what happened prior to the accident, tell the rescue workers, particularly if head and neck injuries are likely (as would be the case if the child was diving when the accident occurred).
- Keep the child warm, especially if he was in cold water. Wrap him in towels or a blanket until medical personnel arrive.

PREVENTION

The vast majority of drowning accidents among children occur in their own family's or a friend's pool. These could be avoided if self-closing, self-latching doors were installed in homes and on gates in the fences around pools. Most children ages four and younger who drown in swimming pools are out of adult sight for less than five minutes and were last seen inside the house. Most are in the care of one or both parents at the time of drowning. Sturdy, childproof pool covers and alarms on doors leading to the pool area—or even an alarm that sounds when someone enters the water—are also appropriate safety measures. Swimming lessons for children can be a worthwhile investment, but they do not substitute for safety measures and attentive adult supervision. Parents need to teach their children the importance of swimming only when supervised and the necessity of life jackets when boating. Older children and adolescents should be warned explicitly of the risks of alcohol or drug consumption while swimming or boating.

When young children are around water, they must always be supervised by an adult. Parents and teens should strongly consider becoming certified in CPR. Poolside telephones are helpful because they allow adults to answer the phone while continuing supervision. They also can speed the process of calling for help if an accident occurs.

RATES OF SURVIVAL

The chances of surviving submersion are not significantly affected by the type of water (saltwater, freshwater, or pool water with chemicals). How long a child can survive without oxygen depends on many other factors, including age, previous health, the water temperature, and the speed and effectiveness of the rescue effort. Children under age five have an advantage because of a nerve reflex that causes the heart to slow down and blood to be diverted to the brain and heart. Younger children usually survive if submersion lasts less than three minutes and may survive a submersion lasting up to ten minutes if the water temperature is 50° to 60°F (10° to 16°C). In general, cold water temperatures improve survival chances.

EAR PAIN AND INJURY

A blow to the side of the head that results in significant swelling or bleeding from the outer ear, bleeding from the ear canal, or loss of hearing should be evaluated by a physician as soon as possible. Ear pain that is not associated with trauma usually arises from infection of the ear canal or middle ear and will also need medical assessment (see "ear infections," Reference Section, page 657).

Removing Objects from the Ear

Occasionally a child will insert a small object (such as a bead or a bean) into an ear and cannot remove it. Less commonly, a small insect may crawl into a child's ear canal. While the sensations experienced by the child can be annoying, neither of these situations poses a threat to hearing, and both parent and child should try to remain calm.

Treatment   It may be possible to remove the object or insect at home by following these steps:

- If an insect has entered the ear canal, put a few drops of oil (mineral, baby, or vegetable) or peroxide in the ear canal.
- If you can see the object or insect in the ear, carefully remove it with tweezers—but only if it is clearly visible at the opening of the ear canal.
- If you cannot see the object clearly or if it is deeper within the ear canal, tilt your child's head to the side of the injured ear.
- If this doesn't work, leave the ear alone. Attempting to remove the object may damage the ear. Seek medical attention as soon as possible.

ELECTRIC SHOCK

Most electric-shock incidents involving children occur in the home through contact with electrical outlets, cords, or appliances. Infants and toddlers are particularly at risk of shock from biting electrical cords or inserting objects into electrical sockets. Most of these shocks cause minor injuries or burns unless the child is standing in water when the contact is made.

Serious injury or death from electric shock (electrocution) usually results from direct contact with high-voltage wires that have fallen during storms, or it may occur when children climb a power pole and touch an electric box or wire. Electric shock is always possible during an electrical storm, particularly if persons are on or in water or take shelter under trees or near any other structures that will conduct electricity from a lightning strike.

Treatment

- Break the child's contact with the electrical source using a nonconducting object, such as a wooden stick. Do not touch the victim until you are certain he is no longer in contact with the source of electricity. If possible, turn off the source of electricity.
- If the child is not breathing, begin rescue breathing or CPR (see page 836).
- Call 911 if there is any change in consciousness or breathing. Even if a child or adolescent appears and feels normal after an electric shock, his physician should be contacted immediately for advice, or he should be checked at the nearest emergency department.

PREVENTION

- Cover all electrical outlets with safety plugs when infants and toddlers are in the house.
- Unplug bathroom and other small appliances when they are not in use.
- Keep electrical cords out of children's reach.
- Teach children to never touch any electrical equipment while in the bathtub or use any electrical appliance or equipment when standing on a wet surface.
- Warn older children to stay away from outdoor electrical wires. This includes avoiding any fallen wires and staying off poles that hold power lines or electric boxes.
- Keep children inside during electrical storms. *At the first sign of lightning, get them out of swimming pools, rivers, or ponds, whether they are swimming or in a boat.* Teach children not to seek shelter under trees when there is lightning but to go to the nearest indoor shelter. If there is no indoor shelter nearby, show them how to minimize contact with the ground by crouching down and balancing on heels or toes.

EYE INJURIES See also "eye care and concerns," Reference Section, page 663

In general, any direct injury to the eye—cut or puncture, blow with a ball or fist, or debris in the eye—should receive immediate medical attention if there is significant pain, blurring, or loss of vision. If pain is minor and no serious injury is obvious, contact the doctor to determine whether your child should be seen in an emergency facility or the doctor's office.

Treatment

- Until it is seen by a doctor, keep the eye closed. This is a natural response to eye injury and helps reduce discomfort.
- If the eye has been penetrated or cut open, take the child directly to the emergency room. If there is fluid oozing from the eye, transfer the child lying flat on his back so additional fluid will not escape.
- Hold a simple shield, such as a paper cup, over the eye to protect it—but don't exert any pressure on the eye.

Chemicals in the Eye

Treatment

Take prompt action whenever any chemical has splashed into the eye. Although many materials will cause only minor irritation, some can result in serious injury or blindness if not attended to immediately.

Immediately flush the eye with lukewarm water. A gentle flow of water should run continuously into the affected eye(s). Hold the child under a tap or hose, or carefully pour water from a glass or pitcher into the eye(s) with the child lying down. If only one eye is involved, hold the child on her side with the affected eye down so none of the chemical can accidentally flow into the other eye. You will probably need to have another adult hold the eye open while you pour the water. You should continue irrigation for at least fifteen to thirty minutes, then seek medical attention as soon as possible. If possible, call the child's physician or ophthalmologist while the irrigation is under way, and be prepared to give as much information as possible about the chemical that was splashed into the eye.

Alkaline materials can penetrate deeply and cause serious damage. Examples of alkaline materials are drain cleaners, oven cleaners, and bleach. Look for these words on product labels:

- Lye
- Sodium hydroxide
- Potassium hydroxide
- Ammonia
- Calcium oxide
- Trisodium phosphate
- Wood ash

Acids tend to cause more localized tissue damage but can still cause significant injury. Examples of acids are automobile battery fluid, toilet-bowl cleaners, and swimming pool acid. Look for these words on product labels:

- Sulfuric acid
- Hydrochloric acid
- Phosphoric acid
- Hydrofluoric acid
- Oxalic acid

Less dangerous chemicals should be washed out of the eye also. Most of these materials will cause only mild redness, stinging, and temporary swelling involving the conjunctiva (the thin, clear tissue lining the white surface of the eyeball and inner surfaces of the eyelid). Irrigation will lessen the irritation and probably prevent the child from rubbing the eye and aggravating the soreness. Examples of less dangerous chemicals include food, alcohol, and household soaps.

FAINTING See also "Loss of Consciousness," page 827

Common situations in which fainting might occur include the following:

- A traumatic or anxiety-provoking situation—such as having blood drawn or witnessing an alarming event
- Standing for long periods of time with the knees locked, especially on a hot day
- An acute illness, especially when there has been loss of fluid through vomiting or diarrhea

- Standing up suddenly after lying down or squatting, especially when a person is hot or mildly dehydrated
- Standing in a hot, crowded area where there is little fresh air

Symptoms

Warning signs for fainting include the following:

- Paleness in the face
- Cold, clammy skin
- Dizziness
- Nausea
- Blurred vision
- Unusually rapid or slow pulse
- Feelings of anxiety or panic
- Numbness or tingling in the fingers or toes

Treatment

If you notice these warning signs or your child feels that she is about to pass out, have her lie down immediately, and if possible, elevate her feet. Do not allow her to stay upright because this can deprive her brain of needed oxygen. If she loses consciousness, take these steps:

- Lay the child on the floor on her back. If possible, raise her legs a few inches.
- Make sure that her airway is clear and that she is breathing.
- Loosen any tight clothing to make certain she is comfortable and able to breathe easily.
- If you are inside a building, open the windows to circulate fresh air.
- If your child vomits while unconscious, turn her head to the side and wipe out her mouth.
- Keep her chin up to prevent her tongue from obstructing her throat.
- If the child remains unconscious for more than one or two minutes, or if she displays any unusual movements or behavior during or after the episode, call for medical help immediately.

If the episode passes within fifteen minutes, emergency medical attention may not be necessary. However, fainting may be a sign of a more significant condition (such as anemia or pregnancy). If your child has fainted for no apparent reason or has repeated fainting episodes, contact her physician for further advice. In addition, a sudden loss of consciousness without any of the symptoms described above is not likely to be a fainting episode and should be evaluated immediately.

HEAD AND NECK INJURIES

Most childhood bumps on the head do not cause significant damage, although many result in a lump or "goose egg," which may alarm parents when it appears soon after the accident. This localized collection of blood, called a hematoma, is not unusual because of the abundant blood supply in the scalp. The lump will gradually decrease in size in a matter of days, although local discoloration may persist for weeks.

Children and adolescents can suffer neck injuries ranging from minor muscle strain to life-threatening cervical (neck) fractures as a result of trauma in which the neck is forcefully bent or twisted. These can occur in situations such as falls, contact sports, excessively rough play, trampoline injuries, or diving accidents. Children who are properly secured in car seats are less likely than adults to suffer neck strain injuries in auto accidents.

Treatment | **of a head bump**

- Typically a child will cry for a few minutes after bumping his head. He will need comforting and reassurance; a cold pack gently applied to the point of impact may help reduce local swelling.
- If the pain continues after fifteen or twenty minutes, acetaminophen (such as Tylenol) in a dose appropriate for the child's size may help. Do not give aspirin because it inhibits blood clotting. Stronger pain medication (such as codeine) might cause drowsiness, which could make evaluation of his condition more difficult later on.
- Over the next few hours he may complain of a little dizziness, nausea, and fatigue. He may throw up once or twice and want to lie down or nap. It is not necessary to try to keep him awake, but after an hour or so make sure he can be awakened without difficulty.
- Watch his progress over the next twenty-four to forty-eight hours because in very rare instances a blow to the head results in bleeding within the skull. This complication is commonly associated with increasing headache, repeated vomiting, and/or (most important) difficulty arousing the child. Observe his daytime behavior for possible signs of trouble (see page 826), and awaken him when you go to bed and once again three or four hours later. Make sure that he can be fully awakened, that he has normal strength and movement of arms and legs, and that he talks appropriately with you (or, if he is too young to talk, that he interacts normally in other ways).

Treatment | **of a minor neck strain**

- If your child has suffered a neck injury and you are not certain how serious it might be, *treat it is as if it might be serious* (see page 826).
- A minor muscle strain of neck muscle will cause some degree of pain, spasm, and stiffness. Acetaminophen or ibuprofen in appropriate doses (see charts on pages 609 and 688) can help relieve pain that can cause more spasm.
- Application of cold packs for no more than twenty minutes three or four times per day can be helpful during the first day or two after the injury. After two days, a warm pad applied for fifteen or twenty minutes may be more helpful.
- If minor neck pain isn't improving after three days, call your child's physician for further advice.

Symptoms

of more serious injury

While most bumps on the head or neck strains will not need medical attention, you should contact your child's doctor if one or more of the following occur:

- There is loss of consciousness, even if it lasts only a few seconds. A child who remains unconscious for more than a few minutes after a head injury should be seen by a doctor immediately. If there is any possibility of a neck injury, he should not be moved until he has been properly immobilized using a backboard and neck brace provided by an emergency transport team.
- The child is confused or disoriented following the accident or cannot remember what happened. If any alteration or loss of consciousness occurs following a blow to the head, the child is said to have a concussion. While a concussion does not necessarily indicate permanent damage to the brain or skull, closer observation at home or in the hospital will usually be recommended for at least one to two days following the injury.
- The child becomes increasingly difficult to arouse.
- The child is younger than twelve months of age.
- Crying continues for more than ten minutes after the injury.
- The child complains of persistent or worsening headache. In an infant or toddler who is too young to say what is bothering him, this may be manifested by ongoing irritability.
- The child vomits more than three times during the twenty-four hours after the accident.
- A seizure occurs (see "seizures," page 833, and Reference Section, page 713).
- There is a cut on the head (or elsewhere) that may require suturing.
- Clear or bloody fluid is draining from the nose or ears.
- You have any questions or concerns about the injury or your child's behavior.
- Neck pain is severe.
- The child complains of numbness or tingling in the arms or upper back.

Treatment

for more severe head or neck injury

If your child appears to have had a more severe head or neck injury, keep him as still as possible, especially his head and neck. Check for loss of consciousness by calling the child's name or tapping his chest. If he has lost consciousness, check his breathing as well. If he is not breathing, start rescue breathing or CPR immediately, but be careful not to move the head or neck while doing so (see page 836).

If the child was not unconscious for more than a few seconds and if he is not complaining of any headache or neck pain, it is probably all right to let him move. However, if he complains of neck pain or if you are concerned that he might have hurt his neck, *do not move him.* A neck injury that might not be apparent could lead to paralysis if he is improperly moved. Call 911 and have medical personnel evaluate him and transport him to the hospital using appropriate immobilization techniques.

LOSS OF CONSCIOUSNESS See also "Fainting," page 823, and "Head and Neck Injuries," page 824

Loss of consciousness in infants and children is most commonly caused by direct trauma to the head. But other conditions and illnesses can cause this event, including fainting episodes, seizures, severe allergic reactions, accidental or intentional drug ingestion, and diabetes. Losing consciousness is potentially very significant, even if it is brief and appears to resolve completely, and it should be discussed with (and possibly evaluated by) a physician.

Treatment

Check breathing. If the child is not breathing, start rescue breathing or CPR immediately (see page 836). Any apparent loss of consciousness can be confirmed by calling the child's name, gently shaking her (unless there is concern about head or neck injury), or tapping her chest. An unconscious child will not respond.

Whenever a child has lost consciousness, it is important to consider the possibility of a head injury. If there is any evidence that this has occurred (such as bleeding or visible swelling), keep the head and neck immobilized and call 911 for transport to an emergency facility.

MUSCLE STRAINS AND CRAMPS

Muscle strains and cramps can result from vigorous physical activity and exercise.

Strains

A strain is an injury in which muscle fibers are pulled, stretched, or torn during physical activity.

Treatment

- Do not massage the muscle; let it rest.
- Elevate a strained arm or leg to prevent swelling.
- Apply a cold cloth or compress to the muscle. Wrap ice in a clean cloth and apply to the injury for a maximum of twenty minutes every hour. Repeat intermittently for twenty-four hours.
- After twenty-four hours, use a warm wet compress to soothe the muscle.
- Ibuprofen or acetaminophen can help ease pain and reduce swelling.

Cramps

Cramps—painful and usually sudden spasms of one or more muscles—can occur following overworking of a muscle, or they may happen spontaneously during sleep.

Treatment

- If your child has a cramp, help him gently stretch out the muscle immediately. Massage the knotted muscle for several minutes.
- Follow the massage with a warm bath, a warm wet compress, or a heating pad.

NOSEBLEEDS

Nosebleeds can have a variety of causes, including nose picking, dry weather, or trauma (such as being hit in the nose).

Treatment

Nosebleeds usually do not require medical attention. If your child gets a nosebleed, follow these steps:

- Have the child lean over a sink or sit in a chair with her head bent slightly forward to prevent the blood from running down the throat.
- Have the child blow her nose once into tissue or toilet paper to remove any clotted blood. If any blood has run into the mouth, have the child spit it out. (Swallowing the blood can irritate the stomach.)
- Apply pressure with the child's thumb and forefinger, pinching the nose near the opening of the nostrils (not high on the bridge of the nose) for five minutes or more. If your child cannot apply pressure, do it for her.
- After five minutes, slowly remove your fingers. If the nose continues to bleed, repeat for ten more minutes.
- If the child's nose continues to bleed for more than twenty minutes, or if the nosebleed was the result of a fall or blow to the face, contact your physician.

Objects in the Nose

If you have small children, it may only be a matter of time before you will be called upon to remove a toy or other small object from your child's nose.

Treatment

Before seeking medical treatment, try to remove the object by following these steps:

- Calm the child, and ask her to breathe through her mouth.
- Hold a tissue up to the child's nose and have her blow her nose.
- If the object is visible and can be grasped easily with tweezers, you can attempt to remove it with a gentle pull.
- If the object does not come out easily or it has been inserted far into the nose, or if your child is struggling and cannot hold completely still, do not try to remove it. (Doing so could damage the inside of the nose.) Contact your child's physician.

OVEREXPOSURE TO HEAT OR COLD

Hypothermia

Hypothermia, or low body temperature, results from prolonged, unprotected exposure to a cold environment. Immersion in cold water causes much greater loss of body heat than exposure to air the same temperature and thus can cause hypothermia (defined as an internal body temperature below 95°F, or 35°C) within minutes. Wearing wet clothes in a cold environment also increases heat loss and the likelihood of hypothermia. Small children and infants are especially prone to hypothermia.

Our physiological functions, metabolism, and central nervous system can perform properly only within a very narrow temperature range. As the body loses heat, several internal responses attempt to maintain the internal or core temperature as close to 98.6°F (37°C) as possible. Blood flow is diverted to the upper body to preserve heat within the brain, heart, lungs, and other vital organs. The hands, feet, arms, and legs become cold first, but our limbs are designed to tolerate this decrease in temperature fairly well. Shivering (rapid involuntary contractions of muscles) generates heat to preserve core body temperature.

Symptoms

- Numbness and/or weakness
- Lethargy
- Sleepiness
- Confusion
- Loss of coordination
- Staggering
- Inappropriate behavior

Treatment

- Move victim to a warm area. If this is not possible, shelter him from the wind, change any wet clothing, and put him in a sleeping bag if one is available. An adult lying in the same sleeping bag may provide additional heat for the child. Give the victim something warm to drink, if he is able to drink and if it is available.
- If available, use an electric blanket, or apply warm compresses to the center of the body—neck, chest, and groin—but not to the arms or legs. Massaging or rubbing the body is not helpful.
- If symptoms persist, if there is any loss of consciousness, or if there has been an immersion in near-freezing water, call 911 or take the victim to the nearest emergency room immediately.

Frostbite

This freezing injury to skin occurs most often in windy or wet conditions. It typically affects areas of the body that are exposed or have a limited blood supply, such as the nose, ears, fingers, and toes. Frostbitten fingers or toes usually appear flushed. If the frostbite is severe, the affected skin will become hard, white or mottled, and numb.

Treatment

As soon as you recognize any change in local skin color, especially in a vulnerable area, after being outdoors, take the following steps:

- Bring the person in from the cold as quickly as possible and remove any wet clothing.
- If signs of hypothermia are present, take appropriate action, as described in the previous section.
- "Thaw out" the frostbitten part of the body by immersing it in warm but not hot water or applying warm, moist compresses to it. Use a bathtub

if multiple areas are involved. Do not use a heat lamp or electric heater, which might overheat and actually burn frostbitten skin.
- Numbness will usually disappear and the normal skin color will return within a half hour. Pain may be felt as the affected areas rewarm; acetaminophen may be given if needed.
- Keep the rest of your child's body comfortable with blankets or other warm clothing.
- Do not massage or rub snow on frostbitten areas of the body—this can cause damage to local tissue.
- Seek medical attention. This is particularly important if skin color and sensation have not returned to normal after twenty to thirty minutes or if blisters develop in the frostbitten areas.

PREVENTION

The primary means of preventing hypothermia or frostbite is to dress appropriately for cold weather. Additional helps include the following:

- Because a significant amount of heat is lost from the surface of the head, and because ears and fingers are particularly vulnerable to frostbite, make sure your child wears a hat or ear protection and mittens outdoors in cold weather.
- Multiple layers of clothing help prevent loss of body heat. Since wet clothing significantly increases heat loss, the outermost layer should be waterproof.

Hyperthermia

Hyperthermia is an increase in the internal or core body temperature resulting from circumstances such as strenuous exercise or exposure to high environmental temperatures. (Fever, which is by far the most common cause of temperature elevation, is discussed in the Special Concerns section "When Your Child Has a Fever," page 241.) The body responds to this heat stress with mechanisms designed to maintain core temperature close to 98.6°F (37°C). The respiratory rate will increase, which causes heat to be lost from the lungs, and sweat will evaporate from the skin, which helps cool the body.

If the environmental temperature is higher than body temperature, the only way heat can be lost from the body is through evaporation. In high-humidity conditions, sweat does not readily evaporate, thus slowing the cooling process even more. Dehydration increases the risk of hyperthermia, as do certain medications that may reduce the body's ability to sweat.

Hyperthermia can take the following forms:

Heat Syncope (Heat Fainting)

Heat fainting is fairly common and typically occurs when a person must stand for a prolonged period in a hot environment. For example, a marching-band member standing at attention for an extended time on a hot day would be a candidate for this problem. In this condition, blood pools in the legs, causing blood pressure to drop until the person feels faint.

Treatment
- Move the person to a cooler location.
- Have the person lie down.
- Elevate the legs.
- Give liquids.

Heat Exhaustion

Heat exhaustion is more serious than heat syncope but milder than heatstroke (see below), and the body temperature may or may not be elevated.

Symptoms

- Nausea
- Vomiting
- Fatigue
- Headache

Treatment

Heat exhaustion can progress to heatstroke if not treated properly, but symptoms should resolve within one hour with proper treatment. Follow the same treatment as given above for heatstroke. If signs and symptoms of more serious trouble develop—confusion, impaired coordination—call 911 or go immediately to the nearest emergency room.

Heatstroke

This is the most severe form of hyperthermia and can occur because of extremes in temperature and very strenuous exercise. The body temperature often climbs above 105°F (41°C), sometimes with an absence of sweating.

Symptoms

- Confusion
- Impaired coordination
- Rapid or shallow breathing
- Rapid heartbeat
- Loss of consciousness

Treatment

Heatstroke is a medical emergency that should be treated immediately. Call 911, and while waiting for help to arrive, do the following:

- Remove the victim's clothing.
- Move her to a cooler environment.
- Blow air on her with a fan while spraying her with a mist of water.
- Give her liquids. If the person cannot take enough liquid by mouth, she will need intravenous fluids.
- Apply cold packs to the groin or the armpits.

POISONING

A child who has ingested a toxic substance or an excessive amount of a therapeutic medication may or may not be able to tell you what has happened; this will depend on the child's age, her condition after the episode (alert, drowsy, or unconscious), and her emotional state.

Symptoms

Indications that your child has swallowed a toxic substance or an overdose of medication could include the following:

- Sudden illness for no apparent reason
- Close proximity to a potentially toxic substance, such as a household cleaning product or a medication—especially if the container is open and pills or liquid are spilled
- Unusual behavior
- Unusual liquids, stains, or powder on the skin, clothing, or around the mouth
- Dizziness, weakness, stupor, confusion, or coma
- Blurry vision, double vision, or a change in the normal size of the pupils
- Rapid or very slow heart rate
- Fever, headache, irritability
- Rash or changes in skin color (blue, flushed, or pale)
- Depression or unusual shifts in mood
- Ringing in the ears
- Coughing, chest pain, or difficulty breathing, with or without increased noise during breathing
- Nausea, vomiting, abdominal pain or cramping, or diarrhea
- Twitching muscles or unexplained muscle pain or cramping
- Excessive saliva
- Inability to control urination or bowel movements
- Loss of appetite
- Abnormal breath odor

Treatment

- Check the child's responsiveness and breathing, and begin rescue breathing or CPR if necessary (see page 836). If CPR has been initiated, have someone call 911. If you are alone, call 911 after you have carried out CPR for approximately two minutes.
- If CPR is not needed, call your child's physician, the nearest emergency room, or a local poison-control center. If you can't find a number for a poison-control center, call 800-222-1222.
- If the child is having seizures, protect him from injury (see next page).
- If the child vomits, try to protect the airway. Position him so that whatever is vomited will exit away from the mouth and not accidentally be inhaled into the airway. If necessary, gently remove any remaining material from his mouth.
- If the skin was exposed to a toxic substance, remove all contaminated clothing and wash skin, hair, and nails.
- If the child has been exposed to fumes, remove him from the area in which the fumes are present.
- If the material went into the eye, irrigate it thoroughly with tap water (see "Chemicals in the Eye," page 822).
- Take the substance and its container with you to the doctor's office or emergency room, and be prepared to answer some questions: Where

was the child found? What and how much was ingested? When did symptoms (if any) begin? Did symptoms begin gradually or abruptly? What treatment was done at home and when?

- *Do not* wait for dramatic signs of illness before seeking medical assistance.
- *Do not* give anything as an antidote or attempt to neutralize a poison unless you have been told to do so by a physician or poison control center.
- *Do not* attempt to give the child anything by mouth if he is unconscious.
- *Do not* rely on the label of a medication or other substance to tell you whether or not it is potentially hazardous.
- *Do not* induce vomiting (see below).

WARNING REGARDING IPECAC

For decades parents were advised to have ipecac, a medicine that induces vomiting, available in case a child swallowed a poisonous substance. However, over the past several years medical professionals have expressed some serious reservations about this routine advice. One major concern is that a host of materials and objects may cause considerable harm as they pass from stomach to mouth during vomiting. In addition, the idea of using ipecac was largely based on intuition rather than actual scientific studies, and more recent research doesn't support the notion that children who receive ipecac at home have better outcomes than those who don't. *As a result, the American Academy of Pediatrics now recommends that ipecac not be used routinely as an intervention at home following accidental ingestion of a toxic substance.* If you have any old syrup of ipecac at home, you should flush it down the toilet.

SEIZURES

A seizure is a sudden abnormal surge of electrical activity in the brain, with manifestations that may range from subtle lapses in attention to terrifying convulsions.

Symptoms

These vary according to the type of seizure. See "seizures," Reference Section, page 713.

Treatment

If your child is having a seizure, take the following steps:

- Gently lay her on a soft surface, such as a bed or carpet, away from any hard objects. Position her head to the side so that any saliva (or any material that comes up if she vomits) can drain from the mouth.
- If her mouth is empty, don't put a finger, stick, or spoon in it because this may damage her teeth or cause her to vomit. If she has anything in her mouth, gently remove it with your finger. Do not try to pour a liquid into her mouth.
- Since she cannot swallow her tongue, don't try to grab it with your fingers.
- Don't restrain the child.

- Do not immerse her in a tub of water, even if she has a fever.
- If you can, time the seizure's length, and carefully observe your child's movements during the episode.
- If the seizure ends within five minutes, call your child's physician immediately for further advice.
- Call 911 for emergency medical assistance for any of the following situations:
  - If the seizure lasts for more than five minutes. (Even if the seizure ends before help arrives, allow the paramedics to assess your child.)
  - If your child is having difficulty breathing.
  - If your child has fallen or hit her head during a seizure.
  - If your child is unconscious or unresponsive for more than a few minutes after a seizure ends. (Calling 911 may not be necessary, however, if your child has a known seizure history with a pattern of sleeping or sluggishness immediately after previous seizures.)
  - If your child has never had a seizure before.

WOUNDS AND WOUND CARE

Bruises and Hematomas

Bruises (also called contusions) usually form a bluish discoloration at the site of the injury and fade from blue to green to yellow over one to two weeks.

A hematoma ("goose egg") is a collection of blood and swelling in the skin or just underneath it. Depending upon its size and location, this swelling will go down in one to ten days.

Treatment
- Rest the injured area for a few days.
- Apply ice intermittently to the injured area for a few days. The ice can be applied for twenty minutes every two to four hours and will help limit bleeding into the tissues. If your child won't allow you to put ice on the bruised area, it will still heal fairly quickly in most cases.

Abrasions

Abrasions (scrapes) are broad areas of superficial skin damage; they seldom result in any deep, underlying tissue damage and rarely leave a significant scar. They heal quickly and usually do not become infected.

Treatment
- Cleanse the wound gently with warm, soapy water to remove any dirt and debris. A painless antiseptic such as hydrogen peroxide can help cleanse an abrasion.
- Apply an antibiotic ointment such as a neomycin-polymyxin mixture (Neosporin and other brands) or one prescribed by your child's physician. Cover the wound with a nonstick dressing to keep it clean.
- Change the dressing once or twice daily until the wound is no longer moist and sensitive.

Lacerations

A laceration (a cut) can range from a minimal break in the skin surface that requires only a brief cleansing and a day or two of a simple dressing, to a long, gaping wound that requires extensive repair. A deep laceration may damage tendons, nerves, joints, or other underlying tissues. It may also contain dirt or other foreign material that can lead to infection. Because of these potential complications, deep wounds should be examined by a physician to determine appropriate treatment.

Treatment

First aid for lacerations that might require sutures (stitches) includes the following:

- Apply steady pressure with clean gauze or washcloth to stop the bleeding.
- Keep the area clean.
- Rinse with clean water if available.
- Keep the wound covered with a sterile bandage, or at least a clean cloth, until it can be examined by a medical professional.
- A laceration should be closed within twelve to twenty-four hours, or sooner if the laceration is on the face. The sooner the wound is treated, the less likely it will become infected. If a laceration is not sutured, the consequences are usually not serious; but healing could take longer, and the resulting scar is likely to be wider or more prominent.
- Sometimes lacerations are deep enough to involve injury to a nerve or tendon. For this reason, any laceration that looks deep should be examined and cleaned by your child's physician or another medical professional.

WHEN SUTURES ARE NOT USED

Some minor lacerations may be closed with adhesive strips or glue. Also, with some contaminated lacerations or certain types of animal or human bites, the physician may not use sutures because closing the wound could increase the risk of infection. In such cases the wound will be left open, but it will gradually heal as the body's repair processes close the cut.

CONCERNS ABOUT TETANUS

Any laceration, puncture, bite, abrasion, or burn should prompt a review of a child's tetanus immunization status. Tetanus is a potential threat following any wound, but it is a greater concern following punctures or contaminated wounds. If a child is on schedule for his or her immunizations or is fully immunized, no tetanus update will be needed. Otherwise a tetanus booster should be given. (You can learn more about tetanus and the immunizations that protect against it in "Immunizations—Which Ones, Why, and When?" beginning on page 741.)

SIGNS OF INFECTION

Signs and symptoms of infection include local pain, swelling, and redness, which may spread over a large area around the wound. There may also be fever. Inflammation of local lymph channels may form red streaks that extend away from the wound. Some bacteria cause the production of discolored drainage (pus). If a wound appears to be developing an infection, see a physician. Mild heat on the affected area, rest, elevation of the affected area (if an arm or leg), and antibiotics will most likely be recommended.

THE IMPORTANCE OF FOLLOW-UP

Be sure to obtain specific wound-care instructions before leaving the office or emergency facility. In general, if sutures or sterile strips have been used, the wound should be kept dry for a few days. This will mean that the child should not go swimming or soak the wound while bathing. In some cases, the physician may instruct you to clean the wound and apply fresh dressings. He or she should also tell you when the strips or bandages should be removed. A follow-up appointment is usually required when stitches need to be removed.

EMERGENCY

Cardiopulmonary Resuscitation (CPR) and Choking Emergencies

It is highly recommended that parents and teenagers take a Red Cross class in first aid and cardiopulmonary resuscitation (CPR), and then take a refresher class every two years. For those who have completed this training, the following material is a review of the basic steps for assisting a choking victim and for performing CPR.

CARDIOPULMONARY RESUSCITATION (CPR): NEWBORN TO ONE-YEAR-OLD

1. Check to see if the baby is conscious.
- Tap his shoulder.
- Do not shake his head and neck.

2. If there is no response, shout for help.
- As soon as help is available, have the person call 911. If you are alone, start CPR and give five cycles (about two minutes) of thirty compressions and two breaths, then call 911. If there is no indication of a traumatic injury, you can carry a baby to the phone with you. In most situations the dispatcher can assist you with CPR instructions.

3. Roll the baby onto his back if he is not in that position already.
- Support his head and neck, keeping them in a straight line with his back.
- Lay the baby on a firm surface.

4. Check to see if he is breathing.
- Gently tilt his head back and lift his chin to open the airway.
- Put your head near the infant's mouth and nose.
- For three to five seconds, look, listen, and feel for breathing.
  (a) Is the chest rising?
  (b) Can you hear breathing sounds?
  (c) Can you feel air moving against your face?

Tilt head back and lift chin. (See 4.)

5. If you can't see, hear, or feel the baby breathing, you must immediately begin breathing for him (rescue breathing).
- Make a tight seal with your lips around the baby's nose and mouth. If you have difficulty making a tight seal over the nose and mouth, try either mouth-to-mouth or mouth-to-nose ventilation. If you use mouth-to-mouth, pinch the nose closed; if mouth-to-nose, close the mouth. In either case, be sure that the chest rises when you give a breath.

Make tight seal around nose and mouth. (See 5.)

- Give two breaths:

  (a) Breathe into the baby for about one second, watching for the chest to rise. If the chest does not rise, make sure the airway is open and try again.

  (b) Pause to let the air flow out, and then give another breath.

6. Position your fingers on the baby's chest.
- With one hand, keep the baby's head tilted back.
- Place two fingers of your other hand on the center of the breastbone, just below the level of the nipples.

7. Compress the baby's chest using two fingers.
- Push the breastbone straight down to approximately one-third to one-half the depth of the chest.
- Give thirty compressions at the rate of one hundred per minute. (This is faster than one per second, so it should take a little less than twenty seconds.)

Compress chest using 2 fingers (See 7.)

8. After you have given thirty compressions, give two full breaths.
- Make a tight seal with your lips around the baby's nose and mouth.
- Give two full breaths for one second each, watching for the chest to rise. If the chest does not rise, make sure the airway is open and try again.

9. Continue cycles of thirty compressions and two breaths until the baby begins to move, another rescuer takes over, or emergency medical personnel arrive and assume care.

Make tight seal around nose and mouth. (See 8.)

CARDIOPULMONARY RESUSCITATION (CPR): ONE- TO EIGHT-YEAR-OLD

1. Check to see if the child is conscious.
- Tap his chest or shoulder.
- Do not shake his head and neck.
- Call out to him, "Are you okay?"

2. If there is no response, shout for help.
- As soon as help is available, have the person call 911. If you are alone, start CPR and give five cycles (about two minutes) of thirty compressions and two breaths, then call 911. If there is no indication of a traumatic injury, you can carry a small child to the phone with you. In most situations the dispatcher can assist you with CPR instructions.

3. Roll the child onto his back if he is not in that position already.
- Support his head and neck, keeping them in a straight line with his back.
- Lay the child on a firm surface.
- Open his shirt if possible.

4. Check to see if he is breathing.
- Kneel next to his head.
- Tilt his head back and lift his chin to open the airway.
- Put your head near the child's mouth and nose.
- For five seconds, look, listen, and feel for breathing.
  (a) Is the chest rising?
  (b) Can you hear breathing sounds?
  (c) Can you feel air moving against your face?

5. If you can't see, hear, or feel the child breathing, you must immediately begin breathing for him (rescue breathing).
- Pinch his nose shut using two fingers.
- Make a tight seal with your lips around the child's mouth.
- Give two full breaths.
  (a) Breathe into the child for about one second, watching for the chest to rise. If the chest does not rise, make sure the airway is open and try again.
  (b) Pause to let the air flow out, and then give another breath.

6. Position your hands on the child's chest.
- Place the heel of the hand on the breastbone in the center (middle) of the chest between the nipples and then place the heel of the second hand on top of the first so that the hands are overlapped and parallel.
- Don't allow your fingers to rest on the child's chest. Point your fingers upward (away from the body), or interlock the fingers of your two hands.
- As an alternative, in a small child you can use the heel of one hand to compress the chest.

7. Compress the chest by pressing straight downward.
- Use your body weight, not your arm muscles.
- Keep your arms straight, with elbows locked.
- Lean over with your shoulders over your hands.
- You should move straight up and down, not rock back and forth.
- The breastbone should depress approximately one-third to one-half the depth of the chest.
- Give thirty compressions at the rate of one hundred per minute. (This is faster than one per second, so it should take a little less than twenty seconds.)

8. After you have given thirty compressions, give two full breaths.
- Gently tilt the child's head back to open the airway.
- Pinch his nose shut with your fingers.
- Make a tight seal with your lips around the child's mouth.
- Give two full breaths for one second each, watching for the chest to rise. If the chest does not rise, make sure the airway is open and try again.

9. Continue cycles of thirty compressions and two breaths until the child begins to move, another rescuer takes over, or emergency medical personnel arrive and assume care.

1. Check to see if the victim is conscious.
- Tap his chest or shoulder, or give his body a gentle shake.
- Do not shake his head and neck.
- Call out to him, "Are you okay?"

2. If there is no response, shout for help.
- As soon as help is available, have the person call 911. If no one else is available to call 911, quickly make the call. In most situations the dispatcher can assist you with CPR instructions. If there is reason to believe the victim isn't responding because of respiratory arrest—for example, a child pulled from a swimming pool—begin CPR for five cycles (about two minutes) and then call 911.

3. Roll the person onto his back if he is not in that position already.
- Support his head and neck, keeping them in a straight line with his back.
- Lay him on a firm surface.
- Open his shirt if possible.

4. Check to see if he is breathing.
- Kneel next to his head.
- Tilt his head back and lift his chin to open the airway.
- Put your head near the person's mouth and nose.
- For five seconds, look, listen, and feel for breathing.
  (a) Is the chest rising?
  (b) Can you hear breathing sounds?
  (c) Can you feel air moving against your face?

Tilt head back and lift chin.
(See 4.)

5. If you can't see, hear, or feel the victim breathing, you must immediately begin breathing for him (rescue breathing).
- Pinch his nose shut using two fingers.
- Make a tight seal with your lips around the victim's mouth.
- Give two full breaths.
  (a) Breathe into the victim for about one second, watching for the chest to rise. If the chest does not rise, make sure the airway is open and try again.
  (b) Pause to let the air flow out, and then give another breath.

6. Kneel beside the victim, halfway between his head and chest so you can move quickly between giving breaths and compressing the chest.

Make tight seal over victim's mouth.
(See 5.)

7. Position your hands on the victim's chest.

- Place the heel of the hand on the breastbone in the center (middle) of the chest between the nipples and then place the heel of the second hand on top of the first so that the hands are overlapped and parallel.
- Don't allow your fingers to rest on the victim's chest. Point your fingers upward (away from the body), or interlock the fingers of your two hands.

8. Compress the chest by pressing straight downward.

- Use your body weight, not your arm muscles.
- Keep your arms straight, with elbows locked.
- Lean over with your shoulders over your hands.
- You should move straight up and down, not rock back and forth.
- The breastbone should depress one and a half to two inches (about 4 to 5 cm).
- Give thirty compressions at the rate of one hundred per minute. (This is faster than one per second, so it should take a little less than twenty seconds.)

Position hands on victim's chest. (See 7.)

9. After you have given thirty compressions, give two full breaths.

- Gently tilt the victim's head back to open the airway.
- Pinch the nose shut with your fingers.
- Make a tight seal with your lips around the victim's mouth.
- Give two full breaths for one second each, making sure the chest rises with each breath. If the chest does not rise, make sure the airway is open and try again.

10. Continue cycles of thirty compressions and two breaths until the victim begins to move, another rescuer takes over, or emergency medical personnel arrive and assume care.

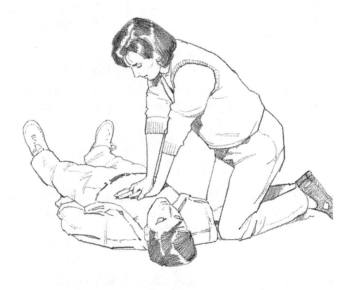

Compress chest, using body weight. (See 8.)

CHOKING EMERGENCIES: NEWBORN TO ONE-YEAR-OLD

1. **Determine if the baby is choking.**
   - If there is forceful coughing or the baby can cry, do not interfere.
   - If she is unable to cry, cough, or breathe, or if she is coughing very weakly, have someone call 911 and take immediate action (step two and following).

2. **Position the baby facedown on your forearm.**
   - Support the baby's head and jaw as you turn her facedown.
   - Position her so that her head is lower than her chest.

3. **Give five back slaps.**
   - Use the heel of your free hand.
   - Strike forcefully between her shoulder blades.

4. **Turn the baby onto her back.**
   - Support the baby's head and jaw as you roll her over.
   - Rest her back on your thigh.

5. **Give five thrusts to the chest.**
   - Place two fingers in the center of her breastbone (just below the level of the nipples).
   - Thrust downward quickly with enough force to dislodge the object.

6. **Repeat steps two through five.**
   - Turn the baby facedown.
   - Give five back slaps.
   - Turn the baby on her back.
   - Give five chest thrusts.

7. **Repeat this sequence until the baby begins to cough or breathe, she coughs up the object, or she becomes unconscious.**

If the baby is or becomes unconscious:

8. **Have someone call 911 for help if this has not been done already.**

9. **Roll the baby onto her back.**
   - Support her head and neck, keeping them in a straight line with her back.
   - Lay the baby on a firm surface.

10. **Clear any material from the baby's mouth.**
    - Use the fingers and thumb of one hand to grasp and lift the baby's lower jaw and tongue.
    - If you see an object in the mouth or throat, remove it. Be careful not to push any object or food farther down the airway.

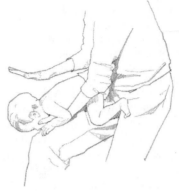

Position baby face down on forearm. (See 2 & 3.)

Give chest thrusts using 2 or 3 fingers. (See 5.)

Clear material from baby's mouth. (See 10.)

11. Check to see if she is breathing.
- Gently tilt her head back and lift her chin to open the airway.
- Put your head near the baby's mouth and nose.
- For three to five seconds, look, listen, and feel for breathing.
  - (a) Is the chest rising?
  - (b) Can you hear breathing sounds?
  - (c) Can you feel air moving against your face?

12. If you can't see, hear, or feel the baby breathing, you must immediately begin CPR (see page 836). Remember to give two breaths before starting chest compressions. The chest compressions may dislodge the object, so you should check the mouth with each attempt to position the airway as you continue CPR. If the object is visible and loose, remove it. Be careful not to push any object or food farther down the airway.

13. If you succeed in opening the airway and you can inflate the baby's lungs, check to see if she is breathing on her own. If not, continue CPR.

Check to see if baby is breathing. (See 11.)

Make tight seal around nose and mouth. (See 12.)

CHOKING EMERGENCIES: ONE-YEAR-OLD TO ADULT

1. Determine if the person is choking.
- If there is forceful coughing or the person can speak, do not interfere.
- Ask the person if he is choking.
- If he is unable to speak or cough, have someone call 911 and take immediate action (step 2 and following).

2. Get behind the victim and position your hands.
- Wrap your arms around the victim's waist.
- Make a fist with one hand.
- Place the thumb side of your fist against the middle of the victim's abdomen—just above the navel but below the rib cage.
- Grab your fist with your other hand.

3. Give abdominal thrusts.
- Quickly pull your fist inward and upward into the abdomen.
- If the victim is pregnant or too big to reach around the abdomen, give chest thrusts instead.
  - (a) Place your fist against the center of the breastbone.
  - (b) Grab your fist with your other hand, and give thrusts into the chest.
- Continue thrusts until the object is forced out of the victim's airway, or the victim becomes unconscious.

Wrap arms around victim's waist. (See 2.)

If the victim is or becomes unconscious:

4. Have someone call 911 for help if this has not been done already.

5. Roll the person onto his back if he is not in that position already.
- Support his head and neck, keeping them in a straight line with his back.
- Lay the victim on a firm surface.
- Open the victim's mouth with your thumb and index finger. If the object is visible and loose, remove it. Be careful not to push any object or food farther down the airway.

6. Check to see if he is breathing.
- Kneel next to his head.
- Tilt his head back and lift his chin to open the airway.
- Put your head near the person's mouth and nose.
- For five seconds, look, listen, and feel for breathing.
  (a) Is the chest rising?
  (b) Can you hear breathing sounds?
  (c) Can you feel air moving against your face?

7. If you can't see, hear, or feel the victim breathing, you must immediately begin breathing for him (rescue breathing).
- Tilt the victim's head back.
- Pinch his nose shut using two fingers.
- Make a tight seal with your lips around the victim's mouth.
- Give two full breaths.
  (a) Breathe into the victim for about one second, watching for the chest to rise.
  (b) Pause to let the air flow out, and then give another breath.

Tilt head back and lift chin. (See 6.)

If the breaths will not go in:

8. Tilt the head farther back and try again.
- Pinch his nose shut using two fingers.
- Make a tight seal with your lips around the victim's mouth.
- Give two full breaths.

Make tight seal over victim's mouth. (See 7.)

If the breaths still will not go in, the airway is probably blocked.

9. Begin CPR. (See CPR, pages 837 and 839.) The chest compressions may dislodge the object, so you should check the mouth periodically as you continue CPR. If the object is visible and loose, remove it. Be careful not to push any object or food farther down the airway.

10. If you succeed in opening the airway and you can inflate the victim's lungs, check to see if he is breathing on his own. If not, continue CPR.

Safety—Indoors and Outdoors

SAFETY: INDOORS

- Never step away when your baby is on a high surface such as a changing table or countertop.
- Keep the sides of a baby's crib raised.
- If an infant seat is used outside the car, place it on the floor.
- Avoid baby walkers.
- Install safety gates (not accordion-style) to guard stairways.
- Lock doors to dangerous areas such as the basement and garage.
- Check the stability of drawers, tall furniture, and lamps before a baby becomes mobile.
- Remove tablecloths that might be within the reach of a baby or toddler.
- Make sure any windows above the first floor of a multistory house are closed or have screens or guards that cannot be pushed out.
- Don't underestimate the climbing ability of a toddler.
- Remove or pad low furniture with sharp corners, such as coffee tables, in your child's living and playing areas.
- Place safety latches on all drawers and cabinets that are off-limits.
- Move anything dangerous—cleaning products; plumbing, gardening, painting, refinishing, and agricultural chemicals and supplies; knives and other sharp utensils; and medicines—to high cabinets that are latched.
- Make knives off-limits to a child until he is old enough to learn (and demonstrate) how to use them correctly.
- Put covers on unused electrical outlets.
- Keep electrical cords out of the reach of children.
- Remove all poisonous plants from the home.
- Put the number of the nearest poison-control center (or 800-222-1222) on or near all phones. Call if a child puts something in his mouth that might be poisonous.
- Purchase or place all medicines in containers with safety caps and store out of reach of children. Remember: There's no such thing as a "childproof" cap.
- Do not transfer toxic substances to bottles, glasses, or jars, especially if those containers originally contained familiar liquids for drinking (such as juice).
- When leaving your children with a babysitter, leave emergency phone numbers, a permission slip for emergency care, and insurance information. (Or designate whom the sitter should call.) Make certain the sitter knows the address and phone number of your home in case she needs to provide this information to emergency personnel.

Prevention of Choking Accidents

- Keep small, hard objects away from small children. This includes hard candy, nuts, popcorn, hot dogs, chewing gum, and hard fruits and vegetables.
- Cut food into small pieces.
- Remove small toys or hanging mobiles from the crib before the baby is able to reach them.
- Use only unbreakable toys that have no sharp edges or small parts that can come loose.
- Do not allow electrical or hanging cords within reach of a crib or a toddler's play area.
- Do not allow an infant to wear a necklace or a young child to play with any cord or string around the neck.
- Keep plastic bags and balloons out of reach of all children. If inhaled, a popped or deflated balloon in a small child's mouth could easily obstruct his airway.

Fire and Burn Prevention

- Never eat, drink, or carry anything hot when you are near or holding a baby or a small child.
- Don't cook when your child is at your feet. Use a playpen, high chair, or crib as a safety area for small children while you are preparing food.
- Use the rear burners on your stove, and keep the pan handles out of reach.
- Check formula, food, and drink temperatures carefully.
- Keep hot appliances and cords out of the reach of children.
- Do not allow your child to use the stove, microwave, hot curlers, curling iron, or steam iron until she is old enough to learn how to do so safely.
- Install and maintain smoke detectors in accordance with fire regulations in your area. If they are not wired directly into your home's electrical system, check smoke detectors monthly and replace batteries annually.
- Provide nonflammable barriers around heating surfaces and fireplaces.
- Teach your child to drop and roll on the ground if her clothing catches fire.
- Have your heating system checked annually.
- If there are any tobacco smokers in the family, they should not be allowed to smoke inside the home.
- Keep matches and lighters out of the reach of children.
- Have a working fire extinguisher near the kitchen, but instruct your child not to play with it. However, older children and adolescents should be taught how to use it in an emergency.
- Do not permit your child to possess or play with fireworks.

SMOKE DETECTORS

Roughly four hundred thousand residential fires occur in the United States each year, causing more than 3,100 deaths, 14,000 injuries, and more than $6 billion in damage. As deadly as the heat itself can be, the main cause of injury and death in residential fires is not the flames but the inhalation of smoke and toxic fumes. All too often, sleeping victims of fire are overcome by smoke before they ever wake up. Properly installed and maintained home smoke detectors could prevent many of these deaths.

Smoke detectors are considered the best and least expensive early-warning systems because they can alert people in a home before the fire ignites, before the concentration of smoke reaches a dangerous level, or before a fire becomes extremely intense. In the United States 96 percent of homes now have at least one smoke alarm, and half of deaths in home fires occur in the 4 percent of homes that have no smoke alarms.

SMOKE DETECTOR

Smoke detectors can be wired directly into a home's electrical system, or they may be battery powered, in which case fresh batteries should be installed at least once a year. Several safety organizations suggest designating a day each year to replace all of the smoke detector batteries in your home. (New Year's Day or the Fourth of July—holidays often celebrated with the discharge of fireworks, legal or otherwise—would be easy days to remember.) Smoke alarms are designed to "chirp" repeatedly when battery levels are low. This is meant to be annoying, and you must resist the urge to remove the battery simply to stop the chirping. Once the chirping starts, don't remove the battery until you're about to replace it—and do so promptly.

Each smoke detector should be tested regularly in accordance with the manufacturer's recommendations to ensure it is operating properly. Because their efficiency decreases over time, you should replace your smoke alarms every ten years. If you or someone in your home is hearing impaired, install smoke alarms with strobe lights.

At least one detector should be installed on each floor of a multistory home, preferably near a bedroom so that sleeping residents will be given early warning in the event of a fire. Local fire regulations or building codes may specify that more smoke detectors must be installed for a particular home's floor plan.

Fire and Disaster Preparation

Hopefully you will never have to deal with a major fire in your home, but some basic preparation can prevent confusion and panic should one occur. To keep your family safe, draft an escape plan using these tips from the National Fire Protection Association:

- Draw a floor plan of your home, marking the locations of all exits from each room (including windows). Also note the location of each smoke alarm.

FIRE ESCAPE ROUTE

- Make sure that everyone recognizes the sound of the smoke alarms and understands what to do when they hear an alarm sound. Make sure that no escape routes are blocked, that windows open easily, and that adults and children alike know how to open them.
- If you have windows covered by security bars, make sure that they have quick-release mechanisms on the inside, and that everyone in the house knows how they operate.
- Discuss how pets will be evacuated. Children must be taught that they are not to jeopardize their own escape from a fire while trying to find and remove a frightened and potentially uncooperative animal.
- If you have a multistory home—especially one with upstairs bedrooms—invest in one or more chain ladders, and learn how to deploy them for a window escape if a fire prevents the use of the stairs.
- Agree on a meeting place that is far enough away from your house to be safe. In case of a fire, everyone should go immediately to that place after getting out of the house so that you can be certain each family member has been safely evacuated.

- If you live in an area where 911 service is not available, make sure that everyone in your house memorizes the local emergency-response phone number. Get everyone out of the house before you stop to call the fire department.
- If you live in an apartment building, know your building's evacuation plan and the location of emergency exits. During a fire, use the stairs, not the elevator.
- Remind everyone to stay low to the ground when smoke is present and to avoid opening any doors that are hot to the touch.
- Explain to younger children what firefighters look like in their full gear. Unless prepared ahead of time, children might be frightened by firefighters' bulky shapes, face masks, axes, and other tools. Hiding from them could be disastrous.
- Make sure your house number is clearly visible from the street, and consider having the number painted on the curbside as well.
- After you have reviewed these details, practice your plan by holding a number of family fire drills until everyone's response appears to be brisk and consistent. Then hold one more drill late at night, after everyone has gone to sleep (pick a weekend night for this), to be sure that family members can awaken and respond appropriately.

While you are talking about your family's response to a fire, you should also go over contingency plans for any possible natural disaster (earthquake, flood, tornado, hurricane) that might occur where you live. Give instructions about whom you or your children might contact in case communications are disrupted. (It may be easier to get in touch with a relative across the country, whether using cell phones or landlines, who could serve as a communication center for the family.)

Water and Bathtub Safety

- Turn down your water heater to 120°F (49°C) or less.
- Make sure that an adult—not another child—bathes a baby.
- Remain in the room during every second of a child's bath. Have everything you'll need available at the tub before you start.
- Install strips with a roughened surface or lay a rubber mat in the bathtub to prevent slips and falls.

Firearms

- Any guns kept in the home should be unloaded and locked up, with ammunition locked in a separate location. Use trigger locks.
- Keeping a handgun for protection is dangerous to your family.
- Teach your children never to touch any gun they might find. If they see or hear about a gun at school, tell them they should tell an adult immediately.
- Nongunpowder firearms (BB or pellet guns) should not be considered toys and are not recommended for children.
- Remove all firearms from your home if anyone living with you—especially a teenager—is dealing with depression. A person who turns a firearm on himself in a moment of despair will almost certainly die, or at best sustain a terrible injury.

- Before allowing a mobile baby or a young child to explore the great outdoors around your home, take a child's-level survey of any area she might reach. If she's a skilled crawler, keep in mind how fast she can move while your attention is diverted.
- Check the lawn for mushrooms—if you are not absolutely certain that they are nontoxic, get rid of them; anything a young child finds will likely go straight into her mouth.
- Make sure that potentially hazardous items, such as garden tools, insecticides, or fertilizer, are not accessible to children.
- Older children should not use garden, hand, or power tools until you teach them to use them correctly and safely. Give them detailed instructions (including demonstrations if appropriate) and safety precautions; they should repeat back to you both directions and cautions before they are allowed to handle any potentially hazardous equipment.
- Protective eyewear must be worn if the use of any tools will produce flying debris. In addition, ear protection should be used when using loud power tools.
- Don't forget to apply sunscreen with a sun protection factor (SPF) rating of 15 or more if a child is going to be outdoors for any length of time, especially between the hours of 10 a.m. and 3 p.m.—even on a hazy or overcast day. This is particularly important at higher altitudes or around lakes and seashores, where the sun's ultraviolet light (which provokes the burn) can reflect off of water and sand. Special caution is needed for infants, because a baby's skin can become sunburned after as little as fifteen minutes of direct exposure. Sunscreens containing the UV-protecting ingredient known as PABA shouldn't be used on a baby's skin till after six months of age, and possibly later. Occasionally a baby's skin will be irritated by PABA, so you may want to avoid sunscreens containing this compound. If you take your baby outdoors for any length of time, keep her in the shade or use an umbrella, and make sure that her skin is covered with appropriate clothing (including a hat or bonnet) if some sun exposure is unavoidable.

Weather Safety

- Dress your child appropriately for outdoor activities, allowing for adjustments if the weather changes.
- Carry rain gear in your car.
- Apply sunblock (SPF 15 to 45, depending on skin type) before you or your child go outside.
- Take and use hats and sunglasses.

Water Safety

- If you have a swimming pool, it should be completely surrounded by fencing. The fence should be at least four feet high, should not be climbable, and should have a self-closing and self-latching gate. The gate should lock so that toddlers cannot gain access to the pool by themselves. If your yard contains a spa, it should be securely covered when not in use. Gate alarms, pool alarms, and automatic pool covers can also reduce the risk of accidents. Pool alarms sound whenever someone or something enters the water; these alarms can sound inside the house as well.
- Do not leave buckets filled with water in any area where a toddler might play.
- Prohibit swimming in fast-moving water such as a creek, river, or canal.
- Permit diving only after the depth of the water has been checked and your child has been taught how to dive correctly.
- Never leave your child unsupervised when he is in, on, or around water.
- Keep rescue equipment at the waterside, and take CPR training.

Bicycle Safety

- Make sure your child takes a bike-safety class, or teach him the rules of the road yourself.
- Stick to bicycle paths whenever possible.
- Children under age six should not ride on the street.
- Make sure that the bicycle is the right size (take the child along when you buy it). When sitting on the seat with hands on the handlebars, the child should be able to touch the ground with the balls of his feet. When straddling the center bar with both feet flat on the ground, there should be at least one inch of clearance between the bar and the child's crotch.
- Do not buy a bicycle with hand brakes until the child is able to grasp with sufficient pressure to use them effectively.
- Keep the bicycle in good repair, and teach your child how to fix and maintain it.
- Insist that your child wear a bicycle helmet, and always wear one yourself (see below).
- Discourage your child from riding at night. If it is necessary for him to do so, be sure that the bicycle is properly equipped with lights and reflectors and that your child wears reflective or at least bright clothing.

Bicycle Helmets and Other Safety Gear

Helmets are designed to absorb the impact of a direct blow to the skull, and they do their job well. Research shows that wearing a helmet when riding a bicycle can reduce the risk of sustaining a head injury by 85 percent and the risk of brain injury by up to 88 percent. When choosing a bicycle helmet, select one that meets or exceeds standards set by the U.S. Consumer Product Safety Commission (CPSC). A sticker inside the helmet should provide this information.

A bike helmet should fit securely and squarely and should not tilt toward the back of the head. The strap should fit comfortably but not loosely under the chin. As your child grows, the helmet he wears will need to be sized upward accordingly. Bicycle helmets contain a foam lining that compresses to absorb the force of a head impact. Once the foam is compacted, the helmet loses much of its ability to absorb further impacts and is unsafe to use. Replace the helmet if it is ever involved in a crash.

Wearing a helmet when riding a bicycle is not just important for children. Adults need to wear a helmet when riding too, both for their own safety and to model this behavior for younger ones. Like wearing a seat belt while riding in a car, wearing a helmet is one of those behaviors that is caught more than taught. When children see parents strap on a helmet, they will be much more likely to do likewise.

In addition to helmets for bicycling, make sure that your child uses wrist guards, elbow and knee pads, and a helmet when in-line skating or skateboarding (see page 361).

Finally, provide appropriate protective equipment for any sport in which your child participates. Make sure it is worn at practices as well as at games.

Pedestrian Safety

- Provide a play area that prevents balls and riding toys from rolling into the street.
- Prohibit riding of toy vehicles, tricycles, and bicycles in or near traffic or on driveways.
- Hold a young child's hand when walking near traffic.
- When crossing the street, teach and model safety measures: Stop at the curb and look left, right, then left again before entering the street. Use marked crosswalks and obey pedestrian light signals.
- Plan walking routes so that crossing heavy traffic is minimized.

Seat Belts and Car Seats

Over the last twenty years, widespread use of seat belts has led to a steady reduction in traffic fatalities. Proper use of seat belts and car seats decreases the risk of serious injury or death by as much as 50 percent. But in the United States, the leading cause of death in people under age thirty-five continues to be motor-vehicle-related injuries. Most of these individuals were not properly restrained by seat belts or car seats.

Safety on the Road

- Parents and children should wear their seat belts. Do not start the car until everyone is secured in an infant or child seat or properly belted.
- Never hold a child in your lap when you are riding in a car.
- A child under twelve should never be placed in the front seat of an automobile with a passenger-side air bag because deployment of the bag can cause fatal injuries in a young passenger—even during a minor accident.
- For children under forty pounds (18 kg), use a car safety seat approved for your child's age and weight in accordance with the manufacturer's directions. (Make sure you have a safety seat for your infant's first ride home from the hospital.) The seat should be secured in the rear seat of the vehicle. An infant should face backward until she is at least one year of age and weighs more than twenty pounds (9 kg). (See "Car Seats" in chapter 2, starting on page 51, for a number of important details about the proper use of infant car seats.)
- Children weighing more than forty pounds should be properly secured in a booster seat. The National Highway Traffic Safety Administration (NHTSA) recommends that children remain in booster seats until they are eight years old or at least four feet nine inches tall (57 inches, or 145 cm). In order to graduate from a booster seat to a regular shoulder/lap belt, your child must be tall enough to sit without slouching, with feet flat on the floor, knees comfortably bent over the edge of the seat, and back against the seat. The lap belt must be able to fit low and tight across the upper thighs (not the abdomen), and the shoulder strap should rest across the chest and over the shoulder. *The shoulder strap should never rest under her arm or behind her back.*
- During the transitional phase from booster seat to adult shoulder/lap belt, your child may fit properly in the restraint system of one vehicle but not another. Check your child's fit in every vehicle she rides in. When in doubt, use a properly secured booster seat.
- If your child takes off his seat belt or gets out of the car seat while you are driving, pull over safely and stop the car. Do not attempt to deal with this problem (or any other) while driving.
- Insist that your child wear a seat belt, no matter whose car she rides in.
- Never leave your child unattended in a car.
- Never transport a child in a cargo area that is not properly equipped to carry passengers (specifically, the back of a station wagon, van, or pickup truck).
- Do not allow a child or adolescent younger than sixteen to operate a motor vehicle, including a motorcycle, motorbike, trail bike, or other off-road vehicles. An adolescent sixteen years old or older may operate one of these vehicles only if he is licensed and properly trained and has demonstrated appropriate responsibility.
- Be very cautious about allowing your child to ride as a passenger on a motorcycle, motor bike, trail bike, or off-road vehicle. Insist on a proper helmet, slow speed, and a mature, sober driver.

Additional Resources

Books, journals, and organizations are listed alphabetically and in categories.

Books marked with the symbol ‡are out of print but may still be available through online booksellers or at your local library.

Some organizations on the list are secular. These are marked with an asterisk (*). Inclusion on this list does not necessarily constitute an endorsement by Focus on the Family of an organization's material content or viewpoint. It would be wise to investigate any organization prior to using it as a resource.

For more information on resources or materials, call 800-A-FAMILY.

Abuse

Boundaries: When to Say Yes, When to Say No to Take Control of Your Life by Dr. Henry Cloud and Dr. John Townsend. Grand Rapids, Mich.: Zondervan, 1992, rev. ed. 2002.

Caring for Sexually Abused Children: A Handbook for Families and Churches by Dr. R. Timothy Kearney. Downers Grove, Ill.: InterVarsity, 2001.

Childhelp*
15757 N. 78th St.
Scottsdale, AZ 85260
480-922-8212
Hotline: 800-422-4453
http://www.childhelp.org
Provides counseling, referral, and reporting services concerning child abuse.

Child SHARE
Joanne Feldmeth, Executive Director
1544 W. Glenoaks Blvd.
Glendale, CA 91201
877-957-4452
http://www.childshare.org
This agency was set up to recruit, train, and support families or individuals who will provide quality care for abused, neglected, or abandoned children. It also offers a monthly newsletter and other materials.

Door of Hope: Recognizing and Resolving the Pains of Your Past by Jan Frank. Nashville: Thomas Nelson, 1995.

Love Must Be Tough: New Hope for Marriages in Crisis by Dr. James Dobson. Sisters, Ore.: Multnomah, 2004.

‡*Pain and Pretending* by Rev. Rich Buhler. Nashville: Thomas Nelson, 1991.

Addictions

see also Substance Abuse

Breaking Free: Understanding Sexual Addiction and the Healing Power of Jesus by Russell Willingham. Downers Grove, Ill.: InterVarsity, 1999.

Celebrate Recovery
25422 Trabuco Road #105-151
Lake Forest, CA 92630
949-581-0548
http://www.celebraterecovery.com
An international ministry started at Saddleback Church in Southern California in 1991, Celebrate Recovery teaches eight biblically based recovery principles to bring freedom from addictive, compulsive, and dysfunctional behaviors. Celebrate Recovery publishes books and visual materials, organizes conferences and training seminars, and promotes recovery ministries in churches.

Deceived by Shame, Desired by God by Cynthia Spell Humbert. Colorado Springs: NavPress, 2001.

Gambling: Risky Business (VHS). Ventura, Calif.: Gospel Light, 2000.

‡*Healing Life's Hidden Addictions* by Dr. Archibald Hart. Ann Arbor, Mich.: Servant, 1990.

Hope, Help, and Healing for Eating Disorders: A New Approach to Treating Anorexia, Bulimia, and Overeating by Dr. Gregory L. Jantz. Colorado Springs: Shaw, 2002.

Living with Your Husband's Secret Wars by Marsha Means. Grand Rapids, Mich.: Revell, 1999.

‡*The Love Hunger Action Plan* by Dr. Sharon Sneed. Nashville: Thomas Nelson, 1993.

Adoption, Infertility, and Miscarriage

"Adoption Options: Fact Sheet for Families"
http://www.childwelfare.gov/pubs/
f_adoptoption.cfm
This information sheet is available from the Child Welfare Information Gateway, a service of the U.S. Department of Health and Human Services. It lists organizations that provide assistance to potential adoptive parents, including those who want to know about adopting special-needs children. Also listed are adoption search organizations, Canadian and international adoption information, and helpful resources.

Adoptive Families*
39 West 37th St., 15th Floor
New York, NY 10018
646-366-0830
http://www.adoptivefamilies.com
This national adoptive parent organization serves parents who have adopted, or who are waiting to adopt, children from all countries. It is an umbrella organization for over three hundred adoptive parent support groups. The group does not discuss adoption in general, but it can provide information about adoption issues, health insurance equity, and adoption procedures. A free general information booklet for prospective adoptive parents is available, as well as a bimonthly magazine called *Adoptive Families*.

Baptist Children's Homes and Family Ministries
354 West St.
Valparaiso, IN 46383
219-462-4111
http://www.baptistchildrenshome.org
This organization exists to assist churches and communities, through the care and counseling of children and adults, to care for the fatherless (see James 1:27). It sponsors group homes for children in three states and offers counseling and referral services to unwed mothers; it also offers adoption and foster-care services.

Bethany Christian Services

901 Eastern Ave. NE

PO Box 294

Grand Rapids, MI 49501-0294

Main office: 616-224-7610

Refugee Service Center: 616-224-7540

24-hour pregnancy help line: 800-238-4269

http://www.bethany.org

This privately licensed, Christian child-welfare and adoption agency offers pro-life pregnancy counseling, temporary foster care, help with international adoptions, and alternative living arrangements for pregnant women. A listing of locations in different states is available. Spanish editions of some of their brochures are available on their Web site.

‡*Brian Was Adopted* by Doris Sanford. Sisters, Ore.: Multnomah, 1989.

Christian Family Care Agency

3603 North Seventh Ave.

Phoenix, AZ 85013

602-234-1935

http://www.cfcare.org

CFCA serves families in crisis through counseling, pregnancy assistance, foster care, and adoption.

Empty Arms: Hope and Support for Those Who Have Suffered a Miscarriage, Stillbirth or Tubal Pregnancy by Pam Vredevelt. Sisters, Ore.: Multnomah, 2001.

Empty Womb, Aching Heart: Hope and Help for Those Struggling with Infertility by Marlo Schalesky. Minneapolis: Bethany, 2001.

The Family Network, Inc.

820 Bay Ave., Ste. 206

Capitola, CA 95010

831-462-8954

http://www.adopt-familynetwork.com

This ministry assists with home studies and family assessment for adoption, placement services for domestic (in the United States) and international adoptions, professional pro-life pregnancy counseling, and postplacement supervision. It also offers services in Spanish.

Holt International Children's Services

PO Box 2880

Eugene, OR 97402

541-687-2202

http://www.holtintl.org

This nonprofit organization works to unite homeless children from foreign countries with adoptive families in the United States.

‡*How to Adopt a Child: A Comprehensive Guide for Prospective Parents* by Connie Crain and Janice Duffy. Nashville: Thomas Nelson, 1994.

I'll Hold You in Heaven: Healing and Hope for the Parent Who Has Lost a Child through Miscarriage, Stillbirth, Abortion or Early Infant Death by Jack Hayford. Ventura, Calif.: Regal, 2003.

Loved By Choice: True Stories That Celebrate Adoption by Susan Horner and Kelly Fordyce Martindale. Grand Rapids, Mich.: Revell, 2002.

‡*Major League Dad* by Tim and Christine Burke. Colorado Springs: Focus on the Family, 1994.

National Council for Adoption*

225 N. Washington St.

Alexandria, VA 22314-2561

703-299-6633

http://www.ncfa-usa.org

This organization serves as a clearinghouse of information on the issue of adoption. It is able to process Spanish correspondence.

Shaohannah's Hope

44180 Riverside Parkway

Lansdowne, VA 20176

http://www.shaohannahshope.org

Founded by Steven Curtis and Mary Beth Chapman, this organization is dedicated to helping prospective adoptive parents overcome financial barriers associated with adoption. It also works to engage the church to care for orphans and provides a variety of resources for individuals and churches.

Share Pregnancy and Infant Loss Support

St. Joseph Health Center

300 First Capitol Dr.

St. Charles, MO 63301-2893
800-821-6819
636-947-6164
http://www.nationalshareoffice.com
This Catholic organization provides a strong, supportive atmosphere through mutual self-help groups where people can share their experiences, thoughts, and feelings regarding the loss of an infant after birth through miscarriage or some other reason. It publishes a bimonthly newsletter and offers some materials in Spanish.

Stepping Stones
Dr. John and Sylvia Van Regenmorter
616-224-7488
http://www.bethany.org/step
Stepping Stones, a ministry of Bethany Christian Services, is a bimonthly newsletter that covers issues of infertility and miscarriage. The Regenmorters are also available for speaking.

Twenty Things Adopted Kids Wish Their Adoptive Parents Knew by Sherrie Eldridge. New York: Dell, 1999.

The Whole Life Adoption Book: Realistic Advice for Building a Healthy Adoptive Family by Jayne E. Schooler. Colorado Springs: Piñon Press, 1993.

Death
Caring for Your Aging Parents: When Love Is Not Enough by Barbara Deane. Colorado Springs: NavPress, 1989.

Empty Arms: Hope and Support for Those Who Have Suffered a Miscarriage, Stillbirth or Tubal Pregnancy by Pam Vredevelt. Sisters, Ore.: Multnomah, 1995.

How to Help a Heartbroken Friend: What to Do and What to Say When a Friend Is Going Through Tough Times by David Biebel. Pasadena, Calif.: Hope, 2004.

‡*The Life and Death Dilemma: Families Facing Health Care Choices* by Joni Eareckson Tada. Grand Rapids, Mich.: Zondervan, 1995.

Safe in the Arms of Jesus by Robert Lightner. Grand Rapids, Mich.: Kregel, 2000.

‡*Sunrise Tomorrow: Coping with a Child's Death* by Elizabeth Brown. Grand Rapids, Mich.: Revell, 1988.

Through a Season of Grief: Devotions for Your Journey from Mourning to Joy by Bill Dunn and Kathy Leonard. Nashville: Thomas Nelson, 2004.

When God Doesn't Make Sense by Dr. James Dobson. Carol Stream, Ill.: Tyndale House, 1993.

Depression
‡*Beyond the Hidden Pain of Abortion* by Patricia Bigliardi. Lynnwood, Wash.: Women's Aglow Fellowship, 1994.

Broken Children, Grown-up Pain: Understanding the Effects of Your Wounded Past by Paul Hegstrom. Kansas City, Mo.: Beacon Hill, 2006.

Conquering Depression: A 30-Day Plan to Finding Happiness by Mark A. Sutton and Bruce Hennigan. Nashville: Broadman & Holman, 2001.

‡*Dark Clouds, Silver Linings* by Dr. Archibald Hart. Colorado Springs: Focus on the Family, 1994.

‡*Door of Hope: Recognizing and Resolving the Pains of Your Past* by Jan Frank. Nashville: Thomas Nelson, 1995.

In the Pit: A Testimony of God's Faithfulness to a Bipolar Christian by Nancy L. Hagerman. Belleville, Ont.: Essence, 2003.

‡*Living through the Loss of Someone You Love* by Sandra Aldrich. Ventura, Calif.: Regal, 1990.

Tame Your Fears: And Transform Them into Faith, Confidence, and Action by Carol Kent. Colorado Springs: NavPress, 2003.

Unmasking Male Depression by Dr. Archibald Hart. Nashville: W Publishing, 2001.

Unveiling Depression in Women: A Practical Guide to Understanding and Overcoming Depression by Dr. Archibald Hart and Dr. Catherine Hart Weber. Grand Rapids, Mich.: Revell, 2002.

Disabilities and Diseases

American Association of the Deaf-Blind*
8630 Fenton St., Ste. 121
Silver Spring, MD 20910-3803
Phone: 301-495-4403
TTY: 301-495-4402
http://www.aadb.org

American Cancer Society*
1599 Clifton Rd. NE
Atlanta, GA 30329-4251
404-320-3333
800-227-2345
http://www.cancer.org

American Council of the Blind*
1155 15th St. NW, Ste. 1004
Washington, DC 20005
202-467-5081
800-424-8666
http://www.acb.org

American Diabetes Association*
1701 N. Beauregard St.
Alexandria, VA 22311
800-342-2383
http://www.diabetes.org
Provides free literature, newsletters, and information on diabetes health education and support-group assistance.

American Epilepsy Society*
342 N. Main St.
West Hartford, CT 06117-2507
860-586-7505
http://www.aesnet.org

American Heart Association*
7272 Greenville Ave.
Dallas, TX 75231
800-242-8721
http://www.americanheart.org

Asthma and Allergy Foundation of America*
1233 20th St. NW, Ste. 402
Washington, DC 20036
202-466-7643
800-727-8462
http://www.aafa.org

Attention Deficit Disorder Association*
15000 Commerce Parkway, Suite C
Mount Laurel, NJ 08054
856-439-9099
http://www.add.org

Autism Society of America*
7910 Woodmont Ave., Ste. 300
Bethesda, MD 20814-3067
301-657-0881
800-328-8476
http://www.autism-society.org

Blind Childrens Center*
4120 Marathon St.
Los Angeles, CA 90029-3584
323-664-2153
http://www.blindchildrenscenter.org
This organization deals primarily with blind children, from birth through elementary school.

Brokenness: How God Redeems Pain and Suffering by Lon Solomon. Potomac, Md.: Red Door Press, 2005.

Braille Bibles International
PO Box 378
Liberty, MO 64069-0378
800-522-4253
http://www.braillebibles.org
This organization makes the Bible accessible to the visually impaired. It offers the King James Version in Braille, large print, and in audio format.

Children and Adults with Attention Deficit/Hyperactivity Disorder (CHADD)*
8181 Professional Pl., Ste. 150
Landover, MD 20785
301-306-7070
http://www.chadd.org
This nonprofit, parent-based organization was formed to help parents and teachers of children with ADHD. There are two hundred chapters in the United States. The organization has a yearly national conference and offers a monthly newsletter and additional resources on the subject.

Coping with Cancer (and Other Chronic or Life-Threatening Diseases) by John E. Packo. Camp Hill, Pa.: Christian Publications, 1991.

Deaf Missions

21199 Greenview Rd.
Council Bluffs, IA 51503-4190
Phone/TTY: 712-322-5493
http://www.deafmissions.com

This organization was set up to provide visuals and train workers to help bring the gospel to deaf people. It offers Bible camps and college extension classes, a quarterly newsletter called *Deaf Missions Report*, as well as more frequent e-mail updates. Daily devotions are filmed in sign language and distributed via VHS, DVD, CD, and on the Internet.

Exceptional Parent magazine*

EP Global Communications
551 Main St.
Johnstown, PA 15901
877-372-7368
http://www.eparent.com

Each January issue is an annual resource guide that includes comprehensive directories of organizations, associations, products, and services. It can be purchased separately as well.

Finding Strength in Weakness by Lynn Vanderzalm. Grand Rapids, Mich.: Zondervan, 1995.

First Candle/SIDS Alliance*

1314 Bedford Ave., Ste. 210
Baltimore, MD 21208
410-653-8226
800-221-7437
http://www.firstcandle.org

Provides literature and referrals on SIDS as well as information on support groups.

The Food Allergy and Anaphylaxis Network*

11781 Lee Jackson Hwy., Ste. 160
Fairfax, VA 22033-3309
800-929-4040
http://www.foodallergy.org

Friendship Ministries

2215 29th St. SE #B6
Grand Rapids, MI 49508
888-866-8966
http://www.friendship.org

Canada:
PO Box 27009
Kitchener, ON N2E 3K2
888-649-5555
http://www.friendshipgroupscanada.org

For Spanish materials:
Amistad
2215 29th St. SE #B6
Grand Rapids, MI 49508
800-333-8300, ext. 835
http://www.ministerioamistad.org

Organized to promote spiritual development for people with mental disabilities, this ministry offers religious educational curricula and provides assistance to churches to reach and teach people with mental disabilities.

Handi*Vangelism

Timothy D. Sheetz, Director
PO Box 122
Akron, PA 17501-0122
717-859-4777
http://www.hvmi.org

This Christian ministry to disabled individuals provides seminars, conferences, literature, periodicals, support groups, and counseling. It helps the local church include the disabled in their programs and operates Handi*Camp, an overnight camping program for physically or mentally disabled children, teens, and adults.

‡*I'll Love You Forever* by Norman and Joyce Wright. Colorado Springs: Focus on the Family, 1993.

In the Pit: A Testimony of God's Faithfulness to a Bipolar Christian by Nancy L. Hagerman. Belleville, Ont.: Essence, 2003.

Joni and Friends

PO Box 3333
Agoura Hills, CA 91376-3333
Phone: 818-707-5664
TTY: 818-707-9707
http://www.joniandfriends.org

The purpose of this Christian ministry is to bring together disabled people and local congregations through evangelism, encouragement, inspiration, and practical service. Joni Eareckson Tada offers seminars and conferences for churches and has her own radio show. Resources and referrals for families with disabled members are available.

Juvenile Diabetes Research Foundation International*
120 Wall St.
New York, NY 10005-4001
800-533-2873
http://www.jdrf.org

Answers questions and provides brochures on juvenile diabetes, and gives referrals to physicians and clinics.

LUNG LINE*
A service of the National Jewish Medical and Research Center
800-222-5864
http://www.njc.org/contact/lung/index.aspx

This information service answers questions about asthma, emphysema, chronic bronchitis, allergies, juvenile rheumatoid arthritis, smoking, and other respiratory and immune system disorders. Questions are answered by registered nurses.

National Association for Down Syndrome*
PO Box 206
Wilmette, IL 60091
630-325-9112
http://www.nads.org

This organization offers resources on Down syndrome, in both English and Spanish. Additional services are provided for the local Chicago area.

National Association for Parents of Children with Visual Impairments*
PO Box 317
Watertown, MA 02471
800-562-6265
http://www.spedex.com/napvi

National Captioning Institute*
1900 Gallows Rd., Ste. 3000
Vienna, VA 22182
Voice/TTY: 703-917-7600
Phone: 800-533-9673
TTY: 800-950-0958
http://www.ncicap.org

This organization provides information on telecaption decoders, which pick up closed-captioned messages for the hearing impaired on videos and television. It also provides information on audio-link, an infrared system that greatly enhances sound.

National Dissemination Center for Children with Disabilities*
PO Box 1492
Washington, DC 20013
800-695-0285
http://www.nichcy.org

National Down Syndrome Society*
666 Broadway
New York, NY 10012
800-221-4602
http://www.ndss.org

National Federation of the Blind*
1800 Johnson St.
Baltimore, MD 21230
410-659-9314
http://www.nfb.org

This national federation was set up to integrate the blind into society on a basis of equality by removing legal, economic, and social discrimination and by educating the public. It publishes a monthly newsletter on issues related to the blind. One of its divisions, the National Organization of Parents of Blind Children (http://www.nfb.org/nopbc), provides support and information to parents of children with serious visual impairments.

National SIDS/Infant Death Resource Center*
8280 Greensboro Dr., Ste. 300
McLean, VA 22102
703-821-8955
http://www.sidscenter.org

National Organization for Rare Disorders (NORD)*
555 Kenosia Ave.
PO Box 1968
Danbury, CT 06813-1968
203-744-0100
800-999-6673
http://www.rarediseases.org

A Special Kind of Love: For Those Who Love Children with Special Needs by Susan Titus Osborn and Janet Lynn Mitchell. Nashville: Broadman & Holman, 2004.

Tourette Syndrome Association, Inc.*
42-40 Bell Blvd., Suite 205
Bayside, NY 11361
718-224-2999
http://www.tsa-usa.org
The purpose of this national association is to educate patients and their families about the disease called Tourette syndrome and to provide support groups. They also publish a quarterly newsletter.

When God Doesn't Make Sense by Dr. James Dobson. Carol Stream, Ill.: Tyndale House, 1993.

When Your Doctor Has Bad News: Simple Steps to Strength, Healing, and Hope by Dr. Al B. Weir. Grand Rapids, Mich.: Zondervan, 2003.

Drug Abuse
see Addictions and Substance Abuse

Faith and Family Life
‡*Faithful Parents, Faithful Kids* by Greg Johnson and Mike Yorkey. Carol Stream, Ill.: Tyndale House, 1993.

Faith Training by Joe White. Colorado Springs: Focus on the Family, 1995.

‡*Family Shock: Keeping Families Strong in the Midst of Earthshaking Change* by Gary R. Collins. Carol Stream, Ill.: Tyndale House, 1995.

Fuel: 10-Minute Devotions to Ignite the Faith of Parents and Teens by Joe White. Colorado Springs: Focus on the Family, 2003.

‡*Home with a Heart* by Dr. James Dobson. Carol Stream, Ill.: Tyndale House, 1996.

How to Lead Your Child to Christ by Robert Wolgemuth. Carol Stream, Ill.: Tyndale House, 2005.

Lead Your Teen to a Lifelong Faith by Joe White and Jim Weidman. Carol Stream, Ill.: Tyndale House, 2005.

Parents' Guide to the Spiritual Growth of Children by Focus on the Family. Edited by John Trent, Rick Osborne, and Kurt Bruner. Colorado Springs: Focus on the Family, 2003.

Parents' Guide to the Spiritual Mentoring of Teens by Focus on the Family. Edited by Joe White and Jim Weidman. Colorado Springs: Focus on the Family, 2001.

‡*Parents Resource Bible* (TLB). Carol Stream, Ill.: Tyndale House, 1995.

Sacred Parenting: How Raising Children Shapes Our Souls by Gary L. Thomas. Grand Rapids, Mich.: Zondervan, 2004.

Seven Habits of a Healthy Home: Preparing the Ground in which Your Children Can Grow by Bill Carmichael. Camp Sherman, Ore.: VMI Publishing, 2002.

Soundbites from Heaven: What God Wants Us to Hear When We Talk to Our Kids by Rachael Carman. Colorado Springs: Focus on the Family, 2005.

Spiritual Milestones: A Guide to Celebrating Your Child's Spiritual Passages by Jim and Janet Weidmann and J. Otis and Gail Ledbetter. Colorado Springs: Chariot/Victor, 2001.

Teaching Kids about God: An Age-by-Age Plan for Parents of Children from Birth to Age Twelve. Edited by John Trent, Rick Osborne, and Kurt Bruner. Carol Stream, Ill.: Tyndale House, 2003.

Teaching Your Child How to Pray by Rick Osborne. Chicago: Moody, 2002.

Tender Mercy for a Mother's Soul: Inspiration to Renew Your Spirit by Angela Thomas. Colorado Springs: Focus on the Family, 2006.

‡*Together at Home* by Dean and Grace Merrill. Carol Stream, Ill.: Tyndale House, 1996.

Why Christian Kids Rebel: Trading Heartache for Hope by Tim Kimmel. Nashville: W Publishing, 2004.

Finances

Cents and Sensibility: How Couples Can Agree About Money by Scott and Bethany Palmer. Colorado Springs: Life Journey, 2005.

Crown Financial Ministries
PO Box 100
Gainesville, GA 30503-0100
770-534-1000
800-722-1976
http://www.crown.org
This ministry offers biblically based financial advice and study materials for all ages on the biblical approach to stewardship and money management.

Debt-Proof Your Marriage: How to Achieve Financial Harmony by Mary Hunt. Grand Rapids, Mich.: Revell, 2004.

Ronald Blue & Co.
1100 Johnson Ferry Rd. Center II, Ste. 800
Atlanta, GA 30342
404-705-7000
800-841-0362
http://www.ronblue.com
This group offers advice about investments and handling money.

Splitting Heirs: Giving Your Money and Things to Your Children without Ruining Their Lives by Ron Blue and Jeremy L. White. Chicago: Northfield, 2004.

Taming the Money Monster: Five Steps to Conquering Debt by Ron Blue. Colorado Springs: Focus on the Family, 2000.

Total Money Makeover: A Proven Plan for Financial Fitness by Dave Ramsey. Nashville: Thomas Nelson, 2003.

Your Kids Can Master Their Money: Fun Ways to Help Them Learn How by Ron Blue, Judy Blue, and Jeremy White. Colorado Springs: Focus on the Family, 2006.

Home Schooling
see also Schools, Education, and Related Issues

Christian Home Educators Association of California (CHEA)
PO Box 2009
Norwalk, CA 90651-2009
562-864-2432
http://www.cheaofca.org

Christian Home Educators of Colorado
10431 South Parker Rd.
Parker, CO 80134
720-842-4852
http://www.chec.org
This organization provides training and resources for home-schooling parents, support groups and seminars, curriculum manuals, and updated information on legislative and legal issues, through a monthly newsletter.

Help for the Harried Homeschooler: A Practical Guide to Balancing Your Child's Education with the Rest of Your Life by Christine M. Field. Colorado Springs: Shaw, 2002.

Help! I'm Married to a Homeschooling Mom: Showing Dads How to Meet the Needs of Their Homeschooling Wives by Todd Wilson. Chicago: Moody, 2004.

Homeschooling on a Shoestring: A Jam-Packed Guide by Melissa L. Morgan and Judith Waite Allee. Colorado Springs: Shaw, 2000.

‡*The How and Why of Home Schooling* by Ray E. Ballmann. Wheaton, Ill.: Crossway, 1995.

‡*Raising Achievers: A Parent's Plan for Motivating Children to Excel* by Dr. Nita Weis. Nashville: Broadman & Holman, 1995.

So You're Thinking About Homeschooling: Fifteen Families Show You How You Can Do It! by Lisa Whelchel. Sisters, Ore.: Multnomah, 2005.

‡*A Survivor's Guide to Home Schooling* by Luanne Shackelford and Susan White. Wheaton, Ill.: Crossway, 1988.

The Ultimate Guide to Homeschooling by Debra Bell. Nashville: Tommy Nelson, 2005.

Love and Marriage

5 Essentials for Lifelong Intimacy by Dr. James Dobson. Sisters, Ore.: Multnomah, 2005.

Becoming a Couple of Promise by Dr. Kevin Leman. Colorado Springs: NavPress, 1999.

Blueprints for a Solid Marriage: Build, Remodel, Repair by Dr. Steve Stephens. Colorado Springs: Focus on the Family, 2006.

Boundaries in Marriage by Dr. Henry Cloud and Dr. John Townsend. Grand Rapids, Mich.: Zondervan, 2002.

Complete Guide to the First Five Years of Marriage: Launching a Lifelong, Successful Relationship by Focus on the Family. Edited by Phillip J. Swihart and Wilford Wooten. Colorado Springs: Focus on the Family, 2006.

Divorce-Proof Your Marriage: 6 Secrets to a Forever Marriage by Dr. Gary and Barbara Rosberg. Carol Stream, Ill.: Tyndale House, 2003.

FamilyLife

PO Box 7111
Little Rock, AR 72223
800-FL-TODAY
http://www.familylife.com

This organization presents marriage and parenting seminars throughout the United States.

Focus on the Family

Colorado Springs, CO 80995
719-531-5181
800-A-FAMILY
http://www.family.org

The Gift of Sex: A Guide to Sexual Fulfillment by Dr. Clifford and Joyce Penner. Nashville: W Publishing, 1981.

Healing the Hurt in Your Marriage by Dr. Gary and Barbara Rosberg. Carol Stream, Ill.: Tyndale House, 2004.

‡*Holding On to Romance: Keeping Your Marriage Alive and Passionate after the Honeymoon Years Are Over* by Dr. H. Norman Wright. Ventura, Calif.: Regal, 1992.

How to Bring Out the Best in Your Spouse by Dr. H. Norman Wright and Dr. Gary J. Oliver. Ann Arbor, Mich.: Vine Books, 1996.

Incompatibility: Still Grounds for a Great Marriage by Chuck and Barb Snyder. Sisters, Ore.: Multnomah, 1999.

The Language of Love: How to Be Instantly Understood by Those You Love (with study guide) by Gary Smalley and Dr. John Trent. Colorado Springs: Focus on the Family, 1988, 1991, 2006.

Love and Respect: The Love She Desires, the Respect He Desperately Needs by Dr. Emerson Eggerichs. Colorado Springs: Integrity, 2004.

The Love List by Drs. Les and Leslie Parrott. Grand Rapids, Mich.: Zondervan, 2002.

Marriage Masterpiece: A Bold New Vision for Your Marriage by Al Janssen. Colorado Springs: Focus on the Family, 2001.

‡*Marriage Savers: Helping Your Friends and Family Avoid Divorce* by Michael McManus. Grand Rapids, Mich.: Zondervan, 1993, rev. ed. 1995.

Marriage Under Fire: Why We Must Win This Battle by Dr. James Dobson. Sisters, Ore.: Multnomah, 2004.

Men: Some Assembly Required by Chuck Snyder. Colorado Springs: Focus on the Family, 2001.

‡*More than You and Me* by Kevin and Karen Miller. Colorado Springs: Focus on the Family, 1994.

‡*Powerful Personalities* by Tim Kimmel. Colorado Springs: Focus on the Family, 1993.

‡*Romancing the Home: How to Have a Marriage That Sizzles* by Dr. Ed Young. Nashville: Broadman & Holman, 1993.

Safe Haven Marriage: Building a Relationship You Want to Come Home To by Dr. Archibald Hart and Dr. Sharon Hart Morris. Nashville: W Publishing, 2003.

Saving Your Marriage Before It Starts: Seven Questions to Ask Before—and After—You Marry by Drs. Les and Leslie Parrott. Grand Rapids, Mich.: Zondervan, 2006.

‡*The Second Decade of Love* by Greg Johnson and Mike Yorkey. Carol Stream, Ill.: Tyndale House, 1994.

The Two Sides of Love by Gary Smalley and Dr. John Trent. Colorado Springs: Focus on the Family, 1990.

What Wives Wish Their Husbands Knew about Women by Dr. James Dobson. Carol Stream, Ill.: Tyndale House, 1975.

Men

Bringing Up Boys by Dr. James Dobson. Carol Stream, Ill.: Tyndale House, 2005.

Developing the Leader within You by John Maxwell. Nashville: Thomas Nelson, 1993, 2005.

Fatherless America: Confronting Our Most Urgent Social Problem by David Blankenhorn. New York: Harper Perennial, 1996.

‡*The Five Key Habits of Smart Dads: A Powerful Strategy for Successful Fathering* by Paul Lewis. Grand Rapids, Mich.: Zondervan, 1996.

For Men Only: A Straightforward Guide to the Inner Lives of Women by Shaunti and Jeff Feldhahn. Sisters, Ore.: Multnomah, 2006.

‡*God of My Father: A Son's Reflections on His Father's Walk of Faith* by Dr. Larry Crabb Jr. and Lawrence Crabb Sr. Grand Rapids, Mich.: Zondervan, 1994.

Healing the Masculine Soul: How God Restores Men to Real Manhood by Gordon Dalbey. Nashville: W Publishing, 2003.

The Hidden Value of a Man: Created to Lead, Empowered to Succeed by Gary Smalley and Dr. John Trent. Colorado Springs: Focus on the Family, 2005.

‡*If I'm Not Tarzan and My Wife Isn't Jane, Then What Are We Doing in the Jungle?* by Steve Farrar. Sisters, Ore.: Questar, 1992.

Raising a Modern-Day Knight by Robert Lewis. Colorado Springs: Focus on the Family, 1999.

‡*The Sexual Man: Masculinity without Guilt* by Dr. Archibald Hart. Dallas: Word, 1993.

Straight Talk to Men: Timeless Principles for Leading Your Family by Dr. James Dobson. Sisters, Ore.: Multnomah, 2004.

Parenting
see also Single Parenting

7 Solutions for Burned-Out Parents by Dr. James Dobson. Sisters, Ore.: Multnomah, 2004.

‡*1001 Ways to Help Your Child Walk with God* by Kathie Reimer. Carol Stream, Ill.: Tyndale House, 1994.

Adolescence Isn't Terminal by Dr. Kevin Leman. Carol Stream, Ill.: Tyndale House, 2002.

‡*As You Leave Home: Parting Thoughts from a Loving Parent* by Jerry Jenkins. Colorado Springs: Focus on the Family, 1993.

Blended Families: Creating Harmony as You Build a New Home Life by Maxine Marsolini. Chicago: Moody, 2000.

The Book of Virtues edited by William J. Bennett. New York: Simon & Schuster, 1994.

‡*Books That Build Character: A Guide to Teaching Your Child Moral Values through Stories* by William Kilpatrick, Gregory Wolfe, and Suzanne M. Wolfe. New York: Simon & Schuster, 1994.

Bringing Up Boys by Dr. James Dobson. Carol Stream, Ill.: Tyndale House, 2005.

Bringing Up Kids without Tearing Them Down by Dr. Kevin Leman. Colorado Springs: Focus on the Family, 1995.

‡*Children of Divorce: Helping Kids When Their Parents Are Apart* by Debbie Barr. Grand Rapids, Mich.: Zondervan, 1992.

The Children's Treasury of Virtues edited by William J. Bennett. New York: Free Press, 2000.

Complete Guide to Family Health, Nutrition, and Fitness by Dr. Paul C. Reisser. Carol Stream, Ill.: Tyndale House, 2006.

Complete Marriage and Family Home Reference Guide by Dr. James Dobson. Carol Stream, Ill.: Tyndale House, 2000.

Creative Correction: Extraordinary Ideas for Everyday Discipline by Lisa Whelchel. Carol Stream, Ill.: Tyndale House, 2000.

‡*Daddy, I'm Pregnant* by a dad named Bill. Sisters, Ore.: Questar, 1988.

‡*Decent Exposure: How to Teach Your Children about Sex* by Connie Marshner. Brentwood, Tenn.: Wolgemuth & Hyatt, 1988.

The DNA of Parent-Teen Relationships: Discover the Key to Your Teen's Heart by Gary Smalley and Dr. Greg Smalley. Carol Stream, Ill.: Tyndale House, 2005.

‡*Dr. Dobson Answers Your Questions* by Dr. James Dobson. Carol Stream, Ill.: Tyndale House, 1982, 1992.

Effective Parenting in a Defective World by Chip Ingram. Carol Stream, Ill.: Tyndale House, 2006.

‡*Faithful Parents, Faithful Kids* by Mike Yorkey and Greg Johnson. Carol Stream, Ill.: Tyndale House, 1993.

Family and Home Network*
PO Box 545
Merrifield, VA 22116
703-352-1072
http://www.familyandhome.org

Family University
PO Box 500050
San Diego, CA 92150-0050
858-513-7150
http://www.smartfamilies.com
This organization, which offers a variety of resources, is designed to attract men into fellowship and to equip fathers for successful family living.

‡*The Five Key Habits of Smart Dads* by Paul Lewis. Grand Rapids, Mich.: Zondervan, 1994.

Focus on the Family
Colorado Springs, CO 80995
719-531-5181
800-A-FAMILY
http://www.family.org

Giving Your Child the Excellence Edge: 10 Traits Your Child Needs to Achieve Lifelong Success by Vicki Caruana. Carol Stream, Ill.: Tyndale House, 2004.

Got Teens? Time-Tested Answers for Moms of Teens and Tweens by Jill Savage and Pam Farrel. Eugene, Ore.: Harvest House, 2005.

Growing Compassionate Kids: Helping Kids See Beyond Their Backyard by Jan Johnson. Nashville: Upper Room, 2001.

Guiding Your Family in a Misguided World by Dr. Tony Evans. Colorado Springs: Focus on the Family, 1991.

Hearts at Home
   1509 N. Clinton Blvd.
   Bloomington, IL 61701
   309-828-6667
   http://www.hearts-at-home.org
This group offers education and encouragment to women who desire to be better equipped for the profession of motherhood.

Hide It in Your Heart: Creative Ways for Families to Explore God's Word by Gloria Gaither and Shirley Dobson. Sisters, Ore.:, Multnomah Gifts, 2005.

Home Court Advantage: Preparing Your Children to Be Winners in Life by Dr. Kevin Leman. Carol Stream, Ill.: Tyndale House, 2005.

‡*How to Parent Your "Tweenager": Understanding the In-Between Years of Your 8- to 12-Year-Old* by Dr. Mary Manz Simon. Nashville: Thomas Nelson, 1995.

‡*The Hurting Parent* by Margie Lewis and Gregg Lewis. Grand Rapids, Mich.: Zondervan, 1988.

‡*Keeping Your Family Together When the World Is Falling Apart* by Kevin Leman. Colorado Springs: Focus on the Family, 1993.

The Key to Your Child's Heart by Gary Smalley. Nashville: W Publishing, 2003.

Let's Make a Memory by Shirley Dobson and Gloria Gaither. Nashville: W Publishing, 1994.

Life on the Edge by Dr. James Dobson. Sisters, Ore.: Multnomah, 2004.

Making Kids Mind without Losing Yours by Dr. Kevin Leman. Grand Rapids, Mich.: Revell, 2005.

The Mommy and Daddy: Practical Tips for New Parents from Parents Who've Been There by Karen Hull. Grand Rapids, Mich.: Zondervan, 1986.

A Mother's Manual for Holiday Survival by Kathy Peel and Judie Byrd. Colorado Springs: Focus on the Family, 1991.

A Mother's Manual for Schoolday Survival by Kathy Peel and Joy Mahaffey. Colorado Springs: Focus on the Family, 1990.

A Mother's Manual for Summer Survival by Kathy Peel and Joy Mahaffey. Colorado Springs: Focus on the Family, 1989.

National Center for Fathering
   PO Box 413888
   Kansas City, MO 64141
   913-384-4661
   800-593-3237
   http://www.fathers.com
This group helps organize seminars for fathers on the local-church level. It also provides Bible study materials, curriculum, and other fathering resources.

National Organization of Mothers of Twins Club, Inc.*
   PO Box 700860
   Plymouth, MI, 48170-0955
   248-231-4480
   http://www.nomotc.org
The purpose of this organization, with more than 475 local chapters across the country, is to offer support to parents and to research and educate the public about twins. It offers a quarterly newsletter and free brochures.

The New Dare to Discipline by Dr. James Dobson. Carol Stream, Ill.: Tyndale House, 1992.

The New Hide or Seek: Building Confidence in Your Child by Dr. James Dobson. Grand Rapids, Mich.: Revell, 2001.

The New Strong-Willed Child by Dr. James Dobson. Carol Stream, Ill.: Tyndale House, 2004.

Parenting at the Speed of Life: 60 Ways to Capture Time with Your Kids by Rick Osborne. Carol Stream, Ill.: Tyndale House, 2004.

Parenting Isn't for Cowards by Dr. James Dobson. Sisters, Ore.: Multnomah, 2004.

‡*Parenting Passages* by David Veerman. Carol Stream, Ill.: Tyndale House, 1994.

Parents' Answer Book by Dr. James Dobson. Carol Stream, Ill.: Tyndale House, 2003.

Parents in Pain by Dr. John White. Downers Grove, Ill.: InterVarsity, 1979.

Preparing for Adolescence: How to Survive the Coming Years of Change by Dr. James Dobson. Ventura, Calif.: Regal, 1978, 1989, 1999.

‡*Raising Them Right* edited by Mike Yorkey. Colorado Springs: Focus on the Family, 1994.

Right from Wrong by Josh McDowell and Bob Hostetler. Dallas: Word, 1994.

The Smart Stepfamily: Seven Steps to a Healthy Family by Ron L. Deal. Minneapolis: Bethany House, 2006.

Sticking with Your Teen by Joe White with Lissa Halls Johnson. Carol Stream, Ill.: Tyndale House, 2006.

Stress and Your Child by Dr. Archibald Hart. Nashville: W Publishing, 2005.

Trend-Savvy Parenting by Mary Manz Simon. Carol Stream, Ill.: Tyndale House, 2006.

The Way They Learn by Cynthia Ulrich Tobias. Colorado Springs: Focus on the Family, 1994.

When Good Kids Make Bad Choices: Help and Hope for Hurting Parents by Elyse Fitzpatrick and Jim Newheiser, with Dr. Laura Hendrickson. Eugene, Ore.: Harvest House, 2005.

When You Feel Like Screaming: Help for Frustrated Mothers by Dr. Grace Ketterman and Pat Holt. Colorado Springs: WaterBrook, 2001.

Your Child Video Seminar: Essentials of Discipline by Dr. James Dobson. Colorado Springs: Focus on the Family, 2005.

Pro-Life Materials

Answering the Call: Saving Innocent Lives One Woman at a Time by John M. Ensor. Colorado Springs: Focus on the Family, 2003.

Bethany Christian Services

901 Eastern Ave. NE
PO Box 294
Grand Rapids, MI 49501-0294
Main office: 616-224-7610
Refugee Service Center: 616-224-7540
24-hour pregnancy help line: 800-238-4269
http://www.bethany.org

This privately licensed, Christian child-welfare and adoption agency offers pro-life pregnancy counseling, temporary foster care, help with international adoptions, and alternative living arrangements for pregnant women. A listing of locations in different states is available. Spanish editions of some of their brochures are available on their Web site.

Care Net

44180 Riverside Parkway, Suite 200
Lansdowne, VA 20176
703-478-5661
Pregnancy support hotline: 800-395-HELP
http://www.care-net.org

Care Net is a network of more than nine hundred pregnancy-resource centers in the United States and Canada. This organization provides a bimonthly newsletter and offers a postabortion Bible study entitled *Women in Ramah*.

Pro-Life 101: A Step-by-Step Guide to Making Your Case Persuasively by Scott Klusendorf. Signal Hill, Calif.: Stand to Reason, 2002.

Saving Levi: Left to Die, Destined to Live by Lisa Misraje Bentley. Colorado Springs: Focus on the Family, 2007.

Why Pro-Life? Caring for the Unborn and Their Mothers by Randy Alcorn. Sisters, Ore.: Multnomah, 2004.

Safety

Complete Guide to Family Health, Nutrition, and Fitness by Paul C. Reisser, MD. Carol Stream, Ill.: Tyndale House, 2006.

Consumer Product Safety Commission*

4330 East West Hwy.
Bethesda, MD 20814
800-638-CPSC
http://www.cpsc.gov

Answers questions and provides materials on consumer product safety, including product hazards, product defects, and injuries sustained while using products. It deals with products used in and around the home (but not automobiles, foods, drugs, cosmetics, boats, firearms, and pesticides, which are the responsibility of other agencies).

National Fire Protection Association*

1 Batterymarch Pk.
Quincy, MA 02169-7471
617-770-3000
http://www.nfpa.org

Provides literature on fire safety and fire codes and standards.

National Safety Council*

1121 Spring Lake Dr.
Itasca, IL 60143-3201
800-621-2855
http://www.nsc.org

Provides posters, brochures, and booklets on safety and the prevention of accidents.

Vehicle Safety Hotline*

National Highway Traffic Safety Administration
888-327-4236
http://www-odi.nhtsa.dot.gov/home.cfm

Provides information and referrals on the effectiveness of occupant-protection devices such as safety belts and child safety seats; also gives information on auto recalls, auto-crash test results, tire quality reports, and other auto safety top-ics. Staffed by experts who investigate consumer complaints and provide assistance to resolve problems. Reports safety defects and gives referrals to other government agencies for consumer questions on warranties, service, and auto safety regulations.

Schools, Education, and Related Issues

see also Home Schooling

Association of Christian Schools International

PO Box 65130
Colorado Springs, CO 80962-5130
719-528-6906
800-367-0798 (orders only)
http://www.acsi.org

The largest Christian school organization in the world, ACSI holds annual nationwide conventions for educators, administrators, and parents, in addition to providing a wide variety of services for teachers and administrators. It also lists referrals for Christian boarding schools.

Blind Childrens Center*

4120 Marathon St.
Los Angeles, CA 90029-3584
323-664-2153
http://www.blindchildrenscenter.org

This organization deals primarily with blind children, from birth through elementary school.

Bringing Out the Best in Your Child: 80 Ways to Focus On Every Kid's Strengths by Cynthia Ulrich Tobias and Carol Funk. Ann Arbor, Mich.: Vine Books, 1997.

Center for Education Reform*

1001 Connecticut Ave. NW, Ste. 204
Washington, DC 20036
202-822-9000
http://www.edreform.com

This nonprofit organization is dedicated to fostering positive education reform through the charter-school movement. It provides a wealth of information about charter schools.

Children and Adults with Attention Deficit/Hyperactivity Disorder (CHADD)*
8181 Professional Pl., Ste. 150
Landover, MD 20785
301-306-7070
http://www.chadd.org

This nonprofit, parent-based organization was formed to help parents and teachers of children with ADHD. There are two hundred chapters in the United States. The organization has a yearly national conference and offers a monthly newsletter and additional resources on the subject.

‡*Christian Colleges and Universities* by the Council for Christian Colleges and Universities. Peterson's Guides, 2002.

Christian Educators Association International
PO Box 41300
Pasadena, CA 91114-8300
888-798-1124
http://www.ceai.org

This national organization has local chapters for educators and parents and keeps members informed on issues affecting education. It offers a nationwide prayer network, conferences, curriculum, and liability coverage comparable to NEA. Legal advice is available to members.

Christian Schools International
Dave Koetje, President/CEO
3350 E. Paris Ave. SE
Grand Rapids, MI 49512-3054
616-957-1070
800-635-8288
http://www.csionline.org/

Offers an extended catalog of resources and publications for curriculum and administration of schools. This organization's membership includes about five hundred Reformed Christian schools around the world, representing more than one hundred thousand students.

Council for Christian Colleges and Universities
321 Eighth St. NE
Washington, DC 20002
202-546-8713

http://www.cccu.org

Provides a complimentary list of, and general information on, Christian colleges and universities for those interested in Christian higher education.

‡*Creating a Positive Public School Experience* by Eric Buehrer. Nashville: Thomas Nelson, 1994.

Eagle Forum
Phyllis Schlafly, President
PO Box 618
Alton, IL 62002
618-462-5415
http://www.eagleforum.org

This well-known national pro-family organization is concerned with legislation and policy-making at the local, state, and national levels.

Educational Guidance Institute*
Onalee McGraw
PO Box 1127
Front Royal, VA 22630
540-635-4420
http://www.educationalguidance.org

Offers a support system to parents, educators, community leaders, and policy makers, gives seminars and conferences, and covers the *Teaching the Whole Person about Love, Sex and Marriage* abstinence-based sex-education curriculum.

Every Child Can Succeed: Making the Most of Your Child's Learning Style by Cynthia Ulrich Tobias. Colorado Springs: Focus on the Family, 1999.

The Foundation for American Christian Education
PO Box 9588
Chesapeake, VA 23321-9588
800-352-3223
http://www.face.net

This organization provides research, documentation, and a publication of America's Christian history and government. It also offers seminars, conferences, and curriculum for Christian schools and home schoolers.

Foundation for Thought and Ethics

PO Box 830721

Richardson, TX 75083-0721

http://www.fteonline.com

This Christian ministry offers a list of resources on intelligent design, publishes a periodic newsletter, and holds seminars and conferences.

Gateways to Better Education

PO Box 514

Lake Forest, CA 92609-0514

949-586-5437

http://www.gtbe.org

Parents with children in public schools will find assistance in evaluating programs and school curricula. A complimentary quarterly newsletter is available, and seminars and conferences are offered.

‡*Helping Your Child Succeed in Public Schools* by Cheri Fuller. Colorado Springs: Focus on the Family, 1993.

How to Stay Christian in College by J. Budziszewski. Colorado Springs: THINK Books, 2004.

How to Stay Christian in High School by Steve Gerali. Colorado Springs: THINK Books, 2004.

‡*How to Survive Middle School* by Rick Bundschuh. Grand Rapids, Mich.: Zondervan, 1991.

Learning Disabilities Association of America*

4156 Library Rd.

Pittsburgh, PA 15234-1349

412-341-1515

http://www.ldanatl.org

Formerly the Association for Children with Learning Disabilities. This organization is set up to define and provide solutions for learning problems such as dyslexia and ADHD. It also provides referral information and offers several publications regarding learning disabilities. Conferences for parents, teachers, and other professionals are available as well.

Moms in Touch International

PO Box 1120

Poway, CA 92074-1120

858-486-4065

800-949-6667

http://www.momsintouch.org

This group was set up as a support base for schools. Mothers meet weekly to pray for their children, teachers, and administrators. They publish a newsletter called *Heart to Heart*.

National Right to Read Foundation*

PO Box 560

Strasburg, VA 22657

http://www.nrrf.org

This is a nonpartisan organization dedicated to the elimination of illiteracy through the use of phonics and values-based literature.

School Choices: What's Best For Your Child by Jan Sheble. Kansas City, Mo.: Beacon Hill, 2003.

So You're Thinking About Homeschooling: Fifteen Families Show You How You Can Do It! by Lisa Whelchel. Sisters, Ore.: Multnomah, 2005.

Surviving Middle School: How to Manage the Maze by Sandy Silverthorne. Cincinnati, Ohio: Standard, 2003.

Teachers Saving Children*

PO Box 125

Damascus, OH 44619-0125

330-821-2747

http://www.teacherssavingchildren.org

The primary purpose of this organization of pro-life teachers and other concerned citizens is to establish respect for all human life from conception to natural death, especially among professional educators' organizations.

U.S. Charter Schools*

http://www.uscharterschools.org

This Web site provides information about the charter-school movement. It includes information on how to start a charter school as well as information for parents considering a charter school for their child.

The Way They Learn by Cynthia Ulrich Tobias. Colorado Springs: Focus on the Family, 1994, 1998.

‡*Welcome to High School* by Diane Eble, Chris Lutes, and Kris Bearss. Grand Rapids, Mich.: Zondervan, 1991.

Sex Education and Sexual Health

‡*Almost 12: The Story of Sex* by Kenneth N. Taylor. Carol Stream, Ill.: Tyndale House, 1995.

A Chicken's Guide to Talking Turkey with Your Kids about Sex by Dr. Kevin Leman and Kathy Flores Bell. Grand Rapids, Mich.: Zondervan, 2004.

‡*Decent Exposure: How to Teach Your Children about Sex* by Connie Marshner. Brentwood, Tenn.: Wolgemuth & Hyatt, 1988.

The Medical Institute for Sexual Health*
    1101 S. Capital of TX Hwy.
    Bldg. B, Ste. 100
    Austin, TX 78746
    512-328-6268
    http://www.medinstitute.org
Science clearly shows that the behavior choices necessary for optimal health are sexual abstinence for unmarried individuals and faithfulness within marriage. The Medical Institute is a science-based organization that is committed to teaching people how to make good choices and adopt healthy behaviors that enable them to achieve their highest potential.

Preparing for Adolescence: How to Survive the Coming Years of Change by Dr. James Dobson. Ventura, Calif.: Gospel Light, 2006.

‡*Sex, Lies, and—the Truth* by Rolf Zettersten. Carol Stream, Ill.: Tyndale House, 1994.

‡*Sex: What You Don't Know Can Kill You* by Dr. Joe S. McIlhaney Jr. with Marion McIlhaney. Grand Rapids, Mich.: Baker, 1997.

Single Parenting

Boundaries: When to Say Yes, When to Say No to Take Control of Your Life by Dr. Henry Cloud and Dr. John Townsend. Grand Rapids, Mich.: Zondervan, 1992, 2002.

Changes That Heal by Dr. Henry Cloud. Grand Rapids, Mich.: Zondervan, 1992.

‡*Children of Divorce: Helping Kids When Their Parents Are Apart* by Debbie Barr. Grand Rapids, Mich.: Zondervan, 1992.

‡*Faithful Parents, Faithful Kids* by Greg Johnson and Mike Yorkey. Carol Stream, Ill.: Tyndale House, 1993.

The Financial Guide for the Single Parent by Larry Burkett. Chicago: Moody, 1997.

Going It Alone: Meeting the Challenges of Being a Single Mom by Michele Howe. Peabody, Mass.: Hendrickson, 1999.

Helping Children Survive Divorce: What to Expect, How to Help by Dr. Archibald Hart. Dallas: Word, 1997.

Moms on the Job: 7 Secrets for Success at Home and Work by Sabrina O'Malone. Carol Stream, Ill.: Tyndale House, 2006.

The Single Dad's Survival Guide: How to Succeed as a One-Man Parenting Team by Mike Klumpp. Colorado Springs: WaterBrook, 2003.

The Single Mom's Guide to Finding Joy in the Chaos by Elsa Kok Colopy. Grand Rapids, Mich.: Revell, 2006.

Successful Single Parenting by Gary Richmond. Eugene, Ore.: Harvest House, 1998.

What Children Need to Know When Parents Get Divorced by William L. Coleman. Minneapolis: Bethany House, 1998.

Spiritual Training

‡*1001 Ways to Help Your Child Walk with God* by Kathie Reimer. Carol Stream, Ill.: Tyndale House, 1994.

Discipleship Journal
> PO Box 35004
> Boulder, CO 80323-4470
> Subscriber services: 800-877-1811
> http://www.navpress.com/Magazines/
> DiscipleshipJournal/

This Christian-growth periodical, published by NavPress, challenges believers to develop a deeper relationship with God. Call or write for subscription information.

FaithTraining: Raising Kids Who Love the Lord by Joe White. Colorado Springs: Focus on the Family, 1998.

The Family Book of Christian Values: Timeless Stories for Today's Families by Stuart and Jill Briscoe. Elgin, Ill.: Cook, 1995.

Guiding Your Family in a Misguided World by Tony Evans. Colorado Springs: Focus on the Family, 1999.

Parents' Guide to the Spiritual Growth of Children by Focus on the Family. Edited by John Trent, Rick Osborne, and Kurt Bruner. Colorado Springs: Focus on the Family, 2003.

Teaching Kids about God: An Age-by-Age Plan for Parents of Children from Birth to Age Twelve. Edited by John Trent, Rick Osborne, and Kurt Bruner. Carol Stream, Ill.: Tyndale House, 2003.

YouthWalk
> Walk Thru the Bible Ministries
> 4201 N. Peachtree Rd.
> Atlanta, GA 30341-1207
> 770-458-9300
> 800-877-5539
> http://www.youthwalk.org
> http://www.walkthru.org

YouthWalk is a daily devotional for teens in junior high and high school.

Stress

After the Boxes Are Unpacked: Moving On After Moving In by Susan Miller. Colorado Springs: Focus on the Family, 1998.

But Mom, I Don't Want To Move! Easing the Impact of Moving on Your Children by Susan Miller. Carol Stream, Ill.: Tyndale House, 2004.

Margin: Restoring Emotional, Physical, Financial, and Time Reserves to Overloaded Lives by Dr. Richard Swenson. Colorado Springs: NavPress, 2004.

Moms on the Job: 7 Secrets for Success at Home and Work by Sabrina O'Malone. Colorado Springs: Focus on the Family, 2006.

The Overload Syndrome: Learning to Live within Your Limits by Dr. Richard Swenson. Colorado Springs: NavPress, 1999.

Stress and Your Child: The Hidden Reason Why Your Child May Be Moody, Resentful, or Insecure by Dr. Archibald Hart. Nashville: W Publishing, 2005.

When Good Kids Make Bad Choices: Help and Hope for Hurting Parents by Elyse Fitzpatrick and Jim Newheiser, with Dr. Laura Hendrickson. Eugene, Ore.: Harvest House, 2005.

When You Feel Like Screaming: Help for Frustrated Mothers by Dr. Grace Ketterman and Pat Holt. Wheaton, Ill.: Shaw/WaterBrook, 2001.

Women and Stress: A Practical Approach to Managing Tension by Jean Lush with Pam Vredevelt. Grand Rapids, Mich.: Revell, 1997.

Substance Abuse

see also Addictions

Al-Anon and Alateen*
> 1600 Corporate Landing Pkwy.
> Virginia Beach, VA 23454-5617
> 757-563-1600
> 888-425-2666
> http://www.al-anon.alateen.org

Provides printed materials on alcoholism, aimed specifically at helping families, as well as support meetings that are held all over the country.

Celebrate Recovery

25422 Trabuco Road #105-151
Lake Forest, CA 92630
949-581-0548
http://www.celebraterecovery.com

An international ministry started at Saddleback Church in Southern California in 1991, Celebrate Recovery teaches eight biblically based recovery principles to bring freedom from addictive, compulsive, and dysfunctional behaviors. Celebrate Recovery publishes books and visual materials, organizes conferences and training seminars, and promotes recovery ministries in churches.

‡*Healing Life's Hidden Addictions* by Dr. Archibald Hart. Ann Arbor, Mich.: Servant, 1990.

Lighthouse Link

800 W. State Street
Suite 302
Doylestown, PA 18901
215-340-2686
Urgent Help Line 877-562-2565
http://www.lighthousenetwork.org

Lighthouse Link, an arm of Lighthouse Network, helps individuals find Christian service providers who deal with mental health and substance abuse issues. They work to match clients with the most appropriate care provider and also offer assistance in understanding the treatment process and in navigating the health system.

Mothers Against Drunk Driving*

511 E. John Carpenter Frwy., Ste. 700
Irving, TX 75062
800-438-6233
http://www.madd.org

This well-known group offers resources on alcoholism, drunk driving, and victim assistance.

National Clearinghouse for Alcohol and Drug Information*

PO Box 2345
Rockville, MD 20847-2345
24-hour hotline: 800-729-6686
TDD: 800-487-4889

Spanish: 877-767-8432
http://ncadi.samhsa.gov

Offers information and technical assistance to schools, parent groups, business and industry, and national organizations in developing drug-abuse prevention activities. Does not provide crisis counseling, intervention, treatment, referral, or information on the pharmacology or criminal aspects of drugs.

National Council on Alcoholism and Drug Dependence*

244 East 58th St., 4th Floor
New York, NY 10022
212-269-7797
800-622-2255
http://www.ncadd.org

Refers people to local affiliates, and provides written information on alcoholism and teenage drinking problems.

National Institute on Drug Abuse Helpline*

800-662-4357
http://www.drugabuse.gov

Provides general information on drug abuse and on AIDS as it relates to intravenous drug users. Also offers referrals.

National Runaway Switchboard*

3080 N. Lincoln Ave.
Chicago, IL 60657
773-880-9860
800-786-2929
http://www.1800runaway.org

This twenty-four-hour service allows runaway children to leave messages for parents, and vice versa. Materials and referrals are available.

Overcomers Outreach, Inc.

PO Box 922950
Sylmar, CA 91392-2950
818-833-1803
800-310-3001
http://www.overcomersoutreach.org

This organization is designed to address problems of alcoholism and drug dependency within churches.

Parenting the Wild Child by Miles McPherson. Minneapolis: Bethany House, 2000.

Parents in Pain: Overcoming the Hurt and Frustration of Problem Children by Dr. John White. Downers Grove, Ill.: InterVarsity, 1979.

PRIDE Youth Programs*
4 West Oak St.
Fremont, MI 49412
231-924-1662
800-668-9277
http://www.prideyouthprograms.org
Formerly Parents Resource Institute for Drug Education. This organization offers helpful resources regarding drug problems. Parents may become better informed about the biological impact of drugs.

SoberRecovery*
Mulligan Group
c/o SoberRecovery
15265 Alton Pkwy., Ste. 400
Irvine, CA 92618
http://www.soberrecovery.com
An online community and resource site that refers adolescents and adults to local facilities for help.

Surviving the Prodigal Years: How to Love Your Wayward Child Without Ruining Your Own Life by Marcia Mitchell. Seattle, Wash.: YWAM, 1999.

Teen Challenge
PO Box 1015
Springfield, MO 65801
417-862-6969
http://www.teenchallengeusa.com
Well-known for its effectiveness, this organization provides a broad scope of help and information in every area of drug and alcohol abuse.

Wild Child, Waiting Mom: Finding Hope in the Midst of Heartache by Karilee Hayden and Wendi Hayden English. Colorado Springs: Focus on the Family, 2006.

Teens

2 Die 4: The Dangerous Truth about Following Christ by Ryan Dobson with Brian Smith. Sisters, Ore.: Multnomah, 2004.

2 Live 4: Why Did You Think You Were Here? by Ryan Dobson with Marcus Brotherton. Sisters, Ore.: Multnomah, 2005.

Airborne: Getting Your Faith Off the Ground by Jose Zayas. Carol Stream, Ill.: Tyndale House, 2005.

‡*Answers to Tough Questions Skeptics Ask about the Christian Faith* by Josh McDowell and Don Stewart. Nashville: Thomas Nelson, 1980.

Anybody Got a Clue About Guys? A Young Woman's Guide to Healthy Relationships by Susie Shellenberger. Ventura, Calif.: Regal, 2004.

Bloom: A Girl's Guide to Growing Up by Susie Shellenberger. Colorado Springs: Focus on the Family, 2003.

Boom: A Guy's Guide to Growing Up by Michael Ross. Colorado Springs: Focus on the Family, 2003.

‡*Cars, Curfews, Parties and Parents . . . 77 Pretty Important Ideas on Family Survival* by Susie Shellenberger and Greg Johnson. Minneapolis: Bethany House, 1995.

How to Live with Your Parents without Losing Your Mind by Ken Davis. Grand Rapids, Mich.: Zondervan, 1988.

‡*I Only See My Dad on Weekends: Kids Tell Their Stories about Divorce and Blended Families* by Beth Matthews, Andrew Adams, and Karen Dockrey. Elgin, Ill.: Chariot Family, 1994.

Life on the Edge: The Next Generation's Guide to a Meaningful Future by Dr. James Dobson. Sisters, Ore.: Multnomah, 2004.

Pure Excitement: A Godly Look At Sex, Love and Dating by Joe White. Colorado Springs: Focus on the Family, 1998.

Stand: Core Truths You Must Know for an Unshakable Faith by Alex McFarland. Carol Stream, Ill.: Tyndale House, 2005.

Women

Blessing Your Husband by Debra Evans. Colorado Springs: Focus on the Family, 2003.

Capture His Heart: Becoming the Godly Wife Your Husband Desires by Lysa TerKeurst. Chicago: Moody, 2002.

Dreams of a Woman: God's Plan For Fulfilling Your Dreams by Sharon Jaynes. Colorado Springs: Focus on the Family, 2004.

Focus on the Family Women's Study Series (designed for group study), Ventura, Calif.: Gospel Light, 2004–2005.
> #1: *Women of Worth*
> #2: *Healing the Heart*
> #3: *Balanced Living*
> #4: *The Blessing of Friendship*
> #5: *Experiencing Spiritual Growth*
> #6: *Created Beautiful*
> #7: *Women of Purpose*
> #8: *Divinely Designed*
> *Focus on the Family Women's Series Ministry Guide*

For Women Only: What You Need to Know about the Inner Lives Of Men by Shaunti Feldhahn. Sisters, Ore.: Multnomah, 2004.

The Friendships of Women by Dee Brestin. Colorado Springs: Life Journey, 2005.

Gentle Passages: Guiding Your Daughter into Womanhood by Robin Jones Gunn. Sisters, Ore.: Multnomah, 2002.

Moms on the Job: 7 Secrets for Success at Home and Work by Sabrina O'Malone. Colorado Springs: Focus on the Family, 2006.

Professionalizing Motherhood: Encouraging, Educating, and Equipping Mothers at Home by Jill Savage. Grand Rapids, Mich.: Zondervan, 2001.

Tender Mercy for a Mother's Soul by Angela Thomas. Colorado Springs: Focus on the Family, 2006.

When Mothers Pray by Cheri Fuller. Sisters, Ore.: Multnomah, 1997.

Who Holds the Key to Your Heart? by Lysa TerKeurst. Chicago: Moody, 2002.

Women And Stress: A Practical Approach to Managing Tension by Jean Lush and Pam Vredevelt. Grand Rapids, Mich.: Revell, 1997.

Endnotes

Note: All information from Web sites was originally accessed between February 2006 and December 2006. Links have been updated whenever possible.

Chapter 1: Preparing for Parenthood

1. March of Dimes and International Food Information Council Foundation, "Healthy Eating During Pregnancy," January 2003, http://www.ific.org/publications/brochures/pregnancybroch.cfm.
2. American College of Obstetricians and Gynecologists, "ACOG Issues Guidance to Ob-Gyns on Impact of Obesity During Pregnancy," news release, August 31, 2005, http://www.acog.org/from _home/publications/press_releases/nr08-31-05-2.cfm.
3. Institutes of Medicine, Subcommittee on Nutritional Status and Weight Gain During Pregnancy, *Nutrition During Pregnancy* (Washington DC: National Academic Press, 1990).
4. Centers for Disease Control and Prevention, "Chronic Disease Prevention: Preventing Smoking During Pregnancy," http://www.cdc.gov/nccdphp/publications/factsheets/Prevention/smoking .htm.
5. American Cancer Society, "Women and Smoking," February 13, 2006, http://www.cancer.org/ docroot/PED/content/PED_10_2X_Women_and_Smoking.asp?sitearea=PED; Mark E. Anderson, Daniel C. Johnson, and Holly A. Batal, "Sudden Infant Death Syndrome and Prenatal Maternal Smoking: Rising Attributed Risk in the Back to Sleep Era," *BMC Medicine* 3 (2005), http://www .pubmedcentral.nih.gov/articlerender.fcgi?artid=545061; KidsHealth, "Sudden Infant Death Syndrome (SIDs)," Nemours Foundation, http://kidshealth.org/parent/general/sleep/sids.html.
6. John L. Carroll and Ellen S. Siska, "SIDS: Counseling Parents to Reduce the Risk," *American Family Physician* 57, no. 7 (April 1, 1998), http://www.aafp.org/afp/980401ap/carroll.html.
7. March of Dimes, "Drinking Alcohol during Pregnancy," August 2002, http://www.marchofdimes .com/professionals/14332_1170.asp.
8. Ibid.
9. Familydoctor.org, "Pregnancy: Taking Care of You and Your Baby," American Academy of Family Physicians, July 2005, http://familydoctor.org/053.xml.
10. Ronald A. Black and D. Ashley Hill, "Over-the-Counter Medications in Pregnancy," *American Family Physician* 67, no. 12 (June 15, 2003), http://www.aafp.org/afp/20030615/2517.html.
11. National Library of Medicine and National Institutes of Health, *MedlinePlus Medical Encyclopedia*, s.v. "Rubella," June 16, 2005, http://www.nlm.nih.gov/medlineplus/ency/article/001574.htm.
12. Centers for Disease Control, National Immunization Program, "Varicella Vaccine—FAQs Related to Pregnancy," February 15, 2001, http://www.cdc.gov/nip/vaccine/varicella/faqs-clinic-vac-preg .htm.
13. U.S. Food and Drug Administration, Center for Food Safety and Applied Nutrition, "*Toxoplasma*: Frequently Asked Questions," *Food Safety for Moms-to-Be: While You're Pregnant,* October 31, 2005, http://www.cfsan.fda.gov/~pregnant/whiltoxo.html.
14. National Library of Medicine and National Institutes of Health, *MedlinePlus Medical Encyclopedia*, s.v. "Listeriosis," October 27, 2005, http://www.nlm.nih.gov/medlineplus/ency/article/001380 .htm; United States Department of Agriculture, Food Safety and Inspection Service, "*Listeriosis* and Pregnancy: What Is Your Risk? Safe Food Handling for a Healthy Pregnancy," September 2001,

http://www.fsis.usda.gov/OA/pubs/lm_tearsheet.pdf; United States Food and Drug Administration, Center for Food Safety and Applied Nutrition, "*Listeria*: Frequently Asked Questions," *Food Safety for Moms-to-Be: While You're Pregnant*, http://www.cfsan.fda.gov/~pregnant/whillist.html.

Chapter 2: Developing a Birth Plan and Preparing the Nest

1. Lay midwives do not have a nursing degree. They may or may not have formal training, a state license, or physician backup. Skill levels vary, and health-care professionals generally have serious qualms about their capabilities should any problem develop.
2. J. P. Rooks et al., "Outcomes of Care in Birth Centers: The National Birth Center Study," *New England Journal of Medicine* 321, no. 26 (December 28, 1989):1804–1811.

Chapter 3: The Moment Arrives

1. UrologyHealth.org, Pediatric Conditions: Abnormalities, "Undescended Testis," American Urological Association, August 2003, http://www.urologyhealth.org/pediatric/index.cfm?cat=01&topic=178.
2. U.S. Preventive Services Task Force, "Newborn Hearing Screening: Recommendations and Rationale," *American Family Physician* 64, no. 12 (December 15, 2001), http://www.aafp.org/afp/20011215/us.html.

Special Concerns: Sexually Transmitted Infections

1. Z. A. Brown et al., "Neonatal Herpes Simplex Virus Infection in Relation to Asymptomatic Maternal Infection at the Time of Labor," *New England Journal of Medicine* 324 (1991):1247–1252, quoted in Caroline M. Rudnick and Grant S. Hoekzema, "Neonatal Herpes Simplex Virus Infections," American Family Physician 65, no. 6 (March 15, 2002), http://www.aafp.org/afp/20020315/1138.html; Richard Fischer, "Genital Herpes in Pregnancy," *eMedicine*, February 15, 2006, http://www.emedicine.com/med/topic3554.htm.
2. Fischer, "Genital Herpes in Pregnancy."
3. AIDS InfoNet, "Pregnancy and HIV," Fact Sheet 611, April 17, 2005 (updated April 5, 2006), http://www.aidsinfonet.org/factsheet_detail.php?fsnumber=611&newLang=en.

Special Concerns: Birth Defects and Prenatal Testing

1. Arnold Christianson et al., *Executive Summary: March of Dimes Global Report on Birth Defects* (White Plains, N.Y.: March of Dimes Birth Defects Foundation, 2006), 2.
2. American College of Obstetricians and Gynecologists, *Planning for Pregnancy, Birth, and Beyond* (New York: Signet, 1994), 94.
3. American Association of Pro Life Obstetricians and Gynecologists, "Perinatal Hospice: Comprehensive Care for the Family of the Fetus with a Lethal Condition," April 24, 2002, http://www.aaplog.org/perinatalhospice.htm.

Special Concerns: Baby Blues, Postpartum Depression, and Postpartum Psychosis

1. E. C. Clay and D. A. Seehusen, "A Review of Postpartum Depression for the Primary Care Physician," *Southern Medical Journal* 97, no. 2 (2004):157–161.

Special Concerns: The Premature Infant

1. B. Byrne and J. J. Morrison, "Preterm Birth," *Clinical Evidence* 10 (2003): 1700–1715. Cited in WebMD, "Preterm Labor—Cause," http://aolsvc.health.webmd.aol.com/hw/being_pregnant/hw222259.
2. National Library of Medicine and National Institutes of Health, *MedlinePlus Medical Encyclopedia*, s.v. "Premature Infant," http://www.nlm.nih.gov/medlineplus/ency/article/001562.htm.

Chapter 4: The First Three Months, Part One

1. American Academy of Pediatrics, "Policy Statement: Breastfeeding and the Use of Human Milk," *Pediatrics* 115, no. 2 (February 2005): 496–506, http://aappolicy.aappublications.org/cgi/content/full/pediatrics;115/2/496.
2. Ibid.
3. P. S. Corso et al., "Cost of Illness in the 1993 Waterborne Cryptosporidium Outbreak, Milwaukee, Wisconsin," *Emerging Infectious Diseases* 9, no. 4 (April 2003), http://www.cdc.gov/ncidod/EID/vol9no4/02-0417.htm.
4. Isadora B. Stehlin, "Infant Formula: Second Best but Good Enough," *FDA Consumer Magazine* (June 1996) http://www.fda.gov/fdac/features/596_baby.html; AskDrSears.com, "A Word about Bottle-Feeding," http://www.askdrsears.com/html/0/T000100.asp.

5. B. D. Schmitt, "Formula (Bottle) Feeding," McKesson Provider Technologies, see http://www.med.umich.edu/1libr/pa/pa_formula_hhg.htm, (last modified March 2, 2006).

Chapter 5: The First Three Months, Part Two

1. Mayo Foundation for Medical Education and Research, "Caring for Your Baby's Umbilical Cord," http://www.mayoclinic.com/health/umbilical-cord/PR00046.

2. National Institute of Child Health and Human Development, Health Information and Media, SIDS: Back to Sleep Campaign, "A Frequently Asked Question about Bed Sharing," http://www.nichd.nih.gov/sids/FQ_bed_sharing.cfm (last modified September 15, 2006).

3. Consumer Product Safety Commission, "CPSC Cautions Caregivers about Hidden Hazards for Babies on Adult Beds: Reports of More Than 100 Deaths from 1999–2001," http://www.cpsc.gov/CPSCPUB/PUBS/5091.html.

Chapter 7: Six to Twelve Months

1. Edward Christophersen, "Burn Safety: Hot Water Temperature," McKesson Provider Technologies, http://www.med.umich.edu/1libr/pa/pa_hotwatr_hhg.htm.

2. Centers for Disease Control and Prevention, "Insect Repellent Use and Safety," August 2005, http://www.cdc.gov/ncidod/dvbid/westnile/qa/insect_repellent.htm.

3. U.S. Food and Drug Administration, "Insect Repellent Use and Safety in Children," September 2005, http://www.fda.gov/cder/emergency/repellants.htm.

4. Jonathan Eig , "Sippy Cups Draw Fire for Speech Slurs, Cavities," *Wall Street Journal*, February 12, 2002, http://www.mindfully.org/Plastic/Sippy-Cups-Slur-Speech12feb02.htm.

Chapter 8: Twelve to Twenty-Four Months

1. Burton L. White, *Raising a Happy, Unspoiled Child* (New York: Simon and Schuster, 1994), 161.

Special Concerns: Child Abuse and Neglect

1. C. T. Lung and D. Dara, "Current Trends in Child Abuse Reporting and Fatalities: The Results of the 1995 Annual Fifty-State Survey" (Chicago: National Committee to Prevent Child Abuse); U.S. Department of Health and Human Services Administration for Children & Families, *Child Maltreatment 2004*, (Washington, DC: U.S. Government Printing Office, 2006), http://www.acf.hhs.gov/programs/cb/pubs/cm04/summary.htm.

2. Bureau of Justice Statistics, U.S. Department of Justice, "Prison and Jail Inmates Report High Rates of Physical and Sexual Abuse before Their Confinement," news release, April 11, 1999, http://www.ojp.usdoj.gov/bjs/pub/press/parip.pr.

3. Child Welfare Information Gateway, *Child Sexual Abuse: Intervention and Treatment Issues* (Washington, DC: U.S. Department of Health and Human Services, 1993), http://www.childwelfare.gov/pubs/usermanuals/sexabuse/sexabuseb.cfm.

4. U.S. Department of Health and Human Services Administration for Children & Families, *Child Maltreatment 2004*.

Chapter 9: Two-Year-Olds

1. Burton L. White, *The First Three Years of Life* (New York: Fireside Books/Simon and Schuster, 1995), 342.

Chapter 11: Ages Five through Eleven

1. E. McCray et al., "The Epidemiology of Tuberculosis in the United States," *Clinics in Chest Medicine*, 18, no. 1 (1997): 99–113, quoted in A. F. Jerant, M. Bannon, and S. Rittenhouse, "Identification and Management of Tuberculosis," *American Family Physician* 61, no. 9 (May 1, 2000): 2667–2678, 2681–2682; Centers for Disease Control and Prevention, "Leading Causes of Death, 1900–1998," http://www.cdc.gov/nchs/data/dvs/lead1900_98.pdf.

2. Centers for Disease Control and Prevention, "Reported Tuberculosis in the United States, 2004," http://www.cdc.gov/nchstp/tb/surv/surv2004/default.htm.

3. J. B. Banks, "Does Screening for Tuberculosis in Children Decrease Morbidity or Mortality?" *American Family Physician* 69, no. 6 (March 2004): 1479–1480. See also Commonwealth of Massachusetts Department of Public Health, "Update on Screening Infants and Children for Tuberculosis in Massachusetts," November 2001, http://www.mass.gov/dph/cdc/tb/tbscreenupdate.htm.

4. Subcommittee on Chronic Abdominal Pain, American Academy of Pediatrics, "Chronic Abdominal Pain in Children," *Pediatrics* 115, no. 3 (March 2005): 812–815, http://pediatrics.aappublications.org/cgi/content/full/115/3/812.

5. Darren Waters, "What Happened to Dungeons and Dragons?" *BBC News Online*, April 26, 2004, http://news.bbc.co.uk/2/hi/uk_news/magazine/3655627.stm.

6. "Global Potter Sales Top 300m Mark," *BBC News*, October 4, 2005, http://news.bbc.co.uk/1/hi/entertainment/arts/4308548.stm; http://www.ipl.org/div/farq/bestsellerFARQ.html.

Special Concerns: Attention Deficit/Hyperactivity Disorder (ADHD)

1. J. Biederman et al., "Family-Genetic and Psychosocial Risk Factors in DSM-III Attention Deficit Disorder," *Journal of the American Academy of Child and Adolescent Psychiatry* 29, no. 4 (1990): 526–533. Cited in National Institute of Mental Health, "Attention Deficit Hyperactivity Disorder," 2006, http://www.nimh.nih.gov/publicat/adhd.cfm#ref06.

2. The MTA Cooperative Group, "A 14-Month Randomized Clinical Trial of Treatment Strategies for Attention-Deficit Hyperactivity Disorder (ADHD)," *Archives of General Psychiatry* 56 (1999):1073–1086, quoted in National Institute of Mental Health, "Attention Deficit Hyperactivity Disorder," 2006.

3. National Institute of Mental Health, "Attention Deficit Hyperactivity Disorder."

Special Concerns: The Overweight Child and Teenager

1. Institute of Medicine of the National Academies, "Childhood Obesity in the United States: Facts and Figures," fact sheet, September 2004, http://www.iom.edu/Object.File/Master/22/606/FINALfactsandfigures2.pdf, from Jeffrey P. Koplan, Catharyn T. Liverman, and Vivica I. Kraak, eds., Committee on Prevention of Obesity in Children and Youth, Institute of Medicine of the National Academies, *Preventing Childhood Obesity: Health in the Balance* (Washington, DC: The National Academies Press, 2005), http://www.nap.edu/catalog/11015.html; National Center for Health Statistics, "Prevalence of Overweight among Children and Adolescents: United States, 2003–2004," http://www.cdc.gov/nchs/products/pubs/pubd/hestats/overweight/overwght_child_03.htm.

2. R. Sinha et al., "Prevalence of Impaired Glucose Tolerance among Children and Adolescents with Marked Obesity," *New England Journal of Medicine* 346 (2002): 802–810, quoted in Alison G. Hoppin, "Assessment and Management of Childhood and Adolescent Obesity," *Medscape.com*, June 25, 2004.

3. M. H. Fishbein et al., "The Spectrum of Fatty Liver in Obese Children and the Relationship of Serum Aminotransferases to Severity of Steatosis," *Journal of Pediatric Gastroenterology and Nutrition* 36 (2003): 54–61, quoted in Hoppin, "Childhood and Adolescent Obesity."

4. Institute of Medicine, "Childhood Obesity in the United States."

5. A. Fowler-Brown, and L. Kahwati, "Prevention and Treatment of Overweight in Children and Adolescents," *American Family Physician* 69 (2004): 2592–2598.

6. K. E. Rhee et al., "Parenting Styles and Overweight Status in First Grade," *Pediatrics* 117, no. 6 (June 2006): 2047–54, http://pediatrics.aappublications.org/cgi/content/abstract/117/6/2047.

7. "Effects of Decreasing Sugar-Sweetened Beverage Consumption on Body Weight in Adolescents: A Randomized, Controlled Pilot Study," *Pediatrics* 117 (March 2006): 673–680.

Special Concerns: Eating Disorders

1. Anorexia Nervosa and Related Eating Disorders, Inc., "Statistics: How Many People Have Eating Disorders?" http://www.anred.com/stats.html; National Eating Disorders Association, "Statistics: Eating Disorders and Their Precursors," http://www.nationaleatingdisorders.org/p.asp?WebPage_ID=320&Profile_ID=41138.

2. M. Makino et al., "Prevalence of Eating Disorders: A Comparison of Western and Non-Western Countries," *Medscape General Medicine* 6, no. 3 (2004): 49, *Medscape.com*.

3. Elanor Taylor, "Totally in Control: The Rise of Pro-ana/Pro-mia Websites," Social Issues Research Centre, July 11, 2002, http://www.sirc.org/articles/totally_in_control2.shtml.

Special Concerns: Education Issues

1. National Center for Education Statistics, U.S. Department of Education, "Homeschooling in the United States: 2003," http://nces.ed.gov/pubs2006/homeschool.

2. National Center for Learning Disabilities, "LD at a Glance," http://www.ncld.org/index.php?option=content&task=view&id=448.

Special Concerns: Divorce and Its Effect on Children

1. Judith S. Wallerstein and Sandra Blakeslee, *Second Chances: Men, Women, and Children a Decade after Divorce* (New York: Ticknor and Fields, 1989).

2. Judith S. Wallerstein, Julia M. Lewis, and Sandra Blakeslee, *The Unexpected Legacy of Divorce: A 25 Year Landmark Study* (New York: Hyperion, 2000).

Chapter 13: The Adolescent Years, Part Two

1. Pornography statistics come from Donna Rice Hughes, "Recent Statistics on Internet Dangers," ProtectKids.com, http://www.protectkids.com/dangers/stats.htm, and TopTenREVIEWS, "Pornography Statistics 2007," Internet Filter Review, http://internet-filter-review.toptenreviews .com/internet-pornography-statistics.html.
2. Senate Committee on Commerce, Science and Transportation, *Hearing on the Science behind Pornography Addiction and the Effects of Addiction on Families and Communities* (testimony of Dr. James B. Weaver III given on November 18, 2004), http://commerce.senate.gov/hearings/testimony .cfm?id=1343&wit_id=3913.

Special Concerns: Bullying: Neither Right nor a Rite of Passage

1. Health Resources and Services Administration, "All About Bullying," part of the organization's "Stop Bullying Now!" online campaign, http://stopbullyingnow.hrsa.gov/adult/indexAdult.asp?A rea=allaboutbullying; National Youth Violence Prevention Resource Center, "Bullying Facts and Statistics," http://www.safeyouth.org/scripts/faq/bullying.asp.
2. Jaana Juvonen, Sandra Graham, and Mark A. Schuster, "Bullying among Young Adolescents: The Strong, the Weak, and the Troubled," *Pediatrics* 112, no. 6 (December 2003): 1231–1237, http:// pediatrics.aappublications.org/cgi/content/abstract/112/6/1231.
3. Tonja R. Nansel et al., "Bullying Behaviors among U.S. Youth: Prevalence and Association with Psychosocial Adjustment," *Journal of the American Medical Association* 285, no. 16 (April 25, 2001): 2094–2100, cited in http://www.safeyouth.org/scripts/faq/bullying.asp.
4. B. Vossekuil et al., *The Final Report and Findings of the Safe School Initiative: Implications for the Prevention of School Attacks in the United States* (a report from the U.S. Department of Education, Office of Elementary and Secondary Education, Safe and Drug Free Schools Program, and U.S. Secret Service, National Threat Assessment Center, May 2002).

Special Concerns: The Teenage Driver

1. Centers for Disease Control and Prevention, "Death: Preliminary Data for 2004," table 7, *National Vital Statistics Reports* 54, no. 19 (June 28, 2006), http://www.cdc.gov/nchs/fastats/deaths.htm.
2. National Highway Traffic Safety Administration, "Motor Vehicle Traffic Crash Fatality Counts and Estimates of People Injured for 2005," DOT HIS 810 639, August 2006.
3. National Highway Traffic Safety Administration, *Saving Teenage Lives: The Case for Graduated Driver Licensing*, http://www.nhtsa.dot.gov/people/injury/newdriver/SaveTeens/Index.html.
4. National Highway Traffic Safety Administration, "Motor Vehicle Traffic Crash Fatality Counts, 2005."
5. National Highway Traffic Safety Administration, *Traffic Safety Facts 2002*, table 81, http://www-nrd .nhtsa.dot.gov/pdf/nrd-30/NCSA/TSFAnn/TSF2002Final.pdf.
6. Centers for Disease Control and Prevention, "Youth Risk Behavior Surveillance–United States 2005," *Morbidity and Mortality Weekly Report* (June 9, 2006), http://www.cdc.gov/MMWR/preview/ mmwrhtml/ss5505a1.htm.
7. Anita Smith, "Putting Science into Practice: Tips for Parents on Teen Driving," *The Youth Connection* (a bimonthly publication of the Institute for Youth Development) 3, no. 2 (March–April 2000), http://www.youthdevelopment.org/download/news0300.pdf.
8. Allan F. Williams, "Teenage Drivers: Patterns of Risk," *Journal of Safety Research* 34 (2003): 5–15, http://www.nsc.org/public/GDL/williams.pdf.
9. Centers for Disease Control and Prevention, "Youth Risk Behavior Surveillance—2005."

Special Concerns: A Parent's Guide to Teen Sexuality

1. B. O. Boekeloo and D. E. Howard, "Oral Sexual Experience among Young Adolescents Receiving General Health Examinations," *American Journal of Health Behavior* 26, no. 4 (July–August 2002): 306–314.
2. William D. Mosher, Anjani Chandra, and Jo Jones, "Sexual Behavior and Selected Health Measures: Men and Women 15–44 Years of Age, United States, 2002" (data are from the 2002 National Survey of Family Growth), *Advance Data for Vital and Health Statistics*, no. 362 (Hyattsville, Md.: National Center for Health Statistics, 2005), http://www.cdc.gov/nchs/data/ad/ad362.pdf.

3. M. A. Schuster, R. M. Bell, and D. E. Kanouse, "The Sexual Practices of Adolescent Virgins: Genital Sexual Activities of High School Students Who Have Never Had Vaginal Intercourse," *American Journal of Public Health* 86, no. 11 (1996): 1570–1576.

4. P. F. Horan, J. Phillips, and N. E. Hagen, "The Meaning of Abstinence for College Students," *Journal of HIV/AIDS Prevention and Education for Adolescents and Children* (1998): 51–66.

5. K. Page-Shafer et al., "Risk of HIV Infection Attributable to Oral Sex among Men Who Have Sex with Men and in the Population of Men Who Have Sex with Men," *AIDS* 16, no. 17 (2002): 2350–2352; Scott Gottlieb, "Oral Sex May Be Important Risk Factor for HIV Infection," *British Medical Journal* 320 (February 12, 2000): 400, cited in "The Facts about Oral Sex and STDs," Medical Institute for Sexual Health.

6. For statistics on teenage pregnancy, see the Alan Guttmacher Institute, "U.S. Teenage Pregnancy Statistics with Comparative Statistics for Women Aged 20–24" (February 19, 2004), http://www.agi-usa.org/pubs/teen_stats.html. See also Joyce Martin et al., "Births: Final Data for 2002," *National Vital Statistics Report* 52, no. 10 (Hyattsville, Md.: National Center for Health Statistics, 2003) and the National Campaign to Prevent Teen Pregnancy, "Fact Sheet: How Is the 34% Statistic Calculated?" (February 2004), http://www.teenpregnancy.org/resources/reading/pdf/35percent.pdf. The last two resources are cited in Patricia Sulak and Sarah Herbelin, "Teenagers and Sex: Delaying Sexual Debut," *The Female Patient* 30, no. 4 (April 2005): 29–35.

7. Rebecca Maynard ed., *Kids Having Kids: A Robin Hood Foundation Special Report on the Costs of Adolescent Childbearing* (New York: Robin Hood Foundation, 1996), 1, 12.

8. Tom Wolfe, *Hooking Up* (New York: Picador USA, 2000), 3–16.

9. Norval Glenn and Elizabeth Marquardt, *Hooking Up, Hanging Out, and Hoping for Mr. Right: College Women on Dating and Mating Today* (New York: Institute of American Values, 2001), see http://www.iwf.org/campuscorner/hookingup.asp.

10. Michael A. Fletcher, "Campus Romance, Unrequited," *Washington Post,* July 26, 2001.

11. A detailed review of this phenomenon, and practical steps toward emotional healing after abortion, may be found in the book *A Solitary Sorrow* by Teri K. Reisser (Shaw/WaterBrook Press, 2000).

12. Lee Warner, Robert A. Hatcher, and Markus J. Steiner, "Male Condoms," table 9-2, in *Contraceptive Technology,* 18th edition, ed. Robert A. Hatcher et al. (New York: Irvington Publishers, 2004), 226.

13. M. J. Steiner et al., "Contraceptive Effectiveness of a Polyurethane Condom and a Latex Condom: A Randomized Controlled Trial," *Obstetrics and Gynecology* 101, no. 3 (March 2003): 539–547; "Workshop Summary: Scientific Evidence on Condom Effectiveness for Sexually Transmitted Disease (STD) Prevention," National Institute of Allergy and Infectious Diseases, National Institute of Health, Department of Health and Human Services, http://www.niaid.nih.gov/dmid/stds/condomreport.pdf; Ron G. Frezieres et al., "Evaluation of the Efficacy of a Polyurethane Condom: Results from a Randomized, Controlled, Clinical Trial," *Family Planning Perspectives* 31, no. 2 (March/April 1999): 81–87; M. Macaluso et al., "Mechanical Failure of the Latex Condom in a Cohort of Women at High STD Risk," *Sexually Transmitted Diseases* 26, no. 8 (September 1999): 450–458; J. Thomas Fitch et al., "Condom Effectiveness: Factors That Influence Risk Reduction," *Sexually Transmitted Diseases* 29, no. 12 (December 2002): 811–817.

14. Karen R. Davis and Susan C. Weller, "The Effectiveness of Condoms in Reducing Heterosexual Transmission of HIV," *Family Planning Perspectives* 31, no. 6 (November/December 1999): 272–279.

15. Saifuddin Ahmed et al., "HIV Incidence and Sexually Transmitted Disease Prevalence Associated with Condom Use: A Population Study in Rakai, Uganda," *AIDS* 15, no. 16 (November 9, 2001): 2171–2179; Jared M. Baeten et al., "Hormonal Contraception and Risk of Sexually Transmitted Acquisition: Results from a Prospective Study," *American Journal of Obstetrics and Gynecology* 183 (August 2001): 380–385; Lee Warner et al., "Condom Effectiveness for Reducing Transmission of Gonorrhea and Chlamydia: The Importance of Assessing Partner Infection Status," *American Journal of Epidemiology* 159 no. 3 (February 1, 2004): 242–251; Judith Shlay et al., "Comparison of Sexually Transmitted Disease Prevalence by Reported Level of Condom Use among Patients Attending an Urban Sexually Transmitted Disease Clinic," *Sexually Transmitted Diseases* 31, no. 3 (March 2004): 154–160. King K. Holmes, Ruth Levine, and Marcia Weaver, "Effectiveness of Condoms in Preventing Sexually Transmitted Infections," *Bulletin of the World Health Organization* 82, no. 6 (June 2004): 454–461.

16. Julie Gerberding, *Report to Congress: Prevention of Genital Human Papillomavirus Infection* (Atlanta: Centers for Disease Control and Prevention, January 2004). On pages 15–16 of this report,

Dr. Gerberding says, "The cumulative body of available scientific evidence suggests that condoms may provide some protection in preventing transmission of HPV infection but that protection is partial at best. The available scientific evidence is not sufficient to recommend condoms as a primary prevention strategy for the prevention of genital HPV infection"; Lisa Manhart and Laura Koutsky, "Do Condoms Prevent Genital HPV Infection, or Cervical Neoplasia? A Meta-Analysis," *Sexually Transmitted Diseases* 29, no. 11 (November 2002): 725–735.

17. Robert T. Michael et al., *Sex in America: A Definitive Survey* (Boston: Little, Brown and Company, 1994), 124.

Special Concerns: Sexually Transmitted Infections (STIs) among Adolescents

1. H. Weinstock, S. Berman, and W. Cates, "Sexually Transmitted Diseases among American Youth: Incidence and Prevalence Estimates, 2000," *Perspectives on Sexual and Reproductive Health* 36, no. 1 (2004): 6–10.

2. Harrell W. Chesson et al., "The Estimated Direct Medical Cost of Sexually Transmitted Diseases among American Youth, 2000," *Perspectives on Sexual and Reproductive Health* 36, no. 1 (January–February 2004): 11-19, http://www.guttmacher.org/pubs/journals/3601104.pdf.

3. W. E. Stamm, "Diseases Due to Chlamydia," in David C. Dale ed., *Infectious Diseases: The Clinician's Guide to Diagnosis, Treatment, and Prevention* (New York: WebMD, 2003), 478–489.

4. Centers for Disease Control and Prevention, "Chlamydia Fact Sheet," April 2006, http://www.cdc.gov/std/chlamydia/chlamydia.pdf.

5. Centers for Disease Control and Prevention, "Gonorrhea Fact Sheet," December 2002, http://www.cdc.gov/std/Gonorrhea/gonorrhea.pdf.

6. Centers for Disease Control and Prevention, "Pelvic Inflammatory Disease Fact Sheet," December 2003, http://www.cdc.gov/std/PID/pid.pdf.

7. L. Westrom and D. Eschenbach, "Pelvic Inflammatory Disease," in K. K. Holmes et al., *Sexually Transmitted Diseases*, 3rd ed. (New York: McGraw-Hill, 1999), 783–809.

8. D. T. Fleming et al., "Herpes Simplex Virus Type 2 in the United States, 1976 to 1994," *New England Journal of Medicine* 337, no. 16 (October 16, 1997): 1105–1111, and S. Brunton, "Genital Herpes and the Primary Care Practitioner," *Medscape*.

9. Z. A. Brown et al., "Neonatal Herpes Simplex Virus Infection in Relation to Asymptomatic Maternal Infection at the Time of Labor," *New England Journal of Medicine* 324 (1991): 1247–1252, quoted in Caroline M. Rudnick and Grant S. Hoekzema, "Neonatal Herpes Simplex Virus Infections," *American Family Physician* 65, no. 6 (March 15, 2002), http://www.aafp.org/afp/20020315/1138.html; Richard Fischer, "Genital Herpes in Pregnancy," *eMedicine*, February 15, 2006, http://www.emedicine.com/med/topic3554.htm.

10. Hillard Weinstock, Stuart Berman, and Willard Cates, "Sexually Transmitted Diseases among American Youth: Incidence and Prevalence Estimates, 2000," *Perspectives on Sexual and Reproductive Health* 36, no. 1 (January–February 2004): 6–10, http://www.guttmacher.org/pubs/journals/3600604.pdf.

11. Cheri Peyton et al., "Determinants of Genital Human Papillomavirus Detection in a US Population," *Journal of Infectious Diseases* 183 (2001): 1554–1564.

12. Julie Gerberding, *Report to Congress: Prevention of Genital Human Papillomavirus Infection* (Atlanta: Centers for Disease Control and Prevention, 2004); Rachel L. Winer et al., "Condom Use and the Risk of Genital Human Papillomavirus Infection in Young Women," *New England Journal of Medicine* 354, no. 25 (June 22, 2006): 2645–2654; Lisa Manhart and Laura Koutsky, "Do Condoms Prevent Genital HPV Infection, External Genital Warts, or Cervical Neoplasia?" *Sexually Transmitted Diseases* 29, no. 11 (November 2002): 725–735.

13. A. B. Moscicki, "Cervical Cytology Screening in Teens," *Current Women's Health Reports* 3, no. 6 (2003): 433–437; G. Y. Ho et al., "Natural History of Cervicovaginal Papillomavirus in Young Women," *New England Journal of Medicine* 338, no. 7 (1998): 423–428.

Special Concerns: Tobacco, Alcohol, and Drug Abuse—Resisting the Epidemic

1. American Lung Association, "Smoking and Teen Fact Sheet," http://www.lungusa.org/site/pp.asp?c=dvLUK9O0E&b=39871; Centers for Disease Control and Prevention, "Youth Risk Behavior Surveillance–United States," *Morbidity and Mortality Weekly Report* 55 (June 9, 2006), http://www.cdc.gov/MMWR/preview/mmwrhtml/ss5505a1.htm; Centers for Disease Control and Prevention, "Boyz II Men—Teen and Tobacco Facts Not Fiction."

2. Campaign for Tobacco-Free Kids, "Smoking and Other Drug Use," http://www.tobaccofreekids.org/research/factsheets/pdf/0106.pdf.

3. D. E. Nelson et al., "Trends in Smokeless Tobacco Use Among Adults and Adolescents in the United States," *American Journal of Public Health* 96, no. 5 (2006): 897–905.

4. American Medical Association, "Brain Damage Risks," (report on alcohol's adverse effects on the brains of children, adolescents, and college students; last updated October 2004), http://www.ama-assn.org/ama/pub/category/9416.html.

5. Editorial, "Break Needed from Alcohol Ads," *American Medical News*, February 2003.

6. Ibid.

7. Ibid.

8. Centers for Disease Control and Prevention, "Quick Stats: Underage Drinking," http://www.cdc.gov/alcohol/quickstats/underage_drinking.htm; Centers for Disease Control and Prevention, "Youth Risk Behavior Surveillance—United States 2005," *Morbidity and Mortality Weekly Report* (June 9, 2006).

9. Centers for Disease Control and Prevention, "Youth Risk Behavior Surveillance—2005."

10. Task Force of the National Advisory Council on Alcohol Abuse and Alcoholism, *A Call to Action: Changing the Culture of Drinking at U.S. Colleges* (April 2002), 4.

11. The Partnership for a Drug-Free America, "Generation Rx: National Study Confirms Abuse of Prescription and Over-the-Counter Drugs," news release, May 15, 2005, http://www.drugfree.org/Portal/DrugIssue/Research/Teens_2005/Generation_Rx_Study_Confirms_Abuse_of_Prescription#.

12. Ibid.

13. National Institute on Drug Abuse, "Hallucinogens and Dissociative Drugs," NIH Publication No. 01-4209 (March 2001).

Special Concerns: Recognizing Depression and Preventing Suicide in Children and Adolescents

1. American Academy of Child and Adolescent Psychiatry, "The Depressed Child," http://www.aacap.org/page.ww?section=Facts+for+Families&name=The+Depressed+Child.

2. National Mental Health Association, "Adolescent Depression: Helping Depressed Teens," http://www1.nmha.org/infoctr/factsheets/24.cfm.

3. Centers for Disease Control and Prevention, "Youth Risk Behavior Surveillance–United States 2005," *Morbidity and Mortality Weekly Report* (June 9, 2006).

4. Centers for Disease Control and Prevention, "Suicide: Fact Sheet," http://www.cdc.gov/ncipc/factsheets/suifacts.htm.

5. National Institute of Mental Health, "Questions and Answers about the NIMH Treatment for Adolescents with Depression Study (TADS)," http://www.mentalhealth.gov/healthinformation/tadsqa.cfm.

6. In December 2004, the New York State Office of Mental Health issued a letter to parents about the FDA warning about anitdepressant use in children and adolescents. The letter covers these guidelines for patient monitoring, as well as other information on children and antidepressants. See http://www.omh.state.ny.us/omhweb/advisories/parentltr.htm.

Reference Section

1. C. A. Adebamowo et al., "High School Dietary Intake and Teenage Acne," *Journal of the American Academy of Dermatology* 52, no. 2 (February 2005): 207–214.

2. In 2003, over 4,099 deaths were attributed to asthma; of these 154 occurred among children younger than fifteen. American Lung Association, "Asthma and Children Fact Sheet," August 2006.

3. American Heart Association, "Cholesterol and Atherosclerosis in Children," citing guidelines given in National Heart, Lung, and Blood Institute, *NIH Parents' Guide: National Cholesterol Education Program*, NIH Publication no. 93-3102, September 1993.

4. Caleb K. King et al., "Managing Acute Gastroenteritis among Children: Oral Rehydration, Maintenance, and Nutritional Therapy," *Morbidity and Mortality Weekly Report* 52 (November 21, 2003): 1–16, http://www.cdc.gov/mmwr/preview/mmwrhtml/rr5216a1.htm.

5. American Academy of Family Physicians and the American Academy of Pediatrics, "Diagnosis and Management of Acute Otitis Media," March 2004, http://www.aafp.org/online/en/home/clinical/clinicalrecs/aom.html.

6. March of Dimes, "Drinking Alcohol during Pregnancy," August 2002, http://www.marchofdimes.com/professionals/14332_1170.asp.

7. Ibid.

8. Centers for Disease Control and Prevention, "Salmonellosis," (October 31, 2006) http://www.cdc.gov/ncidod/dbmd/diseaseinfo/salmonellosis_g.htm.

9. Glaucoma Research Foundation, "Does Your Child Have Glaucoma?" http://www.glaucoma.org/learn/does_your_child.html.

10. Donald W. Lewis, "Headaches in Children and Adolescents," *American Family Physician* 65, no. 4 (February 15, 2002): 625–632, 635–636, http://www.aafp.org/afp/20020215/625.html.

11. National Kidney Foundation, "Hemolytic-Uremic Syndrome," http://www.kidney.org/kidneydisease/fs/showFS.cfm?id=72; William Shapiro, "Hemolytic Uremic Syndrome," *eMedicine*, http://www.medscape.com/files/emedicine/topic238.htm.

12. Anthony Fiore et al., "Prevention of Hepatitis A Through Active or Passive Immunization," *Morbidity and Mortality Weekly Report* 55 (May 19, 2006): 1–23, http://www.cdc.gov/mmwr/preview/mmwrhtml/rr5507a1.htm.

13. National Network for Immunization Information, "Vaccine Information: Hepatitis B," http://www.immunizationinfo.org/vaccineInfo/vaccine_detail.cfv?id=4.

14. Noriko Satake, "Acute Lymphoblastic Leukemia," *eMedicine*, http://www.emedicine.com/ped/topic2587.htm (updated July 2006).

15. National Network for Immunization Information, "Vaccine Information: Pertussis (Whooping Cough)," http://www.immunizationinfo.org/vaccineInfo/vaccine_detail.cfv?id=22; National Center for Health Statistics, *Health, United States, 2006*, table 51, http://www.cdc.gov/nchs/hus.htm; David S. Gregory, "Pertussis: A Disease Affecting All Ages," *American Family Physician* (August 1, 2006), http://www.aafp.org/afp/20060801/420.html.

16. National Network for Immunization Information, "Vaccine Information: Smallpox," http://www.immunizationinfo.org/vaccineInfo/vaccine_detail.cfv?id=26.

17. Eugenio D. Beltrán-Aguilar et al., "Surveillance for Dental Caries, Dental Sealants, Tooth Retention, Edentulism, and Enamel Fluorosis—United States, 1988–1994 and 1999–2002," *MMWR Surveillance Studies* 54, no. 3 (August 26, 2005): 1–44, http://www.cdc.gov/mmwr/preview/mmwrhtml/ss5403a1.htm.

18. Daniel J. Dire, "Tetanus," *eMedicine*, http://www.emedicine.com/EMERG/topic574.htm (updated October 2004).

19. MayoClinic.com, "Tuberculosis," December 21, 2006), http://www.mayoclinic.com/health/tuberculosis/DS00372; World Health Organization, "Tuberculosis Fact Sheet," http://www.who.int/mediacentre/factsheets/fs104/en/; Centers for Disease Control and Prevention, "Questions and Answers about TB 2005," http://www.cdc.gov/nchstp/tb/faqs/qa.htm.

Immunizations—Which Ones, Why, and When?

1. Anthony E. Fiore, "Prevention of Hepatitis A through Active or Passive Immunization," *Morbidity and Mortality Weekly Report* 55 (May 19, 2006): 1–23.

Some ABCs of Good Nutrition

1. Blake Sperry Bowden and Jennie M. Zeisz, "Supper's On! Adolescent Adjustment and Frequency of Family Mealtimes" (paper presented at American Psychological Association meeting, Chicago, August 16, 1997), http://www.sciencedaily.com/releases/1997/08/970821001329.htm.

Index

age 4 years 324
age 5 years 348
in adolescence 458
Duchenne muscular
dystrophy 702
ductus arteriosus 18
duloxetine 576
dust mites 625–626
DVDs 310–311, 368–370
adolescents and 485
in infancy 194–195
dysentery 657
dysmenorrhea 448, 657
dyspepsia 657
dysplastic hip 768
dyspnea 657
dysuria 731

E

ear, nose, and throat (ENT)
specialist 687
ear, removing object from 821
earbuds, hearing loss and 490
eardrum, perforation of 658–659
ear infections 657–659
ages 5 to 11 years 350–351
bottle feeding and 133
cigarette smoke and 15
during infancy 183
in newborns 139
ear pain and injury 821
ear thermometer 135, 243
earwax 640
eating disorders 401–405
causes 403–404
prevention 404–405
pro-ana/pro-mia Web sites
and 404
treatment 404–405
eating habits
ages 12 to 24 months 226–
230
age 2 years 299–301
ages 3 to 4 years 325–327
ages 5 to 11 years 345–346
as contributor to weight
problems 391
establishing healthy 391–394,
785
eclampsia 659
E. coli 668

Ecstasy. *See* MDMA
ectopic pregnancy 89, 608, 659
eczema 613, 615–616
of breasts 128
edema 659, 709, 732
education issues 194–195,
407–415
Edward syndrome. *See* trisomy 18
Effexor 576
effusion 658, 659
electrical burns 816
electric shock 821–822
electroencephalogram 716
embolism 659
emergency care 795–850
emesis 660
emotions
in 2-year-olds 312–315
in adolescents 474–475
in early adolescents 471–473
in school-age children 364–
367
in toddlers 231–235
empty nest 475–478
encephalitis 660, 697, 745
encopresis 648, 660
endocarditis 660
endocrine glands 676
endocrine system 442
endometriosis 450, 608, 660
endometrium 444, 448, 660
enema 660
engorgement, of breasts 120
enuresis. *See* bed-wetting
epididymis 442, 675
epidymitis 675
epidural anesthetic 46, 68
epiglottis 651
epiglottitis 651, 660, 721
epilepsy 713
during pregnancy 21
idiopathic 713
epinephrine 660, 799
EpiPen 799
episiotomy 39
Epstein-Barr virus (EBV) 699
Epstein's pearls 64
equipment, for newborn 46–55
erythema infectiosum. *See* fifth
disease
erythema marginatum 710
erythema migrans 695

erythema toxicum 64
erythromycin 611, 623
escitalopram 576
esophagus 660
esotropia 662
essential fatty acid 8
estimated average
requirement 773
estrogen, role in menstrual
cycle 448
ethmoidal sinuses 719
eustachian tube 133, 350, 658,
660
examination, of newborn 69
exanthem 660
excoriations 615
exercise
ages 5 to 11 years 354–357
during pregnancy 11–14
exocrine glands 676
exotropia 662
expectorant 660
experimentation, with drugs 563
extracurricular activities
ages 5 to 11 years 358–359
in adolescence 469–470
quitting 358
exudate 699, 720
eye
care and concerns 660–665
chemical injury 663, 822
exam 348
foreign object in 663–664
infections 664
injuries 822–823
of newborn 63
eye injuries 663, 822–823

F

failure to thrive 282, 665
fainting 665, 717, 823–824
during pregnancy 14
faith, encouraging in children
and adolescents 337–340,
588–594
fallopian tubes 445
famciclovir 541
"family bed." *See also* co-sleeping
ages 12 to 24 months 231
family counseling 367
family physicians 36

benefits 498
limits and expectations 499–500
monitoring use of 371
pornography and 486–488
risks 498–499
intoeing 706, 766–767
intradermal testing 614
intrauterine growth restriction 14
intussusception 607, 690, 744
ionizing radiation, during pregnancy 19–20
ipecac 224–225, 833
iris 660
iritis 664–665
iron 690
deficiency 620, 690
during pregnancy 10
in formula 134
irresponsibility in children 264
irritability, dealing with in children 366–367
irritable bowel syndrome 352
isoniazid 610
isotretinoin 611

J

jaundice 542, 633–634
hepatitis B and 75
in newborns 138–139
jellyfish stings 808
jock itch (tinea cruris) 691
joint injury 760, 812–814
jugular 691
juice consumption
during infancy 207
in childhood 779–780
junk foods 326
juvenile onset diabetes.
See diabetes mellitus, type 1
juvenile rheumatoid arthritis (JRA) 665, 761–762, 766

K

Kaposi's sarcoma 685
Kawasaki disease 691
keloid 691
ketamine 558–559

ketones 635
ketoprofen, for menstrual cramps 449
kidney disease 732–733
during pregnancy 21
kitchen safety 198–200
Klonopin 552
knee pain 765–767
knock-knee 691, 766
kreteks 548
kyphosis 691, 770

L

lab tests, during pregnancy 20–21
labia 672, 691
of newborn 65
labor/delivery/recovery (LDR) room 42–43
labyrinth 691
labyrinthitis 659
lacerations 691, 835
lacrimal gland 661
lacrimation 692
lactation consultant 130
lactose 131, 692
in breast milk 114
lactose intolerance 607, 617, 692
in infants 131, 186
Lamaze, Fernand 45
Lamaze method 45
language development
ages 6 to 12 months 195–196
ages 12 to 24 months 222–223
age 2 years 295
ages 3 to 4 years 331–333
lanugo 63
in anorexia nervosa 402
laryngitis 686, 692, 721
laryngotracheobronchitis 650
larynx 649
lavage 692
laxatives
abuse of in bulimia nervosa 403
use during pregnancy 19
layette 47
lazy eye 164
lead poisoning 692–693

learning, early in life 407–408
learning disabilities 414
lecithin/sphingomyelin (L/S) ratio 93
Legg-Calvé-Perthes Disease 768–769
leg pain 769
lens 661, 693
lesion 693
let-down reflex 119
lethargy 693
leukemia 242, 638, 693
leukopenia 693
leukotriene inhibitors 627
levalbuterol 626, 799
Lexapro 576
lice 693–694
lichenification 615
ligaments 694, 759
limping 352, 769
during infancy 194
linolenic acid 8
lipoma 694
liquid nitrogen 737
Liquiprin 246
listeriosis, during pregnancy 24
listlessness, in newborns 137
Little League baseball 356
lockjaw 694
Lomotil 669
Loratadine 614
lorazepam 552
lordosis 695
Lortab 552
loss of consciousness 827
LSD (lysergic acid diethylamide) 557–558
lumbar 695
lumbar puncture 698, 716
luteal phase, of menstrual cycle 445–447
luteinizing hormone 445
Luvox 576
lying, in preschoolers 339–340
Lyme disease 695–696, 762, 805
lymphadenopathy 696
lymph nodes 638, 696
lymphocytes 684
lymphoma 638

M

macula 696
macronutrients 772
magnetic resonance imaging
    (MRI) 696, 697
    during pregnancy 19
make-believe
    age 2 years 308–309
    ages 3 to 4 years 334–335
*Making Children Mind without
    Losing Yours* 367
malaria 696
malignancy 696
malignant melanoma 634
malleolus 696
malocclusion 696
Maltsupex 649
malunion 696
mammary glands 117
mandible 696
manic-depressive disorder.
    See bipolar disorder
Mantoux test 347
marijuana 549–554
    use during pregnancy 16
marital relationship, during
    newborn period 110–111
marriage, preparation for 601–
    603
marriage maintenance
    during children's
        adolescence 480
    while children are
        young 316–318
marrow 620, 696
martial arts 357
mastitis 128, 696
mastoiditis 659, 696–697
masturbation 375–376, 697
maternal-fetal medicine
    specialist 36
maxilla 697
maxillary sinuses 719
MDMA (Ecstasy) 555–556
    use during pregnancy 17
mealtimes
    ages 6 to 12 months 209–210
    ages 12 to 24 months 226–228
    ages 3 to 4 years 325–327
    avoiding power struggles 301,
        326–327

measles 697, 745
    immunization 22
meatal stenosis 734
meatus 734
meconium 122
media concerns
    adolescents and 483–488
    ages 5 to 11 368–371
    daily limits 356
medical supplies, ages 1 to 3
    months 138
medication
    breastfeeding and 116
    during labor 66–67
melanin 697
memories, making with
    children 586–587
menarche 443
meninges 137, 697
meningitis 348, 697–698, 745,
    748
    bacterial 743
    Haemophilus influenzae
        type B 742
    in newborns 137
meningococcus 748
meningococcus
    immunization 458, 748
    ages 11 to 12 years 348
meniscus 698
menorrhagia 698
menses 448
menstrual cramps 448–450, 608
menstrual cycle 444–448
menstrual period
    first 375
    irregular 450–452
mental retardation 415
mercury in fish 8–9
mercury in vaccinations 752
mercury thermometers, danger
    of 243
mesenteric adenitis 607, 624
Metadate 552
Metamucil 649
metastasis 638
metatarsal 698
metatarsus adductus (curved
    foot) 764, 766
metered dose inhalers
    (MDIs) 626

methadone, use during
    pregnancy 17
methamphetamine 555, 559
methylphenidate 384, 552, 729
microcephaly 698
micronutrients 772
middle ear 139
Midol, for menstrual cramps 449
migraine headache 350
milia 64, 698
miliaria 698
milk consumption
    ages 12 to 24 months 226
    age 2 years 300
    ages 3 to 4 years 325–326
minerals, in breast milk 115
miserable malalignment
    syndrome 767
mittelschmerz 445, 608, 698
MMR (measles/mumps/rubella)
    immunization 22, 697, 745,
        751
    age 4 to 6 years 324
    booster 347, 458
molars 723
mold 626
molding 62
mole 698
mometasone 627
Moms In Touch
    International 409
money, teaching children and
    adolescents about 597–600
Mongolian spots 64, 634
mononucleosis 699–700, 720
monounsaturated fatty acids 785
monsters, fear of in
    preschoolers 329–331
montelukast 627
mood swings, in early
    adolescence 471–473
moral values 365–371
    passing on to children and
        adolescents 594–597
Moro reflex 65
mother/son relationship 482
motion sickness 700
motorbikes 361
motorcycles 361
motor skills, ages 12 to 24
    months 225

Motrin 18, 246, 449, 644, 658, 678, 689, 701
mountain sickness, acute 618
mouth, care and concerns 700–702
movement
of newborns 165–166
of preschoolers 324
movies
adolescents and 485
ages 5 to 11 years 369–370
mucocutaneous lymph node syndrome 691
Mucomyst 609
mumps 702, 745
immunization 22
muscle strains and cramps 827
muscular dystrophy 702
mushrooms, wild 201
music
adolescents and 483–485
bedtime alternatives 296
music lessons, ages 5 to 11 years 358–359
myalgia 702
myocardial infarction 642
myoclonic seizures 714
myopia (nearsightedness) 662–663, 702
myositis 702
MyPyramid.gov 777
MySpace.com 497, 500

N

N-acetylcysteine 609
nail-biting 703
nail care and concerns 702–703
naproxen
for menstrual cramps 449
use during pregnancy 18
naps
ages 12 to 24 months 231
age 2 years 296
narcolepsy 703
narcotics, use during pregnancy 17
nasal saline solution, use during infancy 183
nasal sprays, use during pregnancy 18–19

nasolacrimal duct 661
obstruction of 662
National Academies 772
National Health and Nutrition Examination Survey (NHANES) 388
National Newborn Screening and Genetics Resource Center 70
National Youth Violence Prevention Resource Center 504
natural childbirth 44–46
nausea 703
nebulizer 703
neck injuries 824–826
neck pain, in children 769–770
negativism, in toddlers 234–235, 312–315
neglect, of children 282–285
neonatologist 37
neoplasm 638, 704
neuralgia 704, 747
neural tube defects 9, 11
neuritis 704
neurofibromatosis 634, 704
neuroma 704
neutrophil 704
nevus 634, 704
giant pigmented 634
newborn
bathing 147–148
behavior of 149–150
body movements of 165–166
body temperature of 144–145
clothing for 47–48
colic 160–163
crying in 160–163
daily routines 113
dressing and undressing 144–145
feeding 113–134
growth of 165–166
head support for 144, 166
hearing in 164–165
illness in 138–140
physical appearance 62–66
preventing infection in 167
reflexes of 65–66
sense of smell in 165
siblings and 112–113, 166–167
single parent and 111–112
skin conditions 149

sleep 150–159
socializing in 165
supplies and equipment for 48–55
touch, sense of 165
vision in 164
New Dare to Discipline, The 367
nicotine
effects of 547–549
effects on fetus 14–15
use during pregnancy 14–15
nightmares 297–298
night terrors 297, 718
nipples
shape of 117
soreness while nursing 125–129
nitrates, avoiding in infant's food 132, 178
nits 693–694
nizatidine, use during pregnancy 19
nocturia 704
nocturnal emission 375, 442
node 704. *See also* lymph nodes
nondisplaced fracture 758
non-insulin-dependent diabetes. *See* diabetes mellitus, type 2
nonionizing radiation, during pregnancy 20
nonprescription drug abuse 552–553
nonunion 704
Norco 552
norovirus 671
nose
of newborn 64
removing object from 828
nosebleeds 828
nuchal thickness ultrasound 92
Nuprin 449
nurse-midwife, certified (CNM) 36
nursemaid's elbow 761
nurse practioner 36–37
nursery school. *See* preschool
nursing. *See* breastfeeding
nutrition 771–785
during pregnancy 6–10
Nutrition Facts label (on food packaging) 775–776
nystatin 639

O

obesity
   during pregnancy 10–11
   in childhood or
      adolescence 395–399
object permanence 196–197,
   224–225
obsessive-compulsive disorder
   (OCD) 404, 576
obstetrician/gynecologist 36
occiput 704
occlusion 726
ocular 704
off-road vehicles, safety
   concerns 361
omega-3 fatty acids 8, 785
omega-6 fatty acids 785
omphalocele 90
open adoption 78, 515
open fractures 758–759
open reduction (of bone) 758
opiates 552
oppositional behavior, in
   toddlers 234–235
optic nerve 660
oral contraceptives. See birth
   control pills
oral rehydration solutions
   (ORS) 655, 735
oral sex, adolescents and 512
orchitis 745
orifice 704
orthodontist 726
orthopaedics 757
Orudis 449
Osgood-Schlatter's disease 766
osteochondritis dissecans 766
osteoma 704
osteomalacia 704
osteomyelitis 704, 763
osteopathy 36
osteoporosis 451, 704
otitis externa 621, 657, 704
otitis media 621, 645, 658, 704
   in newborns 139
outtoeing 767
ova 444
ovaries 444–447
overbite 726
overweight, child or adolescent
   387–399

   causes 390–391
   consequences 389–390
   help for 395–399
   prevention 391–394
ovulation 445
oxybutynin chloride 632
oxycodone 552
OxyContin 552
oxytocin 115–116

P

pacifiers 126–127, 129, 155
pads, for menstrual flow 446–
   447
pain, in bones or joints 351–354
palate 658, 704
pallid breath-holding spell 636
pallor 704
palpate 704
palpitation 704
Panadol 246
pancreatitis 745
papilloma 686, 704
Pap test (smear) 456–457
   during pregnancy 21
   thin prep 456
papule 704
paraplegia 704
parasite 704
parental survival skills, with
   adolescents 478–494
parenteral 704
paresis 704
paresthesia 705
parochial school. See school,
   private
paronychia 703
paroxetine 454, 576
paroxysm 705
parvovirus, during pregnancy 24
patella 705
patient-controlled analgesia
   (PCA) pump, after cesarean
   delivery 68
pauciarticular juvenile
   rheumatoid arthritis 761–762
Paxil 454, 576
PCP. See phencyclidine
peak flow meter 625
pedestrians, safety concerns 362

Pedialyte 655
pediatrician 37
pediatric ophthalmologist 661
pediculosis. See lice
pedodontist 306
peer pressure
   drug abuse and 546
   helping child resist 378
peer relationships, during
   adolescence 468–469, 483
pelvic exam 456–458
pelvic inflammatory disease 540
peptic ulcer 705
peptic ulcer disease 606–607
Percocet 552
Percodan 552
perforation 705
performing arts, ages 5 to 11
   years 358–359
pericarditis 705
perinatal hospice 96–97
periorbital cellulitis 719
periosteum 705, 757
peripheral 705
peritonitis 623–624
peritonsillar abscess 729
permissiveness 262–263
persistent urethral valves 734
pertussis (whooping cough) 347,
   705, 741
pes cavus. See high-arched foot
pet, death of 434–435
petechiae 705
petit mal seizures 714
pharyngitis 620, 720
phencyclidine 558–559
phenylephrine 644, 719
phenylketonuria (PKU) 69, 131
   artificial sweeteners and 18
   breastfeeding and 116
phenytoin 610
phlegm 705
photophobia 698, 705
photosynthesis 786–787
phototherapy 139, 633–634
physical development
   ages 3 to 6 months 171–173
   ages 6 to 12 months 191–193
   ages 12 to 24 months 220–
      226
   age 2 years 294
   ages 3 to 4 years 323–325

in adolescence 442–444, 468
physical fitness
    ages 5 to 11 years 354–357
    encouraging 356–357
physician
    choosing a 37–42
    family 36
    working with 38–39
physician assistant 36–37
physiologic jaundice 633
phytochemicals 7–8, 781
PID. *See* pelvic inflammatory
    disease
pigeon toes. *See* intoeing
pimples. *See* acne
pinkeye 183, 647
pinna 706
pinworms 619, 706
pituitary 444
pityriasis rosea 706
PKU. *See* phenylketonuria.
placebo 707
placenta 447
placental abruption 17
plantar 707
plantar warts 736
plasma 707
Plastibell 148
platelets 707
play groups, toddlers and 311–
    312
playmates
    age 2 years 309–312
    ages 3 to 4 years 336–337
    toddlers and 236–237
playtime, ages 12 to 24
    months 236–237
Plugged In magazine 370
plumbism 707
PMS. *See* premenstrual syndrome
pneumococcal conjugate vaccine
    (PCV) 743
pneumococcus 743
pneumonia 608, 621, 645, 707
    during infancy 184
    in newborns 137
pneumothorax 707
Poison Control Center 225
poisoning 831–833
    preventing in toddlers 225–
        226
    responding to 224–225

poison ivy/oak/sumac 707–708
polio 708, 743, 744
polio booster, age 4 324
polio immunization 743–744
    age 5 years 347
pollens 626
polyarticular juvenile rheumatoid
    arthritis 761–762
polycystic ovary syndrome 451
polydactyly 708
polyp 708
polyuria 733
pool safety 820
pornography, adolescents
    and 486–488
portion sizes 391
postictal 714
postinflammatory
    hyperpigmentation 707
postpartum blues 100
postpartum depression 100–101
postpartum psychosis 101
potty training. *See* toilet training
praise, for good behavior 268–269
prayer
    at bedtime 230–231
    for adolescents 478, 494
    for children 204, 265
preeclampsia 659
pregnancy in teenagers 513–516,
    530–534
pregnancy resource center 31,
    111–112, 143, 233
premature infants 103–106
premenstrual dysphoric disorder
    (PMDD) 452
premenstrual syndrome
    (PMS) 452–454
prenatal care 6–26
prenatal screening 20–22
prenatal testing 97–98
    response to abnormal
        results 97–98
prenatal vitamins 9–10
preparing for adolescence 376–
    378
preschool 336–337
    2-year-olds and 312
    evaluating 336–337
prescription drug abuse 552–553
prickly heat 698
primary-care physicians 37

primary teeth 306, 723
private school. *See* school, private
profanity 328–329
progesterone 444, 451
    supplemental for
        premenstrual
        syndrome 454
projectile vomiting 734–735
    in newborns 140
prolactin 117, 119
prolapse 708
prostaglandins 448–449
prostate 442
protein hydrolysate formulas 131
protein intake 774
    during pregnancy 7
proteinuria 708
Proventil 626
Prozac 454, 576
pseudoephedrine 644, 719
psychoprophylaxis 45
psychosis 575
ptosis 708
pubertal development
    in boys 442–443
    in girls 443–444
puberty 344–345
    discussing with child 375–
        378
    onset of 375–376
pubic lice 694
pubis 708
public school. *See* school, public
Pulmicort 627
pulmonary edema 618
punishment, behavioral
    exceptions 268
pupil 661, 708
purpura 708
purulent 708
pustule 609, 708
pyelonephritis 607, 732
pyloric stenosis 140, 708–709,
    734
pylorus 140

Q

quadriceps 708
quadriplegia 708
quad screen 92

temperature
  axillary 135
  measuring 135, 243–244
  of newborn 144–145
  rectal 135, 136
temporal 726
temporomandibular (TMJ) 680
Tempra 246
tendonitis 353, 726, 761
tendons 726, 761
testicles 672
  changes during puberty 442
tetanus 726–727, 741, 835
tetanus immunization
  age 5 348
  booster during
    adolescence 458
tetracycline 611, 621, 696
THC (delta-9-
    tetrahydrocannabinol) 549
theophylline 627
thermometer
  mercury 135
  rectal 135
  types 135, 243
thimerosal, immunizations
  and 752
third-degree burns 815–816
three-day measles. See rubella
thrush 127, 639, 700, 727
  inflamed nipples and 127
thumb-sucking 727
thyroid 727
tibia 727, 757, 766
ticks 727–728
  bites 762, 805
tics 718, 728
time-outs 271–272
tinea versicolor 728
tinnitus 729
T lymphocytes 740
tobacco use 547–549
  chewing 548–549
  during pregnancy 14–15
  quitting 14–15
  smokeless 548–549
toe-walking 767
Tofranil 632
toilet training 238, 301–305
  ages 3 to 4 years 327
tolerable upper intake level
    (UL) 773
tolterodine 632

tongue-tie 701
tonic neck reflex 166
tonsillectomy 729
tonsillitis 620, 720, 729
tonsils 729
tooth decay, in bulimia
    nervosa 403
torsion 766
torticollis 769
touch, guidelines for dating
    524–525
touch, sense of in newborns 165
Tourette syndrome 718, 729
toxic shock syndrome
    (TSS) 446–447
toxin 729
toxoplasmosis, during
    pregnancy 23–24
toys, ages 6 to 12 months 196–
    199
trachea 649–650
tracheitis 721
training of children 259–275
tranquilizers 552
transient synovitis 762
traveler's diarrhea 668
tretinoin 610
triamcinolone 627
triceps 729
triple screen 92
trisomy 729
trisomy 18 91
  prenatal testing for 92
tuberculosis (TB) 212, 346–347,
    729–730
  breastfeeding and 116
  risk factors 346–347
  testing 346, 347, 458
tub safety 847
tumor 638
Turner syndrome 730
Tylenol 608–609
  fever and 246
  for menstrual cramps 449
  overdose 18, 608–609
  use during pregnancy 18
tympanostomy 659
type 2 diabetes 389
typhoid fever 730

U

U.S. Consumer Product Safety
  Commission (CPSC) 361
ulcer 730. See peptic ulcer
  disease
ultrasound, during
  pregnancy 19, 88–90
umbilical cord 62
umbilical hernia 684, 730
unconjugated estriol 91
underage drinking 550, 551
underbite 726
undescended testicle 64
upper-respiratory infections 643–
    646
  ages 3 to 6 months 182–185
  ages 5 to 11 years 350
ureter 730, 731
urethra 731
urethritis 731, 732
urinalysis 347
  during pregnancy 20
urinary tract care and
  concerns 731–734
urinary tract infections 303, 304,
    308, 607, 621, 731–732
urinary urgency 734
urticaria (hives) 613, 616, 734
uterus 444, 445
uvula 734

V

vaccinations. See immunizations
vaccines. See immunizations
vagina 65, 445
  changes during puberty 443
vaginal discharge 308
vaginosis, bacterial 74
  during pregnancy 21
valacyclovir 541
Valium 552
Valtrex 541
values
  instilling in school-age
    children 371
  instilling in adolescents 594–
    597
vaporizer 183
varicella. See chickenpox

Varicella-zoster immune globulin (VZIG) 641–642
varicella immunization 349, 458–459, 747
Varivax 642
vasopressin 630
vegetables, benefits of in diet 781–782
Venlaxafine 576
Ventolin 626
vernix 62
vertigo 659, 734
Vicodin 552
video games 311, 370
videos 368–371
    adolescents and 485
videotaping, during delivery 44
viral meningitis. *See* aseptic meningitis
viruses 734
vision
    ages 3 to 6 months 172–173
    ages 6 to 12 months 194
    ages 12 to 24 months 221–222
    in newborns 164
visual acuity 661
vitamin/mineral supplementation
    ages 12 to 24 months 228
    ages 5 to 11 years 346
    during pregnancy 9–10
    to relieve premenstrual syndrome 453
vitamins 772
    B12, during pregnancy 8
    C (ascorbic acid) 645
    D, breastfeeding and 115
    in breast milk 115
    K 62, 71

vitiligo 734
vitreous humor 661
vocal cord paralysis 686
vocalization, ages 6 to 12 months 195–196
vomiting 734–736
    during infancy 186, 187
    in newborns 140
vulva 674, 736

W

walker, baby 180
walking
    ages 12 to 24 months 221
    during pregnancy 11–12
    in infancy 193–194
warts 736–737
water heater 200
water safety 848
    ages 6 to 12 months 200
    ages 5 to 11 years 362–363
water skiing, during pregnancy 13
weaning 228–230
weight
    age 6 months 181
    ages 12 to 24 months 220–221
    age 2 years 294
    ages 3 to 4 years 323
    control in children and adolescents 391–394
    excessive 395–399
    loss, in children and adolescents 399
weight gain, during pregnancy 12–13

West Nile virus 201
wet dream. *See* nocturnal emission
whiplash 737
whirlpools, use during pregnancy 20
White, Burton L. 236, 312
whitehead 609
whole grains, benefits of in diet 780–781
whooping cough (pertussis) 348, 705, 741
    booster 458
work, paying children and adolescents for 598
working mothers 319
    considerations 248–251
worldview, developing in adolescence 470–471

X

X-linked genetic disorders 86–87
X-rays, during pregnancy 19–20
Xanax 552
Xopenex 626, 799

Z

zafirlukast 627
Zantac 19
zinc, during pregnancy 8
Zoloft 454, 576
Zovirax 541, 641
Zyrtec 614, 798

Metric Conversion Charts

VOLUME

¼ tsp	1.25 ml
½ tsp	2.5 ml
1 tsp	5 ml
1 Tbsp	15 ml
¼ cup	60 ml
⅓ cup	80 ml
½ cup	120 ml
⅔ cup	160 ml
¾ cup	180 ml
1 cup	240 ml

WEIGHT

1 oz	28 g
2 oz	57 g
3 oz	85 g
4 oz	113 g
5 oz	142 g
6 oz	170 g
7 oz	198 g
8 oz	227 g
16 oz	454 g
32 oz	907 g

TEMPERATURE CONVERSION:
Fahrenheit/Centigrade

°F	°C	°F	°C
97.0	36.1	101.4	38.6
97.5	36.4	101.6	38.7
98.0	36.7	101.8	38.8
98.2	36.8	102.0	38.9
98.4	36.9	102.2	39.0
98.6	37.0	102.4	39.1
98.8	37.1	102.6	39.2
99.0	37.2	102.8	39.3
99.2	37.3	103.0	39.4
99.4	37.4	103.2	39.6
99.6	37.6	103.4	39.7
99.8	37.7	103.6	39.8
100.0	37.8	103.8	39.9
100.2	37.9	104.0	40.0
100.4	38.0	104.2	40.1
100.6	38.1	104.4	40.2
100.8	38.2	104.6	40.3
101.0	38.3	104.8	40.4
101.2	38.4	105.0	40.6

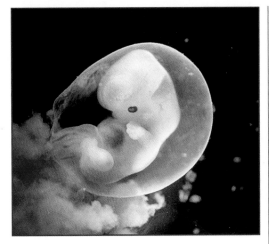

APPROXIMATELY 5 WEEKS

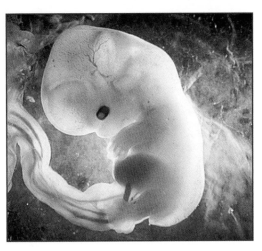

APPROXIMATELY 6 WEEKS

Six weeks after the union of father's sperm and mother's egg, the baby's heart is beating 140 to 150 times per minute. Small buds, which will soon become arms and legs, have sprouted. The large blood vessel in the umbilical cord is carrying oxygen-rich blood from the placenta to the baby, while the two smaller vessels take waste products back to the placenta.

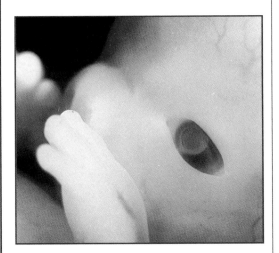

APPROXIMATELY 8 WEEKS

Two weeks later (8 weeks after conception), fingers and toes have formed; bones, hair, and nails have yet to develop. Tiny muscles are beginning to create body movements, but these cannot be felt by the mother. New nerve cells in the brain are being produced at the astonishing rate of 100,000 per minute.

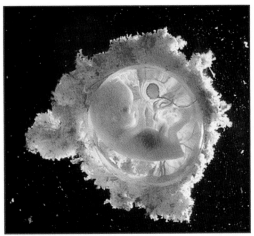

APPROXIMATELY 12 WEEKS

At 12 weeks after conception, all the internal organs and tissues are formed, and the heartbeat may be heard using an electronic listening device. The baby is seen here suspended in amniotic fluid. The irregular tissue surrounding the baby is called the chorionic sac, which attaches to the placenta.

APPROXIMATELY 16 WEEKS

Sixteen weeks after conception, the baby is kicking, turning the head, making facial movements, swallowing, hiccuping, sleeping, and waking. Within the next two weeks the mother will begin to feel movements within her. These will feel faint and almost fluttery at first but will become much stronger in the coming weeks.

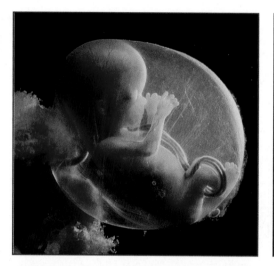

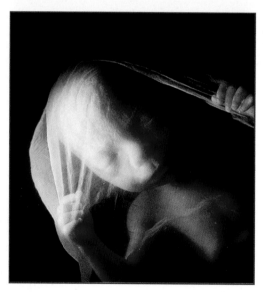

APPROXIMATELY 18 WEEKS

By 18 weeks the baby is approximately 9 inches long and is stretching, turning, and grasping. A finger touching the lips may set off a sucking reflex.

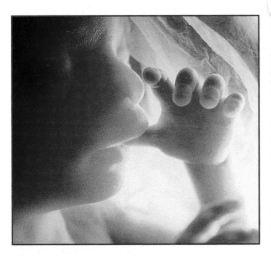

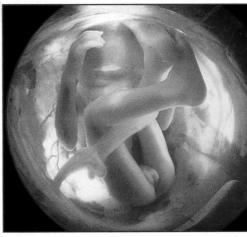

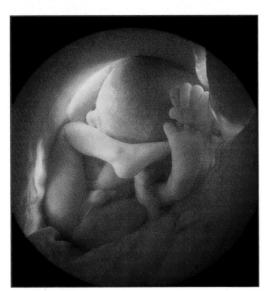

8TH MONTH

As the time of birth approaches, the baby's weight is rapidly increasing, and space within the amniotic sac is becoming more cramped. Stretching and kicking movements are much more forceful. The eyes are now opening and closing. Within a few more weeks, this new person will be ready to be welcomed into the world.

THE EYE

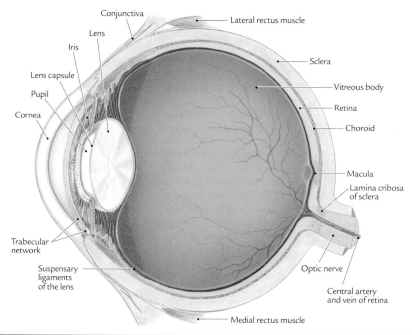

Conjunctiva
Lens
Iris
Lens capsule
Pupil
Cornea
Lateral rectus muscle
Sclera
Vitreous body
Retina
Choroid
Macula
Lamina cribosa of sclera
Trabecular network
Suspensary ligaments of the lens
Optic nerve
Central artery and vein of retina
Medial rectus muscle

THE EAR

Pinna
Semicircular canals
Vestibule
Nerves carrying impulses to the brain
Vestibular
Facial
Cochlea
Cochlear
Stapes (stirrup)
Malleus (hammer)
Incus (anvil)
Tympanic membrane (eardrum)
Tympanic cavum (middle-ear cavity)
External acoustic meatus (ear canal)
Eustachian tube

THE TEETH

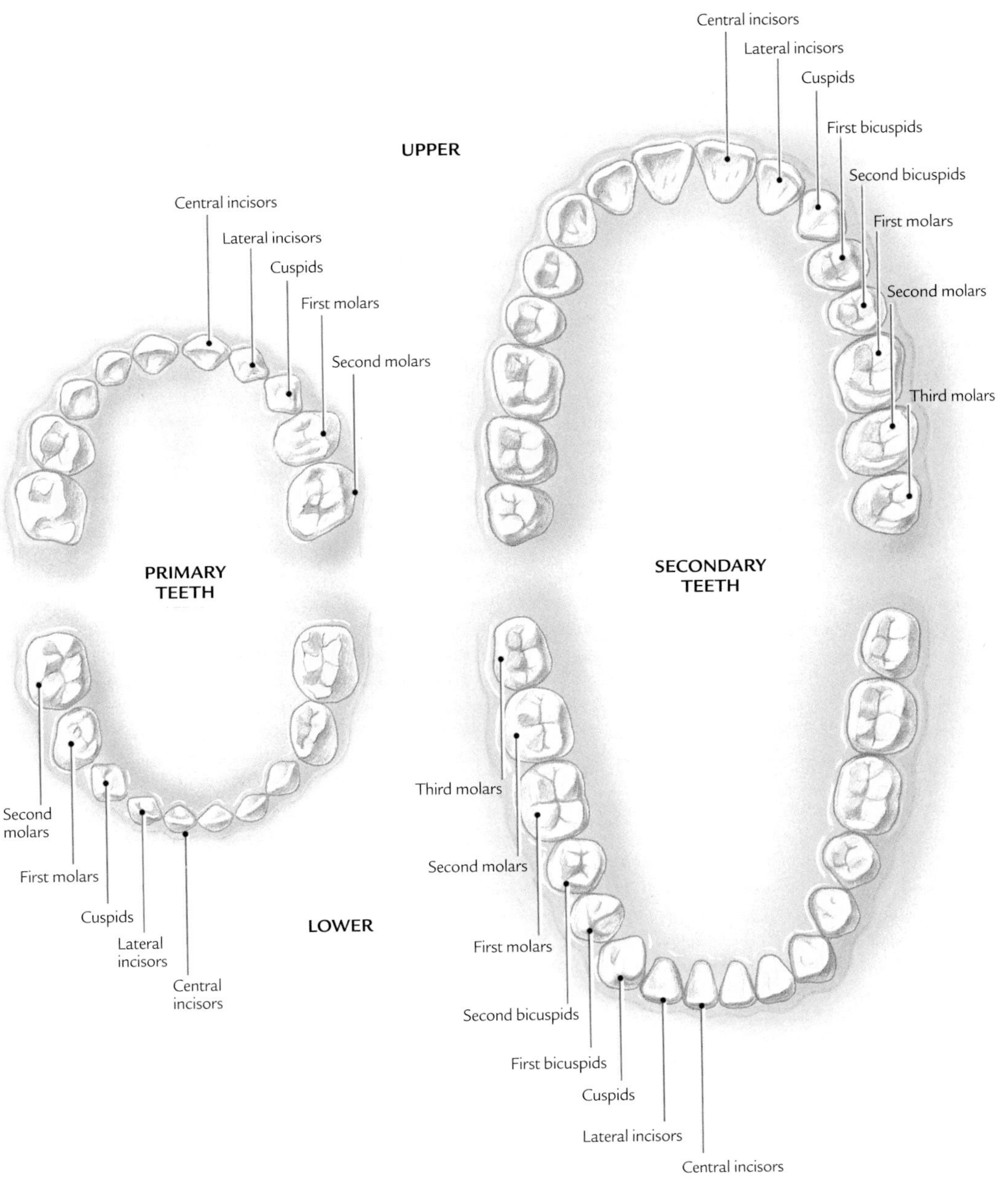
UPPER
Central incisors
Lateral incisors
Cuspids
First molars
Second molars
PRIMARY TEETH
Second molars
First molars
Cuspids
Lateral incisors
Central incisors
LOWER
Central incisors
Lateral incisors
Cuspids
First bicuspids
Second bicuspids
First molars
Second molars
Third molars
SECONDARY TEETH
Third molars
Second molars
First molars
Second bicuspids
First bicuspids
Cuspids
Lateral incisors
Central incisors

One size doesn't fit all

USDA's new MyPyramid symbolizes a personalized approach to healthy eating and physical activity. The symbol has been designed to be simple. It has been developed to remind consumers to make healthy food choices and to be active every day. The different parts of the symbol are described below.

ACTIVITY

Activity is represented by the steps and the person climbing them, as a reminder of the importance of daily physical activity.

MODERATION

Moderation is represented by the narrowing of each food group from bottom to top. The wider base stands for foods with little or no solid fats or added sugars. These should be selected more often. The narrower top area stands for foods containing more added sugars and solid fats. The more active you are, the more of these foods can fit into your diet.

PROPORTIONALITY

Proportionality is shown by the different widths of the food group bands. The widths suggest how much food a person should choose from each group. The widths are just a general guide, not exact proportions. Check the Web site for how much is right for you.

MyPyramid.gov
STEPS TO A HEALTHIER YOU

PERSONALIZATION

Personalization is shown by the person on the steps, the slogan, and the URL. Find the kinds and amounts of food to eat each day at MyPyramid.gov.

VARIETY

Variety is symbolized by the 6 color bands representing the 5 food groups of the Pyramid and oils. This illustrates that foods from all groups are needed each day for good health.

GRADUAL IMPROVEMENT

Gradual improvement is encouraged by the slogan. It suggests that individuals can benefit from taking small steps to improve their diet and lifestyle each day.

USDA

U.S. Department of Agriculture
Center for Nutrition Policy
and Promotion
April 2005 CNPP-16

USDA is an equal opportunity provider and employer.

GRAINS   VEGETABLES   FRUITS   OILS   MILK   MEAT & BEANS

MyPyramid ^{For Kids}

Eat Right. Exercise. Have Fun.

MyPyramid.gov

Grains Make half your grains whole	**Vegetables** Vary your veggies	**Fruits** Focus on fruits	**Milk** Get your calcium-rich foods	**Meat & Beans** Go lean with protein
Start smart with breakfast. Look for whole-grain cereals. Just because bread is brown doesn't mean it's whole-grain. Search the ingredients list to make sure the first word is "whole" (like "whole wheat").	Color your plate with all kinds of great-tasting veggies. What's green and orange and tastes good? Veggies! Go dark green with broccoli and spinach, or try orange ones like carrots and sweet potatoes.	Fruits are nature's treats – sweet and delicious. Go easy on juice and make sure it's 100%.	Move to the milk group to get your calcium. Calcium builds strong bones. Look at the carton or container to make sure your milk, yogurt, or cheese is lowfat or fat-free.	Eat lean or lowfat meat, chicken, turkey, and fish. Ask for it baked, broiled, or grilled -- not fried. It's nutty, but true. Nuts, seeds, peas, and beans are all great sources of protein, too.

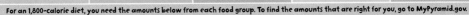

For an 1,800-calorie diet, you need the amounts below from each food group. To find the amounts that are right for you, go to MyPyramid.gov.

Eat 6 oz. every day; at least half should be whole	Eat 2 ½ cups every day	Eat 1 ½ cups every day	Get 3 cups every day; for kids ages 2 to 8, it's 2 cups	Eat 5 oz. every day

◇ Oils Oils are not a food group, but you need some for good health. Get your oils from fish, nuts, and liquid oils such as corn oil, soybean oil, and canola oil.

Find your balance between food and fun

- Move more. Aim for at least 60 minutes every day, or most days.
- Walk, dance, bike, Rollerblade – it all counts. How great is that!

Fats and sugars — know your limits

- Get your fat facts and sugar smarts from the Nutrition Facts label.
- Limit solid fats as well as foods that contain them.
- Choose food and beverages low in added sugars and other caloric sweeteners.

MyPyramid.gov
STEPS TO A HEALTHIER YOU

TEAM
NUTRITION USA
teamnutrition.usda.gov

...artment of Agriculture
and Nutrition Service
September 2005
FNS-381

USDA

...is an equal opportunity provider and employer.

A7

SMALL OBJECT TESTER

CABINET SAFETY STOPS

NASAL ASPIRATOR

SAFETY SCISSORS

ORAL SYRINGE

CORNER CUSHIONS

OUTLET PLUGS

NAIL CLIPPERS

MEDICINE SPOON

RECTAL THERMOMETER

CABINET SLIDE LOCKS

ORTHODONTICALLY APPROPRIATE PACIFIERS

INFANT CAR SEAT/CARRIER

REVERSIBLE BABY PACK/ CARRIER

BABY BACKPACK (for infants who have achieved head control)